TOURING GUIDE TO BRITAIN was edited and designed by
The Reader's Digest Association Limited, London

First Edition Copyright © 1992
The Reader's Digest Association Limited, Berkeley Square House,
Berkeley Square, London W1X 6AB

Copyright © 1992 Reader's Digest Association Far East Limited

Philippines Copyright © 1992 Reader's Digest Association Far East Limited

Printed in Britain
ISBN 0 276 42031 4

READER'S DIGEST

TOURING GUIDE TO BRITAIN

Published by The Reader's Digest Association Limited
LONDON · NEW YORK · SYDNEY · CAPE TOWN · MONTREAL

CONTENTS

CONTRIBUTORS

Editor John Palmer
Art Editor Gay Burdett
Cartographic Editor Peter Gutteridge

WRITERS
John Booth
John Burke
Anthony Burton
Bernard Dumpleton
Ross Finlay
Anne Gatti
Minna Lacey
Robert MacDonald
John Man
Ron Mellor
Keith Spence

ARTISTS
Richard Bonson
Leonora Box
Kevin Dean
Colin Emberson
Nicolas Hall
Jim Robins
Gill Tomblin
Barbara Walker

Cover pictures, from top to bottom:
Elmley Castle village, Hereford and Worcester;
HMS *Victory*, Portsmouth Harbour;
Windmill at Lytham, Lancashire;
Lindisfarne Castle, Northumberland.

Page 1 The Summer Smoking Room, Cardiff Castle.
Pages 2-3 Scott's View, looking towards the Eildon Hills.
Pages 4-5 Ludlow and the Clee Hills, Shropshire.
Page 6 Gardens of Pitmedden, Grampian.

HOW TO USE THE BOOK

Use the map location key on the right to find
the map relevant to your tour. If you are looking for
a specific place then use the gazetteer
between pages 288 and 319. On the maps, all the
places printed in solid black type are well
worth a visit. Those that are more prominently
displayed in bold type are described in the
text next to each map. The symbols (below) used on
the maps also appear alongside the gazetteer
entries and the text entries. Both gazetteer and text
entries have map references for easy location.

Motorway . . . . ▬▬▬	Airport, other aerodrome . . . . . ✈
A road . . . . ▬▬	National boundary . . . . . ▬ ▬ ▬
B road . . . . ▬	County boundary . . . . . . ▬ ▬ ▬
Minor road . . . . ▬	Canal . . . .
Car ferry . . . . 🚗	Long-distance path . . . .

🏘	Village entry in text	🐾	Zoo
O	Other attractive place	🐟	Aquarium
π	Ancient monument	🦋	Butterfly centre
✳	Hill-fort	🐦	Bird collection
🐎	Roman remains	🐐	Rare breeds collection
⊛	Later historical feature	🐴	Horse or pony centre
⚔	Battle site (with date)	⚙	Water mill
†	Cathedral	✗	Windmill
†	Church of special interest	🗼	Lighthouse
⚜	Abbey, priory, etc	🚂	Heritage railway
🏰	House or castle with interesting interior	✪	Industrial feature
🏛	House or castle in ruins	Ω	Theme or leisure park
❀	Garden	✍	Craft centre
♣	Arboretum	🏺	Pottery
♘	Wooded area	🍇	Vineyard, winery
⚘	Country park	🍺	Brewery, distillery, cider press
⚘	Nature trail	▌	Literary association
≗	Beauty spot	🎭	Theatre
🦶	Beach	⚓	Maritime museum
▲	Hill or mountain peak (with height in feet)	Y	Aircraft museum
✳	Viewpoint	🔫	Military museum
		🚜	Farm museum or working farm
	Scenic area	🚌	Motor museum
		🏭	Open-air museum
☆	Other natural feature	🏛	Other museum or art gallery
🍃	Nature reserve or sanctuary	⌂	Picnic site
✦	Wildlife park	⃞	Tourist or visitor information centre

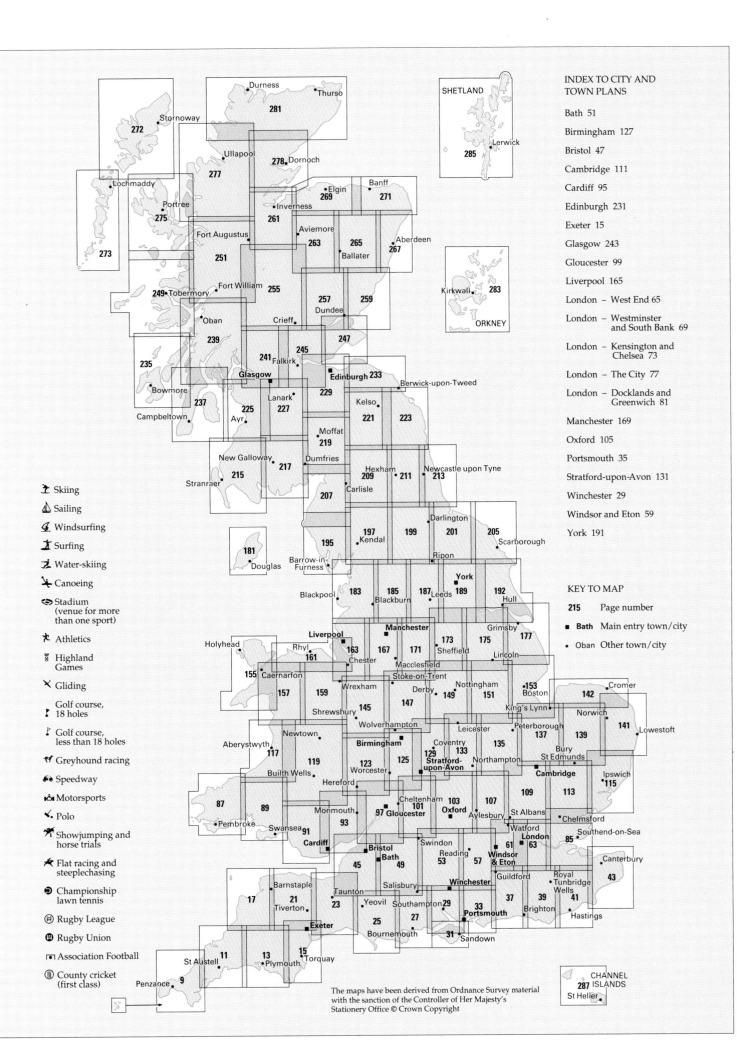

KEY TO MAP

215   Page number

■ Bath   Main entry town/city

• Oban   Other town/city

Skiing

Sailing

Windsurfing

Surfing

Water-skiing

Canoeing

Stadium (venue for more than one sport)

Athletics

Highland Games

Gliding

Golf course, 18 holes

Golf course, less than 18 holes

Greyhound racing

Speedway

Motorsports

Polo

Showjumping and horse trials

Flat racing and steeplechasing

Championship lawn tennis

Rugby League

Rugby Union

Association Football

County cricket (first class)

The maps have been derived from Ordnance Survey material with the sanction of the Controller of Her Majesty's Stationery Office © Crown Copyright

Cadgwith ⌂☆ Eb
Fishing village squeezed into a narrow valley. Cottages built of local serpentine stone cluster around the beach. Artists paint the crab and lobster boats crowding the tiny harbour. Devil's Frying Pan lies south, a hole 200ft deep where the sea foams over a mass of stone and shingle.

Camborne ⌂✿❋⚒ De
Once the heart of Cornwall's tin and copper industries. Rocks and minerals display at the world-famous School of Mines. Engineering relics on adjoining sites near Redruth: beam engine at East Pool Whim, and water pumping engine at Taylor's Shaft – the largest and latest left in Cornwall. Remains of Iron Age fortress on hill of Carn Brea mix with 5000-year-old Stone Age settlements. Shire Horse Farm and Carriage Museum includes heavy horses, ploughing and haymaking.

Carn Euny ⋔ Ac
Iron Age village of 1st century BC. Traces of houses with living-rooms and storerooms opening off a central courtyard. Remains are built round a 2nd-century fogou, or underground chamber, thought to be for storage, defence or religious ritual.

Chacewater ⌂✿ Ee
Steam pioneer James Watt installed his first new pumping engines here at Wheal Busy copper mine in 1777. Stone-built engine-house, smithy and cottages are still in fairly good repair.

Chapel Porth ❀✿❋ Df
Cove reached by a narrow lane from St Agnes. Natural history and industrial archaeology blend along a two hour nature trail with buzzards, jackdaws and ravens. Remains of Wheal Coates mine lie below St Agnes Beacon.

Chysauster ⋔ Bd
Well-preserved homes of Iron Age farmers perch high on the Gulval Downs. Now open to the sky, four pairs of oval stone houses front England's oldest

MAJESTIC PENINSULAR CORNWALL

The granite mass of Land's End tumbles into the sea at the end of the Cornish peninsula, the farthest point west on the mainland of England. In the south, palm trees grow in sheltered coves, while in the north, black cliffs defy the Atlantic. Above all, this is an area steeped in legend, with tales of shipwrecks, smugglers and strange happenings in the subterranean world of the tin miners.

identifiable village street. Each house has several rooms opening onto a central courtyard, with a small garden. Entrances face north-east away from the winds.

Constantine ⌂ Ec
Stands above the woods and quiet creeks of Helford river. Granite from a nearby quarry made London's original Waterloo Bridge. Pixies Hall lies north; underground passage once part of prehistoric fortification. Entrance to remains through Bosahan Farm.

FISHING VILLAGE *Coverack offers good angling for bass and pollack. Boats can be hired.*

Coverack ⌂ Eb
Quaint seaside village with fishing harbour overlooks a sand-and-shingle bay. One of many Cornish villages where smuggling once supplemented the fishing industry.

Falmouth ⚓⛵⌂ Fd
Holiday resort with fine natural harbour. Cliff walks offer views of waters of Carrick Roads and Falmouth Bay. Star of the Maritime Museum's collection is the retired steam tug *St Denys* with exhibitions on board. Coastal fortress of Pendennis Castle, built in the 1540s by Henry VIII, dominates headland.

Glendurgan Gardens ✿ Ec
Rolling down in bursts of colour to Helford river, tropical succulents and exotic shrubs flourish in a temperate climate. Rhododendrons, magnolias, hydrangeas as well as aloes and persimmons.

Godolphin House ⌂ Cd
Early Tudor and Elizabethan country mansion, built around two courtyards on the slopes of Godolphin Hill. Striking north front embellished with stately granite columns.

Goonhilly Downs ✿⚘ Ec
Bleak and eerie downs are brightened by gorse in spring, and heathers in late summer. Giant dish aerials of Goonhilly Earth Station point skywards; the satellite communications station is lapped about by moorland that provides a nature sanctuary for plants and animals.

Gweek ⌂ Ec
Wooded creek-side port with old quays, once bustling with trade and smuggling activity. Surrounding area was well known to the writer Charles Kingsley. Nearby is seal sanctuary on the Helford river.

WILD HEADLAND *The ruined tin mine of Botallack near St Just clings to the cliffs above a rock-torn sea.*

collection of exotic and tender plants at Trengwainton includes rhododendrons and Australian *Dicksonia antarctica.*

Mousehole ⌂⚓ Bc
Picturesque village with narrow streets leading to a snug harbour, draped with nets and crowded with fishermen. Cornwall's main fishing port for many years.

Mullion ⌂⚓ Db
Peaceful village and old-world harbour. Tunnel through rocks leads to a small beach at low tide. Walk southwards over Mullion Cliff to Predannack Head for commanding view over Mount's Bay. Pass through part of Lizard National Nature Reserve for wide range of heathland and cliff-top plants. Birds include kittiwakes, guillemots, razorbills and shags.

Newlyn ⌂ Bc
Bustling harbour crammed with trawlers. Oldest pier dates from the Middle Ages. New fish quay, opened in 1981, serves busy fish market. Artists have painted Newlyn for decades, and local art gallery has exhibitions of modern paintings and sculptures.

Pendeen ⌂✿❋ Ad
Remote and prosperous tin-mining village on granite-strewn moors. Museum at Geevor Tin Mine and a Mineral and Mining Museum in the village. To the east are Chun Castle, the remains of an Iron Age village, and a quoit or stone tomb.

Penzance ⌂⚓⛵⌂ Bc
Popular resort facing St Michael's Mount across sweep of Mount's Bay. Summer ferry plies between mainland and Isles of Scilly. Birthplace of Sir Humphry Davy, inventor of the miner's safety lamp, whose statue stands outside Market House. Fanciful 1820s Egyptian House in Chapel Street is a National Trust information centre. Subtropical plants near the seafront at Morrab Gardens.

Poldark Mine ✿ Dd
Worked since Roman times and now an underground museum. Experience how tin was mined by candlelight a century ago. Steps descend to a depth of 200ft where chambers contain mining relics. Back on the surface, Cornish beam and hoisting engines, and amusements at Ha'penny Park with boats and mini-car race track.

Porthcurno ⌂♥❋☆ Ac
Home of the Minack open air theatre, constructed on the cliffs with the sea below for a backdrop. On opposite side of bay and a short walk from Treen, Treryn Dinas is a sea-girt Iron Age fort perched on a jagged headland.

Porthleven ❀⚘ Dc
Small town with a surprisingly big harbour set between steeply enclosing wooded hills. Beyond lies the Penrose estate, where a partly 17th-century manor house overlooks The Looe freshwater lake. Grand woodland walks.

St Agnes ⌂♀❋☆ Ef
Patchwork of tiny fields dotted with remains of local mining industry surround the town.

COASTAL DEFENCE *Pendennis Castle, near Falmouth, has fine views across Carrick Roads.*

Helford ⌂ Ec
Creek-side village straight from a picture postcard with thatched roofs, whitewashed walls and gardens bright with flowers. Ferry link to Helford Passage has operated since Middle Ages.

Helston ⌂ Dc
Old stone houses jostle with modern buildings in this market town. Annual Flora Day celebrates the coming of summer with a 'Furry Dance', held on or near May 8. Important port until the 13th century, when a bank of sand and shingle (the Loe Bar) silted up the harbour mouth.

Isles of Scilly ⛵✿⋔⚓▦ Bb
Remote granite islands, islets and rocks, said to be all that remains of King Arthur's legendary Lyonnesse – a kingdom engulfed by the sea. Mild winters yield daffodils in December, and flower-growing is the main source of income. Sea birds, dolphins and seals abound.

Land's End ♀ Ac
Fist of wave-lashed granite tumbling into the sea at the end of Penwith peninsula. Westernmost point of English mainland with Heritage Centre, Cornish cream fudge, craft shops and England's last postbox. Fine view out to sea of Longships lighthouse.

Lizard ⌂♛☆ Db
Narrow lane leads along a windy plateau to a tongue of rocks, marking southern tip of mainland Britain. Spectacular views of Mount's Bay at Lizard Point. On road to nearby Church Cove, ancient church of St Wynwallow has woodwork from the wreck of a Portuguese treasure ship. Cliffs 200ft high rise on either side of Kynance Cove, where sea birds nest in caves, and Devil's Bellows fissure spits out clouds of spray.

Madron ⌂✿⋔✿ Bd
Church of St Maddern was once the parish church of Penzance. Wishing well and ancient chapel along field path to north-west. Men-An-Tol stone, 3 miles off the Morvah road, was the entrance to a prehistoric tomb. Unsurpassed

Watch for grey seals swimming off St Agnes Head. Model dinosaurs and a haunted house at St Agnes Leisure Park.

St Ives 🏛⛱☐ Ce

Stone cottages tumble over each other in a maze of narrow streets. Old-world charm lured artists to this town and famous names include painter Ben Nicholson, sculptress Dame Barbara Hepworth, and potter Bernard Leach. Examples of their work at the Penwith Gallery, Barbara Hepworth Museum and Leach Pottery.

St Just 🏛✿⛩ Ad

Westernmost town in England, rich in antiquities, and a medieval church, and an amphitheatre by Bank Square. A narrow lane twists down to Porth Nanven cove then 1¼ mile walk northwards to Cape Cornwall and its derelict tin mine.

St Levan ⛪ Ac

Finely carved pews inside medieval church dedicated to St Levan, said to have landed at the nearby beach in the 6th or 7th century. Celtic cross outside is older than the church itself.

St Michael's Mount ⛪ Cc

Small granite island rises like a giant sandcastle 300ft from the waters of Mount's Bay, crowned by a 14th-century castle; once a monastery and now a mansion owned by the National Trust. Legends of King Arthur abound. Linked by low-tide causeway or ferry to Marazion, mainland village set among winding streets and palm trees.

Trelissick Garden ❀❦ Fd

Hanging woods sweep down to the water's edge of Carrick Roads, on an estate that is almost made an island by the River Fal and its creeks. Landscaped in the 1820s by Ralph Allen Daniell, who laid out the carriage drives along which a Woodland Walk now runs. A steep, narrow lane from Feock village leads to Loe Beach, launching site for small boats. King Harry Ferry lies across sprawling arm of the River Fal.

Truro ✝🏛✿☐ Fe

The three great spires of Truro Cathedral rise dramatically above a cluster of narrow streets filled with elegant Georgian houses. Inspired by medieval architecture, yet only built at the turn of the century. In the Middle Ages, Truro controlled the country's thriving tin industry. Impressive displays of Cornwall's history at County Museum. A cattle market every Wednesday; river cruises daily in summer.

Zennor ⛪🏛⛩ Bd

Village named after St Senara, with a legendary mermaid carved on seat in the Norman church. Wayside Museum in a disused mill has relics of local life over the last 5000 years. Half a mile northwest is wild and lonely Zennor Head. Half a mile south-east, seven stones capped by a massive slab form the largest Stone Age burial chamber in the country, called Zennor Quoit.

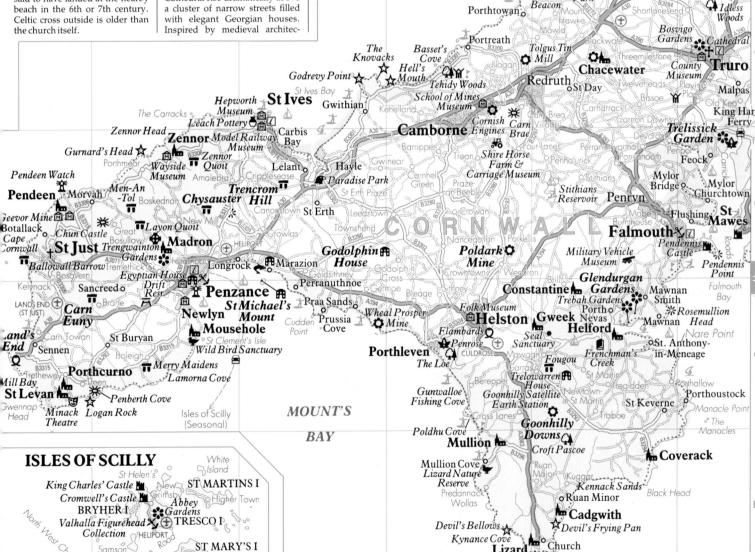

ISLES OF SCILLY

LAND OF ARTHURIAN LEGEND

The old smugglers' coves and pirate villages of Cornwall's southern coast blend into the grand houses, subtropical gardens and mining towns and villages inland, whose industrial prosperity once financed their construction. Ancient Bodmin Moor with its granite tors and tricky marshes sweeps down to the rugged Atlantic coast, where safe, sandy beaches are favoured by surfers and bathers.

Altarnun ⚓🏛 Ef
Stone cottages face an ancient packhorse bridge, linking village to 15th-century church, known as 'Cathedral of the Moors'. Carved bench-ends depict local characters of the time. John Wesley often stayed at a house in Trewint, now a Methodist museum.

Blisland ⚓ Ce
Cluster of Georgian houses and cottages surround village green. Norman and medieval church has richly carved and painted interior. The medieval stone-slab clapper bridge at Bradford, and elaborate rock carvings at Pendrift, celebrate Golden Jubilee of George III.

Bodmin ⚓🏛✝🏛 Cd
Streets of brownstone and granite buildings cluster on edge of Bodmin Moor. Church of St Petroc (15th century) displays the saint's casket, said to contain his bones. Traditional animal breeds at nearby Bodmin Farm Park.

LOW TIDE *The retreating waves at Bedruthan Steps near Mawgan Porth reveal majestic rock stacks. The central formation is known as Queen Bess Rock.*

Bodmin Moor
⚓🏛✝🏛🏛 De
Rolling landscape, scattered with granite boulders, forms the 'roof' of Cornwall. Hut circles, sacred sites and giant tors lie below. Brown Willy, 1375ft, the highest point in Cornwall. Jamaica Inn at Bolventor was made famous by Daphne du Maurier.

Boscastle ⚓ Cg
Graveyard for many ships running for north coast haven. Blowhole in cliffs sends spray booming across harbour in rough weather, echoing up the slate-cottaged village street.

Camelford 🏛🏛 Df
Site of King Arthur's Camelot, according to local legend. Reputed scene of the king's last battle near Slaughter Bridge against Modred, his rebellious nephew. The North Cornwall Museum displays aspects of Cornish life, from fancy lace bonnets to early vacuum cleaners.

Cheesewring ☆ Ee
Remains of engine and boiler houses recall tin and copper-mining days. Mysterious stones nearby: Cheesewring rockpile is a natural phenomenon, while Hurlers megalithic stone circles are said to be men turned to stone for not observing the Lord's Day.

Colliford Lake ⚓🏛 De
Romantic kissing gates, wild and domestic animals, lakeside plants and birdlife. A mile away, Dozmary Pool is where legend tells that Sir Bedivere surrendered King Arthur's sword Excalibur to an emerging hand in the water.

Delabole Slate Quarry ✪ Cf
Largest slate quarry in England, 500ft deep and 1 mile in circumference, worked continuously since Elizabethan times.

Fowey ⚓🏛🏛 Dc
Narrow streets run steeply down to the quays in busy china clay port. Sailors hailed as 'Fowey Gallants' featured in many medieval campaigns. Sir Arthur Quiller-Couch (1863-1944) used Fowey in his novels, and lived at The Haven. Path from Readymoney Cove leads to ruins of St Catherine's Castle, built by Henry VIII.

Lanhydrock 🏛 Cd
Sycamore and beech avenue leads to 17th-century house, rebuilt in grandiose style after 1881 fire. Fine Victorian living in 36 'upstairs' and 'downstairs' rooms.

Lanreath ⚓🏛 Dc
Minor mysteries of country life and language explained in Farm and Folk Museum. For example, 'Codd bottle' invented by Hiram Codd and used for soft drinks, gave rise to 'Codd's wallop'. Craftsmen's tools, farm implements and household equipment.

Lansallos ⚓ Dc
Fascinating 14th-century church in an isolated hamlet; base of pulpit is a pinnacle brought down by lightning in 1923.

Looe ✝🏛 Ec
On sides of a narrow estuary, East and West Looe are joined by a Victorian bridge. West Looe clusters round quayside church of St Nicholas. East Looe has 16th-century guildhall, now a museum. Sanctuary for Amazon woolly monkeys 2 miles east.

Mawgan Porth ☆ Ad
Rocky cove hides remains of a 5th-century settlement. Two miles of sand at Watergate Bay, ideal for surfers. Nearby, steep and slippery Bedruthan Steps, legendary stepping stones of a giant, plunge down from the cliff top to beach.

Mevagissey 🏛⚓ Cb
Ancient fishing port with narrow streets and bustling harbour. Folk museum housed in boatyard recreates old Cornish kitchen with giant cider press. Model railway with more than 2000 models.

Nare Head ✻ Ba
Excellent viewpoint. Between the headland and Veryan, impressive Bronze Age mound of Carne Beacon is legendary burial place of a Cornish king and his ship.

Newquay 🏛⚓Q🏛 Dd
Originally a pilchard port, now popular resort. Beaches, zoo, swimming pools, aquarium and museum. Huer's House, 18th-century pilchard lookout.

Padstow ✝⚓🏛⚓ Be
Picturesque fishing port. The 15th-century church looks down over crooked streets, with houses dating from Middle Ages. May Day celebrations include the famous 'Obby 'Oss.

NAVY DAYS *Nelson's ships once lay off St Just-in-Roseland.*

Pencarrow House 🏛 Ce
Elegant Georgian country mansion, set in 50 acres of woodland gardens, ancestral home of the Molesworth-St Aubyn family. It houses fine collection of paintings, furniture and china.

Polkerris ⚓ Cc
Curving harbour wall, built to embrace a fishing fleet when Polkerris was a port, provides safe bathing. Striped 1832 mariners' beacon crowns Gribben Head.

Polperro ⚓✻ Ec
Strung along a narrow combe, whitewashed houses squeeze together in a fishing village with streets so narrow that traffic is banned. Smuggling museum in cellar of an old cottage. Seafood restaurants and craft shops.

Port Isaac ⚓ Bf
Boats, nets and lobster pots crowd a little harbour. A stream runs through the village between the slate-hung houses with their charming shell-decked gardens. Squeezibelly Alley is one aptly named narrow lane.

Probus ⚓🏛✿ Ab
The 16th-century church has Cornwall's tallest tower; gargoyles lurk beneath pinnacles and hound hunts fox across tower's north face. Garden displays and a children's nature trail at the County Demonstration Gardens. Rare trees and shrubs from around the world in adjoining Trewithen Gardens.

Roche ⚓✻ Bd
Snakes and angels' heads entwine on a Norman font at Church of St Gonandus. A 15th-century hermit's cell and ruined chapel of St Michael crown nearby Roche Rock. Fine view of moorland.

St Austell ✝✻ Cc
Market town and centre of china-clay industry, with a Georgian Quaker Meeting House and an Italianate town hall. Port of Charlestown lies east, dating from 18th century. Anchors and naval guns stand outside visitor centre. Shipwreck display inside.

St Cleer ⚓🏛 Ed
Granite 15th-century building near churchyard houses holy well. A mile north, King Doniert's Stone is thought to record death of a 9th-century Cornish king. A mile north-east is Trethevy Quoit, a prehistoric burial chamber.

St Just-in-Roseland ⚓ Aa
Surrounded by subtropical trees and shrubs, weathered grey stones of 13th-century church look down over a tiny creek. Path through churchyard is flanked by granite tablets carved with verses.

St Keyne ⚓🏛 Ed
Village with one of Europe's finest 'automatic' musical instrument collections. Fairground organs, pianos worked by perforated paper rolls, and a Wurlitzer organ at Paul Corin museum.

St Mawes ⚓🏛 Aa
Fashionable yachting resort. Sheltered harbour becomes a floating forest of masts during holiday season. Castle shaped like a clover leaf built by Henry VIII.

St Neot ⚓ Dd
Attractive village with a church noted for 15th and 16th-century stained glass. Creation window depicts stories of Adam and Eve. Holy well in nearby meadow reached by a riverside path.

St Newlyn East ⚓🏛⚓ Ac
Slumbering village of brown coloured stone high above Newquay. Church of St Newelina, restored 1883, has splendid interior. Engine house of East Wheal Rose Mine once contained the Great Hundred-Inch pumping engine, Cornwall's biggest. Lappa Valley Railway travels along one of Cornwall's oldest track beds.

Tintagel ⚓🏛🏛⚓✻☆ Cf
Legendary seat of King Arthur; ruins on Tintagel Head are of a castle built for Earl of Cornwall in 1145, and of a Celtic monastery. Stained-glass windows of Victorian King Arthur's Hall tell his story, and paths descend to Merlin's Cave. Magical St Nectan's Glen has waterfall and tea garden.

Trenarren ✻ Cb
Secluded hamlet in wooded valley below Black Head, reached by a quarter-mile walk, passing pleasant gardens of stone-built houses and cottages. Stone stile at far end leads to a sheltered cove.

Trerice 🏛 Ac
Authentic Elizabethan manor house, tree-hidden in sheltered valley. Sparkling, mullioned hall window – 576 panes of mostly 16th-century glass. Façade has highly decorative gables.

Trevose Head ✻ Ae
Toll road leads 250ft above sea to a gleaming lighthouse, built 1847 and open to public. Views stretch from St Ives to Lundy Island. Constantine Bay to the south has a vast stretch of sand, ideal for surfing.

NO HIDING PLACE *Veryan's round houses were built without corners to thwart the devil.*

Veryan ⚓ Ba
Quiet village famous for five round, 'Devil-proof' houses, built in early 19th century. Locals believed Satan could not hide in a house without corners.

Wadebridge Be
Oldest working road bridge in Britain, built 1485; piers said to be built on woolpacks. River Camel seen at its best in long walk to Padstow along path following abandoned railway line.

Wheal Martyn ✪ Cc
Built on the site of two old china clay works, Wheal Martyn China Clay Museum tells history of the county's largest industry. Includes Cornwall's largest working water wheel (35ft diameter), pottery and nature trail.

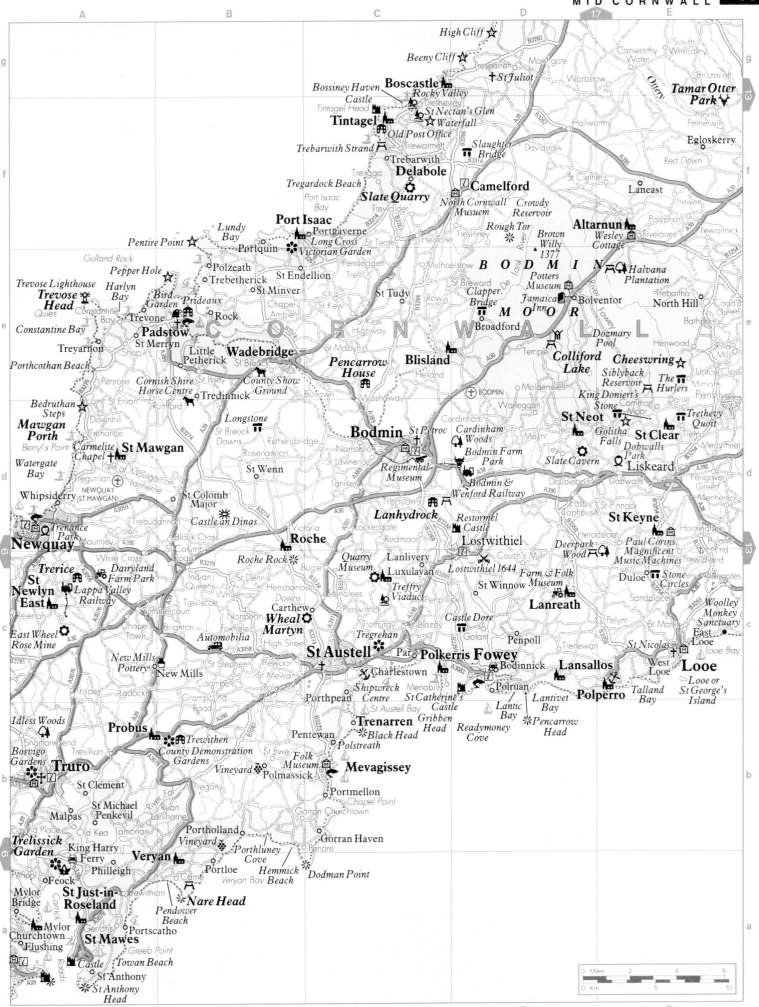

High Cliff · Beeny Cliff · St Juliot · Canworthy Water · Warbstow · Egloskerry · Tamar Otter Park · Ottery · Marhamchurch · Hallworthy · Davidstow · Red Down · Laneast

Boscastle · Bossiney Haven · Castle · Tintagel Head · Rocky Valley · Trethevy · St Nectan's Glen · Waterfall · Old Post Office · Tintagel · Trebarwith Strand · Trewarmett · Trebarwith · Slaughter Bridge · Delabole · North Cornwall Museum · Camelford · St Clether

Tregardock Beach · Slate Quarry · Port Isaac Bay · Trewalder · Crowdy Reservoir · Rough Tor · Brown Willy 1377 · Altarnun · Wesley Cottage · Fivelanes · Polyphant · Trewassick

Lundy Bay · Pentire Point · Portgaverne · Port Isaac · Long Cross · Victorian Garden · St Teath · Helstone · Michaelstow · BODMIN · Potters Museum · Jamaica Inn · Bolventor · North Hill · Trebartha

Pepper Hole · Polzeath · Portquin · Trebetherick · St Endellion · St Minver · St Kew Highway · Row · Clapper Bridge · MOOR · Broadford · Halvana Plantation · Trevose Lighthouse · Trevose Head · Harlyn Bay · Bird Garden · Prideaux · Trevone · Rock · St Kew · Chapel Amble · Temple · Dozmary Pool · Cheesewring · The Hurlers · Penslynn

Constantine Bay · Padstow · St Merryn · Little Petherick · Wadebridge · St Breward · St Mabyn · Blisland · Helland · Colliford Lake · Siblyback Reservoir · King Doniert's Stone · Trethevy Quoit · St Clear

Treyarnon · Porthcothan Beach · Cornish Shire Horse Centre · Tredinnick · County Show Ground · Burlawn · Washaway · Cardinham · St Neot · Golitha Falls · Dobwalls Park · Liskeard

Bedruthan Steps · Mawgan Porth · Carmelite Chapel · St Mawgan · Longstone · St Breock Downs · Rutherbridge · BODMIN · St Petroc · Cardinham Woods · Bodmin Farm Park · Slate Cavern

Watergate Bay · Whipsiderry · Trenance Park · St Colomb Major · Castle an Dinas · St Wenn · Regimental Museum · Bodmin & Wenford Railway · Restormel Castle · St Keyne · Paul Corin's Magnificent Music Machines · Duloe · Stone Circles

Newquay · Trerice · St Newlyn East · Dairyland Farm Park · Lappa Valley Railway · St Dennis · Roche · Roche Rock · Lanhydrock · Lanlivery · Lostwithiel · Deerpark Wood

East Wheel Rose Mine · Quarry Museum · Luxulyan · Treffry Viaduct · Lostwithiel 1644 · Farm & Folk Museum · St Winnow · Lanreath · Stone Circles · Woolley Monkey Sanctuary East

New Mills Pottery · New Mills · Carthew · Wheal Martyn · Automobilia · Castle Dore · Penpoll · St Nicolas · East Looe

St Austell · Charlestown · Par · Polkerris · Fowey · Bodinnick · Lansallos · West Looe · Looe · Looe or St George's Island

Idless Woods · Bosvigo Gardens · Truro · Probus · Trewithen County Demonstration Gardens · Shipwreck Centre · St Catherine's Castle · Polruan · Polperro · Talland Bay

Trenarren · Black Head · Pentewan · Polstreath · Gribben Head · Readymoney Cove · Lantivet Bay · Pencarrow Head

Trelissick Garden · King Harry Ferry · Philleigh · Veryan · Portholland Vineyard · Portluney Cove · Folk Museum · Polmassick · Mevagissey · Portmellon · Chapel Point · Gorran Haven · Hemmick Beach · Dodman Point

St Just-in-Roseland · Nare Head · Pendower Beach · Portscatho · St Mawes · Castle · St Anthony · St Anthony Head · Greeb Point · Towan Beach

Mylor Bridge · Mylor Churchtown · Flushing · Feock

Miles 0 2 4 6 · Km 0 5 10

Antony ⌂♨ Cc
Village within strolling distance of Torpoint ferry. Antony House is where Richard Carew wrote his *Survey of Cornwall* in 1602. Furnishings, books and portraits bring to life the Carew family.

Bere Ferrers ⌂ Cd
Remote village, famous for its silver mines in the Middle Ages, situated on the River Tavy. Poignant tombstones in peaceful churchyard by river bear the inscription 'Cholera 1849'. The 14th-century church has an exquisite knight's tomb, Norman font and original glass.

Bolberry Down ☆ Ea
Expanse of turf, gorse and bracken standing 400ft above sea level, with superb views along coast to mouth of English Channel. Fortified during the Iron Age, Bolt Tail headland has witnessed many shipwrecks.

Brent Tor ✝ Cf
Stout tower of 12th-century St Michael of the Rock dominates the skyline, standing 1130ft up on a windswept volcanic crag. Stiff walk to summit offers one of the West Country's broadest views.

Buckland in the Moor ⌂ Fe
Thatched, stone-built cottages perch on slopes above River Dart. No numbers on church clock, instead letters spell out MY DEAR MOTHER – a memorial placed there by a local landowner, William Whitley, in the late 1920s.

DEVON THATCH *Tiny Buckland in the Moor slumbers among groves of beeches in sheltered hollows.*

Buckland Monachorum ⌂✿🏛 Cd
Pleasant village where Sir Francis Drake made his home in 1581 after circling the globe. Once a 13th-century monastery, Buckland Abbey still has the bones of a church. Fine Jacobean panelling and Armada relics in the Great Hall, including Drake's Drum.

Castle Drogo 🏛 Fg
Melodramatic castle, designed by Lutyens and completed 1930, surrounded by miles of woodland walks above wild Teign gorge. Fierce heraldic lion guards tower entrance to a world of vaulted ceilings and arched passages.

Chagford ⌂ Ff
Tudor and Georgian houses cluster round a 16th-century bridge over the Teign. Name means 'ford in a gorse-covered country'.

Cotehele House 🏛✄ Cd
One of England's finest medieval and Tudor manor houses, home of the Edgcumbe family for 600

DARTMOOR'S BARREN BEAUTY

Granite rocks and tors, rearing up from barren bogs and heather moors, cover the surface of Dartmoor. Once home of many thriving prehistoric communities, it is now an area of charming villages, old churches and wild lanes. Tumbling moorland streams and rivers are crossed by bridges built in medieval times. Southwards is the historic port of Plymouth, cradle of Britain's maritime greatness.

MOORLAND WATER *Burrator Reservoir in Dartmoor's heart glimmers behind Sheepstor village, near Meavy.*

years. Rooms decorated with tapestries and furnishings dating from 16th century. Warehouse museum at the nearby Cotehele Quay recalls bustling days of river transport in the early 1800s.

Dartmeet 🚶🏛 Ee
Famous Dartmoor beauty spot where East and West Dart rivers meet. Medieval rough-stone bridge crosses bubbling East Dart.

Dartmoor Wildlife Park ⋎ Dc
Gaze in safety at lions, tigers, pumas and timber wolves, or have a 'close encounter' with gentler creatures such as lambs, rabbits, calves and raccoons. Birds of prey and hawking demonstrations.

Dewerstone Rock ☆ Dd
Craggy rib of granite frowns down upon a wooded boulder-strewn gorge. Fine views at meeting of Plym and Meavy rivers.

Drewsteignton ⌂ Fg
Picture-book village of thatched cottages perched above the Teign gorge, spanned by Tudor bridge.

Grimspound 🏛 Ff
Well-preserved Bronze Age village, huddled in a fold of the moor. Sherlock Holmes hid here in the *Hound of the Baskervilles*.

Launceston 🏰🏛🚂 Bf
Hilly old-world market town and ancient capital of Cornwall. Medieval remains include ramparts of a 13th-century castle. Lavish carvings cover Church of St Mary Magdalene, and elegant Lawrence House is a local history museum. See 100-year-old locomotives at the Steam Railway.

Lydford 🚶🏰⌂ ⋎ Df
Secluded village dominated by a castle built in 1195; it was used to imprison offenders against local forest and Stannary laws. Dramatic walk beside seething waters at eerie Lydford Gorge, thickly wooded with oaks and dense with ferns. White Lady waterfall slides 100ft down a rocky chute to join River Lyd below. Good place for spotting herons, dippers and woodpeckers.

Meavy ⌂🚶 Dd
Tiny, timeless village in a fold of the moors. Shattered remains of a leaning oak, said to be Devon's last 'dancing tree', was focal point for pagan rites. A Tudor house, adjoining church, belonged to the Drake family. Dartmoor's diverse scenery is strikingly apparent at Burrator Reservoir.

Merrivale Hut Circles 🏛 De
Hallowed stone coffins at an ancient hut site recall a time when prehistoric tribes lived here.

Morwellham 🚶⌂ Cd
Britain's greatest copper port until 1900, revived as a living museum where staff play the part of Victorian workers. Meet the local blacksmith and call in at a miner's cottage. Restored quays and a Victorian farmyard with old-fashioned animal breeds.

Mount Edgcumbe 🏛⋎ Cc
Landscaped park covering 865 acres of formal gardens with temples and a ruined folly, unspoilt coast and scenery. Miles of footpaths and spectacular views over Plymouth Sound. House dates from 1547; gutted by incendiary bombs in 1941, rebuilt in 1958-60.

National Shire Horse Centre
🐎 Dc
Mighty Shires parade three times daily; shining horse brasses and decorated show harnesses on display in the Old Stables, dating back to 1772. Potters and saddlers work in craft centre, Old English game fowl in aviary, and nature trail along Yealm.

Newton Ferrers ⌂ Db
Eye-catching old houses add character to a narrow street running down to Yealm estuary, in a setting of great beauty. Fine cliff-top walks and fishing trips.

Plymouth
🏛🏰✝🖾🎨⋏ Cc
Naval city famous for intrepid seafarers, much rebuilt since the war. Barbican's historic Sutton Harbour still recalls old Plymouth, watched over by a Royal Citadel. Old warehouses on the quayside are now bustling shops and restaurants. Elizabethan house, furnished in period style with a staircase built around an old ship's mast, evokes life in the days of Drake. Merchant's house is a museum of city's social history. Dominated by John Smeaton's 1759 Eddystone lighthouse, the Hoe provides panoramic views of Plymouth Sound, and is where Drake played bowls before defeating the Spanish Armada in 1588.

Postbridge 🏛 Ee
Hamlet noted for medieval stone-slab bridge. Broadun Ring lies 1¼ miles north-west; a prehistoric walled pound enclosing group of hut circles, probably used to pen sheep and cattle. South, Broadun Pound is the largest known prehistoric enclosure on Dartmoor.

Rame Head ✳ Cb
Lofty headland crowned by a ruined chapel, offers breathtaking views; Plymouth and Devon to the east, Whitesand Bay to the west.

St Germans ⌂🏛 Bc
Colour-washed cottages and gabled almshouses overlook small village harbour. Norman church, built on the site of a Saxon cathedral, has Norman doorway and fine east window designed by Pre-Raphaelite artist Burne-Jones.

Saltash 🏛✿ Cc
Gateway to Cornwall spanned by Brunel's railway bridge (1859) and Tamar road bridge (1961). Narrow streets, riverside walks, and part-Norman church.

Saltram House 🏛 Dc
Magnificent mid-18th-century mansion with Tudor and Stuart remains. Lavish interior demonstrates skills of such artists as designer Robert Adam and painter Sir Joshua Reynolds. Great Kitchen contains relics of downstairs life two centuries ago.

Tamar Otter Park ⋎ Ag
Otters play in natural enclosures, and deer roam free along a nature trail with picnic areas. Peacocks and a waterfowl lake.

Tavistock Ce
Market town with largely Victorian character. Sir Francis Drake was baptised in the parish church. Victorian Gothic buildings of sea-green volcanic stone, and ruins of 10th-century Benedictine abbey.

Wembury ⌂⋏ Db
Church on the cliff edge with tiny, romantic churchyard inclining to sea. Bay is a marine conservation area where a rich variety of plants and creatures inhabit a tidal strip.

Widecombe in the Moor
⌂🏛 Fe
Old Uncle Tom Cobleigh and all ride for ever on the elaborately carved sign on the green. It commemorates *Widdicombe Fair*, the song that made the village famous. Fair still held on second Tuesday in September.

SEVEN UP *The old song is recalled by Tom Pearce's overladen, plodding mare at Widecombe in the Moor.*

Wistman's Wood ⋎⋏ Ee
Twisted trunks and gnarled branches of centuries-old oaks force through the lichen-covered rocks in an eerie remnant of the ancient Dartmoor Forest. Now an 8 acre nature reserve.

Yelverton 🏛 Dd
Unusual Paperweight Centre houses a kaleidoscopic array of antique and modern glass paperweights from around the world.

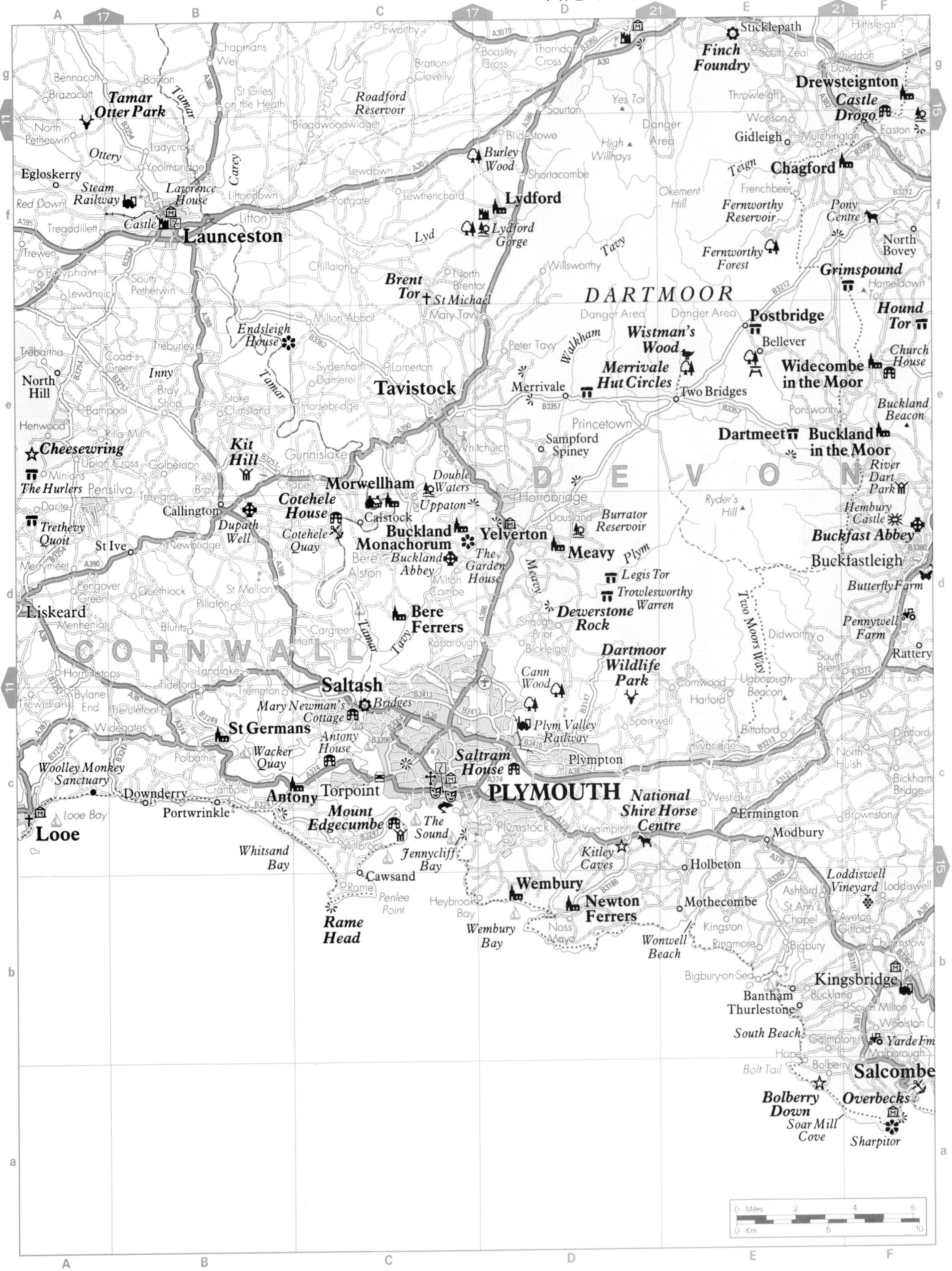

A 17 B C 17 D 21 E 21 F

g

Eworthy
Chapmans Well
Boasley Cross
Thornbury Cross
A3079
Bennacott
Brazacott
Boyton
St Giles on the Heath
Bratton Clovelly
A30
Sourton
Yes Tor
Stickepath
Finch Foundry
South Zeal
Hittisleigh
Whiddon Down
Tamar Otter Park
North Petherwin
Ottery
Ladycross
Yeolmbridge
Broadwoodwidger
Roadford Reservoir
Bridestowe
High Willhays
Danger Area
Throwleigh
Gidleigh
Murchington
Down
Easton
Drewsteignton
Castle Drogo

f

Egloskerry
Red Down
A395
Tregadillett
Trewen
Steam Railway
Lawrence House
Litton
Litttondown
Lewdown
Lewtrenchard
Potgate
Burley Wood
Shortacombe
Okement Hill
Wonson
Chagford
Frenchbeer
Fernworthy Reservoir
Pony Centre
North Bovey
Castle
Launceston
Lifton
Lyd
Lydford
Lydford Gorge
Willsworthy
Tavy
DARTMOOR
Fernworthy Forest
Grimspound
Hameldown Tor

e

Trebartha
North Hill
Henwood
Rilla Mill
Bathpool
Brent Tor
† St Michael
North Brentor
Mary Tavy
Endsleigh House
Milton Abbot
Sydenham Damerel
Lamerton
Tavistock
Peter Tavy
Walkham
Wistman's Wood
Merrivale Hut Circles
Merrivale
Two Bridges
Princetown
Sampford Spiney
Danger Area
Ponsworthy
Postbridge
Bellever
Widecombe in the Moor
Hound Tor
Church House
Buckland Beacon
Dartmeet
Buckland in the Moor

d

Cheesewring
Minions
The Hurlers
Pensilva
Darite
Trethevy Quoit
St Ive
Merrymeet
A390
Pengover
Quethiock
Kit Hill
St Ann's Chapel
Gunnislake
Calstock
Morwellham
Cotehele House
Cotehele Quay
Callington
Dupath Well
Newbridge
Pillaton
St Mellion
Double Waters
Uppaton
Bere Alston
Buckland Monachorum
Buckland Abbey
Milton Combe
The Garden House
Yelverton
Horrabridge
Dousland
Meavy
Burrator Reservoir
Ryder's Hill
Whitchurch
DEVON
River Dart Park
Hembury Castle
Buckfast Abbey
Buckfastleigh
Butterfly Farm

Liskeard
Menheniot
Blunts
Cargreen
Roborough
Plym
Legis Tor
Trowlesworthy Warren
Dewerstone Rock
Shaugh Prior
Bickleigh
Dartmoor Wildlife Park
Cornwood
Harford
Ugborough Beacon
Two Moors Way
Didworthy
South Brent
Pennywell Farm
Rattery

c

CORNWALL
Tideford
Landrake
Hatt
Saltash
Bridges
Mary Newman's Cottage
Tavy
Cann Wood
Plym Valley Railway
Plympton
Sparkwell
Bittaford
Ivybridge
North Huish
Bickham Bridge
Diptford
Bere Ferrers
Woolley Monkey Sanctuary
Downderry
Portwrinkle
Crafthole
St Germans
Wacker Quay
Antony House
Antony
Torpoint
Saltram House
PLYMOUTH
Plymstock
Plympton
National Shire Horse Centre
Ermington
Modbury
Holbeton
Brownston
Westlake

Looe
Looe Bay
Millbrook
Mount Edgecumbe
The Sound
Jennycliff Bay
Whitsand Bay
Cawsand
Rame
Penlee Point
Heybrook Bay
Kitley Caves
Mothecombe
Kingston
Ringmore
Bigbury
Loddiswell Vineyard
Loddiswell
Aveton Gifford
Churchstow

b

Rame Head
Wembury
Wembury Bay
Noss Mayo
Newton Ferrers
Wonwell Beach
Bigbury-on-Sea
Ashford
St Ann's Chapel
Kingsbridge
Bantham
Thurlestone
Buckland
South Milton
Woolston
South Beach
Galmpton
Malborough
Yarde Fm
Salcombe
Hope
Bolberry
Bolberry Down
Bolt Tail
Soar Mill Cove
Overbecks
Sharpitor

a

0 Miles 2 4 6
0 Km 5 10

SUNNY COAST AND RUGGED MOOR

The palms that flourish along the sun-trap curve of the South Devon coast give way to gorse and bracken on the windswept heights of Dartmoor, where weird formations of raw granite strike through the thin soil. Man has lived on coast and moor for thousands of years in caves, abbeys, castles – and some of the prettiest villages in Britain.

A La Ronde 🏠 Df
French name for an 18th-century cottage designed with echoes of a medieval Italian church by two English spinsters. Narrow stairway above octagonal hall contains Gothic grottoes. Note Regency furniture and seaweed collages.

Ashburton 🏛 Ad
'Gateway to Dartmoor'. Fine 17th and 18th-century slate-hung buildings include a shop with slates patterned like playing cards left over from a previous existence as a gaming house.

Becka Falls ☆ Af
Clear brook waters cascade for 70ft over a jumble of boulders, forming tree-fringed pools ideal for paddling.

Berry Pomeroy Castle 🏰 Bd
Romantic double ruin: Elizabethan mansion enclosed by ruined walls, towers and gatehouse of a 13th-century castle. The castle was built by the Pomeroy family who came over in 1066 with William the Conqueror.

beyond. Great Hall with carved Renaissance screen; chapel, and buttery and kitchen still with original contents. Surviving 15th-century east wing makes this one of the best examples of domestic Gothic in the West Country.

Brixham 🎣🏛⚓ Cc
Ancient fishing port, still busy. Town museum includes maritime mementos. Aquarium displays living examples of creatures for which local fishermen risked life and limb. Replica of Drake's ship *Golden Hind* is floating museum, moored to quay.

Raleigh. Water power at the Otterton Mill Centre, local flavour at the Fairlynch Arts Centre.

Cockington 🏠 Bd
Perfect Devon village. Old Forge (14th century) sells horse brasses; Old Mill, beside the village pond, sells cream teas.

Compton Castle 🏠 Bd
Buttressed walls pierced by arrow slits, and chutes once used to shower intruders with stones. Home of the Gilberts, of whom Sir Humphrey founded Britain's first American colony in 1583.

Dawlish ⚓🏛 Ce
Regency and Victorian houses turn their backs on the sea to face Dawlish Water where black swans swim. North is Dawlish Warren, a 500 acre nature reserve.

Dittisham 🏠 Bc
Famed for plums and cider. Stone and thatch cottages climb steeply from Dart estuary at its widest point, where ferry crosses river. Church with Norman font and carved pulpit.

Dunsford 🏠⚓ Bf
Village in Dartmoor National Park with thatched cottages and parish church with striking monument to Sir Thomas Fulford. Nature reserve runs for 2 miles along south bank of River Teign.

Exeter 🏛⚓✝🎣♕ Cg
Bold remnants of Roman town walls, a Guildhall dating from 1160, and a Maritime Museum on England's first ship canal. The Royal Albert Memorial Museum lives up to its name – a Victorian confection in cream and buff stone; gallery of superb Exeter silver. Rougemont House displays costumes and lace in Georgian rooms. Network of medieval passages under city once carried water; now dry, and can be toured. Norman cathedral with two massive towers rising from a green traffic-ringed oasis. Worn stone angels outside on the west front and coloured musical angels inside on the Minstrels' Gallery.

Exmouth 🏛 Df
Holiday resort, popular since 18th century. Badly damaged in last war but some historic buildings survive, including terrace of Georgian houses. Long sandy shore, files of neat beach huts and splendid promenade. Working exhibits at The Country Life Museum.

by floodlight. Flint axes and tools found here, now displayed in Torquay Museum.

Kingsbridge 🏛🏠 Ab
Old town with Georgian houses and Elizabethan arcade. Victorian building with onion-shaped clock tower serves as town hall, theatre and market. Miniature railway takes passengers on a half-mile journey.

Lustleigh 🏠 Af
Creeper-clad cottages of Dartmoor granite thick with thatch hem in 13th-century church in matching stone. Inside recline effigies of knights and a lady.

WARM SPOT *Lustleigh huddles in on itself, a shelter from the moor.*

Newton Abbot ⚓✝ Be
A 'new town' that is seven centuries old; part of it once belonged to Torre Abbey, hence the name 'Abbot'. Lone tower of St Leonard's Church stands in centre; rest demolished in 1836. Earls of Devon built Devon Square and Italian-style Courtenay Park in mid-19th century.

Overbecks ❀🏛 Aa
Olives, palms and the camphor tree all flourish in gardens which bring a Mediterranean touch to the Kingsbridge estuary. In the house are collections of birds' eggs, butterflies and shells.

Paignton 🏠🏠 Bd
Sewing-machine tycoon Isaac Singer built 100-room Oldway Mansion, partly modelled on Versailles. Zoological and botanical gardens cover 75 acres.

Powderham Castle 🏠 Cf
Grandiose, converted castle with portraits of the Courtenays, Earls of Devon, who have lived there for 600 years.

Prawle Point ☆ Aa
Southernmost tip of Devon. Prawle is derived from the Old English for 'lookout' – splendid viewpoint for Channel shipping, migrant birds, and butterflies.

Salcombe 🎣 Aa
Winding creeks and inlets round a fine natural harbour. Americans who sailed from Salcombe for the Second World War D-Day landings are commemorated by a plaque in Normandy Way.

Shaldon 🏠⚓ Ce
Colour-washed cottages line a maze of narrow streets above the Teign estuary. Ness Cove reached

WALKING COUNTRY *A couple of miles east of Salcombe harbour, the South-West Coast Path provides magnificent views along the cliffs towards Pig's Nose, Ham Stone, Gammon Head and Prawle Point.*

Bicton Park ❀ Df
Visit the past, present and future in a single afternoon: the past in World of Yesterday museum; the future in World of Tomorrow display; the present on a train ride taking visitors through woods and gardens.

Bovey Tracey 🏠✝🏛♕⛪ Be
Little town, pronounced 'buvvy'. Restored water wheel stands near 15th-century parish church, founded as penance by one of Thomas Becket's murderers; beautiful rood screen and Jacobean monuments. Second parish church, on other side of river, is Victorian Gothic with lovely mosaics. Longhorn cattle and Exmoor ponies at Parke Rare Breeds Farm.

Bradley Manor 🏠 Be
Medieval house lies in the Lemon valley and stands in sweeping parkland with open country

Brunel Atmospheric Railway ♕ Cf
Pump house at Starcross recalls Isambard Kingdom Brunel's Atmospheric Railway. Built in 1840s; trains powered by atmospheric pressure and vacuum created in pipe between rails. Railway relics and working model powered by vacuum cleaners – on which visitors may ride.

Buckfast Abbey ✝ Ad
Just six monks built this lofty replica of a 12th-century Cistercian abbey. It took them 31 years. Fine mosaic floors and a magnificent altar. Today's monks make wine, extract honey, and sell both.

Budleigh Salterton 🏛🏛 Df
Holidaymakers rub shoulders with fishermen as they land catches at this 19th-century resort. Red cliffs fringe moors enclosing thatched manor house at Hayes Barton, birthplace of Sir Walter

Dartington Hall ❀♕ Ad
Beautiful terraced gardens open to public, as is the Cider Press Centre, now home to craft shops.

Dartmouth 🏛♕⛵🏛 Bc
Warships, trawlers, yachts and ferries fill the Dart estuary. Britannia Royal Naval College crowns the scene. A 15th-century castle guards the harbour entrance. Dartmouth Museum, in elegant 17th-century house, has displays honouring Devon's mariners – Drake, Raleigh, Gilbert – and the Pilgrim Fathers. Local hero Thomas Newcomen, of steam engine fame, has a building to himself.

Dart Valley Railway 🚂⛪ Ad
Puffing engines and gleaming coaches keep the steam age alive between Totnes and Buckfastleigh. Exotic butterflies and moths at Buckfast Butterfly Farm.

DARTMOUTH'S DEFENCE *The castle's hulk still stands solidly at the harbour's mouth.*

Kent's Cavern ☆ Cd
Some 250,000 years ago, primitive man occupied these caves. Now modern man can see their beauty

by Smugglers' Tunnel. Above the tunnel entrance is Shaldon Wildlife Trust, home for small mammals and exotic birds.

Slapton Ley ☙ Bb
Wildfowl and rare marsh birds find sanctuary in 270 acre freshwater lake, shut off from sea by Slapton Sands. Monument commemorates 639 US soldiers killed when German E-boats ran into a force using sands to rehearse Normandy landings.

Stoke Gabriel ⛪ Bc
Hillside village has medieval church with Norman tower reached by cobbled walk beyond local inn. Enormous yew tree propped up in churchyard is said to be about a thousand years old.

Teignmouth 🏛 Ce
Small ships negotiate swift currents to reach the quay, from which Dartmoor granite was shipped to build old London Bridge in 1831. Victorian and Regency houses overlook beach of dark red sand crossed by a pier.

Topsham 🏛 Cf
Pink and white cottages with Dutch gables and bow windows line narrow streets of village on peninsula in the Exe estuary. Museum features ecology of estuary and history of shipbuilding in this former port.

Torquay 🏛 ☙ ⚓ ☆ Cd
Palm trees and a mild climate give Torquay a Mediterranean atmosphere. Yachts and cabin cruisers crowd the harbour first developed when monks from Torre Abbey built a quay. Abbey, now incorporated in a Georgian mansion, houses art gallery. Tithe barn held Armada prisoners in 1588.

Totnes 🏰 🏛 ⚓ Bd
Tudor boom town on the River Dart where locals dress the part each summer Tuesday. Lovingly restored Elizabethan merchant's home is Totnes Museum.

Tuckenhay ⚓ Bc
A 'new town' with restored cottages and warehouses, founded in 1806 by a Mr Tucker to mill paper and ship roadstone. He also built a gasworks – a year before London did.

Ugbrooke House 🏛 Be
Ancestral home of the Lords Clifford of Chudleigh. Built towards end of 18th century by Robert Adam in romantic castle-like style. Magnificent collection of embroidery, portraits, silverware, uniforms and furniture.

Wheel Craft Centre 🏛 Be
Outbuildings around courtyard of old flour mill at Chudleigh now converted into workshops. Visitors can see craftsmen and craftswomen making stained glass, pottery, furniture, jewellery, shoes and clothes – all for sale. The 20ft diameter water wheel and mill machinery are all in working order.

Yarner Wood ☘ ☙ Ae
Nature trails thread 370 acres of bird-haunted oak woodland patched with moorland.

Appledore ⚓ De
Pretty as its name. North Devon Maritime Museum charts a nautical past but traditions continue, particularly shipbuilding. Rivers Taw and Torridge meet here creating a muddy estuary. A ferry sails to Instow opposite.

Barnstaple ⛪✤ Ee
Ancient 'capital' of North Devon. Partly 14th-century parish church has twisted wooden spire; colonnaded Queen Anne's Walk, built 1609, is where merchants sealed deals. Museum of local life housed in a 14th-century chapel.

Bideford ⛪ Dd
Busy quay but not as booming as in Elizabethan times. Steep, narrow medieval streets such as Gunstone and Buttgarden. Medieval bridge across the Torridge has 24 arches. Horwood, 3 miles away, has an interesting church with 15th-century glass.

Braunton †⛪⚓ De
Carved 16th-century bench ends in St Brannock's Church are among finest in country. To the south-west are Braunton Burrows nature reserve, a lunar landscape of sand dunes noted for rare plants, and the 3 mile stretch of Saunton Sands.

Buck's Mills ⚓ Cd
Narrow street of whitewashed cottages facing a shingle beach. Curious ivy-covered outcrops on the hillside are legacy of 19th-century lime kiln.

Bude ⛪✿⚓ Bb
Extensive sands and white-topped waves make Bude a surfer's paradise. Local museum tells dramatic story of 19th-century shipwrecks. Walks by Bude Canal, once navigable for 35 miles. Bude Castle, built 1830, is council offices.

SHOW PLACE *The cobbled main street of Clovelly drops steeply to the edge of the sheltered harbour.*

Clovelly ⚓⚒ Cd
Perfect Devon village oozes charm as thick as clotted cream. Cottages decked with flowers line steep, narrow streets where donkeys and sledges are only traffic. Half-mile hike to harbour. A hill-fort stands on cliffs 400ft above sea.

Coombe Valley ⚓✤ Bc
Tranquil wooded country around thatched hamlet of Coombe, with nature trails and disused water mill of 1842. Stream meanders to pebbled bay at Duckpool.

ROCKY RAMPARTS ABOVE THE SEA

The coast from Ilfracombe to Bude is a spectacular sequence of towering cliffs. While the shoreline is often rocky, there are also long stretches of hard, flat sand where surfers ride the Atlantic rollers and the bucket-and-spade brigade dig in. Just behind the cliffs are sheltered valleys where thatched villages slumber, historic towns and remote stretches of moorland.

HANGMAN'S VIEW *Boats anchor in Water Mouth, watched over by the rounded 716ft hump of Little Hangman.*

Crackington Haven ⚓ Aa
Staggering views from cliff path above shingle and sand beach. Ancient graves in St Genny's churchyard are a reminder of men and ships lost over the centuries on this spectacular but cruel coast.

Croyde ⚓⛪ De
Thatched cottages shelter behind dunes. Unusual gem, rock and shell museum includes giant clams from South Pacific. Miles of sand at Woolacombe and Putsborough reveal why this is called the Golden Coast.

Docton Mill ✿✤ Bd
Gardens and woodlands surround a working water mill from 1249, with streams, ponds, shrubs and a bog garden.

Frithelstock ⚓✤ Dc
Cheeky carvings on parish church's medieval pews show two priests sticking out their tongues. North Devon's only monastic ruin lies next to the church; the west front of a 13th-century Augustinian priory.

Great Torrington ✿ Dc
Ancient market town on a cliff top above River Torridge. Superb views across Devon countryside in an area made famous by Henry Williamson's book *Tarka the Otter*. Charming market square. Glassware blowing at Dartington Glass. Viewing gallery and displays.

Hartland ⚓ Bd
Pretty village of stone-and-slate cottages lies 3 miles inland between two wooded valleys. Clock above chapel door is dated 1622 – the oldest in North Devon.

Hartland Abbey ⛪ Bd
Remains of a 12th-century monastery, greatly added to in later periods. Given by Henry VIII to William Abbott, 'seargeant of ye cellar' in 1546. Still a private home, in same family.

Hartland Point ☆ Bd
Sheer, 325ft cliff on coastline battered by Atlantic gales. Spine-tingling, even when the sea is benign. Known to Romans as the 'Promontory of Hercules'. Toll path leads to lighthouse.

Hartland Quay ⚓⚓ Bd
At foot of fearsome cliffs is 16th-century harbour. Museum tells of smuggling and seafaring. Nearby in Stoke is St Nectan's Church, whose 128ft tower was a landmark for sailors. Path leads to Speke's Mill Mouth, a bay with a waterfall cascading to pebble beach.

Hele ⚓⛪ Ef
Fully restored water mill, dating back to 1525, produces stoneground flour for sale. Hele Bay, less crowded than nearby Ilfracombe, has a shingle-scattered sand beach, flanked by rocks.

Henna Cliff ☆ Bc
Highest sheer drop of any sea cliff in England, apart from Beachy Head. Views north beyond Hartland Point and Lundy Island to Pembroke coast, and south-west along Cornish coast.

Ilfracombe ⛪⚓⚒ Ef
Busy resort around old harbour with a dash of elegance. Former life recalled in medieval Chapel of St Nicholas, where a light has guided mariners for some 650 years. Exhibits at Ilfracombe museum range from a turtle to a turret clock. Armour and period furniture at romantic 11th-century Chambercombe Manor. Shingle beaches. Base for golfing, boating and fishing.

SAFE HOME *Ilfracombe's hill-top Chapel of St Nicholas has burned a guiding light for sailors for 650 years.*

Jungleland ✿ Ee
See familiar domestic pot plants such as cacti, rubber trees, cheese plants and weeping figs growing under glass.

Launcells ⚓ Bb
Village in fold of an elmy valley boasts one of Cornwall's least spoiled church interiors. Rustic and unrestored, St Andrew has richly carved bench ends and 15th-century tiles.

Lee ⚓ Df
Wooded combe with houses tucked in canyons or on valley peaks, in sight of Morte Point headland. Church of St Matthew, built 1837, has interior full of black, Jacobean carved oak.

Lundy Island ⚓⛴ Af
Puffin island with grey seals, sika deer, wild goats and Soay sheep. Cliffs soaring to 400ft with superb views of England, Wales and the Atlantic. The island boat sails from Bideford.

Marhamchurch ⚓ Bb
Hill-top village of whitewashed stone piled about a glorious 14th-century church, with cleverly constructed chequerboard slate floor.

Marwood Hill ✿ Ee
Home-grown beauties such as roses and arum lilies vie for attention with Australasian exotica in a garden created by damming a stream to form a series of lakes.

Millook Haven ☆ Ab
The strata of the cliffs above the small cove have been forced into contorted undulations. Cliff-top walks among dwarf oaks from here to Chipman Strand.

Mortehoe ⚓ Df
Village set on a steep hill above Woolacombe. Its 13th-century church has bench ends carved with sea monsters. Path leads to jutting headland of Morte Point, towering above treacherous reefs and once haunt of wreckers.

Morwenstow ⚓ Bc
Isolated village, also known as Hawker Country after its 19th-century eccentric poet-priest, Robert Stephen Hawker (1803-75). Ancient church, sheltered by wind-bent trees. Vicarage chimneys are copies of church towers.

Rosemoor ✿ Ec
Lady Anne Palmer spent 30 years creating fine garden around her country home. Splendid roses.

Stratton Bb
Narrow streets of thatched cottages swing steeply uphill. Near top is one of the West Country's most typical inns, *The Tree*; it dates from 13th century and has timbers taken from shipwrecks.

Tamar Lakes ⚓ Bc
Placid man-made inland waters. Upper Lake reservoir with surrounding woods. Lower Lake is reed-wrapped and wilder, now a wildfowl reserve. Bench ends in handsome church at nearby Kilkhampton depict country life.

Tapeley Park ✿ Dd
Exquisite William and Mary house faces the sea over terraced Italian gardens with rare plants and woodland walks. Fine 18th-century ceilings and collections of porcelain and furniture.

Water Mouth ⛪ Ef
Castellated Watermouth Castle, built 1825, overlooks narrow inlet, bright with boats. Streams flow seawards over sand-and-shingle beach. Wealth of entertainment at the castle, including model railway, cycle museum, smugglers' dungeons, mechanical music demonstrations, and display of cider-making equipment.

Welcombe ⚓⚓ Bc
Handful of Tudor cottages in the furthest corner of Devon, remote bleak hills and thickly wooded valleys. Tiny church has a screen with primitive carvings, probably the oldest in country. Rough beach and spectacular rocky coast at Welcombe Mouth.

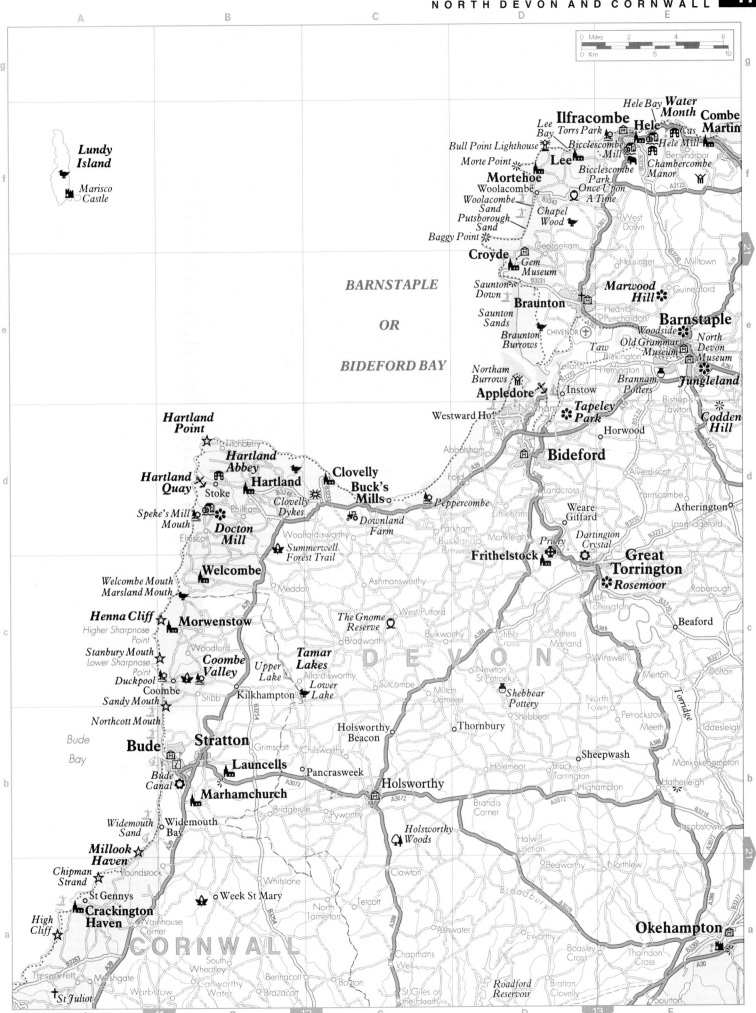

Lundy Island

Marisco Castle

BARNSTAPLE

OR

BIDEFORD BAY

Hele Bay **Water Month**
Ilfracombe **Hele** **Combe Martin**
Lee Bay Torrs Park
Bull Point Lighthouse Bicclescombe Mill Hele Mill
Morte Point **Lee** Bicclescombe Park Chambercombe Manor
Mortehoe Berrynarbor
Woolacombe Once Upon A Time West Down
Woolacombe Sand *Chapel Wood*
Putsborough Sand
Baggy Point *Marwood Hill* Guineaford
Croyde Gem Museum
Saunton Down **Barnstaple**
Braunton Heanton Punchardon Woodside North Devon Museum
Saunton Sands CHIVENOR Old Grammar Museum **Jungleland**
Braunton Burrows Taw Brannam Potters **Codden Hill**
Northam Burrows
Appledore Instow
Westward Ho! **Tapeley Park** Horwood
Abbotsham **Bideford** Alverdiscott
Hartland Point Ford Landcross Weare Giffard Atherington
Titchberry
Hartland Abbey Priory Dartington Crystal
Hartland **Clovelly** **Buck's Mills** Peppercombe **Frithelstock** **Great Torrington**
Hartland Quay Stoke Parkham *Rosemoor*
Clovelly Dykes Littleham
Philham Buckland Brewer Roborough
Speke's Mill Mouth Woolfardisworthy *Downland Farm* Monkleigh
Elmscott **Docton Mill** Meddon Ashmansworthy Beaford
Summerwell Forest Trail Winswell Merton Dolton
Welcombe Mouth **Welcombe** Bulkworthy Stibb Cross Peters Marland
Marsland Mouth West Putford Newton St Petrock
Henna Cliff **Morwenstow** *The Gnome Reserve* Shebbear North Torridge Petrockstowe
Higher Sharpnose Point Woodford Bradworthy Sulcombe Milton Damerel Shebbear Pottery Meeth
Stanbury Mouth **Coombe Valley** Upper Lake **Tamar Lakes** North Town
Lower Sharpnose Point Lower Lake Alfardisworthy Iddesleigh
Duckpool Coombe Slibb Kilkhampton Holsworthy Beacon Holemoor Sheepwash
Sandy Mouth Chilsworthy Black Torrington Highampton Hatherleigh
Northcott Mouth Grimscott Chilsworthy Brandis Corner
Bude Bay **Bude** **Stratton** Pancrasweek **Holsworthy** Pyworthy Halwill Junction Beaworthy Northlew
Bude Canal **Launcells** Bridgerule
Marhamchurch *Holsworthy Woods* Clawton
Widemouth Sand Widemouth Bay Whitstone Clawton
Millook Haven Poundstock Week St Mary Telcott North Tamerton Ashwater **Okehampton**
Chipman Strand
High Cliff **Crackington Haven** St Gennys Wainhouse Corner Chapmans Well Boasley Cross
Tresparrett Marshgate South Wheatley Canworthy Water Bennacott Brazacott St Giles on the Heath Bratton Clovelly Sourton
St Juliot Warbstow Roadford Reservoir

CORNWALL

D E V O N

MOORS OF MYTH AND LEGEND

Though skirted, even invaded, by modern highways, the deeper fastnesses of Dartmoor, Exmoor and Bodmin Moor are joyous places, each responding with its own subtle blend of prehistoric past and wilderness present.

'The long slopes beneath me were all golden green on one side and grey shadow on the other. A haze lay low upon the farthest skyline, out of which jutted the fantastic shapes of Belliver and Vixen Tor. Over the wide expanse there was no sound and no movement. The barren scene, the sense of loneliness and the mystery . . . all struck a chill into my heart.' Thus Dr Watson sketched in the background to that most famous of Holmesian adventures, *The Hound of the Baskervilles*, at the same time imprinting the brooding topography of Dartmoor on the imagination of the world.

In certain of its moods, it is not an unfair picture. The extensive granite plateau of Dartmoor, a separate, untamed country within Devon, is an ancient volcanic region whose highest peaks have been scoured and eroded into the startling profiles of the tors; some, like Yes Tor, still rising to over 2000ft. About them are the peaty bogs, whose streams feed the rough pastures that never dry out.

The intimate charm of Exmoor

With its surround of big, bosomy pastures, based on sandstone foundations and green as any in Ireland, Exmoor presents a cosier, more intimate image to the casual visitor. East of Challacombe Common, however, there is an eerie, pathless wilderness called The Chains, a string of quaking, bottomless bogs, every bit as sinister as those of Dartmoor. Few go there, apart from the ghosts of Bronze Age settlers, whose burial mounds rumple the ground nearby. More often lingering in photograph

ANCIENT CROSSING *A few miles from Dulverton lies Tarr Steps, the remarkably well-preserved clapper bridge over the River Barle, built in either medieval or prehistoric times.*

albums and affections are the uplands of the Exmoor coast, the great bastions admired by Charles Kingsley, rising 'sheer upwards from the sea a thousand feet'.

While Dartmoor makes its visitors uneasy with tales of the Baskerville hound, Exmoor thrills them with R.D. Blackmore's *Lorna Doone*. She is most eagerly sought at Oare church, where she was supposedly shot by Carver Doone on her wedding day. Her memory lingers on elsewhere, up and down the valley of the Badgworthy Water.

With its granite tors and drifting mists, the 80sq miles of Bodmin Moor are rather like a microcosm of Dartmoor. It is a land of unfenced roads and granite-walled, slate-roofed cottages, beside which sheep graze. But

LEGENDARY SITES *R.D. Blackmore's romantic heroine, Lorna Doone, was supposedly shot at the altar of Oare church (above). It is also said that she lived in the farm in Malmsmead (right) after her marriage to Jan Ridd.*

THE HOUND OF THE BASKERVILLES

Conan Doyle Uniform Edition

WILDLIFE HAVEN *Magnificent, panoramic views from Wootton Courtenay look out towards Porlock Bay, around which rare plants flourish in the mild climate and wintering wildfowl return year after year to feed.*

HAUNTING TALES *Hound Tor is the source of the mysterious Baskerville legend of Conan Doyle. Black hell-hounds were seen racing across the moor in 1677, after the death of a local tyrant.*

if it's legend you seek, then Bolventor is your goal. Nearby lies deep Dozmary Pool, which hid the water nymph who received Excalibur from Sir Bedivere after the death of King Arthur. By the Bodmin-Launceston road is Jamaica Inn, the inspiration for Daphne du Maurier's tale of wreckers and murder.

For a rich sample of the area, visitors can explore the country around St Cleer, named after the Celtic saint whose holy well can still be seen. There, atop a tor, is the Cheesewring, a natural heap of boulders, from which you can look across Cornwall to the Atlantic coast. Nearby is the Caradon copper mine, a hundred years ago the richest in the world. Now it is deserted and the doleful stacks of its engine house stand lonely against the horizon.

Other parts of the area conjure up more cheerful images. From the central granite plateau, little streams frolic down through their courses to join the Camel, Lynher, Tamar and Fowey rivers – the last with its impressive Golitha Falls. And many of the stone and slate villages are joined by unexpectedly pretty lanes, running deep between banks of hazel, fuchsia and honeysuckle.

MOORLAND GREEN
The dark green fritillary is identified by the patches of olive-green present on the underside of its hind-wings. It lays its eggs on leaves of the dog violet.

HAUNT OF THE DOONE OUTLAWS

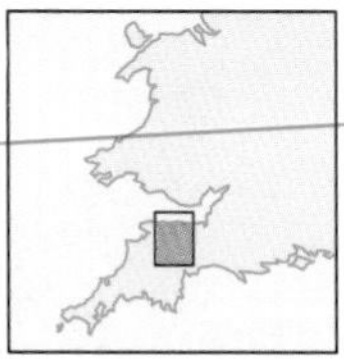

Rocky bays surrounded by some of Britain's highest cliffs stare out towards the mountains of South Wales. In the valleys, thatched cottages shelter in the green-wooded combes beneath the moor – this is the countryside that inspired the story of Lorna Doone. Farther south, rich, red farmland with tranquil villages and imposing manor houses tells of centuries of prosperity.

Arlington Court 🏛 Bf
Victorian atmosphere recalls Rosalie Chichester who inherited 1822 mansion in 1865, aged 15. Clothes, model ships and sea shells everywhere. Her step-nephew Francis Chichester, the lone round-the-world yachtsman, often visited as a child. Model of his *Gipsy Moth IV* on display, and a painting by William Blake called *Cycle of the Life of Man*. Wild and domestic animals in park.

Badgworthy Water ≈ ▮ Cf
Beautiful Exmoor valley and heart of Doone country. Memorial to author R.D. Blackmore beside water. Crumbling ruins of old Badgworthy village in Hoccombe Combe, where outlaws lived.

Bampton ⌂ Ed
Market town on edge of Exmoor with graceful street of Georgian houses. Church is 14th to 15th century. Churchyard has two handsome yew trees, about 500 years old, encircled by stone seats. Exmoor pony fair each October.

Bickleigh ⌂ 🏛 ▣ Eb
Stuart farmhouse and medieval gatehouse surround peaceful courtyard and the 11th-century chapel of a vanished Norman castle. Museum includes gadgets used by spies in World War II. Craft workshops at Bickleigh Mill and rare breeds in adjoining heritage farm.

OUTLAWS' RETREAT *The original Doone gang is said to have had a hideout in the lovely valley of Badgworthy Water, concealed by high moors.*

Brendon ⌂ Cf
Showpiece village consisting of whitewashed thatched cottages in wooded combe, where East Lyn river is crossed by medieval packhorse bridge. Path to Brendon Common leads south.

Brompton Regis ⌂ 🐦 ♣ Ee
Tiny, remote village which Ghida, mother of King Harold, refused to surrender to William the Conqueror's forces in 1068. Views from 15th-century church. Rainbow trout rise for flies in nearby Wimbleball Lake.

Chargot Wood 🌳 Ee
Tranquil Exmoor wood, reaching more than 1000ft above sea-level, with striking views north towards wooded Croydon Hill and Luxborough valley. Kennisham Wood, west, has engine-house remains from disused iron mine.

Chulmleigh † ♜ Bc
Small, hilly town above Little Dart with 15th-century church noted for 38 carved wooden angels on its roof. Barnstaple Inn dates from 1633. Remains of 17th-century Stone Castle 1 mile east.

Codden Hill ✻ Ad
Gorse and bracken-covered hill, 629ft high, is surmounted by Codden Beacon with views over Taw estuary towards Atlantic.

Combat Vehicles Museum ⛟ Bd
Second World War vehicles and rural bygones. First self-propelled armoured vehicle to land in Normandy on D-Day, and a Churchill 'Crocodile' infantry tank, among the exhibits.

Combe Martin ⌂ 🦌 🍷 Af
Old silver and lead mining village turned tourist centre. Horse and cart rides at Bodstone Barton Working Farm and Country Park. Otters, falconry and model railway at Wildlife Park and Monkey Sanctuary. Rare carvings in 13th-century church. Unusual Pack of Cards Inn built as a gambler's tribute to good fortune in 1626.

Crediton † Db
Cathedral city for Devon and Christian centre in Saxon times. Reputed AD 680 birthplace of St Boniface, who converted the Germans. Cathedral-like church is mainly 15th century. Chapter House has Cromwellian relics, including buckskin coat and boots, almost good as new.

Cruwys Morchard † Dc
Parish without a village, 700ft up where road runs through a beech wood. Perfect for quiet walks. Holy Cross Church has Georgian screen, among finest in Devon.

EXMOOR GEM *The tiny church at Culbone dates from the 12th century.*

Culbone † Df
Favoured by poet Coleridge, medieval church reached by 2 mile track from Porlock Weir. Said to be smallest in regular use in England. Measures 34ft by 12ft and seats 30. Oak, beech and alder crowd the wooded combe.

Cullompton † ❖ Fb
Orchards and vineyards surround town, centre of local cider industry. Victorian houses blend with Georgian survivors of 1839 fire. Wagon roof runs length of St Andrew's Church, rebuilt 1430.

Dulverton ⓘ ♣ Ed
Market town of narrow, medieval streets spreading around arched stone bridge – one of the oldest on Exmoor. Exmoor House, a former Victorian workhouse, is home to National Park Centre.

Dunkery Hill ✻ Ef
Highest point on Exmoor at 1705ft. Wild, treeless hill yields fine views of surrounding heathland and wooded valleys below.

Dunster ⌂ 🏛 ▣ Ef
Wide main street of old-world houses and 17th-century Yarn Market. Exmoor forms backdrop to the village, which includes a packhorse bridge, water mill, 11th-century castle and 1000-year-old yew in churchyard. Fine carved rood screen in mainly 15th-century church.

Finch Foundry ⚙ ⛩ Ba
Three mighty water wheels still drive the forges, grindstones and polishing wheels which turned out tools for Devon's farmers and miners until 1960.

Fursdon House 🏛 Eb
Family home of the Fursdons, in residence here for over 700 years. Manor house rebuilt 1732 has Regency library, family tree, portraits and costume collection.

Heddon's Mouth ☆ ♣ 🐚 Bf
Surf glistens on cove's secluded shore beneath towering cliffs where River Heddon meets the sea. Short path from Hunter's Inn runs down steep, wooded valley. Cliff-top walk to Woody Bay passes limekiln and site of 1st-century Roman fort.

Killerton 🏛 Eb
House built 1778, occupied by Acland family for 150 years. Fine furniture and paintings. Theatre costume collection with items dating from the 18th century.

Knightshayes Court ✿ Ec
Flamboyant Gothic façade of gargoyles and gables complements grandiose interior of house built for Heathcoat-Amorys in 1870. Paintings by Constable, Turner and Rembrandt. Topiary in the gardens includes a hunting scene.

Lynmouth ⌂ ▣ Cf
Fishing village refuge for poet Shelley and his child bride in 1812. Devastated by floods in 1952, but 18th-century quay and houses survived. Cliff railway links hilltop Lynton where the museum records local history.

Minehead 🚂 Ef
Ebbing tide leaves this popular resort half a mile from the sea. Oldest part, Quay Town, dates back to 1616. Steam and diesel trains ride 20 mile track to Bishop's Lydeard on the West Somerset Railway. Walks on North Hill.

Morchard Bishop ⌂ Cb
Village of thatched cottages and 18th-century houses, that once belonged to Bishops of Exeter.

North Devon Farm Park 🚜 Be
Rare breeds of cattle, sheep, poultry and waterfowl roam 25 acres.

WORKING WATERS *A 17th-century mill still grinds flour in the beautiful village of Dunster.*

Okehampton ▣ ♜ Aa
Small market town and a main centre for exploring Dartmoor. Remains of fine 14th-century castle with a Norman keep. Parish church with windows by Victorian artist William Morris. Handsome 17th-century town hall. Old three-storey mill houses Museum of Dartmoor Life.

Parracombe ⌂ Bf
Narrow road leads to village in steep little valley. Hidden away is remarkable Church of St Petrock, lovingly restored though no longer used. Dates from late 11th century with unspoilt 18th-century interior.

Porlock ⌂ Df
Old, mellow village set in a natural bowl, flanked by wooded hills with spectacular views. Descend Porlock Hill to whitewashed cottages. Boats bob in 17th-century gated Porlock Weir.

Sampford Courtenay ⌂ Bb
Village of cob and thatch cottages. Norman font in St Andrew's Church where prayer book rebellion began on Whit Monday 1549, in protest against the service being read in English instead of Latin.

Selworthy ⌂ ✻ Ef
Tree-canopied lane leads to village of thatched cottages, centred round a green. Pale and pristine Church of All Saints has 16th-century pulpit and three lavishly carved wooden barrel roofs.

Simonsbath ⌂ Ce
Highest village on Exmoor at 1100ft; small with some attractive whitestone cottages. Footpath opposite inn follows river into heart of moor.

South Molton † ▣ 🚜 Cd
Fine Georgian and Victorian houses in hilly market town, where almost every street has moorland views. The 15th-century church has medieval stone pulpit and handsome figure carvings in the nave.

Stoke Pero † Df
Isolated church – one of Exmoor's highest – is believed to stand on moor's earliest Christian site. Birdwatching from common overlooking the sea; rare visitors include merlins, Montagu's harriers and golden plovers.

Tiverton ▣ ♜ † 🦌 ❖ ⓘ Ec
Wool town of 1200s, revived with lace and spinning in 19th century. Local history in town museum includes relics of Great Western Railway. Arms, armour, and clock collections at Tiverton Castle, built 1106. Horse-drawn passenger narrowboats ply canal.

Valley of Rocks ☆ Cf
Valley remarkable for eroded limestone pinnacles with such names as the Devil's Cheesewring, Ragged Jack and Castle Rock. Drop of 800ft from Castle Rock to Bristol Channel is one of Britain's highest sea cliffs.

Watersmeet ≈ 🏛 Cf
Wooded gorge with beautiful walks where East Lyn river meets the Hoaroak Water. National Trust information centre housed in Victorian fishing lodge.

Winsford ⌂ ⛩ ☆ Ee
River Winn joins the Exe in this village of packhorse bridges with handsome thatched inn. Hill-top church of Norman origin with 90ft tower. Caractacus Stone at Spire Cross commemorates a mystery man; dated from between 5th and 7th centuries.

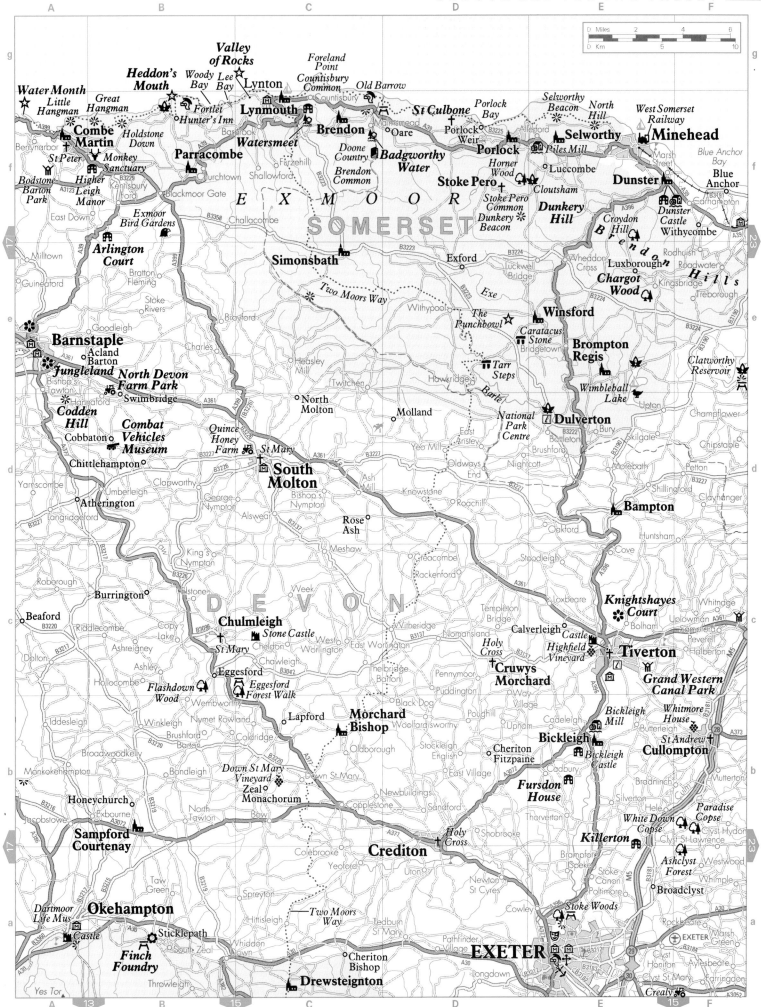

Miles 0 2 4 6
Km 0 5 10

g

Water Month
Little Hangman
St Peter
Bodstone Barton Park
Higher Leigh Manor
Combe Martin
Holdstone Down
Great Hangman
Monkey Sanctuary
Heddon's Mouth
Woody Bay
Lee Bay
Valley of Rocks
Fortlet
Hunter's Inn
Lynton
Lynmouth
Watersmeet
Brendon
Foreland Point
Countisbury Common
Countisbury
Old Barrow
St Culbone
Porlock Bay
Porlock Weir
Selworthy Beacon
North Hill
West Somerset Railway
Minehead
Blue Anchor Bay
Blue Anchor
Marsh Street
Carhampton
Dunster
Dunster Castle
Withycombe

f

Berrynarbor
St Peter
Parracombe
Churchtown
Blackmoor Gate
Shallowford
Furzehill
Barbrook
Mannacott
Oare
Badgworthy Water
Doone Country
Brendon Common
Stoke Pero
Horner Wood
Cloutsham
Stoke Pero Common
Dunkery Beacon
Porlock
Piles Mill
Luccombe
Selworthy
Allerford
Dunkery Hill
Croydon Hill
Rodhuish
Roadwater
Treborough

EXMOOR
SOMERSET
Exmoor Bird Gardens
Arlington Court
Bratton Fleming
Stoke Rivers
Simonsbath
Challacombe
Brayford
Two Moors Way
Exford
Luckwell Bridge
Wheddon Cross
Luxborough
Chargot Wood
Kingsbridge
Brendon Hills
Clatworthy Reservoir

e

Barnstaple
Acland Barton
Jungleland
Bishop's Tawton
Codden Hill
Cobbaton
Combat Vehicles Museum
Chittlehampton
Goodleigh
Charles
Heasley Mill
Twitchen
North Devon Farm Park
Swimbridge
North Molton
Molland
Withypool
Exe
The Punchbowl
Caratacus Stone
Bridgetown
Winsford
Brompton Regis
Wimbleball Lake
Upton
Champflower
Chipstable

d

Yarnscombe
Atherington
Umberleigh
Langridgeford
Quince Honey Farm
South Molton
St Mary
Clapworthy
George Nympton
Bishop's Nympton
Alswear
Ash Mill
East Anstey
Oldways End
Nightcott
Brushford
National Park Centre
Dulverton
Battleton
Bury
Skilgate
Morebath
Shillingford
Clayhanger
Bampton
Petton
Huntsham

c

Beaford
Riddlecombe
Ashreigney
Dolton
Roborough
Burrington
Copy Lake
Elstone
Chulmleigh
Stone Castle
St Mary
Cheldon
Westof Worlington
Chawleigh
Week
East Worlington
Nomansland
Witheridge
Templeton Bridge
Loxbeare
Bolham
Calverleigh
Castle
Highfield Vineyard
Knightshayes Court
Whitnage
Uplowman
Sampford Peverell
Halberton
Tiverton

b

Monkokehampton
Honeychurch
Exbourne
Hollocombe
Ashley
Winkleigh
Brushford Barton
Coldridge
Broadwoodkelly
Iddesleigh
Flashdown Wood
Eggesford
Eggesford Forest Walk
Nymet Rowland
Wembworthy
Lapford
Morchard Bishop
Woolfardisworthy
Black Dog
Puddington
Pennymoor
Cruwys Morchard
Holy Cross
Poughill
Way Village
Cadeleigh
Upham
Stockleigh English
Cheriton Fitzpaine
Cadbury
Bickleigh
Bickleigh Mill
Butterleigh
Whitmore House
Grand Western Canal Park
St Andrew
Cullompton
Bradninch
Mutterton

Down St Mary Vineyard
Zeal Monachorum
Down St Mary
Bondleigh
North Tawton
Bow
Coldridge
Oldborough
Stockleigh Pomeroy
Sandford
Newbuildings
Copplestone
Fursdon House
Thorverton
Silverton
Hele
Killerton
White Down Copse
Paradise Copse
Clyst Hydon
Clyst St Lawrence

a

Dartmoor Life Mus
Sampford Courtenay
Jacobstowe
Exbourne
Okehampton
Castle
Finch Foundry
Sticklepath
South Zeal
Throwleigh
Yes Tor
Taw Green
Whiddon Down
Hittisleigh
Spreyton
Colebrooke
Yeoford
Uton
Crediton
Holy Cross
Shobrooke
Newton St Cyres
Tedburn St Mary
Pathfinder Village
Cheriton Bishop
Drewsteignton
Longdown
Brampford Speke
Stoke Canon
Poltimore
Cowley
Stoke Woods
EXETER
EXETER
Rockbeare
Marsh Green
Clyst Honiton
Aylesbeare
Whimple
Broadclyst
Ashclyst Forest
Westwood
Clyst St Mary
Farringdon
Crealy

DEVON

Two Moors Way

Aisholt ⌂ Bf
Thatched cottages and 14th-century church in out-of-the-way valley. Footpath crosses Aisholt Common to Wills Neck, highest point in the Quantocks (1260ft) with superb views to Exmoor and South Wales.

Axminster ⌂ Db
Narrow Georgian and early Victorian streets converge at centre of bustling market town, birthplace of hand-tufted Axminster carpets. Bells in 13th-century St Mary's would ring when each carpet was finished. Tools of the trade at Axminster Museum.

Axmouth ⌂ Cb
Quiet resort of colour-washed cottages, once a thriving port. Waterfowl haunt muddy flats of estuary. Nearby Dowlands Cliffs were the scene of a cliff fall in 1839.

CHALK FACE *Pale cliffs soar to 426ft at Beer Head.*

Beer ⌂ Ca
Lively fishing village and resort nestles under sweep of Beer Head chalk cliffs, once the favoured haunt of smugglers. Model and miniature railways. Pleasure gardens with some 80,000 plants.

Bicknoller Hill ✳ Bf
Fine vantage point from which to enjoy Wordsworth's 'Smooth Quantock's airy ridge'. Iron Age settlement of Trendle Ring on south-west slopes. Sweeping panoramas from nearby 1018ft Beacon Hill.

Black Down Hills ✳ Bd
Quiet backwater where heather and gorse-clad hilltops descend through high-hedged lanes to secluded wooded valleys. Duke of Wellington's monument, a giant obelisk, stands at highest point surrounded by a nature reserve, from where there are views across country to town of Wellington.

Branscombe ⌂ Ba
Beautiful village of flint and stone thatched cottages and 15th-century smithy. St Winifred's Church dates from 12th century. Fine cliff-top walk from Branscombe Mouth to Beer Head.

Bridgwater ⌂ Cf
Georgian houses and renovated docks are reminders of earlier pretensions to rival Bristol as a port, as is the Bridgwater and Taunton Canal. Church with

DEEP COMBES AND GENTLE HILLS

Between the airy heights and narrow wooded combes of the Quantocks and the crumbling chalk cliffs of the southern coast lies a rural landscape of great charm. The rich and rolling farmlands, shared by Somerset and Devon, are dotted with ancient market towns, as well as many a village of mellow stone and thatch clustered round a graceful church tower.

15th-century spire atop tower where Monmouth sighted loyalist troops before Battle of Sedgemoor in 1685. Battle relics and seafaring memorabilia housed in house where Admiral Blake was born.

Broadhembury ⌂ Bc
Tidy, timeless village of thatched and cob-walled cottages. Towering above is Hembury Fort, finest prehistoric earthwork in Devon.

Broadwindsor ⌂ Ec
Steeply terraced village with 17th-century cottages and houses. One bears a plaque commemorating the night Charles II slept here in 1651. The Church of St John the Baptist has 15th-century tower and parapet carved with grotesque figures, and Jacobean pulpit.

Chard ⌂ Dc
Highest town in Somerset, where two streams flow along a High Street lined with stone buildings. The 16th-century court house is really a group of Elizabethan houses. Ancient water wheel and millstones still grind at 19th-century Hornsbury Mill, an Aladdin's cave of bric-a-brac.

Charmouth ✳ Db
Good hunting ground for fossil collectors, the cliffs of Black Ven are now part of a 161 acre nature reserve. Charles II took refuge at the Queen's Arms Inn when forced into hiding in 1651.

Clapton Court ❀ Ec
Rare and unusual trees, shrubs and plants in 10 acres of formal and woodland gardens. Streams lined with Asiatic primulas. Largest ash in England, more than 200 years old.

HALLOWED STONES *Cleeve Abbey's gatehouse survives intact.*

Cleeve Abbey ✚ Ag
Odours of antiquity and sanctity pervade well-preserved 13th-century buildings of Cistercian monastery set in broad valley.

Combe Florey ⌂ Bf
Sandstone village where Sydney Smith, one of England's greatest wits, and novelist Evelyn Waugh lived. Medieval Gaulden Manor has splendid Tudor plasterwork.

Combe Sydenham Hall ⌂ Af
Elizabethan mansion displays a meteorite that was mistaken for a cannonball when it fell from the sky, convincing Elizabeth Sydenham, later wife of Sir Francis Drake, to cancel her wedding to a rival suitor. Beautiful gardens.

Cothelstone ⌂ Bf
Pretty pink cottages and a fine Elizabethan manor house. The church has 15th-century glass depicting St Dunstan and the pincers with which he tweaked the devil's nose. Ruined 18th-century folly on Cothelstone Hill.

Cricket St Thomas ✚ Dc
Georgian estate used in the TV series *To the Manor Born*, surrounded by 1000 acre wildlife park. Attractions include a work-ing dairy factory, heavy horse centre, woodland railway and country life museum.

Culm Valley ⌂ Ad
Clear waters tumble past quiet hamlets. Kingfishers, dippers, snipe and woodcock inhabit Lickham Common Nature Reserve. Stupendous views at Culmstock Beacon and from Black Down Common. Coldharbour Mill has a working museum.

East Lambrook Manor ❀ Ed
Idyllic Elizabethan cottage garden surrounds 15th-century house of glowing Ham stone. Vibrant colours, rare plants, nursery and fish garden.

East Quantoxhead ⌂ Bg
Tranquil corner of Somerset with village duck pond set against backdrop of a church and partly Jacobean Court House. Footpath leads to rocky beach at Kilve Pill and ivy-clad ruins of old chantry.

Forde Abbey ✚ Dc
Fine Tudor stonework and notable collection of tapestries adorn 12th-century Cistercian abbey set in pleasant gardens.

Fyne Court ❀ Cf
Headquarters of Somerset Trust for Nature Conservation and visitor centre for the Quantocks. Nature trails, with nearly every native British shrub and tree.

Golden Cap ✳ Eb
A band of golden sandstone fringed with bright yellow gorse gives highest cliff on south coast (626ft) its name. Part of a 2000 acre National Trust estate.

Grand Western Canal Park ⌂ Ad
Restored canal, sole relic of a grandiose scheme to link Taunton to the south coast, now forms a country park. Horse-drawn boats carry passengers along part of the tranquil waterway.

Hestercombe ❀ Ce
Wide views from terraced gardens, laid out by Sir Edwin Lutyens and Gertrude Jekyll, in grounds of 1870 mansion.

Ilminster ✚ Dd
Market town founded in Saxon times, with charming Georgian houses and a 15th-century minster with imposing tower.

Lyme Regis ⌂ Db
Medieval port, rich with memories of the past, already old when King Edward I used its harbour during wars against the French. Massive breakwater, known as The Cobb, features in John Fowles's novel *The French Lieutenant's Woman*. It was a seaside resort in the 18th century; novelist Jane Austen had a seafront cottage. Fossil collections at the Philpott Museum, and fossil outings at Dinosaurland.

Nether Stowey ⌂ Bf
Place of pilgrimage for lovers of the Romantic poets. Visit cottage where Coleridge wrote *The Ancient Mariner*. Hold a young lamb or milk a sheep at Quantock Sheep Milking Centre.

Quantock Hills ⌂ Bf
Ancient ridgeway follows crest of heather-clad hills – Will's Neck (1260ft) and Robin Uprights Hill (1170ft) highest points. Red deer shelter in deep, wooded valleys, wild ponies and sheep graze the uplands. Good walking country.

Sidmouth ⌂ Ba
Soaring cliffs enclose resort, rich in Georgian and Regency architecture. Duke and Duchess of Kent stayed in 1819 with the infant Queen Victoria, at Woolbrook Cottage, now Royal Glen Hotel. Vintage toy and train museum.

Taunton ⌂ Ce
County town with a cruel and bloody history; scene of bitter struggles during Civil War of 1642-9. Restored Norman castle contains county and regimental museum. Churches of St Mary's and St James are noted for splendid towers. Traditional taste of Somerset at Sheppy's Cider.

West Sedgemoor Nature Reserve ✳ De
Wetland and woodland where curlews, black-tailed godwits, redshanks and snipe breed. Winter visitors include large numbers of lapwings and occasional Bewick's swans. Important spring passage site for whimbrels.

Whitchurch Canonicorum ⌂ Eb
The jewel of Marshwood Vale, the only English parish church that claims to house the bones of its patron saint, St Wite; kept in a tomb pierced by holes through which medieval pilgrims placed crippled limbs in hopes of a cure.

PROTECTIVE BARRIER *Calm anchorage for the local fishing fleet lies inside The Cobb breakwater at Lyme Regis.*

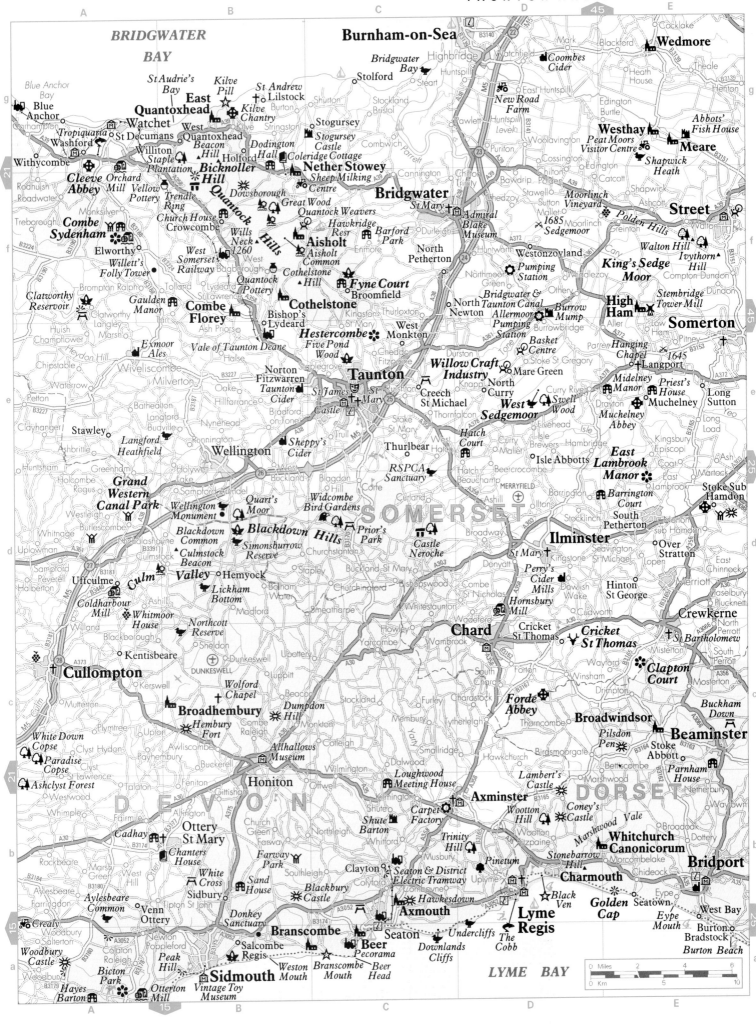

BRIDGWATER BAY

Burnham-on-Sea

Blue Anchor Bay
Blue Anchor
Withycombe
Tropiquaria
Washford
Cleeve Abbey
Combe Sydenham
Elworthy
Willett's Folly Tower
Clatworthy Reservoir
Gaulden Manor
Combe Florey
Exmoor Ales
Stawley
Langford Heathfield
Grand Western Canal Park
Wellington Monument
Uffculme
Coldharbour Mill
Whitmoor House
Culm Valley
Lickham Bottom
Kentisbeare
Northcott Reserve
Cullompton
Broadhembury
Hembury Fort
White Down Copse
Paradise Copse
Ashclyst Forest
Cadhay
Ottery St Mary
Chanters House
Honiton
Aylesbeare Common
Venn Ottery
Woodbury Castle
Bicton Park
Hayes Barton
Sidmouth
Peak Hill
Salcombe Regis
Weston Mouth
Otterton Mill
Vintage Toy Museum
Branscombe
Branscombe Mouth
Beer
Beer Head
Pecorama
Seaton
Axmouth
Undercliffs
Downlands Cliffs
The Cobb
Lyme Regis
Black Ven
Charmouth
Golden Cap
Seatown
Eype Mouth
West Bay
Burton Bradstock
Burton Beach

LYME BAY

St Audrie's Bay
Watchet
St Decumans
Williton
Orchard Mill
Yellow Pottery
Trendle Ring
Church House
Crowcombe
Wills Neck 1260
West Somerset Railway
Quantock Pottery
Bishop's Lydeard
Hestercombe
Five Pond Wood
Vale of Taunton Deane
Norton Fitzwarren
Taunton Cider
Wellington
Sheppy's Cider
Quart's Moor
Widcombe Bird Gardens
Blackdown Hills
Simonsburrow Reserve
Prior's Park
Culmstock Beacon
Blackdown Common
Hemyock
Dunkeswell
Wolford Chapel
Dumpdon Hill
White Cross Sidbury
Sand House
Donkey Sanctuary
Blackbury Castle
Allhallows Museum
Loughwood Meeting Centre

East Quantoxhead
Kilve Pill
Kilve Chantry
West Quantoxhead
Beacon Hill
Staple Plantation
Bicknoller Hill
Dowsborough
Great Wood
Quantock Weavers
Hawkridge Resr
Barford Park
Aisholt
Aisholt Common
Cothelstone Hill
Fyne Court
Broomfield
St Andrew
Lilstock
Holford
Dodington Hall
Coleridge Cottage
Nether Stowey
Sheep Milking Centre
Stogursey
Stogursey Castle
Combwich
Cannington
Chilton Trinity
Bridgwater
St Mary
Admiral Blake Museum
North Petherton
North Newton
West Monkton
Creech St Michael
Taunton
St James
Castle
St Mary
Bradford on Tone
Trull
Stoke St Mary
Thurlbear
RSPCA Sanctuary
Corfe
Curland
Castle Neroche
Broadway
Buckland St Mary
Churchstanton
Churchinford
Yarcombe
Upottery
Stockland
Membury
Wambrook
Chard
Chardstock
Wilmington
Dalwood
Hawkchurch
Lambert's Castle
Axminster
Carpet Factory
Shute Barton
Trinity Hill
Pinetum
Seaton & District Electric Tramway
Colyford
Colyton
Uplyme

Highbridge
Coombes Cider
New Road Farm
East Huntspill
Huntspill Levels
Woolavington
Cossington
Chedzoy
Westonzoyland
Pumping Station
Bridgwater & Taunton Canal
Allermoor Pumping Station
Burrow Mump
Burrowbridge
Basket Centre
Stoke St Gregory
Mare Green
North Curry
Willow Craft Industry
West Sedgemoor
Swell Wood
Curry Rivel
Drayton
Muchelney
Muchelney Abbey
Isle Abbotts
Barrington Court
South Petherton
Ilminster
St Mary
Donyatt
Perry's Cider Mills
Hornsbury Mill
Combe St Nicholas
Cricket St Thomas
Forde Abbey
Thorncombe
Birdsmoorgate
Marshwood
Marshwood Vale
Whitchurch Canonicorum

Wedmore
Coombes Cider
Westhay
Abbots' Fish House
Meare
Shapwick Heath
Moorlinch Vineyard
1685 Sedgemoor
Moorlinch
Polden Hills
Street
Walton Hill
Ivythorn Hill
King's Sedge Moor
Compton Dundon
High Ham
Stembridge Tower Mill
Somerton
Hanging Chapel
1645
Langport
East Lambrook Manor
Midelney Manor
Priest's House
Muchelney
Long Sutton
Long Load
Kingsbury Episcopi
Stoke Sub Hamdon
Over Stratton
East Chinnock
Merriott
Crewkerne
St Bartholomew
Misterton
South Perrott
Clapton Court
Broadwindsor
Buckham Down
Beaminster
Pilsdon Pen
Stoke Abbott
Parnham House
Bridport
Chideock
Eype

SOMERSET

DEVON

DORSET

0 Miles 2 4 6
0 Km 5 10

Abbotsbury ⚓ ✝ ❀ ❤ Bc
Quiet village of thatched cottages in sheltered green valley. Benedictine monks built remaining 15th-century tithe barn, and created the famous Abbotsbury Swannery. Exotic plants and trees in Sub-Tropical Gardens.

Athelhampton ⌂ Dd
Gracious family home built 1485. Magnificent Great Hall with original timbered roof and 10 acres of gardens with fountains. Nearby village of Puddletown is Hardy's 'Weatherbury'. Superb oak roof in nave of 15th-century church.

Beaminster ⌂ ❀ Ae
Small town loved by Hardy. Market cross stands in square of handsome 18th-century houses. Elizabethan Parnham House, rescued by John Nash in 1810, now home to John Makepeace's furniture workshops. Stately terraced gardens at nearby Mapperton House.

Bere Regis ⚓ Ed
Essential port of call for Hardy devotees as Saxon church houses D'Urberville family tombs. Tess buried here too. Richly decorated oak ceiling a gift from Cardinal Morton, Henry VII's chancellor.

Black Down ❀ Cc
Hill-top obelisk commemorates Dorset's other famous Hardy; Sir Thomas Masterman Hardy, captain of Nelson's flagship HMS *Victory* at Battle of Trafalgar.

HARDY'S WESSEX

From the hill claimed to be the site of King Arthur's Camelot, winding lanes lead south into Thomas Hardy's Wessex, a patchwork of farms, heathland and prehistoric earthworks. Peaceful villages of honey-coloured stone lie snugly in this landscape. Pounding seas have carved magnificent sculptures out of the cliffs and thrown up Chesil's great barrier of shingle.

Brympton d'Evercy ⌂ ❀ Bf
Stately home, successfully added to over the centuries. Attractive blend of contrasting styles. Cider making displays in 14th-century priest house. Garden with large pool and long terrace.

Cadbury Castle ❀ Cg
Steep path from village of South Cadbury leads to huge grassy plateau of an ancient hill-fort; traditional site of Camelot, seat of King Arthur's court. Ramparts thrown up by legendary defenders from Iron Age to Saxon times still form a green wall encircling 18 acre fort.

Cerne Abbas ⚓ ⛪ Ce
Half-timbered Tudor houses back on to stone cottages. Gatehouse and tithe barn remain from substantial 10th-century abbey. Chalk giant, 1500 years old and 180ft from head to foot, still looks down from hill above village. Naked figure thought to be a pagan fertility symbol.

East Coker ⚓ Bf
T.S. Eliot's ancestral village, celebrated in his poem *Four Quartets*. His ashes lie in church where local hero William Dampier, the 17th-century pirate, explorer and captain, RN, is buried.

Fiddleford Manor ⌂ Ef
A 14th-century house, altered in early 16th century. Intricately carved oak beams in Great Hall and upstairs sun room.

Fleet Air Arm Museum 🛩 Bg
Climb aboard Concorde and inspect more than 50 other historic aircraft, from World War II carrier biplanes to Argentinian fighters from the Falklands campaign.

Higher Bockhampton ⚓ ❀ ⌂ Dd
Ten-minute stroll through the bluebell woods leads to Hardy's birthplace, a thatched cottage built by his grandfather in 1800. Simple whitewashed rooms and inspiring views over heathland.

Lulworth Cove ☆ Eb
Near West Lulworth is Lulworth Cove where two arms of Portland and Purbeck stone embrace the sea. Walk west leads to limestone sea arch of Durdle Door. Attractive village of East Lulworth has 1786 Rotunda, first Roman Catholic church built after Reformation. From car park between two villages, tanks can be observed in action on Defence Ministry land.

Lytes Cary Manor ⌂ Bg
Restored medieval manor, the ancestral home of 14 generations of Lytes. Great Hall built in 15th century with minstrels' gallery. Tudor dining room and parlour with ornate panelling.

Maiden Castle ❀ ☖ Cc
Iron Age hill-fort with extensive earthworks enclosing some 120 acres. Destroyed by Romans in AD 43; skeletons of defending Britons found in excavations. Foundations of a Romano-Celtic temple lie on the summit.

Moreton ⚓ Ec
Centrepiece of riverside village is Church of St Nicholas. Bombed in 1940, new clear glass windows engraved with festive images by Lawrence Whistler. T.E. Lawrence (of Arabia) buried nearby.

Okeford Fitzpaine ⚓ Ef
Timeless, thatched village owes its name to Fitzpaine family of 14th-century lords. Church overlooks 18th-century rectory. Old parish fire engine in purpose-built shelter. Fine views from Okeford and Bulbarrow Hills.

VILLAGE CHURCH *St Andrews dates from 14th century, overlooking cottages of Okeford Fitzpaine.*

Powerstock ⚓ ❀ Bd
Winding lanes thread terraces of handsome stone houses, perched at strange angles. Topmost is gargoyled Norman church. All overshadowed by Eggardon Hill and its Iron Age fort.

Shaftesbury ⌂ ▢ ❀ Eg
Town built on edge of 700ft plateau features in Hardy's novels under old name of 'Shaston'. Handsome buildings in the High Street, including stone-built Mitre Inn. Tiled and thatched cottages on steep, cobbled Gold Hill.

Sherborne ✚ ⛪ ⌂ ❀ ▢ Cf
Town with abbey dating mainly from 15th century. Two castles: ruined 12th-century Old Castle; and Sherborne Castle built by Sir Walter Raleigh in 1594, lake and gardens by Capability Brown.

Sparkford Motor Museum 🚗 Cg
Mecca for car and motorbike enthusiasts. Over 200 gleaming models from 1905 Daimler to sleek 150mph E-Type Jaguar.

Tolpuddle ⚓ Dd
Village green sycamore is where six farmworkers (the 'Tolpuddle Martyrs') met in 1834 to propose formation of a trade union. They were arrested and convicted as a 'secret society'.

Weymouth ⌂ ✿ ❤ ⚓ ▢ Cb
Roman port now modern ferry terminal. Sheltered sandy beach where George III bathed. Safe boating in bay, overlooked by Lodmoor Country Park. Sealife Centre and Tropical Bird Park. Radipole Lake bird reserve with nature trails. Shipwreck Centre on Custom House Quay.

Yeovil ✝ ⌂ ▢ Bf
Modern town where gloves have been made for centuries. Gloving tools, Roman finds and historic firearms in museum. Church, 14th century, flooded with light from 18 vast windows.

CHALK WALLS *The rippling downland flanks of 827ft high Eggardon Hill rise to an Iron Age hill-fort and Bronze Age barrows on the summit.*

Blandford Forum ✝ ⌂ 🚗 ▢ Ee
Handsome Georgian town that rose from ashes of 1731 fire; rebuilt with chequered brick and stone. Former leper hospital now local history museum. Royal Signals Museum at nearby Blandford Camp tells history of army communications, from carrier pigeons to long-range technology.

Bovington Tank Museum 🚗 Ec
Largest collection of armoured vehicles in the world. Tons of metal giants and a tank simulator.

Bridport ⌂ ◀ ▢ Ad
Ropemakers' town with wide streets, once used for drying and twisting hemp. Still Britain's main producer of cords and twines, but now made of synthetics such as nylon. Fishermen's cottages and fine Georgian town hall. Rope industry museum.

Chesil Beach ◧ Cb
Billions of pebbles form immense bank of shingle, 40ft high in places, stretching for 10 miles from Abbotsbury to Portland. Moonfleet Hotel, 1603, in East Fleet village features in J. Meade Falkner's *Moonfleet* tale.

Cloud's Hill ⌂ Ed
T.E. Lawrence (of Arabia) made this sparsely furnished cottage his 'earthly paradise'. Just as he left it the day he was killed on his motorbike in 1935.

Dorchester ⌂ 🚗 ☖ ⌂ Cd
Busy market town steeped in history. Hardy's 'Casterbridge' and home for many years. County Museum has a reconstruction of his study and collection of manuscripts. Roman remains include amphitheatre adapted from Stone Age circle, and villa with mosaics. Smith's Arms in Godmanstone, 5 miles north, Britain's smallest pub.

Isle of Portland Cb
Dorset's Rock of Gibraltar. Windswept limestone peninsula juts 4 miles into Channel. Pitted with quarries – Portland stone still extracted. Naval harbour overlooked by castle built by Henry VIII. Ruined Rufus Castle, Norman built, lies above Church Ope Cove. Portland Museum in Easton. Old lighthouse near Bill, now a bird-watching station. Good bathing for careful swimmers at Church Ope Cove.

DORSET AUTHOR *A life-size statue of Thomas Hardy stands in Dorchester.*

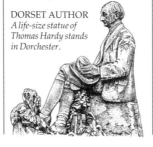

Milton Abbas ⚓ Ee
Peaceful village of whitewashed thatched cottages built in 1770s to replace the original; pulled down by Earl of Dorchester because it spoiled the view from his Gothic-style mansion (now a school). Abbey church, dating back to 14th century, restored in 19th century by Sir Gilbert Scott, architect of London's Albert Memorial.

Minterne ❀ Ce
Acres of wild shrubs and rare trees surround privately owned house in hamlet of Minterne Magna; ablaze with rhododendrons and azaleas in early summer. The house is not open to the public.

Montacute House ⌂ Bf
Golden stone turrets and gables embellish this outstanding Elizabethan mansion. Original panelling, carvings, plasterwork and stained glass. Long Gallery, 172ft, now a portrait gallery.

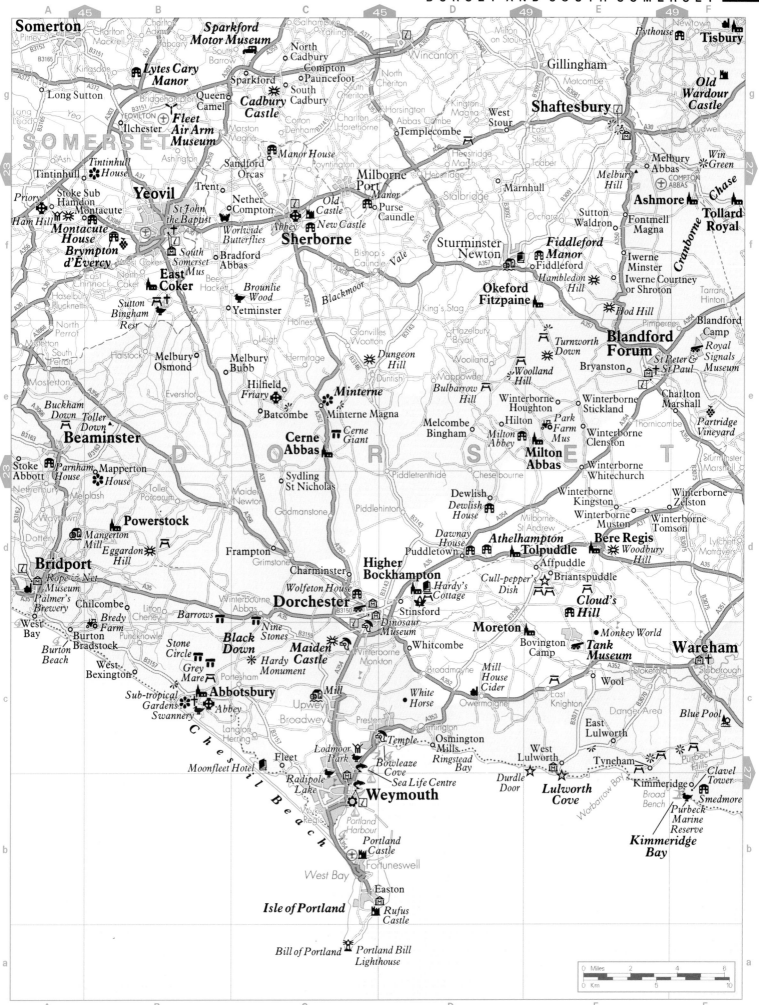

Somerton

Sparkford Motor Museum

Lytes Cary Manor

Long Sutton
Ilchester
Kingsdon
Charlton Mackrell
Pitney
Charlton Adam
Babcary
North Barrow
South Barrow
Sparkford
Queen Camel
North Cadbury
Compton Pauncefoot
South Cadbury
Galhampton
Yarlington
North Cheriton

Cadbury Castle

Fleet Air Arm Museum

Milborne Port

Gillingham

Tisbury

Old Wardour Castle

Pythouse
Newtown

Shaftesbury

SOMERSET

Tintinhull House
Tintinhull
Ash
Stoke Sub Hamdon
Montacute
Ham Hill
Priory

Yeovil

St John the Baptist

Montacute House
Brympton d'Evercy

East Coker

Sandford Orcas
Trent
Nether Compton
Worlwide Butterflies

Sherborne
Old Castle
New Castle
Abbey

Purse Caundle
Manor

Sturminster Newton

Melbury Abbas
Melbury Hill
Win Green

Compton Abbas

Ashmore
Tollard Royal

Cranborne Chase

Fiddleford Manor
Fiddleford

Okeford Fitzpaine

Iwerne Minster
Iwerne Courtney or Shroton
Tarrant Hinton

Hambledon Hill
Hod Hill

Blandford Camp
Royal Signals Museum

Blandford Forum

St Peter & St Paul

Bryanston

Charlton Marshall

Partridge Vineyard

South Somerset Mus
Bradford Abbas
Beer Hackett
Brounlie Wood
Yetminster

DORSET

Melbury Osmond
Melbury Bubb
Hilfield Friary
Batcombe

Minterne
Minterne Magna

Dungeon Hill

Woolland Hill
Bulbarrow Hill

Turnworth Down

Winterborne Houghton
Hilton
Winterborne Stickland

Winterborne Clenston

Winterborne Whitechurch

Beaminster
Buckham Down
Toller Down

Stoke Abbott
Parnham House
Mapperton House
Melplash
Netherbury

Cerne Abbas
Cerne Giant

Sydling St Nicholas

Melcombe Bingham

Milton Abbey

Milton Abbas

Park Farm Mus

Winterborne Zelston

Winterborne Tomson

Winterborne Kingston
Winterborne Muston

Powerstock
Mangerton Mill
Eggardon Hill

Frampton
Grimstone

Maiden Newton
Toller Porcorum

Piddletrenthide
Cheselbourne

Dewlish
Dewlish House

Dawnay House

Athelhampton

Tolpuddle
Woodbury Hill

Bere Regis

Bridport
Rope & Net Museum
Palmer's Brewery
Chilcombe
Bredy Farm

West Bay
Burton Beach
Burton Bradstock
West Bexington

Charminster
Wolfeton House

Higher Bockhampton

Dorchester
Barrows

Puddletown
Hardy's Cottage

Stinsford
Dinosaur Museum

Cull-pepper's Dish
Affpuddle
Briantspuddle

Cloud's Hill

Moreton

Monkey World

Wareham

Stone Circle
Black Down

Maiden Castle
Nine Stones

Hardy Monument
Grey Mare

Abbotsbury
Sub-tropical Gardens Swannery
Abbey

Portesham

Mill

Upwey
Broadwey
Langton Herring
Fleet

Moonfleet Hotel

Chesil Beach

Whitcombe

Winterborne Monkton

White Horse

Broadmayne
Owermoigne

Mill House Cider

Bovington Camp

Tank Museum

East Knighton
Wool
Stokeford

Danger Area

Blue Pool

Temple
Lodmoor Park
Bowleaze Bove
Sea Life Centre

Osmington
Preston
Osmington Mills
Ringstead Bay

West Lulworth
Durdle Door

Lulworth Cove

East Lulworth

Tyneham

Clavel Tower

Kimmeridge
Broad Bench
Smedmore
Purbeck Marine Reserve

Kimmeridge Bay

Radipole Lake

Weymouth

Portland Castle
Fortuneswell

West Bay

Isle of Portland

Easton
Rufus Castle

Bill of Portland
Portland Bill Lighthouse

Miles
Km

A SPIRE ABOVE THE MEADOWS

Salisbury cathedral's spire soars heavenwards, and the cliffs at Durlston Head rise dramatically above the sea. Between them sprawl a royal forest and hills of Purbeck and Chilmark stone, quarried to grace fine buildings in towns and villages made prosperous by wool. The ancient ports of Swanage and Poole contrast sharply with Bournemouth's piers and public gardens.

Ackling Dyke ✿※ Be
Wild flowers and butterflies along one of Britain's finest stretches of Roman road, leading across 8 miles of downland to Iron Age hill-fort of Badbury Rings.

Alderholt Mill ☑ Ce
Working water mill on 14th-century site. Milling demonstrations held on Sunday afternoons. Art exhibitions, glass engraving and crafts.

Ashmore ⛪ Ae
Magnificent views from highest (700ft) village in Dorset. Thatched cottages and houses of grey-green stone, 18th-century Old Rectory and part-medieval church overlook duck pond.

Avon Forest Country Park ☂♿☕※ Cd
Country park with 580 acres of heathland and pine woodland. Guided walks and visitor centre with wildlife displays. Birds include Dartford warbler.

Ballard Down ※ Bb
Heady Dorset downland. Walk west 2 or 3 miles for views of Corfe Castle. Go east to the coast for cliffs and offshore rock features.

Bolderwood Grounds ♿♀♣ Dd
Waymarked walks through Douglas firs, Californian redwoods, Japanese cedar and Norway spruce. Deer sanctuary with viewing platform and arboretum.

Bournemouth ⛪♿☑ Bc
Miles of sandy beaches, 2000 acres of parks and gardens, and two piers. Paintings and oriental objects in the Russell Coates Art Gallery and Museum. Casa Magni Shelley Museum devoted to poet and named after his Italian home.

Breamore ⛪⊞⛲※ Ce
Tudor village with Saxon church. Tapestries, art and antiques in Breamore House, completed 1583, occupied by Hulse family since 1748. Medieval 'miz-maze'

cut in turf on Breamore Down may mark the course of a religious ritual or folk dance.

Brownsea Island ♥♣ Bb
Heath and woodland nature reserve, reached by ferry from Sandbanks or Poole Quay. Home of red squirrels and second-largest heronry in Britain, sika deer, water birds and waterfowl. Bird hide and guided walks.

Burley ⛪※※ Dd
Scattered village near western edge of New Forest with attractive cottages, antique shops and village pub. One mile north-west lies Castle Hill, an Iron Age fortress; remains of its earthworks can be traced among gnarled trees on summit.

Christchurch ✝⛪⛲✿♥☑ Cc
This largely Edwardian town still retains its Saxon street plan. Ancient priory church, founded 1094, has blend of styles from Saxon to Renaissance, and memorial to poet Shelley. Tower holds 12 bells, two cast in 1370, all still rung regularly. Ruins of castle keep built around 1100. Red House Museum has some geology exhibits and wildlife displays. Tricycle museum, Saxon water mill and marsh nature reserve.

Compton Acres ✿ Bb
Individual gardens including Roman, Italian, Palm Court, Rock and Water, Woodland Walk, and Heather Dell. Fine Japanese garden complete with pagoda.

CASTLE RUINS *Ancient villainies haunt the stones of Corfe.*

Corfe Castle ⛪⛫☑ Ab
Centuries of cruelty in this fortress began with murder of 18-year-old King Edward the Martyr in 978, and ended with castle being wrecked by Cromwellians in 1646. Remains dominate a village of grey-stone houses, many built with stone taken from ruined castle, and lending uniformity to the whole village.

Cranborne ⛪✿ Be
Brick and timber Stuart and Georgian houses line twisting byways of this market village; former seat of Chase Court controlling hunting rights in Cranborne Chase until 1102. Outstanding 13th-century church has barrel roof and wall paintings. Manor House, home of the Marquesses of Salisbury, dates back to 1208. Historic gardens open in summer.

Cranborne Chase ※※ Ae
Lonely remnant of a royal hunting forest, once the bloody haunt of poachers and smugglers. Win Green Hill with clump of trees on 910ft summit gives fine views.

Dinton ⛪⊞ Bg
Village with three fine houses: early Tudor Little Clarendon; Lawes Cottage, home of John Milton's composer friend William Lawes; and 19th-century Philippes House with Grecian façade.

Dorset Cursus �🏛 Ae
Neolithic earthworks; two parallel banks flanked with barrows stretching several miles. Probably a religious ceremonial route.

Durlston Country Park ☂ Ba
Superb stretch of countryside and cliff; carved stone globe placed on cliff top in 1887 weighs 40 tons. Portland Stone Trail passes Tilly Whim quarry caves (now closed), colonies of gulls and shags, and fossil-rich Durlston Bay.

Fifield Bavant ⛪⊛※ Bf
Chequered flint and stone walled church contends for 'smallest church in England' title at 35ft long. During First World War, Kitchener's New Armies trained at nearby Fovant and cut regimental badges in hillside chalk.

Hengistbury Head ♥※ Cc
Spit of land 2 miles long, with spine of low hills between mudflats and beaches. Important archaeological site, wildlife conservation area and leisure centre. Land-train runs to tip. Nature trail through grasslands and woods. Observation point for bird life.

Holt Heath ♿ Bd
Covering 2000 acres; one of the largest Dorset heaths. Paradise of unusual plants, birds and animals, including marsh gentian, Dartford warbler and sand lizard.

Kimmeridge Bay ⊞ Aa
Sweep of shingle beach overlooked by 19th-century folly of Clavell Tower. Oil discovered here in 1958, extracted by 'nodding donkey' pump. Low, fossil-rich cliffs yield giant ammonites. Nearby Smedmore House built by Sir William Clavell in 1630s.

Knoll Gardens ✿ Bc
More than 300 species of plants in rare, worldwide collection among waterfalls, rockeries and woodland glen, covering 6 acres.

Knowlton Circles ⏛ Be
Remains of a Norman church stand in centre of 800ft diameter Stone Age circle, largest of three in a row. Church said to have been built to counter the rings' power.

Old Wardour Castle ⛫ Af
Beside a placid lake stand remains of castle, destroyed by exploding gunpowder in 1643. Site exhibitions in landscaped grounds.

Poole ⛵⛪♣♨⛫☑ Bc
Flourishing port and market town since 13th century. History told in three museums. The Guildhall Museum in Market Street has audiovisual presentation built up from collections of old photographs. Maritime Museum off the quay has lively displays on such themes as the Spanish Armada. Scalpen's Court medieval merchant house in High Street, full of domestic items; kitchen complete with cooking and cleaning equipment from medieval times.

Rockbourne ⛪♿⛪※ Ce
Village with one long street, consisting of Tudor and Georgian houses and splendid thatched cottages. Those on north side are reached across little bridges spanning a brook. Grouped around a courtyard are remains of Roman villa. Museum displays finds which include mosaics.

Salisbury ✝⛪⊞♥ Cf
Charming 13th-century cathedral city on rivers Avon, Bourne, Nadder and Wylye. Early Gothic cathedral, with England's tallest spire at 404ft, has 1386 clock claimed to be world's oldest working clock. Cathedral includes stone taken from original Norman cathedral built on hill top called Old Sarum, north of city. Library treasures include an original of the Magna Carta. Fine buildings within Cathedral Close include Bishop's Palace and 18th-century Mompesson House. The grid streets contain black-and-white half-timbered houses such as 16th-century Joiners' Hall. In King's House, Salisbury and South Wiltshire Museum contains important prehistoric remains.

VAULTED GLORY *A fine fan-vaulted ceiling graces the Chapter House in Salisbury Cathedral.*

Studland ⛪♥☆ Bb
Unspoiled village with restored Norman church. Nature trails cover dunes, woodland and swamp with wildfowl, butterflies and lizards. Agglestone boulder said to have been dumped by the devil on his way to drop it on Salisbury Cathedral. Sandy beach.

Swanage ⛪☂⛫☑ Ba
Town Hall's façade taken from London's Mercer's Hall, and Wellington Clock once adorned London Bridge. Old Tithe Barn Museum contains town relics. King Alfred beat Danes in 877 naval battle in bay. Good bathing at this seaside resort.

Teffont Evias ⛪✿ Ag
Delightful village in the Nadder Valley; houses, approached by bridges over the Teff stream,

GREEN PEACE *The church and manor at Teffont Evias rise from tranquil meadowlands by the River Nadder.*

mostly built from local Chilmark stone. Church with tall, slim steeple, rebuilt 1820s, retains Elizabethan tombs. Nearby Teffont Magna has church with 13th-century bell on windowsill.

Tisbury ⌂⛪ Af
Village on steep slope above River Nadder. Fine panelling and carved roof distinguish 12th-century church where Rudyard Kipling's parents are buried. Partly 17th-century almshouses, and 200ft tithe barn at Place Farm, with fort-like gatehouse.

Tollard Royal ⌂ Ae
Old capital of Cranborne Chase tucked away in a wooded hollow. Peaceful place of pink cottages submerged in billows of thatch. King John's 13th-century house was once occupied by 'father of archaeology' General Augustus Pitt-Rivers, 1827-1900.

Wareham ✝⌂ Ab
Market town with spacious Georgian main street. Saxon church has sculpture of T.E. Lawrence (of Arabia) by Eric Kennington. Lawrence died in Dorset, and Wareham museum has records of his life. Overlooking Old Quay, St Mary's Church contains marble coffin of Edward the Martyr, who was murdered in Corfe in 978.

Wilton ✝⌂⚜ Bg
Crowded little town that has played many roles in its long history – Saxon capital, medieval monastic centre, and one of England's first manufacturing centres. Severe, early 18th-century Market Hall in Market Place. Italian-style Church of St Mary and St Nicholas built 1842 with separate bell tower, mosaics, coloured marbles and medieval stained glass. Wilton House, home of the Earls of Pembroke, stands on site of an abbey founded by Alfred the Great. House destroyed by fire in 1647 and reconstructed by Inigo Jones; fine furniture and paintings. Royal Wilton carpet factory, established 1655, set round courtyard.

Wimborne Minster
✝⌂⚜⛪⚐�︎ Bc
Twin-towered Minster dominates town. Its varied architecture reflects 1000 years of history. Astronomical clock shows earth as centre of universe; library (1686) has antique books secured by chains. Heritage Trust exhibitions in Market House. Richly furnished 17th-century Kingston Lacy House, 3 miles north-west, has landscaped gardens and paintings by Rubens, Titian, Velàzquez, and Tintoretto.

Woodgreen ⌂ Ce
Stout hedges keep ponies out of this typical brick-and-thatch New Forest village. Hall has unique murals depicting rural life in the 1930s. Footpath to The Drove, avenue of ancient oaks.

Worth Matravers ⌂ Aa
Purbeck marble quarried here for centuries; story told in Coach House Museum of quarrying. Norman Church of St Nicholas noted for nave, chancel and windows. Coastal path has splendid view of St Aldhelm's Head.

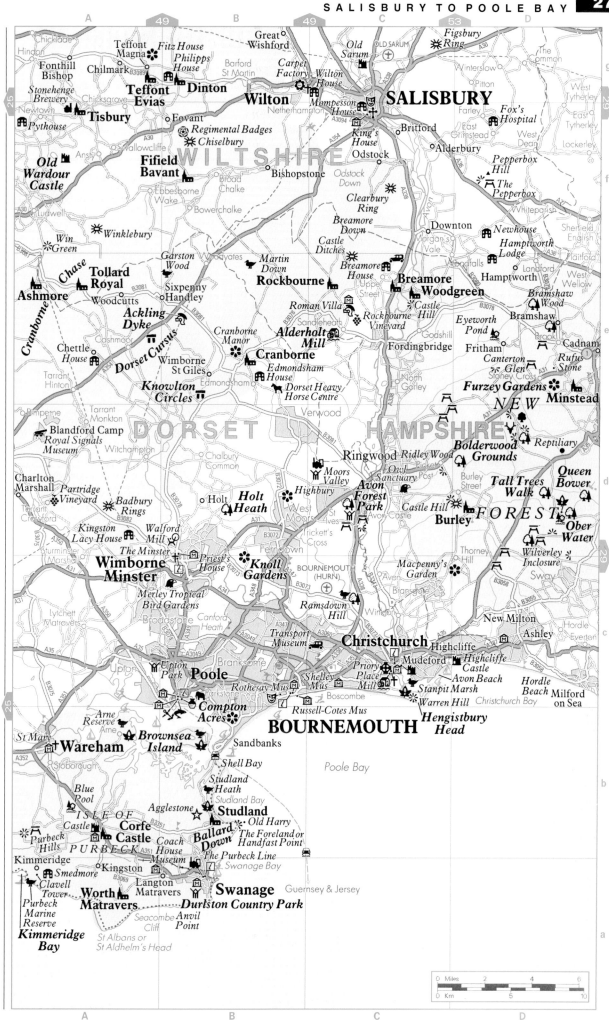

The Alresfords 🚶🏛🅿 De
Causeway crosses 12th-century pond from Old Alresford – where heroic Admiral Rodney lies buried near 18th-century church – to New Alresford where lime trees front Broad Street's colour-washed Georgian houses. Footpath along River Itchen passes watercress beds.

Avington 🏛🏛 De
Nell Gwynne, Shelley family and Dukes of Chandos all lived at Park Mansion; originally 16th century but remodelled late 17th century. Ballroom has magnificent painted ceiling in gold plaster-work. Georgian church of 1770 between house and village.

Beaulieu 🚶♦🏛🚗♦☑ Bb
Attractive village of red-brick Georgian cottages, dominated by Palace House, originally 14th-century Great Gatehouse of Cistercian abbey. Now home to Lord Montagu and National Motor Museum with 200 historic motor vehicles, monorail and Cistercian cloisters. Parish church was abbey refectory.

THE NEW FOREST OF THE NORMANS

Two great cities dominate this area – Winchester, Saxon and Norman capital of England for centuries, and Southampton, once a Norman seaport and still a busy maritime centre. Trout streams and rivers flow down to inlets on the Solent, while the wooded glades and heaths of the New Forest – in fact the oldest of England's great forests – are home to deer and ponies.

Brown. Exhibition recalls Lord Mountbatten's career as statesman, sailor and sportsman.

Bucklers Hard 🚶✂⚓ Ca
Once a busy 18th-century naval shipyard. Life-size effigies and vivid tableaux tell village story in Maritime Museum.

Exbury Gardens ❀ Cb
A paradise for rhododendron lovers, begun by Leonard de Rothschild after World War I. Now contains 1200 varieties among maze of paths in 200 acre woodland. Fine camellias, azaleas, magnolias. Plant centre.

Keyhaven 🚶🕊 Ba
Bird sanctuary; winter visitors include Brent geese, shelduck, teal, dunlin and lapwing. Walk along pebble spit or take ferry to Hurst Castle, built by Henry VIII but now with Victorian façade. Excellent views from Solent Way, running above marshes.

Lymington ✝❀🕊 Ba
Busy port and yachting centre on estuary of Lymington river; ferry to Isle of Wight. Walks along Park Shore and Needs Oar Point take in North Solent Nature Reserve, with Britain's largest colony of black-headed gulls.

by car. Special attractions are the Asiatic lions, smaller and much rarer than African varieties; only 300 now survive.

Mid-Hants Railway 🚂 Ee
Restored steam train runs 10 miles through farmland and up the steep inclines between New Alresford and Alton. Called the 'Watercress Line' as it was once used by growers to get produce to market. Stops at two stations, both restored to their former steam-age glory.

Minstead 🚶❀🎣🅰 Ac
Village set in maze of lanes with 13th-century church where Sir Arthur Conan Doyle (creator of Sherlock Holmes) is buried in churchyard. One mile north-west, Rufus Stone marks presumed spot where William II was killed by an arrow while hunting in 1100. Fine oaks in nearby Canterton Glen.

Mottisfont Abbey 🏛❀ Bd
National Trust house converted from medieval monastery where all is not what it seems; painted 'illusions' by Rex Whistler include ornamental plaster-work and alcoves. Cedar trees, lawns and romantic walled rose garden.

New Forest Butterfly Farm 🦋 Bb
Multicoloured butterflies hover among tropical plants inside huge greenhouses. Bees hum in cottage garden, while scorpions and tarantulas lurk behind glass in the insectarium. Dragonfly pond, aviary and horse-drawn wagon rides through surrounding 2000 acre woodlands.

Ober Water 🎣❀🅰 Ab
Walks laid out by Forestry Commission to show 'secrets' of New Forest, starting at Puttles Bridge or Whitefield Moor. Easy strolls along banks of the peat-stained stream, stocked with trout. Woodpeckers among oaks and Scots pines of Aldridge Enclosure.

Ovington 🚶 De
Small village attractively situated on south bank of River Itchen, where it is joined by two other streams, the Candover and the Alre. There is a 400-year-old village inn with a low-ceilinged bar and huge log fireplaces at either end of it.

Paulton's Park 🦩🏛 Bc
Pink flamingos browse in wildfowl lake; rare breeds graze in paddocks with llamas and wallabies; and large aviaries house exotic birds. Romany Museum depicts nomadic gypsy life and Village Life Museum features workshops and tools of blacksmith, carpenter and dairymaid.

Portchester 🏰⚓ Eb
Situated on Portsmouth Harbour with remains of notable Norman castle, built by Henry II inside walls of Roman fort. Henry V marshalled forces here for 1415 expedition to Agincourt. Norman church originally part of 1133 Augustinian priory.

Queen Bower 🦌 Ab
Magical glade with gnarled oaks and beeches, much loved by Queen Eleanor, wife of Edward I. After heavy rain, creamy torrent surges over banks where Ober Water and Lymington river meet at bridge forming swampland of pools and islands.

Romsey ♦🏛☑ Bd
Small market town with large abbey, founded 907 and enlarged in 12th century; now recognised as one of Europe's finest Norman buildings. Treasures span the centuries; Anglo-Saxon Crucifixion sculpture and richly coloured Edwardian east windows. Lord Mountbatten is buried in the south transept.

VINTAGE CARS *Beaulieu's Motor Museum possesses an outstanding collection of history-making vehicles.*

Beaulieu Heath 🅰 Bb
Yellow blaze of gorse alternates in summer with dark heather on sandy heath, reaching from Southampton almost to Lymington. River Beaulieu crosses heath to become tidal at Beaulieu.

WILD HORSES *New Forest ponies run free on Beaulieu Heath.*

Bishop's Waltham 🏰 Dc
Grey ruined walls outline vast area once covered by palace of Bishops of Winchester, built 1135 and victim of civil war. Dower House displays recount its history. The High Street has 18th and 19th-century buildings, and Victorian lamppost topped by bishop's mitre.

Broadlands 🏛 Bd
This 16th-century house – transformed into Palladian masterpiece by Henry Holland for Palmerston family in 18th century – now home of Mountbatten family. Fine plaster-work, sculpture, pictures and furniture. River Test runs through grounds by Capability

Farley Mount Country Park 🦌 Cd
Roman road from Winchester to Salisbury cuts through downs in 1000 acre park. Rare plants, waymarked woodland walks, and prehistoric burial ground. Views from 572ft Beacon Hill.

Furzey Gardens ❀ Ac
Informal, pesticide-free gardens created in 1920s. Trees from Australia and South America, azaleas, heathers and self-seeding wild flowers co-exist on hillside site with New Forest views, carp-stocked lake and doves.

Gosport ✂🏛☑ Ea
Watch ships in Portsmouth harbour from Ferry Gardens. Royal Navy Submarine Museum has salvaged 1901 *Holland I* and 1817 wooden-walled HMS *Foudroyant*. Fishing by pier.

Hillier Gardens and Arboretum ❀♣ Bd
Over 10,000 different species of shrubs and trees offer all-season colour in extensive gardens.

Hinton Ampner 🏛 Dd
Fine Tudor farmhouses surround secluded village. National Trust Manor House rebuilt in 18th century has Regency furniture, paintings and porcelain.

Hursley 🚶🏰 Cd
Tudor-like village with one street. Richard, son of Oliver Cromwell, buried in churchyard near the poet and theologian John Keble. Remains of 1138 Merdon Castle in Hursley Park.

Lyndhurst ✝🏛☑ Ab
Ancient capital of the New Forest with largely 17th-century Queen's House, home of Lord Warden of the Forest, used as meeting place for governing 'Verderers'. Multicoloured church, built in 1860s, has windows by Burne-Jones and Morris. Alice (Hargreaves) of *Alice in Wonderland* lies in churchyard.

Marwell Zoo 🐘 Dd
Breeding centre for endangered species and one of Britain's largest zoos. Explore 100 acres on foot or

ALL SHIPSHAPE *Tidy Georgian cottages line the street at Bucklers Hard, where Nelson's* Agamemnon *was built.*

Soberton 🏛 Ec

Peaceful Meon Valley village. Church on hill has flint 16th-century tower decorated with demons and gargoyles, built by a butler and dairymaid according to commemorative plaque. Chancel has rare altar cloth of 1645.

Southampton
🏛⚔🏌🏛☑ Cc

Port with rich seafaring history, and former home of great passenger liners. The Pilgrim Fathers set sail for America from here in 1620 – memorial in Mayflower Park. Norman city walls and towers remain, while historic buildings house various collections: furniture in restored Merchant's House of 13th century; local history in 14th-century Guildhall; archaeological finds in 15th-century God's House Tower; domestic bygones and toys in 16th-century Tudor House with secret garden; the Maritime Museum in 18th-century Wool House has *Titanic* display and 22ft model of the liner *Queen Mary*. Sandringham 'Beachcomber' flying boat is pride of Hall of Aviation.

Spinners ❀ Ba

Azaleas, rhododendrons, blue poppies and primulas flourish in garden created by owners.

Tall Trees Walk ♤ Ab

New Forest showpiece. Avenue, 1½ miles long, passing among awesome redwoods and wellingtonias that soar to dizzying 160 ft. Diversions to Black Water and to Brock Hill.

Tichborne 🏛 De

Village with partly Norman parish church, having many monuments to local Tichborne family who lived here from 1135. Tichborne Dole ceremony held every year on March 25, when flour is distributed to villagers; custom started in 1150 by Roger de Tichborne.

Titchfield ✚☙ Db

Little village, once a seaport. Ruined Place House built 1537-42 from an abbey by Earl of Southampton. Charles I spent last night of freedom there in 1647. Redbrick Georgian cottages line main street. Part-Saxon church. Nature reserve at Titchfield Haven (by permit), winter home to wigeons.

Twyford 🏛 Cd

Benjamin Franklin and Alexander Pope both associated with this pretty village. Franklin wrote two parts of his autobiography at Twyford House, while Pope was expelled from school for lampooning a teacher.

Upper Hamble Country Park
🏛 Cc

Hampshire farm life from 1850-1950 re-created in museum with sparsely furnished farmhouse and 18th-century barn. Shaded river walks and paths across open fields with saddleback pigs and shorthorn cattle.

Warsash 🏛☙ Cb

Yachting centre where low tide reveals shipwreck, cannon, and musket balls. Ferry to Hamble with yachts and 13th-century church. Shore walk of 4 miles to Hill Head for beach fishing.

ARTHURIAN ENIGMA *The Round Table in Winchester's Great Hall is of unknown origin.*

Wickham 🏛 Dc

Georgian houses of red and grey brick surround square. Mill next to bridge built from timbers of American frigate *Chesapeake*, captured in 1813. Town was birthplace in 1324 of William of Wykeham who founded Winchester College public school and New College, Oxford.

Winchester
✝🏛⚒🏛☑☑ Cd

Royal capital of Saxon Wessex, and of England, until late 12th century. Fine medieval Great Hall is sole remnant of castle, begun 1067 and rebuilt by Henry III; regarded as King Arthur's Camelot by Tudors, complete with a Round Table. Barracks house museum of Royal Hussars, with real tanks and lifelike model horses. In Romsey Road, museum of Royal Green Jackets. Cathedral begun 1079 for William the Conqueror has medieval wall paintings. Contains shrine of St Swithun, tombs of William Rufus and Jane Austen, and bones of pre-Norman kings, including Canute. Pilgrims Hall has one of England's oldest hammerbeam roofs, built about 1290. Winchester College, 1382, one of Britain's oldest public schools. Pupils known as Wykehamists after founder, William of Wykeham.

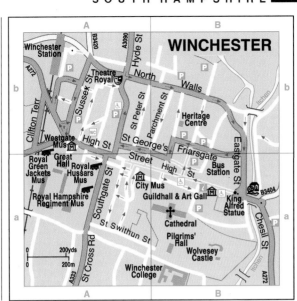

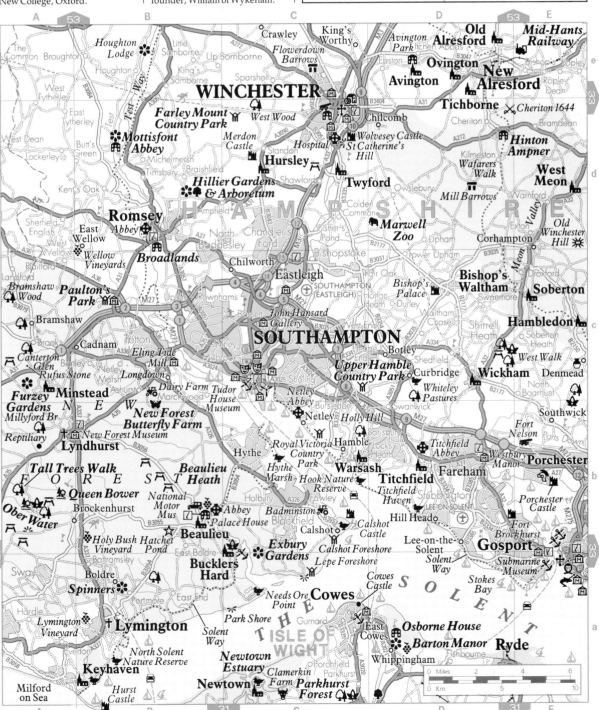

SUMMER RESORT OF ROYALTY

Sandy bays, high cliffs and sheltered creeks fringe England's second smallest county. Inland, the River Medina flows through a gently sloping downland, dotted with farms, woods and attractive little villages. The Victorians built forts along the coast to guard against invasion from the Continent, and Queen Victoria and Prince Albert made the island their summer home.

Alum Bay ✿✿✳ Ab
Multicoloured sands streak lofty cliffs above a pebbly beach, reached by steps or chairlift. Glassblowing in cliff-top glassworks and boat trips to view The Needles rocks.

Appuldurcombe House ▥ Ca
Gaunt shell of baroque mansion in parkland laid out by Capability Brown. Built in 1701 by Sir Robert Worsley with giant pilasters and magnificent pavilions on either side. Museum tells history of the house.

Arreton Manor ▦✿ Cb
Exhibitions of Victorian lace and fashion in Jacobean house with fine panelling and period furniture. National Wireless Museum includes sets dating back to the First World War.

Barton Manor ✿✿✿ Cc
Vines flourish on estate once owned by Queen Victoria. Wine tastings are held in outbuildings built by Prince Albert, who laid out 20 acre gardens. Old photographs give fascinating glimpse of royal visitors.

Bembridge ✿✿ Db
Natural harbour crammed with yachts and houseboats. Lifeboat pier dominates the sandy beach. England's oldest working telephone box, dating from 1921, stands in Foreland Road. Local shipwreck relics in the Maritime Museum. Well-preserved windmill (1700) outside village.

Bembridge Down ✳ Db
Deserted Victorian fort on 343ft summit overlooks Sandown Bay, Bembridge harbour and Hampshire coast. Obelisk is a memorial to 1st Earl of Yarborough.

Blackgang Chine ✿✿ Ba
Named after local band of smugglers this chine or cleft now hosts Fantasy Theme Park; includes a maze, fairy castle, jungle trail, full-size replicas of dinosaurs, 75ft whale skeleton and an Indian camp. Views of cliffs and rocks that have claimed 180 ships since 1750.

Brading Roman Villa ✿ Cb
Grain-drying oven identifies 3rd-century villa as centre of a Roman agricultural estate. Superb mosaic floors, some with underfloor heating. Museum with Roman coins, pottery and wall paintings.

Brighstone ▮ Bb
Chalk-built thatched cottages and a post office with roses round the door stand three-quarters of a mile from the sea. Plaque in 12th-century church records that three rectors became bishops, as does the Three Bishops pub.

Brook Chine ✿ ✿ Ab
Ravine cut into the island's south cliffs; 'chine' coming from Saxon word 'to crack'. Rough path from hamlet of Brook leads down to sheltered sandy beach.

POET'S VIEW *Alfred Lord Tennyson often walked past Arched Rock in Freshwater Bay, then on to distant Tennyson Down which was named after him.*

FIT FOR A KING *Charles I was imprisoned by Parliamentarians at 12th-century Carisbrooke Castle in the months before his execution in 1649. He tried to escape through a window in the Great Hall but became wedged in between the bars.*

Calbourne ▮ Bb
Peacocks strut on banks of the Caul Bourne, which powers a 17th-century water mill still grinding corn. Outbuildings display domestic bygones. Stone cottages with colourful gardens line stream in Winkle Street.

Carisbrooke Castle ▥▦✿ Bb
Imposing Norman and Tudor castle on ridge above Newport. Superb views from keep where Charles I was imprisoned shortly before 1649 execution. Donkeys operate a 16th-century treadwheel drawing water from a well. Governor's House contains Isle of Wight Museum, with Stuart relics and Tennyson memorabilia.

Cowes ▦✿▤ Bc
Victorian and Edwardian shops line narrow streets behind a wide esplanade. Cowes Castle is home of Royal Yacht Squadron and starting point for races. Boat-yards edge the River Medina. Regattas every summer weekend; Cowes Week is first one in August.

Culver Cliff ✳ Db
Culver Down ends in a 300ft chalk cliff overlooking Sandown Bay. Nesting site for many sea birds. Superb views across Sandown Bay from Culver Down.

Freshwater Bay Ab
Sheer cliffs pierced with caves embrace a tiny cove. Stag Rock, Arched Rock and Mermaid Rock lie off rugged foreshore which extends west to The Needles.

Godshill ▮▦▦✿ Cb
Two picturesque villages in one – the second, a model, stands in vicarage gardens. More miniatures in the Toy Museum, including dolls and clockwork toys. Talking cockatoos in aviaries at Old Smithy Garden. Deadly piranha fish at Natural History Centre's tropical aquarium.

Haseley Manor ▦ Cb
Built in the 11th century as a royal residence for King Harold. Tudor timbers lie behind splendid Georgian façade. Rooms feature tableaux of costumes from medieval to Victorian times. The grounds include a 'have-a-go' pottery.

Isle of Wight Steam Railway ▤ Cc
Vintage locomotives, restored to original livery, puff along the track through woodland and meadows between Havenstreet and Wooton. Museum illustrates the island's railway history.

Isle of Wight Zoo ▮ Db
Rare and endangered animals in granite fort on Sandown's seafront. Includes venomous snakes, exotic birds and big cats.

Luccombe Chine ✿ ⌂ Ca
Leads down 300 steps to beach; coastal walk 1 mile to Luccombe village and Old Shanklin.

Mersley Down ✳ Cb
Switchback road running westward behind Brading climbs to 420ft, offering views across Solent to Sussex coast.

Morton Manor ▦ Db
Tudor house with Georgian furniture. Elizabethan sunken garden, rose garden and ornamental ponds. Adjoining vineyard grows seven varieties of grapes.

Mottistone ▮ Bb
Walnut trees ring an old well on village green. Beautiful Tudor manor house, home of island's Lord Lieutenant, can be seen from Military Road. Path from 12th to 14th-century church leads to great pillar of the Long Stone, part of a Stone Age long barrow.

Needles Old Battery ✿✿✳▥ Ab
Amusements in Needles Pleasure Park on cliff top above Alum Bay. Chairlift descends 165ft to bay. Footpath leads to Old Battery, a restored Victorian fort overlooking The Needles – three chalk pinnacles standing in sea – remnants of a ridge that once joined Isle of Wight to mainland.

Newport ✿✿✿✿ Cb
Island capital at the head of the River Medina. Town has some attractive 17th-century houses. Old docks now host pleasure craft and a Georgian quayside warehouse has an arts and crafts centre. Guildhall built by Regency architect John Nash, with clock tower commemorating Queen Victoria's Golden Jubilee. Roman villa in Cypress Road has restored rooms and bathhouse, including hypocaust. Museum contains array of excavated finds.

Newtown ▮▦✿ Bc
Tranquil village with 18th-century Old Town Hall. Once the flourishing port of Francheville, destroyed by French raiders in 1377, and rebuilt as Newtown. Noah's Ark House was the village inn until 1916.

Newtown Estuary ✿ Bc
Windswept marshes border a maze of shallow creeks and Newtown river estuary. Waders, wildfowl and Canada geese frequent 800 acre reserve.

Nunwell House ▦ Cb
Part Jacobean and part Georgian mansion in parkland and gardens reflecting five centuries of island history. Family militaria collection and island Home Guard Museum.

DISCREET DIP *Queen Victoria's bathing machine at Osborne was used to transport her down to the sea.*

Osborne House ▦ Cc
Italianate summer home designed by Prince Albert in the 1840s for Queen Victoria. Ornate rooms are stuffed with royal presents;

private apartments exactly as the queen left them when she died in 1901. Horse-drawn carriage ride to Swiss Cottage, built in grounds for Victoria's children.

Parkhurst Forest 🐿 ✿ Bc
Ancient hunting forest of 1000 acres, some parts have been replanted. Waymarked walks through woodlands inhabited by red squirrels.

Ryde 🏛 ✿ Cc
Half-mile 1813 pier spans broad sands, and 1880 electric railway links Ryde to Shanklin. Streets of mainly Victorian and Edwardian architecture rise steeply from seafront. Gardens and miniature golf in Appley Park.

St Boniface Down ✳ Ca
Highest point on the island, rising to 785ft. Superb viewpoint on Isle of Wight's south-east coast, extending from St Catherine's Point to Culver Cliff.

St Catherine's Hill ▲ 🏯 Ba
Summit (780ft) crowned by ruins of St Catherine's Oratory, built as a lighthouse in 1323. 'Salt Cellar' circle of bricks was to be a second lighthouse; work began in 1785 but never finished. Path over St Catherine's Down passes ball-topped column, commemorating 1814 visit of Russia's Alexander I. South lies 1840 lighthouse at St Catherine's Point.

St Helen's 🏯 Db
Houses in a medley of styles stand around large green. On the seafront, whitewashed ruined tower of 12th-century priory serves as a landmark for sailors.

St Lawrence 🏯 ⚘ Ca
Norman Old Church is one of the smallest in Britain. Old Park estate is situated on 6 mile ledge formed by landslides known as the Undercliff. Wooded scenery houses walk-through aviaries, with over 300 exotic birds.

Sandown 🏛 🐾 ✳ 🎫 Cb
Popular resort in island's largest bay. Six miles of safe, golden sands and a pier theatre. Geology museum explores island fossils, housed in Sandown library.

Shanklin Chine ☆ Cb
Leafy winding glen with marked nature trail leading up to Shanklin town centre set on cliffs above sheltered sands and pier. Crab Hotel, one of the Isle of Wight's prettiest inns is in Old Shanklin.

Sir Max Aitken Museum 🏛 Bc
Nautical paintings, figureheads, models and memorabilia housed in old sail-loft at Cowes.

Tennyson Down ✳ 📓 Ab
Dramatic chalk ridge rises 480ft above Freshwater Bay. Monument to Victorian poet, Alfred Lord Tennyson, who used to walk here. Fine views of Portland Bill and Southampton Water.

Totland 🏯 Ab
Sea wall, 1 mile long, fringes steep sand and shingle beach. Safe bathing, good fishing and boat trips to Alum Bay and The Needles from the pier.

Ventnor 🏛 ✳ Ca
Terraces zigzagging below St Boniface Down add a continental air, while sheltering downs provide a mild climate. Subtropical plants in Botanic Gardens and smuggling museum on seafront.

Whale Chine ☆ Ba
Steep ravine with 126 wooden steps down to secluded 2 mile shingle beach. Good fishing and fossil hunting.

Yafford Mill 🏭 Bb
Water wheel still turns at this 19th-century grain mill. Rare breeds of farm animals and old farm tools on view. In spring bluebells line the mill stream, home to moorhens and ducks.

HARBOUR HOME *Fishing boats and yachts secure in the Yar estuary.*

Yarmouth 🏯 🏯 ⚘ Ab
Neat town and busy harbour, below Henry VIII's castle. Coastal defence displays in Gunners' Lodgings. Nature trail by River Yar begins near the Lymington ferry port.

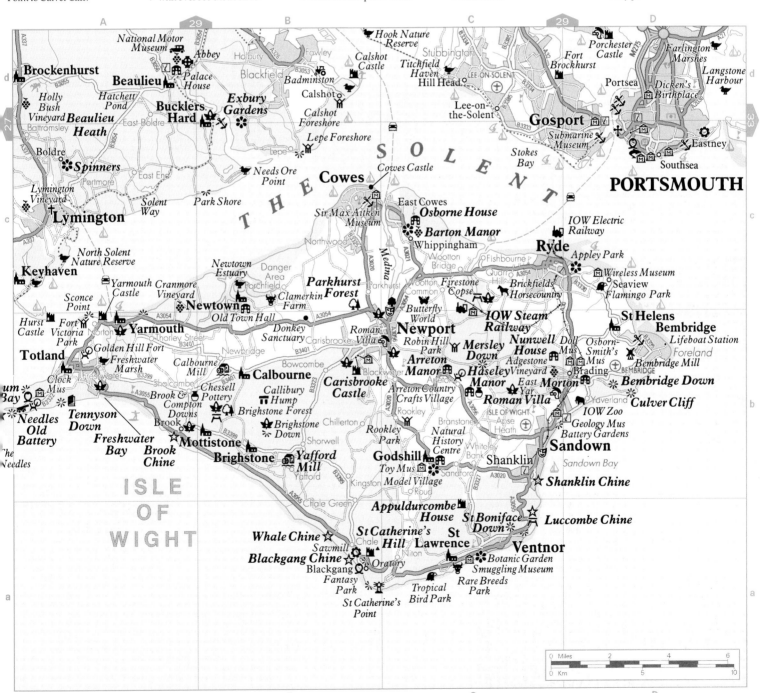

AROUND THE ROTHER VALLEY

The benign bulk of the South Downs links Hampshire and West Sussex, and acts as a protective presence between sea and hinterland. Early people built hill-forts and buried their dead in the high places; the Romans came and left their orderly mark on towns such as Chichester. Today, the peaceful pleasures of yachting, fishing, walking and bathing are pursued.

Apuldram Cc
Ancient parish on the salt flats of Chichester harbour with 13th-century church and 15th-century Rymans manor, privately owned. Haven for wildfowl such as Brent geese and shelducks.

Beacon Hill Cd
High on the South Downs, 793ft. Traces of Iron Age dwellings and hill-fort on 80 mile South Downs Way between Hampshire border and Beachy Head in Sussex.

Bignor Dd
At foot of South Downs, village of farm buildings and timbered cottages set around four lanes. Large Roman villa here has 65 rooms with superb mosaics. Roman Stane Street, built between Chichester and London, runs nearby. Three-mile stretch can still be walked, as sound as when legions marched along it. At Bignor Hill 1¼ miles south is late Stone Age enclosure, one of largest camps with causeway in Britain.

Birdham Cc
Watch boats in the 1000 berth Chichester Yacht Basin. Church, 16th century, has small door, so shaped to keep out the Devil.

Bosham Bc
Beautiful Bosham – pronounced 'Bozzom' locally – with closely packed thatched and tiled cottages, surrounded by creeks of Chichester harbour. Sailing is main preoccupation; landlubbers visit the Saxon Church of Holy Trinity, which contains panel of Bayeux Tapestry. King Harold said to have prayed there before Battle of Hastings, 1066.

Bow Hill Cd
There are more than 200 recorded prehistoric burial mounds in Sussex. Bronze Age sites here, at Barrow Cemetery, are among county's best-preserved. Some of the best scenery of the South Downs round about the hill.

surrounded by city walls; Norman cathedral; 15th-century market cross; and Georgian houses. Local history in the District and Guildhall Museums. Period furniture, paintings and porcelain in Pallant House Gallery, a restored Queen Anne town house. The Festival Theatre, built 1962, holds yearly summer season of theatre. Harbour bird life includes black-tailed godwits, sanderlings, Brent geese and redshanks.

Dell Quay Cc
Main commercial harbour for Chichester in 18th century after the Chichester Channel silted up, now dedicated to sailing for pleasure. Specialist nursery, Apuldram Roses, has 250 varieties.

SEA PICTURE *Among Fishbourne's mosaic floors is this winged boy, who sits astride a dolphin.*

Fishbourne Cc
Step back almost 2000 years to what was once a sumptuous Roman palace of four wings around a formal garden, largest Roman building found in Britain. Discovered in 1960 by workmen laying water pipe. One wing conserved with replica of Roman dining room, and formal garden re-created. Notable 1st-century floor mosaics.

Goodwood House Cc
Seat of the Dukes of Richmond and Gordon, built of Sussex flint in late 18th century. Priceless collection of paintings, Louis XV furniture, and Sevres porcelain. Dressage Centre plays host to equestrian events. Sweeping views from nearby 'Glorious Goodwood' racecourse.

Hambledon Ad
Red-brick Georgian village was early home of cricket; cricket club (founded 1760) evolved laws of modern cricket. Bat and Ball Inn built in 17th century. George Hotel was 18th-century coaching stop. Vineyard on Windmill Down. Bury Lodge, to south, has remains of Roman villa.

Haslemere Cf
Prosperous commuter town; earlier affluence recalled in Georgian buildings. Church has stained-glass memorial to the poet Tenny-

son. Home of Dolmetsch family, makers of harpsichords and other early musical instruments.

Hayling Island Bc
Marshy island shaped like an inverted 'T', edged with safe sands and grassy dunes. Amble along old railway line from West Town along western shore; wide range of waders and wildfowl. Holiday resort, with water sports from westernmost point.

Hollycombe Steam Collection Ce
Woodlands and gardens where steam age is celebrated. Visitors can travel by steam train, listen to a steam organ, and marvel at the power of a paddle steamer.

Kingley Vale Cd
Nature reserve, 360 acres, in chalk valley with finest yew woods in Europe. Some trees almost 500 years old. Orchids, deer and more than 70 species of birds.

Langstone Bc
Tiny fishing village. Medieval port has picturesque waterside inns and the Langstone Mill. Overlooks low-lying marshy coast; officially designated Area of Outstanding Natural Beauty. Roman causeway crosses to Hayling Island. A mile east, ruins of 16th-century Warblington Castle and Saxon church with 14th-century wooden porch.

Midhurst Ce
Old market town on Rother with 15th-century coaching inn, The Spread Eagle, and fine half-timbered houses. Curfew still rung there at 8pm every evening in parish church.

Pagham Cb
Village retains its identity despite the embrace of burgeoning Bognor. Sea wall around harbour overlooks shingle beach and tidal mud flats, now a 1000 acre reserve containing more than 200 species of birds such as oystercatchers and shelducks. Rich in butterflies and moths. At southern end of harbour is Church Norton, with tiny chapel of St Wilfrid, 7th-century missionary.

Petersfield Be
Market town with handsome Georgian houses in Sheep Street and The Spain, names which recall the medieval woollen trade between England and Spain. In early 19th century, town was

VILLAGE SCENE *The zigzag path up the slopes of Selborne Hanger has good views of the village of Selborne.*

Black Down Df
Highest point in Sussex at 919ft, it rises from wooded plateau of 500 acres. Nature trail through Scots pine and oak woods where deer can be seen. Spectacular views of South Downs. Tennyson spent last years at his summer retreat Aldworth House, now a hotel, on east side of Black Down.

Bognor Regis Db
Sedate resort, granted 'Regis' title after George V convalesced here in 1928. Retains its identity despite being part of an extensive 7 mile stretch of seaside resorts. Good sands and safe beach. At eastern end is Felpham, with winding streets and flint cottages, where William Blake, visionary poet and artist, lived.

Buriton Be
Sleepy Hampshire village where Edward Gibbon, author of *The Decline and Fall of the Roman Empire* spent his boyhood in Georgian manor, still standing. On clear days, sea can be viewed from 888ft Butser Hill.

Butser Ancient Farm Bd
Replica Iron Age farm built with techniques used 2300 years ago; thatched house, stockaded bank and ditch and fields of crops planted at that time; working replicas of kilns and a loom.

Chichester Cc
History has left this city many legacies: orderly four-quarter layout from original Roman plan,

Denmans Dc
Series of ornamental gardens created on 19th-century estate. Walled, water and wild, each with an individual character. Teas, plants, dried flowers, herbs and other country produce on sale in old dairy and other buildings on former Home Farm.

East Meon Ae
Charming village on River Meon fished by that 'compleat angler', Izaak Walton, as it is by modern anglers. Brick and flint bridges, and thatched cottages. Norman Church of All Saints with magnificent font in black Tournai marble carved with Creation, Temptation and Expulsion from Eden. Courthouse of 14th century can be visited by appointment.

SHOW HOUSE *A 16th-century farmhouse forms part of a miniature village at the Weald and Downland Open Air Museum, in parkland near Singleton.*

staging post from London to Portsmouth; Red Lion Hotel was coaching inn. Lead equestrian statue of William III, erected 1812, in town square. Bear Museum and Doll's Hospital has collection of antique toys.

Petworth De

Timber-framed houses in a town that huddles close to the walls of 17th-century Petworth House, built by the Duke of Somerset. Magnificent 'natural' setting in 2000 acres created by Capability Brown, inspired the painter Turner, who had a studio there. Many of his works and those of Holbein, Rembrandt, Hals, Van Dyck, Titian and Gainsborough can be seen in the house.

Queen Elizabeth Country Park Bd

Walking, picnicking and grass-skiing in 1400 acres of working countryside, downland and woodlands. Demonstrations of forest and agricultural activities.

Selborne Bf

Pioneer naturalist Gilbert White (1720-93) would find his village unchanged although The Wakes, his home, is now a museum and library devoted to his work and to local hero Captain Oates, Antarctic explorer. Ancient yew tree, surrounded by a seat, stands outside the Norman church. Painted vans, Romany history, crafts and workshops in Romany Folklore Museum. Rising steeply above village is beech-clad Selborne Hanger where White made most of his detailed observations. At top is a monolith known as the Wishing Stone.

Singleton Cd

Weald and Downland Open Air Museum just outside village has historic buildings from medieval times until 19th century; local finds rescued from destruction include timber-framed medieval houses, Tudor market hall, village school and working water mill. Displays of crafts such as charcoal burning and flour milling.

ROOFTOP VIEW *South Harting's distinctive church spire is sheathed in bright green copper shingles.*

South Harting Bd

Village with wide main street lined with 17th-century and Georgian houses. Church of St Mary and St Gabriel is cruciform, with spire of green copper shingles. Slender memorial in churchyard by sculptor and typographer, Eric Gill. Parish stocks and whipping post with three sets of wrist irons outside churchyard gate.

Southsea Ab

Part of the City of Portsmouth; a holiday resort since Victorian times with a sand and shingle beach. Castle, built by Henry VIII, in 1545, now a museum with displays illustrating Portsmouth's development as a walled military garrison and naval base. Three sea forts visible from castle; the *Mary Rose*, Henry VIII's ship, sank at base of one of them in 1545.

Steep Be

Village on a ledge in the hill contours – and it is steep. Partly Norman church stands at the end of a tunnel of yew trees leading from lych gate; built to shield coffin and bearers from rain while awaiting priest. Cottage of Edward Thomas, poet, killed in action in France (1917); memorial stands on hill opposite.

Tangmere Dc

During 1940 Battle of Britain, fighter planes took off from local airfield; now aviation museum. Displays include one on intrepid Lysander pilots who flew secret agents in and out of Occupied Europe. Later exhibits from Falklands campaign. Battle of Britain Hall displays remains of aircraft, personal effects, photographs and paintings as lasting reminders of critical 1940 air battles. Museum extension includes reconstruction of famous 'Dambusters' raid.

Uppark Bd

Red-brick Queen Anne mansion overlooking landscaped gardens and South Downs with original furnishings and portrait collection. Well-preserved ceremonial rooms. Finest room is the Salon which has enormous portraits of George III and his queen, Charlotte. Once home of Emma, Lady Hamilton, Nelson's mistress.

West Dean Gardens Cd

Huge mock-baronial flint mansion of West Dean House, built by James Wyatt in 1804, has superb 35 acre gardens. Formal, wild and sunken gardens, colonnaded pergola draped with roses, honeysuckle and clematis, orangery and summerhouses. Lawns shaded by magnificent cedars of Lebanon. House, built entirely of flint in 1804, now used as college of arts and crafts; not open to the public.

West Meon Ae

Old village with timbered cottages and gabled roofs; burial place in 1832 of Thomas Lord, founder of Lord's cricket ground in London. Guy Burgess, the defector, also buried there.

West Itchenor Bc

Former commercial port, now sailing village on the Chichester Channel beach of hard shingle, from which boats can be launched at any state of the tide.

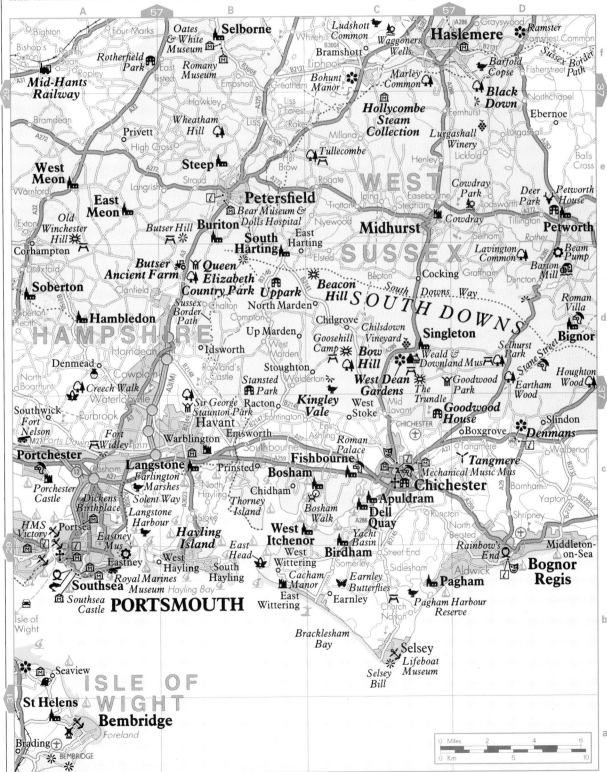

Australian Settlers Memorial Ab
Chain-link sculpture commemorates sailing of first convict ships to Australia in 1787.

City Museum 🏛 Cb
Displays of local history, including domestic life in Portsmouth. Furniture, glass and ceramics dating from the 17th century onwards. Also contemporary crafts and changing exhibitions.

BRITAIN'S MIGHTY NAVAL BASE

Portsmouth's great dockyard is a treasure house of Britain's maritime naval history. From here great fleets set sail to make Britain the most powerful seafaring nation in the world. The Royal Navy is smaller now, but numerous museums – including three of Britain's greatest warships – help to maintain the maritime atmosphere and traditions of the past.

Porter's House Ad
Oldest building in dockyard, dating from 1708.

Quebec House Ab
Weather-boarded house built in 1754 as sea-bathing centre is now private house.

Round Tower Ab
Built in 1415 to defend harbour entrance, tower stands at end of town's defences.

ON ACTIVE SERVICE *Guns on her deck as they were when Nelson's crew lived and fought there, HMS* Victory *is now the longest-serving warship in the world, as she is still in commission as a flagship.*

Mary Rose Exhibition ⚓ Ad
Exhibition features objects recovered from Henry VIII's warship – sunk in Solent in 1545 – including bronze guns, backgammon board and fiddles, pipes and drums of ship's band. Displays re-create shipboard life.

Mary Rose Ship Hall ⚓ Ae
Houses the part of the hull raised from seabed off Portsmouth in 1982. The timbers reveal skill of Tudor shipwrights.

Nelson Statue Ca
Statue faces beach where Nelson stood on English soil for last time before embarking on HMS *Victory* for Trafalgar.

Portsmouth Cathedral ✝ Bb
Church of St Thomas of Canterbury founded in 1185, but much of medieval building destroyed during Civil War. Choir and tower rebuilt during Restoration, and octagonal cupola and lantern added in 1703. Church was made a cathedral in 1927. Tomb of unknown sailor from the *Mary Rose* commemorates all those who died when ship sank.

Royal Naval Museum ⚓ Ad
Museum illustrates story of Royal Navy from Tudor times onwards, concentrating on lives and possessions of ordinary officers and seamen. Relics of Lord Nelson, figureheads and displays of naval history from Trafalgar to Falklands. Housed partly in three Georgian storehouses.

SAILORS' BEACON *For centuries the lantern above the cupola of the cathedral has been the first sight of home that sailors have seen on their return to Portsmouth from the sea.*

Commissioner's House Bd
Building constructed around 1785 for royal visitors is now Admiralty House, distinguished residence of the Commander-in-Chief, Naval Home Command.

Dockyard Apprentice Museum ⚓ Ce
Museum is part of Unicorn Training Centre. Models of ships used to illustrate building and repairing of naval vessels. Displays of tools and photographs of dockyard.

Double Ropehouse Ad
Longest building in the world when it was built in 1776 for making and storing naval ropes, after earlier wooden buildings had been destroyed by fire.

Garrison Church ✝ Bb
Founded in 1212 as hospice, and reduced to roofless remains by bombing during Blitz. Scene of marriage of Catherine of Braganza and Charles II in 1622.

Guildhall Cd
Built in 1890, fronted by columns and guarded by stone lions. Interior was reconstructed after being burnt out during 1941 air raid.

HMS Victory ⚓ Ae
Admiral Lord Nelson's flagship, restored as she was at Battle of Trafalgar, still serves as flagship to the Commander-in-Chief, Naval Home Command. Plaque on quarterdeck marks where Nelson fell. In his cabin – which in action became part of gun deck – is portrait of his only child, Horatia, by his mistress Lady Hamilton.

WARRIOR AT REST *The ship that almost overnight made other warships obsolete, HMS* Warrior, *has been restored to her former glory.*

HMS Warrior ⚓ Ad
World's first iron-clad warship restored to state of her heyday. Launched at Blackwall on River Thames in 1860, *Warrior* was the fastest, largest, strongest and best armed warship in the world. Her 36 guns were mounted on single gun deck 100ft longer than that of any other vessel. But *Warrior* never fired a shot in anger, and within ten years she was obsolete. For years she was used as an oil fuel hulk, until in 1979 she was rescued and restored. Four vast decks are filled with Victorian naval artefacts and personal possessions of the crew; newly carved, 12ft long figurehead.

High Street Bb
Heart of Old Portsmouth, lined by historic buildings. In Buckingham House, Charles Villiers, 1st Duke of Buckingham, was assassinated in 1628 by a discontented soldier discharged from the duke's service. Portsmouth Grammar School was erected as Cambridge Barracks in 1856. George Court has the stone head of the arch of the former George Hotel; inscription records that Nelson passed through archway on his way to join *Victory* before Trafalgar.

Landport Gate Bc
Refurbished in 1698, only gateway from the old town walls still standing in its original position.

Lombard Street Bb
Lined with fine houses whose 17th-century façades show Dutch or Flemish influence.

HOME FROM THE SEA *Spectacularly raised in 1982 after 437 years underwater, the hull of* Mary Rose *is kept constantly moistened in its exhibition hall to preserve its timbers.*

LADIES ABOARD *A dainty shoe, a manicure set, wooden combs, a pomander and a purse are among the items found on* Mary Rose.

EYES FRONT *Figureheads from long-dead warships on show at the Royal Naval Museum include bold faces from HMS* Caradoc, Benbow *(centre) and* Hibernia.

St George's Church † Bd
Built in 1753 in American colonial style from dockyard timber. Rebuilt in stone after bombing.

Sally Port Ab
Ancient gateway through which passed sailors setting off to war, and convicts bound for penal colony at Botany Bay.

Spice Island Ab
Small peninsula with sea defences and views over harbour was formerly area of inns and brothels which lay outside 17th-century city walls.

Square Tower Ab
Built in 1494 to protect dockyard, tower has been carefully restored. Gilded bust of Charles I.

Unicorn Gate Ce
Town gate built in 1778 and re-erected on its present site in 1865.

Victoria Park 🦅 Cd
The city's oldest park, with celebrated displays of plants, and aviary containing variety of wild and exotic bird species.

Additional Places of Interest Outside the City Plan.

D-Day Museum, Clarence Esplanade 🏛
Sights and sounds of Allied invasion of Normandy on June 6, 1944. Overlord Embroidery, 272ft long, portrays Normandy landings and took seven years to create. Wartime scenes re-created include air-raid shelter, troops in forest camp and landing craft approaching beaches. Also has display of military vehicles such as Sherman tank, and artillery.

Charles Dickens' Birthplace Museum, Old Commercial Road 🏛
Georgian house where Charles Dickens was born in 1812 – was then 1 Mile End Terrace – now 393 Old Commercial Road. Furnished in early 19th-century style, reflecting comparative affluence of the writer's parents. Museum contains numerous items associated with novelist, including several first editions in extensive library of his works. Also has couch on which he died in June 1870.

Lumps Fort
Bold remains of early 19th-century gun battery. Building now contains a public rose garden within its walls.

Natural History Museum, Eastern Parade 🏛
Museum illustrates geology and natural history of area and includes the reconstruction of a dinosaur iguanodon, ice caves, fossils, audiovisual displays and freshwater aquaria. Butterfly House contains British butterflies in free flight.

Pyramids Centre, Southsea
Leisure complex has palm trees and warm pools with rolling waves, water slides, fountains, bubblers and geysers.

Royal Marines Museum, Eastney 🗡
History of Royal Marines from 1664 to present day illustrated with displays and exhibits set in original Artillery Officers' Mess. Medal room contains Royal Marines' ten Victoria Crosses. Outside are helicopter and Falklands Landing Craft.

St Mary's Church, Fratton Road, Kingston †
Flint building dating from 1889 with tall pinnacled tower was once parish church for whole of Portsea Island, and one of the largest in England.

Sea Life Centre, Clarence Esplanade ⛲
Displays of marine life, with hundreds of creatures including giant octopus, rays, eels and sharks. An Ocean Reef display contained in 13ft deep enclosure with toughened glass walls.

Southsea Castle 🔫
Castle was built in 1545 by Henry VIII as part of chain of coastal forts. Museum covers city's naval and military history.

Spitbank Fort
In Solent off Southsea Castle: one of four forts built on the seabed by Lord Palmerston in the 1860s. Has 15ft thick walls, 400ft deep well, muzzle-loading cannon with barrels weighing 38 tons, maze of passages and Victorian kitchen. The other forts are visible from coastal defences.

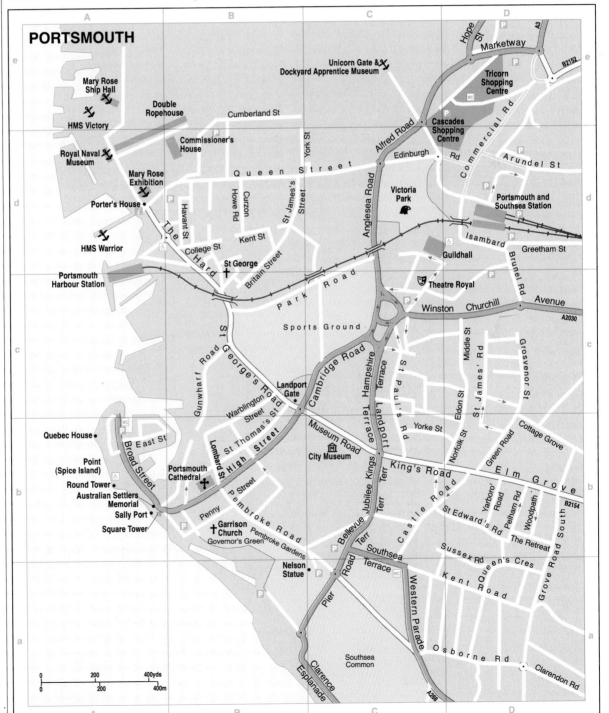

Abinger Common ⚓ ♒ Cf
Stocks on village green, overlooked by church dating from 12th century. Path leads past grounds of Abinger Manor where a small shelter covers remains of a pit-dwelling occupied about 4000 BC; perhaps the oldest man-made dwelling in Britain.

Amberley ⚓ ✦ 🏰 Bc
Village sprawling on low ridge overlooking 30 square miles of grazing marshes watered by the Arun; ideal for walkers. Ruined castle built 1380 for Bishops of Chichester, Norman church and thatched cottages. Museum of local industry in massive former chalk quarry.

Arundel
✝🏰🏛🚂✦✿☑ Bb
Famous castle completed after Norman Conquest to defend Arun valley, one of six regions of Sussex in Norman times; ancestral home of Dukes of Norfolk. Contains period furniture and paintings by Van Dyck, Gainsborough and Reynolds. Flanked by majestic 19th-century cathedral and 14th-century parish church. Toy and Military Museum in a Georgian cottage. Swans, ducks and geese breed in Arundel Wildfowl and Wetlands Trust.

Bletchingley ⚓ Eg
Broad main street lined with timbered and tile-hung houses. Norman and 15th-century church has impressive life-size effigy of Sir Robert Clayton, Lord Mayor of London (1680). Fine village inn, White Hart, built 1388.

Box Hill ♈ ⚓ ♒ ❄ Cg
Popular viewpoint and picnic spot since reign of Charles II, named after box trees that grew there; some remain on flanks. Easy walk to 563ft summit for view of South Downs. More than 800 acres of woods and chalk downland.

Bramber ⚓ 🏰 🏛 🏛 Cc
Gaunt tower on moated hill is all that remains of days when this village was a Norman stronghold. St Mary's is a 15th-century timber-framed house with rare panelling and topiary garden.

Brighton 🏛🏛❄✦🏛☑ Eb
Culture and candy floss in fashionable 19th-century resort. Graceful Georgian and late-Victorian houses co-exist with onion-domed Royal Pavilion; built 1783 for Prince Regent and enlarged by John Nash in 1812. Antique bargains in The Lanes. Porcelain, history and art displays in Museum and Art Gallery. Booth Museum of natural history includes bones of a dinosaur. Promenade and piers; electric railway, theatre and sea-life centre.

Brockham ⚓ Cf
One of Surrey's prettiest villages, set against backdrop of North Downs. Triangular green with white-stone Victorian church has striking Last Supper wood carving behind altar.

Chiddingfold ⚓ Ae
One of the largest Wealden villages with green, duck pond, and 14th-century Crown Inn where Edward VI once stayed.

CHALK HILLS NEAR THE SEA

The heights of Box Hill and Leith Hill rise above the North Downs to overlook commuter country and large tracts of richly wooded countryside, which conceals a string of peaceful villages. To the south is rich farmland and the lovely valley of the Arun. Farther on, over the South Downs, lies the coast with its many resorts, some tranquil, and others bursting with life.

FLOODLIT FANTASY *Domes and minarets at Brighton's Royal Pavilion imitate Indian palace architecture.*

Chilworth Manor ✿ Bf
Gardens laid out in 17th century on site of 11th-century monastery; walled garden, spring flowers, shrubs and herbaceous borders.

Cissbury Ring ❄ Cb
Impressive Iron Age hill-fort covering 60 acres, built about 300 BC. Site previously used by Stone Age man to mine flints; burial mounds remain.

Clandon Park 🏛 Bg
Italianate splendour in house built (1731-5) for Lord Onslow by a Venetian architect. Magnificent interiors; museum of the Queen's Royal Surrey regiment; collections of porcelain and jade.

Clayton ⚓ Ec
Two 19th-century windmills, Jack and Jill, stand above village. Tunnel House, a 19th-century folly built in shape of Tudor fortress when railway was excavated under the Downs, includes the tunnel-keeper's cottage.

FOLLY *A railwayman's cottage lies between the tunnel's castellations above the track at Clayton.*

Cowfold ⚓ Dd
Compact village at a crossroads. Church of St Peter (13th century) has fine stained glass and 10ft brass figure of Thomas Nelond, Prior of Lewes, who died 1429.

Cuckfield 🏛 Ed
Prosperous 13th-century village, now a town, situated near Haywards Heath. Many old buildings remain along the winding High Street. Museum displays relics of old village.

Devil's Dyke ❄ Dc
Deep hollow on the Downs above Brighton with wide views across the Weald from hill-fort above dyke. According to legend, Devil dug dyke to flood the Weald with the English Channel, and frustrate growth of Christianity.

Dorking 🏛 Cf
Medieval market town overlooked by Box Hill and North Downs. Good centre for touring. High Street follows route of Roman Stane Street. Saxons lived here and Danes raided. Charles Dickens stayed at 400-year-old White Horse Inn.

Ewhurst ⚓ Bf
Attractive village below Surrey hills. Church with fine Norman doorway, and village sign erected to mark 1953 Coronation. Good starting point from which to explore Pitch or Holmbury Hills.

Friday Street ♒ Cf
Tiny hamlet with pine-clad hills and tranquil lake. Water once powered bellows of 17th-century ironworks in surrounding forests.

Stephen Langton Inn named after King John's Archbishop of Canterbury, born here 1150.

Godalming 🏛 Af
Old wool town with narrow streets, half-timbered houses and inns of Tudor and Stuart days. King's Arms had Peter the Great as paying guest in 1698; and Tsar Alexander I dined in 1816.

Guildford
🏛🏛⚓🏛✦✿✝☑ Ag
Modern business and shopping centre, once a stopping place for medieval pilgrims travelling to and from Canterbury. Past and present architecture mingle, from surviving keep of Henry II castle to modern cathedral built 1936-61. Museum in Quarry Street, famous theatre, and art exhibitions in Guildford House Gallery.

High Beeches ✿ De
Woodland gardens with fabulous leaf colour in autumn. Also water gardens and wild-flower meadow which is a magnet to butterflies.

Horsham ✦ 🏛 ☑ Ce
Tree-lined Causeway, paved with Horsham slabs, has 16th and 17th-century houses. Timber-framed Tudor Causeway House museum has costumes, toys and archaeological and agricultural displays. This remains a venerable market town, despite development.

Hydon's Ball ♒ Ae
Wooded hill, 586ft, with views over 125 acres of wood and heath owned by National Trust. Memorial to Octavia Hill on summit, one of the Trust's founders.

Legh Manor ✿ Dd
Splendid 16th-century timber-framed house. Influential landscape gardener Gertrude Jekyll helped to design garden.

Leith Hill Tower ⚓ ❄ Cf
Hill is highest point in south-east England (965ft) with sweeping views. Tower at top, 64ft high, built by local landowner Richard Hull in 1766. He was buried upside-down beneath tower, believing that world would spin round so that on Judgment Day he would be facing his Maker.

Leonardslee ✿ Dd
Blazing spring colour provided by rhododendrons, azaleas and magnolias. Valley with lakes and waterfalls. Wallabies and sika deer introduced in 19th century by creator, Sir Edmund Loder.

Littlehampton 🏛 ✦ Bb
Seaside resort and yachting centre with all-weather funfair, bustling harbour, promenade and expanse of sand. Museum in sea captain's house tells of port's history.

Newlands Corner ⚓ ♒ Bf
Lofty viewpoint on North Downs. From large car park here on the road to Merrow and Guildford, there are impressive views across wooded slopes of the Weald towards South Downs, with North Downs Way climbing up from sheltered valley below.

Nymans ✿ Dd
Enchanting garden full of surprises and unexpected vistas. Worldwide collection of rare trees, shrubs and plants.

Outwood ⚓ ✦ Ef
Locals have bought flour from black-and-white working windmill at Outwood since 1665, and patronised 16th-century Cock Inn with equal loyalty.

POST MILL *Outwood's extremely well-preserved windmill turns on a central post to catch the wind.*

Parham 🏛 Bc
Twenty gardeners once tended grounds of this Elizabethan mansion. Now there are only four, but the results are just as charming. Turf and brick maze, woodland and pleasure gardens enhanced by statues and a lake. Portraits and furniture in house, heart of which is Great Hall.

Polesden Lacey 🏛 Cg
Elegant Regency house where society spent leisurely weekends in Edwardian times, including

Edward VII, Paintings and porcelain inside. Delightful walled gardens and rose garden.

Reigate †🏛🔺 Dg
Spruce commuter town with open spaces. Early 18th-century market house, and castle mound under which run medieval tunnels. On Reigate Heath stands a converted 18th-century windmill in which church services are held once a month. Ancient Pilgrims' Way follows base of Reigate Hill; good views from summit.

Shere 🏛🔺🏚🎣 Bf
Tranquil village on River Tillingbourne under North Downs. Pretty old cottages with black-and-white half-timbering and overhanging first storeys; some dating from 16th century. Lych gate, designed by Sir Edwin Lutyens in 1902, leads to Church of St James (dating from 1190) with Norman tower and characteristic pointed arches of Early English style. A mile west, tree-encircled water of Silent Pool is where King John is said to have alarmed a peasant girl bathing naked; she panicked, slipped and drowned.

Shoreham-by-Sea 🛥†⚓ Db
Commercial harbour and seaside resort. Old Shoreham was stranded a mile inland when harbour silted up in 11th century, so new Shoreham was built. Both have fine Norman churches. Marlipins museum in new Shoreham has maritime exhibits, such as model ships and paintings.

Sompting 🏛 Cb
Church of St Mary at foot of Downs has unique Saxon tower with four-gabled spire known as a 'Rhenish Helm', reminiscent of those in Rhine valley.

Stopham 🏛 Bc
Village near River Arun, crossed by medieval seven-arched bridge built by Barttelot family, whose memorial brasses and tombs dominate the church.

Vann ✿ Ae
Garden of contrasts with stately yews, tranquil water and cottage informality. Tudor house with later additions.

West Grinstead 🏛🏚✠ Cd
Well-preserved village with fine Norman church. At nearby Shipley, working mill contains memorabilia of past owner, writer Hilaire Belloc.

Winkworth Arboretum ♣ Af
Wide open spaces with views over North Downs. Nearly 100 acres of hillside cloaked with azaleas and bluebells, rare trees and shrubs. There is also a lake. Best seen in spring and autumn.

Worthing 🏛🐚ℹ Cb
Large seaside town with 5 mile seafront, gardens, pier and some Regency houses and squares. Museum and Art Gallery has local archaeology, social history, costumes, paintings and watercolours of 19th and 20th centuries. West Tarring is Worthing's 'village within a town'; country pub, village store, little church and 15th-century cottages.

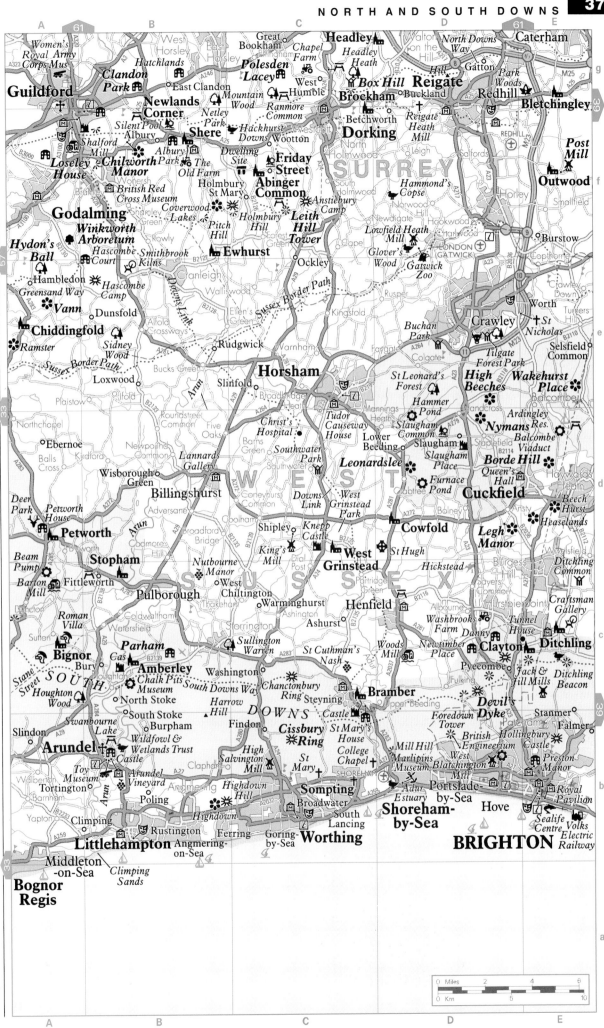

Alfriston Cb
Carefully preserved village in the Cuckmere Gap with 14th-century church and clergy house. Star Inn, 15th century, with much carving, has a ship's figurehead.

Ashdown Forest Be
Now more heath than forest, covering some 14,000 acres. Refuge for badgers and fallow deer. Woodland birds include blackcap, willow warbler, nightjar, nightingale and woodcock.

Beachy Head ☆ Ca
Windswept headland with sheer 534ft drop to the wave-lashed lighthouse below. Open, grassy chalkland where sea birds and hang-gliders ride the air currents. Mile-long clifftop nature trail.

Bentley Wildfowl Collection and Motor Museum Bc
More than 100 species of geese, swans and ducks roam parkland. Motor museum with changing assembly of vintage and veteran cars, formal garden, picnic spot and woodland walk.

Birling Gap Ca
Steep wooden steps lead down cliff to shingle beach. Smugglers landed contraband here and took it to ancient Tiger Inn in nearby village of Eastdean, with flint cottages and Norman church.

STEAM UP *The Bluebell Railway follows old Southern Region line.*

Bluebell Railway Ad
Steam engines pant on 5 mile line between Horsted Keynes and Sheffield Park with period railway station. Collection of locomotives and rolling stock dating between 1865 and 1958.

WHERE FORESTS ONCE STOOD

A green landscape of substantial towns and tiny villages, steeped in history that began long before the Normans came. The forest of Anderida has long since receded, used as fuel for the iron industry in centuries past. Where it stood, a rich country undulates south through gentle farmland, culminating in the great sweep of the chalk cliffs of Beachy Head and the Seven Sisters.

Borde Hill ❀ Ad
The Azalea Ring comes to vivid life in late May; South Lawn has mountain plants from Burma. Walks in surrounding woodland where every copse has its own colony of exotic trees and shrubs.

Charleston Farmhouse Bb
Country home of artist Vanessa Bell; sister of writer Virginia Woolf and one of the Bloomsbury Group of artists and writers. Fireplaces, cupboards and every possible surface decorated by the artist. Visitors here included T.S. Eliot and E.M. Forster.

Chartwell Bg
Sir Winston Churchill's family home for more than 40 years. His presence can still be felt everywhere; in his studio and in the grounds he planned with a painter's eye – a blend of lawns, lakes and flowers. Wide views across the Weald.

Chiddingstone Cf
Authentic Tudor village with half-timbered houses and 14th-century church, featured in many period films. Battlemented castle is a bit of a fraud; a 19th-century Gothic whim around 17th-century mansion containing relics of the Stuarts and a collection of Japanese works of art.

Ditchling Ac
Village best known for 16th-century Anne of Cleves' house. Other treasures in the narrow lanes include old candlemaker's workshop and the 17th-century red-brick Old Meeting House where dissenters gathered.

QUIET CORNER *Lavender and roses lend their old world enchantment to the yew-hedged gardens at 14th-century Penshurst Place.*

Eastbourne Da
Elegant Victorian town planned by 7th Duke of Devonshire. Seaside sun trap, sheltered by bulk of Beachy Head. Spacious promenade with colourful flower beds, bandstand and theatre.

East Grinstead Ae
Commuter town and shopping centre. Antiquity is evident in wide High Street, with terrace of half-timbered buildings. Sackville College almshouses, built 1617, echo the theme in mellow stone.

Emmetts Garden ❀ Bg
Hillside garden of tree shapes formed by low-spreading and rounded specimens, contrasting with taller trees, including 100ft wellingtonia. Planted some 700ft above sea level. Spectacular autumn foliage.

Firle Place Bb
Set in parkland below 713ft Firle Beacon; home of the Gage family for 500 years. Impressive art collection includes works by Rubens and Guardi.

Fletching Bd
Almost as old as neighbouring Ashdown Forest; one village inn dates from 1150. The 13th-century church remembers great and small; Simon de Montfort prayed here before winning the Battle of Lewes in 1264. Peter Donet, a glover, has 1450 brass memorial.

Forest Row Be
Modern village on hillside above the River Medway in Ashdown Forest. Good centre for exploration; country walk along old railway line between East Grinstead and Groombridge.

Glynde Place Bb
Tucked away in the Downs, 16th-century flintstone manor house has collections of paintings and porcelain. Glyndebourne Opera House within singing distance.

Godstone Ag
Brick frontages disguise far older village buildings. In the Middle Ages a centre for the iron industry; two ancient inns still flourish. Bay Path leads to nature reserve with more than 100 bird species.

Groombridge Ce
Terrace of 18th-century tile-hung cottages and 16th-century inn, grouped around sloping green in this attractive village. Brick-built church dates from the early 17th century. Newer part of the village lies across the river.

Hartfield Be
Village with two ancient inns, 13th-century church and houses built between 16th and 18th centuries. A.A. Milne lived here; Pooh and Christopher Robin played Poohsticks in neighbouring Ashdown Forest.

Haxted Mill Bf
Water mill beside River Eden drove millstones to grind flour from the 16th century until 1945. Wheel is now turning again, and the timbered building is a water-power museum.

Hever Castle Bf
Famous 13th-century childhood home of Anne Boleyn, wooed, won and executed by Henry VIII. The American William Waldorf Astor restored it in 1903, creating a spectacular Italian garden containing statuary from Roman to Renaissance times.

Horsted Keynes Ad
Old village with spacious green, edged with inns and houses. Once a centre of the medieval iron industry, now popular as the northern station of Bluebell Line.

Ightham Mote Cg
Perfect medieval moated manor house in secluded valley. Hall built 14th century with chapel and carved staircase. Stonework in courtyard forms a Tudor rose.

Lewes Bc
County town of East Sussex on steep hill overlooking River Ouse. Crammed with fine buildings of all periods; medieval streets and Georgian houses, surmounted by a Norman castle.

Mayfield Cd
Busy village on a ridge with panoramic views and fine main street. Timbered Middle House dates back to 1576. Opposite is 13th-century Church of St Dunstan. Attractive walk from High Street through riverside scenery to Broad Oak hamlet.

SAFE RETREAT *Michelham Priory shelters behind an 8 acre moat.*

Michelham Priory ❀ Cb
Moat surrounding 13th-century Augustinian priory powers old water mill, still used by monks. Church and cloisters long gone, but gatehouse, Tudor wing and Elizabethan Great Barn remain.

Newhaven Bb
Best known for Newhaven-Dieppe ferry. Newhaven fort overlooks the harbour, built in 1860s as a coastal defence; now a museum with barrack rooms. Bridge leads across the moat to Castle Hill Coastal Park, rising 190ft above River Ouse with panoramic views.

RAMBLERS' DOWNS *Superb views from the turf-topped chalk hills above Alfriston attract numerous walkers.*

Penshurst Place Cf
One of the great houses of England, set in rolling parkland. Vast Great Hall, built 1340, has timber roof carved with life-size figures. Impressive apartments, armour collection, toy museum and adventure playground.

Pevensey Castle Db
Mighty Roman fort, already old when William the Conqueror landed on Pevensey Beach in 1066. The Normans built a powerful stone fortress, still impressive with walls 12ft thick. Nearby Mint House is where Norman coins were produced.

Rottingdean Ab
Seascape and Downland with rocky beach and flintstone houses grouped around large pond. Poet and novelist Rudyard Kipling once lived here, and is remembered in a small museum which also has an antique toy collection.

Royal Tunbridge Wells Ce
Life in the fashionable 18th-century spa town is re-created in an exhibition at The Pantiles; 17th-century arcade where a spring was discovered in 1606. The 17th-century Church of King Charles the Martyr has baroque ceiling. Curious common in town centre has sandstone outcrops.

Seven Sisters Park Ca
Wildfowl seek winter refuge in this beautiful area where the South Downs end in sheer white cliffs and the Cuckmere river meanders to the sea.

Sheffield Park Bd
Grand-scale gardening; 120 acres of trees and shrubs around five lakes threaded by walks with shimmering vistas, laid out 1775.

Telscombe Bb
Secret, serene village with old flintstone church, and population of fewer than 50 people. Approached by high downland road with superb views.

Tonbridge Cf
Urban sprawl hides a historical gem; 13th-century castle remains surrounded by walks. River cruises on the Medway.

Tudeley Df
Past and present converge in Church of All Saints, mentioned in the Domesday Book. Magnificent stained-glass windows by 20th-century artist Marc Chagall.

Wakehurst Place Ae
Garden for all seasons with rare and exotic trees and shrubs. Walks through wooded valley, lakes and bog garden.

Westerham Bg
Market town dominated by statues of two great figures; General Wolfe, victor of Quebec, and Sir Winston Churchill. Wolfe is also remembered at Quebec House and 16th-century manor house called Squerryes Court.

Wilmington Cb
No one knows the identity of the 240ft Long Man of Wilmington, cut into the Downs. Possibly the work of Iron Age man.

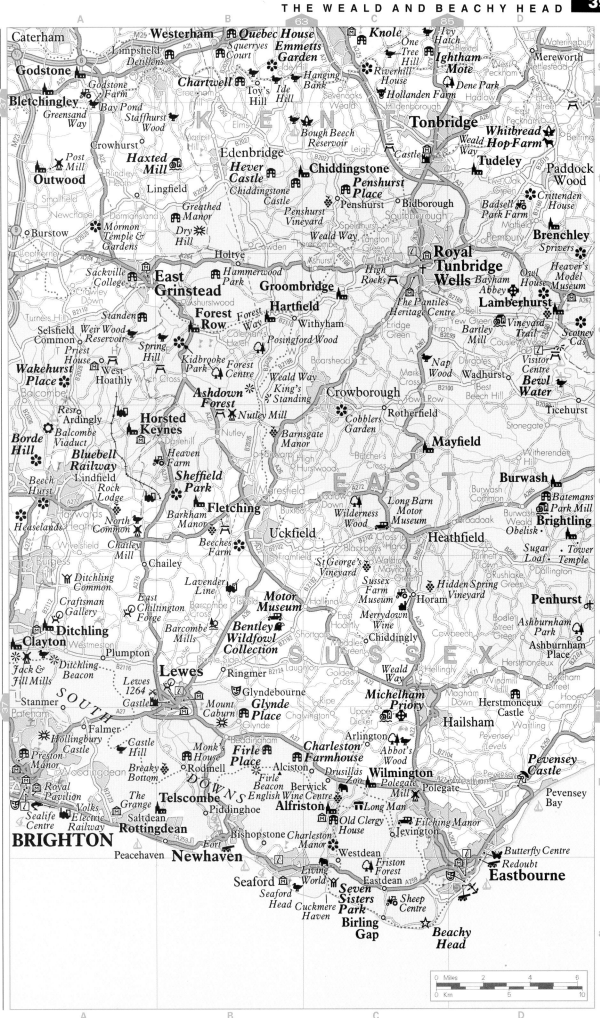

THE GARDEN OF ENGLAND

This is a landscape of timbered and tile-hung villages and comfortable, welcoming towns. The Wealden Forest has fallen prey to the shipwright, the iron furnace and the great storm of 1987, but blossom-filled orchards, hop gardens and white-cowled oasts have taken its place. Ancient towns and harbours of the coast, no longer threatened by invaders, are places of unspoiled charm.

Appledore 🏠 Dd
Royal Military Canal, built 1804 round rim of Romney and Wall- and Marshes as defence against Napoleon, echoes turbulent past of quiet village and 13th-century port. Tiny 22ft stone chapel is all that remains of Horne's Place; manor house besieged by Wat Tyler's angry peasants protesting at 14th-century poll tax.

Ashford 🏛🚂🅿 Ef
Railways brought prosperity to ancient market town; opening of Channel Tunnel promises more. Medieval core of half-timbered, overhanging houses, and some Georgian buildings remain. The Intelligence Corps Museum gives some fascinating insights into the art of counter-espionage.

Battle 🏛⚔🗡 Bc
Battle of Hastings fought on slopes below town. On site of his victory, William the Conqueror built an abbey; high altar marks where Harold fell. Little but foundations and monks' dormitory survive.

Beckley Children's Farm 🐄 Cd
Farmer's daily round of ploughing and scattering, milking and harvesting, for children to see and do on working farm dating back to Saxon times. Rare breeds, working blacksmith and theatre.

Bedgebury National Pinetum ♠ Be
Broad avenues, streams and ridges thread beneath lofty spread of Europe's foremost collection of conifers. Azaleas and rhododendrons add colour.

Bewl Water ♥ ⛺❄🅿 Ae
Trout fishing, birdwatching, passenger cruises, picnics and promenades around flooded valley of River Bewl; largest body of inland water in the south-east.

Biddenden 🏠 Ce
Exquisite village of medieval and Tudor houses, tithe barn, green and pond. Beautiful 17th-century tiled, timbered and gabled Old Cloth Hall was once headquarters of local cloth trade. All Saints' Church has noble 15th-century tower and contains fine Tudor brasses. Village sign commemorates unusual local heroines, Siamese twins Eliza and Mary Chulkhurst. Born about 1100, joined at hip and shoulder, the 'Biddenden Maids' survived for 34 years and bequeathed 18 acres of land to the poor.

Bodiam Castle 🚜🏛🏰 Bd
Picture-book castle with rounded corner towers, battlements, portcullis and moat. Built 14th century and remarkably intact. Airy views from roof across surrounding parkland scattered with handsome oaks. Restored traction engines on display at Quarry Farm Steam Museum.

Boughton Monchelsea Place 🏛 Bf
Battlemented Elizabethan manor house of cool grey Kentish ragstone. Superb views across deer park to hazy expanse of Weald. Tudor kitchens, displays of carriages and farm implements.

DREAM CASTLE *A wide, still moat reflects the well-preserved fortress of Bodiam, which was never assaulted by an enemy.*

Brenchley 🏠 Af
Half-timbered Tudor cottages set in fruit orchards surround village green. Solemn avenue of ancient yews (350 years old) leads to restored 13th and 14th-century church. Marle Place, 16th-century tiled and half-timbered mansion, has herb nursery.

Brightling 🏠 Ad
Strange obelisks, domes, towers and a peculiar cone known as the Sugar Loaf are scattered around this quiet village; follies of 19th-century eccentric 'Mad Jack' Fuller, local squire and MP. He was buried under churchyard pyramid 60ft high; local legend claims he sits in top hat and tails holding a bottle of claret.

Burwash 🏠🏛 Ad
Warm timber, tile and brick in tree-lined village of 16th and 17th-century houses. Bateman's Jacobean mansion was Rudyard Kipling's home from 1902 to 1936; his study, gardens, water mill (still grinding flour) and one of the first water-driven turbines to produce electricity are all preserved. Garden views of Pook's Hill.

Camber Castle 🏰 Dc
Squat ruins of Henry VIII castle today guard caravan parks and holiday beaches of Camber Sands across the Rother estuary.

Carr Taylor Vineyards ❖ Cc
Wines can be seen in production, and tasted in celebration of return of the vine to southern England.

Charing 🏠🏰 Df
Georgian and Tudor houses line single main street. Remains of a medieval archbishop's palace where Henry VIII stayed in 1520. The original 13th-century church burned down in 1592; rebuilt with ragstone tower.

Cranbrook ✝🏛🗡 Be
Imposing medieval church built by Flemish weavers recalls once-flourishing cloth trade in this small town with harmonious mix of buildings. Towering 72ft windmill, built 1814, still grinds corn.

Finchcocks 🏛 Be
Sound of music pervades baroque red-brick mansion, home of historic collection of early keyboard instruments; regular concerts.

Godinton Park 🏛 Df
Impressive Jacobean mansion, rich in carved panelling, portraits, fine furniture and china. Formal gardens and remains of great Domesday Oak, said to have split asunder in 1939 as Chamberlain announced war.

Goudhurst 🏠❖ Be
Village on a steep hill with old inns, elegant houses, and gazebo. St Mary's Church, dating from 13th century, has monuments of local Culpeper family.

Hastings 🏰🏛🗡⛵☆🅿🏖 Cb
Fish stalls and net sheds of old Hastings contrast with modern pier and promenade. Ruins of William the Conqueror's castle brood above. Embroidery (243ft) displayed in town hall is modern rival to Bayeux Tapestry. Pottery, ironwork and ceramics in Art Gallery and Museum. Story of fishing industry in Museum of Local History; Fisherman's Museum in converted chapel. Denizens of the deep in walk-through ocean tunnel at Sea-Life Centre.

Hawkhurst 🏠 Be
Pretty village green framed by old inns, church and cottages, many associated with infamous Hawkhurst Gang of 18th-century smugglers. Highgate on hill above is newer, with 18th-century weather-boarded houses enlivening shopping precinct.

Horsmonden 🏠❖ Bf
Orchards and hop gardens crowd assortment of Kentish houses round village green. At Gun Inn, John Browne made guns for Charles I, Cromwell, British Navy and the Dutch. Dark waters of furnace pond are relic of Wealden iron industry. Sprivers Gardens, set in 108 acre park surrounding 18th-century mansion, contain rare plants, temples and garden statuary.

Hothfield Common ♥ Df
Heathland with trails and views across Weald. Tree-creepers, woodpeckers and yellowhammers fly amongst ancient beech, oak and sweet chestnut trees.

Iden Croft Herbs ❖ Bf
Famous herb gardens fill the air with heady fragrance. Culinary, medicinal, aromatic and decorative herbs for sale.

Lamberhurst 🏠❖❖ Ae
Ancient centre of iron industry. Visit vineyard beside the village green. Ingenious displays in Heaver's Model Museum and Craft Centre in converted oasthouse. Smugglers used Owl House and warned of approaching excisemen by hooting.

Leeds Castle 🏰❖ Cg
Kings and modern statesmen have trodden floors of lake-bound castle whose history goes back 1000 years. Rich furnishings and paintings; aviary and maze in sublime setting of Capability Brown landscaped grounds.

Northiam 🏠🏛 Cd
Straggling village with white weatherboarded cottages surrounding ancient oak on village green, said to be 1000 years old. Queen Elizabeth rested under tree in 1573 on her way to Rye. Fine timber-framed manor house at Great Dixter dates back to 1460; restored by Sir Edward Lutyens in 1911. Splendid garden.

Penhurst ✝ Ac
Tiny hamlet with timeless church and manor farm. Ashburnham chapel has tombs of family that owned nearby Ashburnham Place. Lumps of iron and stray cannonballs litter countryside around Ashburnham Forge; one of the last foundries in Sussex until closure in 1820s.

Pett Level Cc
Waders and waterfowl frequent Colonel Body Memorial Lakes; protected by stern sea wall and beach of shingle which is constantly washed to the west by sea and daily returned by lorry.

Pluckley 🏠 Df
Village on ridge above River Beult, said to be most haunted in England. Ghosts now joined by livelier presence of Ma and Pop Larkin, whose TV comedy saga *The Darling Buds of May* was filmed here. Narrow windows on houses called 'lucky Derings' after Royalist member of local Dering family who escaped through one.

Rolvenden 🏠🏛🏛 Ce
Village where Francis Hodgson Burnett, author of *The Secret Garden*, lived at Great Maytham Hall, later rebuilt by Lutyens. Motoring memorabilia in C.M. Booth Collection includes 1904 Humber tri-car and Morgan three-wheel cars.

CHURCH CLOCK *Cherubs strike the quarter hours at St Mary's, Rye.*

Rye ✝🏛🏛🅿 Dd
Worn cobbles, timbered houses and church with Burne-Jones window. Grim 12th-century Ypres Tower, built to defend ancient port, now houses local museum with smuggling and pottery displays. Lamb House was home of American novelist Henry James. Mermaid Inn was haunt of smugglers who sat with loaded pistols, openly defying the local excisemen.

Rye Harbour 🏚 ⚓ Dc
Quiet fishing village on broad expanse of shingle at mouth of Rother. Noted for bird life; divers, wildfowl, waders and breeding terns. Nature reserve has hides.

Scotney Castle Gardens ❀ Be
Romantic landscaped gardens, awash with roses and flowering shrubs, set around moated ruins of 14th-century castle.

Sissinghurst Castle Gardens ❀ Ce
One of the loveliest gardens in England, created as a series of 'outdoor rooms' around the gatehouse of decayed Tudor mansion, by Harold Nicolson and Vita Sackville-West in 1930s.

Smallhythe Place 🏚 Cd
Half-timbered 15th-century yeoman's house is museum of theatrical relics and shrine to memory of Ellen Terry, the Shakespearean actress who lived here from 1900 until her death in 1928.

KENTISH COTTAGE *Wooden weatherboarding is characteristic of many old Smarden houses.*

Smarden 🏚 ⚓ Cf
Ancient market and centre of wool trade with superb half-timbered, weather-boarded houses. Mainly 14th-century church nicknamed 'Barn of Kent' because of 36ft wide roof span over nave unencumbered by supporting pillars.

Stone in Oxney 🏚 Dd
Lonely marshland village lies beneath huge skies on one-time island of Oxney. Roman altar stone beneath 15th-century tower of church.

Tenterden† 🏚 ⚓ Ce
Market town with wide, tree-lined main street and Elizabethan and Georgian houses. Church of St Mildred (15th century) has 100ft tower. Mementos of hop picking and weaving days in the local museum. Steam nostalgia at Kent and East Sussex Steam Railway.

Whitbread Hop Farm 🐴 ⚓ Af
Largest hop gardens in Kent, once bustling with pickers on working holiday from London's East End. Museum, nature trails and mighty Whitbread shire horses.

Yalding 🏚 Ag
Two long stone medieval bridges lead into wide curving street of mellow brick and timber houses, where Teise and Beult flow into the Medway, in heart of Kent's hop-farming country. Warde's Moat is picturesque vicarage encircled by water.

Barfrestone ✝ Ce

Tiny hamlet near North Downs Way whose 12th-century church is decorated with carvings of animals, men and angels – perhaps finest Norman stonework in England. No tower, but church bell hangs from churchyard yew.

CHRIST IN GLORY *Superb stone carvings adorn the door of St Nicholas' Church at Barfrestone.*

Broadstairs 🏛 🏰 ⌇ Df

Picturesque seaside resort rings safe sands of Viking Bay. Dickens everywhere; he wrote *David Copperfield* at Bleak House; now the Dickens and Maritime Centre. Dickens House Museum in home of Mary Strong; original of Betsey Trotwood. The Crampton Tower Museum recalls work of Victorian engineer T.R. Crampton. North Foreland lighthouse guides sailors past the Goodwin Sands.

The Butterfly Centre ❦ Cd

Kaleidoscope of rare and exotic butterflies. Scarlet mormons, Rajah Brooks and plain tigers, fly free in tropical greenhouse.

Canterbury

🏛 ✝ 🏰 ⌇ Be

Bell Harry Tower, 500 years old, soars over one of world's great cathedrals, mother church of Anglican faith. St Augustine re-established Christianity here in 6th century, and the murder of Thomas Becket made it important shrine. Wartime bombs destroyed one-third of old city centre, but plenty survives; medieval streets, stretches of city wall, ruins of Norman castle and St Augustine's Abbey. Heritage Museum offers audiovisual look at past. Pilgrims Way follows footsteps of Wife of Bath and others, in re-creation of Chaucer's *Canterbury Tales*.

Chilham Castle Gardens ❀ Ae

Ancient wisteria and old roses in gardens surrounding Jacobean mansion and ruined Norman keep. Landscaped by Capability Brown. Falconry, heronry and jousting. Pretty Kent village.

Crabble Corn Mill 🏭 Cd

The water mill still produces stoneground flour, as it did when built in 1812 to feed the hungry garrison of Dover Castle.

Deal 🏛 🏰 🏭 ✕ ⌇ De

Quiet fishing port retaining 18th-century charm. Henry VIII built splendid Tudor-rose shaped Deal Castle; only battered stones remain of sister Sandown Castle. Naval communication displays in 19th-century Time Ball Tower, and seafaring history in Town Hall and Maritime Museum.

Dover 🏛 ⚓ 🏰 ⌇ Dd

Busiest passenger port in the world. Soaring white cliffs are enduring symbol of island Britain.

WHITE CLIFFS OF DOVER

Formidable white cliffs, where the chalk hills of the North Downs reach the sea, have served as a bulwark against foreign invaders from time immemorial. Today they overlook the most crowded shipping lanes in the world. The lonely flatland of Romney Marsh lies south, gradually reclaimed from the sea since Roman times, now a land of tiny villages set among water meadows.

Romans bequeathed lighthouse and 'Painted House'; Saxons the Church of St Mary-in-Castro; Normans and English kings built castle. Grand Shaft staircase was part of port's defences against Napoleon. Labyrinth of tunnels in Hellfire Corner below castle, was nerve centre for evacuation of Dunkirk and Battle of Britain. White Cliffs Experience, in the Market Centre, re-creates whole rich pageant. Churchill's War Rooms at Hellfire Corner in grounds of forbidding castle.

Folkestone

🏛 🏰 ❀ ❦ ☆ ⌇ Cc

Town and beach of this elegant resort, unperturbed by busy Channel port, are separated by 200ft cliff. To the east, landslips created tumbled terrain of The Warren, secluded haven for chalkland butterflies. Eurotunnel Exhibition Centre tells story of the Channel Tunnel with models.

Fordwich 🏰 Be

Church, Tudor houses and old inns beside the Stour, mark site of medieval port. Smallest town hall in England has stocks outside, and ducking stool inside for nagging wives.

Goodnestone Park ❀ Ce

Walled rose garden, fine trees, wide views and shades of Jane Austen, whose brother Edward married daughter of the house.

Graveney Marshes ❦ Af

Vast expanse of flats on estuary of River Swale, home of wild flowers, flocks of wildfowl and wading birds; part of South Swale Nature Reserve.

Hawkinge 🏰 Ⓨ Cd

RAF fighter station at forefront of Battle of Britain, now museum. Holds the largest assembly of remains of British and German aircraft that took part in struggle.

MAKING PROVISIONS *Crabble Mill supplied Dover Castle garrison with flour in Napoleonic times.*

Howletts Zoo Park 🐾 Be

Famed for gorillas, tigers and other endangered species such as dhole, bongo and Calamian deer. Fine captive breeding record.

Hythe 🏛 🏰 Bc

Sedate seaside resort, separated from medieval port by tree-lined stretch of Royal Military Canal. Crypt of the mainly 13th-century church has yielded a macabre and mysterious collection of human skulls and thigh bones of 12th-14th century origin. At Saltwood Castle nearby, the murderers of Thomas Becket plotted how to rid Henry II of his 'upstart priest'.

INVASION SHORE *Fishing boats line the beach at the Cinque Port of Hythe, once among the key medieval ports charged with defence of the south coast.*

Lydd ✝ ❦ Ab

Cluster of old houses and guildhall set in strange hinterland of scrub and shingle. Church, 14th century, known as 'Cathedral of Romney Marsh'. Superb bird reserve at Dungeness nearby.

Lympne 🏰 🏛 ❀ 🐾 Bc

Roman *Portus Lemanis* now represented only by chunks of Roman masonry tumbling down hillside. Views of Romney Marsh from medieval Lympne Castle. Port Lympne is a large 1911 Dutch-style mansion; now extension of Howletts Zoo Park, offering safari trails and walks.

Margate

🏛 ⚓ 🏰 ♨ ❀ ⌇ Dg

Bracing resort with generous sands and bustling funfair at Bembom Brothers Theme Park. Shell grotto, aquarium, caves carved from chalk 1000 years ago, Town Hall local museum, and Draper's Mill of 1850. A 13th-century monks' kitchen, refectory and dormitory are preserved at Salmestone Grange.

Mersham 🏰 🏭 Ac

Norman church of St John the Baptist has west window unique for its tracery, with some original glass from 1400s. Swanton Mill, nearby 17th-century water mill.

Minster 🏰 ⚓ Df

Peaceful town set among fruit farms. Hallowed ground for more than 1300 years; abbey today is convent for Benedictine nuns. Norman crypt and arch with 12th and 13th-century additions; 15th-century choir stalls. The nearby Church of St Mary was founded in 1150 by Canterbury monks.

Mount Ephraim ❀ ❖ Af

Cool Edwardian elegance in 7 acre gardens with rose terraces, lake, extensive Japanese rock garden, herbaceous border, wide variety of shrubs. Small woodland area with rhododendrons.

Paddlesworth 🏰 Bc

Narrow lanes climb steeply to little village on panoramic perch, with one of England's smallest churches, 56ft long by 11ft wide, dating back to Saxon times.

Parsonage Farm 🐖 Bd

Pigs, cattle and rare breeds of sheep nurtured on working family farm. Museum, farm trail and local crafts.

Quex House 🏰 Cf

Regency home of the late Major Percy Powell-Cotton, big game hunter turned a conservationist. Museum houses collection of Chinese porcelain, African ethnography and stuffed animals.

Ramsgate 🏛 ✕ ⚓ ❀ 🐚 ⌇ Df

Funfairs and amusement arcades disguise a more serious town, centred on busy harbour and nearby Channel ferries. Shipwrecks and local history at East Kent Maritime Museum. Model village on cliff-top promenade and historic cars in West Cliff Hall.

Richborough Castle 🏰 Df

Ruins of Rutupiae, Roman fortress built to guard Wantsum Channel from Saxon raiders; lies incongruously in the shadow of Richborough power station. Museum of Roman relics.

Romney, Hythe and Dymchurch Railway

🚂 Aa-Bc

One-third size copies of original steam locomotives ply 14 miles of world's smallest public railway across Romney Marsh, from Hythe to Dungeness.

St Margaret's at Cliffe

✝ ☆ ❀ Dd

White weather-boarded houses look out over Channel and Goodwin Sands. Norman church has stained glass commemorating victims of 1987 Zeebrugge disaster. Cliff-top walks along Saxon Shore Way to Dover Patrol Memorial, north, and South Foreland Lighthouse, south. Winston Churchill, cast in bronze, stands amid flowers in The Pines gardens.

Sandling Park ❀ Bc

Formal and woodland gardens ablaze in spring with rhododendrons, azaleas and magnolias.

Sandwich 🏛 ❦ ⌇ De

Town with medieval winding streets, gateways, churches and houses. Queen Elizabeth I wined and dined at Old House. Guildhall has Elizabethan interior and local history museum. Walk along coast with golf courses to shingle, dunes and salt marsh of Sandwich Bay Nature Reserve. Waders, waterfowl and wild flowers.

Shakespeare Cliff ☆ ❖ Dc

Dizzying 350ft chalk headland, described by Edgar to his blinded father Gloucester in *King Lear*. Old 1880 Channel Tunnel workings, and tons of spoil from modern counterpart, at foot.

Walmer Castle 🏰 De

Henry VIII Tudor-rose shaped fort, converted in 18th century as official residence of Lords Warden of Cinque Ports. Mementos of famous occupants such as William Pitt and the Duke of Wellington; original 'Wellington Boot' on display. Gardens were laid out by Lady Hester Stanhope, Pitt's niece, in 1805.

Wealden Woodlands 🦌 ❦ Bf

Close encounters with fallow and sitka deer, foxes and owls; nature trails, butterfly centre, rare breeds and farm animals to feed.

Wingham 🏰 🐾 Ce

Wide tree-shaded high street on busy main road with handsome houses, two 13th-century inns, and largely 13th-century church. Exotic calls resound from Wingham Bird Park, with walk-through aviaries of rare birds.

Wye ✝ 🏛 ⊛ Ad

Small town on North Downs Way, full of spacious Georgian houses; chalk crown carved out of hillside commemorates coronation of Edward VII in 1902. Wye College has some 15th-century buildings. Museum at Brook displays farm implements in 14th-century barn.

Wye and Crundale Downs Nature Reserve ❦ ☆ Ad

Devil's Kneading Trough, valley formed by ice 10,000 years ago, offers superb views and absorbing walks through some of finest chalk grassland in southern England. Rich in orchids.

A map of Canterbury and East Kent. Labels include:

Warden Point, Warden, Leysdown on Sea, Isle of Sheppey, Shell Ness, South Swale Reserve, Oare Meadow, Graveney Marshes, Faversham, Mount Ephraim, Mount Ephraim Gardens, Sheldwich, Perrywood, North Downs Way, Chilham, Chilham Castle, Jullieberries Grave, Molash, Challock Lees, Boughton Aluph, Boughton Lees, King's Wood, Crundale Downs, College, Wye, Wye Downs, Brook, Ashford, Mersham, Swanton Mill, Hamstreet Woods, Newchurch, Romney Marsh, St Mary in the Marsh, Ivychurch, Brenzett, New Romney, Romney, Hythe & Dymchurch Railway, Lydd, Lydd-on-Sea, Denge Marsh, Danger Area, Dungeness Reserve, Power Station, Dungeness, Greatstone-on-Sea, Littlestone-on-Sea, St Mary's Bay, Dymchurch, Martello Tower, Burmarsh, Hythe, Lympne, Lympne Castle, Port Lympne Zoo Park, Claycocks, Brockhill Park, Sandling Park, Paddlesworth, Stanford, Intime Designs, Brabourne Lees, Stowting, Rhodes Minnis, West Wood, Denslow, Stelling Minnis Mill, Stelling Minnis, Elham Valley, Parsonage Farm, The Butterfly Centre, Hawkinge, Kent Battle of Britain Museum, Eurotunnel Exhibition, Castle, Sandgate, Rotunda Theme Park, Folkestone, The Warren, Abbot's Cliff, Great Farthingloe, Shakespeare Cliff, Capel-le-Ferne, Alkham, Crabble Corn Mill, Painted House, Knights Templar Church, Dover, Dover Castle, Pharos, Maison Dieu House, Kearsney Abbey, Lydden, Lydden Down, St John's Commandery, Swingfield, Ottinge, Wootton, Shepherdswell, Eythorne, Elvington, Tilmanstone, Eastry, Northbourne Court, Three Corners, St Nicholas of Ash, Woolage Green, Denton, Barham, Bishopsbourne, Bridge, Patrixbourne, Bekesbourne, Adisham, Goodnestone Park, Chillenden, Barfrestone, St Margaret's at Cliffe, St Margaret's Bay, The Pines, South Foreland, Kingsdown, Saxon Shore Way, Bockhill, Walmer Castle, Deal, Deal Castle, Time Ball Tower, Sandown Castle, Sandwich, Sandwich Bay, Sandwich Bay Reserve, Saxon Shore Way, St Clement's Bird Observatory, Saxon Shore Way, Woodnesborough, Worth, Staple, Wingham, Wingham Bird Park, Howletts Zoo Park, Goodnestone, Corn Dollies Workshop, Wickhambreaux, Stodmarsh, Fordwich, St Augustine's Abbey, Canterbury, Castle, Chartham, Chartham Hatch, Blean, Blean Bird Park, Church Wood, Ellenden Wood, Wealden Woodlands, Whitstable, Clapham Hill, Yorkletts, Seasalter, The Castle, Herne Bay, Bishopstone Glen, Herne, Herne Mill, Hoath, Reculver, St Mary's, Regulbrium Fort, St Nicholas at Wade, Sarre, Sarre Windmill, Boyden Gate, Upstreet, Hersden, Westbere, Sturry, Preston, Elmstone, Ash, Richborough Castle, Richborough Port, Minster, Abbey, Monkton, Manston, Acol, Quex House, Crampton Tower Museum, Salmestone Grange, Pegwell Bay, Model Village, Ramsgate, Margate, Bembom Brothers, Tudor House, Cliftonville, Kingsgate, Shell Grotto, Draper's Mill, North Foreland, Bleak House, Dickens House Museum, Broadstairs, Westgate on Sea, Strait of Dover, English Channel.

Roads marked include: A2, A28, A252, A251, A20, A256, A257, A258, A259, A261, A299, A253, M20.

Avon Valley Railway Ef
The majesty of steam celebrated in collection of working steam trains, including 126 ton LMS Stanier Black Five locomotive rescued from a scrapheap.

Axbridge Cd
Timbered houses and a splendid Perpendicular church hem a spacious market square. King John's Hunting Lodge, an early Tudor merchant's house, now a local history museum.

Banwell Bd
Victorian folly – decayed octagonal tower – guards south-eastern approach to village. Church, among finest in region, has 15th-century Flemish stained glass. Butstone House in High Street has lump of rock set into pavement, once used to bounce carriage wheels away.

Blaise Castle House Df
Popular refuge from crowded Bristol. Castle House Museum in 1798 mansion has displays, ranging from costumes to chocolate packaging. Orangery by John Nash, who also designed rustic cottages at Blaise Hamlet.

LONELY LIMESTONE HILLS

Only a few miles separate the docks and industry of Avonmouth from the spectacular gorges, solitary heights and subterranean labyrinths of the Mendip Hills. Farther south are the flat, mysterious landscapes of the Somerset Levels, once an inland sea but now fringed by ancient towns and villages. Here at Glastonbury, according to legend, is where King Arthur is buried.

Burnham-on-Sea Bc
Bucket-and-spade beaches surround Victorian resort and spa. Fishing, sailing and water-skiing. Medieval church, built on sand, has leaning tower. Altarpiece by Grinling Gibbons, designed by Sir Christopher Wren for James II's chapel in Whitehall Palace.

Burrington Combe Cd
Cavers and tourists throng ravine where Stone Age man made a home. Reverend Augustus Toplady felt inspired to write 'Rock of Ages' hymn in Aveline's Hole. Iron Age earthworks at Dolebury Camp provide wide views and access to Black Down, highest point of Mendips at 1067ft.

Clevedon Cf
Comfortable resort with sedate Victorian atmosphere, and links with the poets Samuel Taylor Coleridge and Lord Tennyson. Fine 14th-century manor house, Clevedon Court, home of Tilton family since 1709.

Cranmore Ec
Age of steam lovingly re-created by East Somerset Railway in Victorian engine shed. Trips along 2 mile track. Giant 140 ton Black Prince is largest working steam locomotive in Britain.

Crook Peak Bd
Tormentil, wild thyme, rock-roses, bee orchids and white horehound, among lime-loving plants on 628ft hill overlooking the Somerset plain.

Downside Abbey Ed
Abbey Church of St Gregory the Great built of vast proportions; soaring Gothic arches of the nave are contained within a total length of 328ft. Completed between 1880 and 1925. The village, Stratton-on-the-Fosse, is also home of Roman Catholic public school.

Flax Bourton De
St Michael and the Dragon in mortal combat decorate the Norman arch of the church. Track leads from village south to wooded Bourton Combe, nearly 600ft up. Flax once grown alongside footpath leading back.

Glastonbury Db
Arthur's legendary Avalon. He and Guinevere are said to be buried among romantic 13th-century abbey ruins, and where Joseph of Arimathea planted seeds of English Christianity. St Michael's Chapel pierces skyline above Glastonbury Tor, where Holy Grail is said to rest below the Chalice Spring. A 14th-century tithe barn houses Somerset Rural Life Museum, with farmhouse kitchen and cider-making.

High Ham Cb
Tranquil village of tall trees, creamy-grey stone houses and gracious 14th to 15th-century church with amusing use of gargoyles. Stembridge Tower Mill, dating from about 1820, is last thatched windmill in England.

King's Sedge Moor Cb
Former marsh, partially drained over the centuries. Now cut by maze of drainage ditches (rhines) through the peaty land. Its willows used for basketry. Herons, snipe, redshanks and yellow wagtails among the many wetland breeding birds. Monmouth's rebels fought and lost against forces of James II in 1685 in Battle of Sedgemoor, the last on English

soil. Memorial stone stands near Bussex Rhine, where heaviest fighting occurred.

Meare Cc
Lakeside settlement until the Middle Ages. Manor house, 14th century, was a summer retreat for the Abbots of Glastonbury. Curious Fish House used to store salted fish for the monastic table.

Pilton Dc
Haphazard assortment of greystone cottages on either side of a stream. Church, 12th century, houses collection of early musical instruments. Vineyards.

Priddy Dd
Lonely village high up on limestone plateau, dominated by prehistoric burial mounds of Priddy Nine Barrows. Wooded chasm of wild and unspoiled beauty at impressive Ebbor Gorge.

Priston Mill Ee
Imposing 25ft diameter water wheel still grinds wholewheat flour and oats in mill. Children's adventure playground.

Shepton Mallet Ec
Delightful maze of lanes, weavers' cottages and grand owners' houses recall 17th-century boom days of the wool industry. The Shambles, once a medieval meat market, stands in the square, as does 50ft Market Cross, erected in 1500.

Somerton Ca
Ancient capital of Wessex, situated on the River Cary. Medieval marketplace with market cross and 17th-century former town hall, elegant town houses and church with fine early 16th-century timber roof.

OCTAGON *Somerton's shapely market cross dates from 1673.*

Stanton Drew De
Three great stone circles – one the second largest (after Avebury) in Britain – mark important Bronze Age religious site. Stones said to be a petrified wedding party – the bride, parson and guests.

Street Cb
Shoe-making town, indissolubly linked with the Clark family,

whose Quaker convictions are manifest in the Friends' Meeting House and absence of pubs. Museum with a remarkable collection of footwear from Roman times onwards. South-east of the town, on nearby Windmill Hill, is monument to Admiral Lord Hood (1724-1816), scion of successful naval family.

Wedmore Cc
Fine buildings, including Victorian private houses in an ancient village. Modern stained glass in partly 12th-century St Mary's church tells tale of King Alfred, who signed treaty of AD 878 here following his defeat of the Danes at the Battle of Ethendune.

HYMN IN STONE *The cathedral at Wells is among Britain's finest.*

Wells Dc
England's smallest city, medieval in essence. West front of cathedral built around 1230, displays superb collection of statuary. Inside, jousting knights emerge from a clock on the quarter hour. One of England's oldest inhabited houses, Bishop's Palace; moat has swans which ring bell for food. Chapter House and Vicar's Close among many fine buildings.

Westhay Cc
Archaeology, history and wildlife of Somerset Levels exhibited at the Peat Moors Visitor Centre.

Weston-super-Mare Be
Promenade and piers in a traditional resort; once a fishing village. Local history trail to Weston Woods and Worlebury Camp, site of Iron Age massacre. Mendip minerals, indoor nature trail and period amusement machines at Woodspring Museum.

Willow Craft Industry Ba
Tour here follows willows from vast tank in which they are boiled, to workshop where craftsmen weave baskets. Visitor centre illustrates history of the wetlands of Somerset Levels. Allermoor Pumping Station at nearby Burrow Bridge has engines used for draining marshes in 1860s.

Wookey Hole Dc
Primeval mystery in an eerie network of underground rivers and pools. Caves have yielded Ice Age animal bones and 2000-year-old human remains. Museums in old mill buildings display fairground relics and demonstrate handmade paper-making. Complex owned by Madame Tussaud's; small waxworks exhibition.

SCENIC WONDER *Slicing through the Mendips for over a mile, Cheddar's dizzying gorge is an astonishing natural showpiece.*

Bleadon Hill Bd
Exhilarating climb and magnificent views. Solitary stack of Brent Knoll lies south, main bulk of Mendips lies east. Walk along ridge for vista of Bristol Channel, Brean Down and mountains of South Wales.

Brean Down Ad
Iron Age farms and a Roman temple mark the springy turf of this exposed headland. Ruined fort was built in 1867 as defence against France. Peregrine falcons and autumn migrants at bird sanctuary. Colourful exotic species at Tropical Bird Gardens.

Brent Knoll Bd
Formed like a spadeful of earth, flung by the Devil as he dug out the Cheddar Gorge. Iron Age fort at summit. Intriguing church in village, where carved bench ends tell a story of local, medieval intrigue involving an abbot of Glastonbury.

Castle Cary Eb
Old town of honey-coloured stone and good Cheddar cheese. Lockup of 1779 behind market hall once catered for Sunday-school truants.

Cheddar Gorge Cd
Awesome gash in the Mendip Hills, with cliffs towering to nearly 500ft and a fairyland of stalagmite-filled caves. Famous 'Cheddar Man', a 10,000-year-old skeleton discovered in Gough's Cave, on display in adjoining museum. Some 200 species of wild flowers and trees in Black Rock Nature Reserve at head of gorge; including Cheddar Pink, found nowhere else in the world.

Chew Magna De
Pink shop fronts, banks and pubs line the raised pavements surrounding triangular green. South, Chew Valley Lake is in fact a modern reservoir, and a mecca for birdwatchers and fishermen.

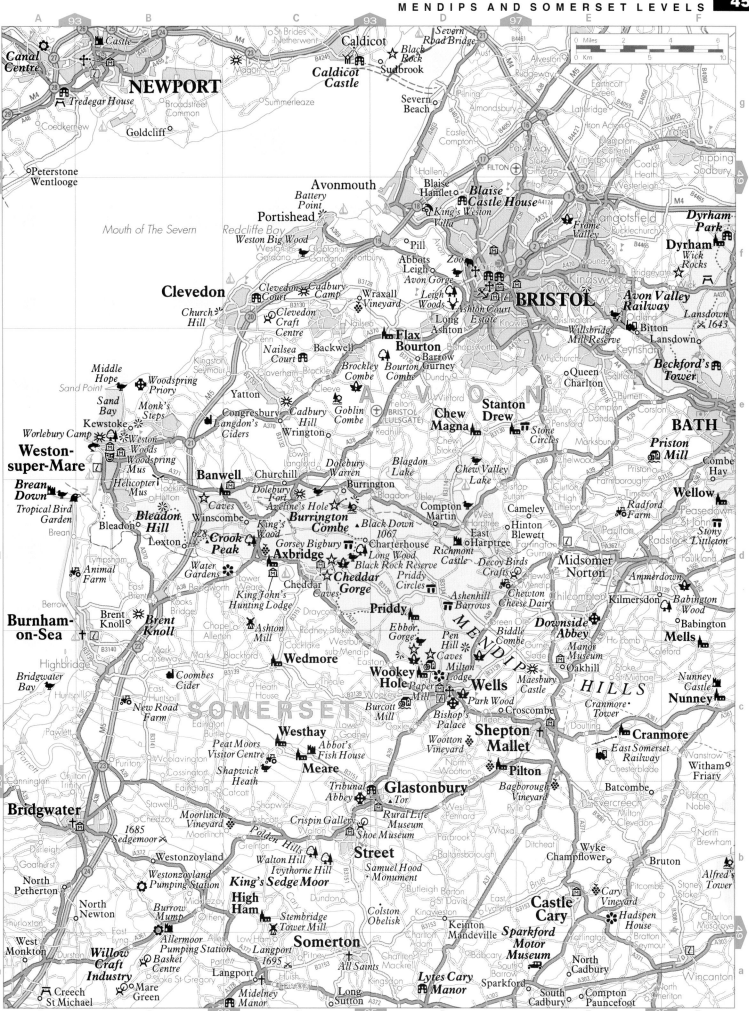

All Saints Church Cc
Church dates from early 12th century, but rebuilt in 18th and 19th centuries. Fine effigy of local philanthropist, Edward Colston, lies inside. Now an environmental study centre.

Arnolfini Gallery 🏛 Bb
Built in the 19th century as tea warehouse, now displaying modern art. Museum café and bar, with tables out on wharf, is favourite summer meeting place for Bristolians.

Bank of England, Bristol Branch Cc
Original mix of classical and Renaissance styles marks this distinguished 1850s building, by C.R. Cockerell. Cockerell became architect to the Bank of England in 1833, following Sir John Soane.

Brandon Hill Ab
Footpaths ascend grassy knoll rising over city, providing fine views. Hill topped by 105ft Cabot

ENGLAND'S ANCIENT PORT

The city thrived from Norman times as one of the great ports and trading centres of Britain. Water still gives it a unique character – whether it is the drama of the Avon Gorge, or the old dock areas at the very heart of the city. Despite heavy war damage, many outstanding buildings remain, from the Norman based cathedral and Georgian terraces to great Victorian public buildings.

and varied industrial history. Dockside has impressive working steam crane and there are rides on steam railway and world's oldest working tug, *Mayflower*.

Broad Street Cc
Narrow street with notable collection of historic buildings. Council House on corner, built by Robert Smirke in 1827, was once the centre of city administration. Nearby plaque marks site of the High Cross, which stood at heart of the medieval town. The Grand

Boxkite and models of locomotives. Fine arts collection includes 14th and 15th-century Italian paintings along with Dutch, Flemish and German art of 16th and 17th centuries.

Corn Street Cc
Street where Bristol merchants 'paid on the nail', outside the old Exchange. These 'nails' are bronze tables on which cash deals were made, dating from the 16th century. Street also known for its coffee houses and banks.

Georgian House 🏠 Ab
House, 18th century, built for wealthy sugar merchant, John Pretor Pinney. House retains original features like a housekeeper's room and plunge bath.

SS Great Britain ⚓ Aa
First propeller-driven ocean vessel, built by Isambard Kingdom Brunel in 1845. Ship was towed back from abandonment in Falkland Islands to Bristol, where it was built.

Harvey's Wine Museum 🏛 Bb
Wine has been stored in these cellars since medieval times. Museum displays collection of wine-related artefacts ranging from antique bottles to corkscrews. Note its collection of 18th-century drinking glasses.

Jacob's Well Ab
Well first recorded in 1042; soon after, it was used to fill ritual bath of local Jewish community. It was only recently rediscovered, along with oldest Hebrew inscriptions known in Britain.

John Wesley's Chapel ✝ Cc
Oldest known Methodist Chapel, built by Wesley in 1739 and rebuilt by him in 1748. Chapel and living quarters are preserved as they were in his day.

King Street Cb
Cobbled street with fine historic buildings, laid out in 1663 outside city wall. Theatre Royal, opened 1766, dominates this street of inns and restaurants. Merchant Venturer's Almshouses on corner, have provided homes for retired mariners since 1699. The Bunch of Grapes Inn has been here since 1762, but present building dates from early 19th century.

Lewins Mead Unitarian Chapel ✝ Bc
Rare example of early nonconformist chapel. First built 1694, it

was rebuilt in classical style in 1791. Chapel stands on site of old Frome Bridge, but river now flows unseen beneath street.

Llandoger Trow Cb
Handsome, timber-framed inn, built in 1664; named after a barge that sailed between Bristol and Wales. Thought to be Spyglass Inn of Stephenson's *Treasure Island*. Also considered to be place where idea for *Robinson Crusoe* was first thought out.

Lloyds Bank Cc
Ornate Venetian-style building, dating from 1854, renowned for its magnificent, restored frieze by John Thomas.

HOME TO STAY *Brunel's pioneer ship, SS Great Britain, back in Bristol from the Falkland Islands.*

Lord Mayor's Chapel ✝ Bb
Small church was originally part of 13th-century St Mark's Hospital. Designated as official civic church in 1722, it features Flemish stained glass and Spanish tiles.

Maritime Heritage Centre ⚓ Aa
Dockside museum tells story of Bristol shipbuilding over past 200 years. Modern display techniques bring port's past back to life.

Neptune Statue Bb
Cast lead figure of Neptune, dating from 1723; positioned here since 1949. Statue commemorates Bristol's seafaring history.

Queen Square Cb
Bristol's first square, named after Queen Anne's visit in 1702. Statue of William III on horseback in centre of green.

CHAPEL OF THE THREE KINGS OF COLOGNE *The chapel adjoins Foster's Almshouses, founded by John Foster, who became mayor of Bristol in 1481. The buildings were reconstructed in the 19th century, in Burgundian-Gothic style.*

Tower, built to commemorate John Cabot's 1497 voyage to North American mainland.

Bristol Cathedral ✝ Bb
Founded 1140 as Abbey Church of St Augustine, on legendary site where St Augustine met early Christians in the 7th century. Building retains Norman chapter house with spectacular carving. Choir, dated 14th century, has notable capitals and unique vaulting design. Ruined nave was rebuilt in 19th century by G.E. Street, masterfully imitating design of choir. Elder Lady Chapel has a beautiful arcade with distorted carved figures. Eastern Lady Chapel has fine window with original glass *c.* 1340.

Bristol Industrial Museum 🏛 Ba
Museum set among tall cranes and wharves of floating harbour. Exhibits explain Bristol's complex

Hotel, built 1869, has impressive Renaissance-style façade.

Christchurch ✝ Cc
Impressive late 18th-century church, known for beautiful Georgian interior. Escaped bomb damage in World War II by the strength of its walls. Two colourful quarterjacks, dating from 1728, strike clock bell each ¼ hour. These quarterjacks and gilded dragon weather-vane survive from old parish church.

Christmas Steps Bc
Steps built in 1699 through what used to be a steep short cut to now-vanished river. Old houses, shops and gas lamps remain.

City Museum and Art Gallery 🏛 Ac
Bristol University and its Refectory surround fine gallery buildings in classical style. Collection includes replica of the Bristol

Edward Everard Building Bc
Magnificent Art Nouveau-style building of 1900. Colourful figures in ceramic tiles illustrate revival of craftsmanship, in 19th century.

Exploratory Hands-On Science Centre Db
Museum housed in mock-medieval station, by great engineer, Brunel. Scientific hands-on exhibits include a gyroscope and arch-building experiments.

Floating Harbour
Created in 1809-10, harbour is so-called because ships can stay afloat whatever the tide, secure behind lock gates. Boat trips and ferries available.

Foster's Almshouses Bc
Victorian buildings designed in Burgundian-Gothic style. The Chapel of the Three Kings of Cologne lies beside Almshouses, founded in the 15th century.

PIONEER PLANE *Full-size replica of the 1910 Bristol Boxkite biplane, suspended from a ceiling in the City Museum and Art Gallery.*

HISTORIC INN *King Street is renowned for the handsome Llandoger Trow, thought to be the Spyglass Inn of R.L. Stevenson's* Treasure Island.

DECORATIVE FOUNTAIN *Set in the wall of St Nicholas Market is an ornate Victorian drinking fountain.*

St Nicholas Market Cc

Covered market built in 1745 to clear street stall clutter in the narrow streets. Building reconstructed in 1850 to original Palladian style. It is still in use and no longer limited to selling fruit and vegetables. Area is liberally supplied with pubs, including The Rummer, on site of city's oldest inn, The Green Lattis.

Temple Church ✝ Db

Large building in Perpendicular style, on site of Knights Templar church dating from the 12th century. Present construction, which has leaning tower, was built in the 15th century. It then succumbed to World War II bombing raids, but shell of building has been preserved.

Temple Meads Station Db

Brunel's old terminus lies near main station building, with an elegant, iron-arched roof dating from 1865-78.

Theatre Royal ♜ Cb

Theatre has been in continuous use since opening in 1766, the longest performing run in Britain. Its elegant façade is even older, originally part of Hall of the Guild of Coopers, built in 1743. Theatre was modelled on Wren's Drury Lane Theatre, London. Home of Bristol Old Vic since 1946.

University Tower Ac

Local landmark, 215ft high, financed by tobacco magnates G.A. and H.H. Wills, as a memorial to their father. Construction of neo-Gothic tower started in the 19th century, but only completed in 1925.

Victoria Rooms Ac

Sumptuous classical building with restored Corinthian portico; former public hall and political meeting place in the 19th century. Now part of the university. Outside is a fine statue of Edward VII, by Edwin Rickards.

The Watershed Bb

Once these were transit sheds, holding goods waiting to be transferred from ships to trains. Now they house an arts complex, shops and bars, bringing new life to the old docks.

STRIKING FAÇADE *Carrara marble-ware tiles decorate Edward Everard's former printing works.*

Welsh Back Cb

Ships have unloaded here since medieval times, when the quay was part of original port, by the River Avon. Old warehouses still line waterfront, including the Granary, built in 1871. Unusual brick style of the Granary is unique to city, popularly known as 'Bristol Byzantine'.

Red Lodge ♨ Bc

Red stone house with garden, once lodge of Great House, a Tudor mansion now vanished. First floor has oak-panelled rooms, plaster-work ceilings and beautiful stone chimneypiece. Upper rooms are hung with 17th and 18th-century paintings.

St Bartholomew's Hospital Ac

One of city's oldest buildings, founded as an almshouse for the poor in the 13th century. Sections of original hospital survive inside. In 1532 it became home of Bristol Grammar School.

St George's, Brandon Hill Ac

Classical-style church known for excellent acoustics, which gave it a new lease of life as a concert hall. Little has had to be changed to adapt building to its new role.

St John's Gate Bc

Effigies of Brennus and Belinus, mythical kings said to be founders of Bristol, look down from their niches above city's last medieval gate. Church of St John the Baptist was built into wall. Nearby is 600-year-old St John's Conduit.

St Mary Redcliffe Church ✝ Ca

Entered through an ornate Norman porch, church has 292ft spire and an interior full of superb detail, including over a thousand carved roof bosses.

St Michael's Hill Bc

Street climbs up from city, lined with fine 17th and 18th-century buildings, including Colston almshouses. Last walk for some Bristolians on their way to the old gallows on hill.

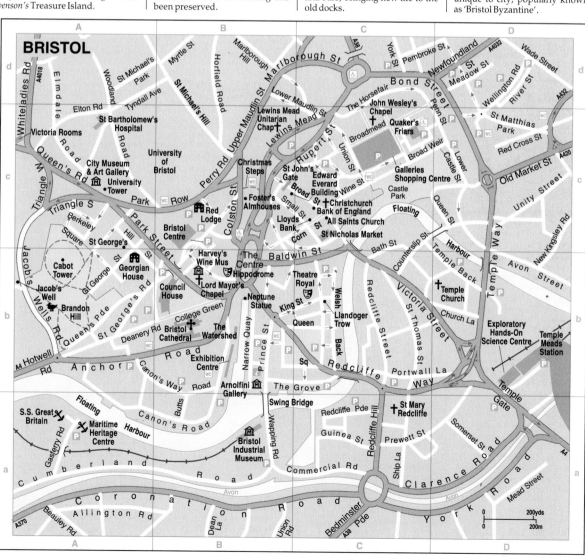

BRISTOL

Avebury ⚏🚏🏚🏛 De
Important stone circle dating from 1800 BC rings village of thatched cottages, Norman church and Elizabethan mansion. Alexander Keiller Museum has finds from here and nearby West Kennet Long Barrow, Silbury Hill, the Sanctuary and Windmill Hill Neolithic camp of 2500 BC.

Barbury Castle ❊☗ Ef
Iron Age hill-fort with two ditches and a rampart covering some 12 acres. Stands on top of Marlborough Downs on the Ridgeway, a prehistoric track running 250 miles from South Devon to The Wash.

Beckford's Tower 🏛 Ae
Climb 156 steps up this 154ft tower for views of Bath. Built 1827 in Italianate style for Sir William Beckford. His collection of paintings and furniture is displayed in the museum below.

Bowood House 🏛 Cf
Adam south front, orangery and mausoleum at this noble house standing in 1000 acres. Contains 5000 volume library and family chapel. Capability Brown gardens have Italianate cascade, serpentine lake and Doric temple.

Bradford-on-Avon ✝🏛☗✿🖾 Be
Houses of Bath stone built between 16th and 18th centuries rise steeply above River Avon in town made prosperous by Dutch weavers. Rediscovered Saxon church by Town Bridge has fish-shaped weather vane called Bradford Gudgeon. A meadow walk leads to stone-walled, 14th-century tithe barn, one of the largest in England.

Bratton Castle ❊ Cd
Double-walled Iron Age hill-fort covering 25 acres on 755ft Westbury Hill. White Horse carved in hillside chalk in 1778.

Broadleas ✿ De
Magnolias, sanguinarias, and a beautiful blue-flowered foxglove tree are among plants that flourish on greensand with views over Bath. Dell shrubbery, walled rose garden and teas.

Calne ✝✿🚋 Df
Once prosperous weaving town which turned to bacon curing. Parish church arcades date from 1160 and Lansdowne Arms has old brewhouse in yard. Attwell-Wilson Motor Museum displays enthusiasts' vehicles including Rolls-Royces, Cadillacs, Model T Fords and elegant little Singer.

Castle Combe ⚏ Bf
Often hailed as England's prettiest village. Lies in hollow, approached through deep, tree-shaded valley. Parking restricted, visitors expected to leave cars at top of village. Bridge looks up a street of stone cottages to Market Cross and Castle Hotel. Weavers House was once lived in by the Blanket brothers who may have taken their name from the bed covering. St Andrew's Church, with 1434 tower built by local cloth merchants, is richly decorated in stone and wood. North aisle has 13th-century tomb of Sir Walter de

DOWNLANDS HOME OF EARLY MAN

The rolling Marlborough Downs sweep towards the Vale of Pewsey, and farther south lie the open grasslands of Salisbury Plain. Civilisation here stretches back to before 2000 BC, taking in the Iron and Bronze Ages. Many centuries later, the wealth from medieval wool and corn was used to build towns and villages such as Bradford-on-Avon and Castle Combe.

Dunstanville, who built the long-vanished castle which gave the village its name.

Chippenham✝ 🏛🖾 Cf
Town of gabled, Cotswold-stone houses with 15th-century town hall sporting wooden turret. Hungerford Chapel of parish church has many monuments of the 15th century; some date back to the 13th century. Yelde Hall Museum in former 15th-century town hall has archaeological and photographic displays.

Claverton Manor 🏛 Ae
Greek-revival house, built 1820, home to American Museum featuring history and art of American people, including Wild West and Red Indian collections. Grounds contain reproduction of George Washington's flower garden.

Corsham Court 🏛 Bf
Elizabethan manor, altered in 18th and 19th centuries, with gardens by Capability Brown. Houses the Methuen collection of paintings, furniture and china, including Lippi's *Annunciation* (1463). Flemish gabled houses in village street.

Devizes ✝🏚✿♻🖾 De
Market town with two 12th-century churches, 15th-century castle, 16th-century timbered buildings, and elegant Georgian houses. Bronze Age artefacts in Archaeological Museum, and warehouse exhibition tells the story of the locks along Kennet and Avon Canal.

Dyrham ⚏🏛 Af
Church of St Peter, 13th century, contains effigies of mourning children and flamboyant heraldry. Dyrham Park mansion, built between 1692 and 1704 in baroque style, has Delft china, tapestries, paintings and books.

Edington ⚏ Cd
Tiny village with grand cruciform Church of St Mary, St Katherine

MELLOW CHARM *Castle Combe is threaded by the little Bybrook.*

PLACE OF PRAYER *Medieval pilgrims bound for Glastonbury used to pray in the chapel on the bridge at Bradford-on-Avon.*

and All Saints, built 1352. Battlemented tower and 17th-century plaster ceiling.

Fyfield Down ✩ Ef
Natural downland source of many Stonehenge stones and one of the finest prehistoric landscapes in Britain. Paths across outlines of rectangular Celtic fields, in an area farmed since 700 BC.

Great Chalfield Manor 🏛 Be
Moat encircles polished yellow stone house from 1480, remarkable for exterior detail, as well as outbuildings and parish church. House has two-storey Great Hall.

Heale House ✿ Eb
Eight acres of grounds, where streams run between trees. Hedge of musk roses, tunnel garden, apple tree avenue, wild water garden, and Japanese Tea House. Charles II hid in the house in 1651.

Iford Manor ✿ Bd
Tudor house with 18th-century façade and Italian gardens by Edwardian landscape architect Harold Peto. Colonnade, cloisters, pools and statuary.

Lackham Agricultural Museum ♻ Cf
Old farm buildings set in Lackham College grounds display agricultural items. Rhododendron walk, riverside and woodland trails. Flower, fruit and vegetable gardens, and glasshouse orchids. Picnic areas and farm animals.

Lacock ⚏🏛🏛 Ce
Ancient village with winding streets, greystone houses (none later than 1800) and half-timbered cottages. Abbey was England's last religious house to be dissolved; a house since 1540. Home of photographic pioneer Fox Talbot with museum of his work.

Longleat 🏛♈ Bc
Seat of the Marquess of Bath; grounds landscaped by Capability Brown, now safari park roamed by lions. Elizabethan mansion has drawing-room ceiling copied from St Mark's Cathedral in Venice. Maze, miniature railway and butterfly garden.

Malmesbury ✚🏛🏛🖾 Cg
Town of water and bridges, almost encircled on its hill by River Avon. Cotswold-stone houses of 17th and 18th century line streets. Notable Tudor market cross and impressive Norman Abbey with fine carvings on south porch.

Marshfield ⚏ Af
One of Britain's longest high streets, almost a mile long, with almshouses of 1619, Georgian houses, and parish church with spectacular tower.

Mells ⚏ Ac
Village of thatched cottages round small greens. Works by Burne-Jones, Lutyens and Munnings decorate 15th-century church. Great tower has faceless clock that chimes and plays hymns.

Nunney ⚏🏚 Ac
Steep descent through woodland reveals remains of 14th-century moated fortress, modelled on Bastille in Paris, demolished in Civil War. Church contains cannonball which helped with demolition.

Rode Tropical Bird Gardens 🐦 Bd
Open-air aviaries among trees and lakes house cranes, flamingos, macaws, peacocks and penguins.

Sheldon Manor 🏛 Bf
Stone manor house of 1659 with two-storey 13th-century porch. House is all that remains of an abandoned medieval village.

Stonehenge ☗ Ec
Ancient stone circles of massive proportions, perhaps built for sun worship. Monument axis points towards sunrise at summer solstice. Begun about 3000 BC as a ditch-and-bank circle, and remodelled with bluestones and sarsen stones over next 1300 years.

Stourhead 🏛✿ Ab
Stately Palladian house built 1722 for the banker Henry Hoare; paintings, sculptures, Chippendale furniture and Gibbons woodcarving. Pleasure garden one of earliest and best examples of English landscaped garden, with temples, grottoes and lakes.

Swindon 🏛☗⚙♻🏛🖾 Eg
Largest town in Wiltshire, built on prosperity of Great Western Railway. Old Swindon, on hill overlooking town, has Brunel's village for railway workers and museum in former Wesleyan chapel.

Underground Quarry Centre ○ Be
Labyrinth of galleries and tunnels tell story of Bath stone, from rock face to finished building. Reached by long flight of steps. Sturdy shoes essential.

Warminster 🖾 Bc
Former wool and corn town with 17th and 18th-century houses, whose mullioned windows rise above modern shop fronts. High gateways to Anchor, Bath Arms and Old Bell inns recall days as stopping places for coaches.

Wellow ⚏ Ad
Old farm buildings surround village square with 13th-century dovecote. Good woodwork in St Julian's Church dating from 1372. Rare mural painting in 1440 Hungerford Chapel.

West Kennet Long Barrow ☗ Ee
Prehistoric burial place where massive sarsen stones guard the largest chambered tomb in England. Nearby Silbury Hill is a prehistoric man-made mound standing 130ft high, dating from at least 2500 BC.

BLACK AND WHITE *Wootton Bassett's town hall dates from 1700.*

Wootton Bassett 🏛☷ Dg
Old market town with 18th-century buildings. Half-timbered town hall contains original stocks, ducking stool and antique fire engine. Lydiard Park has fine rooms dating from the 1740s, and extensive grounds.

Yarnbury Castle ❊ Dc
Iron Age hill-fort covering 28 acres; entrance through lofty double earth ramparts. Superb views over Salisbury Plain.

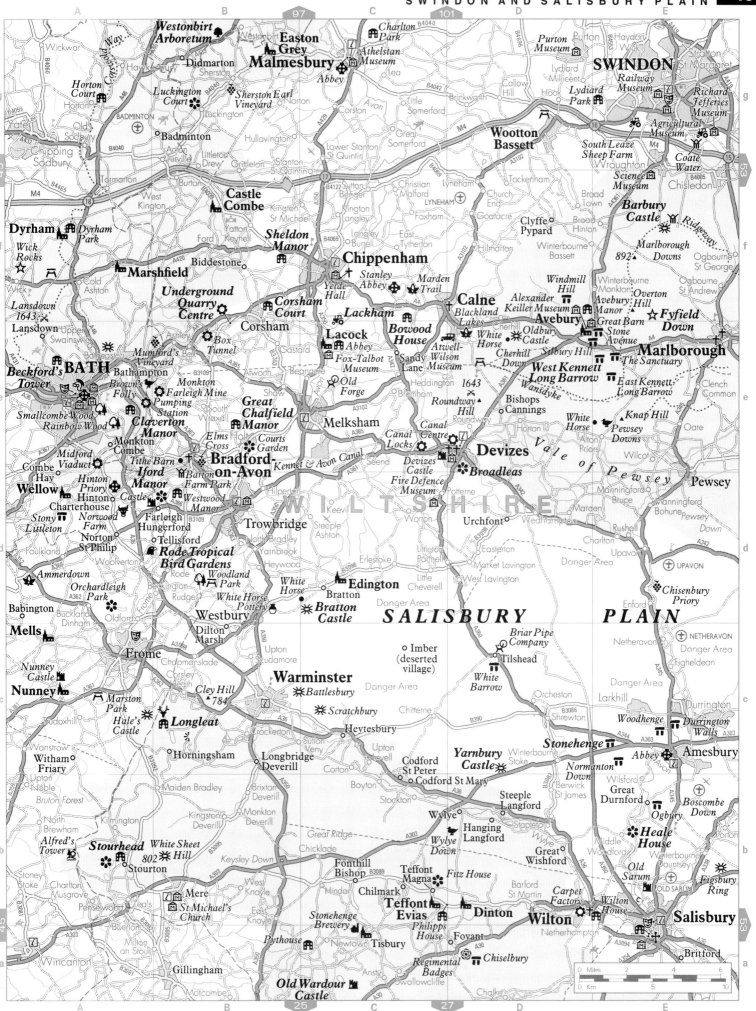

ELEGANT CITY OF GOLDEN STONE

The healing hot springs of this fascinating city have always been a magnet to the rich. Aquae Sulis became a prosperous spa in Roman times, an achievement repeated centuries later when Beau Nash and the two John Woods created a golden-stoned city of polite society and classical elegance. This blend of Roman and Georgian splendour gives Bath the air of a living museum.

STONE GRACE *The building of Bath Abbey spanned four centuries.*

Abbey ✤ Cb
Building in Perpendicular Gothic style, with 162ft high tower, flying buttresses and fan vaulting, was begun in 1499 on site of original abbey founded by local king, Osric, in about AD 680. Each of west front turrets decorated by carving of angels ascending and descending ladder reaching to heaven – commemorating vision that led Bishop King to build church. Many large windows in in Bath. Built in two blocks with magnificent collection of rooms. Largely destroyed by fire in 1942, but later restored.

Bath Industrial Heritage Centre ✿ Bd
Reconstructed workshops of family firm which was in operation from 1872 to 1969. Founder, J.B. Bowler, was engineer, plumber, gas fitter and bell hanger – and maker of aerated water. During firm's existence, nothing was thrown away, allowing for exact reconstructions. Much of ancient machinery still works, including soda fountain. Centre also has displays tracing story of golden Bath stone from which much of city is built.

The Circus Bc
Masterpiece of John Wood the Elder (1704-54) consists of three arcs, each with 33 houses, built round a circular open space. Building started in 1750. Façades of arcs ornamented with three classical 'orders' of Doric, Ionic and Corinthian columns. Plaques mark houses once occupied by famous former tenants including the explorer David Livingstone, empire builder Clive of India, and artist Thomas Gainsborough.

Cross Bath Bb
One of three places where Bath's hot springs emerge – at end of colonnaded Bath Street. More than 800 years old, bath was favoured by nobility during 18th century.

people who lived here were 18th-century novelist Jane Austen and the anti-slavery campaigner William Wilberforce.

Guildhall Cb
Built in 18th century by Thomas Baldwin, Guildhall has banqueting room with chandeliers and portraits of George III and Queen Charlotte by Reynolds. Claimed to be finest room in Bath.

Henrietta Park Cc
Small park contains special scent garden for the blind.

Herschel House and Museum 🏛 Ab
Displays on Sir William Herschel (1738-1822), German-born musician and astronomer who lived in house and made his own reflecting telescope, with which he discovered planet Uranus in 1781. Appointed private astronomer to George III in following year.

Holburne Museum 🏛 Dc
Palladian mansion at end of Great Pulteney Street, originally built in 1796 as Sydney Hotel. Now houses collections by Sir Thomas Holburne of silver, porcelain, glass, bronzes, furniture and 18th-century English paintings. Pictures by Stubbs, Zoffany, Gainsborough and Allan Ramsay. Museum also contains works by 20th-century British artist-craftsmen specialising in woven and printed textiles, furniture, pottery and calligraphy.

Market Cb
Built on site of medieval slaughterhouse and meat market, facing River Avon. Has 12-sided domed and glazed interior, and 18th-century 'nail' where deals were struck – hence expression 'cash on the nail'.

Museum of Bookbinding 🏛 Ca
Museum has displays tracing history of bookbinding and contemporary practices of craft. Exhibits include reconstruction of 19th-century bindery and some outstanding examples of binding.

Museum of Costume 🏛 Bd
Housed in Assembly Rooms, museum is one of the largest of its kind in the world. Displays devoted to fashionable dress for men, women and children from Tudor times to present day. It includes over 200 dressed figures – placed in period settings – as well as about 1000 other items of costume, accessories and jewellery. The collection is kept up to date with annually selected 'dress of the year'.

Museum of English Naive Art 🏛 Bd
The only museum of its kind in this country, housed in Old School House next door to Countess of Huntingdon's Chapel. Entertaining collection of paintings dating from 18th and 19th centuries depicts ordinary people, pursuits and incidents with direct and charming simplicity. Also on display are shop and inn signs – and collection of weather vanes. Shop sells reproductions of the paintings on display.

Parade Gardens Cb
Gardens contain imaginative floral displays. Across the river is a maze with Gorgon centrepiece repeated from Roman Baths.

Pulteney Bridge Cc
City's only work by Robert Adam; elegant bridge has three classical arches spanning River Avon and is lined with shops on either side of roadway. Designed in 1771, it was inspired by medieval Ponte Vecchio in Florence. At time of building, it was feared that narrow 30ft width would not allow air to circulate, and that smoke would become a problem.

Pump Room Bb
Handsome room, dating from 1796, is supported by 16 fluted columns and has windows overlooking steaming waters of King's Bath. Lit by immense chandelier, it also contains statue of Beau Nash, pair of original sedan chairs, and superb clock, 10ft high and made in 1709 by Thomas Tompion. Visitors can sample health-giving Bath water from small fountain, or enjoy Bath buns and coffee while trio plays classical music. Pediment outside is carved with motto 'Water is Best'.

FLORENCE ON AVON *Pulteney Bridge, designed by Robert Adam in 1771 and lined with shops, was inspired by Florence's Ponte Vecchio and named after William Pulteney, 1st Earl of Bath.*

abbey – glass is nearly all modern. Altar-tomb of Bishop Montagu stands on north side of nave. Tablet in south aisle to Beau Nash (1674-1762), who established Bath as fashionable spa.

Abbey Church House Bb
Elizabethan mansion with gabled roof was built around 1570. One of city's few pre-Georgian buildings still standing.

Assembly Rooms Bd
One of Bath's grandest public buildings, and once considered the most elegant in Europe. Erected 1769-71 by architect John Wood the Younger (1728-81), for public breakfasts, fancy-dress balls, card games and other social activities. Total cost of £20,000 made it most expensive building

Bath Postal Museum 🏛 Bc
Housed in the first-ever post office to issue the Penny Black postage stamp, on May 2, 1840. Original 1840 appearance of office has been reproduced. Displays show how letter writing has evolved, from clay tablets of Sumerians to today's electronic methods.

Building of Bath Museum 🏛 Bd
Craftsmen who have shaped Bath provide focus of exhibition showing how city was transformed in 18th century. Tools, fragments of buildings and pattern books are among exhibits. Models include a large-scale reconstruction of entire city. Museum is housed in restored Georgian Gothic chapel built in 1765. Research and educational facilities available.

East Gate Cb
Only surviving medieval gateway into the city, with narrow walls bearing the scrapes and chipping caused by generations of horse-drawn vehicles. A plan shows how small the old city was.

Fashion Research Centre Bc
House on Circus contains extension of Museum of Costume. Students and public can consult books on history of costume and textiles, periodicals, old photographs and archives. Also study collection of costume.

Great Pulteney Street Cc
Long and dignified street, designed by Thomas Baldwin, is lined by classical-style buildings; none of which date from later than 18th century. Among the famous

BATHING IN THE ROUND *The large circular bath, in the Roman Baths Museum, is one of several of different sizes and temperatures.*

FROZEN IN TIME *The Industrial Heritage Centre includes 'Mr Bowler's Business', a factory virtually unchanged since Victorian times.*

SOBER CURVES *Classical houses in honey-coloured stone ring a clump of plane trees in The Circus, designed by John Wood the Elder in the 1750s.*

Queen Square Bc
First great project of John Wood the Elder, started in 1728 when city was still basically medieval. Wood himself lived in square. Obelisk was erected by Beau Nash in 1738 in honour of Frederick, Prince of Wales.

River Avon Towpath Cb
Walk gives views of Bath at its most Florentine, with domes, spires, colonnades and Pulteney Bridge, where water slides over shallow weirs.

BLOOD-CURDLER *A Romano-Celtic Gorgon's head glares down in the Roman Baths Museum.*

Roman Baths and Museum Bb
Vying with Hadrian's Wall as greatest memorial to Roman Britain is Aquae Sulis spa resort, built round hot spring which still produces water at 46.5°C (116°F). Latin name means 'waters of Sul', Sul being name of a local Celtic god. Roman buildings were about 20ft below present street level. Romans called it Aquae Sulis Minerva, after their own goddess of healing. Principal feature is Great Bath – open-air bath, formerly roofed, 70ft long, 30ft wide and 5ft deep, still fed through Roman plumbing from the hot spring. Pool's original lead lining is still intact. Roman-looking statues round bath were added in 19th century. Roman Museum occupies site of actual centre of Aquae Sulis. Displays of archaeological findings include carved head of Minerva, and Romano-Celtic Gorgon's head built into reconstructed temple pediment. Collection of objects dropped into the sacred spring include coins, jewels and pewter tablets inscribed with prayers imploring the help of the gods. Computer graphics show what Roman baths and temple would have looked like from different angles. Near Great Bath lies King's Bath –

nothing like Great Bath in size, but focal point of Roman city, built around hot spring to create head of water to feed baths complex. Supposedly used by medieval monarchs – hence name.

Royal Crescent Ad
World's first crescent, which inspired many successors. It was built by John Wood the Younger in the 1770s, and comprises sweep of 30 impressive houses fronted by 114 massive Ionic columns. No.1 has been restored and furnished in late 18th-century style – classified as World Heritage Building. Details, including sewing put aside and letters left unfinished, give lived-in feeling. There is background music of period. Kitchen museum of brass and pewter utensils in basement. Crescent faces down grassy slope to Royal Victoria Park.

Royal Victoria Park Ac
Magnificent expanse of grass and trees, stretching south and west of Royal Crescent.

RPS National Centre of Photography Bc
Treasures of Royal Photographic Society are displayed in octagonal 18th-century former chapel, which still features gallery and ornate plaster-work. Displays trace history of photography from earliest days to present. Exhibitions of work by major photographers include classics of newspaper photography.

Sally Lunn's House Cb
Bath's oldest house, built in 1482, still produces famous buns to Sally Lunn's original 1680s recipe. Cellar contains kitchen museum, and reveals traces of building's Roman, Saxon and medieval foundations. Collection of clay pipes on display.

Saracen's Head Bc
In Broad Street, city's most ancient inn – two-storeyed, gabled building, dating from 1713, with sash windows.

Sydney Gardens Dd
Graceful 18th-century park stands on banks of Kennet and Avon Canal, which is crossed by Chinese-style bridge. Laid out as Bath's equivalent of Vauxhall Gardens, in London, it was described at the time as 'the most spacious and beautiful Public Garden in the kingdom'. In her youth, novelist Jane Austen lived with her parents in Sydney Place, on south side of gardens.

Theatre Royal Bb
Restored historic theatre completed in 1805 and incorporating parts of a building of 1720 which was Beau Nash's first house; Nash later moved to house next door. Has own theatregoer restaurant and Japanese restaurant.

Upper Borough Walls Bb
Reconstructed wall on site of defences of medieval city, small portion of which remains.

Victoria Art Gallery and Museum Cb
Exhibitions drawn from gallery's collections include 17th to 20th-century paintings, prints and drawings, ceramics, glass and watches; also old topographical views of Bath.

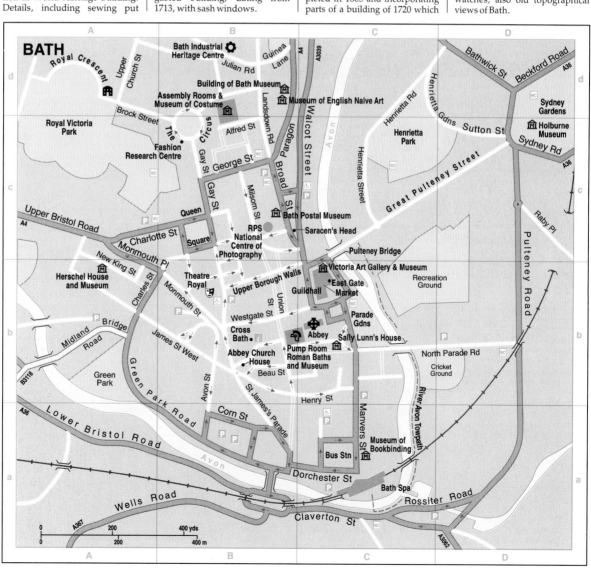

AIRY HEIGHTS OF THE RIDGEWAY

From their trading route along the crest of the Berkshire downs, ancient Britons looked down on a sea of forest and scrub. Now walkers on the Ridgeway Path view a tamed landscape, dotted with pretty villages and prosperous market towns, where racehorses pound the turf. Bronze Age burial mounds, and ancient woods where Norman kings once hunted deer, recall other dwellers.

Aldermaston ⋔ Ed
Hillside village overlooking River Kennet. Former manor house at top of main street and 17th-century coaching inn at bottom. Colourful tapestry of painted walls and stained-glass windows in medieval church.

Andover ⋔⚲ Cb
Busy shopping centre with remains of an old market town. Museum of the Iron Age displays finds from local digs.

Ardington ⋔⚏⚲ Df
Pleasant village with 12th-century church. Ardington House (18th century) has majestic staircase with twisted oak balusters. Craft workshops at Home Farm.

Ashdown House ⚏✳⚲ Bf
Tower-like four-storey white house built by Lord Craven around 1660. Enormous staircase from ground to roof with wide views over downs.

Basildon Park ⚏ Fe
Georgian mansion in 400 acres of hilly parkland overlooking the Thames valley. Elegant octagonal drawing room and decorative Shell Room.

Beale Bird Park ⚶ Fe
Flamingos, peacocks and an especially noted collection of ornamental pheasants share this spacious meadowland reserve beside the Thames. Boat trips and riverside walks. Craft centre and adventure playground.

Bucklebury Common Ed
Sandy heathland where royal hunting horn once sounded. Mile-long avenue of gnarled oaks, said to have been planted during the reign of Elizabeth I, and two medieval fishponds.

Burghclere ⋔✝ Dd
Ancient village in shadow of Watership Down, where villagers once spun wool and extracted lime for nearby market towns. Artist Stanley Spencer spent six years there creating war murals for Sandham Memorial Chapel.

Crofton Beam Engines ⚙ Bd
World's oldest working beam engines housed at Crofton pumping station on Kennet and Avon canal. Installed (1815 and 1845) to pump water to upper level of canal. Narrowboat trips during steam weekends.

Danebury Ring ✳⍍ Ca
Well-preserved ramparts of vast Iron Age fort, with views across to grandstand of Stockbridge's 19th-century racecourse. Nature trail.

Didcot ⚙ Eg
Hissing steam engines from old Great Western Railway brought back to life at 16 acre Railway Centre. Reconstructed Victorian station and occasional dining in luxury saloon carriages.

East Garston ⋔ Ce
Secluded village of timber-framed cottages with sloping walls and brightly patterned tiles. Each whitewashed cottage along road leading to church has a bridge over the River Lambourn. Large flint-built Norman church.

East Hendred ⋔ Df
A 'Best Kept' village with black-and-white cottages and handsome pubs. One of England's oldest timepieces in church; 1525 faceless clock even plays a hymn.

Froxfield ⋔ Bd
Cheery quadrangle of former almshouses overlooks neat brick-and-flint cottages. Hounds of Hell are said to chase ghost of Wild Darrell – 16th-century owner of Littlecote House who murdered a baby – across the fields around Froxfield on moonlit nights.

SUMMER PAGEANT *Holiday craft pass in a seemingly endless procession through Goring Lock.*

Goring ✝⚙ Ff
Riverside town where early travellers had to ford turbulent waters at Goring Gap. Now has weirs, locks and towpaths; wooden bridge connects it to Streatley. Church is 12th century.

Great Bedwyn ⋔ Bd
Unspoilt village was once Saxon city. Past recalled by malthouse with kiln tower, stonemason's yard with early stonework, and 11th-century church with tomb of Sir Henry Seymour, father of Henry VIII's third wife, Jane.

Hawk Conservancy ⚶ Cb
Chance to see eye-to-eye with large number of birds of prey; some bred for release. Injured birds also cared for.

Highclere Castle ⚏ Dc
Victorian mansion built for 4th Earl of Carnarvon. Fifth Earl, sponsor of Tutankhamun expedition, buried on top of Beacon Hill nearby. Egyptian finds in castle.

Hungerford ⚓ Cd
Anglers and antique buyers rub shoulders in gracious High Street. Fine Georgian inns and houses recall days as market centre, and coaching stop for travellers on London to Bath run.

Inkpen and Walbury Hills ✳⍍ Cd
Highest chalk hills in England, thrusting up to almost 1000ft. Replica of 17th-century gallows on Inkpen, along with Stone Age chieftain's tomb. Outline of Iron Age fort on summit of Walbury.

Lambourn ⋔ Ce
Training centre for racehorses. Jockeys exercise their mounts within sight of over 20 Bronze Age burial mounds. Market town has traditional saddlers, 12th-century church and Victorian almshouses.

Longstock ⋔ Ca
Hampshire village with one winding street and colour-washed period houses. Circular thatched huts along banks of River Test – used by anglers.

Marlborough ✝ Ad
Colonnaded High Street is one of widest in country; with Jacobean and Georgian buildings, and back alleys with medieval cottages. Handsome 15th-century church with curfew bell. Arched bridge leads to famous public school and ancient mound of Maerl's Barrow.

Newbury ⚏✕⚲⚲ Dd
Once famous for Tudor cloth workshops, and now a thriving horseracing centre. Handsome Jacobean Cloth Hall houses museum with artefacts, Civil War relics and vintage cameras. To north is 14th-century gatehouse of Donnington Castle, defended by Royalists during Civil Wars.

Savernake Forest ⚲⍍ Bd
Once a hunting ground for Norman kings, now a haven for deer, wild birds and rare plants. Capability Brown designed Grand Avenue of statuesque beeches.

Snelsmore Common Country Park ⍍ De
Nature trail across 146 acre aromatic heathland slopes. Includes wetland area of peaty bog with insect-eating sundews.

Streatley ⋔✳ Ef
Georgian houses line sloping street to banks of Thames. Climb hill behind town for splendid views over locks, weirs and moored boats. Wooden bridge links town to Goring.

Wallingford ⚏⚓⚲ Ff
Market town and riverside resort. Strategic crossing point of Thames, with towpath walks and fine Georgian houses. Saxon stonework in St Leonard's Church, portraits by Gainsborough in Town Hall. Steam railway runs 1¼ miles between here and village of Cholsey.

The Wallops ⋔⍊ Ba
Trio of villages along Wallop Brook. Over Wallop church has 15th-century font. Home of RAF training since 1940, Middle Wallop aerodrome has Museum of Army Flying. Nether Wallop's craftsmen make cricket bats from local willows. Pyramid-shaped tomb of eccentric 1700s doctor outside 14th-century church.

Wantage ⚏ Cf
Birthplace of King Alfred, whose statue stands in marketplace. Buildings span the centuries, and one street is cobbled with sheep's knuckles. History of the Vale of the White Horse recounted in Vale and Downland Museum.

Watership Down ⚶⚲ Ec
Beauty spot that inspired Richard Adams' novel about a community of rabbits. Also used by ramblers and for training racehorses.

Wherwell ⋔⚶ Cb
Fine thatch abounds in this showpiece village of timbered cottages; roofs, doors, windows and walls draped in mantles of straw.

Whitchurch ⚙ Db
Small riverside town with Silk Mill, where garments are woven using traditional techniques. Rare Saxon tombstone in churchyard.

Whitehorse Hill ✳⍍⍍ Cf
Britain's oldest chalk horse gallops across hillside; perhaps carved by Iron Age Celts. Iron Age camp of Uffington Castle crowns

DOWNLAND TROUGH *A curious natural hollow, known as the Horse's Manger, lies under White Horse Hill.*

RIDGEWAY BURIAL *Wayland's Smithy, a prehistoric barrow, lies 1½ miles west of White Horse Hill.*

the hill. Eight skeletons discovered in Stone Age burial chamber, or long barrow, at Wayland's Smithy, named after mythical blacksmith. The Ridgeway Path runs along top of hill, once prehistoric route for driving animals and goods and now path for long-distance walking.

Yattendon ⋔ Ee
Village square is surrounded by fine 17th and 18th-century brick houses. Jacobean pulpit in 15th-century church. Poet Robert Bridges buried there.

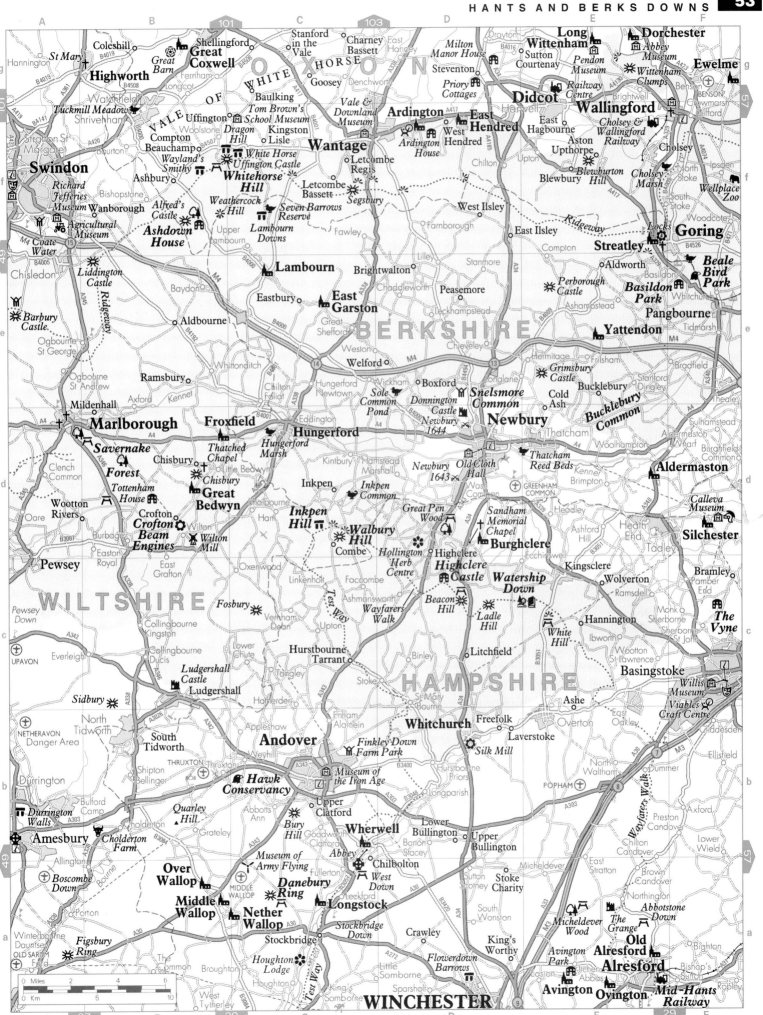

FLINT TOOLS AND STONE CIRCLES

Rolling grasslands, a patchwork of fields and picturesque villages are characteristic of England's downs. The country's first permanent inhabitants settled here, clearing the beech forests to start farming.

The long white line of Dover's cliffs has for centuries been the first sight of England gained by travellers crossing the Channel from France; and the mighty promontory of Beachy Head and graceful chalk cliffs forming the Seven Sisters are familiar landmarks to seafarers. The chalk downland that creates these spectacular coastal sights dominates the whole of south and south-east England, as well as much of the eastern coast. Centring on Salisbury Plain, it radiates eastward to form the North and South Downs and north-east to become the Chilterns and uplands of East Anglia.

The first settlers in the region were Stone Age immigrants who crossed from the

WHITE GIANT *The 180ft long figure at Cerne Abbas may have been associated with fertility rites.*

Continent on the land bridge that now lies beneath the English Channel. Traces of their great trade routes that crisscrossed the whole of southern England can still be seen, among them the Berkshire Ridgeway and its extension the Icknield Way, which runs from Salisbury via the Chilterns to the Norfolk coast. There is also the North Downs Way, heading east from Salisbury Plain to reach the coast at Folkestone.

STONE AGE TOOLS *Wooden hoe, stone axe and flint-toothed sickle.*

Chalk is permeated with flint, which flakes readily and can be chipped into shape with comparative ease. Stone Age man knew this and used flint to create primitive axes, bludgeons and scrapers.

Using the primitive tools available, early man built massive defensive earthworks on many of the prominent hilltops across southern

England. At Cissbury, in Sussex, Iron Age man raised a gigantic hill-fort beside a Stone Age flint mine. One of the largest earthwork fortifications in Europe is Maiden Castle in Dorset, which has an outside perimeter of more than 2 miles. Other notable hill-forts include Old Sarum near Salisbury and Devil's Dyke, high on the South Downs near Brighton.

Henges and chalk figures

The rulers who organised their tribes to produce such enormous earthworks also built religious monuments that have stood for thousands of years. The most striking of these are the stone circles of Stonehenge and Avebury, possibly the greatest Stone Age constructions in the world. The builders of these monuments also left the downland scattered with their tombs – from the huge West Kennett Long Barrow to Kit's Coty, Kent, probably the burial place of a minor chieftain. Equally awe-inspiring are the huge chalk figures cut out of the hillside turf, which stand out for miles around. Examples of these include the White Horse at Uffington in Oxfordshire, the Long Man at Wilmington on the Sussex Downs and Dorset's Cerne Abbas Giant, at the western end of the chalkland.

Since chalk is too soft to provide building material for anything more substantial than farm walls, chalk country never developed any distinctive architectural style. However, it was used internally in churches, as at Boxley church in Kent, on the Pilgrims' Way. Here, the pillars and arches of the nave are made of chalk.

Flint, on the other hand, is much more durable, and can be seen combined with brick in houses and boundary walls in every chalkland village. On churches, squared flints were used to create attractive diaper patterning that enlivens their towers and porches. An outstanding example is the magnificent 15th-century church at Long Melford in Suffolk, renowned for its distinctive flintwork.

The downland chalk was ideal for early farming communities, since it was well drained and good for grazing. Iron Age farming techniques can be viewed today at an experimental farm on Butser Hill, near Petersfield, Hampshire, which examines

CANTERBURY TRAIL *During the Middle Ages, many groups of pilgrims followed the North Downs Way, heading for Canterbury. Chaucer's Canterbury Tales depicts a typical journey.*

crops and animals of the period.

There are few industrial processes native to the chalklands of southern England. For many centuries, the chalk itself was quarried and burnt to produce agricultural lime. Large chalk pits can be seen today on the North Downs around Box Hill; and on the West Sussex Downs, old quarrying methods are illustrated in Amberley Chalk Pits Museum, converted from a former quarry.

The latest by-product of the downlands is very much of the 1990s. The broad white 'skirt' of chalk stretching below the cliffs along the coast between Dover and Folkestone has been excavated from the Channel Tunnel.

NOCTURNAL HUNTER

Badgers are among many animals, such as moles, hedgehogs and hares, that live on the downs. They leave their woodland or hedgerow homes, known as setts, at night to hunt for food. They feed on earthworms, mice, snails, berries and grass.

RING OF STONE *Stonehenge may have been used as a giant astronomical clock.*

HOLY CUP *Pilgrims to Canterbury could buy flasks supposed to contain the diluted blood of Thomas Becket.*

CHALK WHITE *Where the plough has turned the South Downs near Wilmington, the underlying nature of the land becomes obvious. The fine grass of the downlands is the result of centuries of sheep grazing.*

Aldershot ⛳ 🚆 Cb
Military centre with army displays. Museums explain history of Airborne Forces, Dental, Transport, Veterinary, Nursing and Medical Corps. Coarse fishing on the Basingstoke Canal, with one of Europe's largest artificial ski slopes nearby.

Alton ✝ 🏛 Ba
Town at source of River Wey. St Lawrence's Church is largely 15th century, but has tower dating from 1070. Church door has bullet marks from battle that took place here during Civil War. Alton station is terminus for steam railway. Allen Gallery has large display of English ceramics and pottery from 1550 to present. Curtis Museum has displays illustrating local life – exhibits on 19th-century botany, and dolls and dolls' houses.

Ascot Dd
Wide, modern streets spill out to famous racecourse, site of Royal Ascot race week held each June; started by Queen Anne in 1711. Good centre for drives and walks in nearby Windsor Great Park.

Basing House 🏚 Ac
Ruined house, once the largest private house in Tudor England. Destroyed by Cromwell's troops in 1645. An exhibition in 19th-century Lodge House explains its history. Set in peaceful village.

Beaconsfield ❀ ♖ Dg
Elegant town with old inns, timbered cottages and many creeper-clad 17th-century houses; Georgian centre recalls its importance as main staging post on London to Oxford road. Surrounding countryside was once a haunt of highwaymen.

Bekonscot Model Village ❀ Dg
Oldest model village in the world; brainchild of London accountant Roland Callingham. The 1½ acre period piece recalls Britain in the 1920s with lakes, zoo, airport, coal mine and a racecourse. Working models include a model railway with 22 locomotives.

Bray 🏠 De
Delightful Thameside village, every street lined with black-and-white cottages and houses. Local 16th-century vicar, Simon Aleyn, was famous for living through four reigns and adjusting his religion to suit each monarch. Monkey Island, half a mile downstream, has 18th-century lodge decorated with unusual paintings of monkeys in costume.

RIVERSIDE AND HILLSIDE

Much of Berkshire and parts of Buckinghamshire, Hampshire and Surrey serve as a commuter dormitory, but the area is still one of great beauty, with historic houses, parks and gardens. The Thames sweeps eastwards in broad graceful curves, cutting through the beechwood-clad Chiltern Hills. To the south, lie the Surrey heathlands and grass-covered heights of the North Downs.

RED AND GREEN *Chiltern beeches in autumn colours and velvet lawns surround the brick-fronted house at Stonor.*

Burnham Beeches ⛲ 🎪 Df
Gnarled beeches form grotesque shapes; remnants of an ancient forest that once covered Chiltern Hills in prehistoric times. Silver birches add a lighter touch. Numerous paths through 600 acres with open patches of heath.

Chawton 🏠🏛 Ba
Jane Austen's House was built 1645 as a posting inn and altered in 1809 when she came to live and write here. Exhibition of her life and works includes letters and documents. Garden with picnic area. Novelist's mother and sister buried in church.

COMMANDING POSITION *From the formal gardens at Cliveden there are sweeping views of the wooded reaches of the Thames in the valley below.*

Chobham Common ❧ Dd
Nature reserve comprising wet and dry heathland; noted for rare insect life, including one species of spider found nowhere else in the British Isles.

Clewer Village ✝ De
Once independent village has long since been swallowed up by Windsor, but 11th-century parish church is the oldest building in the area. Saxon lettering on font.

Cliveden Reach ⚓ Df
Beautiful stretch of the Thames, dominated by Italianate house set on cliffs. Built 1851 by Sir Charles Barry; later sold to millionaire Astor family. Now a hotel with grounds open to public. Woodland walks, Victorian fountain, and Japanese pagoda.

Cookham 🏠🏛 Cf
Riverside village of red-brick cottages set on a green. Gallery devoted to local painter Stanley Spencer (1891-1959) in King's Hall. Below Cookham Bridge are attractive backwaters with boathouses; one belongs to Keeper of the Royal Swans. Formosa Island has 50 acres of green woodlands.

Courage Shire Horse Centre 🐎 Ce
Working stable founded to preserve the shire breed from extinction. Fine collection of mighty animals and farrier's workshop.

Devil's Punch Bowl ☆ ❀ ❋ Ca
Deep and spectacular valley, attributed to work of the devil; really chiselled out of sandstone hillside near Hindhead by rain and wind. More than 2 miles long and half a mile wide, its slopes plunging 350ft to stream flowing into River Wey. Superb views from 900ft summit of Gibbet Hill on north side, where 1851 granite cross marks spot where a gibbet once stood. Here, until late 18th century, hanged criminals were left as a warning. Sailor's Stone is where sailor was murdered in 1786; a curse is laid on anyone who moves the stone.

SILENT PRAYER *Ewelme's tomb effigy of the Duchess of Suffolk.*

Ewelme 🏠 Ag
Most picturesque of Chiltern villages with group of 15th-century buildings. Church notable for the tomb of Chaucer's granddaughter, Alice, Duchess of Suffolk. Her double effigy – in life and death – is an excellent example of medieval craftsmanship and is perfectly preserved. Font has finely carved pyramidal cover. School in use since 1437.

Farnham 🏰 ♖ ⛲ 🏛 ▨ Cb
Tudor and Georgian houses flank 12th-century Norman castle; keep open to public. Town museum has reminders of 17th and 18th-century life. Road east leads along Hog's Back; 500ft chalk ridge overlooking North Downs Way.

Frensham 🏠 ❧ ⛵ ☆ Cb
Great Pond is one of the largest lakes in southern England; good for sailing, fishing and bird-watching. Church has medieval 'witch's cauldron' used by Mother Ludlam who lived in a cave nearby. Good views from hills known as The Devil's Jumps.

Hambleden 🏠 Bf
Brick-and-flint village noted for grand 14th-century church. Picturesque square with pump beneath spreading chestnut tree. This is a good base for exploring the Chilterns.

REGATTA BANKS *St Mary's overlooks the houses at Henley.*

Henley-on-Thames ✝ ♖ Bf
Royal Regatta in July makes this little town a Mecca for rowers. Five-arched 18th-century bridge spans river between wooded hillside and old town. Church of St Mary, with 16th-century tower, connects to timbered Chantry House built 1400.

Loseley House ▥ Db
Elizabethan mansion built 1561 by Sir William More, cousin of Sir Thomas More. Fine ceilings and panelling. Home to the healthy Loseley dairy products.

Maidenhead ⚓ ♛ ▨ Cf
Notorious champagne-and-high-society town in the 1920s and 30s, where theatre folk had homes by the river. River steamers and regatta recall lavish lifestyle. Balustraded road bridge and Brunel's 1838 railway bridge are classics.

Mapledurham House ▥ 🏠 Ae
Elizabethan red-brick mansion with superb oak staircase and glorious grounds leading down to Thames. Used by John Galsworthy as Soames Forsyte's country house in *The Forsyte Saga*.

Marlow ♛ Cf
Riverside town with 1836 suspension bridge, Georgian houses and beautiful lawns of Compleat Angler Hotel.

Marlow Reach ⚓ Cf
Fine beechwood walks in Quarry Wood, inspiration for menacing Wild Wood explored by Mole in Kenneth Grahame's book *Wind in the Willows*.

Medmenham 🏠 Cf
Dog and Badger Inn (1390) makes good base for riverside walks. Ruins of 12th-century abbey became meeting place of 18th-century Hell Fire Club, notorious group of rakes and gamblers.

Odiham ⛪ Bc
Georgian façades have been grafted onto earlier timber-framed houses in the wide High Street. Stocks in square still claim to 'encourage virtue and discourage evildoers'. Church Bible of 1578 quaintly recounts that Adam and Eve wore breeches.

Reading 🏛 ♨ ☑ Be
Noted for university and industrial base. Made rich by cloth trade in Middle Ages, then with the building of railway and canal. Rural life recalled in University Museum; industrial life in Blake's Lock Museum, and Roman history in Reading Museum.

Silchester 🏛 ♣ ☑ Ad
Rich wool-trading town in Roman times called *Calleva Atrebatum*. Origins recalled by 2 mile section of wall and site of amphitheatre. Calleva Museum displays Roman pottery and other remains.

Stonor Park 🏠 Bf
Still with its 12th-century heart intact, house is now a jumble of styles: Tudor, Georgian, mock-Gothic. Seat of the Stonor family for 800 years. Garden overlooks a deer park.

Stratfield Saye House 🏠 Ad
Bought by Duke of Wellington in 1817 out of his Waterloo victory money, and filled with paintings and gifts from European royalty. A stone marks the grave of the Iron Duke's horse, Copenhagen.

Swallowfield Park 🏠 Bd
Landscaped gardens with shrubs, roses and ancient yew-tree walk. House built 1690 for 2nd Earl of Clarendon; much remodelled in 18th century.

Thursley 🏠 ☙ Da
Tiny village in the middle of a huge common. Wild and mysterious nature reserve; woodland, heath and bog. Birds include the Dartford warbler and occasional Montagu's harrier, merlin, osprey and peregrine.

Tilford 🏠 🏛 Cb
Long, six-arched medieval bridge crosses River Wey at this village, leading to triangular green faced by houses, cottages and an inn dating from 1700. Tilford Institute dates from 1893, an early work by Sir Edwin Lutyens.

The Vyne 🏠 Ac
Three wings form an E-shaped Tudor mansion, set by a lake adjoining River Loddon. Superb interior decoration including Tudor chapel and long gallery.

Windsor Great Park ☙ ❀ De
Remnant of a royal hunting forest with ancient oaks, good walks, and polo most summer weekends. At south-east corner, park stretches into Savill Gardens, famed for rhododendrons, and Valley Gardens famed for heathers. Both flank artificial 160 acre lake of Virginia Water.

Windsor Safari Park ☙ De
A mile long route takes visitors among lions, zebras, giraffes and other African animals. Attractions include Seaworld complex with killer whales.

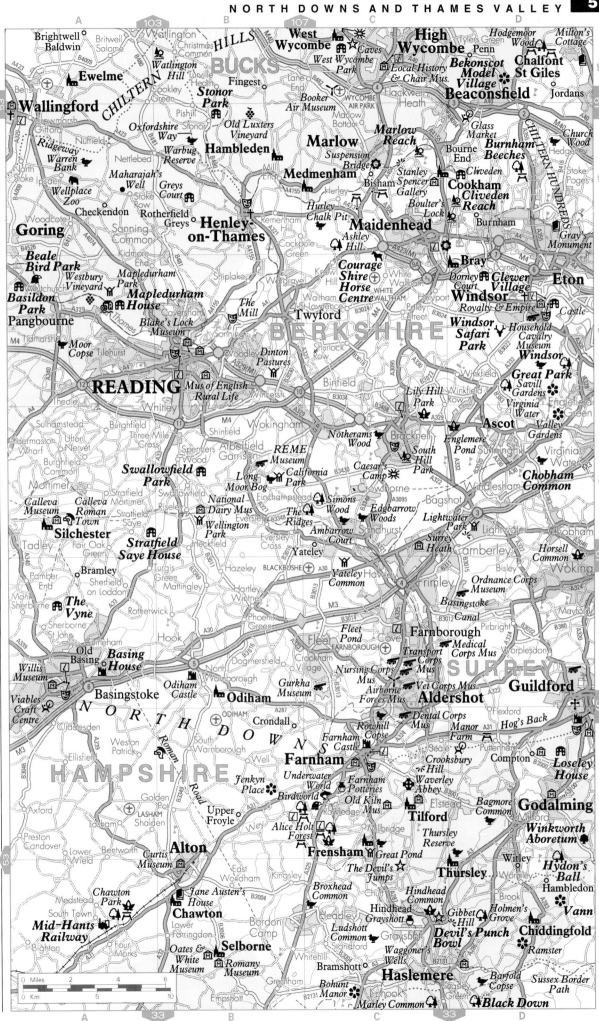

Albert Memorial Chapel Bc
Within Windsor Castle precincts, chapel built by Henry VII and converted by Queen Victoria as memorial to her husband, who died in 1861. Inside is monument of Prince Consort, showing him clothed in full armour.

Brass Rubbing Centre Bb
In St John the Baptist's Church, reproductions of brasses from all over southern England, with instructions and materials for taking rubbings.

Brunel Railway Bridge Ac
Built by Isambard Kingdom Brunel, a rare example of a bowstring bridge, so called because the horizontal tie between the bases of the arch looks like the string of a bow.

ROYAL HOME ON THE THAMES

A school and a castle are responsible for the worldwide fame of Eton and Windsor, which face each other across the Thames. There is a wealth of history to be discovered by the visitor, and a wander down the side streets reveals some unexpected treasures. And for open space, there is the extensive parkland alongside Windsor Castle and walks along the river.

Eton College Chapel † Be
One of finest examples of Perpendicular architecture. Planned by Henry VI as the choir of a church to rival Canterbury – but only the choir was completed, in 1483. Interior has 15th-century narrative wall paintings showing scenes of miracles.

Guildhall Bb
Building in classical style begun by Sir Thomas Fitch, and completed by Sir Christopher Wren in 1689. Inside Corn Exchange area are four pillars which do not reach ceiling – a joke by Wren in response to councillors' insistence on supporting columns which

GRACEFUL HALL *The open area below Windsor's Guildhall Chamber was once a corn market.*

Long Walk Ca
Tree-lined avenue 3 miles long, and laid out in 1685, runs from Windsor Castle's George IV Gateway across part of Home Park and into the 4000 acres of Windsor Great Park. Rises at southern end to Copper Horse – a statue of George IV on horseback, erected in 1831.

Nell Gwynne's House Bc
House, dating from 17th century, built by Charles II for his mistress, orange seller Nell Gwynne. Her son, the Duke of St Albans, inherited house, marked by a decorative plaque.

Promenade Bc
By Windsor Bridge, starting place for boat trips in summer along the River Thames. Journeys upstream

go to Maidenhead, Cookham and Marlow, and those downstream to Runnymede and Staines.

Queen Charlotte Street, Windsor Bb
Shortest street in Britain.

Queen Mary's Dolls' House Cc
Within Windsor Castle, Dolls' House was designed by Sir Edwin Lutyens and presented to Queen Mary as a token of the nation's goodwill. It is 8ft by 5ft, a scale of one-twelfth life size. Walls hung with miniature paintings; library has books specially written by Rudyard Kipling and others.

Queen Victoria Statue Bc
Bronze statue designed by Sir Edmund Boehm, with marble plinth – erected at top of High Street, near castle entrance, to commemorate Queen's Golden Jubilee in 1887. Contained within marble plinth is complete set of coins of Queen Victoria's reign.

Royal Mews Bb
In stables and courtyard, a display of royal carriages, many still taken out on ceremonial occasions such as State visits. There is a miniature barouche given to the young Prince Edward by Queen Adelaide in 1847, and a model of Burmese, the horse once ridden by the Queen at Trooping the Colour. Also on show are riding equipment, paintings and drawings. Adjoining exhibition shows gifts presented to royal family on state tours.

Royalty and Empire Exhibition Bc
Life-size tableau, including replica of train and waxworks of Queen Victoria, her daughter Empress Frederick of Germany, and a guard of honour more than 70 strong which depict start to Queen's Diamond Jubilee

ROYAL WINDSOR *At the head of the tree-fringed Long Walk, the King George IV Gateway leads into Windsor Castle's State and Private Apartments. The Round Tower, with the Union Flag fluttering above it, dates from the 12th century.*

Chariott's Charity Bb
Gothic-style almshouses built in 1863 from money left in Joseph Chariott's will.

Curfew Tower Bc
Tower, built 1227, houses eight chapel bells, and medieval vaulted dungeons with secret passages through 13ft thick walls.

Duffey's Old Bakery Ab
Little has changed in working bakery, built 1839, where visitors can watch bread being baked in original coal-fired ovens.

Eton College Be
School founded by Henry VI in 1440; the College Hall and kitchen still survive from the original buildings. Buildings around the school yard and part of cloisters are also 15th century. Lupton's Tower, also overlooking school yard, completed in 1520. Statue of Henry VI stands in yard. Twenty Prime Ministers listed among old boys. Desk panel in Upper School has names of statesmen Walpole and Pitt the Elder carved on it, amongst those of other schoolboys. College houses Museum of Eton Life.

Frogmore House Da
Built 1618 by Hugh May, architect to Charles I; has been home to three of England's queens. Façade is decorated with seven bays and Tuscan columns. Mural, 17th century, uncovered during recent redecoration. Landscaped gardens include Royal Mausoleum built by Queen Victoria for Prince Albert and herself.

SCHOOL WALLS *Behind Eton's stern battlemented towers, two pinnacled turrets rise above Lupton's Tower, built in 1520 by Provost Roger Lupton.*

Wren knew to be unnecessary. Paintings in the Guildhall Chamber include portraits of Elizabeth I and Elizabeth II.

High Street, Eton Bd
Timber-frame buildings dating back to 16th century mix with Georgian shop fronts along narrow street leading south from Eton College. Victorian pillar box in shape of Doric column.

Home Park
Lying in shadow of Windsor Castle, a public open space situated between King Edward VII Avenue and Thames. Used by sports clubs, and venue for events such as Royal Windsor Horse Show and Windsor Championship Dog Show.

Household Cavalry Museum Aa
Exhibits include ceremonial uniforms and regalia, weapons, equipment and pictures, covering history of Life Guards, Royal Horse Guards and 1st Royal Dragoons from time of Charles II to age of motorised transport. Armoured World War II vehicles outside in yard.

KING'S CHAPEL *The 15th-century chapel was part of Henry VI's original foundation of Eton. The mighty organ was added in 1887.*

RED AND GOLD LIVERY *State landaus are on display at the Royal Mews.*

Windsor Castle Precincts Bc

Access to England's largest castle, established by William the Conqueror, is through Henry VIII Gateway, bearing Henry's coat of arms and that of his first wife, Catherine of Aragon. Immense courtyard of Lower Ward is flanked by St George's Chapel, Albert Memorial Chapel, grace-and-favour homes, Curfew Tower and 19th-century Guardroom with guard-changing ceremony in the morning. On mound is Round Tower, started by Henry II and added to by George IV.

Windsor Castle State Apartments ♯ Cc

Built by Edward III in 14th century, and later restored and embellished by Charles II and George IV. Apartments have painted ceilings, panelled walls, Adam fireplaces, classic furniture and priceless paintings and drawings, including works by Michelangelo, Leonardo da Vinci, Raphael, Rubens, Canaletto and Van Dyck. Queen's Presence Room remains as decorated in 1675-83 for Charles II, with a ceiling painted by Neapolitan artist Antonio Verrio, and walls adorned with tapestries and royal portraits. Suit of armour made for Henry VIII in 1540; military relics include bullet that killed Admiral Lord Nelson.

Windsor Riverside Station Bc

Station has ornate iron and glass train shed. Station buildings are Tudor in style and have royal waiting room.

CASTLE HOMES *St George's priests live in Horseshoe Cloister.*

celebrations in 1897. Audiovisual exhibition recalls heyday of British Empire. Display on Queen Elizabeth II's reign illustrates monarchy in modern age.

St George's Chapel ✝ Bc

Finest example of Perpendicular architecture in England. Building started in 1477 by Edward IV for Knights of the Garter and burial place of royalty. Much 16th-century sculpture, as well as 19th-century monument to Princess Charlotte. Banners of Knights of the Garter hang over their helms in choir. Stained-glass west window depicts kings, popes, saints and ordinary citizens.

St John the Baptist's Church ✝ Bb

Founded 1168, Windsor's parish church was rebuilt in early 19th century. Sculptured angels playing musical instruments can be seen beneath vaulting of apse. Painting of *The Last Supper* said to be by 17th-century artist Franz de Cleyn. On south side of chancel is royal pew, with carved sides by Grinling Gibbons.

Swan Upping Ceremony

Thames tradition dating back to Tudor times, annual marking of new cygnets to indicate ownership. Skiffs carry Swankeepers up river in third week of July to record birds' numbers and nick their beaks once or twice to mark ownership by either of two City livery companies; swans left unmarked belong to Queen.

The Thames

Riverside walks offer views of Eton on the west bank of the Thames and Windsor Park east, as well as boats and locks on river. Alexandra Gardens has lawns and colourful flowerbeds.

Theatre Royal ♜ Bc

Theatre built in opulent style just before World War I to replace original theatre of 1793.

Three Tuns Bb

Built 1518 as the Guildhall of the Holy Trinity, building now a pub and is oldest of a number of 17th and 18th-century buildings in Windsor's Old Town.

Windsor Bridge Bc

Cast-iron bridge, built 1824, links Eton to Windsor; now used only by pedestrians.

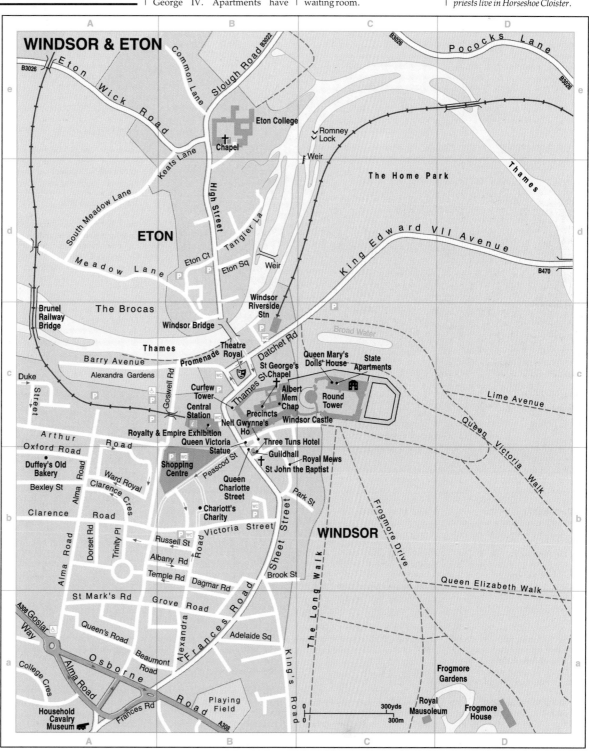

WINDSOR & ETON

ETON

WINDSOR

The Home Park

Eton College
Chapel
Romney Lock
Weir

B3026
Eton Wick Road
Common Lane
Slough Road B3002
Pococks Lane
B3026
Thames

Keats Lane
South Meadow Lane
High Street
Tangier La
King Edward VII Avenue
B470

Meadow Lane
Eton Ct
Eton Sq
Weir
Lime Avenue

The Brocas
Windsor Riverside Stn
Broad Water
Queen Victoria Walk

Brunel Railway Bridge
Windsor Bridge
Thames
Datchet Rd

Thames
Promenade
Theatre Royal
Queen Mary's Dolls' House
State Apartments

Barry Avenue
Alexandra Gardens
St George's St
Albert Mem Chap
Round Tower

Duke Street
Curfew Tower
Precincts
Windsor Castle

Central Station
Nell Gwynne's Ho
Three Tuns Hotel

Arthur Road
Oxford Road
Royalty & Empire Exhibition
Queen Victoria Statue
Guildhall
Royal Mews
St John the Baptist

Duffey's Old Bakery
Peascod St
Frogmore Drive

Bexley St
Ward Royal
Shopping Centre
Queen Charlotte Street

Clarence Road
Clarence Cres
Chariott's Charity
Victoria Street
Park St

Alma Road
Dorset Rd
Trinity Pl
Russell St
Road
Sheet Street

Albany Rd
Temple Rd
Dagmar Rd
Brook St

St Mark's Rd
Grove Road
The Long Walk
Queen Elizabeth Walk

Goslar Way
Queen's Road
Alexandra Road
Frances Road
Adelaide Sq

A306
Alma Road
Osborne Road
Beaumont Road
Playing Field
King's Road

College Cres
Household Cavalry Museum
Frances Rd
A308
Frogmore Gardens
Royal Mausoleum
Frogmore House

Goswell Rd
Broad Water
0 300yds / 300m

GRAND HOUSES, GREAT GARDENS

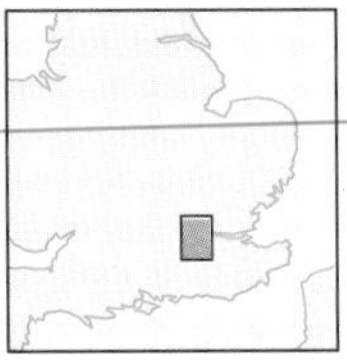

Artists, authors and fashionable society have long enjoyed the pleasures of the parks and heaths that relieve west London's urban sprawl. Noblemen built their palaces and planted gardens here, along the banks of the River Thames. To the south, fine viewpoints offer the opportunity to enjoy some real countryside among the wooded hills that sweep across north Surrey.

Barnet De
Variety of walks through woodland of Monken Hadley Common. Hadley Green, at village of Monken Hadley, is surrounded by 18th-century houses. Obelisk on green marks site of Battle of Barnet, Yorkist victory in 1471, when Earl of Warwick was killed.

Carshalton Db
Older part of suburb, grouped around two ornamental ponds, includes 18th-century Greyhound Inn and several old houses whose grounds can be visited.

Chertsey Bb
Riverside town with commons, unspoilt woodland and seven-arched bridge stretching over river. Bell in church commemorates woman who saved lover from execution at curfew by preventing curfew bell from ringing.

Chessington World of Adventures Cb
Zoological gardens encompass several 'worlds', including an American frontier town, Norman castle, and Fifth Dimension world – behind a computer screen. Safari Skyway monorail offers panoramic views.

LIFE AFLOAT *Narrowboats lie moored along Regent's Canal, an ideal place for walking, jogging or fishing.*

Chiswick Dc
Residential area fashionable in the 17th and 18th centuries. Houses lining riverside Chiswick Mall include Kelmscott House, once home of Pre-Raphaelite artist and author William Morris.

Chiswick House Dc
Palladian villa in Burlington Lane built in early 1700s, with interior decoration by William Kent. The 80 acre grounds include nature trails and Italian gardens. Nearby summer home of artist William Hogarth contains many examples of his paintings and engravings.

Claremont Landscape Garden Cb
National Trust has restored this earliest surviving English landscape garden. Work of Sir John Vanbrugh, Charles Bridgeman, William Kent and Capability Brown complete with lake, island pavilion and amphitheatre.

Epsom Db
Expanse of hawthorn, birch and gorse at Epsom Common. Handsome High Street recalls town's 17th-century heyday as spa resort where Charles II and Samuel Pepys stayed. Bridlepath leads along old Roman road to Box Hill viewpoint. Downs are where Derby has been run since 1780.

Fenton House Dd
William-and-Mary style house, built 1693, has collection of early keyboard instruments, including Handel's harpsichord.

Freud Museum Dd
Home of Sigmund Freud, founder of psychoanalysis, from 1938-9; now houses museum displaying his personal effects, including the famous couch.

Ham Cc
Residential area between Richmond Park and river. Bridlepath over Ham Common leads to Ham House, 17th-century mansion famous for decorative work and restored 17th-century garden.

Hampstead Dd
Fashionable high-society spa resort in 18th century. Many streets and houses have survived from that time; Church Row is Hampstead's most enchanting street. Hampstead Heath covers 720 unspoilt acres.

Hampton Court Palace Cb
Magnificent red-brick Tudor palace built by Cardinal Wolsey and handed to Henry VIII after completion in 1520. Extensions commissioned from Sir Christopher Wren by William III in 1689. Collection of furniture, huge tapestries and paintings by Titian, Tintoretto, Holbein and Lely. Astronomical clock of 1540 in Clock Court still announces time, date, phases of moon and state of tide at London Bridge. Great gatehouse is of Henry's time. Well-kept gardens include maze.

Headley Da
Wide expanse of wooded heath just south of Headley forms Headley Heath. Wildlife abounds; picnic area located beside ancient Brimmer Pond. Accessible by footpaths and riding tracks.

Highgate Dd
Older part on twin hill to Hampstead retains village atmosphere, particularly The Grove with its 17th and 18th-century houses. Near foot of Highgate Hill, Dick Whittington's cat sits on stone marking spot where Whittington heard Bow Bells recalling him to London. Highgate Cemetery has graves of famous people such as Karl Marx and George Eliot.

Keats House Dd
Home of poet John Keats from 1818 until his death in 1820, and place where he wrote his famous *Odes*. Manuscripts, letters and personal relics.

Kenwood House Dd
This 17th-century house was remodelled by Robert Adam in 1760s and left to nation in 1927. Paintings include works by Van Dyck, Franz Hals, Vermeer, Gainsborough and a self-portrait by Rembrandt. In summer orchestras perform in grounds.

Kew Gardens Cc
Royal Botanic Gardens begun in 1759 when Princess Augusta, mother of George III, had private garden laid out. Now covers 300 acres and has more than 25,000 species and varieties of plant with royal buildings, statues, glasshouses and 18th-century pagoda.

Kew Bridge Steam Museum Cc
Features beam engines that pumped west London's water until 1944. Machinery can be seen 'in steam' most weekends.

Leatherhead Ca
Attractive old town with narrow streets and gabled houses. Buildings range from partly 12th-century church to 20th-century Thorndike Theatre – opened 1968. West lie wooded Bookham and Banks Commons, abounding in bird life.

London Zoo Dd
One of world's most representative collections of animals. Aquarium, insect house, reptile house, aviary, small-mammal house – including nocturnal section – as well as larger mammals and apes. Children's Zoo has rabbits, pigs, ducks, sheep, cows and ponies.

Marble Hill House Cc
Villa built 1720s for George II's mistress, Henrietta Howard. Remains of 18th-century Orleans House nearby now an art gallery decorated in the baroque style.

Osterley Park House Cc
Elizabethan mansion turned into 18th-century villa by Robert Adam. Set in park with temples, lakes, orangery, stables and nature trails. Richly decorated interior with Georgian furniture, wall paintings and sculptures.

Regent's Canal Dd
Planned in 1812 to link Grand Union Canal with River Thames at Limehouse. Officially now part of Grand Union Canal though generally still called by its original name. Attractive walk along towpath through Regent's Park and Little Venice.

Regent's Park Dd
One of the largest parks in London. Acres of playing fields, shady avenues, lake for sailing, boating pond for children and beautiful gardens.

Richmond upon Thames Cc
Gatehouse of Henry VII's 'Rychemonde' palace still stands on green. Georgian houses in Maids of Honour Row. Deer roam in Richmond Park – 2400 acres of plantations and heath.

Ripley Ba
Coaching village of half-timbered houses and inns. Royal Horticultural Society gardens a mile north-east at Wisley. Rock garden, wild garden and redwoods.

Royal Air Force Museum De
Two hangars dating back to 1915. Displays cover history of aviation and RAF. Aircraft such as Sopwith Pup, Spitfire, Typhoon and Lancaster. Battle of Britain exhibits.

Runnymede Bc
Temple near spot where King John sealed 1215 draft of Magna Carta. Kennedy Memorial stands on land given to American people by people of Britain. Memorial to those Allied airmen who have no known grave gives a commanding view of Windsor Castle.

Stoke D'Abernon Ca
Life-size effigy of Sir John D'Abernon in St Mary's Church dates from 1277, the oldest monumental brass in England. South wall dates from 7th century, built with bricks from Roman villa.

GRAND SCALE *The glass dome of the conservatory at Syon Park covers 3000sq ft. Inside, birds fly free.*

Syon House Cc
Robert Adam redesigned 1547 mansion in 1762. Syon Park, laid out by Capability Brown in 18th century, includes Great Conservatory, motor museum, rose garden, butterfly house, art and garden centre.

Wimbledon Common Dc
Walking and riding over 1045 acres of natural heath. Iron Age fortification mound at south-west corner. Windmill built 1817 is now museum of windmill history.

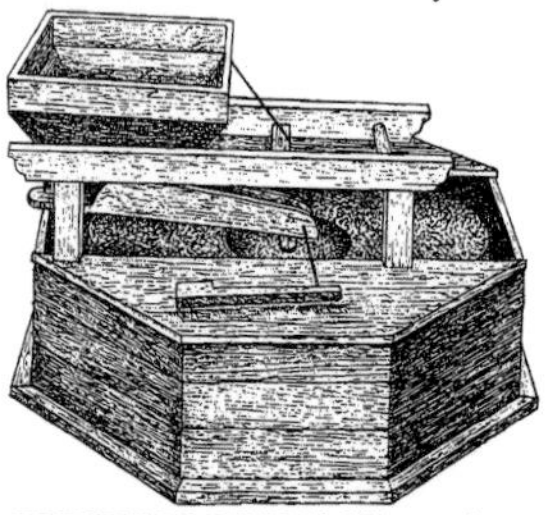

GRINDING CORN *Millstone in Wimbledon Windmill Museum.*

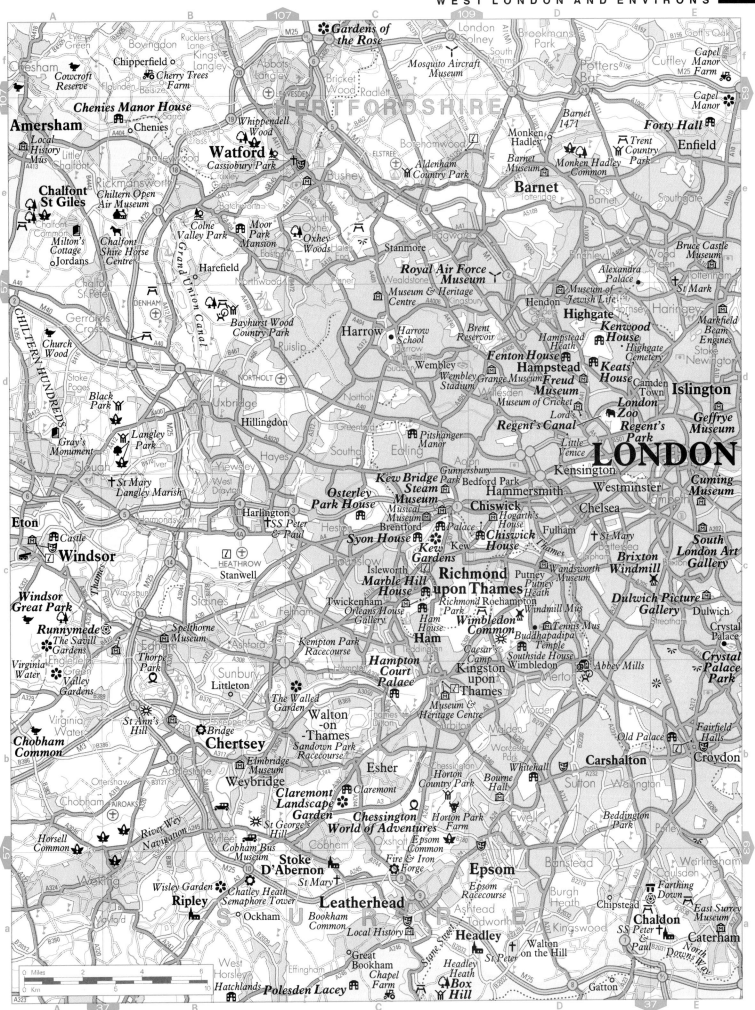

Gardens of the Rose

Mosquito Aircraft Museum

London Colney

Brookmans Park

Goff's Oak

Cuffley

Capel Manor Farm

Capel Manor

Chesham

Bovingdon

Chipperfield

Kings Langley

Abbots Langley

Bricket Wood

Radlett

Monken Hadley

Barnet 1471

Barnet Museum

Monken Hadley Common

Trent Country Park

Forty Hall

Enfield

Cowcroft Reserve

Cherry Trees Farm

Flounden

Belsize

Leavesden

Chenies Manor House

Whippendell Wood

Borehamwood

Elstree

Aldenham Country Park

Monken Hadley

Bruce Castle Museum

Amersham

Local History Mus

Little Chalfont

Chenies

Chandler's Cross

Watford

Cassiobury Park

Bushey

Edgware

Finchley

Alexandra Palace

St Mark

Chalfont St Giles

Chiltern Open Air Museum

Rickmansworth

Croxley Green

Batchworth

South Oxhey

Oxhey Woods

Stanmore

Royal Air Force Museum

Hendon

Golders Green

Museum of Jewish Life

Highgate

Kenwood House

Highgate Cemetery

Markfield Beam Engines

Stoke Newington

Chalfont Common

Milton's Cottage

Chalfont Shire Horse Centre

Jordans

Moor Park Mansion

Harefield

Northwood

Pinner

Hatch End

Wealdstone

Museum & Heritage Centre

Kingsbury

Brent Reservoir

Hampstead Heath

Fenton House

Hampstead

Keats' House

Freud Museum

Camden Town

London Zoo

Regent's Canal

Regent's Park

Islington

Geffrye Museum

Chalfont St Peter

Gerrards Cross

Denham

Bayhurst Wood Country Park

Harrow

Harrow School

Harrow on the Hill

Sudbury

Wembley

Grange Museum

Wembley Stadium

Willesden

Museum of Cricket

Lord's

Little Venice

LONDON

Kensington

Westminster

Cuming Museum

Church Wood

Black Park

Langley Park

Gray's Monument

St Mary Langley Marsh

Uxbridge

Hillingdon

Hayes

Southall

Ealing

Pitshanger Manor

Acton

Gunnersbury Park

Bedford Park

Hammersmith

Chelsea

Eton

Castle

Windsor

Slough

Iver

West Drayton

Harlington

SS Peter & Paul

Heston

Kew Bridge Steam Museum

Musical Museum

Brentford

Osterley Park House

Syon House

Palace

Kew Gardens

Kew

Chiswick

Hogarth's House

Chiswick House

Fulham

St Mary

Battersea

Wandsworth

Putney

South London Art Gallery

Brixton Windmill

Windsor Great Park

Runnymede

The Savill Gardens

Virginia Water

Valley Gardens

Heathrow

Stanwell

Wraysbury

Staines

Isleworth

Hounslow

Twickenham

Marble Hill House

Orleans House Gallery

Richmond upon Thames

Richmond Park

Roehampton

Putney Heath

Windmill Mus

Wimbledon Common

Caesar's Camp

Buddhapadipa Temple

Southside House

Wimbledon

Tennis Mus

Wandsworth Museum

Dulwich Picture Gallery

Dulwich

Crystal Palace

Crystal Palace Park

Chobham Common

Thorpe Park

Spelthorne Museum

Egham

Englefield Green

Feltham

Ashford

Sunbury

Littleton

Kempton Park Racecourse

Ham House

Ham

Teddington

Kingston upon Thames

Merton

Morden

Streatham

Virginia Water

St Ann's Hill

Bridge

Chertsey

Shepperton

The Walled Garden

Walton-on-Thames

Sandown Park Racecourse

Esher

Hampton Court Palace

Museum & Heritage Centre

Thames Ditton

Surbiton

Malden

Worcester Park

Whitehall

Carshalton

Sutton

Wallington

Beddington Park

Old Palace

Fairfield Halls

Croydon

Woking

Horsell Common

Chobham

Fairoaks

Addlestone

Ottershaw

Elmbridge Museum

Weybridge

Claremont

Claremont Landscape Garden

Horton Country Park

Bourne Hall

Ewell

Purley

Wisley Garden

Ripley

Ockham

River Wey Navigation

Byfleet

Cobham

Cobham Bus Museum

St George's Hill

Chessington World of Adventures

Horton Park Farm

Epsom Common

Fire & Iron Forge

Epsom

Epsom Racecourse

Burgh Heath

Banstead

Coulsdon

Warlingham

Farthing Down

Chipstead

East Surrey Museum

Caterham

Stoke D'Abernon

St Mary

Leatherhead

Local History

Ashtead

Tadworth

Kingswood

Chaldon

SS Peter & Paul

Wisley

Chatley Heath Semaphore Tower

Bookham Common

Headley

Headley Heath

Box Hill

North Downs Way

West Horsley

Effingham

Great Bookham

Chapel Farm

St Peter

Walton on the Hill

Gatton

Polesden Lacey

Hatchlands

HERTFORDSHIRE

SURREY

CHILTERN HUNDREDS

Grand Union Canal

Thames

0 Miles 2 4 6

0 Km 5 10

JEWELS IN AN URBAN SPRAWL

From the City eastwards, Greater London spreads outwards in a vast sprawl of concrete and brick. To the south lie the downs of Kent, while to the north, ancient Epping Forest still holds its own against the advance of urban development. The eastern extremities of Greater London touch the marshy shores of the Thames Estuary as the river nears the end of its journey to the sea.

Barking 🏛 Cd
Arcades and food halls at the Edwardian-style shopping centre of Vicarage Fields. Displays on local history at 17th-century Valence House Museum where exhibits include Roman pottery and Anglo-Saxon ornaments.

Bethnal Green Museum of Childhood 🏛 Bd
One of the world's greatest collections of toys and games, set up in 1872. Fine display of dolls' houses illustrates domestic life over the centuries. Contains everything from toy soldiers and Teddy Bears to children's clothes.

Bow ✝ Bd
Church in Bow Road is sole relic of the medieval village that once surrounded it. Two mills preserved in Three Mill Lane recall early industrial London: derelict House Mill is dated 1776; Clock Mill beside it dates from 1817.

Brixton Windmill 🛆 Bc
Five-storeyed brick tower with white sails at Blenheim Gardens. Built to grind corn in 1816, it recalls a rural past when Lambeth had a dozen mills. Worked by wind and later gas engine.

Chaldon 🏛 Ba
Church of St Peter and St Paul dates from 11th to 13th centuries. Rare mural dating from the Middle Ages is an allegorical 'doom' painting depicting the *Ladder of Human Salvation*.

Chingford 🏛🔾 Be
Queen Elizabeth's Hunting Lodge in Ranger's Road was built by Henry VIII in 16th century. Today it houses Epping Forest Museum. Superb views over east London from nearby Chingford Plain and Pole Hill. Large reservoirs fed by River Lea.

Chislehurst Caves ☆ Cb
Miles of man-made caverns and passages, hewn out of chalk over 8000 years. Prehistoric fossils and Druid altar remains can be seen. Caves served as hiding place for Royalists during Civil War, and as air-raid shelter in World War II.

Crystal Palace Park Bc
High plateau named after immense glass and iron structure designed for 1851 Great Exhibition, later destroyed by fire. Plaster monsters are sole exhibition survivors. Intimate children's zoo has animal paddocks, aviaries and monkey island.

FOREST HISTORY *Henry VIII's grand Hunting Lodge, in Chingford, houses the Epping Forest Museum.*

LAST OF THE EVENING SUN *Sunlight flickers through the trees by the Connaught Water in Epping Forest – one of the oldest forests in Europe.*

Cuming Museum 🏛 Bc
Archaeological finds reveal story of Southwark's past; from fragments of a Roman boat to sculpture from a medieval priory. Curious collection of objects associated with the superstitions of London.

Dartford ♘🏛 Dc
Once an important Roman station by a crossing of the Darent. Gateway and remnants of a priory founded by Edward III lie near railway station. Royal Victoria and Bull Hotel dating from 1703 is one of the few surviving galleried inns in Britain.

Downe 🏛 Cb
Secluded village of flint cottages on a ridge of North Downs. Mainly 18th-century Down House was home of Victorian naturalist Charles Darwin for 40 years until his death in 1882. Restored as it was in his time.

Dulwich Picture Gallery 🏛 Bc
England's first purpose-built art gallery dates from 1811, designed by Sir John Soane. Some 300 British and European pictures within, including works by Gainsborough, Rembrandt, Rubens and Canaletto.

Eltham 🏛 Cc
Palace here was favourite country residence of English kings from Henry III to Henry VIII. Rebuilt this century, it retains stone bridge over moat and banqueting hall's magnificent 15th-century oak roof.

Epping Forest 🏛🔾 Ce
One of Europe's oldest forests. Labyrinth of footpaths and bridleways, crisscrossed by roads, covering some 6000 acres. Conservation Centre at High Beach makes a good starting point for walks. Wild plants and flowers lie scattered beneath ancient oaks and grand beeches.

Eynsford 🏛 Db
Village with medieval houses, ruins of a Norman castle, and 15th-century bridge across the River Darent. Lanes and paths lead south through downland villages to join the North Downs Way near Wrotham.

Forty Hall 🏛 Be
This charming Jacobean country estate built 1629-32, houses local museum and art gallery. Parkland walks and gardens. Avenue of limes originally planted during reign of Charles I.

Geffrye Museum 🏛 Bd
Housed in former almshouses in Kingsland Road. Display of British front rooms through the ages, with period furniture and fine furnishings.

Hall Place 🏛✿ Dc
Tudor and Jacobean mansion set in landscaped gardens beside River Cray. Grey masonry laid around 1540, red brick added a century later. Museum covers geology, archaeology and natural history of Bexley.

Horniman Museum 🏛 Bc
Eccentric oddities are the booty of a tea merchant's travels in the 1870s. Frederick J. Horniman collected arts and crafts, weird and wonderful musical instruments, and natural history specimens; from Peruvian whistling pots to Egyptian mummies.

TIBETAN TREASURE *Tibet's Goddess of Holy Life, Usnisavijaya, at the Horniman Museum.*

Islington Bd
Fashionable residential area in 18th and 19th centuries, as it is again today. Village atmosphere lives on in streets and squares, described in works of Dickens. Canonbury Square recalls late Georgian Islington. Browse or buy trinkets in Camden Passage, an alley with antique shops.

Knole 🏛 Da
Deer park surrounds fascinating country palace, built in mid-15th century by Archbishop of Canterbury. Portraits, tapestries and fine furniture inside.

Lee Valley Park 🛶 Bf
Recreational area along River Lea. Cruises and boat hire at Broxbourne Boat Centre, farm animals and rural crafts at Hayes Hill Farm. Every sport imaginable at

Pickett's Lock leisure centre and wildlife displays at Waltham Abbey Countryside Centre.

Lullingstone Castle 🏛 Db
Mainly 18th-century house with gate tower dating from 15th century. Drawing room has splendid Elizabethan ceiling. Staircase with shallow treads was built with an overweight Queen Anne in mind.

Lullingstone Roman Villa 🔾 Db
Remarkable Roman villa in Lullingstone Park reveals life of domestic luxury 1800 years ago. Well-preserved remains include baths, underfloor heating, and an early Christian chapel.

North Woolwich Old Station Museum 🏛 Cd
Story of Great Eastern Railway (founded 1839) and docklands rail system, in restored Victorian station at Pier Road. On show is oldest surviving GER steam train.

Passmore Edwards Museum 🏛 Cd
Late Victorian building in Romford Road dedicated to biology and history of Essex. Churchyard of St Mary Magdalene is unusual natural history reserve, in nearby Norman Road, East Ham.

Quebec House 🏛 Ca
Jacobean home celebrates life of General James Wolfe, killed while commanding 1759 British force that took Quebec.

Rainham 🏛✝ Dd
Late Norman Church of St Helen and St Giles dates from 1170. Fragments of 13th and 14th-century wall paintings. Wren-style red-brick Rainham Hall in the Broadway was built 1730.

South London Art Gallery 🏛 Bc
Leading figures in the art world lent support to this purpose-built gallery in Peckham Road, opened 1891. Prints and works by British artists from 1700 to present day. Includes works by Ford Madox Brown and Lord Leighton.

William Morris Gallery 🏛 Be
Decorative works of a Victorian master craftsman, exhibited in his boyhood home. Wallpapers, textiles, carpets, furniture, stained glass and ceramics that revolutionised 19th-century taste.

PALACE GROUNDS *Deer graze in parkland outside Knole in Kent.*

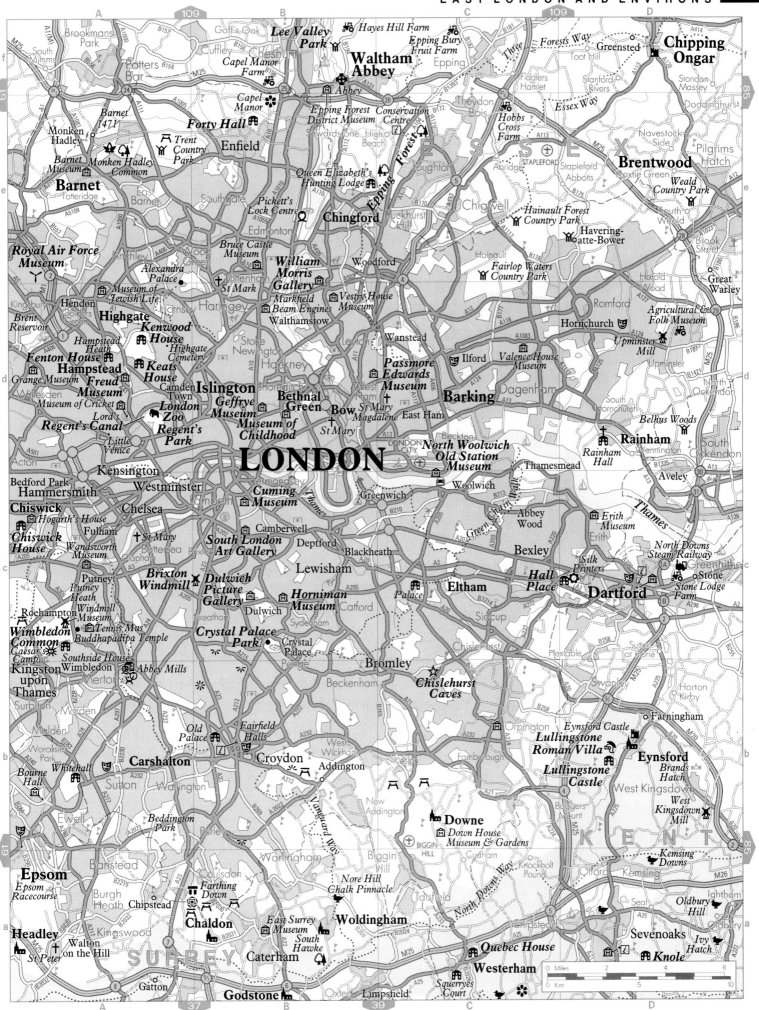

Brookmans Park
South Mimms
Potters Bar
Cuffley
Golf's Oak
Hayes Hill Farm
Epping Bury Fruit Farm
Epping
Lee Valley Park
Capel Manor Farm
Waltham Abbey
Abbey
Greensted
Chipping Ongar
Stondon Massey
Doddinghurst

Monken Hadley
Barnet 1471
Trent Country Park
Capel Manor
Epping Forest Conservation District Museum
Centre
Theydon Bois
Hobbs Cross Farm
Stapleford
Stanford Rivers
Navestock Side
Pilgrims Hatch

Barnet
Monken Hadley Common
Barnet Museum
Totteridge
East Barnet
Southgate
Enfield
Forty Hall
Queen Elizabeth's Hunting Lodge
Epping Forest
High Beach
Loughton
Abridge
STAPLEFORD
Stapleford Abbotts
Brentwood
Coxtie Green
Weald Country Park
South Weald
Brook Street

Royal Air Force Museum
Hendon
Finchley
Alexandra Palace
Pickett's Lock Centre
Edmonton
Chingford
Buckhurst Hill
Chigwell
Hainault Forest Country Park
Havering-atte-Bower
Harold Wood
Great Warley

Kingsbury
Brent Reservoir
Colinindale
Museum of Jewish Life
Highgate
Hornsey
Haringey
Bruce Castle Museum
Tottenham
St Mark
William Morris Gallery
Markfield Beam Engines
Woodford
Wanstead
Fairlop Waters Country Park
Romford
Hornchurch
Agricultural & Folk Museum
Upminster Mill

Fenton House
Hampstead
Hampstead Heath
Kenwood House
Keats House
Highgate Cemetery
Stoke Newington
Vestry House Museum
Walthamstow
Leyton
Ilford
Valence House Museum
Dagenham
Upminster

Grange Museum
Museum of Cricket
Lord's
Freud Museum
Camden Town
London Zoo
Regent's Park
Islington
Geffrye Museum
Shoreditch
Hackney
Bethnal Green
Museum of Childhood
Bow
St Mary
St Mary Magdalene
West Ham
East Ham
Passmore Edwards Museum
Barking
South Hornchurch
North Ockendon

Regent's Canal
Little Venice
Acton
Kensington
Westminster
LONDON
Bermondsey
LONDON CITY
North Woolwich Old Station Museum
Beckton
Thamesmead
Rainham Hall
Rainham
South Ockendon
Aveley

Hammersmith
Bedford Park
Chiswick
Chiswick House
Hogarth's House
Fulham
Chelsea
Cuming Museum
Lambeth
Thames
Greenwich
Woolwich
Abbey Wood
Green Chain Walk
Bexley
Erith
Erith Museum
Thames
North Downs Steam Railway
Greenhithe
Stone

Putney
Wandsworth Museum
Battersea
Clapham
Brixton
Camberwell
South London Art Gallery
Deptford
Blackheath
Lewisham
Palace
Eltham
Hall Place
Silk Printers
Stone Lodge Farm
Dartford

Roehampton
Putney Heath
Brixton Windmill
Dulwich Picture Gallery
Dulwich
Streatham
Horniman Museum
Catford
Sidcup
Chislehurst

Wimbledon Common
Caesar's Camp
Windmill Museum
Tennis Mus
Buddhapadipa Temple
Crystal Palace Park
Crystal Palace
Sydenham
Penge

Kingston upon Thames
Surbiton
Southside House
Wimbledon
Abbey Mills
Merton
Morden
Chislehurst Caves
Swanley
Horton Kirby
Farningham

Malden
Worcester Park
Old Palace
Fairfield Halls
West Wickham
Orpington
Eynsford Castle
Lullingstone Roman Villa
Eynsford
Brands Hatch
West Kingsdown

Carshalton
Sutton
Wallington
Beddington Park
Purley
Croydon
Addington
New Addington
Warlingham
Lullingstone Castle
West Kingsdown Mill

Epsom
Epsom Racecourse
Ewell
Banstead
Burgh Heath
Chipstead
Downe
Down House Museum & Gardens
BIGGIN HILL
Cudham
Baggers Mount
Knockholt Pound
Otford
Kemsing
Kemsing Downs

Headley
Walton on the Hill
St Peter
Kingswood
Coulsdon
Farthing Down
Chaldon
Nore Hill Chalk Pinnacle
Tatsfield
Ightham
Oldbury Hill

Gatton
Caterham
East Surrey Museum
South Hawke
Woldingham
Quebec House
Westerham
Squerryes Court
Sevenoaks
Knole
Ivy Hatch

Godstone
Limpsfield
Oxted
Crockham

SURREY
KENT
ESSEX

Miles 0 1 2 3 4 5 6
Km 0 5 10

Admiralty Arch Da
Terminal point of The Mall at western side of Trafalgar Square; built 1911 by Sir Aston Webb as part of the national monument to Queen Victoria. It is really a screen with five arches: one for ceremonial processions when the wrought-iron gates are opened; two for everyday traffic; two for pedestrians. Above and beside the arches are offices belonging to the Ministry of Defence.

THE WEST END

Some of England's finest architecture can be found among the Georgian squares and terraces that lie between Mayfair and Holborn. Handsome buildings house museums and art galleries with the treasures of the world's civilisations. Treasures of a different kind can be found in shops of world renown that cater for every taste, from suits and souvenirs to diamonds and caviar.

GRAND ENTRANCE *Massive curved Admiralty Arch is named after the adjoining Admiralty buildings. A ceremonial gateway leads to Buckingham Palace along the pink-surfaced, royal processional road of The Mall.*

All Saints Church † Bc
Gothic-revival church, built by William Butterfield in 19th century, has 227ft high slate spire. Granite, marble, alabaster and tiles enhance interior. Tile panel of Nativity decorates north aisle.

All Souls Church † Bc
Portico of Corinthian columns supports squat spire of church designed by John Nash in about 1822. Building disguised bend in great Nash road scheme linking Regent's Park to Piccadilly.

Bedford Square Cc
Three-storey houses surround busy Georgian square, last in Bloomsbury still intact. Central house on each side is stuccoed and pilastered, while wrought-iron balconies decorate other houses.

Berkeley Square Bb
Elegant-fronted terrace houses mix with modern buildings in bustling 1730s square – most of it expensive office space. Plane trees in centre date from 1789.

Bloomsbury Cd
Iron balconies and stucco façades embellish the Georgian terraces, with London University's Senate House overshadowing all.

Bond Street Bb
Actually two streets, Old and New Bond streets, developed from late 1600s onwards. Noted for galleries, art dealers, exclusive shops and auctioneers Sotheby's.

British Museum 🏛 Dc
One of the world's largest collections of antiquities, housed in imposing neoclassical building by Robert Smirke, 1824. Exhibits include Rosetta Stone, which provided clue to translating Egyptian hieroglyphs, Elgin Marbles from Parthenon, Magna Carta, and first draft of *Alice in Wonderland*.

EGYPTIAN ART *A wall painting from a tomb of around 1400 BC shows fowling in the marshes, from the British Museum Collection.*

Burlington Arcade Bb
Regency arcade containing many high-quality shops. Among them is famous tobacconists H. Simmons, founded in 1838. Beadles recruited from ex-servicemen ensure that old rules forbidding singing, running and the carrying of open umbrellas or large parcels are still adhered to.

Carlton House Terrace Ca
Giant Corinthian columns and balconies enhance two terraces designed by John Nash in 1830s.

Cavendish Square Bc
Jacob Epstein statue stands on delicate bridge joining elegant houses of 18th century. Statue of George Bentinck erected in 1851. Nearby lies St Peter's Chapel, built by James Gibbs in 1721.

Charing Cross Db
Junction of Strand and Whitehall, where village of Charing lay in medieval times. Edward I placed cross here in 1290, to mark resting place of funeral cortege of his queen, Eleanor. Station noted for roof; single great arch designed by John Hawkshaw in 19th century.

Christie's Ca
World-famous fine-art auctioneers, founded by James Christie in

MARKET CONCERT *Street performers entertain regularly in and around the restored Covent Garden Market, a lively place to stroll and shop.*

1766. Firm moved to present address in King Street in 1823. Façade of building dates from 1893-4, though rest was reconstructed after World War II bombings. Experts value items ranging from toys to African masks. Regular auctions and public viewing throughout year.

Covent Garden Db
Street entertainers and stall owners vie with designer shops, restaurants and pubs for the attention of shoppers and tourists. Restored Victorian market buildings remain on square designed by Inigo Jones.

Dickens House 🏠 Ed
Family portraits, letters, first editions and some of the author's own furniture adorn Dickens' last surviving London home. *Nicholas Nickleby, Oliver Twist* and later chapters of *Pickwick Papers* were written here in just two and a half years. The house was bought by the Dickens Fellowship in 1924.

Fitzroy Square Bd
Built between 1790s and 1820s, square is now pedestrian precinct. Blue plaque identifies No. 21 as home of Lord Salisbury, Prime Minister. Giant columned centrepieces embellish east and south terraces, designed by Adams brothers in 1790s. George Bernard Shaw lived at No. 29 in 1883-98 when he was the music and drama critic for several newspapers and a writer of political tracts.

Gray's Inn Ec
One of four Inns of Court, founded 14th century, though now mostly reconstructed. Statue of Francis Bacon stands at centre of South Square. Wrought-iron gates to gardens date from early 18th century. Hammerbeam roof and late 16th-century screen enhance hall where Shakespeare's *Comedy of Errors* was first performed. Chapel built in 1315 and rebuilt 1689. East window commemorates four archbishops of Canterbury. Stained-glass windows removed before building was bombed in 1941; rebuilt and enlarged after World War II.

Grosvenor Square Ab
Large 18th-century square – once the grandest of all London addresses; fashionable residences of wealthy. American Embassy building dominates; designed by Eero Saarinen 1960.

Guinness World of Records Cb
Trivia exhibition from *Guinness Book of Records* at The Trocadero. Life-size models and latest in audiotechnology. Achievements from all around the world. The categories include entertainment, sports, human, animal and planet earth. Stand next to the world's tallest man.

Hanover Square Bb
Brick houses surround German-style square built by the Earl of Scarborough in 1717.

Haymarket Theatre 🎭 Cb
Designed by John Nash in 1821, theatre has large pedimented portico. Interior decorated in deep blue, gold and white.

Jermyn Street Cb
Fashionable restaurants and clothing shops mingle in historic street dating from 1680s. Plaque shows site of house where Isaac Newton stayed.

Jewish Museum 🏛 Cd

First permanent collection of Jewish items opened to public in England. Collection contains over 1000 exhibits relating to Anglo-Jewish history, including Venetian ark dating from 1500s, and 18th-century Torah bells.

ROOMS AT THE INN *The barristers' and solicitors' chambers at Lincoln's Inn date from the 1600s.*

Leicester Square Cb

Cinemas and clubs dominate former grazing ground, where Earl of Leicester's town house stood in 17th century. Busts of Hogarth, Reynolds, John Hunter and Newton, and statue of Charlie Chaplin, stand in square.

Lincoln's Inn Ec

One of four Inns of Court – brick buildings date from 15th century. Chapel has windows commemorating renowned benchers and treasurers from medieval times to present day. Old Hall, dating from 1490, contains 17th-century oak screen and Hogarth painting.

Lincoln's Inn Fields Ec

Spacious square with lawns, footpaths and shady trees. Bounded on three sides by terraced rows of 18th and 19th-century houses; on fourth side by red-brick buildings of Lincoln's Inn. Anthony Babington was hung, drawn and quartered here in 1586 for plotting to overthrow Elizabeth I. Pavilion in middle has floor plaque marking site of 1683 beheading of William Lord Russell for plotting to assassinate Charles II.

COVENT GARDEN *One of London's most historic and elaborate theatres, the Royal Opera House seats an audience of 2000 and was built in 1858 by Edward Barry. It is home to the Royal Ballet and Royal Opera companies.*

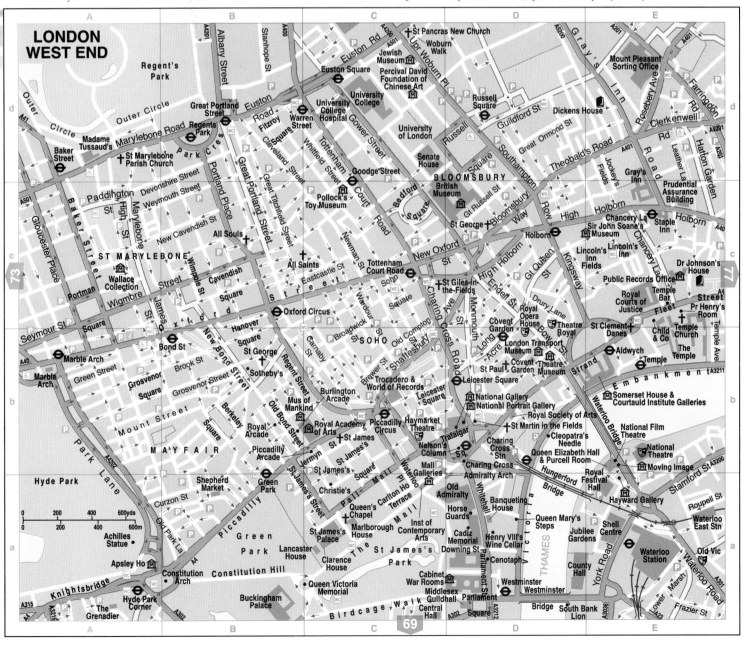

London Transport Museum Db
Old trams, steam engines and buses make up historical display of transport development. Photographs and posters enhance educational exhibits.

Madame Tussaud's Ad
Waxworks founded in 1835 features hundreds of lifelike images of celebrities and historic figures such as Michael Jackson, Boris Becker, Martin Luther King, Napoleon and the Royal Family. Chamber of Horrors features models of infamous murderers, and displays on methods of execution. History of waxworks, how wax models are made, and workings of animatronics.

Marlborough House Ca
Much enlarged Wren mansion, built for Duchess of Marlborough in 1709. Murals depict Duke's victories in early 18th century. Painted ceiling by Gentileschi dates from 1636.

Mayfair Bb
London's wealthiest area, marked by fashionable shops and restaurants, large office blocks and luxurious flats and apartments. Much of 18th-century layout of streets and squares remains, though modern buildings are more prominent.

Museum of Mankind Bb
Tribal masks, figures and jewellery feature in large collection of items from indigenous peoples of Africa, North and South America, Australia and parts of Europe and Asia. Exhibits were part of British Museum, but in 1970, due to lack of space, they were moved to present 19th-century building.

National Gallery Db
Collection of over 2000 paintings dating from 13th to 20th centuries includes works by Velàzquez, Hans Holbein, Leonardo da Vinci, Constable, Seurat, Rembrandt and Turner. Gallery designed by William Wilkins and built 1832-8.

National Portrait Gallery Db
Gallery contains some 10,000 likenesses of famous British men and women, 1000 of which are shown at any one time. Portraits on view include Chaucer, Oliver Cromwell, Nell Gwynne, Florence Nightingale, Charles Darwin and Beatrix Potter.

Old Admiralty Building Da
Naval accommodation, built by Thomas Ripley in 18th century, incorporates interior features of earlier building designed by Christopher Wren.

Oxford Street Bc
London's most famous shopping street stretches from Marble Arch to St Giles Circus. Stores mingle with established fruit stalls and shops for souvenirs and fashion. Selfridges neoclassical department store, founded 1908, has impressive food hall.

Pall Mall Ca
Elite clubs and offices occupy buildings of street laid out during 17th century. Pedimented portico fronts former United Services

TREASURE HOUSE *The National Gallery in Trafalgar Square, founded 1824, has 2000 European paintings. The interiors have been restored to their original splendour with red damask walls, stencilling and gilding.*

Club, designed by John Nash. Schomberg House, dating from 1698, retains original façade.

Park Crescent Bd
Terraced houses, rebuilt with original Nash façades after World War II, form semicircle next to Regent's Park.

Percival David Foundation of Chinese Art Cd
Collection of Chinese porcelain – from Sung, Ming and Ch'ing dynasties – which was presented to University of London by Sir Percival David in 1951.

Piccadilly Ba
Shops, clubs and hotels line old highway out to western suburbs. Hatchard's bookshop founded in 1797; Simpson's classic British fashion; Fortnum and Mason department store renowned for its culinary wonders – established 1707 by one of Queen Anne's footmen, with ornate clock added 1927.

Piccadilly Arcade Cb
Bow-fronted windows display broad array of quality goods in arcade designed by G. Thrale Jell early this century.

Piccadilly Circus Cb
Busy crossroads where Regent Street meets Piccadilly. Eros statue built as memorial to Lord Shaftesbury, designed by Alfred Gilbert in 1893.

Pollock's Toy Museum Cc
Collection of toys, dolls and miniature theatres dating from Victorian times to present day. Museum in two small adjoining houses dating from 1760.

Portman Square Ac
Courtauld Institute of Art housed in 18th-century mansion at No. 20, built by Robert Adam. Nearby is Heinz Gallery, founded 1971, which has changing exhibits of architectural drawings.

Queen's Chapel † Ca
Carved roof adorns olive-green chapel designed by Inigo Jones for the Infanta of Spain, who was intended to marry Charles I.

Regent Street Bb
Broad shopping street designed as approach to Carlton House, where Prince Regent once lived. Liberty store opened in 1875, famous for printed fabrics; early

supplier was William Morris. Veeraswamy's, one of London's first Indian restaurants, at No. 99.

Rock Garden Db
Covent Garden burger café. Tables under arches have good view of market place. Bands play in converted warehouse that claims to have hosted rock's elite.

Royal Academy of Arts Cb
Exhibitions held in Renaissance-style mansion, built by Earl of Burlington in 1664. Grand staircase leads to galleries. Bronze statue of Joshua Reynolds in courtyard. Academy founded in 1768.

Royal Arcade Bb
High ceilinged Victorian arcade in classical style; made 'Royal' as Queen Victoria bought her riding skirts from Brettel's.

Royal Courts of Justice Ec
Law courts occupy Portland-stone building dating from 1874. Central hall has vaulted arcade over 200ft long. Small display of legal costumes near entrance.

Royal Opera House Db
Building, designed by E.M. Barry in 1858, has pillared portico. Frieze of literary figures by John Flaxman survives from earlier theatre on site.

Royal Society of Arts Db
Giant Ionic columns frame the entrance of building designed by Adams brothers in 18th century. Primary purpose of society is promotion of arts.

St Clement Danes † Ec
RAF church contains memorials to and mementos of the wartime squadrons: 17th-century original was built by Christopher Wren; destroyed by fire in 1941. Restored panelling and tunnel vault follow the original design. Preserved pulpit by Grinling Gibbons. The carillon rings out 'Oranges and Lemons' nursery rhyme.

St George's, Bloomsbury † Dc
Corinthian columns decorate entrance to church designed by Nicholas Hawksmoor in 18th century. George I statue surmounts stepped steeple. Plastered ceiling adorns interior.

CLASSIC STYLE *Luxury shops are enclosed in the Royal Arcade of 1879, which lies between Old Bond Street and Albemarle Street.*

St George's, Hanover Square † Bb
Corinthian portico stands at entrance to 18th-century church. Two cast-iron dogs guard main door, added in 1940.

St Giles-in-the-Fields † Cc
Church, founded in 12th century, rebuilt by Henry Flitcroft 1731. Monuments include effigy dating from 1645 and Romanesque altar. Actor David Garrick married here (1749); architect John Soane buried here (1837).

St James's Church † Cb
Parish church designed by Christopher Wren in 1676 has spacious interior with ornate plaster-work and vaulting. Pelican sits atop altar by Grinling Gibbons.

St James's Square Cb
Georgian town houses, 19th-century residences and modern offices surround square planned by Henry Jermyn in 17th century. Statue of William III on horseback stands in middle of square.

St James's Street Ca
This old-world street is renowned for its exclusive gentlemen's clubs. Shops include wine merchant, hatter and shoemaker.

St Martin-in-the-Fields † Db
Church built by James Gibbs in 1722-6. Octagonal lantern tower is surmounted by layered steeple. Corinthian portico supports a triangular pediment embellished by George I's coat of arms.

St Marylebone Ac
Former borough that stretches from Regent's Park to Oxford Street. Most complete grid layout of streets in London can be found around Cavendish Square.

WET-WEATHER FRIEND *Fine shopfront of New Oxford Street umbrella-makers reflects over 150 years of craftsmanship within.*

St Marylebone Parish Church † Ad
Church built 1817; Corinthian portico and bell tower with cupola supported by gilded caryatids.

St Pancras New Church † Cd
Ionic portico and terracotta caryatids adorn Greek-style church built in 1819-22.

St Paul's Church † Db
Church, built by Inigo Jones dates from 17th century. Restored interior reveals a carved wreath by Grinling Gibbons. Memorials pay tribute to famous actors.

Shepherd Market Ba
Pavement cafés give a Mediterranean air to the narrow cobbled lanes where small market once flourished. Crewe House stands in nearby Curzon Street; designed by Edward Shepherd in 1730.

Sir John Soane's Museum 🏛 Ec
Museum established by Sir John Soane in house he had built for himself in 1812. Collection of books, antique furniture, drawings and paintings – including Hogarth's *The Rake's Progress*.

Soho Cb
Bustling, cosmopolitan district famous for its foreign restaurants, many pubs and shops – as well as its brash nightlife. Gerrard Street is heart of Chinatown, focus of best Chinese cuisine. Ornamental gateways and benches, pagoda-style telephone boxes. Grocers' stores feature exotic foodstuffs.

Somerset House 🏛 Eb
Building of Portland stone designed by William Chambers in 18th century. Statue of George III stands in vast courtyard 120yds long by just over 100yds across. Palladian façade overlooks river. Oceanic carving decorates Strand front where Courtauld Institute Galleries are housed. Galleries house art collection created early this century by textile magnate Samuel Courtauld and feature postimpressionist paintings.

Sotheby's Bb
World-renowned fine-art auctioneers. Founded 1744 as book auctioneers by bookseller and auctioneer Samuel Baker. First Sotheby, Baker's nephew John, joined firm in 1776. Large variety of antiques sold at regular sales throughout year.

Strand Db
Nobility lived here in medieval times. St Mary-le-Strand Church of 1714 dominates island in road.

WREATH *Carving by Grinling Gibbons in St Paul's, Covent Garden.*

Theatre Museum 🏛 Db
Old flower market houses collection of costumes, props, puppets and photographs portraying history of theatre.

Theatre Royal Drury Lane ♕ Dc
Theatre in Georgian building has domed hallway. Eastern façade decorated with Ionic pillars. Theatre has been home to many famous musicals, including *Show Boat*, *The King and I*, *My Fair Lady*, *Hello Dolly*, *A Chorus Line* and *Miss Saigon*.

MUSEUM POSTER *Rivalry between bus and tube in 1910.*

Trafalgar Square Db
Statue of Admiral Horatio Nelson (1758-1805) on top of 170ft high column in famous square named after Nelson's naval defeat of Napoleon in 1805. Area was originally the mews for royal hawks, then royal stables; cleared 1830 for John Nash's grand plan. At base of column are four bronze lions by Sir Edwin Landseer, added 1868. Fountains by Lutyens added 1939. Statue of James II stands in front of National Gallery and to east is statue of George Washington.

Trocadero Cb
Two acre shopping and entertainment complex with food from around the world, arcade games, bumper cars and laser guns.

University College Cd
Corinthian portico stands at entrance to college designed by William Wilkins in 1827. Building houses Flaxman Sculpture Galleries and renowned Egyptian antiquities. The clothed skeleton of philosopher Jeremy Bentham on display in hallway.

University of London Cd
Colleges and institutes are housed in large modern complex, and spread throughout 18th and 19th-century houses in local streets and squares.

Wallace Collection 🏛 Ac
Magical museum renowned for 18th-century French paintings and furniture, set out in palatial Hertford House; constructed by 4th Duke of Manchester in 1776 and remodelled by Sir Richard Wallace in 1872. Canalettos, Sèvres porcelain, Renaissance armour and grandfather clocks are also on display.

BUS STOPPED *A K-type motor bus in the London Transport Museum helps tell the story of the world's largest urban passenger system.*

POLITICAL ARENA *Trafalgar Square is a venue for frequent political demonstrations.*

Waterloo Place Ca
Street designed by Nash as triumphal approach to Carlton House. Classical façade distinguishes the Athenaeum designed by Decimus Burton. Statues surround 124ft high Duke of York column; statue paid for by contributions of one day's pay from every man in the British army.

Woburn Walk Cd
Delightful little L-shaped street of Regency shops, constructed 1822. Black-and-white bowfronted windows as pristine as the day they were put in; balconies filled with geraniums. Eastern pavement was built well above road to protect shopfronts from fast-moving carriages. A plaque at No. 5 says W.B. Yeats lodged there.

TICKET TROPHY *An ornate box office from the Duke of York's Theatre stands in the Theatre Museum's entrance hall, Covent Garden.*

Achilles Statue Ad
Statue by Richard Westmacott cast from a captured French cannon and then dedicated to Duke of Wellington from 'the women of England'.

Albert Embankment Dc
Riverside walk about a mile long from Lambeth Palace in north to Vauxhall Bridge in south was constructed during 19th century. Plenty of seating available, with benches raised on plinths so River Thames can be easily viewed over river wall. Wall decorated with iron lamp standards in the shape of dolphins.

Apsley House 🏛 Ad
Paintings, porcelain, gold and silver, field marshal's batons and other memorabilia adorn Duke of Wellington's town house, built in 18th century. Waterloo gallery, added in 1829, contains portrait of Wellington by Goya, as well as *Water Seller of Seville* by Velàzquez. Large chandelier hangs from moulded ceiling. Huge nude statue of Napoleon stands at foot of Grand Staircase. Table in Dining Room has silver-gilt centrepiece of cavorting nymphs. Plate and China Room has ornate silver-gilt shield presented to Wellington by City bankers after the Battle of Waterloo.

Archbishop's Park Ec
Park comprises 20 acres of gardens, walks, shrubberies and flower borders, and also a children's play area.

Banqueting House Dd
Hall, built in classical style, survives from Whitehall Palace designed in 1619 by Inigo Jones. Chamber, 110ft long by 55ft high and wide, has painted ceiling by Peter Paul Rubens depicting divine right of kings – commissioned by Charles I in 1635.

Belgrave Square Ac
Elegant square, designed by George Basevi and built by Thomas Cubitt, is home to many foreign embassies.

Birdcage Walk Cc
Paths skirt southern edge of St James's Park. Birdcages lined walk during reign of Charles II.

Broad Sanctuary Dc
Area beside Westminster Abbey where right of sanctuary could once be claimed – right abolished by James I in 1623. Abbey buildings facing Broad Sanctuary house large brass-rubbing centre.

Buckingham Palace Bc
Palace rebuilt from former Buckingham House of 1703. John Nash started rebuilding for George IV in 1825, but first monarch to live there was Queen Victoria in 1837. Façade added in 1913. Palace has some 600 rooms and gardens covering more than 40 acres. Changing of the Guard takes place daily.

Cabinet War Rooms 🏛 Dd
Warren of nearly 70 rooms – 19 of which are open to public – extends for 3 acres underground, used for top-level meetings during World War II. Brown linoleum floors, metal furniture and army cots

WESTMINSTER AND SOUTH BANK

The past is everywhere in this ancient corner of the capital. At every turn there is something to admire, from the splendour of Westminster Abbey to the perfect proportions of a Georgian terrace. Here too is the political heart of the nation, where laws are made in the Houses of Parliament and executed by the government ministries and departments around Whitehall and Victoria.

CLASSICAL CHAMBER *The nine huge panels in the ceiling of the Banqueting House in Whitehall were painted by the Flemish artist Rubens.*

make up spartan furnishings. Names of ministers remain at their places on cabinet table. Map Room much as it was during war – maps on walls with graphs and marker pins. Scrambler telephone gave Churchill direct line to the White House. Churchill's bedroom, from which live radio broadcasts were made, adjoins Map Room.

ROYAL HOME *Buckingham Palace is the monarch's London residence.*

Cadiz Memorial Dd
French cannon stands on base of winged dragon. Cannon recovered after lifting of siege of Cadiz in 1812 and presented to Prince Regent by grateful Spaniards.

The Cenotaph Dd
Portland-stone memorial to dead of World Wars I and II, designed by Sir Edward Lutyens and unveiled in 1920.

Central Hall Cc
Though built 1912, hall is classical in style. Dome is third largest in London. Hall used for concerts and meetings, and can seat 2000.

Chelsea Bridge Ba
Suspension bridge links Chelsea and Battersea. Built in 1934, it replaced 19th-century bridge.

Clarence House Cd
White stucco home of Queen Mother; built by John Nash in early 19th century.

Constitution Arch Bc
Also known as Wellington Arch, and originally erected near Duke's home at Apsley House in 1828, but

moved to top of Constitution Hill in 1883. Arch designed by Decimus Burton, but bronze of chariot and figures on top are by Adrian Jones.

Constitution Hill Bd
Charles II said to have taken constitutional walks along tree-lined road – hence name.

County Hall Dd
This massive Renaissance-style building was designed by Ralph Knott in 1908 to house London County Council. Other buildings added later.

Downing Street Dd
Only Nos 10, 11 and 12 remain of houses built by George Downing in 1720. No.10 has been Prime Minister's official residence since 18th century.

Eaton Square Ac
Built in 1826, square has been home to many famous people, including Prince Metternich and Prime Ministers Stanley Baldwin and Neville Chamberlain.

Ebury Street Bb
Mozart family stayed at 180 Ebury Street in 1764-5, and the young Wolfgang Amadeus wrote his first two symphonies here.

Green Park Bd
Royal park of 53 acres originally planned by Charles II. Expanses of grass and large groups of trees compensate for lack of flower beds and water features.

The Grenadier Ac
Old pub where Duke of Wellington is said to have played cards – celebrated in Duke of Wellington memorabilia. Sentry box stands outside pub.

Guards' Chapel ✝ Cc
Military chapel built 1963 to replace 19th-century chapel destroyed in World War II. Only mosaic-lined apse remains of the earlier chapel. Regimental standards in cloisters. Opposite is museum containing uniforms, paintings and dioramas illustrating history of various guards regiments from English Civil War to Falkland Islands War.

Hayward Gallery 🏛 Ed
Gallery holds exhibitions of paintings and sculptures.

Henry VIII's Wine Cellar Dd
Vaulted cellar supported by pillars, a fragment of old Whitehall palace lying beneath Ministry of Defence. Accessible with written permission from Department of Environment.

Horse Guards Dd
This Palladian-style guardhouse was designed by William Kent in 18th century.

Houses of Parliament
Officially named New Palace of Westminster, stands on site of principal royal residence from time of Edward the Confessor to Henry VIII. Present Gothic-style buildings constructed between 1840 and 1860 by Sir Charles Barry and A.W. Pugin, and comprise central hall and corridor with Houses of Lords and Commons on either side. Interior of House of Lords decorated in scarlet and gold, with canopied gold throne from which monarch addresses lords and commoners. House of Commons destroyed during World War II and restored by Sir Giles Gilbert Scott. Although 635 members are elected, seating is only available for 437. Clock

RINGING THE CHANGES *VIP telephones in the Cabinet War Rooms. Churchill's scrambler phone, foreground, had a direct line to the White House.*

Tower at end of House of Commons famous for Big Ben, massive bell inside tower. Tower is 316ft high. Clock completed in 1859. Clock mechanism weighs 5 tons, dials are 223ft in diameter, minute spaces 1ft square and minute hands 14ft long. Next to Clock Tower is Westminster Hall, which survives from original Palace; built as a banqueting hall by William Rufus in 1097. Statue of Oliver Cromwell stands outside.

Hungerford Bridge Dd

Bridge, sometimes known as Charing Cross Bridge, was built 1864. Views from bridge take in Cleopatra's Needle, Royal Festival Hall and the City. Near bridge on Embankment side is plaque to librettist W.S. Gilbert.

Hyde Park Corner Ac

Statue of Duke of Wellington astride favourite horse, Copenhagen, stands on island at centre of traffic junction.

Imperial War Museum 🏛 Ec

Museum, housed in building of 1812-15, has displays covering Britain's wars since 1914. Two gigantic naval guns – each weighing 100 tons – stand before portico. Displays include reconstructions of 1914 recruiting office and trench system. Other exhibits include Spitfire from World War II, one of 'little ships' from evacuation of Dunkirk, Lawrence of Arabia's Arab headgear and rifle, and original surrender document of all German forces in World War II. Museum's art galleries house paintings of battle scenes by well-known artists.

Institute of Contemporary Arts Cd

Institute holds exhibitions of works by international contemporary artists and new British painters, experimental theatre and art films, talks and conferences.

Jewel Tower Dc

In precincts of Westminster Abbey, tower is part of original Palace of Westminster, dating from 1365. Now houses relics of old palace discovered during local excavations.

Jubilee Gardens Dd

Walk from Hungerford Bridge to Westminster Bridge through gardens gives views of River Thames and Houses of Parliament. Paved gardens are on site of 1951 Festival of Britain, and were opened in 1977 as part of Queen's Silver Jubilee.

Lambeth Bridge Dc

Red and black, five-arch bridge built between 1929 and 1932 to replace earlier one connecting City of Westminster and Lambeth. Bridge was designed by Sir George Humphries.

RULING THE NATION *The New Palace of Westminster, otherwise known as the Houses of Parliament. On the right of the picture stands Big Ben; the name refers to the enormous bell in the clock tower – not to the clock itself.*

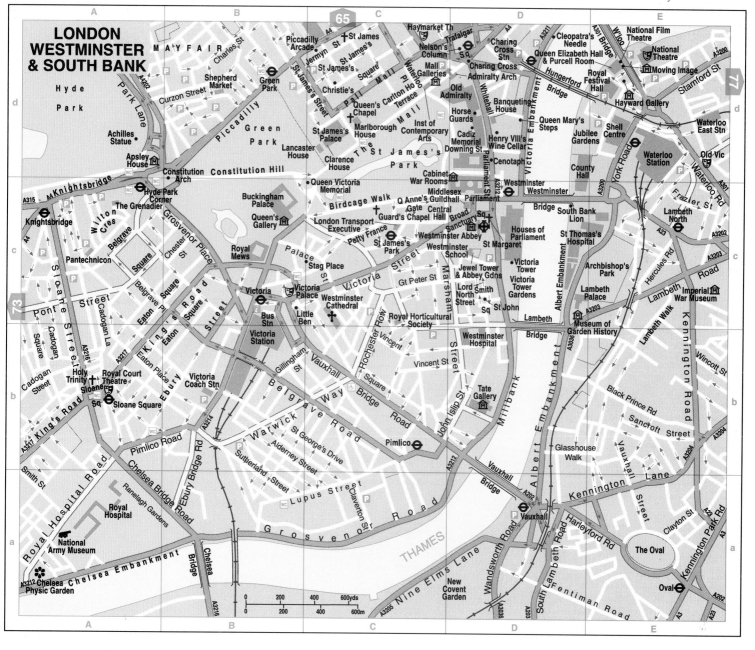

RELICS OF THE PAST *Tombs at Westminster Abbey include, top to bottom, the wife of Edward Talbot, Lady Burghley and Thomas Cecil, Earl of Exeter.*

Middlesex Guildhall Dc
Turreted and decorated with stone figures, hall was built between 1906 and 1913 in Gothic style. Quarter Sessions held here.

Museum of Garden History 🏛 Dc
Housed in 19th-century church, museum commemorates father and son, John Tradescant, gardeners to Charles I. Small 17th-century garden featuring plants brought to Britain by Tradescants from their world travels is behind church. These include yuccas, lilacs and honeysuckle. Collection of Victorian gardening tools also on display. Churchyard has graves of the two Tradescants and of Captain Bligh of mutiny on the *Bounty* fame.

Museum of the Moving Image 🏛 Ed
Interactive, chronological guide to the moving image, from Chinese shadow puppets to television and video production.

Pantechnicon Ac
Only front remains of former Pantechnicon in Motcomb Street, once an area of warehouses and salerooms covering 2 acres and built 1830.

Parliament Square Dc
Great figures of House of Commons depicted here in statuary outside scene of their former triumphs and, also, their disasters. Churchill, Disraeli, Canning and Peel strike variety of poses in square first laid out in 1750, but reconstructed number of times since. Other statues include Jan Smuts and Richard the Lionheart.

Parliament Street Dd
Thoroughfare through heart of Westminster, laid out in mid-18th century and widened in 19th century. Widest street in London.

Petty France Cc
Best-known for Passport Office in Clive House, but worth visit for its urban domestic architecture.

Queen's Gallery 🏛 Bc
Gallery housed in south wing of Buckingham Palace holds paintings, drawings and furniture from Royal Collection.

Queen Victoria Memorial Cc
Unveiled in 1911, memorial is 82ft high and carved from single block of marble. Seated Queen Victoria is surrounded by several allegorical figures representing charity, truth, progress, peace and other idealistic concepts.

Royal Festival Hall Ed
Only permanent building built for 1951 Festival of Britain. Open design allows views of Thames. Concert hall can seat 3000 and stage can accommodate more than 100 players and singers.

Royal Horticultural Society Cc
Regular flower shows held at headquarters of society, which has one of largest horticultural libraries in world.

QUIET HAVEN *The peaceful cloisters at Westminster Abbey date back to the 13th century. Here the Abbot washed the feet of 13 old men each Maundy Thursday – as Christ washed his disciples' feet at the Last Supper.*

Lambeth Palace Dc
Official home of Archbishop of Canterbury since 13th century. Tudor gateway dates from 1495 and Great Hall from 1660. Hall is 93ft long and has hammerbeam roof. Chapel, much restored, dates from around 1230 and features modern stained glass by Powell and Edwards. Crypt under chapel, built around 1200, has Purbeck marble pillars.

FACE IN THE WALL *16th-century monument at St Margaret's Church.*

Lambeth Walk Ec
Street made famous in Cockney-style song of 1930s, *Doing the Lambeth Walk*. Market held here daily. Plaque marks spot where Charlie Chaplin lived.

Lancaster House Cd
Large 19th-century mansion designed by Benjamin Wyatt for Duke of York. One of finest surviving examples of Victorian

architecture in London. Two-storey Corinthian portico; baroque interior. Marble staircase leads to gallery decorated with painted ceilings and mirrors.

Little Ben Bc
Smaller, 30ft high, version of Big Ben outside Victoria Station. Famous meeting place since 1890s, although it was removed in 1964 but returned to traditional home in 1981.

London Transport Executive Cc
Headquarters of London Transport Executive, built in 1920s, are decorated with statues by Jacob Epstein, Henry Moore and Edward Gill.

Lord North Street Dc
Elegant street of Georgian houses dating from 1722.

The Mall Cd
Processional approach to Buckingham Palace, set out in 1910 to replace earlier mall dating from 17th century. Present route links the Victoria Memorial to Admiralty Arch.

Mall Galleries 🏛 Cd
Galleries of Federation of British Artists housed in Carlton House Terrace. New work exhibited by member art societies such as Royal Institute of Oil Painters.

National Film Theatre Ed
Film centre has two cinemas, seating 466 and 162. Home of London Film Festival. Secondhand book market held outside.

National Theatre 🎭 Ed
Three theatres – Olivier, Lyttleton and Cottesloe – make up National Theatre. Building designed by Sir Denys Lasdun and opened in 1976. Backstage tours.

New Covent Garden Da
Market transferred from Covent Garden – where it had been since 1670 – to present site in 1974.

Old Vic 🎭 Ed
Among great theatres of London. Opened in 1818, restored in 1980s. During first half of this century it was centre of Shakespearean theatre, ballet and opera.

The Oval Ea
Headquarters of Surrey County Cricket Club since 1848. Scene of first cricket Test Match – between England and Australia in 1880.

Queen Anne's Gate Cc
Thoroughfare that was originally two streets built in early and late 18th century and separated by dividing wall – Queen Square, dating from 1704, and Park Street, built around late 18th century. Statue of Queen Anne stands on dividing wall. Blue plaques adorning many of the houses in this area indicate number of past distinguished residents, including the philosopher John Stuart Mill and statesmen Lord Palmerston, Lord North and Sir Edward Grey.

Queen Elizabeth Hall and Purcell Room Ed
Built in 1967, Queen Elizabeth Hall can seat 1100. Purcell Room, which seats 370, used principally for chamber music and soloists.

Queen Mary's Steps Dd
Steps and part of terrace designed by Christopher Wren in 1691 for Mary II were excavated in 1939. Nearby is statue of General Gordon of Khartoum.

Royal Mews Bc
Coach houses and stable designed by John Nash and completed in 1825. Great royal coaches such as Gold State Coach built for George III in 1762 – used at coronations – and Glass Coach – used for royal weddings – housed here. Panels of Gold State Coach painted by Cipriani. Fleet of over 20 cars includes Phantom Six Rolls-Royce. Stables are used by Windsor Grey and Cleveland Bay carriage horses.

St James's Palace Cd
Built by Henry VIII in 16th century. Tudor brick towers and turrets enhanced by Wren additions. Chapel Royal, famous for church music, built about 1532. Painted ceiling commemorates Henry VIII's marriage to Anne of Cleves.

St James's Park Cd
Coots, grebes, ducks and geese inhabit capital's oldest royal park. Created by Henry VIII in 1532, it covers 90 acres. John Nash landscaped lake and gardens in the

PICTURE THIS *The dome-roofed Tate Gallery was built on the site of Millbank Penitentiary by sugar magnate and philanthropist Sir Henry Tate. It was opened in 1897, with a collection of 67 paintings and three sculptures.*

19th century. Island in lake is preserved as breeding ground for waterfowl. Modern bridge over lake has views of Buckingham Palace and Whitehall.

GREEN PEACE *St James's Park is popular among Westminster office workers for lunchtime relaxation.*

St John's Church, Smith Square Dc
Early 18th-century church with four ornate towers. Sometimes known as Queen Anne's Footstool, as queen is reputed to have designed it herself, using an upturned footstool as her model. Restored after World War II, and reopened as concert hall in 1969.

St Margaret's Church † Dc
Built 1486-1523, has been parish church for House of Commons since 1614. East window, dating from 1501, shows Henry VIII and Catherine of Aragon beside Crucifix. Memorial window to poet John Milton, who was married here. Modern windows created in 1967 by John Piper replace those blown out during World War II. Monuments include Sir Walter Raleigh, printing pioneer Sir William Caxton, and Yeoman of the Guard who died at 94 in 1577.

St Thomas's Hospital Dc
Red and white hospital overlooking River Thames was built in 1871. Nurses from St Thomas's are known as Nightingales, after Florence Nightingale.

Shell Centre Ed
Built in 1962, when it was one of largest buildings in the world. Building is 26 storeys high, has more than 7000 windows and covers 7½ acres.

South Bank Lion Dc
Statue of lion on tall plinth stands on the site of the now-defunct Lion Brewery.

Stag Place Bc
Statue of stag by E. Bainbridge Copnall, completed in 1962, marks site of Stag Brewery, which closed in 1959 after a history of brewing dating from 1800s.

BRONZE CAST *The sculpture* The Burghers of Calais *by Rodin stands in Victoria Tower Gardens.*

Tate Gallery 🏛 Db
Sugar magnate, Sir Henry Tate, funded building in 1897. Houses two main collections, Historic British Collection with paintings dating from 16th century to about 1900, and Twentieth Century Collection with works by Matisse, Miró and Picasso and taking in Dada, Minimal Art and Pop Art. Rodin's *The Kiss* stands just inside entrance. Also works by artists such as Hogarth, Gainsborough, Reynolds, Blake, Gaugin, Van Gogh, and David Hockney. On east flank stands Clore Gallery, with 300 oil paintings and some 30,000 watercolours, prints and sketches by Turner.

Vauxhall Bridge Da
Bronze figures representing subjects such as science and education decorate turn-of-the-century five-arch bridge. Built to replace earlier bridge.

Victoria Embankment Dd
Promenade follows River Thames from Westminster Bridge to Blackfriars Bridge. Lining route are iron lampposts decorated with dolphins, and benches with sphinxes at each end. Statues along embankment include Cleopatra's Needle and bomb-damaged lions, Queen Boudicca, poet Robert Burns and Brunel.

Victoria Palace ♥ Bc
Theatre, built 1911, has been home to shows such as *Me and My Girl*, *The Crazy Gang* and *The Black and White Minstrel Show*.

Victoria Station Bb
Built in 1870s. Originally two stations side by side – London, Brighton and South Coast, and London, Chatham and Dover.

Victoria Tower Dc
Rising 336ft above River Thames, tower houses parliamentary archives and 3 million documents including House of Commons legislation from 1547.

Victoria Tower Gardens Dc
Gardens, much enjoyed by tourists, has views across River Thames to Lambeth Palace. Bronze statue of suffragette Emmeline Pankhurst and a cast of *The Burghers of Calais* by Rodin. Gothic-Revival drinking fountain in children's play area.

Waterloo Bridge Ed
White, five-arched bridge faced with Portland stone.

Waterloo Station
Frieze of heroic figures – memorial to staff killed during World War I – decorates arch at entrance to station. First opened in 1848, the station was almost totally rebuilt in 1922. Now major terminus for Channel Tunnel rail link.

Westminster Abbey ✠ Dc
Original abbey built by Edward the Confessor in about 1050, replacing the little timber church of St Peter's. Rulers of England have been crowned here since William the Conqueror in 1066. Present buildings constructed between 13th and 16th centuries. West towers, designed by Wren and Hawksmoor, were built during 18th century. Portrait of Richard II, dating from 14th century, hangs near west door. Memorials to Lloyd George, Clement Attlee, David Livingstone, Isaac Newton and Winston Churchill to be found in Chapel of St George. Also grave of Unknown Warrior of World War I, surrounded by poppies. North transept has statues of Pitt, Gladstone, Castlereagh and Disraeli. South aisle contains Poets' Corner, including tomb of Geoffrey Chaucer. St Edward the Confessor Chapel contains shrine to the saint. Coronation Chair stands here, carrying Scotland's Stone of Scone on shelf beneath seat. All around are tombs of medieval kings and queens. Henry VII Chapel has fan-vaulted ceiling, and banners of Knights Grand Cross of the Order of the Bath. Tombs of Henry VII, Mary Tudor and Elizabeth I here. Abbey plate, mostly 17th century, is displayed in Pyx chamber.

Westminster Abbey Gardens Dc
At 900 years, probably oldest of London's gardens. Originally physic garden of Benedictine community that flourished here when abbey was built.

Westminster Abbey Museum 🏛 Dc
Below abbey, in 110ft long 11th-century room, are many of abbey's treasures, notably reproductions of coronation regalia and wax effigies of monarchs.

Westminster Bridge Dc
Seven-arch bridge, built by Thomas Page and Charles Barry in 1862, is over 80ft wide. Views of River Thames, Houses of Parliament, Victoria and Albert Embankments and County Hall.

Westminster Cathedral † Cc
Built in 1903 of red brick with bands of Portland stone in Byzantine style, the Catholic cathedral is 360ft long and 156ft wide. Nave is widest in England, and interior is decorated with mosaics. Visitors can take lift to top of bell tower, 284ft high, from which there are views stretching to Greenwich and Highgate.

Westminster School Dc
Housed in number of buildings within precincts of abbey. Oldest part dates from 11th century and housed school's only classroom from 1602 to 1884.

Whitehall Dd
Government buildings line broad highway running from Houses of Parliament to Trafalgar Square. Relics of Tudor royal residence, Whitehall Palace, remain in surrounding buildings.

Wilton Crescent Ac
Georgian and Regency houses line crescent, now home to many foreign embassies.

EASTERN NAVE *Built in 1903 and decorated with mosaic and marble, the nave in Westminster Cathedral is the widest in England.*

Albert Bridge Da
Distinctive suspension bridge, built 1873, illuminated at night. Wrought-iron bars suspend deck from decorative cast-iron towers.

Albert Memorial Cd
Elaborate monument surrounds 14ft bronze figure of the Prince Consort. Built in early 1870s by Sir George Gilbert Scott, memorial has marble frieze depicting poets, architects, artists and composers. Ornate pinnacles and cross adorn neo-Gothic spire.

ALBERT MEMORIAL *The monument overlooks another memorial, the Royal Albert Hall.*

KENSINGTON AND CHELSEA

Royal Kensington, famous for its museums and mansions, changed from rural village to smart residential area in the 19th century. Members of the royal family live in Kensington Palace, birthplace of Queen Victoria, at the heart of Kensington Gardens. Chelsea, former focus of new ideas and fashions, has attracted many great artists and writers, such as Augustus John and Oscar Wilde.

Scout Movement's founder, whose aim was 'to promote good citizenship in the rising generation'. Displays illustrate life of Baden-Powell from days as officer in Boer War to time as chief of Boy Scout organisation. Hat and uniform are among exhibits.

Battersea Park Ea
Popular park laid out in 1846, on site of wasteland where fairs were held with horse and donkey races. Facilities for tennis, football, hockey, with fishing and boating on lake. Children's zoo, deer park. Ornate Japanese peace pagoda overlooks Thames.

Bayswater Bf
One of the first of the great department stores, Whiteley's, is now a cosmopolitan jumble of cafés, restaurants and shops, with London's first multiplex cinema.

Bonhams Dd
Fine art auctioneers, founded in 1793. Values anything from teddy bears and cameras to oriental pots and Old Masters. Regular viewing in four galleries.

British Library National Sound Archive Dd
Dating from 1893, Queen Anne-style building has display showing history of recording. Research centre has over 45,000 hours of recorded material including an endless variety of music, sound effects and fascinating examples of local dialects.

Brompton Cemetery Bb
Domed octagonal chapel built in mid-19th century survives from earlier development by Benjamin Baud. Graves include those of Emmeline Pankhurst, suffragette leader; Sir Henry Cole, organiser

Carlyle's House 🏠 Da
Fine example of an 18th-century town house built in 1708; still much as it was when Scottish writer Thomas Carlyle, known as the 'Sage of Chelsea', lived here from 1834 to 1865. Charles Dickens, Robert Browning and Alfred, Lord Tennyson all came to visit Carlyle in this house. Displays include the desk at which Carlyle wrote his books, and an early piano played by Chopin.

Chelsea Db
Began life as a fishing village. Henry VIII had a riverside residence here in Tudor times. Later frequented by 'Bohemian' residents such as Whistler and Oscar Wilde; Chelsea achieved colourful notoriety in Victorian times. Still considered one of London's most exclusive residential areas.

Chelsea Embankment Ea
Wide riverside road, opened in 1874, running directly from Chelsea Bridge to Albert Bridge. Embankment Gardens flourish on land reclaimed from the muddy river foreshore.

Chelsea Old Church ✝ Da
Fine church dating from Norman times, reconstructed in 1950s after severe damage in World War II. Sir Thomas More's south chapel survives intact, built as his private place of worship in 1528. Treasures include six chained books donated by Sir Hans Sloane, whose grave is in the churchyard.

Chelsea Old Town Hall Db
Hall built in 1886, extended by L.R. Stokes in 1906. Early 20th century murals, painted by several artists, illustrate Chelsea's connection with science and the arts. Mural on literature nearly destroyed in 1914 because it depicted Oscar Wilde. Hall now used for antique, design and craft fairs throughout year.

Chelsea Physic Garden ❀ Eb
Exotic trees, shrubs and herbs line Britain's second oldest botanic garden, founded by the Worshipful Society of Apothecaries in 1673. Covers 4 acres. First English cedar trees were planted here in 1683. Still a botanic laboratory; plants and seeds are exchanged with gardens throughout the world. Country's earliest rock garden is made of building stone from the old Tower of London and Icelandic lava.

Chenil Galleries Db
Distinguished antique stalls that specialise in fine furniture, 17th and 18th-century paintings, Art Nouveau and Art Deco objects, porcelain and antique toys.

Cheyne Walk Da
A fine row of early 18th-century houses, many with wrought-iron fences and gates. Henry VIII's Manor House, built in 1537, once occupied the site of Nos 19 to 26. Several 19th-century authors and artists lived here including Dante Gabriel Rossetti at No.16, one of the founders of the Pre-Raphaelite Brotherhood of writers and artists. There is a quiet street of unspoilt terraces in Cheyne Row, developed in 1708.

Commonwealth Institute Ad
Oddly shaped modern building, with five-peaked green copper roof on glass curtain walls, opened in 1962. Circular galleries arranged by country or region, aim to promote mutual understanding between peoples of the Commonwealth. Colourful samples of diverse cultures include a towering model of a dancer from West Africa, a Manx cross and a festival dragon from Hong Kong. Water-lily gardens in the Sri Lanka exhibition dominated by a serene Buddha. Learn to play the sitar; sit astride a snowmobile; or shop for craftwork.

Crosby Hall Da
Remarkable medieval hall, formerly part of a City mansion of 1466. In 1483, Richard, Duke of Gloucester held court in the hall; hence its mention in William Shakespeare's *Richard III*. Burnt down in the 17th century, the great hall survived and was rebuilt in Chelsea in 1910.

Earl's Court Bb
Vibrant and cosmopolitan area that originated in 1155 when Lord de Vere of the Manor of Kensington became Earl of Oxford. His manor court house once stood near site of the underground station. Home of a vast exhibition hall that covers over 18 acres. Lively shops and restaurants in Earl's Court Road.

Fulham Road Cb
Road stretches from Brompton Road, across Fulham Broadway to Fulham Palace Road. Lined by smart boutiques, cafés and restaurants. Michelin House stands at eastern end.

CHELSEA PHYSIC GARDEN *Britain's second oldest botanic garden was founded in the 17th century.*

Geological Museum 🏛 Dc
The story of the Earth is told with gemstones, crystals and minerals, including diamonds from Siberia and lapis lazuli from Afghanistan. Some superb models and special effects, including an earthquake simulator. Worlds apart, a delicate 330 million-year-old fossil of a fern from Scotland shares the museum with a piece of the Moon, collected by the *Apollo* astronauts in 1972.

INTERIOR DESIGN *View inside the magnificent 19th-century Brompton Oratory, looking north. Until Westminster Cathedral was opened in 1903, the Oratory was the centre of Roman Catholic activity in London.*

All Saints Church ✝ Dd
Church built in 1840s, to designs of Vulliamy, with Italian-style west front by C. Harrison Townsend. Corinthian columns in iron mark interior, decorated in Arts and Crafts style by Heywood Sumner. Now part of Russian Orthodox Church.

Antiquarius Db
Well-known indoor antiques market selling china, glass, books and jewellery in over 150 stalls.

Baden-Powell House Museum 🏛 Cc
Building designed by Ralph Tubbs in 1961; commemorates the

Turkish baths in the Victorian Porchester Baths. Ice-skating farther along Queensway.

Beauchamp Place Ec
Well-preserved brick terraces line street, developed in late 18th century. Immaculate shopfronts display designer clothes, shoes, silver and antiques.

The Boltons Cb
Palatial mansions occupy two facing crescents, designed by George Godwin in the 1850s. St Mary's Church stands in central gardens. On site of Bousfield Primary School is former home of children's author Beatrix Potter.

of 1851 Great Exhibition and first director of Victoria & Albert Museum; Dr Benjamin Golding, founder of Charing Cross Hospital; and Francis Fowke, architect of the Royal Albert Hall.

Brompton Oratory ✝ Dc
Roman Catholic church in flamboyant baroque style, designed in the late 19th century by Herbert Gribble, based on the Church of Chiesa Nuova in Rome. Impressive Italian altarpiece; also marble statues of the apostles from Siena Cathedral. Oratory was once the centre of Roman Catholic activity in London until Westminster Cathedral was opened in 1903.

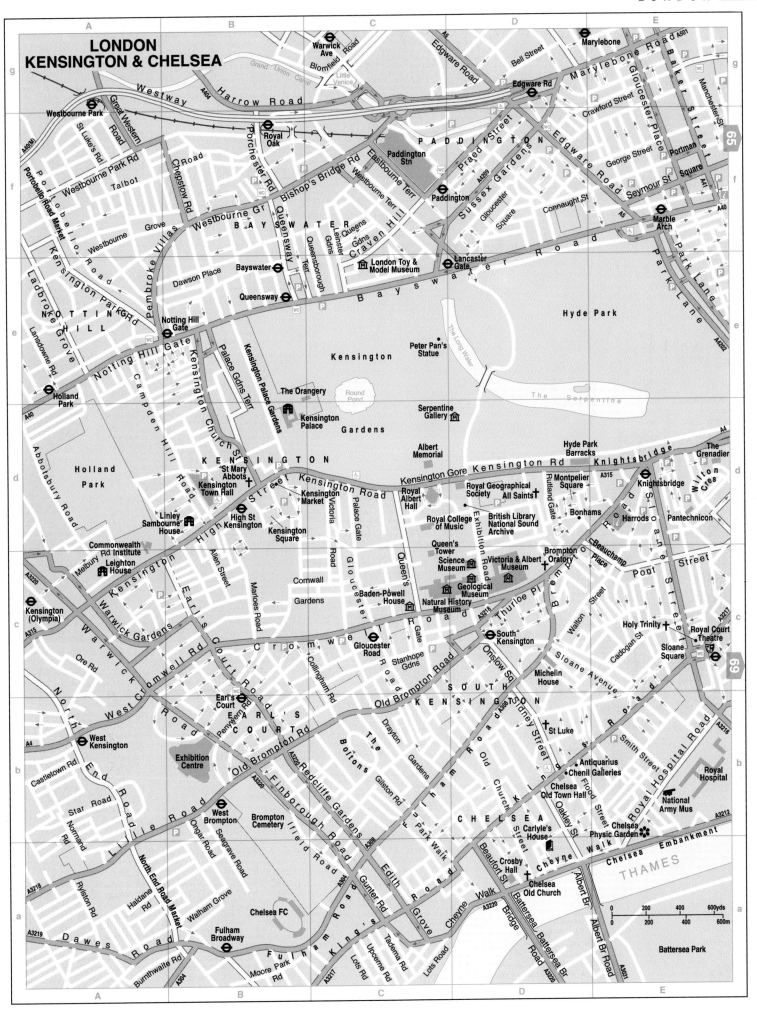

**LONDON
KENSINGTON & CHELSEA**

Harrods Ed
Grand terracotta brick building with towers and cupolas. Houses the most famous and one of the largest department stores in the world, employing around 5000 staff. Originally a small grocery bought by wholesale tea merchant Henry Charles Harrod in 1849, the store now has over 60 fashion departments. Opulent displays of fruit, flowers, meat and confectionery in renowned food hall. Other departments specialise in anything from silverware to cosmetics and furniture.

Holland Park Ad
Formal parkland, opened in 1952. Peacocks cry out amongst wild flowers and grasses in shaded woodland areas. Adventure playground for children is renowned for its rope-swings and climbing structures. Holland House, built 1606, was fashionable meeting place in the 18th century. Heavily bombed in World War II, the surviving wing is now part of Youth Hostel.

Holy Trinity Church ✝ Ec
Designed by John Dando Sedding in 1890, the church has richly decorated interior, inspired by William Morris's Arts and Crafts Movement. Large east window was made by Edward Burne-Jones and William Morris.

WATER SPORT *For centuries the Serpentine in Hyde Park has been used for boating and swimming.*

ROYAL STYLE *The court dress collection in Kensington Palace spans 200 years of fashionable society.*

'HARRODS SERVES THE WORLD' *So claimed an advert in* The Daily Telegraph *in 1894. The store now has 300 departments.*

Hyde Park De
Once the haunt of deer, boar and wild cattle and former hunting ground of Henry VIII, acquired from Westminster Abbey in 1536. Elizabeth I hunted in Hyde Park and inaugurated military reviews that were held here for centuries. Opened to public in 1637, site of Great Exhibition in 1851. Merges to west with Kensington Gardens, together covering 630 acres and forming the largest open space in inner London. Now has boating and swimming in the Serpentine, horse-riding along Rotten Row – former haunt of highwaymen and duellers – and art appreciation in Serpentine Gallery.

Hyde Park Barracks Dd
Tower block, 1970s, by Sir Basil Spence marks headquarters of the Household Cavalry Regiment. Every morning the cavalry rides down through Hyde Park to Buckingham Palace.

Imperial College, Queen's Tower Cc
Green copper dome crowns 280ft tower, relic of demolished Collcut buildings, put up to mark Queen Victoria's Golden Jubilee in 1887. Panoramic view of South Kensington from top of tower.

Kensington Bd
Spacious white stuccoed houses overlook immaculate gardens in London's royal suburb; famous for large and elegant department stores. Present borough formed in 1965 by a merger with Chelsea.

Kensington Market Bd
Labyrinth of stalls on three floors that sells secondhand clothes, shoes and accessories. Strong emphasis in styles from the 1940s and 1950s. Also includes work by new designers.

Kensington Gardens Ce
Once part of Kensington Palace, magical glades laid out in their present form by George II; scarred by the great gale of October 1987. Designed by Sir George Frampton in 1912, Peter Pan's statue was erected overnight to surprise local children; the pipes are said to disappear regularly.

Kensington Palace ⌂ Bd
Bought as a royal residence by William III in 1689, who engaged Wren and Hawksmoor to enlarge it. Queen Victoria lives on in a bedroom filled with her favourite paintings and souvenirs, and the cot once occupied by each of her nine children. An illusionist gallery painted by William Kent on the walls of the King's Staircase is decorated with realistic figures, who lean over the balustrades and peer at you.

Kensington Palace Gardens Be
Broad tree-lined street of enormous 19th-century mansions, developed by James Pennethorne. Once nicknamed Millionaire's Row, road is now home to several embassies.

Kensington Square Bd
Handsome 18th-century houses surround square, laid out by Thomas Young, where several distinguished writers and artists once lived. Philosopher John Stuart Mill resided at No.18, and Edward Burne-Jones at No.41. Thackeray wrote *Vanity Fair* in Young Street, adjacent to square.

King's Road Db
Considered to be the backbone of Chelsea, stretching from Sloane Square to Fulham. Once the royal route to Hampton Court, adopted by Charles II in the 17th century. Fashion focus of the 1960s, later centre for the punk rock scene, the King's Road still thrives from antiques and clothes.

Knightsbridge Ed
Once a small village by the Westbourne river, this elegant district is famous for Harrods department store, where a visit to the food hall is a feast for the eyes. Luxury restaurants and clothes shops mingle with smart antique shops. Hyde Park Hotel dates from 1888.

Leighton House ⌂ Ac
Grand house built 1866 for celebrated Victorian artist, Lord Leighton. Oriental tiles and elaborate stained-glass windows decorate an exotic Arab Hall with mosaic floor and fountain. Collection of Pre-Raphaelite and High Victorian paintings. Works by Leighton and Burne-Jones.

EASTERN DELIGHTS *Exotic Leighton House, built for and partly designed by Victorian artist Lord Leighton, is now a museum and art gallery.*

Linley Sambourne House ⌂ Bd
Renowned *Punch* cartoonist and illustrator Edward Linley Sambourne lived in this Victorian house, completed in 1874. William Morris furnishings still remain. Drawings by Sambourne and fellow artists line the walls.

Little Venice Cg
Magnificent white stucco villas overlook colourful narrowboats in western end of Regent's Canal (now part of the Grand Union Canal). Stroll along towpath and watch boats moor at the Pool. Artists inspired by area include Lucien Freud and Feliks Topolski.

London Toy & Model Museum ⌂ Ce
Summer model boat regatta and a teddy-bear's picnic in a museum where Paddington Bear has his own display. Impressive dolls' room and models galore; toy cars, soldiers, cowboys and Indians, farms and scenes from *Little Red Riding Hood*.

Marble Arch Ef
Monument, 19th century, built next to the site where highwaymen were once hanged. On a small traffic island at the junction of Bayswater Road and Edgware Road, a plaque marks the spot where the Tyburn gallows once stood. Original gateway to Buckingham Palace, Marble Arch was moved to Hyde Park Corner in 1851; now purely ornamental.

Michelin House Dc
Bright, flamboyant Art Nouveau building, once the English headquarters of the French tyre manufacturer. Coloured tiles depict early motoring rallies on building restored in 1985 by Sir Terence Conran. Now houses contemporary furnishings shop, offices, restaurant and oyster bar.

Montpelier Square Dd
Elegant balconies enhance neat brick and stucco houses on site of former fields, owned by wealthy Huguenots in the 18th century. Network of attractive squares, streets and alleyways lie nearby.

National Army Museum ⚔ Eb
Brick and concrete blockhouse defended by a Centurion tank houses galleries that tell story of the British army since 1485. The sullen rumble of artillery adds atmosphere to a full-scale section of trench. Noisy evocation of the Dunkirk beaches. Relics include Marlborough's gold-embroidered saddlecloth and order responsible for the 1854 charge of the Light Brigade. Military paintings, a full range of uniforms, and a staggering array of arms.

Natural History Museum ⌂ Cc
The lofty halls of Waterhouse's impressive neo-Gothic building provide nearly 4 acres of gallery space, with 50 million exhibits. Story of evolution from dinosaurs to man, bones of mammoths in the Fossil Galleries, a 91ft long model of a blue whale in the Whale Gallery, and spiders in the Creepy-crawlies Gallery. Computerised audiovisual displays.

DESIGN FOR LIVING *Once the English headquarters of a French tyre manufacturer, the brightly coloured Art Nouveau Michelin House on Fulham Road was built in 1910. Tyres appear throughout in the patterning and structure.*

MILITARY MUSIC *A 1911 side drum at the National Army Museum.*

North End Road Market Aa
Wide range of goods sold in bustling market. Anything from exotic foods and cheap plants to clothes and kitchenware.

Notting Hill Ae
Home to Europe's biggest street party every August, the Notting Hill Carnival was founded as a local fair in 1966. One of London's best street markets can be found in Portobello Road. Cosmopolitan shops and restaurants around Ladbroke Grove. Stylish residential areas were laid out during the 19th century.

The Orangery, Kensington Gardens Be
Grinling Gibbons carving adorns restored Orangery by Nicholas Hawksmoor, dating from 1704. Said to be where Queen Anne hosted summer parties amongst orange and myrtle trees.

Paddington Df
Tall Victorian houses along wide boulevards distinguish historic London area. Railway terminal and canal junction; Paddington Canal linked to Regent's Canal. All now part of Grand Union Canal. Once used to transport market produce to London in the early 19th century.

Paddington Station Cf
Ornate metalwork embellishes 19th-century station designed by Isambard Kingdom Brunel. Cast-iron pillars support roof made of iron and glass.

Portobello Road Market Af
Streets surrounding Portobello Road are alive with the hubbub of London's most diverse Saturday market. Stalls focus on antique china, clocks, silverware, furniture and bric-a-brac.

Royal Albert Hall Cd
Tier upon tier of boxes and galleries in a magnificent oval concert hall, planned by Prince Albert and built as his memorial. Completed in 1871, a terracotta frieze outside illustrates man's progress in the arts. Inside, the guided tour includes view of Royal Box and perhaps a rehearsal.

Royal College of Music Cd
Victorian red-brick building with ornate gables and pepper pot towers houses Museum of Instruments. Impressive collection includes Handel's spinet and Haydn's clavichord.

Royal Court Theatre ♻ Ec
Opened in 1888, theatre became focus for new drama in the early 20th century. Venue for George Bernard Shaw premières, under his direction. Rebuilt 1952, the theatre continues to encourage experimental plays.

Royal Geographical Society Dd
Splendid red-brick headquarters of a private society founded in 1830, dedicated to exploration and discovery. Over 800,000 maps, a fine collection of paintings, and 19th-century travel photography by Society fellows.

Royal Hospital Eb
Inspired by Louis XIV's Hotel des Invalides in Paris, Charles II founded a hospice for retired soldiers in 1681 with Sir Christopher Wren as architect. Over 400 Chelsea Pensioners still live here. Gibbons's statue of Charles II is decorated with oak leaves every June, to commemorate his escape from Oliver Cromwell's troops by hiding in an oak tree.

St Luke, Chelsea † Db
One of the first neo-Gothic churches, designed by John Savage in 1819. Impressive tower and porch, and a roof of fine stone vaulting. Here, novelist Charles Kingsley held a lectureship, and Charles Dickens married Catherine Hogarth in 1836.

St Mary Abbots † Bd
Spire of 280ft crowns fine 19th-century church, built on site of 11th-century church.

Science Museum ⌂ Dc
Opened in 1857; all-embracing panorama of science through the ages. Interactive displays recount discoveries and inventions, from the Industrial Revolution to the Space Age. Holograms, space exploration and a gallery on nutrition. Measure your heartbeat, shake hands with yourself and star in your own special effects video. Also includes Vickers Vimy aircraft, which made the first transatlantic flight in 1919.

Serpentine Gallery ⌂ Dd
Temporary exhibitions of modern art held in former tea-house designed by Sir Henry Tanner. Galleries look out onto beautiful surroundings of Kensington Gardens and Hyde Park.

Sloane Square Ec
Originally named after Sir Hans Sloane – the eminent physician, President of the Royal Society and Lord of the Manor of Chelsea in the 18th century. War memorial to both world wars stands in centre, near bronze *Venus Fountain* statue of 1951. Peter Jones department store lies on corner, founded by a Welsh cloth merchant in 1877.

South Kensington Dc
Workers' cottages in mews and back streets are now luxurious white-fronted residences. Contains a wealth of museums, developed from profits of the Great Exhibition of 1851.

Victoria & Albert Museum ⌂ Dc
Seven miles of galleries form the world's largest decorative arts museum. National collections in a gentle ambience, from watercolours to wallpaper. Fashions come and go in the Dress Collection, while lasting treasures include Medieval and Byzantine art, an array of oriental carpets, Chinese thrones and samurai swords. Designed by Sir Aston Webb. Queen Victoria laid the foundation stone in 1899.

WEEKEND BARGAINS *Every Saturday, Portobello Road in Notting Hill is the setting for one of London's most popular marketplaces.*

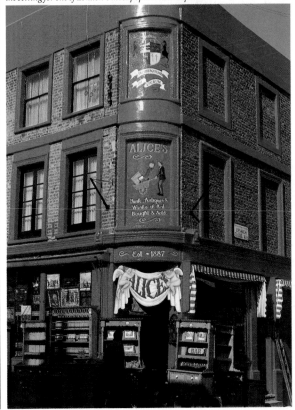

THE CITY OF LONDON

The centre of Britain's financial and commercial power is a curious mixture of the old and the new. Seen from the River Thames, the vast dome of St Paul's still dominates the famous 'Square Mile', but taller modern buildings now stand alongside Wren's churches. Just downriver is the squat mass of the Tower of London, symbol of the City's invincibility since the days of William the Conqueror.

All Hallows Barking by the Tower † Db
Church rebuilt in 1958 after being bombed in World War II, still has Anglo-Saxon arch dating from AD 675. Inside are font cover attributed to Grinling Gibbons, brasses, wall tablets and sword rests. Undercroft contains historic objects, documents.

Anchor Bankside Ca
Riverside inn, rebuilt 18th century, has minstrels' gallery, oak beams and fugitive cubbyholes. Collection of Elizabethan objects, viewing platform, model of Globe Theatre and flood mark in bar.

Apothecaries Hall Bb
Great Hall, built 1670 and renovated 1780, is headquarters of Society of Apothecaries. Entrance

Also St Giles Cripplegate Church, dating from 1090, Museum of London and Guildhall School of Music and Drama.

Barbican Centre for Arts and Conferences 🏛 🎭 Cd
Built on area that was severely damaged during World War II.

Romanesque columns of west railway bridge of 1862 still stand. East railway bridge, built 1884-6, leads to Blackfriars Station.

Broadgate Dd
Contemporary office development covering 29 acres – largest single development in City.

Cheshire Cheese Ac
Ancient, oak-beamed pub lists 15 reigns of its existence outside, as well as celebrated writers who came there such as Mark Twain, Dickens and Yeats.

City Temple † Ac
City's only English Free Church, built 1874 and rebuilt in 1958 after being badly damaged during World War II bombings, contrasts modern interior including theatre with Victorian Palladian exterior.

Clerkenwell Green Ad
On western side of green is old Middlesex Sessions House, built 1782. The green also hosts Marx Memorial Library, once London Patriotic Club, centre for Victorian radical politics.

Clink Street Ca
Site of prison called The Clink, commemorated by plaque under railway arches. Remains of 12th-century Windsor Palace, with Great Hall's rose window, have been excavated. Two 19th-century warehouses have been refurbished. Trading schooner, *Kathleen and May*, built 1900, can be visited at St Mary Overy Dock.

Clink Museum 🏛 Ca
Reconstruction of degrading conditions endured in Clink Prison; prison cells, torture instruments, and working armoury based on Henry VIII's original.

Cockpit Bb
Inn, famous for cockfighting in 16th century, decorated to recreate cockpit. Original spectators' gallery has been restored.

College of Arms Bb
Home of Royal Heralds was probably established by Edward I in 13th century. Restored building is 17th century. Contains charters, rolls and records saved from two great City fires. College examines pedigrees, and designs and grants new coats of arms.

Custom House Db
Early 19th-century headquarters of Collector of Customs for the Port of London. Building replaced earlier one by Thomas Ripley, burnt down 1814. Robert Smirke built notable neoclassical façade extending 1190ft, and Long Room where ships' masters and agents registered cargoes.

Dr Johnson's House 📖 Ac
Home of critic and lexicographer Dr Samuel Johnson from 1748-59. House, dating from 17th century, contains many relics from Dr Johnson's life, including first edition of the *Dictionary*, portrait by Barry, portrait of his companion, Boswell, by Reynolds and a collection of 18th-century prints.

Fleet Street Ac
Centre of Britain's newspaper industry until the 1980s. Former Daily Express building of 1931, and Daily Telegraph offices of 1928, still stand. Reuters/Press Association building, designed by Lutyens, dates from 1935. El Vino's wine bar is haunt of barristers and journalists.

General Post Office Bc
Portland-stone Royal Mail headquarters designed by Tanner in 1895. Carved heads of past postmasters general are above entrance doors. Plaque records Marconi's first radio transmission in 1896. Foundation stone of nearby GPO laid by Edward VII in 1905. Statue of Sir Rowland Hill, founder of Penny Post in 1840, stands outside.

George and Vulture Db
Restored 18th-century pub used by Charles Dickens as setting in *Pickwick Papers*.

George Inn and Yard Ca
National Trust inn, rebuilt 1676, has panelled rooms and galleried and cobbled courtyard.

Giltspur Street Bc
Gilded figure of *Fat Boy* on corner of Cock Lane marks point where Great Fire of London allegedly stopped. Bronze figure, *Peace*, 1873, by J.B. Philip, stands in fountain in public gardens.

Golden Lane Bd
Prize-winning city housing estate surrounding four courts was designed by three architects: Chamberlain, Powell and Bonn. Built 1955-62. Cripplegate Institute stands nearby, rare survivor of World War II.

Guildhall Cc
Original building where Court of Common Council meets. Dates from 1411, restored 1952 after damage in Great Fire and Blitz. Walls, porch and crypt survive from original building. Corporation Art Gallery has paintings of great state occasions over last 100 years. Library contains first folios of Shakespeare's plays. Guildhall Art Library includes paintings and drawings of old London. Limewood statues of Gog and Magog, legendary giants whose warlike exploits resulted in founding of New Troy, stand here.

Guildhall Clock Museum 🏛 Cc
One of Britain's most important horologic collections, housed in Guildhall Library. Comprises collections of Clockmakers' Company, Antiquarian Horological Society and Osborne Index of Watch Makers.

Guys Hospital Ca
Vast 1000-bed hospital tower unit retains iron railings and gateway of 1725 building. Palladian-style original courtyard has allegorical figures. Sculptures also include Lord Nuffield and founder, Thomas Guy. Chapel contains basrelief memorial to Guy.

HMS Belfast ⚓ Da
World War II cruiser, now floating museum. A marked route shows every aspect of ship. Bridge,

GAME MARKET *Leadenhall Market takes its name from the lead roof of a mansion which stood on the site in the 14th century. People coming from outside London were allowed to sell their poultry here. It now specialises in game.*

via arch topped by red and gold coat of arms leads to secluded courtyard and hall. Interior has panelling and portraits, including one by Reynolds.

Bank of England Cc
'The Old Lady of Threadneedle Street' holds nation's gold supply and issues banknotes. Building begun by Sampson in 1734, reconstructed by Soane in 1788 and rebuilt by Herbert Baker in 1920s and 30s. Figures on bronze doors and façade by Wheeler include 'Old Lady'. Figure of Ariel on dome. Mosaic floor in entrance hall is by Boris Anrep.

Bank of England Museum 🏛 Cc
Museum has displays illustrating bank's 300-year-old history.

Bankside Gallery 🏛 Bb
Modern art gallery is owned by two Royal Societies – Royal Water Colour Society and Royal Society of Painter-Printmakers.

Barbican Cd
Site of ancient City gate, now has tower blocks, 40 storeys and 400ft high; and Barbican arts centre.

Includes library, art gallery, three cinemas, concert hall and two-theatre base for the Royal Shakespeare Company.

Billingsgate Db
Building, designed by Sir Horace Jones to house fish market, opened in 1877. It has mansard roofs and pavilions at either end surmounted by dolphins on weather vanes.

Bishopsgate Institute Dc
Romanesque building houses charitable activities of St Botolph Without Bishopsgate. Contains reference library of London history, lecture hall and collection of prints and drawings.

Black Friar Bb
Only Art Nouveau pub in London, built in 1875 and remodelled in 1905 by H. Fuller Clark. Mosaics and carved figures by Henry Poole cover outside. Interior decorated in multicoloured marble with bronze figures of monks at work.

Blackfriars Bridge Bb
Cast-iron road bridge opened by Queen Victoria in 1869. Cast-iron

Numerous pieces of sculpture include giant chess set, and 5 ton bronze Venus by Botero.

Cannon Street Station Cb
Walls and two riverside towers remain of Hawkshaw's original 1866 building. Rest of station remodelled during 1960s.

Central Criminal Court Bc
Best known as Old Bailey, present Portland-stone building dates from 1907 and was extended in 1972. Height from ground to head of gold-leaf statue of Justice with sword and scales is 212ft. Large entrance has figures of Truth, Justice, and Recording Angel above it. Interior dominated by mural and marbles.

Charterhouse Bd
Carefully restored 16th-century manor house buildings include 1571 Elizabethan Great Hall.

Cheapside Cc
Street largely destroyed during World War II, but three shops from 1687 still stand. No.73, attributed to Wren, has 17th-century staircase. Saddlers' and Mercers' halls have been restored.

operations room and fire-control equipment all at action stations readiness. Below decks, model figures help illustrate life at sea, including sleeping, eating and medical attention.

Holborn Viaduct Ac

Bronze statues commemorating Agriculture, Commerce, Science and Fine Arts line 1000ft long road viaduct dating from 1896. Two-and-a-half Italian Gothic houses remain of four which once stood at the viaduct's corners.

Inner Temple Ab

One of the Inns of Court. Neo-Georgian hall by Sir Hubert Worthington dates from 1955. King's Bench Walk, laid out by Wren, is lit by gas lamps.

Jamaica Wine House Db

Wine house on site of Jamaica Coffee House, centre of Jamaican trade from 1670s. Established as wine house in 1869. Early coffee percolator can still be seen.

WREN WAY *Inner Temple's King's Bench Walk was designed by Wren.*

Leadenhall Market Db

Buildings dating from 1881 stand on site of 14th-century market.

Leather Lane Ad

Street of pubs, off-licences and cafés is site of general market.

Liverpool Street Dc

Street built in 1829. Rebuilt Liverpool Street Station has elements of original 1874 building. Great Eastern Hotel, with glass-domed restaurant, dates from 1884. Nearby inn, Dirty Dick's, takes name from suitor who ceased cleaning the place after his fiancée's death.

Lloyd's Dc

Startling steel-and-glass building of 1986, designed by Richard Rogers. Houses firm of world-famous underwriters. Exhibition traces history and trading activities can be viewed. Heysham's neoclassical underwriting room, 1957, houses Lutine Bell recalling Lloyd's maritime origins. Still rung to signal marine news.

Lloyd's Shipping Register Db

Columned, turreted building decorated with Art Nouveau figures and friezes and topped by gilded weather vane in shape of ship.

FRENCH BELL *The Lutine Bell at Lloyd's, rung once for bad news, twice for good, belonged to a French frigate called La Lutine, captured in 1793.*

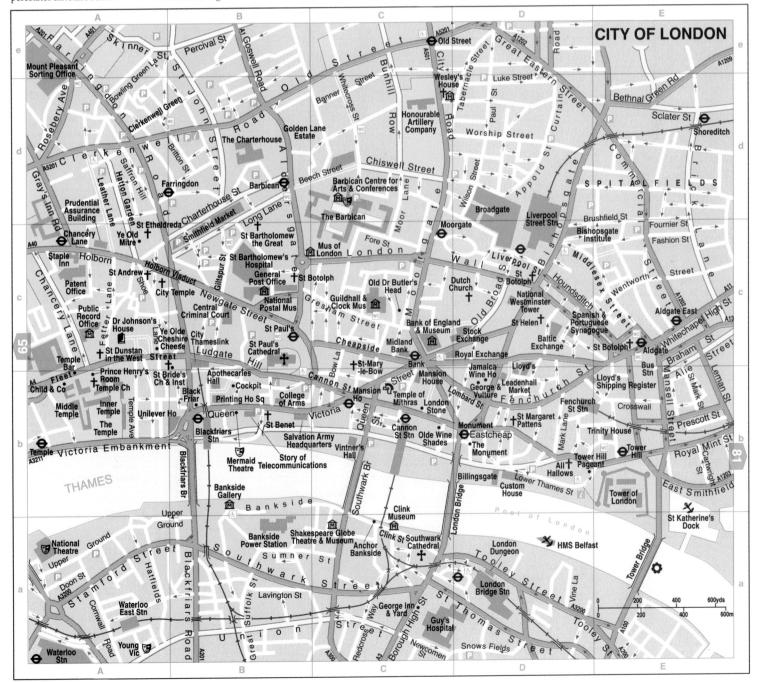

CITY OF LONDON

CITY SKYLINE *The dome of St Paul's Cathedral still dominates the City from almost any viewpoint.*

Lombard Street Db
Financial centre of London in Middle Ages. Colourful signs outside banks resemble the inn signs of medieval times.

STREET OF GOLD *A gilded grasshopper is among several distinguishing signs hanging outside banks in Lombard Street.*

London Bridge Cb
Three-arched, concrete bridge, built 1972, stands on site where Romans built first bridge in AD 100. Good views of Tower Bridge, Tower of London and River Thames. Nearby London Bridge Station rebuilt in 1970s to replace its 1849 predecessor damaged during World War II.

London Dungeon Da
A gruesome medieval horror museum on site of premises occupied by Roland Topcliffe, royal torturer to Elizabeth I. Displays include Queen Boudicca's death-dealings, headless Mary, Queen of Scots and numerous hangings, rackings and boilings.

London Stone Cb
Roughly shaped, round-topped stone with pair of grooves on top set into wall of Bank of China. Origins unknown, but possibly Roman milestone which once symbolised power in City.

London Wall Walk
Walk of 1¾ miles from Tower to Museum of London takes in 21 descriptive panels along line of old City wall. Remains of Cripple-gate Roman fort, outcrops of Roman wall and modern office blocks at Barbican can be seen along way.

Mansion House Cb
Palladian-style official residence of the Lord Mayor of London, designed by George Dance the Elder in 1739-53. Pediment sculptures symbolic of City opulence. Suite of 18th-century staterooms, including 88ft long Egyptian Hall, have chimneypieces of marble and stone, paintings, tapestries, and gold telephone given in 1936 to mark the millionth made. Tours of the staterooms are by appointment only.

Mermaid Theatre Bb
Modern theatre forming part of new office block. Original theatre, begun in 1959, housed in disused Victorian warehouse.

Middlesex Street Ec
Best known as 'Petticoat Lane' street market. Original market has spread into Club Row – specialising in birds and fish – and Brick Lane – noted for furniture and electrical equipment.

Middle Temple Ab
One of the Inns of Court. Restored hall, dating from 1562, has hammerbeam roof and heraldic glass, and contains royal portraits. Library, founded 1641, now housed in 1956 building; previous building was destroyed during Blitz. Has 16th-century globes showing heaven and earth. Gatehouse dates from 1684.

Midland Bank Cc
Bank's head office (1924-39) housed in building designed by Lutyens, Gotch and Saunders. Impressive marble public halls well worth a look.

Monument Db
Fluted Doric column topped by golden globe rising from flames designed by Wren to commemorate Great Fire of 1666. Completed in 1677, spiral staircase of 311 steps leads to 202ft high balcony. Views from balcony over City. Panels at base record story of fire. Basrelief of Charles II giving City protection.

representing its changing face over centuries. Illuminated tableau of Great Fire of 1666. Royal memorabilia. Leatherwork shows craft from original guilds including Roman footwear, ancient purses and saddlery.

National Postal Museum Bc
One of world's great philatelic collections displayed in purpose-designed museum, established in 1965. Phillips Collection covers 19th-century British stamps. Post Office's own collection goes from original Penny Black to present day, incorporating some 250,000 stamps world wide, including all stamps issued under British Post Office control since 1840. Proof of first printing plate for Penny Black also on display.

National Westminster Tower Dc
Bank's headquarters, 600ft high with 52 storeys, completed in 1980. Original design by Richard Seifert, but later redesigned to include City of London Club which became listed building after construction of tower had started.

CATHEDRAL CHOIR *The gilded ceiling of St Paul's Cathedral illuminates the choir below, with its finely carved stalls by Grinling Gibbons.*

Mount Pleasant Sorting Office Ae
One of largest letter-sorting offices in world, directing more than 3 million items per day.

Museum of London Bc
Built on top of west gate of Roman fort, museum incorporates old Guildhall and London Museums, and Museum of Leathercraft. Displays include relics of London since Roman days, with galleries

Old Doctor Butler's Head Cc
Inn founded in 17th century and rebuilt after Great Fire and again after World War II. Founded by court physician to James I.

Old Mitre Ac
Tavern built by Bishop of Goodrich in 1546 for use of servants. Inscribed mitre on side of inn records this fact. Small rooms and dark wall panelling preserved. It is said Elizabeth I drank here.

Olde Wine Shades Cb
Claimed to be London's oldest wine house, dating from 1663 – date found on cistern in garret. Early Victorian frontage has been well preserved. Interior noted for its low ceilings.

Patent Office Ac
Late 19th-century building houses offices which have over 40,000 applications for patents annually.

Prince Henry's Room Ab
Upstairs room in 17th-century tavern, has Tudor panels with ornate strapwork, Jacobean ceiling with centre decoration of Prince of Wales feathers, and initials PH. Filled with Samuel Pepys mementos.

Printing House Square Bb
Henry Moore's huge sundial dominates forecourt of 1960s building designed by Llewellyn Davies. Now home to Continental Bank House.

Prudential Assurance Building Ac
Last of London's great Gothic-revival buildings. Red-brick and terracotta structure has gables, lancet windows and central tower with pyramid roof – designed by Waterhouse in 1879. Museum covers history of early Holborn and of industrial life assurance.

Public Record Office Ac
Historic documents displayed in small museum housed in grand neo-Gothic building of 1851-71. Exhibits, some dating from the Norman conquest, include the Domesday Book – written in the 11th century, log of HMS *Victory* and Shakespeare's will.

Royal Exchange Cc
Present building opened in 1844 after 300 years of trading on site. Classical building, designed by Tite, has Turkish pavement and wall scenes of London's history.

St Andrew, Holborn † Ac
Sculpted charity schoolboys stand above entrance to Wren church of 1687 – restored after wartime damage. Interior is panelled and has Corinthian columns and green-and-gold ceiling with stained-glass lunette. Pulpit dates from 1752.

St Bartholomew's Hospital Bc
London's oldest hospital was founded 1123. Reconstructed in 1730-66 by Gibbs. Great staircase has Hogarth murals. Great Hall contains portraits by Holbein, Kneller, Reynolds and Millais. Pathological museum.

St Bartholomew the Great † Bc
Founded in 1123 on land granted by Henry I for church of which present building was chancel and hospital. Tower dates from 1628. The clerestory, in Perpendicular style, dates from 1405.

St Benet's Welsh Church † Bb
Church built by Wren in 1677 has red-brick tower and white quoins. Topped by lead cupola, lantern and spire. Carving of Charles II's Royal Arms over tower door.

St Botolph's Church, Aldersgate † Bc
Church rebuilt by Nathaniel Wright in 1788-91. East window, by John Pearson, depicts *The Agony in the Garden*. Front of church was stuccoed in 1831.

St Botolph's Church, Aldgate † Ec
Present church was built in 1744. Renatus Harris organ of 1676. Plague pits in churchyard.

St Botolph without Bishopsgate † Dc
Much restored church, rebuilt in 1725-8. East window depicts *The Risen Christ*.

St Bride's Church † Ac
Layered spire, 226ft high, rises above this Wren church completed in 1703. Crypt reveals Roman and Saxon remains.

St Bride's Institute Bc
Complete history of letterpress printing and lithography in building opened for technical education in 1891. Types, presses, blocks and plates feature among equipment on display.

St Dunstan in the West † Ac
Gothic-revival, octagonal church, built 1829-33, has 130ft tower. Includes monuments and bells from earlier church.

St Etheldreda's Church † Ac
Built as chapel in 1793. Crypt dating from 1251. Cloister was added in 1373.

St Helen's Church † Dc
Said to have more monuments than any other London church. Choir stalls date from 15th century and font from 17th. Memorial window to Shakespeare.

BRIDGE OF SIZE *The Act authorising the building of Tower Bridge stipulated an opening span with 200ft clear width and headroom of 135ft.*

destroyed in Great Fire of 1666. At centre of cathedral is great dome, painted with incidents in life of St Paul. Viewing gallery offers broad views of City. Whispering Gallery is reached by 259 stairs; acoustics

Salvation Army Headquarters Bb
Building on two ground levels was opened by Queen Elizabeth, Queen Mother, in 1963.

Shakespeare Globe Theatre and Museum ⛪ Ca
Replica theatre to replace original version, dating from 1599, where Shakespeare's plays were first performed. Museum on site of 16th-century bear-baiting ring illustrates London and theatre of Shakespeare's time. Displays include collection of old Bankside entertainment material and replica of 1616 stage.

Smithfield Market Bc
London's premier wholesale meat market housed in glass, iron-framed building with domed towers, dating from 1868.

Southwark Cathedral † Ca
Last of four churches on present site – earlier ones destroyed by fire. Wide variety of stonework characterises this early 13th-century building, which was parish church until 1905. Early English choir, French Gothic vaulting, shafts and ribs. Present nave dates from 1897. Impressive oak effigy of knight dates from about 1275. Three-tiered stone altar screen above High Altar was donated by the Bishop of Winchester in 1520.

Spanish and Portuguese Synagogue Dc
Rectangular building dating from 1701 has two tiers of windows, flat ceiling and three galleries. Contains handwritten scrolls, raised Tebah and brass chandeliers.

Spitalfields Ed
Georgian buildings flank Fournier and Elder streets. Building at corner of Fournier Street and Brick Lane built as Huguenot chapel in 1743, later used as synagogue, now mosque.

Staple Inn Ac
Row of half-timbered houses, built 1586-96, houses Institute of Actuaries. Arched entrance leads to inn, which surrounds central courtyard. Hall has original hammerbeam roof. Nearby Great Hall of Barnard's Inn has panelling and heraldic stained glass.

Stock Exchange Dc
Trading activities of largest Stock Exchange in Europe take place in 1972 stone and glass buiding.

Story of Telecommunications Bb
Exhibition at Baynard House displays telecommunications technology from inventions of Bell and Marconi to microwave towers, optical fibre and satellite transmissions. Forecourt contains sculpted pillar by Kindersley.

Temple Bar Ab
Dragon mounted on pedestal marks boundaries of cities of London and Westminster. Bar stood here from 1301 to 1672.

Temple Church † Ab
Round church, dating from 1185, is finest monument in England to Knights Templar. Design combines Gothic and Romanesque characteristics. Inside, Purbeck marble pillars support arches. Church has been completely restored over years.

Temple of Mithras ⚱ Cb
Roman temple to Persian god, Mithras, dates from 2nd century – excavated in 1954.

Tower Bridge ✥ Ea
Gothic-towered, hydraulically opening road bridge has been world landmark since 1894. High-level footbridge is reached by lift or 200 steps. Museum has diagrams, models, films and original equipment which lifted 1100 ton bascules until 1976. Panoramic views from walkway.

Tower Hill Pageant Db
Electronic aids tell 2000 year story of River Thames' part in London's development as city and port. Computer-controlled cars take

visitors through tableaux depicting different periods in London's history. The waterfront Finds Museum displays objects dating back to Roman times, uncovered in local excavations.

WHITE TOWER *The Norman keep in the Tower of London.*

Tower of London Eb
Medieval fortress dominated by White Tower dating from 1097. Crown Jewels housed here. Chapel Royal dates from 1520. State enemies were brought through Traitors' Gate for execution. The presence of the Tower's ravens is believed to guarantee its invincibility.

Trinity House Eb
Headquarters of the organisation responsible for coastal navigation, including lights, buoys, pilots, housed in 18th-century building. Rebuilt Ionic pillars and interior under fine weather vane.

Unilever House Bb
Vast, pillared stone building designed by Lomax-Simpson and completed in 1931 carries huge sculptures by Reid-Dick.

Vintners' Hall Cb
Hall, rebuilt 1671, contains panelled courtroom of City Company of Wine Importers. Staircase dating from 1673 leads to 19th-century drawing room.

Wesley's House † ⛪ Cd
Restored Methodist church built in 1778. Contains pulpit from which John Wesley preached. Wesley's tomb is in graveyard. Next door is 18th-century house in which Wesley lived for 12 years – now museum containing much original furniture.

METHODIST MUSEUM *Wesley's House contains many original items of furniture belonging to John Wesley, the founder of Methodism.*

CORONATION CHAPEL *Medieval monarchs spent a night of prayer before their coronation in St John's Chapel in the Tower of London.*

St Margaret Pattens † Db
Black polygon spire rises from square tower to gilded weather vane. Inside is reredos carved with fruit and flowers.

St Mary-le-Bow Church † Cc
Famous for Bow Bells. Church restored after World War II bombing of Wren's design, which incorporated Saxon and Norman church ruins. Weather vane is 8ft 10in long dragon.

St Paul's Cathedral † Bc
Cathedral stands 365ft high and 515ft long. It was designed by Wren after previous cathedral was

allow whisper uttered on one side to be clearly heard on other – more than 100ft away. Choir stalls carved by Grinling Gibbons. Statue of St Paul by Francis Bird is 12ft high. High altar was consecrated in 1958, after previous one was damaged by bombing in 1940. Memorials include those of Nelson and Wellington. In south aisle is artists corner, with monuments to Blake, Landseer, Reynolds and Turner. Chapel dedicated to 28,000 fallen United States servicemen. Wren's epitaph, in Latin, is beneath dome: 'Reader, if you seek his monument, look around you.'

All Saints Church † Dd
Ionic columns support portico at entrance to 19th-century church built of Portland stone. Designed by Charles Hollis, it was damaged during Blitz and restored in 1950s.

Amicable School House Bc
Doorway of three-storey, 18th-century school is crowned with carvings of two schoolchildren.

Angel Inn Bc
Riverside pub, dating from 16th century; balcony has views up Thames to Tower Bridge. Trap door in kitchen used by smugglers.

Ballast Quay Eb
Terrace of early Georgian houses facing River Thames. Number 21 was the harbourmaster's office in 19th century.

Billingsgate Fish Market Dd
Wholesale and retail market moved in 1982 from City to new 13½ acre site in West India Docks. Original market bell was also moved. Clock in centre of main market is copy of one that stood in old market.

Brunel's Engine House ✿ Bc
Former pump house at entrance to world's first underwater tunnel – built by Marc Brunel between 1824 and 1843 to connect Rotherhithe with Wapping. History of tunnel and restored steam engine displayed in pump house.

Burrells Wharf Db
Wharf was site of launching of Isambard Brunel's huge iron ship *Great Eastern* in 1858.

Butler's Wharf Ac
Bermondsey riverside warehouses have been converted into speciality shops, workshops, leisure facilities and housing.

Canary Wharf Dc
Vast modern office blocks, including 800ft high No.1 Canada Square, the United Kingdom's tallest building, tower above waters of West India Docks. When completed, it will be Europe's largest commercial development, providing some 12 million square feet of offices, shops, restaurants and leisure facilities.

Charlton House Ga
Jacobean red-brick house built for tutor of James I's son Henry, and now used as community centre and library. Orangery, stables and park survived World War II Blitz, but north wing of house had to be completely rebuilt.

Cherry Garden Pier Ac
Recently landscaped pier. Old riverside dock buildings are being converted for housing.

Coldharbour Dc
Street on riverfront flanked by 19th-century houses where many officials of West India Company once lived. Nelson said to have stayed at No.3.

Cutty Sark ⚓ Db
Launched in 1869, was fastest tea clipper in her time, able to achieve 363 miles a day, now restored as museum. Ship has hull 212ft long and mainmast 145ft high. The 10 miles of rigging and crosstrees

THE DOCKLANDS AND GREENWICH

The vast system of docks that had made London the world's largest port during the 19th century fell into disuse after the 1960s, but developments in the 1980s have now turned the area into a major business and leisure centre. Careful restoration has, however, ensured that many of the old dockland buildings will remain as reminders of London's busy trading past.

TALL STOREY *Canary Wharf in West India Docks includes the country's highest commercial building, and has its own piazza and waterside walks.*

once carried nearly an acre of sail. Naval memorabilia and world's largest collection of painted figureheads are on display.

CUTTY SARK *Ship once sped from Shanghai to London in 107 days.*

Cutty Sark Tavern Eb
Bow-windowed pub built in 1804 on site of much earlier inn.

Design Museum 🏛 Ac
Bright-white museum on Butler's Wharf devoted to 20th-century mass-produced goods from children's toys to cars and furniture. Displays explain how and why mass-produced consumer goods work and look as they do and how design contributes to quality of daily life. One gallery for displays of latest consumer products around the world.

Docklands Light Railway
Overground light railway which links Bank and Stratford with Island Gardens at tip of Isle of Dogs. First phase of the railway opened by HM The Queen in 1987. Terminus is at Island Gardens, and architecture influenced by curving lines of Old Royal Observatory across river.

Docklands Visitor Centre ☑ Dc
Information and exhibition centre. Operates regular coach tours, helicopter rides and river cruises.

Dreadnought Seamen's Hospital Da
Building was designed in 1763 by James 'Athenian' Stuart. Hospital is now closed.

East Greenwich Pleasaunce Fb
Royal Naval burial ground since the 19th century, to which many bodies from old Infirmary Burial Ground attached to the Naval Hospital were moved.

East London Mosque Ae
Modern mosque where more than 3000 Muslims worship at regular Friday service.

Fan Museum 🏛 Da
Two restored town residences house 2000-strong collection of 17th and 18th-century fans and fan leaves in what is said to be world's only museum devoted entirely to fans.

Financial Times Building Ed
Award-winning building by Nicholas Grimshaw makes original use of glass and aluminium. Printing presses viewed through 320ft long walls of glass.

Gipsy Moth IV ⚓ Db
Ketch, 53ft long, was home to then 66-year-old Francis Chichester for 226 days while he singlehandedly circumnavigated the world during 1966-7.

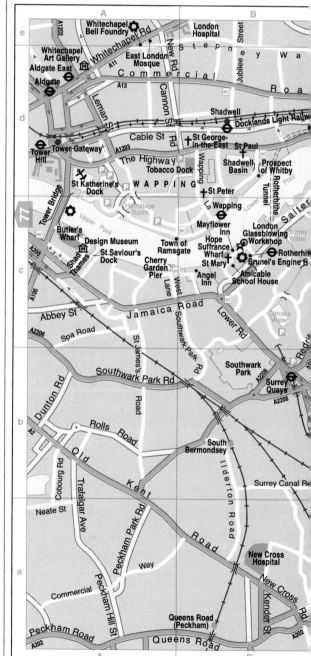

COOL SHOW
A delicately made 18th-century fan in the Docklands Fan Museum.

The Grapes Cd
Public house with good views of River Thames, where Charles Dickens gathered material and drew inspiration for his novel *Our Mutual Friend*.

Greenland Dock Cc
Built in 1700s, dock is largest surviving stretch of water belonging to once-extensive Surrey Docks. Entrance lock still has many original features. Now popular venue for water sports.

Greenwich Markets Da
Stalls along Burney Street sell antiques, while covered market off Nelson Road and William Walk sells craft goods. Weekends only.

Greenwich Park Ea
Park comprises 180 acres of flower gardens, chestnut avenues and woods sloping down from Greenwich Hill towards River Thames. Area laid out for Charles II by Le Nôtre, landscape gardener to Louis XIV of France. Panoramic views from top of hill across Docklands to City.

Greenwich Pier Db
Landing stage for river bus from Westminster, Charing Cross or the Tower of London.

Greenwich Theatre Ea
Restored old music-hall theatre now houses gallery, restaurant, jazz club and theatre.

Greenwich Tunnel Db
Foot tunnel linking Greenwich with Isle of Dogs. Built between 1897 and 1902 by Sir Alexander Binnie for dockers working in West India Docks.

The Gun Dc
Pub which took its name from opening of West India Docks Import Dock in 1802, when first ship *The Henry Aldington* fired her guns as she hauled into view.

Hope Suffrance Wharf Bc
Craft workshops have brought life back to several 19th-century warehouses in notable conservation area of Rotherhithe.

Island Gardens Db
Gardens, covering 2½ acres, have been open to public for nearly 100 years. Christopher Wren thought this was the best viewpoint for Greenwich Hospital, now Royal Naval College.

Lavender Pond Pump House and Nature Park Cd
Site of old Lavender Dock pumping station is now preserved as 2½ acre refuge for wildlife.

FORM FOLLOWS FUNCTION *See how everyday objects can be made more comfortable and beautiful at the Design Museum, part of Butler's Wharf.*

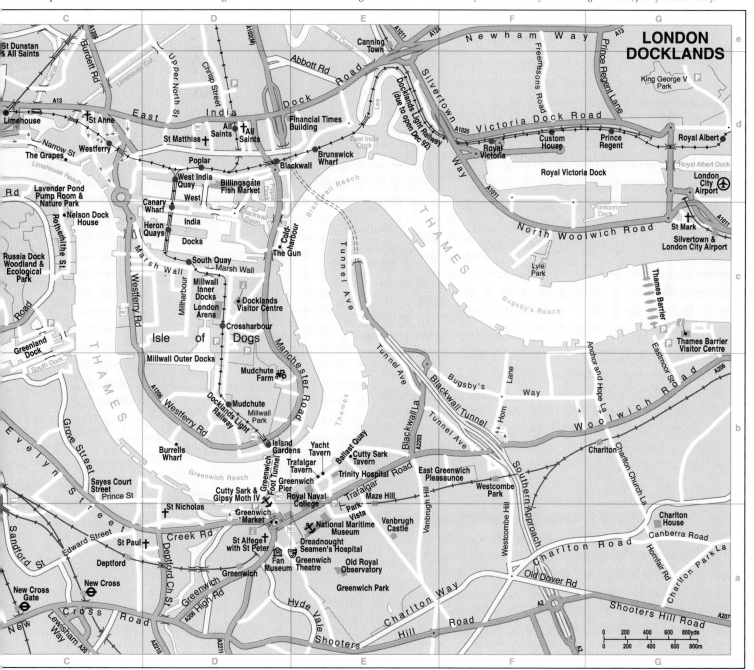

STAR GAZING *The Old Royal Observatory and, in the centre of the picture, Flamsteed House, home of the English astronomer John Flamsteed, who became the first Astronomer Royal in 1675.*

London Arena Dc
Concert venue for popular and classical music, sports and exhibitions centre. Seating 12,000, it stands on site of former Olsen Line shed at Millwall Docks. Opened in 1989.

London Glassblowing Workshop Bc
Riverside craft workshop where original, hand-blown glass objects are produced, from paperweights to water jugs and vases. Constantly changing exhibits on display in showroom are for sale to the public.

London Hospital Ae
Started as 30 bed infirmary in Moorfields in 1740 and moved to present site in 1759, to become one of the finest buildings of its time. Largely rebuilt since World War II.

Mayflower Inn Bc
Public house, jutting into and offering fine views up and down the River Thames. Dates in part from the 16th century. Said to have been named after the *Mayflower*, the ship in which Pilgrim Fathers set out on historic voyage to New World in 1620. Relevant mementos dating from 17th century on display; licensed to sell British and American stamps.

Millwall Docks Dc
Docks constructed in 1868 to accommodate ships carrying grain from Baltic. Offices of *The Daily Telegraph* and associated newspapers have most up-to-date printing works in world.

Mudchute Farm Db
Pergolas lead to park large enough to hold riding school, farm animals, apple orchard and allotments. Vegetables grown on mud dredged from nearby Millwall Dock and left to settle and dry in special beds – hence unusual name of farm.

National Maritime Museum Ea
Museum incorporates Palladian villa – earliest English example of Palladian architecture – known as Queen's House, built for James I's wife, Anne. Famous Tulip Staircase still stands exactly as Inigo Jones designed it. Displays and models arranged in chronological order trace Britain's maritime history from Tudor times to the 19th century. Large collection of portraits and seascapes, including some by Turner, Hogarth and Reynolds. Nelson's bloodstained uniform is showpiece of Battle of Trafalgar display. Preserved navigational instruments and charts. Barges once belonging to Mary II and Frederick Prince of Wales can be seen in Barge House.

Nelson Dock House Cc
Mansion and dry dock, dating from 18th century, owned by shipbuilders and named in early 1800s after Battle of Trafalgar.

New Cross Hospital Ba
Built in 1877 specifically to treat people who had contracted smallpox – endemic at the time. Now attached to Guy's Hospital.

Old Royal Observatory Ea
Observatory designed by Sir Christopher Wren in 1675. Brass rail marks spot through which Greenwich Meridian runs. Meridian Building contains array of historic telescopes, including largest refracting telescope in United Kingdom. Red ball on roof of building lowered from top of mast each day at 1pm Greenwich Mean Time as time check for vessels on River Thames. Caird Planetarium offers astronomical lectures to the public. House of Astronomer Royal John Flamsteed shows his living quarters furnished with 17th-century belongings, and galleries where he used to work.

Park Vista Ea
Road flanked by several buildings dating back to the 18th century, including the Plume of Feathers public house.

Prospect of Whitby Bd
Said to be oldest Thames-side pub – dating from 1520 – with original, early 16th-century panels, beams and flagstones still intact. Has

Russia Dock Woodland and Ecological Park Cc
Part of Surrey Docks filled in and transformed into the country's largest man-made ecological park. Special features include 65ft high artificial hill, woodland, footpaths, ponds, scrub, grassland and wetland.

St Alfege with St Peter Church † Da
Church designed by Nicholas Hawksmoor and built on site of much earlier one. Altarpiece by Sir James Thornhill was restored after World War II. The church

SAILOR'S PRAYER *The chapel at the Royal Naval College at Greenwich was destroyed by fire in 1779 and redesigned by James 'Athenian' Stuart.*

nautical pictures and souvenirs. Excellent views across river from terrace. Artists Whistler and Turner were customers.

Rotherhithe Street Cc
One of London's longest riverside streets, fringed with 19th-century warehouses. Had water on both sides until Surrey Docks filled in during 1970s.

Rotherhithe Tunnel Bd
Tunnel, built between 1904 and 1908 to link Rotherhithe with Shadwell, extends 4860ft.

Royal Naval College Eb
Formerly Royal Hospital for Seamen, buildings were designed by Sir Christopher Wren and Nicholas Hawksmoor, commissioned by William and Mary. Hospital closed in 1869 and Royal Naval College moved to this site four years later. Refectory, known as Painted Hall, and Chapel were both furnished with cupolas. Walls of Painted Hall are painted to give illusion that pillars support roof. College is now used as naval university for NATO officer training.

Royal Victoria Dock Fd
Windsurfing boards, canoes and sailing boats have replaced ocean-going ships in one of London's largest docks, opened in 1855.

Major commercial, residential and leisure developments have been planned for area.

registers, which can be viewed by appointment, give fascinating picture of London life in the 17th and 18th centuries.

St Anne's Church † Cd
Stepped, square tower of Docklands' major church can be seen for miles and is distinctive landmark around Limehouse area. Designed by Nicholas Hawksmoor in early 18th century, built between 1712 and 1730. Interior destroyed by fire in 1850, severely damaged by bombs in World War II, but recently noted for its award-winning restoration. Organ, built for Great Exhibition of 1851 in Hyde Park, is one of the best examples of its kind.

St Dunstan and All Saints Church † Ce
Saxon stone rood is all that remains of earliest church in Stepney, rebuilt in 10th century by St Dunstan. Altered in 15th century and refaced in 19th.

St George-in-the-East Church † Bd
One of Nicholas Hawksmoor's best-known churches – built 1711 – with massive 160ft tower and windows by Joshua Reynolds. Interior burned out in World War II and restored in 1960s. Churchyard laid out as public garden in 1886.

DRINK AND BE MERRY *Dwarfed by the adjacent converted warehouse, the Prospect of Whitby dates back to the early 16th century and is probably the oldest pub along the River Thames.*

NEW MOORINGS *Pleasure craft now fill St Katherine's Dock.*

St Katherine's Dock ⚓ Ad

Thomas Telford's only completed London project, opened in 1828 and spreading over some 25 acres, was first dock to be redeveloped and is now established as one of London's most popular waterside attractions. Quayside buildings occupied by shops, housing, offices, restaurants and pubs, look out at flotilla of bobbing yachts, barges and motorboats. Only original building still standing is 'I' Warehouse, designed by George Aitchison. Other historical features are bowfronted dockmaster's residence, eastern dock footbridge, recessed moorings in dock walls and original bollards at dock entrance. Italianate Ivory House converted into flats and shopping arcade. Historic Ship

ART IN THE STREETS *A brightly coloured mural on a wall at Tobacco Dock shows a typical street scene from the area's busy past.*

Collection at east basin includes lightship, Thames sailing barges and Captain Scott's *Discovery*. Scott's quarters on *Discovery* and those of his officers and scientists have been preserved, together with relics of expedition.

St Mark's Church ✝ Gc

Church designed by S.S. Teulon in 1862 and damaged by fire in 1981. Now being restored as museum of Victorian life.

St Mary's Church ✝ Bc

Brick church, built 1710 on site of medieval church, has octagonal obelisk spire. Huge pillars, supporting barrel roof, are ships' masts encased in plaster. Master of *Mayflower* buried here. His grave disappeared when church was rebuilt, but monument erected to him in 1965.

St Matthias's Church ✝ Dd

Said to be oldest complete building in Docklands – built in 1654 as private chapel for East India Company. Given medieval look in 19th century by S.S. Teulon. Now closed.

St Nicholas's Church ✝ Da

Church, dating from 17th century, built on site of Saxon one. Pillars of entrance gate crowned with laurel-wreathed skulls symbolising victory over death. Interior carvings by Grinling Gibbons. Cherub supporting Jacobean pulpit is thought to have been ship's figurehead.

St Paul's Church, Deptford ✝ Da

Well-restored baroque church designed by Thomas Archer and built 1712-30. Semicircular, porticoed entrance. Huge pillars support intricately carved ceiling.

St Paul's Church, Shadwell ✝ Bd

Brick church, built 1819-20 on site of 17th-century predecessor, erected as thank offering for military victory at Waterloo.

St Peter's Church ✝ Bd

Gothic-style church opened in 1856 to serve area's cholera-ridden poor, but never completed. Restored in 1956. Richly decorated Victorian interior.

St Saviour's Dock Ac

Dock is conservation area where several disused Victorian granaries and mills still stand.

Sayes Court Street Cb

Street where diarist John Evelyn lived, in Sayes Court. Part of Evelyn's gardens converted into public recreation ground, still used today.

Shad Thames Ac

One of few areas in London where Victorian riverside warehouses – linked by bridges and walkways – can still be seen.

Shadwell Basin Bd

New houses now surround basin originally built in mid-18th century. Basin is particularly popular at weekends with tourists and sailing enthusiasts.

Southwark Park Bb

Opened to public in 1869, 63 acre park was formerly an area of market gardens.

Thames Barrier Gc

Movable 1705ft wide barrier built between 1975 and 1982 to protect London from the kind of floods that drowned 14 people in 1928. Barrier comprises curved gates, supported on concrete piers, which can be lowered onto river bed to allow ships to pass over the top of them.

Thames Barrier Visitor Centre ℹ Gc

Videos, working model and an audiovisual presentation in centre illustrate important historical role of capital's river and explain construction of Thames Barrier. Cruise around vast steel gates of barrier takes about 25 minutes. Hallett's painting *Panorama of Bath* stands in rotunda nearby.

Tobacco Dock Bd

Huge complex of shops and entertainments built around 19th-century warehouse once used for storing tobacco. Includes replicas of two 16th-century sailing ships.

Town of Ramsgate Ac

Historic riverside pub with garden where, at low tide, the post can be seen where condemned pirates and thieves were chained up until the tide washed over them three times. Pub's cellars doubled as dungeons where convicts were held before being deported to Australia.

Trafalgar Tavern Eb

Pub with view over River Thames was used by Charles Dickens as setting for *Our Mutual Friend*. Cast-iron balconies were restored in the 1960s.

Trinity Hospital Eb

Almshouses, dating from 17th century, built by the Earl of Northampton. Part of his tomb lies in chapel, which has 16th-century Flemish stained glass.

Vanbrugh Castle Ea

Castle built during early 1700s in medieval style. Designed by architect and playwright Sir John Vanbrugh. Now converted into residential flats.

Wapping Ad

Name said to derive from Saxon settlement of 'Waeppa's people', but this is probably a region to the north of today's Wapping in area which later became known as Wapping Stepney or St-George-in-the-East. New hamlet in parish of Whitechapel called Wapping-on-the-Wose developed when this area of the river began to be built up, and Wapping acquired its narrow, serpentine shape as it followed the River Thames. In 18th century Dr Johnson recommended people to 'explore Wapping' to see 'such modes of life as very few could imagine', a reference to its squalid housing conditions. Population fell from 6000 in 1801 to about 2000 in 1881. Bomb damage in World War II, and closure of docks, wharves and warehouses left area derelict – now recovering fast with major new developments and public gardens on former wasteland. With the demise of Fleet Street, several newspapers are produced here, including *The Times*, *The Sun*, *The Daily Telegraph* and *Today*.

MODERN ARCHITECTURE *The Storm Water Pumping Station on the Isle of Dogs is the winner of several architectural design awards.*

West India Docks Dc

Docks on Isle of Dogs cover some 54 acres of water – designed by William Jessop to be used by merchants of West India Company from 1802 onwards. Docks closed in 1980 and now heart of Docklands' business. Original gateposts frame north-west entrance. Mercury satellite dish stands at Heron Quays.

Whitechapel Art Gallery 🏛 Ad

Turreted Art Nouveau building where sculptor Barbara Hepworth and painter David Hockney first exhibited their work. Mosaic above door is by Walter Crane. Specialises in avant-garde exhibitions. Wholefood restaurant.

Whitechapel Bell Foundry ⚙ Ae

Bells have been cast by this foundry since 1570, and in Georgian buildings on this particular site since 1738. Include Liberty Bell, Bow Bells and Big Ben.

Yacht Tavern Eb

Pub, bombed in World War II, has been rebuilt and furnished with nautical memorabilia.

LONDON'S SHIELD *The distinctive curved metal gates of the Thames Barrier are regularly lowered to the river bed so that ships can pass over them.*

THE THAMES ESTUARY

Harbours, dockyards, old forts and castles line the wide estuary of southern England's great river. They are a reminder of the area's maritime past. Marshland bordering the estuary has been reclaimed for industry and agriculture but much still remains the preserve of wildlife, while the creeks and inlets of the Medway, Blackwater, Crouch and Swale provide havens for yachts and pleasure craft.

Aylesford ⌂✚ Ca
Old houses tumble down steep hillside to Medway, spanned by medieval bridge. Carmelite friary, founded 1284, noted for pottery made by monks. On downs to north, three upright stones and 10 ton capstone form Kit's Coty House, a 4000-year-old Neolithic burial chamber.

Birling ⌂ Bb
Green slopes of North Downs curve down behind little village with 12th-century church. Good starting point for walks along North Downs Way to Trottiscliffe and Neolithic Coldrum Stones, or to Trosley Country Park and wooded North Downs scarp.

Brentwood ⌘ Ae
First staging post on old coaching road from London; fine inn remains in High Street. Good walks through Weald and Thorndon parks with lakes.

Burnham-on-Crouch ⌂ Ee
Quayside, boatyards and old inns echo with nautical talk in the 'Cowes of the east coast'. Georgian High Street with Victorian clock tower. Imposing headquarters of the Royal Corinthian and Royal Burnham Yacht Clubs.

Chatham ⚓⚓⌂☑ Cb
Explore birthplace of Britain's great fighting ships at The Historic Dockyard; Georgian and early Victorian dockyard with galleries, demonstrations and craft show. Audiovisual presentation at Visitor Centre where models trace dockyard's 400-year history. Ropery is one of the longest brick buildings in Europe, almost a quarter of a mile. Napoleonic fortress of Fort Amherst, built 1756.

Chelmsford ✝⌂✿☑ Cf
County town of Essex. Cathedral Church of St Mary the Virgin built around 1420. County Museum contents range from art to militaria. Essex Regiment Museum in same building. Fine Victorian railway viaduct.

Cobham ⌂⌂ Bb
Favourite haunt of Charles Dickens; part of *Pickwick Papers* was written in the Leather Bottle Inn. Medieval brasses in church. Fine plasterwork ceiling in 17th-century Owletts mansion.

AUTHOR'S INN *Cobham's Leather Bottle Inn was a haunt of Dickens.*

HEATHER MIXTURE *Conifer spires and cushions of colourful heathers blend together attractively at Great Comp garden in Kent.*

Danbury Common ✿⌘✝ Cf
This medieval common land has remained unchanged for 1000 years. Heather, gorse, bracken, maze of paths and Napoleonic fortifications. Church has notable 13th-century wooden effigies.

Elmley Marshes ✔ Eb
Lagoons, creeks and mud flats beside River Swale play host to thousands of wintering wildfowl. Visit RSPB centre at Kings Hill Farm, about a mile from hides overlooking bird haunts.

Faversham ⚓⌂⌂☑ Fb
Pretty port and market town full of listed buildings, where pilgrims lodged on way to Canterbury. Wooden pillars support 1574 Guildhall and covered market. Chart Mills claims to be world's oldest gunpowder factory. Fleur de Lis Heritage Centre in converted 15th-century inn tells of local lore and landscape. Maison Dieu at Ospringe is early 16th-century building, with displays of Roman burial objects found locally.

Goldhanger ⌂ Ef
Pleasant sea-wall walks lead to unspoilt centre of overgrown farming and fishing village; 500-year-old Chequers Inn has medieval court room.

Gravesend ✝⌘⚓⌂☑ Bc
Walkways and picnic sites on Gordon Promenade overlook busy traffic on Thames. Statue in St George's churchyard marks death of Red Indian princess, Pocahontas, in 1617. Milton Chantry has been chapel of medieval leper hospital, barracks, tavern and arts centre. Wartime bombs recalled in subterranean magazines of 18th and 19th-century New Tavern Fort. Long-distance walkers can embark on Saxon Shore Way and Weald Way from here.

Great Comp ✿ Ba
Outstanding 7 acre garden with lawns, terraces, woodland paths, rare trees and shrubs.

Ingatestone ⌂ Be
Tudor, Georgian and Victorian houses, set off by church's noble red-brick tower. Ingatestone Hall is ancestral home of Petre family, built by Sir William Petre in 1545.

Leigh-on-Sea ⌘✔ Dd
Old fishing village where jellied eels and cockles from Maplin Sands are brought daily to the stalls in cobbled high street. Fine seaside walks.

Maidstone ⌂☑ Ca
Kent's county town with tranquil riverside heart. Fine grey-stone medieval group beside the Medway includes 14th-century Archbishop's Palace, where old stables house antique carriages.

Maldon ✕✝⌂ Df
Beautiful town where fishing boats and stately old Thames barges throng the Hythe. Houses from medieval times line High Street, rising to 13th-century church with triangular tower.

The Mallings ⌂⌘✿☑ Ba
Twin villages, East and West, with Georgian-brick and white-stucco houses. West Malling has impressive Norman keep known as St Leonard's Tower. Startled Saint Inn portrays St Leonard encircled by Spitfires, recalling use of nearby airfield during Battle of Britain. Grotesque faces adorn the 600-year-old tombstones at Norman Church of St Mary.

Marsh Farm Park ⌘ De
Cattle, sheep and pigs on 320 acres of misty marshland between South Woodham Ferrers and River Crouch. Picnic sites, walks.

Meopham Green ⌂⌘✕ Bb
Wide village green was site of the first recorded cricket match in 1778, between local team and Chatham. Converted oast house and restored 1801 smock mill.

SAXON STONES *The church at Minster is among Kent's finest.*

Minster ⌂✚ Ec
Village centre clusters round ancient Church of St Mary and St Sexburga, founded AD 674, one of England's oldest places of Christian worship. Saxon stonework and fine brasses. Abbey gatehouse next to church houses museum of Sheppey history.

Museum of Kent Rural Life ⌂ Ca
Rural life in bygone Kent is brought to life in old farm buildings and fields. Grazing livestock, beehives and herb garden.

Rochester ⌂⌂⌂✝⌂ Cb
Dickens spent much of his childhood here and made it background for many scenes in *Great Expectations* and *Pickwick Papers*. Mr Pickwick stayed at the Royal Victoria and Bull Hotel; Mr Jingle explored Norman castle and cathedral standing side by side above River Medway; both owe their origins to Bishop Gundulf, William the Conqueror's bishop-architect. A Charles Dickens Centre is housed in a 16th-century mansion with relics of the novelist. Old city within medieval walls has richly gabled houses and inns with cobbled lanes.

Sittingbourne ⌂✕ Eb
Thames and Medway barges once made this a busy harbour town; Dolphin Yard Sailing Barge Museum beside Milton Creek recalls great days of noble sailing barges that traded on Thames.

Southend-on-Sea ✿⌂⌂☑ Dd
Funfairs and illuminations at one of Britain's largest seaside resorts, with longest pier in the world at 7000ft. Popular in 19th century, it grew rapidly during Victorian times. In oldest part of town, Prittlewell Priory public park has remains of 11th-century Cluniac priory lurking behind early 19th-century façade. Southchurch Hall – medieval house in moated gardens at heart of modern Southend – survives from 13th century.

Throwley ⌂⌂ Ea
Church with fine 16th and 17th-century tomb chests. Belmont mansion, 18th century, overlooks unspoilt countryside and houses superb collection of clocks.

Tilbury Fort ⌘ Bc
England's best surviving example of 17th-century military engineering, dating mostly from 1670s, with ingenious triple moats surrounding fort on three sides. Small military museum.

Two Tree Island ✔ Dd
Twin towers of ruined 13th-century Hadleigh Castle stand sentinel over windswept salt marsh, mud flats and grassland of nature reserve in Leigh marshes. Lonely haunt of Brent geese and other wintering wildfowl.

Upper Upnor ⌂⌂ Cc
Little village of weatherboarded cottages sloping gently down to water. Restored castle, built 1559, has exhibits from Medway's embattled past.

Wat Tyler Park ⌘ Cd
Dedicated to people of Essex and Kent who took part in 1381 Peasants' Revolt. Water sports and motorboat museum.

Writtle ⌂⌂ Bf
Village with one of the loveliest greens in Essex: duck pond; Tudor and Georgian houses; church and inn. Nearby 400 acre Hylands Park has woods and lakes.

THAMES TRADERS *Hythe Quay at Maldon is lined with traditional cargo vessels which take part in annual sailing-barge races.*

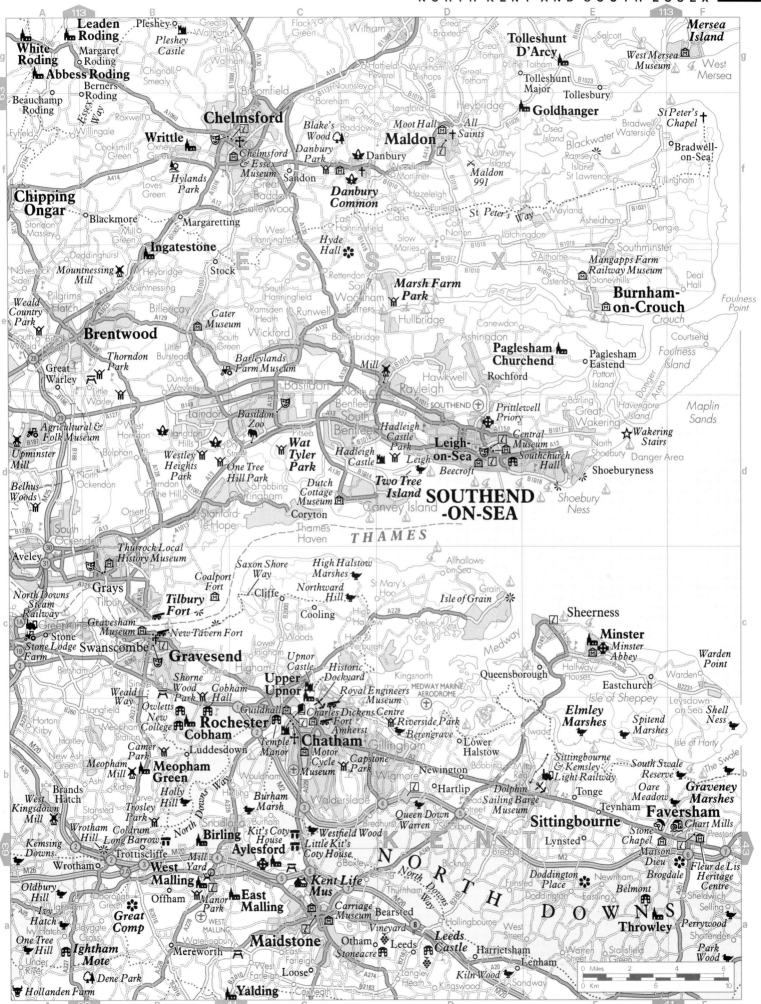

PEMBROKE'S RUGGED PENINSULA

The towering cliffs, sandy coves and thrusting headlands of the Pembroke coast have an unsurpassed beauty, and are of special interest to the naturalist. Though less mountainous than other parts of Wales, the inland scenery is no less impressive, with moorlands rising gently to the Preseli hills. Stone Age forts and Norman castles reflect the area's ancient history.

Abercastle ⛺🏛 Be
Old warehouses and lime kiln recall days when rocky inlet was a coastal trading port, dating back to Tudor times. Old cottages overlook narrow harbour and grey-sand beach. Short walk westwards to Carreg Samson, a Stone Age burial chamber.

Amroth ⛺❀ Eb
Starting point for 168 mile Pembrokeshire Coast Path. Petrified stumps of a forest, drowned 1000 years ago, can be seen on the beach at low tide.

Bosherston ⛺ Ca
Village claims that a dying King Arthur disposed of Excalibur here. White water lilies pave 80 acres of interconnecting ponds, crossed by footbridges; winter haunt for waders and wildfowl.

Caldey Island ✠ Ea
Island with a thriving monastery, reached by boat from Tenby, where Cistercian monks make chocolate, cream and yoghurt. Splendid views of seal colonies from the hill.

SANDSTONE CATHEDRAL *Quietly hidden away in a deep, grassy hollow, St David's is a treasure chest of medieval architecture.*

Cardigan ✝🌀 Ef
Market town at mouth of River Teifi. History goes back as far as 1136. Major port in later centuries. Old quayside warehouses around 12th-century bridge, overlooked by ruined medieval castle.

Carew Castle ⛺🏛 Db
Magnificent ruins of 13th-century castle built by Sir Nicholas de Carew, with Tudor additions. Note striking stone-mullioned windows. Rise and fall of tide on Carew river powers 19th-century tidal mill; only Welsh mill of its kind intact.

Carningli Common ✳ De
Moorland of heather and gorse climbs to rocky peak 1138ft above Newport Bay. Iron Age fort encloses foundations of beehive-shaped huts. Views look across to Cardigan Bay, Cemaes Head and Fishguard.

Cemaes Head ☆ Eg
Awe-inspiring cliffs rise 550ft from sea. Striped dips and peaks formed by layers of mud and sand compressed over millions of years. Astonishing effects best seen at Pen-yr-afr to south-west.

Cenarth ⛺🌀🐟 Ff
River Teifi thunders towards an 18th-century bridge in a series of dramatic waterfalls. Old-world mill, stony cottages and restored smithy. Centre of 'coracle' building – curious fishing craft also used for racing.

Cilgerran ⛺🏛 Ef
Set in beautiful wooded gorge; village is one long street. Romantic 13th-century castle ruins perched on wooded bluff above River Teifi, inspired one of Turner's finest works. Bison, wild boars and other rare breeds at Cardigan Wildlife Park. Safari area.

FISH SIGN *A salmon adorns walls of stone-built Cenarth house.*

Llawhaden ⛺🏛 Dc
Dramatic ruins of 13th-century castle, once a safe refuge for the Bishops of St David's, stands on 200ft wooded bluff above waters of Eastern Cleddau. Decorated archways, vaulted storage rooms, great hall and kitchens survive.

Manorbier ⛺🏛 Da
Limestone ruins of moated 12th-century fortress crown steep sandstone spur above Manorbier Bay. Inner court intact, with vast gatehouse, hall and chapel.

Marloes ⛺🐦 Ab
Superb 1 mile stretch of firm, boulder-strewn sands, backed by rugged cliffs. Gateholm Island accessible at low tide.

Martin's Haven 🏛✠ Ab
Steep-sided valley where Stone Age tribe built a defensive earthwork. Western promontory is a deer park with 1½ mile walk across gorse and heather.

Milford Haven ⚓⛵ Cb
Natural beauty and industrial activity combine in a splendid 20 mile harbour, hailed by Nelson as best in the world. Surrounded by 70 miles of sheltering coastline, and sailed by giant oil-tankers. Refinery lights at night make for a dramatic skyline.

Minwear Wood 🌀🏛 Dc
Red oaks and conifers are winter roosting haunt for migratory starlings, and badgers roam after dark. Wood once supplied fuel for Black Pool ironworks. Attractive Black Pool Mill stands at northeast corner.

Mynydd Preseli ✳▲ Ee
Peaks of shattered rock rise to 1760ft at Foel Cwmcerwyn, with views across Pembroke peninsula as far as Devon coast. Here, massive stone blocks were prised from the hillside and used to build Stonehenge, 240 miles away.

Nevern ⛺✠ De
Tranquil village in secluded valley washed by River Nyfer. Cottages on banks linked by medieval bridge. Norman church with a richly carved Celtic cross and so-called 'Bleeding Yew' that drips a blood-red sap.

Pembroke ⛺🏛 Cb
Small town with one of the largest and most impressive Norman castles in Britain, standing on promontory in Pembroke river, ringed with walls and towers. Keep is 75ft high. Reputed birthplace of Henry VII in 1457.

Pen Caer ✳✳ Bf
Rugged, windswept peninsula of volcanic rock crowned by an Iron Age fort. Cliffs tower to 400ft at Pwllderi. Exhilarating walk to Strumble Head lighthouse.

Pendine ⛺ Fb
Six miles of hard flat sand where many land-speed record attempts were made in 1920s, including Sir Malcolm Campbell who pushed record to 146.16 mph in 1924.

Picton Castle ✿🏛 Dc
This 12th-century castle houses the Graham Sutherland Gallery; frequent visitor and artist of Pembrokeshire coastline (1903-80). Twisted trees on banks of Eastern Cleddau appear in his paintings.

Ramsey Island Ad
Holy island created in legend by 6th-century Breton saint, Justinian, who axed it from the mainland to ensure solitude. Summer boat trips from Porthstinian. Watch sea for bobbing seals.

ROCK SPURREY *This pretty herb abounds on Pembroke's cliffs.*

St Brides Haven 🐦 Ac
Remote cove of red-speckled sand. Ruined lime kiln and rusted mooring rings recall days of coastal trade until late 19th century. Churchyard of Norman St Bride has tombs set in cliffs.

St David's ✝⛺✠🐦 Ad
Britain's smallest city. Secluded cathedral founded by St David in 6th century lies in hollow. Bones in casket behind the High Altar are believed to be his. Present cathedral begun in 12th century. Ruined medieval Bishop's Palace.

St Florence ⛺🏛 Db
Timeless little village with unexpected origins; Norman kings

encouraged people from Flanders to settle here during 12th century. Set in tangle of narrow lanes, quaint cottage near church has two enormous Flemish-style chimneys. Several buildings have stone-framed doorways with pointed arches. Parish church, 12th century, has tall, plain tower.

Saundersfoot Eb
Broad quays, where coal was once loaded for export, form fine Welsh yachting centre. Wide sands sheltered from westerly winds. Coastal path leads to seaside hamlet of Wiseman's Bridge.

Skomer Island 🐦 Ab
Nature reserve, 720 acres, for hundreds of thousands of sea birds; puffins, razorbills, guillemots, kittiwakes, shags and fulmars. Watch for grey seals sprawled on rocks. Two miles south, red-sandstone mass of Skokholm is another island sanctuary.

A

Lleithyr Farm Museum
St David's Head ✳
Whitesands Bay
St Non's Chapel
Porthstinian
St David's
St Justinian
Bishop's Palace
Farm Park
Marine Life Centre
Ramsey Island
Skomer Island 🐦
Martin Haven
Wooltack Point
Deer Park
Gateholm Island
Skokholm Island
PEMBROKESHIRE

Dinas Head ✳✝ Df
Once an island, an immense table of rock forms the headland, ending in 465ft high cliffs. Path leads to pretty cove of Cwm-yr-Eglwys, which has remains of a small church, destroyed by hurricane in 1859.

Elegug Stacks ☆ Ca
Massive limestone pillars owe their Welsh name to nesting guillemots ('heligog' in Welsh). Official bird sanctuary, also famous for razorbills, kittiwakes and fulmars. Arched Green Bridge of Wales rock lies west.

Fishguard 🌀✳ Ce
Picturesque port where boats ride at anchor in bay surrounded by steep cliffs. Stone recalls last invasion of British soil; in 1797 French invaders surrendered here after mistaking local women in red dresses for red-coated soldiers.

Freshwater West Ba
Beautiful sandy beach edged by rocks. Wind-blown dunes cover Stone and Bronze Age sites. The 60-year-old headland hut was used for drying seaweed to make South Wales delicacy, laver bread.

Tenby ✝🏛⛺🏛✠ Eb
Resort with beautiful harbour overlooked by Georgian and Regency buildings. Medieval castle ruins and town walls. Church dates from 13th century.

Whitesands Bay Ad
One of the finest surfing beaches on the Welsh coast. Said to be spot from where St Patrick sailed to Ireland; memorial tablet next to car park marks site of his chapel.

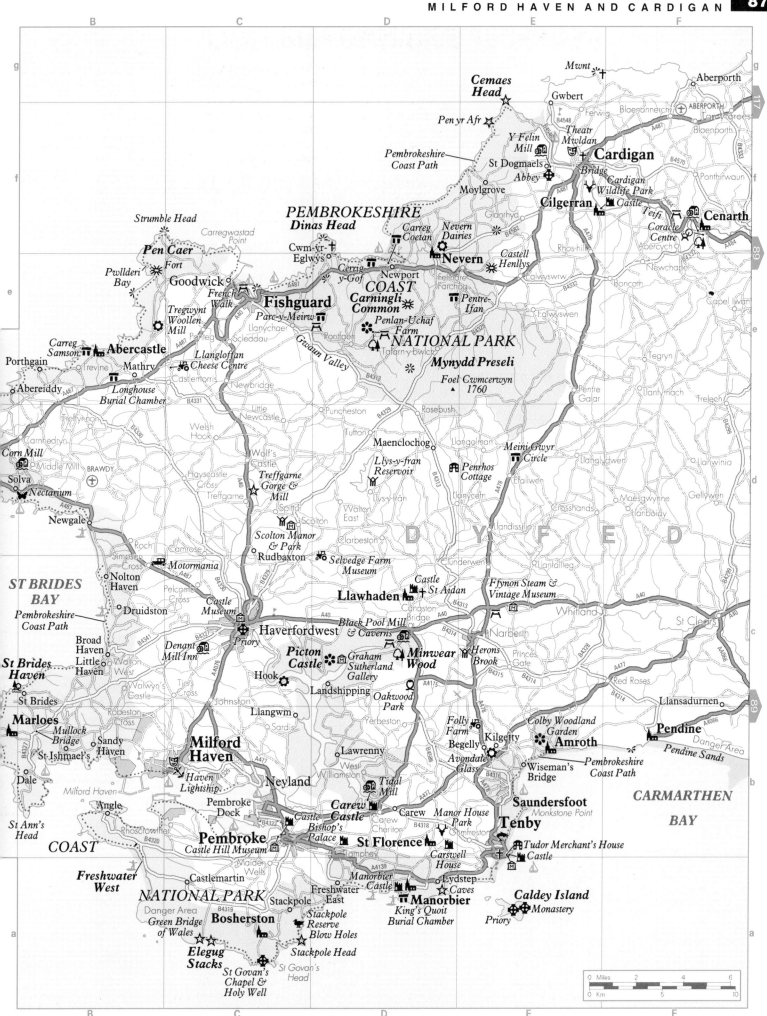

117

89

89

g

f

e

d

c

b

a

B   C   D   E   F

Mwnt — Aberporth
Gwbert — ABERPORTH
Blaenannerch
Blaenporth
Ponthirwaun

Cemaes Head
Pen yr Afr
Y Felin Mill
Theatr Mwldan
St Dogmaels
Abbey
Cardigan
Bridge
Cardigan Wildlife Park
Teifi
Cilgerran Castle
Coracle Centre
Cenarth
Aberçych
Newchapel

Pembrokeshire Coast Path
Moylgrove
PEMBROKESHIRE
Dinas Head
Cwm-yr-Eglwys
Carreg Coetan
Nevern Dairies
Castell Henllys
Glanrhyd
Rhos-hill
Eglwyswrw
Eglwyswen
Boncath
Capel Iwan

Strumble Head
Carregwastad Point
Cerrig y-Gof
Newport
Nevern
COAST
Pentre-Ifan
Felindre Farchog
Llanfyrnach

Pen Caer
Fort
Pwllderi Bay
Goodwick
French Walk
Fishguard
Parc-y-Meirw
Carningli Common
Penlan-Uchaf Farm
Tafarn-y-bwlch
NATIONAL PARK
Mynydd Preseli
Pentre Galar
Tegryn

Tregwynt Woollen Mill
Pantteg
Llanychaer
Rhosfach
▲ Foel Cwmcerwyn 1760

Porthgain
Carreg Samson
Abercastle
Trevine
Mathry
Longhouse Burial Chamber
Llangloffan Cheese Centre
Castlemorris
Newbridge
Llanwinio

Abereiddy
Treffgarne
Welsh Hook
Little Newcastle
Tufton
Maenclochog
Llangolman
Meini Gwyr Circle
Etailwen
Llandissilio
Crosshands
Llanboidy
Maesgwynne
Gellywen

Carnhedryn
DYFED

Corn Mill
Middle Mill
BRAWDY
Hayscastle Cross
Wolf's Castle
Treffgarne Gorge & Mill
Llys-y-fran Reservoir
Penrhos Cottage
Llandeloy
Crundale
Llandissilio

Solva
Nectarium
Simpson Cross
Treffgarne
Spittal
Llys-y-fran
Clarbeston
Ffynnon Steam & Vintage Museum
Whitland
St Clears

Newgale
Roch
Camrose
Scolton
Walton East
Llandissilio

Motormania
Nolton Haven
Pelcomb Cross
Scolton Manor & Park
Rudbaxton
Clunderwen
Llanfallteg

ST BRIDES BAY
Druidston
Castle Museum
Selvedge Farm Museum
Clunderwen

Pembrokeshire Coast Path
Broad Haven
Little Haven
Walwyn's Castle
Tiers Cross
Denant Mill Inn
Priory
Haverfordwest
Black Pool Mill & Caverns
Castle St Aidan
Llawhaden
Clanaston
Narberth
Princes Gate
Red Roses
Llansadurnen

St Brides Haven
St Brides
Picton Castle
Graham Sutherland Gallery
Minwear Wood
Herons Brook
Marloes
Mullock Bridge
Sandy Haven
St Ishmael's
Hook
Johnston
Landshipping
Oakwood Park
Folly Farm
Begelly
Kilgetty
Colby Woodland Garden
Amroth
Pendine
Danger Area
Pendine Sands

Dale
Milford Haven
Neyland
Llangwm
Sardis
Yerbeston
Avondale Glass
Wiseman's Bridge
Pembrokeshire Coast Path

Angle
St Ann's Head
Haven Lightship
Pembroke Dock
Lawrenny
West Williamston
Saundersfoot
Monkstone Point
CARMARTHEN BAY

COAST
Rhoscrowther
Pembroke
Castle Hill Museum
Castle
Bishop's Palace
Carew Cheriton
Tidal Mill
Carew Castle
Carew
Manor House Park
Gumfreston
Tenby
Tudor Merchant's House
Castle

Freshwater West
Castlemartin
NATIONAL PARK
Stackpole
Freshwater East
Green Bridge of Wales
Bosherston
Stackpole Reserve
Blow Holes
Manorbier Castle
Maiden Wells
Hundleton
Lamphey
St Florence
Carswell House
Lydstep
Caves
Manorbier
King's Quoit Burial Chamber
Caldey Island
Monastery
Priory

Elegug Stacks
St Govan's Chapel & Holy Well
St Govan's Head
Stackpole Head

0 Miles 2 4 6
0 Km 5 10

A COAST OF GOLDEN SANDS

Broad, sandy beaches line Carmarthen Bay, pierced by the wide estuary of the Taf and Tywi rivers. Inland the Tywi flows through fertile valleys, east of which lies the brooding 2632ft Black Mountain. The rocky fist of the Gower peninsula is a secluded world of its own – a land of limestone cliffs, remote bays and mile upon mile of golden sands.

Brechfa ⚓ ⥥ Df
Trout-filled River Cothi flows through this village of stone cottages with creeper-clad pub and Victorian church, hemmed in by dense conifer forests. Ty Mawr, 16th-century manor, now a hotel.

Burry Holms ✳ Cb
Small island off Rhossili Bay with Iron Age fort, reached on foot, two hours each side of low water. Ruins of 12th-century church dedicated to 6th-century hermit, St Cenydd.

Carmarthen ⛪ ⚜ 🏛 ☑ Ce
Town on a bluff above the Tywi, dominated by ruined Norman castle. Site of a Roman amphitheatre off Priory Street, and Roman relics in Carmarthen Museum, east of town.

Carn Goch ✳ Ee
High ridge on which stands an Iron Age hill-fort. Y Gaer fawr, 'The Big Fort', housed tribe and cattle in times of attack. Y Gaer fach, 'The Small Fort', was an outer defence.

Carreg Cennen Castle ⛪ Ed
Crumbling walls of 14th-century fortress on edge of 300ft precipice. Beneath, 1500ft long tunnel leads to cave in cliff. Valley views through tunnel holes.

Caswell Bay ⥥ Da
Sandy bay beneath a shrubby headland. Nearby Bishop's Wood Nature Reserve has cliffs, woods and open grassland. Good variety of birds and mammals breed here.

Cefn Bryn ✳ Da
Bracken-clad ridge of red sandstone with views across Bristol Channel to Exmoor. Footpath leads to 609ft summit.

Cwm Lliedi Country Park ⥥ Dc
Woodlands on the banks of Cwm Lliedi Reservoir, in bowl of landscape known locally as 'Swiss Valley'. Footpath around shore.

Cynwyl Elfed ⚓ 🏛 Be
Village of slate rooftops and colour-washed cottages, set in wooded hills. Chapel of 1792 and 14th-century church restored in Victorian times. Nearby Y Gangell farmhouse has museum commemorating best-known Welsh hymn writer, Reverend H. Elfed Lewis, born there in 1860.

Dolaucothi Gold Mines ⚒ ⥥ ⥥ Ef
Romans mined for gold in hills east of the village. Mines reopened in 1870 and worked until 1938. Exhibition centre of 1930s mining equipment; guided tours of underground workings.

Felin Geri 🏛 Bg
Stone-ground flour is milled in this restored 16th-century water mill on tributary of the River Teifi. Craft workshop and museum of country life.

Ferryside ⚓ Bd
Peaceful coastal village on banks of River Tywi with scenic coast-hugging railway line. Captivating views from beach. Tywi flows through sandbanks and cockle and mussel beds into shimmering Carmarthen Bay.

Gower Farm Museum ⚓ Ca
Old farm buildings house relics of farming life on Gower, including household items, agricultural implements and family life memorabilia spanning 100 years. Farm trail through modern farm.

Gwili Railway ⚞ Ce
Steam trains on standard-gauge railway run through rural setting beside Gwili river. Picnic area and nature trail at Llanwynfan Cerrig.

Kidwelly ✝ ⚓ ⚜ 🏛 Cc
Town dominated by well-preserved 12th-century castle with massive towers. Below, 14th-century bridge spans the little Gwendraeth Fach river. Gothic church dates from late 13th century; once served a Benedictine monastery. Industrial museum displays 18th-century machinery used for tinplate manufacturing.

POET'S CORNER *Dylan Thomas's boathouse in Laugharne, where he wrote much of his best poetry.*

Laugharne ⚓ ⚓ 🏛 Ad
Village with old harbour, where poet Dylan Thomas lived for 16 years; buried in churchyard.

Llandeilo ⛪ Ee
Terraces of houses and cottages stand above 19th-century stone bridge spanning turbulent waters of the Tywi. Romantic ruins of ivy-clad Dynevor Castle on cliff above river. Massive keep dates from 13th century.

Llangennith ⚓ Cb
Springs bubble up from the village green surrounded by gleaming whitewashed cottages. College Farm stands on site of 6th-century monastery founded by St Cenydd. Church lych gate has carved scenes of saint's life.

Llanmadoc Hill ✳ Cb
Sheep and ponies wander over slopes of hill, 609ft above the sea. Superb views over Gower. Iron Age hill-fort, The Bulwark; also scattered cairns marking Bronze Age burial sites.

Llanrhidian ⚓ ⥥ Db
Town on a steep slope overlooking wilderness of tidal salt marsh and sandbanks. Sheep and ponies graze on manna-grass (tamarisk), sea lavender and marsh mallow. Waders and wildfowl abound. Small World Pony Centre breeds miniature ponies at Llwyn-y-Bwch Farm.

Maesllyn Woollen Mill Museum ⚒ ⥥ Bg
Flannel and tweed are produced on the renovated 19th-century machinery in this mill, built 1881. Early hand-operated looms and audiovisual display. Woollen clothes and rugs for sale.

The Mumbles Ea
Seaside resort with wide expanse of sand, lined with hotels, pubs and amusement arcades. Fine views of Swansea Bay from high headland of Mumbles Head.

Museum of Welsh Woollen Industry 🏛 Bf
Ancient and modern weaving methods can be seen in this mill, founded 1900. Story of Welsh woollen industry, spinning and weaving demonstrations, and factory trail around sites.

Newcastle Emlyn ⛪ ⥥ Bg
Small town of elegant buildings, colourful cottages and 1860 town hall. Ruined 15th-century castle stands on grassy hillock above River Teifi.

Oxwich ⚓ ⛪ ⥥ Ca
Village of stone cottages. Church of St Illtyd on rocky ledge above sea dates from 12th century. Oxwich Castle is ruined 1541 manor house. Rare birds and plants at Oxwich Bay, with sand dunes and woodland trails.

Oystermouth Castle ⛪ Ea
Ruined castle built 1280 with walls of pale grey, local limestone. Gatehouse, chapel and great hall top a grassy mound.

Park Woods ⥥ ⛩ ☆ Db
Green Cwm valley runs through Forestry Commission woods. Road for walkers passes Parc le Breos prehistoric burial chamber, covered by 70ft long mound of stones, and Cathole Cave where remains of prehistoric animals have been found.

Paxton's Tower ⛪ Dd
Triangular tower built in 1811 by Sir William Paxton as memorial to Lord Nelson. Breathtaking view of Tywi valley.

Pembrey Country Park ⥥ ⥥ ⥥ ☆ Cc
Grasslands and woodlands, with waymarked nature trails. Forest peters out into magnificent beach.

Pennard ⚓ ⛪ Da
Shifting sands of Pennard Burrows have swallowed most of the original village, leaving surviving Pennard Church (dating from around 1195), and ruined Norman castle, over a mile apart.

Port-Eynon ⚓ ☆ Ca
Enchanting village set in sandy bay, backed by dunes. Culver Hole – cave in cliffs sealed with 60ft wall – is of unknown origin.

Pumsaint ⚓ Eg
Village by bridge over River Cothi. 'Five Saints' stone, near Ogofau Lodge to south-east, is legendary spot where five saints once sheltered from storm. Local church also dedicated to them.

Rhossili ⚓ Ca
Colour-washed cottages perch on cliffs above sandy beach. Church has memorial to Edgar Evans, who died on Scott's 1912 expedition to South Pole. Footpath leads to Rhossili Bay; loved by Dylan Thomas for its wild grandeur.

Swansea ✿ ⛪ ⚔ 🏛 ☑ Eb
Second-largest city in Wales, after Cardiff. Modern shopping centre and large market replace the buildings devastated in Second World War. Maritime and Industrial Museum includes lightship, veteran vehicles and locomotives. Local archaeology and natural history at the university museum. Bishop Henry de Gower built a castle in about 1330. Mostly destroyed during Civil War; ruins tower above the Strand.

Threecliff Bay ⛪ Da
Cliffs and fortresses, eroded by time, overlook a beach cut by Pennard Pill stream. Remains of a castle mound on western side of valley, and 13th-century Pennard Castle ruins to the east.

Weobley Castle ⛪ Cb
Late 13th-century castle, partly destroyed by Owain Glyndwr in rebellion of 1400, and rebuilt as a manor house in late 15th century. Towers and walls enclose the courtyard. Honeycomb of rooms.

Whiteford Sands ⥥ Cb
Secluded sands reached by footpath from Llanmadoc. Dunes behind beach form Whiteford Burrow National Nature Reserve. Plenty of oystercatchers, dunlins, knots, golden plovers, turnstones and redshanks.

Worms Head ☆ ⥥ Ba
Rugged 1 mile promontory is reached by a cliff-top walk from Rhossili. Rocky causeway joins head to mainland, passable only at low tide. At seaward end are natural arch of Devil's Bridge and Blow Hole, through which sea roars in spectacular fashion.

ROCK TRIO *Three fang-like craggy rocks, through which the sea has cut a natural arch, give Threecliff Bay its name.*

PREHISTORIC TOMB *Some two dozen skeletons were found in the Park Woods burial chamber.*

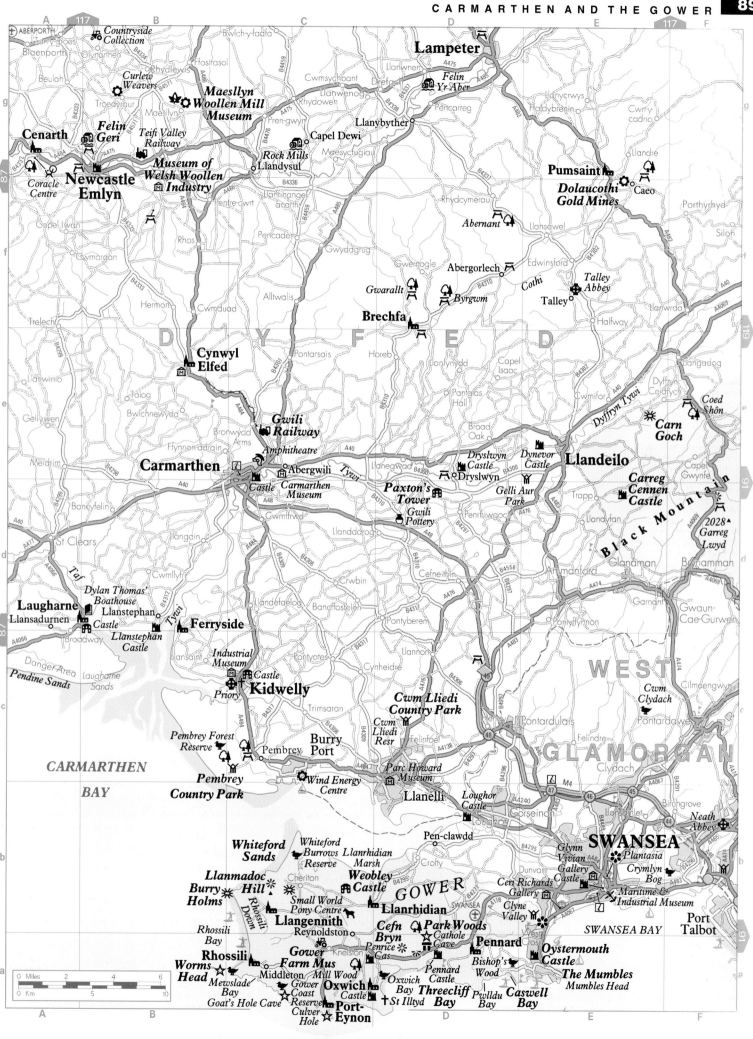

ABERPORTH
Aberffrwd
Blaenporth
Beulah
Troedyraur
Glynarthen
Countryside Collection
Rhydlewis
Curlew Weavers
Maesllyn
Maesllyn Woollen Mill Museum
Felin Geri
Teifi Valley Railway
Cenarth
Coracle Centre
Newcastle Emlyn
Museum of Welsh Woollen Industry
Capel Iwan
Cwmmorgan
Hermon
Trelech
Llanwinio
Llanwinio
Meidrim
Gellywen
St Clears
Laugharne
Llansadurnen
Llanstephan
Broadway
Castle
Danger Area
Pendine Sands
Laugharne Sands
CARMARTHEN BAY

Bwlch-y-fadfa
Ffostrasol
Pren-gwyn
Rhydowen
Llandysul
Rock Mills
Capel Dewi
Maesycrugiau
Llanfihangel ararth
Pentre-cwrt
Rhos
Pencader
Gwyddgrug
Alltwalis
Cwmduad
Bronwydd Arms
Ffynnon ddrain
Bwlchnewydd
Talog
Cynwyl Elfed
Gwili Railway
Amphitheatre
Carmarthen
Abergwili
Castle
Carmarthen Museum
Cwmffrwd
Llangain
Cwmllyfri
Llansaint
Ferryside
Llanstephan Castle
Dylan Thomas' Boathouse
Tywi

Lampeter
Drefach
Cwmsychbant
Llanwenog
Pencarreg
Llanybyther
Maesycrugiau
Pontarsais
Llanegwad
Horeb
Llanfynydd
Llanddarog
Cwmffrwd
Pentre-cwrt
Brechfa
Gwernogle
Gwarallt
Abergorlech
Byrgwm
Cothi
Edwinsford
Talley
Talley Abbey
Halfway
Pumsaint
Dolaucothi Gold Mines
Caeo
Porthyrhyd
Siloh
Llanwrda
Llangadog
Coed Shôn
Dyffryn Tywi
Carn Goch
Capel Gwynfe
Llandeilo
Carreg Cennen Castle
Trapp
Llandyfan
Black Mountain
2028 **Garreg Lwyd**
Brynamman
Gwaun-Cae-Gurwen

DYFED

Rhydcymerau
Llansawel

Dryslwyn Castle
Dryslwyn
Dynevor Castle
Gelli Aur Park
Penrhiwgoch
Cefneithin
Ammanford
Garnant
Pantyffynnon

Crwbin
Bancffosfelen
Pontyberem
Llannon
Cynheidre
Pontyates
Paxton's Tower
Gwili Pottery
Llanddarog
Trimsaran
Kidwelly
Priory
Castle
Industrial Museum
Pembrey Forest Reserve
Pembrey
Burry Port
Pembrey Country Park
Wind Energy Centre
Cwm Lliedi Country Park
Cwm Lliedi Resr
Felinfoel
Pen-clawdd
Parc Howard Museum
Llanelli
Loughor Castle
Gorseinon
Loughor
Crofty
Dunvant

WEST GLAMORGAN

Cwm Clydach
Cwm Clydach
Pontardawe
Clydach
Felindre
Birchgrove
Neath Abbey
SWANSEA
M4
Glynn Vivian Gallery
Clyne Valley
Ceri Richards Gallery
Cefn Bryn
Park Woods
Cathole Cave
Penrice Gas
Plantasia
Crymlyn Bog
Maritime & Industrial Museum
SWANSEA BAY
Port Talbot
West Cross
Bishop's Wood
Pennard
Pennard Castle
Oystermouth Castle
The Mumbles
Mumbles Head
Caswell Bay
Pwlldu Bay

CARMARTHEN BAY

Whiteford Sands
Whiteford Burrows Reserve
Llanrhidian Marsh
Weobley Castle
Llanmadoc Hill
Burry Holms
Cheriton
Small World Pony Centre
Llanrhidian
GOWER
Rhossili Down
Llangennith
Reynoldston
Rhossili Bay
Knelston
Middleton
Mill Wood
Gower Farm Mus
Rhossili
Worms Head
Mewslade Bay
Goat's Hole Cave
Oxwich
Oxwich Castle
Culver Hole
Port-Eynon
St Illtyd
Threecliff Bay
Oxwich Bay

0 Miles 2 4 6
0 Km 5 10

Aberdare ✿ De
One-time coal-mining centre at the head of the Cynon valley. Tramway bridge dated 1811 crosses the Cynon river. Victoria Square has statue of Griffith Rhys Jones, conductor of South Wales Choral Union in 1872.

Aberdulais Falls ☆ Ae
Surging waters of the River Dulais thunder through a boulder-strewn ravine. Visitor centre illustrates time when the falls powered a copper-smelting works.

Afan Argoed Country Park ⛺⚑血🏕 Bd
Scenic vale of woods, moorland and streams, Iron Age forts and settlements among hillside farms. Trails start from Countryside Centre, which houses Welsh Miners' Museum, with pit gear and simulated coal faces.

Black Mountain ☀🏕▲ Af
Scattered treeless peaks soaring to more than 2000ft stretch northwards from Ammanford. Highest peak, 2630ft Fan Brycheiniog, gives enormous views, south to Exmoor, north to Cader Idris.

Brecon Mountain Railway 🚂 Df
Vintage steam engines resplendent in polished maroon livery draw carriages along 2 mile narrow-gauge track in foothills. Panoramic views of Pontsticill Reservoir and 2907ft Pen-y-Fan.

Bridgend 🏰 Cc
Market town straddling the River Ogmore, where the Ogmore, Garw and Llynfi valleys meet. Ruined Norman castle stands on wooded hill above the town.

Coity 🏰🏰 Cc
Village of pale grey-stone houses dominated by ruined 12th-century castle. Effigies of de Turbervilles, builders of the castle, lie in 14th-century church.

Cowbridge Cb
Handsome Norman market town, known as capital of the Vale of Glamorgan, still bustling with trade. Remnants of medieval wall and 13th-century gateway.

Craig Cerrig-Gleisiad ☆ ☙ Cg
Crag, 2000ft high, sweeps round in a three-quarter-mile crescent carved by glaciers. Footpath leads across hollow below.

Craig-y-nos Country Park ⛺♣☆ Bf
Ornamental grounds of 19th-century Gothic mansion, with aboretum and walks by River Tawe. Nearby are spectacular Dan-yr-Ogof Caves, a labyrinth of underground chambers including Cathedral Cave, 70ft high and 160ft long.

Dyffryn Gardens ✿ Db
Landscaped gardens with 50 acres of rare and exotic plants, lily ponds, fountains and statuary. Hothouses contain orchids, palms and cacti.

Ewenny Priory ♣👑 Cb
Wooded lane from village leads to remains of priory founded in 1141 by Maurice de Londres. Massive

AROUND THE RHONDDA VALLEY

The valleys running down from the edge of the Brecon Beacons have taken on a new face with the decline of the coal-mining industry. Grass-covered slag heaps blend with the encircling hills, and terraces of neat houses with brightly painted doors and windows are set like jewels in the hillsides. There are many fine and mostly secluded beaches lining the cliff-backed coast.

walls date from 13th century. Church vault has tomb slabs with Norman inscriptions.

Glamorgan Nature Centre ☙ Bc
Headquarters of the Glamorgan Wildlife Trust, set in oak woodlands beside willow-fringed Park Pond. Displays cover the wildlife of the three Glamorgans.

Kenfig Pool and Dunes ☙ Ac
Underground springs feed lake surrounded by some 100 acres of dunes. Observe wintering duck and whooper swans from hide.

Llantrisant ☙血 Dc
Normans built the ivy-covered 'Tower of the Raven' on a steep hillside above the town. Parish church contains 7th-century 'Resurrection stone'. Town home of the Royal Mint – guided tours in summer.

Llantwit Major ✝ Ca
Village of narrow streets with attractive stone-built whitewashed buildings. St Illtyd founded a monastery here in 5th century. St Illtyd's Church stands on site and has 1000-year-old stone font. Stream runs through village to beach of sand and shingle.

Margam Country Park ⛺♣☀血 Bc
Peaceful 850 acre park with many treasures: Iron Age hill-fort; ruined 12th-century monastery; restored abbey church with windows by William Morris; country house with magnificent 327ft long orangery and parkland decorated with more than 40 sculptures. Margam Stones Museum has inscribed stones and crosses dating from 5th to 11th centuries.

CELTIC PATTERNS *Margam Abbey collection of Celtic crosses and carved stones includes this decorative 10th-century Conbelin cross.*

Merthyr Mawr 🏰🏰 Bb
Thatched stone cottages cluster around the village green and a medieval bridge crosses the Ogmore river. Ruined oratory has pre-Conquest memorials. Close by are ruins of 12th-century Ogmore Castle, and Candleston Castle, a 15th-century fortified manor house.

Merthyr Tydfil ✿血☑ De
Industrial town in heart of the Rhondda, with history of ironworking dating back to 16th century. Mock-Gothic Cyfarthfa Castle houses museum and art gallery with exhibits relating to town's history.

Morlais Castle 🏰 De
Beneath grass-covered mounds and rock-cut ditches lies all that remains of this 13th-century castle. Basement has central pillar and spectacular vaulted arches.

Nash Point ⚓ Ca
Headland with fine views of Gower coast and hills of Devon and Somerset. Two lighthouses, one disused, one working. From cliff top, series of paths follow steep valley down to tiny beach.

Neath ⚓♣血✿ Ad
Town dating back to Roman times; Roman fort of Nidum. Ruins of Norman castle and 12th-century abbey. Five miles north is Cefn Coed Colliery Museum, with re-created mining gallery.

Penscynor Wildlife Park ⅄ Ad
Bird and animal species from all over the world live on a 16 acre wooded hillside. Chimpanzees, penguins and friendly deer. Tropical birds, trout ponds and aquarium.

Pen y Fan ▲ Dg
The whole glory of the Brecon Beacons lies spread out below the 2907ft summit. Top gives fine views that take in Malvern Hills, Bristol Channel and mountains of mid-Wales. Valley below holds small lake, Llyn-cwm-llwch, trapped by glacial rubble.

Porthkerry Country Park ⛺⚓ Da
Imposing, 18-arch 19th-century railway viaduct spans a valley of limestone cliffs, wooded hills and pebble beach. Nature trails and woodland nature reserve.

Pont Melin-fach ☆⚓🏕 Cf
Waters of the River Neath cascade over waterfalls into deep pools. Footpath from Pont Melin-fach, 'Bridge by the Little Mill', follows river downstream, with fine views of falls, pools and caves.

St Hilary 🏰🏰 Db
Quiet and pretty village of pale limestone houses centred around Norman church. Footpath leads to Beaupre Castle; splendid 16th-century mansion with Italianate gatehouse and porch.

St Lythans 🏛✿ Db
Hamlet and Neolithic burial chamber with sturdy stone pillars and capstone. Close by is Tinkinswood tomb, of similar date, 2500 BC, with 40 ton capstone. Bones of 50 people found in it.

Seawatch Centre ☀✿ Ca
Watch the shipping in the Bristol Channel from a 'ship's bridge' in a converted coastguard station. Plot their course on radar and listen in to radio messages.

CABLES AT REST *Massive winding engine preserved at Neath's Cefn Coed Colliery Museum.*

Southerndown 🏰☑ Bb
Cliffs of layered limestone and shale tower above a shingle beach. Footpath leads to Ogmore-by-Sea, on estuary of Ogmore river.

Taf Fawr Valley ⚑☀🏕 Cf
Glorious scenery below 1400ft pass narrowing to sandstone and limestone crags. Three reservoirs set among forests. Garwnant Forest Centre has waymarked trails among the glades.

Taf Fechan Valley ⚑🏕☆ Df
Chain of man-made lakes runs down valley. Woodland trails thread through hillside; one leads to crest of Brecon Beacons.

Vale of Neath Be
Waterfalls, streams and limestone gorges. Merlin Cwrt has 80ft fall. Pontneddfechan has 50ft; possible to walk behind arc of water.

Wales Aircraft Museum ⅄ Da
More than 30 propeller and jet aircraft on display, including Vulcan and Canberra bombers and US Airforce jets.

Welsh Hawking Centre 🦅 Da
Free-flying birds of prey, including kestrels, buzzards, owls and eagles. Displays and nature trail.

Ystradfellte 🏰☆ Cf
Village on River Mellte, with colourful houses grouped around 12th-century church. Mellte flows through Porth yr Ogof cave and over waterfalls.

HIGH TOPS *Carreg Lwyd (2021ft) is one of the highest points in the range of hills known collectively as Black Mountain.*

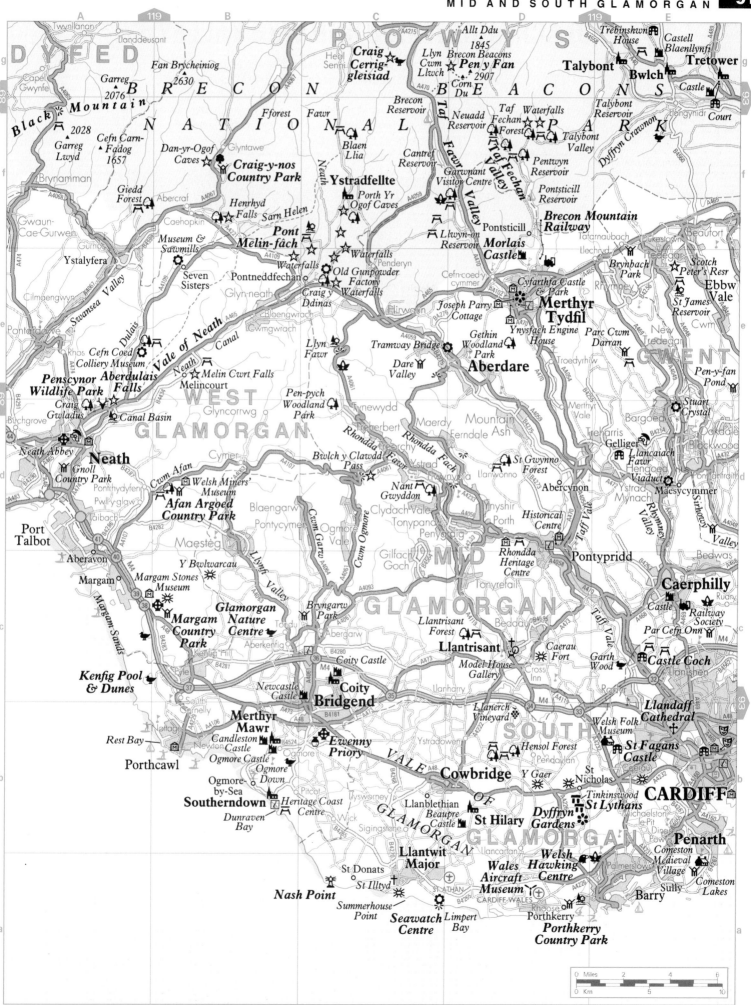

DYFED

BRECON NATIONAL BEACONS

POWYS

Twynllanan
Llanddeusant
Capel
Gwynfe
A4069
Garreg 2076
Gwynfe
Fan Brycheiniog 2630
Black Mountain
Garreg Llwyd 2028
Cefn Carn-Fadog 1657
Dan-yr-Ogof Caves
Craig-y-nos Country Park
Glyntawe
Fforest Fawr
Heol Senni
Craig Cerrig-gleisiad
Allt Ddu 1845
Brecon Beacons
Llyn Cwm Llwch
Pen y Fan 2907
Corn Du
Trebinshwn House
Castell Blaenllynfi
Talybont
Bwlch
Tretower
Castle
Llangynidr
Court

Brynamman
Giedd Forest
Abercraf
Caehopkin
Henrhyd Falls
Sarn Helen
Ystradfellte
Porth Yr Ogof Caves
Blaen Llia
Brecon Reservoir
Cantref Reservoir
Neuadd Reservoir
Garwnant Visitor Centre
Taf Fechan Forest
Taf Waterfalls
Pentwyn Reservoir
Talybont Reservoir
Talybont Valley
Dyffryn Crawnon

Gwaun-Cae-Gurwen
A474
Ystalyfera
Museum & Sawmills
Pont Melin-fâch
Waterfalls
Pontneddfechan
Glyn-neath
Old Gunpowder Factory
Craig y Ddinas
Waterfalls
Penderyn
Llwyn-on Reservoir
Pontsticill
Brecon Mountain Railway
Morlais Castle
Pontsticill Reservoir
Tatarnaubach
Llechrvd
Dukestown
Brynbach Park
Scotch Peter's Resr
St James Reservoir
Beaufort
Tredegar
Ebbw Vale

Seven Sisters
Glyn-neath
Blaengwrach
Cwmgwrach
Hirwaun
Cefn-coed-y-cymmer
Cyfarthfa Castle & Park
Joseph Parry Cottage
Merthyr Tydfil
Ynysfach Engine House
Parc Cwm Darran
New Tredegar
GWENT

Swansea Valley
Rhos
Cefn Coed Colliery Museum
Pontardawe
Cilmaengwyn
Dulais
Vale of Neath
Neath Canal
Blaengwrach
Llyn Fawr
Tramway Bridge
Gethin Woodland Park
Troedyrhiw
Aberdare
Dare Valley
Pen-y-fan Pond
Stuart Crystal

Penscynor Wildlife Park
Aberdulais Falls
Melin Cwrt Falls
Melincourt
Pen-pych Woodland Park
Tynewydd
Treherbert
Maerdy
Ferndale
Mountain Ash
Merthyr Vale
Bargoed
Oakdale
Blackwood

Craig Gwladus
Canal Basin
Buchgrove
Neath Abbey
Gnoll Country Park
Neath
Glyncorrwg
WEST GLAMORGAN
Rhondda Fawr
Bwlch y Clawdd Pass
Cymer
Ystrad
Treorchy
Rhondda Fach
Llwynypia
St Gwynno Forest
Llanwonno
Abercynon
Treharris
Llancaiach Fawr
Hengoed Viaduct
Gelligaer
Llanfrlnfraith
Maesycymmer

Port Talbot
Aberavon
Margam
Cwm Afan
Welsh Miners' Museum
Afan Argoed Country Park
Blaengarw
Pontycymer
Blaengwynfi
Llynfi Valley
Cwm Garw
Cwm Ogmore
Nant Gwyddon
Clydach Vale
Tonypandy
Penygraig
MID
Gilfach Goch
Ynyshir Porth
Tonyrefail
Historical Centre
Rhondda Heritage Centre
Pontypridd
Caerphilly
Castle
Railway Society
Par Cefn Onn

Margam Stones Museum
Maesteg
Margam Nature Centre
Margam Country Park
Bryngarw Park
Abergarw
Aberkenfig
Tondu
GLAMORGAN
Llantrisant Forest
Beddau
Llantrisant
Caerau Fort
Garth Wood
Castle Coch
Llanishen

Kenfig Pool & Dunes
Margam Sands
Kenfig Hill
Pyle
Coity Castle
Newcastle Castle
Coity
Bridgend
Model House Gallery
Cross Inn
Llanharry
Llanharan
Llanerch Vineyard
Welsh Folk Museum
SOUTH
St Fagans Castle
Llandaff Cathedral
CARDIFF

Rest Bay
Porthcawl
Heritage
Newton
Merthyr Mawr
Candleston Castle
Ogmore Castle
Ewenny Priory
Ogmore
Ystradowen
Hensol Forest
Pendoylan
Y Gaer
St Nicholas
Tinkinswood
St Lythans
Dyffryn Gardens
Michaelston-le-Pit

Southerndown
Ogmore Down
Ogmore-by-Sea
Heritage Coast Centre
Pitcot
Tysworney
VALE OF GLAMORGAN
Cowbridge
Llanblethian
Beaupre Castle
St Hilary
Wick
Sigingstone
Llantwit Major
Llancarfan
GLAMORGAN
Wales Hawking Centre
Penarth
Comeston Medieval Village
Comeston Lakes
Sully

Dunraven Bay
St Donats
St Illtyd
Nash Point
Summerhouse Point
Seawatch Centre
Limpert Bay
Wales Aircraft Museum
CARDIFF-WALES
Rhoose
Porthkerry
Porthkerry Country Park
Barry

0 Miles 2 4 6
0 Km 5 10

Abergavenny ⛰✝🏛 Ce
Spectacular mountain ranges encircle this market town on the River Usk. Labyrinth of narrow streets, some with Tudor buildings, testifies to town's long history, linked to fortunes of ruined 11th-century castle. Castle now houses collection of old farming equipment. Museum in 19th-century hunting lodge traces town's history.

Angiddy Ironworks ⚙ Ed
One-time scene of 16th-century iron-making in the Angiddy Valley near the Cleddon Falls. Buildings include charcoal house, blast furnace and casting house.

Blaenavon ⚙⛏ Bd
Ironworks from 18th century, and Big Pit Mining Museum, in a real mine worked until 1980. Descend 300ft in cage to bottom of shaft and experience life as a miner; safety helmet and lamp provided. Pithead baths and changing rooms on surface, and history of the Big Pit.

Bwlch ⛰⛏ Af
Village set in gap high in hills. Fragments of wall and tower are only remains of Castell Blaen-llynfi, formidable stronghold of Llywelyn the Great.

Caerleon ⚓🏛 Cc
Site of Roman fortress of Isca, built AD 75, which housed the 6000 men of the 2nd Augustan Legion. Excavations include gladiatorial amphitheatre and bath house. Relics displayed in Legionary Museum in High Street.

STRONGHOLD *Caerphilly's 13th-century castle has its own leaning tower – 12ft off the vertical.*

Caerphilly ⛰⛏ Ab
Town famous for its cheese and 13th-century castle. Cheese is now made elsewhere, but almost intact castle, with massive walls and wide moat, still dominates town on 30 acre site.

Caerwent Dc
Well-preserved remains of Roman town of Venta Silurum surround the village. Walls, 15ft high in places, remains of two houses and a temple.

Caldicot Castle 🏛⚔ Db
Restored 11th-century castle, with imposing gatehouse and keep, in parkland. Museum houses furniture, costumes, rural craft tools and small collection of relics from Nelson's flagship, *Foudroyant*. Medieval banquets are staged throughout the year in candlelit Great Hall.

BLACK MOUNTAINS AND WYE VALLEY

North of the industrial valleys the Brecon Beacons National Park is edged by the Black Mountains, rising to 2660ft at Waun Fâch and spilling over to the gentler hills around the Wye Valley. Great castles are legacies of Llywelyn the Great's fierce resistance to the English, and monastic settlements embody the solitude sought by the Augustinian and Cistercian orders.

Castell Coch 🏛 Ab
Late 19th-century castle – a rich mixture of Victorian Gothic fantasy and fairy tale – in a steep-sided, wooded gorge. Built in rose-coloured stone, which gives the castle its name, meaning 'Red Castle'. Rooms surrounding the small courtyard contain elaborate carvings and mouldings.

FACE OF TIME *The Roman ivory plaque was found at Caerleon.*

Chepstow 🏛⚓⛏🏛 Ec
Twisting medieval streets lie beyond 13th-century wall and gateway of this town on banks of River Wye. Norman castle stands on limestone cliffs at water's edge. River spanned by graceful bridge, built by John Rennie in 1816. Museum covers history of area from Roman times.

Clydach Gorge 🐾 Be
Beeches and waterfalls provide setting for what is now known as the Fairy Glen, once an industrial area. The 19th-century Clydach Ironworks have recently been excavated and restored.

Crickhowell ⛰⛏ Be
Pleasant village in the Usk valley at foot of Black Mountains. Long 16th-century bridge with 12 arches one side, 13 on the other. Fine Georgian houses, fragments of a castle, gateway of a long-vanished manor house, and 14th-century church with elaborate tombs and memorials.

Cwmcarn Forest Drive ⚓🐾🌲 Bc
Scenic drive travels 7 miles through 10,000 acres of dense woodland, giving superb views of Ebbw Forest. Car parks en route with waymarked footpaths and climb to top of Twmbarlwm, where ancient hill-fort looks out over Bristol Channel. Nature trail from visitor centre follows stream.

Fourteen Lock Canal Centre ⚙ Bb
Section of the Monmouthshire and Brecon Canal with 72 locks and intricate network of channels, sluices, ponds and weirs. Exhibition traces history of canal; provides facts and figures about locks and water storage system. Waymarked canal-side walks.

SHELTERED VALLEY *Talybont lies gently enfolded by green velvet slopes, while the sterner hills of the Brecon Beacons frown beyond.*

Llandaff Cathedral ✝ Aa
Founded 6th century and built of wood, replaced in 12th century by Norman stone, and reconstructed in 1957. Aluminium sculpture of Christ by Sir Jacob Epstein.

Llangattock ⛰ Be
Village with tiny stone-paved square, old weavers' cottages and 16th-century church. Limestone crags of Mynydd Llangatwg rise 1735ft south of village.

Llangorse ⛰ Af
Black Mountains tower above this village of stone cottages. Nearby Llangorse lake is largest stretch of natural water in South Wales.

Llanthony Priory ✟ Bf
Ruins set among silent hills, founded by Augustinians in 1108; existing priory dates from 1175. Pointed Early English archways and decorative stonework.

Monmouth ⛰⚓🏛 Ee
Elegant buildings of many eras enclose Agincourt Square, including early Georgian Shire Hall. Henry V born in ruined castle in 1387; adjoining Great Castle House dates from 1673. Fortified Monnow Bridge dates from 13th century. Museum has relics belonging to Lord Nelson.

Newport ⛰✝🏛🏛 Cb
Industrial town and port on the Usk. Cathedral has Norman work and modern window by John Piper. Museum houses Roman artefacts and art gallery.

Offa's Dyke Ed-Bg
Earthwork constructed in the 8th century as English-Welsh border by King Offa of Mercia; 168 miles in length.

Penarth Aa
Seaside resort with shingle beach, promenade and pier pavilion. Yachts and pleasure craft bring colour to docks.

Penhow Castle 🏛 Dc
Oldest inhabited castle in Wales. Restored 15th-century Great Hall, 12th-century bedchamber and Victorian housekeeper's room.

Pontypool ⚙ Bd
Valley Inheritance exhibition centre in former Georgian stable block of Pontypool Park House. Industrial relics tell story of valleys. Torfaen Trail of History includes ironworkers' cottages.

Raglan Castle ⛏ Dd
Romantic ruins of 15th-century moated fortress with massive hexagonal keep, two courtyards

and double-fronted gatehouse. Surrender of castle to Parliamentarians in 1646 marked end of Civil War.

St Fagans Castle 🏛⛏ Aa
Many-gabled 16th-century mansion where rural buildings of bygone days, brought from all over Wales, have been re-erected in surrounding parkland. Cottages, farmhouses, corn mill, tannery and craft workshop.

Sugar Loaf ▲☀ Be
Conical mountain standing to the north-west of Abergavenny. Green flanks gashed with red sandstone; patched with bracken and gorse. Path to 1995ft summit from car park. Panorama below of Ysgyryd Fawr, Malverns and Cotswolds east, Black Mountains mass north, gentle Usk skirting Brecon Beacons west, and glimpse of the Severn south.

Talybont ⛰ Af
Waterway of Monmouthshire and Brecon Canal cuts through village, supported by huge retaining walls. Built between 1797 and 1812 to carry lime, coal and wool. Lime kiln remains near stone bridge south of the village. Pleasant towpath walks.

Tintern Abbey ✟ Ed
One of the finest relics of Britain's monastic age. Massive vaulted and arched remains in splendid setting, commanding floor of Wye Valley. Traceried windows stand out against the wooded hills. Founded 12th century by Cistercian monks, rebuilt 13th century and suppressed by Henry VIII in 1536. History told in exhibition.

Tretower ⛰⛏🏛 Af
Circular keep surrounds a cylindrical tower in ruins of Norman castle. Nearby Tretower Court, family home of poet Henry Vaughan, is fortified 14th-century manor house with courtyard overlooked by open gallery.

Usk ⛰🏛⚓ Cd
Small market town dominated by ruined 12th-century castle. Gwent Rural Life Museum in old Malt Barn. Church of St Mary (13th century) has fine medieval woodwork and Tudor rood screen. Castle-like building in Maryport Street was county jail, built 1841.

Wentwood ⚓🌲 Dc
Forest gives splendid opportunities for observing wildlife. Fallow deer, badgers, foxes. Banks of daffodils in spring. Three-mile Gray Hill Countryside Trail with Neolithic stone circles.

White Castle ⛏ Ce
Ruined, moated castle on a windswept hilltop, one of the 'Three Castles of Gwent' – a triangle of fortresses protecting border against the Welsh. Dates from 12th century; strengthened by Edward I a century later.

Wolvesnewton ⛰🏛⚓ Dc
Model Farm Folk Museum with horse-drawn wagons and Victorian cottage bedroom, housed in buildings of 18th-century model farm created by Duke of Beaufort. Antique toys and craft workshops in mill courtyard.

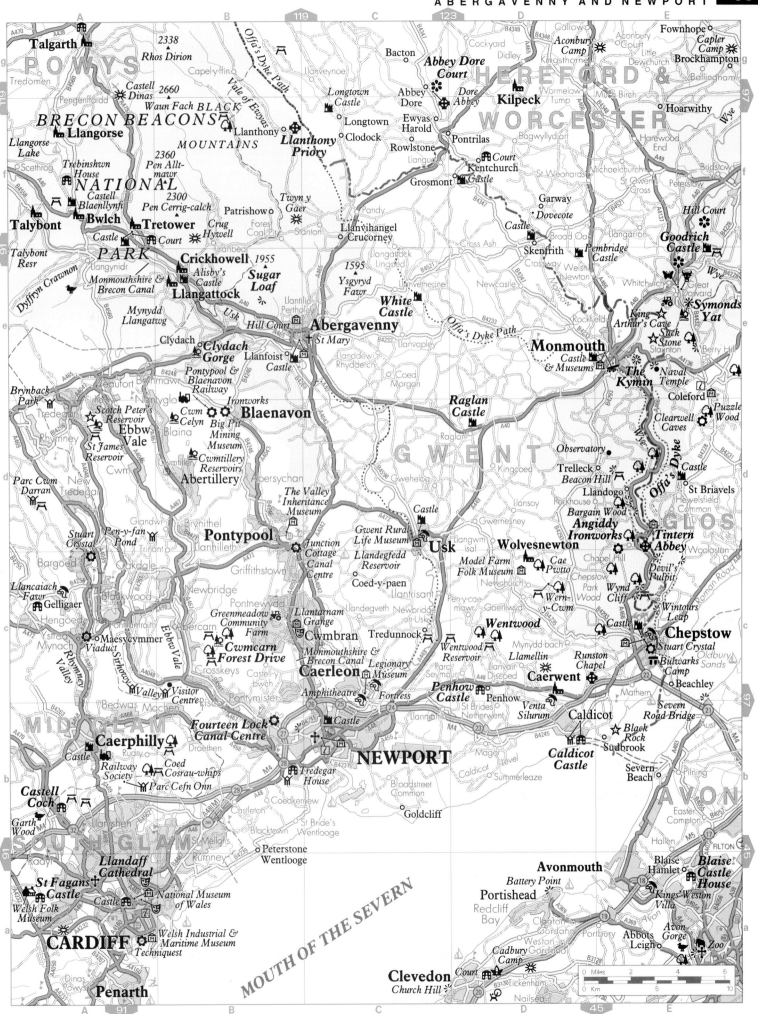

Talgarth

POWYS

2338
Rhos Dirion

Castell
Dinas 2660
Waun Fach **BLACK**

BRECON BEACONS
Llangorse

Llangorse
Lake

Trebinshwn
House

NATIONAL

2360
Pen Allt-
mawr

2300
Pen Cerrig-calch

Castell
Blaenllynfi

Talybont
Bwlch

Tretower

Talybont
Resr

PARK

Castle Court

Crickhowell

Dyffryn Crawnon

Monmouthshire &
Brecon Canal

Crug
Hywell

1955
**Sugar
Loaf**

Llangattock

Mynydd
Llangatwg

Clydach
Clydach
Gorge

Llanfoist

Pontypool &
Blaenavon
Railway

Offa's Dyke Path

Vale of Ewyas

Llanthony

Llanthony
Priory

MOUNTAINS

Patrishow

Twyn y
Gaer

Forest
Coal Pit

Stanton

Llanvihangel
Crucorney

1595
Ysgyryd
Fawr

Bacton

Abbey Dore
Court

Longtown
Castle

Longtown

Clodock

Rowlstone

Abbey
Dore

Dore
Abbey

Ewyas
Harold

Pontrilas

Grosmont

Court
Kentchurch
Castle

HEREFORD &

Cockyard
Didley

Aconbury
Camp

Much Birch

St Weonards

Garway
Dovecote

WORCESTER

Fownhope

Capler
Camp

Brockhampton

Hoarwithy

Harewood
End

Kilpeck

Hill Court

**Goodrich
Castle**

Monmouth
Castle
& Museums

Skenfrith

Pembridge
Castle

Cross Ash

Newcastle

**White
Castle**

Hill Court
Abergavenny
St Mary

Llanfoist
Castle

Offa's Dyke Path

**Raglan
Castle**

Raglan

GWENT

Wye

Whitchurch

King
Arthur's Cave

Great
Doward

Staunton

**Symonds
Yat**

Suck
Stone

Berry
Hill

Coleford

Naval
Temple

**The
Kymin**

Clearwell
Caves

Puzzle
Wood

GLOS

Observatory

Trelleck

Beacon Hill

Llandogo

Bargain Wood

**Angiddy
Ironworks**

Castle

St Briavels

**Offa's
Dyke**

**Tintern
Abbey**

Devil's
Pulpit

Wynd
Cliff

Wintours
Leap

Castle

Chepstow

Brynback
Park

Tredegar

Scotch Peter's
Reservoir

Ebbw
Vale

St James
Reservoir

Cwm
Celyn

Blaina

Blaenavon

Big Pit
Mining
Museum

Cwmtillery
Reservoirs

Abertillery

The Valley
Inheritance
Museum

Parc Cwm
Darran

New
Tredegar

Stuart
Crystal

Bargoed

Llancaiach
Fawr

Gelligaer

Maesycwmmer
Viaduct

Caerphilly

Castle

Railway
Society

**Castell
Coch**

Garth
Wood

SOUTH GLAM

CARDIFF

Penarth

Pen-y-fan
Pond

Pontypool

Junction
Cottage
Canal Centre

Griffithstown

Newbridge

Greenmeadow
Community
Farm

**Cwmcarn
Forest Drive**

Crosskeys

Abercarn

Llantarnam
Grange

Cwmbran

Monmouthshire &
Brecon Canal

Caerleon

Amphitheatre

Visitor
Centre

Pontymister

**Fourteen Lock
Canal Centre**

Coed
Cosrau-whips

Parc Cefn Onn

Llandaff
Cathedral

Castle

St Fagans
Castle

Welsh Folk
Museum

National Museum
of Wales

Welsh Industrial &
Maritime Museum
Techniquest

MID GLAM

Machen

Bedwas

Draethen

**Gwent Rural
Life Museum**

Castle

Usk

Llandegfedd
Reservoir

Coed-y-paen

Model Farm
Folk Museum

Wolvesnewton

Cae
Pwtto

Wern-
y-Cwm

Wentwood

Wentwood
Reservoir

Llanmellin

Legionary
Museum

Tredunnock

Fortress

**Penhow
Castle**

Penhow

Venta
Silurum

Caerwent

Runston
Chapel

Bulwarks
Camp

Caldicot

**Caldicot
Castle**

Black
Rock

Sudbrook

Severn
Road Bridge

Severn
Beach

AVON

NEWPORT

Castle

Tredegar
House

Goldcliff

St Bride's
Wentlooge

Peterstone
Wentlooge

MOUTH OF THE SEVERN

Avonmouth

Battery Point

Portishead

Redcliff
Bay

Blaise
Hamlet

**Blaise
Castle
House**

Kings Weston
Villa

FILTON

Avon
Gorge

Zoo

Abbots
Leigh

Cadbury
Camp

Clevedon
Church Hill

Bute Docks, Cardiff Bay
Docks comprising five large basins, planned by Marquis of Bute in 19th century. Once-busy shipping centre for transportation of iron and coal; now populated by pleasure craft. Museums illustrate industrial past.

Bute Park Ac
Formal parkland and natural riverside unite in stretch of open land more than 2 miles long on east side of the River Taff, near city centre. Includes the remains of the old Blackfriars Priory.

126 Bute Street, Cardiff Bay Eb
Victorian warehouse turned into arcade of shops, all with maritime theme, and dockland pub.

CAPITAL CITY OF WALES

Although its history dates back many centuries, the capital of Wales is essentially a young city. Before the 19th century, Cardiff was little more than a village, but the opening of the docks for exporting iron and coal rapidly increased its prosperity. Today its broad streets, elegant buildings and a wealth of parklands help to give Cardiff the cosmopolitan air that it deserves.

Cardiff Bay Visitor Centre Fa
Silvery, tube-shaped building used as showcase for developments in Cardiff Bay. Display includes a model of the bay, and video wall with 15 screens. Visitors can enjoy spectacular views across the inner harbour.

FAIRY-TALE SCENE *The spires and battlements of Cardiff Castle.*

Cardiff Arms Park Ba
One of the most famous rugby grounds in the world, set un-usually in the heart of the city, only a few hundred yards away from Cardiff Castle. Shared by Cardiff Rugby Club and National Stadium, it accommodates nearly 50,000 people. Clubhouse has trophy room with photographs, presentation items given to the Welsh Rugby Union and other relics of more than 100 years of rugby history.

Cardiff Castle Bb
Castle is part Roman fort, part medieval castle and part 19th-century mansion. A Roman fortress begun in AD 76 was rebuilt in the 3rd century with walls 10ft thick. A 270ft portion of wall can be seen inside castle. A Norman lord, Robert Fitzhamon, built a timber fort on a huge mound in 1091; this was replaced by a stone keep in the 12th century, and strengthened and extended over the years against Welsh attacks.

GOTHIC DETAIL *The Winter Smoking Room, designed by William Burges, in the clock tower of Cardiff Castle. Its walls are covered with tiling and murals.*

After centuries of neglect, castle was restored and rebuilt in 1865 by William Burges, in Gothic, Arab and classical Greek styles. Entrance Hall has Welsh oak table and statues of English monarchs who have possessed the castle. Arab Room, in mock-Moorish style, has gilded ceiling and chimneypiece of white alabaster inset with lapis lazuli. Banqueting Hall has gold-embellished timber-vaulted ceiling and murals. Chaucer Room has stained-glass windows depicting *The Canterbury Tales*. Summer Smoking Room has silver, copper and brass depiction of world inlaid in floor and chandelier representing the sun. William Burges also designed castle's clock tower. Burges's sketches and drawings of his ideas for apartments are on display. Castle is home to two impressive military museums; The Welch Regiment Museum and 1st The Queen's Dragoon Guards Museum.

Cathays Park Bc
Land bought before Cardiff officially made capital of Wales now houses Civic Centre, built 1897, which contains some of Europe's finest neoclassical buildings round a central garden. Law Courts, completed in 1906, have recessed façade and eight-columned portico topped by two

cupolas. Other nearby buildings of note include the University of Wales Registry and the Mid Glamorgan County Hall.

City Hall Cc
Hall built in 1905 of Portland stone in Renaissance style, topped by ornate 194ft clock tower and dome bearing a fierce Welsh dragon. Interior noted for the spectacular Marble Hall, with its columns of Siena marble, housing several statues of Heroes of Wales – including St David, patron saint of Wales, Owain Glyndwr, country's last national leader, and Henry Tudor, Welshman who became Henry VII of England. The Assembly Hall has an impressive decorated ceiling, and contains many fine portraits. Council Chamber is marked by oak panelled walls, and four marble pillars supporting the building's great dome.

Gorsedd Gardens Cc
Circle of stones erected to proclaim holding of National Eisteddfod here in 1899 gives gardens their name. Fine statues include one of David Lloyd George, Prime Minister of Britain from 1916 to 1922. View through the trees takes in handsome Park House, designed by William Burges, in a lively neo-Gothic style with French influences.

Kingsway Underpass Cb
Underpass was once Glamorgan Canal and ledge along one side was the towpath. Canal paddle gear can be viewed at the end of the tunnel. On surface, at corner of Queen Street, is fine statue of Aneurin Bevan, Labour MP for Ebbw Vale from 1929 to 1960 and Minister of Health from 1945 to 1951.

Morgan Arcade Ca
Arcade, built in late 19th century, is Italian in style with fine gabled glass roof supported on iron arches, and attractive Venetian windows on first floor. Noted for several well-preserved Victorian shop fronts.

National Museum of Wales Cc
Museum in same white Portland stone as remainder of the Cathays Park buildings, with imposing pillared façade and 90ft high dome. Contains exhibits on wide range of themes, including geology, archaeology and natural history. Art collection contains works by Welsh artists such as Richard Wilson and Augustus John, as well as many paintings by French impressionists and post-impressionists. These include Renoir, Monet, Cézanne and Pissarro. Also paintings by Botticelli, El Greco, Lawrence, Constable, Turner, Van Gogh and Utrillo. Bronze cast of Rodin's *The Kiss* stands in main hall. Section tells history of Wales from ancient past to present day. Prehistoric sculptured stone from Bryn Celli Du dates from 1700 BC. Dolgellau chalice and paten – so named because they were discovered by chance at roadside near Dolgellau in 1890 – among earliest examples of church plate in Britain, made about 1250. Pre-Norman Gallery contains 6th-century jewellery. Celtic Metalwork Gallery has replicas of outstanding examples of Celtic craftsmanship, such as Ardagh Chalice and Cross of Cong. Industrial section has displays on mining – including simulated coal mine – electricity, oil refining and iron, steel and tin-plate manufacture. Upper gallery has ceramics collection including examples of Swansea porcelain.

New Theatre Cc
Theatre built at beginning of this century by Robert Redford, business manager to the D'Oyly Carte Opera Company. Built in red brick and Bath stone the theatre was

TREASURE TROVE *The National Museum of Wales houses a wealth of exhibits, from impressionist drawings and paintings to Swansea porcelain.*

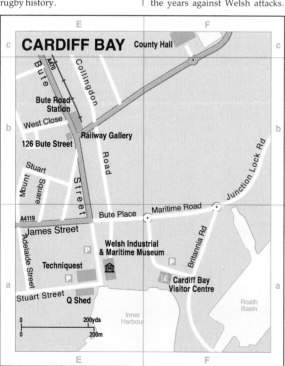

CARDIFF BAY

County Hall

Bute
Collingdon
Bute Road Station
West Close
Railway Gallery
126 Bute Street
Stuart
Mount Square
Stuart Street
A4119
James Street
Adelaide Street
Techniquest
Welsh Industrial & Maritime Museum
Bute Place
Maritime Road
Junction Lock Rd
Britannia Rd
Cardiff Bay Visitor Centre
Roath Basin
Q Shed
Stuart Street
Inner Harbour

0   200yds
0   200m

completed in only six months. It has recently been restored to its Edwardian splendour, both inside and out. The Welsh National Opera Company usually performs four Cardiff seasons a year at the New Theatre, and drama, ballet and musicals are also staged here.

Q Shed, Cardiff Bay Ea
Built as Q Warehouse in 1860, with stone surrounding an iron frame; later brick replaced the

Royal Arcade Ca
Built 1856, the oldest shopping arcade in Cardiff; some early shop fronts survive. Glass roof on ornate iron arches lets in light and keeps out weather.

St David's Centre Cb
Shopping precinct, much of it under cover. Adjoining it is St David's Hall, a new 2000 seat concert hall with frequent concerts by the BBC Welsh Symphony Orchestra.

St John's Church ✝ Cb
Parish church dates from 1453, with 130ft tower, added 1473. Herbert Chapel has monument to two brothers, Sir William Herbert, Keeper of Cardiff Castle, who died in 1609, and Sir John Herbert, private secretary to Queen Elizabeth I, who died in 1617.

Sophia Gardens Ab
Open area next to River Taff, on opposite bank from Bute Park, has concert pavilion.

Techniquest, Cardiff Bay Ea
Centre entertains and educates visitors with scientific displays and experiments; active, 'hands-on' participation is encouraged. A seemingly solid triangle of beams at entrance to building is in fact an optical illusion.

War Memorial Bc
At the centre of Cathays Park, a circular colonnade of Corinthian columns surrounds a sunken court, where there are fountains and bronze sculptures depicting a soldier, a sailor and an airman offering up wreaths to a winged messenger of victory.

Welch Regiment Museum Bb
Dioramas and displays in Black and Barbican towers of Cardiff Castle tell story of regiment founded in 1719. Items of interest include Colour of 4th Regiment of American Infantry, taken at Fort Detroit in 1812, and collection of Welsh insignia. Numerous relics of the Crimean War, in which the regiment played an important part; these include the colours carried at the Alma and at Inkerman, and captured Russian drums. Japanese machine gun captured in Burma in World War II. And from Korean War a Russian machine gun. Museum buildings include working portcullis.

WELSH FIRE *A fierce dragon, the emblem of Wales, crowns the great dome of the City Hall.*

Welsh Industrial and Maritime Museum 🏛 Ea
Museum tells story of Welsh industry. Hall of Power contains engines and heavy machinery – including triple-expansion steam engine, beam engine and turbo-alternator – once used in ships, mines and power stations and now restored to working order. Transport exhibits include horse-drawn trams and replica of Trevithick's steam locomotive. Outside are locomotives and cranes, and collection of boats including pilot's cutter, Bristol Channel tug and narrowboat.

HEROES IN STONE *Life-size marble statues of Hywell the Good (left) and Boudicca in Cardiff City Hall.*

stone, and building became a booking hall for paddle-steamer trips. Now the original frame has been re-used to house a modern dockland exhibition hall, presenting the long and fascinating story of seaborne traffic and its passengers around and beyond the coast of Wales.

EDWARDIAN FACE *The New Theatre, with its imposing twin towers, has been restored to the splendour of its heyday in the 1900s.*

1st The Queen's Dragoon Guards Museum Bb
Unit formed in 1969 by amalgamation of two cavalry regiments has a museum in Cardiff Castle. Both regiments were raised in 1685; the display shows a soldier of the period, and one of 1690 at the Battle of the Boyne. There are relics of the Battle of Waterloo, and VCs won for bravery during Indian Mutiny.

Queen's West Centre Cb
Modern shopping centre at heart of city, based on light and airy atrium and crisscross grid motif.

Railway Gallery, Cardiff Bay Eb
Former headquarters of Taff Vale Railway now holds series of displays on railways in Wales. Outside are ten steam engines of the Wales Railway Centre.

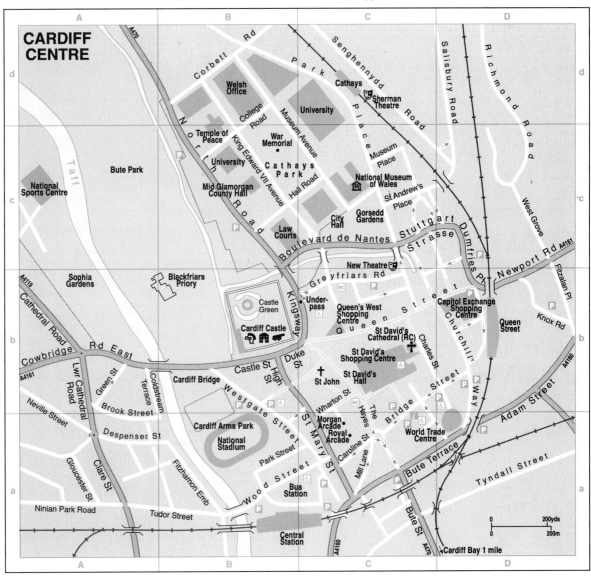
CARDIFF CENTRE

ALONG THE SEVERN VALLEY

The impressive scarp of the Cotswold Hills, dissected by secluded valleys and streams, forms the eastern boundary of the Vale of Berkeley. To the west, the Wye valley cuts its way through wooded hills beyond the Forest of Dean. The Severn wanders south through the Vale of Gloucester, where it broadens into a wide estuary with one of the largest tidal ranges in the world.

Berkeley Castle ⚐ Bb
Medieval fortress keeps watch beside the Severn; Berkeley family home for more than 800 years. Chilling cell where Edward II was brutally murdered in 1327. Cromwell left his mark on ramparts – huge breach in wall from Civil War. Museum in nearby Chantry devoted to 18th-century physician Edward Jenner, who developed smallpox vaccination.

Birdlip Hill ❈ Ed
Vale of Gloucester unfolds beneath Cotswold scarp; forming a timeless picture of green fields, threaded by winding River Severn and framed by the distant blue Welsh hills.

STOREHOUSE *Bredon's great barn has two half-timbered porches.*

Bredon Hill ❈ ❦ ⊛ Eg
Lonely Cotswolds outcrop rising to 961ft, where A.E. Houseman's *Shropshire Lad* listened to church bells ringing. Gothic folly on slopes has views of Avon valley. Iron Age and Roman fortifications can be traced in the turf. Village has black-and-white cottages, 12th-century church, and large 14th-century barn – 132ft long.

Cheltenham 🏛 ⃞ Ee
Anglo-Saxon market town transformed into elegant Regency resort with discovery of medicinal springs. Waters still flow in Pittville Pump Room. Art Gallery and Museum houses costume and jewellery collections. The Holst Museum has memorabilia in Regency house where composer of *The Planets* suite was born in 1874. Cheltenham International Festival of Music held annually in the Town Hall.

The Duntisbournes ⃫ Ec
River Dunt burbles through Cotswold valley, past four greystone hamlets and two villages. Norman church at Duntisbourne Leer, where stream runs down village street, and partly Saxon church at Duntisbourne Rouse.

Easton Grey ⃫ Da
Charming, informal huddle of grey-stone houses beside ancient five-arched bridge spanning infant River Avon. Easton Grey House, a gracious early 18th-century mansion, is last of a succession of manorial seats.

Forest of Dean ⌔ ❦ ❈ ✿ ⊼ ☆ 🏛 ⃫ ⃞ Bd
Wild, remote area of ancient forest covers hills between rivers Severn and Wye. Husbanded for cen-turies to provide game, timber, charcoal and coal. Watch for fallow deer, stoat, weasel, fox, and several species of bat. Occasional otter and polecat. Birds include tree pipit, whinchat, linnet, nightjar, goldcrest, redstart, and woodpeckers. Breeding hawfinch and crossbill. Dean Heritage Museum in mill near Cinderford tells Forest story. Vast chambers and passages at Clearwell Caves were hacked out by ancient Britons mining for iron ore. Forest Railway preserves section of old Severn and Wye line.

Frampton on Severn ⃫ Cc
Riverside village where ducks and weekend cricketers mingle on one of England's largest greens, surrounded by Georgian houses and half-timbered buildings. Bell Inn conveniently sited for cricketers and supporters. Outstanding house on green, screened by trees, called Frampton Court. Built in the Palladian style in the 1730s. The 14th-century Church of St Mary is reached by footpath across water meadow. Sharpness Canal beside it links Gloucester with River Severn. Sight of seagoing vessels passing within a few feet of church tower is an occasional attraction.

Golden Valley ⌔ Dc
Hanging beechwoods clothe the steep slopes where River Frome and Thames and Severn Canal wind down from Sapperton, passing steep terraces and old woollen mills of Chalford in Stroud valley.

Goodrich Castle 🏰 ⊼ Ad
First mentioned in a document of 1095, but existing buildings are all later. Ruin set on red sandstone bluff above the Wye. Important Welsh Border castle in 12th and 13th centuries, now looking much as Cromwell's forces left it in 1646.

Great Witcombe Villa ⌔ Ed
Once home to Roman gentleman of leisure, looking out over vales of Gloucester and Berkeley close to modern Cotswold Way. Fine renovated mosaic pavements and bath house.

Highmeadow Woods ⌔ ❈ Ad
Sun-dappled glades and quiet trails crisscross vast expanse of broad-leaved and evergreen trees above Wye valley. Entrancing walks in all directions; one to Suck Stone, huge sandstone fragment 60ft long by 40ft wide, said to be largest boulder in country.

How Caple Court ✿ Bf
Formal Edwardian terraced gardens in idyllic Wye valley. Restored sunken Florentine garden with plants for sale.

The Kymin ❈ Ad
Round House pavilion of 1794 on wooded 800ft hill, where gentry dined and admired the views. Curious Naval Temple added in 1800 to celebrate victories of Nelson and other naval heroes.

Little Dean Hall ⚐ Bd
Hiding behind 17th-century Jacobean façade, this may be Britain's oldest lived-in house. England's only known remains of a Saxon hall in basement, and restored major Roman temple in grounds. Spine-chilling 'Ghost Tour' and breathtaking 'Panoramic Walk' for views.

Lydney Park ✿ 🏰 ⌔ Bc
Woodland, lakes, fine shrubs and trees provide setting for ruined 12th-century castle and remains of Roman temple.

May Hill ❈ Be
Pine-topped hill soaring to 971ft on western edge of Vale of Gloucester, first planted in honour of Queen Victoria's Golden Jubilee. May Common is wild and windy grassy heath with superb views over ten counties.

Misarden Park ✿ Ec
Elizabethan mansion above infant River Frome has essentials of an English country garden, with its traditional roses, wisteria-hung arbours, spring bulbs, rockeries, yew topiary and terraced lawns.

Much Marcle ⃫ ⚐ ⊣ Bf
Peacefully set amid gentle hills, famous for Hereford cattle and cider. Mainly 13th-century church has imposing tombs, carved effigies, and 1000-year-old yew fitted with seats. Historic house, Hellens, begun in 1292, is mainly 16th century with a dovecote built in 17th century.

Newent ⌔ ❦ ⌔ 🏛 Ce
Wild daffodils grow thickly around this old market town in spring, set in rolling countryside. The 16th-century timber-framed market hall is well preserved. Several 18th-century houses and medieval spired church. Lead removed from church roof by Royalists in 1644 during Civil War, to make bullets to repel Roundhead attacks. It collapsed in 1674 destroying nave; rebuilt when Charles II granted wood from Forest of Dean. Falconry centre has one of world's largest collections of birds of prey, with free-flight displays. Butterfly Centre.

SILKEN WYE *Seen from Symonds Yat Rock, the river winds its curving course below autumn-tinted Coppet Hill.*

Prinknash Abbey ✿ ⌔ Dd
Modern buildings provide startling contrast with 14th-century Old Abbey in thriving Benedictine foundation, famous for pottery. Peacocks, black swans and medieval fishponds in Bird Park.

Ross-on-Wye ✝ ⌔ 🏛 ⃞ Ae
Attractive market town rising on red sandstone cliffs above River Wye. Tall spire of St Mary's dominates steep, winding streets with black-and-white buildings.

Sapperton ⃫ Ec
Good walks and fine crafts in pretty village at head of Frome valley. Home of leading members of William Morris's Victorian Arts and Crafts Movement.

Slimbridge Wildfowl and Wetlands Trust ❦ Cc
Created by the late Sir Peter Scott; largest, best and most famous collection of ducks, geese and swans in the world. Vast migratory flocks of wild geese bring echoes of Arctic north in winter. Flamingoes and tropical house with hummingbirds.

Symonds Yat ☆ ❈ Ad
Views over horseshoe bend in River Wye from towering rock where peregrine falcons breed. Footpaths lead to gaunt Seven Sisters Rocks and King Arthur's Cave – lair of mammoth and prehistoric man. Ferry across river to village and Wye Valley Visitor Centre featuring mazes and Butterfly House.

Tewkesbury ✿ ✕ 🏛 ⃞ Df
Ancient town of black-and-white houses and inns, where Lancastrians were defeated during Wars of the Roses. Impressive abbey with 132ft high Norman tower.

Westbury Court ✿ Cd
Stately, formal gardens with still waters, clipped yew hedges and geometric flowerbeds in late 17th-century Dutch style.

Westonbirt Arboretum ✿ Da
Finest collection of temperate trees in Europe. Founded 1829 for private enjoyment, now Forestry Commission centre. Year-round delight, from bluebell spring to autumn fire of maple glade.

Painswick ⃫ ❈ Dc
Cotswold mason's art seen at its best in hilltop village of gables, stone-tiled roofs and pale grey-gold houses, dating back to 14th century. Churchyard has tombs of wealthy wool merchants, and curious iron stocks by wall, shaped like a pair of spectacles. Peal of 12 bells in 15th-century church is one of finest in west.

ODDITY *Painswick's stocks are unusual in that they are made of iron.*

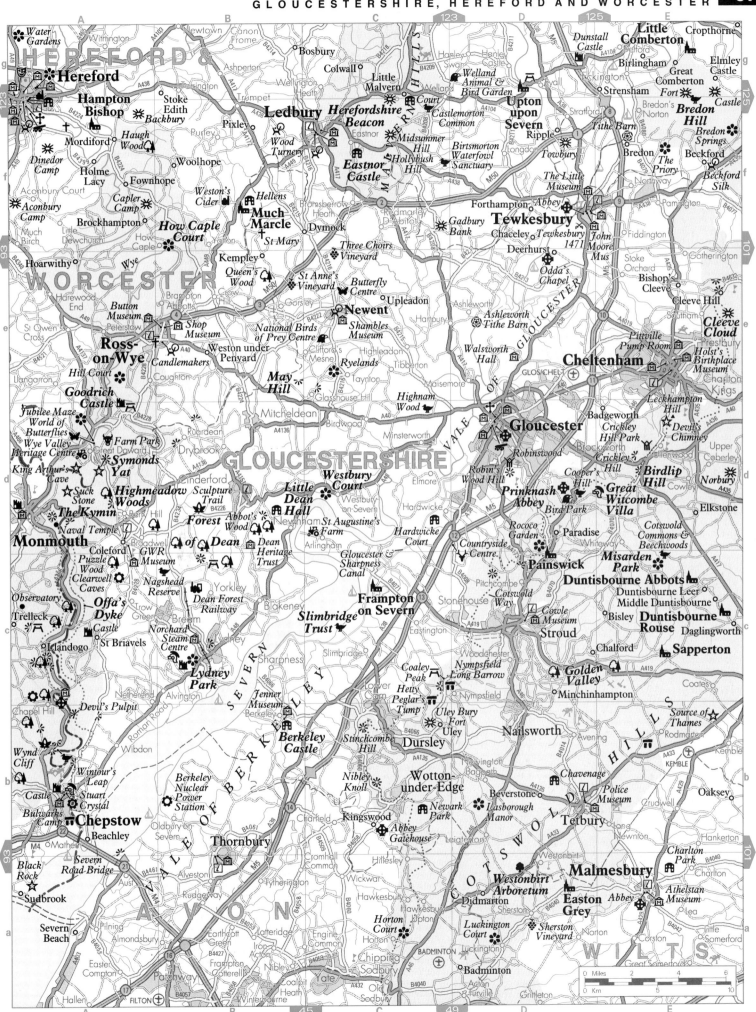

Antique Centre Ab
Converted 19th-century warehouse. Ground floor has open display area; four upper floors set out as arcades of little shops.

The Bastion Cb
Place where two sections of original Roman wall meet. Built in 3rd and 4th centuries, more recent structure consists of massive stone blocks. Semicircular tower added in 13th century.

HISTORIC CITY ON THE SEVERN

The ancient Roman town of Glevum flourishes still as the city of Gloucester. The city's long history is much in evidence in a wealth of historic buildings dominated by an impressive Norman cathedral. The docks, set along the River Severn and for so long the key to Gloucester's prosperity, have taken on a new role as a tourist attraction, with restaurants, an antique centre and museums.

PERFECTLY PRESERVED *With its timber roof and vast nave, Blackfriars still maintains much of its 13th-century character. The cloisters and several surrounding buildings are also still standing.*

Bishop Hooper's Lodging ⌂ Bb
This timber-frame house, built between 15th and 16th centuries, said to be place where the Protestant bishop spent night before martyrdom in 1555. Building now houses museum illustrating social history, local customs, traditions, crafts and agriculture of region. Displays include Victorian school room and farming machinery, information on port of Gloucester and Civil War. First floor has funnel-shaped baskets and nets used for different methods of fishing on Severn through the centuries. Top floor exhibits tell story of brass pin making.

Blackfriars ✠ Bb
Church, built in 13th century and still in good condition, has vast timber roof rising some 60ft above nave measuring 90ft by 55ft, with limestone rubble walls. Cloisters and the surrounding buildings still survive.

The Cross Bb
The tower of 15th-century St Michael's Church, all that remains of four churches that stood here.

East Gate Cb
Underground exhibition chamber displays the remains of Roman gate towers, medieval wall and moat excavated from this site.

Fleece Hotel Bb
This 12th-century barrel-vaulted undercroft belongs to house that stood on site before hotel. Much of present building is 16th century.

Fountain Inn Bb
Dates from 17th century. On front is basrelief of William III, who is claimed to have ridden horse up inn's stairs.

Gloucester and Sharpness Canal Aa
Britain's first ship canal, started 1793 and opened in 1827. Much as it was during last century. Mostly used by pleasure boats today.

Gloucester Cathedral ✝ Bc
Begun in 1089, replacing earlier abbey. Norman nave, lined with piers supports Romanesque triforium and clerestory. Two west bays in nave date from 1421-37. Transepts and choir, remodelled in 14th century, are among earliest examples of Perpendicular architecture. Reredos is Victorian, as are sub-stalls. Restored stalls, dating from 14th century, sport misericord grotesques. East window, dating from 14th century and largest stained-glass window in Britain at 72ft by 38ft, depicts the Coronation of the Virgin – created as memorial to those who died at Battle of Crécy in 1346. Cloisters, also from 14th century, have earliest surviving fan vaulting, and, down south walk, carrels – miniature studies used by monks for reading and working. Organ case, dating from 1663 is oldest in any English cathedral. Elaborately carved alabaster tomb of Edward II, dating from 14th century, stands in north arcade of presbytery, next to tomb of King Osric, who founded first abbey in AD 681. Tomb of Robert, Duke of Normandy, son of William the Conqueror, is carved from oak and dates from 12th century. In north ambulatory stands small cross carved in 1951 by Col. Carne, VC, during captivity in Korea. Bell tower contains heaviest medieval bell in England. Exhibition depicts complete history of Gloucester Cathedral since monastic times.

Gloucester City Museum and Art Gallery ⌂ Cb
Museum, built on excavated part of Roman wall, has variety of displays illustrating archaeology, natural history and geology of area. Bones of mammoth, wild ox and giant deer can be seen along with Roman mosaics, sculptures, coins, pottery and other objects in archaeology section. Birdlip mirror, dating from about AD 25, is one of finest examples of Celtic bronze craftsmanship in Britain. On first floor, hall with plasterwork ceiling contains Georgian furniture, clocks, pottery, silver, ceramics, glass, costume, and an extensive collection of barometers. Paintings by Breugel, Gainsborough, Lawrence, Walter Sickert, Turner and Wilson Steer. Temporary art exhibitions held throughout year.

Greyfriars ✠ Bb
Empty arches and walls of nave and north aisle all that survive of 16th-century church. Adjoining Greyfriars House built in the late 18th century.

TO SITA *Tombstone of Thracian cavalryman Rufus Sita is in the Gloucester City Museum.*

Guildhall Cb
Renaissance-style building dating back to the 19th century is now a lively arts centre with cinema, theatre, dance, exhibitions and arts workshops.

BEAUTY TURNED TO STONE *Fan tracery gives the stone ceiling in Gloucester Cathedral's Great Cloister a surprisingly delicate appearance.*

HOUSEHOLD NAMES *Brand names of the 19th and 20th centuries adorn re-created shop windows at Robert Opie Collection.*

REEL WORLD *Beatrix Potter's cover picture is also the sign for the House of the Tailor of Gloucester.*

House of the Tailor of Gloucester ⌂ Bb
House used by Beatrix Potter to illustrate story of mice who helped tailor. Now a museum devoted to world of Beatrix Potter and her associations with Gloucester. Working models of sewing mice can be seen among large collection of memorabilia.

Llanthony Priory ✠ Aa
Founded in 1136, all that remains are few collapsed walls, arches and a restored timber-frame building. Priory later used as farmhouse and carp pond created round it – now a much-valued wildlife habitat.

Mariners' Chapel † Ba
Built in 1849 to cater for visiting seamen. War poet Ivor Gurney played organ here. Chapel still holds services.

National Waterways Museum ⌂ Aa
Old, seven-storey Llanthony Warehouse, with iron columns and timber beams, now houses museum explaining 200 year history of Britain's canals and inland waterways. Series of dioramas, photographs, audiovisual displays and computer games show how canals were dug and their waters controlled. Items include working engines, scale models, machinery and complete reconstruction of lock and lock gate. Other exhibits illustrate lives and working conditions of canal folk. Warehouse still has spiral chute down which sacks of grain were sent from top floor to bottom. On one floor are chains, ropes, hoists and pulleys used to unload barges. Reconstructed engineer's workshop has power hammers and cutting tools, and blacksmith can be seen at work. Outside are replica canal maintenance yard and canal craft of all kinds, including traditional narrowboats and working steam dredger. Restored oil-engine, built around 1929, stands in yard and drives belts and shafts for engineer's workshop.

New Inn Bb
Timber-framed house round courtyard with galleries on upper floor. Actually new about middle of 15th century and originally built to accommodate pilgrims flocking to see tomb of Edward II at Gloucester Cathedral. Lady Jane Grey said to have been proclaimed queen here in 1553. Carved angle-post at corner.

The Quay Ab
Docking place for vessels before ship canal was built. Dates back to early medieval times, but no longer in use.

Regiments of Gloucestershire Museum ⌂ Mx
Museum housed in early 19th-century Custom House with colonnaded front. Displays show 300 year history of Gloucestershire Regiment and the Royal Gloucestershire Hussars, covering all aspects of soldiering from family life of 200 years ago to life in trenches during World War I. Photographs and archive film bring story up to present, including regiment's participation in Korean War.

Robert Opie Collection ⌂ Aa
Housed in six-storey Albert Warehouse of 1851, nearly 300,000 items trace changes in packaging and advertising of everyday commodities during 19th and 20th centuries. Tins, cartons, packets and posters advertise brands such as Vita-Wheat, Bovril and Oxo. Continual screening of TV advertisements of the last 30 years.

St Bartholomew's Ac
Almshouses built in Gothic style in 1780 on site of earlier hospital. Now houses various shops.

St John's Church † Bb
Oldest part of church is 14th-century tower and spire. Church stands in St Lucy's Garden, once part of abbey precinct.

St Mary-de-Crypt Church and School † Bb
Norman cruciform church with tall central tower and high-arched windows from Perpendicular period. Inside are brasses, 17th-century pulpit and 17th and 18th-century monuments. School added to north end of church in 16th century.

St Mary-de-Lode Church † Bc
Church has low Norman chancel and stands on site of Roman building.

St Mary's Gateway Bc
Western entrance to original abbey, now cathedral, precinct is a 13th-century building with Norman vaulting. Houses on either side stand exactly on line of precinct wall. Some parts of the wall can be seen by standing in St Mary Street.

ABBEY GATE *St Mary's Gateway, probably the old abbey almonry, leads to the cathedral precinct.*

St Nicholas's Church † Bc
Medieval church has Norman south door and tall, leaning Perpendicular spire.

CHARMING CHIMES *Assorted figures above the watchmaker's in Westgate Street strike bells to tell the time to passers-by.*

St Oswald's Priory ✠ Bc
Oldest religious building in Gloucester after the cathedral. Arch in north nave arcade may date from 10th century.

Spa Road Ba
Road once led to spa which no longer exists, though the gardens where it stood have survived.

Transport Museum ⌂ Bb
This collection of horse-drawn vehicles, including fire engine, can be seen from road outside.

The Treasury, Gloucester Cathedral Bc
Collection of plate from all over diocese. Pieces date from before Conquest to 20th century. Treasury was provided by the Goldsmiths Company in 1977.

Westgate Street Bb
Contains some of city's finest old houses, sometimes behind newer façades. No. 26 has Georgian façade with carved timber-frame building behind it. Recently restored No. 66 dates from 16th century. Above watchmaker's are five figures striking bells – Father Time, John Bull, Scotsman, Welsh woman and Irish girl.

Ye Olde Fish Shoppe Cb
Perhaps the only timber-framed fish-and-chip shop in Britain. Building is early 16th century.

NET PROFITS *This group of traps for elver, eel and salmon is part of a display of local fishing methods through the ages at Bishop Hooper's Lodging.*

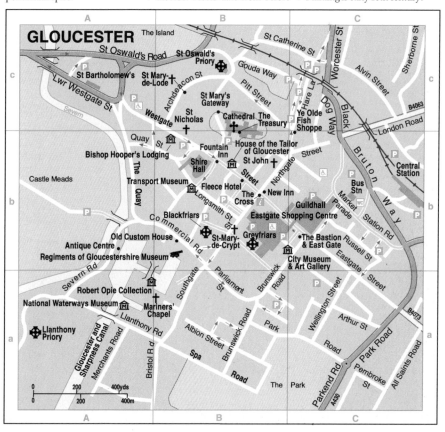

GLOUCESTER

VILLAGES OF GOLDEN STONE

Wool and stone give the Cotswold Hills their unique and distinctive character. Medieval merchants, rich from the fleece of sheep, built great manor houses and noble churches. Little villages grew up along the rushing streams that powered the mills which produced woollen cloth. And the grey-gold radiance of Cotswold stone bound all into a harmonious whole.

COTSWOLD COTTAGES *Famous group of mellow-stone river-front houses in Bibury's Arlington Row.*

Barnsley House Bc
Variety and enchantment in 4 acres of land around 17th-century house, created by gardening writer Rosemary Verey. Doric temple and lily pond, herb and knot gardens. Laburnum tunnel provides a blaze of bold colour in early June.

Batsford Arboretum Cf
Informal gardens laid out in 1880s by eccentric Lord Redesdale, furnished with oriental trophies. Garden centre and adjacent Cotswold Falconry Centre, with over 70 species of birds of prey.

Belas Knap Be
Closely cropped turf disguises brooding bulk of 5000-year-old Neolithic long barrow, high above Vale of Sudeley. Burial chambers have yielded remains of over 30 people, guarded by false entrance built to mislead tomb robbers.

Bibury Cc
Said by Victorian artist William Morris to be the most beautiful English village. Showpiece is Arlington Row's group of 17th-century weavers' houses. Cloth was fulled at Arlington Mill, now a rural and craft museum. Next door is a trout farm. Exceptional church, part Saxon.

Bourton-on-the-Water Ce
River Windrush, spanned by five stone bridges, flows along main street of this Cotswold town with many attractions. Perfect miniature Model Village made from local stone. Exotic birds in Birdland Zoo Gardens and rare species of fowl at Folly Farm. Village Life Exhibition in Old Mill includes Edwardian village shop. Cotswold Motor Museum in old barley mill recalls early days of motor transport.

Broadway Bf
Charming village with warm stone buildings and antique shops. Lygon Arms (16th century) was a resting place for both Charles II and Cromwell. Museum of toys has 600 teddy bears.

Broadway Hill Cf
Folly tower (1799) crowns second highest point in Cotswolds; 1024ft above sea level. Observation room yields panoramic views, much admired by Victorian artist and craftsman William Morris, who spent his holidays here. Morris exhibition in tower. Rural walks in country park.

Burford Dd
Ancient wool town on River Windrush with wealth of antique shops and 15th and 16th-century houses. Tolsey Museum of local history in 16th-century merchants' meeting place; fascinating Norman and Gothic church. Nearby Cotswold Wildlife Park is one of England's foremost wild animal collections.

Buscot Park Db
Restored 18th-century Adam-style house with fine furniture, silver, porcelain and paintings, including *Legend of the Briar Rose* series by Burne-Jones. Village, woods, farmland and Thameside walks on vast 4000 acre estate.

Chedworth Roman Villa Bd
Comfortable property of a Romanised Briton built AD 180-350 for a rich landowner. Equipped with hot-air underfloor heating and two forms of bath. Relics reveal building with three wings enclosing rectangular courtyard. Bath suites and one dining room are particularly well preserved, with good mosaics. Water shrine still filled by ancient spring which supplied fresh water. Display of household objects in museum.

Childswickham Bf
Cotswold stone lends warmth to houses on attractive green. Village cross oddly surmounted by 18th-century urn, put there after Puritans damaged original cross.

Chipping Campden Cf
Dark, golden-stone High Street buildings span 500 years. Mainly 15th-century church has 14th-century chancel and excellent brasses. Town's finest building is the Jacobean Market Hall (1627) with cobbled floor and magnificent oak timbers.

Chipping Norton Ee
Old wool town with 17th-century Cotswold stone buildings. Guildhall windows show its Tudor origins. Church with 15th-century nave and brasses. Tweed made at Bliss Mill until 1980.

Cirencester Bc
Second-largest city in Roman Britain lies buried beneath today's modern shopping centre. Little survives; remains of amphitheatre and section of city wall. Corinium Museum has collection of Roman antiquities. Fine parish church is largest in Gloucestershire. Cirencester Park has 3000 acres of park, woodland and farms.

Cleeve Cloud Ae
Highest point of the Cotswolds, 1083ft above sea level, with Cheltenham spread below. This airy upland remains one of the most breathtaking viewpoints anywhere in England. The remains of an Iron Age hill-fort defend a modern golfing green.

Cornwell De
Curious but charming 'ideal' village of stone-and-slate cottages. Rebuilt in 1930s by Sir Clough Williams-Ellis (famous architect of Portmeirion) who also restored 18th-century manor house and beautiful landscaped gardens.

Cotswold Farm Park Ce
Some 50 acres of small fields on high plateau among Cotswold hills comprise living museum of English agriculture, where rare breeds of farm animals are bred. Fenced walkways give close access to such unusual varieties as Longhorn cattle, Shetland geese, Gloucester Old Spot pigs and Cotswold Lion sheep – the breed from whose fleece Cotswold wealth was founded.

Cricklade Bb
Only Wiltshire village on River Thames – a mere channel at this point. Main street has good 17th and 18th-century houses. Church has cathedral-like turreted tower, built 1553, with Norman features and heraldic work.

Fairford Cc
Market Place surrounded by old stone buildings, including Bull Hotel; famous posting house in stagecoach days. Elegant 15th-century church has superb set of stained-glass windows tracing Bible story.

Gloucestershire and Warwickshire Railway Bf
Railway is restored section of old Cheltenham to Honeybourne line. Gleaming steam locomotives take passengers from Toddington station on 6 mile round trip to Winchcombe.

Great Coxwell Barn Db
One of best surviving tithe barns in the country, built in mid-13th century of stone and timber by Cistercians of Beaulieu Abbey. Vast scale (152ft long and 48ft high) is an awesome reminder of medieval monastic wealth.

Hailes Abbey Bf
Cistercian abbey founded 1242 by Richard, Earl of Cornwall, became gentleman's residence after Dissolution, and a ruin in 1800. Reminders of former splendour in adjoining museum.

Hidcote Manor Cg
Influential British garden, laid out by Major Lawrence Johnston, who bought 17th-century estate in 1905. The formal layouts with informal planting evoke a pleasing turmoil of cottage gardens. Clipped box and yew hedges surround a series of gardens, each with its own theme.

Highworth Cb
Gracious old town and coaching centre atop 400ft hill. Houses around Market Place represent 17th and 18th-century domestic architecture at its elegant best.

Kelmscot Db
Scattered greystone village. The leader of the Arts and Crafts Movement, William Morris, lived at Elizabethan Kelmscott Manor from 1871 to 1896; he is buried in local churchyard.

Kiftsgate Court Cg
Beautiful gardens in grounds of Georgian manor house. Rare plants and old-fashioned roses, among them 'Kiftsgate', claimed to be the most rampant rose.

Lechlade Db
Attractive village of wide Georgian streets at watery crossroads where Leach and Coln join swelling Thames. Lovely 15th-century church with noble tower and spire, inspired Shelley's *Summer Evening in a Churchyard*.

MILL STREAM *An early 19th-century corn mill in Lower Slaughter.*

Lower Swell Ce
River Dikler flows past lovely old bankside cottages and working smithy in this village. Georgian pillar on green, topped by an urn. Fine examples of Norman carving in church.

Minster Lovell Ed
Stone and thatched cottages, 500-year-old-inn, church, dovecote and ruined 15th-century manor beside River Windrush.

Moreton-in-Marsh Df
Ancient market town with Cotswold houses and coaching inns lining wide main street. Opposite Market Hall, 16th-century curfew tower has original bell which rang until 1860.

Northleach Cd
Former market town with ancient stone cottages, some dating from 17th century. Church, endowed by wool merchants in 15th century, has beautiful south porch with weather-worn statues, spacious nave with octagonal pillars, fine brasses and much else. Austere Northleach House of Correction (1791) re-creates former

prison atmosphere in surviving cell block and court room. Remainder houses Cotswold Countryside Collection, illustrating history of Gloucestershire rural life.

Rollright Stones ⊓ Df
Mysterious eroded relics of Neolithic burial site are legendary petrified remains of king, army, and knaves, frozen by a witch.

Sezincote ⌂ Cf
Moghul palace with minarets and onion domes, built 1805 by Sir Charles Cockerell of East India Company. Emulated by Prince Regent in Brighton Pavilion and celebrated by Sir John Betjeman in *Summoned by Bells*. Exotic gardens laid out by Sir Humphry Repton, with fountains, Hindu statuary and Persian garden.

Sherborne ⌂ Cd
Hamlet of stone cottages strung out along Sherborne Brook. Church replete with monuments to Dutton family, once owners of neighbouring Sherborne House, whose park has good views over Windrush valley.

The Slaughters ⌂ Ce
Tucked away in a wooded vale, beautiful Cotswold village of Upper Slaughter has cottages dating from 16th, 17th and 18th centuries, and charming Elizabethan manor house. Neighbouring village of Lower Slaughter has ancient stone bridges and one of the last traditional Cotswold blacksmith's works.

Snowshill Manor ⌂ Bf
Eccentric craftsman, Charles Wade, restored this 17th-century house containing bewildering array of objects he bequeathed to National Trust in 1951. Samurai armour rubs shoulders with Jacobean furniture, old bicycles, compasses and mousetraps.

KNIGHT'S BELL *One of the many curios at Snowshill Manor.*

Stow-on-the-Wold ✝⊡ Ce
Antique shops and art galleries squeeze around market square with medieval stocks.

Sudeley Castle ⌂ Be
Medieval fortress with ruined banqueting hall and tomb of Catherine Parr, sixth wife of Henry VIII. Restored 19th century.

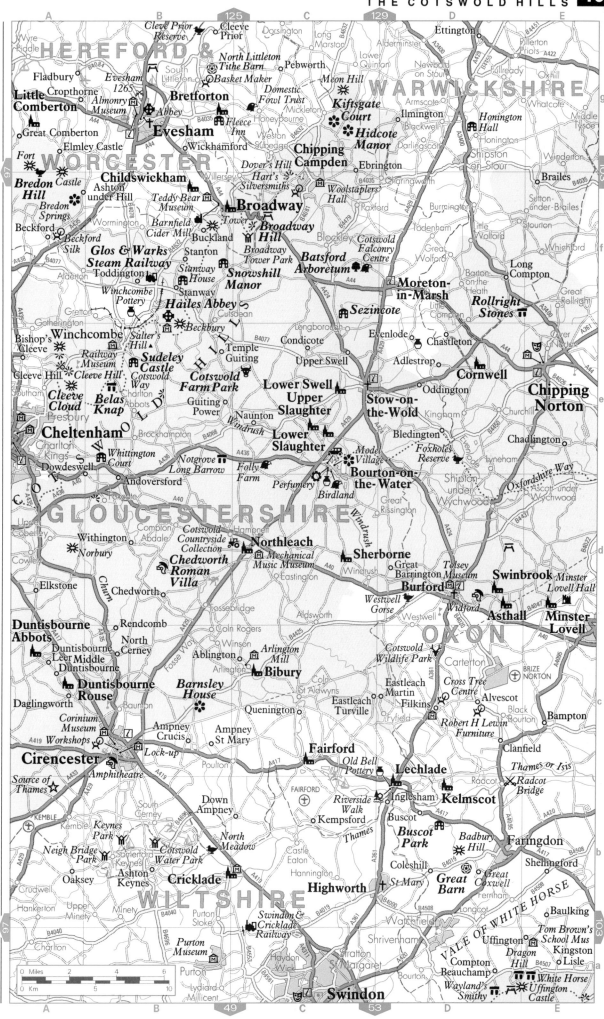

THE HEART OF OXFORDSHIRE

Market towns and villages sit comfortably in a gentle landscape of woods and fields. Local materials give character to the buildings: the golden stones of the Cotswolds; the richer, darker shades of Northamptonshire ironstone; and the warmth of brick, tile and timber to the east. There is everything from the simple charms of a thatched cottage to the baroque splendour of Blenheim Palace.

Abingdon ✿ ♥ ⌂ ☑ Ba
Handsome old houses lead down to Thames. Remains of a Saxon abbey gateway and beautiful 15th-century Long Alley almshouses. Town Hall, 17th century, houses local history museum. Converted jail now a sports centre.

Aston Rowant ⌓ ♥ Ea
Chalk downland, scrub and beech nature reserve on Beacon Hill, with views across Vale of Aylesbury. Look out for fox, badger and deer. Good bird life including uncommon hawfinch.

Aynho ⛪ Ce
Village on a hill where apricot trees grow against cottage walls and gardens burst with petunias. Houses of rich, local stone cluster round hall, rebuilt after Civil War. Church rebuilt in 1725 still has 14th-century tower.

Banbury ⌂ ☑ Bf
Market town and old coaching centre, made famous by nursery rhyme. Market cross of rhyme destroyed in 1602, replaced in 1860. Coaching inns and grand houses still stand.

Bladon ⛪ Bc
Ancient village of stone cottages, where Sir Winston Churchill and his wife lie buried in simple graves at 19th-century Church of St Martin – by north wall of tower. Alongside are his parents, Lord and Lady Randolph Churchill.

Blenheim Palace ⌂ Bc
Built in 1704 for John Churchill, 1st Duke of Marlborough, and birthplace (1874) of Sir Winston

over parkland. Nearby 14th-century church has life-size effigy of Sir John de Broughton, builder of original manor house.

ENTRANCE *Broughton Castle's gatehouse was built about 1405.*

Buckingham ✿ De
Ancient market town, first granted charter by Alfred the Great. Largely rebuilt after 1725 fire; mainly Georgian – even the old jail is elegant. Chantry Chapel still has fine Norman doorway.

Claydon ⛪ ⌂ Bf
Intriguing collection of local memorabilia at Claydon's Granary Museum; everything from beer-pump handles to gas masks.

The Claydons ⛪ ⌂ Ed
Steeple, Middle, East and Botolph Claydons were once manors belonging to 2nd Earl of Verney. He built Claydon House at Middle Claydon in 1752. One room contains Florence Nightingale museum – her sister married former owner Sir Henry Verney.

Cogges Manor Farm Museum ⛪ Ab
Medieval manor house and farm buildings close to church are open-air museum of farming and countryside – history of Cogges village over 1000 years

Deddington ⛪ ⌂ Be
Golden-brown ironstone houses line broad main street and market square. Medieval hall, old inns and fine 13th-century church.

Dorchester ⛪ ⌂ Ca
Abbey Church of St Peter and St Paul dates from 1170. Has 14th-century stained-glass window representing Tree of Jesse and 12th-century lead font. 14th-century gabled building houses village museum. George Hotel, in main street, is 15th century.

Edgehill ✕ Af
Walkers stroll where Charles I's army gathered for battle. Folly tower built a century after the king first raised his standard in 1642; now part of Castle Inn.

Enstone ⛪ ⛏ Ad
Old villages and older stones. Neat Enstone and Church Enstone face each other across gentle Glyme valley. South of Neat Enstone is Hoar Stone Chambered Barrow, a Neolithic burial chamber.

Eynsham Bb
Market town of faded glories. Old town houses built with stones from former abbey, 14th-century cross, arcaded hall in square. Nearby Thames crossed by handsome 1777 toll bridge.

Farnborough Hall ⌂ ☞ Bf
Italianate house, largely rebuilt in 18th century. Principal rooms contain Italian paintings and sculptures. Landscaped terrace with two temples and an obelisk.

Great Tew ⛪ Ad
Mellow stones, roofs of thatch and stone slate, in green setting of encircling trees. Many cottages built by Lord Falkland in 17th century. At top of village, ornate arch frames 14th-century church with battlemented tower.

Islip ⛪ Cc
Best known village on edge of Ot Moor, and 1004 birthplace of Edward the Confessor. Main street of crooked stone houses, cottages and inns, climbs hill from bridge over reedy River Ray.

Kingston House ⌂ Ba
Charles II manor house, surrounded by attractive gardens and park. House features magnificent cantilevered staircase.

Long Wittenham ⛪ ⌂ Ca
Attractive village and good starting point for walk to Wittenham Clumps, topped by Iron Age fort. Pendon Museum of Miniature Landscape and Transport has model countryside and railway.

STONE VISAGE *A Dorchester Abbey corbel bears a benefactor's face.*

North Leigh Roman Villa ⛏ Ac
Patterned mosaic floors, luxurious bath house and extensive servant quarters hint at prosperity of Roman settlers who came here to farm in second century AD.

Rousham Park ⌂ ✿ Bd
Formal classical temples and statues combine with soft contours of Cherwell valley to create one of the best of all early English gardens; William Kent's perfect setting for handsome 17th-century house.

Shotover Country Park ♥ Cb
Wild landscape at the edge of a city. Trails lead through ancient woodland, heath and marshy valleys in 360 acre park. Bird-rich scrub, variety of insects, fallow and muntjac deer. To east of park lies Wheatley, with curious old pyramid-shaped lock-up.

Stanton Harcourt ⛪ ⌂ Bb
Thatched cottages spread out along winding country road. Parts of ruined manor date back to 12th century; old kitchen, Tudor gatehouse and tower where Alexander Pope translated *The Iliad* in 1718. Medieval church has mementos of Harcourt family.

Stoke Bruerne ⛪ ⌂ Eg
Canal village with cottages, whitewashed bridge, inn and colourful narrowboats. Museum,

contained in converted 19th-century grain warehouse tells story of waterways and rural life.

Stowe ✿ De
Best British garden for follies; profusion of classical temples, pavilions, monuments, arches and bridges. Laid out in 18th century by Capability Brown and William Kent.

Sulgrave Manor ⌂ Cf
Home of George Washington's ancestors; modest 16th-century manor house built by Lawrence Washington; buried in 14th-century church.

Thame ⌂ ☑ Eb
The Spread Eagle, made famous in John Fothergill's *An Innkeeper's Diary*, is just one of many inns in this old market town. High Street has 16th-century almshouses.

Towcester ✝ ⌂ Df
The Romans came through on Watling Street and Charles Dickens's *Mr Pickwick* stayed at the Saracen's Head. Chained books in church and racecourse on outskirts of town.

Upton House ⌂ Af
Mansion dating from 1695, remodelled this century but retains classical elegance. Superb art collection includes works by Canaletto, El Greco and Stubbs.

Waddesdon Manor ⌂ ✿ ☞ Ec
Unique French-style château with fairy-tale towers, built 1874-89 for Baron Ferdinand de Rothschild. Porcelain collection, royal furniture and French 18th-century art. Gardens with fountains and statuary. Deer enclosure and aviary with rare birds.

Warmington ⛪ Bf
Buildings of local honey-coloured stone nestle under steep slopes of Edge Hill. Village green and duck pond, 17th-century inn and medieval church combine to create traditional village scene. Several troops killed in Civil War battle of 1642 lie buried in churchyard.

Winslow ⌂ Ed
Old town rich in thatched cottages and in narrow, twisting lanes. Winslow Hall dates from 1700, possibly designed by Wren. Town square inn, The Bell, said to have been a Dick Turpin haunt.

Witney ✝ ⌂ ☑ Ac
Market town famous for blankets. Mills spread down Windrush valley and soaring church spire seen for miles. Unusual Butter Cross, 17th-century, has clock-turret and sundial.

Woodstock ⌂ ⌂ ☑ Bc
Market town of old houses, some with newer, 18th-century façades. Oxfordshire County Museum explains local history. Leather Glove Workshops in Harrison's Lane welcome visitors. Triumphal Arch stands at end of Park Street.

Wytham ⛪ ✿ Bb
Village of grey-stone cottages, surrounded by woods, overlooks River Thames. Lane leads to river where 12th-century hospice now houses popular riverside inn.

CALM WATERS *The Thames flows broad and serene past Abingdon, whose early importance was as a river port and crossing place.*

Churchill. Designed by Vanbrugh in full baroque grandeur, surrounded by Capability Brown's beautiful 2000 acre parkland. Fine paintings, furniture, china and tapestries. Churchill exhibition.

Brill ⛪ ✕ Dc
Picturesque village where 17th-century windmill looks out over green and square, surrounded by red-brick houses.

Broughton Castle ⌂ Be
Moat and battlemented gatehouse disguise elegant country mansion, enlarged in 16th century from a manor house dating back to 1300. Parapet walk with fine views

Burton Dassett ✝ ♥ Bg
Moorland with grassed-over iron-ore quarries, providing sheltered picnic spots. On 630ft Magpie Hill, view indicator identifies landmarks as distant as Malverns and Clee Hills. Hillside All Saints' Church has white interior, 14th-century carvings of animals and foliage, and floor that slopes 15ft from door to chancel.

Charlbury ⌂ ♥ Ac
Small town on tree-clad ridge with honey-coloured stone houses. Museum has displays of local bygones, including penny-farthing bicycle, spinning wheel and agricultural implements.

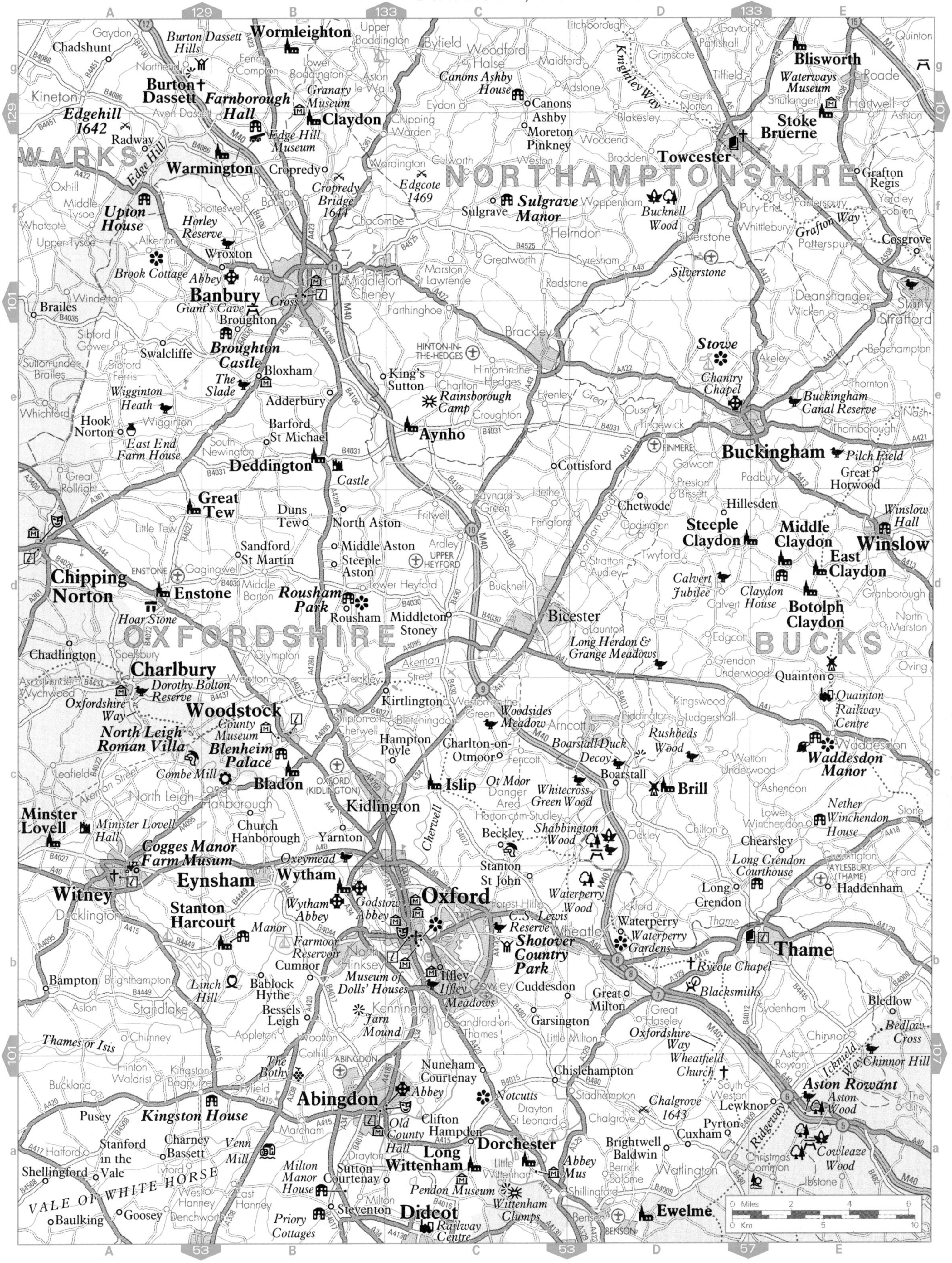

129
133
133
107
101
101
107
53
53
57
A
B
C
D
E
g
f
e
d
c
b
a
Gaydon
Chadshunt
Burton Dassett Hills
Wormleighton
Upper Boddington
Byfield
Woodford Halse
Litchborough
Gayton
Pattishall
Quinton
Blisworth
Northend
Fenny Compton
Lower Boddington
Aston le Walls
Canons Ashby House
Maidford
Grimscote
Knightley Way
Tiffield
Waterways Museum
Roade
Kineton
Burton Dassett
Farnborough Hall
Granary Museum
Claydon
Eydon
Canons Ashby
Adstone
Greens Norton
Shutlanger
Hartwell
Ashton
Edgehill 1642
Avon Dassett
Edge Hill Museum
Chipping Warden
Moreton Pinkney
Blakesley
Stoke Bruerne
Radway
Woodend
WARKS
Edge Hill
Warmington
Cropredy
Wardington
Culworth
Weston
Bradden
Towcester
NORTHAMPTONSHIRE
Grafton Regis
Oxhill
Cropredy Bridge 1644
Edgcote 1469
Middle Tysoe
Upton House
Shotteswell
Great Bourton
Sulgrave
Sulgrave Manor
Wappenham
Bucknell Wood
Pury End
Paulerspury
Yardley Gobion
Whatcote
Horley Reserve
Chacombe
Helmdon
Whittlebury
Grafton Way
Upper Tysoe
Alkerton
Silverstone
Potterspury
Cosgrove
Wroxton
Greatworth
Syresham
Brook Cottage
Abbey
Marston St Lawrence
Silverstone
Banbury
Middleton Cheney
Radstone
Deanshanger
Winderton
Cross
Brailes
Giant's Cave
Farthinghoe
Wicken
Stony Stratford
Broughton
Brackley
Sibford Gower
Swalcliffe
Broughton Castle
HINTON-IN-THE-HEDGES
Stowe
Akeley
Beachampton
Sutton-under-Brailes
Sibford Ferris
Bloxham
King's Sutton
Hinton-in-the-Hedges
Chantry Chapel
Thornton
The Slade
Charlton
Wigginton Heath
Adderbury
Rainsborough Camp
Evenley
Great Ouse
Buckingham Canal Reserve
Whichford
Croughton
Hook Norton
Wigginton
Barford St Michael
Aynho
Tingewick
Nash
Thornborough
East End Farm House
South Newington
FINMERE
Buckingham
Pilch Field
Deddington
Castle
Cottisford
Gawcott
Great Horwood
Great Rollright
Preston Bissett
Padbury
Baynard's Green
Hethe
Great Tew
Chetwode
Hillesden
Little Tew
Duns Tew
North Aston
Fritwell
Fringford
Godington
Steeple Claydon
Middle Claydon
Winslow Hall
Winslow
Sandford St Martin
Middle Aston
Ardley
UPPER HEYFORD
Twyford
East Claydon
Steeple Aston
ENSTONE
Gagingwell
Roman Road
Stratton Audley
Calvert Jubilee
Chipping Norton
Middle Barton
Rousham Park
Lower Heyford
Bucknell
Claydon House
Granborough
Enstone
Calvert
Botolph Claydon
Hoar Stone
Rousham
Middleton Stoney
Bicester
Launton
North Marston
OXFORDSHIRE
BUCKS
Long Herdon & Grange Meadows
Edgcott
Chadlington
Spelsbury
Glympton
Akeman Street
Grendon Underwood
Oving
Charlbury
Wootton
Tackley
Quainton
Ascott-under-Wychwood
Dorothy Bolton Reserve
Kingswood
Quainton Railway Centre
Oxfordshire Way
Woodstock
Kirtlington
Weston-on-the-Green
Woodsides Meadow
Piddington
Ludgershall
County Museum
Shipton-on-Cherwell
Bletchingdon
Arncott
North Leigh Roman Villa
Hampton Poyle
Charlton-on-Otmoor
Boarstall Duck Decoy
Rushbeds Wood
Waddesdon
Blenheim Palace
Fencott
Wotton Underwood
Waddesdon Manor
Leafield
Combe Mill
OXFORD (KIDLINGTON)
Islip
Ot Moor Danger Area
Boarstall
Brill
Ashendon
Bladon
Whitecross Green Wood
Long Hanborough
North Leigh
Kidlington
Cherwell
Horton-cum-Studley
Lower Winchendon
Nether Winchendon House
Stone
Minster Lovell
Minster Lovell Hall
Church Hanborough
Yarnton
Beckley
Shabbington Wood
Oakley
Chilton
Chearsley
Cogges Manor Farm Musum
Oxeymead
Long Crendon Courthouse
Cuddington
Stanton St John
AYLESBURY (THAME)
Ford
Witney
Eynsham
Wytham
Oxford
Waterperry Wood
Long Crendon
Haddenham
Ducklington
Wytham Abbey
Godstow Abbey
Forest Hill
C.S. Lewis Reserve
Ickford
Waterperry
Stanton Harcourt
Manor
Wheatley
Thame
Shotover Country Park
Waterperry Gardens
Farmoor Reservoir
North Hinksey
Rycote Chapel
Bampton
Brighthampton
Cumnor
Museum of Dolls' Houses
Iffley
Iffley Meadows
Cowley
Cuddesdon
Great Milton
Blacksmiths
Linch Hill
Bablock Hythe
Bessels Leigh
Kennington
Jarn Mound
Garsington
Great Haseley
Sydenham
Bledlow
Aston
Standlake
Sandford-on-Thames
Oxfordshire Way
Bledlow Cross
Thames or Isis
Chimney
Appleton
Wootton
Little Milton
Chinnor
Cothill
Wheatfield Church
Aston Rowant
Chinnor Hill
Icknield Way
Hinton Waldrist
Kingston Bagpuize
The Bothy
ABINGDON
Nuneham Courtenay
Chislehampton
South Weston
Aston Rowant
Buckland
Fyfield
Abbey
Notcutts
Stadhampton
Chalgrove 1643
Lewknor
Aston Wood
The City
Abingdon
Drayton St Leonard
Pusey
Kingston House
Marcham
Clifton Hampden
Chalgrove
Pyrton
Ridgeway
Cuxham
Stanford in the Vale
Charney Bassett
Venn Mill
Old County Hall
Dorchester
Brightwell Baldwin
Cowleaze Wood
Hatford
Drayton
Long Wittenham
Abbey Mus
Christmas Common
Shellingford
Lyford
Sutton Courtenay
Milton Manor House
Little Wittenham
Berrick Salome
Watlington
Stoke
VALE OF WHITE HORSE
West Hanney
East Hanney
Milton
Pendon Museum
Shillingford
Ibstone
Baulking
Goosey
Denchworth
Steventon
Didcot
Wittenham Clumps
Ewelme
Priory Cottages
Railway Centre
Benson
BENSON
Miles
Km
0
2
4
6
0
5
10

ANCIENT AND MODERN UNITED

A beautiful city whose dreaming spires, echoing quads and cloistered lawns contain a timeless beauty. Oxford grew into a world-famous seat of learning after the first colleges were founded in the 13th century. Each has its own unique appeal, and among them are to be found many more venerable attractions, all enclosed within the peaceful courses of the rivers Thames and Cherwell.

All Souls College Cb
Graduate college, founded 1438 as memorial to Henry V and heroes of Agincourt. Sir Christopher Wren designed sundial on library. Medieval hall is well-preserved.

Ashmolean Museum 🏛 Bc
Britain's oldest public museum, opened 1683, has a fine collection of paintings and relics from past civilisations. These include gold and enamel jewel believed to have belonged to King Alfred, lantern carried by Guy Fawkes and riches from Egypt and the Aegean.

Balliol College Bc
Planned as a penance by John de Baliol in 1263 after he had insulted the Bishop of Durham by calling him names. Doors in one corner of Front Quad were charred by the fire which put Bishops Latimer and Ridley to their deaths.

Bate Collection of Historical Instruments 🏛 Ca
Wide-ranging collection of wood-wind, brass and percussion instruments, including a full Javanese gamelan orchestra.

Beaumont Street Bc
A tablet outside No. 24 marks the site of former Beaumont Palace, birthplace of Richard the Lion-heart. The street was laid out between 1828 and 1837.

Bodleian Library Cc
Founded in 1598, it receives a copy of every book published in Britain and now has more than 5 million volumes. Incorporates the 1444 Duke Humfrey's Library which originally housed rare manuscripts given by the duke, the youngest son of Henry IV.

TRANQUIL STUDY *The 'dreaming spires' on the horizon provide a calm backdrop to Christ Church meadow.*

PEDAL POWER *A cyclist passes under Hertford College's Bridge of Sighs.*

Botanic Gardens ✿ Db
Britain's oldest, founded in 1621 by Henry Danvers, Earl of Danby, to grow plants for scientific study. Has pools, herbaceous borders and rock gardens. Glasshouses of exotic plants line River Cherwell.

Brasenose College Cb
The front facing Radcliffe Square and a knocker over the college gate date from the college's foundation in 1509. The roof of the chapel and a kitchen range off the hall are 15th century.

Bridge of Sighs Cc
A copy of the famous Venetian bridge was built in 1913 - 14 to link the north and south quadrangles of Hertford College.

Broad Street Bc
Blackwell's Children's Bookshop was the first of its kind in Britain. It remains the largest stockist of children's books in the country, and also has cassettes and toys. Remains of the old city wall can be seen from the first floor.

Carfax Tower Bb
All that remains from the 14th-century Church of St Martin, standing above the city's ancient crossroads: the name Carfax is derived from the Latin *quadrifurcus*, 'four-forked'. Gilded quarterboys strike the quarter hours, and there are fine views of the colleges from the top of the tower.

Christ Church ✝ Bb
Founded by Cardinal Wolsey in 1525, the college has Oxford's largest quadrangle and medieval hall. The chapel, formerly the church of a 12th-century priory demolished during the building of the college, serves as Oxford's cathedral and is the smallest in England. The chief glory is the vaulted choir.

Christ Church Meadow Ca
Site of the city's first settlement, an ox-drovers' fording place on the Thames in Saxon times. Has good views of the city's skyline.

Christ Church Picture Gallery 🏛 Cb
Most impressive array of paintings and drawings of any college in Oxford, with emphasis on 14th to 17th-century Italian work. Exhibits selected from large collection include drawings by Rembrandt, Da Vinci, Michelangelo, Titian, and Rubens. Also has portraits by Reynolds, Gainsborough, Lely and others of former college members, on show in college dining hall and normally open to public.

Church of St Michael ✝ Bc
The 11th-century tower is the oldest building in Oxford, and east window has city's oldest stained glass, from about 1290. In 1606 William Shakespeare stood beside font as a godfather.

Clarendon Building Cc
Former home of University Press, designed by Wren's most outstanding pupil, Nicholas Hawksmoor, and erected 1711-15.

Corpus Christi College Cb
Founded in 1517. In the centre of Front Quad stands Turnbull Sundial, with 27 separate sundials, topped by a pelican with a bleeding heart. Only college to retain its founder's plate; other colleges gave theirs to help Charles I. Fellows' Quad is Oxford's smallest.

Divinity School Cc
Oldest lecture room in university, hardly altered since completion in 1490. Has the first book printed in England by Caxton, and an exquisite vaulted ceiling.

Holywell Music Room Cc
Oldest concert hall in Europe belongs to the university's music faculty and has been in almost continuous use since 1748.

Magdalen College Db
Buildings little changed since they were erected towards end of 15th century. Majestic square tower with peal of ten bells; some of city's finest gargoyles; deer park and walks alongside Cherwell.

Martyrs' Memorial Bc
Victorian Gothic memorial commemorates Bishops Latimer and Ridley, burned at the stake for their Protestant faith in 1555, and Archbishop Cranmer who met with the same fate in 1556.

Merton College Cb
First residential college, founded 1264. Part enclosed by old city wall, and some of original structure survives. Gave university one of its characteristic features, the quadrangle. Chapel has 13th-century stained-glass windows.

Merton College Library Cb
Oldest college library in England, built 1370s. Relics include an astrolabe – medieval instrument used for astronomical calculations – thought to have belonged to Geoffrey Chaucer.

Museum of the History of Science 🏛 Cc
Early astronomical, mathematical, optical and scientific instruments; also a blackboard used by Einstein in 1931 lecture at Oxford.

Museum of Modern Art 🏛 Bb
A leading European visual arts centre, it includes international 20th-century painting, sculpture, architecture and photography.

Museum of Oxford 🏛 Bb
Housed in Victorian town hall, tells story of city and university with relics, photographs, models and reconstructed interiors from 16th century to present day.

FACE OF WOE *A gargoyle adorns a wall along New College Lane.*

New College Cc
City wall serves as boundary to the attractive gardens of college, founded by the Bishop of Winchester in 1386; his jewelled crosier is in chapel. Much Gothic work survives.

New College Lane Cc
A collection of modern gargoyles featuring humans and animals mixes horror with humour.

Oriel College Cb
Founded 1324 and refounded two years later by Edward II, the first royal foundation in Oxford. No medieval structures survive.

Oxford Castle 🏰 Ab
St George's Tower and the Mound rise above river, all that remain of Norman castle built around 1071. Both visible from Paradise Street.

Pitt Rivers Museum 🏛 Cd
More than 14,000 items of world-wide ethnology and archaeology. Folk life section and musical instrument collection.

Queen's College Cb
Named after Queen Philippa, wife of Edward III. Her chaplain founded college in 1341, although present buildings date from the 18th century. Design of college considered to be an unrivalled example of Palladian style.

DOCTOR'S GIFT *Dr John Radcliffe left funds to build the circular library.*

Radcliffe Camera Cb
Impressive circular building completed in 1749 as England's first round library, with tall Corinthian columns supporting a parapet topped by a dome and lantern.

St Edmund Hall Cb
Last surviving medieval hall dates from 1238. Front quadrangle still has original well in its centre.

St John's College Bc
The front quadrangle was part of the original college founded in 1437 especially for Cistercian monks. Canterbury Quad is elegantly arcaded, and behind the college stretch 5 acres of gardens, designed by Capability Brown.

Sheldonian Theatre Cc
Designed by Wren in 1664 and still used for university functions. Based on a Roman theatre, it is semicircular and fronted with classical pilasters and columns. Superb city vistas from cupola.

The Oxford Story Bc
Life-size models of great Oxford men and women help to re-create eight centuries of the university's past in an exhibition of sights, sounds and smells.

Tom Tower Bb
Octagonal tower designed by Wren in 1682 capping gateway of Christ Church. The 7 ton bell, Great Tom, is rung 101 times every night at 9.05, the old signal for the closing of the college gates.

Trinity College Bc
Founded in 1555 by Sir Thomas Pope, whose alabaster tomb is in the chapel, it incorporates parts of the 14th-century Durham College. The gardens have a 1713 Lime Walk and a quadrangle designed by Wren.

Turl Street Bc
The heart of collegiate Oxford, flanked by three colleges – Exeter, founded in 1314, Jesus (1571) and Lincoln (1427).

University Church of St Mary the Virgin ✝ Cb
Restored mainly 15th-century church, with 13th-century north tower and a bold 14th-century spire. Gargoyled and pinnacled tower gives one of best panoramas over the colleges. Baroque south porch of about 1637 has 'barley-sugar' twisted columns.

University College Cb
Front quadrangle has memorial to poet Shelley, depicted after his death by drowning. College founded 1249. Shelley was most famous son, though sent down for distributing atheist pamphlet.

University Museum 🏛 Cd
Natural history museum includes the university's zoology and geology collections dating from the 17th century onwards.

Wadham College Cc
Founded by Nicholas Wadham and completed in 1613, four years after his death. Noted for its well-laid-out and secluded gardens.

Worcester College Ac
Founded in 1714 on site of Benedictine college, from which row of monks' cottages survives. Library has original designs and drawings by Inigo Jones, and extensive gardens are noted for the lake.

PEACEFUL OASIS *Wadham College was named after its founder, a Somerset squire. It was built in its entirety early in the 17th century, and is little changed. The Chapel and Hall are notably well-preserved, and there are secluded gardens.*

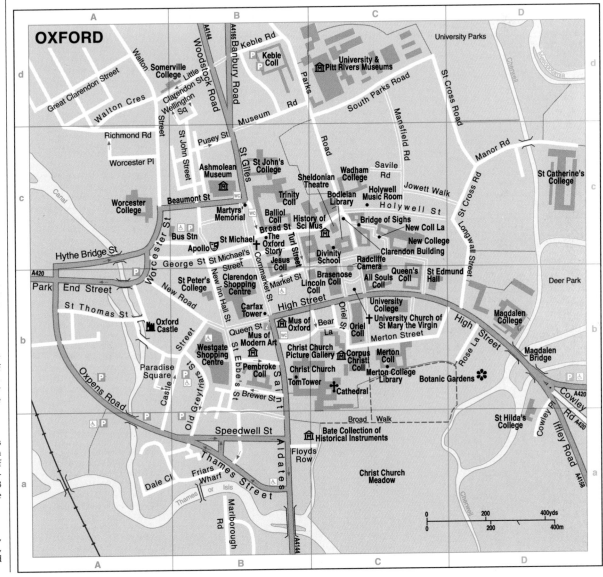

Amersham ✝ 🏛 Ca
Town High Street has Georgian houses, gabled and timbered inns, cobbled courtyards leading to thatched cottages. Market Hall and almshouses both date from 17th century. Church dates from 1140, restored 19th century, with fine brasses and monuments.

Ascott 🏠 Bd
Mock-Tudor hunting lodge built 1870 to take Anthony de Rothschild's collection of English and Italian paintings, French and Chippendale furniture, and Chinese porcelain. Fine gardens with immense topiary sundial.

Ashridge Park ❀ ⚘ Cc
Top of 108ft tall Bridgewater Monument peeps above this forest; erected 1831 in memory of canal pioneer, 3rd Duke of Bridgewater. Climb 172 steps to top, or follow walks through woods. Look for fallow and muntjac deer. On eastern side, Gothic revival Ashridge House (now a college) begun 1808 by James Wyatt. Set in fine gardens landscaped by Humphry Repton and Capability Brown.

Aylesbury ✝ 🏛 ☑ Bc
Buckinghamshire's county town, rich in narrow Tudor alleyways, courtyards, and some good 17th-century houses. Church of St Mary's dates from 13th century; restored 1848. King's Head Inn founded 1386 has medieval gateway and 15th-century stained glass. County Museum housed in interesting group of 18th-century buildings, with Rural Life Gallery.

Bedford 🏛 ☖ ☑ Df
Town where author John Bunyan lived, and was imprisoned for his religious beliefs in the 1660s and 1670s. Meeting House of 1849 stands on site of barn where he preached; adjoining Bunyan Museum has personal relics. Costumes and toys, ceramics and glass, English watercolours and modern sculpture in Cecil Higgins Art Gallery. Local and natural history displays in Bedford Museum.

PILGRIM ON THE CHALK HILLS

Preacher and writer John Bunyan was born in Bedfordshire in 1628; the area across which Christian walked in The Pilgrim's Progress. *Although much of Buckinghamshire is now a commuting area, many villages retain their traditional Chiltern character. Everywhere has a peaceful charm – from the valley of the Ouse to the Dunstable Downs, with their rich wildlife.*

Berkhamsted 🏰 ✝ ☑ Cb
Country town on Grand Union Canal, where William the Conqueror accepted English throne in 1066. Norman castle was a favourite royal residence until time of Elizabeth I – now in ruins. The 13th-century Church of St Peter has window dedicated to poet and hymn writer William Cowper, born at Berkhamsted Rectory in 1731.

Biddenham 🏠 Df
Quiet village of colour-washed cottages; some of them splendidly thatched. The larger houses date mostly from 19th century, including a fine merchant's house. The Church of St James (12th century) has a Jacobean screen.

Bromham Mill 🏛 Dg
Restored water mill beside River Ouse with countryside exhibition centre. Part brick-built around 1700 and part stone-built in 1858. Picnic in surrounding water meadow, where dragonflies and kingfishers can be seen.

Chalfont St Giles 🏠🏛 Ca
Village where poet John Milton escaped London's Great Plague to complete *Paradise Lost* and begin *Paradise Regained*. His 16th-century cottage has personal relics and manuscripts. Chiltern Open Air Museum, set in Newland Park, has rural life displays.

Chenies Manor House 🏠 Da
Brick-built manor owned by Russell family (Earls and Dukes of Bedford) from 1526 until 1955.

Tudor gardens with old-world flowers, 400-year-old lawns, sundial and ancient well.

Coombe Hill ❀ ⚘ Bb
One of the highest points in the Chilterns at 852ft. Magnificent views of neighbouring ridges and Vale of Aylesbury. Monument perched on hillside commemorates those Buckinghamshire men who died in the Boer War.

Dunstable Downs ❀ ⚘ Dc
Intoxicating views over the Vale of Aylesbury from these rolling stretches of grassland. Lanes lead south-east to Whipsnade Heath, where in 1930s a local landowner planted trees that matured into a 'Tree Cathedral' with nave, cloisters and chapels. Fairy flax and chalk milkwort among rare plants to be found on downs. Wild birds include whinchats and warblers.

Elstow 🏠 Df
Author John Bunyan born a mile east in Harrowden (1628) and spent childhood in this village. Behind Norman church, cloisters and fishponds remain from nunnery founded by William the Conqueror's sister. Fine late 15th-century Moot Hall was a meeting place for Bunyan's followers; now contains rural life exhibition.

Hanslope 🏠 Bf
Village centred around small square, overlooked by stone-built thatched cottages; several with 17th-century date stones. Landmark church has 186ft steeple. Inside, long staves with claw-like

heads were used for pulling thatch from burning houses before days of fire brigades.

Hemel Hempstead ✝ ☑ Db
Old town in a valley in the Chilterns formed by the River Gade. St Mary's Church is mainly Norman. Tudor cottages and 17th and 18th-century buildings in High Street. New town added in 1947.

MARKET HOUSE *This is one of High Wycombe's few old buildings.*

High Wycombe 🏠🏛 ☑ Ba
Largely industrial town with a few old buildings: 13th-century church; Guildhall dating from 1757; Little Market House from 1604. Late 17th-century Castle Hill House, set in grounds of medieval motte and bailey, houses Chair Museum telling story of High Wycombe furniture industry.

Hughenden Manor 🏠 Ba
Home of Benjamin Disraeli from 1847 until his death in 1881; Prime Minister of Great Britain under Queen Victoria. He 'gothicised' a plain Georgian building, adding Jacobean-style parapets.

Ivinghoe Beacon ❀ Cc
Chalk hillside with paths to summit; one of several beacon points established during reign of Elizabeth I to summon men in case of Spanish invasion. Wild flowers include thyme and rock-roses.

Luton ⊕ ☖ 🏠 🏛 ☑ Dd
Once a straw hat and lace-making centre; now famous for automobiles and airport. Social and natural history displays in Luton Museum and Art Gallery, housed in Victorian mansion with extensive parkland. Horse-drawn carriages in the Mossman Exhibition.

Luton Hoo 🏠 Ec
Large stone mansion surrounded by 1200 acre Capability Brown park. Begun 1767 by Robert Adam, it owes its present appearance to diamond tycoon, Sir Julius Wernher, who bought it in 1903. Full of family treasures: Renaissance jewels; French furniture, porcelain and tapestries; Russian items by Fabergé.

Marston Moretaine 🏠 Cf
Judgment Day came to Church of St Mary (rebuilt 1445) when a magnificent Doom wall painting

was uncovered in 1969; depicting Christ sending people to heaven or hell as they rise from graves.

Princes Risborough Bb
Town with thatched cottages and brick market house with arcades. Owned by National Trust, 17th-century manor is open only by written appointment from tenant.

Redbourn 🏠 Dc
Village High Street stretches along part of Roman Watling Street; Roman bricks were re-used in Norman tower of St Mary's Church. Nave and aisle are also Norman. Redbourn Common is edged with timber-framed, thatched and Georgian houses.

Sharpenhoe Clappers ⚘ 🌲 Dd
Crooked finger of low hills stretch across Bedfordshire plain, rising to 525ft at Sharpenhoe, crowned by Clappers Wood. Road leads up from the village to National Trust car park for footpaths through wooded glen and hedgerows.

Stagsden Bird Gardens 🐦 Cf
Breeding and conservation centre specialising in pheasants, waterfowl and poultry. More than 150 species, many of which are rare.

Stewartby Lake ⛵ Df
Disused claypit covering 287 acres forms centre for bankside walks and birdwatching. Sailing at the Water Sports Club.

Tring 🏛 Cc
Small market town with Zoological Museum crammed with hundreds of stuffed species. One mile north, Tring Reservoirs National Reserve is home to many water birds, including great crested grebe, heron and pochard.

DISRAELI'S DREAM *Sloping park and woods of Hughenden Manor.*

Turvey 🏠 ⛵ Cg
Curious effigy of Jonah and the Whale near a 13th-century stone bridge. Saxon Church of All Saints, restored by Sir George Gilbert Scott during 19th century, has 12th-century font and 14th-century wall painting. Numerous brasses from 15th century onwards.

Watford ✝ ⛲ 🏛 Da
Dormitory town with 1539 flint-built parish church containing 17th-century pulpit. Cassiobury Park belonged to Earls of Essex; mansion no longer exists, but the grounds are a public park with walks along Grand Union Canal and River Gade. Narrowboat trips depart from Ironbridge Lock. West lies the Whippendell Wood with nature trail.

TRANQUIL TURVEY *On a sultry summer's day, the tree-shaded banks of the River Ouse provide a cool resting place.*

Wendover Woods
Bb

Part of Chiltern Forest (and highest part of Chilterns at 876ft) blanketing steep ridges of Boddington, Haddington and Aston hills. Aston Hill is starting point for waymarked walks and trails.

Weston Underwood
Bg

Stone gateway, built 1700, forms entrance to village with thatched cottages, barns and manor. Home of the poet William Cowper (1731-1800), whose house is still there. Birds and animals in natural settings at Flamingo Gardens and Zoological Park.

West Wycombe
Ba

Village of fine 15th to 18th-century houses. Hill-top church surmounted by golden ball inside which members of notorious Hell Fire Club used to meet – a fraternity of knights founded 1746 by Sir Francis Dashwood (1708-81). He built adjacent mausoleum in 1763, and the Palladian mansion of West Wycombe Park in 1750. Rooms are superbly decorated with painted ceilings by Borgnis. Humphry Repton landscaped the grounds with lake and temples. Caves in hill are where Hell Fire Club conducted secret revels; tableaux recall Dashwood and his time.

Whipsnade Zoo
Dc

Open-air zoo on Dunstable Downs where 2000 animals roam 500 acre park. Rarities include herd of white rhinoceroses and breeding group of Przewalski's wild horse. Sea lions and other water mammals on display.

Whitchurch
Bd

Delightful village of half-timbered cottages and a fine church with 15th-century painting. Novelist Jan Struther, of *Mrs Miniver* fame, lived here and wrote her patriotic sketches about village life in the early days of Second World War. Her house, The Priory, is now a hotel.

Woburn
Ce

The Dukes of Bedford once owned a tenth of the county; many cottages still have the carved monogram 'B' and a coronet on their façades. Original Woburn Abbey (founded 1145) passed to them at the Dissolution. Present building owes its appearance to 18th-century dukes who transformed it into a palatial country mansion. Crammed with paintings, furniture, porcelain and silver collected by Dukes of Bedford over past 250 years. The 3000 acre park, landscaped by Humphry Repton, has rare Chinese Père David's deer. Elephants, lions and giraffes in Woburn Wild Animal Kingdom.

Wrest Park
De

Estate of the de Grey family, first Earls – then Dukes – of Kent, from 1280 until family died out. Present house, built 1835, now an agricultural college. Staterooms can be seen. Unusual gardens with canals, star-shaped pavilion, pagan altar, Chinese bridge and paths leading to summerhouses. Represents 150 years of garden design, starting with the formality of the early 1700s and ending with French-style symmetry in early Victorian times.

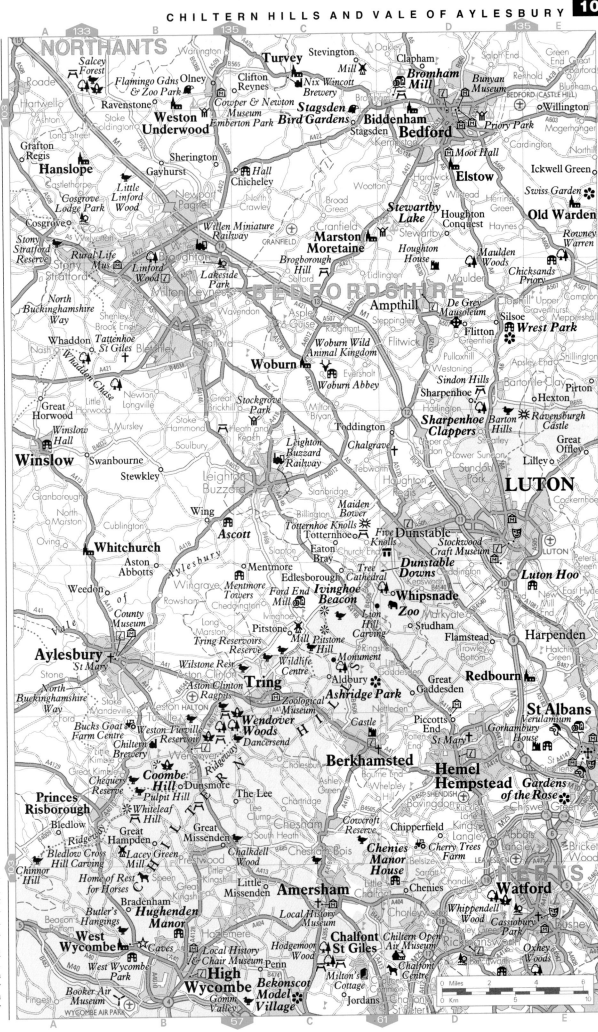

LEAFY LANES AND ANCIENT ABBEY

Advancing north from London, the Romans founded a hillside city at present-day St Albans and a town at Cambridge. Later, across the gentle chalk uplands of Hertfordshire and west Essex, forests were cleared for market towns and villages, many of which remain unspoilt, their houses embellished with decorative plasterwork. Farther north, fenland has been drained to create fertile farms.

Anglesey Abbey Eg
Tudor manor house built around 12th-century abbey ruins. Lord Fairhaven landscaped 100 acres of fenland. Tree-lined avenues, thousands of spring bulbs, elegant statues. House contains fine paintings and furniture.

Audley End Ed
Village mainly Georgian, with Jacobean almshouses. House (1603) built for 1st Earl of Suffolk. Grand entrance hall and staircase. Much fine decorative work by Adam; elegant 18th-century furniture. Classical grounds.

Ayot St Lawrence Ab
Peaceful village where George Bernard Shaw made his home, scarcely altered since death in 1950; typewriter still sits on study desk and hats still hang in hall. Ruined 14th-century church and 18th-century Grecian-style successor, timber-framed cottages, and 17th-century Old Rectory.

Benington Lordship Gardens Bc
Hill-top gardens designed around 18th-century manor house with Norman keep. Rock, water, and walled kitchen garden. Brilliant beds of roses.

Bishop's Stortford Dc
Busy market town with fine 15th-century church. Cecil Rhodes (British imperialist who became prime minister of Cape Colony in 1890) born at Old Vicarage; now Memorial Museum and Commonwealth Centre.

Chipping Ongar Ea
A 50ft mound marks site of 11th-century castle. Main street fronted by houses dating from 1624. Nearby Greensted has historic Saxon church with nave wall made of oak logs.

Clavering Dd
Village of old cottages with moat encircling meadow where Sheriff of Essex built castle in 1052. Church dates from 14th century. One of Britain's smallest houses stands beside river.

Docwra's Manor Ce
Exotic and familiar plants spill out of raised beds, stone troughs and old sinks in 2 acres of inventive garden design.

Duxford De
Airfield has seen real and screen action; now belongs to Imperial War Museum. Superb collection of historic aircraft from First World War fighters to first Concorde ever flown.

Fowlmere De
Oasis for resident warblers and kingfishers in 85 acre fen reed bed with boardwalks and hides. Stop-over for migratory birds.

Furneux Pelham Dc
Largest of three Pelham villages once owned by Norman family in heart of rolling wheatfields. Mainly 15th-century church, gloriously restored, has windows by Morris and Burne-Jones. Footpaths connect to Stocking Pelham with thatched pub, and Brent Pelham with medieval stocks and whipping post.

OLD PALACE *The original Tudor building where Elizabeth I lived as a child still stands next to Hatfield House.*

Gardens of the Rose Aa
Said to be world's greatest rose collection; 12 acre garden with some 30,000 types grown by Royal National Rose Society.

Grantchester Df
Pretty village of thatch, timber and plaster beside River Cam has captured hearts of many writers; Chaucer, Milton, Byron, and Rupert Brooke who wrote poem *The Old Vicarage, Grantchester.* Vicarage still stands.

Hatfield Forest Eb
Over 1000 acres of ancient woodland, once royal hunting ground. Nature walks and coarse fishing. Look for Canada geese, pochards and tufted ducks in winter.

Hatfield House Ba
Superb red-brick Jacobean mansion built by Robert Cecil, 1st Earl of Salisbury, between 1607 and 1611. Marble Hall with richly carved oak ceiling; Grand Staircase with heraldic beasts; Long

TIMELY WARNINGS *Sombre mottoes adorn St Mary's clock at Furneux Pelham.*

Gallery with gold-leaf ceiling. West Gardens re-created in 17th-century formal style.

Hertford Cb
Attractive county town with many fine buildings faced with decorative plasterwork. Some of the most interesting are in Salisbury and Parliament squares. Present castle is 15th-century gatehouse to demolished Norman castle. Old Verger's House, timber-framed, dates from 1450.

Ickleton De
Normans made use of Roman tiles and columns when building unusual parish church. Remarkable interior; arcades resting partly on Roman monolith columns. Strange beasts carved on pews and churchyard wall.

Ickwell Green Ae
Pretty village built around vast green with maypole, still used for May Day festivities. Brightly painted cottages and old forge with horseshoe-shaped doorway, the 17th-century workshop of Thomas Tompion – father of English clock-making.

Knebworth House Bc
Ancestral home of Lytton family. Gothic towers and turrets, and Tudor Great Hall behind Victorian embellishments. Library doors masquerade as bookshelves. Set in 250 acres of formal gardens and deer park.

Mole Hall Ed
Unusual mixture of animals from home and abroad, including wallabies, chimps and otters. Wildfowl nest in moat of 13th-century manor house. Butterfly pavilion.

Much Hadham Db
Showpiece village, for centuries the country seat of the Bishops of London. Their palace, near 12th-century church, is mainly Jacobean. Main street of Elizabethan cottages and Regency houses.

Newport Ed
Once a 13th-century market town. Red-brick Monk's Barn in main street was 15th-century 'holiday' retreat for monks. Three late medieval houses by green; church has rare altar chest.

Old Warden Ae
Lord Ongley built roomy thatched cottages for tenants in 19th century. Veteran motor cars in Shuttleworth Collection, and historic aircraft that fly above Biggleswade Airfield on summer weekends. Old Warden Park has romantic Swiss Garden.

Prior's Hall Barn Ed
Splendid aisled barn built from unseasoned oak beams, little altered since 14th century. Scars of original wattle and daub in posts and studs.

St Albans Aa
Commuter town where Romans built city of *Verulamium* by River Ver; walls, amphitheatre, and centrally heated mosaic floors preserved. Christian martyr St Alban beheaded on hill where imposing cathedral now stands.

St Neots Ag
Magnificent church tower soars above market square framed by Georgian houses backing onto Great Ouse. Riverside terrace at 17th-century Bridge Hotel.

Saffron Walden Ed
Unspoilt town dominated by 193ft spire of Essex's largest church. Saffron crocus brought prosperity for 400 years; grown for yellow dye used to colour cloth and cakes. Tangle of 15th and 16th-century timber-framed buildings, decorated with elaborate plasterwork known as 'pargeting'.

Sandy Ae
Headquarters for RSPB with adjoining 104 acre reserve. Formal gardens lead into parkland, woodland and heathland. Trails offer chance to see some of 100 species, including Britain's three native woodpeckers.

Stansted Mountfitchet Ec
Busy town where Norman family built motte-and-bailey castle. Destroyed by King John, now re-created with giant catapult, thatched falconry and white-washed Grand Hall. Row of well-preserved 16th-century houses below. Restored tower windmill of 1787 up Chapel Hill.

Waltham Abbey Ca
Church is all that remains of huge abbey founded by King Harold. Norman nave and aisles, 14th-century south chapel, 16th-century west tower. Plain slab said to mark Harold's tomb.

WATER IMAGE *Waltham Abbey's ancient gatehouse stands reflected in a tributary of the Lee.*

Wandlebury Df
Gog Magog Hills are crowned by Iron Age fort, whose ramparts enclose 15 acres. Nearby building is stable block of now-demolished mansion. Famous Arab stallion buried beneath central arch in 1753. Nature trail in grounds.

Ware Cb
Important medieval malting and milling centre, whose famous 'Great Bed of Ware' is now in Victoria and Albert Museum. Mainly 14th and 15th-century church has fine 1400 font. Lady Jane Grey proclaimed Queen at Ware in 1553. Council offices occupy remains of Franciscan priory.

Wimpole Hall Cf
Generations of owners, including Kipling's daughter, have rebuilt and added to 17th-century central block to create magnificent stately home. Capability Brown and Humphry Repton remodelled original gardens of 3000 acre estate. Museum of farming equipment and rare breeds farm.

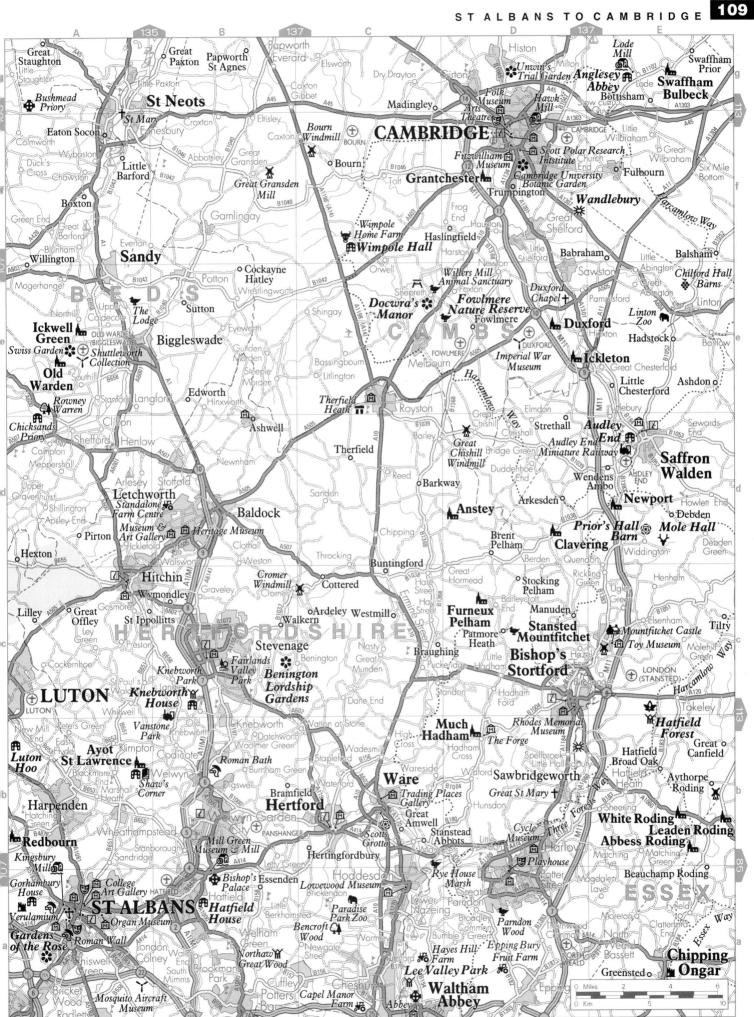

FENLAND SEAT OF LEARNING

Here, in a tranquil rural setting, lies a city of colleges founded as acts of piety by or for the personal glorification of each founder. The city's winding streets are lined with old houses and shops and even older colleges and churches, while the gently flowing River Cam, shaded by trees, provides a serene accompaniment to the architectural splendours.

The Backs Ad
Green expanse of lawns beside River Cam is ideal for strolling, viewing some of finest buildings in Cambridge, or just lounging while college and city clubs hold their 'Bumps' rowing races. In summer, there are leisurely parades of punts. Elegant bridges, shaded by weeping willows, link colleges to The Backs.

Cambridge and County Folk Museum ☖ Ad
Former White Horse Inn houses a huge array of items collected from city and surrounding countryside. This includes trade tools, domestic crafts, toys, furniture and farm equipment.

Christ's College Bc
Founded in 1440s as a teachers' college known as God's House, it was once the poorest of colleges. In 1505 it was reformed by Lady Margaret Beaufort, whose arms and statue stand high in turreted gatehouse. The chapel has an oriel

Downing College Cb
It took two centuries to complete work allowed for in 1749 will of Sir George Downing. Main building begun by William Wilkins in 1807, who decided upon Greek style and an arrangement of blocks more open than traditional pattern of courts. Though his plan could not be completed for lack of funds, his successors used the same classical style in detail and layout, up to completion of chapel in 1953 and Kenny Court in 1963. Style is unique in Cambridge.

Gonville and Caius College Bc
Founder Edmund Gonville's 1348 buildings have been considerably altered. Dr John Caius's further endowment in 1557 added a second court with three gates to symbolise students' progress. Two remain: 'Virtue' leads to

founded 1816 by 7th Viscount Fitzwilliam, who left university £100,000, library and art collections. Interior rich in marble and rococo adornments.

Kettles Yard Art Gallery ☖ Ad
Collector Jim Ede, who lived here, bought works of 20th-century artists, which can be seen among his furnishings and belongings.

King's College Ac
Founded in 1441 by Henry VI, though most of the building is of much later date. James Gibbs designed the Fellows' Building in 1724, but the Victorians returned to medieval themes.

King's College Chapel † Ac
Henry VI's Gothic masterpiece, begun 1446 and completed 1515 under Henry VIII. Its superb fan-vaulted ceiling is 80ft high and stretches nearly 300ft.

King's Parade Bc
Former high street of Cambridge, lined with buildings of different periods, heights and styles; the oldest is 16th century, but those of the 18th and 19th set the mood.

Little St Mary's Church † Bb
An elaborately decorated church dating from 14th century, also called St Mary the Less.

Magdalene College Ad
First court built late 1400s as Buckingham College for Benedictine monks. At Dissolution of Monasteries Henry VIII gave college to his Lord Chancellor, Baron Audley of Walden, who refounded it 1542 as 'The College of St Mary Magdalene'.

Mathematical Bridge Ab
Constructed 1749 from straight timbers to form graceful arch over the River Cam at Queens' College. Screws or bolts used only at main joints. Rebuilt of teak in 1904 to the original design.

Pembroke College Bb
Chapel built 1663-5 was the first completed design by Christopher Wren. His uncle, Bishop Wren of Ely, had given university £5000 to pay for it. The college was founded 1347 by widowed Countess of Pembroke. Some of the medieval building survives.

Pepys Library Bd
Samuel Pepys (1633-1703) left 3000 books, including six volumes of diary written in shorthand, to his old college. Library contained in bookcases he designed himself.

Peterhouse Bb
Oldest college in Cambridge was founded in 1284 by Hugh de Balsham, Bishop of Ely, for a Master and 'fourteen worthy but impoverished Fellows'. Hall is only building to retain some of the original masonry, though it was heavily restored in the 1870s.

Queens' College Ac
Margaret of Anjou, Henry VI's queen, refounded St Bernard's 1448 as Queen's College. Edward IV's queen, Elizabeth Woodville, became patroness. Support of both queens acknowledged in spelling *Queens'*. Old Court, completed 1449, is almost unaltered example of medieval brickwork.

MILITARY MONKS *Crusaders built the Norman Round Church.*

The Round Church † Bd
Circular Church of Holy Sepulchre built around 1130 by crusading monastic order in imitation of original Holy Sepulchre in Jerusalem. Carvings of demons and Norman warriors on walls. North aisle and chancel are 14th century. Heavily restored 1841-3.

WOODEN WONDER *This elaborate coat of arms in Wren's library at Trinity College was created from limewood by master carver Grinling Gibbons.*

LAWN IDYLL *Spaciousness and peace linger over the greensward at St John's, a college where the building styles and additions cover every century since its foundation in 1511.*

window through which Lady Margaret joined in services from rooms in Master's Lodge. Fellows' Building (1643) is the university's first in classical style.

Clare College Ac
Founded 1326, destroyed by fire and refounded 1338 by Lady Elizabeth de Clare. Again burnt down 1521, rebuilt between 1638 and 1715 by Thomas and Robert Grumbold, master masons. It has the air more of a palace than a college, with gardens noted for their beauty. Graceful wrought-iron gates give access to Clare Bridge, built 1640 and oldest across Cam.

Corpus Christi College Bc
Where rival Oxford has quads, Cambridge has courts, and oldest of all is here, built in 14th century. Corpus Christi was founded by the townspeople of Cambridge. Dramatists Christopher Marlowe and John Fletcher studied here.

Eagle Inn Bc
This 17th-century coaching inn that became a public house still has its external gallery, which used to provide a draughty route for guests to reach bedrooms.

Emmanuel College Cc
Founded by Sir Walter Mildmay (Chancellor of the Exchequer to Elizabeth I) in 1584. Mixture of styles and origins make harmonious whole. Sir Christopher Wren designed the chapel and its colonnade in 1666. St Andrew's Street façade is Georgian.

Fitzwilliam Museum ☖ Bb
Corinthian portico is feature of entrance to one of Europe's major treasure houses. Large collections of antiquities from Egypt, Greece and Rome. English and Chinese pottery and porcelain. Paintings span the centuries from early Italian to Pre-Raphaelites and French Impressionists. Museum

Caius Court, while successful students pass under 'Honour' on their way to receive degrees.

Great St Mary's Church † Bc
Tower of 15th-century university church gives wide views over city and countryside. Clock chimes were the pattern for Big Ben's chimes at Westminster.

Hobson's Conduit Ba
Gullies lining Trumpington Street are survivors from a 17th-century scheme to bring water to the city from springs south of Cambridge. An ornate fountain-head on the west side of the road is named after Thomas Hobson (1544-1631). Customers at his livery stable always had to take horse nearest door, hence 'Hobson's Choice'.

Jesus College Cd
Spacious college with extensive grounds. Converted in late 1400s

AERIAL FANTASY *Glorious fan tracery in the soaring roof of King's College Chapel, one of the finest examples of Perpendicular architecture in England.*

St Bene't's Church ✝ Bc
City's oldest building dates from early 11th century. Parish clerk Fabian Stedman invented art of change ringing after studying the variations possible on a given number of bells. Wrote first book on bell-ringing 1668.

St Botolph's Church ✝ Bb
Mainly 14th-century church with two sundials stands just inside site of former city gate. West tower dates from about 1400. Elaborate wooden font cover and canopy recently restored in opulent and glowing colours.

St John's College Bd
Charter granted 1511, two years after death of founder, Lady Margaret Beaufort. Turreted three-storey Gate Tower of 1516 in red brick dressed with stone bears her statue and Tudor and Beaufort coats of arms. Behind college, Cam spanned by covered New Bridge of 1831, known as Bridge of Sighs.

Scott Polar Research Institute ⌂ Ca
Displays on life of Captain Robert Falcon Scott, who perished with his four companions on return journey from South Pole in 1912. Records and souvenirs of polar expeditions, section on scientific explorations and displays of Eskimo soapstone carvings.

Sedgwick Museum of Geology ⌂ Bc
A million animal and plant fossils and collections of rocks, stones and marbles. Dr John Woodward's geological collection in original 18th-century cabinets.

Senate House Bc
University 'parliament' meets every fortnight in James Gibbs's 1722-30 building with its Corinthian columns and pilasters. Students also gather here in June to receive their degrees.

Sidney Sussex College Bd
Founded 1594, Tudor brickwork cemented over in the early 19th century. Oliver Cromwell student here 1616. What is believed to be his embalmed head buried 1960 in a secret place in ante-chapel.

GATEWAY STATUE *The statue of Henry VIII, founder of Trinity College in 1546, dates from 1615.*

Trinity College Bd
Gilded clock on chapel tower of Great Court strikes each hour twice. Undergraduates try to run round the 2 acre court while it strikes 12 twice – they have to cover the 380yds in 43 seconds. Statue of founder, Henry VIII, above gates holds chair leg – a joke

played by students last century. Library designed by Sir Christopher Wren 1676-95.

Trinity Street Bd
Rich array of architecture; from jettied and timber-framed Tudor with pargeting, leaning over pavement, to elegant Georgian red-brick façades.

University Botanic Gardens ✿ Ca
Founded 1761 for research. The present 40 acre site was purchased in 1831 and opened in 1846; it contains an impressive rockery and a scented garden.

University Museum of Archaeology and Anthropology ⌂ Bc
Collections built up with finds from around world, but still a strong emphasis on prehistoric inhabitants of the Cambridge area. Material about peoples of America, Africa, Oceania and South-East Asia.

VENETIAN ECHO *The 1831 Bridge of Sighs spans the Cam, leading from St John's College to The Backs. It was inspired by its Venetian namesake.*

University Museum of Zoology ⌂ Bc
Sections on all types of animals. Even extinct species are here. Designed for student research, but of great value to the public.

Whipple Museum ⌂ Bc
Early scientific and surveying instruments, ranging from old astronomical telescopes to early electrical apparatus. Housed in original Cambridge Free School.

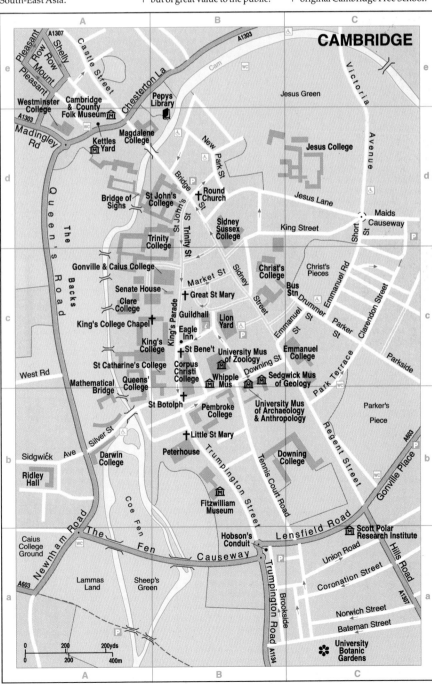

Abberton Reservoir Eb
Popular nature reserve for winter wildlife, especially ducks. Osprey visit in spring and autumn.

Bildeston Ee
Medieval wool centre with multi-coloured Tudor houses. Ghostly footsteps at The Crown, said to be a haunted pub.

Boxford Ee
Thatched cottages and willows on banks of Lambourn river, where magnificent water mill still turns. Medieval murals in church.

Braintree Cc
Lively market town made rich from wool and textiles; story told in Town Hall's Heritage Centre. Ancient houses in every street and striking courtyard in partly medieval Swan Hotel.

Castle Hedingham Cd
Village dominated by towering Norman keep of Hedingham Castle, built around 1140 by the De Vere family who lived there for 500 years. Well-preserved banqueting hall and minstrels' gallery.

Cavendish De
Broad, slanting village green backed by 14th-century church and restored almshouses. Old Rectory (16th century) serves as headquarters of Sue Ryder Foundation for the Sick and Disabled, with museum.

Chelsworth Ee
Timbered cottages, 14th-century church, and 18th-century double-humped bridge straddling River Brett. Village much admired by poet Julian Tennyson, grandson of Lord Tennyson.

Clare Ce
Ornately plastered 15th-century Ancient House stands near Clare Priory, founded in 13th century. Locals protested when 1865 railway station cut through remains of Norman castle. Station now stands abandoned below ivy-choked keep in Clare Castle Country Park.

Coggeshall Dc
Medieval wool and cloth village noted for merchants' houses with fine woodcarving. Finest example is Paycocke's House, dating from 1500, with local lace display.

Colchester Fc
Ancient town on site of Roman city, founded in AD 50. Massive Norman castle keep, built 1076 on base of Roman Temple of Claudius, houses collection of Roman antiquities. Impressive ruins of St Botolph Priory.

Colne Valley Railway Cd
Vintage steam trains take passengers along lovingly restored section of Old Colne Valley and Halstead Railway. Wildlife conservation area with picnic site.

Copford Green Ec
Remote Norman church with medieval murals. Framed fragments of human skin on wall served as grim warning in 9th and 10th centuries, when sacrilegious Danes were flayed alive.

A PAINTER'S PARADISE

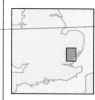

The hills and river valleys surrounding the Suffolk-Essex border open up to magnificent skies, captured in paintings by Constable and Gainsborough. Timbered houses, moated manors, and fine church towers enrich towns and villages which prospered from wool and weaving in medieval times. Out of town, winding lanes lead to rivers, creeks and reservoirs teeming with wildlife.

ARTIST'S INSPIRATION *The church tower at Stoke-by-Nayland, near the market town of Nayland, appears in many of the paintings by John Constable.*

East Anglian Railway Museum Ec
Handsomely restored locomotives puff and steam in Victorian country station.

Finchingfield Bd
Much photographed village with haphazard grouping of medieval cottages, Georgian houses, winding lanes and green. Church with Norman tower crowns hill.

Great Bardfield Bd
One of three Bardfield villages huddled by River Pant, with medieval and Georgian houses, restored windmill, and mainly 14th-century church. Cottage museum and village lock-up.

Halstead Dd
Historic water mill overlooks River Colne, built for corn in 1788 and converted for silk weaving by Samuel Courtauld in 1825. Walled garden surrounds Blue Bridge House displaying 17th and 18th-century European furniture. Flint church (14th to 15th century) has imposing monuments and tombs.

Haughley Park Fg
Small red-brick mansion of 1620. Mock-Elizabethan trimmings. Set in gardens and woodland.

Kersey Fe
Peaceful village of red-tiled houses on steep slope descending to ford, rising again to summit of Church Hill. Wooden panels in south porch roof of 14th-century church are masterpieces of 15th-century craftsmanship.

Lavenham Ee
Resplendent Suffolk wool town reflects the prosperous Middle

DOORWAY FIGURE *A carved effigy adorns the late 15th-century De Vere House in Lavenham.*

Ages – telegraph lines hidden underground to preserve character of over 300 listed buildings. Tudor houses sag with age, and cathedral-like church on hill is greatest of all East Anglia's medieval 'wool' churches. Old Wool Hall now part of Swan Hotel. Museum of weaving industry displayed in Tudor Guildhall.

The Layers Eb
Two 'Layer' villages and one hamlet within 2 miles of each other: Layer Breton with remote church set in heath; Layer-de-la-Haye with fine views over the wildfowl haunt of Abberton Reservoir; and Layer Marney with red-brick tower gatehouse – only completed part of a 16th-century mansion – decorated with terracotta shells and dolphins.

Long Melford De
Main street of village runs along former Roman highway. Pepperpot towers distinguish 16th-century mansion of Melford Hall, where Elizabeth I dined in 1578. One room features paintings by Beatrix Potter, once a frequent visitor. The 16th-century Bull Inn is reputed to be haunted. Holy Trinity Church, famed for its flintwork, has 1496 Lady Chapel and medieval stained glass. Moated manor of Kentwell Hall has Tudor-rose maze, and rare breeds of domestic farm animals.

Nayland Ed
Compact, drowsy little market town with a jumble of colour-washed dwellings and 15th-century Alston Court. Church dates from 1400 and houses one of Constable's rare religious paintings. Nearby village of Stoke-by-Nayland regarded as heart of 'Constable Country'. Largely 15th-century church features in several of his paintings.

Nether Hall Ce
Sumptuous merchant's house built during 15th-century heyday of Suffolk wool trade, now a wine production centre. Vineyard trail and wine tasting.

Polstead Ed
Scene of famous 'Red Barn Murder' in 1827; Maria Marten murdered by her lover William Corder and found buried in a barn. Her cottage still stands in Marten's Lane. His farm is in village centre.

The Rodings Ab
Eight villages and hamlets (Abbess, Aythorpe, Beauchamp, Berners, High, Leaden, Margaret and White Roding) strung along valley of River Roding. Mostly picturesque with old churches, moated halls, half-timbered cottages and comfortable pubs.

Saling Hall Bc
Church and old village horse pond lie within grounds. Original house built 1570, altered in 1698 by lawyer Martin Carter who built beautiful walled garden.

Stebbing Bc
Well-preserved buildings date from Middle Ages, and handsome 18th-century water mill straddles brook. Great Mount earthwork is site of castle built by Ranulf Peveral in 1086. Moated Porter's Hall on Stebbing Green is early 17th-century farmhouse.

Sudbury De
Birthplace of painter Thomas Gainsborough in 1727. Half-timbered Gainsborough's House dates from 1480, with added Georgian front. Now a museum with portraits and landscapes illustrating artist's career.

Terling Cb
Village with immaculate green, colour-washed cottages, and Tudor manor house preserved opposite 13th-century church. Fine dairy farm run by Lord Rayleigh family, who live at Terling Place. Windmill at Flacks Green.

Thaxted Bd
Tudor houses jumble around stately 1400 Guildhall. Magnificent church dates from 14th century, with towering 180ft spire and airy interior. Elegant red-brick Clarence House, built 1715, is where composer Gustav Holst worked on part of *The Planets*. Well-preserved tower windmill dating from 1804 has museum of rural life.

QUIET CORNER *A row of red-brick almshouses leads to Thaxted's windmill, preserved as a museum.*

Tolleshunt D'Arcy Eb
The 14th-century church houses fine brasses commemorating family who gave their name to village. Moated manor house, built by D'Arcy family in 1500, was without a bridge until 1585.

Wickhambrook Cf
Scattered village noted for restored Gifford's Hall, gabled and timber-framed manor house dating from 1480.

Woolpit Eg
Recorded in Domesday Book as 'Wolfpeta', a pit in which wolves were trapped. Legend dating from 12th century tells of two children with green bodies who came to live here saying they came from mysterious land called St Martin. Ancient dwellings of late medieval and Tudor design, 400-year-old Swan Inn. Church dates from 11th century.

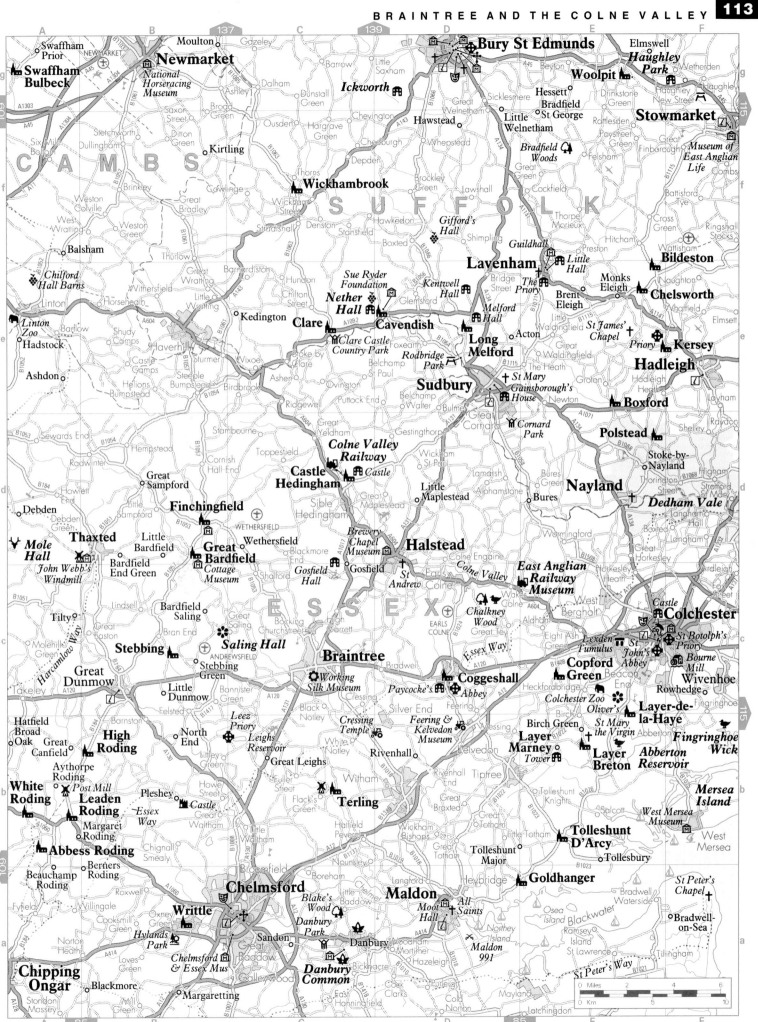

A map of Braintree and the Colne Valley region. Key locations shown include:

Cambs/Suffolk area: Swaffham Prior, Swaffham Bulbeck, Newmarket, National Horseracing Museum, Moulton, Gazeley, Ickworth, Bury St Edmunds, Haughley Park, Elmswell, Woolpit, New Street, Stowmarket, Museum of East Anglian Life, Wickhambrook, Lavenham, Guildhall, Little Hall, The Priory, Monks Eleigh, Bildeston, Chelsworth, Sue Ryder Foundation, Kentwell Hall, Brent Eleigh, Nether Hall, Clare, Cavendish, Melford Hall, Long Melford, Acton, St James' Chapel, Priory, Kersey, Hadleigh, Clare Castle Country Park, Rodbridge Park, Sudbury, Gainsborough's House, St Mary, Boxford, Polstead, Cornard Park, Stoke-by-Nayland, Nayland, Dedham Vale, Bures.

Essex area: Colne Valley Railway, Castle Hedingham, Castle, Little Maplestead, Finchingfield, Sible Hedingham, Great Maplestead, Thaxted, Mole Hall, John Webb's Windmill, Great Sampford, Little Bardfield, Great Bardfield, Cottage Museum, Wethersfield, Gosfield Hall, Gosfield, Brewery Chapel Museum, Halstead, St Andrew, Colne Valley, East Anglian Railway Museum, Chalkney Wood, Colchester, Castle, St Botolph's Priory, St John's Abbey, Lexden Tumulus, Bourne Mill, Wivenhoe, Rowhedge, Stebbing, Saling Hall, Braintree, Working Silk Museum, Coggeshall, Paycocke's, Abbey, Copford Green, Colchester Zoo, Oliver's, Layer-de-la-Haye, Fingringhoe Wick, Great Dunmow, Little Dunmow, Leez Priory, Cressing Temple, Feering & Kelvedon Museum, St Mary the Virgin, Layer Marney, Tower, Layer Breton, Abberton Reservoir, High Roding, North End, Leighs Reservoir, Great Leighs, Rivenhall, Birch Green, White Roding, Post Mill, Leaden Roding, Pleshey, Castle, Essex Way, Terling, Witham, Mersea Island, West Mersea Museum, Abbess Roding, Tolleshunt D'Arcy, Tollesbury, Goldhanger, St Peter's Chapel, Chelmsford, Writtle, Hylands Park, Blake's Wood, Danbury Park, Moot Hall, All Saints, Maldon, Bradwell Waterside, Bradwell-on-Sea, Chipping Ongar, Blackmore, Danbury Common, Sandon, Danbury, Maldon 991, St Peter's Way.

MARSHY CREEKS, REEDY RIVERS

Tides on the Essex and Suffolk coast wash around yacht moorings, flat marshes and oyster beds. Thriving ports jostle with seaside playgrounds. Inland the River Stour runs through chalky lowlands; the spaciousness of its lush valley was an inspiration to the painters Constable, Gainsborough and Munnings. This is a popular area for birdwatchers and other nature lovers.

Aldeburgh † 🏛 Ee
Georgian houses line main street of seaside town, home of annual music festival established in 1948 by composer Benjamin Britten and singer Peter Pears. Church (14th–16th century) has brasses and John Piper window commemorating Britten. Half-timbered 16th-century Moot Hall, now a museum, fronts shingle beach.

Beth Chatto Gardens ❀ Ab
Mediterranean and moisture-loving plants flourish in what was once a wilderness of dry gravel slopes with a waterlogged hollow; created in 1960s by Beth Chatto.

Brightlingsea † Aa
Medieval port on Colne estuary, once an associate member of the Cinque Ports, now yachting centre. Medieval Jacobes Hall, now a hotel. Church, with 94ft tower, contains tiled plaques in memory of local men who died at sea. Headquarters of the Smack Preservation Society; fine old Essex fishing boats that race here each year in September.

Dedham Vale Ac
Bordering the River Stour from Flatford to Nayland, this is known as 'Constable country', where water mills and willow-fringed streams inspired the artist.

Dunwich 🏠🏛 Eg
Relentless erosion of wind and tide caused this town to be lost beneath the waves, after destruction by 1326 storm. Only small village, ruins of leper chapel, and medieval friary remain. It is said that submerged church bells ring out storm warning. Excellent museum on town's history.

Flatford Mill 🕍 Ac
Unchanging scenery of willows, shimmering meadows and winding stream, as painted by Constable in early 19th-century. Close to wooden bridge over Stour, 17th-century family water mill featured in *The Hay Wain*. Upstream, thatched 16th-century Bridge Cottage was home of friend Willy Lott; now houses exhibition.

Framlingham 🏰❀ Cf
Market town with a patchwork of architectural periods dating from 12th century. Victorian pillar box in Double Street. Castle dating from 1100 was largely rebuilt in 16th century, and has walk linking nine of the towers, two ditches and lower court beside artificial lake. Church contains splendid mid-16th century Howard monuments and helmet of Thomas Howard, victor at Flodden.

Great Bromley 🏠 Ab
Quiet village with 15th-century Church of St George. Fine west tower, south porch with flushwork panelling, a clerestory to the nave and a double hammerbeam roof. A priest is remembered in a 15th-century brass.

Great Glemham 🏠 Df
Church of All Saints, though restored in 19th century, contains fragments of medieval stained glass and seven sacrament font.

Hadleigh † 🔲 Ad
Town of colour-washed houses with decorative plaster-work on walls (pargeting). Fine Georgian and medieval buildings, including 15th-century Guildhall. St Mary's Church contains handsome 18th-century organ case, brasses and memorials.

streets and 17th-century treadmill crane on The Green. Restored 19th-century fortress, Harwich Redoubt, was defence against invasion by Napoleon.

Helmingham Hall❀ Be
Tudor house with moated gardens, herbaceous borders and rare roses. Safari ride takes visitors through deer park.

Heveningham Hall 🏛 Dg
Georgian mansion built in 1780 as Vanneck family home. Exterior designed by Sir Robert Taylor. Interior by James Wyatt contains some of his best surviving work. Grounds by Capability Brown.

Ipswich 🏛†🏚🏛🔲 Bd
County town of Suffolk; major shopping centre with 12 medieval churches. Christchurch Mansion of 1548 houses splendid collections of decorative art.

John Western Reserve ☞ Cb
Walk along 70ft high fossil-rich cliffs, and through grassland and thickets to see migrating birds. Butterflies include Essex Skipper.

Kyson Hill 🕍 Cd
Excellent birdwatching from this 4 acre finger of National Trust land projecting into River Deben.

Manningtree ❀ Bc
Pretty Georgian town, famous for its swans and sailing barges. Once a busy port and 17th-century headquarters of Matthew Hopkins, the 'Witch Finder General' who terrorised East Anglia.

Mersea Island 🎠🏛 Aa
Winding lanes cross open countryside, joined to mainland by Strood causeway. West Mersea has fresh oysters and attractive old fishing cottages. Country park at Cudmore Grove.

Minsmere ☞ Ef
Major bird reserve, nesting places for over 100 species. Breeding birds include avocets, bitterns, nightjars and nightingales.

Needham Market † 🏚 Ae
Graceful town with Georgian houses in High Street, made prosperous by agriculture. Church of St John the Baptist (15th century) has superb hammerbeam roof.

Orford 🏠🏰 Ee
Quiet village of brick-and-timber buildings with magnificent 12th-century castle built by Henry II. Dunwich Underwater Exhibition.

Otley Hall 🏛 Ce
Fine linen-fold panelling, good hall screen and Jacobean wall decorations are outstanding features of this 16th-century house. Magnificent gardens.

Pin Mill 🕍🏚 Cc
River Orwell beauty spot where barges race in July, and where refreshments are served direct to boats at high tide from Butt and Oyster Inn. Access on foot to Pin Mill and Old Wharf.

St Osyth 🏠❀ Ba
Waterside village with imposing range of monastic buildings. Priory dates from 12th century, founded by St Osyth, wife of a 7th-century East Anglian king. Peacock and deer in grounds.

Saxtead Green 🏠✖ Cf
Superb example of an 18th-century Suffolk post mill, in full working order, with three-storey roundhouse, sails and fantail.

Snape 🏠♻🏛 De
Unique among villages as an international centre of music. Composer Benjamin Britten and tenor Peter Pears founded annual Aldeburgh Festival in 1948, which moved here in 1967 when superb concert hall complex was created within a former malt house. Summer trips on River Alde, and riverside walks by reed beds.

Stowmarket 🏛🔲 Ae
Small market and industrial town with open-air Museum of East Anglian Life. Steam engines and rides on vehicles drawn by Suffolk Punch horses.

CURIOSITIES *A windmill and 'House in the Clouds', an old water tower, loom over Thorpeness.*

Thorpeness 🏠✖☞ Ee
Eccentric holiday village planned around specially dug 65 acre lake, and laid out before World War I. Houses in many styles.

390th Bomb Group Air Museum Υ Df
In restored World War II control tower of old US airfield outside Parham; dedicated to Allied airmen who gave their lives. Items on display include material recovered from crashed planes.

Walton on the Naze ♻❀✖☞ Cb
Popular for bathing and fishing with long, 800ft pier. Salt marshes behind town, rich in bird life. Great Naze Tower warns mariners of treacherous West Rocks.

Westleton Heath ☞ Ef
Sandy heaths, woodland, heather and bracken. Bird life includes stone curlews, nightjars, red-backed shrikes and woodlarks.

LANDMARK *A stumpy disused lighthouse in Harwich is known as the old 'Low Lighthouse'.*

BUILT TO LAST *Hugh, 12th-century Earl of Norfolk, began the great curtain wall at Framlingham Castle, which survives intact today.*

Butley Priory ❀ Dd
Medieval gatehouse with stone heraldic decoration incorporating arms of 12th-century England and France. Gateway flanked by buttresses was once part of an 1171 Augustinian priory.

Clacton-on-Sea ☞🔲 Ba
Jolly Victorian seaside resort with long sandy beach, lively pier with wide range of entertainments, children's zoo, Ocean World and pseudo-medieval Moot Hall – all created since 1860. The older buildings include three Martello towers, built against Napoleonic invasion.

Cotton 🏠🏛 Af
Mechanical Music Museum in reconstructed cinema displays nostalgic collection of musical machines, including Wurlitzer theatre organ, street pianos, polyphones, musical boxes and dolls.

Dedham 🏠 Ac
Memory of Constable lingers in attractive village, where he went to Elizabethan Free Grammar School. St Mary's Church appears in – and contains – some of his paintings. The painter Sir Alfred Munnings lived at Castle House: many of his works are on display.

Dunwich Heath ☞ Fe
Wildlife finds refuge among rushes and grasses of 215 acres of coastal heathland called Sandlings; also sandy cliffs and a mile of pebble beach.

East Bergholt 🏠❀ Ac
Heart of Constable country and still an unspoilt village. Painter born here in 1776 in house near parish church. Only an outbuilding remains – converted since into a private cottage – but plaque identifies the site.

Felixstowe 🔲🏚 Dc
Family seaside resort doubles as one of Europe's largest container ports. Seaside Felixstowe has Victorian atmosphere with bathing huts, seafront gardens and red-shingle beach with pier. Landguard Fort dates from 1718.

Fingringhoe Wick ☞❀ Aa
Disused gravel pit near estuary of River Colne, now one of the richest wildlife sanctuaries in Essex. Noted for Brent geese, dunlins and curlews in winter. Visitor centre incorporates 19th-century farm buildings; displays illustrate wide range of Essex wildlife. Several nature trails including one for disabled.

Harwich 🏰🔲 Cc
Ship-spotter's paradise and port from where Edward III's fleet set out to destroy the French at Sluys in 1340. Associations with famous seafarers Raleigh, Drake, Frobisher and Nelson. Now an important car ferry port to Hook of Holland. Medieval cobbled

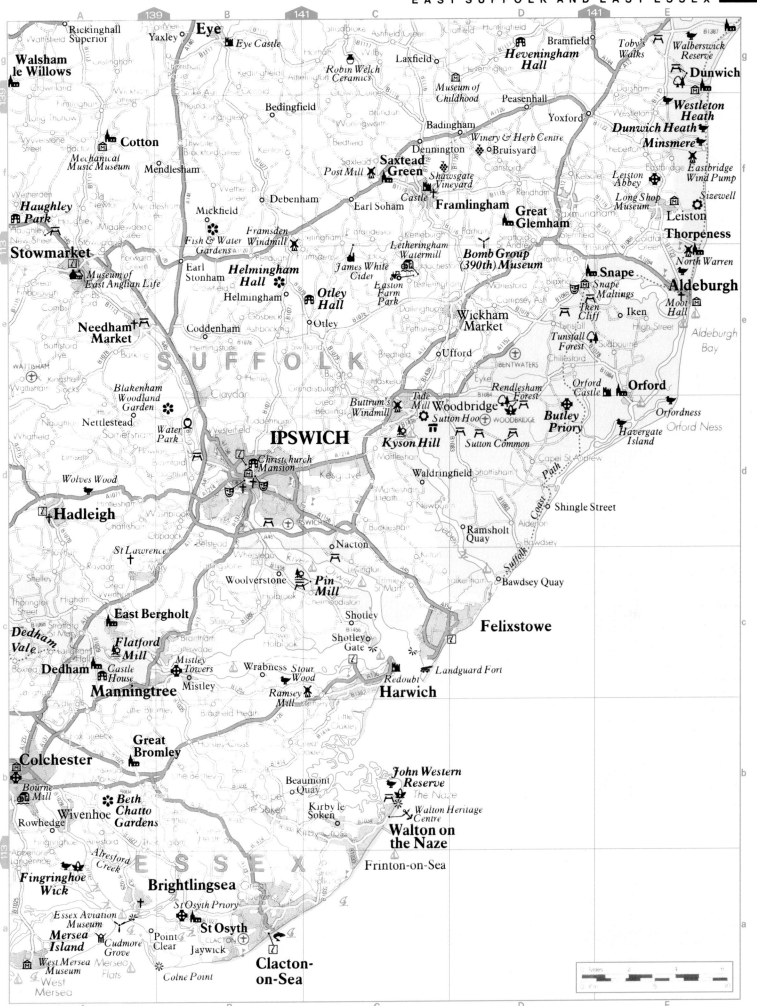

139 141 141

Rickinghall Superior
Walsham le Willows
Yaxley
Eye
Eye Castle
Wattisfield
Cotton
Mechanical Music Museum
Mendlesham
Bedingfield
Robin Welch Ceramics
Laxfield
Heveningham Hall
Bramfield
Toby's Walks
Walberswick Reserve
Dunwich
Westleton Heath
Museum of Childhood
Peasenhall
Yoxford
Dunwich Heath
Minsmere
Badingham
Winery & Herb Centre
Dennington
Bruisyard
Saxtead Green
Post Mill
Shawsgate Vineyard
Eastbridge Wind Pump
Sizewell
Leiston Abbey
Long Shop Museum
Leiston
Earl Soham
Castle
Framlingham
Great Glemham
Thorpeness
Haughley Park
Mickfield
Framsden Windmill
Letheringham Watermill
Stowmarket
Debenham
Bomb Group (390th) Museum
North Warren
Museum of East Anglian Life
Earl Stonham
Helmingham Hall
James White Cider
Snape
Snape Maltings
Aldeburgh
Fish & Water Gardens
Otley Hall
Easton Farm Park
Iken Cliff
Iken
Moot Hall
Needham Market
Helmingham
Coddenham
Otley
Wickham Market
Aldeburgh Bay
Blakenham Woodland Garden
Ufford
Tunstall Forest
Nettlestead
S U F F O L K
Rendlesham Forest
Orford Castle
Orford
Water Park
Buttrum's Windmill
Tide Mill
Woodbridge
Orfordness
Wolves Wood
IPSWICH
Sutton Hoo
Butley Priory
Orford Ness
Christchurch Mansion
Kyson Hill
Sutton Common
Havergate Island
Hadleigh
Waldringfield
Ramsholt Quay
Shingle Street
St Lawrence
IPSWICH
Nacton
Bawdsey Quay
Woolverstone
Pin Mill
Shotley
Felixstowe
East Bergholt
Shotley Gate
Dedham Vale
Flatford Mill
Mistley Towers
Wrabness
Stour Wood
Dedham
Castle House
Mistley
Ramsey Mill
Redoubt
Landguard Fort
Manningtree
Harwich
Great Bromley
Colchester
Bourne Mill
John Western Reserve
The Naze
Beth Chatto Gardens
Beaumont Quay
Walton Heritage Centre
Wivenhoe
Kirby le Soken
Walton on the Naze
Rowhedge
E S S E X
Frinton-on-Sea
Fingringhoe Wick
Alresford Creek
Brightlingsea
St Osyth Priory
Essex Aviation Museum
St Osyth
Mersea Island
Cudmore Grove
Point Clear
Jaywick
West Mersea Museum
Colne Point
Clacton-on-Sea
West Mersea

Aberaeron Cc
Ranks of colourful Regency houses give a Mediterranean flavour. Yachts and fishing fleet shelter in harbour at Aeron river mouth. Harbour-side aquarium.

Aberdyfi Ef
Attractive seaside resort at mouth of River Dyfi with wide beach. Maritime museum in old warehouses on jetty. Quiet streets and squares of houses, built for sea captains, behind busy seafront.

Aberystwyth De
Coastal resort and university town where three million books are housed in National Library of Wales. Library treasures on show. Aberystwyth Yesterday recalls town's past. Ruined castle, cliff railway and camera obscura.

Borth Ef
One-street village resort with picturesque cottages. Three-mile stretch of golden sands, north. Raccoons and friendly farm animals at the Animalarium. Creepy-crawly section and reptile house.

Bwlch Nant Yr Arian Forest Fe
Forest visitor centre with magnificent views down valley to Aberystwyth and Cardigan Bay. Imaginative displays introduce the Rheidol Forest, surrounding landscape and local history.

Castell y Bere Eg
Impressive 13th-century mountain stronghold of Llywelyn the Great. Ivy-covered ruin stands on rocky outcrop, commanding views of Dysynni valley and Cadair Idris.

HIDDEN FORTRESS *Trees hide the ruins of Castell y Bere from the road.*

Centre for Alternative Technology Fg
Disused slate quarry housing Centre for Alternative Technology. Displays explain how energy can be supplied by sun, wind and water.

Clarach Bay De
Pleasant sand-and-shingle beach. Chalets and caravans crowd the bay; walkers can explore rock pools or follow cliff-top trails to Borth and Aberystwyth.

Corris Fg
Steep-sided slopes filled with fir trees rise above village of slate cottages. Museum recalls time of Corris's narrow-gauge railway that carried slates from local quarries, with relics and memorabilia.

MOORLANDS AND FINE BEACHES

Desolate moorlands rise to the Cambrian Mountains, wild and barren hills that reach a height of 2000ft or more in places, and fast-flowing rivers descend through thickly wooded valleys to the sea. The 40 mile sweep of Cardigan Bay is remote and secluded, with some of Britain's finest beaches and quiet seaside towns standing at the mouths of river estuaries.

SEASIDE RESORT *Once the centre of a busy shipbuilding industry, Aberaeron is now a bustling holiday resort.*

Cwmtudu Bb
Secluded shingle beach reached by narrow lanes leading to car park and steep path. Edged by cliffs with caves and rock pools. Remains of old lime kiln on shore.

Devil's Bridge Fd
River Mynach cascades 300ft into a dark ravine; christened the 'dread chasm' by poet William Wordsworth. Village remarkable for its three bridges, piled one on top of another across the Mynach gorge. Medieval stone 'Bridge of the Evil One', 1753 bridge for horse-drawn traffic, and road bridge dating from 1901.

Felin Crewi Mill Fg
Millstones driven by a cast-iron water wheel grind corn in restored 18th-century mill. Products from mill's flour can be sampled at café.

Furnace Ef
Water wheel driven by waterfall on the Einion river drove bellows of an 18th-century ironworks in the village. Ironworks splendidly restored. Lovely walks beside river and through ravine.

Lampeter Da
Coaching inns and Georgian and Victorian buildings line main streets of this market town. St David's University College of 1822 stands around quadrangle with clock tower and fountain.

Llanddewi Brefi Eb
Village of patriarchal legend. St David addressed a turbulent meeting here in AD 519; ground said to have risen beneath his feet. Church of St David, built around 12th-century tower, stands on site of meeting place.

Llanegryn Dg
Church of St Mary and St Egryn has magnificently carved rood screen with patterns of diamonds, flowers, berries and vines; said to have been rescued from Cymer Abbey during Dissolution.

Llangranog Bb
Pretty little village with sandy beach, bounded by rocky headlands. Cliff-top walk leads to National Trust headland, Ynys-Lochtyn, with spectacular views.

Llanrhystud Dc
Small village on River Wyre with two pleasant sand-and-shingle beaches at low tide. Southern one has car park, northern one reached by walk down lane from church. Green mound is site of 12th-century castle.

Llansantffraed Dc
Village reached by lane from neighbouring Llanon on main coast road. Handsome little St Bride's Church, with tower and purple slate-faced walls, stands by bridge crossing Peris stream.

Llyn Brianne Reservoir Ga
Waters from the Llyn Brianne reservoir race down a 1312ft spillway to join River Tywi in a deluge of spray. Reservoir 4 miles long with scenic road on eastern side.

Machynlleth Fg
Victorian Gothic clock tower with pinnacles, spire and four-faced clock straddles main street. Building in Maengwyn Street stands on site of first Welsh Parliament held by rebel leader Owain Glyndwr in 1404. Exhibition devoted to Owain's life and times.

Nant-y-Moch Reservoir Fe
Man-made lake supplying water for Rheidol hydroelectric power scheme. Stone dam 172ft high.

New Quay Bb
Stone quay of 1835 shelters harbour of this port, where harbour dues and tolls are still displayed. Life of resort probably inspired Dylan Thomas's *Under Milk Wood.*

Plynlimon Fe
Peat-carpeted massif rising to 2469ft, highest peak in the Cambrian Mountains. Source of the rivers Wye, Severn and Rheidol. Path to summit from road 2 miles north of Ponterwyd.

Ponterwyd Fe
Village on gorge above River Rheidol. Nearby is Llywernog Silver Lead Mine Museum, on site of 18th-century mine. Restored buildings and water wheels surrounded by pine woods. Miner's trail and prospector's tunnel.

WATER POWER *Re-created water wheel turns at Llywernog mine.*

Pontrhydfendigaid Fc
Traditional Welsh community, with slate-roofed Victorian and Edwardian cottages. The stone humpbacked bridge gives village its name: 'The bridge of the blessed ford.' Close by is striking archway and ruins of 12th-century Strata Florida Abbey.

Rheidol Power Station Fd
Nerve centre of hydroelectric power scheme, harnessing waters of Nant-y-Moch and Dinas rivers. Guided tours. Downstream are spectacular Rheidol Falls.

Tal-y-bont Ee
Village was a wool centre during 18th and 19th centuries. Nearby are tweed mills, at bridge over River Leri.

Tregaron Eb
Small market town, once staging post for drovers crossing bleak Abergwesyn Pass.

Tregaron Bog Ec
Vast peat bog forms Cors Caron National Nature Reserve. Disused railway line leads to observation point. Otters, polecats, marsh birds, hen harriers and merlins.

Tywyn Dg
Trains of the Talyllyn Narrow Gauge Railway start the journey at this pleasant seaside resort. Tywyn's Wharf station houses Narrow Gauge Railway Museum. St Cadfan's Church has 7ft high stone with possibly 7th-century Welsh inscription.

Vale of Rheidol Railway Ed
See the lovely Vale of Rheidol from narrow-gauge line between Aberystwyth and Devil's Bridge. Trains climb along ledge cut into side of valley, giving spectacular views of Rheidol river below.

Wallog De
Secluded beach of sand and shingle. Finger of shingle stretching out to sea is said to be dyke of Cantref-y-Gwaelod, legendary drowned city beneath the waters of Cardigan Bay.

Ynyslas Ef
Site of Dyfi National Nature Reserve. Vast stretch of dunes, salt marshes and sands; haven for rabbits and good hunting ground for foxes, weasels and stoats. Views across Dyfi estuary.

Ysbyty Cynfyn Fd
Village with 19th-century church. Churchyard walls use stones and site of prehistoric stone circle.

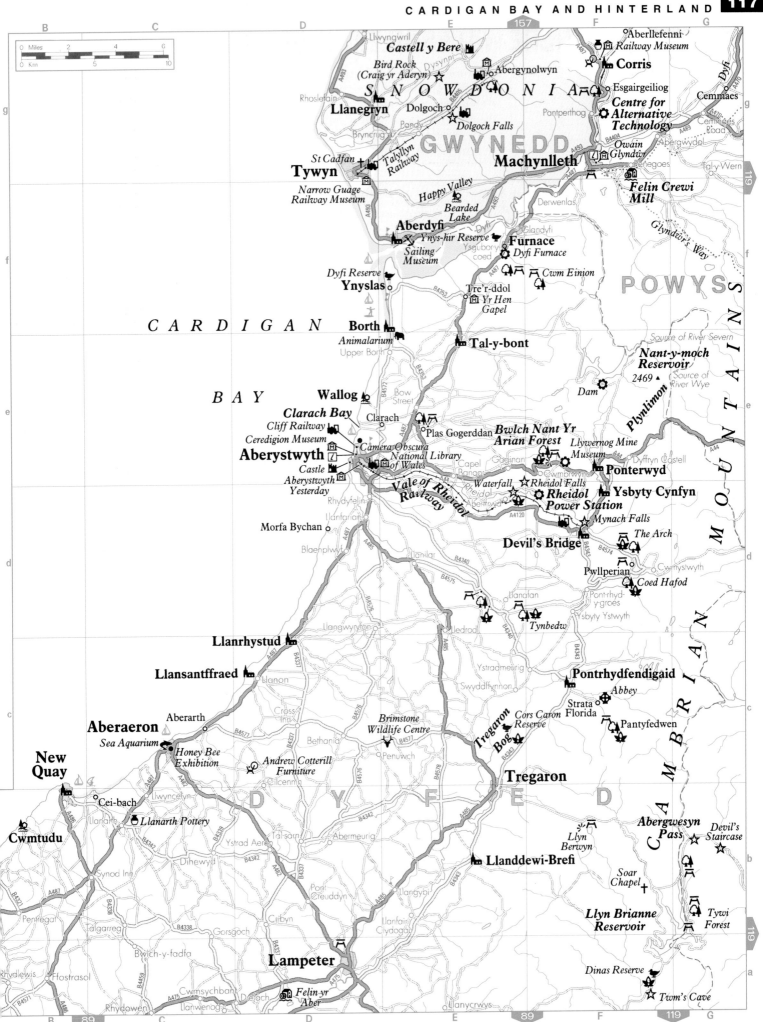

Miles 0 2 4 6
Km 0 5 10

Llwyngwril

Castell y Bere

Bird Rock
(Craig yr Aderyn)

Rhoslefain

S N O W D O N I A

Abergynolwyn

Llanegryn

Dolgoch

Bryncrug

Pandy

Dolgoch Falls

G W Y N E D D

St Cadfan

Talyllyn Railway

Tywyn

Narrow Guage Railway Museum

Happy Valley

Bearded Lake

Derwenlas

Aberdyfi

Ynys-hir Reserve

Sailing Museum

Glandyfi

Furnace

Dyfi Furnace

Ysgubor-y-coed

Dyfi Reserve

Ynyslas

C A R D I G A N

Tre'r-ddol

Yr Hen Gapel

Borth

Animalarium

Upper Borth

Tal-y-bont

Bow Street

B A Y

Wallog

Clarach Bay

Clarach

Plas Gogerddan

Bwlch Nant Yr Arian Forest

Cliff Railway

Ceredigion Museum

Aberystwyth

Camera Obscura

National Library of Wales

Capel Bangor

Goginan

Llywernog Mine Museum

Ponterwyd

Castle

Aberystwyth Yesterday

Vale of Rheidol Railway

Waterfall

Rheidol Falls

Rheidol Power Station

Ysbyty Cynfyn

Mynach Falls

Morfa Bychan

Llanfarian

Rhydyfelin

Aberffrwd

Devil's Bridge

The Arch

Blaenplwyf

Llanilar

Pwllperian

Coed Hafod

Cwmystwyth

Llanrhystud

Llangwyryfon

Lledrod

Llanafan

Pont-rhyd-y-groes

Llansantffraed

Llanon

Ystradmeurig

Ysbyty Ystwyth

Tynbedw

Cross Inn

Brimstone Wildlife Centre

Swyddffynnon

Pontrhydfendigaid

Abbey

Strata Florida

Aberaeron

Aberarth

Sea Aquarium

Bethania

Penuwch

Cors Caron Reserve

Tregaron Bog

New Quay

Honey Bee Exhibition

Andrew Cotterill Furniture

Cilcennin

Tregaron

Cei-bach

Llwyncelyn

D Y F E D

Llanarth

Cwmtudu

Llanarth Pottery

Synod Inn

Tal-sarn

Ystrad Aeron

Abermeurig

Llanddewi-Brefi

Abergwesyn Pass

Llyn Berwyn

Devil's Staircase

Penfrgat

Dihewyd

Soar Chapel

Pont Creuddyn

Llyn Brianne Reservoir

Tywi Forest

Gorsgoch

Llanfair Clydogau

Llangybi

Cribyn

Lampeter

Rhydlewis

Ffostrasol

Bwlch-y-fadfa

Cwmsychban

Drefach

Llanwenog

Llanycrwys

Felin yr Aber

Dinas Reserve

Twm's Cave

P O W Y S

Owain Glyndwr

Machynlleth

Felin Crewi Mill

Tal-y-Wern

Glyndŵr's Way

Aberllefenni

Railway Museum

Corris

Esgairgeiliog

Cemmaes

Centre for Alternative Technology

Abergwydol

Cemmaes Road

Cwm Einion

Source of River Severn

Nant-y-moch Reservoir

Source of River Wye

2469

Dam

Plynlimon

Dyffryn Castell

C A M B R I A N   M O U N T A I N S

Pantyfedwen

WHERE WALES MEETS ENGLAND

A land of black-and-white houses, border castles and Hereford cattle, where English is the common language, merges with the very Welsh county of Powys, a land of old spa towns. To the north-west, hills merge into the great moorlands beyond the Elan Valley. East of the moorlands, steep and narrow valleys divide a succession of rounded hills that stretch to the English borderlands.

Abbey Cwmhir ✛ ⚘ Df
This ruined Cistercian 'Abbey in the Long Valley' lies below hills of 1500ft. Sacked by Henry III in 13th century and destroyed by 14th-century Welsh hero Owain Glyndwr, who thought monks were English soldiers in disguise.

Abbey Dore Court ✿ ⚘ Gb
Walled and riverside 4 acre garden; notable fern border, herb garden, sedum and euphorbia collections. The nearby Cistercian abbey church is 12th century.

Abergwesyn Pass ☆ Bd
Narrow pass between Tregaron and Abergwesyn called The Devil's Staircase. Steep hairpin bends rise and fall in roller-coaster style through wild moorland with views that go on for ever.

Berriew ⌂ Ei
Prettier than any picture postcard with black-and-white timbered houses clustered around church. Gardens crammed with colour.

Bishop's Castle ☷ ◢ Gg
Border town in lush country of streams and water meadows. Little remains of the castle built by the Bishop of Hereford in 1127 but there are three Tudor houses including the House on Crutches, its overhanging upper storey supported by posts. Three Tuns inn, 17th century, has own brewery.

Brecon ✛ ⚏ ⌂ ☒ Da
Touring centre for Brecon Beacons which rise to 2096ft. Narrow streets full of craft and antique shops dominated by massive bulk of medieval cathedral. Brecknock Museum's exhibits include a traditional Welsh kitchen.

Bronllys ⌂ ☷ Eb
Castle built in 13th century in an unsuccessful attempt to control troubled borders. Standing on a hill apart from the village, single round tower is reminiscent of a huge chimney.

Bucknell ⌂ ✳ Gf
Rustic architecture in a peaceful corner among wooded hills. Norman church and Gothic 19th-century railway station. Neighbouring hill of Coxhall Knoll is crowned with the remains of an Iron Age fort.

Builth Wells ⚞ ⚒ ☷ Dd
Approached by ornate 18th-century bridge across stretch of River Wye. Fashionable spa town in early 19th century; now headquarters of Royal Welsh Show held each summer, when town explodes in glorious pageant. Ruins of 11th-century castle.

Chirbury ⌂ Fh
Harmonious blend of mellow brick and black-and-white cottages in glowing green landscape of Welsh borders. Evidence of antiquity in 13th-century church. School and Chirbury Hall both 16th century.

Clun ⌂ ☷ ⌂ Gg
Sleepy village with dramatic ruin of a Norman castle, although settlement dates from Bronze Age. Prehistoric relics in Clun Town Trust Museum, housed in Georgian town hall.

CLUN CASTLE
The ruined Norman keep lies half on and half off an earlier Norman motte.

Clun Forest Fg
Remote part of Shropshire, once a royal hunting ground though much has been replanted. Wide moorlands where plovers call, buzzards soar and hardy Clun sheep graze.

Clyro ⌂ ⚘ ⌂ Fc
Snug village, sleepily unaware of its fame from diaries of Francis Kilvert, curate from 1870 to 1872. His former home has a gallery of contemporary art.

Dorstone ⌂ ⚏ Gc
Oliver Cromwell was listed among the guests at 500-year-old Pandy Inn in this immaculate village of stone cottages around a green. Arthur's Stone, burial chamber from 3000 BC, stands on Dorstone Hill. Glorious views stretch across the Wye Valley.

Eardisley ⌂ Gc
This straggling medieval village closely hugs its one main street. Many small black-and-white cottages. Church has one of Britain's finest Norman fonts and earliest-known tombs – that of Edward Fitz-John Fiest, from 11th century.

Elan Village ⌂ ⚏ Ce
A 'model' settlement built 1906-9 to house waterworks maintenance staff in Elan Valley. Beautifully designed grey-stone houses arranged around greens and beside wooded river bank. Water fed to Birmingham from four dams through 73 mile aqueduct. Visitor Centre tells the story of water in the valley.

Golden Valley Gb
River Dore winds its way for 10 miles between villages of Dorstone and Pontrilas along this beautiful Golden Valley, where cornfields, orchards and rich grass meadows are flanked by Black Mountains on the west, and gentle hills on the east.

Gregynog ⚏ ⚘ Dh
Black-and-white house built 19th century on a site inhabited since 12th century. Woodland walks and nature trail in 750 acres of grounds. Famous for displays of azaleas and rhododendrons.

Hay Bluff ▲ Fb
Feel almost airborne on the 2220ft summit of the Black Mountains with views at every turn: Brecon Beacons, Malvern Hills, distant Snowdon, Offa's Dyke and misty lands of Hereford and Worcester.

Hay-on-Wye ☷ ⌂ Fc
Paradise for book lovers in peaceful market town that has become a world famous second-hand book centre. Almost every building bulges with bargains – more than a million titles.

Hergest Croft ✿ Fd
Elizabethan mansion surrounded by 50 acres of gardens. The old-fashioned kitchen garden is a delight. Azaleas, shrubs, woodland walks where rhododendrons grow to 30ft.

Hopton Castle ⌂ ☷ Gf
Village and ruins of Norman castle lie in a hollow among gentle wooded hills. Scene of a famous siege in the Civil War when Roundheads surrendered and were butchered to a man.

Knighton ⌂ Ff
Rural market town in Teme Valley, home of Offa's Dyke Heritage Centre which tells history of this great 8th-century defensive rampart and ditch dug between England and Wales. Long-distance footpath of 168 miles follows part of the Offa's Dyke route.

Llandeilo Graban ⚘ Ec
Tree-lined road beside River Wye is now a wayside nature reserve following old railway line along a green valley, where trees overhang meandering river. Rich in bird life.

Llandovery ☷ Ab
As pretty a place as it was when admired by 19th-century writer George Borrow. Cobbled market square, Georgian façades and a ruined medieval castle.

Llandrindod Wells ⚘ ⚒ ⌂ ☒ De
Elegant Victorian spa town where visitors can still take the waters for gout or rheumatism as 80,000 visitors a year did in its heyday. Spacious parks; also a museum with collection of old bicycles.

Llangurig ⌂ Cf
Tiny 900ft hill village lies in a lovely setting on the Upper Wye, noted for sheep-rearing. Single street with two welcoming inns.

Llyn Clywedog ⚘ ⚘ ✳ ⚏ Bg
Huge dam created in 1968, tallest in Britain at 237ft, solved Severn Valley flooding problems and created opportunity for water sports. Scenic walks through breathtaking country.

Montgomery ✳ ☷ ⌂ Fh
Site of Neolithic, Iron Age, Roman and medieval fortifications, this small town now has a comfortably placid air. Bow-windowed Georgian houses and cobbled pavements are dominated by a 13th-century ruined castle.

Old Radnor ✛ Fd
Church in the hamlet below Old Radnor Hill has many treasures: Megalithic stone that has been a font for 1200 years, Tudor organ case and carved oak screen.

Presteigne ✛ ⌂ Ge
Small market town that once boasted 30 inns. Medieval Duke's Arms, and the Radnorshire Arms with secret passages and a priest chamber, still remain. Flemish tapestries woven in 16th century, in part-Saxon church.

ST ANDREW'S *Saxons, Normans, Tudors and Georgians have all left their mark in Presteigne's church.*

Radnor Forest ☆ Ee
A huge rock 'dome' made up of several rolling hills about 2000ft high, and deep valleys known as 'dingles'. Haunt of badgers.

Rhandirmwyn ⌂ ☆ ⚘ ⚘ Ac
Isolated village of farms. Twm Shon Catti, 16th-century outlaw, hid in Twm's cave in nearby Dinas Hill, now a bird reserve.

Stiperstones ☆ ⚘ Gh
Jagged rocks mark the spine of the heather-dark ridge in this wild country. The Devil is said to sit at the curious rock formation when cloud hides the ridge.

Talgarth ☷ ✛ Eb
Busy Victorian town with a web of narrow streets; clock tower above town hall was built to mark Victoria's Golden Jubilee in 1887.

Y Gaer ⚘ Da
Romans built their great fort here in AD 75. Largest of its type in Wales, covering 5 acres.

Y Pigwn ⚘ Bb
Roman legions marched along the high track between Trecastle and Llandovery in about AD 50. Evidence of their camps at 1353ft.

POWYS PEAKS *Hedged fields in the Usk valley stop abruptly at the foot of the Brecon Beacons, the highest mountains in South Wales.*

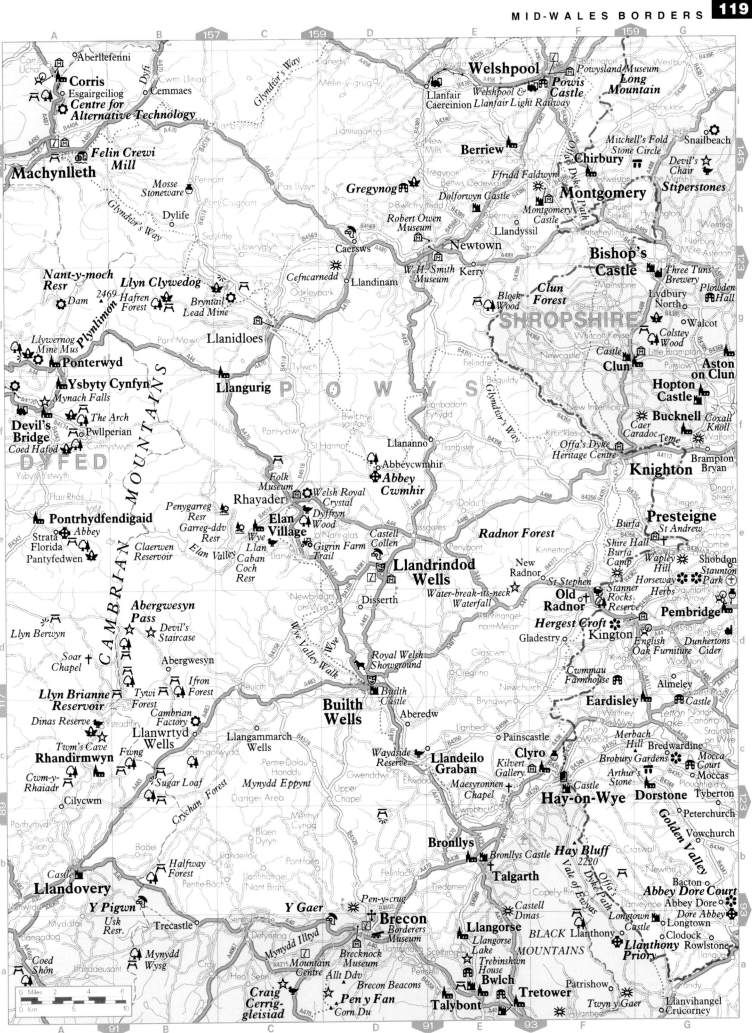

Aberllefenni
Corris Uchaf
Corris
Esgairgeiliog
Centre for
Alternative Technology
Cemmaes
Dyfi
Cwm-Llinau
Llanerfyl
Glyndŵr's Way
Mélin-y-grug
Buttington
Welshpool
Powysland Museum
Westbury
Powis Castle
Welshpool & Llanfair Light Railway
Long Mountain
B4386
Hope
Brockton

Machynlleth
Felin Crewi Mill
Mosse Stoneware
Pennant
Plas Llysyn
Berriew
Brooks
Ffridd Faldwyn
Priestweston
Chirbury
Mitchell's Fold Stone Circle
Snailbeach
Devil's Chair
Stiperstones

Gregynog
Robert Owen Museum
Dolforwyn Castle
Abermule
Montgomery
Montgomery Castle
Church Stoke
Hyssington
Norbury

Nant-y-moch Resr
Llyn Clywedog
Hafren Forest
Bryntail Lead Mine
Caersws
Newtown
W.H. Smith Museum
Kerry
Llandyssil
Sarn
Bishop's Castle
Three Tuns Brewery
Lydbury North
Plowden Hall
Walcot

2469
Plynlimon
Dam
Cefncarnedd
Llandinam
Clun Forest
Block Wood
Mainstone
SHROPSHIRE
Colstey Wood
Newcastle
Whitcott Keysett

Llywernog Mine Mus
Ponterwyd
Llanidloes
Llangurig
P O W Y S
Beguildy
New Invention
Clun
Castle
Little Brampton
Aston on Clun

Ysbyty Cynfyn
Mynach Falls
The Arch
Pwllperian
Pant-y-dwr
St Harmon
Llanbadarn Fynydd
Knucklas
Caer Caradoc
Hopton Castle
Coxall Knoll

Devil's Bridge
Coed Hafod
DYFED
Ysbyty Ystwyth
Ffair-Rhos
Folk Museum
Rhayader
Welsh Royal Crystal
Dyffryn Wood
Llananno
Llanbister
Dolau
Offa's Dyke Heritage Centre
Knighton
Bucknell
Teme
Walford
Brampton Bryan

Pontrhydfendigaid
Strata Florida
Abbey
Pantyfedwen
Penygarreg Resr
Garreg-ddu Resr
Elan Village
Gigrin Farm Trail
Wye
Llan
Abbeycwmhir
Abbey Cwmhir
Castell Collen
Crossgates
Penybont
Radnor Forest
Kinnerton
Presteigne
St Andrew
Burfa
Shire Hall
Burfa Camp
Combe

CAMBRIAN MOUNTAINS
Claerwen Reservoir
Elan Valley
Caban Coch Resr
Llandrindod Wells
Disserth
Water-break-its-neck Waterfall
New Radnor
St Stephen
Old Radnor
Stanner Rocks Reserve
Herbs
Wapley Hill
Horseway
Shobdon
Staunton Park
Pembridge

Llyn Berwyn
Abergwesyn Pass
Devil's Staircase
Soar Chapel
Abergwesyn
Hergest Croft
Gladestry
Glascwm
Kington
English Oak Furniture
Dunhertons Cider
Almeley

Llyn Brianne Reservoir
Dinas Reserve
Ystradffin
Twm's Cave
Ifron Forest
Tywi Forest
Cambrian Factory
Royal Welsh Showground
Cregrina
Newchurch
Cwmmau Farmhouse
Eardisley
Castle
Letton

Rhandirmwyn
Cwm-y-Rhaiadr
Cilycwm
Fwng
Llanwrtyd Wells
Cefn-gorwydd
Beulah
Builth Wells
Builth Castle
Aberedw
Painscastle
Bryngwyn
Clyro
Kilvert Gallery
Merbach Hill
Bredwardine
Brobury Gardens
Arthur Stone
Mocca Court
Moccas
Dorstone
Tyberton

Castle
Llandovery
Y Pigwn
Usk Resr.
Trecastle
Sugar Loaf
Llangammarch Wells
Pentre-Dolau-Honddu
Wayside Reserve
Llandeilo Graban
Gwenddwr
Upper Chapel
Maesyronnen Chapel
Erwood
Maesyronnen
Hay-on-Wye
Peterchurch
Vowchurch

Halfway Forest
Mynydd Eppynt
Danger Area
Blaen Dyryn
Bronllys
Bronllys Castle
Hay Bluff 2220
Golden Valley
Bacton
Newton

Coed Shôn
Mynydd Wysg
Mynydd Illtyd
Brecknock Museum
Mountain Centre
Allt Ddu
Pen-y-crug
Y Gaer
Borderers Museum
Brecon
Talgarth
Castell Dinas
Longtown Castle
Abbey Dore Court
Abbey Dore
Dore Abbey

Craig Cerrig-gleisiad
Pen y Fan
Corn Du
Brecon Beacons
Heol Senni
Trebinshwn House
Talybont
Bwlch
Tretower
Twyn y Gaer
Llangorse
Llangorse Lake
BLACK MOUNTAINS
Llanthony
Llanthony Priory
Rowlstone
Patrishow
Llanvihangel Crucorney

Miles 0 2 4 6
Km 0 2 4 6 8 10

ENGLAND'S WESTERN HILLS

'On Wenlock Edge the wood's in trouble; His forest fleece The Wrekin heaves;
The gale, it plies the saplings double, And thick on Severn snow the leaves.'
– a tribute to the western hills from A.E. Housman's *A Shropshire Lad*.

STARK CONTRAST *Stone-built Butter Cross Museum frames Tudor-style Broad Street, Ludlow.*

From Somerset's Mendips, by way of the Cotswolds, the Malverns and the Shropshire uplands, a great crescent of hills curves for more than 100 miles up the western flank of England, looking over to the loftier, wilder mountains of Wales. Even so, the English hills are wild enough to have kept many of the latest agricultural practices at bay. Their very nature makes them inaccessible to modern farming machinery, so you can still see the patchwork of small fields, hedges and copses that once patterned the face of rural England.

These less-worked lands carry a richer wildlife than much of the rest of Britain. The grassy tops are scoured by buzzards and kestrels, while underfoot lies a tapestry of wild flowers. The limestone hills reveal rare pasque flowers in spring and many species of orchids in summer. The harder rocks, like those of The Long Mynd, support heather which in turn supports grouse, merlins and curlews.

The first settlers took refuge in the caves that line the deep limestone gorges of the Mendips: Cheddar and Ebor and Burrington Combe. And it is the caves that still draw people to the Mendips today, to see how our predecessors lived more than 30,000 years ago. In today's gentler climate the Cheddar Gorge is still a refuge – for one of Britain's rarest wild flowers, the Cheddar pink.

But for all their history and natural beauty, the Mendips are famed for one thing above all else: Cheddar cheese. Once made locally, it is now produced throughout the world.

Cotswold and Malvern hills

North of the Mendips lie the Cotswolds, a vast plateau of limestone stretching over 50 miles from Bath to Chipping Campden. It is veined with valleys cut by some of the most beautiful rivers in England, containing some of the most beautiful villages, all built of local Cotswold stone.

From the 961ft summit of Bredon Hill you can look back to the Cotswolds proper and ahead to the windswept humps of the Malverns. The 9 mile long Malvern spine is formed from some of the oldest and hardest rock in Britain, thrust high above the surface about 300 million years ago and since worn down to the smooth contours seen today.

JAGGED TOR *Cranberry Rock (above) is one of the rugged outcrops on the treacherous quartzite ridge known as the Stiperstones.*

The Malverns provided the inspiration for the poets A.E. Housman and William Langland – author of the 14th-century epic, *Piers the Plowman*. The composer Edward Elgar also loved the Malverns, and is buried in the churchyard at Little Malvern.

One of the most memorable landmarks of the region is the extensive dyke, built by Offa, the King of Mercia in AD 757-796. It runs 140 miles from Chepstow in the south to Prestatyn in North Wales. The 10 mile stretch through Clun Forest is the highest and best preserved part of the whole dyke.

On the map, Clun Forest looks like the palm of a hand with five hill ranges running north-east as fingers. Looking out beyond Ludlow, the Clee hills form the thumb, with 1790ft Brown Clee at its extremity. The forefinger of the Shropshire 'hand' is Wenlock Edge, a 16 mile long

PASQUE FLOWER

coral reef left high and dry by a tropical sea that vanished about 400 million years ago. Its limestone has been quarried over the centuries, first for building stone, more recently for road stone and unofficially for fossils.

The steep north-western face – the Edge itself – looks over well-farmed Ape Dale to the Caradocs, a 10 mile long mountain range in miniature with half-a-dozen separate summits linked by a web of tracks and footpaths.

The wildest of the western hills, The Long Mynd, forms the third finger of the hand. Much of it is heather-clad moorland, home to grouse, merlins, curlews and sheep. Deep, narrow valleys carve into the ridge and carry bubbling streams down to the plain. The scarce bog pimpernel, butterwort and mosses colour the banks of the streams.

If The Long Mynd is the wildest range in the western curve, the final range, the Stiperstones,

is probably the weirdest. The jagged, white rocks that thrust up at odd angles from the ridge can be seen as the spinal crest of some prehistoric monster, or the ruins of some long-vanished civilisation. Certainly the Devil has long been associated with the area, and one particularly striking outcrop is credited with being his chair.

MURDER AND DECEIT

Legend has it that in AD 794, King Offa of Mercia promised his daughter's hand in marriage to King Ethelbert of East Anglia. On the eve of his wedding day, King Ethelbert was beheaded by the scheming Offa.

SAXON LINE *Offa's Dyke was the first official border between the English and the Welsh.*

ETHELBERT *Brass rubbing in Hereford Cathedral.*

MINE SPOIL *White calcite, debris from Roman lead mining, is found scattered north of the Stiperstones.*

ANCIENT OUTCROP *Underlying the sheep-grazed slopes of the Malvern Hills is a backbone of crystalline rock some 600 million years old.*

THE WELSH MARCHES

Ruined castles in the border country and Iron Age and Roman hill-forts recall a turbulent battle-scarred past. Now the landscape is peaceful, with comfortable small towns and villages. Hereford cattle graze in pastures beside apple orchards and hop gardens, and the quiet harmony is echoed in the music of Elgar, who was greatly influenced by the country of his childhood.

HOMELY CASTLE *One of England's finest fortified manor houses, Stokesay was built to withstand attack from Welsh raiders. However, the timbered Jacobean gatehouse could never have resisted serious assault.*

Acton Scott Historic Working Farm ♨ Bf
Noble shire horses draw ploughs in this re-creation of a 19th-century farm. Red-haired Tamworth pigs, Longhorn and Shorthorn dairy cows. Country skills such as butter-making are demonstrated by experts.

Aston on Clun ⌂ Af
Village below benign, broad-backed Hopesay Hill, set in unchanging farming country. A black poplar, the Arbor Tree, is festooned with bunting each May, still celebrating nuptials of an 18th-century landowner.

Broadfield Court ⚘ Cc
Large country estate, just outside village of Bodenham. House built in 1300s, expanded 1500s. Stone terrace, walled garden and vineyards producing Broadfield Court fine wine.

Bromfield ⌂ Be
Ruins of a Benedictine priory in water meadows where the Rivers Onny and Teme converge. Beside it is the massive presence of St Mary's Church with 13th-century tower, and a chancel ceiling painted with Biblical texts.

Bromyard ⌂☑ Dc
Medieval market town with streets lined with half-timbered buildings. Nearby Lower Brockhampton Manor is a stout house built for a squire, with a galleried dining hall, tilting timbers and a buckled roof of fine old tiles.

Brown Clee Hill Cf
Highest point in Shropshire, almost 1800ft. Sandstone formation with fine views and nature trail winding through woods.

Burford ⌂⚘ Cd
Village beside gentle River Teme. Graceful 18th-century Burford House stands in gardens full of shrubs and flowers, especially clematis. Tiny Norman church.

Clungunford ⌂ Be
Quiet little village with Saxon origins and scattered cottages. Clungunford House is a fine Georgian mansion. Humble 'Thatched Cottage' was probably built in 14th century as a farm labourer's home. Church of St Cuthbert dates from 13th century.

Croft Ambrey ☀ Bd
Iron Age hill-fort of 550 BC with ramparts and ditches, crowning windswept escarpment. From the fort it is claimed that 14 counties can be seen.

Croft Castle ⚑ Bd
Dusty-pink medieval walls and turrets enclose a fanciful Georgian interior. Spacious parkland with stretch of Spanish chestnuts more than 350 years old. Home of Croft family from 11th to 20th centuries. Bircher Common, on estate, is patchwork of bracken, gorse and grassland covering 1300 acres.

Dudmaston ⚑ Ef
Manor house of 18th century. Garden boasts trees, shrubs and landscaped waterfalls. Important art collection of Dutch 17th-century painters and moderns such as Matisse.

Eardisland ⌂ Bc
Cottage gardens border River Arrow as it meanders through this sleepy village. Moated motte of an old castle adjoins medieval St Mary's Church, with 15th-century carvings. Staick House beside two-arch bridge is a black-and-white manor with gables and lattice windows. Burton Court has 14th-century Great Hall and a costume collection.

Eastnor Castle ⚑ Ea
Despite its air of medieval impregnability, this castle was built in 1814 when there was a passion for the Gothic style. Collections of armour, tapestries and paintings in six large rooms.

Great Malvern †⌂☑ Eb
Fashionable spa town in last century with echoes of that period. The water is still popular. Greatest treasure is the 11th-century church with 15th-century stained glass, among best in Britain.

Hampton Bishop ⌂ Ca
Serene village street lined with thatched houses and pretty gardens. Norman church with striking black-and-white belfry.

Hereford
†⌂⚑🚂⚘🖼☑ Cb
Cathedral city, once Saxon capital of West Mercia. Treasures in superb 11th-century cathedral include brasses, ancient books and famous AD 1300 Mappa Mundi world map. Museum and distillery trace history of cider-making. Jacobean Old House furnished in 17th-century style. Local history exhibits in museum.

Herefordshire Beacon ☀ Eb
Isolated Iron Age fort covering 32 acres, with splendid views from 1115ft summit. Known as British Camp, 2000 people may have lived here in ancient times. Giant's Cave on Broad Down, below, said to have sheltered Welsh prince fleeing English in 1405.

Hopesay Common ⚹ Af
Snug green lanes cross the undulating landscape up to windswept shoulder of Hopesay Hill with its grazing sheep and ponies. Iron Age forts on neighbouring hills were links in a defensive chain. Brooding trees include ancient hollies and ash.

Kilpeck ⌂ Ba
Hamlet with Norman church, unchanged since 1100s. Intricate carvings on south door show tree of life, dragons and angels. Outside frieze has some 70 carvings of human and animal heads.

Kinver Edge ✿ ☀☀ Ff
Dramatic cliff springing from wooded heathland offers views of the Clees, the Cotswolds, the Malverns and the Clents. Caves in the sandstone may have been used by prehistoric man. One, Holy Austin Rock, was a hermitage.

CARVED ARCH *Strange motifs adorn the little church at Kilpeck.*

Ledbury ⌂⚘☑ Ea
Comfortable, quietly prosperous market town. Many fine Tudor houses with overhanging gables, and 17th-century market hall supported by chestnut pillars.

Leominster †⌂☑ Cc
Red Hereford cattle are exported from this old market town. Magnificent church of St Peter and St Paul built from 12th century on site of nunnery founded before 9th century. Intricately timbered 1663 town hall. Folk Museum.

Lower Broadheath ⌂⌂ Fc
Trim Georgian house facing Malvern Hills was 1857 birthplace of English composer Sir Edward Elgar, who drew inspiration from his surroundings. Memorabilia of the man and his life.

Ludlow ⚑⌂†☑ Ce
One of Britain's loveliest towns. Harmonious mix of medieval, Tudor, Stuart and Georgian buildings. Dominating all is 11th-century castle, rivalled only by huge 15th-century church. Poet A.E. Housman (1859-1936) is buried in churchyard.

Pembridge ⌂⚘♨ Ac
Tiny medieval village surrounded by meadows and orchards. On hill above 16th-century market hall, sparse remains of motte-and-bailey castle adjoin churchyard.

Ravenshill Wood ♈⚘✿ Ec
Some 30 kinds of native trees. Carefully marked paths into woods and to summit with views. Warblers and wetland birds. Badgers and foxes abound.

Severn Valley Railway 🚂 Ef
Giants of the steam age pant along 16 mile track, through lovely countryside between Kidderminster and Bridgnorth. Large collection of locomotives.

Stokesay Castle ⚑ Bf
Fortified manor house whose timbered additions give a cosy, rather than a defensive air. Almost unchanged after 750 years, Great Hall with solar chamber is one of the country's finest. Church nearby is 17th century with texts painted on walls.

Tenbury Wells ⌂☑ Cd
Old market town on sparkling River Teme, hemmed in by apple orchards and hop gardens. The 18th-century church has a 12th-century tower with Norman windows. Many half-timbered and Georgian houses and a Tudor inn, The Royal Oak.

Wenlock Edge ✿⚘♈ Bf
Phenomenal limestone escarpment, remarkably regular in height and dark with trees, runs for 16 straight miles.

Weobley ⌂ Bc
Graceful spire of Norman church dominates gentle valley in which this ancient village (pronounced Webley) lies. Unsurpassed collection of black-and-white buildings with huge timber frames that overhang the streets. Red Lion Inn is 14th century.

Wernlas Collection ⚹ Be
Colourful collection of hens, from Rhode Island Reds to black-and-gold German Vorwerks. Rare farm animals such as primitive native sheep from the island of North Ronaldsay in Orkney. They graze almost entirely on seaweed.

MAGPIE TOWN *Ledbury boasts beautiful black-and-white buildings.*

West Midlands Safari Park and Leisure Centre ⚹ Fe
Wild African animals look thoroughly at home in 200 acres of green countryside. Amusement park and cinema.

Worcestershire Beacon ☀ Eb
Highest point of Malvern Hills at 1394ft. Staggering views as far as the Mendips in Somerset.

Wyre Forest ♈⚘✿ Ee
Remnant of a much larger royal hunting ground. Fallow deer and several species of bat. Birds include sparrowhawk, woodcock, tawny owl and kestrel.

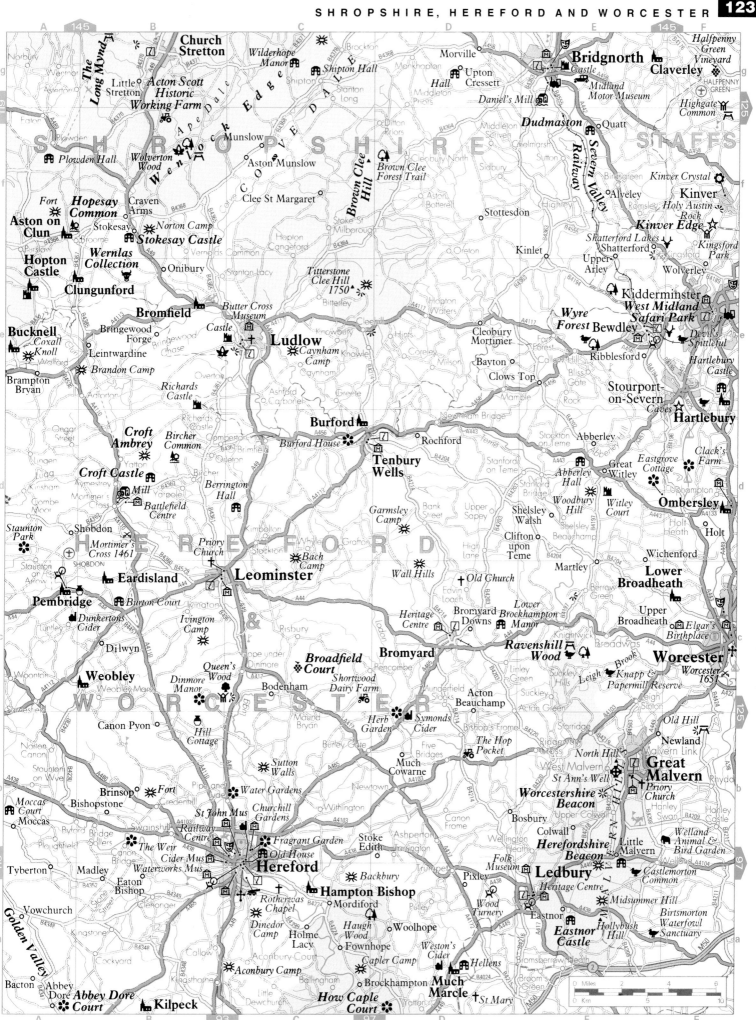

Map region labels and place names:

SHROPSHIRE
STAFFS
HEREFORD
WORCESTER

The Long Mynd · Church Stretton · Wilderhope Manor · Shipton Hall · Morville · Bridgnorth · Claverley · Halfpenny Green Vineyard · Highgate Common · Halfpenny Green

Little Stretton · Acton Scott Historic Working Farm · Upton Cressett · Hall · Castle · Midland Motor Museum · Daniel's Mill · Quatt

Plowden Hall · Wolverton Wood · Munslow · Aston Munslow · Brown Clee Hill · Brown Clee Forest Trail · Dudmaston · Kinver Crystal · Kinver

Hopesay Common · Craven Arms · Stokesay · Clee St Margaret · Stottesdon · Holy Austin Rock · Kinver Edge

Aston on Clun · Fort · Stokesay Castle · Norton Camp · Shatterford Lakes · Shatterford · Kingsford Park

Hopton Castle · Wernlas Collection · Onibury · Titterstone Clee Hill 1750 · Cleobury Mortimer · Upper Arley · Wolverley

Clungunford · Bromfield · Butter Cross Museum · Castle · Ludlow · Bayton · Clows Top · Kidderminster · West Midland Safari Park · Bewdley · Devil's Spittleful

Bucknell · Coxall Knoll · Bringewood Forge · Leintwardine · Caynham Camp · Knowbury · Ribblesford · Hartlebury Castle

Brampton Bryan · Brandon Camp · Richards Castle · Stourport-on-Severn · Hartlebury · Caves

Croft Ambrey · Bircher Common · Burford · Burford House · Rochford · Abberley · Clack's Farm

Croft Castle · Mill · Battlefield Centre · Tenbury Wells · Garmsley Camp · Abberley Hall · Great Witley · Eastgrove Cottage · Ombersley

Staunton Park · Shobdon · Berrington Hall · Woodbury Hill · Witley Court · Holt Heath · Holt

Mortimer's Cross 1461 · Priory Church · Bach Camp · Wall Hills · Clifton upon Teme · Martley · Wichenford

Eardisland · Leominster · Old Church · Lower Brockhampton Manor · Lower Broadheath · Elgar's Birthplace

Pembridge · Burton Court · Dunkertons Cider · Ivington Camp · Heritage Centre · Bromyard Downs · Ravenshill Wood · Upper Broadheath · Worcester

Weobley · Dinmore Manor · Queen's Wood · Broadfield Court · Bromyard · Acton Beauchamp · Knapp & Papermill Reserve · Worcester 1651

Canon Pyon · Hill Cottage · Bodenham · Shortwood Dairy Farm · Herb Garden · Symonds Cider · The Hop Pocket · Old Hill · Newland

Brinsop · Fort · Water Gardens · Sutton Walls · Much Cowarne · North Hill · Great Malvern

Bishopstone · St John Mus · Churchill Gardens · Worcestershire Beacon · St Ann's Well · Priory Church

Moccas Court · Moccas · Railway Centre · Fragrant Garden · Old House · Stoke Edith · Bosbury · Colwall · Welland Animal & Bird Garden

Tyberton · The Weir · Cider Mus · Waterworks Mus · Hereford · Backbury · Herefordshire Beacon · Little Malvern · Ledbury · Castlemorton Common

Madley · Eaton Bishop · Rotheras Chapel · Hampton Bishop · Mordiford · Pixley · Folk Museum · Heritage Centre

Vowchurch · Dinedor Camp · Holme Lacy · Woolhope · Wood Turnery · Eastnor · Midsummer Hill · Birtsmorton Waterfowl Sanctuary

Bacton · Abbey Dore · Abbey Dore Court · Kilpeck · Aconbury Camp · Capler Camp · Weston's Cider · Hellens · Much Marcle · Eastnor Castle · Hollybush Hill

How Caple Court · Brockhampton · St Mary

Golden Valley

FARMLAND AND FACTORIES

It may look as if the urban mass of Birmingham (see pages 126-7) dominates everything, but even here there are delights to be discovered; unspoilt oases of green among the concrete. All around is a landscape rich in history, whether it be a mighty cathedral, stately home, half-timbered cottage or factory where two centuries ago needles were made to the throb of the water wheel.

Alcester Cc
In Roman times, market town at meeting point of two roads and two rivers, Arrow and Alne. Now homely black-and-white Tudor houses sit alongside Georgian red brick. Town hall built 1618.

Aston Hall Cg
Riot of gables, arches, octagonal chimneys and domes. One of the last great Jacobean houses built in England, completed in 1635 for Sir Thomas Holte. The interior has superb plaster-work. Arcaded oak panelling in 135ft Long Gallery. Cantilevered oak staircase has intricately carved balustrade.

Avoncroft Museum of Buildings Bd
Collection of historic buildings spanning seven centuries of English history – from working windmill and chain-making shop to 1946 prefab – dismantled and rebuilt here. Also display of carts and caravans.

Barber Institute of Fine Arts, Birmingham University Cf
European paintings from the 13th century to the present day, including works by Rubens, Gainsborough and Degas. There are also medieval ivories, antique bronzes and furniture.

Bidford-on-Avon Dc
Known to William Shakespeare as 'drunken Bidford' on strength of his experiences during nights out at Falcon Inn with companion Ben Jonson. Eight-arched stone bridge built 15th century.

Birmingham Botanical Gardens Cf
Paths wind among shrubs, trees and rose gardens, while exotic orchids flourish in glasshouses and banana trees spread their branches over a lily pond.

Birmingham Nature Centre Cf
Natural-seeming habitat created from ponds, streams and rocky outcrops is home to wild animals from Britain and Europe, such as lynx, beaver, badger and otter, as well as the wild birds and insects which arrive as welcome visitors.

Birmingham Railway Museum Df
Impressive collection of working steam locomotives, including *Clun Castle* and *Kolhapur*. Saloon carriage from royal train built for Edward VII and Queen Alexandra. The travelling post office ambushed by the Great Train Robbers can also be seen.

Blakesley Hall Df
Inventory of 1684 listed everything in this timber-framed 16th-century house. It was used as guide to restock contents and re-create world of 300 years ago. Painted Chamber decorated with 16th-century wall paintings rediscovered in 1950s.

Bournville Cf
Cadbury brothers created model estate for their workers after setting up chocolate factory in 1879. Now home to Cadbury World, presenting story of chocolate from its origin in tropical rain forest to final packaged sweet.

Bretforton Cb
Documented history goes back to Saxon deed of 714. Church with medieval carvings dates from 12th century; Fleece Inn – owned by National Trust – and manor house date from 14th century.

Broadfield House Glass Museum Af
Georgian mansion records glass-maker's art from Roman times to present, showing examples of the region's best work.

Bromsgrove Be
Light industrial town with dignified Georgian houses and 16th-century grammar school. Church tower dates from 14th century. Monuments in churchyard, with remarkable verses, to railwaymen killed in locomotive explosion.

Castle Bromwich Hall Df
Early Jacobean mansion, bought in 1657 by Sir John Bridgeman, who added the Restoration-style porch. Gardens restored to period style and open to public.

Chaddesley Corbett Ae
Half-timbered cottages and 14th-century Talbot Inn. St Cassian's Church, mainly 14th century with Norman nave and 12th-century font, dedicated to martyred teacher murdered by pagan pupils. Harvington Hall nearby has moat and secret passages and priests' hiding holes.

Clent Hills Be
Grassy hills of up to 1000ft, woods and farm land covering more than 500 acres and criss-crossed with footpaths and bridlepaths. Magnificent views of Black Country, Cotswolds, the Malverns and Kinver Edge. High Harcourt Farm has been restored as a countryside interpretation centre.

Cotwall End Nature Centre Bg
Butterflies and 80 species of wild birds throng to 15 acres of grass and woodland. Collection of British wild and domestic animals and waterfowl.

Coughton Court Cd
Imposing gatehouse to early 16th-century mansion where wives of 1605 Gunpowder plotters are said to have heard of plot's failure. Secret compartments under floor of Tower Room were used for hiding priests in times of trouble.

Droitwich Ad
Visitors to the spa baths can float in buoyant brine pumped up from lake over bed of rock salt deposited 200ft under town. Heritage centre tells story of salt industry. Church of Sacred Heart and St Catherine has walls and ceiling covered with striking mosaics.

BOAT TRIPS
Barges give trips at Dudley's Black Country Museum.

Dudley Bg
Zoo set in woods and gardens. Chair lift up to remains of 13th-century castle. Victorian village re-created in Black Country Museum standing on banks of canal, from which tram takes visitors past small colliery and replica of world's first steam engine. Working chain shop at Mushroom Green.

Evesham Cb
Market town of fruit-growing district. Gatehouse and bell tower remain from Benedictine abbey and form spectacular group with Norman All Saints and St Lawrence's parish church. Rambling, half-timbered almonry museum in Vine Street, dating from 14th century, has Roman, Saxon and medieval remains.

Feckenham Cd
Timber-framed cottages and red-brick Georgian houses in wide main street. Carved figures of angels playing musical instruments look down on nave of partly 13th-century church. Shurnock Court, 16th-century farmhouse, 1 mile east.

Forge Mill Cd
National Needle Museum in 18th-century water mill where needles were cleaned and sharpened. Original machinery still intact and working. Adjoins remains of 12th-century Bordesley Abbey.

Hagley Hall Bf
Palladian mansion built by Lord Lyttelton 1754-60 with Italian rococo plaster-work and collection of furniture and paintings. Ionic temple, rotunda and fake Gothic ruins in landscaped park.

Hanbury Hall Bd
Red-brick Queen Anne house built around 1701 for barrister Thomas Vernon. Interior decoration commissioned 1710 from Sir Thomas Thornhill; staircase murals and ceiling painted with scenes from mythological subjects. Other rooms contain some fine plaster-work.

Hartlebury Ae
Only moat remains of castle which was home of Bishops of Worcester for 1000 years. Present mansion built 1675. North wing houses county museum. Red sandstone tower of St James's Church soars over village. Off the A4025 road is the Hartlebury Common nature reserve and beyond it are Stone House Cottage Gardens, next to Stone Church.

Inkberrow Cc
In 1582 Shakespeare stayed at Old Bull inn, model for Ambridge pub in *The Archers* radio serial. Village green, 12th-century church and timber-framed houses.

King's Norton Ce
Patrick Collection displays 80 years of motoring history in large halls with period settings, and exhibits including 1934 Singer Le Mans and Aston Martin Zagato.

Lickey Hills Be
Country park offers birdwatching, bowls, golf, skiing or simply walks through the woods and meadows. Junior nature trail.

Little Comberton Bb
St Peter's Church with 500-year-old tower, 18th-century manor and medieval dovecote. Great Comberton – actually smaller – has yellow-stone Norman church set in narrow, leafy lanes.

Ombersley Ad
Village of black-and-white timber-framed houses, with its partly 15th-century pub. Clack's Farm garden, created for BBC-TV programme *Gardener's World*.

Perrott's Folly Cf
In 1758 John Perrott built this 96ft high tower for no apparent reason, though modern tourists appreciate the view from the top.

Pershore Bb
Market town with fine Georgian houses, set among fruit farms. Some parts of abbey, originally Norman, survived to serve as parish church, mostly in Early English style. Norman font, and monument bearing arms of Thomas Hazelwood – died 1624. College of Horticulture now Royal Horticultural Society Centre.

Ragley Hall Cc
Grey-stone house designed 1680 in Palladian style; 1750 baroque plaster-work; modern mural of *The Temptation* by Graham Rust on view in south hall took 14 years to complete. Country trail.

RIVERSIDE SETTING *The colours of sunset warm the scene as the River Avon meanders slowly past Evesham Abbey.*

Sandwell Valley ⌖⌖⌖ Cg
Farmland and woods with 1400 acres of open space and nature trails. Rare breeds farm and ruins of 1180 priory.

Sarehole Mill ⌖ Df
This 18th-century water mill has two working wheels – one for grinding corn and one for tools.

Selly Manor ⌖ Cf
A half-timbered 14th-century manor house furnished in period style. Near is 13th-century Minworth Greaves cruck cottage.

Spetchley Park ⌖ Ac
Deer park, lake with wildfowl and 30 acres of gardens with rare plants, shrubs and trees.

Stourbridge ⌖⌖⌖ Bf
Centre of crystal glass production. Visitors can watch it being made at Stuart Crystal's 18th-century Redhouse Cone, only traditional glass furnace in area and now museum. Old canal warehouse has been restored as arts centre.

Tardebigge Locks ⌖ Bd
Longest flight of locks in Britain: 30 strung out along 2 miles. Part of the 30 mile long Worcester and Birmingham Canal system.

Upton upon Severn ⌖⌖ Ab
A town with Tudor and Georgian buildings. Oldest building is the massive 14th-century Bell Tower with copper cupola, all that remains of the Church of St Peter and St Paul.

Weoley Castle ⌖ Cf
Excavations of this 13th-century manor-house ruin revealed an older house. Museum on site.

KINGS' WAY *Statues of Charles I and Charles II flank the entrance to Worcester's Guildhall.*

Worcester
✝⌖⌖⌖⌖ Ac
Cathedral tower, 14th century, dominates city's setting by banks of River Severn. Cathedral was started in 1084 and has wealth of fine carvings, depicting everything from tournament scene to naked woman on goat. Among many memorable old buildings are 15th-century Commandery, once almshouse for aged and poor, now visitor centre, and well-restored 18th-century Guildhall with displays of armour from Battle of Worcester in 1651. Dyson Perrins Museum shows local porcelain from 1751 to present day. Tours of Royal Worcester factory.

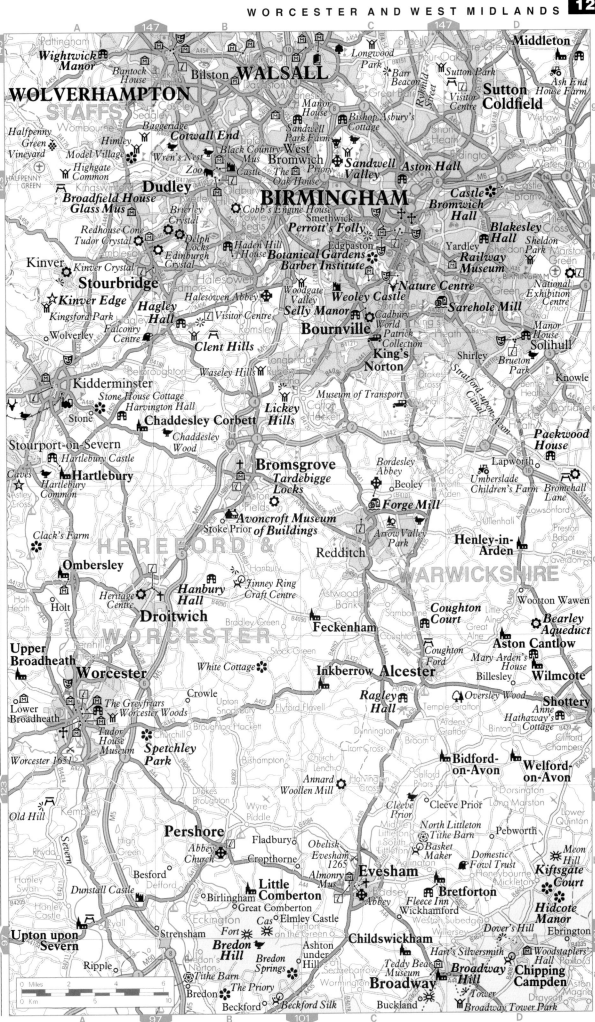

'CITY OF A THOUSAND TRADES'

The Industrial Revolution of the 19th century promoted the growth of Birmingham until the city became Britain's second largest; its prosperity was based on factories, hundreds of small workshops and a huge network of canals, all of which helped in the production of everything from buttons to steam engines. Grand public buildings express a sense of civic pride in a city which is still growing.

Assay Office Bc
Founded 1773, office is still in use. Red-brick building bears royal coat of arms. Objects made with precious metals in Jewellery Quarter are hallmarked here to indicate their origin.

Birmingham and Fazeley Canal De
From city's centre, this canal heads downhill through 13 locks within its first 1½ miles. It passes old factories and warehouses and then under more recent tower blocks. Restored towpaths make canal walking easier and safer.

Birmingham Hippodrome ♥ Cb
One of the largest theatres outside London, with 1950 seats, it houses extravagant opera and ballet productions, as well as West End musicals. Also home to The Birmingham Royal Ballet, formerly the Sadler's Wells Royal Ballet. Opposite the theatre, on Hurst Street, is the new Arcadian Shopping Centre, with piazza, cinema and hotel.

Birmingham Museum and Art Gallery 🏛 Cc
Buildings dating from 19th century hold painting collection strong on Pre-Raphaelites, and sculptures by Rodin, Epstein and Henry Moore. Industrial Gallery houses applied arts. Prize work in European section is Bellini's altarpiece, *Madonna and Child*. Museum also features local and natural history, and archaeology.

Birmingham Repertory Theatre ♥ Bc
Original theatre, now a mile away, dates back to the turn of the century – this second building, next to the International Convention Centre on Centenary Square, opened in 1971. Main house seats 900, and smaller studio 200. Sets and costumes for theatre's own productions made in-house. Actors and actresses to launch careers here include Lord Olivier,

Sir Ralph Richardson, Dame Peggy Ashcroft, Dame Edith Evans and Richard Chamberlain.

Broad Street Bc
Bronze statue of three key figures in Birmingham's industrial success stands in street. It depicts Matthew Boulton and James Watt, first major manufacturers of steam engines, consulting with gas lighting inventor William Murdoch. Opposite is Centenary Square, displaying fountains and modern sculptures symbolising the city's past, present and future. Square is flanked by International Convention Centre and the new Birmingham Repertory Theatre.

BANKSIDE STROLL *Gas Street Basin is the centrepiece of the city's celebrated canal-side walk.*

The Bull Ring Cc
Markets have been here since 12th century. Now a shopping centre surrounded by multi-lane ring road. Together with the large cylindrical office block known as Rotunda it serves as familiar landmark, although Rotunda is to be demolished and The Bull Ring redeveloped in the late 1990s.

Central Library Bc
Enormous modern library houses more than 1,000,000 books. Its celebrated Shakespeare Collection is the largest in Britain, with over 50,000 items.

Council House Cc
Building of late 19th century modelled on Italian Renaissance architecture from Florence and Sienna. Its tall clock tower is known as 'Big Brum'.

Curzon Street Station Dc
Station was designed by architect Philip Hardwick for George Stephenson's London and Birmingham Railway. Today it serves as offices.

Gas Street Basin Bc
Old canal basin in heart of city is home to varied collection of traditional, colourful canal boats. Renovated with attention to historical detail, basin is now the highlight of the canal-side walk. Part of a canal system that has been used to transport goods from the mid-18th century.

Great Western Arcade Cc
Victorian arcade squeezes in amongst modern stores. Wooden-fronted stores and restaurants are adorned with wrought-iron railings, lanterns and brightly painted arches.

Gun Barrel Proof House Dc
Establishment opened in 1813 to test thousands of locally produced guns. Still serves this purpose, but

now only about 60,000 pieces are proved yearly, down from as many as 1,000,000 in years past.

The Hall of Memory Bc
Small octagonal temple sits in a wide formal garden, surrounded by buildings important to city life, including administrative offices of Baskerville House. Inside hall, rolls of honour list local soldiers who died in two world wars.

MODERN CITYSCAPE *Sculptures and fountains in Centenary Square complement the impressive new International Convention Centre*

Ikon Gallery 🏛 Cb
Modern gallery in John Bright Street, showing fine art and sculpture by present-day artists. All aspects of contemporary art are explored; the gallery shows films, holds discussions, and stages performances relevant to the exhibitions. Sometimes shows work by local artists.

International Convention Centre Bc
Modern conference centre built in heart of city, officially opened in 1992. Home to arts as well as business – its Symphony Hall, with 2200 seats, is base to the City of Birmingham Symphony Orchestra. Outside centre in Centenary Square are several specially commissioned sculptures depicting the city's industrial history. Next to the Birmingham Repertory Theatre. Close by is National Indoor Arena, part of the same complex, with sports of all kinds.

James Brindley Walk Bc
Brindley was engineer who built first Birmingham Canal in 1760s. Street bearing his name leads down to restored canal area with waterside pub, shop, old toll-house and wharves.

Jewellery Quarter Bd
An area of not only jewellers' shops, but also small workshops where craftsmen shape gold and silver into settings for precious stones. At its centre stands ornate Chamberlain Clock.

Museum of Science and Industry 🏛 Bc
A 125 ton steam locomotive is just one example of museum's displays of Birmingham's industrial past. Equally grand is its 1873 lighthouse optic, surrounded by machines that made everything one could possibly need, from tricycles to buttons.

National Indoor Arena Bc
Opened in 1991, arena near International Convention Centre hosts all kinds of sporting events and world championships, especially for indoor athletics and gymnastics. Ice skating possible using portable ice mat. Occasionally stages rock concerts. Seats 13,000.

Old Crown Db
Oldest secular building in the city. Largely rebuilt in the late 1970s, though outside appearance is of a modern pub. Inside some of the

beams and one wall remain from the original 15th-century timber-framed inn that was once part of large medieval house built around an enormous courtyard.

St Chad's Cathedral ✝ Cd
First Roman Catholic Cathedral built after Reformation, designed and built by Pugin and finished in 1841. Medieval-style interior is enhanced by 16th-century pulpit and 15th-century statuary. Relics of St Chad, who died in AD 672, also housed here; their story told in stained glass.

St Martin's Church ✝ Cc
Birmingham's oldest building sits in Bull Ring area. Church dates from 13th century but appears to be more recent as it was extensively restored in 19th century.

St Martin's Rag Market Cb
Popular covered market with approximately 500 stalls offering new and secondhand goods, including everything from bric-a-brac to more valuable antiques.

St Paul's Square Bd
Part of Georgian town planning, was built as complete unit in 18th century. St Paul's Church stands in centre. Inside are numbered box pews, which were 'sold' to pay for church. Among the box-holders were pioneering engineers Matthew Boulton (owner of box number 23), James Watt (little-used box number 100), and several local jewellers from the

LUCKY THIRTEEN *From the mid-18th century this flight of 13 consecutive locks, known as Farmer's Bridge Steps, once slowly raised canal barges by 40ft into the heart of industrial Birmingham. It is now mainly used for sightseeing trips.*

Jewellery Quarter who gave St Paul's Church its irreverent nickname of the 'jewellers' church'.

St Philip's Cathedral ✝ Cc

Designed by Thomas Archer and finished in 1715, building is prime example of English baroque architecture, with superb stained-glass windows by Burne-Jones, who was born in Birmingham and later christened in this cathedral. Memorials include those to Colonel Frederick Burnaby, the war correspondent and balloonist who died in 1885.

Stratford House Da

Timber-framed farmhouse stands incongruously in Birmingham's bustling city centre. House was built at beginning of 17th century,

at a time when the city was just a small market town with a population of scarcely 2000.

Town Hall Cc

Built in 1830s by Joseph Hansom, famous for his Hansom cab design. Building was originally intended as a concert hall rather than a seat of civic government. Standing aloft on a platform supported by tall arches, building's design was clearly inspired by classical Roman architecture.

Worcester and Birmingham Canal Ba

Canal's towpath provides good walk past university and botanical gardens to city centre. At this point, canal junction is marked by small island.

SOMETHING OLD, SOMETHING NEW *The Great Western Arcade is the Victorian predecessor of the modern shopping mall.*

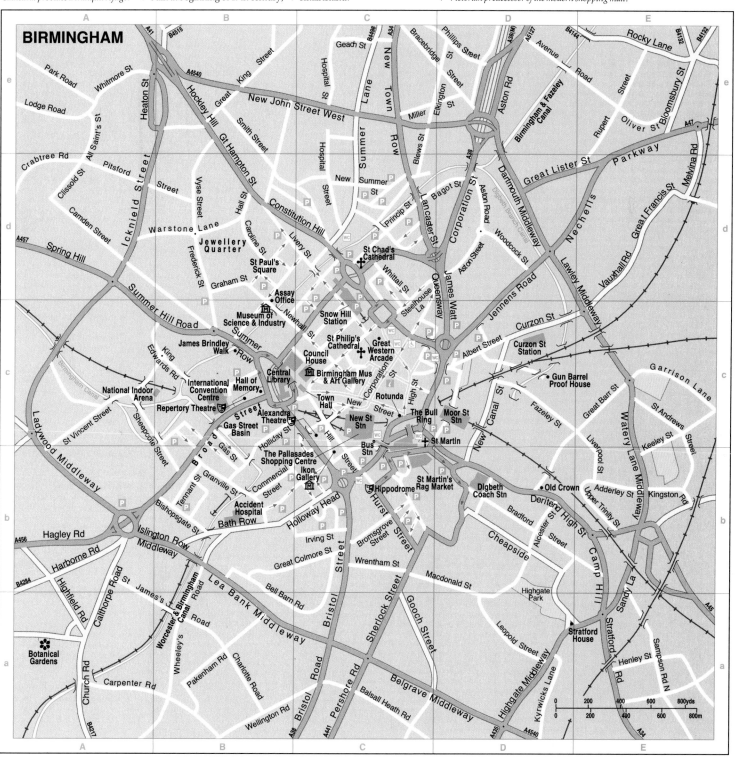

THE HEART OF ENGLAND

This is indeed the heart of England, for Meriden claims to be the country's geographical centre. It is a heart which beat throughout the ravages laid upon it by Saxons and Normans, the Wars of the Roses and wartime bombs. This is Shakespeare country, where the willow-lined River Avon meanders slowly along a broad, well-pastured valley and through the Forest of Arden.

Alvecote Priory ✣ ✿ ⌂ Bg
Ruins of Benedictine priory beside Coventry Canal. Waymarked walks lead along canal bank and Alvecote Pools, flooded coal mines now with nature trail rich in bird and plant life.

Arbury Hall ⌂ Ce
Elizabethan Hall transformed into 18th-century Gothic-style mansion. Luxurious rooms described in *Mr Gilfil's Love Story* by George Eliot, born on estate, 1819. Landscaped gardens and 17th-century chapel with fine plaster ceiling.

Aston Cantlow ⌂ Ac
Shakespeare's parents reputedly married at 13th-century St John the Baptist's Church in 1557. Picturesque inn and 16th-century half-timbered Guild House add to village charms.

Baddesley Clinton ⌂ Bd
Outstanding medieval moated house, little changed since 1634. Tall, handsome gatehouse is only entrance in sheer walls rising from broad moat. Great Hall has fine fireplace with massive carved stone chimney piece.

Bearley Aqueduct ✿ Ac
England's longest iron aqueduct, 475ft. Built 1813, carries Stratford-upon-Avon Canal across valley, road and railway line.

Berkswell ⌂ ⌂ Bd
Warwickshire's best Norman church, 12th-century pink stone St John the Baptist's. Beautiful double crypt and unusual timbered porch. Ancient Bercul's well gave village name. Russian Crimean War cannon guards 16th-century Bear Inn.

Berkswell Mill ✹ Bd
Four-storey tower mill with 60ft sails, restored with most of original machinery. Built 1826, last used for grinding corn in 1948.

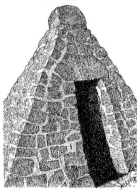

WELL OF HOPE *Stone cairn marks the spring on Bosworth Field from which Richard III quenched his thirst.*

Bosworth Field ⚔ ⌂ Dg
Flags of opposing armies still fly where Richard III fell to forces of Henry Tudor, future Henry VII, in 1485. Drama re-created in Battlefield Visitor Centre at Ambion Farm. Battle trails take in such crucial places as where Richard was killed.

Charlecote ⌂ ⌂ ✣ ⌂ Bb
Avenue of limes leads from old village to Charlecote Park, massive Elizabethan mansion built 1558. Rooms arranged as they were 150 years ago. Landscaped

CASTLE-TOP VIEW *Towers and turrets of Warwick Castle soar high above the River Avon. The Beauchamp family built most of the present structure.*

deer park, brew house with original brewing equipment and coach house with historic carriages.

Coleshill † Ae
Pretty town on steep hill above River Cole, crossed by medieval five-arched bridge. Pillory, stocks and whipping post near church.

Coventry
† ✿ ✣ ♉ ✿ ⌂ ⌂ Ⓩ Cd
A phoenix from the ashes, Coventry is a modern city which has risen from wartime rubble. Its 1962 cathedral, in bold pink-grey sandstone, stands next to the blackened ruins of 14th-century predecessor. Inside is Sutherland's immense 'Christ in Glory' tapestry and a charred cross made from roof beams of destroyed cathedral. Historic buildings include 14th-century St Mary's Guildhall, 13th-century Holy Trinity Church and timber-framed Ford's Hospital founded 1509. Herbert Art Gallery and Museum features British artists and city history. Museum of British Road Transport has cycles, motorcycles and commercial vehicles. Toy Museum is housed in part of 14th-century friary. Canal walk passes canal museum, former buildings

of Daimler Motor Company – which opened in 1896 – and old weaving works.

Drayton Manor Park ♞ Ag
Leisure park and open-plan zoo in 160 acres of parkland.

Hartshill ✹ Cf
Hartshill Hayes Country Park encompasses 136 acres of hilltop and woodland. Waymarked trails and panoramic views.

YEW AVENUE *The shadows of carefully shaped cones of yew stripe the walk to Tudor Packwood House. The trees represent Christ and His disciples.*

Hatton ⌂ ✹ Bc
Hatton Country World has craft village, rare breeds farm, vintage farm machinery and nature trail to Hatton Locks, there are 21 locks – longest flight in Britain – carrying Grand Union Canal uphill towards Birmingham.

Hawkesbury Junction ✿ Ce
Elegant cast-iron bridge, built 1836, spans junction between Oxford and Coventry canals.

Henley-in-Arden ⌂ Ac
Walking base among undulating country beside River Alne. Long main street has oak-timbered buildings, Blue Bell Inn and Guildhall all dating from 15th century. Earthworks, near 12th-century St Nicholas' Church, are sole remains of Norman Beaudesert Castle.

Kenilworth Castle ⛫ Bd
Dramatic ruins of Norman stronghold with imposing outer walls and red-sandstone keep. Built 12th century, later additions include great banqueting hall, 16th-century gatehouse and well-preserved stables.

Kingsbury Water Park ✹ Bf
Warwickshire's 'little lake district', 20 former gravel pits bustling with watersports in landscaped park. Woodland and waterside footpaths and nature reserve with trails and hides.

Lunt Roman Fort ⚲ Cd
Impressive reconstruction on site of AD 60 original. Has gateway erected in original post holes and fenced ring in which battle horses trained. Reconstructed granary displays finds from site.

Marton ⌂ ⌂ Dc
Collection of local memorabilia forms Museum of Country Bygones; tools, dairying implements and agricultural machinery. Bridge across River Leam has 15th-century masonry.

Meriden ⌂ ✣ Be
Village green has 15th-century wayside cross, which claims to mark centre of England, and monument honouring cyclists who died in both world wars. Forest Hall is 18th-century home of Woodmen of Arden, country's oldest archery society.

Midland Air Museum ✈ Cd
Open-air exhibits include only Lockheed Starfighter displayed in country, a huge Vulcan bomber, and work of Coventry-born jet engine pioneer Sir Frank Whittle.

Napton on the Hill ⌂ ✹ Dc
Saxon hillside village overlooking Oxford Canal. On hilltop are 12th-century St Lawrence's Church and restored windmill dating from the 19th century.

National Motorcycle Museum ⌂ Be
More than 800 machines displayed in varied theme halls. One of the halls traces 'Sixty Glorious Years' of mechanical development, 1902-61, another has on and off-road racing bikes and record-breakers.

Packwood House ⌂ Ad
Trees of remarkable Yew Garden clipped to represent persons involved in Sermon on the Mount. Fine Tudor house, with modified interior, has superb oak floor in Hall, oak-floored and panelled Long Gallery and timber-roofed Great Hall added 1925-31.

Royal Leamington Spa
✿ ✣ ✹ ⌂ Ⓩ Cc
Popular spa town made 'Royal' after Queen Victoria visited in 1838. Royal Pump Rooms built 1814 over one of town's seven springs. Regency and Victorian terraces overlook Jephson Gardens with bordered walks, tropical bird aviary and lake.

Ryton Gardens ✿ Dd
National Centre of Organic Gardening. Extensive vegetable, rose and herb gardens, shrub walk and fruit trees all grown without chemicals. Demonstrations of composting and natural pest control and weed killing.

Shottery ⌂ Ab
Anne Hathaway's Cottage and other thatched, timber-framed buildings carefully preserved as they would have been before she married Shakespeare in 1582.

Southam † Dc
On old Wales-London cattle droving road, where Charles I stayed before Battle of Edgehill, 1642. St James' Church has handsome timber roof, octagonal spire and 14th-century tower.

Stoneleigh ⌂ Cd
Timber-framed houses and cottages run down to River Sowe. Red-sandstone St Mary's Church, Norman, has monuments to Leigh family.

Stretton-on-Dunsmore ⌂ Dd
Low, brick bridges cross stream on triangular green surrounded by timber-framed houses and red-brick farm buildings. On Dunsmore Heath, astride Roman Fosse Way.

Tamworth 🏰🏛🅿 Bg

Historic Saxon capital of Mercia. Fine Norman motte-and-bailey castle spans centuries – keep, tower and herringbone curtain wall from 1180s, Tudor timber-framed Great Hall and Jacobean apartments decorated with wood-work and heraldic frieze. Castle Museum of local history includes models of Tamworth's Saxon fortifications and ancient silver pennies from Tamworth Mint.

Warwick 🏰🏛🚂🅿 Bc

Majestic 14th-century castle has massive walls, towers and turrets reflected in River Avon. Waxwork tableaux depict history. Magnificent state rooms and dungeon with grisly torture instruments. Finest buildings are timber-framed almshouses (1383) of Lord Leycester Hospital, precariously leaning over cobbled pavement, and 1720's Court House. Oken's House (1550) has fascinating Doll Museum. Market Hall (1670) displays geology, history and natural history of Warwickshire, and 17th-century St John's House has reconstructed Victorian rooms and Royal Warwickshire Regimental Museum. Superb 15th-century Beaumont Chapel of St Mary's Church has monuments to Earls of Warwick and Leicester.

Welford-on-Avon 🏠 Ab

Half-timbered, thatched cottages with attractive gardens are looped round by the River Avon. Riverside footpath through willow-hung water meadows.

Wellesbourne Mill 🏭 Bb

Restored wooden water wheel powers grindstones to produce flour. Secluded setting with mill pond and water meadow conservation area.

MARY ARDEN'S HOUSE The Tudor home of Shakespeare's mother is a perfectly preserved museum piece.

Wilmcote 🏠🏛 Ab

Typical timber-framed Tudor farmstead, once the home of Mary Arden, Shakespeare's mother. Dairy, dovecote and outbuildings, preserved in almost original condition, now house collection of country bygones.

Wormleighton 🏠 Db

Twists and turns of James Brindley's pioneering contour cutting allows 18th-century Oxford Canal to follow the natural curves of landscape. Best seen from Wormleighton Hill.

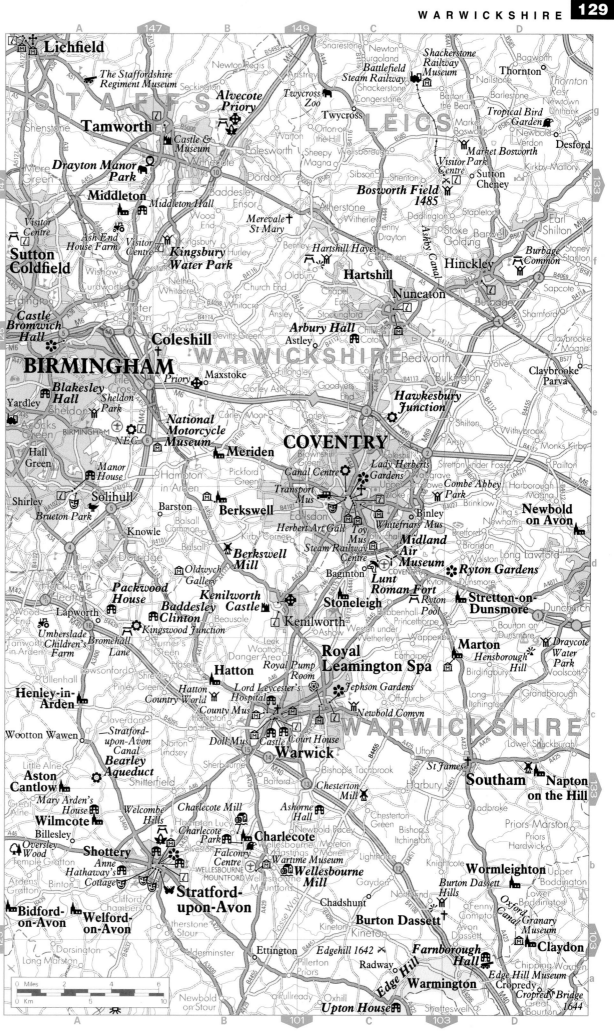

BIRTHPLACE OF THE BARD

Renowned as the birthplace of Shakespeare, this well-preserved market town is a showcase of Tudor architecture, its broad streets lined with half-timbered houses. Although thousands of people flock to Stratford every year to trace Shakespeare's life, the town has retained its character and is a rewarding place to visit quite apart from its literary associations.

American Fountain Ac
Gothic clock-tower and drinking fountain in the centre of Rothermarket, presented by a citizen of Philadelphia to mark Queen Victoria's Golden Jubilee in 1897. Fountain was unveiled by actor Henry Irving and inscriptions on it include line from *Timon of Athens*: 'Honest water which ne'er left man i' the mire.'

Bancroft Gardens Bb
Sweeping lawns beside Avon and canal basin of 1816, with brightly painted narrowboats and a riverside footpath. Gower Memorial is 1888 life-size bronze of Shakespeare by Lord Ronald Gower; small figures of Hamlet, Lady Macbeth, Falstaff and Prince Hal symbolise philosophy, tragedy, comedy and history.

Brass Rubbing Centre Ba
A rubbing table and walls hung with replica brasses in the former conservatory of Charles Edward Flower, local brewer and founder of the Memorial Theatre.

Bridge Street Bb
Street lined by pleasant houses, many having bay windows and elegant porticoes.

Church Street Ab
Georgian buildings include a row of timber-framed almshouses, the Guildhall and Guild Chapel.

Clopton Bridge Cb
Stone bridge with 14 pointed arches, built by local merchant Sir Hugh Clopton in the 1480s. Clopton also built New Place, and was Lord Mayor of London in 1492. Tower at end of bridge was tollhouse, added in 1814.

Falcon Hotel Bb
Dating from around 1500, and containing panelling from its former neighbour, New Place.

Great Garden ✿ Bb
Originally orchard and kitchen garden belonging to New Place.

ELIZABETHAN SPLENDOUR *Ornate half-timbering at the High Street's Garrick Inn, built in the late 16th century.*

Lawns with clipped hedges, and a mulberry tree said to have been grown from a cutting planted by Shakespeare.

Guild Chapel ✝ Bb
Begun in 1269 although the nave, tower and porch were rebuilt in 1495 by Sir Hugh Clopton. Vivid medieval wall paintings of the Last Judgment on arch above 13th-century chancel. Chapel still used by the grammar school for morning service.

Guildhall Bb
King Edward VI School, which Shakespeare attended, on upper floor. Ground floor, used by travelling actors, was where he probably saw his first play. Almshouses adjoining Guildhall were built by Guild of the Holy Cross in 15th century.

Hall's Croft 🏠 Aa
Splendid Tudor town house of Shakespeare's eldest daughter Susanna after she married Dr John

Hall. One of Stratford's finest Tudor buildings, with oak framing, an overhanging upper storey and a many-gabled roof. Interior has collection of rare Tudor and Jacobean furniture. Period room is reconstructed as a doctor's dispensary. Spacious walled garden, with sundial in an arbour.

used for baptism survives. In front of altar is Shakespeare's simple gravestone, with an inscription beginning: 'Good frend, for Jesus sake forbeare, To digg the dust enclosed heare.' A bust of Shakespeare was erected by his family in 1623. His wife Anne and eldest daughter Susanna lie beside him. Misericords, dating from *c.* 1500, depict birds, bears, angels, unicorns, and a husband birching his wife. Other imaginative carvings show a dromedary, a mermaid and two figures emerging out of shells. Chancel overlooks barges and boats on river. Lime trees in churchyard represent the apostles and the tribes of Israel.

Judith Quiney's House Bb
Long-time home of Shakespeare's younger daughter after her marriage to Thomas Quiney; building now a gift shop.

Knott Garden Bb
Reconstruction of the garden New Place would have possessed in Shakespeare's time, with beds of herbs and flowers interlaced in intricate patterns.

Nash's House 🏛 Bb
Home of Shakespeare's granddaughter Elizabeth Hall after she married Thomas Nash. Rooms furnished with fine Tudor and Jacobean furniture to re-create background of domestic life in Shakespeare's time; also local history museum, with many Roman and Saxon finds.

New Place Bb
Only the foundations remain of Shakespeare's last home, built by Sir Hugh Clopton *c.* 1483. The great poet lived here from 1611 until his death five years later. House pulled down 1759 by the Rev Francis Gattrell, to the rage of

OUR LITTLE LIFE IS ROUNDED WITH A SLEEP *The elegant spire of Holy Trinity Church rises majestically above the graveyard. Here, Shakespeare was brought to be baptised in 1564, and here he was finally laid to rest in 1616.*

GABLED HALL *Beautifully restored timber framing distinguishes Hall's Croft, the house where Shakespeare's eldest daughter Susanna once lived.*

Harvard House Bb
Restored half-timbered town house of Shakespeare's time, with richly carved frontage; birthplace of John Harvard who founded oldest university in America. Nearby, two handsome timbered properties – Tudor House and Garrick Inn – still retain their original splendour.

Holy Trinity Church ✝ Aa
Dating back to early 13th century, this is the church in which Shakespeare was baptised in 1564, and buried in 1616. Font

the town. Access through Nash's House – former site of New Place – now partly occupied by Knott Garden and Great Garden.

The Other Place ♟ Ba
Small theatre which encourages new and experimental drama as well as Shakespearean plays. Educational projects and workshops for children.

Royal Shakespeare Company Collection 🏛 Bb
Theatre museum with a variety of exhibits relating to productions of

POET'S CORNER *Columns of black marble frame Shakespeare's bust in Holy Trinity Church.*

Shakespeare's works. Displays include paintings, manuscripts, scenery, props and old costumes. Explanations on lighting and sound effects. Entrance adjoins Swan Theatre.

Royal Shakespeare Theatre Bb

The red-brick home of the Royal Shakespeare Company seating 1500 people – winning design by Elizabeth Scott in architectural competition of 1928. Building opened 1932, six years after original 1879 Memorial Theatre burnt down. Pleasant gardens and riverside terrace outside. Adjacent Swan Theatre is pure Victorian Gothic; includes museum of stage costumes and scenery.

Shakespeare Centre Bc

Study centre and headquarters of the Shakespeare Birthplace Trust, founded 1847 to preserve the playwright's heritage in and around the town. It houses the Birthplace Library and Royal Shakespeare Library. Glass panels in entranceway depict some Shakespearean characters by J. Hutton.

Shakespeare Hotel Bb

Magnificent ancient inn, three storeys high, with black-and-white timbering; meeting place for centuries of distinguished actors and visitors.

Shakespeare's Birthplace Bc

House little changed since Shakespeare's day, furnished in Elizabethan style. In bedroom is oak bed, a carved chest and 17th-century cradle; on leaded lights of window are signatures of distinguished early visitors. East part of

house contains a museum with rare books and manuscripts including a 1623 first folio of Shakespeare's plays. The garden has a display of the various trees, herbs and flowers mentioned in Shakespeare's works.

Stratford Butterfly and Jungle Safari Ca

Walkways pass pools and waterfalls inside a hothouse where hundreds of moths and butterflies fly among exotic plants, trees and flowers. Spider and insect house.

Stratford Canal Bc

Opened in 1816, this 25 mile long canal connects the Avon Canal with Worcester and Birmingham Canal. Restored south section, running from Bancroft Gardens, is home to handsome narrowboats and pleasure craft. Canal has 36 locks.

Stratford New Lock Ba

Deep lock lies just north of old Stratford to London railway bridge, overlooking Holy Trinity Church. Lock strengthened by steel girder frames to withstand high ground pressures. Handsome narrowboats queue up by the lock side in summer, watched by holiday crowds and picnickers

ROMANTIC VENUE *New plays feature at The Swan Theatre, ideally sited on the banks of the River Avon.*

The Swan Theatre Bb

Shell of old Memorial Theatre, which burnt down in the 1920s, now hosts The Swan Theatre, opened in 1986. Variety of work from Shakespearean tragedies to radical new plays. RSC collection of theatrical paraphernalia on display next door.

ABLAZE WITH COLOUR *Magnificent formal beds in bloom at the Knott Garden, New Place. Bright flowers of different colours interweave with herbs and neatly trimmed box hedges in traditional Elizabethan style.*

Teddy Bear Museum Ac

Hundreds of toys including some of the oldest, most valuable and most unusual teddy bears from around the world. A hall of fame displays both famous bears and bears of the famous.

Town Hall Bb

Built of Cotswold stone in 1767, by Robert Newman – master builder and mason. Restored after a fire in 1946. On wall facing Sheep Street is statue of Shakespeare presented by actor David Garrick in 1769. Facing Chapel Street is legend 'God Save the King', referring to George III, in whose reign Town Hall was built.

Tramway Bridge Cb

Built in 1823 as part of a horse-drawn tramway project to connect Shipston-on-Stour and Moreton-in-Marsh. One of the wagons used is preserved nearby.

White Swan Ac

This timber-framed, 15th-century hotel has a mural with three painted scenes, believed to be 16th century, illustrating story of Tobias and the Angel, from the apocryphal book of Tobit.

World of Shakespeare Bb

Life-size tableaux re-create sights and sounds of Shakespearean England, from the court of Elizabeth I to street slums.

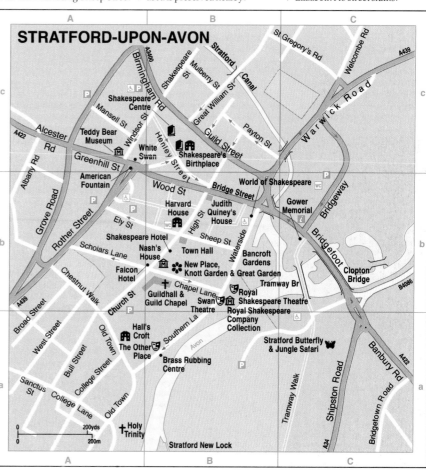

SOME MEN ARE BORN GREAT *Shakespeare's Henley Street home contains the room where he was born, a shrine for thousands of visitors each year.*

Anstey Bf
Old cottages and 14th-century packhorse bridge just 5ft wide. Ned Ludd born here – instigator of Luddite Riots, which opposed job-threatening innovations by smashing new machinery.

Ashby St Ledgers Bb
Narrow, tree-lined roads pass between stone-and-thatch cottages. Medieval Church of St Leodegarius boasts three-tier Jacobean pulpit. Nearby, medieval manor house where local legend maintains Gunpowder Plot was hatched by Robert Catesby in 1605.

Aylestone Bf
Leicester district with medieval bridge nearly 50yds long but only 4ft wide, built to allow packhorse trains across River Soar.

Badby Ba
Thatched, ironstone cottages flank Badby Downs. Parish Church of St Mary, 14th century, on high ground above main street; memorial window shows St George and St Michael slaying two dragons. Gothic-style village hall, now private home, stands in centre of village green. Neighbouring wood becomes mass of bluebells in spring. Nearby Arbury Hill is capped by earthworks of Roman camp. Attractive countryside within walking distance of the village.

Billesdon Df
Large village, some of it dating back to 1650, with mainly 13th-century church. Wooded hill, Billesdon Coplow, has fine views.

Blisworth Da
Village of cottages built from brown ironstone and cream-coloured limestone.

Bradgate Park Bg
Untouched moorland, woods, heath and rocky hills ideal for pleasant walks and picnics. Fallow deer roam park. Ruins of Bradgate House, home of Lady Jane Grey (1537-54), Queen of England for nine days.

FREE RANGING *Fallow deer roam wild in Bradgate Park.*

Braunston Junction Bb
One of the few places where working narrowboats can be seen, carrying cargoes such as sand, gravel and coal. Settlement is at meeting of Grand Union and Oxford canals.

GREEN FIELDS, GRACEFUL SPIRES

Rolling landscapes of rich pastures and patches of woodland stretch between the historic cities of Leicester and Northampton. Hills form a watershed through which runs the Grand Union Canal. Rivers such as the Avon, Nene and Welland start their journeys here, flowing past villages whose cottages of timber and honey-coloured stone are dominated by the graceful spires of their historic churches.

QUIET WATERS *Narrowboat on the Grand Union Canal lies moored below Foxton Locks, Leicestershire.*

Brixworth Dc
Church of All Saints, 7th century, one of finest Saxon buildings in England. Stair turret added 10th century, belfry and spire in 14th.

Burrough Hill Dg
Site of Iron Age hill-fort, with dramatic views from the 690ft summit.

Coton Manor Gardens Cc
Old English garden with lakes, waterfalls and rose beds. Cranes and flamingos dot grounds, which include tropical house with palms and mimosa.

Cottesbrooke Dc
Three-storey pulpit stands in 13th-century Church of All Saints. Rare 18th-century movable, wooden pedestal font can be seen on application.

Daventry Bb
Huge Iron Age camp and Roman excavations lie on nearby Borough Hill, where Charles I's army camped before Battle of Naseby in 1645. Town has pleasant marketplace holding twice-weekly markets. Also 18th-century church and moot hall.

Daventry Park Bb
Country park with 150 species of birds, reservoir for coarse fishing, adventure playground, interpretive centre and picnic areas. Nature trail and hides alongside the reservoir.

East Carlton Park Ed
Peaceful 100 acre park with woodlands and ponds overlooking Welland Valley. Steel Heritage Centre uses models, films and photographs to show making of iron and steel.

Flore Cb
Village with narrow streets and alleyways running between thatched cottages built of limestone and ironstone. South of village, brick bridge crosses River Nene near Mill Farm – pleasant spot with river running through reeds under overhanging trees.

Foxton De
Complex staircase of ten locks built to negotiate 75ft rise in 300yds. Village church, 13th century, contains part of Saxon cross. Nearby manor house is partly medieval.

Great Brington Cb
Russet-coloured church, partly 12th century, stands at north of village. Spencer Chapel added in 1514 contains graves of Spencers, family of Princess of Wales. Family home, Althorp, is nearby: extensive picture gallery with paintings by Gainsborough, Reynolds and Rubens.

Hardingstone Da
Queen Eleanor's Cross, one of 12 memorials erected by Edward I to mark spots where queen's body rested on funeral journey to Westminster Abbey. Church of St Edmund has 13th-century tower.

Holdenby House Cb
Elizabethan garden in grounds of 16th-century house. Charles I was held prisoner here after his defeat at Battle of Naseby. Stream-fed ponds, model railway, museum, donkey rides and pets' corner provide fun for all.

Horninghold Ee
Early 20th-century stone and half-timbered houses blend well with rural setting. Norman Church of St Peter sensitively restored during Victorian era. Walk to Eyebrook Reservoir 3 miles east.

Hunsbury Hill Da
Locomotives and wagons are among exhibits at site of former ironstone workings. Rides on diesel and steam engines in summer. Country park pleasures.

Kirby Muxloe Castle Bf
Fortified manor house, started in 1480, with gun-ports which are among oldest in country. Built of newly fashionable brick. Never completed due to execution of owner, Lord Hastings, in 1483.

Lamport Hall Dc
House built in 17th and 18th centuries with interiors lavishly decorated with paintings, furniture and porcelain. High Room has plaster-work ceiling of cherubs, nymphs, mermen and swans. In grounds, agricultural museum and display of vintage tractors.

Leicester Bf
Cathedral city with 2000 year history, now known for modern university and light industry. Façade of Roman building that housed public baths, now known as Jewry Wall. Jewry Wall Museum has remains of Roman baths and wall paintings. Cathedral originally Norman church; much rebuilding until 19th century. Raised to cathedral status in 1927. Guildhall, begun in 1340 for Corpus Christi Guild, incorporates a library, first recorded in 1587. Belgrave Hall, early 18th century, now a furniture museum. Newarke Houses Museum presents social history of city and county from 1500. Museum of Royal Leicestershire Regiment at Magazine nearby. Display of industrial heritage at John Doran Gas Museum. Leicestershire Museum and Art Gallery contains English paintings, modern art, ceramics and sculpture.

Little Billing Eb
Museum of corn milling in 18th-century mill. Exhibits include eel traps, as millers often paid rent with eels.

Lutterworth Bd
Small town, once important staging post, with half-timbered houses and 18th-century bridge over River Swift. Church much restored in 19th century, but still has 15th-century wall paintings. Monument in church to John Wycliffe, who preached against papal politics and completed first English translation of Bible.

Market Harborough Dd
Market town with wealth of Georgian architecture. Old grammar school, built in 1614, stands on wooden pillars. Church of St Dionysius built in 13th to 15th centuries. Harborough Museum recalls medieval times when town was market and staging post for coaches and wagons.

Medbourne Ee
Jumble of 19th-century houses, with 13th and 14th-century Church of St Giles. Packhorse bridge, 13th century, crosses shallow brook – kingfishers, herons and swifts can be seen from here in summer. Annual Easter Monday 'battle' over small beer barrel between men of Medbourne and those of neighbouring Hallaton.

Naseby Cc
Site of Cromwell's final victory (1645) over Charles I a mile north of village. Battle and Farm Museum combines story of battle and history of local rural life.

Newbold on Avon Ac
Tunnel of old Oxford Canal can be seen near church. Remains of old wharves and bridges survive, but no water. Canal built on straighter line now lies to the north.

Northampton Db
Town well known for shoemaking industry; highlighted at Central Museum and Art Gallery. Large collection of shoes includes Queen Victoria's wedding slippers, ballet shoes of Fonteyn and Nijinsky, and boots made in 1959 for elephant used in re-enactment of Hannibal's crossing of the Alps. Also collections of coins, archaeological finds, pottery, paintings and furniture. Museum of Leathercraft tells story of leather from ancient Egyptian times to today. Abington Park Museum

has reconstruction of 18th-century street and exhibits of toys, agricultural implements and horse-drawn fire engines. Delapré Abbey, former Cluniac nunnery, is Northants Records Office. On southern outskirts is Eleanor Cross erected by Edward I to mark funeral procession of his queen.

Old Dairy Farm Centre ✤ Ca
Working farm near Upper Stowe containing range of craft shops, restaurant and variety of farm animals, including rare breeds.

Pitsford Reservoir ⚓ Dc
Water of 800 acres, with trout fishing, sailing, nature reserve (permit needed), and picnic area.

Queniborough ⌂ Cg
Contrasting collection of houses along main street – brick, tiled, half-timbered and thatched.

Rothley ⌂ Bg
One of village's two greens – Town Green – flanked by some of country's finest timber-framed houses. Weekend steam train from Swithland Reservoir to Loughborough stops at Rothley Station, restored to original 1890s condition with Victorian advertisements and gas lamps.

Rugby ⌂ Bc
Town noted for public school where William Webb Ellis reputedly invented rugby. Tablet on wall near school buildings commemorates this.

Rushton Triangular Lodge ⌂ Ed
Lodge built in 1593 with three 33ft long sides, each with three triangular gables, three floors, a triangular chimney and Latin quotations from the Bible 33 letters long. Erected by Roman Catholic Sir Thomas Tresham to symbolise the Holy Trinity.

TIMES THREE *Triangular Lodge, Rushton, symbolises the Trinity.*

Stanford on Avon ⌂ Bc
Village divided by River Avon, the county boundary of Leicestershire and Northamptonshire. Late 17th-century Stanford Hall has collections of paintings, furniture and costumes. Stables house vintage motorcycles and replica of early flying machine.

Sywell Park ⚓ Eb
Wildlife observation, waterside walks, picnic areas, visitor centre.

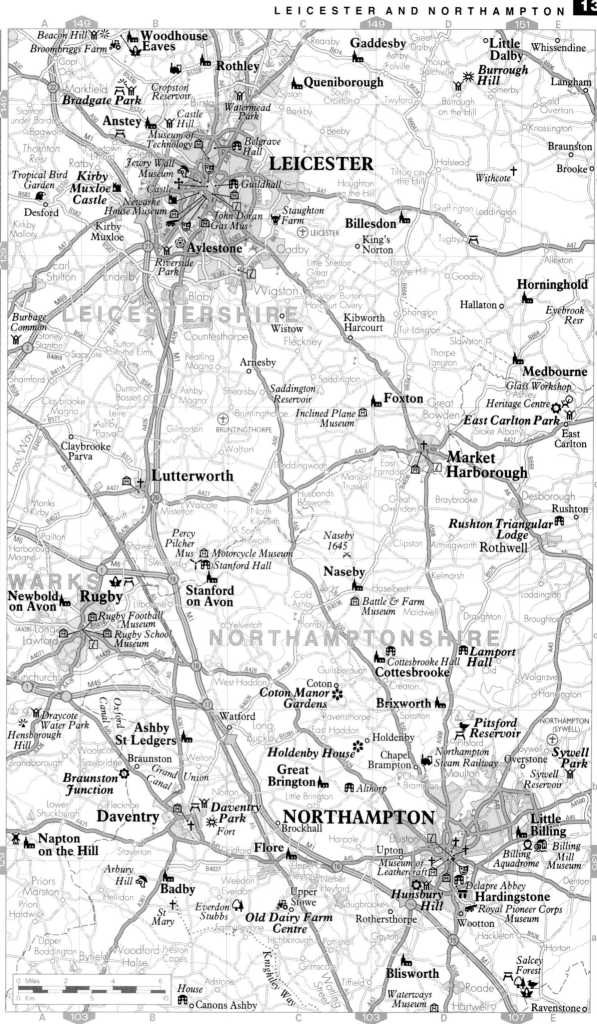

WESTERN APPROACHES TO THE FENS

In this landscape, the rolling farmlands dotted with patches of woodland are broken by rivers – the Welland, the Nene and the Great Ouse – meandering eastwards. It is here that the gentle hills of the Midland shires, Northamptonshire and Leicestershire, give way to the flat Cambridgeshire and Bedfordshire lowlands, with their huge skies and high-banked, reedy dykes.

CHRIST MAJESTIC *The 11th-century relief graces Barnack church.*

Barnack ♟☙✗ Cf
Stone cottages made from local 'Barnack rag', pale grey limestone extracted for the great abbeys of eastern England. Nearby quarry known as Hills and Holes is a maze of grassy holes and hummocks – now a nature reserve.

Boughton House ♙ Ad
Former 15th-century monastery gradually enlarged around seven courtyards. Elegant 17th-century façade imitates a French chateau. Treasure house of fine art with porcelain and silverware.

Burghley House ♙ Cf
Grandest Elizabethan house in the country, with dome towers, slender chimneys and 200ft front of Barnack stone. Named after Elizabeth I's chief minister, Lord Burghley. Rare furniture and 400 Old Masters.

Burley ♟ Ag
Village with superb views, dominated by late 17th to early 18th-century manor house of Burley on the Hill. Norman church, restored in the 19th century, contains 1820 marble figure by sculptor Sir Francis Chantrey.

Castle Ashby ♟✿ Aa
Impressive house with octagonal turrets and ornate 18th-century iron gates. Begun in 16th century and completed by Inigo Jones. Grounds by Capability Brown include woodland walks and lake.

Castor ♟ De
Founded in Roman times, village was a centre of early Christianity. Church with richly carved Norman tower has inscription dedicated in 1124.

Crowland ♟ Eg
Georgian and timber-framed cottages dominated by tower and ruined Norman arch of partly 12th-century Croyland Abbey. Its bells are country's oldest – one dates from 15th century. Town centre includes the 14th-century Trinity Bridge with three linked arches which once spanned now-vanished streams.

Deene Park ♙ Be
Elegant medieval manor house, owned by Brudenell family since 1514, much altered over centuries. Superb grounds with roses, rare trees, shrubs and a lake. Military uniforms and mementos inside.

Edith Weston ♟ Bf
Once the royal domain of Edward the Confessor's queen, Edith. Spired 12th-century church and largest man-made lake in Europe – the 3500 acre Rutland Water. The shoreline forms important nature reserve for waterfowl.

Elton Hall ♙ Ce
Gatehouse and crypt survive from original 15th-century building, destroyed by Cromwell. Present-day house built in late 17thcentury by Sir Thomas Proby, whose family still lives there. Fine library and paintings by Constable and Reynolds.

Felmersham ♟ Ba
Charming old stone-and-thatch houses overlook the River Great Ouse. Unusually lofty Church of St Mary the Virgin, 13th-century, flanked by medieval tithe barn.

Ferry Meadows ♜ De
Water and water sports at this 500 acre country park. Bird sanctuary, adventure playground and miniature steam railway.

Fotheringhay ♟♖ Ce
Tranquil riverside village where visitors can watch ironwork being wrought at forge. Grassy mound marks site of castle in which Mary, Queen of Scots was executed in 1587. Cathedral-like church is local landmark.

Geddington ♟♙ Ad
Village square monument is one of three remaining 'Eleanor Crosses' marking resting places of Queen Eleanor's coffin, wife of Edward I, during its journey from Harby to London in 1290. Church is 14th century and scene of annual May Queen celebrations.

Godmanchester ♙♜ Ec
Ancient town, originally a Roman settlement. Charter dates from 1213. Island Hall, by the river, is a fine 18th-century house with panelled rooms. Carved choir stalls in 13th-century Church of St Mary the Virgin.

Grafham Water ♒ Db
Farmland and woodland nature reserve provide nesting sites for lapwings, skylarks, wagtails, willow warblers and chiffchaffs. Fishing and sailing on reservoir.

Grafton Underwood ♟ Bd
Stream flows along street lined with chestnut trees. Each house reached by small stone bridge. Nearby site of World War II base for US Flying Fortresses.

Harringworth ♟✿ Be
Village built around Church of St John the Baptist, with a 12th-century tower and 14th-century chancel arch and doorway. Fine village cross with 14th-century shaft. Western side of village dominated by Welland Viaduct, built between 1876 and 1878 to carry Midland Railway across Welland valley. Has 82 arches and is three-quarters of a mile long.

Hinchingbrooke House ♙ Ec
Mansion built in 16th century by great-grandfather of Oliver Cromwell on site of nunnery. Finely carved gatehouse may have come from abbey in Ramsey, to north. House now contains a school.

Huntingdon ♙♜♔▨ Ec
Fine Georgian houses form heart of this handsome old town. Birthplace of Oliver Cromwell in 1599, with museum of Cromwellian relics in former grammar school. Other associations include The George, old coaching inn once belonging to Cromwell's grandfather, and All Saints' Church where Cromwell was baptised and his father buried. A 14th-century bridge leads over Great Ouse to twin town of Godmanchester.

Kimbolton ♟ Cb
Village with Tudor manor remodelled in 1707 by Sir John Vanbrugh. Catherine of Aragon was imprisoned here after being divorced by Henry VIII. Now serves as school. Church has some fine monuments.

ARCADE VIEW *An archway leads to the inner courtyard of Kirby Hall.*

Kirby Hall ♖ Be
This largely ruined Elizabethan house is famed for French-style ornateness. Façade and gardens well preserved. Seven-arched arcade leads to inner courtyard, and the roofline is a fascinating panorama of parapets, gables, balustrades and chimneys.

Market Deeping ♟ Dg
Stagecoach travellers once frequented old inns forming the Georgian heart of this grey-stone village. The 14th-century rectory is one of England's oldest.

Nene Valley Railway ♖ De
Reopened 7 mile stretch of the old Northampton-Peterborough line which closed in 1972. It links Wansford and Peterborough and runs several foreign engines.

Oakham ♙✿♜▨ Af
Old market town with 16th-century school. Great Hall is fine remnant of Norman castle – now a courtroom with remarkable collection of horseshoes. Rutland County Museum recalls life when town was capital of county.

Oundle ♜▨▨ Cd
Stone-built town with Georgian houses and two 17th-century inns, looped by River Nene. Buildings of town's public school surround partly 14th-century church. Victorian and Edwardian costumes in Southwick Hall.

Peakirk ♟♜ Df
England's only church dedicated to St Pega has rare 14th-century lectern and paintings. Wildfowl refuge contains flooded gravel pit for several hundred waterfowl, including Hawaiian geese and trumpeter swans.

Peterborough ✝♜▨▨ De
Medieval and Tudor buildings blend happily with modern town. Cathedral is one of England's finest Norman buildings, begun 1118 with magnificent west front of three soaring Gothic arches. City Museum and Art Gallery.

Rockingham Castle ♙ Ae
Twin round towers of the 11th-century castle entrance date from Edward I's time, but much of the interior is Tudor. Fine collection of furniture and English paintings. Garden with 400-year-old yew hedge has splendid views.

Sacrewell Farm and Country Centre ▣♨ Cf
Working mill on site mentioned in Domesday Book. Grounds cover 530 acres, and also include farm buildings containing displays of rural life.

Stamford ♙♜▨▨ Cf
Ancient town, once Fens capital, with traces of Norman castle. Fine Tudor, Queen Anne, Georgian houses, six churches and several inns recall heyday of this former wool centre. Museum has life-size model of England's fattest man, 53 stone Daniel Lambert, who died here in 1809. Victorian steam brewery is preserved as museum.

Uppingham Ae
Small market town rearing above open farmland, renowned for its public school with 16th-century courtyards. Marketplace is mostly Victorian, with fountain and some old-fashioned shops.

Wadenhoe ♟ Cd
Church of Norman origin with unusual gabled roof and good views of the willow-fringed River Nene. Main street is lined with thatched stone cottages.

LOCAL LANDMARK *An outstanding feature of Fotheringhay's church is its magnificent lantern tower and windows.*

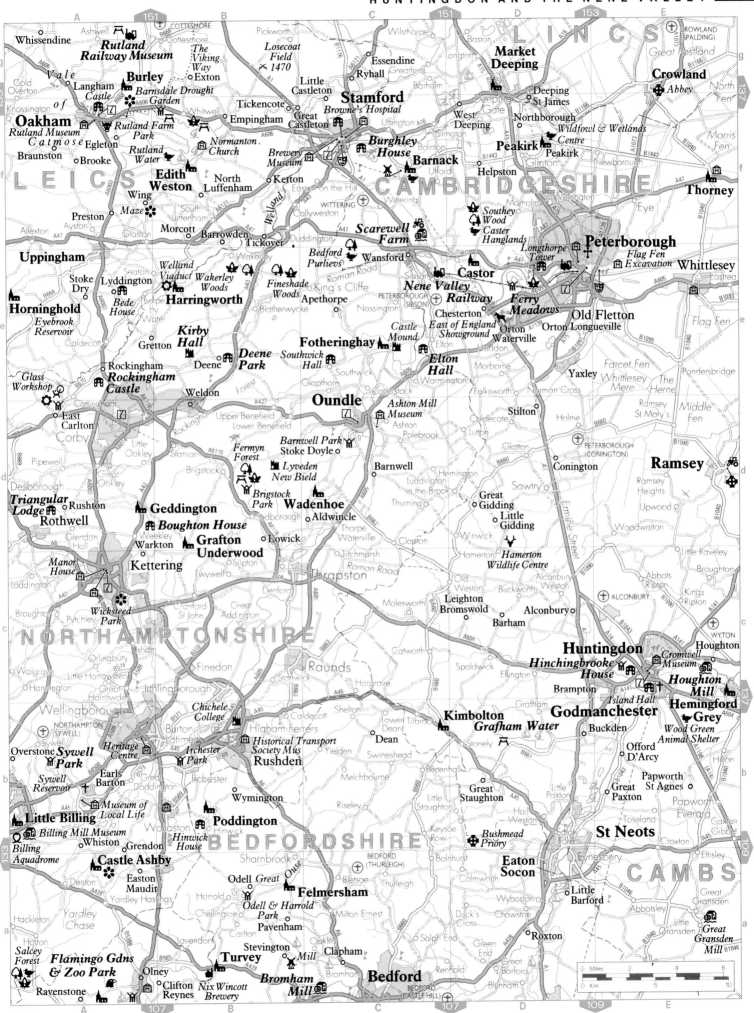

CATHEDRAL ABOVE THE FENS

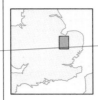

Ely Cathedral stands triumphant over the vast fen fields where sheep and cattle graze on land which has seen Stone Age inhabitants, Roman conquerors, Saxon farmers and Danish marauders. On the coast, King's Lynn developed as a thriving port and market town. This prosperous area has left a legacy of impressive merchants' houses and worthy villages.

Burwell Da
Sprawling fenland village whose history stretches back to Dark Ages. Wide main street with pink-and-white houses dating from 17th and 18th centuries. Solitary post mill and church with soaring octagonal tower. Dried-up moat is all that remains of 12th-century castle, built by villainous Geoffrey de Mandeville.

Castle Rising Castle Eg
Massive Norman keep within equally massive earthworks. Stone staircase leads to arch that once opened into Great Hall. Edward III kept his mother imprisoned here for 30 years, after her part in his father's murder. In village below stand 17th-century almshouses.

Chippenham Ea
Splendid example of a squire's village, built to house his workforce; attractive cottages date from 1800. Chippenham Park Mansion rebuilt 1866 from earlier 17th-century mansion of Earl of Orford.

Conington Ba
Church of St Mary has 14th-century tower, 18th-century nave and late 19th-century chancel. Monuments to Cotton family include one by famous wood-carver Grinling Gibbons.

Denny Abbey Ca
Originally a 12th-century Benedictine abbey; roof remains despite later alterations by Knights Templar and Franciscan nuns.

Devil's Ditch Da
These impressive earthworks run 7 miles and stand 15ft from ditch to bank. Probably built during post-Roman occupation to defend Icknield Way – ancient track from Wash to Salisbury Plain – which served East Anglia for more than 2000 years.

Downham Market Ee
Hill-top market town on River Ouse, where Nelson went to school. Windmill at Denver, 1 mile south, where masts of yachts rise above banks of the sluices.

DAILY GRIND *A mill has stood on this site at Houghton since AD 974.*

Ely Dc
Once known as 'Eel Island'. St Etheldreda founded abbey in AD 670; Norman cathedral built on site in 1083. Norman work survives in west front, nave and transepts. Octagonal lantern tower added in 1322. Cathedral museum tells history of stained glass from medieval to modern times.

BECKONING TOWER *Few other buildings dominate their surroundings in the way that Ely Cathedral does.*

Fenstanton Ba
Landscape genius Capability Brown (1715-83) is buried in 14th-century village church, along with his wife and son. Church stands among colour-washed cottages and Georgian houses. Former lock-up dates from 1650.

Haddenham Cb
Highest fenland village, 120ft above sea level, has air of spacious dignity. Porch House dates back to 1657; Vine House and Limes are 18th century; church built in 13th and 14th centuries.

Hemingford Grey Ab
Village of timber, thatch and brick cottages. Moated Norman manor house said to be oldest inhabited home in England. Upper section of 12th-century church spire came down in 1741 gale; believed to be at bottom of river. Large plane tree planted in gardens of 17th-century Hemingford Grey conference centre was planted in 1702.

Houghton Mill Ab
Massive brick-and-timber water mill on backwater of Great Ouse, ground corn until 1930. Building dates mostly from 17th century. Village green has elaborate 'Gothic' pump. Centre has bow-fronted shops and clock tower.

Isleham Eb
Angels embellish hammerbeam roof of St Andrew's Church, which dates from 14th and 15th centuries. Brasses, monuments and 15th-century eagle lectern.

King's Lynn Ef
Lively port and market town since Middle Ages, known as Bishop's Lynn until Henry VIII took over

manor during 1539 Dissolution. Ornate 1683 Customs House has Charles II statue over doorway. In Market Place, 12th-century St Margaret's Church contains two of England's largest brasses; both 14th century. Victorian Town Hall and 1420 Guildhall have checkerboard flint-square design. North along river, second Guildhall dates from 1407, and is oldest and largest in England. Archaeology and natural history in Lynn Museum. Costumes, toys and domestic items in Museum of Social History.

CUSTOMS HOUSE *Henry Bell's Dutch-style building in King's Lynn.*

Landbeach Marina Ca
Flooded gravel pits for inland water enthusiasts. Fishing, sailing, canoeing, windsurfing and water-skiing. Putting greens and tennis for landlubbers.

Leverington Cf
Parish with noteworthy 17th and 18th-century houses: Hallcroft,

Lancewood and Beechwood with dovecote of 1600. Leverington Hall is part Elizabethan, part built 1660-75, with two chimney breasts, mullioned windows and good staircase.

March Cd
Railway junction by River Nene, where 200 angels are carved in oak in 15th-century St Wendreda's Church. Magnificent west tower and 16th-century brasses.

Methwold Fd
Landmark 14th and 15th-century Church of St George is an architectural wonder; 60ft tower surmounted by 30ft corona and topped by 30ft spire.

Mildenhall Fb
North porch of Church of St Mary and St Andrew is largest in Suffolk. Arrowheads and small shot fired by Cromwell's supporters found embedded in woodwork of angel roof.

Newmarket Ea
Headquarters of British horse racing since 17th century. Two of the turf's most revered institutions: Jockey Club founded 1752 governs every aspect of horse racing; Tattersalls has pristine stabling and sale ring. Beside heath, National Stud houses some of world's finest stallions. National Horseracing Museum has paintings by Stubbs and Munnings. Nell Gwynne's House in Palace Street survived 1683 fire that destroyed most of town.

North Runcton Ef
One of the finest 18th-century churches in Norfolk, built 1703-13 by Henry Bell, designer of King's

Lynn Custom House. Lantern tower, 19th-century chapel, and Florentine paintings.

Ouse Washes Cc
Meadows and ditches rich in plant and animal life. Rivers famous for fish. Vast numbers of winter wildfowl. Black-tailed godwit and ruff among notable breeding birds.

Ramsey Ac
Market town whose grammar school incorporates remaining 13th-century Lady Chapel of medieval abbey. A ruined 1480 gatehouse is one of the most highly decorated in England. Nearby Bodsey House has superb 17th-century chimney-stack.

Reach Da
Village claims to be district's oldest settlement, due to Stone Age flints found in surrounding peat. Charter given by King John grants the right to their own king; chosen at yearly Reach Fair.

St Ives Bb
Market town with pretty houses in The Quay, 15th-century church and six-arch bridge with rare bridge chapel. Local history in Norris Museum includes story of 16th and 17th-century witch trials.

Stretham Db
Village on edge of fens with derelict tower mill and 20ft high cross of 1400. Old Engine House boasts scoop-wheel engine, used for fen drainage in early 19th century.

Swaffham Bulbeck Da
Dutch-style Merchant's House, granary and malt house remain from 17th-century days as inland port. Italian portable altar in 13th-century church is 500 years old. Pew-ends with 15th-century carvings of fabulous beasts.

Thorney Ae
Small island where Saxon rebel Hereward the Wake made his last stand against invading Normans. Saxon abbey rebuilt by Normans in 1085, partly incorporated in the parish church. Yellow-brick houses built in 1850s by Duke of Bedford for estate workers.

Welney Wildfowl Refuge Dd
A haven for nesting wildfowl; famous for its Bewick's swans. Observatory overlooks the swan lagoon, floodlit in winter.

West Walton Cf
Splendid marshland church, noted for angel-carved hammerbeam roof and detached 13th-century tower with early tracery.

Wicken Fen Db
Britain's oldest nature reserve and East Anglia's last stretch of undrained fenland; 600 soggy, peaty acres of old England. Marsh plants, 5000 species of insects and great variety of birds, including warblers and breeding snipe.

Wisbech Cf
Fruit-growing area with distinguished architecture. Impeccable Georgian houses line River Nene. Peckover House (1722) contains rococo wood and plasterwork. Fine Tudor work in Rose and Crown Hotel, dating from 1600.

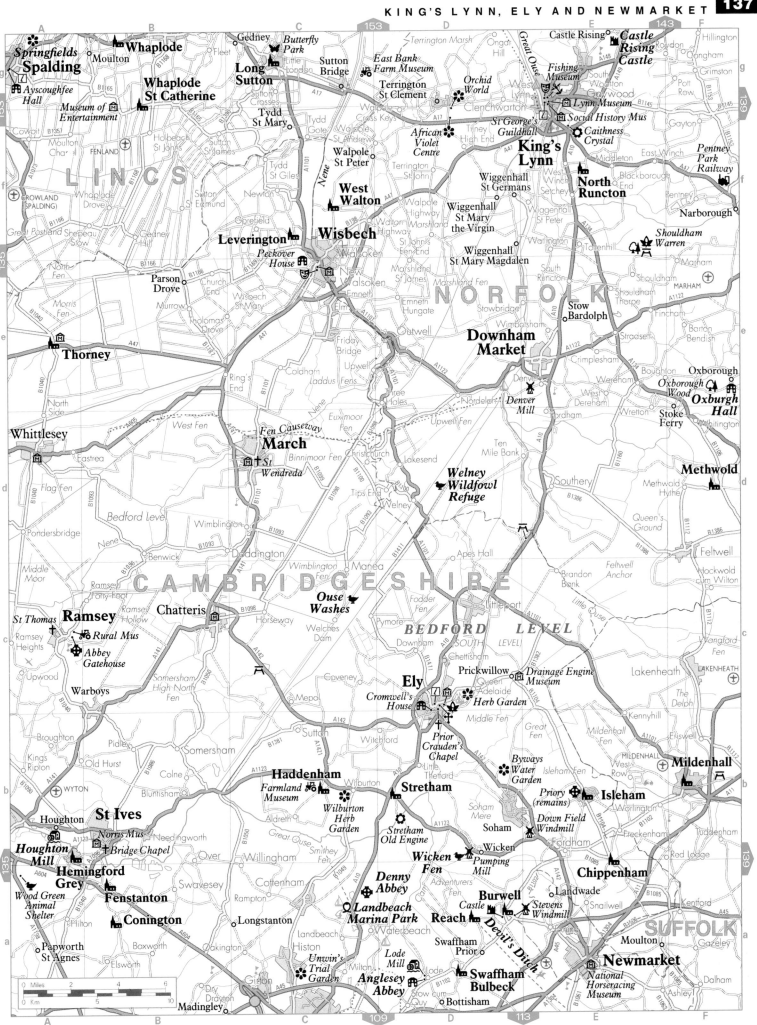

Attleborough  Dd

Pink-washed and plain red-brick houses surround village green. Flint-walled Norman church has 15th-century rood screen, masterpiece of medieval woodcarving. Filigree vaulting and fragments of medieval wall painting.

Bawburgh Ee

Brick cottages line one side of a village green, and look across to a water mill. St Walstan's Well once claimed a miraculous spring with healing properties.

Brandon Ac

Town much admired for buildings made of flint from local mines. Excellent example of flint and red brickwork on 18th-century Brandon Hall.

Bressingham Gardens Dc

Extensive 500 acre nursery makes unusual setting for steam locomotive collection. Over 5000 varieties of alpines, heathers, conifers and perennials. Narrow-gauge railway runs across valley of River Waveney. Splendid Victorian steam roundabout in museum.

Bury St Edmunds Ba

Remains of Saxon King Edmund kept in small monastery here, after he was martyred in AD 870. Abbey ruins include Norman tower and 14th-century Abbey Gate. The 12th-century flint-and-rubble building on Cornhill has been synagogue, tavern and jail. It now houses collections including 'poaching corner' with terrifying mantraps. Theatre Royal (1819) is one of only three surviving Georgian playhouses. On Angel Hill is Queen Anne house.

Castle Acre Bf

Village on ancient Peddars' Way, with huge Norman castle mound and green, entered through 13th-century gate. Remains of priory with fine 12th-century arcading. Painted panels in 13th and 15th-century Church of St James.

Cockley Cley Ae

Reconstructed encampment of Iceni tribe at the time of Queen Boudicca, with watchtowers, drawbridge, chariot house and snake pit, on site of original. Village contains the remains of Saxon church.

THE SOLITUDE OF BRECKLAND

Sandy heaths, huge fields and forest comprise much of this windblown area known as Breckland. It was probably a vast oak forest 4000 years ago and still contains Thetford Forest, the second largest in England. Sparsely populated now, the landscape was more densely inhabited in Roman, Saxon and Norman times, when towns such as Bury St Edmunds and Thetford were founded.

Diss Eb

Twisting streets with Tudor, Georgian and Victorian architecture; busy on Friday market days. Imposing 12th-century St Mary's Church and 6 acre mere, haven for wildfowl.

East Dereham Cf

Site of 7th-century nunnery founded by St Withburga, now occupied by St Nicholas' Church; part Norman with 16th-century bell tower. St Withburga's well found in churchyard. Melancholic poet William Cowper was buried here in 1800. Bishop Bonner's Cottages, with distinctive fruit-and-flower plaster-work, house archaeological museum.

East Wretham Heath Cc

Eerie countryside of reed-fringed meres, haven for waterfowl and waders, and birds such as willow warblers, skylarks, nightingales, nightjars and merlins.

Euston Bb

Village with black-and-white thatched cottages and some flint-and-brick houses. Euston Hall was seat of Dukes of Grafton, begun in 17th century, largely rebuilt in 1902 and reduced to present size in 1955. Grounds laid out in 18th century by William Kent contain mill disguised as a church – thought to be Georgian – and real church dating from 1676. Paintings by Reynolds, Stubbs and Van Dyck.

Eye Eb

Once an island town, granted charter by King John in 1205. Norman castle demolished 1655 by Cromwell's army; stones used to make a 19th-century folly. Church dating from the 15th century has a fine rood screen and flint-and-stone tower. Good 18th-century houses and 16th-century Guildhall.

ABBEY RUINS *Gaunt columns and half-demolished walls loom among the trees in the abbey precinct at Bury St Edmunds.*

Grimes Graves Bc

One of the world's oldest mining areas; Neolithic flint mines begun 2000 BC and rediscovered 1870, cover 34 acres. Shaft with radiating galleries open to visitors.

Ickworth House Ba

Extravagant rotunda house begun about 1794 and completed 1830. Commissioned by eccentric 4th Earl of Bristol and Bishop of Derry, to house his art collection. Sumptuous state rooms with 18th-century and late Regency furniture, silver and pictures. Magnificent grounds landscaped by Capability Brown.

ROTUNDA *The oval house is Ickworth's great curiosity, its wings connected by two curved corridors.*

Ixworth Cb

Small village with grand abbey converted to dwelling house in 16th century; started in 12th century as Augustinian priory and rebuilt over following centuries.

Norfolk Rural Life Museum Cf

Complex in 18th-century red-brick workhouse, tells story of village life in past times with reconstructed workshops. Craftsmen's Row includes smithy, bakery and village store.

North Elmham Cg

Seat of the Bishop of 'North Folk' from AD 600, until moved to Norwich. Ruins of 11th-century Saxon cathedral and 1386 manor house blend in moated enclosure.

Oxburgh Hall Ae

Red-brick, moated manor house, built 1482 by Bedingfeld family, who still live there. Tapestry panels embroidered by Mary, Queen of Scots. Formal French garden. Views from tower.

Pakenham Ca

Village unique for its two working mills: restored 18th-century water mill and five-storey 19th-century tower mill which still grinds corn.

Santon Downham Bc

Modern forestry village at heart of Thetford Forest, with 2 mile long trail leading from Forestry Commission Information Centre.

Stowlangtoft Ca

St George's Church, decorated with flint, noted for wealth of medieval woodcarving and variety of old bench ends. Medieval wall painting of St Christopher and 14th-century font.

Swaffham Be

Town sign features local benefactor John Chapman, 15th-century pedlar who found gold coins in his garden and gave money to parish church. Market Place flanked by graceful 18th-century buildings, Victorian Corn Exchange and old workshops.

Thetford Bc

East Anglian capital of the Danes in 9th century. Extensive ruins of 12th-century priory. Castle Hill has Iron Age earthworks and a Norman castle mound. Church is part Saxon, part Norman. Medieval and Georgian buildings in almost every street; 15th-century Ancient House houses local and natural history museum.

Thetford Forest Bc

Britain's largest pine forest with lime avenue and bird trail where woodlarks and nightingales can be heard. Remains of medieval hunting lodge.

Walsham le Willows Db

Village set in heart of parkland, with timber-framed cottages and a fine confusion of eaves and roof levels. Six Bells Inn derives name from church tower.

West Acre Priory Af

Remains of Augustinian priory founded 1100 extend either side of River Nar; 14th-century gatehouse and parts of church and chapter house.

Weston Longville Ef

Place of pilgrimage for loyal admirers of Parson James Woodforde, renowned good-living author of classic *Diary of a Country Parson*, who lived here from 1776. Rectory was rebuilt last century, but Church of All Saints remains as it was, with its 13th-century tower and 14th-century Tree of Jesse painting.

West Stow Bb

Tiny, attractive village among sandy heaths, with cottages of white Suffolk brick, and Hall notable for sturdy, red-brick gatehouse dating from 1520s. Country park's main attraction is reconstruction of Anglo-Saxon farming settlement, on site of original village established between AD 400 and 650.

Wicklewood Mill De

Striking five-storey windmill, black with white cap, that ground corn until 1942. Restored to working order in 1985.

HOSANNA *Carved angels decorate the roof over the nave of Swaffham's 15th-century church.*

Wymondham Ee

Ancient town centred on wooden 17th-century market cross. Green Dragon pub (15th century) still bears scorch marks from 1615 town fire. Two towers of abbey church compete as they have for 500 years; result of 14th-century dispute over shared use by townspeople and monks. Monks built octagonal tower and put up thick wall to seal off parishioners. Townspeople built larger square west tower 50 years later.

MOATED GRANDEUR *Oxburgh Hall was much rebuilt in the 19th century, but the gatehouse and north front survive from the Middle Ages.*

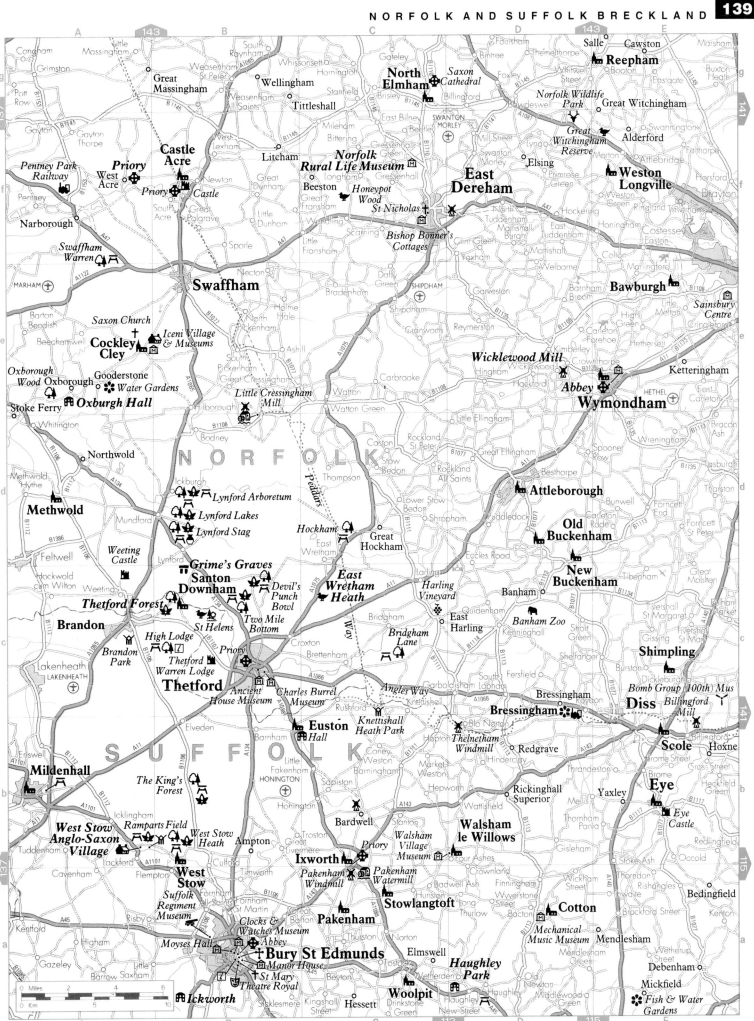

Aylsham ⚓ Af
Market town with splendid old buildings: 16th-century Manor House, Abbots Hall (early 1600s) and Old Hall (1689). Rose-covered grave of the landscape gardener Humphry Repton in 14th-century St Michael's churchyard.

Beccles ⌂ Db
Mellow old town on River Waveney with handsome red-brick Georgian houses. Best-preserved are in Ballygate and Northgate. Gardens run down to waterside, fringed with boathouses.

Berney Arms Mill ✗ Dd
Best and largest of the Norfolk Marsh mills, 70ft high, built 19th-century. Still in working order.

Blickling Hall ⌂ Af
Jacobean 17th-century moated hall with immaculate formal garden. Impressive period-style rooms. Huge tapestry of Russian ruler hangs in Peter the Great Room, Long Gallery has ornate plaster ceiling. Extensive walks, crescent-shaped lake, orangery and temple in grounds.

NORFOLK'S LAKELAND

When medieval man abandoned his peat diggings he left behind miles of waterways for boating enthusiasts and naturalists – the Broads. Proudly surveying them, Norwich Cathedral stands like a king, its sentinels the delightful windmills dotting the landscape. Close by the calm waters of the Broads, the North Sea slowly erodes Lowestoft Ness, Britain's easternmost point.

East Anglia Transport Museum ⌂ Eb
Trams, trolley buses, old cars and commercial vehicles, period street scene and other memorabilia.

Fritton ⚓ ⚜ Dd
St Edmund's Church has Saxon tower and thatched roof. Chancel shows Norman work. Original foundations date from AD 750.

Fritton Lake ⚜ Dd
Water sports and fishing on beautiful 3 mile lake, gardens and woodland walks. The ruins of St Olave's Priory and working wind pump on bank of River Waveney.

tower – topped by an unusual 15th-century octagonal belfry. Immaculate 200-year-old windmill overlooks Horsey Mere; one of the remoter Norfolk Broads.

Kessingland ⚓ ⚜ Eb
Resort town with wide shingle beach and amusements. Suffolk Wildlife and Rare Breeds Park has everything from miniature cows and horses to lynx, leopard and Barbary ape.

Lowestoft ✱ ✗ ⌂ ☑ Ec
Holiday resort and fishing port. South is modern resort with sandy beach and amusement arcades, north is old town with lighthouse and cobbled steps leading down cliffs. The Ness is Britain's most easterly point. Maritime Museum traces seafaring history with model ships and fishing tools.

Mousehold Heath ✱ Bd
Breezy hill across River Wensum takes in Norwich skyline of towers and spires, a fairyland of floodlit stonework at night.

North Walsham † Bg
Fine decorated church in this market town has 15th-century font cover and 17th-century monument to Sir William Paston, who founded the grammar school there in 1606. Market cross dates from 1550.

GRIM WARNING *Elizabethan monument in Norwich Cathedral.*

Norwich † ⌂ ⚘ ⌂ ☑ Bd
East Anglia's flourishing capital has one of the country's most beautiful cathedrals, started between 1094-6. Nave roof and cloisters have bosses painted with Biblical scenes and grotesque creatures. City centre has some 30 medieval churches, dominated by Norwich Castle housing military museum. Death masks of executed prisoners in dungeons. Museums abound: archaeology and art galleries in the castle; medieval Stranger's Hall has period rooms depicting domestic life, from Tudor to Victorian. Unique Mustard Shop has mustard museum.

Otter Trust ⚜ Cb
Otters in near-natural surroundings beside River Waveney at Earsham, bred to protect species from extinction. Woods, lakes with abundant waterfowl, night heronry and nature trail.

Oulton Broad ☆ Ec
Attractive stretch of water for fishing and sailing. Boats can be hired from The Boulevard, walks lead to Nicholas Everitt Park.

Ranworth ⚓ Ce
Steep climb to top of St Helen's Church tower is rewarded by vast Broadland views. Glorious 15th-century rood screen painted with saints, apostles and martyrs.

Ranworth Broad ✿ ☆ Ce
Boardwalk nature trail through woodland and marshland to the floating Broadland Conservation Centre explaining history and wildlife of Norfolk Broads, with birdwatching gallery upstairs.

Raveningham Gardens ✿ Cc
Rare plants, shrubs and trees in gardens surrounding elegant Georgian house.

Reedham ⛴ ⚓ Dd
Nautical village: chain ferry over River Yare is only crossing for 26 miles between Norwich and Great Yarmouth. Flint-walled church stands aloof on ridge behind village. Exotic birds at nearby Animal Park.

St Benet's Abbey ✚ Ce
Romantic ruins of Benedictine monastery (AD 816) surround Georgian windmill. Largely intact gatehouse, outer walls and church foundations. Barn of nearby Horning Hall Farm was chapel of abbey hospice. To the east can be seen large white-painted wind pump at riverside village of Thurne with its staithe, or landing place. The wind pump was built in 1820 and worked for almost 120 years.

Somerleyton Hall ⌂ Dc
Original Elizabethan Hall was rebuilt in 1851 as an Anglo-Italian masterpiece. Luxurious rooms with paintings, carvings and tapestries. Elaborate stable clock made for Houses of Parliament, discarded in favour of today's tower. Gardens, 300 years old, have many ancient trees, maze, lime avenue and rose walk.

Southwold ⌂ Ea
Once a Saxon fishing port, now a charming seaside town. Period houses and Dutch gabled cottages, many painted in pinks and pale blues, are built around nine greens. Whitewashed 1890 lighthouse can be seen from all over town. A ship's figurehead stands outside Park Lane Cottage; more in the Sailors' Reading Room in East Street. Perpendicular Church of St Edmund houses 'Southwold Jack', a 15th-century mechanical figure of armoured foot soldier. When a cord is pulled, his battle-axe strikes a bell.

RED CAP *The male lesser-spotted woodpecker has barred upper parts.*

Strumpshaw Fen ⚜ Cd
Typical fenland country beside River Yare, reed and sedge beds, woodland and marshes and meadows rich in bird life. Hides and footpaths. Steam Museum has engines and small railway.

Sutton Windmill ✗ Cf
Britain's tallest, built 1789, nine storeys with restored sails and grinding machinery. Crafts in adjacent Broads Museum.

Walberswick ⚓ ⚜ Da
Sandy-beached village, popular with sailors. St Andrew's Church stands within ruins of large medieval predecessor.

West Somerton ⚓ De
Stone coffin of 'Norfolk Giant' in churchyard is Robert Hales (7ft 8in, 32 stone), born in village 1820. Norman church has remains of 14th-century wall painting.

NAUTICAL VILLAGE *Once a flourishing port at the mouth of the River Blyth, Walberswick is now popular with small-boat sailors.*

Blythburgh ⚓ ⛵ Da
Once a 15th-century port. Holy Trinity Church dates from 1412, with majestic buttresses, nave and Gothic windows. Benches are carved with Seven Deadly Sins, roof angels and a rare wooden figure, Jack-o'-the-clock, strikes bell to start services.

Bungay ♜ ⌂ Cb
Village dominated by stone towers of 12th-century castle gatehouse and pinnacle of 15th-century St Mary's Church, part of a Benedictine nunnery whose ruined walls are visible in the churchyard. Elegant 18th-century buildings built after 1688 fire.

Bure Valley Railway ⚓ Bf
Narrow-gauge line runs along track bed of old Great Eastern for 9 miles beside River Bure, between Wroxham and Aylsham.

Caister-on-Sea ⚓ ♜ ⚓ Ee
Historic site with remains of 3rd-century Roman town and magnificent ruin of 15th-century Caister Castle with 100ft tower. Museum in the grounds has veteran and vintage cars. Wide sandy beach backed by dunes.

Great Yarmouth
✚ ♜ ✗ ⌂ ☑ ⚓ Ed
Thriving port more than 1000 years ago, now a seaside resort with waxwork museums, model village and amusement arcades. Remnants of Middle Ages include town wall, narrow alleys and 13th-century toll house with sinister dungeons. At South Quay, Elizabethan House is a museum of 19th-century domestic life. Maritime Museum for East Anglia has displays of local seafaring life.

Harleston ⚓ Bb
Mellow village ideal for exploring attractive 14 mile stretch of River Waveney. Nearby rose nursery adds colour in summer.

Hickling ⚓ Df
Boats leave Pleasure Boat Inn quay to explore largest and least spoilt of Norfolk's waterways, Hickling Broad. Rich in birds; renowned area for bitterns and bearded tits. Home to the rare swallowtail butterfly.

Horsey ⚓ Df
Scattered village standing 3-6ft above sea level. Tiny church has thatched roof and Saxon round

GRAND ENTRANCE *The great sweeping façade of Jacobean Blickling Hall with its cupolas, turrets, chimneys and gables is set in formal gardens.*

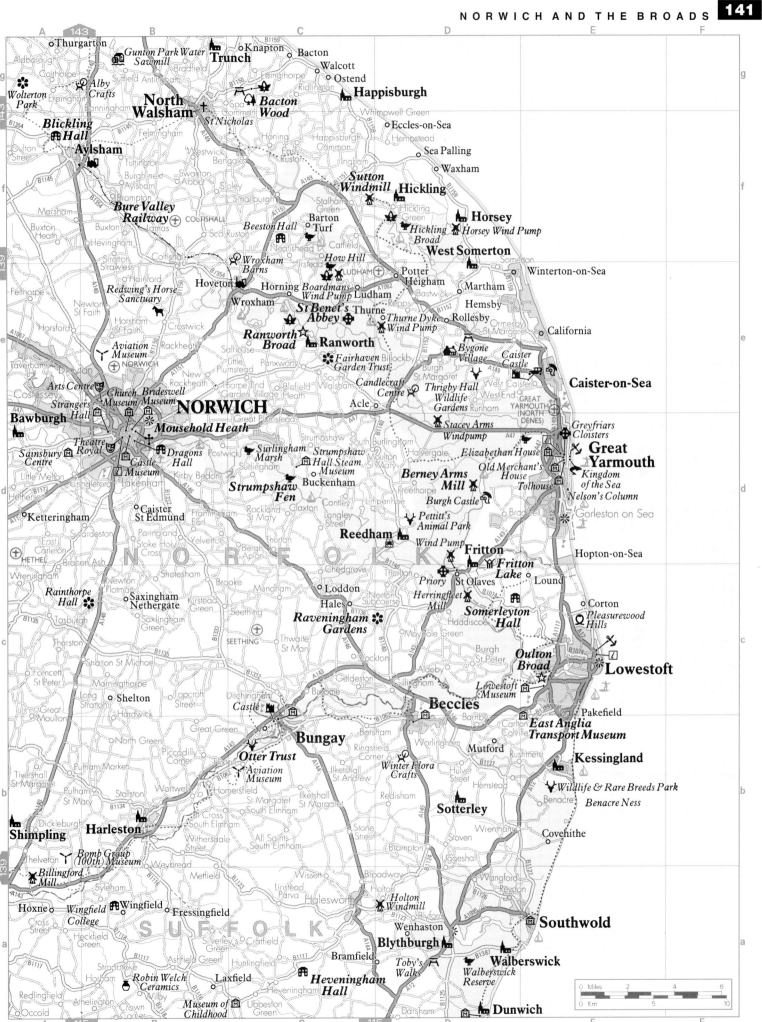

A · B · C · D · E · F

g

Thurgarton
Aldborough
Calthorpe
Wolterton Park
Alby Crafts
Gunton Park Water Sawmill
Knapton
Trunch
Bacton
Walcott
Ostend
Laingthorpe
Ridlington
Whimpwell Green
Happisburgh

f

North Walsham
St Nicholas
Bacton Wood
Felmingham
Suffield Antingham
Bradfield
Honing
Eccles-on-Sea
Hempstead
Sea Palling
Waxham

Blickling Hall
Aylsham
Burgh next Aylsham
Tuttington
Brampton
Buxton
Bure Valley Railway
COLTISHALL
Smallburgh
Stalham Green
Barton Turf
Sutton Windmill
Hickling
Hickling Green
Horsey
Horsey Wind Pump

NORFOLK

Bawburgh

NORWICH

Great Yarmouth

Lowestoft

Beccles

Bungay

Harleston

Shimpling

SUFFOLK

Southwold

Walberswick

Dunwich

| 0 Miles | | 2 | | 4 | | 6 |
| 0 Km | | | 5 | | | 10 |

SALT MARSHES AND SAND DUNES

Church towers, windmills, sand dunes, marshes and pine woods feature on this exposed and sandy coastline, where the agricultural revolution brought prosperity to the great houses, towns and villages. Long-popular resorts such as Hunstanton and Wells retain their Victorian charm, while the quieter villages attract birdwatchers, sealwatchers, anglers and weekend sailors.

Baconsthorpe Castle ⛪ Fb
Medieval fortified manor, built mid-15th century by wealthy lawyer John Haydon. Substantial remains include two huge gatehouses: one commanding the bridge across the moat; the other set farther out with pepperpot tower intact.

Bacton Wood ⚘♣⌂ Hb
Part of Forestry Commission's scattered Wensum Forest, known locally as Witton Wood. Some 30 kinds of trees, from the old-established sweet chestnut and birch to other species from Japan, Corsica, northern Europe. Forest trail leads into the valley. Goldcrests and warblers found in larch woods.

Blakeney ⛪ Ec
Popular sailing village. High Street runs down to the harbour; houses built of rounded flints have brightly coloured doors. At Blakeney Quay, fishing boats bob on tide or sit on mud of channel winding out to sea. Boat service to Blakeney Point Nature Reserve. South of town, vast Early English Church of St Nicholas overlooks marshes and sea, with second tower probably built as shipping beacon. Hammerbeam nave roof carved with angels and 13th-century chancel window.

Blakeney Point ☆ ♥ Ec
Nature reserve reached by boat from Blakeney or Morston, or by 4 mile walk from Cley Eye. Vast spit of shingle and sand, with sand dunes, salt marshes and mud flats on landward side. Seals bask on sandbanks. Typical plants are thrift, sea lavender, sea asters and samphire. Visiting birds include warblers, wheatears, whinchats, bluethroats and pied flycatchers. Common terns, little terns and sandwich terns nest between May and July.

Burnham Overy Staithe ⛪♥ Cc
Little sailing village with extensive views across saltings to Scolt Head Island; reached by 'Cockle Path' track across marshes at low tide. Plaque on house by harbour reads 'Richard Woodget, master of the *Cutty Sark* lived here 1899-1926.' Early 18th-century water mill by River Burn. Church with Norman central tower.

Burnham Thorpe ⛪ Cc
Village green overlooked by brick-and-flint Georgian buildings and 13th-century Church of All Saints. Roadside plaque marks site of rectory where naval hero Horatio Nelson was born in 1758. His father Edmund was village rector until his death in 1802. Church, restored in Nelson's honour in 19th century, has marble bust of him above his father's tomb. Cross and lectern made from timbers taken from HMS *Victory*.

Cley next the Sea ⛪♥✗ Ec
Busy fishing port in Middle Ages until sea retreated leaving half a mile of marshland. Landmark 18th-century tower windmill built on remains of quay. Some 650 acres of Cley and Salthouse Marshes are a nature reserve.

CROMER HERO *Memorial bust commemorates lifeboat coxswain Henry Blogg, holder of three RNLI Gold Medals for bravery.*

Cromer ✝ ⌂ ✗ ☑ Gc
Popular family resort with sandy beach, Pavilion Theatre and Lifeboat Museum. Church tower is tallest in Norfolk at 160ft. Row of Victorian fishermen's cottages forms Cromer Museum, with crabbing industry displays.

Felbrigg Hall ⌂ Fb
Jacobean home of Windham family for three centuries, built around 1620. Furnishings and pictures from 18th century, windows with medieval stained glass, elegant rococo plasterwork and Gothic library. Grounds contain a walled garden, orangery, woodland and lakeside walks.

Glandford ⌂ ⌂ Ec
Village of flint and red-brick houses. Dutch-gabled building built 1915 by Sir Alfred Jodrell of nearby Bayfield Hall, to house vast collection of shells.

Great Bircham Windmill ✗ Bb
Norfolk's finest working corn mill stands on site dating back to the 1700s. Five-floor climb reveals mill machinery and sails. Tours, shop, tearoom and bakery.

Happisburgh ⛪ Hb
Dangerous sandbanks run parallel with the coast about 7 miles offshore. Large green mound north of church said to be mass grave of 119 members of HMS *Invincible*, wrecked 1801. Church, 15th-century, has font of same period carved with lions, satyrs and angelic musicians. The 110ft tower was probably built to serve as a beacon for sailors.

PERFUMED FIELDS *Acres of lavender at Heacham scent the air from June to August.*

Heacham ⛪✿ Ab
Large seaside village with two beaches and good walks along sea wall. On edge of village, Caley Mill is home of Norfolk Lavender; fields are a blaze of colour from mid-June to mid-August. Tours during flowering and harvesting, when lavender is distilled to produce lavender water and soap perfumes. Riverside gardens.

Holkham Gap ♥ Cc
Half-moon sweep of sand with grassy dunes and pine trees growing almost to water's edge; part of

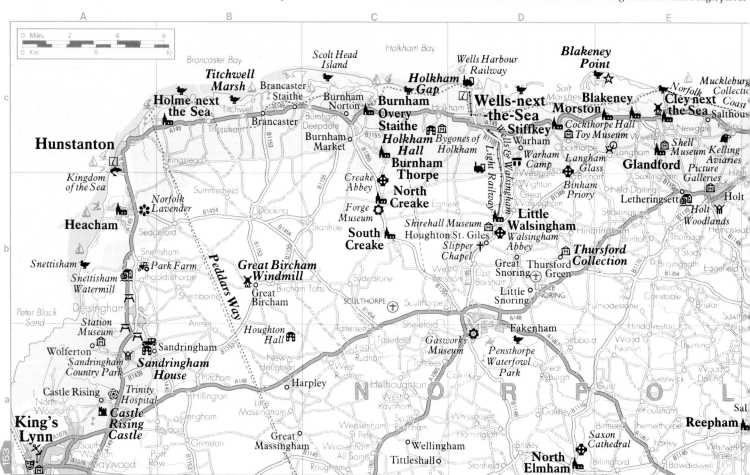

10,000 acre Holkham National Nature Reserve. Lady Ann's Drive at Holkham leads to panoramic views over cove. Red squirrels in woods. Birds include goldcrests, coal tits, green woodpeckers and occasional crossbills.

Holkham Hall 🏛🏰 Cc
Palladian mansion built 1734-62 on fringe of bleak coastal salt marshes by Thomas Coke. Marble, mosaics, monuments and art treasures inside. Paintings by Van Dyck, Rubens and Gainsborough. Lake, woodland and deer park. Bygones collection features thousands of items, from fire engines to farming implements.

Holme next the Sea 🏠🦋 Bc
Village with beach and Holme Dunes Nature Reserve; 500 acres of sand dune and salt marsh. Adjoining Bird Observatory with hides from which warblers, wrynecks, hoopoes, ospreys and sooty shearwaters can be seen. Also rare collared flycatcher and red-rumped swallow.

Hunstanton 🦋📷 Ac
Victorian resort with striped cliffs and miles of sandy beaches. Boat trips to sandbank where seals bask at low tide. Seal observatory and hospital at Kingdom of the Sea, where you can walk under water in a glass tunnel.

Little Walsingham 🏠🏛🚤🌿 Db
Village with tall timbered houses in woodland setting. Medieval place of pilgrimage noted for Shrine of Virgin Mary, founded 11th century. Augustinian friary and Franciscan priory added later;

priory ruins approached by 15th-century gateway in High Street. Square with 16th-century pumphouse on whose roof sits The Beacon, only form of street lighting at the time.

Mannington Hall Gardens ✿ Fb
Set around moated 15th-century house, entered over drawbridge. Extensive lawns enclosed by yew hedges with statuary busts. Hundreds of different roses in Heritage Rose Gardens, lake with stone bridge, woodland paths and nature trails.

Morston 🏠 Ec
Village lane leads down to tidal creek and Morston Quay; extensive foreshore of hard sand where boats ferry passengers to bird sanctuary on Blakeney Point, or to see seals on nearby sandbanks.

North Creake 🏠✿✤ Cb
Changing styles reflected in St Mary's Church, founded 1300, with faded 'Doom' painting over chancel arch, Royal Arms of Charles I above north door, and tasteful 1978 memorial chapel. Abbey fragments remain – it had to close when resident canons died in 1504 plague.

North Norfolk Railway 🚂 Fc
The 'Poppy Line' trains run over restored section of North Norfolk Railway, first opened in 1887. Steam trains and diesel railbuses travel from Sheringham to Weybourne, inland to Holt.

Paston 🏠 Hb
Influential Paston family wrote series of letters that tell about Nor-

COASTAL CHARM *Burnham Overy Staithe, with its annual regatta, is a popular sailing village.*

folk life during Wars of the Roses. Margaret Paston, who wrote most of them, lived at Paston Hall – long since gone – between 1440 and 1484. Church has thatched roof, 14th-century wall paintings and several Paston monuments.

Peddars Way Bb
Prehistoric footpath runs for 50 miles from Knettishall Heath to Holme, passing old towns, villages and countryside. Taken over by Romans as supply route to and

from The Wash; long sections can still be walked through Norfolk farmlands.

Pretty Corner 🌲 Fc
Aptly named ridge running parallel to coast, rising to 300ft in places. Thickly wooded with birch, beech, ash, rowan, pine and fir trees. Wild flowers in profusion: dog violets and orchids. Paths lead into glades of gnarled beeches and dells with tall pines where red and grey squirrels, jays, tits and finches live.

Reepham 🏠 Fa
An 18th-century market town with Georgian houses and half-timbered dwellings, where three churches used to share a single churchyard. Two remain – linked by choir vestry. One has been a ruin since 1543. Sundial over door of Georgian Old Brewery.

Sandringham House 🏰🏛🏠 Aa
Vast royal estate of heathland and forest with red-brick house bought by Queen Victoria for King Edward VII (then Prince of Wales) in 1862. Portraits, sculpture, china, ornaments and furniture on display. Museum of royal cars, country park with footpaths, nature trails, scenic drive, picnic sites. Wolferton station, where once royalty alighted for Sandringham, now houses a museum.

Sheringham 🚤🏊🎠📷 Fc
Busy little resort with old fishing village, small fleet and sandy beach. Sail-powered lifeboat preserved in shed by shore. Regular steam train service from local station with 1887 signal box; vintage carriages and railway relics. A mile inland, 1812 Sheringham Hall set in fine park.

South Creake 🏠 Cb
Village with one of East Anglia's finest churches, dating mainly from 13th and 14th centuries. Medieval hammerbeam roof decorated with carved angels. Unusual brass depicts priest lying

between his parents. Glorious nave, 15th-century rood screen and pulpit.

Stiffkey 🏠🏛 Dc
Straggling village with partly ruined Elizabethan Hall. Church contains Tudor monument and 15th-century brass. Track leads down to Stiffkey Marshes; purple with sea lavender in July. Nearby Cockthorpe Hall Toy Museum contains Kidd family collection, made between 1870-1960.

Thursford Collection 🏛 Db
Exciting museum for steam enthusiasts. Working fairground organs and roundabouts, mighty Wurlitzer cinema organ, barrel organs. Steam railway and play area for children.

Titchwell Marsh 🦋 Bc
Salt and freshwater marshes and reed beds, rich in bird life, such as reed buntings, reed warblers, water rails, wigeons, bearded tits, bitterns, marsh harriers and avocets. Viewing hides, information centre and picnic area.

Trunch 🏠 Gb
Perpendicular Church of St Botolph, famous for rare font canopy standing on eight pillars, carved with foliage. Hammerbeam nave roof decorated with angels. Screen with painted saints of 1502.

Wells-next-the-Sea 🚤🦋📷 Dc
Little town with quay, bustling with cafés, stalls selling sprats and whelks, amusement arcades and fishing boats. Narrow streets and Georgian houses on green. Beach area a mile north, reached by road, on foot along sea wall or by miniature railway. Boating area for canoes and dinghies.

West Runton 🏠🐎 Fc
Sandy beach reached down Water Lane. Road leads up to Beacon Hill, highest point in Norfolk at 329ft. Massive Shires and tiny Shetlands give demonstrations at Norfolk Shire Horse Centre.

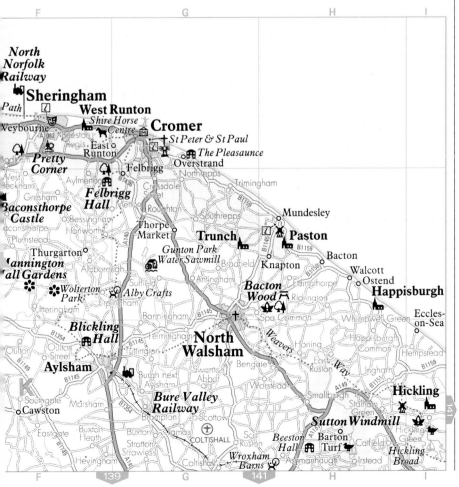

Aerospace Museum ⊤ Eb
More than 60 aircraft, aero-engines and models tell story of military and civil aviation. Second World War exhibits include Field-Marshal Montgomery's Dakota, German 'doodle bug' and the Japanese suicide bomb.

Atcham Cb
On horseshoe bend of Severn, crossed by seven-arched bridge dating from 1769. St Eata Church built with stone from Wroxeter Roman city.

Attingham Park Cb
Grandiose 18th-century mansion in landscaped park. Central portico with 40ft columns rises three storeys. Has fine interior picture gallery and circular staircase.

Boscobel House Fb
From Italian *bosco bello* (beautiful wood), converted 17th-century timber-framed farmhouse. The 'Royal Oak' is said to have sprouted from acorn of tree where Charles II hid after Battle of Worcester, 1651.

Bridgnorth Ea
Split in two by Severn, with Low Town on banks, High Town on 200ft cliff opposite. Keep of ruined Norman castle leans dramatically. Childhood and Costume Museum has interesting doll collection and nearby Midland Motor Museum has more than 100 types of racing cars and motorcycles.

Caer Caradoc ✳ Ba
Hill-fort on rocky ridge, where British chieftain Caractacus is said to have made last stand against Romans in AD 50.

Carding Mill Valley Ba
Secluded valley flanked by The Long Mynd and headed by Light Spout waterfall. Birds, walks and information centre.

Church Stretton Ba
Prettiest of three Strettons in picturesque valley. Half-timbered houses date from town's late 19th-century boom as health resort.

Claverley Ea
Charming village of timber-framed cottages on wooded slope. All Saints' Church, built 1094, has large Bayeux Tapestry-style mural of battling knights.

WINTER RIDGE *A cold sun lights a country lane curving towards the ridge of The Long Mynd, located near Asterton in Shropshire.*

PEACE REIGNS WHERE CHAOS RULED

These tranquil borderlands of meadows, wooded hillsides, lakes and half-timbered villages were once far from peaceful. The Wrekin and Stretton Hills were created by violent volcanoes; hostilities between ancient tribes and invading Romans and, much later, the English and Welsh have also left their mark. Later still, Coalbrookdale was to throb at the heart of the Industrial Revolution.

Colemere Countryside Leisure Area ⊤ Be
Miles of waymarked walks circle 68 acres of water, woodland and flowery meadows.

Corbet Wood ✳ Cd
Trail through wooded hillside nature reserve has good views of surrounding countryside, and passes disused quarry workings.

Earl's Hill ✳ Bb
Wooded nature reserve on site of Iron Age stronghold. Enchanting nature trail ends with spectacular views from summit.

Ellesmere Ae
Centre of Shropshire's 'Lake District'. Story of the seven attractive lakes told in visitor centre near The Mere. Abundant bird life, boating, fishing.

Gnosall Fd
Waterfront area on Shropshire Union Canal is most attractive part of village. Impressive Church of St Lawrence retains some original Norman details.

Goldstone Hall Garden ✳ Ed
Walled garden with glorious flowers and trees and excellent views towards Staffordshire.

Grinshill Cd
Well-kept houses range from Jacobean to Georgian. Overlooked by rocky outcrop which has views of distant North Wales peaks.

Hanmer Be
Anglo-Welsh village next to reedy mere, part of Shropshire's 'Lake District'. Margaret Hanmer married Welsh Prince Owain Glyndwr in village church.

Hawkstone Hall Ce
Listed Georgian mansion with state rooms and winter garden.

WATER'S EDGE *Rhododendrons bloom in an extravaganza of brilliant colour, contrasting strongly with the lily-strewn lake at Weston Park.*

Hodnet ✳ Dd
Village church has unique octagonal tower and 1479 Nuremberg Bible. Magnificent landscaped gardens of Hodnet Hall have lakes and waterfalls set among woodlands and colourful flowers.

CHINA WORKS *A bottle-shaped kiln soars skyward at Iron-Bridge.*

Iron-Bridge Db
World's first bridge of iron, built across Severn 1777-9. Converted worksites along river bank form Ironbridge Gorge Museum celebrating area's industrial heritage: Blists Hill Open Air Museum with re-created 19th-century industrial town; Coalport China Museum; Jackfield Tile Museum; Museum of Iron with furnace Abraham Darby used to first smelt iron ore with coke in 1709.

The Long Mynd Ba
Imposing flat-topped ridge of hills rising to 1700ft. Wild moorland, waterfalls, streams, panoramic views, magnificent walks.

Loppington Bd
Bricks of the 18th-century Loppington Hall contrast with predominant half-timberings. Iron ring where bulls were tethered and baited is Shropshire's last remaining bull ring.

Malpas † Bf
Spreads down hillside from medieval St Oswald's Church, in whose churchyard is motte of 1000-year-old Norman castle built to keep out the Welsh.

Marbury † Cf
Village with 13th-century church, farm, pub and cottages. Overlooks Big Mere, formed at end of Ice Age 20,000 years ago.

Market Drayton † De
Grammar school has desk carved with initials of Robert Clive (Clive of India), born in this attractive market town in 1725. Good views from 14th-century church tower, across river valley.

Much Wenlock Da
Town of narrow streets built around Wenlock Priory, whose history is told in museum. Site of 1850 Olympian Games, forerunner of modern Olympics.

Nesscliffe ✳ Ac
Wooded hill with remains of Iron Age fort and cave said to have been hideout of Shropshire's Robin Hood – 'Wild Humphrey' Kynaston – during 16th century.

Newport † Ec
Church from original Norman 'new town' still stands. Eye-catching Town Hall, built 1860 in Italian style. White windows, facings and pale blue brickwork give it 'Wedgwood' look.

Overton Af
Unspoilt 'capital' of The Hundred of Maelor, narrow strip of Wales which lies between Cheshire and Shropshire. Folklore counts churchyard yews among 'Seven Wonders of Wales'.

Shifnal † Eb
St Andrew's Church, originally Norman, was one of few survivors of 1591 fire which destroyed most of town. Has two chancels and fine monuments.

Shrewsbury Bc
Historic fortress town within loop of River Severn. Castle, rebuilt 13th century to guard Welsh borders, has original gateway of 1083. Attractive alleyways, Georgian terraces and 15th-century half-timbered houses.

Stapeley Water Gardens ✳ Dg
Koi carp and 60 varieties of water lilies thrive in lakes, pools and landscaped waterfalls. Glasshouse has environments ranging from rain forest to palm beaches.

Stretton Hills ☆ Ba
Miniature range of mountains formed 900 million years ago. Ancient tracks climb to give immense views of summits.

Tong Eb
Ornate 15th-century church is 'little Westminster' whose striking effigies and tombs have been compared with those of the famous abbey.

Wem † Cd
Known for strong ales and infamous Judge Jeffreys, Baron of Wem 1685. His house, Lowe Hall, survived 1677 fire which burnt down most of town.

ABBEY RUINS *Wenlock Priory dates back to Norman times.*

Wenlock Priory ⊕ Db
Lovely 11th-century ruins. Wall of priory church towers 70ft over well-kept lawns and elaborate lavatorium, where monks washed.

Weston Park ✳ Fc
Restoration-style mansion, built 1671. Fine pictures and tapestries. Landscaped grounds with lakes, ornamental buildings, nature trails and miniature railway.

Whitchurch † Cf
Known to Romans as Mediolanum, this town lies midway between Deva (Chester) and Uriconium (Wroxeter). It is dominated by St Alkmund's Church, built in Queen Anne style.

The Wrekin ✳ Db
Remote 1334ft hump rising from flat plain, formed 900 million years ago. Earthworks from 2000-year-old tribal capital of the Cornovii. Footpath to top.

Wrenbury † Cf
Village on banks of Shropshire Union Canal near Dutch-style lift bridge; boat-hire centre housed in old mill.

Wroxeter Roman City Cb
Foundations of baths complex of Viroconium, fourth largest city in Roman Britain, founded in 1st century. Site museum.

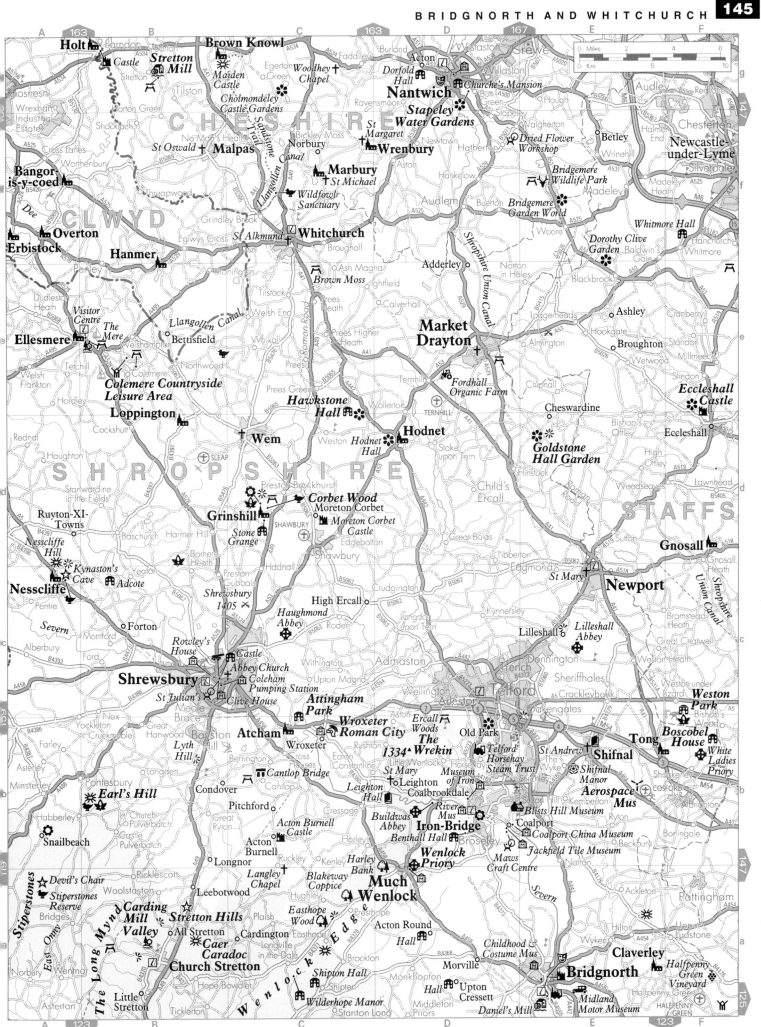

LANDSCAPE OF CONTRASTS

A region of startling contrasts, with scenery ranging from the old royal hunting ground of Cannock Chase to the limestone bluffs of Dove Dale. The industrial heritage is equally varied, offering the bottle kilns of the Potteries and the bottled beers of Burton upon Trent. Among it all survive age-old ceremonies like the Horn Dance, well-dressing and Ashbourne's free-for-all football.

Abbots Bromley Cd
Saxon reindeer horns in St Nicholas' Church used annually in medieval hunting rite. Butter Cross, six-sided timber building, marks 14th-century marketplace.

Alrewas Dc
Tranquil village of pretty gardens and half-timbered, thatched cottages. Merging canals at nearby Fradley Junction recapture magic of old waterways.

Alton Towers Cf
Fun and fantasy world engulf 19th-century Alton Towers, whose restored rooms and landscaped gardens provide relaxing contrast to Corkscrew Rollercoaster, Black Hole and more than 100 other amusements.

Ashbourne Df
Attractive gateway to Peak District with tall-spired church and old almshouses. Three miles separate millwheel spindle and stone plaque – used by locals as goals in their annual football matches.

Bradbourne Eg
Impressive 8th-century Saxon cross and Norman doorway of All Saints' Church are focal points of this remote hillside village.

Burton upon Trent Ed
Historic brewing centre pervaded by scent of hops and malt. Shire horse stables are included among 400 years of brewing heritage in Bass Museum.

Cannock Chase Bc
Heath and forest roamed by fallow and red deer. Country Park with nature reserve, graves of the first Zeppelin crew shot down over Britain and the interesting visitor centre.

Chatterley Whitfield Mining Museum Ag
Real colliery where helmets and lamps are needed to descend to the coal miners' underground world of 1800s. Pit ponies, machinery, railway and steam winding engine.

Cheadle Cf
Set among hills at gateway to wooded Churnet valley, dominated by 200ft steeple of Roman Catholic church.

Cheddleton Bg
Water mills at Flint Mill ground flint for local pottery industry from 1765 to 1963. One still works, other contains exhibits. Railway museum gives steam rides.

Dove Dale Dg
Dramatic tree-clad gorge where River Dove has shaped Dove Dale Castle, Lion's Head, Reynard's Cave and other limestone formations. Where Izaak Walton learnt fly-fishing.

Eccleshall Castle Ad
Nine-sided tower is among romantic 13th-century ruins set in grounds of 1690 William and Mary house. Moat walls now surround formal gardens.

Foxfield Steam Railway Bf
Steam locomotives pull coaches on thrilling 4 mile ride over steep gradients and sharp curves on line once used to transport coal.

Froghall Cf
Pleasure boats and picnickers now line Froghall Basin, terminus of restored Caldon Canal which carried limestone from nearby quarries to Stoke. Great Froghall Plane is 900ft incline of 1802 quarry tramway.

Ilam Park Dg
Lawns sweep down to River Manifold, natural wonder which emerges here after disappearing underground in drier months. Paradise Walk climbs from park to stunning views of moorlands and limestone cliffs.

Ingestre Bd
Classical design of 17th-century St Mary the Virgin's Church most definitely Sir Christopher Wren. Magnificent interior.

Leek Bg
Brindley Mill, fully working 1752 corn mill, built by James Brindley, giant of Industrial Revolution best known for his canals. Museum covers his life.

Lichfield Db
Overlooked by three graceful spires – 'Ladies of the Vale' – and magnificent statued west front of 13th-century cathedral. Dr Samuel Johnson's 1709 birthplace now period-style museum with personal relics. Heritage and Treasury Exhibition covers 2000 years of city history with series of life-like tableaux.

Marston on Dove Ed
Attractive old Derbyshire village in good walking country. Church bell dates from 1366.

Middleton Da
Unspoilt oasis amid industrial sprawl which predates Domesday Book. Middleton Hall, ruined shell of stately mansion, restored with gardens and craft centre.

Moorlands Farm Park Cg
Among more than 70 rare animal breeds are ancient Longhorn cattle, Gloucester Old Spot pigs and pygmy goats.

Moseley Old Hall Bb
Elizabethan house whose interesting links to Charles II include bed and cupboard where he slept and hid after Battle of Worcester 1651. Also letter he wrote to a local who helped him escape to France.

Shallowford Ad
Izaak Walton's Cottage, part of farm owned by author of famed *The Compleat Angler*. Typical 17th-century interior has interesting fishing artefacts.

Shugborough Bd
Doric Temple, Chinese House and Triumphal Arch are among unusual monuments in park of Earl of Lichfield's home. Brewery is one of bygone restorations in County Museum, farm has working corn mill and rare breeds.

Stafford Bd
Impressive Norman castle earthworks, built 1070, include some evidence of original town. Izaak Walton born here 1593, baptised in St Mary's Church font. Ancient High House, largest timber-framed town house in England, built in 1595.

Stafford Doxey Marshes Bd
Wetland nature reserve occupies marsh, meadow and lake and supports rich variety of bird life. Herons haunt the marshes which are also important for breeding redshank, snipe, yellow wagtail and sedge warbler.

Stoke-on-Trent Af
'The Potteries', union of six towns made world-famous by ceramic designers Wedgwood, Spode and others. History of industry and precious collections on display at the Spode Factory and Museum, home of bone china; Coalport Minerva Works; Minton Museum and Factory; The Potteries Centre, covering 25 local pottery and china makers; and City Museum, which also honours local Spitfire designer R.J. Mitchell. Nearby are the parklands, lake and nature reserves of Trentham Gardens.

Sudbury De
Charming red-brick village. Jacobean-style Sudbury Hall, built in 17th-century, has fine plasterwork, woodcarvings, paintings, furniture and modern ceramics. Museum of Childhood has Betty Cadbury collection of playthings past and displays of Victoriana. All Saints' Church built 12th century, has window presented by Queen Victoria.

Sutton Coldfield Da
Medieval market town has magnificent 2400 acre country park nearby with woods, valleys, gorse and heather moors, lakes and bird sanctuaries. Traversed by old Roman Rykind Street.

CHINESE HOUSE *Exotic corner of the Orient at Shugborough.*

Swynnerton Ae
Attractive village on high ground surrounded by woods. St Mary's Church has 8ft high statue of Christ, considered late Norman.

Tissington Dg
Idyllic village enhanced each Ascension Day when its five wells are 'dressed' with Biblical scenes made from flower petals. St Mary's Church has font carved with curious beasts and memorials to FitzHerbert family, builders of Tissington Hall.

FLORAL TRIBUTE *Annual well-dressing ritual at Tissington.*

Tutbury Ed
Overlooked by shattered ruins of 12th-century castle, twice prison of Mary, Queen of Scots. Tutbury Crystal has traditional glassmaking on view. St Mary's Church, founded 1080, has a magnificent doorway.

Wall Roman Site Cb
High walls of exceptional example of Roman town bath-house dominate Letocetum, settlement on road from London to Chester. Museum has excavated finds.

Walsall Ca
Fascinating museums include England's only Lock Museum, Birthplace Museum of *Three Men in a Boat* author Jerome K. Jerome and Canal Museum in former Boatman's Rest and Mission.

Wedgwood Visitor Centre Ae
Craftsmen make Jasper ware for which Josiah Wedgwood is famous. Centre has personal works including 'first edition' Portland Vase of 1793. Also comprehensive collection of early and modern Wedgwood.

Wightwick Manor Aa
Half-timbered manor house, built 1887-93, is awash with work of famous Pre-Raphaelites including wallpapers and fabrics by William Morris, watercolours by Ruskin and Kempe stained glass. Terraced gardens have topiary work and were designed by Victorian flower painter Alfred Parsons.

Wolverhampton Ba
'Capital of the Black Country', a medieval market town made famous by iron and brass foundries. Fine parks, art galleries and museums including extensive collection of English painted enamels at Bantock House Museum.

VALLEY OF DELIGHTS *Mile-long Dove Dale reveals a wealth of scenic attractions, from green, tranquil river banks to limestone pinnacles.*

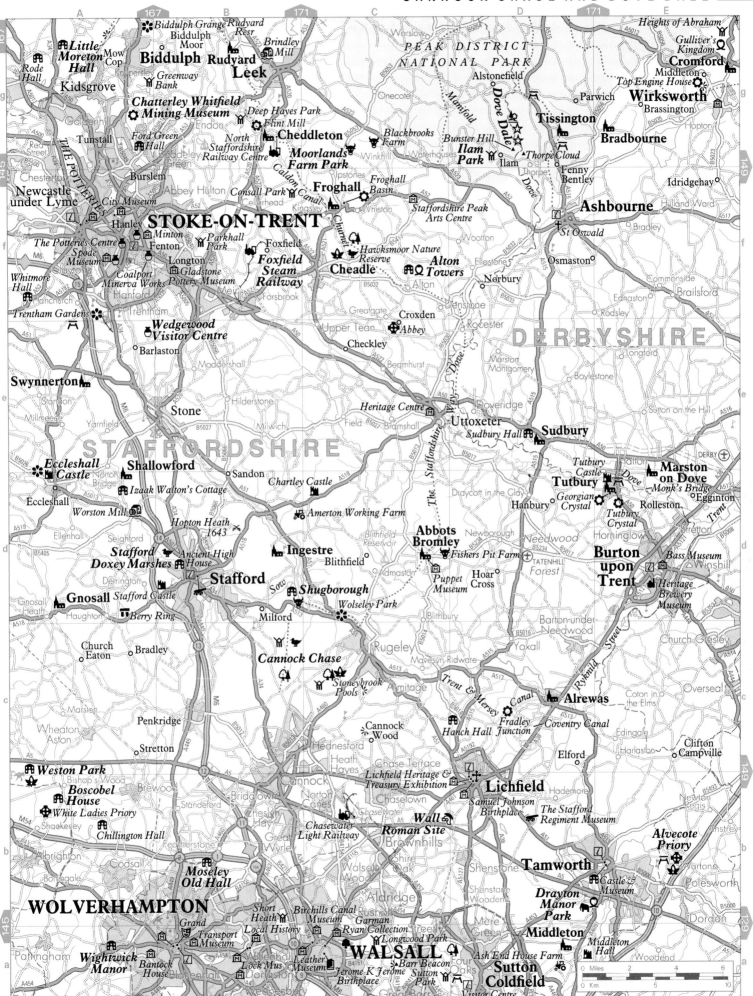

WHERE THREE COUNTIES MEET

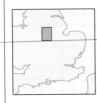

This corner of Derbyshire, Nottinghamshire and Leicestershire runs from the barren heights of the Peak District east and south over rolling farmlands scarred by the Industrial Revolution. Though colliery tips dot the landscape, many now are grass-covered and landscaped. To the south lie the open heathlands of what was once thickly wooded Charnwood Forest.

Ashby-de-la-Zouch Bb
Town has ruined 12th-century castle with impressive Hastings Tower and 15th-century St Helen's Church with 300-year-old finger pillory for those who misbehaved during services. Three miles west, 19th-century Moira Furnace has mining displays.

Black Rock ☆ Af
Steep paths wind up jagged peak to picnic area with views of Matlock and Peak District. At foot is 17½ mile High Peak footpath.

Breedon on the Hill Cc
On limestone bluff above village is Norman Church of St Mary and St Hardulph with remarkable 8th-century Saxon frieze, Iron Age hill-fort and views of Trent Valley.

Calverton Ee
Museum and former knitters' cottages with large windows letting in maximum light mark village's 16th-century growth as stocking knitting centre.

Castle Donington Cc
Attractive town famous for Donington Park motor-racing circuit with its museum of historic Grand Prix cars and racing motorcycles.

Crich Bf
Disused limestone quarry above rural village has National Tramway Museum with 40 models built 1873-1953, reconstructed 19th-century street, and tram rides with views over Derwent Valley.

Cromford Af
Stone village built for workers of Richard Arkwright's first water-powered cotton mills. Original 1771 Cromford Mill now museum on Arkwright and village. Canal restored for leisure use.

Derby Bd
Industrial heritage of cathedral city shown at Industrial Museum housed in Britain's first factory, a silk mill (1717), and in Royal Crown Derby Porcelain museum and factory tour.

Donington le Heath Cb
Medieval manor house has fine oak furniture and herb garden.

Eastwood Ce
D.H. Lawrence born 1885 in red-brick former mining village, set among farmland. Birthplace and other family home, Breach House, restored with furnishings of time.

Elvaston Castle Cd
Country Park with woodland and gardens surround gaunt 19th-century castle (not open). Two acres of estate buildings re-create 1910 community with blacksmith, cobbler, saddler and other types of local craftsmen.

Frisby on the Wreake Eb
Gretna Green of Midlands, 18th-century vicar of St Thomas Becket's Church performed unlicensed marriages. Remains of 13th-century cross stands among brick and wattle-and-daub buildings.

Gaddesby Eb
Medieval St Luke's Church has life-size marble monument of squire Colonel Cheney astride one of four horses which died under him at Waterloo.

Hardwick Hall Cg
Well-preserved Elizabethan mansion in country park, with Elizabethan enclosed garden and rare Whiteface Woodland sheep and Longhorn cattle.

High Peak Junction Bf
Restored railway and canal buildings where 19th-century Cromford and High Peak Railway met Cromford Canal. Horse-

LOCAL HERO *Robin Hood – in effigy outside the castle – defies Nottingham's sheriff of long ago.*

drawn narrowboat trips along waterway and 17½ mile High Peak walking trail.

Holme Pierrepont Ed
Battlemented brick façade added to Tudor Holme Pierrepont Hall in 1800. Fine medieval timber work and original fireplaces. Disused gravel pits are now National Water Sports Centre with sailing, canoeing and angling.

Kedleston Hall Be
Elegant exterior and interiors, unaltered since 1759, mainly work of Robert Adam. Indian silver, ivories, weapons and art collected by Lord Curzon while Viceroy of India, 1898-1905. Fine furniture and collection of Old Masters including Giordano and Lely.

Loughborough Db
Town's famous bell casting evident in World War I memorial's carillon of 47 local bells and in Bell Foundry Museum. Restored Loughborough Central Station is start of Great Central Railway with original Victorian stations, signal boxes, bridges and viaducts on 5 mile line to Leicester.

Matlock Ag
Tourist resort beside beautiful wooded Derwent gorge. Fine views from 750ft Heights of Abraham, reached by cable car, and from terraces below 380ft High Tor. Grounds of Riber Castle (1862) have wildlife park with rare animals including lynx. Mining Museum records local mining since before Romans.

Melbourne Bc
Small town of thatched and whitewashed cottages includes remains of 14th-century castle, swans on Melbourne Pool, and carved pillars in Norman church.

Melbourne Hall Bc
Relics in study belong to Queen Victoria's first prime minister Lord Melbourne, who once lived here. Built in 17th century around medieval house. Grounds with wrought-iron pagoda, woodland walks and 180ft yew tunnel.

Newstead Abbey Df
Home of poet Lord Byron (1778-1824), 12th-century Augustinian priory with stone-vaulted crypt and three magnificent carved and painted 16th-century overmantels. Rare collection of Lord Byron's letters, first editions and manuscripts. In grounds are two mock forts.

Nottingham Dd
Castle on 130ft rock above city, built 1674, now city museum and art gallery. Fragments of original Norman castle in grounds. City's famous fabric features at Lace Centre in medieval Severns building and Story of Nottingham Lace. Brewhouse Yard Museum has 17th-century cottages re-creating 300 years of Nottingham life, and Trip to Jerusalem (1189), said to be England's oldest inn. Museum of Costume and Textiles has styles from 1760-1960, Salvation Army Museum, in the birthplace of founder William Booth. Canal Museum has narrowboats. Man-made caves of Bridlesmithgate and Broad Marsh Centre are 13th century. Green's Mill is operational four-sail windmill with scientific centre telling of former owner George Green, who became brilliant mathematician.

Papplewick Df
Pretty village of pink stone and red-tiled cottages. Fireplace in medieval St James's Church warmed pew of Frederick Montagu, who rebuilt church in Gothic style in 18th century.

Papplewick Pumping Station Df
'Temple' of Victorian engineering. Decorated and carved iron columns, stained-glass windows, ornate lamps and pair of beam pumping engines clad with polished mahogany and brass. Made by James Watt and Co, 1884.

Repton Bc
Capital of the 7th-century Saxon kingdom of Mercia. St Wystan's Church, topped by 212ft spire, has original Anglo-Saxon crypt. Gateway and gatehouse remain of 1172 priory, now Repton School, founded 1557.

Ruddington Dd
Factory and cottage complex in Framework-knitters' Museum re-creates home and working life of 19th-century stocking makers.

Shardlow Cd
Once busy inland port on Trent and Mersey Canal has swapped industrial cargoes for leisure cruising. Fine canal pubs and warehouses, including restored Clock Warehouse (1780). Boat trips can be taken.

Southwell Ff
Beautiful cream-coloured Southwell Minster with slender towers and spires dates from 1108. Exquisite 'Leaves of Southwell' stone carving in Chapter House. Charles I gave himself up to the Scots Commissioners in 17th-century Saracen's Head in 1646.

NORMAN SYMMETRY *The twin towers of Southwell Minster.*

Ticknall Bc
Village of stone-and-brick cottages and farmhouses. Calke Abbey, baroque mansion built 1703 on site of priory, unchanged for 100 years. In landscaped Calke Park with lime tree avenue to ancient oaks and ponds.

Winkburn Ff
Red-brick and pantiled cottages and farmhouses on banks of tiny Wink stream. Village church has box pews, three-tiered Jacobean pulpit and Norman tower.

Wirksworth Af
Small town annually 'dresses' its wells with pictures created from petals, one of crafts and customs explained in Wirksworth Heritage Centre. Tall brick smokestack marks Middleton Top Engine House, built 1825 on Cromford and High Peak Railway. Two cavernous boilers, great pulley wheels which hauled wagons up steep Middleton Incline, and a visitor centre.

Wollaton Hall Dd
Red and fallow deer roam in parkland of Elizabethan house extravagantly designed with cupolas, pinnacles, balustrades and false Dutch gables. Rooms home to Nottingham Natural History Museum, while stable block has Nottingham Industrial Museum.

Woodhouse Eaves Db
Commanding views of Charnwood Forest from craggy Beacon Hill rising 818ft behind village of old thatched and slate-roofed cottages and almshouses. Broombriggs Farm has farm trail with boards explaining local farming.

POWER AT REST *Nottingham's proud industrial past – from lacemaking to pharmaceuticals and tobacco – now lies quiet at Elizabethan Wollaton Hall.*

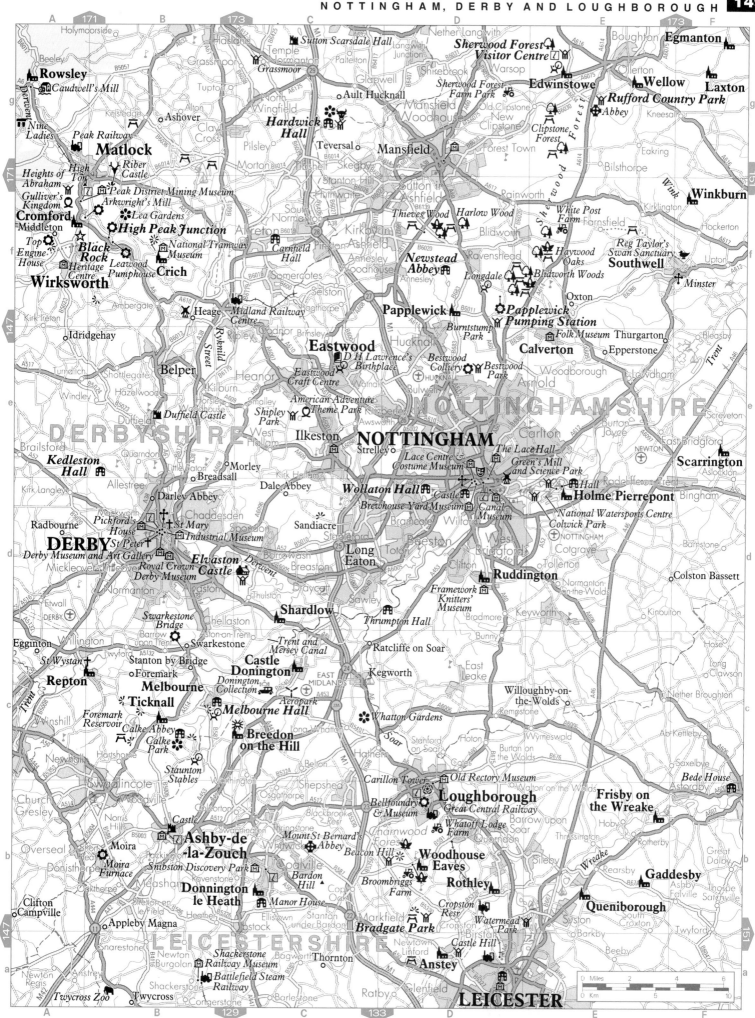

Ancaster Ce
Medieval quarries outside the village provided the honey-coloured stone for many Lincolnshire churches. Ermine Street has traces of Roman camp.

Belton House Cd
Cupolas crown beautiful Restoration mansion; it has been virtually untouched since 1688. Noted for plaster ceilings, woodcarvings, paintings and silverware. Landscaped grounds with formal gardens and orangery.

Belvoir Castle Bd
Romantic battlements and turrets dominate Vale of Belvoir from steep escarpment. Norman fortress rebuilt early 19th century as home of the Duke of Rutland. A treasure house of furniture, paintings by Reynolds and others, and ancient arms.

Billingborough Ed
Rambling fenland village with red-brick houses and old stone buildings, including George and Dragon Inn and 17th-century Old Hall. St Andrew's Church has tall steeple with flying buttresses.

Billinghay Ef
Vicarage Museum in 17th-century 'mud-and-stud' cottage reflects 300 years of village life.

Bottesford Bd
River Devon loops around Leicestershire's highest church spire soaring 207ft above St Mary's. Monuments of Earls of Rutland include curious Witchcraft Tomb of 6th Earl which tells of the Belvoir witches. Market cross, stocks and whipping post are medieval relics.

Bourne Dc
Home town of fenland hero Hereward the Wake, last Saxon noble to resist William the Conqueror. His manor house stood in beautiful park where earthworks of 11th-century castle remain.

Brant Broughton Cf
For centuries the Coldron family has worked wrought iron from small forge. Gates and chandeliers of 13th-century St Helen's Church, topped by 198ft spire, are their handiwork.

Caythorpe Ce
Fine medieval nave is feature of 13th-century St Vincent's Church. Arnhem Aisle has memorabilia of the 1944 battle.

Collingham Bg
Two settlements, each with secluded limestone church, link to form elongated village. Hollow-trunked elm tree, 250 years old, celebrates Bonnie Prince Charlie's defeat at Culloden in 1746.

Colsterworth Cc
Sundial in St John the Baptist's Church cut by nine-year-old Isaac Newton, born in nearby Woolsthorpe Manor. Narrow main street is old Roman road.

Cromwell Ag
More than 1000 dolls, dolls' houses, toys, children's clothing and baby wear revive childhood memories at Museum of Dolls and Bygone Childhood.

ACROSS THE VALE OF BELVOIR

Beneath the limestone ridge of Lincoln Edge soaring church spires, handsome coaching inns on the Great North Road and impressive Belvoir Castle stand amid rich agricultural land. From these surroundings, awash with the warm hues of the local limestone, came Hereward the Wake, Sir Isaac Newton, Margaret Thatcher – and Melton Mowbray pork pies.

ROMANTIC CASTLE *Belvoir's fairy-tale turrets look down from their commanding escarpment onto the rich farmlands of the Vale of Belvoir.*

Denton Bd
Impressive entry to golden-stone village formed by 19th-century gatehouses of former manor. Lake in grounds of present manor fed by spring, St Christopher's Well.

Folkingham Dd
Orange-brick Greyhound Inn was former 17th-century staging post between Lincoln and Peterborough. Governor's House and gateway of 19th-century 'House of Correction' stand on medieval castle site.

Fulbeck Cf
Fulbeck Hall, built 1733, reached by magnificent lime avenue and overlooked by eight pinnacles of 14th-century St Nicholas' Church. Weaving, woodwork and dried flowers are among Manor Stables craft workshops.

Grantham Cd
Richard III signed the Duke of Buckingham's death warrant in 1483 at ancient Angel and Royal, one of historic staging posts on Great North Road. Isaac Newton (1642-1727) carved name at 15th-century grammar school and is featured in museum, along with Margaret Thatcher, born in town

1925. St Wulfram's Church has original Norman pillars and chained library, established in 1598. Oldest book dated 1472.

Grimsthorpe Castle Dc
Medieval castle and Tudor House, remodelled as miniature Blenheim Palace by Sir John Vanbrugh in 1720s. Magnificent arcaded hall with busts and portraits of kings. Parkland was landscaped by Capability Brown.

Heckington Ee
Enormous sails and original 1830 workings stand idle in Britain's last eight-sailed windmill. Exquisite St Andrew's Church was built by 14th-century monks in Decorated style.

ANGELIC HOST *Corbel of Angel and Royal Hotel, Grantham.*

Honnington Camp Ce
Earthworks of Iron Age hill-fort, on slopes of Ancaster Gap.

Irnham Dc
Wooded oasis in flat fenlands. Peaceful village in hollow where ivy-clad willows shade pond waters and waterfall cascades down to trickling stream.

Jubilee Way Ad
Footpath through scenic Vale of Belvoir winds 15 miles between Woolsthorpe and Melton Mowbray. Passes through attractive woodlands under Belvoir Castle and intersects Viking Way.

Little Dalby Ab
Traditional birthplace of Stilton cheese, made by Little Dalby Hall housekeeper in 1720. Virtually untouched by progress: no street names and one made-up road.

Market Overton Bb
Pale stone cottages, grand manor house and trees planted to celebrate Queen Victoria's Golden Jubilee in 1887 line single, winding street of village overlooking Vale of Catmose.

Melton Mowbray Ab
Famous for Stilton cheese, and pork pies which Ye Olde Pork Pie Shoppe has baked since 1850. Pies and cheese celebrated in Melton Carnegie local history museum. Gracious St Mary's Church dates from 1170. Attractive parks and gardens line Eye river banks.

Navenby Cf
Quaint village of stone and pantiled houses. Easter Sepulchre of St Peter's Church compares with that of Lincoln Cathedral. Delicately carved figures include three Roman soldiers.

Newark-on-Trent Af
King John died (1216) in 12th-century Newark Castle, reduced to ragged ruins after Civil War. Immense St Mary's Church, mainly 15th century, has 252ft spire and magnificent carvings. One of last Vulcan bombers is among historic aircraft at nearby Newark Air Museum.

Norton Disney Bf
Church has remarkable double-sided Disney brass depicting 26 members of family, former lords of manor from whom Walt Disney descended. Wooden tablets honour those of 300 and 301 Polish RAF Squadrons killed on duty.

Rutland Railway Museum Bb
Re-created industrial yard and railway siding with 20 steam and diesel locomotives and other rolling stock. Free rides.

Scarrington Ae
Some 35,000 nailed horseshoes form unique, cone-shaped obelisk in this roadside village. Begun by blacksmith in 1946, it is 14ft high with 5ft base. Brick-built Old Hall, with three storeys, dates from early 18th century.

Sempringham Ed
Church of St Andrew has Norman nave arcades and doorways. Former church of nearby abbey, founded 1132 by Gilbertines – only English monastic order.

Sleaford De
Attractive cottages on River Slea beneath one of oldest stone spires in England atop 12th-century St Denys' Church. Grassy hummocks mark Sleaford Castle, where King John's final fever was treated in vain.

Staunton in the Vale Be
Unspoilt rural village huddled around church and hall. Associated with Staunton family since Middle Ages, bullet holes in family residence of Staunton Hall mark their support of Charles I during Civil War.

Threekingham Dd
Supposed site of 9th-century battle in which three Danish kings slain. Three Kings Inn was host to only two kings, John and Henry VIII. Old Hall opposite has whale jawbone gateway.

TOWERING SPIRE *The imposing Church of St Mary dominates the town of Newark-on-Trent.*

Waltham on the Wolds Ac
Charming blue-black pantiles protect cream cottages from frosts brought in by chilly Wash winds. Crumbling 13th-century St Mary Magdalene's Church has woodcarvings of monastic figures.

Witham on the Hill Db
Named in Domesday Book. Bywells Spring gushes out on large village green near covered stocks. Outside village, hollow trunk of 500-year-old Bowthorpe Oak can hold 40 people.

Woolsthorpe Manor Cc
Modest farmhouse where Isaac Newton was born 1642, kept much as it was. Made revolutionary scientific discoveries in study and garden, where an apple tree is descended from tree which prompted law of gravitation.

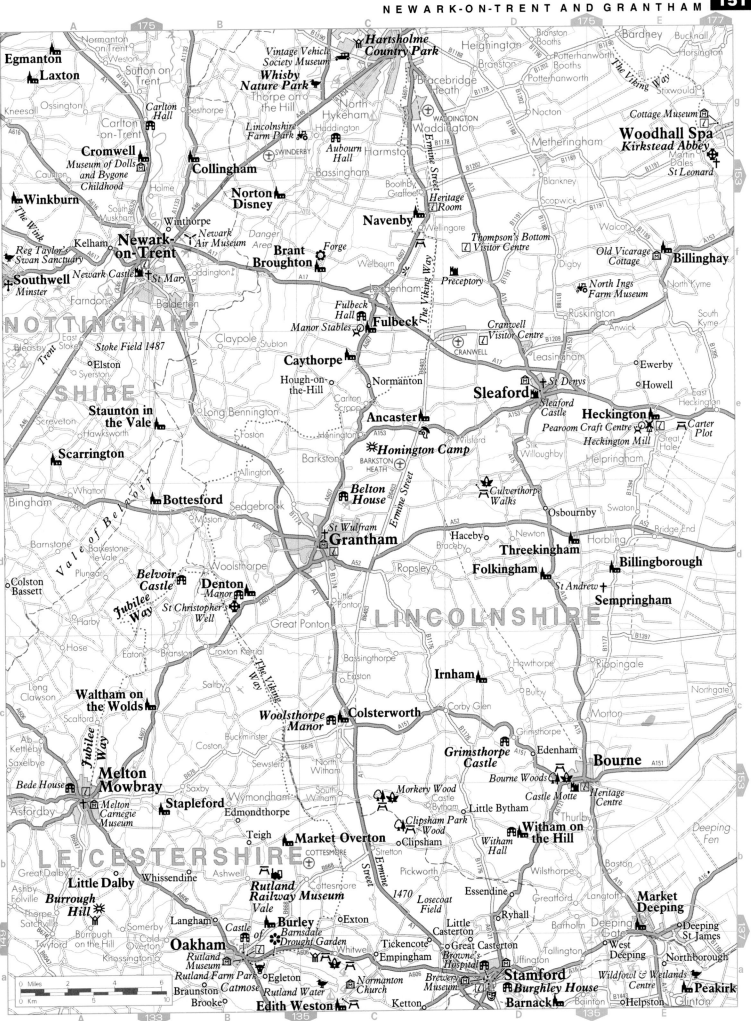

Key locations shown include:

Egmanton, Laxton, Normanton on Trent, Weston, Sutton on Trent, Kneesall, Ossington, Besthorpe, Carlton Hall, Carlton-on-Trent, Winkburn, Cromwell, Museum of Dolls and Bygone Childhood, Caunton, South Muskham, Holme, Collingham, Norton Disney, Winthorpe, Kelham, Newark Air Museum, Reg Taylor's Swan Sanctuary, Newark-on-Trent, Newark Castle, St Mary, Southwell Minster, Farndon, Balderton, Coddington, Brant Broughton, Forge, Bleasby, East Stoke, Elston, Syerston, Stoke Field 1487, Claypole, Stubton, Hough-on-the-Hill, Caythorpe, Fulbeck Hall, Manor Stables, Fulbeck, Staunton in the Vale, Hawksworth, Long Bennington, Foston, Honington, Normanton, Carlton Scroop, Ancaster, Scarrington, Whatton, Allington, Barkston, Barkston Heath, Honington Camp, Bingham, Barnstone, Barkestone-le-Vale, Sedgebrook, Moston, Belton House, Bottesford, Colston Bassett, Plungar, Harby, Woolsthorpe, Belvoir Castle, Jubilee Way, St Christopher's Well, Denton Manor, Great Ponton, Little Ponton, Grantham, St Wulfram, Eaton, Branston, Croxton Kerrial, The Viking Way, Saltby, Bassingthorpe, Easton, Hose, Waltham on the Wolds, Long Clawson, Scalford, Buckminster, Coston, Sewstern, North Witham, Colsterworth, Woolsthorpe Manor, Irnham, Corby Glen, Ab Kettleby, Saxelbye, Jubilee Way, Bede House, Melton Mowbray, Saxby, Wymondham, South Witham, Morkery Wood, Grimsthorpe Castle, Bourne, Bourne Woods, Castle Motte, Heritage Centre, Asfordby, Melton Carnegie Museum, Stapleford, Edmondthorpe, Teigh, Market Overton, Clipsham Park Wood, Clipsham, Castle Bytham, Little Bytham, Witham Hall, Witham on the Hill, Thurlby, Little Dalby, Great Dalby, Whissendine, Ashwell, Cottesmore, Stretton, Pickworth, 1470, Losecoat Field, Essendine, Greatford, Ryhall, Wilsthorpe, Market Deeping, Deeping Fen, Deeping St James, Burrough Hill, Thorpe Satchville, Burrough on the Hill, Twyford, Great Dalby, Langham, Rutland Railway Museum, Burley, Castle, Barnsdale, Drought Garden, Exton, Whitwell, Tickencote, Little Casterton, Great Casterton, Barholm, West Deeping, Deeping Gate, Northborough, Oakham, Rutland Museum, Rutland Farm Park, Egleton, Catmose, Braunston, Brooke, Edith Weston, Normanton Church, Rutland Water, Ketton, Empingham, Tinwell, Browne's Hospital, Brewery Museum, Uffington, Tallington, Barnack, Stamford, Burghley House, Bainton, Helpston, Glinton, Peakirk, Wildfowl & Wetlands Centre

Lincolnshire locations: Harmston, Bassingham, Boothby Graffoe, Navenby, Wellingore, Heritage Room, Leadenham, Welbourn, Preceptory, Cranwell Visitor Centre, Cranwell, Leasingham, Ruskington, North Kyme, Sleaford, Sleaford Castle, St Denys, Heckington, Pearoom Craft Centre, Heckington Mill, Carter Plot, Great Hale, Helpringham, Osbournby, Swaton, Bridge End, Haceby, Braceby, Newton, Horbling, Threekingham, Folkingham, St Andrew, Billingborough, Sempringham, Ropsley, Hawthorpe, Rippingale, Northgate, Morton, Grimsthorpe, Edenham, Hanthorpe, Billinghay, North Ings Farm Museum, Digby, Old Vicarage Cottage, Walcot, Anwick, South Kyme, Ewerby, Howell, East Heckington, Woodhall Spa, Kirkstead Abbey, St Leonard, Cottage Museum, Martin Dales, Bardney, Bucknall, Horsington, Stixwould, Nocton, Metheringham, Scopwick, Blankney

Nottingham: NOTTINGHAMSHIRE, Trent, Vale of Belvoir

LEICESTERSHIRE

Waddington, North Hykeham, Haddington, Aubourn Hall, Swinderby, Lincolnshire Farm Park, Thorpe on the Hill, Whisby Nature Park, Vintage Vehicle Society Museum, Hartsholme Country Park, Heighington, Branston, Bracebridge Heath, Branston Booths, Potterhanworth, Potterhanworth Booths, Ermine Street

Scale: 0 Miles 2 4 6 / 0 Km 5 10

LINCOLNSHIRE'S FENLAND

The rounded chalk hills of the Lincolnshire Wolds descend to a flat farming landscape, broken only by the silhouette of church towers and castles. Tulips, potatoes, onions and wheat flourish on some of the finest agricultural land in Britain, drained and reclaimed from the sea in past centuries and bounded now by protective banks. The marshes that remain are home to numerous wildfowl and waders.

Boston † ⚔ ✗ 🏛 ⓩ Cd
Port since 13th century; still active. Since 14th century, fenland travellers and sailors on The Wash have taken their bearings by 272ft tower of St Botolph's Church, known as Boston Stump. Earliest Pilgrim Fathers were imprisoned in medieval Guildhall (now Borough Museum) in 1607 for trying to emigrate illegally. Later group set sail for America in 1630 and founded city of Boston, Massachusetts. Fydell House (1726) has an American Room and superb plaster-work.

GRINDING POWER Inside the windmill at Burgh le Marsh.

Burgh le Marsh ⚓ ✗ 🏛 Ef
Handsome windmill dating from 1833, unusual because it turns millstones anticlockwise. Lincolnshire Railway Museum, in former Great Northern Railway goods depot, has restored locomotives and waiting room.

Coningsby ⚓ Ƴ Be
Village church clock can be seen for miles across fenlands; 16½ft in diameter, its face has only one hand. Battle of Britain Memorial Flight based at RAF Coningsby has Lancaster bomber, two Hurricanes and five Spitfires.

Croft ⚓ Ef
Marshland church with angels on the corners of the pinnacled tower; original pews with doors; notable brass eagle lectern and fine monuments.

Donington ⚓ ⊛ Bc
Birthplace of explorer Matthew Flinders in 1774, who mapped Australia's coastline in early 1800s. Former village Grammar School, founded 1719 and rebuilt 1812, retains original windows, bell turret and porch. Church spire dates from 14th century. Inside, unusual box-like 'hude' was used to keep the parson dry during rainy funerals.

Fishtoft ⚓ ⊛ ⚲ Cd
Memorial on bank of The Haven marks where earliest Pilgrim Fathers attempted to set sail for America in 1607 from Scotia Creek, until betrayed by ship's captain. Good views of The Wash.

Frampton Marsh ❧ Cc
Dead-end lane parallel with south bank of The Haven leads to field path, then sea bank, with rich farmland behind and wild marsh in front. Good walks lead along the embankment.

Freiston Shore ⚓ Cd
Tiny hamlet popular with birdwatchers, 2 miles from Freiston village; thousands of sea birds flock to creeks and marshes. Footpaths along sea wall lead to Boston and Skegness.

Friskney ⚓ De
Scattered parish in rich farmland, reclaimed from salt marshes by dykes and banks. Church has original 14th-century beamed roof and wall paintings of 1320. Coastal walks along innermost of three sea banks.

Gibraltar Point ❧ ⓩ Ee
Promontory of dunes and salt marshes on the Lincolnshire coast, now 1000 acre nature reserve. Oystercatchers, dunlins and knots roost here, and it is the breeding ground of the rare little tern. Seals bask on offshore sandbanks. Visitor centre and bird observatory.

Gosberton ⚓ Bc
Village mentioned in Domesday Book with church dating from Norman times. Spire decorated with foliage; gargoyles peer from under battlements of tower. Inside, 14th-century effigy of a crosslegged knight.

Great Steeping ⚓ ⚲ Df
Northcote Heavy Horse Centre features shire horses, rare breeds of farm animals, and collection of horse-drawn vehicles.

Gunby Hall ⚔ Df
Grandiose red-brick and stone house built 1700, reputed to be Tennyson's 'haunt of ancient peace'. Portraits by Reynolds hang in oak-panelled drawing room. Gardens ablaze with roses in summer.

Hagworthingham ⚓ ❧ 🎨 ❧ Cf
Craft shop, tea rooms and an exhibition of Lord Tennyson's work and possessions in 17th-century Stockwith water mill. Unusual farm breeds are on show at Lincolnshire Rare Breeds Centre.

Halton Holegate ⚓ Df
Pasture land comes right up to the main street of the village. View of Boston Stump across the fens. Handsome church has 15th-century woodwork, including bench-ends carved with angels, owls and monkeys. Low-beamed Bell Inn may date from 1520; imposing red-brick Old Hall is largely 18th century; and 19th-century St Andrew's Rectory was a regular haunt of Tennyson.

Horncastle ⚲ Bf
Market town, mostly rebuilt 19th century, once famous for annual horse fairs. Fighting Cocks Inn still has cockpit in yard; bull-baiting practised in the Bull Ring until 1835. Square stands in centre of what was once Roman fort of Banovallum; parts of Roman wall survive. Church of St Mary, dating from 13th century, has massive low tower with beacon; noted for brasses and Civil War relics.

Kirkstead Abbey † ⊕ Af
Church of St Leonard was once the 13th-century south chapel of a Cistercian abbey, founded 12th century. Early effigy (1250) of a knight inside.

HIGH AND DRY Common seals often bask off Gibraltar Point.

Long Sutton ⚓ ❧ Db
Village with large indoor tropical gardens, where exotic butterflies fly freely. Outdoors, wild-flower meadows attract native breeds. Church with Early English tower and medieval brass eagle lectern.

Old Bolingbroke ⚓ ⚒ Cf
Demure Wold village where grassy mounds and fragments of walls are all that remain of Bolingbroke Castle; birthplace of Henry IV in 1367. Dating from 11th century, it fell into decay after being captured by Cromwell in 1643. Partly 14th-century church; tower adorned with gargoyles.

Pinchbeck Marsh ⊛ Bb
Restored steam pumping station demonstrates land reclamation projects across fens. Drainage methods explained; also rare collection of hand tools.

Revesby ⚓ ⚔ Cf
Estate village surrounded by woodlands. Deer graze in grounds of Revesby Abbey, once home to naturalist Sir Joseph Banks, who sailed with Captain Cook in 18th century. Present house built middle of last century. Nearby reservoir is a magnet for fishermen and waterfowl.

PEACEFUL HAUNT Gunby Hall, a red-brick and stone mansion built in about 1700, has strong associations with the poet Tennyson.

Sibsey Trader Mill ✗ Ce
Restored brick-built tower mill of 1877; one of the few surviving six-sailed windmills in England. Lincolnshire mill display.

Skegness ❀ ❦ ❧ ✗ ⓩ Ef
Large Victorian houses in leafy avenues lead to grand seaside promenade. Bustling seafront with formal gardens overlooks miles of white sand. Natureland Marine Zoo has tropical house with crocodiles, butterfly house, aviaries and seal hospital. Church Farm Museum, housed in 19th-century farm buildings, decorated in authentic Victorian style. Rural craft workshops in grounds.

Snipe Dales ✗ ❧ ❧ Cf
Reached by footpath from hamlet of Winceby; grassy slopes of this 120 acre nature reserve echo with soft whirring call of snipe and woodcock at dusk. Area hunted by short-eared and barn owls. Wild marsh plants grow in damp valley bottoms. Nearby Slash Hollow was scene of 1643 Battle of Winceby in Civil War.

Spalding ⚔ ❀ ⓩ Bb
Bulb-growing centre, famous for tulips and daffodils. Flower-growing fields stretch for 10,000 acres; visit April and early May. River Welland runs close to the marketplace, dividing town in two, spanned by seven bridges. Church with unusual double aisles is 13th century. Local history museum housed in 15th-century Ayscoughfee Hall.

Springfields Gardens ❀ Bb
Tulips, narcissi, hyacinths, dahlias and roses in 25 acre gardens. Signposted trails weave through woodland scenery to lake and tropical hothouse.

Tattershall Castle ⚔ ⊛ Be
Mighty keep rises 110ft above flat countryside, built by Ralph, Lord Cromwell (1433-43) on site of an earlier castle. Tower has four storeys above basement, each with vast room and massive, carved fireplace. Adjoining 365 acres of parkland form Castle Leisure Park, with fishing, horse riding, pony trekking, nature walks and golf.

Whaplode ⚓ Cb
Splendid Marshland Church of St Mary, largely Norman. Remarkable 17th-century monument to Irby family with reclining effigies and kneeling children.

Whaplode St Catherine ⚓ Cb
Mechanised musical instruments in the Museum of Entertainment, Rutland Cottage, include early pianos, church organs, cinema organs and fairground barrel organs. Phonographs, gramophones and large collection of records from 1900 to 1950s.

Woodhall Spa ⊕ 🏛 ⓩ Af
Town with Victorian pump room built after discovery of medicinal waters in 1821. Remains of medieval hunting lodge near golf course. Unusual for Lincolnshire, this area has stretches of heather, pine and silver birch.

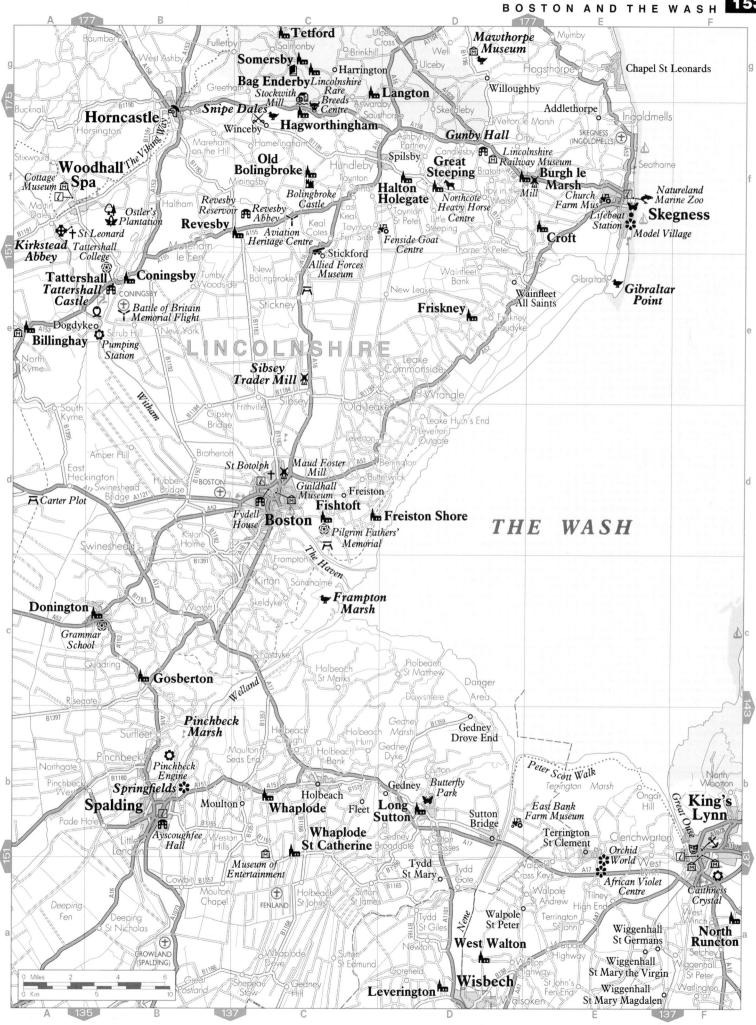

A 177 B C D 177 E F

Tetford
Somersby
Bag Enderby
Snipe Dales
Hagworthingham
Horncastle
Winceby
Harrington
Langton
Lincolnshire Rare Breeds Centre
Stockwith Mill
Mawthorpe Museum
Chapel St Leonards
Willoughby
Addlethorpe
Ingoldmells
SKEGNESS (INGOLDMELLS)
Seathorne

Woodhall Spa
Cottage Museum
The Viking Way
Ostler's Plantation
St Leonard
Revesby
Revesby Reservoir
Revesby Abbey
Old Bolingbroke
Bolingbroke Castle
Spilsby
Gunby Hall
Great Steeping
Halton Holegate
Northcote Heavy Horse Centre
Lincolnshire Railway Museum
Mill
Burgh le Marsh
Church Farm Mus
Natureland Marine Zoo
Skegness
Lifeboat Station
Model Village

Kirkstead Abbey
Tattershall College
Tattershall
Coningsby
Aviation Heritage Centre
CONINGSBY
Stickford
Allied Forces Museum
Fenside Goat Centre
Croft
Wainfleet All Saints
Gibraltar Point

Tattershall Castle
Dogdyke
Billinghay
Pumping Station
Battle of Britain Memorial Flight
New York
LINCOLNSHIRE
Scrub Hill
Friskney
Friskney Eaudyke
Leake Commonside

Sibsey Trader Mill
Witham
Sibsey
Wrangle
Old Leake

Carter Plot
East Heckington
Swineshead Bridge
Hubbert's Bridge
St Botolph
Maud Foster Mill
Guildhall Museum
Fydell House
Boston
Fishtoft
Freiston
Freiston Shore
Pilgrim Fathers' Memorial

THE WASH

Donington
Grammar School
Swineshead
Kirton Holme
The Haven
Kirton
Sandholme
Skeldyke
Frampton Marsh

Gosberton
Welland
Holbeach St Marks
Holbeach St Matthew
Danger Area
Duxmere

Pinchbeck Marsh
Pinchbeck Engine
Springfields
Spalding
Ayscoughfee Hall
Holbeach Clough
Moulton Seas End
Holbeach Bank
Gedney Dyke
Gedney Marsh
Long Sutton
Butterfly Park
Gedney Drove End
Peter Scott Walk
Terrington Marsh
East Bank Farm Museum
North Wootton
King's Lynn

Whaplode
Moulton
Fleet
Gedney
Sutton Bridge
Terrington St Clement
Clenchwarton
Orchid World
Whaplode St Catherine
Museum of Entertainment
Tydd St Mary
Tydd Gote
Sutton St James
Sutton Crosses
Walpole Cross Keys
West Lynn
African Violet Centre
Caithness Crystal

Cowbit
Moulton Chapel
FENLAND
Holbeach St Johns
Tydd St Giles
Walpole St Andrew
High End
Tilney High End
Walton Highway
Wiggenhall St Germans
North Runcton

Deeping Fen
Deeping St Nicholas
CROWLAND (SPALDING)
Great Postland
Shepeau Stow
Gedney Hill
Whaplode Drove
Sutton St Edmund
Gorefield
Newton
West Walton
Walpole St Peter
Terrington St John
Walsoken
Wiggenhall St Mary the Virgin
Wiggenhall St Mary Magdalen
St Peter
Watlington

Leverington
Wisbech

0 Miles 2 4 6
0 Km 5 10

A 135 B 137 C D E 137 F

OVER THE MENAI STRAIT

Thomas Telford's graceful suspension bridge, built in 1826, spans the narrow Menai Strait to join mainland Wales and Anglesey, an island of rugged cliffs, glorious beaches and charming stone-walled villages. To the south, the windswept Lleyn Peninsula thrusts into the Irish Sea, with an almost treeless landscape that is ablaze with the golden yellow of gorse in summer.

Aberdaron ⌂ Ba
Tiny fishing village of white-washed cottages embraced by thumb and forefinger of Lleyn Peninsula. Church of St Hywyn dates from 6th century. Offshore Bardsey Island said to be burial place of many holy men and of King Arthur's wizard, Merlin.

Abererch ⌂ Db
Loop of River Erch enfolds charming winner of many best-kept village awards. Medieval Church of St Cawrdraf has double nave. Nearby Pennarth Fawr is 15th and 16th-century house with heavy roof beams, large fireplace and flagstone floors.

Aberffraw ⌂ ✕ De
Village that was capital of North Wales from AD 870 until 13th century. Norman-style arch in Church of St Bueno said to come from destroyed palace of the Llywelyns. Packhorse bridge crosses River Fraw. Sandy beach backed by dunes.

Anglesey Sea Zoo ◔ Ee
Fascinating aquarium near village of Brynsiencyn. Walk-through tanks, wave tank, touch pools and rock pools. All under cover.

Bangor ✝ ♨ 🏛 Ff
University and cathedral city. Cathedral of St Deinol founded in 13th century and restored in 19th century. Carved oak figure, the Mostyn Christ, dates from 1518. Bishop's garden has collection of every plant mentioned in Bible. Museum of Welsh Antiquities.

Beaumaris 🏰 ✿ 🏛 Gf
Elegant little town dominated by last of Welsh castles built by Edward I in 13th century. Moated fortress whose outer wall boasts 16 towers. Courthouse and jail of 1614 has cells, workroom and preserved treadmill. Victorian toys and music boxes displayed in Museum of Childhood.

Betws Garmon ⌂ Fd
Village on route to Snowdonia National Park. River Gwyrfai cascades over rocks and under picturesque bridge.

Borth-y-Gest ⌂ Fb
Village tucked away in Glaslyn Estuary. According to legend, Prince Madog sailed from here to discover America, 300 years before Columbus. Trim cottages line seafront below towering crags of Moel-y-Gêst.

Bryn Brâs Castle 🏰 Fe
Mock medieval castle built in 1830s. Contains fine stained glass, carved furniture, massive slate fireplace. Extensive grounds with pools and flowering trees.

Bryn Celli Ddu ⎯ Ff
Stone Age burial mound, 4000 years old. Passage leads to 10ft long central chamber, with an upright stone, probably used for sacrificial rituals.

Caernarfon ⚓ 🏰 ✕ ⛴ Ee
Walled town of narrow streets lined with ancient houses, shops and inns. Battlements and towers of Edward I's 13th-century castle command entrance to Menai Strait. Audiovisual display in Eagle Tower tells castle's story. Nearby, remains of 'Segontium' Roman Fort and a museum.

Clynnog-fawr ⌂ Ec
Village of whitewashed cottages centred around church founded by 7th-century St Benno. Present church is 16th century; other saintly sites include St Benno's Chapel and Well.

Criccieth 🏰 Eb
Attractive resort where Liberal Prime Minister and great orator Lloyd George practised as a solicitor. Round towers and ruined walls of 13th-century castle crown the towering headland, dividing town's two beaches.

Holyhead Mountain ⎯ Ch
Highest point on Anglesey at 720ft, with views of the Isle of Man and mountains of Ireland. Evidence of early occupation at Caer y Twr, ancient hill-fort, and Cytiau'r Gwyddelod, where stone foundations of village date back some 1700 years.

Llanaelhaearn ⌂ Dc
Village set in pass between steep hills. Cottages cluster around church dedicated to 6th-century St Aelhaearn, with churchyard containing Celtic headstones and avenue of yews. Iron Age hill-fort crowns peak nearby.

Llanddwyn Bay De
Superb 4 mile stretch of sand backed by dunes. At western end is Llanddwyn Island, a nature reserve where shags and cormorants breed, connected to mainland by narrow neck of land.

Llaneilian ⌂ Eh
Village close to cliffs of Point Lynas and little bay of Porth Eilean. Lighthouse established in 1835. Church, 15th century, contains painted skeleton with motto 'Colyn Angan yw Pechod' – The Sting of Death is Sin.

Llanengan ⌂ Ca
Village church founded in 6th century by St Einion, King of Lleyn. Present church dates from 15th century with double nave and 16th-century tower. Close by is Porth Neigwl, sweeping bay of sand and hazardous rocky cliffs, known as Hell's Mouth.

OLD STATESMAN *Lloyd George mementos abound at Llanystumdwy.*

Llanystumdwy ⌂ ⚰ 🏛 Eb
Place of pilgrimage for admirers of David Lloyd George, Prime Minister of Britain 1916-21. Cottage where he lived as a boy is marked by slate plaque; nearby is a museum dedicated to him. Boulder on banks of River Dwyfor marks his burial place, from which he took the title 'Earl of Dwyfor.'

Moelfre ⌂ ⎯ Fg
Cottages cluster around shingle beach below rocky headland, infamous for being a danger to shipping. Scene of tragic shipwreck in 1859 when *Royal Charter* foundered on rocks.

Mynydd Bodafon ✳ Eg
Heather and bracken carpet a rocky ridge, rising steeply to 548ft. Panoramic views of Anglesey.

Mynydd Mawr ✳ Ba
Dramatic 525ft headland above sheer cliffs at end of Lleyn Peninsula. Views over Cardigan Bay and Bardsey Island, and inland of distant peaks of Snowdonia. Path leads down to St Mary's Well.

Newborough Warren ⌂ ☘ ⌖ ⛺ Ee
Vast wilderness of sand, marram-grass dunes and Forestry Commission plantations. Common birds include curlew, lapwing, oystercatcher and meadow pipit.

Penmon ◉ ✠ Gg
Ruined monastery buildings, dating from 12th, 13th and 16th centuries. Toll road leads to Black Point, with castellated lighthouse and old lifeboat station. Nearby Puffin Island is breeding ground for puffins.

Penrhyn Castle 🏰 🏛 Gf
Elaborate 19th-century mock-Gothic castle built for Pennant family who made fortune from slate. Slate everywhere – floors, fireplaces, staircase – even a slate bed. Houses doll museum, collection of industrial locomotives and variety of stuffed animals.

Plas Newydd 🏰 Fe
Splendid 16th-century mansion built for William Henry Paget, 1st Marquis of Anglesey, and one of Wellington's trusted commanders. Dining room has 58ft long painting full of whimsical references to large Paget family.

Plas-yn-rhiw 🏰 Ca
Late Tudor manor house with Georgian additions, restored to preserve bygone way of life. Gardens and traditional Welsh cottage.

Porthmadog ⚓ ✕ 🏛 Fb
Harbour town on the Glaslyn estuary from where slate was exported. Terminus of 1836 narrow-gauge Ffestiniog Railway; railway museum in harbour station. Maritime museum in old ketch, the *Garlandstone*.

Porth Trecastell ⎯ Df
Sheltered, sandy cove bordered by steep cliffs. Ancient burial chamber on headland with elaborate Stone Age wall carvings.

LITTLE ITALY *The Gloriette in Portmeirion resembles a ducal palace, but is merely a façade.*

Portmeirion ⌂ Fb
Fantasy village at end of peninsula, created by architect Clough Williams-Ellis in late 1920s. Italianate buildings and architectural oddments rescued from various parts of Britain, stand side by side among Mediterranean plants, fountains, statues and waterfalls. Waymarked walks through surrounding woodland.

Pwllheli Db
Seaside town with harbour and long sandy beach. Tall buildings with Victorian and Edwardian upper storeys line the narrow High Street. Georgian arcade and canopied shop fronts.

RAF Valley Df
Watch RAF at work from viewing enclosure beside airfield. Valley is advanced training school for jet pilots, also base for search-and-rescue helicopters and mountain rescue unit.

Red Wharf Bay Fg
Deep, curving bay with vast expanse of sand. Hamlet of cottages protected by sea wall. Walk to north passes limestone bulk of Castellmawr, with ancient fort.

Rhoscolyn ⌂ Cf
Village situated at southern end of Holy Island. Sandy bay, White Cove, and spectacular coastal

WELSH SEASCAPE *The slopes of Yr Eifl look out across Caernarfon Bay towards Anglesey on the horizon.*

...alks along cliffs to Rhoscolyn
...ead and ancient, sacred well of
...ynnon Gwenfaen.

...t Cwyfan's Church † De
...ttle church built 1300 years ago,
...stored 1893. Spectacular setting
...n a rock between two coves,
...orth Cwyfan and Porth China.
...eached by causeway at low tide.

...outh Stack ♥ ☀ Cg
...ocky island with towering cliffs
...eached by pedestrian suspension
...ridge. Puffins, razorbills, ful-
...ars and guillemots nest on
...dges. Lighthouse dates from
...809. Ellin's Tower, a Victorian
...ummerhouse, is RSPB centre and
...arting point for cliff walks. Fine
...iews of Snowdonia and the
...leyn Peninsula.

...raeth Lligwy Eg
...ide, spacious sandy beach
...ffers good swimming. Cliff-top
...alk south to Moelfre and trek
...orth to secluded beach at Traeth
...r Ora. Inland walk passes for-
...fied village of Din Lligwy, major
...oman settlement.

...raeth Penllech Cb
...ath beside stream leads to steep
...avine and sandy beach. Walks
...ver headland to rock, shingle
...nd sandy bay of Porth Ychain.

...r Eifl ☀☀ Dc
...riple mountain peaks crowned
...y hut circles and hill-fort of Tre'r
...Ceiri. Massive walls, 15ft thick,
...ncircle Iron Age fort and some
...50 stone-walled dwellings.

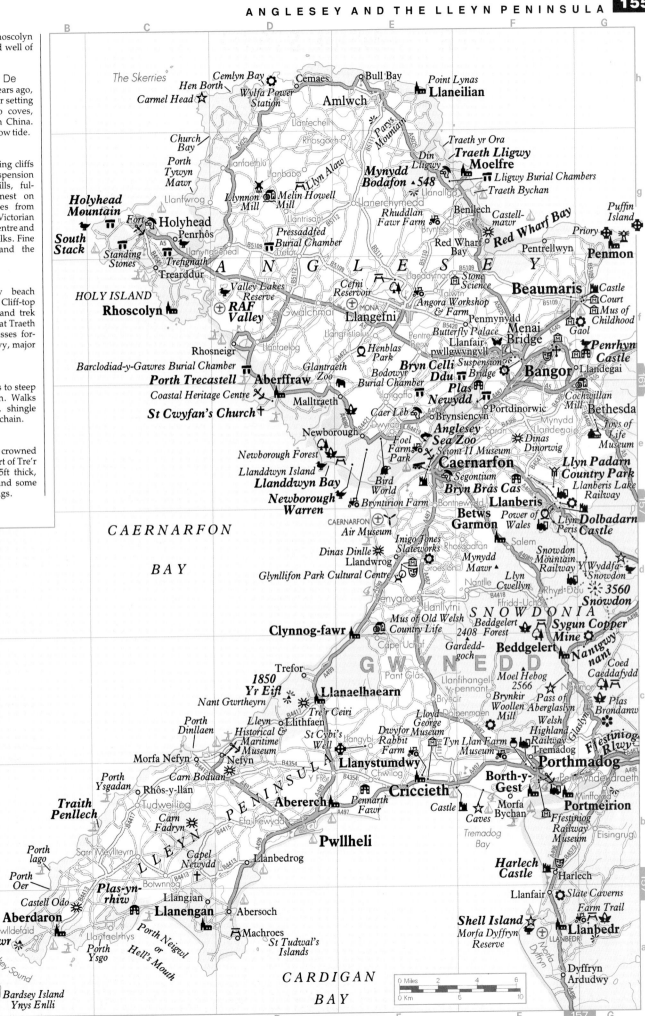

MOUNTAINS OF NORTH WALES

Craggy mountains, steep valleys and jewel-like lakes make up the Snowdonia National Park, whose chief attraction is Snowdon itself. This wild landscape is traversed by winding mountain roads and narrow-gauge railways, but it also has tranquil villages, castles built by Welsh princes who defied the invading English, and mines and quarries where slate, copper and gold were extracted.

Arthog ⚓♨☘ Cb
Small village of terraced houses on south bank of Mawddach estuary. Lakes, and Arthog Falls half a mile away. Good walks into foothills of Cadair Idris.

Bala Lake ⚓⛵ Fd
Largest natural lake in Wales, 4½ miles long, 1 mile wide and 150ft deep. Only home of trout-like *gwyniad* and site of legendary drowned palace. Lakeside steam railway runs between town of Bala and Llanuwchllyn.

Barmouth ⚓ Cb
Busy medieval port, now resort town with sandy beaches and esplanade, and cottages climbing hilly lanes at mouth of Mawddach estuary. The parish church is 13th century, with fine east window and inscribed stones dating from 5th century.

Beddgelert ⚓✿ Be
Riverside village in awe-inspiring mountain landscape between gorge-like Pass of Aberglaslyn, 2566ft Moel Hebog and Snowdon. Good walks abound.

Betws-y-Coed ⚓⛟🏛🌳 Df
Delightful village among conifer-clad crags above confluence of Conwy and Llugwy rivers. Historic bridges, waterfalls, beauty spots, salmon leaps and walks. National Park Visitor Centre.

SAFE PLACE *The name Betws-y-Coed means 'sanctuary in the wood'.*

Blaenau Ffestiniog ⚓✿🏛 De
Surrounding hills clad with vast piles of slate, still mined, with two sites open to public. Terminus of Ffestiniog Railway.

Bontddu ⚓✿ Cb
On edge of Dolgellau Gold Field abandoned early this century. Tramway bridge and remnant of ore-crushing mill remain.

Bwlch y Groes ✳ Fc
'Pass of the Cross', highest mountain road in Wales climbing 1709ft above shores of Llyn Vyrnwy.

Coed-y-Brenin Forest 🎣✿☆☘🌳 Dc
Waterfalls, shady valleys, woodlands, mountain views and 50 miles of forest trails. Wildlife includes buzzards, otters, polecats and fallow deer.

Cwm Bychan ♨ Cd
Lonely lake in centre of rocky amphitheatre. Nearby 'Roman Steps' were added in Middle Ages to ancient mountainside track. Steps climb through beautiful scenery to mountain pass.

WILD COUNTRY *A sweeping view down the Pass of Llanberis extends over glimmering lakes to distant Anglesey.*

Cwm Idwal Nature Trail ☆✿✿ Cf
Two-mile circuit of Llyn Idwal, surrounded by steep slabs of rock and glacier formations including cleft named 'Devil's Kitchen'.

Cymer Abbey ✚ Db
Arched windows and intricately crafted columns are among ruins of 12th-century Cistercian abbey, on river bank where Mawddach and Wnion meet.

Dinas-Mawddwy ⚓🏛 Eb
Attractive, single-street village overlooked by Arans mountains. Fishing, waterfalls. Meirion Wool Mill open to visitors. Brigands' Inn recalls outlaw gang who terrorised area in 11th century.

Dolbadarn Castle 🏰 Bf
Round keep stands among ruins of 12th-century castle, built to defend Llanberis Pass.

Dolgellau ✿ Db
Mighty Cadair Idris looms 2928ft above town on banks of River Wnion. Stone bridge dates from 1638, nave of 1716 St Mary's Church has four oak pillars. Gold was mined locally until 1966.

Dolwyddelan ⚓🏰 Df
Ancient village set among forests, rivers, lakes and mountains. Ruined 12th-century castle outside village has original keep and is said to be 1173 birthplace of Welsh prince Llywelyn the Great. Edward I probably built the western tower. Castle was partially restored in 19th century.

Ffestiniog Railway ⚓ Ce
Original 1860s locomotives and carriages cover 14 miles of captivating scenery on narrow-gauge tracks. Museum at Porthmadog terminus houses retired engines.

Gwydyr Forest 🎣☆🏛♨🌳 Df
Waymarked walks taking in Giant's Head precipice, Swallow Falls and view of Snowdonia at High Parc.

Harlech Castle 🏰 Bd
Largely intact, built in 13th century by Edward I. Formidable walls, towers and gatehouse rise 200ft on rocky spur above dunes. Besieged by Yorkists during Wars of the Roses, when eight-year struggle inspired song 'Men of Harlech'. Views of Snowdon range and Lleyn Peninsula from grey sandstone walls.

Llanbedr ⚓♨ Bc
Village between mountains and sea on swift-flowing Afon Artro. Craft centre outside village. Road through lichen-clad trees leads to jewel-like lake of Cwm Bychan.

Llanberis 🏰♨✿⚓♨ Bg
At foot of Snowdon, narrow-gauge mountain railway and easiest walk to summit. Slate terraces 2000ft high and museum recall the past of Dinorwic Quarry. Llanberis Lakeside Railway.

Llanfachreth ⚓ Dc
Start of 3 mile 'Precipice Walk' on ridge above 800ft drop, with superb views of Snowdonia.

Llechwedd Slate Caverns ✿ De
Journey back to slate-mining from 100 years ago. Vast caverns, 200ft high rock faces and steep tramway leading down to atmospheric underground lake.

Llyn Crafnant Reservoir Dg
Enchanting mile-long lake whose reflections merge with surrounding mountain slopes. Walks to Gwydyr Forest.

Llyn Padarn Country Park ♨✿⚓ Bg
Scenic lakeside railway, hillside oak wood and trail around workings and 50ft deep pool of disused slate quarry.

Maentwrog ⚓ Ce
Attractive alpine-like valley with cottages clinging to steep slope. Church with slate-clad spire and ancient yews.

Mawddach Estuary ✿ Cb
Swirling waters, sandbanks and wooded shoreline, flanked by smooth-sided mountains, form one of the loveliest of British estuaries. Bridge near river mouth gives memorable walk.

Nantgwynant Ce
Wooded valley with tranquil Gwynant and Dinas lakes. Start of Watkin Path's 3300ft climb to Snowdon's summit.

Pass of Llanberis ☆ Cf
Squeezed between Snowdon, Glyder Fawr and Y Garn, spectacular road snakes below vertical

cliffs to 1200ft. Watch climbers tackle Snowdon's ascents from streamside car park or walk to view them from Pyg Track.

Penmachno ⚓✿ Df
Oldest Christian gravestones in Wales, 5th or 6th century. Weaving demonstrations in 18th century woollen mill. Nearby is birthplace of Bishop William Morgan, first to translate Bible into Welsh in 1588.

Shell Island ☆✿ Bc
Sand-dune peninsula covered in more than 200 kinds of shells. Formed in last century when local landowner diverted river.

Snowdon ⚓❋ Cf
Highest mountain in England and Wales with 3560ft summit reached by numerous walks of varying difficulty and by railway from Llanberis. On a clear day, views from top extend to peaks of Lake District, and to Wicklow Mountains in Ireland. April offers good weather; some walkers ascend on September nights, when paths are lit by harvest moon, to watch sunrise from summit.

VINTAGE STEAM *Snowdon's rack-and-pinion system mountain railway still uses Victorian engines.*

Sygun Copper Mine ✿ Ce
Caverns with stalagmites and stalactites, where copper was mined until 1903, have been restored. Artefacts and audiovisual display in visitor centre.

Tomen-y-Mur ⚓ Dd
Site of 1st/2nd-century Roman fort with remains of amphitheatre, bath buildings, parade ground and burial mounds. Motte of early medieval castle stands inside outline of fort.

Torrent Walk Db
Spectacular riverside walk leads 1 mile past waterfalls along steep, wooded banks of the Clywedog.

Vale of Ffestiniog ☆ Ce
Mountain-framed valley is best seen from crag rising behind Ffestiniog church. Nearby, waters of Rhaeadr Cynfal plunge into 200ft ravine.

Ysbyty Ifan ⚓ Ee
Village set in valley, beside River Conwy. Church of St John the Baptist has mutilated effigy of what is said to be Rhys ap Meredydd, Henry Tudor's standard-bearer at 1485 Battle of Bosworth.

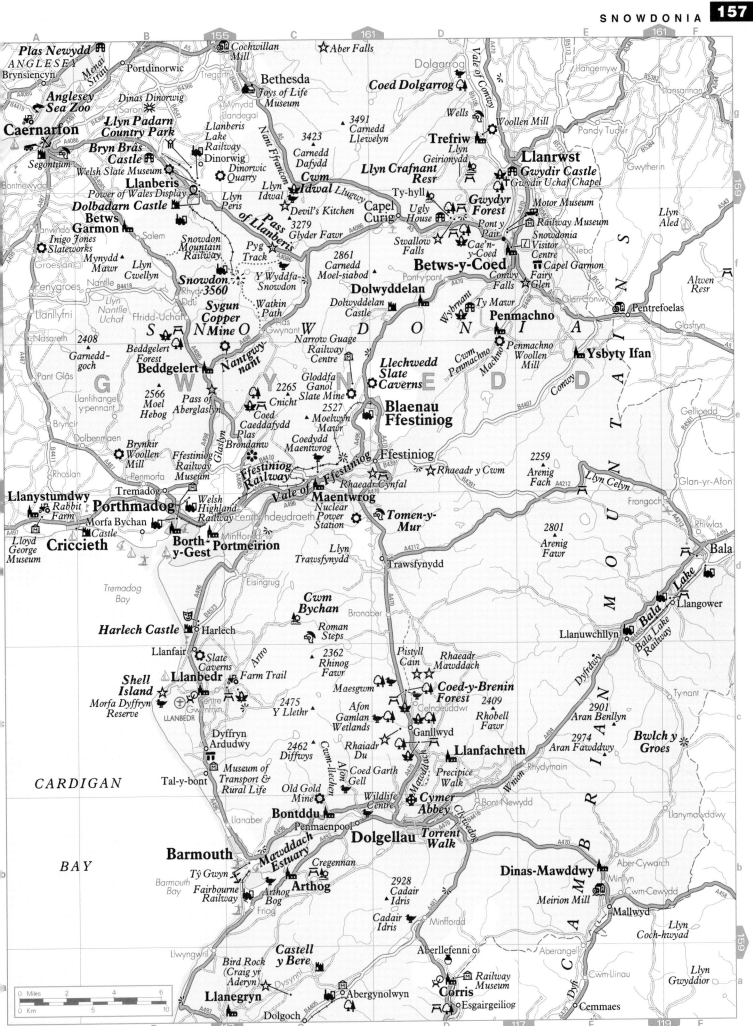

Bangor-is-y-coed ⌂ Ee
Bright little village of brick and sandstone buildings. Medieval five-arched bridge spans River Dee. Basket-making on village outskirts demonstrates traditional willow-weaving skills.

Breidden Hill ❊ Db
Wide-ranging views of Welsh hills and Shropshire plain from the summit, reached by footpath from Criggion. Monument to Admiral Lord Rodney, who routed a French fleet off Cape St Vincent, Dominica, in 1782.

Bwlchgwyn ⌂ 血 Df
Lofty village, one of the highest in Wales, looks across Wrexham to Cheshire. Geological Museum of North Wales contains 600 million-year-old rocks, slate quarry blast furnace, and winding gear from nearby Gresford colliery.

Ceiriog Valley ✿ Dd
Two graceful examples of 19th-century civil engineering: Thomas Telford's aqueduct completed in 1801, carrying Llangollen Canal 70ft above river, overlooked by impressive railway viaduct in use since 1848.

ARTISTRY IN IRON *Chirk Castle's intricate wrought-iron gates were made by two local Welsh brothers, Robert and John Davies.*

Chirk ⌂ 🏰 ⚘ ✿ Dd
Village set in woodland, mountain and river landscape. Nearby castle built by Edward I in late 13th century, still occupied; home of the Myddleton family since end of 16th century. Modernised in 1760s and extended in 1840s. Tapestries, portraits and furnishings on display. Elaborate 18th-century iron gates with ornamental faces lead to 460 acre wooded parkland. In grounds are traces of Offa's Dyke, 8th-century earthwork rampart.

Chwarel Wynne Mine ✿ Dd
Walk through 2½ miles of underground caverns to see how slate was mined and processed from 1750 until 1928. Film in museum tells history of slate industry in North Wales. Tools, photographs and documents displayed.

Clocaenog Forest ⚘ ⳩ ☑ ❊ Bf
Mixed woodland of 15,000 acres, replanted in 1930-4, on high moorland, enclosing Alwen and Llyn Brenig reservoirs. Waymarked walks lead from Bod Petruel Visitor Centre.

Corwen ⚘ ✝ Be
Market town on a stretch of the Dee, renowned for trout and salmon. Fine walks in conifer-clad Berwyn mountains. Partly 13th-century parish church with ivy-clad almshouses of 1750 in churchyard. Area has associations

with Owain Glyndwr; 15th-century hero who led Welsh in rebellion against Henry IV.

Cwm Hirnant ⚘ ⳩ Ad
Valley of dark forests and treeless moorlands threaded by crystal-clear stream. Road climbs 1600ft into Berwyn mountains and descends to Lake Vyrnwy.

Eliseg's Pillar ⳨ De
Ancient memorial stone to Eliseg, 9th-century chief of the house of Powys. Stands on burial mound of 5th or 6th-century chieftain.

Erbistock ⌂ Ee
Scattered hamlet, one of the most enchanting places on the Dee. Boat Inn, dating from the 16th century, clad with rambling roses. Ancient windlass recalls days when travellers were hauled across river in a small boat.

Erddig 🏰 ⳩ Ee
Superbly restored late 17th-century mansion recalls life in a self-contained community. Outbuildings include laundry, joiner's shop, bakehouse and smithy. Ornate furniture, Chinese wallpaper and portraits of faithful servants. Landscaped 150 acre park.

Horseshoe Falls ✿ Ce
Horseshoe-shaped falls across the Dee, man-made in 1801 to divert water to the Llangollen Canal. Reached by short walk along towpath.

Knockin ⌂ Ec
Attractive single-street village of brick, sandstone and timber-framed buildings. Streams at end of street spanned by two 18th-century bridges, each with an old sheep dip. Parish church of St Mary has Norman doorway and 19th-century yellow-brick belfry.

Lake Vyrnwy ⚘ ⳩ Ac
Man-made lake of 1881 when valley of River Vyrnwy was flooded to make a reservoir; superb example of Victorian ingenuity, built to supply water to Liverpool. Five miles long and half a mile wide, encircled by peaks and tall pines. Mock-Gothic tower at water's edge conceals start of 75 mile pipeline. Visitor centre in converted chapel.

Llanarmon-yn-Ial ⌂ Cf
Peaceful village in valley of River Alyn. Limestone cottages and whitewashed inn cluster around double-naved medieval church containing effigy of 14th-century hero Llywelyn ap Gruffydd.

Llanfyllin ⚘ Cb
Steep hills with woodlands and narrow lanes rise on every side of this quiet little town, at junction of Cain and Abel rivers.

Llangollen 🏰 ✿ ⳩ 血 De
Charming town on River Dee hosts Eisteddfod festival each July. Canal Museum devoted to 18th and 19th-century canal system; post-1920 vehicles in motor museum; horse-drawn boat rides along vale. On outskirts lived two 'Ladies of Llangollen', at Plas Newydd, 1780 to 1831.

LADIES' TOWN *Trim, red-brick gables look down on the tumbling River Dee at Llangollen, immortalised by the eccentric 'Ladies of Llangollen'.*

Llangollen Railway ⳩ De
Restored line, once part of Great Western Railway. Steam and diesel locomotives pull passenger trains 2 miles from Llangollen to Berwyn through Dee valley.

Llanyblodwel ⌂ Dc
Village scattered along stretch of River Tanat. Timber-framed buildings – among which is 16th-century Horseshoe Inn – contrast with curious Church of St Michael, rebuilt in 19th century by local vicar, John Parker.

ROMANTIC ENGINEERING *Mock-Gothic tower standing beside Lake Vyrnwy conceals water outlet.*

Llanymynech ⌂ ❊ ⳩ Dc
Limestone cliffs of abandoned quarry rise 500ft above this 'frontier' village; now part of Llanymynech Rocks Nature Reserve. English and Welsh border divides main street. Mock-Norman St Agatha's Church of 1845 has tower with clock face large enough to be seen by quarry workers. Afon Vyrnwy joins Severn nearby.

Llyn Brenig ⚘ ⚘ ⳩ ☑ Af
Reservoir of 919 acres in two valleys high on Mynydd Hiraethog. Visitor centre, nature and archaeological trails.

Long Mountain Da
Historic mount, 1338ft above meandering River Severn. Here Henry Tudor camped in 1485, before crossing border to defeat Richard III at Bosworth and take the English throne.

Meifod ⌂ Cb
Wooded hills shelter this ancient village, a mixture of ivy-clad and whitewashed buildings, many of them Georgian. Medieval church has pre-Norman burial slab and 19th-century stained glass.

Melverley ⌂ Eb
Remote hamlet with early 15th-century Church of St Peter. Timber-framed wattle-and-daub walls, oak beams, tiny tower, lichen-covered tiled roof, Elizabethan altar and Saxon font.

Old Oswestry Fort ❊ Dd
Hill-fort of about 250 BC, with ramparts and ditches covering 56 acres. Main entrance flanked by pits, probably for water storage.

Oswestry ✝ ⳩ ☑ Dc
Border town with several timber-framed houses lining main street: 17th-century Llwyd Mansion, Fox Inn, and Coach and Dogs. St Oswald's Church dates from the 13th century.

Pistyll Rhaeadr ☆ Bc
Highest waterfall in England and Wales. Waters of River Disgynfa cascade 240ft down mossy pine-flanked cliff and through natural arch into deep pool.

Pont-Cysyllte ✿ De
Awe-inspiring aqueduct, 1007ft long, carrying Shropshire Union Canal 120ft above the River Dee. Built between 1795 and 1805 by Thomas Telford.

Powis Castle 🏰 Da
Magnificent 17th-century mansion, began life as 1200 border fortress built of red limestone and known as Red Castle. William, third Baron Powis, who died in 1696, added towers, turrets, battlements and created formal gardens with terraces, statues and clipped yews. Interior contains fine furnishings and paintings.

Ruthin ⚘ ✝ ☑ Cf
Medieval, Tudor, Georgian, Regency and Victorian buildings rub shoulders in this colourful town. St Peter's Church of 1310 has carved oak roof, said to be gift of Henry VII. Fine half-timbered Elizabethan Nantelwyd House in Castle Street was once Assize judge's residence. Modern craft centre with 13 studios producing glass, leather, wood, ceramics, jewellery and textile goods.

Valle Crucis Abbey ✚ De
Roofless but otherwise substantial ruin on wooded slope beside Eglwyseg river. Founded 1201 for Cistercian monks, as second Cistercian abbey in Wales, by Madog ap Gruffyd Maelor, Prince of Powys. In Elizabethan times, following Dissolution of Monasteries by Henry VIII, east range adapted as dwelling house probably used until mid-17th century.

Welshpool 🏰 ⳩ 血 ☑ Da
Lively market town with medieval streets, where elegant Georgian houses mingle with black-and-white timber-framed buildings. Cockfighting cockpit restored to original condition. Waterways exhibition in Montgomery Canal Wharf. Welshpool and Llanfair Light Railway, built early 20th century, runs along restored 8 mile track.

Whittington ⌂ 🏰 Ed
Reputed home of Dick Whittington who left village in 1371 to seek fame and fortune in London. Ruined 13th-century castle with moat and gatehouse and remains of two towers.

World's End ⚑ De
Limestone crags tower above wooded Eglwyseg valley. Remote and beautiful spot with timber-framed, 16th-century manor house. Picnic on broad verges, paddle in rocky stream, and explore nature trail.

Wrexham ✝ 🏰 血 ☑ Ef
Industrial centre of North Wales and important market town. Weekly cattle market provides leather for tanning, town's oldest industry. Church of St Giles (1472) has 135ft steeple – one of the traditional 'Seven Wonders of Wales' – decorated with figures of saints and royalty.

The River Dee threads its way through the steep, wooded Vale of Llangollen, overlooked by mountain ranges with peaks more than 2000ft high. Northwards, the tortuous Horseshoe Pass climbs between Llantysilio Mountain and Eglwyseg Mountain towards the fertile Clwyd valley. To the east, the River Dee loops around Wrexham – market town and industrial capital of North Wales.

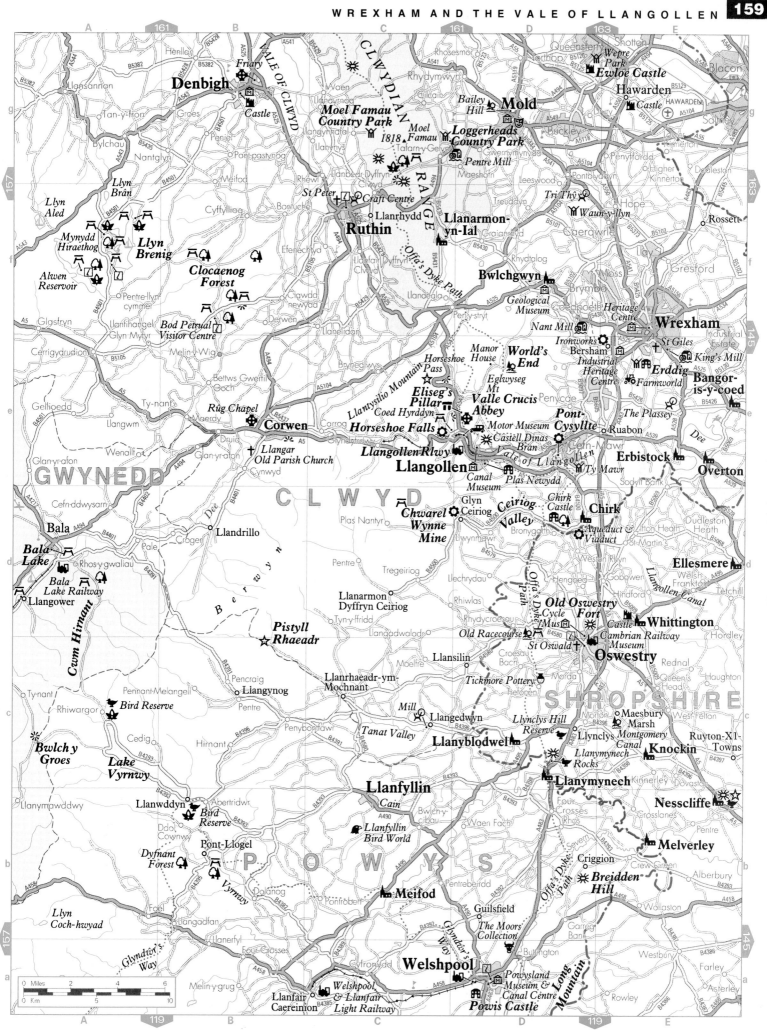

Denbigh
Castle
Friary

VALE OF CLWYD

Moel Famau Country Park
Moel Famau 1818

Loggerheads Country Park
Pentre Mill
Bailey Hill
Mold
Hawarden
Castle
Ewloe Castle
Wepre Park

Tri Thŷ
Waun-y-llyn

St Peter
Craft Centre
Ruthin
Llanrhydd
Llanarmon-yn-Ial

Llyn Bran
Llyn Aled

Mynydd Hiraethog
Llyn Brenig
Alwen Reservoir
Clocaenog Forest

Bwlchgwyn

Bod Petrual Visitor Centre

Geological Museum
Nant Mill
Ironworks
Bersham Industrial Heritage Centre
Heritage Centre
Wrexham
St Giles
Erddig
Farmworld
King's Mill

Manor House
World's End
Horseshoe Pass
Eliseg's Pillar
Eglwyseg Mt
Coed Hyrddyn
Valle Crucis Abbey
Pont-Cysyllte
The Plassey
Ruabon

Rûg Chapel
Corwen
Llangar Old Parish Church
Horseshoe Falls
Llangollen Rlwy
Llangollen
Motor Museum
Castell Dinas Brân
Vale of Llangollen
Ty Mawr
Erbistock
Overton
Canal Museum
Plas Newydd

Bangor-is-y-coed

GWYNEDD

C L W Y D

Bala
Bala Lake
Bala Lake Railway
Llangower

Llandrillo

Glyn Ceiriog
Chwarel Wynne Mine
Plas Nantyr
Ceiriog Valley
Chirk Castle
Chirk
Aqueduct & Viaduct

Ellesmere

B e r w y n

Pentre
Tregeiriog
Llanarmon Dyffryn Ceiriog
Tyn-y-ffridd

Offa's Dyke Path
Hengoed
Gobowen
Llangollen Canal

Cwm Hirnant

Pistyll Rhaeadr

Llansilin
Old Oswestry Fort
Cycle Mus
Castle
Cambrian Railway Museum
Whittington
St Oswald
Oswestry
Old Racecourse

Rhiwargor
Bird Reserve
Pennant-Melangell
Llangynog
Pentre
Llanrhaeadr-ym-Mochnant
Tickmore Pottery

Tyn-tant

Bwlch y Groes
Lake Vyrnwy

Mill
Llangedwyn
Tanat Valley
Llanyblodwel
Llynclys Hill Reserve
Llynclys
Montgomery Canal
Knockin
Ruyton-XI-Towns
Llanymynech Rocks
Llanymynech

S H R O P S H I R E

Llanwddyn
Bird Reserve
Pont-Llogel
Dyfnant Forest

Llanfyllin
Cain
Llanfyllin Bird World

Four Crosses
Nesscliffe
Melverley

Llyn Coch-hwyad

P O W Y S

Vyrnwy
Meifod
Guilsfield
Criggion
Breidden Hill

The Moors Collection

Glyndŵr's Way

Welshpool
Llanfair Caereinion
Welshpool & Llanfair Light Railway
Powysland Museum & Canal Centre
Powis Castle
Long Mountain

0 Miles 2 4 6
0 Km 5 10

Abergwyngregyn
 Ab

Village at mouth of valley and starting point for walks through nature reserve beside swirling waters of Rhaeadr-fawr river. Waterfall at head of valley plunges 120ft from high cliffs.

Bodelwyddan ☖🏛 Eb
Outstanding Victorian church and castle. Church has 202ft spire, ornate pinnacles, and interior decorated with 14 different kinds of marble. Turreted, battlemented castle contains National Portrait Gallery collection with over 200 portraits and photographs from the 19th century, including works by Hunt, Watts, and Sargent. The Williams Hall is authentically decorated in various Victorian styles. Furniture on loan from Victoria and Albert Museum. Magnificent gardens include maze.

Bodnant ✿ Cb
Splendid garden known for its Italianate terraces, lawns, lily ponds, shrubs and mature trees. Remarkable collection of rhododendrons. Garden created by the Aberconway family in years since 1875. Stunning views of Snowdonia from terraces.

Bodrhyddan Hall 🏛 Eb
Handsome, mainly 17th-century mansion. Superb display of 15th-century arms and armour and carved panels from Spanish Armada galleon. Egyptian collection includes ancient mummy, 3000 years old. Garden pavilion built by Inigo Jones in 1612.

Burton ☖✿ Hb
Half-timbered, thatched cottages mingle with Georgian brick houses in winding village street. Footpath to wooded hill with views across Dee estuary.

Bwlch y Ddeufaen ☆ Bb
Steep road to Pass of Ddeufaen hemmed in by boulder walls. Awe-inspiring scenery at pass: wild moorland and rocky gorse-covered slopes.

Coed Dolgarrog 🏞☆ Ba
Woodland of ancient oaks and alders, above gorge with precipitous crags. Nature reserve with multitude of badgers; permit needed to stray from the paths.

Colwyn Bay Cb
Seaside resort sharing 3 miles of sandy beach with Rhôs-on-Sea and Old Colwyn. Promenade with miniature railway. Overlooking bay at Eirias Park, amusements include Leisure Centre and Dinosaur World.

Conwy ☖🏛✿ Bb
One of the best-preserved medieval fortified towns in Britain, with battlemented walls, narrow gateways, and the frowning bulk of Edward I's great castle, built 1283-92. Three bridges: Telford's 1826 suspension bridge, Robert Stephenson's tubular railway bridge of 1848, and modern road bridge. Over 200 listed buildings. Aberconwy House dating from 1300; Elizabethan Plas Mawr, Jacobean and Georgian houses and rows of early Victorian terraces. A quayside cottage is said to be smallest house in Britain.

THE GREEN HILLS OF CLWYD

From the northern end of the Menai Strait to the estuary of the River Dee, the North Wales coast runs in long, sandy stretches broken only by the occasional headland, and punctuated by attractive seaside resorts. Across the Dee estuary the Wirral peninsula is a place of dramatic contrasts; green and peaceful until it spreads to the urban, industrial sprawl of Merseyside.

SPRING COLOUR *Daffodils make a thick carpet in the gardens of Bodnant – a series of terraces stepped into the hillside.*

Denbigh ☖🏛✿ Ea
Ancient market town on steep hillside overlooking the Vale of Clwyd. Medieval town walls are mostly intact. Castle, built 1282 by Edward I, stands 467ft above town on hill. Eight towers and gatehouse remain.

Dyserth ☖✳ Eb
Village at foot of Clwydian hills with waterfall tumbling 60ft down wooded, limestone cliff. Detour north to 500ft peak of Graig Fawr; footpath to summit with views along coast to the Great Orme.

Ellesmere Port 🏊 Ib
Port built by Thomas Telford, where Shropshire Union Canal met River Mersey, and now meets Manchester Ship Canal. Old warehouses and canal buildings house the Ellesmere Port Boat Museum: collection includes narrowboats, pumping engines and boatbuilder's workshop. Canal trips on horse-drawn narrowboat.

CANAL RELICS *Narrowboats lie in Ellesmere Port Boat Museum.*

Ewloe Castle ☖ Ga
Fortress hidden in deep, secluded valley of thick oaks. Begun by Llywelyn the Great about 1210 and completed about 1257 by Llywelyn the Last. D-shaped tower is typical of period.

Felin Isaf Water Mill 🏛 Cb
Superbly restored 17th-century mill tucked away in small valley. Most of machinery dates from

about 1730; mass of cogs, ropes, hatch doors, levers, hoppers and water wheels.

Flint ☖⚒ Gb
Former county town of Clwyd; superseded by Mold. First of a chain of medieval castles built by Edward I, standing on edge of sea. Detached keep was once surrounded by a moat. Much of castle destroyed during Civil War.

Great Ormes Head 🐐✿ Bc
Limestone headland rising 679ft from sea at Llandudno; noted for curly horned wild goats that scramble round rocks and grassland. Nature trail through heathland. Cliff ledges are nesting places for guillemots, razorbills and kittiwakes. Summit reached by car, by Britain's longest cable-car which travels 5320ft, or by a funicular railway built 1877. Splendid views of Snowdonia from the top.

Greenfield Valley Heritage Park ✿🏛 Fb
Park stretching from market town of Holywell down to ruins of historic Basingwerk Abbey by River Dee; founded 1132 by Cistercian monks. Wooded and lakeside walks, five reservoirs and nature trails. Collection of old farm tools and machinery in Abbey Farm Agricultural Museum.

Gwydir Castle ✝🏛 Ba
Romantic Tudor mansion, built 1555 and restored 1940s. Contains manorial courtroom and dungeons, long gallery with fine hammerbeams, and a secret room. Landscaped gardens contain cedars of Lebanon, planted to mark wedding of Charles I in 1625. Just up hill is 17th-century Gwydir Uchaf Chapel, with fine ceiling paintings of angels.

Heswall Gc
Coastal village with winding streets and lanes leading down to foreshore. Miles of saltings on Dee estuary. Four-mile walk along foreshore to West Kirby.

Llandudno 🏛♨☑ Bc
Major Welsh holiday resort in bay flanked by Great Ormes Head and Little Ormes Head. Wide promenade, pier and two beaches. Doll Museum contains over a thousand items, from 16th century to

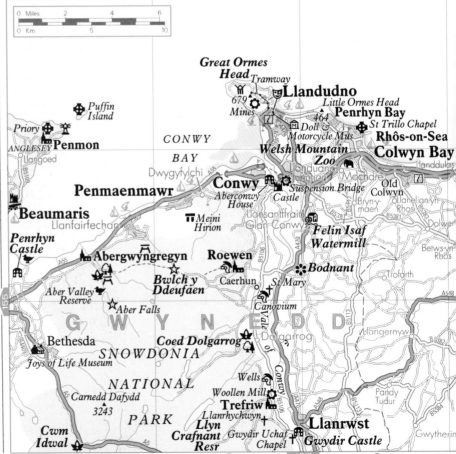

present day, and scale model working railway. Water-skiing, sailing and fishing trips from jetty.

Llanfair Talhaiarn 🏠 Db
Steep hills and hidden valleys enfold dark stone village beside River Elwy. Small square overlooked by church whose origins go back to the 6th century. Because hillside is so steep, one corner of churchyard is on same level as nearby cottage chimney.

Llanrwst Ba
Elegant, 17th-century, three-arched bridge, attributed to Inigo Jones, spans River Conwy in this old market town. Late 15th-century church has magnificent rood screen, and stone coffin said to be that of Llywelyn the Great.

Loggerheads Country Park 🏠 Fa
Peaceful 70 acres of parkland bordered by River Alyn, below conifer-clad slopes of Moel Famau. Pentre Water Mill (19th century) still grinds corn. Abundant bird life includes chiffchaffs, treecreepers, pied flycatchers, skylarks and kingfishers.

Moel Famau Country Park 🏠 Fa
Footpath through woodlands of 2000 acre park leads to 1818ft summit of Moel Famau. Views of Snowdonia, Isle of Man and Pennines. Slopes often hunting grounds of kestrels and buzzards.

Mold 🏰 Ga
County town of Clwyd and busy market town. Interesting features are the High Street's picturesque buildings, and the 15th-century church with animal fresco.

Ness Gardens ❀ Hb
Fine botanic garden run by Liverpool University, on the Wirral peninsula above the Dee. Sweeping lawns, rock, rose and water gardens. Includes outstanding collection of heathers.

Parkgate ⚓ Gb
Village with promenade and old harbour wall overlooking acres of salt marsh; feeding ground for countless birds. Fine views across Dee estuary to mountains of North Wales.

Penmaenmawr ⛏ Bb
William Gladstone often visited this largely Victorian coastal resort, squeezed between mountains and sea. Historic trail leads to hill-top site of Stone Age flint works, 1200ft above town. Views across beach to private Puffin Island, where puffins breed.

Penrhyn Bay Cc
Long, sweeping, sand-and-shingle beach below Little Ormes Head, with sand and rock pools. Walk to 464ft summit for spectacular views.

Point of Ayr ⚓ Fc
Bird reserve of wide sands, mud flats and shingle banks on the Dee estuary. Birds include dunlins, knots and redshanks.

Port Sunlight 🏠🏛 Hc
Victorian soap maker, William Hesketh Lever, founded Port Sunlight factory in 1888 and created this 130 acre garden village for his workers. Centrepiece is classical Renaissance building housing Lady Lever Art Gallery, with outstanding English 18th-century paintings and furniture.

SOAP MAKER'S CREATION *The Dell is one of the delights of William Lever's village of Port Sunlight.*

Prestatyn 🏰 Ec
Popular holiday resort. Central mound of 12th-century castle stands in town centre. Nature trail over hillsides to south of town, where Offa's Dyke Path begins.

Rhôs-on-Sea ⛪ Cc
Pleasant resort at western end of Colwyn Bay sands. Splendid view along coast towards Rhyl. Close to promenade is tiny, stone-built chapel dedicated to St Trillo; only 12ft long and 6ft wide, built in 16th century by same monks who made ingenious fish trap on sands, an enclosure of triangular stone walls, still visible at low tide.

Rhuddlan 🏰🚂 Eb
Massive walls and twin gatehouses of ruined 13th-century castle tower majestically over River Clwyd. One of 15 fortresses built throughout Wales by Edward I, famous for military architecture; exhibition inside. Village has 14th-century church and 16th-century bridge.

Rhyl 🏰🚂 Ec
Brash and breezy resort. Funfairs, boating pools, miniature railway, Butterfly Jungle and Ocean World. Sandy beach and fishing-trip boats in the harbour.

Roewen 🏠🚶 Bb
Romans came here in 1st century AD and drove roads across hills and moors. West of village, Roman road climbs to 1400ft and crosses mountains and moorland scattered with ancient burial chambers and standing stones.

St Asaph 🏠✝ Eb
Britain's smallest cathedral stands on hill beside River Elwy, founded AD 560 by St Kentigern, and rebuilt late 15th century. Village has 14th-century parish church and 17th-century coaching inn. Riverside walks.

Shotwick 🏠 Hb
Village with remote Church of St Michael, mainly 14th-century. Norman doorway, three-decker pulpit, box pews and church-warden's seat of 1673.

Thurstaston 🏠✳ Gc
Hamlet centred on church, hall and several farms. Thurstaston Hill is wilderness of sandstone rocks and sandy trails with fine views across the Dee estuary; perfect for picnics. On top is Thor's Stone, 25ft high pinnacle of weathered red sandstone.

Trefriw 🏠🚶 Ba
Hillside village once popular as Victorian spa. Wells, about 1½ miles north, have old bathhouse and pump room. Church of St Mary founded by Llywelyn the Great early in 13th century. The Trefriw Woollen Mill demonstrates traditional spinning and weaving methods.

Welsh Mountain Zoo 🐾 Cb
Animals and plants from all over the world in splendid mountain setting, 500ft above sea level. Watch feeding of sea lions and free-flying eagle displays. 'Chimp Encounter' features audiovisual display with robot chimpanzees. Breeding programme involves endangered species such as American bald eagle, European otter and Persian leopard.

Wirral Country Park 🏠 Gc
Interesting mixture of tree-covered embankments, cliffs, ponds and mud flats. Wilderness around an abandoned railway encourages wild plants, foxes, badgers and wading birds. Views across River Dee to Welsh hills.

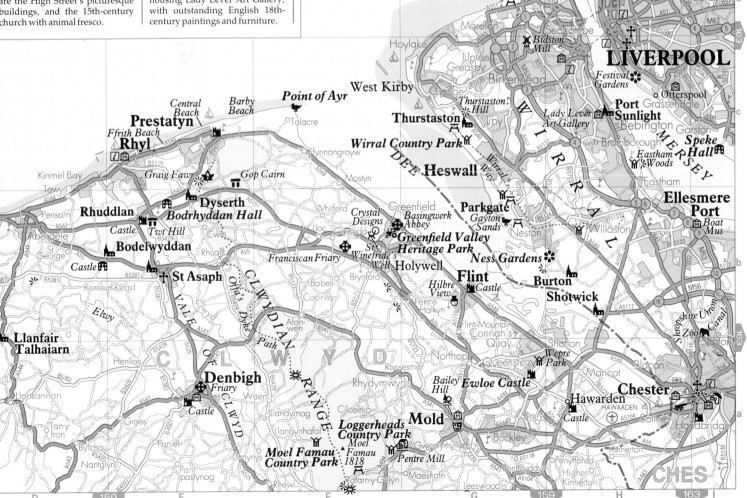

Ainsdale ☙ Bg
Wide variety of animals and plants, including rare natterjack toads and sand lizards, live among Ainsdale dunes. National nature reserve in dunes has 6 miles of marked footpaths.

Aughton ⌂ Bf
Village dominated by St Michael's Church – Norman with later medieval work. Font dates from 15th century. In churchyard stands 1736 sundial. Opposite church is Aughton Old Hall.

Beacon Country Park ❋ ☙ Df
Walk to top of Ashurst's Beacon allows views of Blackpool Tower, Lakeland hills, Welsh mountains and Lancashire Pennines. Visitor centre in park is starting point of many trails leading to picnic sites.

HILL CASTLE *Beeston Castle was built in 1220 by the Earl of Chester.*

Beeston ⌂ 🏰 ⚔ Da
Houses and timber-frame cottages dominated by ruins of castle on Beeston Hill, where party of Royalists held out for six months after Charles I had been defeated in 1645. Museum on site has displays telling stories of castle.

Bootle ✿ Be
Long line of docks, behind massive wall, stretching along Mersey river; built between 1824 and 1860. Many of them still in use.

ACROSS THE CHESHIRE PLAIN

The stark industrial areas of Merseyside towns such as Runcorn and Warrington contrast sharply with the charms of the old, walled town of Chester and the picturesque villages that dot Cheshire's countryside. Iron Age forts, Roman ruins, medieval churches, Tudor cottages and elegant Georgian and Victorian homes are among the many attractive sights to be seen in this historic area.

Brown Knowl ⌂ ❋ Ca
Iron Age hill-fort of Maiden Castle, south of village, is protected by two banks with shallow ditch between to south-east, and by steep slopes on all other sides. Walk from village to castle rewarded with views across Wales and Shropshire.

Bunbury ⌂ 🚢 Da
Village of cottages ranging from timber-framed Tudor to Georgian brick. Church of St Boniface from 14th and 15th centuries – collection of carved alabaster and stone effigies inside. Bunbury Locks on Chester Canal built in 1770s.

Castle Ditches ❋ Db
Iron Age earthworks enclosing the whole 11 acre summit of Eddisbury Hill.

Cheshire Workshops ✍ Da
Ancient art of hand-sculpting candles can be seen here. Wax figurines and wall plaques, as well as wooden name plaques and candle-holders made here. Film explaining candle-making processes shown, and shop sells items from the workshops.

Chester
✝ ⚔ ⌂ 🏰 ✝ ✿ 🚗 ⚓ 🅿 Cb
Town is ringed by medieval walls with Roman and Saxon fragments – walk along them gives views of the city. Eastgate, on site of Roman east gate, rebuilt in 1769 – clock added to celebrate Queen Victoria's Diamond Jubilee in 1897. King Charles Tower – reputed to be place from which Charles I watched defeat of his troops at Battle of Rowton Moor in 1645 – now contains displays of Civil War. Chester Visitor Centre has reconstruction of street in 1850s. Video takes visitors on armchair tour of city and shows history and customs. Opposite centre is site of Roman amphitheatre. Roman archaeological finds, as well as displays on local history, can be seen at Grosvenor Museum. The Rows are two-tier shopping arcades dating from medieval and Victorian times. Cathedral originally built in 10th century as church to house Shrine of St Werburgh, and turned into Benedictine abbey in 1092. Became cathedral in 1541. Part of St Werburgh's Shrine in Lady Chapel; carved 14th-century stalls in choir. Grotesque figure known as Chester Imp in north clerestory of nave. Norman Church of St John the Baptist stands in St John Street. Bishop Lloyd's house in Watergate Street has carvings of Biblical scenes and animals on front. Agricola's Tower on southwest corner of town wall all that remains of Norman castle. Military Museum gives history of regiments historically based in Cheshire. Toy Museum has 5000 items dating from 1830 to present day. Chester Zoo has animals in most natural surroundings possible – tropical house has trees up to 40ft, snakes, lizards and birds.

Crosby Be
Georgian Crosby Hall stands beside old smithy and 17th-century cottages. Regency houses

RIVER CROSSING *Passenger ferries provide an important link across the Mersey, and also fine waterfront views.*

KING'S CORNER *King Charles Tower in Chester's city wall now houses a Civil War museum.*

with wrought-iron balconies and verandahs from time when Crosby was popular seaside resort. Wayside cross marking resting place stands on road along which coffins were carried.

Croxteth Hall 🏰 ☙ Ce
Furnished rooms and costumed figures depict Edwardian house party in 16th-century house. The country park includes walled garden, home farm with livestock, miniature railway, walks and picnic places.

Delamere Forest ⚹ ⅋ 🅿 Dc
Once royal hunting preserve of Earls of Chester – visitor centre has displays of Delamere's history. Forest walks through area, now mostly planted with conifers – noted for kestrels, sparrowhawks, foxes and badgers.

Formby Bf
Norman font in Church of St Luke and cross in churchyard which used to stand on village green are all that remain of old Formby. Town separated from its beach by over a mile of dunes.

Formby Point ☙ Af
Dune reserve and stronghold of rare natterjack toad. Plants include rarities such as dune helleborine and grass of Parnassus. Also red squirrel reserve.

Frodsham ✝ ❋ Dc
Old town with thatched black-and-white cottages and Georgian and Victorian houses. St Laurence's Church dates from 12th century, Old Cottage from 1580, and Bear's Paw Inn from 1632. Extensive views from war memorial near Mersey View Club.

Haigh Country Park ☙ Ef
Park with rambles in woods, ride on miniature railway, miniature zoo, and model village.

Hale ⌂ Cd
Disused lighthouse stands at Hale Head, overlooking mud flats and rock-strewn sand. Southern

façade of now-ruined Hale Hall redesigned by John Nash. Sign of village inn commemorates John Middleton – reputed to be 9ft 3in tall – who defeated James I's champion in wrestling match in 17th century.

Halsall ⌂ Bg
Church of St Cuthbert one of best 14th-century churches in Lancashire. Fifteenth-century octagonal tower with spire and square base. Medieval doorway has original oak door with ornate top.

Helsby ⌂ ❋ Cc
Helsby Hill offers views of surrounding areas. Iron Age hill-fort near summit.

Holt ⌂ ⚔ Ca
Remains of Holt Castle – built by Edward I in 13th century to protect crossing of River Dee – 500-year-old, eight-arch bridge, and church dating from 13th century with elaborate font.

Knowsley Safari Park ✯ Ce
Combination zoo and park with lions, tigers, elephants, rhinos, zebras, camels, wallabies and bison among the many animals.

Little Budworth ⌂ ☙ Eb
Village with old water mill, sandstone Church of St Peter, and almshouses. Paths in nearby country park lead through landscape almost untouched by man – heaths covered by heather, gorse and bracken; bogs with islands of sphagnum moss. Woods of birch trees are noted for their fungi, insects and birds.

Newton-le-Willows ✿ De
Nine-arched Sankey Brook Viaduct – part of the Liverpool-Manchester Railway, opened 1830 – crosses St Helens Canal, opened 1759. First major viaduct built purposely to carry a railway.

Norton Priory Museum 🏛 Dd
Museum on site of remains explains story of priory dating from 12th century, which was turned into Tudor house in 1545 and Georgian mansion in about 1750. Displays show what three buildings looked like and give insight into everyday life of Augustinian canons. Sixteen acres of woodland and gardens include glade with stream and pool, and Victorian rock garden.

Ormskirk ✝ ✿ Cf
Perpendicular Church of St Peter and St Paul had second tower added in 1540 to house bells of Burscough Priory. Inside church, 16th-century Derby chapel houses two coffins of 7th Earl of Derby – beheaded after Civil War for being Royalist. Body in short coffin, head in casket next to it. Ruins of 13th-century Burscough Priory can be seen 2 miles north-east of town. Neo-Gothic Scarisbrick Hall, 3 miles north-west of town, is now school and not open to public. Clock tower erected by Earl of Derby in 1876 stands in shopping precinct.

Parbold ⌂ ❋ Cg
Views of surrounding countryside can be seen from 394ft high Parbold Beacon. Humpback

bridge crosses Leeds and Liverpool Canal next to stump of tower windmill and mill house in Parbold village.

Prescot 🏛 Ce
Prescot Museum of Clock and Watch-making, in 18th-century house, recalls time when area was internationally famous for watch-making. Displays illustrate history of timekeeping and show something of Lancashire clock workers' lives.

Runcorn 🏛 ☑ Dd
Old part of town almost encircled by two canals; Bridgewater Canal built in mid-18th century and Manchester Ship Canal built 150 years later.

St Helens 🏛 De
Pilkington Glass Museum illustrates history of glass-making from Ancient Egypt to today.

Sefton ⛪ Bf
Sixteenth-century Church of St Helen has 14th-century spire. Interior famous for carved wooden fittings. Medieval stained glass in windows; mail-clad effigy c. 1296; 16th-century brasses; and 'Treacle Bible' with mistranslations, corrected in Authorised Version of 1611.

Speke Hall 🏠 Cd
One of the best-preserved half-timbered houses in Britain, built between 1490 and 1612. In cobbled courtyard stand two yew trees over 400 years old.

Standish Dg
Mostly 16th-century St Wilfred's Church has Victorian steeple, Elizabethan pulpit, and two-storey porch. Stocks and town cross stand in square.

Stretton Mill 🏚 Ca
Mill, which belonged to Leche family between 1596 and 1970, now a working museum.

Tarporley ⛪ Db
Tiny village with 1585 Old Manor House, Georgian and Victorian homes, and medieval Church of St Helen which was largely rebuilt in 19th century.

Warrington 🏛 ☑ Ed
Warrington Museum and Art Gallery depicts local history from prehistoric times to present day with displays including Roman items and 18th and 19th-century glass-ware. Over 1000 paintings. Geology and wildlife also covered.

Widnes 🏛 ☑ Dd
The Halton Chemical Industry Museum explains industry's history with photographs, slide shows, life-size reconstructions and working machines. Railway skirts town on tall stone viaduct. Victoria Promenade offers views of River Mersey and bridges.

Wigan Pier ✿ Df
Restored coal-loading pier on canal to Liverpool, immortalised in George Orwell's novel *The Road to Wigan Pier*, has five renovated warehouses, educational centre and exhibition on Wigan in early 1900s. Waterbus goes to old cotton mill with world's largest working mill engine.

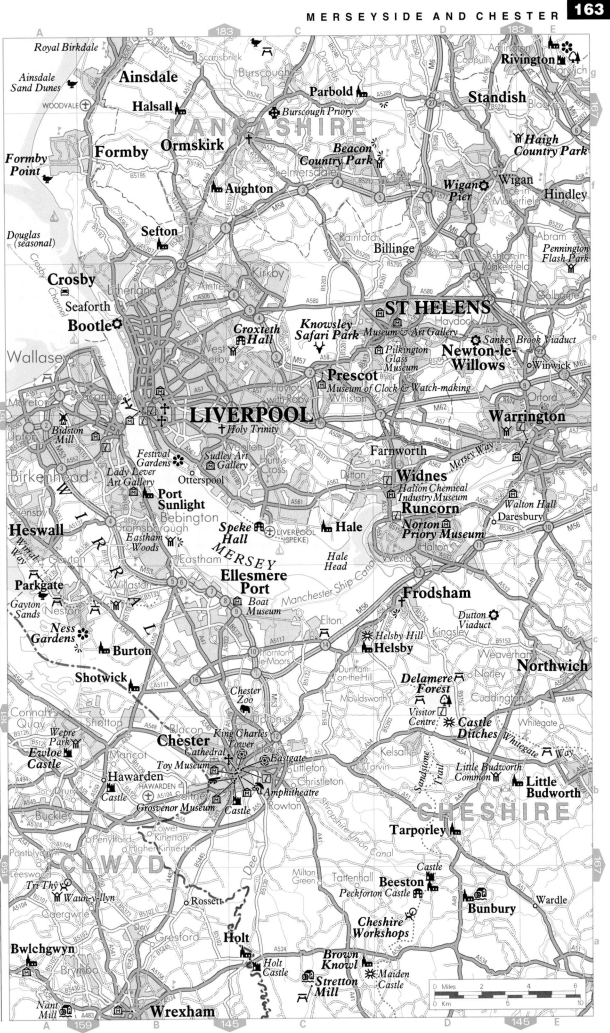

VIGOROUS CITY ON THE MERSEY

People flocked to Liverpool long before the Beatles emerged from The Cavern in the swinging Sixties. Having grown from a sailing village to a prosperous port, millions of emigrants used Albert Docks as a gateway to far-off lands. Today the mighty steamships have gone, but the new dock complex ensures that the perch of the Liver Birds – symbols of the city – remains the heart of Merseyside.

Albert Dock ⚓ 🏛 Ab
Opened in 1846 as England's gateway to New World, Albert Dock is largest group of Grade 1 listed buildings in Great Britain. It fell into disuse but has now been revamped into quayside complex featuring water sports and museums. Alongside Animation World, The Beatles Story, Maritime Museum and Tate Gallery are a number of speciality shops and restaurants.

STILL WATERS *The Spanish brig Maria Asumpta, built in 1858 and now the oldest seagoing sailing ship in the world, calmly sits under Pier Head in Albert Dock – a complex of museums, galleries and Beatles' memorabilia.*

and Hardy appeared here soon after it was opened. Now stages ballet, opera, drama, musicals and concerts.

Liverpool Museum 🏛 Cd
Wide variety of exhibits ranging from dinosaurs to space exploration in museum housing military and transport galleries, planetarium, aquarium and natural history room.

Liverpool Playhouse 🎭 Bc
Britain's oldest working repertory theatre, staging diverse range of shows from popular theatre to Elizabethan drama. Studio produces work by local writers.

Merseyside Maritime Museum ⚓ Ab
Floating exhibits, working displays and craft demonstrations focusing on Liverpool's history of emigration and shipbuilding.

Metropolitan Cathedral of Christ the King ✝ Dc
Unusual Roman Catholic cathedral topped with spiked lantern tower containing 25,000 pieces of stained glass designed by John

Piper and Patrick Reyntiens. Cathedral finally completed in 1960s after three attempts: in 1853 Edwin Welby Pugin designed a cathedral but only Lady Chapel was built. World War II interrupted Sir Edward Lutyen's vast classical domed building, later abandoned because of high cost. In 1959 Archbishop Heenan asked for designs for new cathedral and Sir Fredrick Gibberd's was chosen from 300 entries. Interior contains white marble altar, which stands in centre of large circular nave from which 13 chapels radiate.

Municipal Buildings Bc
Buildings dating from 1866 are supported by massive sandstone pillars, each with different type of carved foliage. Square tower has four clock faces.

Neptune Theatre 🎭 Cc
Traditional proscenium arch civic theatre, built in 1910, offering amateur, professional and children's productions including drama, musicals, opera, variety and puppetry.

Philharmonic Hall Db
The home of the Royal Liverpool Philharmonic Orchestra, rebuilt after 1933 fire destroyed original 1840s building.

Pier Head Ac
Wide, open areas with good views of passing ships are dominated by office-block trio of the Port of Liverpool, Cunard and Royal Liver Building. All were built during Liverpool's Golden Age in early 1900s. Take a passenger ferry for best view of waterfront.

Animation World Ab
Popular cartoon characters such as Danger Mouse, Count Duckula, Big Friendly Giant and characters from Kenneth Grahame's *The Wind in the Willows* are brought to life through series of moving and stationary exhibits. Behind-the-scenes displays of puppetry, model-making, and costume and set design.

Beatles and City Tours, Tourism Board Cc
Details of walking trails around the city centre and bus tours taking in such sights as homes of the band members, Strawberry Field and Penny Lane.

The Beatles Story Ab
Walk-through sight and sound experience following the fab four from childhood to Beatlemania, Flower Power and beyond. Includes reconstructions of The Cavern Club, Abbey Road recording studios and Yellow Submarine. Lies within Albert Dock.

Bluecoat Chambers Bc
Fine Queen Anne building, dating from 1717, with cobbled quadrangle and old garden courtyard. Now houses city's art centre with its own gallery.

Brown, Picton and Hornby Libraries Cd
Permanent exhibitions include rare books and works of art, as well as documents autographed by such notables as Elizabeth I, Nelson and Napoleon.

The Cavern Club Bc
Opened in 1957 as jazz club. The Beatles made their first of 300 performances here in February 1961 and became resident band. Last performance in October 1963, by which time they had become national stars. The Cavern was originally a cellar beneath warehouses in Mathew Street, once centre of Liverpool's fruit market. Demolished in 1973 and used as car park. The second Cavern Club was built in 1984 on site of first, using original bricks. Now live music venue and major tourist attraction, club lies beneath Cavern Walks, shopping centre in Mathew Street.

Church of Our Lady and St Nicholas ✝ Ac
Built in 1360 as city's first parish church, known as 'the Sailors' Church' – but largely rebuilt after World War II. Lantern spire, dating from 1815, still stands, topped with ship weather vane.

Derby Square Bc
The site of the 1230s Liverpool Castle, now marked by the domed Queen Victoria Monument.

Everyman Theatre 🎭 Db
Occupies site of Hope Hall, chapel built in 1837, transformed into music hall, cinema and opened as theatre in 1964.

Exchange Flags Ac
The four naked and chained figures of 1813 Nelson Memorial overlook the former exchange

used by merchants dealing in cotton brought across the Atlantic from the southern states of USA.

The Famous Mersey Ferries Ac
Beautifully restored boats from Europe's oldest ferry service provide the best view of the city's 7 miles of waterfront. Cruises depart hourly.

FAITH IN STONE *The spectacular, ultramodern Metropolitan Cathedral of Christ the King.*

Liverpool Cathedral ✝ Da
Foundation stone of this Anglican cathedral was laid in 1904 by King Edward VII, but building interrupted by two world wars and not completed until 1978. Designed by Sir Giles Gilbert Scott and built in Gothic style from red sandstone, it measures 671ft in length with 330ft tower. Largest cathedral in Britain, containing world's largest church organ.

Liverpool Empire 🎭 Cd
England's largest provincial theatre seating 2340, built in the 1920s as a variety theatre. Laurel

---

THE VIEW INSIDE *The magnificent interior of the Metropolitan Cathedral of Christ the King, with its white marble altar and stained-glass lantern tower.*

Port of Liverpool Building Ac
Building topped by green, lantern-crowned dome and dolphins supporting globes. Marble entrance hall is laid out as compass with surrounding gallery inscribed with text from ship-related psalm.

Queensway (Birkenhead Road) Tunnel Bd
Opened in the 1930s, tunnel passes under the River Mersey from area around the Royal Liver Building to Birkenhead on the other side. Allow around 1½ hours to drive through tunnel during rush hour. Known locally as 'Mersey Tunnel'. Farther from the city centre is another tunnel with same nickname – the Wallasey (King's) Tunnel, opened in early 1970s.

Riverside Walk Aa
Walk offers sights of Mersey ferries, shipyard cranes at Birkenhead and one of the finest urban views in Britain – city climbing up towards Liverpool Cathedral and Metropolitan Cathedral of Christ the King.

Rodney Street Db
Leading away from Liverpool Cathedral is one of the finest groups of Georgian houses in northern England, including 1809 birthplace of former prime minister William Gladstone.

Royal Insurance Building Bc
Built as the company's headquarters from 1896-1903, its tower has a gold sundial on the wall, gilded cupola and panels symbolising aspects of insurance.

PAST THE PORT *A tug sails along the River Mersey; in the background is the Royal Liver Building.*

Royal Liver Building Ac
Built in 1911, Liverpool's famous landmark has twin 300ft towers topped by statues of mythical Liver Birds from which city is said to have taken its name. City's symbol of two birds, probably cormorants holding seaweed – or laver – in their beaks, perch on twin towers. Building also has Britain's largest clock.

St George's Hall Cd
Imposing Greco-Roman building encased in 16 Corinthian columns, each about 60ft high, opened in 1854. Great Hall features pink marble, gold-leaf ceiling and mosaic-effect floor. Designed by Lonsdale Elmes, who was 24 years old when

NEW WORLDS *Exhibits in the Maritime Museum recall that between 1830 and 1930, 9 million Europeans emigrated to America through Liverpool.*

foundation stone was laid in 1838. Finished in 1854, seven years after his death. The columned portico is approached from Lime Street.

Tate Gallery Ab
Only English gallery devoted to modern works, sharing with its London counterpart the National Collection of 20th Century Art.

Titanic Monument Ac
This memorial to engine-room staff of the Liverpool ship now commemorates all engineers lost at sea since it sank in 1912 with the loss of more than 1500 lives.

Town Hall Ac
Home of Lord Mayor of Liverpool, topped by statue of Minerva by Felix Rossi and fronted by Corinthian portico, has been rebuilt around parts of 1754 hall designed by Bath architect John Wood the Elder. Chandeliers in large ballroom were made in 1820 – each is 28ft long and weighs over 1 ton.

Unity Theatre Db
First purpose-built synagogue in Liverpool, dates back to 1857 and converted into theatre in 1950s. Glass frontage now exposed again to reveal arches. Venue for local, national and international small-scale touring companies. Theatre lies in Hope Place, in the centre of Liverpool arts community and between its two cathedrals.

University of Liverpool Art Gallery
Georgian terraced house (outside map area) exhibiting Lucien Freud and contemporaries, Turner and Early English watercolours, drawings, prints, ceramics, silver, glass and Georgian furniture.

Walker Art Gallery Cd
Internationally renowned collection of paintings dating from 14th century to the present, including works by Van Dyck, Rembrandt and Rubens. Particularly large collections of European Old Masters, Victorian, Pre-Raphaelite and modern British works. Also includes eight paintings by George Stubbs, born in Liverpool in 1726. Recently opened Sculpture Gallery received National Art Collections Award in 1989. Originally gift from Sir Andrew Barclay Walker, city's mayor in 1873, who provided money to build gallery.

FAB FOUR *John, Paul, George and Ringo are remembered opposite The Cavern Club in Mathew Street.*

Ye Hole in Ye Wall Bc
Public house once scene of fights between merchant seamen and navy's press gangs. Built 1727 as Quaker meeting house; one of Liverpool's oldest pubs, and last open to men only.

WHERE COTTON WAS KING

From the cotton towns around Manchester to the peaceful villages of Cheshire, all have their own delights. The Industrial Age is marked by disused mills and the engineering feats of James Brindley, while rural landscapes are dotted with glorious Tudor 'magpie' houses. But to prove everything is not rooted in the past, Jodrell Bank brings the space age to the Pennine foothills.

Alderley Edge ☆ Cc
Wooded escarpment of pink sandstone with superb views of Cheshire Plains and Pennines, Bronze Age lead and copper mines, and Wizard Cave where legendary knights on white horses wait to save country.

Arley Hall 🏛 Ad
Gardens of Victorian Jacobean-style mansion have changed little over 150 years. Herbaceous borders, walled, scented, herb and woodland gardens and splendid avenue of hollies clipped into 20ft cylinders. Tudor barn and 15th-century tithe barn survive.

Astbury 🏛 Cb
Small triangular green eclipsed by battlemented St Mary's Church. Took 200 years to build from 13th century, has detached tower and spire and beautiful interior notable for carved, painted roof.

Barton upon Irwell ♦ Be
Revolutionary machinery of Barton Swing Aqueduct carries Bridgewater Canal over Manchester Ship Canal. Built 1894, pivots to allow ships past while gates at each end hold in water.

Biddulph ✿ Ca
Surrounded by lonely Biddulph Moor which rises 1000ft and is source of River Trent. Rare Victorian gardens of Biddulph Grange provide rural world tour with charms such as Egyptian Court complete with topiary pyramids and Sphinx.

Bollin Bank ♦ Bd
Pioneering embankment carrying Bridgewater Canal across valley of the River Bollin; built by James Brindley in 1767.

Bolton 🏛🚋 Bg
Cotton industry revived at Hall-i'-th'-wood, half-timbered home of Samuel Crompton, inventor of the spinning mule (1779). Tonge Moor Textile Museum shows mule with other innovations – Hargreaves' spinning jenny and Arkwright's water frame.

Bramall Hall 🏛 Cd
Attractive Elizabethan half-timbered house noted for remarkable wall paintings of beasts and demons in ballroom. Paradise Room has fine 16th-century plaster-work. Set in gardens, lakes, lawns and woodland.

Brereton Green 🏛 Bb
Bear's Head inn (1615) is exceptional Cheshire 'magpie' house of black timbers, white infill. In contrast, 15th-century St Oswald's Church is gem of pink and grey sandstone. Pleasant walks by tiny River Croco take in insect-trapping sundew flower.

Bridestones 🗿 Db
Burial chamber, forecourt and long gallery among remains of 300ft Neolithic long barrow.

Bury 🏛 Cg
Relics from when regiment held Napoleon prisoner on St Helena feature in Lancashire Fusiliers Museum. Turner, Constable and Landseer are among British 19th-century artists in art gallery and museum's Wrigley Collection.

The Cloud ✻ Db
Enormous 1000ft hill, rising abruptly from Cheshire plain 3 miles east of Congleton. Its heather slopes and granite boulders give wide views from Potteries to Pennines.

Dunham Massey 🏛 Bd
Fallow deer roam parkland of restored Tudor house where 30 rooms recapture life in past centuries. Several relics survive in grounds, including an Edwardian water garden and Elizabethan mill in working order.

Fletcher Moss Botanical Gardens ✻ Ce
Green oasis on Manchester's fringe has sumptuous gardens devoted to flowers, trees and shrubs. Includes orchid and alpine houses and wild garden with roses and other British and European flowers.

Hare Hill ✿ Cc
Walled garden and parklands famed for rhododendrons and azaleas. Footpaths lead to Alderley Edge.

Heaton Hall 🏛 Cf
Landscaped grounds of 18th-century Palladian house has boulder where Pope John Paul celebrated mass in 1982, boating lake and vintage tram service. Painted ceilings and walls in Cupola Room are 'Etruscan' style – popularised after excavation of Pompeii.

Jodrell Bank ♦✦ Bc
Giant 250ft radio-telescope dish towers above the modern astronomy centre. Planetarium, displays on satellite communications and weather monitoring and working space models. Back on earth, arboretum has 20,000 trees and shrubs.

Knutsford ✦🏛 Bc
Contrasting with town's black-and-white houses are flamingos and other exotic birds at Hillside Ornamental Fowl Centre. Fine English painting collection at Tabley House, built 1761.

Little Moreton Hall 🏛 Ca
Dazzling jigsaw of black timber and white plaster, interior just as ornate. Built 15th century within moat. Leaning walls, elegant gables and windows, 68ft Long Gallery with original panelling and floor. Also fine wall paintings and herb and knot gardens.

Macclesfield ♦🏛 Dc
Former silk centre, last hand-loom workshop preserved in Paradise Mill museum, and history of silk told in Heritage Centre. St Michael's Church, reached by 108 steps, still has its medieval battlements, and Christ Church, built 1775-6, has all its original box pews in nave.

Marple ♦ Dd
Delightful riverside town in rocky, wooded ravine. Flight of 16 locks and three-arched aqueduct takes Peak Forest Canal over River Goyt. Fine, curling 'snakebridge', allowed horses across canal without untying towrope. Pleasant woodland and moorland walks with splendid Peak District views.

Marton 🏛 Cb
Charming Church of St James and St Paul, built 1343, proclaims itself 'oldest half-timbered church in use in Europe'. Bull once penned in giant trunk of Marton Oak, split in four by age.

Nantwich 🏛 Aa
Elegant town rebuilt by Elizabeth I who organised nationwide collection after great fire in 1583. Only Churche's Mansion, Sweetbriar Hall and magnificent 14th-century St Mary's Church, noted for 'Green Man' pagan fertility gods, survived 20 day blaze.

Nether Alderley 🏛 Cc
Water mill, 15th century, has Elizabethan woodwork and working Victorian machinery driven by two wheels. St Mary's Church has 14th-century font and a copy of the 1717 'Vinegar' Bible in which misprint reads 'parable of the vinegar', not vineyard.

Northwich ♦🏛 Ac
Towns ending in '-wich' were salt towns, and the story of salt is told in the Salt Museum here. Trade route was River Weaver; later, Trent and Mersey Canal was dug. In 1875 river and canal were linked by Anderton Lift and boats were hoisted up and down.

Oldham 🏛 Df
Many cotton mills still stand, but disused or adapted for other purposes. Art gallery specialises in British art from Early English watercolours to contemporary.

Platt Hall 🏛 Ce
Outstanding collection of male and female fashions from Tudor times to Laura Ashley and Zandra Rhodes, in 1762 textile merchant's home. Surrounding park has Coronation Rose Garden, boating lake and Shakespearean Garden with plants mentioned in plays.

Prestbury 🏛 Dc
Charming village centred on attractive 13th-century church. Restored Saxon cross, stone coffin dated 1250 and carved doorway of Norman chapel in churchyard.

GRINDING RELIC *Millstone at Nether Alderley corn mill.*

Risley Moss 🦋 Ae
Wild country, now tamed. Boggy moorland of Mersey valley includes woodland with grassy glades, ponds and nature trails. Visitor centre tells of Risley Moss and its people.

Rostherne 🏛 Bd
Beautifully kept village. Cottages carved with names of shrubs and trees line road to church with magnificent view over Rostherne Mere (bird sanctuary), whose 100 acres and 100ft depth make it largest and deepest in Cheshire.

Rudyard 🏛 Da
Pretty houses and gardens on wooded banks of reservoir. Walks to caverns, rock formations and Roman copper workings. Origin of Rudyard Kipling's name: his parents became engaged here.

Sale Water Park ⚓ Ce
Former gravel pits popular with anglers, birdwatchers, walkers and boating enthusiasts. Above is impressive embankment built by James Brindley in 1761 to carry Bridgewater Canal.

Salford 🏛 Be
Largest public collection of L.S. Lowry's work in Britain and reconstructed 19th-century street are attraction of Peel Park

ROLLING LANDSCAPE *Magnificent panorama across the fields of Cheshire from The Cloud, just east of Congleton.*

Museum and Art Gallery. Mining museum features pit scenes of 1840s and drift mine of 1930s.

Smithills Hall 🏛 Bg
Medieval manor house on lower slopes of moor. Great hall and adjoining rooms date from 14th century. Later additions include Tudor withdrawing room with exquisite oak panelling. Now a museum surrounded by wooded nature trail.

Stalybridge 🏛 De
Astley Cheetham Art Gallery has collection of medieval and Renaissance paintings. Special section on Harry Rutherford – important painter of the region.

MODEL MILL *Quarry Bank cotton mill, Styal, is now restored.*

Styal 🏛 Cd
Largely unchanged model village of Quarry Bank cotton mill. Mill, founded 1784, restored as working museum with spinning room, weaving shed and giant water wheel. Village retains houses where mill's owner, manager and apprentices lived. Lies in 240 acre country park with varied wildlife and miles of woodland walks.

Tatton Park 🏛 Bd
Sumptuous rooms of 18th-century mansion appeared in television series *Brideshead Revisited*. Exquisite grounds have 1000 acre deer park, Japanese garden with Shinto temple and bathing, fishing and sailing in mile-long Tatton Mere. Waymarked walks include lakeside, woodland, and medieval village trail recalling former village cleared to make room for park. Old Hall still exists with restored pre-Reformation rooms.

Tegg's Nose Park 🏛 Dc
Park extends across ridge of Millstone Grit in Pennine foothills. There are dramatic views over Cheshire Plain, Macclesfield and Manchester. Area dotted with old quarries with geology displays. Waymarked trails start from visitor centre.

Werneth Low Country Park 🏛 De
Dramatic views stretch to mountains 50 miles away in North Wales, and Liverpool's two cathedrals. Memorial marks local men killed in World War II.

Worsley Bf
Birthplace of British canals. James Brindley built Bridgewater Canal to carry coals from Worsley Delph mines to Manchester. Canal was completed in 1761.

TRADE CAPITAL OF THE NORTH

When Flemish weavers came to 14th-century Manchester, the foundations of the North's industrial capital were laid. Their textiles transformed a market town into a thriving boom town at the forefront of the Industrial Revolution. It then developed into England's finest Victorian city. Despite the devastation caused by wartime bombing, many outstanding buildings still remain.

Abraham Lincoln Statue Bc
Statue 13ft high of the former American president, commemorating Manchester's support of the Union cause during the American Civil War.

Air and Space Gallery 🏛 Ab
Covers all aspects of flight and space technology, with special emphasis on the Manchester firm Avro. Exhibition has replica of A.V. Roe's triplane which made the first British powered flight in 1909. Display includes a Spitfire from World War II.

FLIGHTS OF FANTASY *A 1901 triplane and 1950's Shackleton are on show at the Air and Space Gallery.*

Albert Square Bc
Pedestrianised square is overshadowed by 19th-century Albert Memorial, which predates the London version. Statue of former Prime Minister William Gladstone is most impressive among monuments of notable Victorians.

Arndale Centre Cc
One of the largest covered shopping areas in Europe, covering 26 acres. Includes car park, bus terminal and indoor market.

Athenaeum Gallery 🏛 Cb
Palazzo-style building designed by Sir Charles Barry in 1837. Part of the City Art Gallery, housing a number of touring exhibitions throughout the year.

Balloon Street Cd
Plaque on corner with Corporation Street marks site of first manned balloon ascent in 1785, by pioneer James Sadler.

Barton Arcade Bc
One of the most elegant Victorian arcades, built in 1871 with a glazed dome roof and delicate iron tracery. Now a popular and fashionable shopping centre.

Bridgewater Canal Aa
One of Britain's first cross-country canals, constructed in 1758-72 to bring cheap coal from the Duke of Bridgewater's mines.

Castlefield 🚶 ⚓ 🏛 Ab
Britain's first urban heritage park, incorporating the birthplace of the city, canals, museums and a television studio. Reconstructions

and special displays in visitor centre show development of Manchester since Roman times. Railway viaducts cross the land where a Roman fort and settlement once stood. It was then known as 'the castle in the field', which gave area its name.

Castlefield Canal Basin ⚓ Ab
Heart of the canal system which linked city with surrounding cotton-mill towns. Grocers' Warehouse has been reconstructed with boat holes and water wheel for lifting containers of coal up to street level. Waterways and towpaths are being renovated for boating and walking. Historic trail follows Rochdale Canal.

Central Library Bb
Classical building, based on the Pantheon in Rome, designed by E. Vincent Harris in 1934. Largest municipal library in the country, has large domed reading room and Shakespeare Hall has stained-glass window showing the playwright. Outside is a war cenotaph by Lutyens.

CLASSICAL GRANDEUR *A great columned portico distinguishes the Central Library in St Peter's Square.*

Chetham's Hospital Cd
Decorative wooden panelling marks 15th-century manor house, built to house members of the collegiate church. Converted in 1653 to a charity school for the poor, now operating as the Chetham School for children who are musically gifted.

Chetham's Library Cd
The first free public library in England, founded in 1653, occupying the old dormitory of church residence. Contains printed books and manuscripts, and desk used by Karl Marx and Friedrich Engels.

China Town Cc
Heart of Manchester's growing Chinese community, between Oxford and Charlotte streets. Imperial Arch, 30ft high, unique in Europe, is decorated with

ceramics, gold leaf, lacquer and paints. Jasmine, cherry and bamboo surround two pavilions in ornamental gardens nearby. Area also has restaurants, supermarkets and herbalist centre.

Chinese Arts Centre Cb
Includes tea house, craft shop and gallery with changing exhibitions focusing on Chinese art, history and culture.

City Art Gallery 🏛 Cb
Considered Manchester's finest building, designed by Sir Charles Barry in 1825. Contains the city's principal collection of paintings, sculpture, silver and pottery. Superb display of Pre-Raphaelite masterpieces, and development of British painting from the 17th to 20th centuries. Special display about 20th-century painter L.S. Lowry includes reconstruction of his living room and studio.

Corn Exchange Cd
An impressive façade marks glass-domed market hall, dating back to 1903. Now a centre for regular antiques fairs and bric-a-brac sales.

Cornerhouse Cb
Visual arts centre with regular workshops, debates and courses throughout the year. Includes three cinemas which specialise in films not on general release. Galleries hold changing exhibitions of photography, ceramics, painting and sculpture. Also has café, bar and bookshop.

SUNLIT ARCADE *A smart shopping centre now occupies the beautifully restored Barton Arcade – a tribute to Manchester's prosperous past.*

County Court Ab
Grand Georgian house, built in 1770. Former residence of 19th-century free trade reformer Richard Cobden. Later went on to become Owens College, the birthplace of Manchester University. Has been the home of the County Court since 1876.

Courts of Justice Bc
Rebuilt in 1962 to replace 19th-century buildings, bombed during World War II. The Crown Court has sculptures of medieval punishments from the ducking-stool to the rack.

Free Trade Hall Bb
Built in 1865 on St Peter's Field – site of 'Peterloo Massacre' in 1819, in which 11 people died and hundreds were injured after a meeting for political reform was broken up by mounted troops. Hall bombed during war, then rebuilt in 1951 following earlier Palladian style with much original stonework. Home of the renowned Hallé Orchestra which first performed here in 1857.

Granada Studios Ab
Visit downtown New York, the House of Commons and a jungle without leaving Manchester, and still have time to see the Rovers Return in *Coronation Street*. Television studios tour includes explanations of the secrets of show business, lighting techniques and special effects.

Greater Manchester Police Museum 🏛 Dc
Set in a Victorian police station, features a reconstructed charge office of the 1920s, cells and collections of uniforms and equipment. Special section about Victorian detective Jerome Caminoda. By appointment only.

John Rylands Library Bc
Gothic-style building, completed in 1900. Notable watermarking of the red sandstone in entrance hall. Has some of the earliest examples of printed works including a block-print document dated 1423. Special attraction is the 'St John Fragment' – oldest New Testament writing in existence. Changing displays of rare books.

King Street Bc
The 1788 Georgian bank is the pick of this exclusive precinct of handsome shops and offices, running through the centre of the city.

GOTHIC INTERIOR *Manchester's Victorian town hall has been described as a classic of its age. The interior detail reflects the imaginative design of the whole.*

Manchester Cathedral ✝ Bd

Originally collegiate and parish church of St Mary, St Denys and St George in the 15th century, it became a cathedral in 1847. Heavily bombed during the war, but now fully restored. Perpendicular-style building has side chapels and widest medieval nave in Britain. Victoria porch at foot of tower commemorates Queen Victoria's Diamond Jubilee of 1897. Magnificent early craftsmanship in pulpit and choir stalls depicting eagles, lions, dragons, unicorns and bears. Wall posts are supported by angels playing recorders, bagpipes, trumpets and harps. Gilded bronze figure of the Virgin and Child outside the ancient Lady Chapel with its restored 15th-century screen. Treasures include three royal charters and stone carvings.

Manchester Craft Centre ⚑ Cd

More than 20 shops and workshops display crafts made on the premises including textiles, jewellery, ceramics, glass and fashion. Housed within handsome Victorian market buildings, converted from old Smithfield fruit and fish market in 1973.

Museum of Science and Industry 🏛 Ab

Housed on site of world's first passenger railway station – Liverpool Road, a Grade 1 listed building dating back to 1830. Museum illustrates development of science in Greater Manchester, the world's first industrial heartland. Power Hall has mill engines, vintage cars and railway locomotives – all restored to working order. Warehouse Exhibition displays textile, printing and paper-making machinery. Restoration work can be seen in progress in museum workshop.

National Museum of Labour History 🏛 Cb

Social history museum housed in Manchester Mechanics Institute – birthplace, in 1868, of the TUC. Displays show history of trade unions, the Labour Party and women's movements. Includes largest collection of trade union banners in the world.

Piccadilly Gardens Cc

This peaceful haven is one of the most attractive squares in the city, and once the site of Manchester's Royal Infirmary.

Portico Library Cc

Classical-style stone building, dating from 1806, with a distinctive portico of Ionic pillars. Contains rare first editions. First honorary secretary of the library was Peter Mark Roget, who wrote *Thesaurus of the English Language* in the 19th century.

Roman Fort ⚑ Ab

North gate and part of west wall of Roman stronghold of Mancunium have been reconstructed on the original site. Excavations reveal first fort was built from turf and timber in AD 79. A civilian settlement which developed to the north was the birthplace of the city. A guardroom has been furnished as it is thought to have appeared when still in use.

RIVERSIDE SCENE *The winding River Irwell gives excellent views of Manchester Cathedral.*

Royal Exchange ⚜ Bc

Imposing, columned building dating mostly from 1874 was originally built as city's cotton exchange. Its hall has an acre floor space which was once considered 'the largest room in the world', accommodating thousands of cotton traders. Now houses a theatre in futuristic glass and steel structure. Also has craft centre and gallery.

St Ann's Church ✝ Bc

A Wren-style church, made with local Collyhurst stone, founded by Lady Anne Bland in 1712. Georgian interior with fine plasterwork, box pews and Queen Anne altar. Also has a medieval painting by Annibali Caracci.

St John's Street Bb

Beautifully restored Georgian houses mark conservation area. Numbers 8 to 22 are of particular historic interest.

Shambles Square Bc

A medieval shopping place, largely destroyed by wartime bombs. Still standing is half-timbered, 14th-century Wellington Inn, an old shop and house built around 1550. Past residence of poet and essayist John Byrom, who wrote the hymn *Christians Awake* and invented phonetic shorthand. Pub next door, 18th century, is one of oldest oyster bars in England.

Town Hall Bc

Greatly restored Gothic-style building by Alfred Waterhouse, completed in 1877. It covers nearly 2 acres and has 280ft tower with fine peal of 21 bells. The Great Hall has a hammerbeam roof and murals depicting history of city from Roman times to the 19th century. An organ fills the apse at the east end.

Victoria Station Cd

Retains railway pioneer George Stephenson's roof, built in 1844. Two clocks adorn pedimented parapet of façade. Iron canopy along front has destination names in stained glass.

Additional Places of Interest Outside City Plan

Manchester Jewish Museum

Housed in an old Hispanic synagogue, dating from 1874. The lower floor has been restored to its original condition, while upstairs is an exhibition covering 200 years of local Jewish history. Temporary displays and special demonstrations on Jewish crafts and cookery are held.

Manchester Museum

Contains natural history and archaeological antiquities, including renowned collection of Egyptian mummies, and Greek and Roman coins. Also has fossils, plants and special Japanese section. Temporary exhibitions and lectures throughout the year. Vivarium and aquarium.

'MATCHSTICK' FIGURES *Many paintings fill Lowry's lively studio, reconstructed in the City Art Gallery.*

Whitworth Art Gallery

Houses fine collection of English watercolours, from the 18th century to present day. Superb section on ancient textiles includes Coptic robes and cloths.

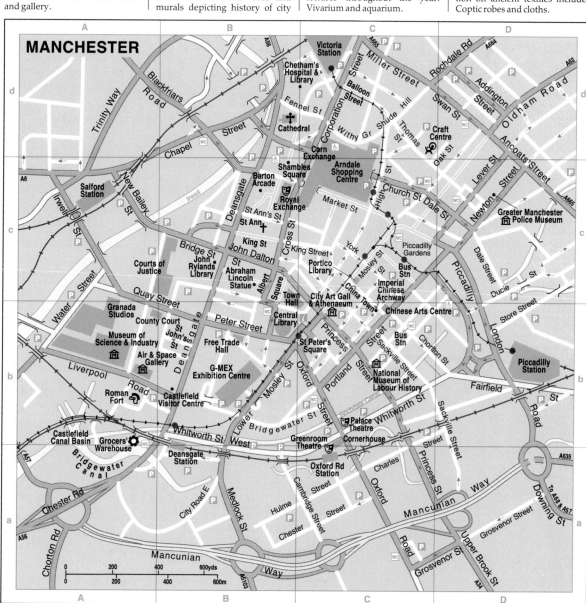

MANCHESTER

SPA TOWN IN THE HIGH PEAK

Although surrounded by industrial centres, the High Peak is as wild and lonely as anywhere in Britain. Man-made lakes and villages of local stone merge with both the peat moorlands of the gritstone Dark Peak and the airy hills of the limestone White Peak with its enchanting caverns. In elegant contrast are the spa town of Buxton and the classical splendour of Chatsworth House.

Arbor Low ⊓ Cb
The 'Stonehenge of the North'. Flattened Stone Age circle of massive stones within 250ft diameter bank, 4000 years old. Bronze Age burial mounds nearby.

Bakewell ⌂ Db
Home of Bakewell tart at heart of Peak. Handsome market town on River Wye with medieval five-arched bridge and Bath House (1697) fed by warm springs. The Old House Museum, with its 16th-century walls of wattle and daub, records local life.

RIVER CROSSING *Bakewell's ancient bridge straddles the Wye.*

Birchover ⌂ ☆ Db
Single street village surrounded by spectacular rocks and tors. Footpath to massive boulders of Row Tor and Eagle Tor, some carved into seats with views of wooded hill and valley below.

Buxton ❀ ⌂ ☑ Bc
Gracious spa town, 1000ft up in Peak District. The 5th Duke of Devonshire built elegant Crescent at end of 18th century, to rival fashionable Bath. Hospital of 1859 has one of the widest domes in the world at 156ft in diameter. Victorian Pump Room houses Micrarium museum where microscopes explore natural world.

Cannon Hall ⌂ ☙ Df
Georgian country house in parkland, with rooms furnished in a variety of styles, from Jacobean to Victorian. Also houses regimental museum of the 13th and 18th Royal Hussars, whose role in 1854 Charge of the Light Brigade is recalled in a series of displays.

Castleton ⌂ ⌂ ☆ Cd
Steep climb is only way to Peveril Castle on sheer rock face above village. Built 1086, keep added 1176. Tight-knit village of pretty cottages, split by tumbling millstream, is perfect centre for exploring the Peak caverns.

Chatsworth House ⌂ Dc
Palatial stately home, largely 17th-century, in grandest of landscaped grounds. Inside are 175 richly furnished and decorated rooms, outside are secluded walks, 290ft jet of Emperor Fountain and Cascade staircase of flowing water.

Chelmorton ⌂ ⌂ Cb
Guided tours of East View and Dale Grange working livestock farms; includes history of the old village and walk along limestone dale to caves, said to be burial ground of Brigantes tribal chief.

MUSIC CENTRE *Domes adorn Buxton's Victorian opera house.*

Cressbrook Dale ✿ Cc
Breathtaking views from winding road through this deep river valley. Imposing 1815 Cressbrook Mill and 18th-century hostel for its apprentices stand near millpond. Road turns through valley to Cressbrook village.

Derwent Edge ☆ Dd
Above Derwent Valley with views of Peak's 7 mile reservoir system; natural-looking lakes set among conifers, crowned by extraordinary weathered rocks.

Edale ⌂ ☑ Cd
Pennine Way starts its gruelling 250 mile trek to Scotland from this unspoilt village between gentle limestone White Peak, and bleak gritstone Dark Peak. Peak District National Park Information Centre has history, archaeology, geology and wildlife displays.

Eyam ⌂ Dc
Plague Cottages, church register and graves of whole families record heroism of moorland villagers in 1665 who stayed isolated for 13 months to prevent disease spreading. Only 83 of 350 survived. Supplies left for villagers at Mompesson's Well east of village.

Glossop ❀ † ⌂ ☑ Be
Two towns in one. Unspoilt 17th-century village with cobbled streets, and industrial 19th-century town with Victorian cotton mills. Remains of Roman fort of Ardotolia. Dinting Railway Centre has locomotives and miniature railway.

Goyt Valley ⌂ ❀ ⌂ Bc
Peaceful walks in steep-sided valley. Peaty moorland, oak and conifer woodlands and Fernilee and Errwood Reservoirs where coal mines, quarries, mill and gunpowder plant once stood.

Grindleford ⌂ Dc
Village with good walking in Hope Valley and the surrounding woods and moorlands. A mile north-east, ancient chapel of Nether Padley was restored in memory of two Catholic priests executed in 1588.

Hathersage ⌂ Dd
Village of legend and literature: Robin Hood's Little John is said to be buried in churchyard, while North Lees Hall is believed to feature in Charlotte Brontë's classic novel *Jane Eyre*.

Kinder Scout ☆ Bd
Bleak 2088ft moorland plateau, highest part of Peak District National Park. Best approached on Pennine Way from Edale or simply viewed from Mam Tor. Kinder Downfall on western edge is spectacular 100ft waterfall.

Ladybower Reservoir ❀ Cd
Thickly wooded shores surround waters under which two villages were submerged 1943. Perfect for walking, picnicking or relaxing.

Lathkill Dale ☙ ✿ Cb
Path through valley follows Lathkill river past trout pools and melancholy remains of lead-mining buildings and corn mill, where it tumbles over 11 weirs.

Longshaw Estate ❀ ⌂ Dc
Moorland, plantations, grazing land and oak-wooded Padley Gorge in country park only 7 miles from industrial Sheffield. Odd rock formations include precariously balanced Rocking Stone.

TRAIL'S BEGINNING *Track in Edale village is the start of the Pennine Way, leading northwards up to the bleak Kinder plateau.*

The Longstones ⌂ Dc
Village and hamlet at foot of 1300ft escarpment called Longstone Edge. Great Longstone climbs gently up a street with some 18th-century houses. St Giles Church, built between 13th and 15th centuries, restored in 1872. Quiet hamlet of Little Longstone has one of finest Peak District views at Monsal Head, high above Monsal Dale with steep, winding gorge.

Lyme Park ⌂ ⌂ Ad
Elegant Palladian exterior conceals Elizabethan mansion overlooking lake and stream on 1220ft Pennine moor. Chippendale parlour chairs upholstered with cloth from cloak Charles I wore at execution in 1649. Extensive gardens and walled country park with ancient limes, red and fallow deer.

Mam Tor ☀ Cd
Seeping water causes cliff face of 'Shivering Mountain' to shift constantly, sending showers of rocks into valley below. Stupendous panoramas, and best ridge walk in Peak District between Edale and Hope Valley. Large Iron Age fort of 1200 BC tops 1700ft summit.

Marsden † ☑ Bg
Canal and Countryside Centre in former keeper's cottage of 3 mile Standedge Tunnel, Britain's longest canal tunnel. Mementoes of Huddersfield Narrow Canal and Pennine countryside displays. Idyllic walk on towpath from Marsden to Slaithwaite.

Miller's Dale Cc
Part of the River Wye valley, named after two great mills built here in the 18th century. Path from Cressbrook leads along quiet river, a stretch known as Water-cum-Jolly-Dale.

Peak Cavern ☆ Cd
Vast entrance, 102ft wide and 60ft high, was carved out by an ancient river. Once the abode of beggars and tinkers, now tourists walk beneath stalactites through tunnels and chambers with names like Pluto's Dining Room, Lumbago Walk, Orchestra Chamber, and Devil's Staircase which leads to the River Styx.

Penistone † Df
Bustling market town with 13th-century church. Cloth Hall and Shambles date from 1768.

Poole's Cavern ☆ Bc
Spectacular limestone cave with illuminated stalactites and stalagmites. Flitch of Bacon is 5ft long stalactite and Poached Egg Chamber has stalagmites stained orange by iron oxide. Visitor centre has Stone Age and Roman relics from cave. Crenellated folly known as Solomon's Temple crowns 1440ft grassy summit of Grin Low. Spiral staircase inside leads to platform with superb views over Buxton.

Rivelin Nature Trail ❀ Dd
Runs through river valley to Rivelin Dams and Redmires Reservoirs before following Roman road to 100ft high Stanage Edge.

The Roaches ☆ Bb
Weirdly shaped mile-long ridge of dark millstone above moorland. Steep climb to top rewarded by fine views to Cheshire and Staffordshire. Colony of wallabies, result of zoo escape, is said to live on nearby Hen Cloud.

Rowsley ⌂ ⌂ ⌂ Db
Paths lead from typical peak village to Haddon Woods and across Derwent River to moors. Haddon

REFLECTED GLORY *Chatsworth, one of the great stately homes of England, was built by William Talman for the 1st Duke of Devonshire.*

Hall, 1½ miles west, is immaculately preserved medieval house with panelled rooms and exquisite tapestries. Chapel and dining room have 12th-century wall and ceiling paintings. Terraced gardens step down to River Wye.

Sheldon ⚒ ✿ Cb
Mine manager's house, two engine-houses and smithy at Magpie Mine, a well-preserved 19th-century lead mine.

Snake Pass ☆ Bc
Road twists up Derwent valley through conifers and barren moorland under Kinder Scout.

Speedwell Cavern ☆ Cd
Impressive Peak District underground chamber, which can be reached only by boat.

Stanton Moor ⊤⊤ ⚐ Db
Gritstone expanse, with spectacular Bronze Age remains of Nine Ladies Stone Circle, which may have surrounded burial mound.

Stoney Middleton ⚒ Dc
Attractive old village with steep, narrow streets, octagonal 18th-century church and nearby 80ft Lover's Leap.

Taddington Moor ⊤⊤ ▲ Cc
Two limestone burial chambers remain of Chambered Cairn, huge barrow built on this limestone ridge 4500 years ago. Highest point Sough Top is 1438ft above windswept pastures boxed with dry-stone walls.

Three Shire Heads ✳ Bb
Meeting place of three counties: Derbyshire, Staffordshire and Cheshire and where five rivers begin. About 2 miles north, Cat and Fiddle Inn is one of England's highest pubs at 1690ft, with panoramic view over moors.

Treak Cliff ☆ Cd
Limestone cliff with network of caverns. Translucent mineral Blue John was mined at Blue John and Treak Cliff caverns, Fossil Cave has remains of sea creatures, Crystallised Cavern sparkles with minerals and Variegated Cavern is multicoloured.

Uppermill ✿ ⚒ ⚐ Af
Former cotton mill in 19th-century industrial village houses Saddleworth Museum, recording life in Pennines 200 years ago with reconstructed clothier's cottage, complete with spinning wheels and looms. Narrowboat trips on the Huddersfield Narrow Canal through countryside and Standedge Tunnel.

Winster ⚒ 🏠 Db
Charming village of pale limestone, creamy sandstone and dark gritstone. Market House has pointed ground floor arches, now bricked in, dating from 15th or 16th centuries. Church has squat 1721 tower, 19th-century cast-iron relief from Da Vinci's *The Last Supper* and fine stained glass.

Youlgreave ⚒ Db
This ancient hilltop village in scenic limestone countryside has Cotswold-looking Old Hall (1650) and Norman All Saints Church with eight-pinnacled tower.

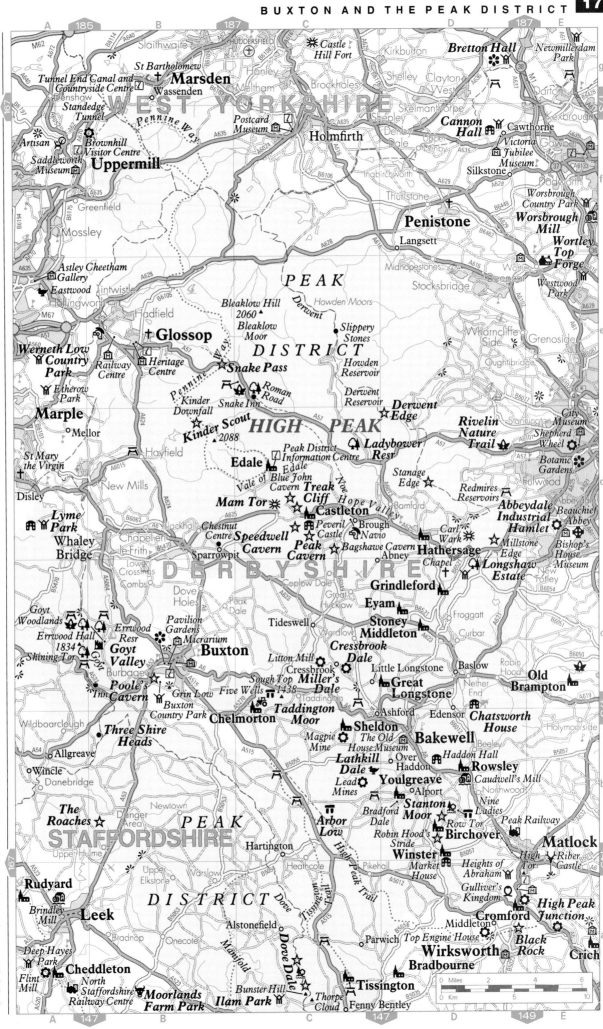

YORKSHIRE'S STEEL HEARTLAND

The area around Sheffield – the city of steel – is dominated by iron and steel industries, part of a long history whose romance lives on in the thrashing of water wheels and the pounding of hammers. There is romance too in the surrounding countryside, in Sherwood Forest, home of legendary Robin Hood, and the Dukeries, an area of vast estates once owned by the aristocracy.

Abbeydale Industrial Hamlet
✿❧🏚 Ac

Spitting, white hot metal, rumbling water wheels and crashing, giant water-powered hammers re-create foundry life as it was in this 19th-century industrial village. Reconstructed forge, counting house, as well as terraced workmen's cottages. Also has demonstrations of scythe making.

IRON REVIVAL *At Abbeydale Industrial Hamlet the 19th century lives again in a reconstruction of the foundry and its busy workshops.*

Adwick le Street ✝ Ce
Industrial town with Norman Church of St Laurence. Contains elaborate tomb of James and Margaret Washington, ancestors of the US president. Coat of arms contains stars and stripes motif later used in American flag.

Barnsley ✿🏚🗌 Ae
Market town founded in Saxon times on River Dearne. Substantial remains of church and gatehouse of Cluniac Monk Bretton Priory, established 1135. Cooper Gallery's collection of European paintings includes several English watercolours.

Blyth 🏚 Dc
Village on banks of winding River Ryton, with remains of Benedictine priory, founded 1088. Norman priory church, now parish church, has splendid nave.

Bolsover Castle 🏰🗌 Bb
Remains of 17th-century mansion on the site of a Norman castle rise above the countryside on a hilltop. The Little Castle is a folly, a fantasy of pinnacles and turrets.

Carlton Marsh ❦ Af
Area of 34½ acres colonised by plants, insects and birds. Old railway embankment is popular breeding ground for whinchats. The southern marsh orchid and other wetland plants thrive round the marshy pools.

Catcliffe ✿ Bc
Brick cone 68ft high and 40ft across visible from miles around, on outskirts of Sheffield. Built in 1740 for glass-making. Workers heated glass in central furnace and then shaped it.

Chesterfield ✝🏚🗌 Ab
This ancient town, now an engineering centre, is famous for its church with a crooked spire. Made of wood covered with lead, the 13th-century spire has warped

9ft out of line and has remained so for 200 years. Peacock Heritage Centre, in 16th-century timber-framed building, tells story of town. Railway pioneer George Stephenson (1781-1848) lived here; his name lives on in Stephenson Memorial Hall, now a theatre.

Clumber Park ✲🗌 Db
The 4000 acre park, half of which is wooded, once surrounded the seat of the Dukes of Newcastle. The house has gone, but the ornate glasshouses and formal gardens survive, including 3 mile Duke's Drive, double avenue of limes. Lake is 2 miles long.

Conisbrough Castle 🏰 Cd
Mighty stone keep rises on a mound above countryside. Once 100ft high, it is now in less lofty ruins but is still one of most impressive Norman castles; six wedge-shaped buttresses visible. Features in Scott's novel *Ivanhoe*.

Creswell Crags ✩🗋🗌 Cb
More than 45,000 years ago Neanderthal man hunted woolly rhinos and bison that lived in caves in these limestone crags. After them, 13,000 years ago, came the 'Creswellians', makers of sophisticated tools and works of art. Visitor centre displays history of the caves' inhabitants. Discovery trail around caves.

Cusworth Hall Museum
✲🏚 Ce
Early Georgian mansion, with Palladian pavilions and elaborate plasterwork, set in grounds noted for exotic trees such as cedars of Lebanon and bamboo. Museum of local history, with special study and games areas for children.

Doncaster ✝🏚🗌 Ce
Ancient settlement, now throbbing industrial town known for butterscotch and annual St Leger horse race, oldest Classic on the calendar, run since 1776 past Italianate grandstand with Venetian windows and Tuscan columns. Georgian Mansion House has grand banqueting hall and elaborate staircase. St George's Church, built 1850s, has pinnacled, 170ft tower. Doncaster Museum and Art Gallery has glassware, ceramics and outstanding Dutch paintings.

Edwinstowe 🏚🗋✲🗌 Da
Village on River Maun, on edge of some of oldest remnants of Sherwood Forest. The Major Oak, in the forest, is said to have sheltered Robin Hood.

Fishlake 🏚 Df
Village with Norman Church of St Cuthbert; richly carved south doorway. Inside are a medieval carved font and elaborate screens.

Hooton Pagnell 🏚 Be
Cottages of grey stone, with pantiled or slate roofs, line sloping streets. Limestone church on grassy bank has 1799 clock face. Nearby Luttrell Hall, once home of local squire Sir Geoffrey Luterel, who commissioned the Luttrell Psalter around 1340, illustrated with village scenes.

Howell Wood Country Park
✲ Be
Planted as woodland for hunting in early 19th century, park is now protected reserve, with about 60 species of breeding birds, such as blackcap, chiffchaff, woodcock and jay; other wildlife includes weasels and brown hares. Two trails, one 1⅓ miles, the other half a mile. Victorian ice house.

carries Chapel of Our Lady of Rotherham Bridge, one of only four such bridges in Britain. All Saints' Church, 15th century, has fine fan vaulting and bench ends; Clifton House, 18th-century mansion, is now town museum, with collection of Rockingham porcelain; York and Lancaster Regimental Museum.

Rother Valley Country Park
✲✿ Bc
Flooded open-cast workings, now pleasure ground for sailing, fishing, rowing or birdwatching for tufted duck, heron or, with luck, osprey. Visitor centre in Bedgreave Mills, once powered by water wheel, then by steam engine, internal combustion engine and now by electricity.

FADED GLORY *The façade of 17th-century Bolsover Castle is now in a partially ruined state. The mansion was built by the Cavendish family on the site of land originally bestowed by William the Conqueror.*

Old Brampton 🏚 Ab
Village of dark stone houses shaded by trees. Partly Norman church with clock depicted with 63 minutes to the hour. Inside the church, 1224 monument to Matilda le Claus portrays her holding heart in hands. Path to woods behind church.

Roche Abbey ✿ Cc
Cistercian abbey founded 1147 in wooded valley with chalk cliffs rising above stream. Transepts show change from rounded Romanesque to pointed, soaring Gothic. Capability Brown used this romantic setting in his landscaping of Sandbeck Hall.

Rotherham ✝🗌🏚🚲 Bd
Saxon market town transformed by Industrial Revolution, though evidence of the past remains. Four-arched stone bridge (1483)

Rufford Country Park ✲ Da
Ruins of 12th-century Cistercian abbey among trees of country park. Woodland walks, lake, formal gardens and sculpture gardens. Stable block remains of 16th-century country manor are now craft centre.

Sandall Beat 🗋 De
Wood on edge of Doncaster planted early in last century, where nightingales can be heard. Reserve of 189 acres includes area of fen where woodcock and grasshopper warbler breed.

Sheffield ✝✿✿🏚 Ac
City of steel, on banks of River Don, set in natural amphitheatre in shadow of moors. Industry thrived here long before Industrial Revolution: Chaucer's miller carried a Sheffield-made knife. Shepherd Wheel, water-powered

cutlery grinding works, was first recorded in documents in 1584. Sheffield Industrial Museum, in former generating station on Kelham Island, dominated by great Bessemer converter used in steel making, portrays industry on grander scale. City Museum displays cutlery and Sheffield plate. Older buildings of interest include Sheffield Cathedral, 15th century, with fine stained glass; Bishop's House, timber-framed yeoman's house built around 1500, is now museum of domestic life of the time. Mappin Art Gallery contains English paintings, with works by Turner, Gainsborough and Constable.

Sherwood Forest Visitor Centre ✲🗌🗋 Da
Story of legendary hero Robin Hood is told with tours along paths and trails in last remnants of ancient woodland, once a royal hunting preserve. He would not have been able to hide long in the much-reduced modern forest.

Sprotbrough 🏚 Ce
Church of St Mary, begun in 12th century, has elaborate rood screen and carved bench ends. Long lake by River Don is home to kingfishers and herons:

Steetley ✝ Cb
Tiny Norman chapel in a field. A mere 52ft by 15ft, it crams in nave, chancel and apse. Derelict after Civil War, but restored in 1880.

Thorpe Salvin 🏚 Cc
Little village with ruined 1570s manor house, once seat of Dukes of Leeds. St Peter's Church has glorious Norman font, cylindrical, with arches, under which carved scenes represent the four seasons and a baptism. South doorway also Norman.

Tickhill ✝🏰 Cd
Battle raged here in the 14th century, when John of Gaunt was governor at the castle, now a ruin. Castle was one of five in England licensed by Richard I for holding tournaments. Today Tickhill is a quiet village with wide main street, 18th-century market cross,

splendid Gothic Church of St Mary, which has one of England's earliest Renaissance monuments, and 13th-century friary ruins.

Wellow ☐ Da

Only village in Nottinghamshire with village green. Handsome Gothic Church of St Swithin with Norman font and 300-year-old wooden-case clock. Village still has old ducking stool.

Wentworth ⌂✿ Ad

Village with working woollen mill and spinning centre. On hilltop is 19th-century Church of Holy Trinity, with Restoration font, early benches and 15th-century screen. It replaces ruined medieval church nearby.

Wentworth Woodhouse
✿ Ad

Set in 150 acres of elegant parkland is 18th-century house built for Marquess of Rockingham, with longest façade in England, at 606ft. With 240 rooms, covers more than 2½ acres; porticoed front flanked by two pedimented buildings, with towers at either end. House private, but path through park is public. Follies.

NEEDLE'S EYE *An 18th-century folly at Wentworth Woodhouse.*

Worsbrough Mill ⌂♜ Ae

Ancient site of corn mill, recorded in Domesday Book. Present 17th-century mill now surrounded by country park. River Dove drives 19th-century water wheel which turns millstones. Second mill, built late 19th century, was worked by steam engine, and by oil engine in 1920s. Reservoir nearby home to waterfowl.

Worksop ✚✝🏠☐ Cb

Old town on River Ryton, with 14th-century priory gatehouse and market cross leading to 15th-century shrine and chapel. Priory has imposing Norman west front and Gothic Lady Chapel. Town is gateway to The Dukeries, grand estates in north of Sherwood Forest. Town museum.

Wortley Top Forge ♜ Ad

Water-powered hammers were pounding iron into cannonballs and nails in the Upper Don valley in 1640s. Now open-air museum, with blacksmith's, joiner's shop and foundry; re-creates life of forge in the early 18th century, still with water wheels and hammers. Worked until 1910, turning out axles for wagons and coaches.

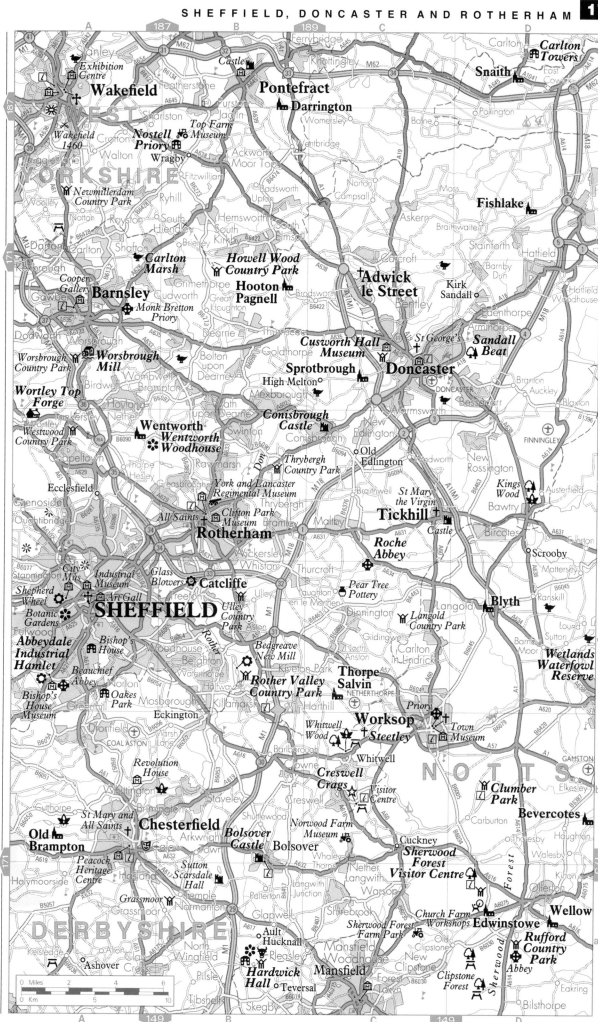

RICH FARMLAND ON THE TRENT

The broad valley of the Trent runs north to the Humber estuary. It passes 200,000 acres of rich fenland, drained in the 17th century, known as the Isle of Axholme. The river parallels a limestone ridge, the Lincoln Edge, and the Roman road of Ermine Street. In the south, the ancient city of Lincoln, with its splendid cathedral, dominates a countryside rich in Saxon and Norman churches.

Alkborough Cg
Village overlooking Trent and Ouse where they form Humber estuary. Medieval maze known as Julian's Bower is cut in turf on escarpment nearby.

TURF LABYRINTH *The maze at Alkborough, known as Julian's Bower, is about 40ft in diameter.*

Barton-upon-Humber Eg
Market town overshadowed by Humber Bridge. Well-preserved Saxon church, St Peter's, has 7th-century tower. St Mary's parish church is Norman with later additions. Georgian Baysgarth Park has museum of local history.

Barton Waterside Eg
Eight-mile countryside project including marshland and lakes formed from clay pits. Information centre in old coastguard station. Five nature reserves.

Bevercotes Ab
More than half a mile of artificial underground galleries form part of National Mining Museum next to Coal Board training centre. Underground canal barge and coal-cutting machines on display.

Blacktoft Sands Cg
Stands of reeds on sandy spit formed where Ouse and Trent meet before flowing into Humber. Nature reserve for waterfowl.

Brigg Ee
Market town built on crossing of River Ancholme, granted charter 1235. Subject of 1907 tone poem *Brigg Fair* by Frederick Delius.

Caistor Fe
Georgian town overlooking lowlands. Name derives from Latin *castrum*, fortified camp. Church of St Peter and St Paul has massive tower with Saxon base.

Church Laneham Cb
Trent-side village church has 11th-century doorway and 13th-century tower, with views to Lincoln Cathedral 6 miles east.

Coates Dc
Small church of St Edith has no aisles. Name derives from Norman south doorway and font, and rare Perpendicular rood screen with gallery.

Crowle Bf
Clearwater Leisure Park has seven lakes available for extensive range of water sports.

Doddington Da
Single street of 19th-century redbrick cottages dominated by 18th-century church and Doddington Hall, 1600 manor. Nature trail.

Egmanton Ba
St Mary's Church has rood screen and pulpit by turn-of-century sculptor Sir Ninian Comper. Norman architecture in nave.

Elsham Hall Country Park Ef
Nature trail through 400 acre woods and gardens with three lakes. Arboretum has 80 varieties of British forestry tree. Craft centre in hall outbuildings.

Epworth Be
The founder of Methodism, John Wesley, born 1703 in Old Rectory, 15th of 19 children. House burned down by mob politically opposed to views of Wesley's father. Rebuilt, and now preserved.

The Fossdyke Db
Still navigable 11 mile canal linking River Witham at Lincoln with Trent at Torksey lock. Once part of Roman water-transport system.

Gainsborough Cc
Market town with 18th-century three-arched bridge across Trent to Nottinghamshire. Old Hall, timber-framed house built 1500, now museum of furniture, paintings and costumes, with exhibition on Richard III.

Gainsthorpe Deserted Village De
Earthwork remains of peasant houses, gardens and streets of abandoned medieval village 5 miles south-west of Brigg.

Gringley on the Hill Bd
Village on 200ft ridge with views in three directions. Early English Church of St Peter and St Paul. Remains of prehistoric fort on Beacon Hill nearby.

Harpswell Dc
Church of St Chad has Saxon tower, Norman font and 14th-century south aisle.

Hartsholme Country Park Da
Former reservoir with lakeside path and nature trail in 100 acre estate. Hartsholme Hall, built 1862, pulled down 1951.

TUDOR SYMMETRY *Doddington Hall's plain but elegant façade.*

GOTHIC SPLENDOUR *Lincoln Cathedral's crossing tower soars above buttresses and traceried windows, a miracle in stone and glass.*

Kirton in Lindsey Dd
St Andrew's Church, restored 19th century, has Early English tower and some Norman work.

Laxton Ba
Village retains medieval strip-farming practice of working three great fields in rotation, dividing two into strips for individual farmers with third left fallow. Restored 12th-century church.

Lincoln Db
Cathedral city with pre-Roman origins and important industrial centre. Newport Arch, straddling main road to north, is only Roman gate still used by traffic in Britain. William the Conqueror's castle on 14 acre site has Norman gateway and walls with three towers. Jew's House and House of Aaron date from 12th century when Jews provided financial services. Triple-towered Norman and Gothic cathedral stands on 200ft limestone plateau among medieval buildings. Usher Gallery has collections of watches, miniatures, porcelain and paintings. Northwards lies Roman Ermine Street.

Lincolnshire and Humberside Railway Museum Dd
Station recalls age of steam with authentic furnishings and sound effects of old engines. Narrow-gauge railway takes visitors to viaduct with views of Trent Valley.

Melton Gallows Ef
Set up opposite Gallows Wood by James I as warning after feud erupted between the Ross and Tyrwhitt families during a hunt.

Nettleton Beck Ee
Beck, or stream, near village of Nettleton winds down to foot of Wolds past old mine workings.

Normanby Hall Cf
Regency house with authentic decorations and furnishings. Fine silver, displays of period dress and uniforms. Deer park and picnic area in 350 acre grounds.

North Leverton Windmill Bc
Built 1813, last working windmill in Nottinghamshire still grinds corn for local farmers.

Sandtoft Transport Centre Be
Built on former RAF wartime airfield, centre has more than 60 trolleybuses operating on their own circuit, including the last one of all, which ceased running in Bradford in 1972.

Scunthorpe Cf
Local ironstone beds transformed hamlet of 100 years ago into steelmaking town. Borough museum illustrates geology, natural history and folk life. Scunthorpe museum has Roman artefacts excavated from nearby villas.

Snarford Ec
St Laurence's Church, begun 12th century, has superb 16th and 17th-century monuments to Sir Thomas de Pol, Sir George de Pol and Robert, Earl of Warwick.

Stow Cc
Saxon and Norman Church of St Mary with 15th-century tower is one of largest pre-Conquest churches in country. Carving of dragon beneath font symbolises defeat of devil.

Thornton Abbey Ff
Moated ruins of Augustinian abbey built 1139. Wealth of abbey shown by 50ft high gatehouse, built 1382 with elaborate system of wall passages and chambers.

Wetlands Waterfowl Reserve Ac
Two lakes and marshland form 32 acre sanctuary for 40 species of duck, 18 species of goose and five species of swan.

Whisby Nature Park Da
Nature trail through 145 acre park with flooded gravel pits, marshland and willow carr (low-lying woodland). Sanctuary for wigeon, teal and duck in winter; for grebe, mallard and warblers in summer. Information centre.

MONASTIC RICHES *Thornton Abbey's substantial 14th-century gatehouse of red brick and stone, hints at the abbey's enormous medieval wealth.*

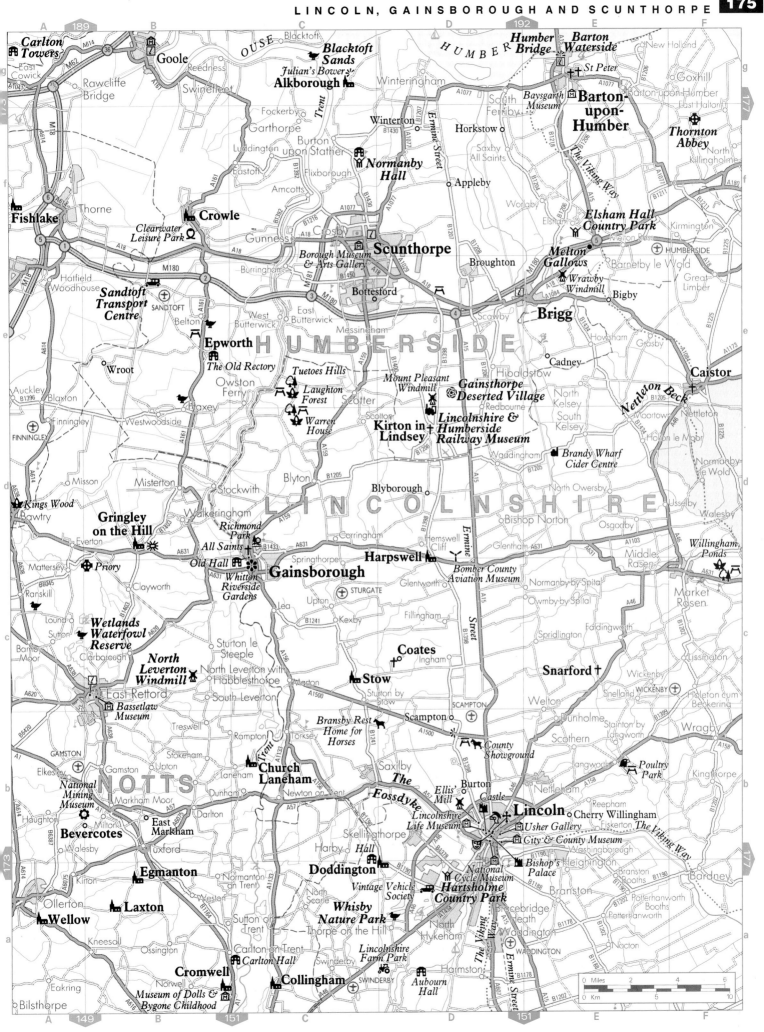

Carlton Towers

Goole

Fishlake

Crowle

Sandtoft Transport Centre

Epworth
The Old Rectory

Wroot

Kings Wood

Gringley on the Hill

Priory

Wetlands Waterfowl Reserve

North Leverton Windmill

National Mining Museum

Bevercotes

Egmanton

Laxton

Wellow

Cromwell
Museum of Dolls & Bygone Childhood

Carlton Hall

Collingham

Blacktoft Sands
Julian's Bower
Alkborough

Normanby Hall

Scunthorpe
Borough Museum & Arts Gallery
Bottesford

Laughton Forest
Warren House

Kirton in Lindsey

Gainsthorpe Deserted Village
Lincolnshire & Humberside Railway Museum

Brandy Wharf Cider Centre

Harpswell
Bomber County Aviation Museum

Coates

Stow

Snarford

Church Laneham

The Fossdyke

Doddington

Vintage Vehicle Society
Whisby Nature Park

Lincolnshire Farm Park

Aubourn Hall

Ellis' Mill
Castle
Lincolnshire Life Museum

Lincoln
Usher Gallery
City & County Museum
Bishop's Palace
National Cycle Museum
Hartsholme Country Park

Humber Bridge
Barton Waterside
St Peter

Baysgarth Museum
Barton-upon-Humber

Thornton Abbey

Elsham Hall Country Park

Melton Gallows
Wrawby Windmill

Brigg

Caistor

Nettleton Beck

Willingham Ponds

Market Rasen

Poultry Park

County Showground

Bransby Rest Home for Horses

HUMBERSIDE

LINCOLNSHIRE

NOTTS

Miles 0 2 4 6
Km 0 5 10

Alford ✠ 🏛 Db

Small town with a house within a house; original timbered manor house of 1540 is encased in red brick in early 18th century. Now a folk museum with Victorian exhibits. 'Heritage Trail' around old town starts here.

STRANGE SAILS *Alford's unusual 1813 windmill has five sails.*

Alvingham 🏠🏛 Cd

Village on old Louth Navigation Canal has only church in Britain dedicated to Saxon St Adelwold. It shares a churchyard with St Mary's, once the chapel of a 12th-century priory. Restored red-brick water mill (18th century) is a working museum.

Animal Gardens ✿ Ec

Conservation centre with successful breeding programme, including desert lynx from Africa and wildcats from highland Britain. Rescue and care of sick and injured animals also undertaken. More than 70 species among 200 inhabitants. Enclosures lie among colourful gardens.

Bag Enderby 🏠 Cb

Oaks and beeches watch over sleepy cottages. Village noted for local greensand stone 'Tennyson Church' where poet's father was rector. Chancel, nave and windows date from 14th century. Tower and porch 15th century.

Binbrook 🏠 Bd

Small village spread over shallow hillside in northern wolds. Square with late Georgian manor house in stone and red brick. St Mary's ironstone tower and broach spire soar above church.

Bluestone Heath Road Bc

Running along crest of Wolds, this 14-mile road gives splendid views over cornfields, hills and valleys. It follows course of an ancient trackway, probably created by early farmers some 4000 years ago. Viewpoint near Belchford overlooks River Waring.

Calceby ✠ Cb

A 'lost village' of the Wolds near south end of Bluestone Heath. Ivy-covered limestone ruin on hilly outcrop was once the parish church. The village mysteriously dwindled away in 1621, with only present farmhouse and scattered cottages remaining.

MARSHES BELOW THE WOLDS

Huge sweeps of sand and salt marsh south of the Humber estuary have become nature reserves, while the dunes and shallow waters attract holidaymakers to the resorts of Cleethorpes and Mablethorpe. Inland, flat pastures give way to the gentle hills of the Wolds, whose broad and lonely horizons played their part in the poetry of Alfred, Lord Tennyson, born in Somersby village.

Chambers Farm Woods 🏕✿🐦🎿 Ab

Almost 1000 acres of fields and woodlands, including ancient Lincolnshire lime woods and undisturbed meadow. Woods are noted for varieties of woodland butterflies such as marbled whites and peacocks.

Claythorpe Water Mill 🏛🐟 Db

Preserved 18th-century water mill in the Lincolnshire Wolds. Its riverside gardens are a bird sanctuary, full of ducks, geese and ornamental waterfowl. Exotic species include storks, ibises and crowned cranes. In the millpond are tame trout which will take food from visitors' hands.

COUNTRY DWELLER *Red-legged partridge may be seen on farm land.*

Cleethorpes ✠🐦 Ce

Popular resort with 3 miles of sandy beach, promenade, short pier and pleasure gardens. Sea withdraws up to a mile at low tide. By boating lake, Jungleland and Mini-Beasts Zoo has a spider display room, and tropical and wild flower gardens. Norman church tucked away in Old Clee.

Donna Nook Nature Reserve 🐦 Dd

Bare dunes back huge expanse of sand, mud flats and saltings. Named after foreign ship wrecked on shore. Partly used as RAF bombing range – closed when red flags fly. Rich and varied plant life. Breeding birds include whitethroats, little grebes and ringed plovers. Winter visitors can include shore lark, twite and Lapland bunting. Watch for grey and common seals on flats.

Donington on Bain 🏠 Bc

Village with access to long-distance wold footpath of Viking Way, running along wooded banks of River Bain. Join path by white-painted mill close to weir. Early English sandstone church.

Grimsby ✄ Bf

Important fishing port and commercial dock, lined with trawlers. Arcaded fish market, where fresh produce auctioned daily, and Victorian warehouses dominated by Dock Tower folly – modelled on

tower of Siena's Palazzo Publico, and used as a guiding landmark for miles out to sea. National Fishing Heritage Centre, devoted to rise of Grimsby as world's largest fishing port in 19th century, recreates trawling life. Inland, old town has fine medieval church, mainly 13th century.

Langton 🏠 Cb

Church of St Peter and St Paul is early 18th century, with steep roof and stubby octagonal tower. Splendid Georgian interior with tiers of inward-facing box pews and three-decker pulpit. Pretty 'roundhouse' cottage nearby has conical thatched roof.

Legbourne 🏠🏛 Cc

Railway Museum here includes restored Great Northern station frontage, fully equipped signal box, railway relics and steam locomotive nameplates.

Louth ✠🏛🎿 Cc

Beautifully preserved Georgian market town straddling River Lud. Church of St James is a 16th-century Gothic masterpiece, with county's tallest spire at 295ft, which can be seen for miles around. Butterfly, moth and fossil collections in Louth Museum.

Mablethorpe ✿🐦 Dc

Once a woodland village that was swamped by sea in Middle Ages; low tide still reveals old wooden stumps of foundations of original medieval dwellings. Now a popular resort with golden sands and lively promenade.

Mawthorpe Museum 🏛 Db

Steam engines, wagons, tractors and agricultural machinery on display. Working fairground organ and model fairground.

Red Hill 🐦✳ Bc

Nature reserve formed by steep hillside overlooking a disused chalk quarry. Lime-loving flowers include kidney vetch and yellow wort. Vetches, clovers and grasses attract many species of butterfly and moth.

Rigsby Wood 🐦 Db

Ash and oak woodland with good range of woodland birds. Woodcock and redpoll are frequent in winter. Plants include early purple orchid, wood anemone and ragged robin.

Saltfleet 🏠 Dd

Small, sleepy village of red-brick cottages, overlooked by derelict windmill. Narrow, muddy har-

bour is estuary of the Great Eau, with moorings for small vessels. Rough track leads to seashore of dunes and mud flats.

Saltfleetby All Saints 🏠 Dd

Lone church with leaning tower rising out of marshland. Airy, well-preserved stone building of Norman origin, but mainly 13th century. Top section of tower added in 15th century.

Saltfleetby-Theddlethorpe Dunes 🐦 Dd

Footpath leads through coastal reserve of dunes, salt marsh and freshwater marsh. Wetlands shelter rare community of natterjack toads; listen for curious churring call on warm evenings. Grey and common seals bask on sandbars. Birds include oystercatchers, redshanks and skylarks. Partly used by Ministry of Defence.

Somersby 🏠 Cb

Peaceful village at foot of Woldsarden Hill where Alfred, Lord Tennyson was born in 1809. The 'silent woody places' in his poem *Maud* recall this boyhood haunt. Father was rector of Somersby and Bag Enderby – rambling rectory now a private house. Memorials to Tennyson in church.

Sutton on Sea Ec

Quieter and more sedate resort than neighbouring Mablethorpe. Residential streets set back behind concrete sea walls. Pleasure gardens line promenade, and golf course follows shore to the south.

Tealby 🏠 Ad

Well-preserved village next to River Rase. Houses of reddish-brown ironstone and beautifully kept gardens. Steep climb to top of 480ft beech-capped Bully Hill, with views of Humber estuary.

Tetford 🏠 Cb

Snug village of red-brick houses and 14th-century church built from local greensand stone. Sundial above porch claims to be 'Redeeming the time because the days are evil'. Dr Samuel Johnson played skittles at The White Hart Inn, and Lord Tennyson attended literary meetings there.

Tetney Haven 🐦 Ce

Small harbour near entrance of disused Louth Navigation Canal, where anglers fish for pike. Little terns nest at Tetney Marshes Nature Reserve in summer; Brent geese winter there. From bridge at Tetney Lock hamlet, 1½ miles south-west, path follows canal for last mile seawards.

Willoughby-Farlesthorpe Nature Reserve 🐦 Db

Disused railway line developed as small reserve with walk along old track. Whitethroats, tits, turtle doves, linnets and redpolls nest here. Winter visitors include finches, fieldfares and redwings.

Wold Newton 🏠✳ Bd

Straggling village buried in woodland and backed by 360ft hill with lovely views over River Humber. Church has Norman chancel arch and font. Stone monument marks the spot where a meteorite fell to earth in 1795. Pheasants and brown hares can often be seen.

WORKING WATER MILL *The restored 18th-century red-brick mill at Alvingham village has an 11ft diameter and 8ft wide water wheel.*

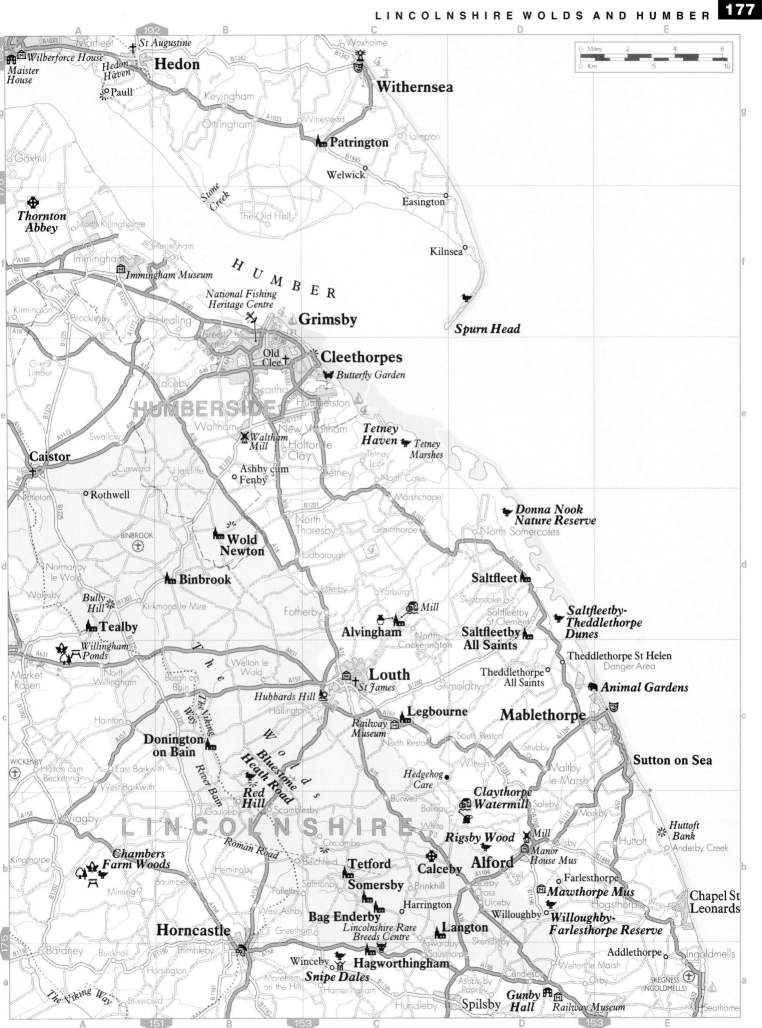

HUMBERSIDE

LINCOLNSHIRE

Maister House
Wilberforce House
St Augustine
Hedon
Hedon Haven
Paull
Marfleet
A1033
Keyingham
Ottringham
Winestead
B1362
A1033

Waxholme
B1242
Withernsea
Patrington
B1445
Welwick
Holmpton
Easington
Kilnsea
Spurn Head
Stone Creek
The Old Hall

Goxhill
Thornton Abbey
A160
A180
Immingham
A180
Immingham Dock
North Killingholme
Immingham Museum
Kirmington
Brocklesby
B1210
B1211
B1173
A18
Great Limber
Healing
H U M B E R
National Fishing Heritage Centre
Grimsby
Cleethorpes
Butterfly Garden

Caistor
Nettleton
Rothwell
A46
A1084
A1173
B1225
Swallow
Cuxwold
Laceby
A46
Scartho
Waltham
New Waltham
Holton le Clay
Humberston
Tetney
Tetney Lock
North Cotes
Tetney Haven
Tetney Marshes

Normanby le Wold
Walesby
Market Rasen
B1203
BINBROOK
Waltham Mill
Ashby cum Fenby
North Thoresby
B1201
Marshchapel
North Somercotes
Donna Nook Nature Reserve

Wold Newton
Binbrook
Bully Hill
Kirmond le Mire
Ludborough
Utterby
Yarburgh
Skidbrooke
Saltfleet
Saltfleetby St Clement
Saltfleetby-Theddlethorpe Dunes

Tealby
Willingham Ponds
North Willingham
Burgh on Bain
Welton le Wold
Fotherby
Mill
Alvingham
North Cockerington
Saltfleetby All Saints
Theddlethorpe St Helen
Danger Area
Theddlethorpe All Saints

The Viking Way
Hallington
Hubbards Hill
Louth
St James
Grimoldby
Animal Gardens
Mablethorpe

WICKENBY
B Holton cum Beckering
East Barkwith
West Barkwith
Donington on Bain
W o l d s
Bluestone Heath Road
Red Hill
Goulceby
Scamblesby
Railway Museum
North Reston
South Reston
Strubby
Maltby le Marsh
Sutton on Sea

Wragby
A158
Kingthorpe
Chambers Farm Woods
Minting
Baumber
River Bain
Roman Road
Hemingby
Belchford
Oxcombe
White Pit
Burwell
Belleau
Saleby
Markby
Claythorpe Watermill
Rigsby Wood
Mill
Alford
Manor House Mus
Well
Huttoft
Huttoft Bank
Anderby Creek

L I N C O L N S H I R E
Baumber
Fulletby
Salmonby
Tetford
West Ashby
Tetford
Somersby
Brinkhill
Harrington
Calceby
Ulceby Cross
Willoughby
Farlesthorpe
Mawthorpe Mus
Hogsthorpe
Willoughby-Farlesthorpe Reserve
Chapel St Leonards

Horncastle
Lincolnshire Rare Breeds Centre
Bag Enderby
Langton
Aswardby
Skendleby
Addlethorpe
Ingoldmells

Bardney
Bucknall
Horsington
Thimbleby
Mareham on the Hill
Winceby
Hagworthingham
Snipe Dales
Hameringham
Ashby by Partney
Candlesby
Orby
Welton le Marsh
Spilsby
Gunby Hall
Railway Museum
Hundleby
SKEGNESS (INGOLDMELLS)
Seathorne

The Viking Way
Stixwould
A1191
Mareham le Fen

A LAND RECLAIMED FROM THE MARSHES

Centuries of effort to reclaim the marshlands and cultivate the area has resulted in a huge network of drains, dykes and canalised rivers, interspersed with rich farmland and havens for wildlife, such as the Broads.

REFLECTED GLORY *Sunlight strikes the stonework on the magnificent west front of King's College Chapel, Cambridge, considered to be the most outstanding building in the University.*

Each year, about the time that dog roses begin to illuminate Cambridgeshire's hedgerows with their wayward gleam, small parties of elderly Americans arrive on pilgrimage. With assurance, they seek out ancient pubs, deep hidden in obscure villages, and can be seen leaning on field gates pointing out to each other some red-brick ruin or oil-stained slab of concrete, cracked and riven by weeds pushing through from below. Men and artefacts alike are survivors of the years 1943 to 1945, when vast areas of these East Anglian flatlands were given over to the 8th USAAF. On them, it occupied nearly 50 airfields, all of whose crews learned to depend upon the landmarks of eastern England. Distinctive from far off were the great medieval spire of Norwich, the octagonal lantern above Ely Cathedral, the truncated tower of Boston and the fretted front of King's College Chapel in Cambridge. The north Norfolk coast, too, was at once recognisable – a dark band of salt marsh fronted by a great pale width of sand.

BIRDWATCHERS' PARADISE
The secluded reed beds which border the quiet waters of Horsey Mere provide an ideal breeding ground for wildfowl and marsh birds. Nelson is said to have learned to sail on the mere.

Inland, the marsh gave way to the long necklace of the Broads, to Breckland and swathes of pine, while beyond was the vast black, green and gold blanket of the fens, ruled into segments by mile upon mile of lodes, canalised rivers and dykes.

People first came to the area about 10,000 years ago, at the end of the last Ice Age. What they found was a vast plain, across which slow-moving rivers meandered to the North Sea. Where the rivers met the sea, rich silts were deposited, while inland the country gradually sank to become fen and peat bog, in which higher ground featured as islands. Over millennia, the sea advanced and rivers changed direction, leaving their old courses as banks of silt in the unstable marsh.

The years around the Norman Conquest saw the establishment of great abbeys on some of the fen islands – at Thorney, Ramsey, Ely and Peterborough. The abbots started draining the fens, bringing hundreds of acres under cultivation, cutting ditches and drains, and building the sea wall to safeguard the

TUDOR CHARM *Little Hall in Lavenham is notable for its well-preserved half-timbering.*

Water, near Great Yarmouth, is bounded by more solid mud flats, creating a haven for waders and wildfowl. Different again are the bordered Broads like Horsey Mere, inhabited by bitterns, herons and spotted flycatchers.

The ever-threatening sea

The struggle between sea and land has been a constant preoccupation in this region. For the sea has remained a persistent threat, gnawing at the land, silting up harbours and actually casting down entire towns, as at Dunwich. Nevertheless, for connoisseurs of coasts, who don't mind the chill wind that seems to blow straight from Siberia, there is none finer in Britain. Once away from the entrances to the beaches, you have all the vast sands to yourself; any other persons present are no more than dots on the horizon. At some places, the tide retreats out of sight, but it also comes in at a fast clip to trap the unwary and flood the creeks of the salt marshes behind. For the untrapped, however, these are also splendid to fossick in, full of samphire and sea lavender, crabs and cockles. And, of course, the shell cases bequeathed by the USAAF.

WINDING WATERWAY *The Great Ouse weaves a serpentine path across the middle of England, before joining the North Sea by King's Lynn. In the last 50 miles, the river drops only 20ft as it drains the flat fens.*

grazing silt lands of the north. Meanwhile, the middle of the fens remained untouched, a strange, ancient world where the fenmen fished, wildfowled, dug peat for fuel and cut rushes to build their huts.

It was not until the 17th century that the next serious attempt was made to reclaim the fens, by the Earl of Bedford. This laid the basis for the huge mesh of drains and ditches that look so bewildering on the ground, but take on the logic of a cobweb from the air. Most spectacular is the Old Bedford river, which captures the waters of the Great Ouse, diverts them around Ely and despatches them to the North Sea. This

was followed 20 years later by the parallel New Bedford river, with The Washes, a wide strip of land in between which takes the surplus water from both in times of flood.

In all the rolling, opulent remainder of East Anglia, you do not meet this sort of thing again until you get to the Broads. Here, as in the fens, there are the same tucked away places married to airy spaciousness, the same uncertainty where land ends and water begins. But there are a greater range of habitats in the Broads. Places like the Bure Marshes, for instance, are more or less liquid mud overlaid by lichens, mosses and swamp grasses, while Breydon

ARCHITECTURAL WONDER *The building work of Ely Cathedral spans many centuries and includes the superb octagonal wooden lantern tower, a masterpiece of Gothic design.*

ISLAND WITH A VIKING PAST

Tailless cats and the annual Tourist Trophy motorcycle races indicate the variety within this green dot in the middle of the Irish Sea. Measuring 32 miles long and 13 miles at its widest point, this delightful mixture of holiday towns and handsome villages, plunging cliffs and sandy beaches, rugged glens and wild moors preserves the rich vein of the island's Celtic and Viking heritage.

Andreas Dd
Carved stones and crosses in church reflect village's close Viking connections. Jagged top of separate tower dates from 1940 when spire was removed, lest it endanger wartime aircraft from nearby airfields. One of few places on island with no sight of sea.

Ballaglass Glen Dc
Stream cascades over rocks and delightful woodland waterfalls. Steep climb up hill above glen to Cashtal yn Ard, Neolithic burial ground dating from 3500 BC.

Ballasalla Bb
Picturesque village beside Silver Burn river. Upstream is cobbled 14th-century Crossag, or Monk's Bridge. Downstream are ruins of Rushen Abbey founded 1134 by Viking Olaf I, King of Man. Walks to popular Silverdale Glen with boating lake and unique water-powered roundabout.

Ballaugh Cd
Humpbacked bridge makes good viewpoint for the Tourist Trophy motorcycle course races.

Blue Point Ce
Easy access to 17 miles of sandy beach and dunes between Peel and Point of Ayre, island's northernmost tip.

PORTLY PUFFIN *Its massive bill makes this bird unmistakable.*

Calf of Man Aa
Puffins, guillemots and razorbills are among large colonies of sea birds living on uninhabited island nature reserve. Also smaller groups of hooded crows and choughs. Boats from Port Erin and Port St Mary cross rock-strewn Calf Sound, overlooked by massive cliff of Spanish Head.

Castle Rushen Ba
Standing on site of an original Viking stronghold, this medieval fortress dates from 1153, and has served many functions: home of the Norse Kings of Man, prison, lunatic asylum, Parliament House and Court of Justice. Four square limestone towers rise 70ft above sturdy curtain wall. One-handed clock on outer wall said to have been presented by Elizabeth I.

Castletown Ba
Limestone town with brightly painted front doors, palm trees and picturesque harbour. Former island capital. In 1874, Manx Parliament moved to Douglas, but Parliament Square remains, and town hall is old Parliament House.

Cregneish Aa
True Manx village standing 450ft above sea level, with magnificent views over land and sea. One of the last places where traditional crofters' skills were practised. Open-air Folk Museum embraces a number of different buildings, including restored cottage of Harry Kelly (crofter who died in 1934) dating from early 18th century. Smithy and weaving shed with demonstrations.

The Cronk Cd
Village notable for 13th-century St Mary de Ballaugh's Church with 10th-century Viking cross. Lane leads to beach and dunes.

Crosby Cb
Hillside village overlooked by St Runius' Marown; typical of the medieval church of Man, stoutly built of rough local stones with cave-like entrance and tiny belfry. Legendary goblin makes sure St Trinian's Chapel stays roofless.

Curraghs Wildlife Park Cd
Llamas, monkeys, parakeets and penguins are among animals from all over the world which mix with indigenous four-horned Loghtan sheep and tailless cats.

Dalby Bb
Eccentric St James' Chapel is built in two tiers on hillside, and doubles as the village hall. At sunset on a clear day, Mourne Mountains can be seen 40 miles across Irish Sea.

Derby Haven Ba
Bay curves to St Michael's Island where old fort has fine coastal views. Greensward on western side of bay was 1627 site of Derby horse race, organised by Earl of Derby. But it was a later Lord Derby whose name was given to present race at Epsom.

Dhoon Glen Dc
Fern-clad glen where fast-flowing stream drops through waterfall with two leaps of 60ft and 70ft, before passing through cliffs to Dhoon Bay. Rustic bridges carry path to shore.

Douglas Cb
Island capital and largest town, spread out along 2 mile curve of Douglas Bay. Promenade overlooks beach with sand exposed at low water. Horse-drawn trams run length of promenade in summer; a service that began in 1876. Terminus of Isle of Man Steam Railway lies near harbour. House of Keys on Prospect Hill is home of the Manx Parliament.

Elfin Glen Dd
Legendary haunt of fairies and elves among woods close to famous Hairpin Corner on Tourist Trophy racing course. Mature hardwoods and conifers. Splendid views over northern plain to Point of Ayre.

Foxdale Bb
Village set in a bowl of hills and fields, with old railway trackway and fading scars of disused lead mines on surrounding hills. Waterfall cascades in Lower Foxdale, where Neb tributary runs under creeper-clad bridge by pretty Mill House. Brownstone cottages lie on hills above.

Glen Maye Bb
Swift stream flows through bridged gorge, waterfall and cliffs to pebbly beach. Fern-filled woodland has oaks and hazels of ancient forest which once covered island. 'Mona-Erin' water wheel provided power for lead mines.

Glen Helen Cc
Paths by rivers Neb and Blaber lead to Rhenass waterfall. Woods planted 1850. Café, restaurant and children's playground.

Glen Mooar Cc
Path leads to high Spooyt Vane, White Spout waterfall. Patrick's Chapel dates back 1000 years and has remains of hermit's cell.

Groudle Glen Db
Trains on the Manx Electric Railway stop here; one of the island's best-known glens. Paths with bridges descend narrow valley through groves of beech, larch and pine, past cliffs and rushing rapids to small stony beach.

Grove Rural Life Museum Dd
Early Victorian house shows life on prosperous 19th-century Manx farm with costume, toy, beekeeping and gardening displays. Original horse-powered threshing mill still in working order.

Isle of Man Steam Railway Cb
Original narrow-gauge engines and coaches transport summer visitors through countryside between Douglas and Port Erin, where Railway Museum illustrates history of line, opened 1874.

Kirk Michael Cd
Picturesque village of colour-washed cottages with stone church. Nearby Bishopscourt was built as fortress before 13th century. It overlooks Bishopscourt Glen with artificial mound topped by French cannons, marking 1760 British victory over French navy. Bishops meditated on carved stone seat in small cave.

Laxey Dc
Compact town with working woollen mill and tiny harbour. Short promenade overlooks sand-and-shingle beach. 'Lady Isabella' is a mighty water wheel, 72½ft across, built 1854 to drain local lead mines. Electric train climbs 4 miles to Snaefell summit.

Manx Electric Railway Db
Journey between Douglas and Ramsey has panorama of Douglas Bay, wooded approach to Groudle Glen and long climb to cliff top above Bulgham Bay. Two of original 1893 cars still used. Museum at Ramsey has historic locomotives and rolling stock.

Manx Museum Cb
All aspects of island life are covered here, and exhibits range from delicate Art Nouveau silver

PEEL CASTLE *Standing on St Patrick's Isle and linked to the mainland, it forms a protective arm around the harbour.*

CREGNEISH COTTAGES *The traditional 19th-century Manx homes of crofters and fishermen can be seen in an open-air folk museum in the village.*

to lumbering 4½ ton skeleton of a sei whale. Large-scale model of a Viking warship with dragon-head prow recalls sea power that once spread fear around coasts of Britain; model built 1939 in Norway.

MIGHTY WHEEL *Laxey's water wheel bears the Manx coat of arms.*

Manx Nautical Museum
✕ Ba
Three-storey boathouse dating from late 18th century is home for this museum, tucked in beside Castletown's harbour. First-floor cabin room, with balcony and wooden railings, resembles cabin of a ship of Lord Nelson's time. Centrepiece is 1791 schooner-rigged yacht, the *Peggy*; last in a local line of clippers made during 17th and 18th centuries.

Marine Biological Station
➳ Aa
A department of the University of Liverpool, where glass tanks display wonders of the deep. Many set at children's eye level. Aquarium and museum cover broad range of marine topics, from giant icebergs to humble cod.

Maughold ⌂✳ Dd
Tiny village with Celtic and Norse monuments from 6th-13th centuries in churchyard Cross House, and remains of three Celtic chapels. Steep path to Maughold Head lighthouse.

Murray's Motorcycle Museum ⌂ Cc
More than 130 motorcycles and 90 years of motoring memorabilia form collection of local enthusiast, Charles Murray. Early machines include 1902 Kerry and 1910 Wynn Ladies' Model. Housed at Bungalow Corner, well-known point on Tourist Trophy course.

Niarbyl Bay ✳ Bb
Tiny sheltered bay guarded by promontory of rocks projecting out to sea. These give bay its name, *niarbyl* being Manx for 'tail'. Footpath climbs round cliff face.

Noble's Park ❀ Cb
Breeding cattery where Manx kittens are born. Tailless cats are unique to Isle of Man, and enjoy official protection. Thought to have been first bred about 300 years ago. Grandstand marks start and finish of Tourist Trophy motorcycle racecourse.

Onchan ⌂⛵ Cb
Small town around Onchan Head, with leisure centre, sports stadium, golf, and boating lake. Pleasant walks to Groudle and

Molly Quirk's glens. Residence of Lieutenant-Governor (Queen's representative) on edge of village. Regular services to Douglas by horse-drawn tram.

Peel ⌂✕ Bc
Old fishing harbour with winding streets and town promenade overlooking sandy beach. Good fishing for mackerel, mullet, skate and conger eel. Boathouse at harbour has Viking longship replica, *Odin's Raven*, which sailed from Norway in 1979 to celebrate Manx Parliament millennium.

Peel Castle ⌂✛ Bc
Vast fortress on St Patrick's Isle, linked to mainland by causeway. Built mostly by the Lords of Man

in the 15th century, on site of an old timber fort. Within its walls, massive Round Tower dates from 10th century, and ruins of St German's Cathedral are 13th century.

Point of Ayre ⛵✿✳⌂ De
The Ayres form 4 mile stretch of coast between Rue Point and Point of Ayre. Road from village of Bridge leads to lighthouse on the point. Two miles west, turning off coast road runs north to visitor centre and Ayres Nature Trail.

Port Cornaa ⚓ Dc
Beautiful cove below Ballaglass Glen where pebble bank holds back stream at high tide to form lagoon. Remains of large lime kiln, hut where telephone cable

once came ashore, and gaunt shell of factory where high explosives were made in late 18th century.

Port Erin ➳⌂⛵✳⌂ Aa
Small resort sheltered by high cliffs of two headlands. Western terminus for Isle of Man Steam Railway, with engines, carriages and signals in Railway Museum. Footpath round Bradda Head gives panoramic views.

Port St Mary ⌂ Ba
Chapel Bay and Bay of Rocks provide firm sandy beaches, safe swimming and easy launching facilities, popular with yachtsmen. The Underway in this former fishing village has fine limestone houses.

Ramsey ❀⛵⌂⌂ Dd
Island's second largest town is dignified resort on sheltered sub-tropical bay, shielded by northern tip of hills to south-west, with two sandy beaches and good fishing from Queen's Pier. Albert Tower commemorates 1847 visit of Victoria and Albert. Mooraugh Park, 40 acres in extent, has a children's playground and boating lake, surrounded by palm trees. Terminus for Manx Electric Railway.

Snaefell ▲✳⛵ Cc
Spiralling mountain railway transports electric train on 4 mile journey from Laxey up to island's highest point, 2036ft above sea level. Journey ends at viewpoint overlooking spectacular scenery.

Abbeystead † De
Hamlet in River Wyre valley noted for honey. One mile outside is Christ Church-over-Wyresdale, known as Shepherds' Church, as porch faces water meadows ideal for grazing.

Arkholme De Dg
Beautifully preserved cottages and stone houses lead to the River Lune in single-street village. Grassy dome near water's edge was site of 12th-century fort. Riverside walk to Hornby Castle.

Beacon Fell Country Park ⚘ ❋ Dd
Coniferous forest and moorland surround fell side with views to Welsh mountains and Lakeland hills. Information centre, nature trails, scenic drive and tawny owls among bird life.

Blackburn 🏛 † Eb
Past prosperity of cotton industry recalled in old mills on Leeds and Liverpool Canal and working models of spinning jenny, spinning mule and flying shuttle in the Lewis Museum of Textile Machinery.

Blackpool ♀ 🏛 ☂ ❋ ⚓ ⛱ Bc
Summer sun and autumn illuminations light up Golden Mile, Pleasure Beach amusement park, three piers, unique trams, Zoo Park and famous 518ft Tower along resort's 7 mile promenade.

SEASIDE JOYS *Traditional merry-go-round gives thrills and fun on Blackpool's Pleasure Beach.*

Bowland Knotts ❋ Ff
Dark crags tower above moorland, Gisburn Forest and Stocks Reservoir. Views across limestone peaks of Whernside, Ingleborough and Pen-y-ghent.

Brindle ⚓ Db
Village clustered around 16th-century St James' Church with five fonts and two original bells.

Browsholme Hall 🏛 Ed
Centuries-old treasures and present-day possessions of Parker family whose ancestors built house in 1507. Fine furniture, stained glass from Whalley Abbey, and neat gardens.

Carnforth ⚒ Cg
Flying Scotsman and more than 30 other steam locomotives at Steamtown Railway Centre. Free train rides, model and miniature railways and other memorabilia.

ALONG THE LANCASHIRE COAST

The three faces of Lancashire – seaside, wild country and industry – are all rolled into one on Lancashire's coast and its hinterland. Millions of holidaymakers continue to seek sun, sand and seaside amusement parks at Blackpool, Morecambe and Southport, while inland the Forest of Bowland provides an untamed wilderness on the doorstep of industrialised Blackburn and Preston.

LIGHT AND DARK *Elaborate black-and-white timbering of Rufford Old Hall stands out dramatically.*

Chingle Hall 🏛 Dc
Britain's oldest surviving brick-built house, said to be haunted by monks. Cross-shaped and moated, built in 1260 around Viking Great Hall (*c.* 700).

Chipping ⚓ Ed
Charming village of cobbled pavements and 17th-century houses above fast-flowing stream. School and almshouses honour benefactor John Brabin, others mark prosperity as wool centre. St Bartholomew's Church has 1450 tower and examples of chair-making craft for which the village is justly famed.

Chorley 🏛 Da
An elegant 17th-century façade fronts Elizabethan Astley Hall maintained as family home of 300 years ago. Ornate plaster ceilings, Tudor carving, tapestries and pic-

STEAM RIDE *Old locomotive in gallant action at Carnforth.*

tures. Nature trail leads through magnificent grounds with lake, woodland and River Chor.

Glasson ⚓ Ce
Boating centre on 18th-century harbour. Lune Estuary Coastal Path follows disused railway line to Lancaster from Conder Green.

Hest Bank ⚓ Cf
Guided walks at low tide from suburb follow ancient 11 mile route across Morecambe Bay to Grange-over-Sands. Do not walk without guide – sands and tides are dangerous.

Heysham 🏛 ✚ † ✿ Cf
Cliff above Old Heysham has ancient body-shaped graves cut in rock and ruined 5th-century St Patrick's Chapel. Saxon St Peter's Church has gravestone carved with bears and Viking figures. Modern Heysham has Isle of Man ferry and guided tours of nuclear power station.

Hindburndale ☆ Ef
Hindburn flows gently through attractive valley until reaching bottom where it tumbles down wooded rapids and waterfalls.

Hoghton Tower 🏛 Eb
Fortified 16th-century mansion on steep, wooded hill with wonderful sea views. Carved oak table and menu from when James I created 'sirloin' in 1617 by knighting his beef. Tudor well-house and dolls' house exhibition.

Lancaster ⚒ 🏛 ☂ ⛱ † ✄ Cf
Roman fort occupied hill where castle stands. Norman keep

Wild West theme park, Central Pier with theatre, dance hall and bars. Illuminations along the promenade in autumn.

Preston ⚒ 🏛 Db
Busy industrial town, grew from inland port to cotton centre after Preston-born Richard Arkwright (1732-92) invented the spinning frame. Harris Museum and Art Gallery has collections ranging from Bronze Age burial urns and Viking coins to 20th-century British paintings.

Ribchester ⚓ ✿ 🏛 Ec
Beneath picturesque riverside village is Roman fort. Massive pillars at White Bull Inn probably from Roman bath-house, part of two granaries and museum with fort relics. Museum of Childhood has working fairground model.

Rivington ⚓ ❋ Ea
Rivington Hall Barn and Great House Barn – fine examples of Saxon 'cruck barns' with roofs supported by huge oak boughs or 'crucks'. Half of old village is under reservoir complex which provides Merseyside with water. Reservoirs best seen from 1190ft Rivington Pike.

Rufford Old Hall 🏛 Ca
Black-and-white timbered manor house, largely unchanged since built in 15th century. Fine hammerbeam roof with carved angels; rare 15th-century carved screen. Brick wing added 1661 contains 16th-century militaria and folk museum. Large garden.

Samlesbury Hall 🏛 Ec
Remarkable 14th-century Samlesbury Hall built in two styles – half red brick, half timbered with quatrefoil design showing white plaster beneath. Handsome interior used for exhibitions, antiques market and craft centre.

Southport 🏛 ⚓ ☂ ✄ ⛱ Ba
Elegant resort with long beach and sand dunes has Victorian pier. Amusement park, zoo, boating lake and Royal Birkdale championship golf course. Steamport Transport Museum has collection of railway engines and vintage road vehicles.

Thornton ✄ Bd
Restored 110ft tall Marsh Mill (1794) has four sets of giant millstones, each 6ft across.

Trough of Bowland ☆ Ee
Wild moorland pass with spectacular views of mountains, streams, valleys and fells of Forest of Bowland. Crossed by winding road and superb walks.

Waddington Fell ▲ Fd
Views across River Hodder to Bowland fells best seen from hill above Walloper Well, a natural spring. Footpaths closed during grouse-shooting season.

Worden Hall 🏛 Db
Charming 18th-century country house, restored after fire, in beautiful grounds.

Wyre Valley † 🏛 De
Gentle wooded valley between wild fells. Riverside walks from dam at Abbeystead Reservoir.

Leyland ⚒ 🏛 Db
'Popemobile' from Pope John Paul II's 1982 British visit and 1896 steam van are part of extensive British Commercial Vehicle Museum. South Ribble Museum in timber-framed Tudor grammar school records local history and archaeology.

Martin Mere ⚓ Ca
Whooper and Bewick's swans fly from Iceland and Russia to artificial lake in wildfowl park, home to thousands of wild and tame birds. Exhibition hall, Norwegian log house with pine walls and sloping turf roof, has history of mere and its wildfowl trust.

Morecambe ♀ ⛱ Cf
Holiday resort on curving 4 mile promenade with panoramic view across Morecambe Bay to Lakeland hills. Seaside amusements,

Lever Park 🏛 ❋ ⚓ Ea
Tree-fringed reservoir, replica ruins of medieval Liverpool Castle and terraced woodland walks in magnificent park and gardens created from fortune William Lever made from Sunlight Soap.

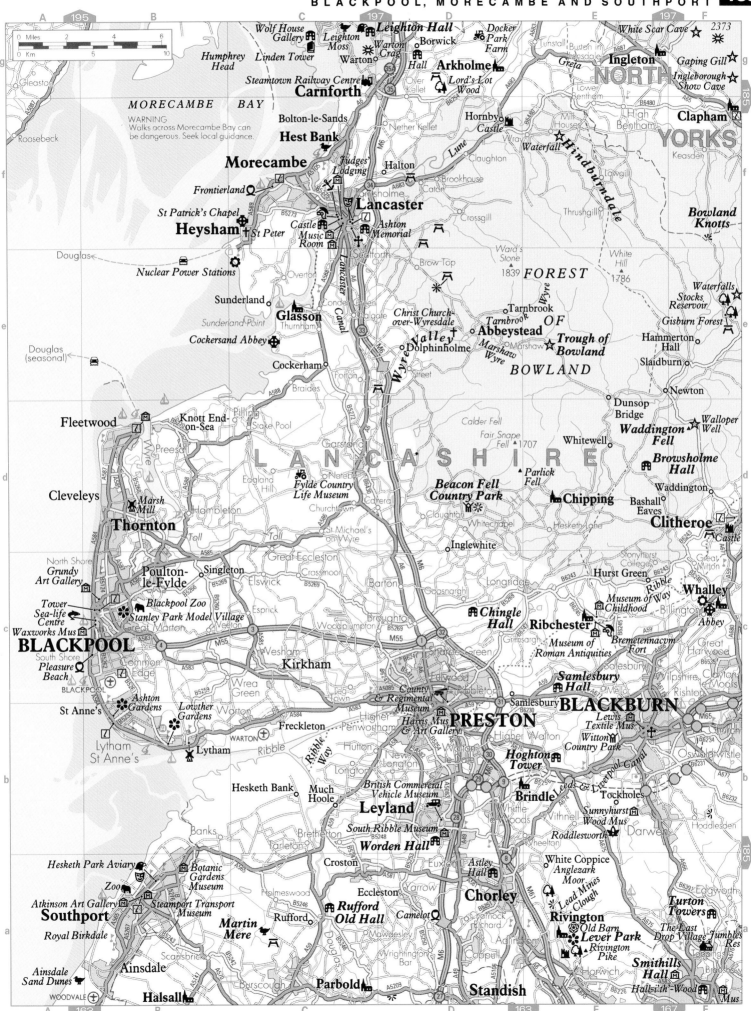

A map of the Blackpool, Morecambe and Southport region of Lancashire, including parts of North Yorkshire.

Locations and features shown on the map include:

Roosebeck, Gleaston, MORECAMBE BAY, Humphrey Head, Wolf House Gallery, Leighton Moss, Leighton Hall, Borwick, Docker Park Farm, White Scar Cave, 2373, Gaping Gill, Ingleborough Show Cave, Ingleton, NORTH YORKS, Clapham

Linden Tower, Warton Crag, Warton, Hall, Arkholme, Lord's Lot Wood, Steamtown Railway Centre, Carnforth, Over Kellet, Nether Kellet, Hornby Castle, High Bentham, Keasden

Bolton-le-Sands, Hest Bank, Morecambe, Frontierland, St Patrick's Chapel, Heysham, St Peter, Judges' Lodging, Halton, Lancaster, Castle, Music Room, Ashton Memorial, Scotforth, Brookhouse, Caton, Claughton, Waterfall, Hindburndale, Howgill, Thrushgill, Bowland Knotts

Douglas, Nuclear Power Stations, Sunderland, Glasson, Thurnham, Conder Green, Galgate, Christ Church-over-Wyresdale, Dolphinholme, Abbeystead, FOREST, Tarnbrook, Marshaw Wyre, Trough of Bowland, Hammerton Hall, Slaidburn, White Hill 1786, Ward's Stone 1839, Brow Top

Douglas (seasonal), Cockersand Abbey, Cockerham, Braides, Pilling, Stake Pool, Garstang, OF, BOWLAND, Newton, Dunsop Bridge, Waterfalls, Stocks Reservoir, Gisburn Forest

Fleetwood, Knott End-on-Sea, Preesall, Hambleton, Eagland Hill, Fylde Country Life Museum, Churchtown, Nateby, Calder Fell, Fair Snape Fell 1707, Whitewell, Waddington Fell, Walloper Well, Browsholme Hall, Waddington

Cleveleys, Marsh Mill, Thornton, Toll, Great Eccleston, St Michael's on Wyre, Beacon Fell Country Park, Parlick Fell, Chipping, Bashall Eaves, Clitheroe, Castle

Grundy Art Gallery, Poulton-le-Fylde, Singleton, Elswick, Crossmoor, Barton, Whitechapel, Hesketh Lane, Stonyhurst College, Great Mitton, Whalley, Abbey

Tower, Sea-life Centre, Waxworks Mus, Blackpool Zoo, Stanley Park Model Village, Great Marton, Weeton, Woodplumpton, Inglewhite, Longridge, Hurst Green, Museum of Childhood, Ribble, Billington

BLACKPOOL, Pleasure Beach, Common Edge, Wesham, Kirkham, Wrea Green, Chingle Hall, Grimsargh, Broughton, Museum of Roman Antiquities, Ribchester, Bremetennacvm Fort, Great Harwood

St Anne's, Ashton Gardens, Lowther Gardens, Warton, Freckleton, Teg Town, Fulwood, Sharoe Green, Ribbleton, Samlesbury Hall, Samlesbury, Mellor, BLACKBURN

Lytham St Anne's, Lytham, Ribble, Ribble Way, Hutton, Higher Penwortham, New Longton, Longton, County & Regimental Museum, Harris Mus & Art Gallery, PRESTON, Higher Walton, Hoghton Tower, Witton Country Park, Lewis Textile Mus

Hesketh Bank, Much Hoole, British Commercial Vehicle Museum, Leyland, South Ribble Museum, Brindle, Tockholes, Sunnyhurst Wood Mus, Roddlesworth, Darwen

Banks, Bretherton, Tarleton, Croston, Worden Hall, Euxton, Astley Hall, White Coppice, Anglezark Moor, Lead Mines Clough, Turton Towers

Hesketh Park Aviary, Zoo, Botanic Gardens Museum, Holmeswood, Eccleston, Yarrow, Chorley, Rivington, Old Barn, Lever Park, Rivington Pike, The Last Drop Village, Jumbles Res

Atkinson Art Gallery, Southport, Royal Birkdale, Steamport Transport Museum, Martin Mere, Rufford, Rufford Old Hall, Camelot, Coppull, Smithills Hall

Ainsdale, Ainsdale Sand Dunes, Scarisbrick, Parbold, Burscough, Standish, Halls 'ith'-Wood Mus, Edgworth

WOODVALE, Halsall

MORECAMBE BAY WARNING: Walks across Morecambe Bay can be dangerous. Seek local guidance.

Scale: 0 Miles 2 4 6 / 0 Km 5 10

LANCASHIRE

Wyre Valley, Lune, Greta

Appletreewick 🏠 Df
Pretty hillside village with old merchants' and yeoman farmers' houses and cottages and fine 17th-century mansions Mock Beggar Hall and High Hall. Beautiful terrace gardens of Parcevall Hall found nearby.

Barley 🏠☑ Bd
Start for easiest route to 1827ft gritstone plateau of Pendle Hill, notorious for group of 17th-century witches. Panoramas over Pennines. Visitor centre in village for walkers.

Bolton Abbey ♥⛪⛪🎋 De
Charming ruins of 12th-century Augustinian priory set among woods, waterfalls and meadows. Eleven paintings on east wall symbolise life of Christ, and lengthened nave is now parish church. Waymarked nature trails.

Bolton-by-Bowland 🏠 Ad
Attractive village of whitewashed houses and two tree-fringed greens by Tosside Beck. Medieval Church of St Peter and St Paul has memorial to 15th-century landowner Sir Ralph Pudsey, his three wives and 25 children.

Burnley 🏛♣🏛 Bc
Memories of 19th-century cotton town in Weavers' Triangle – section of Leeds and Liverpool Canal with textile mills, factories and other canal-side buildings. Towneley Hall, 1½ miles south-east, 14th-century fortified home with Elizabethan and Regency additions. Museum of Local Arts and Crafts in brewhouse.

CANAL-SIDE MEMORIES *The Clocktower Cotton Mill, Burnley, is now a preserved industrial relic.*

Burnsall 🏠 Df
Village green on banks of River Wharfe near massive five-arched bridge. St Wilfrid's Church has 16th-century tower, Norman font, Jacobean pulpit and 10th-century 'hog-back' gravestones. Grammar school building (1602) with gabled porch and mullioned windows now primary school.

Clapham 🏠🏛☆ Af
Four stone bridges cross Clapham Beck mountain stream in village of grey-stone cottages. Walks upstream along banks bushy with acacias and rhododendrons to exotic gardens of Ingleborough Hall, to fantastic stalactites and stalagmites of Ingleborough Show Cave and to Norber Boulders, massive slate blocks perched on limestone pedestals.

UNDER THE LONELY MOORS

This is a countryside of high moorlands, limestone hills, steep-sided valleys and plunging waterfalls. To the north, the lush green splendour gives way to the harsh magnificence of Brontë country. Set amidst this beauty are villages made prosperous by the cotton and wool industries, whose mills, merchants' houses, workers' cottages and places of worship provide a unique charm.

IDEAL RETREAT *Ruins of Bolton Abbey lie on the River Wharfe.*

Clitheroe 🏰🎋☑ Ad
Ancient market town between cliff-top ruins of Norman castle and hillside St Mary Magdalene's Church, built 12th century but mostly 19th century. Water still flows from medieval Heald and Stocks wells.

East Riddlesden Hall 🏛 Dd
Superb 17th-century oak panelling and plaster-work, oak furniture and pewter in Jacobean manor house. Magnificent 120ft long medieval tithe barn.

Gawthorpe Hall 🏛 Bc
Embroidery, lace and costume collections in 17th-century manor house. Built around remains of peel tower, much remodelled in 1850s. Restored Great Barn and Estate Block in gardens.

Giggleswick 🏠 Bf
Peaceful and enchanting Pennine village of stone cottages. Nearby Yorkshire Dales Falconry and Conservation Centre has daily demonstrations, eagle aviaries, vultures and other rare birds.

Grassington 🏠🏛☑ Df
Handsome dales village with medieval bridge across Wharfe and cobbled market square. Two 18th-century lead miners' cottages form Upper Wharfedale Folk Museum recording local domestic and working history.

Hardcastle Crags ☆ Cc
Valley of Hebden Water named from large angular rocks, eroded by river, lining valley sides. Disused Gibson's Mill, old tollbridge and abundant wildlife including kingfishers and dippers.

Haworth 🏛📖 Dc
Two places in one – old hilltop town with Brontë's parsonage home linked by steep, cobbled Main Street to mill town on Keighley and Worth Valley Railway. Parsonage is museum furnished as the Brontë sisters knew it and with many family relics. Museum of Childhood has Victorian and Edwardian dolls, teddy bears and toy trains.

Healey Dell ♦♣⛲ Ba
Towering 200ft long, eight-arched viaduct (1880) above River Spodden forms part of trail through nature reserve in tree-lined valley rich in flowers.

Helmshore Textile Museum 🏛 Ab
Two mill museums in tiny country village. Tall stone mill follows transformation of cotton waste into finished yarn and neighbouring Higher Mill retains water wheel and massive wooden hammers which pounded soaked wool into felt.

Heptonstall 🏠🏛 Cb
Captivating hillside village below Pennine moors with churchyard shared by roofless ruin of 13th-century chapel of St Thomas Becket and 1850s church of St Thomas the Apostle. Grammar

LIMESTONE WILDERNESS *The wild and craggy fastness of Gordale Scar lies about 1½ miles east of Malham Cove.*

school, founded 1642, has some original furniture and village history museum. Foundation stone of octagonal Methodist church laid by John Wesley, 1764, the founder of Methodism.

Hollingworth Lake ⛵☑ Ca
Popular destination since Victorian times, with boat trips, waymarked lake shore trail, bird sanctuary, information centre and Easter funfair.

Keighley 🏛🏛 Dd
Cliffe Castle Museum in magnificent Victorian mansion records history of Airedale, including reconstructed craftsmen's workshops and natural history and geology displays. Finely decorated reception rooms furnished with French furniture and art treasures. Grounds include extensive gardens, conservatory and small aviary.

Keighley and Worth Valley Railway 🚂🏛 Dc
Restored steam line runs through 5 miles of fine Pennine scenery from Haworth to Oxenhope. Edwardian station at Oakworth featured in television drama *The Railway Children*. Steam locomotive museum in Oxenhope and workshops in Haworth.

Kilnsey ☆🎣☑ Cf
Greystone village in base of vast Kilnsey Crag. Church of St Mary rebuilt in 1846 on site of Anglo-Saxon chapel. Medieval features include two massive Norman arches in north side of nave.

Langcliffe Scar ☆ Bf
Craggy headlands of the scar are riddled with caves, most famous of which is Victoria Cave. Remains of Ice Age animals, and Stone Age, Roman and Celtic artefacts excavated from here. Relics from this and other caves are on display at Pig Yard Museum in Settle.

Linton 🏠 Cf
Stone cottages, ivy-clad walls, and immaculate gardens centre on a green overlooked by large 18th-century almshouse, in what was once voted 'Loveliest Village in the North'. St Michael's Church dates back to 14th century and contains fine medieval altar and Jacobean pulpit.

Malham Cove ☆ Bf
Gigantic natural amphitheatre with walls 240ft high, created by earth movements in the Ice Age; home to many plants such as

hart's tongue fern and herb robert. Paths lead to staggering cliffs of Gordale Scar, where waterfalls plunge into ravine 250ft deep. A mile north of cove is Malham Tarn, where Charles Kingsley set opening scenes of *The Water Babies*; large lake with abundant bird life. Information centre at nearby Malham village gives details of walks and drives.

Middle Wharfedale De
Area of glorious fells scenery, best between Ilkley and Grassington, where outlines of outstanding Romano-British field system can be seen.

Penistone Hill Country Park 🐑✳🏛 Dc
Fine views of glorious heather moorland surround marked paths and picnic areas here. Penistone Hill good starting point for walks into Brontë country – Brontë waterfalls for instance.

Rochdale 🏛☑ Ba
Rochdale Pioneers' Memorial Museum commemorates the town's status as birthplace of the Cooperative Movement in the 1840s. Town was famous for making both wool and cotton cloth; 19th-century town hall modelled on Flemish cloth halls. John Bright (1811-89), opponent of Corn Laws, and Gracie Fields (1898-1979), singer, born here. On Blackstone Edge, 2 miles east, one of the best preserved stretches of Roman road in country.

Sabden 🏠✳ Ac
In spring, gorse and aromatic heather buzzing with honey bees line descent to village. From St Nicholas' Church, 1841, azaleas and rhododendrons frame views to Padiham Heights. Breathtaking views of Fylde coast and Lakeland hills from Nick of Pendle.

Settle ☑🏛 Bf
Limestone cliffs overlook this bustling market town with handsome square, multitude of small courts and alleyways contained

y 18th and 19th-century houses.
Museum of North Craven life in
Chapel Street. Excellent centre for
country walks.

Skipton ♙✝🏛 Ce

Two massive stone towers guard
entrance to Skipton Castle,
moated fort boasting 50ft long
banqueting hall, 'shell room' with
walls decorated with seashells,
large kitchen and dungeon. In
front of castle stands Holy Trinity
Church, mostly 14th century.
Market open most days on High
Street. Nearby Craven Museum
displays local history.

Sowerby Bridge Db

Group of late 18th-century warehouses stands in this canal basin
at meeting of Rochdale Canal and
Calder and Hebble Navigation.
Underneath buildings are shipping holes, where barges were
loaded under cover. Basin now
used for pleasure craft.

Stainforth ♙☆ Bf

Charming waterfall tumbles in
wooded ravine just below village's 17th-century packhorse
bridge over River Ribble. Stepping stones at village centre start
longer walk to Catrigg Foss
waterfall.

Troller's Gill ☆ Df

Spectacular but eerie limestone
ravine below Barden Fell, reputedly haunted by a barghest, or
spectral hound. Lead mine at end
of ravine dug by miner named
Troller.

Turton Tower🏰 Aa

Fine Tudor house built around
15th-century peel tower fortified
against Scots. Used as farmhouse
in 18th century and restored as
manor house in 1830s. Now a
museum with fine collection of
armour, Tudor and Victorian furniture, and German chandelier
made from antlers.

Whalley ♙○✤ Ac

Village grouped around 13th-
century Cistercian abbey. Church
of St Mary, also 13th century, has
amusing carved misericords, or
hinged shelves on choir seats,
including one of wife hitting husband with frying pan. Disused
viaduct, 2000ft long with 49
arches, used to carry Blackburn to
Hellifield railway. Ancient corn
mill surrounded by brightly
painted cottages.

Worsthorne ♙ Bc

Extremely pretty village with
17th-century shops and cottages
and small green overlooked by
Victorian church. Walk half a mile
through meadows to equally
charming village of Hurstwood.
House of poet Edmund Spenser,
author of *Faerie Queen*, here. Also,
stable once owned by Richard
Tattersall, founder of Newmarket
sales.

Wycoller Country Park
🏛⚶ Cc

Single-slab or 'clam' bridge, 2000
years old, crosses stream in
depths of ancient hunting forest.
Nearby Wycoller Hall was the original of Ferndean Manor in *Jane
Eyre*. Also 19th-century industrial
village perfectly preserved – no
cars allowed. Three easy walks.

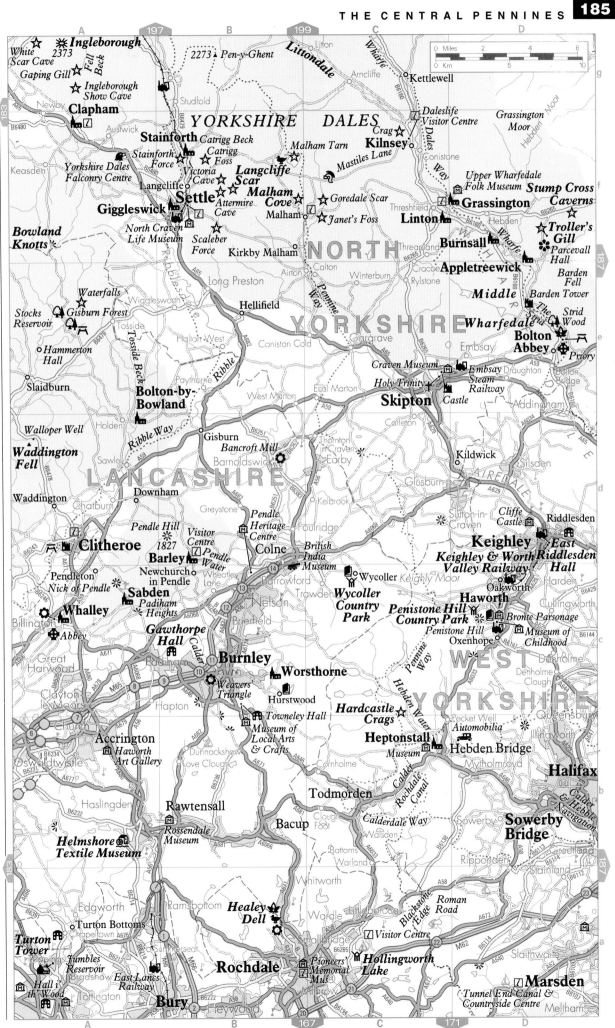

Aldborough Ef
Little village with houses clustered round green and maypole; capital of a Celtic tribe 2000 years ago, then known as Isurium Brigantum. Remains of Roman town wall and mosaic pavements with relics in museum.

Barwick in Elmet Dc
Once a tiny Anglo-Saxon kingdom, village retains extensive remains of earthworks. Festivities held in spring at nearby maypole.

Bingley Bc
Leeds and Liverpool Canal runs through this medieval wool town. Between Three Rise and Five Rise Locks, water level raised by manmade staircase against hillside; magnificent example of late 18th-century canal engineering. Towpath walk, 16th-century church.

Boroughbridge Df
Market town around crossing point of River Ure, with early 19th-century coaching inns. West of town, stone monoliths known as Devil's Arrows formed part of Bronze Age religious site.

Bracken Hall Countryside Centre Bc
Scenery, history and wildlife displays of area at top of Shipley Glen. Nature walks through wide, airy moors. Shipley Glen cable tramway (1895) runs over steepest part of route.

Bradford Bc
City born of the Industrial Revolution with tiers of terraced houses and mill chimneys dotting skyline. Victorian City Hall and opulent Wool Exchange. Industrial Museum in former mill has machinery and locomotives. Unique Colour Museum explores world of dyes and colours. Cartwright Hall offers baroque setting for fine art collection. Bolling Hall Museum in 15th-century manor house has 17th-century oak furniture in period rooms; Chippendale furniture in Georgian wing. More modern delights at National Museum of Photography, Film and Television; IMAX theatre has England's largest cinema screen.

Bramham Park Ed
Queen Anne mansion built 1698–1710, with outstanding French-style formal gardens. Canal, ponds, groves, statues and temples create a miniature Versailles. Waymarked woodland walks.

Bretton Hall Ca
Unusual outdoor art collection in Yorkshire Sculpture Park. Exhibits by Barbara Hepworth and Elizabeth Frink displayed in parkland and formal gardens. Waymarked trails in nearby 96 acre Country Park lead through nature reserve with Canada geese.

Brimham Rocks Cf
Fantastic shapes of moorland sandstone outcrops, carved by Druids according to legend; carved by rain, wind and weather in fact. Splendid situation high above Nidderdale.

Fountains Abbey Cf
Grand, romantic ruins of 12th-century Cistercian abbey, with long line of cloisters extending for

WHERE WEALTH MEANT WOOL

The prosperity of central Yorkshire was built on wool. In the Middle Ages, wool brought wealth to the monks of Fountains Abbey and a living to the village weaver. As the centuries passed, the mills helped villages develop into towns and towns grow into prosperous cities. The profits contributed to the splendours found in many fine country houses that are such a feature of the region.

CISTERCIAN GRANDEUR *Sunlight streams through the impressive ruins of 12th-century Fountains Abbey.*

312ft. Nearby Studley Royal garden, laid out in the 18th century, has follies, temples, waterfalls and statues. Bounded on northern edge by deer park extending 400 acres. Abbey history in Jacobean Fountains Hall.

Golcar Aa
Weaving village of solid stone houses perched on hill above Colne valley. Colne Valley Museum in terrace of weavers' cottages, with hand looms and living rooms where wool was spun before days of steam.

Halifax Ab
Cloth town since 15th century. Wool trade's ancient Piece Hall, rebuilt 1770s, now transformed into textile museum, shops and art gallery. Textile machinery and street scenes re-creating Halifax of 1850s in Calderdale Industrial Museum. Costumes and textiles from around the world in Bankfield Museum. West Yorkshire Folk Museum housed in 15th-century mansion of Shibden Hall. Magnificent Wainhouse Tower of 1875 was built as grand mill chimney, but never used. Reconstruction of Halifax Gibbet, used in executions 13th–17th centuries.

Harewood House Dd
Regal 18th-century house built by John Carr with Woodland Garden, Bird Garden, Penguin Pond, and Paradise Garden with tropical wildlife. Robert Adam designed interiors and Thomas Chippendale made furniture. Spanish Library has Yorkshire landscapes by Turner. Gallery has 76ft long Adam ceiling, with paintings of gods and goddesses.

Harlow Carr Gardens Ce
Cold, exposed site on edge of moors where Northern Horticultural Society manages to grow splendid rhododendrons and heathers. Stream-side gardens.

Harrogate De
Grass and flowerbeds of The Stray surround this spa town. Royal Pump Room Museum (1842) still has old sulphur well, and local history displays include pottery, costumes and Victoriana. English paintings and watercolours in Harrogate Art Gallery.

Horsforth Hall Park Cc
City park with traditional herbaceous borders and bowling green, and unusual Japanese garden.

Huddersfield Ba
Industrial townscape with one of the finest railway buildings in England; designed 1847 in classical style by J.P. Pritchett. Art gallery with works by Gainsborough, Lowry, Turner and Constable. Tolson Memorial Museum in Victorian mansion contains folk life displays, horse-drawn vehicles and numerous toys.

Ilkley Bd
Roman fort that became an elegant 19th-century spa town; retreat for wealthy Bradford wool merchants. Elizabethan Manor House Museum and Art Gallery, on site of Roman fort near exposed section of Roman wall, tells history of town. Moorland walks.

Kirkstall Abbey Cc
Well-preserved 12th-century Cistercian church. Gatehouse now a museum with 18th and 19th-

century cottages, workshops and shops with period furnishings. Items from abbey excavations, costumes from 1760, Folk Galleries with toys, domestic bygones.

Knaresborough De
Market town with narrow streets and Georgian houses, dominated by ruins of Norman castle partly demolished by Roundheads. Steep steps and alleys lead down to River Nidd. Damp and eerie Dropping Well hung with curious objects, solidified by lime in water. Prophetess Mother Shipton said to be born in lane nearby (1488). Old Courthouse, dating from 14th century, has original courtroom preserved.

Leeds Cc
Middle Ages wool centre; sheep on Yorkshire moors still provide wool for spinning and weaving.

MIRROR IMAGE *Lofty rail bridge spans the Nidd at Knaresborough.*

Impressive Town Hall (1858) has Corinthian columns and 255ft clock tower. Corn Exchange of 1861 has huge, domed roof. Ornate shopping arcades built mostly in late Victorian period. Middleton Colliery Railway was first to run steam locomotives in 1812; steam and diesel engines on display. City Museum and Art Gallery has works by Henry Moore, an aquarium, animal and bird tableaux, and a full reconstruction of a Roman kitchen. Outside, the piazza is laid out with large, playable chess sets. Industrial Museum housed in grand 1806 wool mill shows development of textiles and clothing.

STRIKING OUTLAW *Robin Hood Clock in Leeds' Thornton Arcade.*

Newby Hall Df
One of most elegant houses in north of England, dating from late 17th century, but dominant style is 18th century with interiors by Robert Adam. Church (1872) in grounds richly decorated in high Victorian style. Miniature steam railway runs through gardens famed for herbaceous borders.

Nostell Priory Ea
Palladian house designed by James Paine in 1733; each state room a masterpiece with decorations by Robert Adam, wall paintings by Venetian artist Zucchi, and notable collection of Chippendale furniture. Lakeside walks, rose gardens, and 16th-century church in grounds.

Oakwell Hall Cb
Manor house built 1583; visited by Charlotte Brontë in 1830s and used as model for 'Fieldhead' in her novel *Shirley*. Restored and furnished in style of 17th and 18th centuries. Country park with wildlife garden, formal gardens and woodland walks.

Otley Cd
Old town with medieval courts and alleyways. Part-Norman church has scale model of the Bramhope railway tunnel in churchyard; monument to men who died during its construction, 1845–9. Steep wooded hillside of The Chevin rises behind town; forest park with woodland walks.

Pateley Bridge Bf
Little town with street of stone cottages swooping down to bridge over River Nidd. Old workhouse (1863) is Nidderdale Museum, where Dale life is illustrated with domestic, farming and industrial bygones.

Plompton Rocks ☆ De
Massive gritstone rocks, worn by thousands of years of erosion into fantastic shapes. Curious outlines reflected in lake, with stretch of woodland nearby.

Red House Museum 🏛 Cb
Red-brick house built 1660 by cloth merchant, William Taylor. Alterations produced Regency country residence where Charlotte Brontë stayed weekends. House appears as 'Briarmains' in her novel *Shirley*. Now furnished in style of the 1820s with local history displays.

Ripley ☆ 🏛 Cf
Lord of the manor, Sir William Amcotts Ingilby, attempted to remodel Ripley into style of a typical French village in 1827. Yorkshire character prevails in the cobbled square, grey-stone houses and village stocks. Ingilbys have lived here since 1350 in Ripley Castle; rebuilt 1780 with gardens designed by Capability Brown. Arched 15th-century gatehouse and 16th-century tower remain from earlier days.

Ripon 🏛 🏛 † Dg
Cathedral dates from 12th century with Saxon crypt. Liberty Prison dates from 1815 and houses Prison and Police Museum, with police mementos and equipment from 17th century onwards. Town history illustrated in 13th-century Wakeman's House Museum, reputed to be haunted.

Saltaire 🏛 🏛 Bc
Victorian 'factory' village created as alternative to Bradford's 'dark satanic mills' by industrialist Sir Titus Salt (1803-76), where industry and beauty combine in Italian style buildings. Mill (1853) with chimney disguised as Venetian bell tower, now houses works by artist David Hockney. Splendid Classical-style church (1859) by canal, and almshouses modelled on Italian villas. Reed organ collection in Victoria Hall.

Stump Cross Caverns ☆ Af
Underground wonderland of stalactites and stalagmites, probably began forming some 500,000 years ago, discovered mid-19th century. Floodlit paths wind past rocks named after their shapes.

Temple Newsam 🏛 ⚘ ☆ Dc
Elegant Tudor and Jacobean mansion built around 1500 on estate once owned by Knights Templar. Splendid suite of Georgian rooms. Capability Brown landscaped 1000 acre park in 1760s. Seven gardens and Home Farm with rare breeds of livestock.

Wakefield ☆ ⚔ † 🏛 🏛 Db
Georgian houses reflect prosperity of days as centre of clothing trade. Cathedral, founded 13th century, has Yorkshire's tallest spire at 247ft. Medieval bridge over Calder has rare 14th-century bridge chapel. Former Caphouse Colliery is now Yorkshire Mining Museum with underground tours. Art gallery features works by Barbara Hepworth and Henry Moore. Museum features exotic birds and animals collected by 19th-century local naturalist, Charles Waterton.

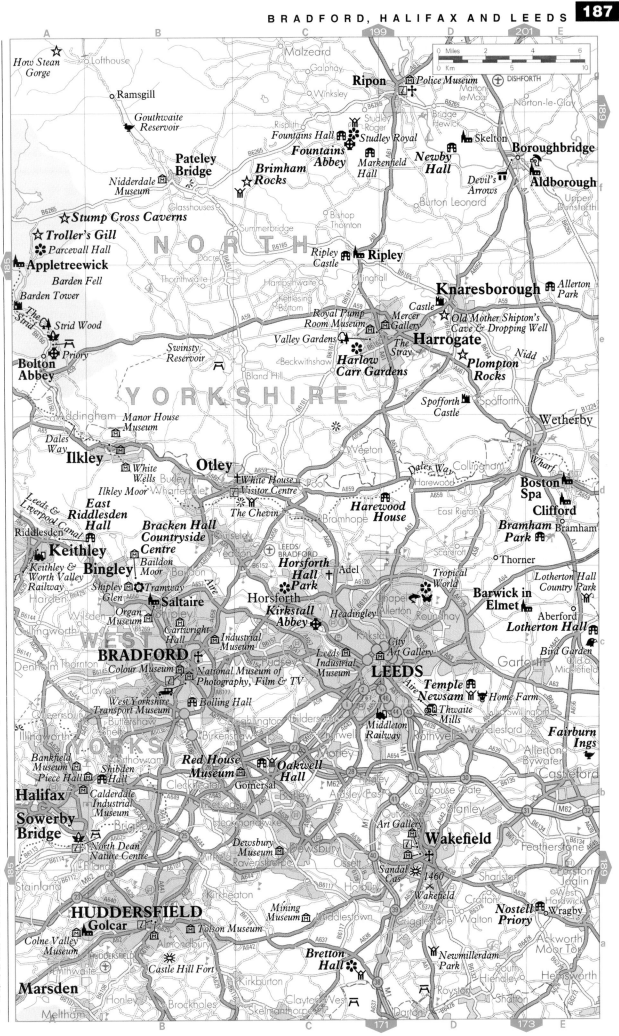

Allerthorpe Common
🦆🌲 Dd

Remnant of once-mighty York Forest – one of few stretches of woodland left around Selby after most of area was farmed. Owned by Forestry Commission, which has laid out picnic site from which paths radiate through woods.

Alne 🏠 Af

St Mary's Church is basically Norman with carved south doorway. West tower has 18th-century additions. The interior contains Norman font and 14th-century effigy of lady.

COUNTRY GARDEN *The west front of Beningbrough Hall provides a backdrop to the parterre.*

Beningbrough Hall 🏛 Be

Life in an English country house is illustrated here, from sumptuous Georgian apartments to a Victorian laundry. Recently restored by the National Trust, the red-brick mansion has fine interior carving and panelling.

Bishop Wilton 🏠 De

Tiny Norman church has rare black-and-white mosaic floor with local bird-like motif. Village centred in region which has many prehistoric burial sites.

Bolton Percy 🏠 Bd

Village's 15th-century church has stained-glass window bearing arms of Bishop Scrope – executed in 1405 by Henry IV for treason.

Bossall † Df

Church of St Botolph, dating from Norman times, has central tower. Font with 18th-century cover may be Norman. Church also contains brass dating from 1454.

Boston Spa 🏠 Ad

Georgian houses survive from time when spa was popular resort. Spa bathhouse now serves as headquarters for angling club. Old bridge crosses River Wharfe. Riverside and woodland walks.

Carlton Towers 🏛 Cb

Victorian Gothic country house, work of 19th-century architect Pugin. Beneath Gothic extravagance lies original Jacobean home of Stapleton family, residents from Norman conquest until the 19th century.

Castle Howard 🏛 Dg

Sir John Vanbrugh's design for 3rd Earl of Carlisle features vast dome above entrance. Paintings include works by Van Dyck, Gainsborough and Reynolds. Grounds contain 70 acre lake.

LANDSCAPE WITH RIVERS

A broad expanse of lowland is dominated by a single river system. The well-watered soil gives rise to rich farmland that makes an idyllic setting for the Vale of York's market towns and villages. In the west is a ridge of limestone, which has been used in many of the area's buildings, from simple cottages to some of the finest ecclesiastical architecture in Britain.

Clifford 🏠 Ad

Village of stone cottages. Roman Catholic church, dedicated to St Edward the Confessor, built in 1845-8 in Romanesque style. Tower added in 1859-66.

Darrington 🏠 Ab

Norman church features unusual arcaded gallery above north chapel and aisle. Cross-legged effigies of knight and lady date from 14th century.

Easingwold † Bf

Small market town of cobbled streets, and weathered red-brick dwellings around a large green. Church, rebuilt in 15th century, contains coffin used to carry poor to their graves.

Eastrington 🏠 Db

Village dominated by St Michael's Church, of Anglo-Saxon origin. Now mostly Norman, church contains 15th-century memorial to judge – depicted wearing armour, robes and pigtail.

Eden Camp 🏛 Dg

Former POW camp houses vivid re-creation of World War II era of British life. Sights, sounds and smells of enemy bombing raids, day-to-day life of rationing and propaganda all portrayed.

Fairburn Ings 🐦 Ab

Shallow ponds and mounds of mining waste serve as a bird reserve hosting 170-80 species. 'Ings', Old Norse for 'meadow', indicates the Viking past.

Hemingbrough 🏠 Cc

Slender, 180ft church spire soars above village of 18th-century houses. One surviving misericord in church is oldest in England, dating from around 1200.

Holme-on-Spalding Moor
🏠†▲ Ec

Monks once kept lookout from church on Church Hill, ringing its bell to guide night travellers through surrounding marshland. Now drained, the area provides grassy picnic spot and views.

Howden † Db

Small market town has some medieval and Georgian houses. Church, dedicated to St Peter and St Paul, has columns in nave dating from 1267.

Kirkham Priory ✚ Df

Augustinian priory on River Derwent, dating from 12th century, has Norman doorway and richly carved 13th-century gatehouse façade. Best view from riverside path near three-arched bridge.

Ledsham 🏠 Ab

Church of All Saints dates from 8th century, with Norman additions. Saxon windows and doorway. Memorials inside include one for an 18th-century philanthropist, Lady Elizabeth Hastings – who died in Ledsham in 1739.

SILENT STONES *The choir of Howden's church collapsed in 1696.*

Lotherton Hall 🏛 🐦 Ac

Edwardian mansion with art, furniture collections. Bird garden designed to re-introduce birds to the wild. Species live in landscaped aviaries or fly free.

Malton †🏛❀ Dg

Old market town surrounds church dating from Norman times. Museum tells town's history from 8000 BC – included are Roman fort remains from AD 70. Stone houses dating from 18th century line main street.

Newton Kyme 🏠 Ad

John Milton read lessons in the 13th-century church, Elizabeth I visited Newton Kyme Hall. Sir Thomas Fairfax's church memorial commemorates his part in the 1704 capture of Gibraltar.

Old Malton 🏠 Dg

Best features are 12th-century church ruins and modern working farm that provides farming lectures and displays.

Pocklington †🏛 Ed

Market town's All Saints' Church, built between 1200 and 1450, has 15th-century tower. Inside is 14th-century churchyard cross. Penny Arcadia houses collection of amusement machines.

Pontefract 🏛🏰 Ab

Georgian houses and shops still survive in town. Castle founded in 11th century – part of 13th to 14th-century great tower and some walls remain.

Selby ✚☑ Cc

Three-towered limestone abbey dates from 1069. Georgian houses can be seen in The Crescent and Market Place.

Sherburn in Elmet 🏠 Ac

Late-Norman church occupies earlier Saxon church site dating from old Kingdom of Elmet days.

Sheriff Hutton 🏠🏰❀ Cf

Village dominated by 14th-century castle ruin – once seat of Richard III. Sheriff Hutton Hall was originally James I's hunting lodge. Grounds open to public.

Skelton 🏠 Be

Church of St Giles, built 1250, is well preserved. Unusually, no later additions were built, making it a rare, single-style structure.

Snaith 🏠 Cb

Large priory church, originally Norman, rebuilt in 13th and 15th centuries when west tower and battlements were added.

Stamford Bridge 🏠✕🍴 De

Site of Harold of England's victory over Harald of Norway in other great English battle of 1066.

Steeton Hall Gateway 🏛 Ac

Small, well-preserved gatehouse, dating from 14th century, stands near South Milford.

Sutton Park 🏛 Bf

Early Georgian house, built 1730, contains furniture by Chippendale and Sheraton. Parkland was designed by Capability Brown – includes lily canal, woodland walks and Georgian ice house.

Yorkshire Museum of Farming 🏛 Ce

Museum set in 8 acres of country park has exhibits illustrating Yorkshire's agricultural heritage. Farm animals and agricultural machinery on display.

FARMING COUNTRY *Farm fields create a colourful patchwork effect along the flat plain of the Vale of York.*

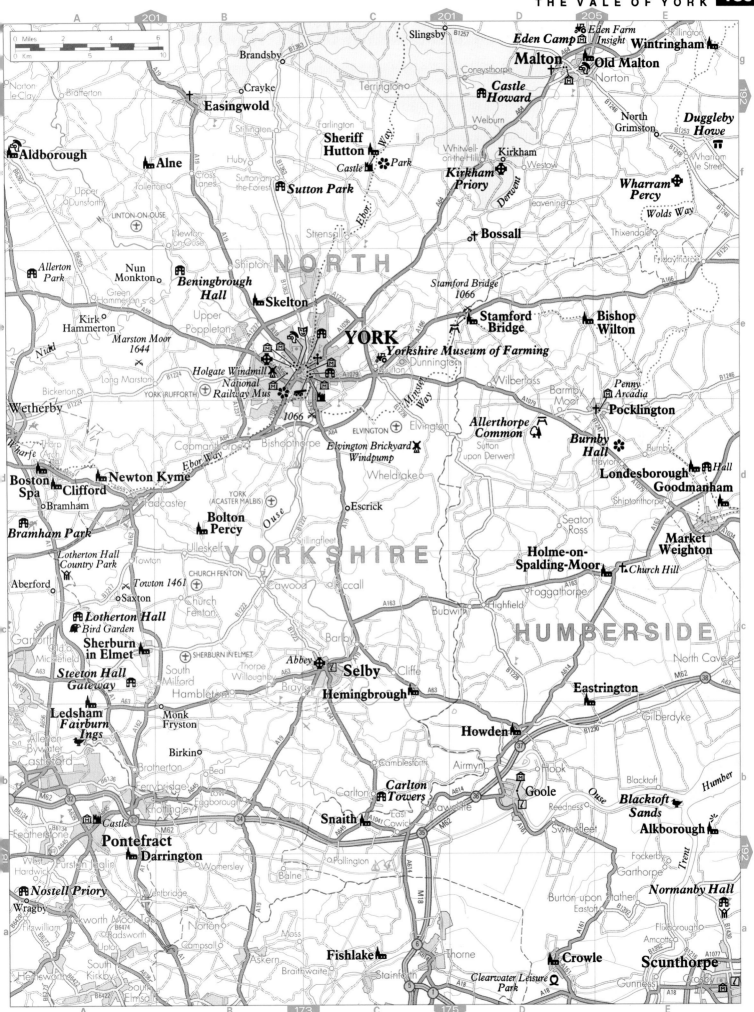

0 Miles 2 4 6
0 Km 5 10

Slingsby

Eden Camp *Eden Farm Insight*

Malton **Old Malton** Norton

Wintringham

Brandsby

Crayke

Easingwold

Terrington

Coneysthorpe

Welburn

North Grimston

Dugglby Howe

Aldborough **Alne**

Farlington

Stillington

Huby

Sutton-on-the-Forest

Sheriff Hutton *Castle* *Park*

Castle Howard

Whitwell-on-the-Hill

Kirkham

Westow

Leavening

Kirkham Priory *Derwent*

Wharram Percy

Wolds Way

Wharram le Street

Brafferton

Norton-le-Clay

Upper Dunsforth

Tollerton

Cross Lanes

LINTON-ON-OUSE

Newton-on-Ouse

Shipton

Strensall

Bossall

Thixendale

Fridaythorpe

Allerton Park

Nun Monkton

Beningbrough Hall

Green Hammerton

Upper Poppleton

N O R T H

Stamford Bridge 1066

Stamford Bridge

Bishop Wilton

Skelton

Kirk Hammerton

Marston Moor 1644

YORK

Yorkshire Museum of Farming

Dunnington

Murton

Wilberfoss

Barmby Moor

Penny Arcadia

Pocklington

Long Marston

Bickerton

Nidd

Holgate Windmill

National Railway Mus

YORK (RUFFORTH)

A1079

Elvington

Allerthorpe Common Sutton upon Derwent

Hayton

Burnby

Wetherby

1066

Copmanthorpe

Bishopthorpe

ELVINGTON

Elvington

Burnby Hall

Londesborough

Wharfe

Thorp Arch

Ebor Way

Elvington Brickyard Windpump

Wheldrake

Seaton Ross

Londesborough **Hall**

Goodmanham

Boston Spa **Clifford**

Newton Kyme

Tadcaster

Bramham

YORK (ACASTER MALBIS)

Ouse

Escrick

Shiptonthorpe

Market Weighton

Bramham Park

Bolton Percy

Ulleskelf

Y O R K S H I R E

Sillingfleet

Holme-on-Spalding-Moor **Church Hill**

Lotherton Hall Country Park

Towton

CHURCH FENTON

Towton 1461

Cawood

Riccall

Foggathorpe

Aberford

Saxton

Church Fenton

H U M B E R S I D E

North Cave

Lotherton Hall *Bird Garden*

Sherburn in Elmet

SHERBURN IN ELMET

Bubwith

Highfield

Garforth

Micklefield

South Milford

Thorpe Willoughby

Barlby

Steeton Hall Gateway

Hambleton

Brayton

Selby *Abbey* Cliffe

Hemingbrough

Eastrington

Gilberdyke

Ledsham **Fairburn Ings**

Monk Fryston

Allerton Bywater

Castleford

Birkin

Beal

Camblesforth

Howden

Airmyn

Hook

Blacktoft

Humber

Nostell Priory

Wragby

Brotherton

Ferrybridge

Knottingley

Eggborough

Carlton

Carlton Towers

East Cowick

Goole

Rawcliffe

Reedness

Swinefleet

Blacktoft Sands

Alkborough

Featherstone

Purston Jaglin

Castle

Pontefract **Darrington**

Womersley

Balne

Snaith

Pollington

Fockerby

Garthorpe

Burton upon Stather

Normanby Hall

West Hardwick

Badsworth

Norton

Moss

Campsall

Askern

Braithwaite

Stainforth

Thorne

Fishlake

Eastoft

Amcotts

Flixborough

Crowle

Scunthorpe

South Kirkby

Clearwater Leisure Park

Gunness

Crosby

STREETS ALIVE WITH HISTORY

England's 'eternal city' is a place of outstanding beauty with its history recorded in the streets, buildings and museums gathered around the mighty Minster. Within York's towering medieval walls is a heart of rich and colourful character, where relics of Roman Eboracum and Viking Jorvik live side by side with re-created Victorian and Edwardian streets.

The ARC Dc
Archaeological Resource Centre with excellent visitor involvement. Try ancient crafts such as stitching a Roman shoe or weaving on a Viking loom, handle artefacts or sieve soil samples.

All Saints, North Street † Bb
Although parts of this church are older, the feature is the 15th-century 'Prykke of Conscience' stained-glass window which depicts the world's last 15 days according to an English mystic.

All Saints, Pavement † Cb
Mainly 15th-century church but the west tower was rebuilt in the early 1800s. Its octagonal lantern was a guide to travellers.

Assembly Rooms Cc
Built 1731-2. The roof of the 112ft long centre hall is supported by 52 Corinthian columns.

Bar Convent Museum 🏛 Ba
Based in the oldest active convent in the country, it features an elegant chapel and a display telling the story of its Sisters.

Bootham Bar Cd
North-west gateway, built in 14th century, has two hanging turrets.

Castle Museum 🏛 Db
Covers 400 years of Yorkshire life and even includes Victorian and Edwardian reconstructed streets, period rooms and the condemned cell in which Dick Turpin spent his final night before being hanged.

Clifford's Tower Db
Keep, 13th-century, of the ruined York Castle. Built by Henry III on the artificial mound of William the Conqueror's wooden tower which guarded the Ouse. Has one of the finest views of the city.

Fairfax House 🏛 Db
One of the greatest examples of a Georgian town house in England, with a superbly decorated exterior and rooms filled with 18th-century furniture and clocks.

Friargate Wax Museum 🏛 Cb
Among the famous and infamous from past and present are world leaders, British monarchs and politicians; also a chamber of horrors. New exhibition of Britain's visual history each year.

BLUE BLOOD *The extravagant interior of Queen Victoria's railway carriage in the National Railway Museum.*

Guildhall Cc
Burnt out in a 1942 air raid but restored to its 15th-century design with a carved timber roof supported by columns made from oak. The Inner Chamber retains its original timbers.

Holy Trinity † Cc
One of the city's most interesting churches, built between 1250 and 1500. Has a rare pitched roof, notable woodwork and some ancient glass.

Impressions Gallery of Photography 🏛 Db
A wide range of modern and historical exhibitions in the first contemporary photography gallery to open outside London. Includes video and computer displays.

DIGGING UP THE PAST *This detail of an animal is from a fragment of a gravestone unearthed at the Viking settlement of Jorvik.*

Jorvik Viking Centre 🏛 Cb
On site of Jorvik, Viking city founded in AD 867. Relics found during excavations used in reconstructions of Viking life.

King's Manor Bc
Mostly Tudor building dating originally from 1270. Initially built as abbot's house, restored in 1960s and now used by university.

Mansion House Cc
Lord mayor's official residence, completed in 1730. It houses a magnificent collection of silver.

Merchant Adventurers' Hall Db
Britain's finest surviving medieval Guildhall, built 1350s. Exhibition describes merchants' wealth and influence at time when York was England's second city.

Merchant Taylors' Hall Dc
Built in the second half of the 14th-century. Has a fine timbered roof and was later used as a theatre.

Micklegate Bar Bb
Principal gateway commanding the southern approaches, where sovereigns were received and the heads of traitors displayed prominently. Two doors, a Norman archway and a pair of impressive turrets still remain.

Monk Bar Dd
The north-east gateway is the tallest and strongest fortress with two square gun ports and turrets. Six figures, 'silent watchers', hold stone missiles.

Multangular Tower 🔯 Bc
Most spectacular remnant of the 1st century Roman fortress-city of Eboracum, later incorporated in the medieval city wall. Chisel marks made by Roman masons can be seen.

Museum Gardens ❁ Bc
Ten acre botanical park on the banks of the Ouse near York Minster, famous for its animals and birds including peacocks and friendly squirrels.

Museum of Automata 🏛 Cb
Unique collection of mechanically animated figures spanning 2000 years from ancient articulated figurines to modern robotics. A video wall display provides a potted history of automata.

National Railway Museum 🏛 Ac
Historic locomotives, rolling stock and railway memorabilia explain the story of railways in Britain. Exhibits include the steam speed record holder *Mallard* and Queen Victoria's plush personal carriage.

Our Lady's Row Cc
Oldest surviving buildings in the city, built in 1316 and more or less in their original condition.

Raindale Watermill 🏛 Da
Corn mill, still working and dating back to 18th century, brought from its original site on the Yorkshire moors and restored.

Regimental Museum ⚔ Cb
History of the 4/7th Royal Dragoon Guards and the Prince of Wales' Own Yorkshire Regiment. Includes uniforms, weapons, medals and pictures.

Roman Bath Inn 🔯 Cc
Has the remains of Roman steam baths, including part of the brick hot-air ducting.

St Anthony's Hall Dc
Two-storey building dating from 15th century. First used as a workhouse and then a jail, school, armoury, and later a meeting place for merchants' guilds.

PALE SPLENDOUR *No less than 52 marble Corinthian columns support the ceiling of the 18th-century Assembly Rooms.*

ANCIENT HISTORY *Remains of the 1st-century Roman fortress Eboracum, which once stood on this site, can be seen at the Multangular Tower.*

St Leonard's Hospital Bc
Remains of a medieval hospital, rebuilt after a fire in 1137.

St Martin-le-Grand † Cb
Partly rebuilt after a 1942 air raid, but maintaining one of England's finest 15th-century windows.

St Mary's Abbey ✤ Bc
Impressive ruins containing much of the later additions to this 11th-century abbey.

St William's College Cd
Overshadowed by York Minster and built in 1453 for its Chantry priests; has a picturesque quadrangle and three well-preserved medieval rooms.

Shambles Cc
Shops lean over the street to keep it shaded and hooks inserted above windows are reminders that this was once a butchers' slaughterhouse and market.

Stonegate Cc
One of the city's best-preserved medieval streets follows earlier Roman road. A carved devil on one building marks site of former printing shop.

Theatre Royal ♟ Cc
Became one of the chief Georgian theatres in the country after opening in 1740. Later rebuilt and then enlarged.

Treasurer's House ⌂ Cd
Surrounded by a walled garden is one of the city's most beautiful buildings, dating from the 1620s. Also has period furniture and collections of pottery, china and antique glass.

Twelfth Century House Cc
Restored remnant of a Norman dwelling, the oldest house in the city. Substantial traces of original still remain.

The Walls
Three miles long and with walks providing superb views of the city. Built by Henry III around 1220, with four principal gateways and 39 towers.

STEPPING BACK IN TIME *Visitors can walk through lifelike replicas of Victorian and Edwardian streets in the Castle Museum.*

MEDIEVAL TOWERS *The Minster dominates the city skyline.*

Walmgate Bar Eb
The south-east gateway has the only complete barbican – the walls and towers guarding its approach – in England.

York City Art Gallery ⌂ Bd
Includes a collection of paintings by European masters from 14th to 19th centuries, and a display of stoneware pottery.

York Dungeon ⌂ Cb
Horror museum set in dark, musty cellars. Life-size tableaux depict medieval death and torture, including the sufferings of Dick Turpin and Guy Fawkes.

York Minster † Cc
Largest medieval cathedral in England, 519ft long with a central roof 198ft high, can be seen from anywhere in the city. Begun in 1220, it took more than 250 years to build. Among its famous stained glass is the tennis-court sized east window. The nave has 100ft high limestone pillars and a rib-vaulted roof.

The York Story Cb
Heritage centre using models, paintings, audiovisual displays and reconstructions to trace the city's life from before the Roman invasion in AD 71.

The Yorkshire Museum ⌂ Bc
Archaeological, local and natural history museum set in spacious Museum Gardens. Has some of the finest Roman, Anglo-Saxon, Viking and medieval treasures discovered in Britain.

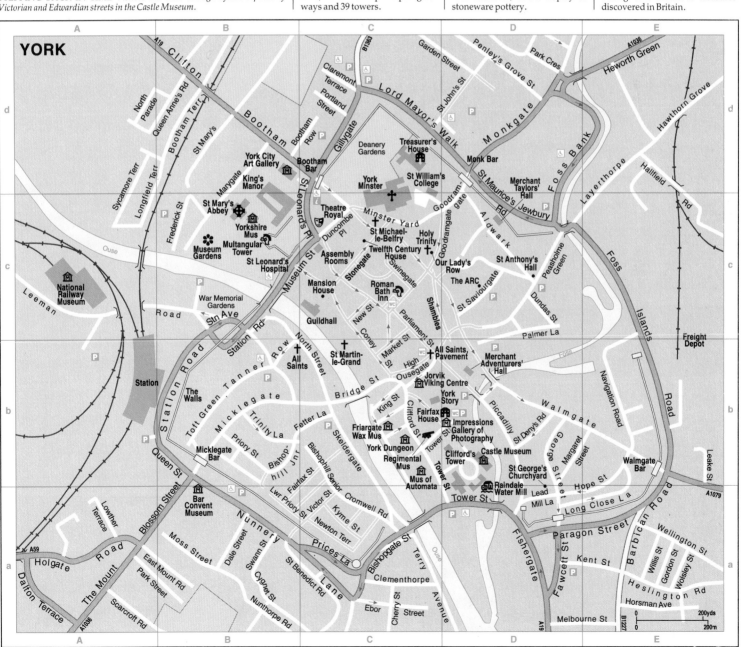

YORK

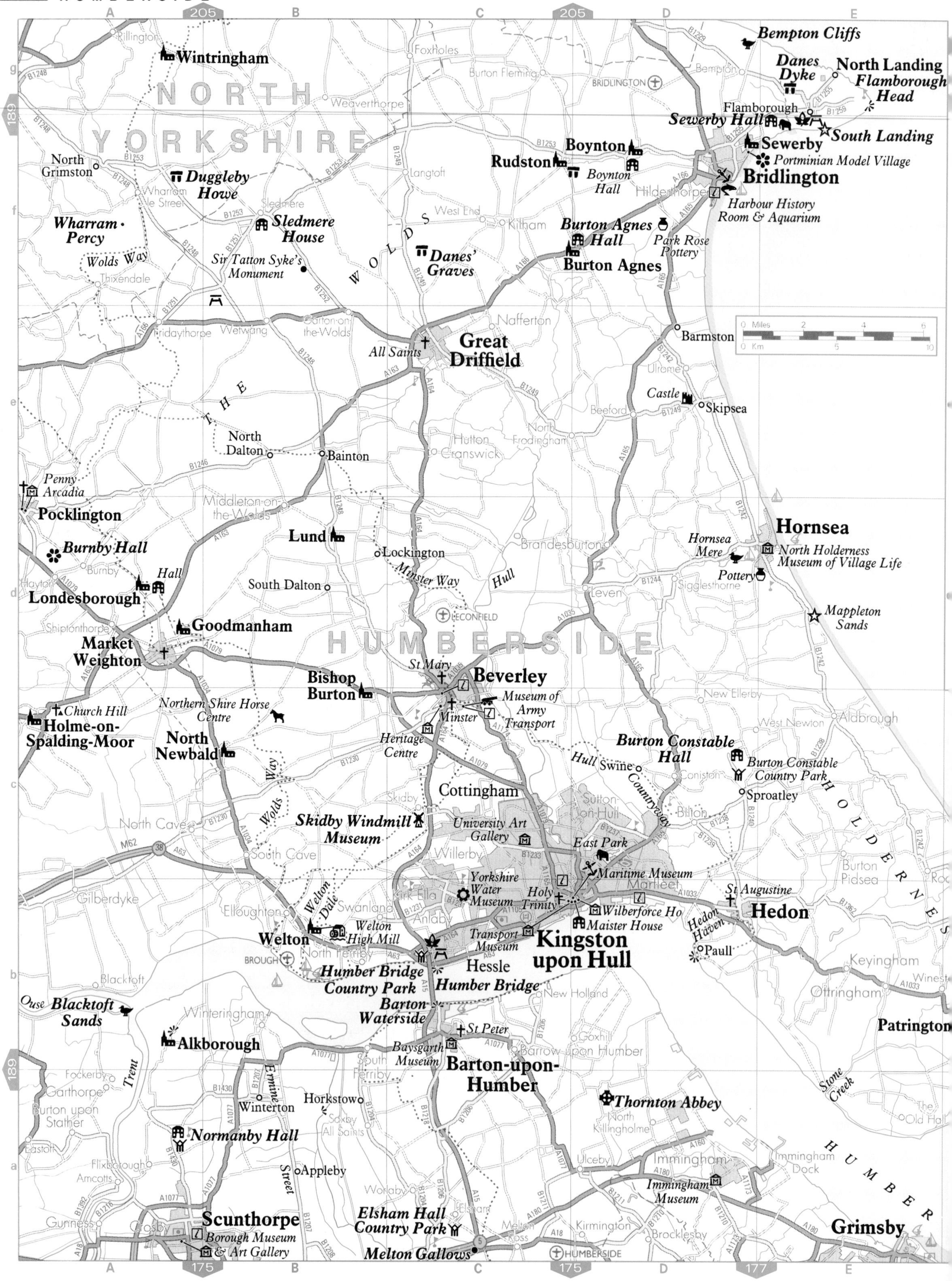

A · 205 · B · 205 · C · D · E

189

g

NORTH

Wintringham

Rillington

Foxholes

Burton Fleming

BRIDLINGTON

Bempton Cliffs

Bempton

Danes Dyke

North Landing
Flamborough Head

Flamborough

Sewerby Hall

Sewerby

South Landing

YORKSHIRE

North Grimston

Duggleby Howe

Wharram le Street

Sledmere

Weaverthorpe

West End

Kilham

Boynton

Rudston

Boynton Hall

Portminian Model Village

Bridlington

Harbour History Room & Aquarium

f

Wharram Percy

Wolds Way

Thixendale

Sledmere House

Sir Tatton Syke's Monument

Langtoft

Burton Agnes Hall

Burton Agnes

Park Rose Pottery

Danes' Graves

THE WOLDS

e

Fridaythorpe Wetwang

Barton-on-the-Wolds

All Saints

Nafferton

Great Driffield

Ulrome

Barmston

Castle

Skipsea

Miles 0 2 4 6
Km 0 5 10

North Dalton

Bainton

Beeford

Hutton Cranswick

North Frodingham

d

Penny Arcadia

Pocklington

Burnby Hall

Burnby

Londesborough

Hall

Hayton

Goodmanham

Shiptonthorpe

Market Weighton

Lund

Lockington

South Dalton

Minster Way

Middleton-on-the-Wolds

Brandesburton

Hull

Leven

HUMBERSIDE

Sigglesthorne

Hornsea

Hornsea Mere

North Holderness Museum of Village Life

Pottery

Mappleton Sands

c

Church Hill

Holme-on-Spalding-Moor

Northern Shire Horse Centre

North Newbald

Bishop Burton

St Mary

Beverley

Minster

Museum of Army Transport

Heritage Centre

Leconfield

New Ellerby

West Newton

Aldbrough

Burton Constable Hall

Hull

Swine

Coniston

Burton Constable Country Park

Sproatley

Bilton

HOLDERNESS

Burton Pidsea

b

North Cave

South Cave

M62

A63

Gilberdyke

Wolds Way

South Cave

Skidby Windmill Museum

Skidby

Cottingham

University Art Gallery

Yorkshire Water Museum

Willerby

Kirk Ella

Anlaby

Maritime Museum

Marfleet

East Park

Holy Trinity

Wilberforce Ho
Maister House

Transport Museum

Kingston upon Hull

Hessle

Hedon Haven

Hedon

St Augustine

Paull

Keyingham

Ottringham

Winestead

Patrington

Welton Dale

Welton

Welton High Mill

Swanland

North Ferriby

Brough

Humber Bridge Country Park

Humber Bridge

Barton Waterside

New Holland

Goxhill

St Peter

Barrow-upon-Humber

HUMBER

Stone Creek

The Old Hall

a

Ouse

Blacktoft Sands

Blacktoft

Winteringham

Alkborough

Garthorpe

Fockerby

Burton upon Stather

Normanby Hall

Winterton

Horkstow

Saxby All Saints

Trent

Ermine Street

Appleby

South Ferriby

Baysgarth Museum

Barton-upon-Humber

Worlaby

Thornton Abbey

North Killingholme

Immingham

Immingham Dock

Immingham Museum

Ulceby

Brocklesby

Scunthorpe

Borough Museum & Art Gallery

Crosby

Flixborough

Amcotts

Elsham Hall Country Park

Elsham

Wrawby

Melton Gallows

Kirmington

HUMBERSIDE

Grimsby

A · 175 · B · 175 · C · 177 · D · E

Bempton Cliffs ❧ Dg
Sea birds wheel and scream about Bempton's chalk cliffs, at 400ft the highest in the country. Visitors to the RSPB's reserve can watch some 33 breeding species, including auks, guillemots, puffins and gannets. There are also 15 butterfly species to be seen.

Beverley ✝ ⬚ ☗ ☖ Cc
Notable buildings include 13th-century Minster, 14th-century St Mary's Church and many Georgian houses. Guildhall's heritage centre illustrates Beverley history. Museum of Army Transport crammed with military vehicles.

Bishop Burton ☖ Bc
Altisdora Pub named after local horse that won 1813 St Leger. In the 19th-century church, bust of Methodism founder John Wesley marks his visit to village.

Boynton ☖☗ Df
Boynton Hall's Strickland family introduced the turkey to England, commemorated by carving of one on 18th-century church's lectern.

Bridlington ❧ ✗ ⬚ Df
Beaches sheltered from north wind by Flamborough Head. Fishing trawlers unload their catch at quayside each day.

Burnby Hall ✿ Ad
Over 50 water-lily varieties grow in garden created around two lakes. Six acres include roses, lilacs and Japanese maples.

Burton Agnes ☖ Df
Cream-washed brick cottages with pantiled roofs surround a placid pond. Part-Norman church entered through tunnel of yews.

Waxholme
Withernsea
Holmpton
elwick
Easington
Kilnsea
Spurn Head

F   G

THE WOLDS AND HOLDERNESS

The views stretch for miles over the Yorkshire Wolds. Quiet villages lie in the shadow of great houses, and there are echoes of a more distant past in prehistoric monuments and burial grounds. The sea is a constant presence; holidaymakers flock to the coast every year, fishing trawlers take on the North Sea daily and merchant ships are constantly in and out of the busy port of Kingston upon Hull.

OLD AND NEW *Early 17th-century Burton Agnes Hall contains a notable collection of Impressionist paintings.*

Burton Agnes Hall ☗ Df
Well-preserved mainly Jacobean house contains picture collection with works by Utrillo, Gauguin, Cézanne and Matisse.

Burton Constable Hall ☗ Dc
Elizabethan brick mansion conceals Georgian interior designed by Robert Adam; furniture by Chippendale, and parkland by Capability Brown.

Danes Dyke � Eg
Deceptive name, as this 2½ mile Stone Age defensive earthwork was finished long before Danes' 9th-century arrival. Part can be explored along nature trail.

Danes' Graves ⊓ Cf
Once numbering 500, remaining burial mounds predate Danish invasion. Thought to be Celtic tribal remains of 2nd century BC.

Duggleby Howe ⊓ Af
Stone Age mound where eight adults and two children were buried with their belongings. Finds include 4000-year-old tools made from antlers of red deer.

Flamborough Head ✳ Eg
Flamborough Head thrusts into the North Sea, which has gouged caves into its chalk cliff faces. Walks over springy turf on headland and to beach below.

Goodmanham ☖ Ad
Norman church stands on 7th-century pagan temple site whose high priest, Coifi, was converted to Christianity in AD 627.

Great Driffield ✝ Ce
Busy market town having large weekly cattle market; known as 'the capital of the Wolds' among

its inhabitants. Look out for 110ft tower of All Saints, landmark visible for miles.

Hedon ✝ Db
Tower of the 12th to 15th-century church soars 128ft above this former port, now silted up.

Hornsea ☖ ◉ ❧ Ed
Seaside town grown up from ancient market town. Hornsea Mere is Yorkshire's largest freshwater lake, attracting anglers, sailors and birdwatchers.

Humber Bridge Cb
World's longest single-span bridge is 1542yds long and has twin towers 533ft high and linking cables 27in thick.

Humber Bridge Country Park ☗ ✿ ⩑ ✳ Cb
Rural retreat of 50 acres with woods, meadows, ponds, picnic area and nature trail.

ERODED CHALK *The cliffs around Flamborough Head have been heavily gouged by sea and wind.*

Kingston upon Hull ⬚ ✗ ☗ ☖ ☗ ✝ Cb
Wilberforce House, home of the anti-slavery activist, now houses museum of his life's work. Holy Trinity Church is largest parish church in England. Maritime museum near former docks area.

Londesborough ☖ ☗ Ad
Bought to foil a rival's rail scheme by 19th-century railway magnate, who extended Londesborough Park in Baronial style.

Lund ☖ Bd
Weathered brick cottages with tiled or slate roofs include fine 18th-century masonry example, Manor House Farm.

Market Weighton ✝ Ad
Birthplace of tallest Englishman recorded, William Bradley, who stood 7ft 9in. His huge chair sits in Londesborough Arms Hotel. He died in 1825 aged 33, as church memorial attests.

North Landing Eg
Open-decked boats offer short sea trips for viewing extraordinary rock formations carved by the North Sea on Flamborough Head.

North Newbald ☖ 🐎 Bc
Reached by a winding lane from Beverley, village has clusters of whitewashed cottages and a fine Norman church. Northern Shire Horse Centre displays this horse breed, vintage farming implements and farmhouse kitchen.

Patrington ☖ Fb
St Patrick's Church is prime example of English Gothic's Decorated period. Among its many treasures are 200 stone carvings of humans and animals on columns.

Rudston ☖ ⊓ Cf
Britain's tallest standing stone, 25ft high and weighing 46 tons, in All Saints churchyard. Testament to skill and religious faith of Neolithic people who erected it.

Sewerby ☖ ✿ Df
Terraced cottages, pub and church sheltered by Flamborough Head. Portminian Model Village set on 1 acre site.

Sewerby Hall ☗ ☖ Ef
Classic Georgian mansion – with fine panelling and cantilevered oak staircase – set in 50 acres of parkland. Amy Johnson Museum celebrates life of the Hull-born aviation pioneer (1903-41). Zoo houses Shetland ponies, deer and wallabies.

Skidby Windmill Museum ✗ Cc
Built 1821, Skidby Mill is only functional East Riding windmill. Inside is museum showing how the mill works.

Sledmere House ☗ Bf
Grey-stone 18th-century mansion houses Sheraton, Chippendale, French period furniture. Turkish Room copies Sultan's Apartments in Valideh Mosque, Istanbul. Park of 2000 acres was laid out by Capability Brown.

WAGONERS' MEMORIAL *Farm drivers from the Wolds are commemorated in this World War I frieze at Sledmere.*

South Landing ☆ Ef
Boulder-strewn beach is popular for sunbathing, as sunlight reflects off chalk cliffs nearby. Choice of walks: either east to Flamborough Head for views, west to Sewerby for pub lunch.

Spurn Head ❧ Fa
Seals, porpoises and birds can be spotted from 3 mile long finger of land. Owned by Yorkshire Naturalists' Trust, it is constantly reshaped by coastal erosion debris and silt from the Humber.

Welton ☖ Bb
Houses built by prosperous 18th-century Yorkshire businessmen. Dick Turpin, captured in 1736, held at Green Dragon Inn.

Wharram Percy ✚ Af
Lost village, victim of 15th-century landlord's decision to switch from arable to sheep farming. Only church ruin remains, 15 minutes' walk from the road's end.

WHERE WORDSWORTH WANDERED

The Lake District lies to the west of the Pennines like a cluster of jewels, its craggy fells and peaceful lakes alive with the beauty that inspired poet William Wordsworth and children's writer Beatrix Potter, who both chose to live here. On its western edge, rivers flow down from the fells to enter the sea. Along their banks stand the remains of ancient castles and monasteries.

Ambleside ☑ ✗ Ee
Busy resort at centre of Lake District, crowded with walkers and teashops. Bridge House, 17th century, perched on bridge over Stock Ghyll, is now a National Trust information centre.

Bardsea ⚓ ☗ Eb
Village of grey-stone houses with 19th-century church overlooking Morecambe Bay. Coastal woodland area of Bardsea Country Park has footpaths by sands. Prehistoric stone circles and temple ruin, west, on Birkrigg Common; Bronze Age implements found there.

Barrow-in-Furness ✪ 🏛 ☑ Da
Red sandstone ruins of Furness Abbey, founded 1123 by King Stephen, include Norman arches. It stands aloof from town, made prosperous by iron and shipbuilding. By 1870 Barrow's steelworks were world's largest.

NORMAN SOLIDITY *Massive arch in Furness Abbey cloisters.*

Boot 🏭 ⚓ Ce
Hamlet set in heart of Eskdale valley where old water mill has ground corn since the 16th century. Terminus nearby of Ravenglass and Eskdale Railway. Popular walking centre with Stanley Force waterfalls nearby.

Bowness-on-Windermere ⚓ ⛴ Fd
Resort on Lake Windermere with quaint, narrow streets and 15th-

century church. World of Beatrix Potter exhibition includes 3-D tableaux, music and videos.

Brantwood 🏠 ❀ ⚓ 🄰 Ed
Coniston home from 1872-1900 of Victorian artist and writer John Ruskin. Built 1797. Study, dining room and bedroom much as he left them, full of drawings and artistic treasures. Nature trail.

Broughton-in-Furness ⚓ Dc
Village with market overlooking Duddon Estuary. Market square has stone-slab stalls and 1766 clock. Broughton tower is 14th-century peel tower, incorporated into 18th-century house.

Cartmel ⚓ ✪ Eb
Ivy-clad walls, old shops and pubs surround village square with 18th-century market cross. Magnificent priory church, founded 1188, has superb stained glass and choir stalls carved with strange creatures. The 14th-century gatehouse was once part of priory.

Coniston ⚓ 🏛 Ed
Village of grey-slate houses, dominated by craggy Old Man of Coniston, towering 2635ft high. Ride lake in stately steam yacht *Gondola*, first launched 1859. Ruskin museum in Yewdale Road describes life and work of Victorian artist with paintings, drawings and personal items. He is buried in Coniston churchyard.

Dalton-in-Furness ✝ 🏠 Db
Birthplace of painter George Romney (1734-1802), whose grave lies in churchyard. Restored 14th-

century tower of Dalton Castle stands in marketplace. St Mary's Church (1882-5) bears witness to wealth created in surrounding iron-ore quarries.

Elterwater ⚓ Ee
Village of green-slate houses gathered about corner shop, pub and green, overlooked by stunning peaks of Langdale Pikes. First-floor galleries on some cottages are where locals spun wool.

Grasmere ⚓ 🏠 🏛 Ec
Poet William Wordsworth lived in Dove Cottage, 1799-1808. Humble interior preserved much as it was. The Grasmere and Wordsworth Museum nearby has manuscripts and relics. Wordsworth is buried in village churchyard along with his family.

Great Urswick ⚓ Db
Cross carved with Nordic runes bears witness to great age of this little village. Mellow stone houses in maze of lanes look out over placid waters of Urswick Tarn.

Grizedale Forest ✱ 🄰 ❀ ☑ Ed
Forest and farmland between Coniston Water and Windermere, run by Forestry Commission. Visitor and wildlife centre, and concert theatre at heart of forest. Red squirrels, roe and red deer.

Hardknott Pass 🔺 De
Hairpin bends and steep gradients make this one of Britain's most spectacular roads. Lonely Roman fort at top, with parade ground and bathhouse.

Hawkshead ⚓ 🏛 Ed
Medieval village with intricate maze of alleys. Church and courthouse, 15th century. William Heelis had his solicitor's office in Thimble Hall when he married Beatrix Potter; now Hall houses exhibition of her life and work.

Hill Top 🏠 🏛 Ed
Scenes from *Peter Rabbit* come alive in 17th-century farm that inspired Beatrix Potter's work. Bought as her retreat in 1905; now preserved by the National Trust.

Holker Hall 🏠 ⚓ Eb
Former residence of Dukes of Devonshire, built 17th century and restored 1873. Woodcarvings by local craftsmen, period furniture and paintings. Attractions include deer park and exhibition of period kitchens.

Kirkstone Pass Fe
Highest road in Lake District with 1489ft summit. Once used by stagecoaches; passengers had to disembark at narrow, twisting section known as 'The Struggle'.

COLD SPOT *Hardy Highland cattle graze below Kirkstone Pass.*

Millom ✝ ⛏ 🏛 Cc
Remains of iron-mine complex behind great sea walls and 14th-century castle ruin in town. Church, 12th century, noted for windows. Folk museum has full-scale model of a miner's cottage.

Muncaster Castle 🏠 ❀ Cd
Home of Pennington family since 13th century, with 19th-century reconstructions. Sanctuary for Henry VI during Wars of Roses, who made a gift of glass bowl known as 'Luck of Muncaster'; replica on display. Owl aviary and rhododendron gardens.

Ravenglass ⚓ 🚂 🏭 ⛴ 🏛 Bd
Seafaring village and site of 4 acre Roman fort with bathhouse. Century-old miniature railway, once used to carry minerals, now takes tourists on scenic 7 mile journey up Eskdale.

Rydal 🏠 🏠 Ee
Stone-and-slate settlement with humpbacked bridge, completely surrounded by high fells. William Wordsworth lived at stone farmhouse called Rydal Mount from 1813 until his death in 1850; still full of his possessions.

St Bees ⚓ ✝ ❀ ⚓ Af
Village in valley south of St Bees Head, whose sandstone cliffs rise to 500ft above shore. Sea birds include kittiwakes, fulmars and black guillemots. St Bee or St Bega is thought to have been Irish princess who set up a nunnery here. St Mary and St Bega is much-restored church of nunnery.

Stott Park Bobbin Mill 🏛 Ec
Sole survivor of local bobbin factories. Opened 1835 and still in working order; now museum of social and industrial history.

Townend 🏠 Fe
Remote stone farmhouse with slate roof, mullioned windows and round chimneys. Built during 1620s for self-sufficient Lakeland farmers, the Browne family; now preserved by National Trust with furniture and utensils assembled over 300 years.

Troutbeck ⚓ Fe
Village of grey-brown stone, with cottages and farms spread along fellside above beck tumbling towards Windermere. Church, twice rebuilt, has east window by Burne-Jones.

Ulverston 🏛 ☑ Db
Old town and port with cobbled streets and market square. Tranquil waters of Ulverston Canal popular with fishermen and walkers. Elizabethan Swarthmoor Hall is former home of George Fox, founder of Quaker religion in 1652. Explorer Sir John Barrow born here 1764; lighthouse memorial on Hoad Hill. Comedian Stan Laurel born here 1890; Laurel and Hardy Museum contains press cuttings, personal possessions and film archive.

Wasdale Head Ce
Hamlet at head of dramatic Wast Water, deepest Lakeland lake at 258ft. Centre for climbing on Great Gable, Kirk Fell, Yewbarrow and Scafell Pike, England's highest peak at 3210ft.

Whitehaven ✪ 🏛 ☑ Af
Once a small fishing community, developed as a port in early 17th century. Wealth of Georgian and Victorian buildings reflect prosperity from coal and iron. Elaborate mines at South Beach recreation area look more like medieval castles: Duke Pit sunk in 1747, and 1840 Welling Pit. Town history outlined in civic hall museum and art gallery.

Windermere ❀ ⚓ ✱ ☑ Fc
Popular, crowded resort with England's largest lake. Footpath from town leads to Orrest Head; famous viewpoint for central lakeland fells. Steamboat Museum has Victorian and Edwardian steamboats, many in working order. Brockhole, north, is National Park Visitor Centre with Living Lakeland audiovisual shows, gardens and woodland.

POET'S COUNTRY *Wooded slopes surround the placid waters of Grasmere, beside which Wordsworth lived.*

A207

Distington
Lowca
Parton
Moresby
Mockerkin
Branthwaite
Cocker
Whinlatter Pass
Braithwaite
B5792
Cars of the Stars Museum
Castlerigg Stone Circle
A207

Whitehaven
Mines
Rowrah
Frizington
Holme Wood
Loweswater
Lanthwaite
Pencil Mus
Fitz Park Museum
Keswick
Friar's Crag
Derwent Water
Dockray
Aira Force
Hallin Fell
A197

Cleator Moor
Burnbank Fell
Carling Knott
Rannerdale
Ard Crags
Newlands Pass
Ashness Bridge
Surprise View
Castle Rock
Great Dodd
Aira Beck
Martindale
Sleet Fell
Dalehead Farm

Crummock Water
Buttermere
Moss Force
Grange
Bowder Stone
Rosthwaite
Lodore Falls
Watendlath
Thirlmere
Glenridding
Lanty's Tarn
Patterdale
Helvellyn 3116
Angletarn Pikes
Angle Tarn
Hartsop

Middleton
Beckermet
Scale Force
Buttermere
Johnny Wood
Seatoller
Watendlath Tarn
Blea Tarn
Stonethwaite
Eagle Crag
WythBurn
Easedale Tarn
Dove Cottage
Grasmere & Wordsworth Mus
Kirkstone Pass

St Bees
SS Mary & Bega
Egremont
Castle
Reserve
Ennerdale Water
Bowness Knot
Ennerdale Forest
Seathwaite
Sourmilk Gill Waterfall
Great Gable 2949
Styhead Tarn
Stickle Tarn
Grasmere
Grasmere
Rydal Mount
Rydal
Rydal Water
Stockghyll Force
Trout-beck

C U M B R I A

Haile
Calder Abbey
Calder Bridge
Sellafield Exhibition Centre
Wellington
Yewbarrow 2058
Wasdale Head
Scafell Pike 3210
Langdale Pikes
Dungeon Ghyll Force
Elterwater
Ambleside
The Struggle
BridgeHo
Stagshaw
Brockhole
Townend

Middleton
Gosforth
Nether Wasdale
Burnmoor Tarn
Eskdale Moor
Hardknott Fort
Cockley Beck
Skelwith Force
Skelwith Bridge
Outgate
High Wray
Orrest Head
Windermere

L A K E
Eskdale Green
Boot
Eskdale Mill
Dalegarth
Hardknott Pass
Wrynose Pass
Little Langdale
D I S T R I C T
Beatrix Potter Gallery
Coniston
Ruskin Museum
Hawkshead
Steamboat Mus
World of Beatrix Potter
Bowness-on-Windermere

Seascale
Holmrook
Gubbergill
Mite
Ravenglass & Eskdale Railway
Esk
Eskdale
Stanley Force
2129
Harter Fell
Dunnerdale Forest
2628
The Old Man of Coniston
Walna Scar Road
Near Sawrey
Brantwood
Hill Top
Visitor Centre
Winster

Ravenglass
Muncaster Mill
Muncaster Castle
Hall Dunnerdale
Seathwaite
G R I Z E D A L E
Satterthwaite
Crosthwaite

Hycemoor
Rainsbarrow Wood
Ulpha
Hoses
F O R E S T
Bowland Bridge

Broughton Mills
Stott Park Bobbin Mill
Finsthwaite
Cartmel Fell

Bootle
Lower Hawthwaite
Water Yeat
Lakeside
Fell Foot Park

Annaside
Annas
Black Combe 1970
Duddon Bridge
Broughton in Furness
Grizebeck
A5092
Gawthwaite
Haverthwaite
Low Wood
High Newton
Witherslack

Whitbeck
Hallthwaites
The Green
A5092
Gawthwaite
Lakeside & Haverthwaite Railway
Newby Bridge

Gutterby Spa
The Hill
Kirkby-in-Furness
Broughton Beck
Penny Bridge
Haverthwaite
Greenodd
Lindale
Hampsfield Fell

Silecroft
Duddon Sands
Askam in Furness
Sandscale Haws
Castle
Millom
Folk Museum
Soutergate
Mansriggs
Arrad Foot
Cartmel
Priory
Holker Hall

Haverigg
Furness Galleries
Laurel & Hardy Museum
Ulverston
Canal Foot
Lakeland Motor Museum
Grange-over-Sands

Dalton-in-Furness
St Mary
Castle
Ireleth
Conishead Priory
Tarn
Flookburgh
Humphrey Head

Great Urswick
Birkrigg Common
Bardsea
Bardsea Country Park
Baycliff

Hawcoat
Stainton with Adgarley
Aldingham
Dendron
Gleaston Mill
Newbiggin

BARROW (WALNEY ISLAND)
Furness Abbey
Rampside
Roosebeck

WALNEY ISLAND
Barrow-in-Furness

Roa Island
Castle
Piel Island
M O R E C A M B E
B A Y

A183

Morecambe
Frontierland
St Patrick's Chapel
Heysham
St Peter
B5273

WARNING
Walks across Morecambe Bay can be dangerous. Seek local guidance.

Miles 0 2 4 6
Km 0 5 10

WESTMORLAND'S FELLS AND DALES

A rich mix of landscapes lies within the area – salt marshes, peaks and fells, and quiet valleys adorned by shimmering lakes. This is a breathtaking place to explore or simply to sit and admire. Its turbulent past is recalled by the castles once laid siege to by Scottish marauders, though any tumult now is confined to the cascading waters of spectacular falls and tumbling rivers.

LAKELAND MAJESTY *Ullswater's grand stretch of tranquil water is surrounded by sweeping, tree-clad slopes.*

Appleby-in-Westmorland Cf
Former Westmorland capital, two towns either side of River Eden. Old was 10th-century Danish village on bluff overlooking new, which grew round 12th-century Norman castle. Restored in 1650s, has original keep and rare breeds farm. Many splendid buildings, Jacobean to Victorian.

Arnside Aa
Pretty resort on sandy estuary crossed by spectacular railway viaduct. Popular with yachtsmen, mud flats for birdwatchers, and wooded hillside of Arnside Knott has good walks and views.

Askham Bf
Immaculate village on steep wooded bank of River Lowther. Upper green has fine views to Lowther Castle and Pennines. Ancient stone circle and burial sites on Askham Fell.

Beetham Aa
Riverside walk leads to Heron Mill, which ground corn 1750-1955. Restored with four pairs of millstones, working machinery and 14ft water wheel.

Brough De
Ruined castle, built by Normans on site of Roman fort, rebuilt in medieval style but gutted by fire. Castle Hotel has original stables and outbuildings, and cobbled courtyard. Stone from Roman fort used in building 11th-century St Michael's Church.

Burton-in-Kendal Ba
Mixture of whitewashed, pebble-dashed and limestone cottages and fine old houses fill narrow alleys and courtyards below wooded slopes of Dalton Crags. Both pubs were coaching inns, and Georgian houses round market square date from when town prospered as corn market.

Cauldron Snout Ef
Highest waterfall in England tumbles spectacularly down eight cascades before final 200ft drop. Footpath follows descent.

Crosby Ravensworth Ce
Prehistoric settlements comprise many ruined huts, one measuring 50ft across. St Lawrence's Church is 'miniature cathedral', much rebuilt since 13th century, in picturesque setting.

Dalemain Af
Country home of Hasell family since 1679. Medieval banqueting hall, Elizabethan wings and Georgian façade. Norman peel tower houses museum of Westmorland and Cumberland Yeomanry.

Dent Db
Picturesque cobbled village overlooking River Dee in small but lovely Dentdale. Famous for hand-knitted woollens, still produced by resident knitters at nearby craft centre.

Hallin Fell Ae
Superb Lakeland panorama from 1271ft summit across Ullswater to peaks of Skiddaw and Helvellyn and south to beautiful valleys. Path to summit from Howtown.

Harter Fell ▲ Ad
Fearsome crags overlooking Haweswater Reservoir and delightful Small Water. Scenic approaches to summit pass tumbling rivers and towering rocks.

Hawes Eb
Among old ways of life illustrated in Upper Dales Folk Museum are local crafts and equipment used for cheese and butter making, sheepshearing and lead mining. Touring centre for upper Wensleydale and nearby waterfalls.

Haweswater Reservoir Ae
Steep mountains surround man-made lake containing drowned village of Mardale, whose ruined Holy Trinity Church can be seen.

THIRST QUENCHER *Granite memorial fountain in Dent commemorates Adam Sedgewick, local pioneering geologist.*

Ingleborough Da
Distinctive flat-topped 2373ft summit crowned by Iron Age hill-fort. Extensive views from hill.

Ingleton Ca
Excellent walking country of Ingleton Glens, with spectacular waterfalls and fine woodland scenery. White Scar Cave under Ingleborough hill has stalactites and two waterfalls.

Kendal Bc
Isolated above 'auld grey town' of fine limestone buildings and narrow, twisting streets is ruined 12th-century castle, birthplace (1512) of Henry VIII's last wife, Catherine Parr. Elegant 18th-century Abbot Hall preserves local traditions in Museum of Lakeland Life and Industry and has art gallery. Among riverside walks is one to Roman fort.

Kentmere Ad
Hidden among attractive fells. Garburn Pass leads to Windermere and has superb views over Troutbeck Valley.

Kirkby Lonsdale Ca
Georgian buildings and quaint cottages combine in riverside 'capital' of Lune valley. Views from churchyard praised by Ruskin as 'naturally divine' and painted by Turner. Riverside walks from medieval Devil's Bridge.

Kirkby Stephen Dd
Brightly painted shops and old coaching inns huddle among attractive cobbled squares above

Eden valley. Inside 13th-century St Stephen's Church is shaft of unique 10th-century cemetery cross of Loki, the Danish Devil.

Leighton Hall Aa
Public rooms of handsome 18th-century building show everyday life in this family home. Extensive grounds include rose garden with sundial dated 1647 and aviary of birds of prey.

Levens Hall Ab
Cones, corkscrews, pyramids and other curious shapes of fantastic 17th-century topiary gardens maintained in original forms. Grey-stone hall built 1250 around peel tower, but mainly Elizabethan with superb plaster-work and carved woodwork. Working steam engine collection.

Lowther Bf
Fairy-tale façade of towers, turrets and battlements, only remnant of 19th-century castle demolished 1957. Lowther Park created 1283 for estate's deer, now country park with nature trails, children's entertainments, rare breeds and red deer whose ancestors roamed original deer park.

Mallerstang Common Dc
Superb walking centre in lonely valley, overlooked by Norman peel tower of ruined Pendragon Castle and 2324ft Wild Boar Fell.

Milburn Cf
In shadows of 2930ft Cross Fell, rising up behind sandstone cottages huddled around spacious

green. Lofty maypole, topped by weathercock, stands on base of long-gone preaching cross.

Penrith Bf
Ruined 14th-century castle and Beacon Hill tower, where warning fires were lit during Border wars. Churchyard of St Andrew's has ancient 'Giant's Grave' where Owen Caesarius, 10th-century Cumbrian ruler, is supposedly buried. Wordsworth educated at Dame Birkett's School, now restaurant, and lived at what is now Town Hall. Penrith Steam Museum has vintage farm machinery and blacksmith's shop.

Ribble Head Da
Man-made spectacle of 24-arched Settle-Carlisle railway viaduct vies with natural wonders of Yorkshire's Three Peaks – 2414ft Whernside, 2373ft Ingleborough and 2277ft Pen-y-ghent. Information centre of Yorkshire Dales National Park.

Sedbergh Cc
Beneath domed peaks of Howgill Fells where Lune and Rawthey rivers meet. Steep paths lead directly above town to Winder, with views of Pennines, Lune valley and Forest of Bowland. Playing fields of public school, founded 1525, flank magnificent Norman St Andrew's Church.

Sizergh Castle Ab
Medieval hall and Elizabethan wings added to peel tower built 1350. Many portraits and relics of Strickland family. Panelling, original fireplaces and windows in tower museum. Queen's Room named after Catherine Parr, sixth wife of Henry VIII. Rock, rose and Dutch gardens in grounds.

PLANTSMAN'S DELIGHT *The rock garden is one of several special gardens at Sizergh Castle.*

Ullswater Af
Lakeland's longest waters after Windermere, stretches 7 miles under wooded fells and 2000ft peaks. Attractive lakeside walks, superb views of lake from Hallin Fell and Pooley Bridge.

Whernside ▲ Db
Craggy 2414ft bulk, highest peak in Yorkshire Dales. Magnificent views of other three peaks, Ingleborough and Pen-y-ghent, and Howgill Moss. Easiest route to summit on well-marked footpath from Chapel-le-Dale.

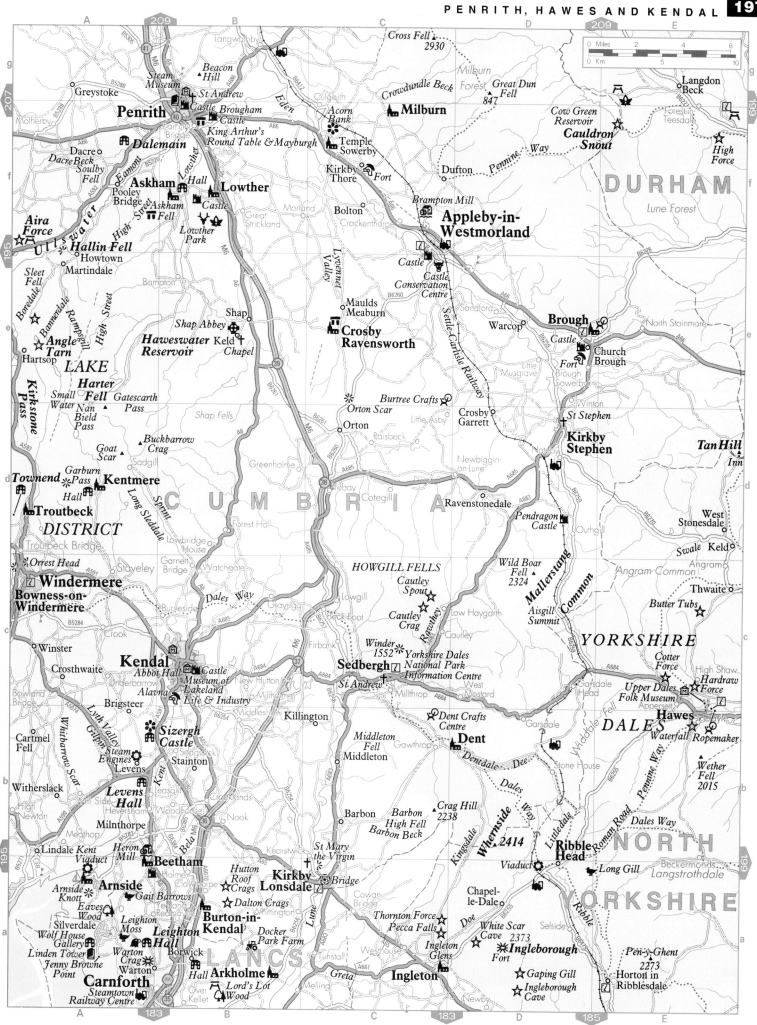

JAMES HERRIOT COUNTRY

Rugged Pennine peaks loom over unspoilt moors and dales, the setting for James Herriot's vet stories. Walkers explore the wild landscape where waterfalls thunder through limestone gorges and drystone walls surround the scattered farmsteads. Ancient drovers' tracks cross a land rich in Roman and Iron Age remains, while the stark outlines of ruined castles and abbeys pierce the horizon.

Arkengarthdale Bd
Moors sweep down from Tan Hill to hamlets along the Arkle Beck. Relics of lead mines line walk from Reeth to Whaw, with fine views over dale.

Askrigg ☆ Bc
TV series based on Herriot novels filmed here. St Oswald's Church, 'Cathedral of Wensleydale', dates from late 15th and early 16th centuries. Coaching inn built in 1767 stands nearby. Short walk leads to Whitfield Gill Force, waterfall that once drove three mills.

Aysgarth ☆ Cb
River Ure cascades over three spectacular falls in tree-lined gorge. Former cotton mill is now carriage museum, and houses restored coaches and wagons.

Bainbridge Bc
Hunting horn blown on village green on dark evenings, tradition from when forest workers had to be guided home. Track by River Bain follows old Roman road. Remains of Roman fort nearby.

GEORGIAN CENTREPIECE *The covered market cross, Barnard Castle, once served as the town hall.*

Barnard Castle Ce
Norman castle ruins perched on rocky crag loom above this market town. Bowes Museum built in style of French chateau by magnate John Bowes in 1869 houses his art collection in 40 rooms. Paintings by Goya, El Greco, Canaletto; furniture, ceramics and other antiques.

Bedale Eb
Imposing parish church dating from Saxon times overlooks town. Bedale Hall, a Georgian mansion, has huge ballroom with finely decorated ceiling.

UNSPOILT RICHNESS *The beautiful valley of Littondale, with its many walks, shows traces of Iron Age farmsteads and animal enclosures.*

Bishop Auckland Ef
Auckland Castle, residence of Bishops of Durham for 800 years, stands on River Wear. Oldest part is St Peter's Chapel, built about 1190 as banqueting hall. Beyond lies 800 acre deer park.

Bowes Be
Stump of 12th-century Bowes Castle keep and a church are set on Roman ramparts. Charles Dickens stayed at Unicorn inn and based Dotheboys Hall in *Nicholas Nickleby* on a local school.

Bowlees Visitor Centre Bf
History and ecology of Teesdale explained in disused chapel close to Low Force waterfalls. Woodland stroll a mile upstream leads to 70ft cataract of High Force.

Buckden Pike ☆ Ba
Bridle path from Buckden and steeper ascent from Starbotton lead to pike's 2302ft summit with splendid views. Bronze Age stone circle at Yockenthwaite.

Castle Bolton Cc
Mary, Queen of Scots was locked up for six months in this 14th-century castle overshadowing stone cottages that fringe village green. Nearby 14th-century church houses local exhibitions.

Constable Burton Dc
Gardens of Constable Burton Hall, built in 1768, noted for alpines, borders and mature trees. Handy for viewing Swaledale and Wensleydale.

Coverdale ☆ Cb
Drovers, miners and monks once crossed these secluded moors. Most dramatic way into dale is from Kettlewell. Flamstone Pin commands views of castles, abbeys, churches and woodland.

RUGGED POWER *The solid stump of Bowes Castle keep was built in more turbulent times to repel Scottish marauders.*

Darlington † Ee
Market town and the birthplace of railways. Museum contains George Stephenson's *Locomotion* of 1825. St Cuthbert's Church is 13th century, 14th-century spire.

QUEEN'S JAIL *Castle Bolton, where Mary, Queen of Scots was imprisoned for six months.*

Escomb † Dg
Well-preserved Saxon church, built with Roman stones, contains 13th-century carving of a knight.

Gainford De
Georgian houses surround handsome village green. Gainford Hall, dating from early 17th century, features high chimneys and gables. Gainford Spa nearby.

Great Whernside ▲ Ca
Dark-grey cottages of Kettlewell huddle below 2309ft Great Whernside. Traces of forestry, mining and cotton weaving still visible on lonely moors.

Grinton Cc
Dead from outlying areas once brought in wicker biers along 'corpse way' to Norman St Andrew's Church, nicknamed 'Cathedral of the Dales'.

Hamsterley Forest Cf
Much of this 5000 acre coniferous forest open to public with waymarked walks, nature trails, picnic spots and 4 mile scenic drive. Visitor centre with local natural history displays.

Jervaulx Abbey Db
Abbot of this now ruined 12th-century Cistercian foundation executed for part in unsuccessful revolt against Henry VIII.

Kiplin Hall Ec
Jacobean manor full of art treasures, where Lord Baltimore, founder of State of Maryland, USA, once lived.

Kisdon Gorge ☆ Bd
Noisy River Swale tumbles through this thickly wooded glen near granite hamlet of Keld.

Leyburn ☆ Dc
Short walk from market hall leads to pine-clad ridge of Leyburn Shawl, where Mary, Queen of Scots is said to have been caught after escaping from Bolton Castle.

Littondale Aa
Network of walks leads through valley, rich in bird life and flowers. Traces of Iron Age farms.

Middleham Db
Georgian houses line market square, overlooked by massive keep, once home of Warwick the Kingmaker and of Richard of Gloucester, later Richard III. Racehorses train on moors.

Middleton in Teesdale Bf
This former lead-mining centre attracts walkers to High Force and Low Force waterfalls. Medieval tombstones in village church.

Piercebridge Ee
Village lies on site of 4th-century Roman fort. Remains of Roman bridge across the Tees.

Raby Castle Df
Deer roam 200 acre park surrounding castle, built for Nevill family in 14th century but heavily restored. Fine collection of paintings, tapestries and porcelain. Handsome display of horse-drawn vehicles in courtyard.

Redmire Cc
Pale stone houses ring green, dominated by gnarled oak and looking out to 1792ft Penhill and bubbling River Ure. Woodland walk from remote Norman church leads to Wensley village.

Richmond Dd
Norman castle with 100ft high keep towers dramatically over the River Swale and cobbled marketplace. Green Howards regimental museum; Theatre Royal, beautifully restored, survives from 18th century. Riverside walks through woodland to 12th-century Easby Abbey.

Romaldkirk Bf
Three village greens with pump and stocks combine with colourful gardens and old houses to make charming whole. Church dating from late 12th century has effigy of knight dated 1304.

Semer Water Bb
Legend tells of drowned city in depths of this lake left over from Ice Age. Remains of 'Iron Age, Celtic and Roman life on shores. Popular for water sports.

Shildon Ef
Restored section of pioneer Stockton and Darlington Railway contains memorabilia of dawn of Steam Age. Walks laid out, leading to Adamson's Coach House, reputedly first railway station in the world.

The Stang ☆ Cd
Walks through forest lead to picnic spots with stunning views of Pennines and Teesdale. From 1550ft cliff edge of Hope Scar, Barnard Castle and Durham Cathedral – and even North Sea – are visible on clear day.

Tan Hill ▲ Bd
Drovers' roads cross 1758ft summit of Tan Hill, haunt of grouse and Swaledale sheep and home of Tan Hill Inn, highest inn in England. Arkengarthdale moor stretches to east and Stonesdale moor to south.

Thorpe Perrow Arboretum Eb
Sixty acres of landscaped grounds contain 1000 species of trees and shrubs. Nearby is Snape Castle, home of Henry VIII's sixth and last wife, Catherine Parr.

West Tanfield Ea
Medieval parish church stands opposite Marmion Tower, 15th-century gatehouse noted for great arch and oriel window. Fine outlook over wooded banks of River Ure.

Witton-le-Wear Dg
Tiers of stone houses perch around Norman church rebuilt in 1902. Dun Cow inn dates from 1799, and Witton Castle by River Wear from 15th century, though largely rebuilt.

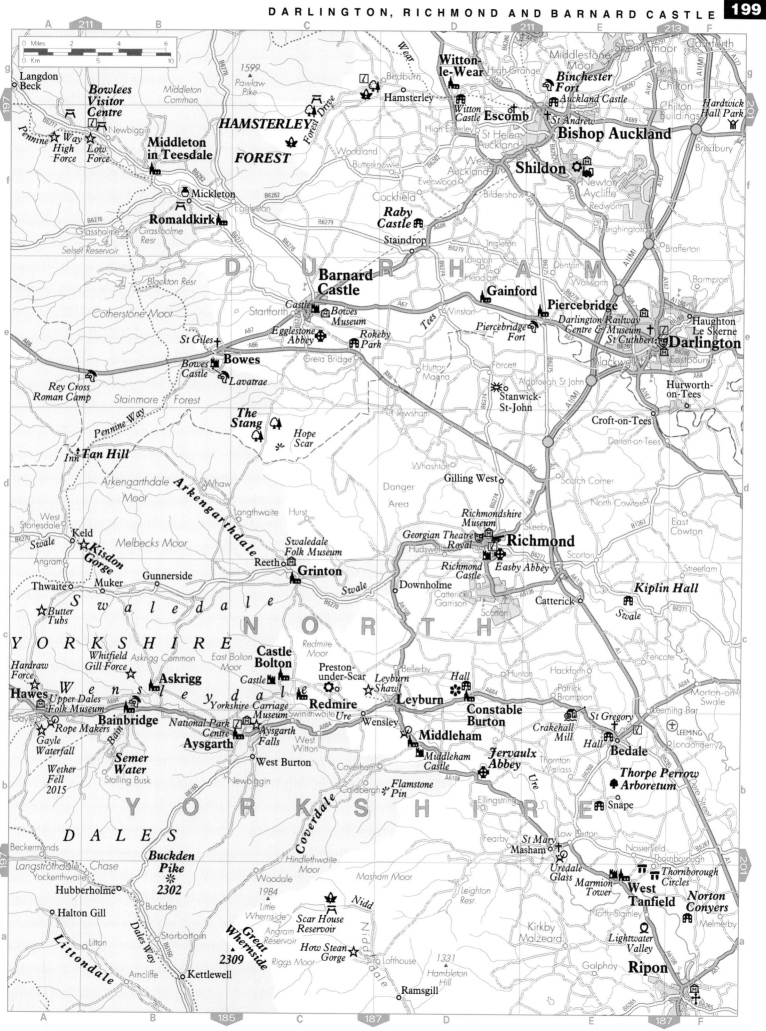

Scale: 0 Miles 2 4 6 / 0 Km 5 10

Grid references at top: 211, 211, 213
Side references: 197, 201
Bottom references: 185, 187, 187, 197, 201

Places and features shown:

Langdon Beck, Bowlees Visitor Centre, Newbiggin, Pennine Way, High Force, Low Force, Middleton in Teesdale, HAMSTERLEY FOREST, Forest Drive, Hamsterley, Witton-le-Wear, Witton Castle, Binchester Fort, Auckland Castle, Escomb, St Andrew, Bishop Auckland, Hardwick Hall Park, Chilton, Middleton Common, Pawlaw Pike 1599, Woodland, Butterknowle, Cockfield, Evenwood, West Auckland, Bildershaw, Shildon, Newton Aycliffe, Redworth, Bradbury, Corntorth

Mickleton, Romaldkirk, Eggleston, Grassholme Resr, Selset Reservoir, Blackton Resr, Cotherstone Moor, Raby Castle, Staindrop, Ingleton, Langton, Headlam, Denton, Walworth, Brafferton, Barmpton

Barnard Castle, Castle, Bowes Museum, Startforth, St Giles, Egglestone Abbey, Bowes, Bowes Castle, Lavatrae, Rokeby Park, Greta Bridge, Gainford, Winston, Piercebridge, Piercebridge Fort, Darlington Railway Centre & Museum, St Cuthbert, Darlington, Haughton Le Skerne, Eastbourne, Hurworth-on-Tees

Rey Cross Roman Camp, Stainmore Forest, Pennine Way, The Stang, Hope Scar, Hutton Magna, Forcett, Newsham, Aldbrough St John, Stanwick-St-John, Blackwell, Croft-on-Tees, Dalton-on-Tees

Tan Hill, Inn, Arkengarthdale, Whaw, Langthwaite, Hurst, Melbecks Moor, Swaledale Folk Museum, Reeth, Grinton, Whashton, Gilling West, Danger Area, Richmondshire Museum, Georgian Theatre Royal, Richmond, Richmond Castle, Easby Abbey, Skeeby, Scorton, Scotch Corner, North Cowton, East Cowton, Streetlam, Kiplin Hall

Keld, Kisdon Gorge, Swale, West Stonesdale, Angram, Thwaite, Muker, Gunnerside, SWALEDALE, YORKSHIRE, Downholme, Catterick Garrison, Scotton, Catterick, Swale, Fencote

Butter Tubs, Hardraw Force, Hawes, Upper Dales Folk Museum, Gayle, Rope Makers, Gayle Waterfall, Wether Fell 2015, Bainbridge, Semer Water, Stalling Busk, WENSLEYDALE, Whitfield Gill Force, Askrigg Common, Askrigg, East Bolton Moor, Castle Bolton, Castle, Preston-under-Scar, Redmire Moor, Yorkshire Carriage Museum, Redmire, Ure, Wensley, Bellerby, Leyburn Shawl, Leyburn, Hall, Constable Burton, Hackforth, Patrick Brompton, Crakehall Mill, Hall, Morton-on-Swale, Leeming Bar, St Gregory, Bedale, Londonderry, Leeming

National Park Centre, Aysgarth, Aysgarth Falls, West Witton, West Burton, Newbiggin, Middleham, Middleham Castle, Coverham, Fervaulx Abbey, Thornton Watlass, Ure, Thorpe Perrow Arboretum, Snape

NORTH YORKSHIRE, DALES, Beckermonds, Langstrothdale, Yockenthwaite, Hubberholme, Halton Gill, Buckden Pike 2302, Buckden, Starbotton, Woodale, Hindlethwaite Moor, Coverdale, Caldbergh, Flamstone Pin, Ellingstring, Fearby, Low Burton, Masham, St Mary, Masham Moor, Leighton Resr, Uredale Glass, Marmion Tower, Thornborough Circles, West Tanfield, Norton Conyers, Nosterfield, Thornborough

Litton, Littondale, Arncliffe, Kettlewell, Dales Way, Little Whernside 1984, Great Whernside 2309, Scar House Reservoir, Angram Reservoir, How Stean Gorge, Nidd, Nidderdale, Riggs Moor, Lofthouse, Ramsgill, Kirkby Malzeard, Galphay, Lightwater Valley, Ripon, Melmerby, Hambleton Hill 1331

ON THE NORTH YORK MOORS

To the south are the heather-covered uplands of the North York Moors National Park, sliced by deep valleys where farmsteads and villages cluster, and where medieval monks built their secluded monasteries. To the north, iron, steel and chemicals dominate the towns along the Tees. The coastline, too, has its contrasts: quaint fishing villages and seaside resorts give way to commercial docks.

Boulby Cliffs ☆ Ee
Highest cliffs on England's east coast stand 666ft above the sea. Footpath to summit with magnificent views along coast.

Byland Abbey ✦ Ca
Cistercian monastery ruins, 12th century; west front of church still stands. Remains include layout of entire monastic site.

Captain Cook Birthplace Museum ⌂ Ce
Museum tells story of Captain James Cook, RN. Cook heritage trail leads from the museum.

Carlton in Cleveland ♙ Cd
Once home to freed Norse slaves, or 'karls'; the town has a Palladian manor house and a Victorian Gothic church.

Coxwold ♙⌂ Ca
Shandy Hall was home to *Tristram Shandy* author Lawrence Sterne. Cobbled streets run alongside 17th-century stone houses.

SHANDY VILLAGE *Coxwold, where* Tristram Shandy *author Lawrence Sterne was curate.*

Danby ♙ Ed
Danby's main street heads toward heather moorlands. Red-stone houses dot landscape.

Danby Rigg ⛏ Ed
Defensive dykes and some 800 cairns constructed c.1000 BC lie in hills above Danby.

Farndale Dc
Valley carpeted with daffodils in spring, locals claim this inspired Wordsworth.

Gilling East ♙◉ Da
Modest cluster of houses and church dominated by Gilling Castle, an Elizabethan great hall with 18th-century façade.

Great Ayton ⌂ Ce
James Cook's boyhood school is now museum. Obelisk of rocks from Point Hicks, first part of Australia sighted on the voyage of discovery, stands on site of his cottage.

Guisborough ✦ De
Augustinian priory founded here in 1119 by Robert de Brus. East end of church, gatehouse and dovecote survive today.

Hambleton Drove Road ⛏⛰☀ Bc
Ancient cattle-driving route is still used today, partly as modern road, partly as green road.

Helmsley ♙⌂ Db
Castle retains the original 11th-century earthworks, later stone walls rising from them. Duncombe Park, built 1713, features terraces, temples, riverside walks.

Husthwaite ♙ Ca
Rare half-timbered Tudor cottage stands in town, church retains some Norman features. Beacon once lit on Beacon Banks to warn of approaching Spanish Armada.

Hutton-le-Hole ♙⌂ Eb
Ryedale Folk Museum holds reconstructed buildings ranging from Elizabethan glass furnace to medieval long-house examples.

Kilburn ♙☀ Ca
Once home to woodcarver Robert Thompson, died 1955, famous for mouse trademark on his carvings. His workshop still functions.

Kilburn White Horse ☀⛏⛰⛰ Cb
In 1857, a Kilburn schoolmaster and pupils cut away turf to form a white horse 314ft long. Nearby, footpaths lead to limestone crags of Roulston Scar and prehistoric Caston Dikes.

Kirkbymoorside ♙ Db
A market every Wednesday for past six centuries. Coaching inns include the half-timbered Black Swan of 1634.

Kirk Dale † ☆ Db
Prehistoric mammoth, lion and hippopotamus remains found in

CONTINUING CRAFT
Woodcarver applies his skill at the Thompson workshop, Kilburn.

cave in 1821. Local church has Saxon sundial built during Edward the Confessor's reign.

Lealholm ♙ Ed
Village set by River Esk. Picnic on riverside green or join locals in a game of quoits.

Marske-by-the-Sea Df
Captain Cook's father was buried here in 1779, just before news of his son's murder in Hawaii reached England. Sandy cliffs overlook fishing boats on beach.

Middlesbrough ⛏⛰⌂ Be
Once famous as an iron and steel-making town. Cleveland Crafts Centre features contemporary ceramics, area art gallery houses 20th-century British art. Note unusual transporter bridge, opened in 1911, across the Tees.

Mount Grace Priory ✦ Bc
Best preserved Carthusian monastery in Britain. One monk's cell restored. Substantial church and cloister remains.

Newburgh Priory ⌂ Ca
Vault under house holds Oliver Cromwell's remains. Twelfth-century priory incorporated in current house. Water garden.

Newham Grange Leisure Farm ⛏ Ce
Rare breeds of farm animals in grounds. Craft demonstrations, farming displays featured.

Northallerton † Ac
The Old Fleece Inn is partly medieval. Church has 15th-century pinnacled tower.

Norton Conyers ⌂ Aa
Medieval house with alterations through 18th century. Said to be inspiration for Thornfield Hall in Charlotte Brontë's *Jane Eyre*.

Nunnington ♙⌂ Da
Nunnington Hall features Jacobean façade, miniature period room collection and 17th-century walled garden.

Old Byland ♙ Cb
Medieval sundial in village church's wall is unusable, as it was installed upside-down.

Ormesby Hall ⌂ Ce
Country house of 18th century with delicate interior wood and plaster-work. Finished in 1770s by Sir James Pennyman.

Osmotherley ♙ Bc
Old market centre set at foot of Cleveland Hills. Stone table where John Wesley preached still stands, as does the Methodist church dating from 1754 – one of England's first.

Redcar ⚓ Df
Popular resort with a racecourse. Museum holds *Zetland*, world's oldest surviving lifeboat, built 1800. Fishing boats line promenade beside amusement arcade.

Rievaulx Abbey ✦❀ Cb
Beautiful and well-preserved ruins of Cistercian abbey, founded 1131, sit in peaceful River Rye valley. Rievaulx Terrace provides walk with views of ruins.

Rosedale Abbey ♙ Ec
Little remains of abbey that gave village its name – present church is Victorian.

Saltburn-by-the-Sea Df
Fishing boats drawn up on beach along Shingle Bay Inn. Climb a path for cliff-top views or walk along the Skelton Beck to amusement park.

Scarth Nick ☆ Bd
A nick in hills between Osmotherley and Swainby. Scarth Wood Moor is start of 39 mile section of Cleveland Way which crosses moors to coast. Superb views.

Skinningrove ♙◉ Ee
Houses cling to sides of deep narrow valley ending at a sandy beach. Stream stained by iron ore waste from steelworks.

Staithes ♙ Ee
Sandstone cliffs rise over valley crowded with the slate-topped houses of village. Young James Cook watched passing ships from the harbour.

Stockton-on-Tees ⌂ Be
Market town made famous in 1825, when Stephenson drove his *Locomotion* for the opening of Stockton and Darlington Railway. Preston Hall Museum features re-created Victorian high street.

Sutton Bank ☀⛰ Cb
Gliders swirl above escarpment that rises 700ft from the Vale of York. Walk leads to the White Horse of Kilburn.

Thirsk ⌂ Bb
Birthplace of Thomas Lord (1755-1822), founder of Lord's Cricket Ground, is now Thirsk museum. Church, 15th century, designed in Perpendicular style.

Urra Moor ⛏ Cd
Escarpment at Urra Moor's edge provides large car park and picnic area with viewpoint. Panorama includes Roseberry Topping.

Yarm ◉ Be
George and Dragon Inn hosted first Stockton and Darlington Railway promoters' meeting in 1820. Railway viaduct over the Tees still towers over town.

SHELTERED HARBOUR *Staithes snuggles comfortably beside its quiet creek, protected by a pair of bluff headlands.*

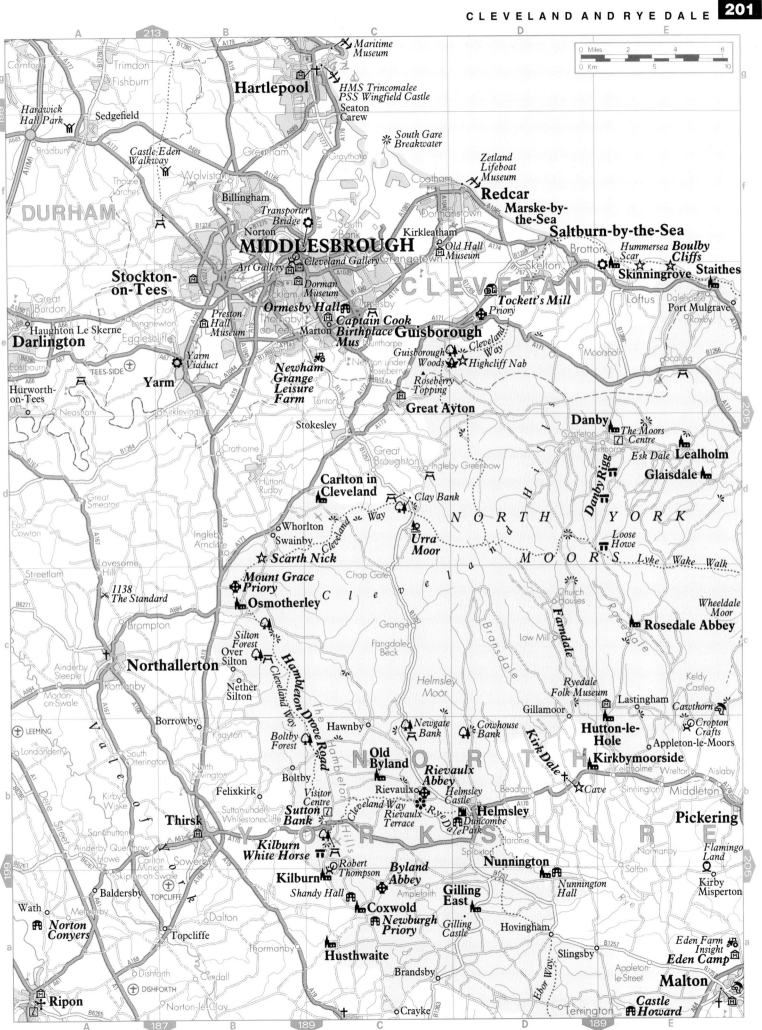

Miles
Km

Hartlepool
Maritime Museum
HMS Trincomalee
PSS Wingfield Castle
Seaton Carew
South Gare Breakwater

Trimdon
Fishburn
Sedgefield
Hardwick Hall Park
Bradbury
Castle Eden Walkway
Thorpe Thewles
Billingham
Wolviston
Greatham
Graythorp
Coatham

DURHAM

Zetland Lifeboat Museum
Redcar
Kirkleatham
Old Hall Museum
Marske-by-the-Sea
Saltburn-by-the-Sea
Brotton
Skelton
Hummersea Scar
Skinningrove
Boulby Cliffs
Staithes
Loftus
Dalehouse
Port Mulgrave
Roxby

Transporter Bridge
Norton
MIDDLESBROUGH
Art Gallery
Cleveland Gallery
Dorman Museum
Stockton-on-Tees
Acklim
South Bank
Grangetown
CLEVELAND
Tockett's Mill
Priory
Guisborough
Moorsholm
Locating

Preston Hall Museum
Ormesby Hall
Marton
Ormesby
Captain Cook Birthplace Mus
Nunthorpe
Newton under Roseberry
Guisborough Woods
Highcliff Nab
Cleveland Way

Darlington
Haughton Le Skerne
Eaglescliffe
Longnewton
Yarm Viaduct
Yarm
TEES-SIDE
Kirklevington
Newham Grange Leisure Farm
Tanton
Roseberry Topping
Great Ayton

Hurworth-on-Tees
Neasham
Crathorne
Hutton Rudby
Stokesley
Great Broughton
Ingleby Greenhow
Danby
The Moors Centre
Castleton
Ainthorpe
Esk Dale
Lealholm
Glaisdale
Danby Rigg

Great Smeaton
Ingleby Arncliffe
Carlton in Cleveland
Clay Bank
NORTH YORK
Cleveland Way
Loose Howe
Wheeldale Moor

East Cowton
Whorlton
Swainby
Scarth Nick
Urra Moor
MOORS
Lyke Wake Walk

Lovesome Hill
Streetlam
1138 The Standard
Mount Grace Priory
Osmotherley
Chop Gate
Cleveland Way
Church Houses
Rosedale Abbey

Ainderby Steeple
Romanby
Northallerton
Silton Forest
Over Silton
Nether Silton
Cleveland Way
Grange
Fangdale Beck
Helmsley Moor
Bransdale
Low Mill
Farndale
Ryedale Folk Museum
Gillamoor
Lastingham
Cawthorn
Keldy Castleo

LEEMING
Londonderry
Borrowby
Knayton
North Kilvington
South Otterington
Boltby Forest
Hawnby
Newgate Bank
Cowhouse Bank
Kirk Dale
Hutton-le-Hole
Cropton Crafts
Appleton-le-Moors

Kirby Wiske
Sandhutton
Old Byland
Rievaulx Abbey
Rievaulx
Helmsley Castle
Beadlam
Cave
Wrelton
Keldholme
Sinnington
Middleton
Aislaby

Morton-on-Swale
Borrowby
Thornton-le-Moor
Felixkirk
Boltby
Sutton-under-Whitestonecliffe
Visitor Centre
Sutton Bank
Cleveland Way
Rievaulx Terrace
Rye Dale
Duncombe Park
Helmsley
Harome
Sproxton
Pickering

Thirsk
Carlton Miniott
Skipton-on-Swale
Sowerby
Kilburn White Horse
Robert Thompson
Kilburn
Shandy Hall
Byland Abbey
Ampleforth
Nunnington
Nunnington Hall
Salton
Normanby
Flamingo Land
Kirby Misperton

Baldersby
Skipton-on-Swale
Sowerby
Coxwold
Newburgh Priory
Gilling East
Gilling Castle
Hovingham
Slingsby
Appleton-le-Street
Eden Farm Insight
Eden Camp

Wath
Memberby
Dalton
Topcliffe
Thormanby
Husthwaite
Brandsby
Malton

Norton Conyers
Dishforth
DISHFORTH
Carlton
Crayke
Terrington
Castle Howard

Ripon
Norton-le-Clay

THE MAJESTIC NORTHERN UPLANDS

'Peace, everywhere serenity, and a marvellous freedom from the tumult of the world.' So said a 12th-century abbot of Rievaulx of his beloved North York Moors, in a description that might equally apply to the moors of Northumbria.

In the beginning, or as near to it as makes little difference, was the inferno. It produced sufficient magma from the earth's surface to create a rough granite plateau maybe 20,000ft high, which was then ground down over millions of years to a tenth of its original height. Glaciers rounded the tops, gouged deep lakes and carved out the beds of the streams that now rush north to feed the waters of the Tweed. They also bequeathed the infamous morasses that are the despair of long-distance walkers over the magnificent crown of the Cheviots.

South of the range, the bedrock is sandstone, the relic of an ancient sea. Darkly blanketed with heather, this area is known locally as the Black Country, not least for the contrast it makes

ROCK OF AGES *The Bride Stones, High Staindale, are formed from layered limestone.*

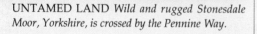

UNTAMED LAND *Wild and rugged Stonesdale Moor, Yorkshire, is crossed by the Pennine Way.*

with the pale, grassy slopes of the Cheviots. Southwards again, there is another geological surprise, the upthrust of a line of volcanic basalt, about which the softer sandstone has eroded away, leaving the glowering bastion of the Great Whin Sill.

From there, up through the Cheviots to the Scottish border, this vast area of moorland has been dubbed the Northumbrian National Park. Its western march is the Kielder Forest Park, the largest man-made forest in Europe, while beyond its eastern boundary is the North Sea.

The Northumbrian moors are associated with the lonely, piping cry of the curlew, quite

properly chosen as the badge of the Park. It shares the skies with swift predators such as hen harriers, peregrine falcons and rare merlins, known for their low, erratic flight.

For a glimpse of nature from the distant past, it is worth making a visit to one of the peat hags. There, among the bog moss grow sundew, cranberry and cotton grass, all cautious colonisers from the era immediately after the last Ice Age. They attract the large heath butterfly, one of the first species to return to Britain as the ice retreated.

The Romans came to Britain around 55 BC and, though they eventually penetrated as far north as Inverness, by AD 105 it was decided that the permanent occupation of what is now Scotland was not worth their while. A frontier was therefore established on the line Solway-Tyne, and substantiated during the reign of Emperor Hadrian, around AD 200, by the building of a great 76 mile wall, stretching across England. This is Hadrian's Wall, which took three legions, some 25,000 men, five years to build. The best of what remains can be seen in the south of the Park, where the engineers cunningly laid the foundations along the edge of Whin Sill crags.

The efforts of the Roman builders, however, were in vain, for in AD 367 the wall and its garrison, depleted by recalls to defend Rome, were overwhelmed by the Picts; and so began hundreds of years of strife along the Scottish borders. Reminders of those troubled times persist in the ruined castles and keeps, and in the villages. Elsdon, for example, has a vicar's peel, or fortified rectory, while more than 100 borderers, killed at the Battle of Chevy Chase, lie in the churchyard. Near Branxton, a cross in a cornfield commemorates 'the brave of both nations' who died in the Battle of Flodden in 1513.

The North York Moors are more beckoning, and encompass a variety of landscapes, each of which interlock and complement the whole. To the north, there is the great sandstone massif of the Cleveland Hills, while the south and west are mainly limestone. There lie the strange, flat-topped, Tabular Hills with their bows pointing northwards like a fleet of aircraft carriers. Then there are the dales, Bilsdale, Rosedale, Farndale

and the rest, cutting deeply into the uplands The floors of the valleys are rich green pasture while on the slopes above, a rising pattern of dry-stone walls carries the eye up to the heather and bracken of the tops.

Though the coast is being noticeably eroded today, it was the shallow seas of 150 million years ago that created the North York Moors, laying down the sediments that form its bedrock. Successive Ice Ages sculpted the land. When the ice departed, its run-off waters scooped out the dales, floored them with rich soils and began the carving of strange

MOORLAND VIEW *Malham Beck lies 280ft below the white limestone rocks of Malham Cove in the heart of the Pennine moorlands. The beck wanders on towards distant Malham village.*

DEATH ON THE MOORS *Thousands died at the Battle of Chevy Chase in 1388. An event before the slaughter is depicted on this carved panel.*

abstract shapes, like the Bridestones above Dovedale Griff, that outcrop here and there on the moors.

The North York Moors remain a monument to those who passed through them. Visitors can still walk along prehistoric tracks like the Hambleton Drove Road. These trails came to be marked by stone crosses, one of which, Lilla's Cross, commemorates a steward who died to save Edwin, King of Northumbria. The 12th century saw the start of many monasteries; Rievaulx, Byland, Mount Grace and Whitby, which even in their ruined state are ornaments of the countryside.

The moors were most populous during the late Stone and Bronze Age, but these early inhabitants cleared the natural vegetation for grazing and planting, leaving the soil thin and acid. New woodlands are now being planted to replace those long lost and, far from being a desert, the present moors are a vivid, living entity. Yet for those who seek its peace, the long-distance walkers on the old trails, there still remains the splendid emptiness, under the great arched dome of the sky.

BORDER LOOKOUT *The best preserved remains of Hadrian's Wall lie near Housesteads, situated in the south of the Northumbrian National Park.*

MERLIN'S MAGIC

The elusive, low-flying merlin, hunting bird of noblewomen in the Middle Ages, is rarely spotted as it scours the open moorland for small birds and rodents.

THE COAST OF CAPTAIN COOK

From the Cleveland Hills, the River Esk cuts a lush valley through the bleak plateau of the North York Moors to Whitby. To the south, streams tumble from the highlands down to the Vale of Pickering and into the River Derwent which flows west from the coast. This stretch of coast is associated with the explorer and navigator Captain James Cook, who lived for some years at Whitby.

Ayton Castle Cb
Remains of fortified medieval tower, built like Scottish peel tower to serve both as house and as fortress. Tower's base is all that is left standing.

Boggle Hole ☆ Cd
Small stream has cut small valley in Robin Hood's Bay cliffs; this valley is one of few ways down to shore. Good walk across rocks to Stoupe Beck Sands during low tide.

Bridestones ☆ ✿ ➹ Bc
Two groups of massive sandstone outcrops, 150 million years old. Surrounding moorland has 300 acre reserve with roe deer, foxes and badgers.

Cleveland Way Db-Ae
Ninety-mile path starts north of Filey and runs 40 miles to Saltburn-by-the-Sea. From here, it runs inland across North York Moors National Park to Helmsley. Coastal stretches trace cliffs, with magnificent views.

Fylingdales Moor Cc
Bleak moorlands dominated by three huge white 'golfballs' of RAF's Early Warning System.

Glaisdale Ad
Iron-smelting centre until ore reserves ran out in 1880s. Single-arched packhorse bridge retains its cobbles. Three-mile walk through River Esk valley ends via stepping stones at Egton Bridge.

Goathland ⌂✿ Bd
Village of mostly 19th-century houses scattered over several

High Hawsker ⌂ Cd
Moorland village noted for handsome stone-built farms. Nearby a curious brick structure encloses spring once used by nuns of Whitby Abbey.

Hole of Horcum ☆ Bc
Natural hollow eroded in heather-covered moorland. Legend tells of a giant, Wade, scooping out the hollow and throwing rock 2 miles east to form Blakey Topping.

Kettleness ⌖ Be
Isolated cliff-top hamlet with relics of disused coastal railway, including red-brick Victorian station. Footpath leads north along railway line to Staithes.

Mallyan Spout ☆ Bd
Seventy-foot waterfall over mossy cliff in Murk Esk valley. Fall is reached by a 20 minute walk down steep, rough track from Mallyan Hotel.

Newton-on-Rawcliffe ⌂ Bc
In farmyard setting, Mel House Bird Garden displays interesting variety of wild and domestic birds, some rare.

North Yorkshire Moors Railway ⌨ Bb
Steam trains of restored railway travel 18 mile run from Pickering to Grosmont through Pickering Castle deer park and past 'golfball' radar domes of Fylingdales. Line was built in 1830s by George Stephenson.

Pickering ⌨⌂⌨ Ab
Originally Celtic town dates from 3rd century BC. Motte-and-bailey castle has Norman remnants. Church has medieval frescoes and effigies. Beck Isle Museum of Rural Life recalls Victorian era with typical printer's shop, outfitters and cobblers.

Raindale ✿⌖ Bc
Marked paths lead through 375 acre Forestry Commission conser-

vation area of old oaks, newly planted pines, spruces and larches. Wildlife includes roe deer and badgers.

Ravenscar ☀ Cd
Rugged headland of Old Peak at Ravenscar is National Trust owned. On peak's 600ft summit is 18th-century Raven Hall, now a hotel, situated on site of Roman signal point.

DUTY FREE Smuggled goods were handled in tunnels beneath the houses of Robin Hood's Bay.

Robin Hood's Bay ⌂⌨ Cd
Fishing village on bay of same name, where legend says Robin Hood repelled Danish invaders. Rock-floored bay is rich in fossils. Smuggling Experience Museum recalls surrounding area's 18th-century smuggling days.

Runswick ⌂ Be
Sand crescent stretches south-east from village set at foot of cliffs. To east, headland called Kettle Ness has Roman lighthouse remains.

Saltwick Bay Ce
Above bay is Whitby High Light and fog signal station. Light has 22 mile range and 'The Hawsker Bull'

foghorn can be heard 10 miles away. Good fossil hunting among bay's rocks.

Sandsend ⌂ Be
Village set around two streams at west end of Whitby Sands. Paths lead into Mulgrave Woods with overgrown ruins of 13th-century fortress and Gothic 18th-century Mulgrave Castle.

Scarborough ⌨⌖⌨⌂⌨ Db
Resort, spa and fishing town with twin bays. Town has theatres, art gallery, and museums of natural, local and archaeological history. Hundreds of oceanic species visible from Sea Life Centre's underwater glass tunnels.

Snainton ⌂⌖ Cb
Mile Bush Open Farm illustrates agricultural past with various farm animals and old implements as part of working farm.

Stoupe Beck Sands Cd
Best stretch of sand in Robin Hood's Bay. Beach road provides view over whole bay.

Thornton Dale ⌂ Bb
Village with variety of architecture. Buildings include 12 dark-stone almshouses built 1656, Tudor thatched cottage, Georgian mansions and medieval church.

Trouts Dale ⌖➹☀ Cb
From River Derwent, road leads up steep valley of Troutsdale Beck with Wykeham Forest to the east. At summit of climb, moors fall away in series of flat plateaux.

Wade's Causeway ⌖ Bc
A 1¼ mile stretch crossing Wheeldale Moor forms Britain's best surviving Roman roadway. Built around AD 80, it was once part of 25 mile stretch. Original gravel surface is gone, but foundation slabs and kerbstones remain.

WHITBY ABBEY German World War I shelling added to the ancient abbey's ruinous state.

Whitby ✿⌖⌂⌨ Be
Former whaling port set on Esk estuary. Cook Museum recalls life and times of explorer Captain James Cook, who lived here 1746-9. St Mary's Church, at top of 199 steps, has 18th-century wooden interior carved by shipbuilders. Sandstone ruins of Whitby Abbey on cliff above port.

Wintringham ⌂ Ba
Norman Church of St Peter has Norman font, medieval screens, 15th-century glass and 17th-century pews.

SPLENDID SWEEP The view north from the headland of Ravenscar takes in the wide crescent of Robin Hood's Bay, once the haunt of smugglers.

Dalby Forest ⌨✿✿➹☀ Bb
Mostly conifer forest with 14 marked paths and 9 mile drive linking Thornton Dale and Hackness. Picnic area at Staindale Lake. Information centre at Low Dalby tells woodland story.

Falling Foss Forest Trail ☆⌖✿➹ Bd
From car park, easy 3 mile woodland trail leads past well-hidden Falling Foss waterfall and ponds.

Filey ⌨✿ Eb
Victorian family resort with 6 miles of sand backed by red clay cliffs. Natural breakwater of Filey Brigg to north provides protection, where walking and fishing is safe at low tide. Avoid Filey Brigg in rough weather. Filey North Cliff Reserve has nature trail.

Forge Valley ✿ Cb
River Derwent valley containing woodland reserve. Hillside features oak, ash and elm, while valley floor has alder and willow trees. Bird life includes nuthatch, great spotted woodpecker, chiffchaff and warbler.

huge, heath-like greens. Centre for moorland and woodland walks and waterfalls.

Grosmont ⌂⌨ Bd
Hillside village is northern terminus for North Yorkshire Moors Railway. Sheds exhibit steam engines and carriages dating back to 1890. Three-mile historical railway trail to Goathland.

Hackness ⌂ Cc
Village at junction of Derwent and several tributaries, site of a monastery in Saxon times. Medieval church has fragments of 8th-century cross. Good centre for walks and forest drives.

Hayburn Wyke ⌖✿ Dc
Steep track through wooded glen leads down to rocky shore. Stream flowing through nature reserve ends in beachside waterfall.

High Bridestones and Flat Howe ⌖ Bd
Bridestones are Bronze Age remains of two 40ft circles of standing stones. Flat Howe, to the east, is a round Bronze Age barrow, or grave mound.

HIKER'S GUIDE This stone post, one of many on the Cleveland Way, acted as a prominent route marker when the path was first defined centuries ago.

Boulby Cliffs

Staithes
Port Mulgrave
Runswick Bay
Dalehouse
Roxby
Hinderwell
Runswick
Kettleness
Goldsborough
Lythe
Mickleby
Newholm
Sandsend
The Dracula Experience
Abbey
Mulgrave Woods
Saltwick Bay
Cook Museum
Whitby
Sneaton

Lealholm
Glaisdale
Egton
Sleights
High Hawsker
Egton Bridge
Grosmont
Fylingthorpe
Robin Hood's Bay
High Bridestones & Flat Howe
Falling Foss
Smuggling Experience Museum
Falling Foss Forest Trail
Boggle Hole
Thomason Foss
May Beck
Stoupe Beck Sands
Beck Hole
Mallyan Spout
Goathland
Ravenscar

Wade's Causeway
Goathland Moor
Fylingdales Moor
Lyke Wake Walk
Staindale
Wheeldale Moor
NORTH YORK MOORS
Hayburn Wyke
Newton Dale Forest Drive
Wykeham High Moor
Cloughton Wyke
Reasty Bank
Cloughton
Crook Ness
Harwood Dale
Blakey Topping
Burniston
Raindale
Hole of Horcum
Langdale Forest
Keldy Castle
Newton Dale Forest Drive
Bridestones
Broxa
Toll
Hackness
Sea Life Centre
Cawthorn
Cropton Crafts
Lockton
Stape Dale
Langdale End
Everley
Scalby
Castle
Newton-on-Rawcliffe
Deepdale Forest
Scalby
Trouts Dale
Scarborough
Castle
Wykeham Forest
Art Gallery
Dalby Forest
Forge Valley
Falsgrove
Middleton
North Yorkshire Moors Railway
Ebberston Hall
Mile Bush Farm
Ayton Castle
Ayton
Eastfield
Cayton Bay
Pickering
Wilton
Ebberston
Ruston
Irton
Osgodby
Thornton Dale
Allerston
Wykeham
Brompton
Wrelton Buscel
Cayton
Cleveland Way
Snainton
Lebberston
Gristhorpe
Flamingo Land
NORTH YORKSHIRE
Willerby
Filey
Kirby Misperton
Flixton
Muston
Great Habton
Staxton
Holiday Camp
Ganton
Hunmanby
Eden Farm Insight
West Heslerton
Wolds
Way
Bempton Cliffs
Eden Camp
Wykeham
Sherburn
East Heslerton
Knapton
Reighton
Speeton
Malton
Old Malton
Rillington
Wintringham
Scampston
Foxholes
Danes Dyke
North Landing
Norton
Weaverthorpe
Burton Fleming
BRIDLINGTON
Bempton
Flamborough

Abbeytown 🏠⛪ Ce
Monks founded Holme Cultram Abbey in 1150, grew grain, raised sheep and cattle and traded in salt from estuary. At the Dissolution of the Monasteries in 16th century, stones were hauled away to build houses. Nave survives as St Mary's parish church. Tomb of Robert Bruce's father in porch.

Aira Force ☆🏞 Fb
Short walk from car park on Ullswater shore leads to where Aira Beck rushes under stone bridge and pours 70ft down green hole.

Angle Tarn ☆ Fa
Remote, trout-filled waters with two small islands in Martindale deer forest. Reached by 1½ mile walk from Dale Head Farm in Bannerdale, south of Ullswater.

Ashness Bridge ⚓☀ Da
Narrow road leads to humpbacked bridge and footpath to Surprise View, where ground falls away to reveal Derwent Water and Skiddaw.

ACROSS THE BECK *Beyond Ashness Bridge lies Derwent Water.*

Bassenthwaite 🏠 Dc
Peace reigns on 4 mile long lake where motorboats are banned. Traces of Roman and Norse settlements round village.

Borrowdale ☆🏞⚓☀ Da
Walking and climbing country dominated by 2949ft Great Gable: 2000 ton Bowder Stone, left behind by Ice Age glacier, perched above Jaws of Borrowdale pass.

Bowscale Tarn ☆ Ec
Walk up fell from Bowscale hamlet in Calder valley to admire cliffs mirrored in black waters.

Burgh by Sands 🏠 Ee
Border outpost built over site of Roman fort which provided stones for St Michael's Church. Edward I died nearby in 1307.

Buttermere ☆ Ca
Walks radiate from this hamlet through woods and meadows, past peaks and waterfalls and round lake. Path from Fish Hotel leads to Scale Force, 2 miles away.

Caldbeck 🏠🏛 Ec
John Peel buried near porch of medieval church after falling from horse in 1854, aged 78. River-powered woollen mills once produced grey cloth for Peel's hunting coats. Wheel still turns on restored 18th-century Priests Mill.

FROM FELL TO FARMLAND

From lofty Helvellyn to the dark waters of Bassenthwaite Lake, the region has all the romantic charm that one expects of the Lake District. But the immemorial peace and beauty so beloved of poets belie a harsher past. To the north, Hadrian's Wall marks an early boundary in what was to be a bitterly fought-over border region, where even the churches were fortified for refuge.

PEACEFUL TARN *The shining waters of trout-filled Watendlath lie cradled by the surrounding friendly hills.*

Carlisle ⊛✝🏛🚂🏰ℤ Ee
Founded by Romans as part of Hadrian's Wall defences. King William Rufus's 1092 sandstone keep changed hands between English and Scots many times, now Border Regiment HQ. Cathedral, originally church of 12th-century Augustinian priory, greatly damaged in Civil War; 15th-century screen survived. Roman road through grounds of 15th-century Guildhall Museum.

Castlerigg Stone Circle ᚦ Db
Bronze Age ring of stones up to 6ft tall set in amphitheatre of hills. Probably 3500 years old.

Cockermouth 🏰🏛🏭 Cc
Poet William Wordsworth born in Georgian house at end of main street in 1770. Art gallery in another Georgian house. Remains of largely 14th-century castle where Cocker and Derwent rivers meet. Toy and doll museum.

Crummock Water ☆ Ca
Romantic setting between high fells gives lake its character. Car parks at Rannerdale and Lanthwaite provide viewing points. Footpath to Scale Force waterfall.

Dalston 🏠 Ee
Colour-washed cottages group round St Michael and All Angels, dating from 13th century, restored in 1890. Dalston Hall, now hotel, built about 1500. Peel tower with turret stands beside it.

Dodd Wood 🏞♣🏛 Db
Roe deer and red squirrels live in woodland, with views over Bassenthwaite lake. Mirehouse (17th

SQUAT POWER *Carlisle's massive Norman keep has watched over the border country since 1092.*

century) on lakeside has associations with Francis Bacon and Lord Tennyson. Has adventure playgrounds for children.

Ennerdale Water 🏞♣☀ Ca
Wild and remote lake with views to towering mass of Pillar, 2927ft. Motor road stops at Bowness Knott, about ½ mile from bank. Footpaths round shore.

Friar's Crag 🏛 Db
Short walk from lakeside Century Theatre to monument where John Ruskin expressed 'intense joy' at view over Derwent Water.

Glenridding 🏠 Ea
Steamers leave for trips round Ullswater. Fell walks lead to isolated Lanty's Tarn; only experienced walkers should carry on to tackle Helvellyn, 3116ft, and its dramatic ridge, Striding Edge.

Grange 🏠 Da
Scree-covered slopes reach almost to edge of village. Through it flows

clear, pebble-bedded River Derwent, crossed by graceful but narrow bridge. Centre for walks.

Hadrian's Wall ♛ Df
Roman soldiers guarded western end of wall at Bowness-on-Solway. Vallum, or defensive ditch, can be seen near Glasson.

Hesket Newmarket 🏠 Ec
Base for exploring hills. Open-sided market building on village green survives from days of sheep and cattle trading.

Holme Wood ♣ Cb
Broad-leaved woodland stretches a mile from edge of Loweswater; at its heart Holme Force tumbles under canopy of oak trees.

Keswick 🏛🎭🏛ℤ🚂 Db
Several museums with variety of displays including lead pencils made here since 16th century, originally with local graphite, relief model of Lake District, works by Lakeland poets, and cars used in films and TV series. Church of St Kentigern mainly 14th to 16th century. Poets Coleridge and Southey lived here.

Lodore Falls ☆ Da
Watendlath Beck drops into Derwent Water near Lodore Swiss Hotel, 'rushing and lushing and brushing and gushing', as described by Southey.

Maryport ℤ✕♛ Bc
Now silted up. Landowner built it in 1749 to ship iron ore, naming it after wife. Maritime museum has tug *Flying Buzzard*, Clyde puffer and *Bounty* mutiny relics.

Newlands Pass Da
Road from Braithwaite runs 3 miles above this green valley and through wild scenery to drop down into Buttermere.

Papcastle 🏠♛ Cc
Site of Roman fort. Stone cottages, gardens bright with flowers, look out over River Derwent.

Rosthwaite 🏠 Da
Grey-slate village, popular with naturalists, where herons stand patiently by the streams. Old oak woods with varied plant life.

Seathwaite ☆ Da
Hamlet at end of narrow road in Borrowdale. Difficult paths to Great Gable, 2949ft; Scafell Pike, 3210ft, and Styhead Tarn, 1600ft, Britain's wettest place with average annual rainfall of 172.9in.

Seatoller ℤ Da
Built for slate-quarry workers at foot of Honister Pass. Houses National Park information centre in converted barn.

Silloth Ce
Named after 'sea laths', granaries built by monks from Holme Cultram. Grain ships still call. Promenade looks out at mountains across Solway Firth.

Stonethwaite Da
Tucked away at end of minor road in Borrowdale, where streams tumble down crags. Old packhorse trail over hills to Grasmere.

Thirlmere ☀🏞 Ea
Dam built in 1879 turned two small lakes into one large one, now fringed by conifer plantation. At southern end is Wythburn church: village lies beneath water.

Thornthwaite 🏛 Db
Car park at Woodend Brow gives wide views of Bassenthwaite Lake, dominated by awesome bulk of Skiddaw, 3054ft.

Threlkeld 🏠 Eb
Famous for fox-hunting and sheepdog trials. Stagecoach travellers used to stay at 17th-century Horse and Farrier Inn.

Watendlath ☆ Da
Whitewashed cottages roofed with grey slate cluster round trout-filled tarn, from which stream passes under humpbacked Ashness Bridge.

Whinlatter Pass ℤ☆♣ Cb
Forestry Commission visitor centre and Noble Knott picnic site are starting points for many marked footpaths.

Workington ♛🏭🏛 Ab
Clothes and furniture in Helena Thompson Museum recall Victorian heyday of port, which still exports coal and steel. Remains of Roman fort. Wooded park round ruins of 14th-century Workington Hall, brief refuge for Mary, Queen of Scots in 1568.

Wythop 🏛🏠🏰 Cb
Grain mills here since medieval times. The present 18th-century building converted to sawmill in 1860, now has museum showing how original mill operated.

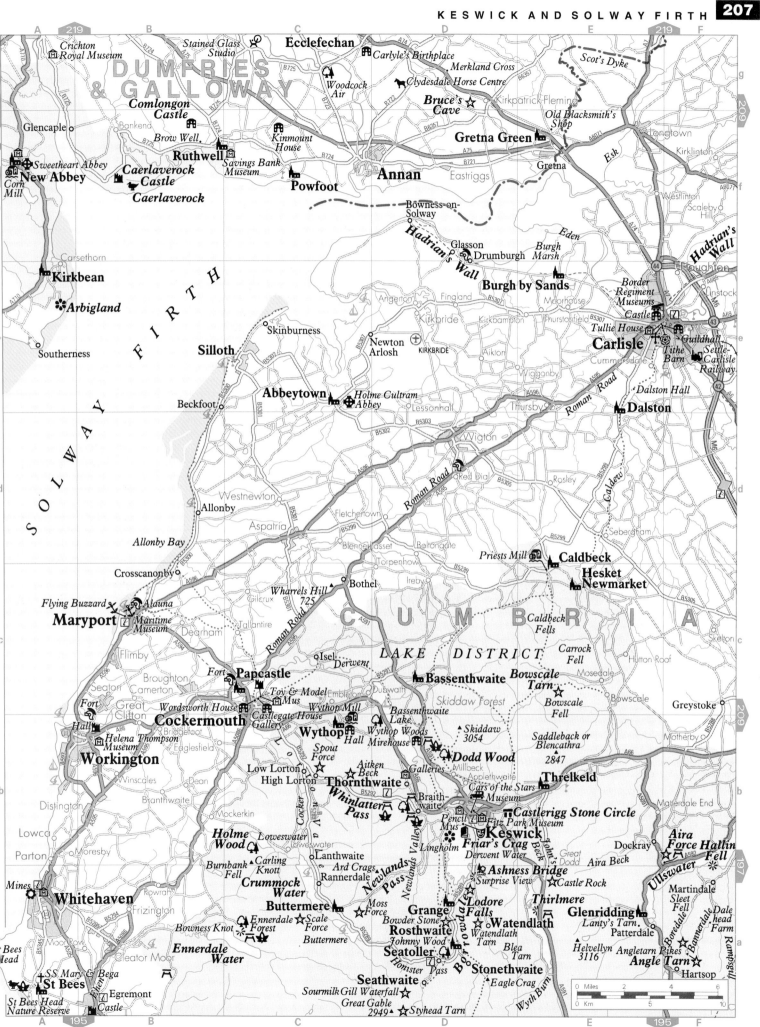

DUMFRIES & GALLOWAY

Crichton Royal Museum
Stained Glass Studio
Ecclefechan
Carlyle's Birthplace
Merkland Cross
Woodcock Air
Clydesdale Horse Centre
Scot's Dyke
Comlongon Castle
Bruce's Cave
Kirkpatrick Fleming
Old Blacksmith's Shop
Glencaple
Bankend
Brow Well
Kinmount House
Gretna Green
Gretna
Longtown
Sweetheart Abbey
New Abbey
Ruthwell
Savings Bank Museum
Annan
Eastriggs
Esk
Kirklinton
Corn Mill
Caerlaverock Castle
Powfoot
Bowness-on-Solway
Westlinton
Caerlaverock
Scaleby Hill
Kirkbean
Hadrian's Wall
Glasson
Drumburgh
Burgh Marsh
Eden
Houghton
Hadrian's Wall
Arbigland
Burgh by Sands
Moorhouse
Border Regiment Museums
Angerton
Finland
Castle
Southerness
Kirkbride
Aikton
Thurstonfield
Tullie House
Carlisle
Guildhall
Carsethorn
Newton Arlosh
KIRKBRIDE
Wiggonby
Cummersdale
Tithe Barn
Settle-Carlisle Railway
Skinburness
Silloth
Lessonhall
Thursby
Roman Road
Dalston Hall
Abbeytown
Holme Cultram Abbey
Wigton
Dalston
Beckfoot
Roman Road
Rosley
Calder
SOLWAY FIRTH
Westnewton
Fletchertown
Red Dial
Caldew
Allonby
Aspatria
Blennerhasset
Boltongate
Sebergham
Allonby Bay
Crosscanonby
Torpenhow
Ireby
Bothel
Priests Mill
Caldbeck
Skelton
Flying Buzzard
Alauna
Wharrels Hill 725
Gilcrux
Hesket Newmarket
Maryport
Maritime Museum
Dearham
Tallantire
CUMBRIA
Caldbeck Fells
Bowscale
Flimby
LAKE DISTRICT
Carrock Fell
Hutton Roof
Isel
Derwent
Moredale
Fort
Papcastle
Bassenthwaite
Bowscale Tarn
Bowscale Fell
Great Clifton
Broughton Camerton
Toy & Model Mus
Embleton
Dubwath
Skiddaw Forest
Greystoke
Fort
Wordsworth House
Wythop Mill
Bassenthwaite Lake
Skiddaw 3054
Saddleback or Blencathra 2847
Hall
Cockermouth
Castlegate House Gallery
Wythop
Wythop Woods
Helena Thompson Museum
Spout Force
Mirehouse
Dodd Wood
Motherby
Workington
Eaglesfield
Millbeck
Appletwaite
Threlkeld
Low Lorton
Aitken Beck
Galleries
Cars of the Stars Museum
Matterdale End
High Lorton
Thornthwaite
Braithwaite
Distington
Whinlatter Pass
Castlerigg Stone Circle
Lowca
Mockerkin
Pencil Mus
Fitz Park Museum
Parton
Holme Wood
Loweswater
Lanthwaite
Friar's Crag
Keswick
Dockray
Aira Force
Hallin Fell
Burnbank Fell
Carling Knott
Ard Crags
Rannerdale
Lingholm
Derwent Water
Great Dodd
Aira Beck
Castle Rock
Ullswater
Martindale Sleet Fell
Mines
Crummock Water
Moss Force
Newlands Pass
Ashness Bridge
Surprise View
Thirlmere
Glenridding
Lanty's Tarn
Dale head Farm
Whitehaven
Buttermere
Grange
Lodore Falls
Watendlath
Patterdale
Bowness Knot
Ennerdale Forest
Scale Force
Bowder Stone
Rosthwaite
Watendlath Tarn
Helvellyn 3116
Angletarn Pikes
Buttermere
Johnny Wood
Blea Tarn
Bees Head
Ennerdale Water
Seatoller
Stonethwaite
Angle Tarn
SS Mary & Bega
Cleator Moor
Honister Pass
Eagle Crag
Hartsop
St Bees
Egremont
Seathwaite
St Bees Head Nature Reserve
Castle
Sourmilk Gill Waterfall
Great Gable 2949
Styhead Tarn
Wyth Burn

0 Miles		2		4		6
0 Km			5			10

Allen Banks ⌖ ☆ Ed
Stands of beech and oak cling to steep banks of ravine cut by River Allen above point where it joins South Tyne. Home of roe deer and red squirrel. Riverside walks. View from top of east bank across Tyne valley to Hadrian's Wall.

Allendale Town ⌖ Ec
Village said to be the exact geographical centre of Britain stands high above wooded gorge of River East Allen. Buildings in golden stone radiate from tree-lined square. Gothic-style St Cuthbert's Church dates from 1807.

Allen Gorge ⌖ ☆ Dd
Tree-lined banks, 250ft high, descend steeply to riverside pathways. Woodland walks lead through magnificent scenery.

HIGH POINT *The spire of Alston's church rises above some of England's steepest streets.*

Alston 🏛 ⛪ ⚓ Db
Said to be England's highest market town at an altitude of nearly 1000ft. Stone houses line steep, cobbled streets. Gossipgate Gaslight Gallery has exhibitions of regional arts and crafts. Narrow-gauge South Tynedale Railway operates trips above valley.

Armathwaite ⌖ ✿ ⚓ Bb
Village clusters round bridge over River Eden. Chapel of Christ and St Mary dates from 17th century. Tower of riverside castle built into Georgian mansion. Eden Valley woollen mill open to public.

Bewcastle ✝ ⚓ Be
Village near 6 acre site of Roman fort, outpost of Hadrian's Wall. Shaft of 1300-year-old cross in churchyard has runic inscriptions and carvings of figures.

Bellingham ⌖ Ef
Small market town whose one-time iron industry provided metalwork for Newcastle's Tyne Bridge. Grey-stone 19th-century buildings flank wide main street. Stone-slab roof of 12th-century St Cuthbert's Church guarded against 16th-century marauders.

Birdoswald Roman Fort ⚓ Cd
Remains of massive gateway, tower and part of Hadrian's Wall stand on 5 acre site guarding Roman bridge over River Irthing. Exhibition displays fort's history and life of garrison.

ALONG THE ROMAN WALL

The forts and mile castles of the great wall built by the Roman Emperor Hadrian between AD 122 and 136 straddle the southern edge of the Northumberland National Park, rearing up from wild, undulating moorland that was once a no-man's-land between England and Scotland. In this barren region, modern man has created mighty pine forests and Europe's largest artificial lake.

Black Middens Bastle House 🏚 Dg
Fortified farmhouse built of stone in 16th century. Livestock accommodation on ground floor, family quarters above.

Brampton ✝ Bd
Market town with cobbled streets and slate-roofed brick buildings. Octagonal Moot Hall, built 1817, has clock tower cum belfry, external staircases and iron stocks. Shop in High Cross Street was Bonnie Prince Charlie's headquarters in 1745.

Brocolitia ⚓ Ee
Roman Wall fort with temple of Mithras, Persian god of light. Replicas of altar, columns and statues – originals in Newcastle Museum of Antiquities.

Cawfields ⚓ 🌲 Dd
Impressive 2 mile section of Hadrian's Wall runs along Great Whin Sill crest. Five-minute walk from picnic site to Roman mile castle at Cawfield Crags.

Chesterholm ⚓ 🏛 Dd
Excavated remains of Roman fort of Vindolanda. Relics galore in museum: letters, boots, sandals, jewellery in remarkably good condition. Replica of Hadrian's Wall section, reconstructed kitchen, Roman milestone still in original position and undamaged.

Corby Castle ✿ Ac
Bulky 13th-century keep with 17th and 19th-century additions. Terraced gardens overlook River Eden with its medieval wood-and-stone salmon traps.

Garrigill ⌖ Db
Stone houses, 1790 church, 1757 chapel set around spacious village green. Lane leads to 2930ft Cross Fell, highest point of Pennines.

Gilsland ⌖ ⚓ Cd
Well-preserved mile castle with 10ft high walls above fast-flowing Poltross Burn. Mile castles were small forts placed along Hadrian's Wall at distances of one Roman mile (1620yds).

Great Salkeld ⌖ ⚓ Ba
Red-sandstone cottages and farmhouses cluster round part-Norman church of St Cuthbert. Norman dog-tooth carving on south doorway. Ivy-clad tower built 1380 as refuge for villagers against border raiders.

Housesteads Roman Fort ⚓ 🏛 Dd
Best-preserved Roman fort in Britain with remains of commanding officer's quarters, barracks, granaries, latrines and hospital within 8ft high walls. Museum houses model of 3rd-century fort.

Hutton-in-the-Forest ⌂ Aa
Mansion with battlemented sandstone towers set in wooded parkland. The south front has a fine, 17th-century classical façade of three storeys, flanked by a 14th-century peel tower and Victorian Gothic tower. The house has a collection of furnishings, paintings and tapestries.

Ireshopeburn 🏛 Ea
Attractive grey-stone houses and cottages stand beside Ireshope Burn. Weavers Forge Cottage, converted 200-year-old smithy, is now workshop selling yarns and hand-woven fabrics.

Killhope Wheel Lead Mining Centre ✿ Eb
Pan for lead or work machinery in restored 19th-century lead-ore crushing mill. Giant water wheel 34ft across, railways, stables, smithy and displays of mining through the ages.

Kirkoswald ⌖ ✿ Bb
Red-sandstone village with 15th-century church, St Oswald's. Late-Victorian bell tower on hill 200yds above church. College, seat of Featherstone family since 1613, was converted from 1450 peel tower. Ruined castle has 13th-century moat.

LINE OF DEFENCE *Hadrian's Wall, built to protect the northern boundary of Roman Britain, stretches for 73 miles.*

Kielder Forest ⌖ ✿ 🌲 🏕 Cg
Britain's largest man-made forest; 125,000 acres of conifers. Visitor centre in Kielder Castle, battlemented hunting lodge built 1775 by Duke of Northumberland – the starting point of forest walks and 12 mile forest drive.

Kielder Water 🏕 ⌖ 🌲 🏕 Cf
Landscaped reservoir, Europe's largest, covering 2684 acres and with 27½ mile shoreline. Created 1976 by damming North Tyne. Southern shore paths link viewpoints and centres for visitors, field studies, fishing and sailing.

HOLY TRIO *These ancient carvings at Housesteads may depict deities.*

Lanercost ✚ Bd
Priory founded 1166, damaged by Scottish raiders in 13th and 14th centuries and abandoned 1536 during Dissolution of Monasteries. North aisle survived and served as parish church until nave restored in 1740. Aisle has windows by Victorian artists William Morris and Edward Burne-Jones.

Naworth Castle ⌂ Bd
Border stronghold built 1335, turned into mansion in 17th century, now home of Earl of Carlisle. Battlemented sandstone towers overlook gatehouse carved with coat of arms. Rooms of castle contain elaborate tapestries.

Nenthead ⌖ 🏛 Db
Lead miners once lived in village, 1450ft up in Pennines and said to be highest in England. Miners' reading room and Miners' Arms pub still exist. Old mine workings along path by River Nent.

North Tyne Road 🌲 🏕 Cf
Scenic drive around the southern shores of Kielder Water. Tracks lead off it to viewpoints, including one to Otterstone Viewpoint on Bull Crag Peninsula with broad panorama of lake.

Once Brewed 🏕 🏛 Dd
History of region since retreat of the Ice Age glaciers displayed in Northumberland National Park information centre. It stands on *vallum* – broad earthwork that probably defined military zone south of Hadrian's Wall.

Roman Army Museum 🏛 Cd
Lifelike figures of Roman soldiers, audiovisual displays and large-scale model of fort create daily life of men who guarded Rome's northernmost outpost.

Talkin Tarn Country Park 🏕 Bc
Lake of 65 acres set in 100 acres of wood and farmland. Nature trail through woodlands starts from Victorian boathouse.

Twice Brewed 🌲 Dd
Spectacular viewpoint on Hadrian's Wall. Three-mile stretch of desolate and rugged countryside leads to Housesteads Roman Fort.

Wade's Road Cd
Straight, switchback road – running parallel to Hadrian's Wall – was built in 1750s.

Wark ⌖ Ee
Grey-stone houses surround village green on River North Tyne. Stone bridge spans wooded banks of stream. Remains of massive Norman castle on bank.

Weardale Museum 🏛 Ea
Rugged past of upper Wear Valley illustrated in High House Chapel, built 1760 and second oldest Methodist chapel still in use. Displays of family life in 1870s, farming, mining and wildlife.

Wetheral ⌖ ✿ Ac
Large stone houses stand around triangular green, dominated by 19th-century chateau-style Eden Bank. Village's 16th-century Church of Holy Trinity has chapel to Howard family.

Whitley Castle ⚓ Cb
Complex system of ditches is sole reminder of Roman fort built in 2nd century and rebuilt in 3rd.

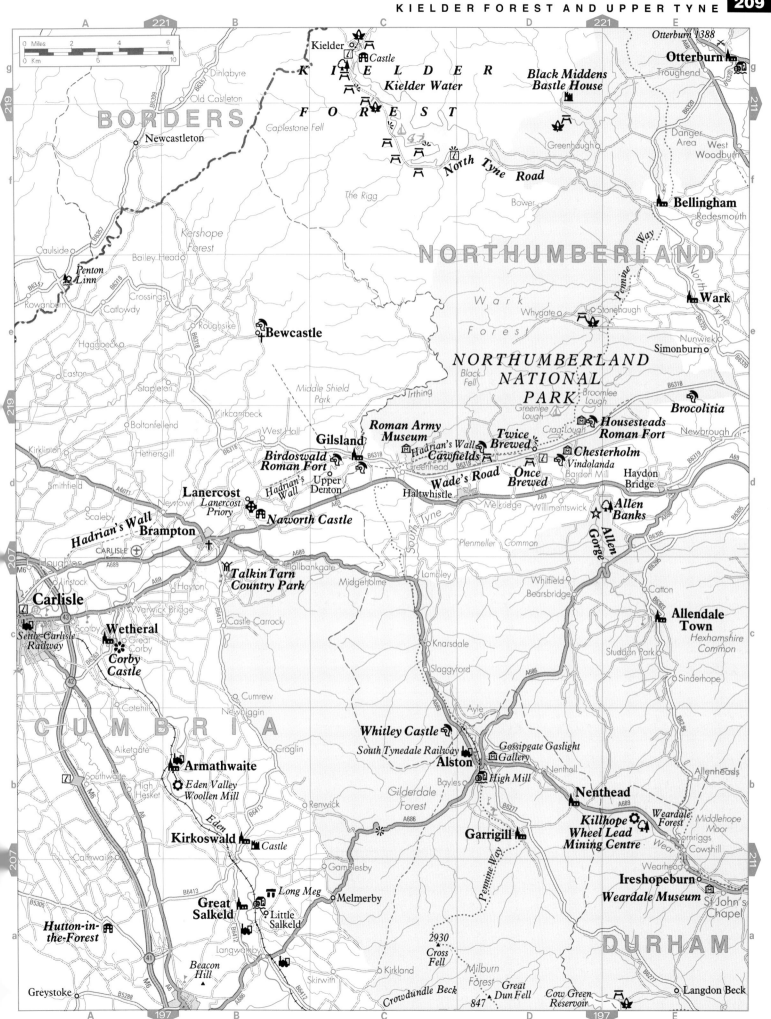

Otterburn 1388
Otterburn
Troughend

Kielder
Castle
Kielder Water

Black Middens
Bastle House

North Tyne Road
Greenhaugh

BORDERS

Newcastleton

Dinlabyre
Old Castleton

Caplestone Fell

The Rigg

Bower

Danger
Area

West
Woodburn

NORTHUMBERLAND

Bellingham
Redesmouth

Caulside

Bailey Head

Kershope
Forest

Pennine
Way

Penton
Linn

Rowanburn

Crossings

Catlowdy

Roughsike

Haggbeck

Easton

Stapleton

Boltonfellend

Wark
Forest

Whygate

Stonehaugh

Wark

Nunwick

Simonburn

Bewcastle

Black
Fell

**NORTHUMBERLAND
NATIONAL
PARK**

Broomlee
Lough

Brocolitia

Middle Shield
Park

Kirkcambeck

West Hall

Irthing

Greenlee
Lough

Crag Lough

Newbrough

Roman Army
Museum

Housesteads
Roman Fort

Hadrian's Wall

Twice
Brewed

Chesterholm

Gilsland

Birdoswald
Roman Fort

Cawfields

Greenhead

Vindolanda

Haydon
Bridge

Kirklinton

Hethersgill

Smithfield

Upper
Denton

Wade's Road

Once
Brewed

Bardon Mill

Haltwhistle

Lanercost

Lanercost
Priory

Hadrian's Wall

Melkridge

Willimontswick

Allen
Banks

Hadrian's Wall

Newtown

Naworth Castle

South Tyne

Brampton

CARLISLE

Plenmeller Common

Allen
Gorge

Scaleby

Houghton

Talkin Tarn
Country Park

Hallbankgate

Midgeholme

Lampley

Whitfield

Bearsbridge

Catton

Carlisle

Warwick Bridge

Hayton

Castle Carrock

Knarsdale

**Allendale
Town**

Hexhamshire
Common

Scotby

Great
Corby

Wetheral

Corby
Castle

Cumrew

Slaggyford

Studdon Park

Sinderhope

Aiketgate

Newbiggin

Cumrew

Ayle

CUMBRIA

High
Hesket

Cotehill

Renwick

Croglin

Knarsdale

Gilderdale
Forest

Whitley Castle

South Tynedale Railway

Gossipgate Gaslight
Gallery

Nenthead

Armathwaite

Eden Valley
Woollen Mill

Alston

High Mill

Nenthall

Allenheads

Southwaite

Weardale
Forest

Middlehope
Moor

Kirkoswald

Castle

Long Meg

Gamblesby

Bayles

Killhope
Wheel Lead
Mining Centre

Sorriggs

Cowshill

Melmerby

Gilderdale
Forest

Pennine Way

Garrigill

Wear

Wearhead

**Great
Salkeld**

Little
Salkeld

Langwathby

Kirkland

Skirwith

Ireshopeburn

Weardale Museum

St John's
Chapel

**Hutton-in-
the-Forest**

Beacon
Hill

2930
Cross
Fell

Milburn
Forest

847

Great
Dun Fell

Cow Green
Reservoir

DURHAM

Greystoke

Crowdundle Beck

Langdon Beck

INTO THE BORDER COUNTRY

Hadrian's Wall marked one of the northern Roman frontiers, and castles, peel towers and fortified manors recall the days of fierce border raids of later centuries. In the last century this was the birthplace of the railways. But now the defences have become museum pieces and once-busy railways have been turned into paths for walkers and trackways for cyclists.

Aydon Castle 🏰 Cd
One of England's finest fortified manor houses, built at end of 13th century. Main feature is Great Hall. Many walks in the area.

Belsay Hall 🏰✿🏛 Ce
Neoclassical building resembling Greek temple. Rooms with decorative friezes and woodwork lead off central courtyard. Extensive grounds include water garden, rhododendron garden and meadow garden of wild flowers.

Binchester Fort 🏛 Ea
Roman cavalry fort with well-preserved hypocausts. Concrete floor of one room is still intact, supported on brick piers – some stamped with name of army unit that made them.

Blanchland 🏠🏚 Bc
Village, 18th-century, was built following ground plan of 12th-century abbey. Post office was once gatehouse, inn was abbot's guesthouse and Church of St Mary was former north transept.

Bolam 🌲✝ Cf
Red squirrels can still be seen in country park surrounding Bolam Lake – an artificial feature created by John Dobson in 1818 which caters for fishing, paddling and boating. Woodlands, lakeside meadows, walks and picnic areas. Birdwatching – birds come close to parked cars and will feed from the hand. Norman Church of St Andrew has tall Saxon tower.

Brancepeth 🏠 Ea
Originally 12th century, Church of St Brandon has west tower and stands in grounds of castle. Chancel rebuilt in 15th century.

Bywell 🏠 Cd
Two churches dominate tiny village – St Andrew's has tower dating from before AD 950, and fragments of St Peter's north wall date back to 8th century. Rare medieval scratch clock on south wall of St Peter's Church. The market cross – a pillar supporting a ball – stands between churches, from days when Bywell was important ironworks centre.

Cambo 🏠 Cf
Hilltop village of 18th-century terraced houses with 19th-century church. Post office housed in medieval peel tower. Village hall was once school where Capability Brown was educated.

Causey Arch ✿ Ec
Oldest surviving railway bridge in the world, built in 1725-6 to facilitate removal of coal from mines in horse-drawn trucks. The single-arch bridge, 100ft long, spans deep, wooded gorge.

ROMAN RELIC *Tablet dedicated to goddess is now in Chesters Museum.*

Chesters 🏛🏚 Bd
Roman cavalry fort, including remains of barracks, stables, commandant's house and bathhouse, on Hadrian's Wall by bank of River North Tyne. Museum has sculptures, including headless statue of goddess standing on cow's back, weapons, jewellery and pottery on display.

Consett 🏚🌲✝ Dc
St Cuthbert's Church, designed by John Dobson, completed 1886 in blend of Gothic Revival and mock Early English styles. Allensford Country Park 2 miles from Consett on River Derwent. Sheltered by woods, paddling pool, play park and picnic sites.

Corbridge 🚩 Bd
Resort town on River Tyne. Peel tower, built in 1300s to protect vicar of Church of St Andrew's from marauding Scots now serves as information centre. Church dates from 13th century.

Corstopitum 🏛🏚🌲 Bd
Roman fort built to guard bridge over River Tyne. Remains of a storehouse, the largest Roman building in Britain. Also ruined temples, granaries and houses. Museum shows archaeological finds, including fountainhead depicting lion devouring stag.

Derwent Reservoir 🌲🐟🌲 Bc
Reservoir, 3½ miles long, set in heather-covered moorland. Picnic sites, walks and a bird hide. Trout-fishing permits available from Utilities Building.

Derwent Walk 🌲 Dc
Open to walkers, riders and cyclists on disused railway line through woodlands and along shoulder of Derwent Valley. Several picnic sites. Forms part of Derwent Walk Country Park.

Ebchester 🏠🏚 Dc
Village built on site of Roman station of Vindomora. Parish church of St Ebba has Roman stone in its walls and Roman altar set into wall of its tower. Ebchester Museum has small collection of finds from Vindomora.

Frosterley 🏠 Ca
St Michael's Church, built 1866, has excellent examples of Frosterley marble – used for centuries to make fonts, tombs and pillars in churches all over the world.

Gibside Chapel ✝ Dc
Gibside Estate is one of the finest examples of Georgian landscaping in Durham, carried out by Lancelot 'Capability' Brown. Gibside Chapel, built in Palladian style, has three-tier mahogany pulpit and box pews.

Hartburn 🏠 Cf
Church of St Andrew dates back to 12th century. Maltese Cross and daggers carved over door indicate association with Knights Templar. Dr Sharpe's Tower, 18th century, built to house village school and schoolmaster, and to stable hearse. Georgian vicarage has 13th-century peel tower.

Heavenfield ✝✗ Bd
Church of St Oswald built in 1737 on site where King Oswald of Northumbria is said to have erected wooden cross before defeat of Welsh and Mercian invaders in AD 634. Battlefield is 2 miles east of Chollerford, marked by tall wooden cross. Information on battle available at church.

Heddon-on-the-Wall 🏠 Dd
The wall is Hadrian's, and a well-preserved 100yd section can be seen. Small hilltop Church of St Andrew has choir dating partially from 680, as well as vaulted Norman sanctuary and 13th-century nave.

Herterton House ✿ Cf
Herterton House, 16th-century farmhouse, surrounded by 1 acre garden laid out in formal 18th-century manner. Flowers, herbs and topiary.

Hexham ✿🌲🏚🚩 Bd
Hexham Abbey built in 12th and 13th centuries over crypt of earlier abbey built by St Wilfrid in AD 674 from stone taken from Roman camp of Corstopitum. Stone seat in choir known as Wilfrid's Throne. Other buildings in town of Hexham include 15th-century moot hall and old jail, built in 1330, which now serves as Border History Museum and tourist information centre.

Kirkwhelpington 🏠 Bf
Small village whose mainly 12th and 13th-century church was heavily damaged in 14th-century border raids and much altered in 18th century. Grave of Charles Parsons, steam-turbine pioneer.

Lanchester 🚩 Db
Massive columns in Norman Church of All Saints taken from nearby Roman fort of Longovicium, porch is made from Roman altar. Stones from fort used to build houses which surround a broad village green.

Leap Mill Farm 🏚 Dc
Well-preserved water mill dating from 18th century with rare breeds of farm animals.

Mickley Square 🏠🏚 Cd
Thomas Bewick, wildlife illustrator, born here in 1753. Family cottage shows examples of his work and still produces hand printing from wooden blocks.

Mitford 🏠🏚 Df
Sited in wooded valleys of Wansbeck and Ford rivers, with ruins of Norman castle. Mitford Hall designed by John Dobson in 1823. Church of St Mary Magdalene, Norman, much restored in 19th century. Bell, which alerted castle opposite during siege by King John in 1215, claimed to be oldest in Britain.

Morpeth 🚩🌲🏚✝ Ef
Busy market town on a loop of the River Wansbeck; gateway to the moors, hills and coast. Museum in refurbished 13th-century chantry contains large collection of bagpipes from Britain and abroad, craft centre and tourist information centre. Church of St Mary the Virgin, mainly 14th century, has stained-glass Tree of Jesse from same period in east window. Town hall was designed by Sir John Vanbrugh in 1714. Unusual 15th-century clock tower in town was once jail; clock still strikes curfew. Stepping stones across the Wansbeck lead to walks beside river, crossed by a number of bridges. Meldon Park, built 1832 by architect John Dobson.

Newburn Hall Motor Museum 🚗 Dd
Museum houses large collection of veteran, vintage and post-vintage cars. Restoration work can be seen in progress.

Ovingham 🏠 Cd
Tall Saxon tower built about 1050 dominates 13th-century Church of St Mary. Fragments of Saxon crosses are displayed inside the church. Monument to the wood engraver Thomas Bewick.

SAFE SEAT
Throne in Hexham Abbey gave right of sanctuary.

TRANQUIL VALLEY *Wolsingham's cottages huddle among Weardale trees, while sheep graze the slopes above.*

Ponteland De
Blackbird Inn was once fortified manor house. Drinks now served in 600-year-old vaulted basement. Church of St Mary has Norman tower and 13th-century chancel. About 3 miles north, Kirkley Hall grounds have ornamental and sunken gardens.

Prudhoe Castle Cd
Nineteenth-century manor house stands hidden behind gatehouse of the ruined 12th-century castle. Rooms of manor house decorated in late Georgian style. Castle's keep still stands.

Shotley Bridge Cc
Bridge in centre of village spans river Derwent, linking Northumberland and Durham. Village famous for sword making in 17th century – sharpening grooves can be seen in some large stones in village. Site of old railway station now picnic spot. Shotley Bridge Heritage Centre has displays of photographs relating to history of Derwentside.

Stamfordham Ce
Huge green surrounded by 18th and 19th-century houses. Jail and lock-up, from days when visiting drovers became too rowdy for peace, still stand. Market cross, built 1735, takes form of arched shelter. Art gallery.

Stanhope Ca
Stump of 250-million-year-old tree outside 12th-century St Thomas's Church. Mock-medieval castle, built 1798, now serves as school. Village is excellent centre for walking – footpaths along rivers and into open moorlands.

Tanfield Railway Ec
Steam engines run on a section of old line. Impressive collection of industrial locomotives includes some more than 100 years old.

Wallington Hall Cf
Built 1688 and extended in the 18th century. Rococo plasterwork, Regency furniture, Pre-Raphaelite paintings, Dutch porcelain. Victorian doll's house in servants' hall has 36 rooms, also electric lights and running water.

Waskerley Cb
Footpath, called Waskerley Way, is all that remains of railway that made Waskerley a rail centre. Main feature is 150ft high viaduct over Hownes Gill.

Whalton Df
Green verges dotted with trees flank main road lined with rows of stone cottages. St Mary's Church dates from 13th century.

Wolsingham Ca
Town of stone cottages, some with slate roofs. Whitfield House was built 1700; restored cottages nearby date from 1677.

Wylam Dd
Birthplace in 1781 of railway pioneer George Stephenson. Plaque depicting early steam locomotive *Rocket* stands at top of hill leading down to village. Cottage where he lived as child in Tyne Riverside Country Park. In Wylam itself is a museum illustrating the village's place in railway history.

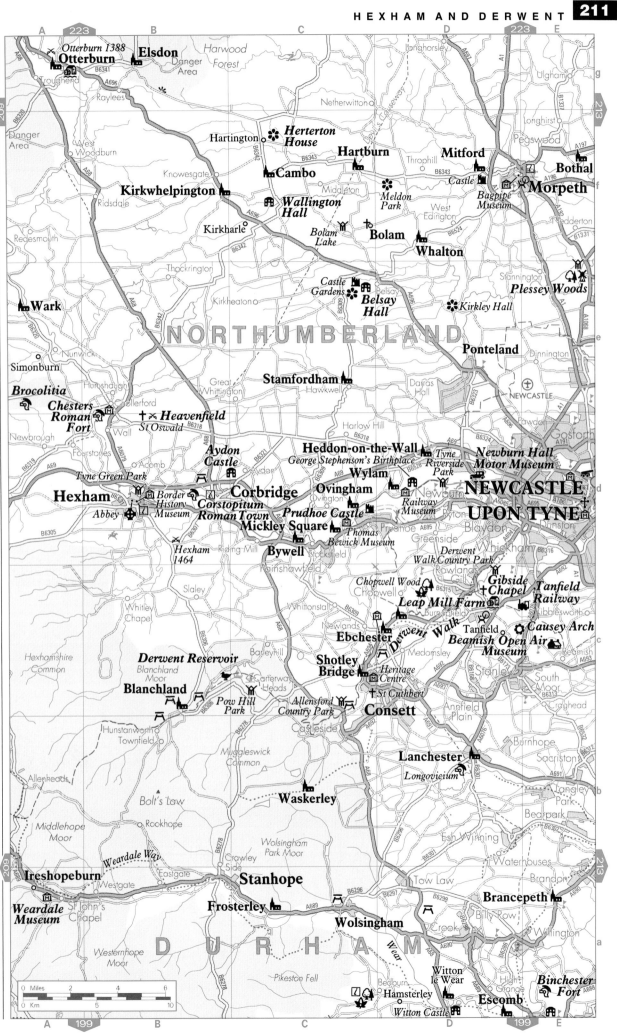

Beacon Hill ☆ Cb
Highest point on Durham coast, preserved by the National Trust. 279ft summit has splendid views, reached by path from wooded Hawthorne Vale.

Beamish Open Air Museum Ac
Turn of century brought back to life on 200 acre site. Re-created 'town' of cobbled streets, old houses rebuilt brick by brick, store stocked with goods of the period. Farmhouse with traditional kitchen, a blacksmith's forge and a steam railway station. Replica of Stephenson's *Rocket* runs to an authentic drift mine with pitmen's cottages nearby.

STEAM DAYS *Replica* Rocket *runs on a pit railway at Beamish museum.*

Blyth Bf
Largely modern town overlooking harbour busy with ships loading coal and unloading timber. Mile-long pier sheltered by rocks. South is 2 mile sandy beach, safe for swimming.

Bothal Af
Village of pale stone houses built towards end of 19th century. St Andrew's Church is partly 9th century. Small, medieval castle has stone soldiers on the battlements; now offices and closed to public.

Castle Eden Dene Ca
Wooded ravine is nature reserve with roe deer and many varieties of trees and birds. Runs from visitor centre at Peterlee to coal-speckled shore south of Horden.

Cullercoats Be
Village's harbour shelters sandy shore with good bathing. Tall tower and spire crown St George's Church, built 1884.

Cresswell Ag
Beach protected from North Sea by outlying reef. Handsome 14th-century peel tower emerges from walled parkland.

Durham Ab
Norman cathedral, containing shrines of Venerable Bede and St Cuthbert, towers above loop in River Wear. Mighty columns and stone-ribbed vaulting. Castle was palace of bishops from 1072 to 1837, now university student residence. Oriental Museum is only one in Britain wholly devoted to oriental art: Chinese ceramics from 2000 BC to 18th century, jade, art of ancient Egypt, Near East and India. Durham Light Infantry regimental museum displays battle relics.

Finchale Priory Ab
Thirteenth-century Wearside ruin on site of hermitage founded by St Godric, a reformed pirate. Cross on floor marks his tomb.

BEAUTY AMID INDUSTRY'S PAST

The rugged coastline around the Tyne estuary bears traces of an industrial past; disused collieries and pit heaps dot the landscape. Yet the coast reveals miles of unspoilt sandy beaches with unusual rock formations and limestone cliffs haunted by thousands of sea birds. Viking invasions forced the monks of Lindisfarne to find a new home, and so Durham was founded.

HALLOWED JAIL *Soaring Durham Cathedral once housed Scottish prisoners taken by Puritans during Civil War.*

Hartlepool Da
Old town on limestone headland facing Hartlepool Bay. Morning fish auction at docks. Medieval town wall with archway; Early English Church of St Hilda built 1189-1239 by family of Robert Bruce. Maritime museum with working model of ship's engine. Paddle steamer *Wingfield Castle*, built here in 1934, used as Humber estuary ferry; and frigate HMS *Trincomalee*, built Bombay 1817, oldest British warship afloat. Both in Jackson Dock.

Haswell Bb
Well-preserved steam-powered colliery engine house, dating from about 1800, has walls nearly 8ft thick.

REST HOME *Durham monks took their sabbaticals at Finchale Priory.*

Houghton-le-Spring Bc
Cruciform Church of St Michael and All Angels with central tower, originally Norman and now mainly 13th-15th centuries, has stone effigies of 13th-century cross-legged knights.

Hylton Castle Bc
Four square turrets and battlements crown impressive castle, built by Sir William Hylton in the 14th century. Medieval heraldry banners on display inside.

Jarrow Bd
Industrial town on banks of Tyne. Saxon Church of St Paul, with some 7th-century stained glass, and remains of a monastery where the Venerable Bede, 'father of English history' who died 735, wrote *Ecclesiastical History of the English People*. Saxon relics in Bede Monastery Museum.

Killingworth Ae
New town with artificial sailing lake. Several buildings have won design awards. Dial Cottage was home to railway pioneer George Stephenson in early 1800s.

Lizard Point Cd
Lizard Point lighthouse, built in 1871 with a circular tower rising 76ft, was one of the first to be equipped with electric light.

Marsden Cliffs Cd
Thousands of sea birds haunt these cliffs. Cormorants nest on Marsden Rock, a natural archway. At cliff foot is Grotto – cave turned into home by 18th-century miner, now a pub. Grotto is reached by lift or by steps from beach.

Monkwearmouth Cc
Benedictine monastery, founded 674, adjoins Church of St Peter. Nearby railway museum recreates steam age in Monkwearmouth Station, built 1848.

Moorhouse Woods Bb
Footbridge from Leamside, north of Durham city, leads to woodland walks beside meandering River Wear.

WAVE-CARVED *Pounding storms have washed away the soft rock, exposing harder stone which forms the 100ft tall 'triumphal arch' of Marsden Rock.*

Newbiggin-by-the-Sea B
Was a grain port in medieval times but is now a haven for a few leisure boats and a fleet of fishing cobbles.

Newcastle upon Tyne Ad
Old port, shipbuilding centre on River Tyne. Ramparts of Norman castle, built 1080, provide views of city's six bridges. Joicey Museum illustrates area's social history. Bagpipe Museum in Black Gate.

North East Aircraft Museum Bc
Collection of 25 aircraft spanning most of aviation history. Relics of RAF and German aircraft which crashed during World War II. Display of military vehicles.

North Shields Bd
Morning fish market on quay. Pioneer locomotives at Stephenson Railway Museum, including *Killingworth Billy* of 1826.

Pittington Bb
Church of St Laurence distinguished by Norman north arcade with twisted columns and zigzag ornament of about 1175. Also has medieval wall paintings and Saxon windows. Effigy of knight dates from 1280.

Plessey Woods Ae
Unusual windmill lies in peaceful woodland setting. Inscription in Bedlington Church commemorates sleepwalker who died while climbing church in 1669.

Rosa Shafto Nature Reserve Aa
Beech, oak, ash and willow trees flourish here. Woodpeckers and warblers can be seen in clearings rich in wild flowers.

Ryhope Engines Museum Cc
Old pumping station houses 19th-century beam engines that delivered water from village well. Sanitary fixtures collection is included in the display.

t Mary's Island ⚓ Be
etty group of houses and light-
ouse built 1898 on burial ground
Tynemouth Priory. Island
ked to the mainland by a
arrow causeway which can be
ossed on foot at low tide.

eaham † Cb
rivately run harbour founded
828 as outlet for Lord Lon-
onderry's coal mines. North of
wn is white mansion of Seaham
all, scene of poet Lord Byron's
815 marriage to Anne Isabella
Milbank. Cliff-top church has
3th-century font and chancel.

eaton Delaval Hall 🏛🎠 Be
alatial 18th-century mansion by
r John Vanbrugh. Interior
cludes superb sculpted chim-
eypiece in Great Hall. Norman
hapel in grounds houses family
ombs and 14th-century effigies.

eaton Sluice ⚓ Be
ir Ralph Delaval built harbour in
660 for export of salt and coal.
ilt-controlling sluice gate at
ver's mouth gave village its
ame, but no longer exists.

South Shields 🏛 Bd
ardens and wooded park slope
own towards mile-long pier. To
he north lie remains of fort of
rbeia, built 2nd century to guard
ast flank of Hadrian's Wall and
upply routes. Beside fort stands
ull-size reconstruction of Roman
gateway. Museum houses Roman
word and jewellery.

Springwell 🚂 Ac
Demonstrations of rope-worked
rains on restored 1¼ mile section
of Bowes railway, which carried
coal to Jarrow for 150 years.

Sunderland ⚙🏛 Cc
Ancient port on River Wear. River
Wear Trail traces the remains of
town's old industries, including
shipbuilding, pottery and glass-
making. Borough Road museum
features local lustre-ware pottery
of 19th century.

Tynemouth ✚🏰⚙🏛 Bd
Seafront dominated by walls of
1090 Norman church, later fortified by Richard II. Timber watch
house of volunteer life brigade
holds small museum illustrating
local offshore wrecks and rescues.

Wallsend 🗝 Ad
Town grew up where Hadrian's
Wall reached sea. Heritage centre
displays finds from fort of Sege-
dunum nearby. Liner *Mauretania*
launched here 1907.

Washington 🏛⚙ Bc
Washington Old Hall, restored
17th-century home of George
Washington's ancestors. Colliery
museum has 19th-century winding engine. Flamingos in 100 acre
waterfowl park.

Whitley Bay Be
Seafront hotels and guesthouses
overlook flower gardens along the
resort's promenade. Sands are
safe for bathing.

Woodhorn 🏛🎵⚙🏛 Af
Colliery museum in country park
has displays on mining and social
history. Medieval bells and Saxon
cross-shaft in church museum.

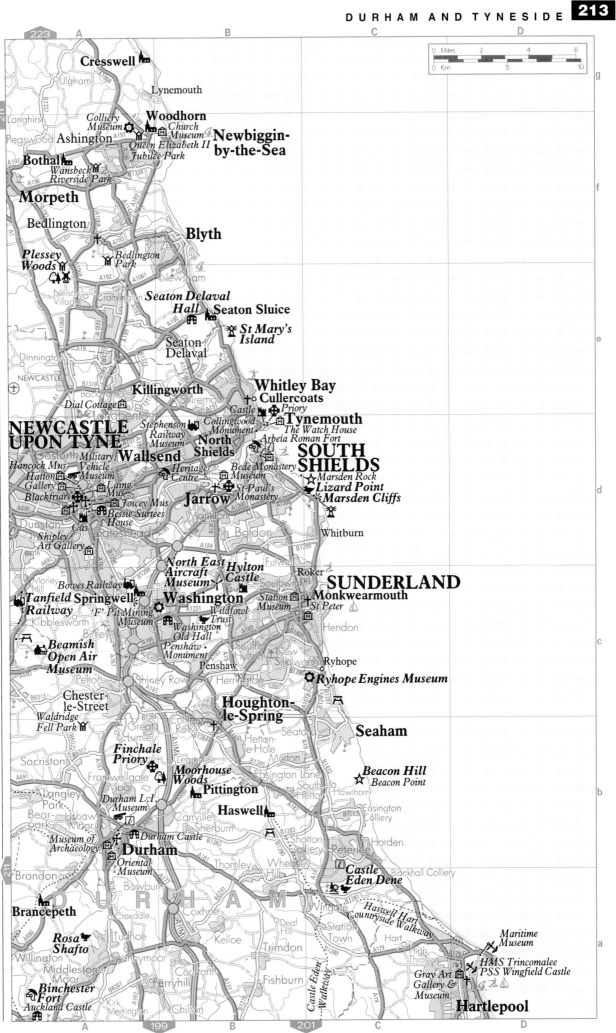

A LAND OF PASTORAL CHARM

Ailsa Craig, the granite plug of an extinct volcano, stands ten miles off the western shore of this land of lochs, moors and high hills in lowland Scotland. Forested uplands cut by ravines form the hinterland to the peninsula of The Rhins, and beneath its rocky spine are gardens where the influence of the mild Gulf Stream allows subtropical plants to grow.

Ailsa Craig 🏰 Bh
Once-volcanic island with 19th-century lighthouse and castle. Its bluish granite is source of stones for curling.

Ardwell Gardens ❀ Cc
Walled garden, hawthorn avenue and wooded walk around 18th-century Ardwell House. The Machars visible across Luce Bay.

Auchenmalg Bay Dd
Sandy bay featuring sea angling and swimming is overlooked by revenue men's barracks of 1820s and by Auchenmalg to the north.

Ballantrae 🏰 Bg
Gaelic for 'village on the shore'. It was 18th-century smugglers' headquarters. River Stinchar's tidal creeks and lagoons provide refuge for terns and other birds.

Barr 🏰 Dh
Remote Carrick Hills village by the Water of Gregg. Red-sandstone church of 1891 now private house.

Cairnsmore of Fleet Ge
Six-mile return walk to 2331ft summit was mentioned in John Buchan's *The Thirty-Nine Steps*. Walk begins near Palnure.

Castle Kennedy Gardens ❀ Ce
Gardens encompassing two castles were laid out by Field Marshal Lord Stair and troops in 18th century. Features terraces, lily pond and separate gardens of Stair family's Castle Lochinch.

Creetown 🏰 Fd
Gem museum has an agate containing drop of water said to be 2 million years old. Granite clock tower commemorates Queen Victoria's 1897 Diamond Jubilee.

Drummore 🏰 Cb
Popular resort, sea angling centre. Seven ancient kingdoms can be seen from Mull of Galloway. Double Dykes crossing the mull believed to be work of Picts.

Galloway Forest Park Fg
Wooded 250 miles of countryside topped by 2766ft Merrick. Lochs include Loch Trool and Clatteringshaws Loch. Features include deer range, wild goat park, forest trails among glens, waterfalls.

FORTRESS FLOWERS *Castle Kennedy Gardens contain woodlands, viewpoints, formal beds and tree-lined avenues.*

Galloway House Gardens ❀ Fc
Laid out in 1740s as pleasure gardens for Galloway House, they include rare handkerchief tree and heronry. Open daily.

Garlieston 🏰 ❀ Fc
Popular fishing centre protected by sea wall, with sea-angling boats for hire. Village's brightly painted houses are best viewed from bay road. Galloway House Gardens 1 mile south.

Girvan 🏰 Ch
Sandy beaches, safe swimming, fishing all attract visitors. Visit boatyard where wooden fishing boats are built, also distillery. Killochan Castle, 16th century, lies 3 miles north-east.

Glenluce 🏰 Cd
Sixteenth-century Castle of Park to the west overlooks village from across Water of Luce. Twelfth-century Cistercian abbey ruins retain chapter house with vaulted ceiling, Gothic windows.

Glen Trool Ff
Go by Water of Minnoch's foaming rapids to reach glen. Road finishes above the waters of Loch Trool, where Bruce Stone marks 1307 rout of English by Robert Bruce's men. For the energetic, a path leads 4 miles to the summit of Merrick's 2766ft, highest point in Southern Scotland.

Glenwhan Gardens ❀ Cd
Hilltop gardens where exotic trees and shrubs flourish in Gulf Stream climate. Views over Luce Bay among rocky outcrops and cascading waterfalls.

Isle of Whithorn Fb
Busy though unspoiled sailing resort. St Ninian landed on grassy peninsula (once the isle) in AD 395 on return from Rome. Iron Age fort, ruined 13th-century chapel.

Kirkmadrine Church † Bc
Tiny, isolated church where three of Britain's earliest known inscribed Christian stones stand. Two, praising 5th-century priests, were being used as gateposts.

Loch Doon 🏰 Fh
Fourteenth-century castle with keep on western shore. It was moved from an islet in loch flooded for hydroelectricity.

Logan Botanic Gardens ❀ Bc
Gulf Stream keeps garden of subtropical trees and flowering shrubs virtually frost-free. Note the avenue of Chusan palms.

Minnigaff 🏰 Fe
Now a suburb of Newton Stewart, though far older. Ruined medieval church, ivy covered; also spacious 19th-century church. Churchyard yew is reputed to be 800 years old.

Monreith 🏰 Ec
Village with safe, sandy beaches. Ruined Kirkmaiden chapel contains local Maxwell family tombs, and plaque to drowned French naval captain washed ashore 200 years ago. Gavin Maxwell otter memorial on headland.

Mull of Galloway Cb
Headland with 250ft cliffs topped by 1830 lighthouse. Views from here of Lake District, Isle of Man and Ireland's Antrim Hills.

Murray's Monument Ff
Obelisk stands above shell of cottage where Alexander Murray was born in 1775. A self-taught shepherd boy, he became professor of Oriental languages at Edinburgh University.

Newton Stewart 🏛 Fe
Small town with museum of local history including farmhouse kitchen and blacksmith's forge. Cree Bridge, built in 1813, backed by riverside gardens.

Palgowan Open Farm Eg
A 7000 acre hill farm offering afternoon tours. Livestock rearing, the making of 24 miles of dry-stone walls explained. Livestock includes shaggy, long-horned Highland cattle, Blackface sheep.

Penkill Castle Dh
Fifteenth-century castle with chesspiece tower, enlarged in 1844 by Spencer Boyd. Mural by William Bell Scott follows curving staircase. Pre-Raphaelite artists including Holman Hunt and Dante Gabriel Rossetti painted here. Visits by appointment only.

Port Logan 🏰 Bc
Port Logan Fish Pond, excavated 1800, served as fresh fish larder for Logan estate owners. Land-hungry feudal laird said to have built up main road above house-top level to drive out locals.

Portpatrick 🏰 Bd
Colour-washed houses line promenade. Ferry link to Ireland before 1862. Irish elopers were married in 17th-century church. Dunskey Castle ruin nearby.

The Queen's Way Ff
Scenic road alongside Galloway Forest Park linking New Galloway and Newton Stewart commemorates Queen's Silver Jubilee 1977. Picnic spots, forest trails.

St Ninian's Cave ☆ Fb
Cave where first Christian missionary to Scotland prayed after arrival in AD 395. Crosses are carved into nearby rock.

Soulseat Loch ❀ Cd
Near loch is promontory site of herb garden, now featuring 100 species set in individual beds. Garden planted beside mounded remains of Soulseat Abbey.

Stranraer 🏛 Be
Seaside resort, ferry terminal for Larne, Northern Ireland. Castle of St John now visitor centre. North West Castle, shaped like a ship, was home of 18th-century polar explorer Sir John Ross.

Torhouse Stone Circle Ed
Sixty-foot diameter Bronze Age circle. There are 19 stones in the circle and three boulders set in line in the centre. It is thought it may have been a burial site. Ruins of Baldoon Castle, 3 miles south-east, the setting for Sir Walter Scott's *The Bride of Lammermoor*.

Whithorn Fc
Twelfth-century priory ruin, said to be built on site of St Ninian's 5th-century church *Candida Casa*, or 'white house', retains barrel-vaulted crypt, roofless nave. Site has been excavated to reveal foundations of Viking trading settlement, and coins and gaming pieces from earlier times.

WHITHORN RELICS *The 5th-century Latinus Stone (right) in abbey museum, is the earliest Christian memorial in Scotland.*

Wigtown 🏛 Fd
Martyrs' Memorial Stone marks spot where two anti-Episcopalian women who refused to recant their religion were, in 1685, tied to stakes in River Bladnoch to drown in rising tide. Working distillery of 1814, creamery, tiny museum.

Wood of Cree Nature Reserve Ef
Stands of fine oak and birch with wide variety of animal, plant life. Marked walks, waterfalls.

BATTLE SITE *Glen Trool, where Robert Bruce ambushed and put to flight 2000 English soldiers in 1307.*

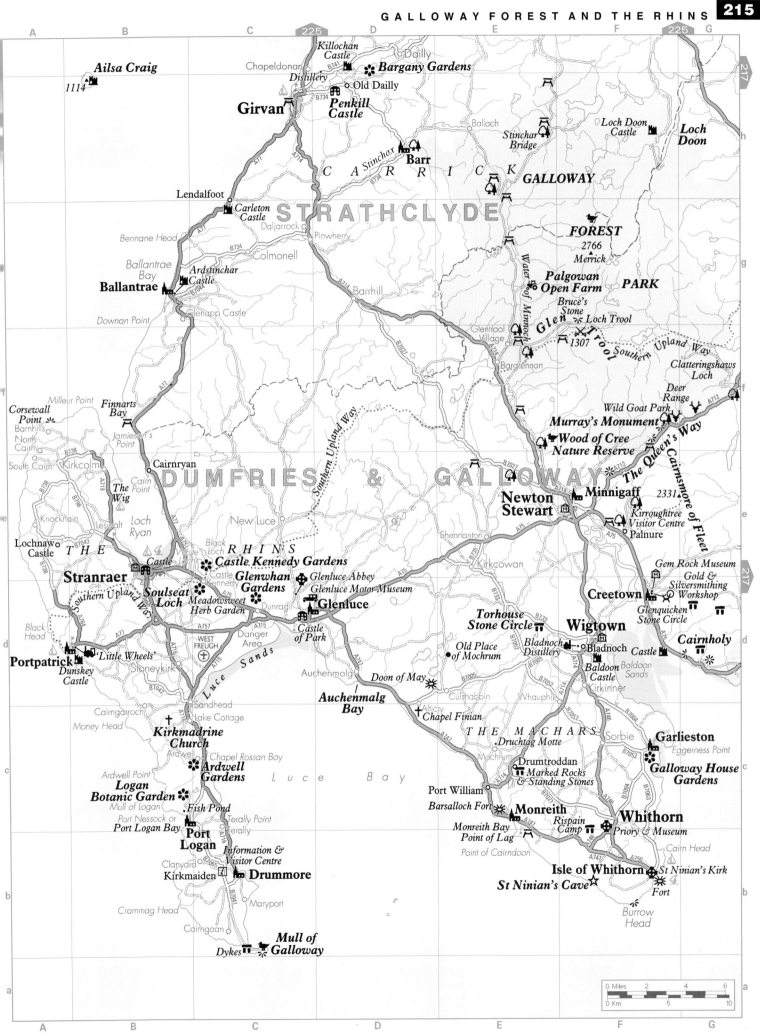

Ailsa Craig
1114

Girvan

Killochan Castle
Chapeldonan
Dailly
Bargany Gardens
Old Dailly
Distillery
Penkill Castle

Barr

Stinchar
CARRICK
GALLOWAY
Balloch
Stinchar Bridge
Loch Doon Castle
Loch Doon

Lendalfoot
Carleton Castle
Daljarrock
Pinwherry
STRATHCLYDE
FOREST
2766 Merrick
Palgowan Open Farm
PARK
Bruce's Stone
Loch Trool

Bennane Head

Ballantrae Bay
Ardstinchar Castle
Ballantrae
Colmonell
Barrhill
Glenapp Castle

Downan Point

Glentrool Village
1307
Glen Trool
Southern Upland Way
Clatteringshaws Loch
Deer Range

Corsewall Point
Milleur Point
Finnarts Bay
Jamieson's Point
Barnhills
North Cairn
South Cairn
Kirkcolm
The Wig
Cairnryan
Cairn Point
New Luce
DUMFRIES & GALLOWAY
Southern Upland Way
Wild Goat Park
Murray's Monument
Wood of Cree Nature Reserve
The Queen's Way
Cairnsmore of Fleet

Loch Ryan

Knocknain
Lochnaw Castle
Leswalt
THE
B718
Stranraer
Castle
RHINS
Black Loch
White Loch
Castle Kennedy Gardens
Glenwhan Gardens
Glenluce Abbey
Glenluce Motor-Museum
2331
Newton Stewart
Minnigaff
Kirroughtree Visitor Centre
Palnure

Soulseat Loch
Meadowsweet Herb Garden
Dunragit
Glenluce
New Luce
Shennanton
Kirkcowan
Gem Rock Museum
Gold & Silversmithing Workshop
Creetown
Glenquicken Stone Circle

Black Head
Portpatrick
Dunskey Castle
'Little Wheels'
Stoneykirk
WEST FREUGH
Danger Area
Castle of Park
Luce Sands
Auchenmalg
Auchenmalg Bay
Torhouse Stone Circle
Old Place of Mochrum
Bladnoch Distillery
Wigtown
Bladnoch
Baldoon Castle
Baldoon Sands
Kirkinner
Cairnholy
Castle

Cairngarroch
Money Head
Sandhead
Lake Cottage
Kirkmadrine Church
Ardwell
Chapel Rossan Bay
Ardwell Gardens
Luce Bay
Chapel Finian
Alticry
THE MACHARS
Druchtag Motte
Sorbie
Garlieston
Eggerness Point
Galloway House Gardens

Ardwell Point
Logan Botanic Garden
Mull of Logan
Fish Pond
Port Nessock or Port Logan Bay
Terally Point
Terally
Port Logan
Information & Visitor Centre
Clanyard
Kirkmaiden
Drummore
Mochrum
Drumtroddan Marked Rocks & Standing Stones
Port William
Barsalloch Fort
Monreith
Monreith Bay Point of Lag
Point of Cairndoon
Rispain Camp
Whithorn
Priory & Museum
Cairn Head

Crammag Head
Maryport
Cairngaan
Cairngaan
Dykes
Mull of Galloway
Isle of Whithorn
St Ninian's Cave
St Ninian's Kirk
Fort
Burrow Head

0 Miles   2   4   6
0 Km   5   10

Arbigland ❀ Eb
Rhododendrons, azaleas and camellias in formal and water gardens with Torbay-like climate. John Paul Jones's Cottage was 1747 birthplace of United States' first naval commander.

Auchencairn Bay Db
Pebble beaches become acres of sand at low tide. Smugglers built 18th-century Balcary House in whitewashed Auchencairn village to store contraband. Footpath beyond bay through woods, farmland and rocky shore leads to spectacular cliffs.

Blowplain Open Farm ⚘ Bd
Guided tours show day-to-day life on stock-rearing hill farm set in rolling countryside.

Broughton House ⛪ Bb
Museum and art gallery in elegant Georgian mansion with sheltered gardens on River Dee. Library has 15,000 books and manuscripts.

Cairnholy ⊓ Ab
Façade of tall standing stones flanks entrance of larger of two Stone Age burial mounds 200yds apart dating from *c.* 3000 BC.

ANCIENT GRAVE *The two burial mounds at Cairnholy may be the graves of a single family.*

Cardoness Castle ⛪ Ab
This well-preserved 15th-century tower house still has original stairway and vaulted basement.

Castle Douglas 🏛☑ Cc
Bronze Age *crannogs* (artificial islands) among islets of Carlingwalk Loch on southern edge of 18th-century weaving and carpet-making centre. Main street has steeple-like clock tower.

Cauldside Burn ⊓ Ab
At head of Cauldside Burn are Bronze Age remains of two cairns, two stone circles and large carved stone block. Larger circle, 70ft across, has ten standing stones.

Dalbeattie ⚘ Dc
Forest walks start from outskirts of silvery-grey granite town in rolling countryside.

Drumlanrig Castle ⛪🐦 Df
Pink-sandstone stately home, 17th century, has art collection as well as personal possessions of Bonnie Prince Charlie. Wooded parkland overlooks upper Nithsdale and old stables now house visitor and craft centre.

Dumfries ⊕🏛🏛 Ed
Former seaport where Robert Burns lived before his death in 1796. House contains personal

NORTH OF THE SOLWAY FIRTH

Tranquillity abounds along the beautiful Nith and its neighbouring valleys, hemmed in by the gentle Galloway Hills and the Solway Firth. The Firth brings a soothing climate to an area where passions once raged – both the fierce passion of clan battles, and the romantic passion of ballad poets. Immortalised in stone are St John the Baptist's chair and the Twelve Apostles.

TREASURE HOUSE *Drumlanrig Castle's richly furnished public rooms contain one of the finest private art collections in Britain – including works by Rembrandt and Holbein – as well as some rare and valuable silverware.*

possessions. Robert Burns Centre recalls his years in Dumfries and his mausoleum is in St Michael's churchyard. Mid Steeple was built in 1707 as courthouse and prison. Bridge dating from 15th century is oldest of five across River Nith, and 18th-century windmill contains camera obscura and local history museum.

Dundrennan Abbey ⊕ Ca
Handsome and substantial Cistercian ruin, founded 1142, where Mary, Queen of Scots spent last night in Scotland, 1568. Murdered bishop and his assassin among many fine memorials.

Durisdeer ⊕ Dg
Dukes of Queensberry mausoleum in 17th-century Durisdeer Church. Monument to second duke (*d.* 1711) and his duchess (*d.* 1709) has them reclining beneath columns and flying cherubs.

Ellisland Farm ⚘🏛 Ee
Farmhouse, built by Robert Burns when he took farm over in 1788, contains museum room. The Granary houses display showing Burns as farmer. Riverside walk. Burns wrote *Tam o'Shanter* here.

Fleet Forest Trails ⚘🏕 Bb
Footpaths and marked walks through oak, ash, beech and sycamore woods.

Gatehouse of Fleet ♦⚘ Bb
Former cotton town is now walking and holiday centre on banks of Water of Fleet. Original gatehouse now houses whitewashed wine bar, and Bobbin Mill Visitor

Centre displays local history and recalls 18th-century prosperity as cotton town.

Kippford ⚓ Db
Village, once smugglers' haunt, now sailing resort, home of Solway Yacht Club. Houses are mixture of old fishermen's cottages and modern bungalows and villas. Low-tide walk from pebble beach to Rough Island bird sanctuary – home of waders, scaups, shelducks and mergansers. Jubilee Path has views to distant Galloway mountains.

Kirkbean ⚓ Eb
Unusual domed parish church of well-kept village has 1826 sundial telling times in such places as Madras, Calcutta and Gibraltar. Font presented by United States Navy in 1945 to honour its first naval commander John Paul Jones who was baptised here.

Kirkpatrick Durham ⚓ Cd
Orderly estate village little changed since it was built in 1785, with 50 houses and number of craft workshops.

Kirkcudbright ✝⛪ⴾ🏛 Bb
Town dominated by St Cuthbert's Church spire, Gothic tower of Tolbooth (1411) and jagged top of 16th-century MacLellan's Castle. Wooded Wildlife Park has eagle, snowy and barn owls.

Lincluden College ⊕ Ed
Red-sandstone remains of 12th-century convent. Fine heraldic decorations. Knot garden has been restored.

Mabie Forest ⚘🏕 Ed
Views of Nithsdale and the Solway Firth can be seen from marked trails that lead through hillside plantations of fir, spruce, oak and beech.

Maxwelton House ⛪ De
Restored 14th to 15th-century house was once home of Annie Laurie, immortalised in Scottish ballad of same name written by her unsuccessful suitor, William Douglas, and later revised. In courtyard is museum of kitchen, dairy and farm implements.

Mote of Mark ☀ Db
Excellently preserved Celtic hillfort of 5th or 6th century, one of most important archaeological sites on Solway Firth. Good views of Cumbrian Hills.

SEASIDE TOWN *Kirkcudbright has many attractions, including river trips and sea fishing.*

Mote of Urr ☀ Dc
Most extensive motte-and-bailey castle in Scotland, dating from 12th century, and built on Saxon or early Norman mound.

New Abbey ⊕⛪🏛 Ec
Grey-stone riverside village with beautiful ruin of 13th-century Sweetheart Abbey, where Lady Devorgilla and embalmed heart of husband John de Baliol are buried. Scottish Baronial mansion, Shambellie House, contains costume museum with women's fashions from 18th century to Edwardian times. Water-powered corn mill, dating from 18th century, is in working order.

New Galloway ⚘ Bd
Angling centre on River Ken has town hall with high clock tower and *jougs*, hinged iron collars in which malefactors were confined. Carved Adam and Eve stone stands in Kells churchyard.

Orchardton Tower ⛪ Db
Round tower house, unique in Scotland, built by John Cairns in the 15th century. Spiral staircase, hidden within double walls, leads to parapet walk.

Palnackie ⚓ Db
Village little changed since days as thriving inland port, with colourwashed houses around harbour, now silted up. Competitors use bare feet and spears to catch fish from mud flats in World Flounder Tramping Championships, off Glen Isle peninsula. Upper floors in two-storey houses were once lodgings for sailors.

Raiders' Road 🏕 Ad
Ten-mile forest drive beside Black Water of Dee, follows route taken by armed cattle thieves in S.R. Crockett's 1894 novel *The Raiders*. Riverside and lochside picnic areas, walks and bronze otter statue. Open June-September, 20mph speed limit.

Thornhill ⚓ Df
Village among attractive shallow hills has two boulevards lined with 100-year-old lime trees planted by 6th Duke of Buccleuch. Tall column erected 1714 supports winged horse, emblem of Dukes of Queensberry.

Threave Garden and Wildfowl Refuge 🏛❀⚘ Cc
Estate surrounding Scottish Baronial Threave House has woodland walks and various gardens including display in spring of 200 daffodil varieties. Observation points overlook refuge along banks of River Dee with wild swans, ducks and geese. On island to north-west is ruined Threave Castle, 14th-century stronghold of feared Black Douglases.

Tongland ⚓♦ Bb
Battlemented and turreted bridge over River Dee, designed by Thomas Telford in 1800s. Guided tours of hydroelectric power station and dam.

Twelve Apostles' Stone Circle ⊓ Ed
Dated 2000 BC, largest diameter stone circle in Scotland. Only 11 stones remain – twelfth removed by locals for building.

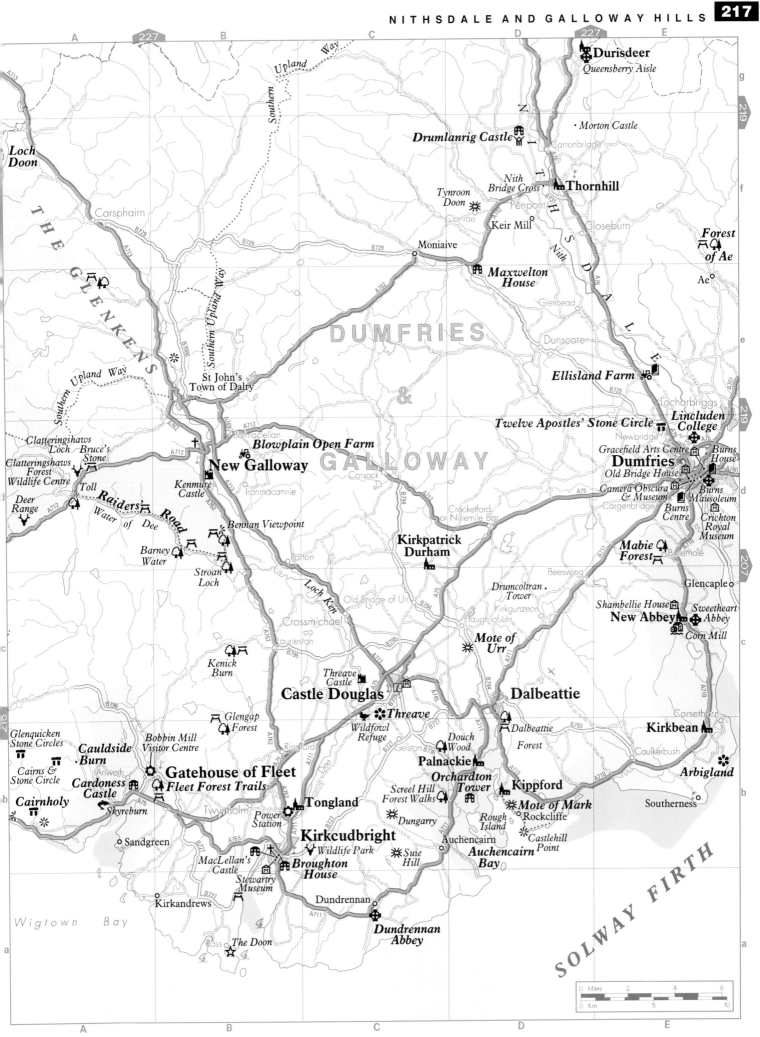

Durisdeer
Queensberry Aisle

Morton Castle

Drumlanrig Castle

Tynroon
Doon

Nith
Bridge Cross

Thornhill

Keir Mill

Closeburn

Forest
of Ae

Moniaive

Ae

Maxwelton
House

Glenhead

Dunscore

Ellisland Farm

Locharbriggs

Twelve Apostles' Stone Circle

Lincluden
College

Newbridge

Gracefield Arts Centre

Burns
House

Dumfries

Blowplain Open Farm

Old Bridge House

Carsack

Camera Obscura
& Museum

Burns
Mausoleum

New Galloway

Cargenbridge

Crichton Royal
Museum

Kenmure
Castle

Ironmacannie

Crocketford
or Ninemile Bar

Burns
Centre

Mabie
Forest

Bennan Viewpoint

Batton

Kirkpatrick
Durham

Drumcoltran
Tower

Buttethole

Barney
Water

Stroan
Loch

Glencaple

Drumgunzeon

Beeswing

Shambellie House

New Abbey

Sweetheart
Abbey

Corn Mill

Kenick
Burn

Loch Ken

Old Bridge of Urr

Haugh of Urr

Mote of
Urr

Crossmichael

Glengap
Forest

Laurieston

Threave
Castle

Castle Douglas

Dalbeattie

Kirkbean

Glenquicken
Stone Circles

Bobbin Mill
Visitor Centre

Ringford

Threave

Wildfowl
Refuge

Douch
Wood

Dalbeattie
Forest

Cauldside
Burn

Anwoth

Gatehouse of Fleet

Fleet Forest Trails

Gelston

Palnackie

Orchardton
Tower

Kippford

Arbigland

Cairns &
Stone Circle

Cardoness
Castle

Skyreburn

Twynholm

Power
Station

Tongland

Screel Hill
Forest Walks

Rough
Island

Mote of Mark

Rockcliffe

Castlehill
Point

Southerness

Cairnholy

Sandgreen

Kirkcudbright

Wildlife Park

Dungarry

Auchencairn

Auchencairn
Bay

MacLellan's
Castle

Broughton
House

Suie
Hill

Kirkandrews

Stewartry
Museum

Dundrennan

The Doon

Dundrennan
Abbey

Wigtown Bay

SOLWAY FIRTH

THE GLENKENS

Loch
Doon

Carsphairn

Clatteringshaws
Loch

Bruce's
Stone

Clatteringshaws
Forest
Wildlife Centre

Deer
Range

Toll

Raiders' Road

Water of Dee

St John's
Town of Dalry

DUMFRIES

&

GALLOWAY

Southern Upland Way

0 Miles 2 4 6

0 Km 5 10

Annan Da
Victorian red-brick houses overlook banks of River Annan, where anglers try for salmon and trout. Dismantled railway, now overgrown, once led to bridge across Solway Firth. Locally born historian, Thomas Carlyle, taught at Annan academy in 19th century.

Barr's Hill ✳ Bc
Network of ditches and huge bank remain from Iron Age hill-fort, built on narrow ridge between Annandale and Nithsdale.

Beattock Hill ✳ Be
Narrow road leads to top of Beattock Hill. Iron Age fort lies near summit, with extensive views over Annandale. In days of steam, trains laboured to climb dramatic 10 mile incline of Beattock Bank.

Bruce's Cave ✩ Db
Steep footpath leads to cave above Kirtle Water where, according to legend, Robert Bruce hid from the English invaders in 1306 and, inspired by a spider trying again and again to spin its web, carried on his struggle for independence.

Burnswark ✳🔥 Cb
Iron Age defences extend 17 acres on windswept hilltop, looking out to Solway Firth and Cumbrian coast. Remains of two Roman siege camps on opposite hillside date from AD 155, and small Roman fort dates from AD 140.

RUINED GLORY *Renaissance carvings survive at Caerlaverock.*

Caerlaverock Castle 🏰 Ba
Triangular fortress on shore of Solway Firth has mysterious origins. Built during 1290s, but whether by English or Scots is unknown. Largely destroyed 1320, rebuilt a few years later and demolished again by Scots in 1357. Pink-sandstone gatehouse survives from castle rebuilt 15th century, reduced to ruins in 1640. Finely carved panels remain from mansion added to building in 1630s by Robert Maxwell, 1st Earl of Nithsdale.

Caerlaverock Nature Reserve 🦆 Ba
Barnacle geese from Spitzbergen and large flocks of pink-footed and greylag geese make this 13,000 acre area of salt marsh and foreshore a notable bird sanctuary. Wild ducks and waders haunt creeks and reed banks. Hides and observation towers.

Comlongon Castle 🏛 Ba
Well-preserved Great Hall, dungeons and fine bedrooms create medieval atmosphere in 15th-century castle on Scottish border. Picnic area and nature trail in surrounding woodland.

SCOTLAND'S SOUTHERN UPLANDS

Remote lochs glitter amongst the gentle hills of Annandale and Eskdale, south of which lie the flat Solway marshes, where sea birds gather on a huge nature reserve. The turbulent history of the borderlands haunts this stretch of countryside. Fortresses and castles stand in ruins after endless raids, and the memory of Robert Bruce – hero king of Scotland – lingers on in the places he visited.

Craigcleuch 🏛 Ec
Scottish Baronial mansion, 19th-century, houses Craigcleuch collection of curiosities found by early Scottish explorers, including carved coral and ivory, African sculptures, Chinese jade animals, prehistoric ornaments and implements. Set in parkland overlooking Esk valley, with views north between 'Gates of Eden' hills.

Devil's Beef Tub ✩✳ Bf
River Annan flows down this 500ft deep hollow among four barren hills which look, according to Sir Walter Scott in his novel *Redgauntlet*, 'as if they were laying their heads together to shut out the daylight from the dark hollow space between them'.

Dryhope Tower 🏰 Dg
Ruins of stout 16th-century tower stand by northern shores of St Mary's loch. Once home of Mary Scott, ancestor of Sir Walter Scott.

Ecclefechan 🏛 Cb
Historian Thomas Carlyle born 1795 in 'Arched House' built by his father and uncle, master masons. Restored as in his day, containing papers and personal belongings.

Ewes ✝ Ed
Hamlet lying at foot of Eskdale hills. A 300-year-old bell hangs in churchyard tree; put there for safety when old church was demolished, stayed when new church was built 1867. Fine views of Ewes Water and Teviotdale.

Forest of Ae 🌲 Ad
Road and waymarked walks wind through woods and hills thick with grass or bracken, sometimes under trees bent over to meet one another. Picnic site beside stream fringed by spruce and alder.

Gretna Green 🏠🏛 Ea
Village close to the border with England where runaway couples could seek quick marriages under easygoing Scottish law at the old tollhouse or smithy, until the custom was banned in 1940. Old Blacksmith's Shop, where weddings were performed by an 'anvil priest', now a museum.

Grey Mare's Tail ✩ Cf
Path leads to foot of this spectacular 200ft waterfall formed by Tail Burn dropping from Loch Skene to join Moffat Water. Area rich in wild flowers has herd of wild goats.

Hoddom Castle 🏰 Cb
Sturdy 16th-century watchtower built by John Maxwell stands on hill above site of 16th-century tower castle. Visitor centre is start of riverside and woodland walks.

LOVERS' TRYST *Runaways headed for Gretna to find wedded bliss.*

Langholm 🏛🏠 Ec
Thriving mills surround this textile centre where River Esk meets Wanchope Water and Ewes Water; spanned by several bridges. Narrow, twisting streets of old part contrast with 18th-century houses of 'new' town across river. Ruined peel tower was home to the Armstrong family, ancestors of astronaut Neil Armstrong – first man on the moon.

Lochmaben 🏰🦆 Bc
Nature reserve surrounds the creeper-clad ruins of a 14th-century castle, reputed birthplace of Robert Bruce. Both James IV and Mary, Queen of Scots visited castle. Look for greylag and pink footed geese in Castle and High tae lochs. Statue near the town hall recalls local man William Paterson, co-founder of Bank of England in 1694.

Megget ✳🏡 Cg
Picturesque valley transformed in 1983 by reservoir, stocked with trout. Picnic areas with good viewpoints. Visitors can walk along top of dam.

Moffat 🏛☸ Be
Sheep-farming centre, symbolised by ram statue in high street. Spring discovered 1633 made it popular spa. Robert Burns among those who came to take waters. Baths Hall of 1827 now town hall. Local crafts thrive at woollen mill.

Powfoot 🏠 Ca
Resort created late 1700s at mouth of Pow Water. Sand yachting on beach. Golf course. Kinmount gardens with lakeside walks and resident geese.

Rammerscales 🏛 Bb
Manor with Palladian frontage built 1760 for Dr James Mounsey, physician to Tsarina Elizabeth of Russia. Annandale views, picnic site, woodland walks and garden.

Ruthwell 🏠🏛 Ca
Church has late 7th-century cross, 18ft high, carved with figures and runic verses from Anglo-Saxon poem *The Dream of the Rood*; possibly written by Caedmon, a 7th-century monk and poet from Whitby in Yorkshire. Small museum commemorates Henry Duncan in cottage where he founded Scottish Savings Bank. Displays include bank archives and room settings of late 18th and early 19th centuries.

St Mary's Loch 🏡 Dg
Sailing and angling centre. Statue of local poet James Hogg (1770-1835) stands above Tibbie Shiels Inn. Single-track road to beauty spot of Talla Reservoir.

St Mungo's Church ✠ Cb
Shell of church lies above River Annan. Mungo was 6th-century 'Apostle of Strathclyde' who became Glasgow's patron saint.

Telford Memorial Ec
Recalls engineer Thomas Telford, born 1757. As apprentice, worked on bridge at nearby Langholm.

Teviothead 🏠 Fe
Hamlet with a churchyard memorial marking mass grave of border outlaw Johnnie Armstrong and 36 of his men, sent to gallows without trial by James V, 1530.

Torthorwald Castle 🏰 Bb
This 15th-century fortress of the Kirkpatricks and later Carlyles is an unsafe ruin. View it from road.

Tweedsmuir 🏠 Bg
Good walking country where Talla Water meets Tweed. Church built in 1874 has war memorial from oak tree planted 100 years earlier by writer Sir Walter Scott. Covenanter's stone of 1685 lies in the churchyard.

GOLDEN HILLS *The Lowthers were known as 'God's Treasure House in Scotland' due to their rich mineral wealth.*

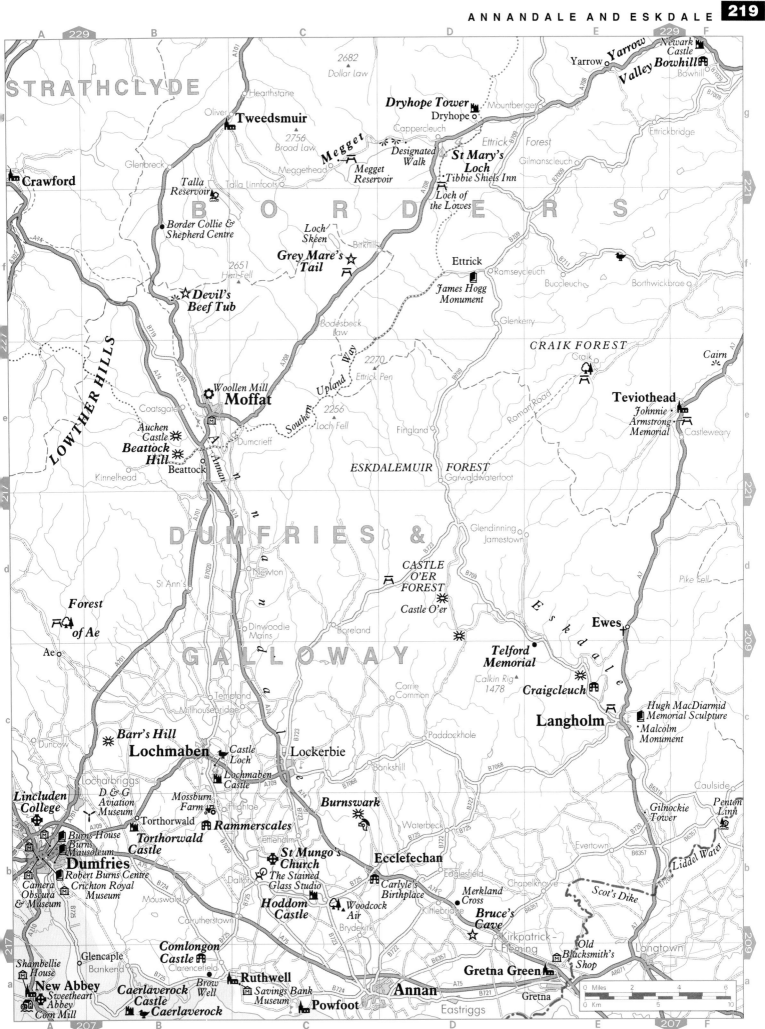

STRATHCLYDE

229

2682
Dollar Law

Hearthstane

Oliver

Tweedsmuir

Yarrow **Yarrow**
Valley *Newark Castle*
Bowhill
Bowhill

229

221

Glenbreck

Dryhope Tower
Mountbenger
Dryhope

Cappercleuch

Ettrickbridge

Crawford

2756
Broad Law

Megget
Meggethead

Designated Walk

St Mary's Loch
Tibbie Shiels Inn

Ettrick *Forest*

Gilmanscleuch

Talla Reservoir

Megget Reservoir

Loch of the Lowes

B709

Talla Linnfoots

B O R D E R S

221

Border Collie & Shepherd Centre

Loch Skéen

Birkhill

Ettrick

Ramseycleuch

Buccleuch

Borthwickbrae

2651
Hart Fell

Grey Mare's Tail

James Hogg Monument

Glenkerry

Devil's Beef Tub

Bodesbeck Law

CRAIK FOREST

Craik

Cairn

221

2270
Ettrick Pen

Roman Road

Teviothead
Johnnie Armstrong Memorial
Castleweary

LOWTHER HILLS

Woollen Mill
Moffat

Southern Upland Way

2256
Loch Fell

Fingland

Coatsgate

Dumcrieff

ESKDALEMUIR FOREST
Garwaldwaterfoot

Auchen Castle

A n n a n

Beattock Hill
Beattock

Kinnelhead

D U M F R I E S &

Glendinning
Jamestown

209

St Ann's

Newton

Ewes

Pike Fell

Forest of Ae

CASTLE O'ER FOREST

Castle O'er

Eskdale

Ae

Dinwoodie Mains

Boreland

Telford Memorial

G A L L O W A Y

Corrie Common

Calkin Rig
1478

Craigcleuch

Templand

Millhousebridge

Hugh MacDiarmid Memorial Sculpture

209

Barr's Hill

Lochmaben
Castle Loch
Lockerbie

Paddockhole

Langholm

Malcolm Monument

Duncow

Locharbriggs

Lochmaben Castle

Bankshill

Caulside

D & G Aviation Museum

Mossburn Farm
Hightae

Torthorwald

B7068

Gilnockie Tower

Penton Linn

Lincluden College

Burns House
Burns Mausoleum

Torthorwald Castle

Rammerscales

Burnswark

Waterbeck

Everton

Dumfries

Robert Burns Centre
Crichton Royal Museum

Dalton

St Mungo's Church

Eaglesfield

Chapelknowe

Scot's Dike

Liddel Water

Camera Obscura & Museum

Mouswald

The Stained Glass Studio

Ecclefechan

Hoddom Castle

Carlyle's Birthplace

Kettleholm

Woodcock Air

Brydekirk

Merkland Cross
Kittlebridge

Old Blacksmith's Shop

Longtown

Carrutherstown

Bruce's Cave

Kirkpatrick-Fleming

Comlongon Castle

Clarencefield

Shambellie House

Glencaple
Bankend

Ruthwell
Brow Well

Gretna Green

Gretna

New Abbey
Sweetheart Abbey
Corn Mill

Caerlaverock Castle
Caerlaverock

Savings Bank Museum

Powfoot

Annan

Eastriggs

Miles 0 2 4 6
Km 0 10

207

207

209

Abbotsford ⌂ Be
Sir Walter Scott's home set above the Tweed. Originally a farmhouse, Scott largely rebuilt it in 1822. Inside are 9000-book library, armour collection, historical relics and paintings.

Addinston and Longcroft Hill-Forts ✷ Bg
Two Iron Age hill-forts built less than a mile apart. They were constructed about 27 centuries ago to protect their makers' settlements.

Ancrum ⌂✕ Cd
Village of stone and stucco houses with 16th-century cross on its green. Border wars victims were said to have sheltered in Ale Water caves nearby. Battle of 1545 on Ancrum Moor between Scots and English still remembered.

Bonchester Bridge ⌂ Bc
Little bridge over Rule Water has single inn set beside it. Bonchester Hill, with traces of ancient hill-fort, overlooks bridge.

Bowhill ⌂ Ad
Georgian mansion frequented by Queen Victoria. Inside are paintings by Canaletto, Gainsborough and Reynolds. Trails explore estate's wooded hills and lochs.

Carter Bar ✷ Cb
Upright boulder marks border between Scotland and England. 1370ft Carter Bar has views of Rubers Law and the Cheviots.

Chew Green ❧ Db
Three Roman earthwork camps and small permanent fortlet; earliest camp dates from AD 80 when Agricola, Governor of Britain, was subjugating fierce local tribes.

Coldstream ⌂✿Ⓐ Ee
Scots killed in 1513 Battle of Flodden Field buried nearby. Coldstream Guards, though not raised here, took their name in memory of marching through here to defeat Richard Cromwell and place Charles II on the throne.

Denholm ⌂ Bc
Village with large green set above salmon-rich River Teviot. Victorian monument honours local scholar John Leyden, plaque honours Sir James Murray, *Oxford Dictionary* editor.

Dryburgh Abbey ✚ Be
Twelfth-century abbey ruin, sacked by English invaders in 14th and 16th centuries. Remains include delicate rose window in west wall. Sir Walter Scott, Field-Marshal Earl Haig are buried here.

Earlston Be
Birthplace of Thomas the Rhymer, 13th-century seer and poet. Wall fragment of his tower remains, hidden behind a café.

Eildon Hills ✷✷ Be
Hills, rich in legend, rise 1385ft over Tweed valley, suitable for climbing. Northernmost summit of three hills held largest Iron Age fort in Scotland, site of a Roman signal station later.

Ferniehirst Castle ⌂▱ Cc
Ancient seat of Kerr family. Story of 16th-century frontier fortress, and history of border region,

---

RIVER VALLEYS ON THE BORDER

The region's gentle, wooded landscape rising to rounded hills is at odds with its violent history – this border country saw numerous clashes between Scots and English, as its ruined castles and abbeys testify. And each year towns like Hawick remember the stormy past with the Common Ridings. Sir Walter Scott made the area famous, drawing his inspiration from the countryside and its people.

are told at information centre, housed in adapted 17th-century stable block.

Floors Castle ⌂ De
Georgian structure with 19th-century turrets and domes. Collections of paintings, porcelain, tapestries and furniture. Walled garden with herbaceous borders and rosebeds.

Galashiels ⌂▱Ⓐ Ae
Tweed and woollen industry centre has produced wool since medieval times. Peter Anderson Museum, Borders Wool Centre tell story of tweeds and tartans. Braw Lads' Gathering re-creates town's past every June.

Greenknowe Tower ⌂ Cf
Sixteenth-century roofless tower built 1581 by James Seton. Clockwise staircase gave retreating defenders advantage of an unhindered sword arm while attacker's would be hindered.

Hawick ✿Ⓐ Bc
Border town famous for knitwear and rugby, largely destroyed by English in 1570. Museum tells knitwear history. Festival of Common Riding every summer recalls past, when townsfolk rode around town ensuring other towns had not encroached on their common land.

Hermitage Castle ⌂ Aa
Fourteenth-century castle on Hermitage Water. Violent history recalls stories of death by boiling, drowning and starvation. Mary, Queen of Scots rode here in 1566 to visit her lover Bothwell, who lay wounded.

The Hirsel ✿ Ef
Country residence of Lord Home, former Prime Minister. Grounds are open to public, stable yard now houses folk museum and craft centre. Picnic site and paths through grounds.

FRENCH INFLUENCE *Kelso Abbey was founded in the 12th century by monks from Chartres.*

Jedburgh ✚⌂Ⓐ Cd
Mary, Queen of Scots stayed here – her house now an information centre. Jedburgh Abbey, founded 1138, with tower and roofless nave. Castle jail converted to museum of Victorian prison life.

Kelso ✚⌂Ⓐ De
Town at confluence of Tweed and Teviot rivers with wide square, elegant houses and five-arched bridge. Kelso Abbey, now in ruins, was founded in 1128 by monks from Chartres, in France.

Kirk Yetholm and Town Yetholm ⌂ Ed
Twin villages in foothills of Cheviots. Town Yetholm is larger, Kirk Yetholm, where gypsy queens were crowned until 19th century, is older. Gypsy Palace, a tiny cottage, still stands.

Lauder ⌂ Bf
Tolbooth and several large inns indicate town's importance in coaching days. Thirlestane Castle, a turreted sandstone mansion, has family portraits by Gainsborough and others. Border Country Life Museum nearby.

Legerwood ⌂ Bf
Church retains much original 12th-century interior. Its Norman arch of red stone is one of Scotland's finest.

Mellerstain ⌂ Ce
Georgian house built by William Adam and his son, Robert. Interior features exquisite ceilings. Italian-style terraced gardens give wide views of the Cheviots.

Melrose ✚⌂✿✿ Be
Town clustered around 12th-century abbey, founded in 1136 for Cistercian monks. Melrose Motor Museum illustrates vintage motoring, railway station is now heritage centre.

Mertoun Gardens ✿ Ce
Walled garden and ancient circular dovecote are featured. Twenty acres of trees, flowering shrubs, herbs and views of nearby river.

Priorwood Garden ✿ Be
Garden specialises in flowers suitable for drying. Unusual strains of

apples are grown, some known since Roman times. Picnic areas and orchard walks.

Roxburgh ⌂ De
Remains of Roxburgh Castle stand above confluence of Teviot and Tweed rivers. Present village, 3 miles south of original site, has views of Kelso.

Rubers Law ✷ Bc
Hill, nearly 1400ft high, is topped by remains of Iron Age fort. Excellent fort site – no attacking party could approach without being detected by defenders.

Scott's View ✷ Be
Sir Walter Scott's favourite prospect allows views of River Tweed curving through woods below peaks of Eildon Hills.

Selkirk ⌂ Ad
Sir Walter Scott sat as sheriff in town courthouse from 1800-32. Halliwell House is now a museum illustrating Selkirk history. The Clapperton Daylight Photographic Studio has photographs which date from the 1860s.

ROUGH FOOTING *An unusual flight of stone steps climbs the wall in Legerwood churchyard.*

Smailholm Tower ⌂ Ce
Five-storey watchtower with 7ft thick walls sits on isolated crag. Surprisingly, it now houses museum of dolls and tapestries rather than more warlike items.

Waterloo Monument Cd
Monument honouring Duke of Wellington is prominent landmark on top of Peniel Heugh Hill. Built in 1815 by Marquis of Lothian and his tenants.

Wilton Lodge Park ✿Ⓐ Ac
Langland family's ancestral home, now containing museum of border history. Wilton Park covers 107 acres and has riverside walks, garden, greenhouses, and scented garden.

Woden Law ✷ Dc
Hilltop of 1388ft once had Roman legions stationed on it; Iron Age people lived there before that. Good walking in the surrounding Cheviot hills.

Woodland Visitor Centre ▱ Cd
Home farm of large country estate 3 miles north of Jedburgh now houses interpretation centre explaining woodland and timber use. Woodland walks, with fine views of Waterloo Monument, accessible by wheelchair.

VICTORIAN GRANDEUR *Floors Castle, built in the 18th century, had many additions made in the 19th century.*

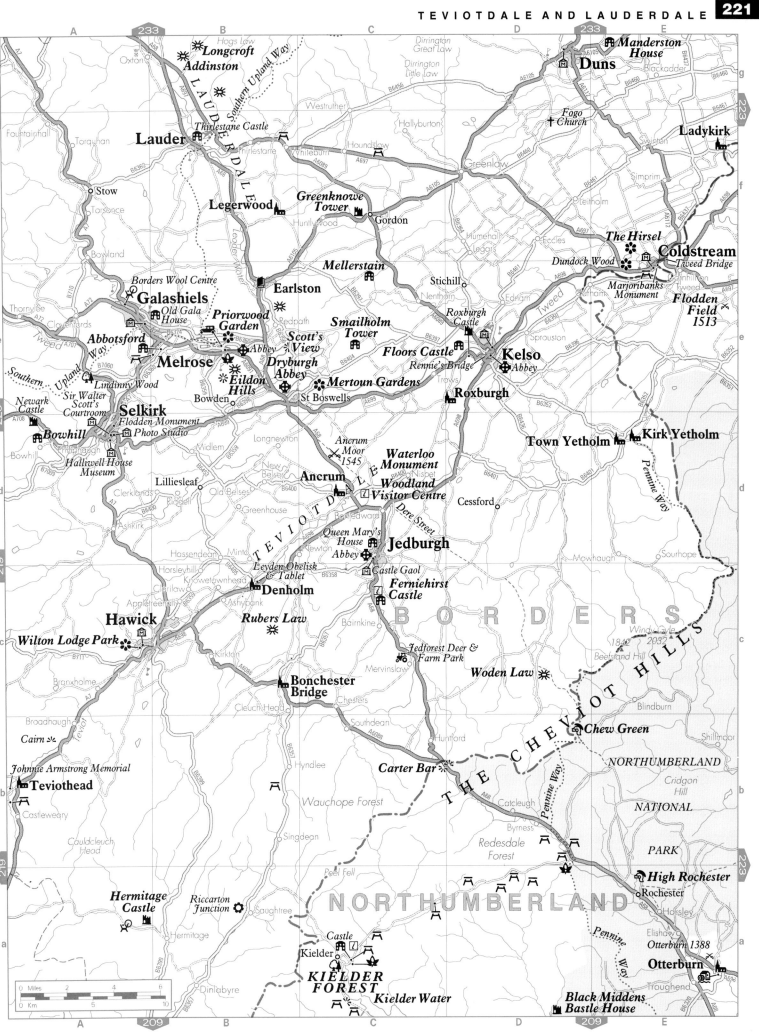

TEVIOTDALE AND LAUDERDALE

Longcroft
Addinston
Hogs Law

Manderston House

Duns

Ladykirk

Oxton
233

LAUDERDALE

Southern Upland Way

Dirrington Great Law
Dirrington Little Law

A6105

Fogo Church

Fountainhall

Torquhan

Westruther

Hallyburton

Houndslow

Greenlaw

Leitholm

Simprim

Lauder
Thirlestane Castle
Thirlestane

Whitburn

A6089

A697

B6460

B6461

The Hirsel
Dundock Wood

Coldstream
Tweed Bridge

Stow

Torsonce

Legerwood
Greenknowe Tower
Gordon

Humehall
Legars
Eccles

Marjoribanks Monument

Flodden Field 1513

Bowland

Borders Wool Centre

Mellerstain

Stichill

Ednam

Sprouston

Galashiels
Old Gala House

Earlston
Redpath

Smailholm Tower

Nenthorn

Roxburgh Castle

Kelso
Abbey

Thornylee

Clovenfords

Priorwood Garden
Abbey

Scott's View

Floors Castle
Rennie's Bridge

Abbotsford
Way

Melrose

Dryburgh Abbey

Trows

Roxburgh

Lindinny Wood
Eildon Hills

Bowden

Mertoun Gardens
St Boswells

Newark Castle

Sir Walter Scott's Courtroom

Selkirk
Flodden Monument
Photo Studio

Longnewton

Ancrum Moor 1545

Waterloo Monument

Town Yetholm

Kirk Yetholm

Pennine Way

Bowhill

Bowhill

Halliwell House Museum

Midlem

New Belses

Ancrum
Woodland Visitor Centre

Nisbet

Cessford

Lilliesleaf

Old Belses

Bonjedward

Greenhouse

Clerklands

Piasell

B6400

TEVIOTDALE

Dere Street

Ashkirk

Hassendean
Minto

Newton

Queen Mary's House
Abbey

Jedburgh

Mowhaugh

Sourhope

Horsleyhill

Leyden Obelisk & Tablet

Castle Gaol

Clarilaw

Knowetownhead

Denholm

Ferniehirst Castle

B O R D E R S

Windy Gyle

Appletreehall

Ashybank

Rubers Law

Bairnkine

1842 2032

Beefstand Hill

Hawick

Wilton Lodge Park

Kirkton

Jedforest Deer & Farm Park

Mervinslaw

Woden Law

THE CHEVIOT HILLS

Branxholme

Bonchester Bridge

Chesters

Cleuch Head

Blindburn

Broadhaugh

Cairn

Cleuch Head

Southdean

Huntford

Chew Green

NORTHUMBERLAND

Cridgon Hill

Johnnie Armstrong Memorial
Teviothead

Hyndlee

Carter Bar

Pennine Way

Catcleugh

NATIONAL

Castleweary

Wauchope Forest

A68

Byrness

PARK

Cauldcleuch Head

Singdean

Redesdale Forest

High Rochester
Rochester

209

Peel Fell

Pennine Way

Otterburn 1388

Hermitage Castle

Riccarton Junction

Saughtree

Castle
Kielder

Otterburn

A696

Hermitage

KIELDER FOREST

Kielder Water

Black Middens Bastle House

Dinlabyre

Troughend

0 Miles 2 4 6
0 Km 5 10

Alnwick Dc
Sedate border town on River Aln, once vital defence against Scots. Formidable 11th-century castle acquired Renaissance-style interior when restored by Percy family in 19th century. Abbot's Tower houses Royal Northumberland Fusiliers Museum. Grateful tenant farmers raised 83ft Percy Tenantry Column on south side of town in 1816 when rents were reduced.

Amble Eb
Former coal harbour, now fishing port of stone cottages and bow-fronted shops. Sandy beaches and dunes form Area of Outstanding Natural Beauty.

Ancroft Bf
Stubby 14th-century tower of St Anne's Church, built as fortress with tunnel-vaulted refuge, is one of area's finest peel towers.

Bamburgh De
Pretty 18th-century cottages, dwarfed by multi-turreted 12th-century castle with huge curtain wall and keep perched on 150ft coastal crag. Battlements provide views to Cheviot Hills in west and to Farne Islands in east. Museum devoted to lighthouse keeper's daughter, Grace Darling, who rowed out with father to rescue shipwreck survivors in 1838.

HEROINE AT REST *The tomb of courageous Grace Darling lies in Bamburgh churchyard.*

Beadnell Ed
Distinctive, fortress-like round towers overlooking tiny harbour are 18th-century limekilns. Two-mile sandy shoreline.

Brinkburn Priory Da
Augustinian priory built 1135 on River Coquet, now ruined except for the church, carefully restored in the 19th century.

Chillingham Cd
Scattering of cottages, flanked by 300 acre park of castle, built in 14th century, noted for its 50-strong herd of unique fierce white cattle descended from prehistoric wild oxen that roamed Britain's forests.

Cocklawburn Beach Cf
Bay of rocks and sandy beaches with nature reserve in dunes.

Coquet Island Eb
Flat-topped, rocky sea bird sanctuary. Lighthouse and monastery ruins. Most southerly breeding ground of eider duck; RSPB boat from Amble runs summer bird-watching trips round island, but landing not allowed.

These empty borderlands are wonderfully varied, with high moors, bare hills, rugged cliffs and swathes of sandy beaches. Offshore islands were for centuries fastnesses of the early Christian faith. Sturdy fortresses and peel towers attest to centuries of struggle between English and Scots, but the region's violent past and savage feuds are remembered in legend only.

FEUDAL MAJESTY *The mighty ruins of Dunstanburgh Castle look out over the sea from a 100ft cliff.*

Craster Ec
Unspoilt fishing village built of local dark whinstone. Noted for oak-smoked kippers. Herrings now bought, not caught locally. Footpath along rocky shore to Dunstanburgh castle.

Doddington Ce
Grouped round ruins of 1584 peel tower. Church has 1826 watch house to guard against body snatchers. Steep scramble up Dod Law scarp to Iron Age hill-fort and views of Cheviots.

Dunstanburgh Castle Ed
Ruins of 14th-century castle set on 100ft cliff and accessible only on foot. Massive keep and long line of towers along wall.

Edlingham Db
Remote moorland village with three substantial monuments. Five-arched bridge of former Alnwick-Coldstream railway line across Edlingham burn stands beside 13th-century castle. Close by is 12th-century barrel-vaulted church with square peel tower and slit windows.

Elsdon Ba
Village scattered round 7 acre green with peel tower and earthworks of Norman castle. Three horse skulls, found in belfry of 14th-century church in 1877, said to protect it from lightning.

Embleton Ed
Bay offers sand and solitude to walkers, and sport for golfers on links. Peel tower incorporated into vicarage next to church.

Etal Be
Single street of whitewashed houses, some thatched, leads to ruined gatehouse of 14th-century castle. Below, on River Till, is weir where salmon leap.

Farne Islands Ee
Two dozen treeless islands, half of them submerged at high tide, form sanctuary where seals breed and sea birds nest. In 676 St Cuthbert built cell on 16 acre Inner Farne; tower of 1500 marks site. Nature walk starts from chapel nearby. Boats from Seahouses also go to Staple Island and Longstone, whose lighthouse was run by William Darling, father of sea-rescue heroine Grace.

TAKING IT EASY *Grey seals on Inner Farne bask on the shingle.*

Flodden Field Ae
Tall cross in field marks site of 1513 Battle of Flodden when English routed Scots. At least 10,000 died; many buried at St Paul's Church, Branxton, nearby.

Glanton Cc
Charming old buildings that formed Britain's first bird research station now house field study museum with history of ornithology, apparatus and literature. View by appointment.

Heatherslaw Be
Working mill and museum of milling machinery. Railway museum with photographs, relics and exhibits: narrow-gauge steam railway runs to Etal.

Hepburn Wood Cd
Conifers and beeches cover sandstone crags edging Hepburn Moor. Waymarked walks include steep one through heather to Ros Castle, Iron Age hill-fort with breathtaking all-round views.

High Rochester Aa
Village green was site of legionary fort overlooking Roman road. Rampart, part of tower and gateway visible. House, in hamlet of Rochester below, partly built of stones from fort. Rounded stones in gable were ammunition for Roman catapults.

Holy Island Df
Incoming tides cut off this ancient monastic site, now paradise for birdwatchers. Romantic castle perched on cone of rock was ruin until rebuilt 1903. Monastery founded 634 by St Aidan, destroyed by Vikings, replaced 1093 by priory and now roofless ruin. Illuminated 7th-century Lindisfarne Gospels now in British Museum; copies kept at St Mary's.

Holystone Bb
Pretty jumble of stone cottages. Footpath to Lady's Well, where St Paulinus in 7th century is said to have baptised 3000 Celtic converts in one day. Holystone Forest, part of Northumberland National Park, lies nearby in wooded valley with waymarked walks past streams and waterfalls.

Howick Hall Ec
Trees in Howick Hall gardens, a mile inland from Howick hamlet, shelter colourful banks of plants

and shrubs. Path runs through wooded valley to shore and Rumbling Kern gully.

Kirknewton Be
Rebuilt Church of St Gregory is of primitive design: walls are so low that transept and chancel appear to be only a vault. Crude carving of Adoration of the Magi. Huge stone to north-east marks 1415 battlefield where 600 Northumbrians defeated 4000 Scots.

Ladykirk Af
Pale pink church with fine carvings and three-storey tower built 1499 by James IV in gratitude for escape from drowning in Tweed.

Norham Bf
Towering over village on loop of Tweed is 90ft wall of ruined Norman keep. Station museum recalls Kelso branch line, county's oldest, with original signal box, booking office and porter's room.

Otterburn Aa
Tweed still made at water mill, open to public, near arched stone bridge over River Rede. Percy Cross to north-west marks 1388 battle of Otterburn where Scots under Earl of Douglas defeated English and captured Sir Henry Percy (Harry Hotspur). Douglas himself was killed.

Rothbury Cb
Elegant market town on steep bank of River Coquet. Mile east is Victorian Cragside House, built by industrialist Sir William (later Lord) Armstrong and probably first house to be lit by electricity. Grounds form country park with 6 mile scenic drive.

Seahouses Ee
Fishing harbour and resort from which boats offer trips to Farne Islands. To north, National Trust dunes and sandy beaches.

Simonside Hills Ca
Wild, heather-clad moorland, conifer-covered slopes and crags popular with rock climbers. Most of Coquet valley visible from 1444ft Tosson Hill.

Warkworth Eb
Horseshoe loop of Coquet enfolds village. At head of main street stands imposing shell of castle, birthplace of Henry Percy (Hotspur), friend and then foe of Henry IV. Cruciform keep, 12th-century Great Hall and gatehouse with vaulted entry. Medieval humpbacked bridge noted for fortified tower. Half mile upstream lies 14th-century hermitage with tiny vaulted chapel cut into cliff.

Wooler Bd
Houses mostly post-1862, when town was burned. Seven hotels and inns cater for hiking and fishing. Near market place is mound of Norman castle which guarded highway to south. Earle Hill Museum contains old domestic and farming equipment.

Yeavering Bell Bd
Iron Age hill-fort with stone wall and remains of 150 huts covers 14 acres on 1182ft summit. Below, by River Glen, stood Gefrin, 7th-century capital of Edwin, first Christian King of Northumbria.

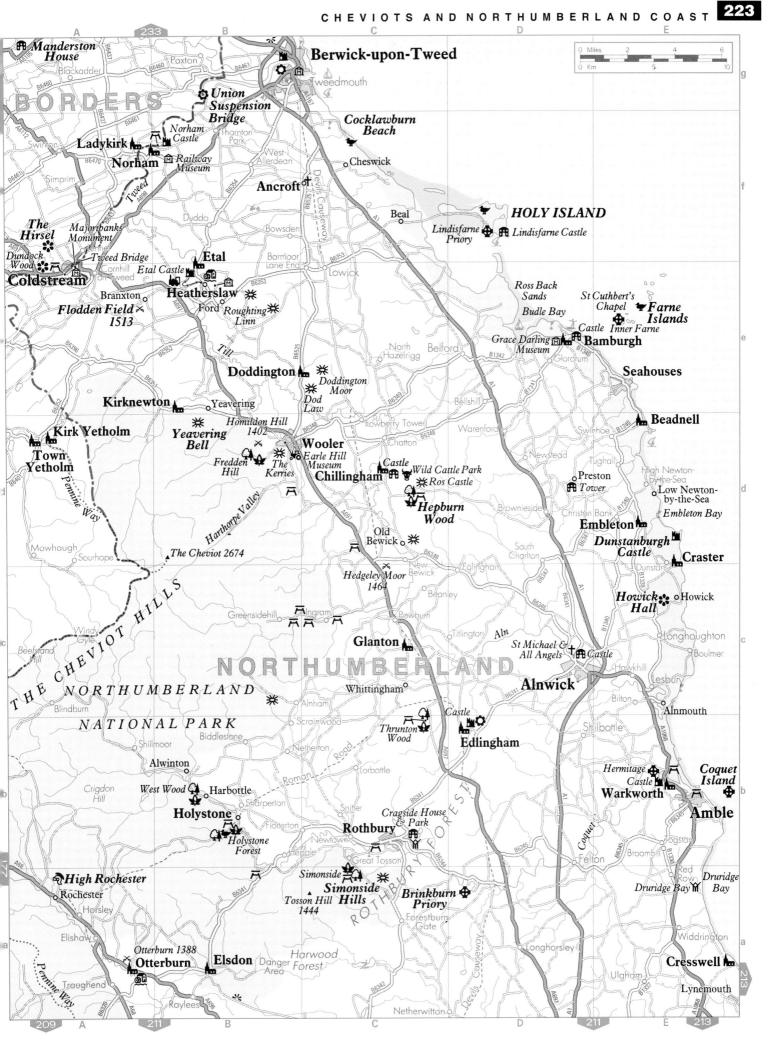

Manderston House
Blackadder
Paxton
Berwick-upon-Tweed
Tweedmouth

BORDERS

Union Suspension Bridge
Norham Castle
Cocklawburn Beach
Ladykirk
Norham
Railway Museum
Cheswick
Thornton Park
West Allerdean
Ancroft
Beal

HOLY ISLAND

Lindisfarne Priory
Lindisfarne Castle
Bowsden
Lowick

The Hirsel
Majoribanks Monument
Tweed Bridge
Dundock Wood
Coldstream
Etal
Etal Castle
Heatherslaw
Branxton
Ford
Roughting Linn
Flodden Field 1513

Barmoor Lane End

Ross Back Sands
Budle Bay
St Cuthbert's Chapel
Farne Islands
Inner Farne
Castle
Grace Darling Museum
Bamburgh

Doddington
Doddington Moor
Dod Law

Belford
Bellshill
Glororum
North Hazelrigg
Seahouses

Kirknewton
Yeavering
Homildon Hill 1402
Yeavering Bell
Fredden Hill
The Kerries

Rowberry Tower
Warenford
Chatton
Swinhoe
Tughall

Beadnell

Kirk Yetholm
Town Yetholm

Harthorpe Valley
Wooler
Earle Hill Museum
Chillingham
Castle
Wild Cattle Park
Ros Castle
Hepburn Wood

Brownieside
Christon Bank
High Newton-by-the-Sea
Preston Tower
Low Newton-by-the-Sea
Embleton Bay

The Cheviot 2674
Old Bewick
New Bewick
Hedgeley Moor 1464

South Charlton
Eglingham
Beanley

Embleton
Dunstanburgh Castle
Craster

Mowhaugh
Sourhope

Greensidehill
Ingram
Powburn
Titlington

Howick Hall
Howick

Windy Gyle
Beefstand Hill

THE CHEVIOT HILLS

NORTHUMBERLAND

Glanton
Whittingham
Alnham
Scrainwood

Aln
St Michael & All Angels
Castle
Alnwick
Howkhill
Lesbury
Longhoughton
Boulmer

Blindburn

NATIONAL PARK
Shillmoor
Biddlestone
Netherton
Lorbottle

Thrunton Wood
Castle
Edlingham

Bilton
Alnmouth

Alwinton
Crigdon Hill
West Wood
Harbottle
Sharperton
Snitter
Flotterton

Cragside House & Park
Rothbury
Newtown

Hermitage Castle
Coquet Island
Warkworth
Shilbottle

Holystone
Holystone Forest
Hepple
Great Tosson

Amble

High Rochester
Rochester
Horsley
Simonside
Simonside Hills
Tosson Hill 1444
Brinkburn Priory
Forestburn Gate

ROTHBURY FOREST
Felton
Broomhill
Red Row
Druridge Bay
Druridge Bay

Otterburn 1388
Otterburn
Elsdon
Harwood Forest
Danger Area

Longhorsley

Cresswell

Elishaw
Troughend
Raylees
Netherwitton
Ulgham
Widdrington
Lynemouth

Pennine Way

COUNTRYSIDE OF ROBERT BURNS

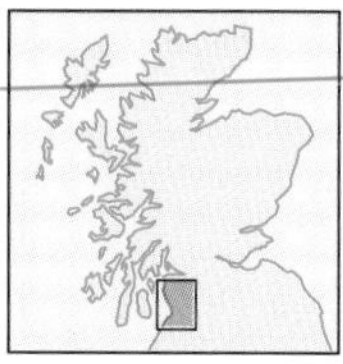

The Gulf Stream's warm currents bring the blessings of a mild climate to the Ayrshire coast, with its holiday resorts dotted among rocky coves and sandy beaches. Inland are lofty hills cut by rivers flowing through wooded valleys. Here, too, are ruined strongholds, reminders of old feuds, and the landscapes, towns and villages that inspired Scotland's national poet, Robert Burns.

Alloway Cb
Burns born in thatched cottage 1759. Some original furniture. Museum has manuscripts, letters. Close by are Auld Brig O' Doon and Alloway Kirk, mentioned in ballad *Tam o'Shanter*, and Burns Monument. The Land o'Burns Centre depicts his life and times.

POET'S BIRTHPLACE *The cottage in Alloway where Burns was born is joined to a Burns museum.*

Ardrossan Be
Town of stone houses planned by Earl of Eglinton in 1805 round sandy South Bay. Terminus for Man and Arran shipping services.

Ayr Cc
Main west coast resort with sandy beaches. Two bridges – 13th-century Auld Brig and New Bridge of 1788 – span River Ayr. Dominated by 1828 Town Buildings, with octagonal turret and 126ft steeple. Burns mementos in Tam o'Shanter Museum.

Bargany Gardens Ba
Azaleas and rhododendrons surround lily pond in woodland setting. Fine trees, rock garden and walled garden. Picnic area.

Craigie Castle Dd
Stonework of 13th-century former Lindsay seat features Gothic ceiling and barrel-vaulted cellar.

Crossraguel Abbey Ba
Ruins of 1244 Cluniac house. Turreted gatehouse, abbot's tower and dovecote are 15th century.

Crosshill Ca
Once prosperous handloom weaving centre beside Water of Girvan. Single-storey cottages line main street.

Culzean Castle Bb
Cliff-top mansion designed by Robert Adam in 18th century for 10th Earl of Cassillis. Lavishly furnished. Oval staircase and round drawing room overlooking Firth of Clyde. Park contains terraced gardens, woodland walks.

Cumbrae Islands Af
On Great Cumbrae, reached by ferry from Largs, is Millport resort with Cathedral of the Isles – Scotland's smallest. Museum and aquarium. Little Cumbrae has lighthouse and ruined castle.

Dalgarven Mill Ce
Water mill housing Ayrshire Museum of Countryside and Costume. Farm machinery, tools, photographs; local costumes.

Dalmellington Da
Former ironworks, now open-air museum. Rows of miners' cottages. Industrial railway centre with locomotives and rolling stock. Visitor centre in old weaver's cottage.

Dunure Bb
Tiny yachting harbour lined with fishermen's cottages. Overlooked by ruined castle where in 1570 4th Earl of Cassillis roasted abbot of Crossraguel alive to make him hand over abbey lands.

Eaglesham Ef
Built 1790s on A-shaped plan by 10th Earl of Eglinton. Streets of weavers' cottages enclose park called the Orry beside river.

Eglinton Country Park Ce
Large park round former Eglinton Montgomery estate. Natural history displays in visitor centre.

Failford Dc
Monument where Burns is said to have parted from Mary Campbell, his 'Highland Mary', after exchanging vows. She died the following autumn.

Fairlie Bf
Hunterston nuclear power station nearby has video displays. Iron ore complex. Boatyard where Sir Thomas Lipton built racing yachts in 1890s. Waterfalls, gardens, nature trails and adventure course at Kelburn Country Centre.

Galston Ed
Red-sandstone buildings include Barr Castle and tower. Church of St Sophia built 1886, in two-coloured brick imitating Haghia Sophia in Istanbul, Turkey.

ROMANTIC GLEN *A richly coloured maple makes a striking feature among rhododendrons and azaleas in tree-lined Bargany Gardens.*

Greenbank Garden Ef
Sixteen acres of walled garden, woodland and picnic area. Garden for disabled.

Heads of Ayr Bb
Cliffs topped with grazing land. Ruined 16th-century Greenan Castle. Inland, picnic areas on Brown Carrick Hill look out to Arran, Ailsa Craig, Kintyre and Firth of Clyde.

Irvine Cd
Miles of beaches. Water sports. Harbourside display of historic vessels. Museum on harbour traces shipbuilding history.

Kildoon Ba
Vitrified Iron Age fort on rocky ridge overlooking Girvan valley.

Kilmarnock Dd
Burns monument in Kay Park houses first edition of his poems. Dick Institute has collection of Scottish broadswords. Restored Dean Castle has arms and armour, musical instruments and country park. Guided tours of Johnnie Walker whisky-bottling plant.

Largs Bf
Yachting centre. Long esplanade and stony beach. Monument to 1263 defeat of Norse fleet. Hill walk to Douglas Park offers panorama over sea and mountains. Italian-baroque Skelmorlie Aisle erected 1636 as mausoleum for Sir Robert Montgomerie.

Lochwinnoch Cf
Colour-washed houses of early 19th century. Cask and barrel-making industry. Sailing and canoeing on loch in Castle Semple country park. Nature reserve.

Mauchline Dc
Museum in house where Burns and wife, Jean Armour, set up home has displays of granit curling stones made locally Poosie Nansie's tavern was th setting for *The Jolly Beggars*.

Maybole Ba
Restored 17th-century Maybol Castle was town house of Kennedy family. Earls of Cassilli buried in 14th-century church now in ruins.

Muirshiel Country Park Cg
Nature trails in broadleave woodland, also conifers an rhododendrons. Waterfall an moorland view from Windy Hill.

Portencross Ae
Hamlet on Farland Head with ruined 15th-century castle an vitrified Iron Age fort.

Prestwick Cc
Promenade runs round curve o Ayr Bay. First Open golf championship played here 1860. Mercat Cross is 13th century, ruined Church of St Nicholas 12th century. Robert Bruce said to have taken waters of Bruce's Well to relieve skin disease.

Rozelle House Cb
Georgian mansion in 96 acre park. Woodlands, sculptured gardens, nature trails, wildfowl pond. Local history displays.

SPORTSMAN'S STONE *Granite curling stones are hand-hewn at Mauchline by local craftsmen.*

Saltcoats Be
Seaside resort. Good fishing. Sea wall built 1686. Harbour contains fossilised trees seen at low tide. Museum in 18th-century church.

Sorn Ec
Village laid out 1770 on Ayr banks. Castle with 15th-century tower: 1650 church has outside staircase.

Tarbolton Dc
Former weaving and mining village. Burns founded Bachelors' Club debating society, now museum with relics of poet.

Troon Cd
Turreted red-sandstone Victorian buildings look across Ayr Bay. Five golf courses. Sandy beach, marina and harbour.

Turnberry Ba
Silver sands backed by dunes run for 1½ miles. Two golf courses. Robert Bruce said to have been born at Turnberry Castle.

WIDE VISTAS *Looking north-west up the dramatic sweep of Calder Glen from Muirshiel Country Park.*

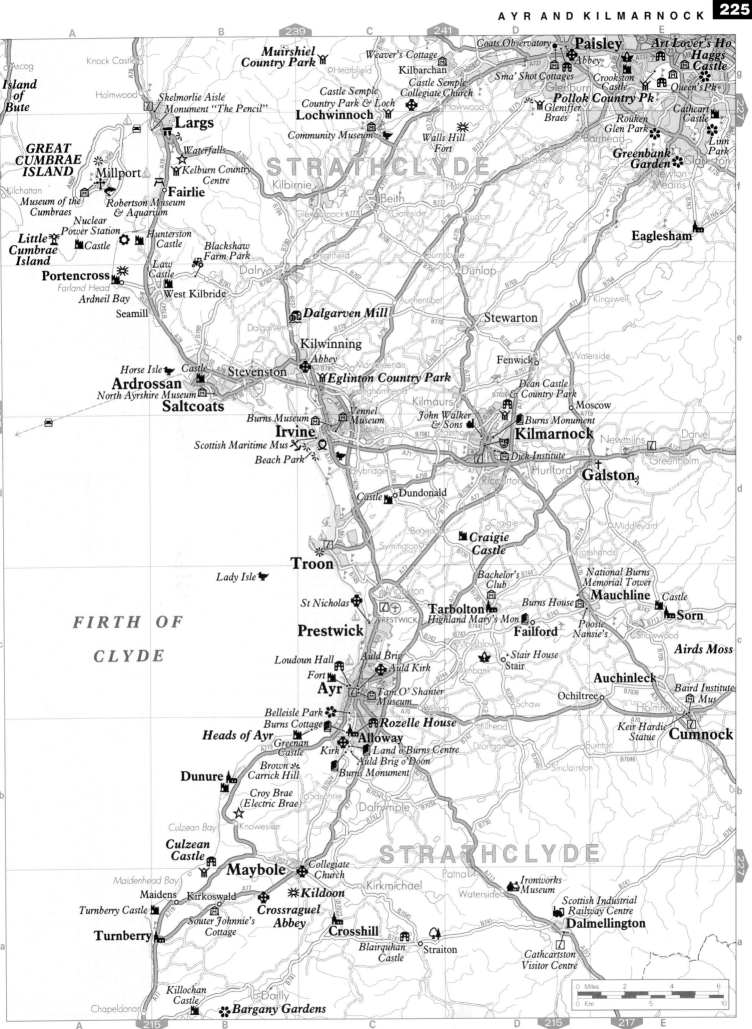

FIRTH OF CLYDE

STRATHCLYDE

Island of Bute

Ascog
Knock Castle
Holmwood

GREAT CUMBRAE ISLAND
Millport
Kilchattan
Museum of the Cumbraes

Little Cumbrae Island
Castle

Portencross
Farland Head
Ardneil Bay
Seamill

Skelmorlie Aisle Monument "The Pencil"
Largs
Waterfalls
Kelburn Country Centre
Fairlie
Robertson Museum & Aquarium
Nuclear Power Station
Hunterston Castle
Law Castle
West Kilbride
Blackshaw Farm Park

Muirshiel Country Park
Heathfield
Weaver's Cottage
Kilbarchan
Castle Semple Collegiate Church
Castle Semple Country Park & Loch
Lochwinnoch
Community Museum
Howwood
Kilbirnie
Beith
Gateside
Glengarnock
Highfield
Dalry

Coats Observatory
Paisley
Abbey
Sma' Shot Cottages
Crookston Castle
Glenburn
Gleniffer Braes
Barrhead
Neilston
Uplawmoor

Art Lover's Ho
Haggs Castle
Queen's Pk
Pollok Country Pk
Rouken Glen Park
Cathcart Castle
Linn Park
Greenbank Garden
Newton Mearns
Clarkston

Eaglesham

Dalgarven Mill
Dalgarven
Kilwinning
Abbey
Stevenston
Horse Isle
Castle
Ardrossan
North Ayrshire Museum
Saltcoats

Eglinton Country Park
Cunninghamhead
Montgreenan
Springside
Burns Museum
Vennel Museum
Irvine
Scottish Maritime Mus
Beach Park

Stewarton
Dunlop
Auchentiber
Fenwick
Waterside
Kilmaurs
John Walker & Sons
Crosshouse
Dean Castle & Country Park
Moscow
Burns Monument
Kilmarnock
Dick Institute
Hurlford
Riccarton
Newmilns
Darvel
Greenholm

Galston

Drybridge
Dundonald
Castle
Symington
Bogend

Craigie Castle
Crosshands
Middleyard

Lady Isle
Troon
Monkton
St Nicholas
Prestwick
Loudoun Hall
Fort
Ayr
Tam O' Shanter Museum
Auld Brig
Auld Kirk

Bachelor's Club
Tarbolton
Highland Mary's Mon
Mossblown
Annbank
Stair House
Stair
Failford
Poosie Nansie's
Shawwood

National Burns Memorial Tower
Mauchline
Castle
Sorn
Airds Moss
Auchinleck
Ochiltree
Baird Institute Mus
Cumnock
Keir Hardie Statue

Belleisle Park
Burns Cottage
Heads of Ayr
Greenan Castle
Kirk
Brown Carrick Hill
Croy Brae (Electric Brae)

Rozelle House
Alloway
Land o' Burns Centre
Auld Brig o' Doon
Burns Monument

Dalrymple
Hollybush
Drongan
Sinclairston
Patna

Culzean Bay
Knoweside
Culzean Castle
Maidenhead Bay
Maidens
Kirkoswald
Turnberry Castle
Souter Johnnie's Cottage
Turnberry
Dailly
Killochan Castle
Chapeldonan
Bargany Gardens

Maybole
Collegiate Church
Kildoon
Crossraguel Abbey
Crosshill
Blairquhan Castle
Straiton
Kirkmichael

STRATHCLYDE

Ironworks Museum
Waterside
Scottish Industrial Railway Centre
Dalmellington
Cathcartston Visitor Centre

0 Miles   2   4   6
0 Km   5   10

GENTLE HILLS AROUND THE CLYDE

The gently rolling, seemingly empty landscape of the Lowther hills makes a tranquil contrast to the busy towns in the north, their prosperity built on textiles and mines. Yet each has its own fascination. While Clydesdale is a rich valley devoted to growing fruit and vegetables, New Lanark is the site of one of the most exciting ventures in Scotland's industrial history.

Airds Moss ✕ Ac
Wild stretch of high moorland where government troops defeated Covenanters in 1680, and leader of the Covenanters – Richard Cameron – was killed. The Cameron Stone monument marks battle site.

Arbory Hill ✳ Ec
Remains of a well-preserved Iron Age fort crown hill on east bank of River Clyde; walled enclosure lies inside ramparts and ditches.

Auchinleck † 🏛 Ac
Two local 18th-century personalities are commemorated in parish church museum with portraits and mementos: James Boswell, biographer and friend of Dr Johnson; and gas-lighting pioneer William Murdoch. Boswell is buried in the family mausoleum next to church.

Barons Haugh Nature Reserve ✿ Cf
Mixed woodland, parkland and freshwater marsh; haunt of dabbling ducks and peregrine falcons. Hides give splendid views of waders.

Carstairs 🏛 Ee
Old village surrounds village green in rich farming country. Rare 15th-century crucifixion stone preserved in vestibule of church, dating from 1794. Wild moorland was invaded by the Caledonian Railway in 1845, and a new village sprang up to house station workers.

Cartland Crags ☆ De
Precipitous cliffs overhang rocky chasm, through which Mouse Water river plunges. Impressive three-arched bridge spans gorge; one of highest road bridges in Scotland, built by engineer Thomas Telford in 1823.

Crawfordjohn 🏛 Dc
Little township at foot of 1400ft Mountherrick Hill. Countryside of grassy hills, described by Dorothy Wordsworth as being 'inhabited solitude' in 1803. Surrounding country was favourite hunting ground of James V.

Cumnock 🏛 Ab
Industrial, market town on Lugar Water. Bust of James Keir Hardie, a founder of the Labour Party, stands outside town hall. Local history displays at Baird Institute Museum. Snuff box collection at Dumfries House, 2 miles west, built by William Adam in 1757 for the 4th Earl of Dumfries.

Lanark. Look for badger, roe deer and red squirrel. Kestrels nest safely on gorge ledges and woodland birds include great spotted woodpecker and willow tits.

Hamilton † 🏛 ☛ Cf
Rare example of attractive industrial town. Octagonal church (1732) designed by William Adam, with Covenanters' monument in churchyard. Hamilton District Museum, housed in 17th-century inn, retains original stables and Assembly Rooms dating from 18th century.

Lamington 🏛 Ed
Small Clydesdale village, transformed in 19th century from a place of 'rotting peat-roofed hovels' into a charming 'new town' by Alexander · Baillie-Cochrane. Robert Burns visited church, with Norman doorway dated 1647. Ruined Lamington Tower carries date of 1589.

Lanark † ☆ ✿ ☑ De
Peaceful market town, declared a royal burgh when David I built 12th-century castle, now vanished. Ruins of 12th-century Church of St Kentigern survive. People's hero William Wallace said to have lived and raised his forces here for Wars of Independence. His statue stands in 1777 parish church.

Lanark Moor Country Park ✿ Ee
Boating and fishing on the loch, picnic areas and golf on shore, good walks through woods.

Leadhills 🏛 Db
Situated 1350ft above sea level, surrounded by bare hills that yielded lead for centuries. Allan Ramsay Library has records and maps of mining ventures. Hill-top graveyard has memorial to John Taylor, who died aged 137, after a century of working in mines. Longevity attributed to fresh uplands air.

TOLBOOTH AT SANQUHAR
The old town hall, built in 1735, now houses the local history museum.

Sanquhar 🏰 🏛 Ca
Town post office, opened in 1763, survives as Britain's oldest post office. Granite monument pays tribute to two declarations made by the Covenanters – in 1680 and 1685 – renouncing their allegiance first to Charles II and then to James VII of Scotland.

Strathaven 🏰 🏛 Ce
Silk-weaving town in the Middle Ages. Some weavers' cottages still line older streets. Powmillon Burn flows through three public parks. Gorge dominated by 15th-century castle ruin, below which Old Town Mill is an arts centre.

Strathclyde Country Park ✿ Cf
Man-made loch, nature trails, fun park and sandy beaches. Extravagant Hamilton Mausoleum, built in the 1840s by 10th Duke of Hamilton. Huge bronze doors and multicoloured marble inside. Make a noise and listen for remarkable echo.

Tinto ✳ Ed
Famous landmark, rising 2335ft. Long climb to summit for views over Lake District and coast of Northern Ireland.

Wanlockhead 🏛 ✿ 🏛 Db
Lonely moorland village, 1380ft above sea level, where gold was once panned from neighbouring streams. Beam pump is a relic of lead-mining days. Disused mine is now part of Scottish lead-mining museum.

MODEL INDUSTRIAL VILLAGE *New Lanark was once the largest cotton-spinning complex in Britain. Behind the workers' houses in the foreground is the school, and to its left the dyeworks and workshop.*

Blackhill ✳ De
Remains of Lanarkshire's largest Iron Age fort, with Bronze Age cairn on summit. Fine views over the Isle of Arran and hills around Loch Lomond.

Blantyre 🏛 Bf
Industrial town and birthplace of explorer Dr David Livingstone; born 1813 in an 18th-century weaver's house in Shuttle Row. Now restored as The Livingstone National Memorial with mementos, including journals, surgical instruments and relics from Africa.

Calderglen Country Park ✿ Bf
Over 300 acres of wooded gorge and parkland with nature trails, woodland, and river with waterfalls. Natural history displays at the Visitor Centre. Children's zoo and adventure playground.

Chatelherault Country Park ✿ 🏛 Cf
Ten miles of woodland and country walks on the edge of Glasgow, where ancient breed of white cattle grazes parkland. Handsome 18th-century lodge, designed by William Adam, once belonged to Dukes of Hamilton.

Craignethan Castle 🏰 De
Fine example of 16th-century military architecture, in picturesque setting above small River Nethan. Stronghold of the Hamiltons, supporters of Mary, Queen of Scots; partly dismantled by her opponents in 1579.

Crawford 🏛 ✿ Ec
Quiet village overlooking grazing land on a bend in the Clyde. Site of Roman fort. Fragment of 16th-century castle lies opposite village across the Clyde.

Dalveen Pass Ea
Wild pass, 1140ft high over Lower Hills from Crawford to Durisdeer; one of the finest viewpoints in the Lowlands.

Douglas † 🏰 Dd
Coal-mining town with fragment of 18th-century castle; model for Sir Walter Scott's *Castle Dangerous*. A coal seam, opened beneath it in the 1940s, reduced it to ruins. Earlier castle on site was stronghold for the warlike Douglas family; clan warriors buried in St Bride's Church.

Falls of Clyde ✿ ☆ ✿ ☑ De
Scottish Wildlife Reserve on both banks of River Clyde, with spectacular falls and woodland walks. Bonnington Linn is most famous fall; beloved of poets and romantic painters. Visitor Centre in the old dyeworks, beside river in New

frame, Richard Arkwright. In 1800, Robert Owen (Dale's son-in-law) managed and improved working conditions, providing schools and homes for workers. Local history exhibits on display in visitor centre.

Lesmahagow ✚ Dd
Small town on edge of moorland, also known as Abbey Green. Priory, founded by Benedictine monks in 1144, no longer stands.

Lowther Hills 🏛 ✿ ✳ 🏛 Db
Quiet hills, frequented by sheep and grouse, overlook the Elvan Water, the Glengonnar, the Wanlock and the Mennock. Once rich in mineral wealth; gold and lead attracted miners for centuries.

New Lanark 🏛 ✿ De
Cotton-mill village of austere buildings, preserved as living museum and memorial to social reform. Village founded 1785 by Glasgow merchant David Dale, and the inventor of a spinning

BEAM ENGINE *A 19th-century wooden pump recalls a rich lead-mining past at Wanlockhead.*

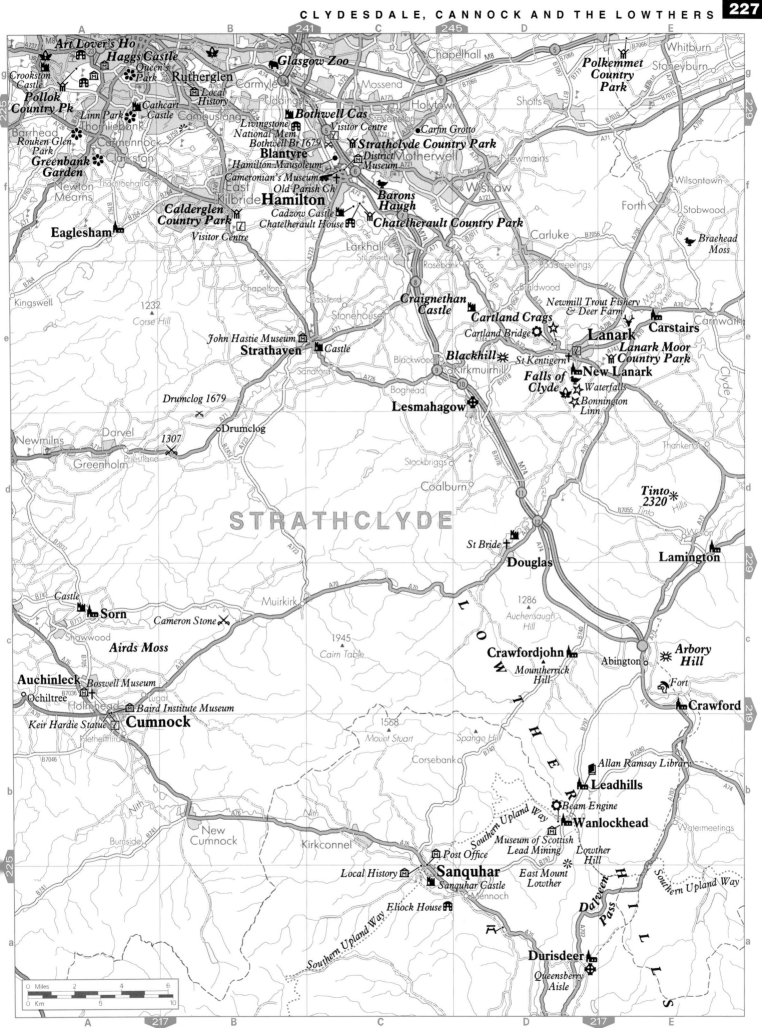

Art Lover's Ho
Haggs Castle
Crookston Castle
Pollok Country Pk
Queen's Park
Rutherglen
Carmyle
Uddingston
Glasgow Zoo
Chapelhall
Mossend
Holytown
Shotts
Stoneyburn
Whitburn
Polkemmet Country Park

Local History
Cambuslang
Linn Park
Cathcart Castle
Thornliebank
Clarkston
Greenbank Garden
Newton Mearns
Thorntonhall

Livingstone National Mem
Bothwell Br 1679
Blantyre
Hamilton Mausoleum
Cameronian's Museum
East Kilbride
Hamilton
Old Parish Ch
Calderglen Country Park
Visitor Centre
Cadzow Castle
Chatelherault House

Bothwell Cas
Visitor Centre
Strathclyde Country Park
District Museum
Motherwell
Carfin Grotto
Wishaw
Newmains
Wilsontown
Forth
Stobwood

Barons Haugh
Chatelherault Country Park
Larkhall
Stutherhill
Rosebank
Carluke
Roademeetings
Braidwood

Eaglesham
Kingswell
Corse Hill
1232
Chapelton
Glassford
Stonehouse
Sandford
Blackwood
Kirkmuirhill
Boghead

John Hastie Museum
Strathaven
Castle

Craignethan Castle
Cartland Crags
Cartland Bridge
Newmill Trout Fishery & Deer Farm
Lanark
St Kentigern
Lanark Moor Country Park
Blackhill
New Lanark
Falls of Clyde
Waterfalls
Bonnington Linn
Carstairs
Carnwath
Braehead Moss

Drumclog 1679
Newmilns
Darvel
Greenholm
Priestland
1307
Drumclog

Lesmahagow
Stockbriggs
Coalburn

STRATHCLYDE

Tinto 2320
Lamington
Wiston
Thankerton

St Bride
Douglas
1286
Auchensaugh Hill

Castle
Sorn
Shawwood
Cameron Stone
Airds Moss

Muirkirk
1945
Cairn Table

Crawfordjohn
Mountherrick Hill
Abington
Arbory Hill
Fort
Crawford

Auchinleck
Ochiltree
Boswell Museum
Lugar
Holmhead
Baird Institute Museum
Keir Hardie Statue
Netherthird
Cumnock
1568
Mount Stuart
Spango Hill
Corsebank

Allan Ramsay Library
Leadhills
Beam Engine
Wanlockhead
Museum of Scottish Lead Mining
Lowther Hill

New Cumnock
Burnside
Kirkconnel
Post Office
Local History
Sanquhar
Sanquhar Castle
Mennoch
Eliock House
East Mount Lowther
Dalveen Pass
Southern Upland Way
Watermeetings

LOWTHER HILLS

Southern Upland Way
Durisdeer
Queensberry Aisle

0 Miles 2 4 6
0 Km 5 10

Almond Valley Heritage Centre 🏛 Be
Museum in restored 18th-century water mill: story of Scottish shale oil; local history displays; and working farm with livestock.

Almondell and Calderwood Country Park ☞ Be
Two adjoining estates form park of woodlands, rhododendrons and azaleas beside River Almond.

Balerno 🏛❀ Ce
Grounds of 17th-century Malleny House famed for shrub roses and yews planted in 1603. 'Doocot' (dovecote) has 915 nesting boxes.

Beecraigs Country Park ☞ Af
Waymarked forest of 700 acres round loch. Park centre has exhibition area and craft displays. Trout and deer farms nearby.

Biggar †🏛♙🏛 Bb
Set around broad main street. Greenhill Covenanters' House is rebuilt farmhouse with displays focusing on troubled 17th century. Gasworks museum tells history of Scotland's only surviving gasworks. Puppet theatre seating 100 people is Victorian theatre in miniature. Moat Park Heritage Centre records local geology and history. Gladstone Court Street Museum displays old shopfronts and interiors.

The Binns 🏛 Bf
Turreted mansion built 1612-30 by ruthless royalist Thomas 'Bluidy Tam' Dalyell on two 'binns' or hills. After the execution of Charles I, Dalyell refused to cut his hair until the monarchy was restored. Fine Scottish furniture.

Blackness 🏛🏰 Bf
Massive 15th-century castle, known as Ship Castle from elongated shape, dominates seaside village. Charming path through woods to Hopetoun House.

Bo'ness ☀🏛🏛♙❀ Ag
Former port and coal-producing town, name contracted from Borrowstounness. Kinneil House has Biblical frescoes and estate history museum in stables. James Watt installed steam pump in cottage

nearby in 1764. On the foreshore is a restored steam railway with veteran rolling stock. Birkhill fireclay mine can be visited.

Broughton 🏛🏛 Cb
Riverside village where author John Buchan spent holidays as child with farmer grandfather. Church restored as John Buchan centre with photographs and mementos. Broughton Place, designed by Sir Basil Spence in 1930s, contains art gallery.

Castlelaw ✳ De
Road climbs to car park and then short walk to Iron Age fort with an underground refuge – passage opens into round chamber lit by windows above.

Cockleroy ✳ Af
Gentle climb from Beecraigs country park to Iron Age fort on 912ft summit. All-round views include Arran, 66 miles away.

Craigmillar Castle 🏰 Df
Extensive 14th-century ruins of favourite retreat of Mary, Queen of Scots. Gunport in tower shows early use of defence artillery.

Cramond ☀🏛 Cf
White 17th-century cottages. Stone steps and alleys lead to anchorage on River Almond. Remains of Roman fort: town was supply depot for Antonine Wall. South is Lauriston Castle with 1590 tower house. Low-tide causeway to Cramond island. Bird sanctuary on Inchmickery.

Crichton Castle 🏰 Ee
Imposing medieval ruins with 16th-century façade overlook Tyne Water. Castle has four kitchens and prison pit below tower.

TIME CAPSULE *In Biggar's Gladstone Court Street Museum visitors can see among other shops a reconstruction of a 19th-century grocer's shop.*

Dalkeith ☞ Ee
Palace remodelled in 18th century stands at end of high street. Park has nature trails and woodland adventure playground.

Dalmeny 🏛†🏛 Cf
Romanesque kirk has fine carving and sculpture. Tudor and Gothic-style Dalmeny House, 1 mile east, built 1817 by Earl of Rosebery, contains Old Masters, French furniture, porcelain, Goya tapestries and Louis XIV carpet.

Dawyck Botanic Garden ❀ Cb
Superb arboretum contains rare mature trees, including the tall, columnar Dawyck beech with its upward-growing branches.

Edinburgh Royal Botanic Garden ❀ Df
Founded 1670. Noted for rock garden, rhododendron walk and arboretum. Tropical house has huge Victoria water lilies from South America.

Edinburgh Royal Observatory 🏛☑ Df
Visitor centre set in a public park explores astronomy and space research. Exciting photographs of deep space. Astronomy shop and Scotland's largest telescope.

Forth Bridges ✿ Cg
Two awe-inspiring bridges linking Edinburgh and Dunfermline were record-breakers when built. Rail bridge of 1890 has three 1700ft spans; suspension road bridge of 1964 is 1½ miles long.

Glentress Forest ❀☞ Dc
Planted on hills of Tweedside, 10,000 acres of spruce, pine and larch. Waymarked walks lead from Glentress village.

Hopetoun House 🏛 Bf
Classical-style mansion built 1699 and enlarged by William Adam. Silk wall coverings, paintings by Canaletto, Titian, Gainsborough.

LANDMARKS IN STEEL AND STONE

Despite industrial development along the busy Forth, much of West Lothian's coastal lands retain their sense of rural solitude and historic charm. Prehistoric remains, medieval strongholds and modern achievements give the area exceptional variety. To the south, away from Edinburgh's teeming streets, the gentle slopes of the Pentland and Moorfoot hills provide superb walking country.

Rooftop observatory with views over Firth of Forth. Grounds include walled gardens, woodland walks and deer park.

Innerleithen 🏛❀ Eb
Small town where Leithen Water meets River Tweed. Robert Smail's Printing Works are reconstruction of Victorian press, including reconstructed water wheel and office containing many historic items.

Inveresk Lodge Garden ❀ Ef
Created by National Trust for Scotland to show range of plants for small gardens. Conservatory and exotic birds collection.

Kailzie Gardens ❀ Db
Tweedside estate of 15 woodland acres. Walled garden with shrub roses. Waterfowl pond.

Kirkliston 🏛🏰 Cf
This 12th-century church has a saddleback tower and fine carved doorway. Niddry Castle ruins 2 miles west – refuge for Mary, Queen of Scots in 1568.

Linlithgow 🏰🏛 Af
Shell of 15th-century palace overlooks lochside town. Medieval St Michael's Church. Museum housed in 1822 stables tells story

of 31 mile Union Canal between Edinburgh and Falkirk; carried on aqueduct 1½ miles south-west of town. Canal trips, boats for hire.

Neidpath Castle 🏛 Dc
Turreted 14th-century stronghold on rock high above Tweed valley. Converted to home in 17th century. Riverside footpaths, roe deer and other wildlife.

Peebles ✿🏛🏛☑ Dc
River Tweed, noted for salmon, rushes through town. where tweeds and knitwear are produced. Cross Kirk is 13th century. Chambers Institute with library and local history museum. The Cornalees Bridge visitor centre records story of former aqueduct.

Prestonpans ✕🏛 Ef
Name recalls priests' salt pans set up in 12th century. Cairn marks Jacobite victory in 1745 uprising. Grim Preston Tower is medieval. Graceful Northfield and Hamilton are 17th-century lairds' houses.

Roslin 🏛🏰 De
Mining village, also spelt Rosslyn, on River North Esk is overlooked by Earl of Orkney's ruined castle. Its 15th-century chapel notable for finely carved Prentice Pillar, named after apprentice mason killed in rage by jealous master.

Scottish Mining Museum 🏛 Ee and Ef
Set in Lady Victoria and Prestongrange collieries, linked by coal heritage trail through old Lothian coalfield. Visitor centre, pithead tour, 1874 beam engine.

Traquair House 🏛 Eb
Dating from 10th century and one of Scotland's oldest inhabited houses: 27 Scottish and English monarchs have stayed there. Iron gates have stayed closed since 1745 pending Stuart return to throne. Tapestries, silver, relics of Mary, Queen of Scots. Riverside walks, maze, craft workshops.

Walkerburn 🏛🏛 Eb
Woollen textiles museum displays history of shearing, spinning, dyeing, weaving and knitting.

YARROW VALLEY *This gentle, open countryside is ideal for long-distance hikes and for shorter walks.*

Yarrow Valley Ea
Wooded valley leads from Yarrow hamlet to wide open pastures and then on to Broadmeadows, Scotland's oldest youth hostel, built in 1931. Footpath joins Southern Upland Way.

SPRING BEAUTY *Thousands of bulbs provide a splendid display and carpet the lawns round the sprawling house at Dawyck Botanic Garden.*

SINGLE HANDED *Linlithgow's intricate market cross was carved by a one-handed mason in 1807.*

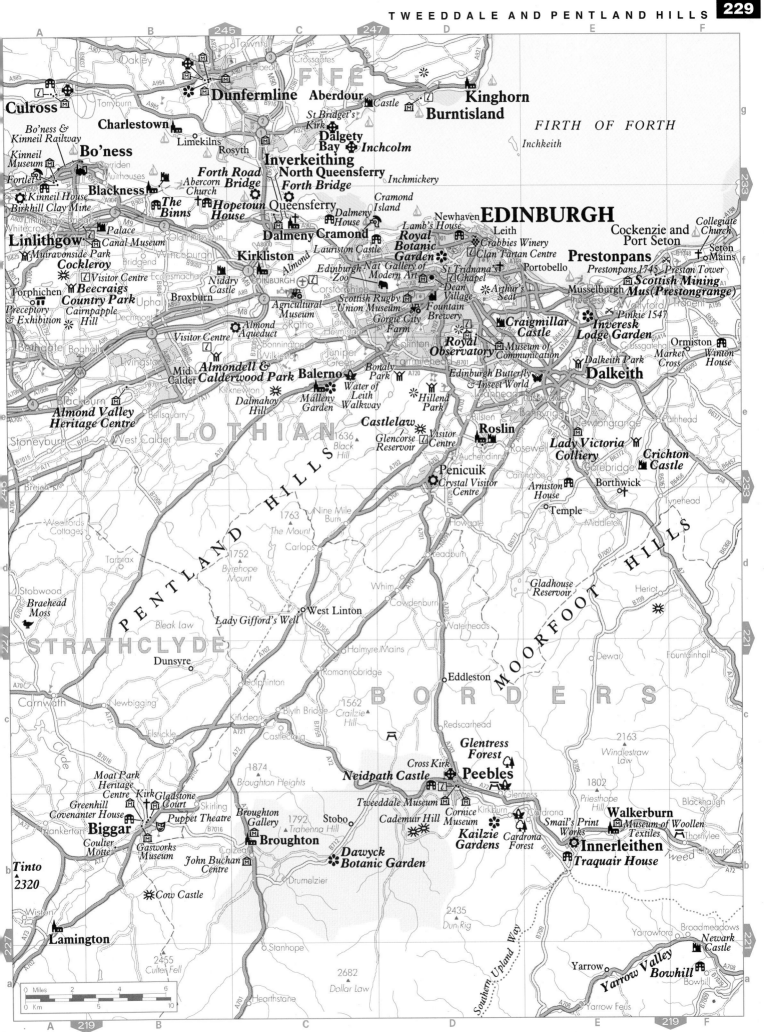

FIRTH OF FORTH

FIFE

Culross
Charlestown
Bo'ness & Kinneil Railway
Kinneil Museum
Fortlet
Kinneil House
Birkhill Clay Mine
Blackness
The Binns
Linlithgow
Palace
Canal Museum
Cockleroy
Visitor Centre
Beecraigs Country Park
Cairnpapple Hill
Preceptory & Exhibition
Torphichen

Dunfermline
Charlestown
Limekilns
Rosyth
Inverkeithing
North Queensferry
Forth Bridge
Forth Road Bridge
Abercorn Church
Hopetoun House
Queensferry
Dalmeny House
Dalmeny
Cramond
Kirkliston
Niddry Castle
Broxburn
Uphall
Almond Aqueduct
Visitor Centre

Aberdour
Castle
Dalgety Bay
Inchcolm
St Bridget's Kirk

Kinghorn
Burntisland

Inchkeith

Cramond Island
Newhaven
Lamb's House
EDINBURGH
Leith
Crabbies Winery
Clan Tartan Centre
Royal Botanic Garden
Edinburgh Zoo
Nat Gallery of Modern Art
Lauriston Castle
St Tridnana's Chapel
Portobello
Dean Village
Scottish Rugby Union Museum
Gorgie City Farm
Fountain Brewery
Arthur's Seat
Royal Observatory
Museum of Communication
Edinburgh Butterfly & Insect World

Cockenzie and Port Seton
Collegiate Church
Seton Mains
Prestonpans
Prestonpans 1745
Preston Tower
Scottish Mining Mus (Prestongrange)
Musselburgh
Pinkie 1547
Wallyford
Inveresk Lodge Garden
Ormiston
Market Cross
Winton House
Dalkeith
Dalkeith Park

Almond Valley Heritage Centre
Mid Calder
Almondell & Calderwood Park
Dalmahoy Hill
Malleny Garden
Balerno
Water of Leith Walkway
Bonaly Park
Hillend Park
Castlelaw
Glencorse Reservoir
Visitor Centre
Roslin
Lady Victoria Colliery
Crichton Castle
Penicuik
Crystal Visitor Centre
Arniston House
Temple
Borthwick

LOTHIAN

PENTLAND HILLS

Braehead Moss
Bleak Law
Lady Gifford's Well
West Linton
Gladhouse Reservoir

STRATHCLYDE
Dunsyre
Newbigging
Carnwath
Dolphinton
Romannobridge
Eddleston

MOORFOOT HILLS

BORDERS

Tarbrax
The Mount
Carlops
Byrehope Mount
Nine Mile Burn
Whim
Cowdenburn
Waterheads
Halmyre Mains
Blyth Bridge
Crailzie Hill
Castlecraig
Redscarhead
Windlestraw Law
Priesthope Hill
Blackhaugh

Glentress Forest
Cross Kirk
Peebles
Neidpath Castle
Tweeddale Museum
Cademuir Hill
Cornice Museum
Kailzie Gardens
Cardrona Forest
Walkerburn
Museum of Woollen Textiles
Smail's Print Works
Innerleithen
Traquair House

Moat Park Heritage Centre
Greenhill Covenanter House
Gladstone Court
Kirk
Skirling
Puppet Theatre
Biggar
Gasworks Museum
Coulter Motte
Broughton Gallery
Broughton
Broughton Heights
Stobo
Dawyck Botanic Garden
John Buchan Centre
Drumelzier
Cow Castle

Tinto 2320
Lamington
Wiston
Culter Fell
Dollar Law
Dun Rig
Stanhope
Hearthstane

Yarrow Valley
Bowhill
Newark Castle
Yarrow
Broadmeadows
Yarrow Feus
Southern Upland Way

Brass Rubbing Centre Dc
Collection of replicas moulded from ancient Pictish stones, rare Scottish brasses and medieval church brasses, with facilities for making rubbings.

Calton Hill Dc
A collection of monuments mark 350ft hill, with magnificent views of castle and Arthur's Seat. Part reproduction of Parthenon, and replica of Lysicrates' monument show why city is known as 'Athens of the North'. Nearby stand City Observatory and monuments to Burns and Nelson.

Camera Obscura Bb
Observation tower near castle, with panoramic views of city. Guide tells story of Edinburgh while visitors watch revolving image of city.

Canongate Kirk † Dc
Restored 17th-century church, built by order of James VII to serve parishioners of Canongate, Palace of Holyroodhouse and Edinburgh Castle. Buried in the churchyard are economist Adam Smith and 18th-century poet Robert Fergusson.

Canongate Tolbooth Dc
Has served as a courthouse and prison since it was built in 1591. Building now houses *The People's Story* – an exhibition which illustrates the life and works of Edinburgh citizens, from late 18th century to present day. Also includes restored prison cell.

Chambers Street Cb
The Heriot-Watt University, founded in 1854, stands among buildings of the University of Edinburgh, founded 1582. Robert Adam designed impressive 'Old College' in 1789.

City Art Centre 🏛 Cb
Converted warehouse with four floors of changing exhibitions and displays from the city's collection of paintings.

Edinburgh Castle 🏰 Bb
Home of Scottish kings and queens from centuries past, dominating the city from its perch of volcanic rock. The Scottish Crown Jewels are kept in the Old Royal Palace, where Mary, Queen of Scots gave birth to future King James VI of Scotland, James I of England. Within castle walls are National War Memorial, 13ft long Mons Meg cannon and the city's oldest building – 12th-century St Margaret's chapel.

Edinburgh Dungeon Ab
An eerie atmosphere is evoked with sounds, smells and settings based on Scotland's history in the 'Historical Torture Museum'.

Edinburgh University Collection of Historic Musical Instruments 🏛 Ca
More than 1000 items including around 350 woodwind instruments, 250 stringed and 150 brass. Also percussion and bagpipes.

Floral Clock Bc
Oldest in the world, built 1903 in Princes Street Gardens. Almost 12ft in diameter and filled with 250,000 flowers.

SCOTLAND'S CAPITAL CITY

History and beauty unite in this proud capital, dubbed 'The Athens of the North'. It is a tale of two cities where a dramatic balance exists between the high, dark buildings of the medieval Old Town and the classical architecture of the Georgian New Town. The Georgian period also saw the city grow as a cultural centre – a tradition kept alive today by the annual summer Edinburgh Festival.

FLOODLIT PAGEANT *The Military Tattoo takes place every summer within the battlements of Edinburgh Castle.*

Georgian House 🏛 Ac
A selection of rooms furnished as they might have been during the city's 'Golden Age' in 1796. China, silver and furniture. Bathroom with mahogany and brass lavatory. House lies in elegantly designed Charlotte Square, which dates from late 18th century.

Gladstone's Land 🏛 Cb
Early 17th-century six-storey tenement, with main floors restored as typical home of the period. Contains remarkable painted ceilings. Copies of 17th-century goods in replica shop booth.

GREYFRIARS BOBBY *The faithful terrier, who guarded his master's grave, is remembered in stone.*

Greyfriars Kirk † Ca
Site of the signing of the National Covenant in 1638, rejecting Anglicanism and asserting Scotland's right to decide its own destiny. Outside is a statue of 'Greyfriars Bobby'; famous Skye terrier who watched over his master's grave in the kirkyard for 14 years.

Holyrood Abbey ✚ Ec
Picturesque ruins of Chapel Royal of Holyroodhouse, founded in 1128 by King David I. Old vault contains the remains of several Scottish monarchs.

Huntly House Museum 🏛 Db
Principal museum of local history, housed in a restored 16th-century town mansion. Includes National Covenant of 1638 and collections of Edinburgh silver and glass.

John Knox House 🏛 Db
Museum in house with numerous gables, outside stair and elaborate carvings, dating from 15th century. Associated with John Knox, Scotland's religious reformer, and James Mossman, goldsmith to Mary, Queen of Scots. Goldsmith's workshop and Knox's library with 'preaching window', from which he is said to have addressed crowds below.

Lady Stair's House 🏛 Cb
Museum devoted to Scotland's greatest literary figures: Robert Burns, Sir Walter Scott and Robert Louis Stevenson. Includes portraits, relics and manuscripts.

Magdalen Chapel † Cb
One of the city's oldest surviving buildings, dating from the 16th century, notable for its stained-glass windows. Now serves as chapel of Heriot-Watt University.

Mercat Cross Cb
Restored cross, containing part of the 14th-century original, is still the appointed place for royal proclamations. Here in 1513 crowds heard of the death of James IV at Flodden Field.

Nelson Monument Dc
Built 1815, 106ft high, with magnificent views over city and Firth of Forth from parapets. Naval flags are flown each year on October 21 to commemorate Nelson's victory and death at Battle of Trafalgar.

North Bridge Cc
Built across the chasm formed when the Nor' Loch was drained in 1760, it divides the Old and New towns. The current cast-iron bridge dates from the 1890s.

Old Tolbooth Cb
Heart-shaped pattern of cobblestones set in pavement, marks site of vanished 15th-century prison, demolished in 1817. It provided the opening scene in Sir Walter Scott's famous romantic novel *Heart of Midlothian*.

Palace of Holyroodhouse 🏰 Ec
The official Scottish residence of the Queen dates from the late 15th century, but was reconstructed for Charles II in the 17th century. Mary, Queen of Scots came here in 1561 and stayed for six tragic years. State apartments house tapestries, paintings and furniture, and the picture gallery has portraits of 89 Scottish kings. Adjoining palace is Holyrood Park, rich in animal and plant life.

Parliament House Cb
Built 1632-9, seat of the Scottish government until Union with England in 1707. Now the supreme law courts of Scotland. Parliament Hall is a Gothic chamber, 120ft long, with a fine hammerbeam roof and portraits by Raeburn. Statue of Sir Walter Scott stands beside library.

Princes Street Bc
Scotland's greatest thoroughfare, built in 1805, famous for its shops, public buildings and spectacular panorama of the Old Town and castle. Its south side is flanked by fine gardens. At one end is the Scott Monument.

Regimental Museum of The Royal Scots ⚔ Bb
Bursting with memorabilia of the British Army's most senior Regular Regiment, formed in 1633. Displays include silver, weapons, medals and campaign relics.

Museum of Childhood 🏛 Db
Fun-filled museum devoted solely to the history of childhood. Vast collection of historic toys, dolls, games, books and costumes.

National Gallery of Scotland 🏛 Bb
Unrivalled collection of Scottish paintings. Also has masterpieces from the Renaissance to 20th century, by artists such as Raphael, Rembrandt and Van Gogh.

National Monument Dc
Twelve Doric pillars, modelled on the Parthenon, commemorating Scottish dead in the Napoleonic Wars. Intended to be a church, but funds dried up two years after work started in 1824.

MINIATURE SHOP *This model of a Victorian-style general store is one of the many evocations of the past to be seen in Edinburgh's Museum of Childhood.*

Register House Cc
Robert Adam building, designed in 1722, has Scottish national archives from the 12th century.

Royal Museum of Scotland, Chambers Street ☖ Cb
Houses the national collections of decorative arts, natural history, geology, science and technology.

Royal Museum of Scotland, Queen Street ☖ Cc
Collection showing History of Scotland from Stone Age to present day. 'Dynasty' exhibition traces 300 years of Scottish rule by Royal House of Stewart.

Royal Scots Dragoon Guards Display Room ⚔ Bb
Founded 1678; pictures, badges, brassware and other relics of this historical regiment.

St Cecilia's Hall ☖ Db
This restored 1762 concert hall now houses the Russell Collection of early keyboard instruments which includes pianos, organs and clavichords.

St Giles' Cathedral ✝ Cb
The High Kirk of Edinburgh, with its famous Crown Spire, dates mainly from the 15th century. The tiny Thistle Chapel is dedicated to the Order of the Thistle, Scotland's highest order of chivalry, and features two carved bagpipe-playing angels.

SOARING NEO-GOTHIC *The Scott Monument rises 200ft above East Princes Street Gardens.*

St John's Church ✝ Ab
Recently restored Gothic-revival church, designed by William Burn in 1817. Interior has fan-vaulted ceiling and outstanding collection of Victorian stained glass. Third World crafts and wholefood sold in 'One World Shop'. Café and bookshop in crypt.

St Mary's Cathedral ✝ Cd
One of largest Gothic churches in Britain since Reformation, built by Sir Gilbert Scott in 1879. Central spire soars 276ft high. Impressive interior contains paintings by Mateo Cerezo and Parmigianino.

Scotch Whisky Heritage Centre Bb
Brings the story of Scotch whisky to life. A barrel car travels through 300 years of history, complete with sound effects and aromas. Whisky tastings by arrangement.

Scott Monument Cc
Marble statue of novelist Sir Walter Scott, born and brought up in the city; a New Town resident for much of his life. Completed in 1844 and designed by George Meikle Kemp, it is a 200ft confection of Gothic spires, crockets, niches and gargoyles. Spiral staircases lead to various levels giving fine views over Princes Street and Old Town, and close-ups of the monument's many statues. These depict characters, some historical, some fictional, from Scott's novels, including John Knox, Ivanhoe and Rob Roy.

Scottish National Portrait Gallery ☖ Cc
More than 2000 portraits of those who have contributed to the history of Scotland since the 16th century; from Mary, Queen of Scots to Robert Burns and Sir Walter Scott. Also has the national collection of photography.

Scottish United Services Museum ⚔ Bb
Displays illustrate the history of all three armed services in Scotland through a collection of uniforms, weapons, equipment, medals, photographs, paintings and personal relics.

Traverse Theatre ♘ Cb
Historic 200-year-old Grassmarket building, one of Britain's most successful theatres for new plays.

Water of Leith Ad
Part of course flows through valley overshadowed by trees and towering houses, to emerge in Leith's western harbour. On both sides of river are immaculate private gardens.

VILLAGE OF DEAN *Edinburgh's winding river, Water of Leith, flows past wooded gardens in the old village of Dean, on its way to the Firth of Forth.*

West Register House Ac
The former St George's Church now houses more modern documents of the Scottish archives. A permanent exhibition on Scottish history includes the 1320 Declaration of Arbroath, asserting independence from England.

White Horse Close Ec
A restored group of buildings includes the former White Horse Inn, dating from 1623, a staging post for coaches to London. Captain Waverley stayed here in *Waverley* by Sir Walter Scott.

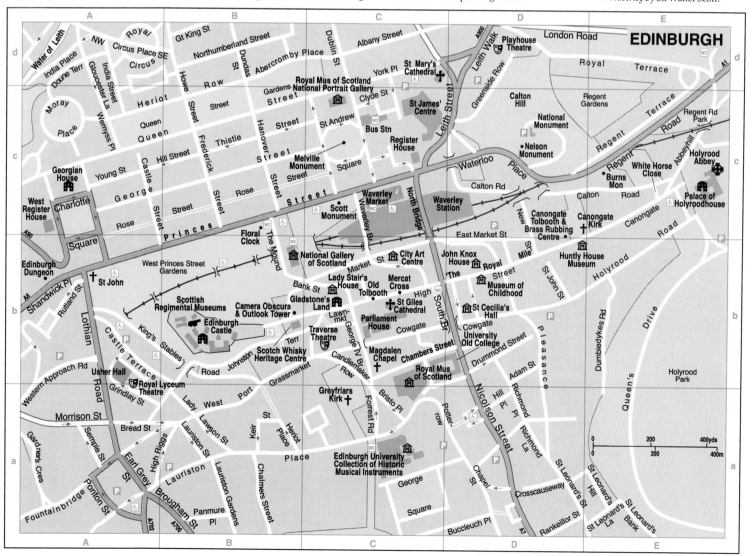

EDINBURGH

Abbey St Bathans Db
Village in secluded valley of Whiteadder Water, with remains of 12th-century Cistercian priory built into parish church. Craft centre and gallery. Riverside and woodland walks; salmon fishing, trout farm and deer. Traces of hill-forts, huts and a Pictish broch.

Aberlady Ac
Neatly restored 17th to 19th-century rubblestone houses line main street. Parish church has 15th-century square tower and pyramidal spire: on pavement outside is a 'loupin-on-stane' mounting stone used by farmers' wives to get on horses. Main road leads to Aberlady Bay, expanse of salt marsh, dunes and creeks.

Ayton Castle Fb
This flamboyant house of red sandstone, in Scottish Baronial style, was built 1846 for governor of Bank of Scotland by James Gillespie Graham. In churchyard are ruins of a pre-Reformation kirk.

Barns Ness Dc
Wildlife preserve, geology trail and limekilns along 2½ miles of coastline where limestone is quarried for local cement works.

Berwick-upon-Tweed Fa
England's northernmost town, with elegant Georgian streets and square dominated by spire of 18th-century town hall. Two mile walk leads round top of Elizabethan walls encircling town. Georgian barracks contain exhibition of British infantry's history. Three bridges span River Tweed: 15-arch Jacobean stone bridge, Robert Stephenson's 1847 railway bridge and A1 road bridge of 1928.

Coldingham Fb
Remains of priory restored 1098 on site of earlier building. Splendid arch rises among scattered gravestones and masonry. Priory choir embodied in parish church.

Cove Dc
Aptly named village with Cornish flavour. Steep track carved out of rock leads down cliffs to harbour where fishing boats shelter.

TIME-WORN *Battered walls of Dirleton Castle hide a prison pit.*

Dirleton Bd
Cottages and houses from 17th, 18th and 19th centuries and 12th-century church line three sides of wide green. On fourth side are ruins of 13th-century castle built on outcrop of rock with drum towers, kitchen, chapel and ruins of Great Hall. Gardens with 17th-century bowling green.

THE RICHES OF LOTHIAN

Castles and great houses, old fishing ports and lovely villages, sandy beaches and a string of golf courses punctuate the coastline bordering Lothian and Borders. This fertile corner of Scotland is rich in agricultural land, with cultivated acres running up the slopes of the gentle, green Lammermuir Hills where sheep graze and skylarks soar, singing above the heather.

TRIBAL LAIR *View of Lammermuirs from slopes of Traprain Law, capital of the Votadini people during Roman times.*

Drem Bc
The Chesters Iron Age fort with multiple ramparts and ditches. Situated unusually in low-lying land beneath a steep scarp.

Dunbar Cc
Red-sandstone tower and scattered ruins of 11th-century castle overlook fishing harbour with cobbled quays, restored warehouses and coastguard station. Mary, Queen of Scots was brought to the castle in 1567 by Earl Bothwell. Lauderdale House, part-extended by Robert Adam, at end of High Street, while at No 126 is a museum dedicated to the conservationist John Muir, who was born there in 1838.

Duns Da
Narrow streets straggle below Duns Law, 700ft. Statue to philosopher John Duns Scotus, born here about 1265. Jim Clark Memorial Room contains trophies of racing driver born at Duns who was twice world champion and died in 1968 racing accident.

Earn's Heugh Eb
Iron Age hill-forts on cliff near St Abb's Head. Banks, ditches and foundations of circular huts.

East Fortune Bc
Museum of Flight on airfield houses Vulcan bomber, 1930 De Havilland Puss Moth and Piper Comanche flown by Sheila Scott, holder of 94 world records in 1970s. Photographs of airship R34 which made first double crossing of Atlantic from here in 1919.

Edin's Hall Db
Substantial remains of Iron Age tower or broch built within ramparts of earlier fort on shoulder of Cockburn Law.

Eyemouth Fb
Cobbled streets, alleys and busy fishing harbour. Georgian Gunsgreen House has secret passages once used by smugglers. Museum relates history of East Coast fishing; tapestry records 23 boats and 129 men lost in 1881 gale.

Garvald Bc
Tucked away in valley beside Papana Water. On church wall are *jougs*, iron collars used on miscreants. Above village is Nunraw, 16th-century tower house built into 19th-century mansion.

Gifford Bb
Laid out by the 2nd Marquis of Tweeddale early in 18th century: 1708 church in wide main street. Avenue of limes to Yester House, built 1745 by Robert Adam.

Gullane Ad
Resort with three golf links, including Muirfield course. Exhibition shows game's development since 15th century.

Haddington Bc
Gracious town of wide streets, dating from 1100s. Town House of 1748; 15th-century church. Home of reformer John Knox. Carlyle's House, named after Thomas Carlyle, has fine façade. Restored rooms of Jane Welsh, who became his wife, in house nearby.

Hailes Castle Bc
Extensive 13th-century ruins on rock above River Tyne include tower, dungeons and chapel.

Innerwick Dc
Village with 1500s farm buildings, Georgian manse, 1700s Gothic church. Ruins of castle destroyed during English invasion 1547.

John Muir Country Park Cc
Expanse of coastal countryside, including 8 miles of sand and salt marsh, named after Dunbar-born conservationist who was father of U.S. National Parks movement.

John Wood Collection Fb
Remarkable photographs from Victorian and Edwardian days on display in garage at Coldingham.

HERB GARDEN *Haddington House grounds are in style of 1600s.*

Taken by John Wood, whose glass-plate negatives were discovered in 1983, 69 years after his death, restored and printed.

Lammermuir Hills Bb
Softly contoured heather and gorse-clad hills run east to west across Lothian. Road climbs through beech woods, past Iron Age hill-fort of White Castle, into rounded summits and deep valleys. Whiteadder reservoir lies in bowl of wooded slopes.

Lennoxlove Bc
Mansion set in woodland looking towards the Lammermuir Hills. Named after Frances Stewart, 17th-century Duchess of Lennox, model for Britannia on coinage. Good rooms, one lined with 17th-century damask. Dutch, Italian and English paintings, porcelain and furniture. Duchess's workbox, inlaid with mother-of-pearl, was gift from Charles II. Mansion is now family home of Dukes of Hamilton. Anteroom has death mask of Mary, Queen of Scots.

Longniddry Ac
Mining village for 500 years until 1920s. Golf links and rocky shore

leading down to Gosford Sands. Gosford House, seat of Earl of Wemyss and designed by Robert Adam in late 18th century, has celebrated marble hall, park and ornamental waters with wildlife.

Luffness Ad

Fortifications, moat and gardens of 1500s castle with 13th-century keep. Built on site of Norse camp.

Manderston House Ea

Edwardian country house built 1901. Marble staircase with silver handrail, ballroom hung with embossed velvet and curtains embroidered in gold and silver. Louis XVI-style furniture. Stables have arched roof, teak stalls and marble floor. Dairy has fountain designed by Italian and French craftsmen to resemble Roman cloister. Garden is entered through gilded gateway that blazes in setting sun. Rare rhododendrons and azaleas.

Myreton Motor Museum Ac

Collection of cars and trucks once in regular use. Vintage cars, motorcycles, Second World War military vehicles, road signs and petrol pumps. Oldest exhibit 1896

Leon Bolle once owned by Charles Rolls, co-founder of Rolls-Royce. All in working condition.

North Berwick Bd

Narrow streets lead down to tiny harbour flanked by fine beaches, with ruined 12th-century Auld Kirk by harbour wall. Safe anchorage for yachts and fishing boats, bathing often dangerous. Golf courses surround village below 613ft volcanic pyramid of North Berwick Law, crowned by watchtower from the Napoleonic Wars and arch of whale jawbones. Tough climb to top with impressive views. Boat trips to islands of Fidra and 350ft Bass Rock.

Oldhamstocks Dc

Village of neat cottages on eastern edge of the Lammermuir Hills, overlooking valley of Dunglass Burn. Village green with mercat cross and 18th-century water pump. Parish church remodelled 1701 from much earlier building.

Pease Bay Dc

Sandy cove with red cliffs at foot of steep Pease Dean: to north-west, Dunglass Burn tumbles through a gorge spanned by three bridges. One is 130ft high, built 1786.

Preston Mill Bc

Restored 1600s water-driven mill with wheel 13ft across. Nearby 16th-century Phantassie Doocot (dovecote) has circular walls with sloping, horseshoe-shaped roof.

St Abb's Head Fb

Spectacular cliff scenery; birds resting on precipitous lava cliffs are the main attraction. Shags, guillemots, kittiwakes, razorbills, fulmars and puffins.

Stenton Cc

Restored *tron*, weighing machine used at wool fairs, on green. Ruined old kirk next to church.

Stevenson House Bc

Mansion house dating mainly from 16th and 17th centuries. Guided tours. Furniture, pictures, china. Landscaped garden.

Tantallon Castle Bd

Cliff-edge ruins of 14th-century castle of 'Red' Douglases. Stairway inside the walls leads to battlements with fine sea views.

Torness Power Station Dc

Most modern nuclear plant in UK produces quarter of electricity used in Scotland. Guided tours.

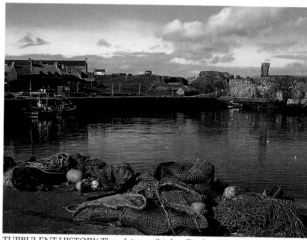

TURBULENT HISTORY *Though tranquil today, Dunbar was the backdrop for Oliver Cromwell's 1650 victory over Scotland's Covenanters.*

Traprain Law Bc

Whale-backed hill 734 ft high with Iron Age fort. Occupied through Roman times and into Dark Ages.

Tyninghame Cc

Pretty 19th-century estate village with cottages smartly uniformed in rose-red stone. Tyninghame

House noted for its beautiful wooded and walled gardens.

Union Suspension Bridge Fa

Links England to Scotland across the River Tweed, 2 miles south of Paxton. Built in 1820 by Samuel Brown; first of its kind in Britain.

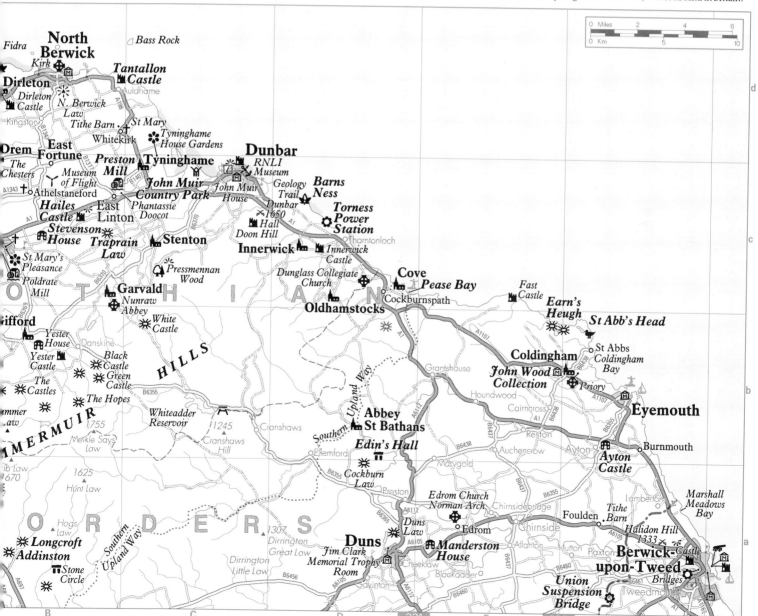

ISLANDS, MOORS AND WHISKY

This Hebridean group includes Islay, Jura, Colonsay, Oronsay and assorted rocky outcrops. The turbulent seas are popular with experienced sailors, while walkers, swimmers and cyclists are drawn to the hills, beaches and countryside. Golden eagles, grey seals and goats are among the abundant wildlife, and subtropical plants grow in the mild climate.

Ardlussa Cemetery Ff
Mary McCrain, said to have lived to 128, buried here. Male ancestor reputed to have reached 180.

Beinn Bheigeir Dc
Island's highest point at 1612ft. From Ardtalla at its foot, path leads to McArthur's Head lighthouse on Sound of Islay.

Beinn nan Gudairean ✳ Cg
Old road at rear of hotel leads to summit of hill and scattered remains of fort. Views of Staffa, Lunga, Mull and peaks of Ben Nevis, Ben Mor and Ben Lomond.

Bowmore ⌂⚓☑ Cc
Council offices, hospital, and fire station located in this harbour village of stone-built houses and modern dwellings. Distillery, established 1779, has excellent reception area. Kilarrow Church built in 1767 is circular in shape.

Bridgend ⌂ Cd
Roads to north, south and west of island meet here at head of sandy sea loch. Viaduct nearby carries private road to Islay House. Hilltop memorial to John F. Campbell, collector of West Highland folklore. Trout fishing in five lochs, sea angling from launches, wildfowling and hind stalking.

Colonsay ⌂⊕✿✳✳✳☆ Cg
Subtropical plants and 150 species of birds flourish in naturalist's paradise. Man first visited island in 7000 BC, and has occupied it since the Middle Stone Age. Walking, fishing, cycling and golf.

Corran Sands Ed
Silver and white sands stretch for 3½ miles beside Jura's only road, which runs for 24 miles from Feolin Ferry to Ardlussa.

Corryvreckan Whirlpool ☆ Fh
Ten-knot tide race in channel between north Jura and Scarba becomes roaring maelstrom of white water. Has claimed many vessels and lives. Best to view an hour or so after low tide.

Dun Ghallain ✳ Cg
Secret cave hiding place of MacFie clan and remains of fort protected by cliffs on two sides.

Dunyvaig Castle ⌂ Db
Ruined fortress dating back to 14th century once belonged to MacDonalds, Lords of the Isles.

Ellister Bird Sanctuary ☙ Bc
Thirty species of ducks, swans and geese in scenic environment near Port Charlotte.

Finlaggan Castle ⌂ Cd
Ancient seat and parliament of the Lord of the Isles, now ruins on island in Loch Finlaggan. Visitor centre at Finlaggan farm.

Grannie's Rock ☆ ⌂ Bd
Rock above Machir Bay sands has profile like old woman gazing out to sea. Ruins of Dun Chroisprig, Iron Age broch, nearby.

Islay ⚓⊕✕⌂☊☆✳☙⌂☂ Cc
Community of 4000 yields £7000 a head annually to Exchequer, largely thanks to whisky industry. Malt dried over local peat, giving unique flavour. Wilder west coast gives way to farms and boggy lowlands. Walking, cycling, sailing.

Jura ⌂☆☊⊕⚓⊙ Ef
Red deer outnumber 250 inhabitants by 20 to one. Standing stones, Iron Age forts and cave-strewn cliffs. Inland, woods give way to moorland heath and scree. One main road.

CUT CORNERS *Bowmore's church is circular, legend has it, so that the Devil cannot hide in the corners.*

Jura House Walled Garden ✿ Dd
Subtropical shrubs and flowers grow abundantly. Views from cliff top and woodland walks.

Kilchattan ⊕ Cg
Remains of medieval church, thought to be dedicated to St Catan, within walled burial ground. Baptist chapel built 1879 near remains of chapel to St Mary.

Kilchiaran ⊕ Bd
Ruins of St Ciaran's Chapel lie by track leading to bay. Oystercatchers and curlews to be seen.

Kildalton ⊕ Dc
Ruined church with 8th-century carved Celtic cross, reached by unclassified road through woods.

Kilnaughton Bay Cb
Unspoiled golden sands 1 mile west of Port Ellen.

Kiloran Bay Cg
Beach backed by sand dunes in which rabbits thrive. Safe surfing in Atlantic rollers. Natural rock pool deep enough for diving.

Kiloran Gardens ✿ Cg
Rhododendrons, palms, mimosa, embothriums and eucalyptus flourish beside native trees, bluebells and meconopsis.

Laggan Bay Bc
The Big Strand, 5 miles of shell sand, stretches to Laggan at northern end where river with salmon and trout flows into sea.

Laphroaig Distillery ⚓ Cb
Established in 1815. One of several distilleries on island which produce distinctively flavoured malts. Traditional malting floor. Visitors by appointment.

Loch Gruinart ☙ Bd
A main wintering ground for Arctic barnacle geese. In 1598 MacLeans of Duart lost clan battle against MacDonalds of Islay, who pursued survivors to their refuge in Kilnave Chapel and burned it. Only one MacLean escaped.

MacFie's Stone ⊕ Cg
Clan chief murdered here in 1623; many clan members visit site. Two carved stones may indicate early Christian burial ground.

The Mill ⌂ Cg
Mill, 19th century – built by Lord Colonsay – now converted to dwelling, but water wheel still in place. Building behind mill said to have been carpenter's shop.

The Oa ✳ Cb
Peninsula of lochs and caves, once used by illicit whisky distillers and smugglers. Topped by Beinn Mhór, 658ft. Monument at Mull of Oa to 650 U.S. servicemen who died when two troopships, *Tuscania* and *Otranto*, sank off the headland nearby in 1918.

Oronsay ⊕ Cf
St Columba said to have landed here on way to Iona in 6th century. Long-horned, black-fleeced wild goats may be descendants of animals from Armada ships wrecked in 1588. Grey seals on rocky islets.

Oronsay Priory ⊕ Cf
Ruins of priory dating from 13th century contain 16th-century Celtic cross and high altar. Stone slabs in graveyard have carved portraits of warriors and saints.

Paps of Jura De
Three conical mountains, highest 2571ft, give views over 100 miles to Isle of Man and Outer Hebrides. Climbers should take care, especially from August to February when deer stalkers abound.

Port Askaig ⌂⚓ Dd
Ferry port from mainland and connecting point for five-minute ferry run to Jura. Post office, hotel, store and a lifeboat station. Safe bathing and sailing.

Port Charlotte ⌂⌂ Bc
Principal village of Rinns of Islay and prosperous farming area. Village creamery takes island's entire milk output, producing cheese sold on mainland and abroad. Museum of Islay Life has displays of local history from prehistoric times. Street names are written in Gaelic – spoken by most villagers. Fishing and sailing.

Port Ellen ⚓ Cb
Chief township built in mid-19th century and car ferry port. Flanked by peat moor used in malt whisky industry. Pier, post office, double-tower lighthouse. Sailing, swimming and Machrie golf course nearby.

Portnahaven ⌂ Ac
Tiny village and neighbouring Port Wemyss stand in treeless area with dramatic cliff scenery and views to Ireland. Village includes post office, store, school and two churches. Offshore is 150ft Isle of Orsay lighthouse.

Riasg Buidhe Dg
Remains of 19th-century homes, earlier chapel and burial ground. Village abandoned in 1918. Inhabitants rehoused at Glassard, near Scalasaig.

Saligo Bay Bd
Atlantic rollers wash great sandy bay dominated by 400ft cliffs. Behind is Loch Gorm, largest freshwater loch on island.

Scalasaig ⌂⚓ Cg
Saithe and mackerel can be caught from the pier – arrival point for Oban ferry. Seafarers use the 19th-century monument to Lord Colonsay as a landmark when anchoring off pier or at Queen's Bay. Village includes hotel and post office/shop.

The Strand ☆ Cg
Mile-wide beach dotted with mussel-growing rocks links two islands at low tide. Cross once stood at centre: any fugitive from Colonsay who passed it was held to be within jurisdiction of Oronsay Priory, and could claim sanctuary from enemies for a year and a day.

SEASIDE ATTRACTION *Glistening waters and pristine sands at Kiloran Bay, Colonsay's most popular beach.*

ARCTIC VISITORS *Barnacle geese from Greenland spend the winter on Loch Gruinart.*

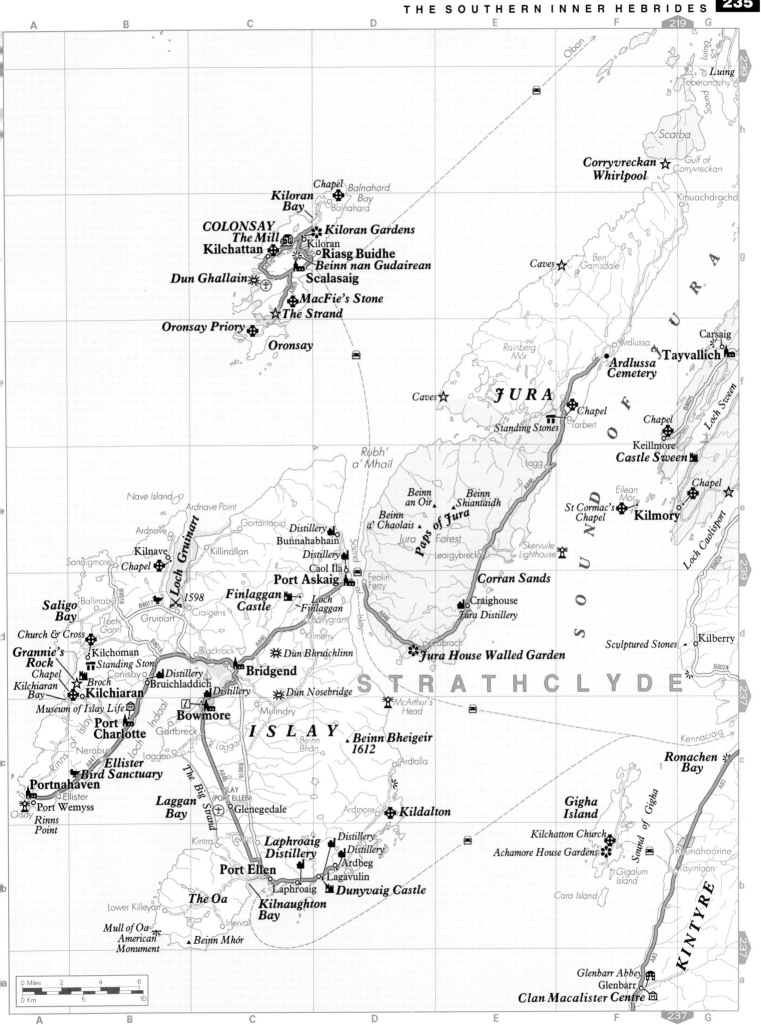

219
239

Oban

Luing
Toberonochy
Sound of Luing

Scarba

**Corryvreckan
Whirlpool** ☆
*Gulf of
Corryvreckan*

Kinuachdrachd

Chapel ✠
*Balnahard
Bay*
Balnahard

**Kiloran
Bay**
COLONSAY
The Mill ✠ **Kiloran Gardens**
Kilchattan ✠ *Kiloran*
Riasg Buidhe
Beinn nan Gudairean
Dun Ghallain ✠ **Scalasaig**

Caves ☆
*Ben
Garrisdale*

MacFie's Stone
☆ **The Strand**
Oronsay Priory ✠
Oronsay

Ardlussa

J U R A

Carsaig
Tayvallich 🏛

*Rainberg
Mór*

**Ardlussa
Cemetery** ●

Caves ☆

J U R A

Chapel ✠
Castle Sween 🏛

Loch Sween

Chapel ✠
Tarbert
Standing Stones 🏛

Castle Sween 🏛

Keillmore

*Rubh'
a' Mhail*

*Beinn
an Oir* ▲
*Beinn
Shiantaidh* ▲
*Beinn
a' Chaolais* ▲
Pups of Jura

*Eilean
Mór*
*St Cormac's
Chapel* ✠
Kilmory

Chapel ✠ ☆

Lagg
Jura Forest

Leargybreck

*Skervuile
Lighthouse* 🗼

Corran Sands
Craighouse
Jura Distillery

*Feolin
Ferry*

Nave Island
Ardnave Point

Ardnave

Gortantaoid
Killinallan

Distillery
Bunnahabhain
Distillery
Caol Ila

Port Askaig
*Loch
Finlaggan*
**Finlaggan
Castle**
Ballygrant

*St Cormac's
Chapel* ✠
Kilmory

Loch Caolisport

Sculptured Stones ●
Kilberry

B8024

Kilnave
Chapel ✠

Loch Gruinart
Sanaigmore

1598 ✗
**Salig o
Bay**

B8017
B8018
Ballinaby
Gruinart
Craigens
Kilmeny

*Loch
Gorm*

**Grannie's
Rock**
Church & Cross
Kilchoman
Standing Stone 🏛
Chapel
**Kilchiaran
Bay**
Broch
Kilchiaran ✠

Conisby
Blackrock
Distillery
Bruichladdich

❋ **Dun Bhruachlinn**
Bridgend

Jura House Walled Garden ❋

S T R A T H C L Y D E

Distillery

Museum of Islay Life 🏛
**Port
Charlotte** 🏛

Nereabus
**Ellister
Bird Sanctuary**

Portnahaven
Ellister
Port Wemyss
Orsay
*Rinns
Point*

❋ **Dun Nosebridge**

Mulindry

Bowmore 🏛
Gartbreck

I S L A Y
*Beinn
Bhán*
**Beinn Bheigeir
1612** ▲
Ardtalla

🗼 **McArthur's
Head**

Kennacraig

**Ronachen
Bay**

Laggan
**Laggan
Bay**
The Big Strand
**ISLAY
(PORT ELLEN)**
Glenegedale ●
Ardmore

Kintra
Cragabus

**Laphroaig
Distillery**
Port Ellen 🏛
Laphroaig

Distillery
Distillery
Ardbeg
Lagavulin
Dunyvaig Castle 🏛

Kildalton ✠

**Gigha
Island**

Kilchatton Church ✠
Achamore House Gardens ❋

Sound of Gigha

*Gigalum
Island*

Rhunahaorine

The Oa
**Kilnaughton
Bay**

Lower Killeyan
Irerval
Mull of Oa
**American
Monument** 🗼
Beinn Mhór ▲

Cara Island

Tayinloan

Glenbarr Abbey 🏛
Glenbarr
Clan Macalister Centre 🏛

K I N T Y R E

237
239
237
237

0 Miles	2	4	6
0 Km	5		10

CLYDESIDERS' PLAYGROUNDS

The isles of Arran and Bute and the peninsula of Kintyre have long been playgrounds for the Scots, particularly the Glaswegians. The topography of each island resembles that of a miniature Scotland – a mountainous north and rolling, pastoral south. Outdoor pursuits include walking, fishing and sailing, while indoor entertainment can be found in Brodick, Campbeltown and Rothesay.

Arran ✿ Ed
Favourite island retreat of Glaswegians, once popular with Scottish monarchs. Fine mountain scenery in north contrasts with lowlands of south. Robert Bruce landed at Lochranza from Ireland in 1306.

Arran Heritage Museum Fd
Brodick croft farm contains a museum of Arran history, geology and archaeology. Authentic rooms exhibit spinning wheels, wooden cradle and other domestic items. Geology section includes amethysts found on local beaches. Picnic area and tearoom.

FARMING PAST *Old equipment is on show at Arran Heritage Museum.*

Auchagallon Dd
Bronze Age monument consists of rounded stone mound surrounded by rough circle of 15 standing stones.

Blackwaterfoot Dc
Hamlet standing amid ancient remains. Robert Bruce may have sheltered at King's Cave, to north, in 14th century. Ponytrekking and golf course nearby.

Brodick Fd
Arran's main port set by sandy Brodick Bay. Goat Fell, at 2866ft, dominates mountain trail. Views of bay and surrounding peaks from String Road, to west.

Brodick Castle and Country Park Fd
Seat of Dukes of Hamilton, built 13th century with later additions. Interior features fine plaster ceilings, furniture, porcelain and paintings. Grounds include 1710 formal garden, Victorian rose garden, nature trail.

Bute Fg
Rolling hills in north descend to quiet sandy beaches. Island separated from mainland by narrow waterway called Kyles of Bute. Popular with Clydesiders.

Campbeltown Cc
Former Celtic capital of Dalriada kingdom, now sailing centre. Stone buildings mark past prosperity from whaling, fishing, coal and distilling. Town centre has richly carved Celtic cross.

Canada Hill Gg
Hill rising above Loch Fad gives panoramic views of Firth of Clyde, Argyll and seven counties from picnic spots.

Carradale Dd
Village with shops, situated on hill above small harbour. Remains of Aird Castle and 1500 BC fort lie nearby. Walks from Forest Centre through 16,000 acre estate have splendid views of Arran and 2366ft Bein Bharrain.

Carradale House Gardens Dd
Forested hills surround 1870 home of novelist and children's writer, Naomi Mitchison. It has a wild garden with pond.

Clan Macalister Centre Bd
Dumbarr Abbey, Gothic-style home of the Macalister chieftain, dates from 1700. Museum includes historic weapons, photographs and other artefacts.

Clauchland Hills Fd
Conifer forests and bracken-covered hillsides are threaded by footpaths, with views of Lamlash and Holy Island.

Corrie Fe
Village at foot of 2866ft Goat Fell. Now-silted harbour was built in 1882 to ship locally quarried limestone. Walk coast to Fallen Rocks or climb to High Corrie hamlet, birthplace of the book publisher Daniel Macmillan.

Dunaverty Rock Ba
Site of old Dunaverty Castle, former Macdonald stronghold. A garrison of 300 were besieged here in 1647 by Covenanters, supporters of English parliament. Every defender was slain on surrender. Known as 'Blood Rock'.

Dun Skeig Cf
Vitrified wall of oval Iron Age fort overlooks Loch Tarbert. Outside fort is a roughly circular dun with thick wall and single entrance.

Gigha Island Bf
Gaelic for 'God's Island', area scattered with fort remains and standing stones. Achamore House Gardens has 50 acres of flowering trees and shrubs. Bicycle hire from post office.

Glen Rosa Ee
Glen climbs from coast to 2618ft Cir Mhor with Glenrosa Water flowing through it. Glacial terrain reveals huge granite boulders.

Holy Island Fd
St Molaise reputedly lived in a cave here and died in AD 639, after accepting 30 diseases at once to avoid purgatory. Visit this cave by boat and see runic inscriptions.

Kildonan Fc
Area of 1869-70 gold rush; prospectors still pan for gold in Helmsdale's tributaries today. Path to promontory with views of rapids and leaping salmon in summer.

Kilmory Cairns Ec
Torrylin, a Neolithic chambered cairn, lies south-west of Kilmory village. Inside were found skeletal remains and a flint knife.

Kintyre Cd
Narrow peninsula of great beauty, connected to mainland by Tarbert isthmus. Long, isolated beaches offer windsurfing and sailing. Grey seals and sea otters.

Lamlash Fd
Boat haven sheltered by Kingcross and Clauchlands points. Arran's largest village with good fishing. Underwater enthusiasts can visit *Derwent* shipwreck in bay, dating back to 1880.

Lochranza Ef
Robert Bruce is said to have lived here in 1306, when he began his struggle for independence. Castle built in 13th century, rebuilt in the 17th century. Village resort has safe bathing facilities with shore or boat fishing.

Machrie Moor Ed
Remains of six 15ft Bronze Age stone circles lie scattered within a mile, south of Machrie. Nearby are traces of Stone Age hut circles and tombs.

Machrihanish Bc
Corn-coloured sands run for 3½ miles along coast. Better to walk this beach than to swim – its undertow is fierce. Golf course and airfield to north.

Mull of Kintyre Aa
Southernmost point of Kintyre Peninsula. Lighthouse built here in 1788. One of the most treacherous points for shipping on the Scottish coast.

Ronachan Bay Cf
Car park overlooking bay provides views of Inner Hebrides across Sound of Jura. Grey seals, largest of British wild mammals, can be seen around offshore reefs.

Rothesay Fg
Scottish kings once holidayed at now-ruined Royal Stuart castle, which overlooks this popular resort. See Bute history museum and magnificent floral displays at Ardencraig Gardens. Swimming from beaches; bicycles and rods available for hire.

Saddell Abbey Cd
Abbey built 1160 by Samerled, liberator of Argyll and Kintyre from Viking control. Amongst remains are tombstones carved between 1300 and 1560 depicting armoured warriors, priests and war galleys. Tower of Saddell Castle stands south-east of village.

LOCHRANZA CASTLE *On the loch shores lie ruins of a bold fortress, where Robert Bruce once lived.*

St Blane's Chapel Ff
Remains of chapel built 1100 and named after Celtic saint who founded monastery here in AD 575. Fine example of Norman arch still stands.

St Mary's Chapel Fg
Remains of late medieval chapel contain recessed canopied tombs with carved effigies of Walter the Steward, his wife Alice and a child. Nearby is the grave of Napoleon's niece Stephanie, who died here in 1885.

Sannox Fe
Deserted in 1823 when villagers were evicted and emigrated to Canada, leaving today's scattered ruins. Cart track leads to spectacular Glen Sannox.

Skipness Df
Sandy beach and tiny village dominated by remains of 13th-century Campbell Castle and chapel. Fortress escaped major conflict, but abandoned in 1700.

Southend Ba
St Columba stepped onto local beach in 6th century to convert Picts to Christianity. He left behind what are said to be his footprints in stone. Traces of Druid altar nearby. St Columba's Well behind churchyard.

Tarbert Dg
Fishing port and resort town on isthmus connecting Kintyre to mainland. Village with shops encircled by hills and overlooked by 14th-century stronghold of Robert Bruce.

Thomson Memorial Seat Fd
Highest point of road from Brodick to Lamlash on Arran. Good views of mountains rising 2800ft to the north; moorland and rolling hills to the south.

ANCIENT DEFENCE *Gigha Island contains several prehistoric sites like this overgrown earthwork and ditch.*

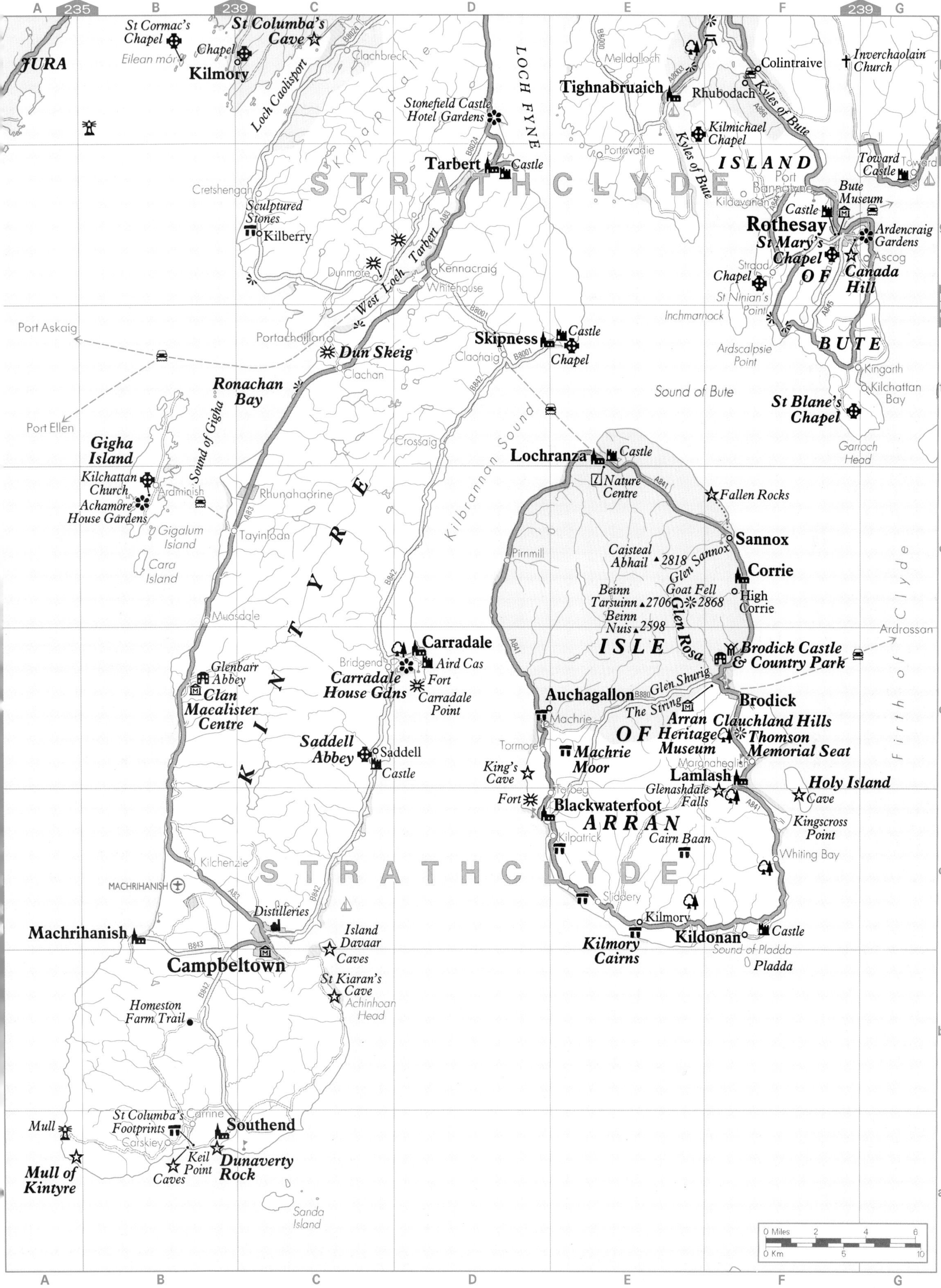

JURA

St Cormac's Chapel
Eilean mór
Chapel
Kilmory
St Columba's Cave
Loch Caolisport
Clachbreck

STRATHCLYDE

Stonefield Castle Hotel Gardens

Tighnabruaich
Melldalloch
Rhubodach
Colintraive
Inverchaolain Church
Kyles of Bute
Portavadie
Kilmichael Chapel
ISLAND
Toward Castle
Toward
Kyles of Bute
Port Bannatyne
Kildavanan
Bute Museum
Castle
Rothesay
St Mary's Chapel
Ardencraig Gardens
Ascog
Straad
Chapel
St Ninian's Point
Canada Hill
Inchmarnock
OF
BUTE
Ardscalpsie Point
Kingarth
Kilchattan Bay
Sound of Bute
St Blane's Chapel
Garroch Head

LOCH FYNE

Tarbert
Castle
Cretshengan

Sculptured Stones
Kilberry
Dunmore
Kennacraig
Whitehouse

Port Askaig
Portachaillan
Dun Skeig
Clachan
Skipness
Castle
Chapel
Claonaig

Port Ellen
Ronachan Bay

Gigha Island
Kilchattan Church
Ardminish
Achamore House Gardens
Gigalum Island
Cara Island

Crossaig

Lochranza
Castle
Nature Centre
Fallen Rocks
Caisteal Abhail ▲2818
Glen Sannox
Sannox
Corrie
High Corrie
Goat Fell
Beinn Tarsuinn ▲2706 ❋2868
Beinn Nuis ▲2598
ISLE
Glen Rosa

Pirnmill

Kilbrannan Sound

Sound of Gigha

Rhunahaorine
Tayinloan
Muasdale

KINTYRE

Glenbarr Abbey
Clan Macalister Centre
Carradale
Bridgend
Aird Cas Fort
Carradale House Gdns
Carradale Point

Saddell Abbey
Saddell
Castle

STRATHCLYDE

Kilchenzie
Distilleries
MACHRIHANISH

Machrihanish
Campbeltown
Island Davaar Caves
St Kiaran's Cave
Achinhoan Head

Homeston Farm Trail

Mull
St Columba's Footprints
Carrine
Southend
Carskiey
Keil Point Caves
Dunaverty Rock
Mull of Kintyre
Sanda Island

Brodick Castle & Country Park
Auchagallon
Glen Shurig
Brodick
Machrie
The String
Clauchland Hills
Arran Heritage Museum
Thomson Memorial Seat
Tormore
OF
Marganaheglish
Lamlash
King's Cave
Machrie Moor
Teleoeg
Glenashdale Falls
Holy Island
Cave
Fort
Blackwaterfoot
ARRAN
Kingscross Point
Kilpatrick
Cairn Baan
Whiting Bay
Sliddery
Kilmory
Kilmory Cairns
Kildonan
Castle
Sound of Pladda
Pladda

Firth of Clyde
Ardrossan

0 Miles 2 4 6
0 Km 5 10

Achnacloich Woodland Garden ✿ Dh
Castellated mansion on promontory among gardens protected by oaks and larches. Views west to Mull and east to Ben Cruachan.

Ardanaiseig Gardens ✿ Eg
Rhododendrons and azaleas set paths ablaze with colour in woodland gardens overlooking Loch Awe. Walled garden, 1 acre, with herbaceous borders.

Ardrishaig Cc
Sailing boats moor in harbour at southern end of 9 mile long Crinan canal, started 1794 by John Rennie to link Loch Fyne with Atlantic Ocean and cut out the 120 mile voyage round Kintyre.

Argyll Wildlife Park ✟ Ee
Thousands of wildfowl feed on the 60 acre reserve, which also has a large collection of owls.

Auchindrain Open Air Museum 🏚 Ee
Restored cottages and barns survive from ancient communal farm worked by families who shared labour. Visitor centre shows life of Highlanders in past centuries.

COUNTRY LIFE *A crofter's cottage at the Auchindrain Folklife Museum evokes the area's rural past.*

Barcaldine ⊖ Di
Crofters' fields surround scattered houses. Huge Douglas firs line paths to Gleann Dubh, where waterfalls plunge. Views of the Western Isles from reservoir.

Benmore ⓗ✿⊖☆ Fc
Dawn redwoods and eucalyptuses line forest paths near Loch Eck. Avenue of 130ft Wellingtonias leads to grounds of Benmore House and botanic garden.

Bonawe ✿ Eh
Restored 1753 charcoal ironworks above Loch Etive. Exhibition of smelting process and local life. Boat cruises leave from pier.

ARGYLL AND THE ROAD TO THE ISLES

Dramatic mountain peaks tower over moors dotted with tumbledown crofts and castles laid waste in clan feuds. Icy streams ripple through wooded glens and into lochs teeming with salmon and trout – the delight of anglers. Golden eagles soar above the rocky crags and red deer roam the moors, near scattered villages haunted by tales of murder and treachery in days gone by.

SLATE WORK *Easdale shows many signs of the former industry – slate walls, quays and roofs.*

Castle Sween ⛰ Bb
Probably Scotland's earliest stone castle, built in mid-12th century. Stronghold of the MacSween family; destroyed in 1647. Ruins retain their original proportions.

Clachan Bridge ✿ Bf
Humpbacked stone 'Bridge over Atlantic', designed by Thomas Telford 1792, links Seil Island to mainland across arm of ocean.

Cornalees ♣ Gb
Footpaths skirt reservoirs and hillside channels built 1827 by Robert Thom to serve textile mills. Visitor centre shows history. Nature trail to Shielhill Glen with waterfall.

Connel ⓗ☆ Dh
Falls of Lora swirl beneath bridge across narrows of Loch Etive. Stained glass in village church depicts bridge and falls.

SALMON WATER *Lochawe, once a fastness for the Highland clans, is now popular with salmon and trout anglers.*

Crarae Glen Garden ✿ Dd
Rare trees and rhododendrons flourish here. Associated garden centre sells shrubs and trees.

Crinan ⓗ Bd
Yachts and fishing boats pass through locks at terminus of Crinan Canal. Duntrune Castle (closed to public) has skeleton of MacDonald piper imprisoned by Campbells in 17th century.

Dunadd Hill-Fort ✳ Cd
Stone walls of ancient fort. Carvings on rock face thought to mark Pictish victory in AD 683.

Dunoon ⓑ⛰ ☆✳ Fb
Resort noted for sandy bays and castle burned in 1685. Hillside statue of Mary Campbell, Burns's 'Highland Mary', who was born here. Holy Loch Farm has rare breeds of cattle and horses.

Dunstaffnage Castle ⛰✿ Ch
Castle remains cling to black crag on or near site of capital of Dalriada, original Scots kingdom. Campbells were castle governors in medieval times. Many buried in roofless chapel in wood.

Easdale 🏛 Bf
Peaks of Dun More look down on old slate quarries. Museum of 1800s industrial and domestic life.

Eredine Forest ⊖ De
Dense forest skirts lochside road, ideal for picnics. View of Innis Chonnell Island with ruins of former Campbell stronghold.

Glen Nant ⊖☆ Eg
Trails explore oak and hazel woods in narrow glen. Charcoal hearths once fuelled Bonawe ironworks nearby.

Helensburgh 🏠 Gc
Fishing, sailing and golf resort, backed by hills and glens. Obelisk memorial to steamship pioneer Henry Bell. Charles Rennie Mackintosh designed moated Hill House in park with 700 deer.

Inveraray ✟🏠🚂🏛 Ee
Hereditary seat of Dukes of Argyll. Campbell chiefs ruled from 15th century in blue-grey castle. Tapestries, paintings and swords on display. Story of Scottish crime and punishment in Inverary Jail, with reconstructed prison cells and torture scenes.

Inverliever Forest ⊖☆✳ De
Switchback road through forest inhabited by deer and badgers. Paths from Dalavich village to waterfalls and hill-top views.

Kilmartin ⓗ🚂 Cd
Bronze Age symbols adorn burial chambers in village. Medieval stone sculptures in churchyard.

Kilmory ✿ Bb
Ruined church contains medieval cross and Celtic grave slabs. Views look across to Paps of Jura.

Kilmory Castle Gardens ✿ Cc
Rare alpines, ferns and rhododendrons line the woodland paths in these gardens started in 1770s.

Kilmun Arboretum ❀ Fc
Pathways weave among pines, hemlocks, cedars, cypresses, dawn redwoods, and eucalyptuses.

Lismore Island ⓗⓑ Ci
Mountains embrace site founded AD 560 by St Moluaig. Parish church set in 13th-century cathedral destroyed in Reformation.

Lochawe ⓗ⛰✿ Fg
Resort overlooks narrow loch with fishing for salmon and trout. Robert Bruce memorial chapel i 1881 St Conan's Kirk. Kilchur Castle, built 1440, on loch shore.

Loch Creran ⬅ Di
Seals gambol in well-lit tanks a Sea Life Centre. Eels, dogfish salmon, cod and bass also o view. Hillside walks above 17th century Barcaldine Castle.

Lochgilphead ⚓✿🚂 Cc
Crescent of stone-built house overlooks loch. Bronze Age carvings on rocks near standing ston at Achnabreck.

Oban ⓑ🚂⚓⛰🏛 ✟⚓⚓✿ Ch
Sheltered bay with fishing boat and Hebrides ferries. Creeper clad ruin of Dunollie Castle former MacDougall stronghold McCaig's Tower above town i Colosseum replica built 1890s.

BUSY PORT *Craft of all sorts moor in Oban's harbour.*

Port Appin ⓗ Di
Whitewashed hamlet has wildlif museum with local nature dis play. Castle Stalker, built 14th century, on offshore island.

Rosneath ⓗ Gc
Sailing centre set among trees Renowned for healing waters o St Modan's Well.

St Columba's Cave ☆ Bb
Cave with rock-shelf and alta associated with St Columba' arrival in Scotland. Occupie since Middle Stone Age.

Strone House Gardens ✿ Ff
Pinetum contains tallest tree i Britain – a 203ft grand fir (*Abie grandis*). Exotic plants and shrubs.

Taynuilt ⓗ Eh
Anglers and walkers converge o village dominated by 3695ft Ber Cruachan. Nelson memorial erec ted in 1805. Woodland natur reserve at Glen Nant.

Tayvallich ⓗ Bc
Natural harbour on shores of Loch a' Bhealaich. Walks lead int Knapdale and west to Carsaig Bay, overlooked by hills of Jura.

Tighnabruaich ⓗ Db
Cottages scattered on hillside of woods and gardens. To the north lies viewpoint of Kyles of Bute and forest trail.

BONNIE BANKS BELOW THE BRAES

The vast expanse of Loch Lomond's waters and the sharp peaks and forest-covered slopes of Trossachs country fulfil a popular ideal of Scotland based on the poems and novels of Sir Walter Scott. To the south lie the remains of the Antonine Wall, built across the narrowest part of Scotland and marking what was the northern extremity of Roman territory in Britain.

Aberfoyle Cf
North of village is Queen Elizabeth Forest Park Visitor Centre, with informative displays. Facilities for forest walks, pony treks, boating and fishing. Old slate quarries and site of Aberfoyle Quarries village on hills above Aberfoyle.

Achray Forest Cf
Part of Queen Elizabeth Forest Park. Achray Forest Drive is a 7 mile route with fine view of Trossachs, and good opportunities for observing wildlife. Picnic sites, parking places and marked paths.

Airdrie Eb
Weavers' Cottages Museum comprises two cottages built 1780. Gives insight into lives of weavers and displays local artefacts. Wide views from Airdriehill.

Antonine Wall Dc
Roman wall built *c.* AD 142 stretching 37 miles from sea to sea at narrowest part of Scotland. Ran from Bowling on the Forth to Bo'ness on the Clyde, and was built of turf and clay on stone base some 14ft wide. May have reached height of 12ft. Huge ditch 12ft deep on north side of wall is still visible in places. Wall had been finally abandoned by AD 214.

Art Lover's House, Glasgow Cb
Charles Mackintosh's largest and greatest domestic design, set in open parkland. Interiors have stone carvings and stained glass.

Balloch Castle Country Park Ad
Public park on southern shore of Loch Lomond covering 200 acres. Nature trails, guided walks, walled garden and picnic lawns with views of loch. Castle, built 1808, contains visitor centre.

Bearsden Cc
Roman bathhouse, used by soldiers stationed on Antonine Wall during 2nd century AD.

Blair Drummond Safari and Leisure Park Ee
Animals can be seen at close quarters from car or bus. Features include monkey jungle, boat trip to Chimp Island and cable car across lake. Other attractions include adventure playground and cinema showing 3-D films.

Bothwell Castle Da
Remains of one of Scotland's finest medieval buildings, built 13th century, stand on crag above River Clyde. Dismantled in 14th century following siege, and later restored by powerful Douglas family after 3rd Earl, Archibald the Grim, acquired it by marriage and made it his seat in 1362.

Callander Df
Holiday resort and base for walks and drives around Trossachs and Loch Katrine, with 18th-century homes around Ancaster Square.

Coatbridge Eb
Summerlee Heritage Trust in West Canal Street is museum of industrial and social history. Working machinery and tramway, excavations of 1835 ironworks and restored canal.

Colzium House Ec
Mansion, 19th century, set in landscaped gardens, contains local history museum. Banqueting hall and two rooms displaying paintings by local artists can be seen. Woodland walks, children's zoo, ruins of castle demolished by Cromwell and picnic areas.

Doune Castle Ef
Moat surrounds well-preserved 14th-century castle of four floors. Gatehouse tower 95ft high. Walk along walls affords good views of surrounding country. Doune Motor Museum contains veteran, vintage and post-vintage cars.

Dumbarton Bc
Castle built above River Clyde in 5th century – only Wallace Tower and some 17th and 18th-century fortifications remain, as well as sundial given to town by Mary, Queen of Scots. Denny Ship Model Experiment Tank is world's oldest – visitors can see wax hull forms being made.

Finlaystone House and Garden Ac
Ten-acre estate has formal garden, woodland walks, picnic sites, play areas and visitor centre. Tours of house can be arranged.

Fintry Dd
Four hamlets in Endrick Valley. Views across Clyde Valley from Lennoxtown road. Loup of Fintry, 90ft waterfall, 3 miles east.

Gartocharn Bd
Footpath up nearby Duncryne Hill allows views of Loch Lomond and its islands.

Glasgow Victoria Park and Fossil Grove Cb
Park contains formal flower garden, arboretum and Fossil Grove, with fossilised stumps of 330-million-year-old trees.

Glasgow Zoo Db
Zoo specialises in big cats and reptiles. Children's showground, long walks, picnic areas.

Haggs Castle, Glasgow Cb
Children's museum in 1585 castle, showing daily life over last 400 years. Landscaped gardens include knot garden.

RIVERSIDE RUIN *The River Clyde flows past the remains of Dumbarton Castle's lower ramparts.*

Inversnaid Af
Views from above Snaid Burn ravine take in 'Arrochar Alps' and narrows of Loch Lomond. From waterfall above tiny harbour, footbridge leads south along West Highland Way, beside loch.

Kirkintilloch Dc
Church of St Mary, built 1644, now restored as centre for exhibitions. Next door is museum of domestic life.

Loch Ard Forest Be
Wildlife includes roe deer, red deer, foxes, wildcats and swans. Large choice of forest trails.

Loch Katrine Bf
Reservoir in Trossachs, surrounded by woodlands. Visitor centre at Trossachs Pier is starting point for walk through woods and departure point for rides in turn-of-the-century steamer.

Loch Lomond Ag-Ad
Largest loch in Scotland – 23 miles long, up to 5 miles wide, and 630ft at deepest point – with 30 islands. Pleasure boats and paddle steamer offer rides.

Luss Ae
Village of stone cottages with rose gardens, next to Loch Lomond. 1875 church has ancient stone font and medieval effigy of St Kessog.

Mugdock Country Park Cc
Ancient woods, open moorland, lochside marshes and remains of 14th-century Mugdock Castle in this 500 acre park.

Old Kilpatrick Bc
Reputed to be birthplace of St Patrick – hence name. Church built 1812 on site of older one.

Paisley Bb
Paisley Museum and Art Gallery houses world famous collection of Paisley shawls and traces development of Paisley pattern. Also collections of local history, natural history, ceramics and Scottish painting. Sma' Shot Cottages restored as typical Victorian millworkers' houses and Weaver's Cottage. Paisley Abbey founded in 1163 – much 14th and 15th century architecture remains, as well as stained-glass windows and one of finest church organs in Europe. Coats Observatory, built 1882, is now one of Scotland's best-equipped observatories.

THREAD MILL *A cotton mill recalls Paisley's days as the world's largest thread-manufacturing centre.*

Palacerigg Country Park Ec
Wildlife such as roe deer, badgers, foxes and stoats roam park, while bison, wolves and lynxes are kept in paddocks. Deer park and children's farm with rare breeds.

Pollok Country Park Cb
Impressive 8000-piece Burrell collection is main attraction of this 360 acre parkland. Items include ceramics, bronzes, Oriental jade, tapestries, silver and glassware, furniture, needlework, prints and paintings. Pollock House, Georgian mansion, has one of finest Spanish painting collections in Britain, with works by Goya and El Greco. Country park centred on Old Stables Courtyard beside a weir on White Cart Water. Interpretation centre illustrates history and wildlife of park.

Queen's View Cd
Viewpoint 12 miles north-west of Glasgow from which Queen Victoria gained her first view of Loch Lomond. Forestry exhibition in visitor centre. Waymarked trails begin at Allean car park, west. Steep circular trail leads down through woods, along lochside.

Rowardennan Forest Ae
Forestry Commission car park starting point for walks through woodland offering views of surrounding mountains. Part of Queen Elizabeth Forest Park.

Strathyre Forest Cg
Visitor centre, situated in extensive picnic area, has display that illustrates working forest. Variety of walks. Part of Queen Elizabeth Forest Park.

BALLAD OF LOCH LOMOND *A Bonnie Prince Charlie supporter awaiting execution is said to have written the song.*

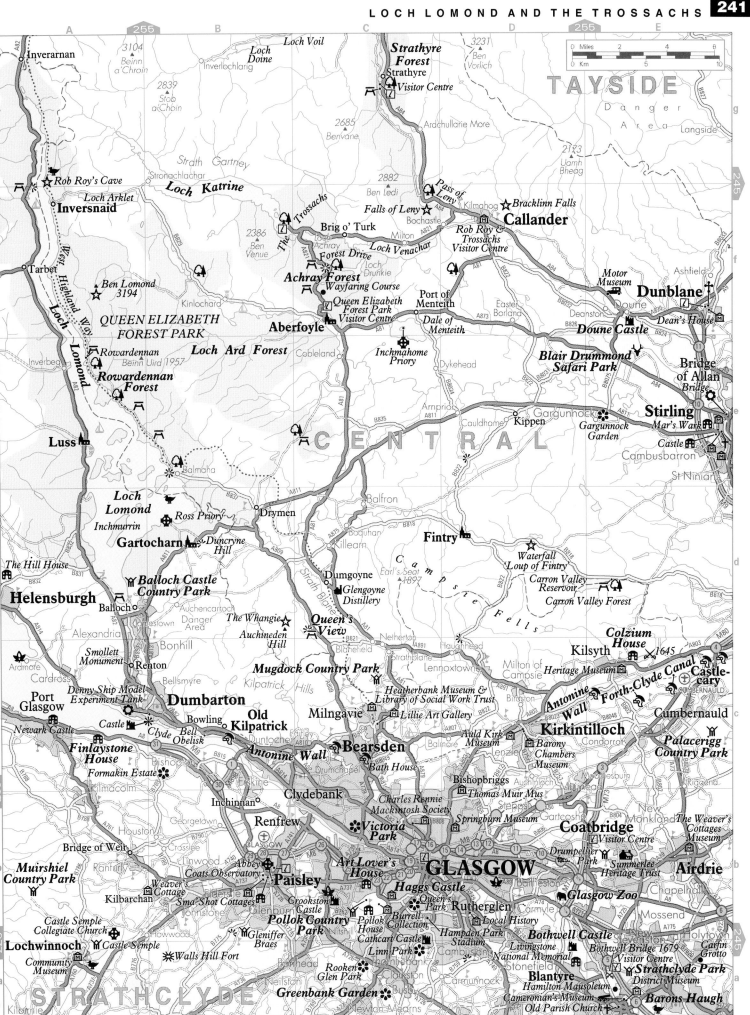

TAYSIDE

Danger Area

Inverarnan

3104 Beinn a'Chroin

Loch Voil

Loch Doine

Inverlochlarig

Strathyre Forest

Strathyre

Visitor Centre

3231 Ben Vorlich

Langside

Ardchullarie More

2839 Stob a'Choin

2685 Benvane

2882

Loch Katrine

Strath Gartney

Stronachlachar

Ben Ledi

Pass of Leny

Kilmahog

Bracklinn Falls

Rob Roy's Cave

Loch Arklet

Inversnaid

2386 Ben Venue

2173 Uamh Bheag

Falls of Leny

Callander

The Trossachs

Brig o' Turk

Milton

Rob Roy & Trossachs Visitor Centre

Tarbet

Ben Lomond 3194

Kinlochard

Forest Drive

Loch Achray

Loch Venachar

Bochastle

Loch Drunkie

Port of Menteith

Motor Museum

Dunblane

Achray Forest

Wayfaring Course

Easter Borland

Doune

Deanston

Dean's House

QUEEN ELIZABETH FOREST PARK

Queen Elizabeth Forest Park Visitor Centre

Aberfoyle

Dale of Menteith

Doune Castle

Loch Ard Forest

Cobleland

Inchmahome Priory

Dykehead

Blair Drummond Safari Park

Bridge of Allan

Bridge

Rowardennan

Beinn Uird 1957

Rowardennan Forest

Arnprior

Cauldhame

Kippen

Gargunnock

Gargunnock Garden

Stirling

Mar's Wark

Castle

Cambusbarron

C E N T R A L

St Ninians

Luss

Balmaha

Loch Lomond

Inchmurrin

Ross Priory

Drymen

Balfron

Fintry

Waterfall 'Loup of Fintry'

Colzium House

Gartocharn

Duncryne Hill

Killearn

Earl's Seat 1897

Carron Valley Reservoir

Carron Valley Forest

Kilsyth

1645

The Hill House

Dumgoyne

Glengoyne Distillery

Campsie Fells

Heritage Museum

Helensburgh

Balloch

Balloch Castle Country Park

Auchencarroch

Danger Area

The Whangie

Auchineden Hill

Queen's View

Blanefield

Strathblane

Netherton

Haughhead

Milton of Campsie

Lennoxtown

Antonine Wall

Forth-Clyde Canal

Castlecary

CUMBERNAULD

Cumbernauld

Alexandria

Bonhill

Bellsmyre

Mugdock Country Park

Kilpatrick Hills

Birdston

Kirkintilloch

Condorrat

Palacerigg Country Park

Smollett Monument

Renton

Heatherbank Museum & Library of Social Work Trust

Auld Kirk Museum

Lenzie

Cardross

Ardmore

Denny Ship Model Experiment Tank

Dumbarton

Bowling

Old Kilpatrick

Duntocher

Faifley

Drumchapel

Bearsden

Lillie Art Gallery

Bath House

Balmore

Barony Chambers Museum

Meiklehill

Auchinloch

New Monkland

The Weaver's Cottages Museum

Port Glasgow

Castle

Bell Obelisk

Clyde

Antonine Wall

Milngavie

Bishopbriggs

Thomas Muir Mus

Stepps

Gartcosh

Muirhead

Riggend

Coatbridge

Visitor Centre

Newark Castle

Finlaystone House

Bishopton

Formakin Estate

Clydebank

Charles Rennie Mackintosh Society

Springburn Museum

Drumpellier Park

Summerlee Heritage Trust

Airdrie

Kilmacolm

Inchinnan

Renfrew

Victoria Park

Bridge of Weir

Georgetown

Muirshiel Country Park

Houston

Crosslee

Tinwood

Ranfurly

Linwood

Abbey

Coats Observatory

Art Lover's House

GLASGOW

Haggs Castle

Battlefield

Glasgow Zoo

Chapelhall

Mossend

Holytown

Kilbarchan

Weaver's Cottage

Sma' Shot Cottages

Paisley

Crookston Castle

Glenburn

Queen's Park

Rutherglen

Local History

Carmyle

Carfin Grotto

Lochwinnoch

Castle Semple Collegiate Church

Castle Semple

Gleniffer Braes

Pollok Country Park

Nitshill

Pollok House

Burrell Collection

Cathcart Castle

Hampden Park Stadium

Hampden Park

Bothwell Castle

Livingstone National Memorial

Bothwell Bridge 1679

Visitor Centre

Strathclyde Park

Community Museum

Walls Hill Fort

Linn Park

Cambuslang

Stonefield

District Museum

Barons Haugh

Barrhead

Rooken Glen Park

Clarkson

Busby

Carmunnock

Hamilton Mausoleum

Blantyre

Cameronian's Museum

Old Parish Church

Kilbirnie

Greenbank Garden

Neilston

Newton Mearns

S T R A T H C L Y D E

West Highland Way

Kinlochard

Inchcailloch

The Barras Eb
World-famous weekend market founded 100 years ago, home to more than 1000 traders.

Blythswood Square Bc
Built round wooded gardens, this was the British starting point for the Monte Carlo Rally. At No. 7 lived Madeleine Smith, accused in 1857 of poisoning her lover in the most notorious of all Glasgow murder cases.

SCOTLAND'S SECOND CAPITAL

Much of the beauty of Scotland's largest city had disappeared under years of smoke and grime, until modern thinking restored the magnificent mix of Victorian elegance and revolutionary Art Nouveau. Against this backdrop, the famed art galleries and museums of Glasgow have ensured that its cultural heritage now stands alongside Athens, Florence and Paris.

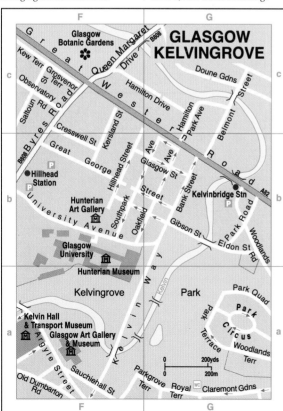

CULTURE CITY *Glasgow's Art Gallery and Museum has collections of paintings and sculpture as comprehensive as any in Europe. Other exhibits include furniture, silver, pottery, glass, porcelain, and European arms and armour.*

Buchanan Street Cc
Upmarket shopping street gives glimpses of opulent past. Elegant 1827 glass-roofed Argyll Arcade, 1891 Clydesdale Bank made of multicoloured sandstone, and replica of an 1851 pendulum swinging from atrium roof.

Carlton Place Ca
City's finest riverside terrace. Restored Georgian buildings look out across public gardens.

Citizens' Theatre ♨ Ca
Originally opened as a music hall in 1878, now a listed building.

City Chambers Dc
Massive 1888 Italian Renaissance-style building with a 240ft tower and opulent interiors full of mosaics and maiolica. The banqueting hall has murals showing the city's history.

Custom House Quay Cb
Part of the Clyde Walkway, designed to give new life to the riverside, enhanced by the suspension bridge and 1848 clipper SV *Carrick* moored nearby.

George Square Cc
Oldest of Glasgow's public squares and heart of the city, named after George III. Laid out at end of 18th century. Probably has more statues than any other square in Scotland, including those of Queen Victoria, Prince Albert, Sir Walter Scott, Robert Burns, William Gladstone, James Watt and Sir Robert Peel.

Glasgow Art Gallery and Museum 🏛 Fa
Britain's finest civic collection of British and European art and a museum featuring a famous array of European arms and armour, Egyptian archaeology and an area devoted to Scottish wildlife.

Glasgow Botanic Gardens ❀ Fc
Covering 40 acres, gardens are famous for plant collections, especially begonias and orchids. Imposing domed glasshouse, the Kibble Palace, houses National Tree Ferns Collection. Herb garden and chronological border showing when plants were first introduced to Britain.

Glasgow Cathedral ✝ Ec
Most complete survivor of the great Gothic churches of south Scotland. Built on or near site of church built in 6th century by St Mungo – the founder of Glasgow. Mainly 13th century, though a fragment dates from late 12th century. Outstanding feature is the fan vaulting around St Mungo's tomb in the crypt. Much fine work in choir, including 15th-century stone screen.

Glasgow Cross Db
Topped by heraldic unicorn, a 1929 replica of the medieval original where Bonnie Prince Charlie was proclaimed Regent.

Glasgow Green Da
A public park since 12th century. Bonnie Prince Charlie reviewed his troops here in 1745 after retreat from England. Monument to Lord Nelson erected 1806 is 144ft high. Memorial to engineer James Watt.

Glasgow School of Art Bd
Completed in 1907, the masterpiece of Charles Rennie Mackintosh who was responsible for everything from the striking exteriors to the interior furniture and fittings.

Glasgow University Fb
A visitor centre gives tours around pinnacled Gothic buildings of this second-oldest university in Scotland, founded 1451. Tower of the main building has magnificent views of the city.

Hunterian Art Gallery 🏛 Fb
The Charles Rennie Mackintosh collection has reconstructions of the architect's house fitted with his own furniture. Main gallery includes Scottish paintings from the 18th century to the present day, and Old Masters.

Hunterian Museum 🏛 Fb
Glasgow's oldest museum, opened in 1807, has a major coin collection going back 2000 years, a history of Glasgow University, fascinating archaeology and geology displays, and a science and astronomy building.

Hutchesons' Hospital Dc
One of the city's most elegant buildings, founded in the 17th century by the brothers George and Thomas Hutcheson, whose statues from the original hospital adorn the façade.

International Stock Exchange Cc
A 'French Venetian' building of 1877, with visitors' gallery.

Merchants' House Cc
Handsome 1874 building with carved female figures supporting bow windows. Home of Glasgow

Chamber of Commerce and fir Merchants' Hall with ancie relics and good stained glass.

Merchants' Steeple Ca
All that remains of old Merchant House built 1651-9. Details i Gothic and Renaissance styl rising in four towers to 164ft.

GOTHIC STRENGTH *St Mungo's Cathedral, with its central tower.*

Mitchell Library Ad
Europe's largest public referenc library has over one millio volumes, including Celtic litera ture, the history of the city an probably the world's larges Robert Burns collection.

Necropolis Ec
Cemetery of 1833 has numerou tombs of illustrious Glaswegian and best view of cathedral.

Park Circus Ga
Curved Victorian terraces on lofty site over Kelvingrove Par with fine views of the university the towering cranes of the Clyd and the Renfrewshire Hills.

The People's Palace 🏛 Ea
Three-storey red-stone building completed in 1897 as a cultura centre for Glasgow's East End. A social history museum with col lections from 1175 to the presen day covering the city's politics industry, art and popular culture It has a purse and ring tha belonged to Mary, Queen o Scots, and an organ built by James Watt. Adjoining Winter Garden i a conservatory housing palms ferns and variety of exotic plants

Provand's Lordship 🏛 Ec
Oldest house in city built 1471 probably for priest in charge o nearby hospital. Mary, Queen o Scots is thought to have stayed here in 1566. Now a museum with furniture and domestic displays dating from 1500 to 1918.

Royal Bank of Scotland Cc
Grecian-style building designed 1827 by Archibald Elliott. Ionic portico on central block linked to two symmetrical buildings by archways with Ionic columns.

Royal Highland Fusiliers Museum ⚔ Ad
Reveals the exploits of the Royal Scots Fusiliers, the Highland Light Infantry and the Royal Highland Fusiliers – formed when the first two merged. Exhibits include medals, uniforms and numerous photographs.

GLASGOW KELVINGROVE

St Andrew's Cathedral Cb
Roman Catholic cathedral built in 1816, one of the city's earliest examples of Gothic Revival-style architecture.

St David's 'Ramshorn' Church † Dc
Impressive church built in 1824. Graveyard contains ornate tombs of many notable citizens including grave of David Dale, creator of New Lanark.

St Enoch's Station Cb
Gem of toytown architecture; most striking station remaining from city's original underground built in 1896, now a travel centre adjoining modern station.

St Vincent Street Church † Ac
Fine example of the work of Alexander 'Greek' Thomson, built in his classical Grecian style in 1859

with magnificent Ionic porticoes, an elaborate tower and brightly painted interior columns.

Scotland Street School Museum of Education Aa
Two reconstructed classrooms in a former school designed by architect Charles Rennie Mackintosh, which opened in 1906.

Stirling's Library Cc
Originally the mansion of 'Tobacco Lord' William Cunningham, built 1775. New building designed by David Hamilton in 1832, adding massive portico and clock tower. Handsome interior.

Templeton Carpet Factory Ea
Exotic Victorian factory designed in the style of the Doge's Palace in Venice with colourful bricks and tiles, arches, pinnacles, turrets, and pointed windows.

The Tenement House Ad
Museum celebrating the lives of ordinary people through the belongings of this tenement flat's occupants from 1911 to 1965, which have been left undisturbed in bedroom, parlour, kitchen and bathroom.

Theatre Royal Cd
Fine Victorian theatre, elegantly restored as home of Scottish Opera. Used by Scottish Ballet.

Tolbooth Steeple Db
Seven storeys and 126ft high; the sole remnant of a 1626 tolbooth. Emblems of St Mungo and royalty decorate lintels.

The Trades House Cc
Glasgow's only major building by Robert Adam, opened 1794. Silk frieze in banqueting hall shows work of city's historic trades.

Transport Museum Fa
Displays of every kind of transport, from horse-drawn vehicles to fire engines and historic Scottish locomotives. Reproduction of a typical 1938 Glasgow street, a collection of model ships and a walk-in car showroom.

JOURNEY'S END A painted gypsy wagon now finds rest in the Museum of Transport in Kelvin Hall.

Tron Steeple Db
Forming an arch over the pavement is the only remnant of a 1637 church, accidentally burnt down by drunken members of the local Hell Fire Club. Church rebuilt behind.

Virginia Street Cb
Built around 1819; the former Tobacco Exchange and Sugar Exchange at No. 33 has a 'pulpit' high on an inner wall from which the auctioneer called for bids when selling shipments newly arrived from America.

Willow Tearoom Bd
Finest of a series designed by Charles Rennie Mackintosh for caterer Miss Kate Cranston. Reopened as a tearoom with reproduction Mackintosh furniture and restored Art Nouveau decorations.

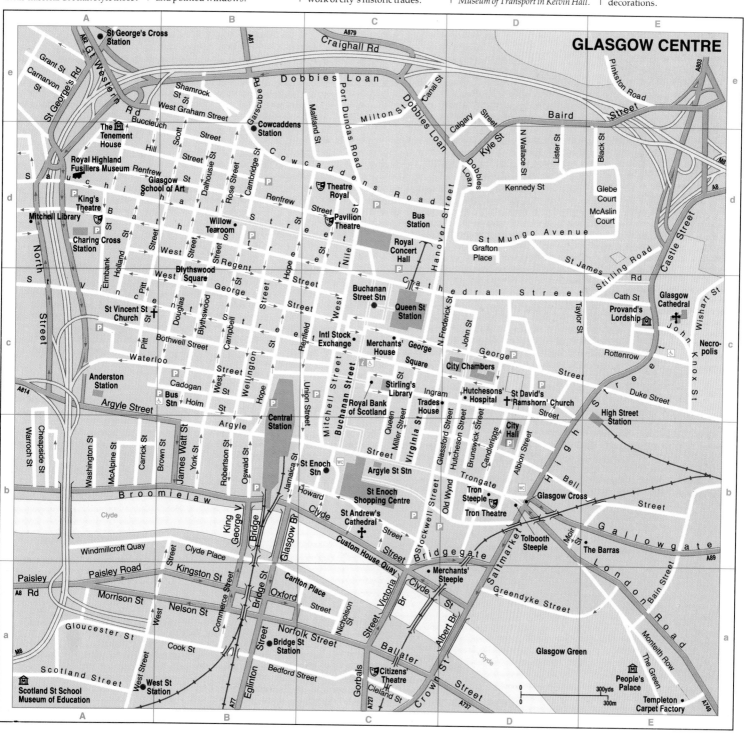

Alva Glen ⚓ Be
Gorge with waterfalls cuts into treeless flanks of Ochil Hills. Approached by a zigzag walk from village of Alva with views of the Forth.

Bannockburn ⚓✕ Be
Village, dating from 19th century, near site of 1314 battle when Robert Bruce's army secured Scottish independence by defeating Edward II's forces. Battle commemorated at Bannock Heritage Centre, on site of Bruce's headquarters. Statue near car park.

Blairlogie ⚓ Be
Village on south slopes of Ochil Hills. Dumyat rises to 1373ft nearby, providing fine views over surrounding villages. Car park on east side is starting point for walks to nearby villages and into Ochils.

Burleigh Castle 🏰 Ef
Ruined fortress, dating from 15th century, was once a Balfour stronghold. Fortress's keep, curtain wall, tower house and gatehouse still remain.

Cambuskenneth Abbey ✠ Be
Abbey founded by David I in 1147, now in ruins. Western doorway and 13th to 14th-century bell tower survive.

Castle Campbell 🏰 Ce
Once headquarters for Earls of Argyll, now in ruins. Courtyard, Great Hall and barrel roof of third floor well worth seeing.

Castlecary ⚑ Ac
Remains of 15th-century tower house. Roman stronghold nearby guarded Antonine Wall, northern boundary of Roman Empire.

Charlestown ⚓ Dd
Model village built between 1756 and 1758 by Earl of Elgin, using wealth from local limestone, coal and salt. Small harbour. White-painted houses surround green.

AROUND THE LOWER FORTH

Pleasure craft now frequent the once-bustling ports of the many small towns and villages that line the banks of the Forth. The handsome 17th and 18th-century houses flanking the winding streets are reminders of former prosperity brought by the coal industry. To the north lie the Ochil Hills, whose wooded slopes provide plenty of opportunities for naturalists and walkers.

Culross ✠⚑🏛☑ Cd
Most complete example of Scottish burgh of 16th and 17th centuries. Coal mining has provided town prosperity. Visitor centre in 17th-century town house has audiovisual presentation. Mine owner George Bruce's Culross Palace, finished 1611, is fine example of rich merchant's home.

CASTLE RUIN *Castle Campbell stands on a spur between two ravines.*

Dalgety Bay ✠ Ed
View from settlement takes in impressive panorama of Firth of Forth, and distinctive landmarks of Edinburgh. Best viewpoint is St Bridget's Kirkyard. Ruined church, dating from 1244, survives as National Monument. Path from church to sandy cove.

Dunblane ✝🏛☑ Af
Town with 16th-century bridge spanning Allan Water. Dunblane Cathedral, mostly 13th century with Norman tower in nave, has six stained-glass south windows and fine interior wood carving. Dean's House of 1624 now houses museum of local history.

Dunfermline ✠🏛✿ Dd
Abbey is originally Norman, with many later styles. Church of 19th century contains grave of Robert Bruce, 14th-century king of Scotland. Birthplace cottage of US millionaire Andrew Carnegie now museum. Library has Burns memorabilia collection.

Falkirk 🏛 Bd
Town made rich by 19th-century iron working. Museum has displays on local archaeology, industry and 1298 battle when English gained brief control of Scotland. Roman fort on well-preserved section of Antonine Wall. Mariner Leisure Centre has pool, wave machine and other amusements.

Forth-Clyde Canal Ac
Canal, closed 1963, now offers recreation. Towing path provides walks through town and country. Excursions by canal boat start from Stables Inn on Glasgow Road near Kirkintilloch.

Gartmorn Dam Country Park ⚑ Ce
Park rich in bird life surrounds Scotland's oldest surviving reser-

voir, built 1713 for Alloa's industries. Former pump house is information centre.

Grangemouth 🏛☑ Cd
Town of low stone houses adjoins one of Europe's largest oil refineries. Museum illustrates town's development as port and shipbuilding centre. The world's first commercially successful steamship was completed here in 1802.

Great Scots Visitor Centre ☑ Cg
In village of Auchterarder, centre has weaving display and last factory steam engine in Scotland. 'Great Scots' display illustrates Scottish history using computerised lighting and special effects projected on huge map.

Inchcolm ✠ Ed
Island in Firth of Forth with ruin of St Colm's Abbey. Includes well-preserved 13th-century octagonal chapter house. Visited by boat from Hawes Pier in Queensferry during summer.

Inverkeithing 🏛 Ed
Old Royal Burgh and modern housing estates separated by steep hillsides. Town's chief activity is ship breaking. Painted Mercat Cross set up 1393. Tower of St Peter's Church, built where St Erat began converting pagans in 744, dates from 13th century.

Kinnesswood ⚓🏛 Ef
Cottage in village is birthplace of 18th-century poet Michael Bruce. Now a museum commemorating man known as 'Gentle Poet of Loch Leven'.

Kinross ✿ Ef
Town on loch with 17th-century tolbooth decorated by Robert Adam. Town cross still displays iron collars that held criminals. Formal gardens of Kinross House noted for yew hedges and roses.

Loch Leven 🦆🏰 Ef
Nature reserve of note for ornithologists. Two islands: St Serf's has 16th-century priory ruin, and Castle Island has Lochleven Castle from which Mary, Queen of Scots made her 1568 escape from imprisonment. Boats go regularly to Castle Island.

Menstrie Castle 🏛 Be
Well-restored 16th-century castle was birthplace of poet and statesman Sir William Alexander, 1567-1640, initiator of British colonisation of Nova Scotia. Nova Scotia Exhibition Room has coats of arms of 109 baronets on display.

Monarch Deer Farm ⚓ Df
Besides red deer herd, farm also has waterfall, waterfowl, rare breeds, riverside walk and picnic

area. Farm shop sells local produce, venison and crafts goods; café sells farmhouse teas.

North Queensferry ⚓ Ed
Town named after Queen Margaret, who used ferry in 11th century. View of 512ft towers of Forth Road Bridge and arching girders of rail bridge. Forth Yacht Marina by bridges.

Ochil Hills Woodland Park ⚑⚓ Be
Mixed woodland including oak, ash, birch and yew. Once part of gardens of long-vanished Alva House, seat of Sir John Erskine.

Polkemmet Country Park ⚑ Cb
Converted stables and barn, once part of nearby mansion, form focal point for woodland walks.

Rumbling Bridge Gorge ✿ De
River Devon flows through 120ft deep chasm crossed by double bridge – lower built in 1713, upper in 1816. Riverside walk leads upriver from bridge – picnic areas have been laid out along walk.

Stirling 🏛🏰⚓⚑ Ae
Stirling Castle stands on 250ft high rock. Most of the main buildings date from 15th and 16th centuries. Church of the Holy Rude dates from 1414, though oldest parts of existing structure date from 1460. Monument commemorating Sir William Wallace's 1297 victory over English was erected in the 19th century. Smith

MUSEUM PIECE *Stirling's castle houses the Museum of the Argyll and Sutherland Highlanders.*

Art Gallery and Museum has a programme of exhibitions on art, history, craft and design. The MacRoberts Arts Centre comprises 500 seat theatre, art gallery and studio.

Tillicoultry 🏛✿ Ce
Clock Mill, dating from 19th century, now information centre, with display of looms and weaving equipment; also craft workshop. Mill Heritage Trail leads to mills in surrounding countryside.

Vane Farm Nature Centre 🦆 Ee
RSPB reserve overlooking Loch Leven is home to many bird species. Old farm building converted for observation has telescopes. Public hide and nature trail along loch.

Westquarter Dovecote Cc
Dovecote dating from 17th century built to house pigeons when they were important meat source. Above doorway is heraldic panel dated 1647, with Sir William Livingstone's coat of arms.

BURGH PORT *The red-roofed houses and narrow streets of Culross, whose fortunes were founded on sea trade and coal.*

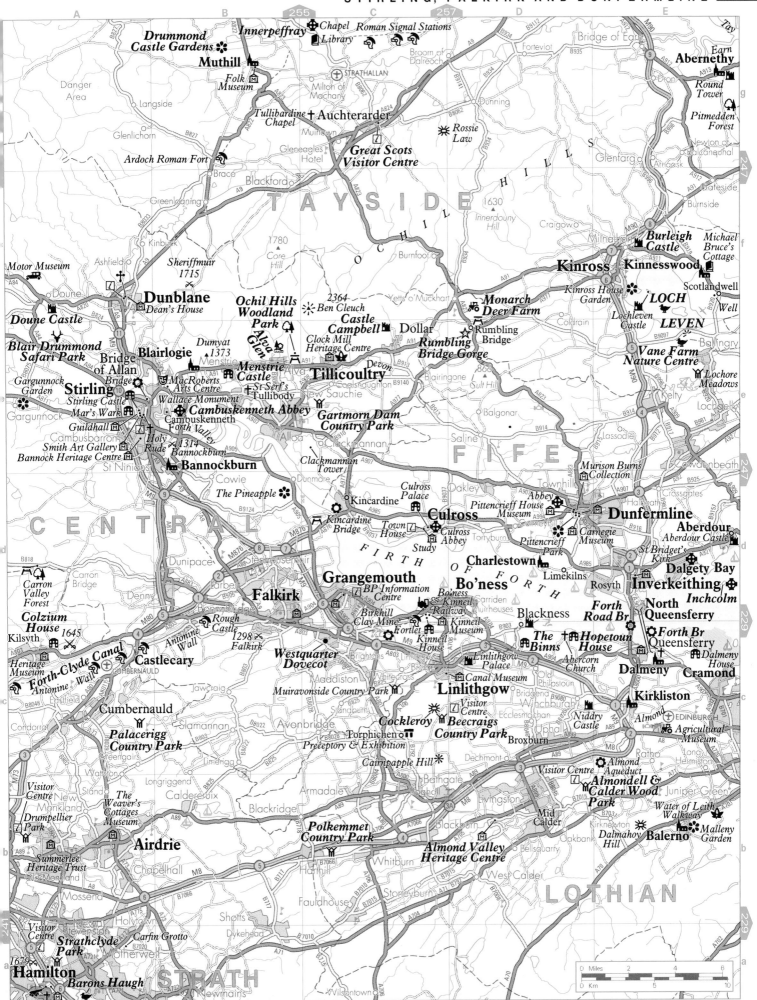

A map of the Stirling, Falkirk and Dunfermline region showing the following labelled locations:

Drummond Castle Gardens
Innerpeffray — Chapel, Library, Roman Signal Stations
Muthill — Folk Museum
Abernethy — Round Tower, Pitmedden Forest
Danger Area
Langside
Tullibardine Chapel — **Auchterarder**
Ardoch Roman Fort
Rossie Law
Great Scots Visitor Centre
Gleneagles Hotel
Blackford
Broom of Dalreoch

TAYSIDE

OCHIL HILLS

Sheriffmuir 1715
Motor Museum
Doune
Dunblane — Dean's House
Doune Castle
Blair Drummond Safari Park
Bridge of Allan
Blairlogie
Gargunnock Garden
Stirling — Stirling Castle, Mar's Work, Guildhall, Holy Rude, Smith Art Gallery, Bannock Heritage Centre
St Ninians
Bannockburn — 1314 Bannockburn
Cowie
The Pineapple

Ochil Hills Woodland Park
Alva Glen
Dumyat 1373
Menstrie Castle — St Serf's, Tullibody
Tillicoultry
Cambuskenneth Abbey — Cambuskenneth, Forth Valley
Gartmorn Dam Country Park
Clackmannan Tower
Clackmannan

Ben Cleuch 2364
Castle Campbell — Dollar
Clock Mill Heritage Centre
Rumbling Bridge Gorge — Rumbling Bridge
New Sauchie

Monarch Deer Farm
Kinross House Garden
Kinross
Burleigh Castle
Kinnesswood — Michael Bruce's Cottage
Scotlandwell, Well
LOCH LEVEN — Lochleven Castle
Vane Farm Nature Centre
Lochore Meadows

FIFE

Saline
Balgonar

Murison Burns Collection

Culross — Culross Palace, Culross Abbey, Town House, Study
Kincardine
Kincardine Bridge

Pittencrieff House Museum
Abbey
Pittencrieff Park
Carnegie Museum
Dunfermline
Aberdour — Aberdour Castle
St Bridget's Kirk
Dalgety Bay
Inverkeithing
Inchcolm
North Queensferry
Forth Road Br
Forth Br
Queensferry
Dalmeny — Dalmeny House
Cramond

FIRTH OF FORTH

Charlestown
Limekilns
Rosyth
Blackness
The Binns
Hopetoun House
Abercorn Church

Bo'ness — Bo'ness & Kinneil Railway, Kinneil Clay Mine, Kinneil Museum, Fortlet, Kinneil House
Grangemouth — BP Information Centre, Birkhill Clay Mine

CENTRAL

Carron Valley Forest
Carron Bridge
Colzium House
Kilsyth 1645
Heritage Museum
Castlecary
Antonine Wall
Forth-Clyde Canal
Dunipace
Larbert
Denny
Falkirk — Rough Castle, 1298 Falkirk
Westquarter Dovecot
Bonnybridge
Brightons

Linlithgow — Linlithgow Palace, Canal Museum, Visitor Centre
Old Philipstoun
Cockleroy
Beecraigs Country Park
Torphichen — Preceptory & Exhibition
Cairnpapple Hill
Muiravonside Country Park

Niddry Castle
Winchburgh
Ecclesmachan
Broxburn
Uphall
Kirkliston
EDINBURGH
Agricultural Museum
Ratho
Almond Aqueduct
Almondell & Calder Wood Park
Visitor Centre
Water of Leith Walkway
Dalmahoy Hill
Balerno — Malleny Garden
Kirknewton
Juniper Green

Cumbernauld
Palacerig Country Park
Slamannan
Avonbridge
Armadale
Blackridge

Airdrie
New Monkland — Visitor Centre
Drumpellier Park
The Weaver's Cottages Museum
Caldercruix
Greengairs
Watston
Longriggend
Limerigg

Polkemmet Country Park
Harthill
Whitburn
Almond Valley Heritage Centre
Bathgate
Blackburn
Livingston
Mid Calder
West Calder
Oakbank
Dechmont

LOTHIAN

Summerlee Heritage Trust
Old Monkland
Mossend
Holytown
Shotts
Dykehead
Fauldhouse
Stoneyburn

Carfin Grotto
Strathclyde Park
1679
Hamilton
Barons Haugh
Motherwell
Newmains
Carluke
Wilsontown

STRATH...

Scale: Miles 0 2 4 6
Km 0 5 10

Aberdour ⛪ Aa
Ruined, 14th-century Aberdour Castle stands among formal gardens dating from 16th century. Stone dovecote, 52ft deep well. Town is popular seaside resort. On Inchcolm Island, 1½ miles from coast, stand ruins of Abbey of St Columba, founded 1123.

Abernethy ⛪ Ad
Village, once Pictish royal capital, dominated by 11th-century round tower 74ft high – one of only two such towers on Scottish mainland. At base is 7th-century stone with Pictish carvings. View from top of tower takes in village, River Tay and Carse of Gowrie.

MYSTIC MARKS *Pictish carvings of 7th century on Abernethy church.*

Anstruther ⛪ Ec
Scottish Fisheries Museum in old town and ecclesiastical buildings, illustrates history of fishing industry. Exhibits include aquarium, reconstructed turn-of-the-century fisherman's cottage, old fishing vessels and North Carr lightship – now a maritime museum. Oldest building of museum is 16th-century Abbot's Lodging. Village has 17th and 18th-century houses in Castle and Shore streets. Arch made from whale jawbone behind house in East Forth Street, Cellardyke.

Balcaskie ⛪ Ec
Classical-style house designed by Sir William Bruce in 17th century. Terraced garden, parkland with splendid view of Bass Rock rising 350ft from sea.

Balmerino Abbey ⛪ Ce
Hilltop ruins of Cistercian abbey founded by Alexander II and his mother Queen Ermyngarde, who was buried beneath high altar. The gardens contain a Spanish chestnut some 425 years old.

Burntisland ⛪ Ba
Sixteenth-century parish church was where Authorised Version of the Bible was proposed in 1601. Inside are panels with paintings of nautical devices and three-sided 17th-century oak pew. Burntisland Edwardian Fair is reconstructed as it was in 1910. Includes local history gallery. Wide sandy beach backed by promenade. Somerville Street has some 17th-century town houses.

Cambo Country Park ⛪ Ed
Park offers woodland walks, adventure play area, nature trail and tame farm animals at Cuddle Corner. Safe, sandy beach has rock pools and birds such as herons and gannets.

ROYAL AND ANCIENT FIFE

The Firth of Forth, the Firth of Tay and the North Sea border Fife on three sides, providing one of Britain's finest stretches of coastline. Between the two great rivers lies a land of gentle hills, cut by the River Eden flowing eastwards to St Andrews. Named after Scotland's patron saint, St Andrews is the home of the world's oldest golf club, the Royal and Ancient, founded in 1754.

Cambo Gardens ✿ Fd
Victorian gardens of 2 acres beside burn spanned by bridges. Lilac walk, box hedges, herbaceous borders, lily pond.

Ceres ⛪ Dd
Medieval Bishop's Bridge leads to Fife Folk Museum, housed in two weavers' cottages and 17th-century tolbooth weigh house. Exhibits portray domestic and agricultural past of Fife, including costumes and needlework. Ceres church, built 1806, has horseshoe gallery. Ceres burn spanned by 17th-century stone bridge. Number of 18th-century stone carvings by local stonemason, John Howie, can be seen around village, including one on wall of man holding jug – last Provost of Ceres, appointed 1578.

The Clink ⛪ Bd
Scenic walks through Pitmedden Forest. Mixture of coniferous and broadleaf trees and variety of shrubs. Views of farming country and Lomond Hills beyond.

Craigtoun Country Park ⛪ Dd
Fifty-acre park of lawns, pastures and woodlands laid out around Melville House, now hospital. Includes Italian garden and Dutch 'village' on island in ornamental lake. Miniature railway, crazy golf, trampolines, boating and picnic areas.

Crail ✝ ⛪ Fc
Fresh crabs, lobsters and sea urchins can be bought at harbour, built of uncemented red boulders. Marketgate lined with 17th and 18th-century houses. Early 16th-century tolbooth has gilded salmon weather vane and Dutch-cast bell of 1520. Collegiate church dates from 12th century and contains Pictish stone slab with cross carved on it. Crail Museum and Heritage Centre outlines history.

Cupar ✿ Cd
Hopetoun Monument 100ft high stands just outside town, built 1826 in memory of 4th Earl of Hopetoun, commander of British Army in Peninsular War. Main street lined with 18th-century houses, and mercat cross dated 1683 stands at one end. South of town is Scotstarvit, five-storey tower built 1579, once home of statesman Sir John Scott.

Dura Den ⛪ Dd
Wooded gorge with ruins of linen and jute mills on banks of stream flowing into River Eden. Near bridge over stream are ruined Dairsie Castle, mostly 16th century, and church dating from 1621 with gargoyles.

Dysart ⛪ Cb
Original buildings restored and new ones built in same style to re-create 17th-century atmosphere in Dysart. Tolbooth was powder magazine in Civil War.

Earlshall Castle and Gardens ⛪ De
House, 1546, with panelled rooms containing fine furniture and porcelain. Painted ceiling in 50ft Long Gallery. Collection of Scottish weapons. Walled garden, yew topiary, nature trail and picnic facilities.

East Wemyss ⛪ ☆ Cb
Red-sandstone castle on cliff top at village's north-eastern end said to be stronghold of Macduff thanes of Fife. Below castle are caves whose walls bear inscriptions indicating occupation from Bronze Age to medieval times. Court Cave has rough depiction of Viking god Thor.

Elie and Earlsferry ⛪ Db
Sheltered bay and red-sand beach are attractions of resort comprising old fishing port, Elie, and market town of Earlsferry. Kirk in Elie High Street dates from 1726. Views of resort and harbour from Chapel Ness, with remains of 1093 chapel. Kincraig Point to south is volcanic plug.

Falkland ⛪ Bc
Falkland Palace, begun in 15th century and completed in 16th, was favourite seat of James V and Mary, Queen of Scots. Grounds, laid out on Stuart plan, include oldest real tennis court in Britain, built 1539.

Heatherall Wood ⛪ Bd
Waymarked walk through early 19th-century wood. Rossie Drain, cut 1740 to drain Rossie loch, runs down western edge of wood.

Hill of Tarvit ⛪ Cd
Mansion expanded in 1904 from building of 1696. Rooms contain 18th-century French and English furniture, tapestries, porcelain and paintings. Walk from gardens leads to summit of Tarvit Hill, with 1897 monument to Queen Victoria's Diamond Jubilee.

Isle of May ⛪ Fb
Island in Firth of Forth with remains of a lighthouse in form of a coal-fired beacon dating from the 17th century.

Kellie Castle ⛪ Ec
Dating from 14th century but largely restored from late 19th century onwards. Includes notable plaster-work in most rooms.

Withdrawing room painted with scenes from reign of Charles II 4 acres of gardens.

Kinghorn ⛪ Ba
Seaside resort with sandy beach and stone buildings. East of town is monument marking spot where Alexander III was thrown from his horse and killed in 1286. Views of Forth.

Kirkcaldy ⛪ Bb
Kirkcaldy Museum and Art Gallery has displays covering history, industries and natural history of region. One display devoted to Adam Smith, political economist. Collection of 18th and 19th-century English and Scottish art. Several houses near harbour date from 15th century, and 17th-century houses in Sailors' Walk have been restored.

Letham Glen Park ⛪ Cc
Lawns and flowerbeds laid out beside a burn. Nature centre houses domestic animals, and information provided in park's wildlife. Trail starting from nature centre leads past remains of only ochre mine in Scotland, and through Sillerhole Glen.

Leuchars ⛪ De
Church of St Athernase has chancel and apse built by a Crusader, Saier de Quinci, in 13th century – one of the best examples of Norman architecture in Scotland. Interior carved with grotesque heads and Crusaders' crosses.

Lower Largo ⛪ Dc
Sandy, rocky beach of one-time fishing hamlet looks across Forth to Lammermuir hills. Statue to Alexander Selkirk, castaway who inspired *Robinson Crusoe*, on site of cottage where he was born in 1676. Upper Largo has 16th-century parish church with a carved Pictish stone in churchyard. Near church are remains of castle of Sir Andrew Wood, Scottish admiral, who died in 1515. Views of Firth from top of volcanic mound of Largo Law; ruins of 18th-century Largo House at bottom.

McDouall Stuart Museum ⛪ Cb
Commemorates explorer, John McDouall Stuart, born in 1815, who made first south-to-north crossing of Australia in 1861.

Markinch ✝ Bc
Church on small hill at end of main street dates from 1788, with late Norman tower, one of only five such towers in Scotland.

Newburgh ⛪ Bd
Prosperous houses of 18th-century merchants line main street of town. Near summit of Ormiston Hill is stump of Mac-Duff's Cross, which medieval murderers could touch to expiate themselves of crime. Remains of 12th-century Lindores Abbey stand on eastern outskirts of town. Image of bear – abbey's symbol – cut into hill opposite.

Norman's Law ☀ Ce
Complex Iron Age hill-fort on 1000ft hill. Comprises stone wall surrounding summit and wall on lower slopes.

CLIFFTOP RUIN *The impressive remains of St Andrews Cathedral; it was sacked in the Scottish Reformation.*

GABLED ELEGANCE *Dutch-style houses at Pittenweem harbour.*

Pittenweem ✿ ☆ Ec
Cave of 7th-century missionary, St Fillan, set in cliffs behind fishing port. Stone bed and spring where he drank still evident. Kellie Lodging, built late 16th-century, in High Street. Dutch-gabled houses surround harbour.

Ravenscraig Castle 🏰 Bb
Commissioned by James II in 1460, one of first castles in Britain built to withstand artillery. Four-storey tower house has 14ft thick walls in places.

St Andrews
🏛 ✝ ✿ ✿ ✿ ✓ Ed
Old Course of Royal and Ancient Golf Club dates from 15th century and is world's oldest. Club is headquarters of world golf and the supreme authority in golfing matters. British Golf Museum opposite has memorabilia dating back to origin of game. Remains of 12th-century cathedral on eastern edge of town. Church and tower of St Rule – who is reputed to have brought St Andrew's bones to Scotland – lie nearby. Ruins of castle, dating from 13th century, include bottle-shaped dungeon. University is oldest in Scotland, founded in 1411. St Salvator's College was founded in 1450, St Leonard's in 1512 and St Mary's in 1537. Town Hall of 19th century contains several relics from the tolbooth it replaced, including executioner's axe and stone dated 1565. West Port, built 1589, was old city entrance. Converted fishermen's houses contain the St Andrews Preservation Trust Museum, with displays on the city's social history. St Andrews Botanic Garden has peat garden and rock garden. St Andrews Sealife Centre is an aquarium, with shark display and outdoor seal pool. Leisure Centre on East Sands. Beaches offer traditional seaside recreation.

St Monance ⚓ ✝ Ec
Church of St Monan has foundation possibly dating from AD 400, but church dates from *c.* 1265. St Monan's cave is nearby.

Scottish Deer Centre ⚲ Cd
Many species of deer, including rare breeds, can be seen during ranger-led tour. Includes Audio-visual show and multi-media exhibition, outdoor adventure-land, maze, treetop walk, farm walk and winery.

Tay Bridges ✓ Ce and De
Newport-on-Tay gives fine views of 2 mile rail bridge – built 1883-7 and longest rail bridge in Europe – and 1½ mile long road bridge opened in 1966.

Tayport ✝ De
The church of Ferry-Port-en-Craig famous for 17th-century tower which lists to one side.

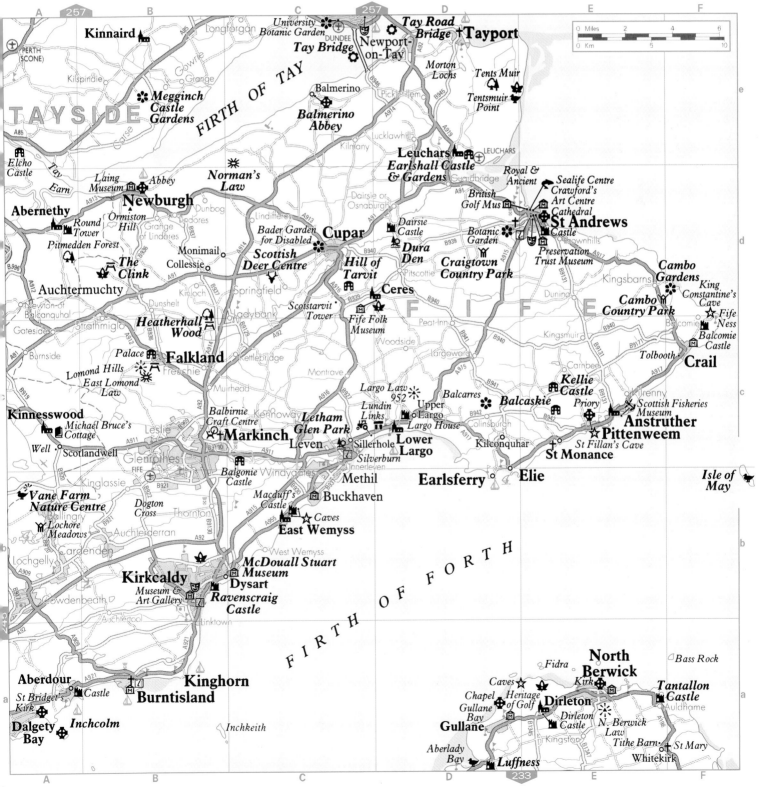

Ardnamurchan Gf
Peninsula tipped by 19th-century lighthouse is westernmost point of British mainland. Ardnamurchan Natural History Centre at Glenbeg has photographic and film displays of local wildlife.

Ardtornish ✿ Id
Woodland garden covering 28 acres on rocky hillside overlooking Loch Aline. Garden is part of Ardtornish Estate which includes Kinlochaline Castle, a 14th-century tower house.

Ardtornish Castle 🏰 Hd
Built about 1340, castle ruin was once seat of Lords of the Isles. Stands on promontory in Sound of Mull, and can be reached by boat across mouth of Loch Aline.

Arisaig 🏠 Hh
Village was base for Bonnie Prince Charlie during 1745 rebellion. Its tiny harbour on sea loch looks out to Rhum and Eigg islands, and the Cuillin hills on Skye. Wonderful views at sunset.

Aros Park 🌲 Ge
Wooded hillside estate on Mull, open to public, with crags and waterfalls above loch. Paths lead down to lochside. Shore path leads along cliff ledge with some dramatic views of Tobermory.

Burg ☆ Fb
Wild area lies along north shore of Mull's Loch Scridain, accessible only at low tide. Area has MacCulloch's fossil tree, claimed to be 50 million years old.

Calgary 🏠 Ee
Village near Calgary Bay of white sand with grassy plains behind. Views from roads to and from bay offer views of Coll and Treshnish islands to west and Skye and Ardnamurchan to north.

FAR PROSPECT *Restored croft on Coll is a reminder of the harsh days of the Highland Clearances.*

Carsaig Arches ☆ Fa
Tunnels that have been eroded in basaltic rock by sea; reached by 3 mile walk from Carsaig and accessible only at low tide. Nun's Cave reputed to be place where Iona nuns sheltered after their expulsion during Reformation.

Castle Tioram 🏰 Hg
Shell of 14th-century MacDonald fortress on small island accessible at low tide. Castle was set ablaze by Jacobite owner during 1715 uprising to prevent it falling into hands of Campbells.

ISLES OF THE INNER HEBRIDES

Mountains, sandy bays and a multitude of islands form landscapes of wild beauty. Mull, in particular, is a jewel of moorlands, forests and cliffs rich in wild flowers nurtured by the Gulf Stream. Largely emptied by the Clearances in the last century, the area is full of history, from early Christian settlement to the 1745 Jacobite rebellion led by Charles Edward Stuart, 'Bonnie Prince Charlie'.

ARDNAMURCHAN VIEW *The distant outline of Ardmore Point on Mull can be seen from Camas nan Geall.*

Coll 🏠 Ce
Island 12 miles long, with dune-laden west coast, craggy east coast and heather-covered interior. Restored Breachacha Castle, 15th century, was once home to the MacLeans. Dr Johnson stayed in its successor, built 1760, which he called a 'tradesman's box'. Shops and craft centre at Arinagour.

Craignure 🏠 Ic
Busy port on Mull connected by car ferry to Oban. Java Point, just north, is starting point for hilly woodland walk with views of Sound of Mull.

Dervaig 🏠 Fe
Outside village is 43 seat Mull Little Theatre, claimed as Britain's smallest professional theatre. Old Byre Museum has audiovisual presentation with displays of animal and bird life of Mull.

Duart Castle 🏰 Ic
MacLean stronghold built in 13th century on a Mull cliff top, giving wide views over the junction of three sea lochs. Name comes from Gaelic *dubh aird*, 'dark headland'. Three centuries of additions have created a total of 100 rooms. Castle was restored early this century and has exhibitions of scouting and family mementos.

Eigg ☆ Fh
Island 4 miles long, with cliff-top walks and sandy bays. Ferries run from Mallaig, Arisaig and Glenuig. Quartzite 'Singing Sands' at Camas Sgiotaig squeak underfoot or moan in the wind. In MacDonalds' Cave, MacLeods suffocated 395 MacDonalds in 1577 by blocking cave with fire.

Glenuig 🏠 Hg
Starting point for summer ferries to Eigg. Rough walks lead west over pass along coast to restored cottages of Smirisary, and south to Loch na Bairness.

Gruline 🏠 Gd
Estate overlooking head of Loch na Keal once owned by Major-General Lachlan MacQuarie, a 19th-century governor of New South Wales. His mausoleum is beside road near head of loch.

Iona ✚ Db
Island, 3 miles long, famous as cradle of Scottish Christianity. St Columba built monastery here in 563. Panoramic views from the highest hill, 330ft Dùn.

NEW LOOK *Duart Castle fell into disrepair until restored to its former 13th-century grandeur in 1912.*

Iona Abbey ✚ Db
Abbey, ruined nunnery, 15th-century cathedral, St Oran's Chapel and graveyard form important Christian historical site, burial place of 48 Scottish kings. Present abbey was built in 13th century and restored between 1938 and 1959. Home of

Iona Community founded 1938. Oldest-surviving relic is 10th-century St Martin's Cross, 14ft high and carved with intricate Celtic designs.

Kinlochaline Castle 🏰 Hd
Tower house of 14th century, restored in 1890. Part of 60sq mile Ardtornish Estate. Fireplace on roof supposedly used to heat water and oil to pour on attackers.

Lochaline 🏠✚ Hd
Port guarding entrance to Loch Aline has car ferry across to Mull. Mining operation on the beach collects sand of special quality for use in optical glass.

Lochbuie 🏠🏰 Hb
Moy Castle, former stronghold of MacLaine clan, is dangerous 14th-century ruin not open to public. Walks along coast pass many caves, including Lord Lovat's Cave 300ft deep, on southern tip of Laggan peninsula.

Loch nan Uamh Hh
Broad bay where Bonnie Prince Charlie landed on July 25, 1745, and from which he left for France a year later after being defeated at Culloden. Cave below Arisaig House said to be where he and his followers sheltered. Cairn on shore commemorates his flight. Glen Beasdale runs down to loch through woods.

Mallaig 🏠 Hi
Road to the Isles and West Highland Railway end at port busy with fishing boats and ferries. Overlooked by 1797ft Carn á Ghobhair, with path from nearby Glasnacardoch up to its summit.

Moidart Ig
Desolate hinterland with six peaks of 2000-3000ft. Road passes Seven Men of Moidart, seven beech trees planted to commemorate the small group who accompanied Bonnie Prince Charlie from France in 1745. There are magnificent views seawards.

Morar 🏠 Hi
Loch Morar, at 1017ft, is the deepest lake in Britain. Like Loch Ness, it supposedly holds a monster, named Morag. Village of Morar, with white quartzite sand beach, stands on narrow neck of land between Loch Morar and the Sound of Sleat.

Mull and West Highland Railway 🚂 Ic
Narrow-gauge railway covers 1¼ miles between Craignure and Torosay Castle at walking pace. Views of sea and mountains.

Salen 🏠 Gd
Ruined pier, stone cottages and craft shops form village on rocky shore of Sound of Mull. Village built about 1800 by Major-General Lachlan MacQuarie, once governor of New South Wales and so-called 'Father of Australia'. Aros Castle ruins to north.

Staffa ☆ Ec
Uninhabited island with many caves, popular tourist site since the 19th century. Fingal's Cave, island's largest, is 227ft long with six-sided black basalt pillars up to 36ft tall. Island visits possible only in good weather.

Tiree ❋✚🏛 Ad
Island swept treeless by winds. Population of 1000 scattered in several villages. Balephuil is protected by Ben Hynish and Ceann á Mhara, headland with two prehistoric forts.

Tobermory ⚓🏛 Ge
Mull's largest resort, built on natural harbour in late 18th century. Wreck of Spanish galleon lies offshore. The Mull Museum illustrates local history. Distillery offers guided tours. Wooded walk north leads to Rubha nan Gall lighthouse.

Torosay Castle 🏛 Ic
Victorian baronial-style mansion near Craignure on Mull, with turn-of-the-century decor. The 12 acre terraced gardens include stylised Japanese garden.

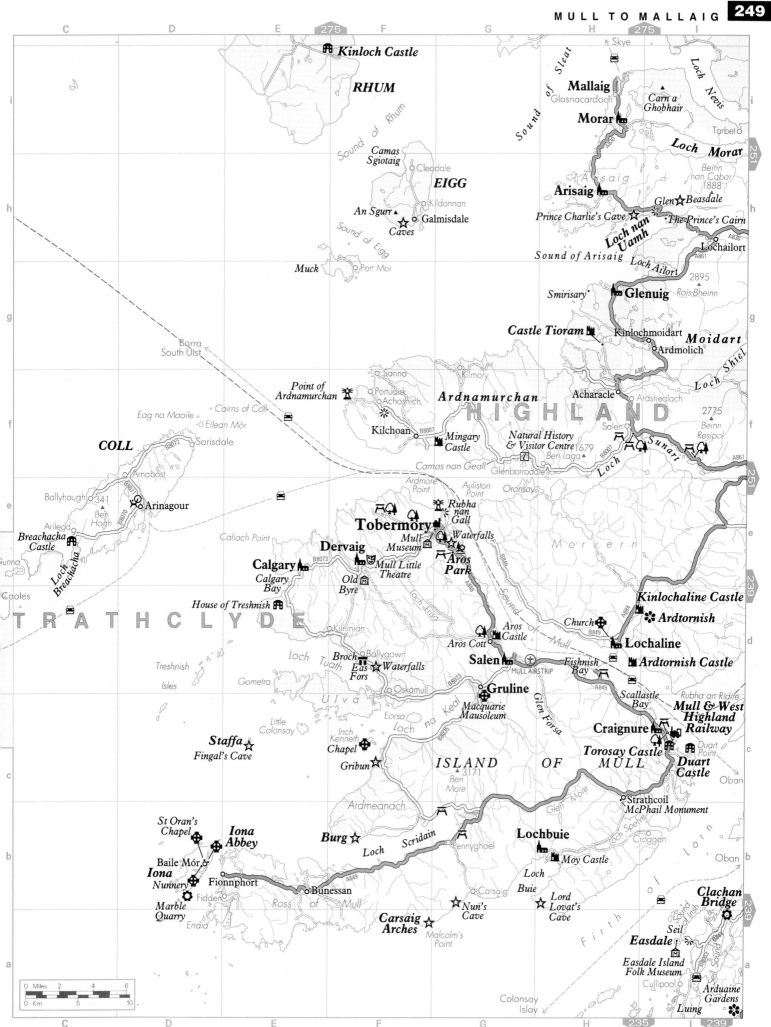

Kinloch Castle

RHUM

Skye

Mallaig
Glasnacardoch

Morar

Carn a Ghobhair

Loch Neuis

Tarbet

Loch **Morar**

Sound of Sleat

Sound of Rhum

Camas Sgiotaig

Cleadale

EIGG

Kildonnan

Beinn nan Cabar
1888

Arisaig

Arisaig

Glen ☆ *Beasdale*

Prince Charlie's Cave

The Prince's Cairn

An Sgurr ▲

Caves ☆ Galmisdale

Sound of Eigg

Loch nan Uamh

Lochailort

A830

A861

Muck

Port Mór

Sound of Arisaig

Loch Ailort

2895

Smirisary

Glenuig

Rois-Bheinn ▲

Point of Ardnamurchan

Sanna

Kilmory

Castle Tioram

Kinlochmoidart

Moidart

Loch Shiel

Portuairk
Achoshich

Ardnamurchan

Ardmolich

Barra South Uist

Cairns of Coll

O Eilean Mór

Kilchoan
B8007

Mingary Castle

Natural History & Visitor Centre

Acharacle

Ardshealach

H I G H L A N D

2775

Salen

Beinn Resipol ▲

COLL

Sorisdale

Eag na Maoile

Camas nan Geall

Ben Laga ▲ 1679

Glenborrodale

Loch Sunart

A861

Ballyhaugh
341

Arnabost
B8072

Ben Hogh ▲

Arinagour

Caliach Point

Ardmore Point

Auliston Point

Oransay

Mervern

Arileod
B8070

B8073

Rubha nan Gall

Tobermory

Mull Museum

Waterfalls

Breachacha Castle

Loch Breachacha

Dervaig

Aros Park

B846

Kinlochaline Castle

Gunna

Caoles

Calgary

Calgary Bay

Old Byre

Mull Little Theatre

A848

Sound of Mull

Ardtornish

Church
B849

Lochaline

S T R A T H C L Y D E

House of Treshnish

Kilninian

Loch Tuath

Ballygown

Broch

Waterfalls

Eas Fors

Aros Castle

Aros Cott

Salen

Fishnish Bay

Ardtornish Castle

Treshnish Isles

Gometra

Loch na Keal

Oskamull

B8073

MULL AIRSTRIP

Scallastle Bay

Rubha an Ridire

Ulva

Eorsa

Gruline

Macquarie Mausoleum

Glen Forsa

Craignure

Mull & West Highland Railway

Little Colonsay

Inch Kenneth Chapel

Staffa

Fingal's Cave

Gribun

ISLAND OF

Ben More ▲ 3171

Torosay Castle

MULL

Duart Point

Duart Castle

Oban

Ardmeanach

Strathcoil
McPhail Monument

Glen More

Firth of Lorn

St Oran's Chapel

Iona Abbey

Glen Spelve

Croggan

Burg ☆

Loch Scridain

Lochbuie

Oban

Baile Mór

Iona

Nunnery

Fionnphort

Moy Castle

Clachan Bridge

Pennyghael

Loch Buie

Marble Quarry

Fidden

Bunessan

Ross of Mull

Carsaig

Lord Lovat's Cave

Seil

Erraid

Nun's Cave

Easdale

Easdale Island Folk Museum

Carsaig Arches

Malcolm's Point

Cullipool

Colonsay
Islay

Luing

Arduaine Gardens

| 0 Miles | 2 | 4 | 6 |
| 0 Km | 5 | 10 | |

RUINED FORTS AND EMPTY GLENS

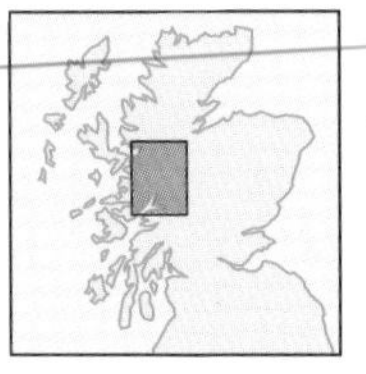

The Great Glen – a chain of narrow lochs marking a giant geological fracture of the land – cuts across a wild and lovely landscape of peaks, lakes and rivers overlooked by Britain's highest mountain, the giant Ben Nevis. Ruined forts and glens emptied by the 19th-century Clearances testify to the violence that marked the slow end of the traditional Highland way of life.

Achnacarry ⌂ Ee
Achnacarry House has been seat of Camerons of Lochiel since 1660. Present building dates from 1802, has Gothic decoration, crenellated parapet and corner turrets. Clan Cameron Museum, housed in reconstructed 17th-century croft house, commemorates role of Camerons in the armed forces.

Ardgour ⚶ ⚘ ☆ ⊞ Cc
Lighthouse marks entrance to Loch Linnhe's tide race. Superb walks in surrounding woods and mountains. Behind Corran village is steep mountain with waterfall known as MacLean's Towel.

Balmacara ❋ ☑ Bi
Access to 6400 acre National Trust estate with woodland walks, lochs and streams. National Trust for Scotland information centre. Lochalsh Woodland Garden was established in 1887 for Lochalsh House. Converted Coach House is visitor centre.

Banavie ○ Ed
Locality near south end of Caledonian Canal, by set of eight locks forming Neptune's Staircase.

Caisteal Grugaig �🏛 Bi
Iron Age Pictish fort, or broch, overlooking bay at junction of Loch Duich and Loch Alsh. Fort has walls 9ft thick and 13ft high, and a huge triangular block above the doorway. Wall chambers, part of staircase and part of gallery also remain standing.

Caledonian Canal Ee
Series of 28 locks and cuts stretching along 22 miles of the Great Glen. Links 45 miles of lochs to create route between east and west coasts, through spectacular scenery of mountains and glens. Built mainly in early 19th century by Thomas Telford.

Eilean Donan Castle ⌂ Bi
MacRae stronghold dates from 13th century. Ruined by naval bombardment in 1719, rebuilt earlier this century. Causeway, three-arched bridge and gateway with portcullis lead through walls up to 14ft thick. Restored chambers, billeting room and banquet hall with furnishings.

Falls of Glomach ☆ Di
Tumbling down 750ft cleft, falls make single leap of 350ft. Among highest falls in Britain. Also 8ft high, and curves from cliff edge to cliff edge. Wall has internal chambers and entrance passage.

STRONGHOLD *Eilean Donan was built to ward off Viking raiders.*

uprising. Scottish crafts and Ben Nevis Exhibition. Three miles east, Nevis Range Gondola takes visitors 1½ miles up mountain.

Glen Affric ⚘ ⌂ ⚲ Ei
Landseer's paintings made glen's woods, crags and tumbling waters famous. Glen links lochs Affric and Beinn a' Mheadhoin (Benevean) and forms part of long-distance path to Kintail. Several one to three-hour walks marked from Dog Falls and car park between lochs Affric and Beinn a' Mheadhoin.

Glen Coe ⚘ ☑ ⌂ ☆ ❋ Eb
Stone cross marks site where 38 Jacobite MacDonalds were murdered by their guests, pro-English Campbells, in 1692. Surrounding mountains provide walks and rock climbs. Visitor centre with story of massacre and local ecology. Glencoe and North Lorn Folk Museum displays clan and Jacobite relics.

Glenelg ⌂ �🏛 Bh
Small harbour at foot of Glen More, backed by hills of Glenshiel Forest. North lie remains of Bernera Barracks, 18th-century English military headquarters. To south are Iron Age Pictish forts Dun Telve and Dun Troddan, best-preserved on Scottish mainland; double walls once 40-50ft high, now only 25-30ft; spiralling galleries and chambers remain.

Glenfinnan ⌂ ⚲ ☑ Be
Fishing village at head of Loch Shiel. Pillar, 65ft high, erected in 1815 to commemorate Bonnie Prince Charlie's 1745 arrival to raise Highland army. Spiral staircase inside pillar leads to parapet with views over Loch Shiel. Visitor centre contains displays on the prince's campaign from Glenfinnan to Derby.

Glen Garry ⚘ ⚘ ⚲ ☆ Eg
In lee of high moorland hills, picnic area at east end of Loch Garry is start of 2 mile long walk through Glengarry Forest to impressive Falls of Garry. Forest comprises mostly conifers.

Glen Moriston ☆ Fh
Cave where Bonnie Prince Charlie hid in 1746 after defeat lies 1 mile west of An Reithe, and can be reached by lengthy walk from the west end of heavily wooded glen. Roadside cairn commemorates Roderick Mackenzie, one of the prince's bodyguards, killed when mistaken for him.

Glen Nevis ⚲ Ec
One of Scotland's loveliest valleys with varied terrain of rivers, crags and steep wooded gullies. At eastern end, flanked by steep tracks, is 1250ft 'water slide', Allt Coire Eoghain, tumbling from flanks of Ben Nevis.

Glen Shiel ⚔ Ch
Road runs through valley with mountains rising over 3000ft on both sides; Five Sisters of Kintail to east and The Saddle to west.

Kyle of Lochalsh ⌂ ⊞ ❋ Ai
Busy little port that expanded when railhead was built in 1897. Now main car-ferry terminus to Skye. From hilltop nearby superb views westwards over Skye.

Loch Morar Bf
The deepest lake in Britain, reaching 1017ft at its eastern end, this glacier-carved loch is 12 miles long. Like Loch Ness, it is said to have a monster – Morag. Morar, hillside village on narrow neck of land above loch, looks across sea towards Rhum and Eigg.

Loch Oich ⌂ Gf
Nearby slopes bear ruin of Invergarry Castle, former Macdonnell stronghold – destroyed by Duke of Cumberland because Bonnie Prince Charlie stayed there before and after his defeat at Culloden. One mile south is Well of Seven Heads, monument erected in 1812 by Alastair Macdonnell to recall revenge taken on seven murderers of his clan in 1660s.

Plockton ⌂ ❋ Bj
White houses line the shore of an inlet in Loch Carron, with gardens and palm trees encouraged by warmth of Gulf Stream. Sheltered anchorage for yachts.

South Ballachulish ⌂ Db
Loch-side village with superb views up Loch Leven. Monument to James Stewart who was wrongfully hanged there in 1752 for murdering a Campbell.

Spean Bridge ⌂ Fe
Hamlet with 1819 bridge over fast-flowing River Spean. Commando Memorial, with Scott Sutherland sculpture nearby, was erected in 1952 to commemorate the commandos trained in surrounding area during World War II.

Strontian ⌂ ⚘ ⚲ ⚲ Bc
Village at mouth of River Strontian is base for salmon and sea-trout fishing. Walks include 7 mile Ariundle Nature Trail, passing old mine workings and derelict village of Scotstown. The village gave its name to the mineral strontianite, from which the element strontium comes.

SILENT WITNESSES *The Three Sisters of Glen Coe loom over the scene of a massacre ordered by William III.*

Locks, built 1822, climb 64ft in 1 mile. Walk of 1½ miles up canal bank leads to Torcastle Farm and ruins of Tor Castle, overlooking River Lochy.

Bealach Ratagain ❋ Ch
Also known as Mam Ratagain Pass. Steep road zigzagging up to 1116ft was for centuries major strategic route through Western Highlands. View from the top over little Loch Shiel, Shiel Bridge and Loch Duich.

Ben Nevis Ed
Britain's highest peak rises 4406ft above sea level. Massive, round-shouldered hulk with steep cliffs on its north face. Rough 5 mile long footpath leads to mountain's summit from Achintree House near Fort William. Initial strenuous climb levels out at 2500ft; summit offers views stretching for more than 100 miles from Great Glen to Atlantic islands.

Corrimony �🏛 Gj
Hamlet on an ancient site, with a chambered cairn, or passage grave, of about 2000 BC. Mound 60ft across contains 23ft long passage into central chamber with fine corbelled roof.

PASSAGE GRAVE *The ancient grave at Corrimony is encircled by 11 standing stones.*

Duirinish Lodge ❋ Aj
Woodland garden with heathers, azaleas and rhododendrons overlooks Skye and Raasay.

Dun Grugaig ⌂ Bh
Remains of Iron Age fort stand on cliff top, above precipitous side of gorge. Protecting wall is 14ft thick, known as The Hidden Falls because of inaccessibility. Best approached along 5 mile track from car park at Dorusduain. Round trip takes five hours.

Fort Augustus ⌂ ⚲ ⌂ ⚕ Gg
Village spanning six locks bringing Caledonian Canal into Loch Ness. Great Glen Heritage Exhibition covers local history. Fort built after 1715 Jacobite uprising named after Duke of Cumberland, Prince William Augustus. Site of fort now occupied by 19th-century St Benedict's Abbey, now a school. Inchnacardoch Forest Trail begins 2 miles from village centre.

Fort William ⌂ ⌂ Ed
Small town at foot of Ben Nevis provides base for climbers planning to scale Britain's highest mountain. Fort built in 17th century, demolished in 1850s. West Highland Museum focuses on regional history, including 1745

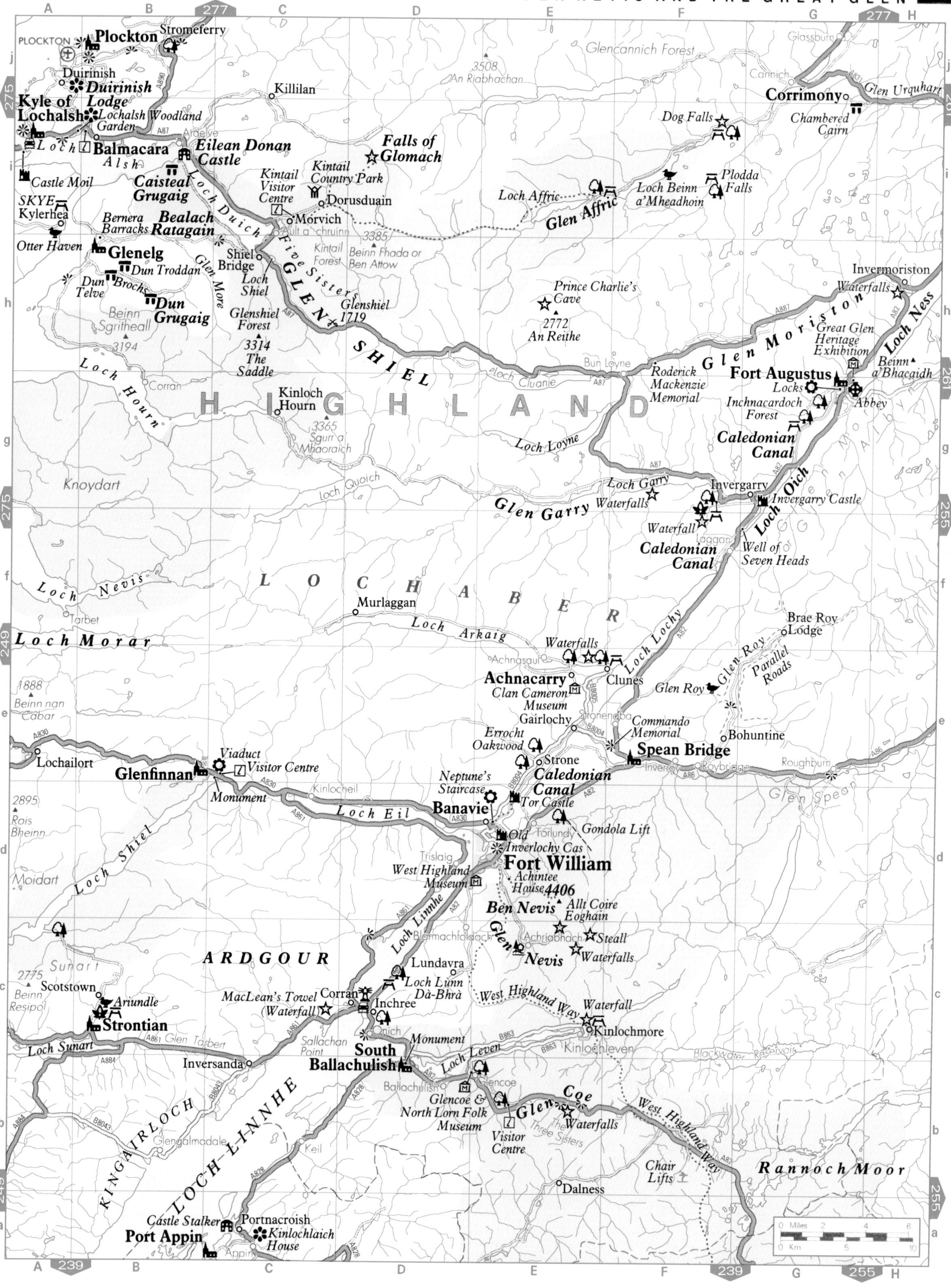

HIGHLAND
LOCHABER
ARDGOUR
Plockton
PLOCKTON
Stromeferry
Duirinish
Duirinish Lodge
Kyle of Lochalsh
Lochalsh Woodland Garden
Balmacara
Loch Alsh
Castle Moil
SKYE
Kylerhea
Otter Haven
Eilean Donan Castle
Ardelve
Caisteal Grugaig
Bernera Barracks
Bealach Ratagain
Glenelg
Dun Troddan
Dun Telve
Brochs
Dun Grugaig
Beinn Sgritheall
3194
Killilan
Falls of Glomach
Kintail Visitor Centre
Kintail Country Park
Dorusduain
Morvich
Ault a' chruinn
Loch Duich
Five Sisters
Kintail Forest
Beinn Fhada or Ben Attow
3385
Shiel Bridge
Loch Shiel
Glen More
GLEN SHIEL
Glenshiel 1719
Glenshiel Forest
3314
The Saddle
Loch Hourn
Corran
Kinloch Hourn
3365
Sgurr a' Mhaoraich
Knoydart
Loch Quoich
Loch Nevis
Tarbet
Loch Morar
1888
Beinn nan Cabar
Glencannich Forest
3508
An Riabhachan
Glassburn
Cannich
Corrimony
Glen Urquhart
Chambered Cairn
Dog Falls
Plodda Falls
Loch Beinn a'Mheadhoin
Loch Affric
Glen Affric
Prince Charlie's Cave
2772
An Reithe
Invermoriston
Waterfalls
Glen Moriston
Great Glen Heritage Exhibition
Loch Ness
Beinn a'Bhacaidh
Bun Loyne
Loch Cluanie
Roderick Mackenzie Memorial
Fort Augustus
Locks
Abbey
Inchnacardoch Forest
Caledonian Canal
Loch Loyne
Loch Garry
Glen Garry
Waterfalls
Invergarry
Invergarry Castle
Loch Oich
Waterfall
Laggan
Well of Seven Heads
Caledonian Canal
Murlaggan
Loch Arkaig
Waterfalls
Achnasaul
Achnacarry
Clan Cameron Museum
Clunes
Loch Lochy
Brae Roy Lodge
Glen Roy
Parallel Roads
Gairlochy
Stronenaba
Commando Memorial
Bohuntine
Erracht Oakwood
Strone
Spean Bridge
Invertoy
Roybridge
Roughburn
Glen Spean
Caledonian Canal
Neptune's Staircase
Banavie
Tor Castle
Gondola Lift
Torlundy
Old Inverlochy Cas
Fort William
Achintee House
4406
Ben Nevis
Allt Coire Eoghain
Steall
Waterfalls
Glen Nevis
Achriabhach
Blarmachfoldach
Lochailort
Glenfinnan
Viaduct
Visitor Centre
Monument
Kinlocheil
Loch Eil
Trislaig
West Highland Museum
2895
Rois Bheinn
Moidart
Loch Shiel
Loch Linnhe
Lundavra
Loch Lunn Dà-Bhrà
West Highland Way
Waterfall
Kinlochmore
Kinlochleven
Blackwater Reservoir
Sunart
2775
Beinn Resipol
Scotstown
Ariundle
Strontian
Glen Tarbert
Loch Sunart
MacLean's Towel (Waterfall)
Corran
Inchree
Onich
Sallachan Point
South Ballachulish
Monument
Loch Leven
Glencoe
Ballachulish
Glencoe & North Lorn Folk Museum
Visitor Centre
Glen Coe
Waterfalls
The Three Sisters
West Highland Way
Inversanda
KINGAIRLOCH
LOCH LINNHE
Glengalmadale
Keil
Chair Lifts
Dalness
Rannoch Moor
Castle Stalker
Portnacroish
Kinlochlaich House
Port Appin
Appin
A87
A887
A82
A86
A830
A861
A884
B8043
B8004
B8005
B863
A828
A831
A890
0 Miles 2 4 6
0 Km 5 10
277
275
261
255
249
239
A B C D E F G H
j i h g f e d c b a

A GRAND AND SAVAGE BEAUTY

The Highlands form a landscape of immense drama and grandeur, with mighty wind-blown heights, forest-lined glens and towering cliffs above lonely lochs.

Some regions merge imperceptibly with their neighbours, but not the Scottish Highlands. Visible for miles across plains and minor foothills, the Highland Boundary Fault is an abrupt start to a landscape of mountains, forests, glens and tumbling rivers.

At Loch Lomond the fault line appears as a row of islands beyond which the loch narrows between peaks. Another force has been at work. A receding glacier gouged out the trough that the waterway now occupies.

As ice sheets thawed, meltwater lakes were periodically dammed by detritus. In Glen Roy the famous 'parallel roads' are the successive hillside shorelines of a prehistoric lake.

But long before the Ice Age, volcanic action created the structure of the Highlands. Some of that activity can be seen today. For instance, in Glen Coe, gullies around Clachaig show where the land surface once collapsed into the molten ferment below.

Elemental forces have created the most varied mountain landscape in Britain. Ben Nevis, at 4406ft the highest of all British summits, rises from a sea loch to a bleak plateau accessible by footpath or by a mountaineers' playground of buttresses and gullies. The 4000ft high Cairngorms form Britain's only extensive sub-arctic plateau. There are Torridon's sculptured sandstone peaks, the grassy summits of the Monadhliaths and the quartzite tops of Beinn Eighe with their illusion of a summer dusting of snow. In Assynt, sugarloaf mountains such as Suilven and Quinag rear up from an undramatic foreground.

On the lower levels the original Caledonian pine forest has largely disappeared. In its place have come spruce and larch plantations. Oak-woods survive, but the most widespread tree cover in undeveloped areas is birch.

The Highlands are home to a wide range of birds and animals – some quite rare. High in the Cairngorms, ptarmigan change to white plumage in time for the winter snows. Dotterels and the rare snow bunting attract keen birdwatchers. Speyside and Deeside pine forests support siskins, crested tits and crossbills. They also shelter the capercaillie, which blunders through the undergrowth as it launches its turkey-like body into the air. Sometimes a golden eagle may be seen soaring high in the skies. Peregrine falcons nest around Aviemore, and elsewhere on Speyside an osprey will swoop on a loch and soar upwards

DUN TELVE BROCH *This ancient fortified dwelling, near Glenelg, shows the skilful dry-stone walling techniques adopted by broch engineers.*

HIGH LIFE *Suilven's sugarloaf peak (above left) has long provided a challenge for climbers. Palm trees (above) flourish in Plockton's mild climate, tempered by the warm waters of the Gulf Stream.*

with a trout in its talons. Britain's largest wild animals, the red deer, summer among the high corries and ridges, slipping quietly down to a river for a drink before nightfall. Roe, fallow and sika deer browse in the woodlands. In Wester Ross there may be a glimpse of a pine marten. Otters frequent the western shores.

Agriculture defers to geology and altitude. Hill farming is the general rule, although there is some arable land in the lower glens. Sheep are the most common livestock, the rams often summered on lusher lowland farms. Crofts are common – smallholdings with a patch of arable ground, a share of hill grazing and access to peat banks for fuel. On a grander scale, timber is a major crop.

GLENCOE MASSACRE *One of many Highland tragedies – desperate survivors of the MacDonald clan fled into the snow-covered hills to escape a punitive force of government troops in 1692.*

MOUNTAIN SETTING *Glen, mountain and loch combine to provide some of Britain's wildest and most magnificent scenery, a spectacular setting for the tiny village of Torridon.*

Enormous acreages are devoted to deer forests or grouse moors, the latter on heather uplands, which burst into purple flower in late summer. Grouse moor management includes the careful burning of sectors of the heather to promote fresh spring growth for the grouse to feed on. The resulting patchwork effect can be seen from many Highland roads, such as the exhilarating climb of Cairn o' Mount in the eastern Grampians.

Standing stones and brochs

One of the most fascinating prehistoric sites in Scotland is the Kilmartin valley in Argyll. Neolithic settlers of the 3rd millennium BC have left burial chambers, standing stones and a cemetery. Close by, the rock outcrop of Dunadd was the coronation place of the kings of Dalriada (modern Argyll). Bronze Age hill-forts include the dramatic Craig Phadrig, just west of Inverness. Characteristic of the Iron Age was the dry-stone broch, a defensive tower with an inner court where livestock could be penned. Good examples survive at Dun Troddan and Dun Telve, south of Glenelg.

In the 18th century General Wade and his successors built a network of military roads,

ISLAND CASTLE *Built as a royal stronghold in the 13th century, Eilean Donan Castle later passed into the ownership of the Mackenzies of Kintail. In the 16th century Clan MacRae became the castle's constables.*

and many survive with modern surfaces. On Thomas Telford's Caledonian Canal, pride of place goes to the Neptune's Staircase locks at Banavie. Early industry made little impression on the Highlands, though charcoal-fired ironworks were tried; one has been well restored at Bonawe, Argyll. Many landowners went in for town planning: Grantown-on-Spey, granite Ballater, the highest village in the Highlands at Tomintoul and the Duke of Argyll's elegant Inveraray are all products of this 18th-century enthusiasm. Ullapool on Loch Broom was laid out in the 1780s by the British Fisheries Society.

Highland castles have an abiding appeal: Eilean Donan, set on a rocky islet in Loch

Duich, is a fine reconstruction of a Mackenzie fortress. Corgarff Castle, guarding the start of the Lecht pass to Tomintoul, declined in status until it housed a haphazard force supposed to keep an eye on whisky smugglers.

Deeside and Donside have the greatest concentration of castles of all styles and ages, from Braemar, stronghold of the Earls of Mar, to Victorian mock-medieval like Balmoral, the Highland residence of the Royal Family.

Balmoral spurred the revival of the Scots Baronial style for castellated mansions. At Craigievar in the 1620s the Bell family of master masons created a vision of towers and turrets, corbels and ornamented roofline, the castle of many people's dreams.

AMONG LOCHS AND GLENS

The glens and hills near Balquhidder, where outlaw Rob Roy spent his last days, mark the beginning of the Highlands proper. Walkers and climbers have a choice of mountain peaks, from Ben Lawers in the south to Schiehallion's snow-capped cone in the centre. Here, too, is a pocket of Scotland's ancient Caledonian forest, and the tree-fringed Loch Tummel so admired by Queen Victoria.

Aberfeldy ⬛◀◆ Fd
General Wade's fine five-arched bridge, built 1733, still spans River Tay, overlooked by kilted figure on monument commemorating Black Watch regiment. Dewar family's distillery open to visitors.

Ben Lawers ✳◆✿☑ Dd
Rising 3984ft over Loch Tay's north shore, entire mountain is national nature reserve. Visitor centre, 1400ft up southern slope, is start of 1½ hour nature trail.

Birks of Aberfeldy ☆✿ Fd
Network of burns cascades over stepped rocks, below Falls of Moness. Footpaths weave their way through birch-clad sides of ravine, and nature trail leads to footbridge above falls.

Blair Atholl ⬛⬛⬛⬛ Ff
Pepper-pot turrets and castellated towers adorn granite buildings of village, which stands at meeting point of several highland glens. Mill dating from 17th century is still in operation on River Garry – its products can be sampled.

Blair Castle ⬛ Ff
Turreted baronial castle, home to Dukes of Atholl. Restored to Gothic style in 1868. Rooms filled with fine furniture, paintings, tapestries, arms, clothes telling story of Highland life from 1500.

Braes of Balquhidder Bb
Steep glens and windswept hills, framed by mountain peaks to north-west. Outlaw Rob Roy lived his last years here; he and other MacGregors are buried in Balquhidder churchyard, his grave marked by slate slab carved with kilted figure.

Castle Menzies ⬛ Fd
Castle built 1488 with later additions, seat of Clan Menzies chief. Two towers and central block with four storeys. Copper cast of Bonnie Prince Charlie's death mask on display. Castle also houses Clan Menzies museum.

Clan Donnachaidh Museum ⬛ Ff
Purpose-built museum housing memorabilia of Donnachaidh clan, which included several families. Relics from Jacobite uprisings of 1715 and 1745, tartans, glass, silver and books. Starting point for walk to Falls of Bruar.

Comrie ✳☆◆⬛ Eb
Resort town at meeting point of two glens. Museum of Scottish Tartans includes reconstructed weaver's cottage and plant dyes. Path up Glen Lednock leads to Deil's Caldron, where river disappears through hole in rock.

Craigower ✳◆ Gf
Marked trail, north of Pitlochry, leads through woods to 1300ft summit of beacon hill. Views from summit across water meadows to Schiehallion's peak.

Crieff ⬛◆☑ Fb
Visitor's centre has two walk-around craft factories, allowing visitors to see pottery and paperweights being made. Octagonal mercat cross stands within iron railing. Old stocks stand near the 17th-century tolbooth.

ROYAL APPROVAL *Queen Victoria praised this view from above Loch Tummel – hence the name Queen's View.*

Drummond Castle Gardens ✿ Fa
Originally laid out in 1600s the gardens were Italianised about 1830. Terraces with geometrically shaped beds, lawns and hedges slope away from medieval keep. John Mylne, Charles I's master mason, created obelisk sundial furnished with 50 different faces.

CASTLE COLOUR *Earl of Perth laid out Drummond gardens in 1630.*

Glengoulandie Deer Park ✿✿ Ee
Red deer, Highland cattle and rare breeds of sheep roam free at foot of Schiehallion peak.

Glen Lyon ⬛⬛ Cd
Castle ruins and standing stones dot steep slopes of Scotland's longest glen. MacGregor's Leap marks spot where ancestor of Rob Roy bounded to safety across ravine. Fortingall is legendary birthplace of Pontius Pilate.

Glenturret Distillery ◀ Fb
Whisky distillery, established 1775, where traditional methods are on display. Samplings of whiskies up to 21 years old are offered. Restaurant and audio-visual theatre.

Innerpeffray ✝◀ Ga
Scotland's first public library still exists. Founded 1691, library now housed in 18th-century building. Rare Scottish books displayed, including pocket Bible taken into battle by Montrose, general who won brilliant victories in Scotland for Charles I. Church nearby dates from 1508.

Kenmore ⬛ Ed
Village on eastern shore of Loch Tay, noted for salmon fishing. Bridge over River Tay here was built by Earl of Breadalbane in 1774. In 1787, Robert Burns wrote verse about view from bridge, copy in Kenmore Hotel.

Killin ⬛⬛☆ Cc
Fishing resort on Loch Tay with walking, climbing, skiing and motoring in surrounding mountains. Finlarig Castle, former Campbell seat built 1609, has beheading pit where crude guillotine, The Maiden, was used. Falls of Dochart rush through town.

Kingussie ◆◀ Ej
Winter sports resort in Spey Valley. Highland Folk Museum complex has Hebridean blackhouse, water-powered clack mill, and 18th-century shooting lodge. Inside are objects of everyday Highland life. Free tours of nearby china factory.

Kinloch Rannoch ⬛ De
Village at eastern end of Loch Rannoch. Car parks around loch provide views of 3554ft Schiehallion peak. Stone cottages, baronial-style hotel, forge and shops.

Loch Faskally ◆✿ Ge
Reservoir created when Tummel was dammed in 1950; breeding site for greylag geese. At southern end, salmon leap up fish pass in season. Forest trails along east and north shores of loch.

Logierait ⬛ Ge
Tummel flows into Tay here in narrow gorge of historic military importance. In local churchyard are three mortsafes (metal frames padlocked round coffins to deter body snatchers).

Melville Monument ✳ Eb
Short detour off Glen Lednock Circular Walk leads to Dunmore Hill, 840ft, with obelisk in memory of Lord Melville. Fine views of Highlands.

NOISY NORSE *Clack mill, named for its sound, and introduced by the Vikings, can be seen at Kingussie Highland Folk Museum.*

Moulin ⬛⬛ Ge
Moulin Inn retains iron rings to which Bonnie Prince Charlie's army tethered their horses on way to battle of Culloden in 1746. Churchyard has two medieval warrior graves. An Caisteal Dubh (black castle) of 1320, now in ruins, was inhabited until 1500 when plague wiped out garrison.

Muthill ⬛⬛ Fa
Village has 15th-century church with 12th-century tower. Local folk museum housed in *c.* 1760 Georgian cottage.

Newtonmore ⬛⬛ Ei
Centre for walking, pony trekking at foot of Monadhliath Mountains and head of Spey Valley. Clan Macpherson Museum displays historical relics including 15th-century bagpipes. Path leads to Loch Dubh by 3087ft Carn Bàn.

Pass of Killiecrankie ✕◆✳☆☑ Gf
River Garry gorge where English were defeated by Jacobites under Bonnie Dundee in 1689. Visitor centre explains battle's history. Soldier's Leap is where English soldier sprang 18ft across ravine to escape his pursuers.

Pitlochry ◆◀✿ Ge
Summer festival at hillside theatre above River Tummel. Highland games take place each September. Scotland's smallest distillery lies north-east of town. Viewing chamber allows public to watch salmon struggling upstream at southern end of Loch Faskally.

Queen's View ✳◆ Fe
Viewpoint of Loch Tummel's wooded valley, with Schiehallion's peak in distance. Named after Queen Victoria's 1866 visit. Four waymarked paths through woodland; picnic spot with loch views. Steep trail to loch shore.

Rannoch Forest ◆ De
Old and new woodlands south of Loch Rannoch. To west are Scots pines, remnant of ancient Caledonian Forest. To east are stands of recently planted larch, pine and spruce. Three marked trails from Carie car park.

Rannoch Moor Ae
About 60sq miles of peat bog with pools, lochs and burns. Haven for wetland birds; treacherous for walkers in places. Surrounded by mountains.

Ruthven Barracks ⬛ Ei
Roadside ruins of English barracks built 1718. Built for troops brought in to control Highlanders after 1715 rebellion, Highlanders captured it 1746 and later blew it up to stop English using it again.

St Mary's ✝ Fe
Church dating from 16th century contains notable 17th-century wooden ceiling. Its 29 painted panels portray Biblical scenes and coats of arms. Panels separated by paintings of fruit, vases of flowers and birds. Now restored.

Weem ⬛ Fd
Village has late 15th-century church housing Menzies family memorials and two crosses from 8th-century monastery.

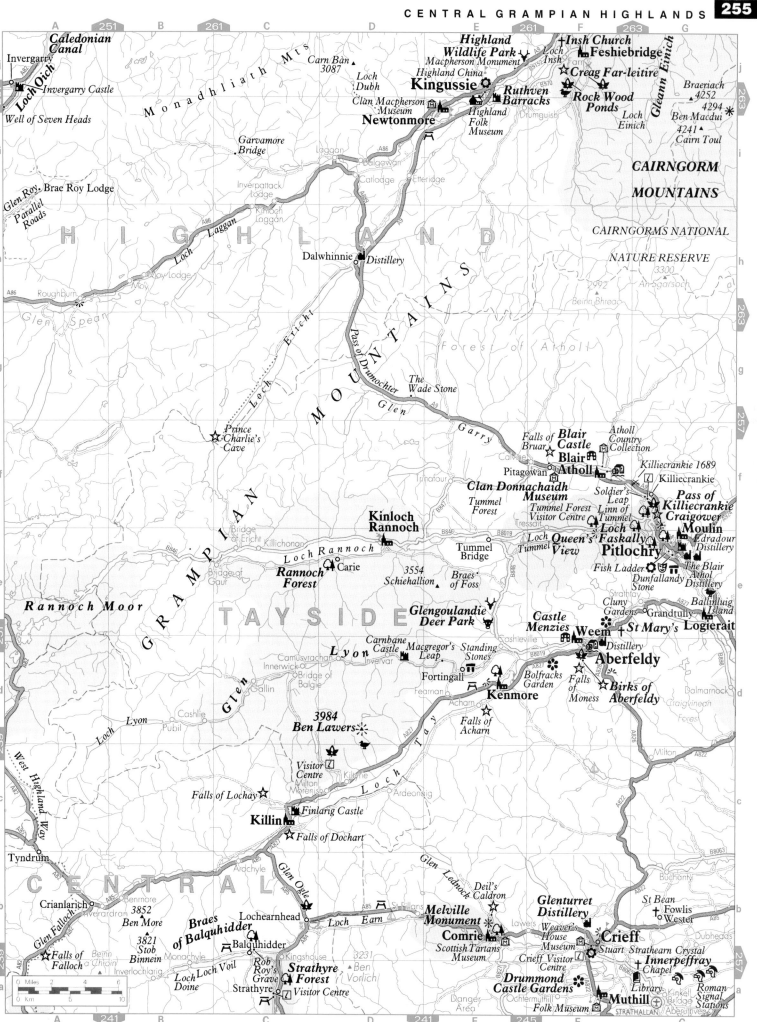

Caledonian Canal
Invergarry
Loch Oich
Invergarry Castle
Well of Seven Heads

Monadhliath Mts

Carn Bàn
3087
Loch Dubh

Highland Wildlife Park
Macpherson Monument
Highland China
Kingussie
Ruthven Barracks
Clan Macpherson Museum
Highland Folk Museum
Newtonmore

✝**Insh Church**
Loch Insh
Feshiebridge
✦**Creag Far-leitire**
Rock Wood Ponds
Drumguish

Gleann Einich
Braeriach
4252
4294
Ben Macdui ✳
4241
Cairn Toul

CAIRNGORM MOUNTAINS
CAIRNGORMS NATIONAL NATURE RESERVE

Garvamore Bridge
Laggan
Balgowan
Inverpattack Lodge
Kinloch Laggan
Catloge
Etteridge

Glen Roy Brae Roy Lodge
Parallel Roads
Moy Lodge
Roughburn
Glen Spean

Dalwhinnie ⊙ Distillery

Forest of Atholl
3300
2992
An Sgarsoch
Beinn Bhreac

H I G H L A N D

Loch Laggan
Loch Ericht
Pass of Drumochter
Glen Garry
The Wade Stone

Prince Charlie's Cave

Falls of Bruar
Blair Castle
Blair Atholl
Pitagowan
Clan Donnachaidh Museum
Tummel Forest
Tummel Forest Visitor Centre
Atholl Country Collection
Killiecrankie 1689
Killiecrankie
Soldier's Leap
Linn of Tummel
Pass of Killiecrankie
Craigower
Moulin
Edradour Distillery

Trinafour
Tressait

Kinloch Rannoch
B846
B8019
Loch Tummel
Queen's View
Loch Faskally
Pitlochry
Fish Ladder
Dunfallandy Stone
The Blair Atholl Distillery

Bridge of Ericht
Killichonan
Loch Rannoch
Carie
Rannoch Forest
Bridge of Gaur

3554
Schiehallion
Tummel Bridge
Braes of Foss

Cluny Gardens
Grandtully
Strathtay
Ballinluig Island
A827

Rannoch Moor

G R A M P I A N

T A Y S I D E

Glengoulandie Deer Park

Castle Menzies
Weem ✝**St Mary's**
Distillery
Aberfeldy
Logierait

Glen Lyon
Camusvrachan
Innerwick
Bridge of Balgie

Lyon
Carnbane Castle
Invervar
Macgregor's Leap
Coshieville

Standing Stones
Fortingall
Fearnan
Acharn

Bolfracks Garden
Falls of Moness
Birks of Aberfeldy
Dalmarnock
Craigvinean Forest

Loch Lyon
Cashlie
Pubil
Glen Lyon
Gallin
Bridge of Balgie

Loch Tay

3984
Ben Lawers ✳
Visitor Centre
Kiltyrie
Milton Morenish
Ardeonaig

Kenmore
Falls of Acharn

Falls of Lochay

Killin
Finlarig Castle
Falls of Dochart

Tyndrum

West Highland Way

C E N T R A L

Ardchyle
Glen Ogle
Glen Lednock
Deil's Caldron

Milton
Buchanty

Crianlarich
Inverardran
3852
Ben More
3821
Stob Binnein
Benmore

Lochearnhead
Loch Earn
St Fillans
Lawers

Glenturret Distillery
St Bean
Fowlis Wester

Melville Monument
Comrie
Weaver's House Museum
Scottish Tartans Museum
Crieff
Crieff Visitor Centre
Stuart Strathearn Crystal
St Bean Chapel

Braes of Balquhidder
Balquhidder
Kingshouse
Monachyle
3231
Ben Vorlich

Rob Roy's Grave
Strathyre Forest
Strathyre
Visitor Centre

Falls of Falloch
Glen Falloch
Loch Doine
Loch Voil
Inverlochlarig
Danger Area

Drummond Castle Gardens
Folk Museum
Library
Kinkel Bridge
Dubheads
Roman Signal Stations
✝**Innerpeffray Chapel**
Muthill
STRATHALLAN
Aberuthven
Ochtertyre

0 Miles 2 4 6
0 Km 5 10

Alyth Dd
Alyth Folk Museum, open only in summer, has collection of agricultural and domestic artefacts.

Baledgarno Dc
Secluded and unsignposted village built on private property. Houses overlook village green split by rushing burn.

Barry Hill De
Remains of Pictish fort on top of hill. Guinevere, King Arthur's queen, is said to have been imprisoned here for loving Pictish prince. View rewards climb.

Birnam Bd
Village, dating from 19th century, on River Tay. Birnam Wood mostly birch and oak. Terrace Walk along right bank of Tay passes oak said to be last survivor of original Birnam Wood featured in prophecy of Macbeth's death.

Blairgowrie and Rattray Cd
Scotland's largest working water wheel on view at Keathbank Mill. Heraldic crests centre here. Two towns linked by 19th-century

WHERE HISTORY AND LEGEND MEET

Fields of raspberries and strawberries stretch between the ancient cities of Perth and Dundee, while farther north wooded glens and tranquil lochs show some of Scotland's wilder side. This is a region rich in history and legend: kings were crowned at Scone, Macbeth scanned Birnam from Dunsinane Hill, Guinevere was imprisoned at Barry Hill, and ghosts still stalk the corridors of Glamis Castle.

Dundee Fc
From Law of Dundee, hill of volcanic rock in centre of town, views of surrounding areas including docks. Iron Age hill-fort and War Memorial here. McManus Galleries have displays of history and art including Dutch, French, Italian and British paintings, and oldest known astrolabe – dating from 1555. Barrack Street Museum has natural history exhibits. Steeple of St Mary's Tower, dating from 16th century, now museum of church and local history. Ruins of Mains of Fintry Castle in Caird Park. Mills Observatory has displays on astrology and space travel, and allows public to use telescopes.

Eassie Ed
Pictish symbol stone in ruins of Eassie church. Cross and figures carved on one side; elephant men and animals on other.

Fowlis Easter Ec
St Marnock's Church dates from 1453 and has medieval painted panels, bronze alms dish and bell dated 1508. Jougs – iron collars for tying up wrongdoers – still hang from oak doors. Nearby Fowlis Castle built early 17th century.

Glamis Ed
Glamis Castle, childhood home of Queen Mother and birthplace of Princess Margaret, reputed to be most haunted stately home in Britain. Six-storey tower built in 15th century, but wings, turrets and castellated parapets added in the 17th century. Collection of tapestries, paintings, furniture and weapons. Parkland and formal garden laid out by Capability Brown; also 21ft high sundial with 84 dials. Angus Folk Museum in Kirkwynd has collection of furnishings, clothes and tools used by local community over last 200 years housed in 19th-century cottages. Glamis Stone nearby has intricate carvings.

Glen Clova Eg
From gentle, forested slopes around village of Clova, glen narrows to wild mountain home of red deer, wildcat and ptarmigan.

Glen Isla Cf
River Isla runs through picturesque valley for 17 miles. Loch fishing, horse riding and cross-country skiing. Highland Adventure Centre at Knockshannach, east of Kirkton of Glenisla.

Glen Prosen Ef
Roadside cairn in memory of Captain Scott and Dr Wilson, who planned their Antarctic exploration at Dr Wilson's home in the glen. Walks through birch woods along glen.

The Hermitage Woodland Walk Bd
Walk leads through wooded area containing numerous exotic trees, beneath 19th-century railway bridge, along River Braan, past 18th-century bridge to folly overlooking waterfall.

Highland Motor Heritage Centre Bc
Classic and vintage cars, costumes and accessories displayed in authentic period settings. Driving game, free slot-car racing and motor heritage videos.

Huntingtower Castle Bb
Remains of castellated mansion consisting of two medieval towers, linked by another tower in

17th century. Ceiling timbers carved with scrolls, fruit and the faces of dragons and other animals. Fragments of colourful wall paintings remain.

Inchtuthil Cc
Ramparts and ditches of timber fortress built by Roman general Agricola in AD 83.

Kindrogan Bf
Three-storey house is the start for Victorian walk which passes wooded river bank where Queen Victoria once took tea, then 4 mile climb up Kindrogan Hill where surrounding mountains are indicated on circular map.

Kinnaird Db
Village overlooking Carse of Gowrie, River Tay and Ochil Hills. Kinnaird Castle dates from 12th century – restored in 1855 and now private home.

Kirkton of Glenisla Df
Ruined Forter Castle stands 4 miles north-west of village. The village itself is on River Isla.

Kirriemuir Ee
Birthplace of author and playwright J.M. Barrie, creator of Peter Pan. His home now houses Barrie Museum. On hill behind the graveyard where Barrie is buried is cricket pavilion with camera obscura. Views north towards highlands and south across Strathmore Valley.

Loch of Kinnordy Ee
Freshwater loch with large numbers of nesting water birds. Observation hides.

Loch of the Lowes Bd
Loch is part of Scottish Wildlife Trust reserve. Hide allows for viewing of water birds and pair of nesting ospreys. Visitor centre has wildlife exhibition and several small aquaria. Woods surrounding centre populated by roe and fallow deer.

Megginch Castle Gardens Db
The grounds of this 15th-century castle have a physic garden, 16th-century rose garden, astrological garden and 1000-year-old yews.

Meigle Dd
Meigle Museum contains 25 Pictish and early Christian carved stones, found in churchyard.

Meikleour Cc
Beech hedge, 100ft high and 580yds long, forms eastern border of Marquis of Lansdowne's home – said to be largest hedge of its kind in world.

Perth Cb
Ancient city, made Royal Burgh in 1210, though few old buildings remain. St John's Kirk consecrated in 1243, but now mainly 15th century. From here, John Knox preached his sermon on idolatry that resulted in church wrecking throughout Scotland. Restored mill from 18th century produces flour and oatmeal in the traditional way. Fair Maid of Perth's House, once home of Catherine Glover, heroine of Sir Walter Scott's novel, now a craft shop. Black Watch Museum and Gallery holds treasures of Highland regiments. Perth Art Gallery and Museum has displays of local history, art, natural history and archaeology. Whisky blending explained at Dewar's distillery. Walk up Kinnoul Hill to folly at top, views of surrounding area.

Pitcairngreen Bb
Village of 18th-century cottages and houses. North-east stands a prehistoric burial mound.

BARRIE RELIC *A plate in the Barrie Museum, Kirriemuir, records places associated with the author.*

Reekie Linn De
Impressive waterfall where River Isla cascades into deep gorge.

Scone Palace Cb
Pink-stone castellated mansion, enlarged in 1803 around 16th-century and earlier buildings. Place where kings of Scotland were crowned. Interior reveals china, ivories, clocks and exquisite French furniture – including Marie Antoinette's writing table. Grounds include pinetum, woodland garden, children's playground and picnic area. Elaborately decorated chapel on Moot Hill in front of palace.

Tealing Fc
Well-preserved example of Iron Age earth house, comprising passage, long gallery and small inner chambers. Close by is dovecote shaped like house, built 1595.

MOUNTAIN AND GLEN *The slopes of Mount Blair rise above Glen Isla, which stretches for 17 miles through the eastern Grampians.*

bridge over River Ericht. North of town, river rushes through 200ft deep gorge overlooked by 17th-century Craighall.

Branklyn Garden Cb
Described as finest 2 acres of private garden in country. Gardeners from all over world come to see collection of plants including rhododendrons, alpines, and herbaceous and peat-garden plants.

Bridge of Cally Ce
Peaceful village in sheltered gorge at meeting place of River Ardle and Black Water. Choice of walks through deciduous forests.

Camperdown House and Country Park Ec
European brown bears, wolves, lynxes, arctic foxes, reindeer, raccoons and golden eagles can be seen at wildlife centre. Other activities include golf, horse riding, tennis and Adventure Park. House has golf museum tracing sport's history.

Traditional methods of sweet making explained at Shaw's Sweet Factory. Frigate *Unicorn*, oldest British-built ship still afloat is now museum for Royal Navy. RRS *Discovery*, Captain Scott's ship, has displays of ship's history, with actors reliving events on board. In suburb of Broughty Ferry, 4 miles east of town, Broughty Castle houses museum of whaling and local life.

Dunkeld Bd
Ruined cathedral dates from 12th century, 14th-century choir now houses parish church. Cathedral and High Streets have restored 17th-century houses, one of which has metal ell, measurement for cloth, on wall. Scottish Horse Museum has memorabilia of one of Scotland's two Highland yeomanry regiments.

Dunsinane Dc
Iron Age hill-fort enclosed by strong rampart – said to be site of Macbeth's castle.

DUKE'S FOLLY *The folly on The Hermitage Woodland Walk was built by the Duke of Atholl in 1758.*

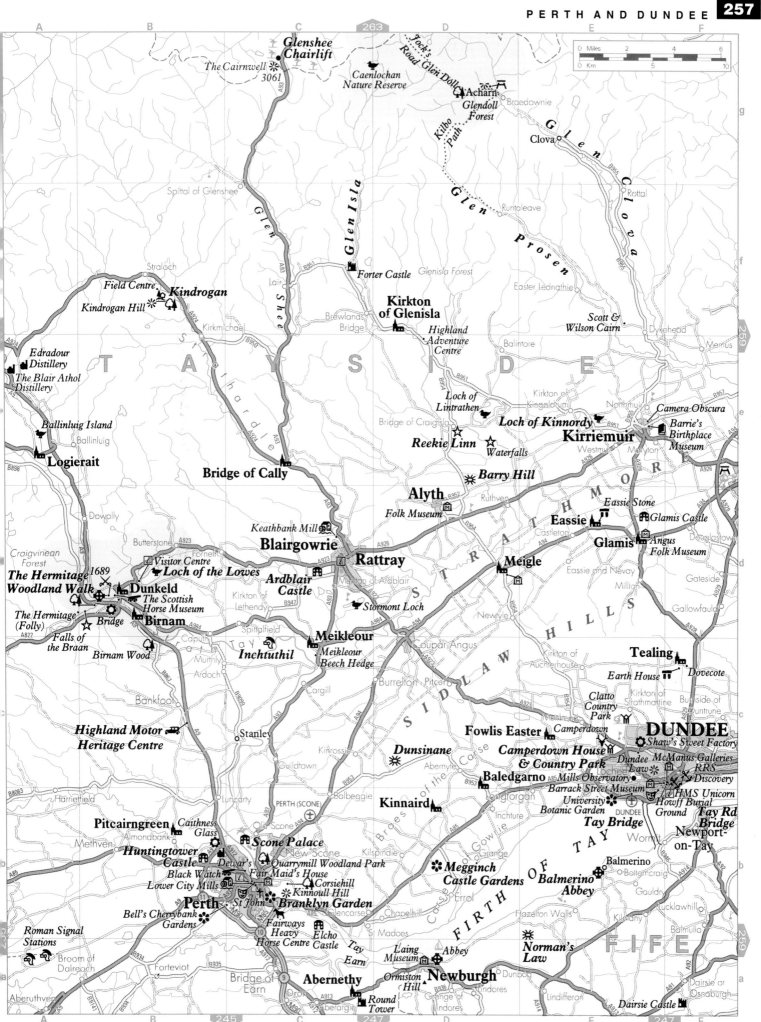

Miles 0 2 4 6
Km 0 5 10

Glenshee
Chairlift

Jock's
Road *Glen Doll*

The Cairnwell
3061

Caenlochan
Nature Reserve

Acharn
Glendoll
Forest

Braedownie

Clova

Rottal

Spittal of Glenshee

Glen Prosen

Glen Clova

Stral och

Field Centre
Kindrogan
Kindrogan Hill

Kirkmichael

Forter Castle

Glenisla Forest

Easter Lednathie

Runtaleave

Kirkton
of Glenisla

Scott &
Wilson Cairn

Dykehead

Brewlands
Bridge

Highland
Adventure
Centre

Balintore

Merlus

Edradour
Distillery
The Blair Athol
Distillery

Loch of
Lintrathen

Kirkton of
Kingaldrum

Northmuir

Camera Obscura

Barrie's
Birthplace
Museum

Ballinluig Island
Ballinluig

Bridge of Craigisla

Loch of Kinnordy

Kirriemuir

Westmuir

Moryton

Logierait

Reekie Linn
Waterfalls

Barry Hill

Ruthven

Eassie Stone
Glamis Castle

Dowally

Bridge of Cally

Keathbank Mill

Alyth
Folk Museum

Castleton

Eassie

Angus
Folk Museum

Glamis

Douglastown

Craigvinean
Forest

1689

Visitor Centre
Loch of the Lowes

Butterstone

Forneth

Blairgowrie

Rattray

Meigle

Eassie and Nevay

Gallowfauld

The Hermitage
Woodland Walk

Dunkeld
The Scottish
Horse Museum

Kirkton of
Lethendy

Ardblair
Castle

Muirton of Ardblair

Stormont Loch

Newtyle

The Hermitage
(Folly)

Bridge

Birnam

Falls of
the Braan

Birnam Wood

Caputh

Spittalfield

Meikleour
Meikleour
Beech Hedge

Inchtuthil

Coupar Angus

Kirkton of
Auchterhouse

Tealing
Earth House
Dovecote

Ardoch

Murthly

Burrelton

Pitcur

Clatto
Country
Park

Kirkton of
Strathmartine

Burnside of
Duntrune

Highland Motor
Heritage Centre

Bankfoot

Stanley

Cargill

Fowlis Easter

Camperdown

DUNDEE

Shaw's Sweet Factory

Dunsinane

Camperdown House
& Country Park

Dundee
Law

McManus Galleries

RRS
Discovery

Luncarty

Abernyte

Baledgarno

Mills Observatory
Barrack Street Museum
University
Botanic Garden

HMS Unicorn
Howff Burial
Ground

Guildtown

Balbeggie

Kinnaird

Inchture

Longforgan

DUNDEE

Tay Bridge

Tay Rd
Bridge
Newport-
on-Tay

Harrietfield

PERTH (SCONE)

New Scone

Braes of the Carse

Gowrie

Wormit

Balmerino

Gauldry

Pitcairngreen
Caithness
Glass

Almondbank

Scone

Scone Palace

Kilspindie

Megginch
Castle Gardens

Balmerino
Abbey

Bottomcraig

Methven

Huntingtower
Castle

Quarrymill Woodland Park
Fair Maid's House
Corsiehill

Black Watch
Lower City Mills

Dewar's

Kinnoull Hill

Branklyn Garden

Perth

St John

Grange

Errol

FIRTH OF TAY

Hazelton Walls

Tucklawhill

Kilmany

Bell's Cherrybank
Gardens

Fairways
Heavy
Horse Centre

Elcho
Castle

Chapelhill

Roman Signal
Stations

Broom of
Dalreoch

Fortevlot

Bridge of
Earn

Tay
Earn

Laing
Museum

Abbey

Dunbog

Norman's
Law

Balmullo

Aberuthven

Abernethy

Round
Tower

Ormiston
Hill

Newburgh

Grange of
Lindores

Dairsie or
Osnaburgh

Dairsie Castle

FIFE

SIDLAW HILLS

STRATHMORE

TAYSIDE

Strathardle

Glen Shee

Glen Isla

FERTILE FARMLAND BY THE SEA

Strathmore's fertile vale with its cattle farms and steep braes divides the Grampian Mountains and Sidlaw Hills from the Firth of Tay and the area's splendid beaches. Wildlife abounds, from wooded watersides to marshy stretches such as Montrose Basin. The remains of rugged castles proliferate, along with intriguing gardens such as Edzell and fine houses like the House of Dun.

Aberlemno ⛪ ⅱ Be
Three carved Pictish stones line roadside of this hamlet. One more in churchyard; carved with Celtic cross and animal decorations. Battle scene on reverse.

DARK-AGE ART *Intricately carved 7th-century cross from Aberlemno.*

Arbroath ⧄ ✦ 🏛 ⛴ ⛵ Cd
Smell of 'smokies' everywhere in this fishing town – haddock smoked over hardwood chip fire. Roofless red-sandstone walls of abbey founded 1178 by King William the Lion, who is buried in front of high altar. Museum in 19th-century tower which used to signal to Bell Rock lighthouse.

Ardestie ⅱ Ac
A well-preserved underground earth house with chambers and passages; homes for 1st and 2nd-century Picts. Another earth house stands 1 mile north.

Auchmithie ⛪ Cd
Village on red-sandstone cliffs with restored cottages and tiny harbour; one of the oldest fishing settlements on Angus coast. Model for 'Musselcrag' in Walter Scott's novel *The Antiquary*.

Boddin Point ☆ De
Low-lying point with fortress-like limekiln on tip. Look for agates among rocks at low tide. Coastal path leads to Elephant Rock: red-sandstone stack in which sea has carved 'legs' and 'trunk'. Fine view across bay.

Brechin ⛴ 🏛 ✝ Cf
Town rising steeply from River South Esk. Red-sandstone cathedral dates from 13th century, now a parish church. Pictish relics, 16th-century font and 17th-century silver inside. Next to it, 87ft high watchtower dates from 11th century.

Bridge of Dun Ce
Spanning River South Esk, squat obelisks guard approaches to this three-arched bridge decorated with Gothic motifs. Built by Alexander Stevens in 1787.

Broughty Castle 🏛 Ac
Perched on a rocky spur above Broughty Ferry harbour, this 15th-century castle was restored in 1860. Now it houses a museum with exhibits of seashore wildlife, Tay's natural history and Dundee's former whaling industry.

Broughty Ferry 🏛 Ac
Built around cottages of old fishing village, this Dundee suburb doubles as a holiday resort with harbour and sea-fishing trips.

Carmyllie ⛪ Bd
Former home of Reverend Patrick Bell, inventor of the reaping machine in 1828. Workshop remains. Church founded 1500.

Caterthun, Brown and White ✳ Bf
Two Iron Age forts: Brown stands alone with six lines of defence, the outermost enclosing an area of 1000ft by 900ft; White, a mile south-west, is a hilltop oval surrounded by two stone walls.

Claypotts Castle 🏰 Ac
Well-preserved late 1500s fortress with towers capped by square garrets. Ground floor dominated by kitchen with vast fireplace and gunport. Sole entrance by small doorway on west front.

Cliffs Nature Trail ❧ Cd
East of Arbroath town, broad esplanade has acres of grass. From northern end, 3 mile nature trail leads along cliff tops, passing stack known as Deil's Heid; one of many oddly shaped rocks. Cave in Carlingheugh Bay leads through to neighbouring bay. Check tide times before venturing in cave.

Crombie Country Park ☗ Bc
Conifer and broadleaf woodland extending for 250 acres, where a Victorian reservoir looks deceptively like a natural loch. Wildlife hides, trails and Ranger Centre with environmental displays.

Damside Garden ✿ Dg
Fragrance fills the air in 8 acres of gardens where history of herbs is explained with Celtic, Roman and monastic displays. Arboretum and tearoom.

NEAT SHRUBS *Edzell Castle's pleasance, an elegant walled garden.*

Edzell Castle 🏰 ✿ Bf
Red-stone ruins of 16th-century castle dominated by square tower house and walls of the Great Hall. The formal 17th-century walled garden has geometric beds. Trimmed boxwood hedges spell out motto: *Dum Spiro Spero* – 'While I Breathe I Hope.'

HOME OF 'SMOKIES' *Fishing gear on the quay at Arbroath, famed for smoked haddock. Scottish independence was proclaimed here in 1320.*

Fasque 🏛 Cg
Castle home of Prime Minister W.E. Gladstone 1830-51. Built 1809, the house looks much as it did in Gladstone's time; still lived in by his descendants. Deer park.

Fettercairn ⛪ ⚖ Cg
Learn how to make malt whisky on a tour of Scotland's second oldest licensed distillery. Arch marks Queen Victoria's 1861 town visit. Shaft of 1670 Kincardine Tower Cross in main square.

Forfar 🏛 ⛺ Ae
Small town where Malcolm III had a castle – destroyed by Robert Bruce; site is marked by 17th-century octagonal turret. Town hall and museum has 'Forfar bridle': medieval iron collar used to gag those about to be executed.

Guthrie Castle 🏛 Be
Built in 15th century on site of earlier fortress. Square tower of 1468 and 19th-century additions. Can be viewed from outside only.

Hill of Finavon ✳ Ae
Remains of ramparted Iron Age fort crown hill with all-round views of countryside. Evidence of metal working and pot making.

House of Dun 🏛 Cf
Handsome house designed by William Adam in early 18th century. Saloon plaster-work depicts armorial bearings, naval and military trophies and mythological scenes. Potting shed contains early 20th-century tools and life-size figure of a gardener at work. Wooded walks through the surrounding parkland.

Johnshaven ⛪ Df
Bustling lobster-fishing port, full of holiday homes, with two-basin harbour. Four mile coastal path runs north to town of Inverbervie, taking in part of disused Montrose to Inverbervie railway track.

Kellie Castle 🏛 Cd
Fine domestic architecture of the 16th and 17th centuries; oldest part dates from 1360. Restored a century ago by Professor Lorimer, whose grandson is the resident custodian. Notable plaster-work and painted panelling. Gardens and tearoom.

Lunan Bay De
Broad sweep of sand, backed by dunes, curves for 6 miles from Lang Craig to Boddin Point. Salmon nets are draped on posts

to dry. Good shore to search for semiprecious stones, such as agate and amethyst.

Milton of Mathers O Df
Ruined cottages stand side by side with modern holiday chalets. Beach of pebbles and rocks. Good walking in woods where there are two streams; one tumbles down 40ft waterfall of Den Finella.

Monikie ⛪ 🏛 ⛵ Ac
Village noted for battlemented 15th-century Affleck Castle, with fine upper hall and vaulted chapel. Waterside walks and boating in country park surrounding reservoir. Beyond Monikie, road runs back towards coast, giving wide views over the sea.

Montrose ⧄ 🏛 ⛴ De
Town with water on three sides. Popular sailing centre with fine beach. Pink-footed geese overwinter on shores. Church steeple soars 220ft above elegant, gable-ended High Street houses, where the narrow, twisting closes have remained unchanged for 200 years. Curfew bell of 'Big Peter' rings from steeple nightly.

Red Castle 🏰 Ce
Short, steep path from Lunan Bay to remains of cliff-top castle, probably dating from the 15th century when it replaced earlier fort built for King William the Lion.

Red Head Dd
One of the most unspoiled spots on Scotland's east coast; 265ft sandstone headland is reached by a bumpy, 1½ mile drive on an unpaved road. Superb view along coast. Path below cliff edge leads to rocky shore.

Restenneth Priory ✦ Ae
Romantic stone ruin surrounded by sloping meadows. Incorporated into remains of Augustinian priory church is porch, possibly dating from 11th century; later heightened to form square tower. Capped by spire in 15th century.

St Cyrus ⛴ Df
Sweep of sand backed by dunes, with cliffs of volcanic rock. Rich in wild flowers, butterflies and moths. Colony of little terns on sand and shingle at the south end. Stonechats, whitethroats and yellowhammers frequent gorse and scrub. Common porpoises sometimes appear offshore and grey seals are seen regularly.

St Vigeans ⛪ ✿ 🏛 Cd
Unexpected gem in dip below modern housing. Small 12th-century church, renovated 19th century, on steep mound dotted with gravestones. Below stands semicircle of red-stone cottages with stone-slabbed roofs.

Tannadice ⛪ Ae
Small village on River South Esk in Vale of Strathmore. Ruined 15th-century stronghold of Finavon Castle, 2 miles south-east.

Turin Hill ✳ Be
Iron Age hill-fort called Kemp's Castle, originally a large enclosure with two ramparts, partly surrounded by stone wall. Replaced by three 'duns' (small hill-forts) later in the Iron Age.

G R A M P I A N

Loch Lee Tarfside
Glen Esk Glenesk
Folk Museum
Clatterin' Brig **Glen of Drumtochty** Auchenblae
Fasque Deer Farm & Park **Catterline**
HOWE OF
Distillery **Fettercairn** THE MEARNS Old Church
Kinneff
Laurencekirk Inverbervie
Damside Garden
Edzell Castle & Gardens Edzell Johnston Tower Hill of Garvock Gourdon
Brown Caterthun Den Finella **Johnshaven**
White Caterthun St Cyrus **Milton of Mathers**
St Cyrus
Brechin **House of Dun**
Cathedral Caledonian Railway
Tannadice Round Tower **Bridge of Dun** William Lamb Memorial Studio
South Esk Montrose Basin **Montrose**
Finavon Castle
Hill of Finavon **Aberlemno** Fishtown of Usan
Sculptured Stones **Boddin Point**
Turin Hill **Restenneth Priory** **Lunan Bay**
Forfar **Guthrie Castle** **Red Castle**
Letham Pitmuies Lunan Water **Red Head**
T A Y S I D E
Auchmithie
Carmyllie **St Vigeans** **Cliffs Nature Trail**
Abbey The Deil's Heid
Arbroath Art Gallery
Crombie Country Park Signal Tower Museum
Affleck Castle **Kellie Castle** Kerr's Miniature Railway
Tealing **Monikie**
Dovecote Monikie Country Park
Earth House Carlungie
Ardestie Carnoustie
DUNDEE
McManus Galleries Danger Area
Claypotts Castle Monifieth
RRS Discovery **Broughty Ferry**
HMS Unicorn **Broughty Castle**
Tay Road Bridge FIRTH OF TAY
Newport-on-Tay Morton Lochs
Pickletillem Tents Muir
Tayport
Tentsmuir Point
Lucklawhill
St Athernase
Earlshall Castle & Gardens
Leuchars LEUCHARS
Guardbridge Royal & Ancient St Andrews Bay
Dairsie or Osnaburgh Sealife Centre
British Golf Museum Crawford's Art Centre
Dairsie Castle Castle **St Andrews**
Botanic Garden Cathedral
Preservation Trust Museum
Brownhills

F I F E

Avoch 🏠 Df

Cottages clustered around small harbour have their gable ends facing the sea so fishing boats can be drawn up between them during rough weather. Easy walk along farm lanes south of village on north side of Munlochy Bay provides views of bay and surrounding mountains.

Beauly ✚🕈🛒 Be

Main street of town dominated by 1905 Boer War memorial and remains of 13th-century Beauly Priory, which contains 16th-century monument to Sir Kenneth Mackenzie. Nearby mud flats home to waders and wildfowl. Walk through Reelig Glen, 3 miles east of Beauly.

Cawdor 🏠🏰 Ee

Cawdor Castle has turreted 14th-century tower with 17th-century additions and still serves as home to Earls of Cawdor. Drawing room has 17th-century fireplace and portrait of Emma Hamilton, Nelson's mistress. Tapestry Bedroom has Venetian bed and 17th-century tapestries portraying Biblical scenes. Three differently styled gardens, nature trails. Castle is scene of King Duncan's murder in Shakespeare's *Macbeth*. Licensed self-service restaurant.

Clachnaharry ✪ Ce

Sea lock built here for Caledonian Canal because North Sea runs out long way at low tide; one of great engineering achievements of the canal-building age. Canal opened in 1822.

Clava Cairns ⊼ De

Cairns dating from late Stone Age surrounded by standing stone circles and hidden by trees. Originally contained domed burial chambers with passage entrances.

Cobb Memorial Bc

Cairn commemorates John Cobb, British racing and motorboat driver who lost his life in 1952 attempting to better world water speed record on Loch Ness. His jet-propelled craft, travelling over 200mph, disintegrated.

Conon Bridge and Maryburgh 🏠 Bf

Two villages joined by bridge at head of Cromarty Firth, built by Thomas Telford in 1809. Walks upstream along river bank.

MONSTER TERRITORY *More sightings of the Loch Ness Monster have taken place near the tiny village of Drumnadrochit than anywhere else on the loch.*

CAPITAL OF THE HIGHLANDS

Highland hills rich in plants and wildlife are a backdrop to the Moray Firth and the sand-and-shingle beaches of the coast. Inverness, 'capital' of the Highlands, stands at the entrance of the man-made Caledonian Canal, which connects Scotland's east and west coasts. On its way, the canal passes through Loch Ness, home of the famous but officially unverified monster.

Craig Phadrig 🕈☀ Ce

Remains of vitrified Iron Age fort – said to have been stronghold of Pictish King Bude – stand atop 556ft hill. Wide views of Moray and Beauly firths, and mountains to west. Varied walks through open woodland.

Creag Far-leitire ☆ Ea

Small ridge rises from woods of pine and birch, and carpets of heather. Old pine trees, well spaced out, as well as denser, younger woods. Views of Inshriach Forest plantations and Spey Valley from summit.

Culloden Muir ⚔🏛 De

Site of last battle fought on Scottish soil – Bonnie Prince Charlie defeated by Duke of Cumberland in 1746. Battlefield restored to 1746 appearance. Visitor centre has audiovisual display of battle. Farmhouse has museum containing historical maps and relics.

BATTLE CAIRN *Culloden's Memorial Cairn was erected in 1881.*

Dingwall 🏛 Bf

Town's oldest building, a former schoolhouse, dates from 1650. Town House, mostly 18th century with older tower, has a museum. Good birdwatching possible from harbour's foreshore.

Divach Falls ☆🕈 Ac

Walk to falls from Lewiston passes old slatted wooden deer leaps. Cataract cascades 100ft down rocky valley of birch and oak.

WATERSIDE RUIN *Urquhart Castle, situated on a promontory on Loch Ness, was blown up in 1692 to prevent it being occupied by the Jacobites.*

Dochfour Gardens ❀ Bd

Terraced gardens stand in 15 acres by Loch Dochfour. Daffodils, trees and rhododendrons; water garden and yew topiary. Kitchen garden with soft fruit in season.

Drumnadrochit 🏠🏛🖼 Bc

Small stone village dominated by Loch Ness Monster trade. Exhibition centre tells of monster sightings and reveals ingenuity of searchers. Visitor centre features film on monster history and myth. Sonar scanning cruises.

Farigaig Forest Centre 🕈🛒 Bc

Converted stone stable houses Forestry Commission Interpretive Centre, demonstrating forest wildlife conservation practices. Walks, picnic areas, car parks.

Feshiebridge Ea

Four-house hamlet stands by bridge over River Feshie rapids. These rapids turn quickly to birch surrounded pools as water makes its way through Glen Feshie.

Fort George 🔫 Df

One of finest artillery fortifications in Europe, completed 1769. Regimental museum of Queen's Own Highlanders has military items covering period from 1778 to present day.

Fortrose ✚ Df

Cathedral, probably destroyed by Cromwell, retains some vaulting. Hill of Fortrose provides views over town and Chanonry Point.

Foyers 🏠☆🛒 Ac

Foyers Falls on eastern shore of Loch Ness. Best places to view falls are from vantage points along path through trees.

Highland Wildlife Park ⅄ Ea

Royal Zoological Society of Scotland park; wildlife includes European bison, mouflon, red deer and birds. Exhibition on 'Man and Fauna in Highlands'.

Dochfour Gardens

Inverness ✪📇🏛🏰✝🕈 Ce

Highland 'capital' on River Ness. Castle Wynd Museum has bagpipes, various Jacobite relics. Abertarff House in Church Street built in 1693. St Andrew's Cathedral built 1866-9.

Insh Church ✝ Ea

Tiny white-painted church dating from 18th century has 8th-century bronze handbell inside.

Kilravock Castle ❀ Ee

Grounds of 15th-century castle contain tree garden with some varieties unique to Britain. Nature trails, guided castle tours.

ROGIE FALLS *Visitors may see salmon leaping the cascade.*

Loch Moy 🖼 Dd

Remains of 14th-century Castle of Moy and obelisk honouring 19th-century Mackintosh chief stand on one of loch's islands.

Loch nan Lann ⚓ Ab

Loch reached by path at foot of Beinn a' Bhacaidh. Stepping stones leading from this loch descend deep gorge to boathouse 600ft below on Loch Ness.

Loch Ness 🕈🛒☆ Ac

Possibly Scotland's most famous stretch of water, renowned for perennial tourist attraction, the Loch Ness Monster. Loch is 24 miles long, about a mile across, and up to 754ft deep. Road from Urquhart Castle to Invermoriston runs alongside wooded slopes of loch; there are plenty of lay-bys and viewpoints.

Nairn 🏛🕈 Ef

Town granted royal charter in 12th century. Laing Hall in King Street houses the Fishertown Museum, which has exhibits on domestic life of town, model boats and collection of photographs and articles on fishing industry. Ornamental gardens just off High Street, and walks along River Nairn. Sandy beaches popular in summer, provide nickname, the 'Brighton of the North'.

Nairn Viaduct ✪ De

Viaduct, 600yds long and 130ft above ground at maximum height, built in 1898 for Highland Railway's route between Aviemore and Inverness through Nairn Valley. Each of the 28 arches has span of 50ft. Arch over river has span of 100ft.

North Kessock 🏠☀🕈🛒 Ce

Iron Age fort tops Ord Hill, overshadowing village of small houses along mud-and-shingle shore. Kessock Bridge replaced ferry route across Beauly Firth. Sea trout angling, bird life along foreshore of firth. Walks through forest along slopes of Ord Hill allow views of firth.

Rock Wood Ponds ⅄❀ Ea

Trail from car park at edge of loch follows 2 mile circular route along deer paths and through open country, providing views of area's many tiny lochs. Bird life includes chaffinches, goldcrests, crossbills and sparrowhawks.

Rogie Falls ☆🕈 Af

Named after Norse for 'splashing, foaming river'. Leaping salmon can sometimes be seen from suspension bridge.

Rosemarkie 🏠⚜☆🏛 Df

Sandstone cliffs dotted with caves face the sea and overlook red-sandstone cottages. Groam House is small museum containing Pictish stone. Footpath starting on road to Cromarty, just north of village, leads along Fairy Glen to two waterfalls. Ledges allow visitors behind falls.

Strathpeffer 🏠🏛⊼ Af

Village, once Victorian health resort with sulphur springs, now famous for doll museum housed in remains of baths complex. Dolls, teddy bears, games and toys spanning 150 years on display, as well as other features of Victorian nursery such as baby clothes, lace and cradles.

Urquhart Castle 🖼 Bc

Jutting out on strategic point into Loch Ness, part of this large often-rebuilt castle ruin dates from Norman times. Blown up in 1692 to prevent Jacobite occupation.

Whitebridge Ab

Humpback bridge, no longer used, built over River Fechlin by General Wade in 1732 to move forces against rebellious Jacobites. Hotel once military rest home.

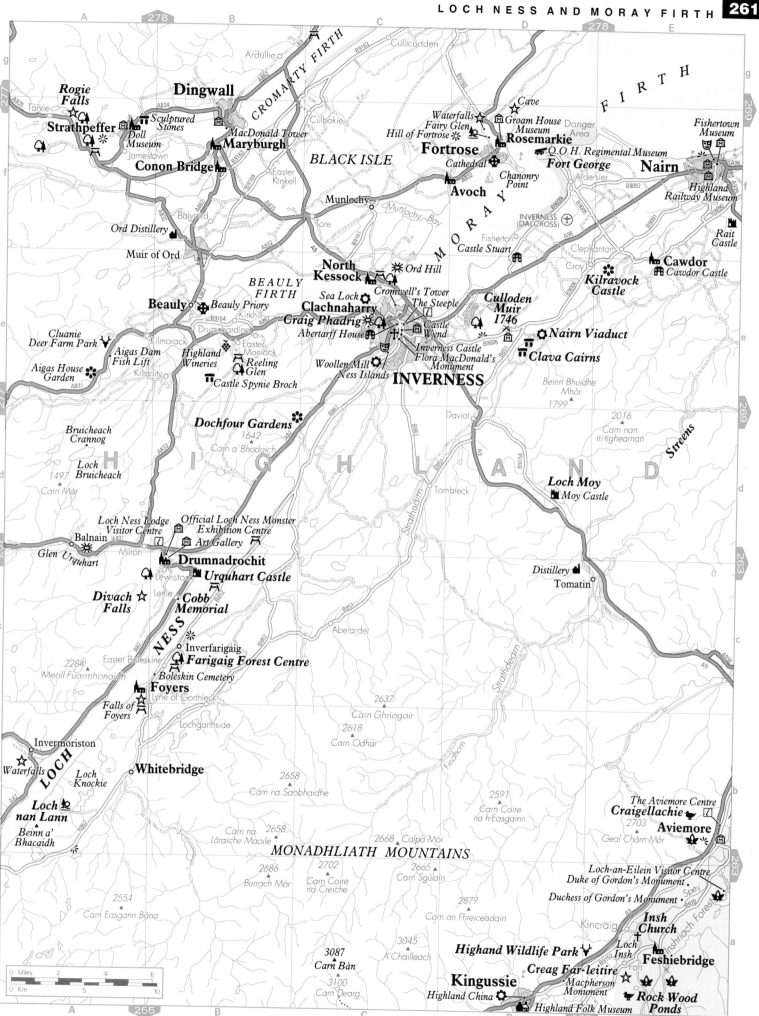

CROMARTY FIRTH

Rogie Falls
Dingwall
Strathpeffer
Sculptured Stones
Doll Museum
MacDonald Tower
Maryburgh
Jamestown
Conon Bridge

Cave
Waterfalls Fairy Glen
Groam House Museum
Danger Area
Hill of Fortrose
Rosemarkie
Fortrose
Cathedral
Q.O.H. Regimental Museum
Fort George
Fishertown Museum
Nairn
Highland Railway Museum

BLACK ISLE

Avoch
Chanonry Point

Rait Castle

Ord Distillery
Munlochy
Tore
Balvaird
Easter Kinkell

Munlochy Bay

INVERNESS (DALCROSS)
Fisherton
Castle Stuart
Clephanton
Croy

Cawdor
Cawdor Castle

Muir of Ord

MORAY

BEAULY FIRTH
North Kessock
Ord Hill
Beauly
Beauly Priory
Kirkhill
Drumchardine
Clachnaharry
Sea Lock
Cromwell's Tower
The Steeple
Craig Phadrig
Abertarff House
Castle Wynd
Culloden Muir 1746
Kilravock Castle
Nairn Viaduct
Clava Cairns

Cluanie Deer Farm Park
Aigas Dam Fish Lift
Easter Moniack
Highland Wineries
Reeling Glen
Kiltarlity
Castle Spynie Broch
Woollen Mill
Ness Islands
Inverness Castle
Flora MacDonald's Monument
INVERNESS

Aigas House Garden

Beinn Bhuidhe Mhòr 1799

Bruicheach Crannog
Dochfour Gardens
1642
Carn a'Bhodaich
Daviot
2016 Carn nan tri-tighearnan
Streens

Loch Bruicheach
1497
Carn Mòr

H I G H L A N D

Tombreck
Loch Moy
Moy Castle

Loch Ness Lodge Visitor Centre
Official Loch Ness Monster Exhibition Centre
Balnain
Art Gallery
Glen Urquhart
Milton
Drumnadrochit
Lewiston
Urquhart Castle
Lenie

Distillery
Tomatin

Divach Falls
Cobb Memorial
Aberarder

NESS

Easter Boleskine
Inverfarigaig
Farigaig Forest Centre
2284 Meall Fuarmhonaich
Boleskin Cemetery
Foyers
Lyne of Gorthleck
Falls of Foyers
Lochgarthside
2637 Carn Ghriogair
2618 Carn Odhar

Strathdearn

Invermoriston
Whitebridge
Loch Knockie
2658 Carn na Saobhaidhe
2591 Carn Coire na h-Easgainn

Waterfalls
LOCH

Loch nan Lann
Beinn a' Bhacaidh
2658 Carn na Làraiche Maoile
2668 Calpa Mòr
2703 Geal Chàrn Mòr

The Aviemore Centre
Craigellachie
Aviemore

2686 Burrach Mòr
2702 Carn Coire na Creiche
2665 Carn Sgùlain
MONADHLIATH MOUNTAINS

2879 Carn an Fhreiceadain
Loch-an-Eilein Visitor Centre
Duke of Gordon's Monument
Duchess of Gordon's Monument
Spey
Kincraig

2554 Carn Easgann Bàna

Insh Church
Loch Insh
Feshiebridge

3045 A'Chailleach
Highland Wildlife Park
Creag Far-leitire
Macpherson Monument

3087 Carn Bàn
3100 Carn Dearg
Kingussie
Highland China
Highland Folk Museum
Rock Wood Ponds

0 Miles 2 4 6
0 Km 5 10

SKI SLOPES OF THE NORTH

Winter sports on the snow-covered slopes of the Cairngorm Mountains have made this part of the Highlands a popular tourist area. In summer, tranquil lochs, woodlands and glens teeming with wildlife attract another group of visitors – those who wish simply to wander through the idyllic scenery and perhaps to glimpse an osprey or a golden eagle.

Aviemore ⌂ ♨ ♿ Ae
Resort catering predominantly for skiing, though there are facilities for golf, squash, riding, curling, and water sports. Cinema, ice rink, saunas, artificial ski slope, go-carts and discos. Also a good summer base for touring in the Spey Valley.

Balmoral Castle ❀ † Ec
Scottish Baronial summer home of Royal Family, rebuilt by Prince Albert from earlier castle in 1859. The 70ft ballroom houses changing exhibits from royal collection. Gardens have rare conifers, Queen Victoria's garden cottage and Queen Mary's sunken garden. Opposite bridge leading to castle's main gate is Crathie Church, built 1895, place of worship for the Royal Family.

Boat of Garten ⌂ ♿ Be
Museum at Boat of Garten station is former waiting room, and has signs, signals and other memorabilia on display. Village name comes from ferry which once crossed River Spey where bridge now stands.

Braemar ⌂ ♿ ⚐ Dc
Village, set among heather-covered hills and where the Clunie Water joins River Dee, famous for Highland Games. Robert Louis Stephenson wrote *Treasure Island* in cottage here.

BUILT FOR DEFENCE *Braemar Castle retains its turrets and star-shaped curtain wall.*

Braemar Castle ⌂ Dc
Built 1628 and largely rebuilt as residence in 18th century, castle has barrel-vaulted ceilings, underground prison, star-shaped curtain wall and central tower with spiral staircase. Interiors fully furnished and containing items of historical interest, including a 52lb cairngorm – a semi-precious stone found in the Cairngorm Mountains.

Cairngorm Mountains ❀ Bd
Chair lifts lead to observation point, short distance from top of Cairn Gorm – mountain from which range gets its name. Paths along range take energetic walkers through moss, campions and creeping rhododendrons. Golden eagles, capercaillies, deer, ptarmigan and wildcats. Awe-inspiring Ben Macdui is highest mountain in range, rising 4294ft.

Cairngorm Whisky Centre ⚑ Be
Whisky-making presentation, the tasting room offering more than 100 brands.

Carrbridge ⌂ ♿ ❀ Bf
Landmark Visitor Centre, popular attraction of this après-ski resort, has audio show of Highland history. Landmark Highland Heritage and Adventure Park has treetop trail, nature trail and sculpture trail with works by Anthony Caro and Eduardo Paolozzi; also steam-powered sawmill. Early 18th-century bridge spans River Dulnain.

Colyumbridge ⌂ Be
Sports complex and hotel attract visitors to this convenient stop-over between Aviemore and Cairngorm chair lifts.

Corgarff Castle ⌂ Ed
A 14th-century tower house, remodelled as fortified military barracks with star-shaped wall in 1748. Restored interior of 200 years ago has musket recesses, wide wooden bunks and large stone fireplaces.

Craigellachie ❧ Ae
Nature reserve to north-west of Aviemore is mainly birch forest on lower slopes. Plants and wildlife include rowans, wych elms, bog myrtles, red grouse, spotted flycatchers. Among rare moths is Kentish Glory (flies March-May). Breeding peregrine falcons nest on imposing granite cliff above Aviemore; kestrels and jackdaws also favour cliffs for nesting.

Gleann Einich Bd
Loch lies at foot of glacial hollow. Reached by good hike from Glenmore Forest Park along tracks once used by cattle thieves.

Glenlivet Distillery ⚑ Df
Guided tours of distillery include free dram. Exhibits of ancient tools and artefacts used in making whisky, and video programme.

Glenlivet Estate ⌂ De
Working Highland estate seen from guided tours in Land Rover, focusing on history, landscape, wildlife and land use.

Glenmore Forest Park ⛺♿❀⚐ Bd
Walking routes lead through pine, spruce and Douglas fir, but one-fifth of park is mountainside above tree line. Wildlife includes roe deer, red squirrels, wildcats, foxes, badgers, golden eagles, whooper swans, ducks, grouse, woodpeckers and Britain's only herd of reindeer.

Glenmuick and Lochnagar Wildlife Reserve ❧ Fb
Walks and trails – some easy, others needing proper equipment – lead through azaleas, red campions, and cranberry and bilberry bushes. Wildlife includes red deer, mountain hares and adders.

Glenshee Chairlift ❀ Da
Ascends Cairnwell mountain from summit of Britain's highest main-road pass, 3061ft.

ANCIENT CROSSING *The single-arched Old Bridge of Carr spans the Dulnain at Carrbridge.*

Grantown-on-Spey ⌂ Cf
Popular ski resort, also famous for trout and salmon fishing in Spey and Dulnain rivers. Old Spey bridge built in 1750.

Kindrochit Castle ♿ ⚐ Dc
Grassy embankments, walls of 11th-century fort. Picnic site.

Loch an Eilein ♿ ❀ ☑ Ad
Remains of 15th-century castle on island in loch surrounded by deep pine and juniper forests. Wildlife includes roe deer, red squirrels, wildcats, whooper swans, herons and crossbills. Remains of stone dam at Milton Burn and site of 18th-century mill, where pine trunks were hollowed out to make water pipes – reminders of time when area had flourishing timber industry. Visitor centre in cottage by loch has small exhibition with displays on the management and conservation of forest.

Loch Garten ❧ Be
Hide and closed-circuit TV allow viewings of pair of nesting ospreys, for a long time extinct in Scotland. Reserve, much of which is Caledonian pine forest, home to roe deer, red deer, wildcats, red squirrels and crossbills.

Lochindorb ♿ Bg
Shell of 14th-century castle, stronghold of Alexander Stewart, 'Wolf of Badenoch', who terrorised Moray lowlands, stands on island in middle of loch. Area has rolling heather landscape with peat stacks and boggy grassland.

PINES BY THE LOCH *The calm waters of Loch an Eilein are surrounded by forests of pine and juniper where wildcats are sometimes seen.*

Loch Morlich ♿ ❀ ⚐ Bd
Inland loch at foot of Cairn Gorm, surrounded by pine, birch, alder, willow and rowan trees. Lies mainly within Glenmore Forest Park. Waymarked walks lead along the shoreline. Wildfowl hides. Osprey sometimes fish here. From Loch Morlich, the River Luineag rushes through banks of tall pines to Spey Valley.

Morrone ▲ ❀ Db
Many walks up this hill; lower slopes clothed with gnarled birch trees. One walk leads to view indicator which identifies view to Cairngorms taking in three of Britain's highest peaks – Ben Macdui, Braeriach and Cairn Toul, all over 4000ft. Tomintoul farm nearby reckoned to be highest in Britain.

Nethy Bridge ⌂ Cf
Village, hub of timber trade during 18th century, has Victorian hotel, remains of Norman castle, old stone cottages and bridge built in 1809. Now centre for skiing, fishing, walking and climbing.

Rothiemurchus ❀ ♿ ⚐ Be
Variety of walks, some ranger guided, lead through farmland, woods, forestry plantations, lochs and heath-clad hills that lie within boundaries of this estate. Two-hour tractor and trailer ride to see red deer, Highland cattle and other animals. Birdwatching with experienced ornithologist.

Royal Lochnagar Distillery ⚑ Ec
Distillery granted royal warrant by Queen Victoria in 1848. It is set amid beautiful scenery, close to Balmoral Castle.

Speyside Garden Heather Centre ❀ Bf
Heather Heritage Centre has exhibition on the historical uses of heather, including thatching, wool dyeing and medicine. Impressive ornamental landscaped gardens display more than 300 heather varieties.

Strathspey Railway ♿ Be
Steam trains travel along line between Aviemore and Boat of Garten, allowing views of woods and cultivated fields in Spey valley. The railway's locomotives and carriages date from Victorian and Edwardian times.

Tamnavulin-Glenlivet Distillery ⚑ ♿ Ef
Visitor centre is in converted old carding mill. Picnic area, walks along River Livet.

Tomintoul ⌂ ⚑ De
Tomintoul Museum has displays on local history, including reconstructed farm kitchen and smithy, wildlife and environment. Picturesque village of limestone houses, built 1776, is highest in Highlands, at 1160ft. Now centre for skiing, shooting and fishing.

Well of Lecht ⚐ Ee
Carved stone monument to General George Wade and team of soldier-builders who opened up Highlands with military roads, intended to pacify the local population. Good views of the surrounding area. Picnic spot.

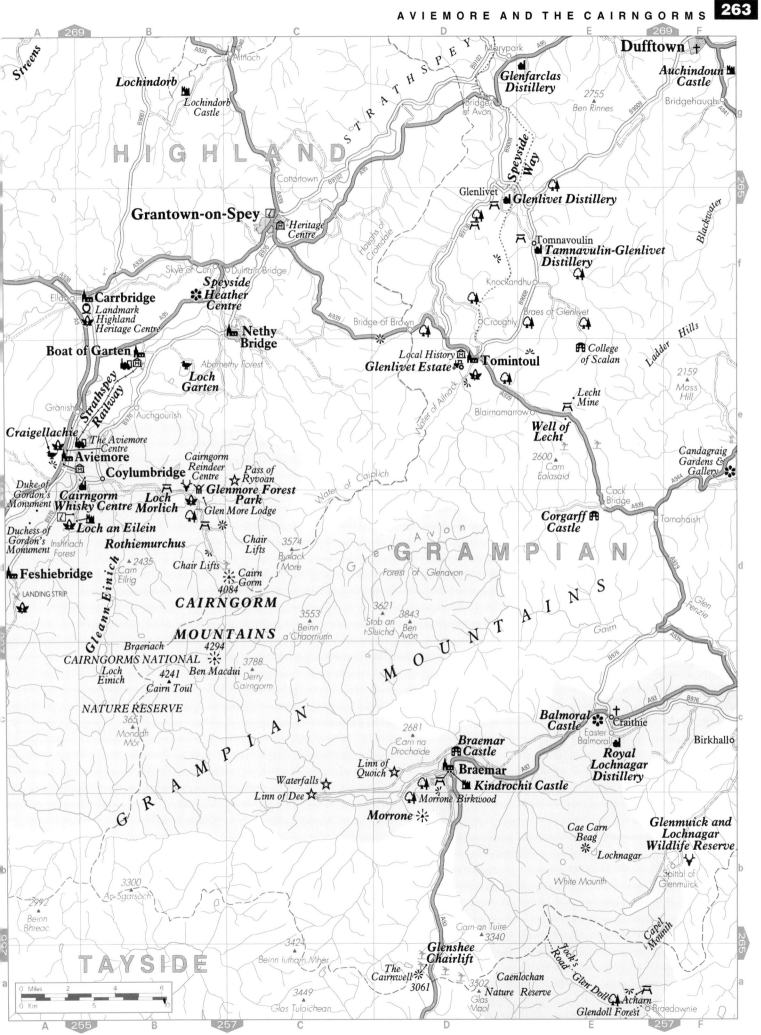

Streens

Lochindorb
Lochindorb Castle

Dufftown †

Glenfarclas Distillery

Auchindoun Castle

2755 Ben Rinnes

Bridgehaugh

Marypark

B9102

A95

A939

Altnoch

B9007

H I G H L A N D

S T R A T H S P E Y

Cottartown

Bridge of Avon

Blackwater

Grantown-on-Spey
Heritage Centre

Haughs of Cromdale

Glenlivet
Glenlivet Distillery

Speyside Way

Skye of Curr
Dulnain Bridge

Tomnavoulin
Tamnavulin-Glenlivet Distillery

Carrbridge
Landmark Highland Heritage Centre

Speyside Heather Centre

Ellan

A938

A95

Knockandhu

Bridge of Brown

Croughly

Braes of Glenlivet

Ladder Hills

2159 Moss Hill

Boat of Garten

Nethy Bridge

Abernethy Forest

Local History
Glenlivet Estate

Tomintoul

College of Scalan

Granish

Strathspey Railway

Loch Garten

Auchgourish

Water of Ailnack

Lecht Mine

Craigellachie

Aviemore

Coylumbridge

Cairngorm Reindeer Centre

Pass of Ryvoan

Glenmore Forest Park

Glen More Lodge

Blairnamarrow

Well of Lecht

2600 Carn Ealasaid

Candacraig Gardens & Gallery

A944

Duke of Gordon's Monument

Cairngorm Whisky Centre

Loch Morlich

Water of Caiplich

G R A M P I A N

Cock Bridge

Corgarff Castle

Tornahaish

Duchess of Gordon's Monument

Inshriach Forest

Loch an Eilein

Rothiemurchus

Chair Lifts

3574 Byrack More

Glen Avon

Forest of Glenavon

A939

Glen Fenzie

Gleann Einich

2435 Carn Eilrig

Chair Lifts

Cairn Gorm

4084

3553 Beinn a'Chaorruinn

3621 Stob an t-Sluichd

3843 Ben Avon

Gairn

B976

Feshiebridge

LANDING STRIP

CAIRNGORM

MOUNTAINS

Braeriach 4294

CAIRNGORMS NATIONAL

Loch Einich

4241 Cairn Toul

Ben Macdui

3788 Derry Cairngorm

G R A M P I A N   M O U N T A I N S

A93

NATURE RESERVE

3651 Monadh Mór

2681 Carn na Drochaide

Balmoral Castle

Craithie

Easter Balmoral

Birkhall

Braemar Castle

Braemar

Royal Lochnagar Distillery

Linn of Quoich

Waterfalls

Linn of Dee

Kindrochit Castle

Morrone Birkwood

Morrone

Cae Carn Beag

Lochnagar

Glenmuick and Lochnagar Wildlife Reserve

White Mount

Spittal of Glenmuick

3300 An Sgarsoch

2992 Beinn Bhreac

T A Y S I D E

3424

Beinn Iutharn Mhor

3449 Glas Tulaichean

Carn an Tuirc 3340

Glenshee Chairlift

The Cairnwell
3061

Caenlochan

3502 Glas Maol

Nature Reserve

Jock's Road

Glen Doll

Capel Mounth

Acharn

Glendoll Forest

Braedownie

| 0 Miles | 2 | 4 | 6 |
| 0 Km | | 5 | |

Aboyne Cc
Gordon stronghold castle, north of village, dates from 13th century. Oldest surviving part is west wing, rebuilt 1671, with two towers and keep. Wooded valley of Glen Tanar, south-west, has fine walks over hills to Glen Mark.

Alford Ce
Network of walks and castle trails surround this market town by the River Don. Green and red engines of Alford Valley narrow-gauge railway carry passengers from reconstructed Victorian station through lush forest. Half-hour trips to Haughton Country Park and on to Murray Park. Vehicles of every description at Grampian Transport Museum, from 19th-century horseless carriages to vintage racing cars. Most cherished exhibit is Craigievar Express; cross between steam engine and three-wheeled cart, built 1895 by local postman.

MOTORISTS' DELIGHT *Two prize items in the Grampian Transport Museum, Alford.*

Auchindoir Bf
A few houses dominated by ruins of St Mary's Church, once one of Scotland's finest medieval parish churches. Carved doorway dates from 13th century.

Ballater Ac
Rolling wooded hills enclose bustling holiday town beneath mighty summit of Lochnagar; founded as 18th-century spa town. Well-trodden path climbs 700ft to Craigendarroch – 'The Hill of Oaks' – with dramatic views of Dee valley. Nearby 18th-century Birkhall is Queen Mother's residence.

Banchory Dc
Little town rising in a series of terraced streets. View of leaping salmon from footbridge at junction of rivers Dee and Feugh. Several easy forest walks and well-marked paths lead up 1000ft Scolty hill.

Barmekin of Echt Ed
Ramparts and stone walls enclose extensive hill-fort, a complex resulting from several phases of Iron Age defence-building.

Bennachie Df
Several peaks are gathered together here, including spectacular 1698ft summit of Mither Tap; granite tor weathered into shattered cliff faces and bare boulders. Four pathways of varying lengths

QUIET FLOW THE DEE AND DON

Pinewood forests open out to the wild Grampian hills, thick with heather, where stone circles and Pictish carvings take the traveller back to ancient times. Winding roads pass a wealth of fairy-tale castles, surrounded by magnificent gardens and waymarked walks. Fishermen line the banks of the Dee and the Don, attractive rivers which thread their way through richly wooded valleys.

start from forest fringe, winding up through lower slopes of pine, spruce and larch to summit ridge, becoming heather tracks with fine views of surrounding area. South, forestry and wildlife displays in Donview Visitor Centre.

Braeloine Interpretive Centre Bc
Glen Tanar's natural history inspires lively display in educational centre, set among picnic areas and waymarked walks.

Bridge of Feugh Ec
Narrow 18th-century bridge, with niches for pedestrians, crosses gorge lined with lilacs, sycamores and beeches. Upstream, the river turns into a torrent, pouring over crags and pools.

Cairn o'Mount Db
Ancient pass through eastern Grampians, with compelling views from 1070ft summit over heathery hills, pine forests, and black mountains beyond. Macbeth and other historic leaders led their armies this way in Scotland's war-torn past.

Castle Fraser Ee
Crow-stepped gables and turrets adorn grand Baronial tower house, built 1575. Stairway from smoking room leads to eerie Green Room, said to be haunted by ghost of a murdered princess. Round tower commands views of wooded parkland with walled formal garden.

Craigievar Castle Cd
Classic example of a Scottish Baronial castle, seven storeys high and virtually unaltered, with fairy-tale turrets, crow-stepped gables, conical roofs, pink walls

and magnificent moulded plasterwork ceilings. Built 1610-26 for Forbes family. Door of musicians' gallery bears arms and initials of first owner; prosperous merchant William Forbes.

Crathes Castle Ec
Pepper-pot towers and square turrets crown grand 16th-century castle, lived in by a single family – the Burnetts – for more than 350 years. Room of Nine Nobles named after ceiling decorations showing great heroes of the past, including Julius Caesar and King Arthur. Formal 18th-century gardens bordered by yew hedges lead to woodland trails with views of the Dee, including one for disabled visitors.

Culsh Earth House Cd
Well-preserved Iron Age earth house with roofing slabs intact, over large chamber and entrance.

Dinnet Oakwood Bc
Wood warblers, spotted flycatcher, jays and great spotted woodpeckers haunt 33 acre oak wood, where rare plants and insects thrive.

Finzean Bucket Mill Cc
Impressive water wheel drives handsome wood-turning mill, built 19th century. Information centre with educational displays.

Glenbuchat Castle Ae
Bold castle ruins on hill approached by twisting paths, once trodden by smugglers carrying tax-free whisky from illicit stills. View from outside only. Z-shaped with round and square turrets, steep gables and tall chimney stacks. Stone inscription above entrance states that it was

DEESIDE OASIS *The June border in the gardens of Crathes Castle contains poppies, lupins and irises.*

built 1590 to mark marriage of John Gordon of Cairnburrow to Helen Carnegie.

Glen Esk Ca
Landscape of cliffs, cascades and weird rock formations. Dramatic pathway joins public road following winding river, ending at Loch Lee. Local folk museum illustrates daily life in glen from about 1800.

Glen of Drumtochty Ea
Mostly Forestry Commission country, with fairy-tale Chapel of St Palladius near Drumtochty Castle. Short walk starts from Mearns Forest car park. Road continues through pretty gorge to Slack Burn and Clatterin' Brig.

Kildrummy Castle Be
Impressive 13th-century ruin. Surviving towers, hall and chapel recall a colourful history. Besieged

1404 and dismantled after 1715 Jacobite Rising. Fine garden sheltered by canopy of beeches.

Knock Castle Ac
Steep track leads to late 16th century stronghold; bare keep is all that remains. Once owned by Gordon family, gruesomely murdered in 16th century.

Leith Hall Cf
White-painted 17th-century mansion, typically Scottish Baronial with 'witch's hat' turrets. Set in series of attractive gardens, each with own theme, divided by hedges and walls. Nature trails through woodlands. Flock of Soay sheep in grounds.

Loanhead Stone Circle Ef
On broad shelf near top of a gentle hill, stone circle with huge horizontal boulder, creates air of Celtic mystery in fields bordering small village of Daviot.

Maiden Stone Ef
Fine example of a Pictish symbol stone near Chapel of Garioch. This beautiful red-granite pillar 10ft high, is carved with men, fish and monsters.

Monymusk De
Village and parish on the Don. Noted for fine ancient church building, incorporating Norman chancel arch and west doorway from former Augustinian priory, dated around 1140.

Muir of Dinnet Bc
Nature reserve with striking landscape, formed by ice and water towards end of the Ice Ages. Lochs are important feeding ground for otters; watch for them on north shore of Loch Kinord near Celtic cross. Foxes, wildcats and red deer visit occasionally. Birds include willow warblers, redpolls, great tits and woodcocks.

Peel Ring of Lumphanan Cd
Tradition has it that Macbeth made his last stand south of Lumphanan village, at Peel Bog, now only a moated medieval earthwork. North on Perkhill, Macbeth's Cairn is said to be where he was killed by Macduff.

Rhynie Bf
Grey village set amid dramatic scenery. Formidable yet beautiful, 15th-century Druminnor Castle is surrounded by barley fields.

Strathdon Ae
River and hill country surrounds this village. Riverside walks along the Don, Scotland's finest trouting stream, fringed by delicate birches and gnarled oaks.

Tap o'Noth Bf
Landmark hill and stunning viewpoint, reached by steep tracks through heather and grasslands. The 1847ft summit is hollow, scattered with remains of an Iron Age fort, enclosing oval basin. Magnificent views of Blackwater and Glenfiddich deer forests.

Tomnaverie Stone Circle Bd
Bold remains of recumbent stone circle lie near village of Aboyne; dating around 1800-1600 BC.

BARONIAL SPLENDOUR *A feature of Craigievar Castle, built in the 17th century, is its decorative ceilings.*

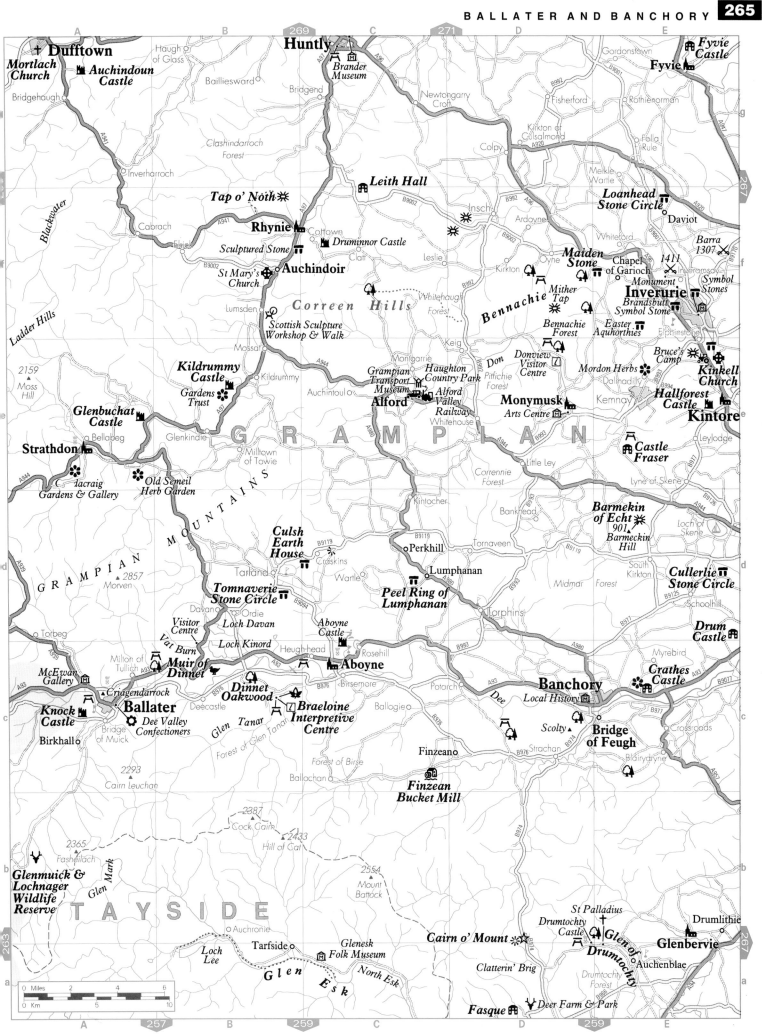

Dufftown
Mortlach Church
Auchindoun Castle
Bridgehaugh
Inverharroch
Blackwater
Ladder Hills
2159 Moss Hill
Glenbuchat Castle
Strathdon
Candacraig Gardens & Gallery
Old Semeil Herb Garden
2857 Morven
GRAMPIAN MOUNTAINS
McEwan Gallery
Knock Castle
Craigendarroch
Ballater
Bridge of Muick
Dee Valley Confectioners
Birkhall
2293 Cairn Leuchan
2365 Fasheilach
Glenmuick & Lochnagar Wildlife Reserve
Glen Mark
TAYSIDE
Auchronie
Loch Lee
Tarfside
Glenesk Folk Museum
Glen Esk
North Esk
2387 Cock Cairn
2433 Hill of Cat
2554 Mount Battock
Fasque
Deer Farm & Park
Cairn o' Mount
Clatterin' Brig
St Palladius
Drumtochty Castle
Drumtochty Forest
Glen of Drumtochty
Glenbervie
Auchenblae
Drumlithie

Haugh of Glass
Bailliesward
Bridgend
Clashindarroch Forest
Cabrach
Flriel
St Mary's Church
Auchindoir
Sculptured Stone
Rhynie
Cottown
Druminnor Castle
Clatt
Lumsden
Mossat
Correen Hills
Whitehaugh Forest
Scottish Sculpture Workshop & Walk
Kildrummy Castle
Gardens Trust
Kildrummy
Glenkindie
Milltown of Towie
GRAMPIAN
Bellabeg
o Glenkindie
Tarland
Culsh Earth House
Craskins
Tomnaverie Stone Circle
Davan
Ordie
Loch Davan
Visitor Centre
Vat Burn
Loch Kinord
Muir of Dinnet
Milton of Tullich
Dinnet
Oakwood
Deecastle
Glen Tanar
Braeloine Interpretive Centre
Forest of Glen Tanat
Ballochan
Forest of Birse
Finzean
Finzean Bucket Mill

Huntly
Brander Museum
Newtongarry Croft
Leith Hall
Tap o' Noth
Insch
B9002
Leslie
Kirkton
Keig
Montgarrie
Haughton Country Park
Grampian Transport Museum
Alford
Alford Valley Railway
Auchintoul
Whitehouse
Wartle
Perkhill
B9119
Lumphanan
Peel Ring of Lumphanan
Aboyne Castle
Heugh-head
Rosehill
Aboyne
Birsemore
B976
Potarch
Ballogie
Finzean

Gordonstown
Fyvie Castle
Fyvie
Fisherford
Rothienorman
Folla Rule
Colpy
Kirkton of Culsalmond
B920
Meikle Wartle
Loanhead Stone Circle
Daviot
Ardoyne
Whiteford
Oyne
Barra 1307
Inveramsay
Chapel of Garioch
1411
Monument
Inverurie
Maiden Stone
Mither Tap
Bennachie
Bennachie Forest
Brandsbutt Symbol Stone
Symbol Stones
Easter Aquhorthies
Bruce's Camp
Kinkell Church
Donview Visitor Centre
Mordon Herbs
Dalmadilly
Hallforest Castle
Monymusk
Arts Centre
Kemnay
Kintore
Leylodge
Castle Fraser
Lyne of Skene
Little Ley
Corrennie Forest
Correnie Forest
Kintocher
Bankhead
Tornaveen
B9119
Torphins
Barmekin of Echt
901 Barmeckin Hill
Loch of Skene
South Kirkton
Midmar Forest
Cullerlie Stone Circle
Schoolhill
Drum Castle
Myrebird
Crathes Castle
Banchory
Local History
Scolty
Bridge of Feugh
Strachan
Blairdryne
Crossroads

0 Miles 2 4 6
0 Km 5 10

269 271
257 259 259
263 267

THE GRANITE CITY AND ITS COAST

Aberdeen Cd
'Granite City', whose speckled grey buildings overlook bustling fishing port and docks. Art gallery focuses on 18th to 20th-century painting and sculpture. Provost Skene's House, built 1545, has fine painted ceilings and local museum. Science and technology discovery centre at the Satrosphere – suitable for all ages.

Balmedie Beach Ce
Shifting dunes border miles of sandy beach, safe for swimming, from River Ythan to River Don. A dozen burns trickle across sands, where birds and plants live.

Bridge of Dee Cd
Graceful seven-arched bridge dates back 400 years. Scene of historic battle in the 17th century.

Brig o' Balgownie Cd
Massive bridge, completed in 1329, spans 62ft in single arch. Bridge crosses deep pool of river and is backed by woods. Closed to motor vehicles.

Brimmond and Elrick Country Park Bd
Park set in rolling countryside of hills and moorland. Guided and marked walks, and picnic area.

Broomend of Crichie Ae
Bronze Age enclosure, over 100ft wide, with external bank and enclosed ditch. It surrounds central stone, a later addition, carved with Pictish symbols.

Camphill Village Trust Bd
Community for people with special needs has workshops producing goods such as soft toys, furniture, metalwork and weaving. Shop sells wholemeal bread, cakes and coffee.

North of Aberdeen, undulating hillsides sweep down to shifting dunes and wide stretches of golden sands. To the south, spectacular rock formations provide sanctuary for thousands of sea birds, and rocky beaches reveal caverns once used by smugglers. Inland, there are numerous castles and country mansions with splendid interiors and furnishings and, in addition, fine gardens.

Catterline Ba
White cottages perch on cliff tops descending steeply to a craggy bay. Short walk along coast leads to Trelong Bay, where kittiwakes and fulmars nest in grass-covered cliffs. Remains of ancient church survive from 12th century.

Collieston Df
Grey-stone houses stand above caves once used by smugglers. Sheltered harbour supported thriving fishing industry. St Catharine's Dub, a rocky headland, takes name from Spanish galleon wrecked there in 1594.

Cove Bay Cd
Road from village approaches harbour set in cliffs. Fishing boats moor here and salmon nets are hung to dry.

Crombie Woollens Visitor Centre Cd
Mill by River Don in Aberdeen has award-winning museum and visitor centre. Cloth, wool and ready-made clothes for sale. Fishing and riverside walks.

Cruickshank Botanic Gardens Cd
Gardens have extensive collections of shrubs, alpine plants, heather and succulents. Rock and water gardens.

Cullerlie Ad
Bronze Age stone circle, 30ft across, with eight boulders around its circumference. Within circle are number of excavated burial chambers.

Downies Cc
Rough road from village leads to cliff-top walk, where views look over to Cammachmore Bay. Steep path descends to rocky cove.

Drum Castle Ad
Antique furniture and paintings enrich castle's interior. Home of Irvine family since 1323, its original keep adjoins Jacobean mansion, built 1619. Extensive grounds border old forest of Drum, where rhododendrons bloom beneath ancient oak and yew trees.

Dunnottar Castle Bb
Steep path from beach climbs solitary rock, crowned by dramatic castle ruin. Cromwell's troops captured this Royalist stronghold after months of siege in 1652. Little-changed dungeon housed 167 covenanters in 1685.

Duthie Park Cd
Park of 50 acres has floral displays in all seasons, including spectacular 'rose mountain'. Children's play area includes trampolines,

swings and boating lake. Modern conservatories, known as Winter Gardens, house exotic plants, flowers, birds, fish and turtles. Cactus house has award-winning cacti and succulents. Bonsai plants and miniature streams in Japanese gardens.

Dyce Be
Incised symbols and carved relief work cover two Pictish stones in St Fergus churchyard, to the north. Standing stone circle, 60ft in diameter, lies 2 miles west.

Findon Cc
Good walk from village leads through fish-farm research station to two rocky coves, and on round cliffs to Portlethen village.

Fowlsheugh Nature Reserve Ba
Two miles of cliffs echo with the calls of kittiwake and guillemot pairs that arrive for summer breeding season. Path to reserve leads from Crawton village.

INSCRIBED TOMBS *Glenbervie churchyard contains a remarkable collection of elaborate memorials to Robert Burns's forebears.*

Glenbervie Ab
Robert Burns memorial cairn lies in scattered parish surrounded by wooded hills. Nearby churchyard holds ornate tombs.

Gordon Highlanders Regimental Museum Cd
Museum has many relics of regiment, first raised by Duke of Gordon in 1794.

Haddo Country Park Bg
Woodland walks span 180 acres rich with wild flowers and plants. Picnic areas and playground.

Haddo House Bg
Fine gardens enclose mansion, designed by William Adam in 18th century for Earl of Aberdeen. Antique works of art, books and ceramics adorn rich interior. Nature trail skirts forest clearings, where roe deer graze.

Hallforest Castle Ae
Ruin of powerful fortress dating from 14th century can be seen from road. Old residence of Keith family, Earls of Kintore.

Hazlehead Park Bd
Largest park in Aberdeen, contains extensive woodland and well-tended rose, heather and azalea gardens. Children's corner has chickens, lambs and rabbits. Walk-in aviary. Adventure playground and bumper-car track. Impressive maze has over a mile of twisting paths.

Hill of Barra Bf
Site of Battle of Barra fought between Robert Bruce and John Comyn in 1307. Comyn is thought to have camped in Pictish fort on hill. Fine views from hill over the Garioch basin.

Inverurie Af
Town museum displays local archaeological and geological finds, including arrowheads, stone axes and flint knives. In cemetery is 50ft mound, the Bass, site of Norman castle. Brandsbutt Stone bears Pictish symbols. Seventeenth-century Scottish poet, Arthur Johnston, was born at Caskieben Castle – now part of Keith Hall.

Kinkell Church Ae
Ruin of parish church, built in 16th century, retains ornate details. Unusually designed sacrament house dates from 1524.

Kintore Ae
External stone stairs enhance elegant town house, built 1737. Old bell chimes in house clock tower with original slate roof. Early Pictish stone stands in churchyard. Well-preserved Balbithan House lies in quiet dell to the north-east, across River Don.

Kirkton of Maryculter Bc
Nursery rhyme and fairy-tale characters greet visitors, young and old, to make-believe garden world of Storybook Glen. Tropical palms and waterfalls enhance landscaped gardens.

Muchalls Cc
Picturesque, white-painted village, dating from 19th century. To north, coast has spectacular rock formations including stacks and deep caverns.

Muchalls Castle Bc
Fine plaster-work distinguishes Great Hall of 17th-century castle. Smugglers' tunnel, now blocked, once led to Gin Shore Cove.

Old Slains Castle Dg
Ruined tower remains from Earl of Erroll's fortress, set above shingle beach. James VI had it destroyed in 1594 after learning of the Earl's plot to land Spanish troops on Scottish coast.

Pitmedden Garden Bf
Formal gardens established in 1675 with central fountain, pavilions and sundials, all laid out in four great rectangles. Box hedges form elaborate designs and Latin mottoes. Museum of Farming Life includes furnished farmhouse.

Portlethen Village Cc
Once-busy fishing village is now community for people employed in Aberdeen. Steep road leads to small cove, hemmed in by cliffs.

HARBOUR LIFE *Yachts are as much a feature of Aberdeen's docks as are the commercial fishing and cargo boats.*

St Machar's Cathedral † Cd
Cathedral founded in 1131, though main part of building dates from 15th century. West front has twin towers. Painted wooden heraldic nave, dated 1520, is in use as parish church.

CROWBERRY *Grouse feed on the black berries of this moorland plant, common at the Sands of Forvie.*

Sands of Forvie Nature Reserve ⚓ ☑ Df
Kittiwakes, terns, geese and ducks find sanctuary in extensive sand and moorland. Butterflies settle on grass-topped dunes and hedgerows in summer. Reserve is home to largest colony of eider duck in Britain. Visitor centre offers an audiovisual display. Nearby lie traces of ancient church, founded in 5th century.

Stonehaven 🏛 ⚓ ⛱ Bb
New town, with amusement park and beach, dominates old town of fishermen's cottages by harbour. Local exhibits found in 16th-century Tolbooth Museum, where Episcopal clergymen were imprisoned in 1748. Panoramic view from war memorial on hill.

Tarves 🏰 🏛 Bg
Gothic and Renaissance styles evident in fine altar-tomb of William Forbes, resident of nearby Tolquhon Castle in 16th century. Tomb lies in Tarves parish church.

Tolquhon Castle 🏰 Bf
Impressive, pink sandstone castle ruins, set in wooded glen. Large quadrangular mansion, built by William Forbes adjoins keep, dating from 15th century, called Preston Tower. Two round towers with grated windows stand beside remains of gatehouse with ornate gunports.

Tolquhon Gallery 🏛 Bf
Work of Scottish artists, including prints, paintings, ceramics and glass, exhibited in changing programme. Sculptures are displayed in garden.

Udny Green 🏰 Bf
Above village is Udny Castle, tower house dating from 14th-century, crowned by ornamental turrets. Churchyard has stone and slate 'morthouse', built 1832, to protect unburied dead from clutches of resurrectionists.

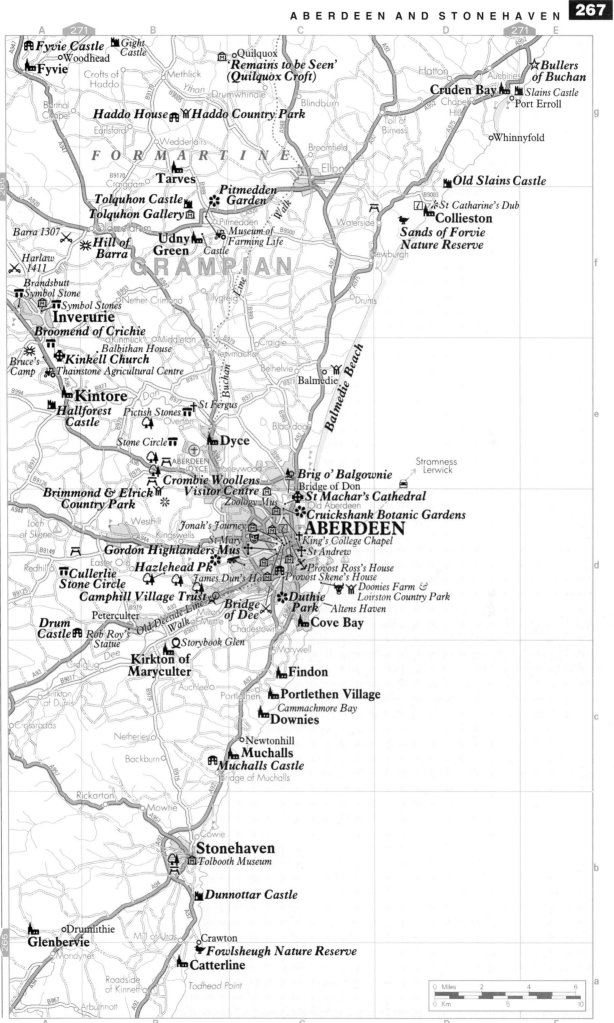

SOUTH FROM THE MORAY FIRTH

Steep red-sandstone cliffs sweep down to sheltered sandy coves and rocky outcrops, where thousands of sea birds flock together. Scattered farmsteads and fishing villages border the fertile land by Moray Firth, known as the 'Granary of the North'. The Spey's soft, peaty waters supply a host of malt whisky distilleries, and its rocky pools are alive with salmon and brown trout.

Archiestown 🏘🏚 Eb
Ladycroft Agricultural Museum, a mile east of Archiestown, displays horse-drawn vehicles, distinctive farm tools.

Ardclach Bell Tower Bb
Two-storey tower built in 1655. Bell tolls to summon locals to church and to warn of danger.

Auchindoun Castle 🏰 Fa
Fortress of clan chief 'Edom o' Gordon' in 16th century tops ancient earthworks. Its cornerstones were taken for use in Balvenie Castle nearby.

Auldearn 🏘🗡 Bc
Castle motte of 12th century overlooks scene of 1645 Civil War skirmish. Restored dovecote on castle mound provides views of Black Isle. Remains of medieval Rait Castle stand nearby.

Aultdearg ☆※🎋 Fc
Earth Pillars, naturally eroded from red sandstone, stand on steep hillside near River Spey.

Balvenie Castle 🏰 Fb
Dry moat surrounds bold, 13th-century castle ruin, noted for its high stone walls and double iron

Burghead 🏚🏰 Dd
Burghead Well, chamber carved into rock, may have served as early Christian baptistry.

Charlestown of Aberlour 🏚 Eb
Old general store has original shop fittings and stock dating from the 1920s.

Craigellachie 🏘 Eb
Thomas Telford's cast-iron bridge of 1815 spans River Spey. Ben Aigan dominates valley.

Culbin Forest 🌲🐦 Bd
Roe deer and capercaillie inhabit forest and salt marsh along coast. Picnic areas near dunes, which cover old village of Culbin.

Dallas 🏘 Dc
Set on River Lossie. US vice-president George Mifflin Dallas, a descendant of Dallas family which owned the village, gave his name to the Texas city in 1845.

Dallas Dhu Distillery 🍶 Cc
Working distillery housed in a Victorian building offers guided tours, videos of whisky making. Impressive shop display of 200 different whiskies.

Darnaway Farm Visitor Centre 🏚 Bc
Old farm tools contrast with a modern dairy viewed from elevated walkway. Afternoon trips explore Darnaway forest and castle. The latter is noted for its magnificent medieval hammer-beam roof in the hall.

Darnaway Forest Walks 🌲 Cc
Deciduous and coniferous woodland crossed with marked paths. Trail from the car park passes by Findhorn Gorge.

Deskford Church ✠ Hd
Noble church ruin bears inscription of founder, Alexander Ogilvy of Deskford, dated 1551.

Drummuir Castle 🏚 Fb
Lantern tower crowns restored castle, built by Duff family in Victorian era. Guided tours of castle and grounds available.

Dufftown ✝🏰🏚🍶 Fa
River Fiddich and Dullan Water converge here. Town clock tower houses museum and information centre. Glenfiddich distillery was founded in 1887.

Duffus 🏘🏰 Dd
Ruin of Duffus Castle, rebuilt of stone in 14th century, stands on a Norman mound. The sounds of modern fighter planes are heard from RAF Lossiemouth.

Elgin ✠🏰🚂🏚 Ed
Settlement featuring remains of Elgin Cathedral, burned by 'Wolf of Badenoch' in 1390. Pictish symbols survive on Celtic cross slab in choir. Old oatmeal mill on River Lossie dates from 13th century.

Findhorn 🏘❀ Cd
Third village of this name; storms buried first one with sand in 17th century while flooding swamped second in 1701. Sea birds feed in tidal bay and organic vegetables flourish at Findhorn Foundation, established 1962.

Findlater Castle 🏰 Hd
Steep path to ruins of cliff-side castle, built by Ogilvy family in medieval times and inhabited until about 1600. Crescent-shaped Sunnyside Beach to the west.

Findochty 🏘 Gd
Village's lower part envelops sandy cove, from which footpath leads to Portknockie. Upper part's skyline dominated by church. War memorial near harbour heads old smugglers' route.

Fochabers 🏘⚙🏚 Fc
Gridiron-pattern village designed in 18th century. Horse-drawn vehicles, model engines re-create past at folk museum, housed in old church. Riverside path from bridge joins Speyside Way.

Fordyce 🏘 Hd
Castle of 16th century lies at heart of conservation village. Impressive canopied tombs housed in small church.

Forres 🏚🏛 Cc
Ancient town among hills. Buildings of many periods include 15th-century market cross and a 19th-century tolbooth. Steep path leads to battlemented 70ft Nelson Tower, which provides views of Moray Firth. Walks south explore riverside and woodland trails.

Glenfarclas Distillery 🍶 Ea
Whisky distillery supplied by soft, peaty water from Grampian Hills. Guided tours, exhibitions and audiovisual displays explain whisky-making process.

Hopeman 🏘 Dd
Fishing village, now water sports and fishing centre. Pleasure boats moor at harbour, village itself is set on slope away from sea.

Huntly 🏰🏚🎋 Ha
Excellent fishing at this meeting place of the rivers Bogie and Deveron. A 17th-century heraldic carving stands over the main door of Huntly Castle, set in lush parkland by Deveron Gorge.

Keith ⚙🍶 Gc
'Auld Brig o' Keith' over River Isla, built 1609, links medieval Old Keith and New Keith (1750) to Fife

BURN'S END *The confluence of the River Findhorn and tidal Findhorn Bay is a rich feeding ground for waders – and a paradise for birdwatchers.*

gates. Triumphant Jacobite troops returned here in 1689 after the Battle of Killiecrankie.

Brodie Castle 🏛 Bc
Family portraits line walls of battlemented tower house built in 1567. Ornate plaster ceiling of flowers and fruit in dining room.

Buckie ✝🐟 Gd
Fishermen moor at Cluny Harbour to sell their catches. Chapel dedicated to fishermen who died at sea. Maritime museum illustrates local fishing industry.

Culbin Sands 🐦 Bd
Ducks, geese, terns inhabit shingle bars along coast. Predatory birds scout acres of salt marsh where waders sift the mud. Stonecrops and lichens thrive on Nairn Old Bar to the west, as well as heathers, crowberries and gorse.

Cullen 🏘✝ Hd
Resort village on two levels, divided by disused viaduct. Distant Sutherland peaks present panorama from Bin Hill. Footbridge leads to golf course and 'Three Kings' rock formations.

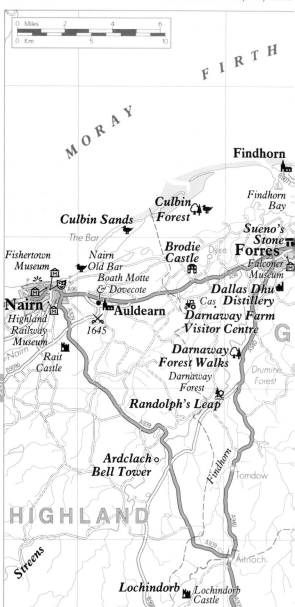

HOT STONE *Heraldic emblems feature above a fireplace among the ruins of Huntly Castle.*

Keith (1817). Milton Distillery, now Strathisla, of 1785, is Scotland's oldest operating malt whisky distillery.

Kingston and Garmouth ⌂ Fd
Local pine forests supplied timber to these two once-flourishing sailing-ship building centres on the River Spey in the 18th and early 19th centuries. Sea birds flock to coastline. Coastal path by sand and shingle beach leads 7 miles west to Lossiemouth.

Lossiemouth ✤⌂ Ee
Bustling fishing port, with sandy beaches good for bathing. Fisheries and Community Museum at harbour includes story of James Ramsay MacDonald (1886-1937), born here, who became Prime Minister in 1924. A 4 mile walk inland leads to ruins of Palace of Spynie, 15th-century fortress of Bishops of Mornay. Good fishing at both riverside and seashore.

Mill of Towie ⌂ Gb
Restored oatmeal mill, built 19th century, stands beside River Isla. Picnic area on river bank nearby.

Mortlach Church ✝ Fa
Well-preserved church stands on an ancient site, founded by St Moluag in 6th century. Pictish stone in the churchyard records Danish defeat.

North East Falconry Centre ☛ Gb
Trained owls, hawks and falcons can be seen in action daily on the flying ground.

Pluscarden Abbey ✤ Dc
Monastic services still take place in abbey founded in 1230 by Alexander II. Badly damaged in 14th century and had fallen into ruin by 1560, but was restored in 1948 by Benedictines.

Portgordon ⌂ Fd
Restored Gollachy ice house, relic of salmon industry, and where fish were once stored, stands on shore of this 18th-century harbour. Dovecote surviving from now-vanished castle nearby can be seen from A98.

Portknockie ⌂ Gd
'Preacher's Cave' on shore was church in 19th century. Foundations of 7th-century Pictish fort perched on promontory overlooking harbour. Cliff-top path to west provides views of the Black Isle.

Randolph's Leap ⌂ Bb
River Findhorn runs through a deep, spectacular sandstone chasm at Randolph's Leap. Beech, larch and oak shade woodland paths above gorge. Floodstones are reminders of the storms of 1829, when waters rose 50ft.

Roseisle Forest ⌁⌂ Dd
Picnic sites line trails through the woodlands. Way-marked paths lead to fine sandy beach lying south of Burghead.

St Ninian's Chapel ✝ Fd
Restored 18th-century chapel; perhaps oldest post-Reformation Catholic church still in use.

Spey Bay ⌂⌂ Fd
Ice house recalls former salmon industry of village at Spey's mouth. Speyside Way starts on east bank. Shorter walk to Garmouth over disused viaduct.

SAFE HAVEN *Portknockie harbour, once busy with fishing vessels, now shelters small craft.*

Speyside Way ☆⌂⌁ Fc
Long-distance 30 mile walk follows fishermen's trails and old railway south. Ospreys fish in river near Fochabers. A marked and well-maintained pathway leads to Ballindalloch.

Streens Aa
Stretch of steeply angled hillsides hold the turbulent waters of River Findhorn in check, like a bridle on a mettlesome horse – Gaelic *srian* means 'bridle'. Grouse moors overlook the Tirfogrean Gully, eroded by swirling currents. Scattered farms are those that survived flooding in 1829.

Sueno's Stone ⌂ Cc
Carvings of warriors and corpses embellish this 23ft monolith east of Forres. It was carved by the Picts around AD 900. Witches' Stone at foot of Cluny Hill nearby marks the place where women accused of practising witchcraft were put to death.

Whiteash Hill Wood ⌁⌂ Fc
Marked paths, called Winding Walks, span stretch of woodland east of Fochabers. Hill's summit provides views of Fochabers and lower Speyside.

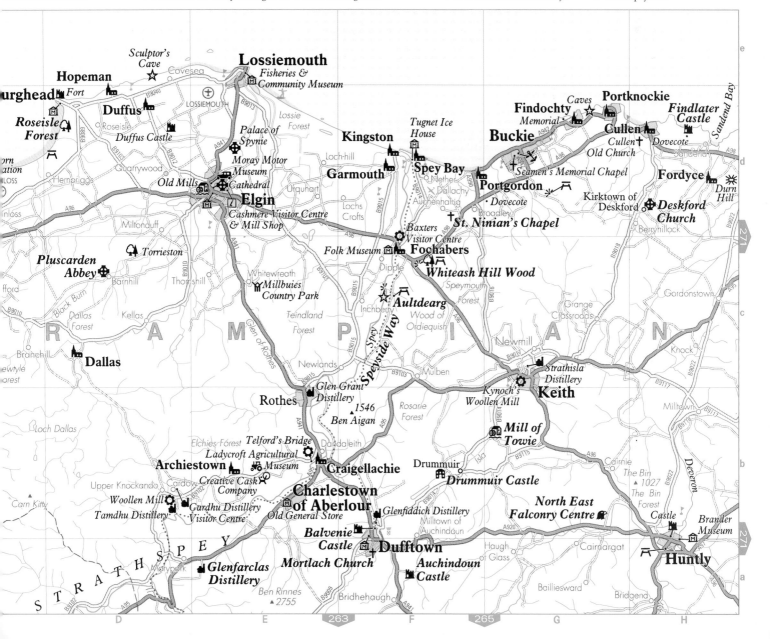

TOWERING CLIFFS OF BUCHAN

Spectacular cliffs around Banff and Buchan shelter secluded, sandy coves, tiny hamlets and the ruins of old fortresses. Precipitous cliff-top paths take in the magnificent Highland scenery and dramatic sunsets that distinguish this section of coast. Old villages bear traces of a prosperous fishing industry in days gone by, and folk museums bring local history vividly to life.

Aberchirder ⌂☗ Cc
Rolling patchwork fields surround gravel approach road, overhung with beech and sycamore. Fine woodland walk leads from village; once the smallest burgh in Banffshire. Founded in 1764.

Aden Country Park ☗ Fb
Estate dating from 18th century with restored farm buildings, ruined mansion, and 230 acres of field, forest and walled nursery garden. Exhibition of local farming life; past and present. Woodland walks by lake and along South Ugie Water; deer, rabbits and foxes often seen.

EXECUTION SITE *Banff's Biggar Fountain stands on the site of the former gallows.*

Banff ⌂🏛 Cd
Ancient fishing port at mouth of River Deveron. Seven-arch bridge spans river. Royal burgh in 1372; fashionable 18th-century wintering resort; now a quiet holiday resort with sandy beaches and sailing centre. Town of architectural surprises: Greek columns, crow-stepped gables, Venetian windows and delicate steeples. Duff House (1725-40), baroque mansion; church dates from 1789. Local history and British bird exhibition in Banff Museum.

Boddam ⌂☗ Hb
Granite fishing village above harbour with massive concrete walls. Dominated by lighthouse on Buchan Ness, dating from 1827. Built by Robert Stevenson, grandfather of author R.L. Stevenson, and linked to mainland by bridge.

Bridge of Alvah ☗ Cd
Walk of 2 miles from Banff's Duff House leads inland through woods beside River Deveron to Alvah Bridge, crossing river 40ft above impressive gorge. Follow path past Mains of Montcoffer and turn north over wooded hill to join main road near Banff Bridge; circular walk of 4½ miles.

Bridge of Marnoch ☗ Cb
Handsome bridge spanning River Deveron. Marnoch Old Church built 1792 with standing stone nearby. Special wool from resident llamas and alpacas sold at Cloverleaf Fibre Stud Farm. Culinary, aromatic and medicinal herbs grown and sold at Old Manse Herb Garden.

Buchan Line Walkway ⚇ Fb
Long-distance footpath created along line of old Buchan railway. Station yard at Maud has been

NARROW FOOTHOLD *The picturesque fishing village of Crovie clings like a limpet to a narrow shoreline facing the open sea.*

landscaped and picnic tables provided. Some of Buchan's best scenery; wildlife abounds.

Bullers of Buchan ☆ Ha
Sea has carved immense rock amphitheatre and cave in cliffs. 'Bullers' probably derived from 'boilers', referring to seething waters. Cliff-top path leads along dizzy knife-edge, 100ft above waves. Gulls, kittiwakes and guillemots scream and wheel in the maze of cliffs and stacks that form the coast.

Cruden Bay ⌂🕮 Ga
Village and Port Erroll harbour are centre of popular holiday area with sandy beaches, dunes and championship golf course. Cruden Water spanned by Bishop's Bridge of 1697. Stark ruins of Slains Castle above gaunt cliffs are thought to have inspired setting for *Dracula*, as author Bram Stoker used to holiday here. Castle built 1664 by Earl of Errol, Great Constable of Scotland.

Delgatie Castle 🏰 Dc
Grand 13th-century home of the Clan Hay. Altered in 16th century with fine painted ceilings dating

from 1570, and collections of paintings and armour. Mary, Queen of Scots visited in 1562; her portrait hangs in her room. The mighty turnpike stair has 97 steps.

Duff House 🏰 Cd
Richly detailed mansion on edge of Banff is one of Britain's finest works of Georgian baroque architecture. Designed by William Adam in 1735 for William Duff, later 1st Earl of Fife. A second classical wing added 1870, then house drifted into decay. It served as a hotel and sanitorium; and housed German prisoners of World War II. Rooms are now restored but mansion still unfurnished and uninhabited. Exhibition on building's history.

Fraserburgh ☗ Fd
Busy fishing port at end of rocky Kinnairds Head, where 1570 castle was converted into 1786 lighthouse; one of Scotland's oldest. Mysterious Wine Tower at head of steep cove has no stairs between its three floors; purpose unknown. Dune-backed sands at Fraserburgh Bay, morning fish market at the quay, and fishing trips from the harbour.

Fyvie ⌂🏰🕮 Da
Resort village in wooded vale of River Ythan, bordered by cornfields and pine forests. Early 19th-century parish church has east window created by American artist, Louis Tiffany, featuring life-size St Michael with flaming sword. Unusual oak pulpit is carved in shape of huge wineglass. Wild path through woods leads to ruins of 16th-century Gight Castle.

Fyvie Castle 🏰 Da
Stately fortress with five great towers named after owners of last 500 years: Preston, Meldrum, Seton, Gordon and Leith. Oldest part dates from the 13th century. Labyrinth of rooms and passages,

rich in Edwardian furnishings and 16th-century tapestries. Great spiral staircase, with 10ft wide steps, rises through five floors.

Gardenstown ⌂⚓ Ed
Busy fishing village clinging to steep hillside above Gamrie Bay, overlooked by Castle Hill of Findon, with good views of the surrounding cliffs. To the west ruined chapel of 1513 said to be on site of older church built to commemorate victory over invading Danes in 1004. Short walk along path from harbour's east end leads to tiny twin village of Crovie.

Glendronach Distillery ⚗ Dc
Fine aromas of malt whisky fill old distillery, founded 1826. Visitor centre, guided tours.

Honeyneuk Bird Park
⚘☙☗ Dc
Rambling wildlife and conservation park housing over 100 species of birds and animals. Special breeding centre nurtures rare species. Pets' corner.

Loudon Wood Circle 🗿 Fb
Forest clearing reveals Buchan prehistoric stone circle – central stone weighs about 12 tons.

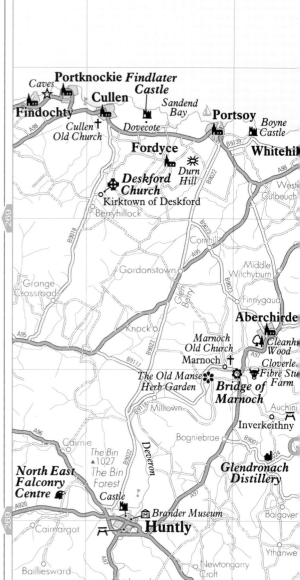

SAFE REST *Gardenstown harbour is protected against all but north winds.*

Longside Gb
Set about with trees and well-kept gardens, village has two contrasting churches and ruins of third. On left of road into village, small Episcopalian church with large bell tower is gem of 19th-century architecture; built of blue-grey stone, with windows by pre-Raphaelite artist Edward Burne-Jones. Spacious parish church dating from 18th century has large gallery. Standing next to it is its ruined 17th-century predecessor.

Macduff Dd
Resort town, formerly known as Doune, with busy fishing harbour, crammed with salmon nets and lobster pots. Boatyard on western side. Hill of Doune, reached by path from east end of Banff Bridge, provides fine views of Deveron estuary and Banff on west side of bridge.

New Aberdour Ed
Single street lined with fishermen's cottages, 1 mile from sea. Steep road leads to pebble beach at mouth of Dour valley, where caverns riddle red-sandstone cliffs. Ruined church of Old Aberdour, among the oldest in north Scotland, has a number of interesting gravestones.

New Deer Eb
Village high street leads to Hill of Culsh, topped by austere monument to a local landlord. Fine view over hills of Buchan and towards Bennachie hills.

Northfield Farm Museum Ec
Old farm tools, beautifully restored stationary engines and various household items recall agricultural life in Victorian times.

Pennan Ed
Tiny one-street village with stone cottages and harbour. To the west, the road plunges down to Cullykhan Bay, where waves pound into huge clefts and caves. To the east, sheer cliffs of red sandstone provide nesting sites for numerous sea birds. Cliffs pitted with caves and tunnels, accessible at low tide.

Peterhead Hb
Busy port with some 400 fishing boats and lively fish auctions each morning. Pink-granite town clusters around huge harbour that took more than 70 years to build, beginning in 1886. Ruined pre-Reformation church of St Peter stands among gravestones on South Road. Arbuthnot Museum in St Peter Street features display on local history. Trout fishing in River Ugie.

Portsoy Bd
Thriving resort and haven for pleasure craft, with restored 17th and 18th-century harbour warehouses. Look for souvenirs made from local red and green marble. Coastal walks lead west to Sandend Bay, and east to ruined 16th-century Boyne Castle.

Remains to be Seen Ea
Museum in Quilquox featuring period clothes and fine display of porcelain. Special gardens were planted by an ornithologist to attract variety of birds. Children's play area.

Rosehearty Fd
One of Scotland's oldest seaports, surrounding peaceful harbour used by inshore fishermen. Open-air sea-water swimming pool, and golf course. Small museum has displays on local history. Impressive ruins of Pitsligo Castle, half a mile south, date from 1424. Pitsligo Church, 8 miles south-west, noted for richly carved gallery.

Sandhaven Fd
Sleepy old fishing village where seals can be watched from rocky shoreline. Sea walls, battered by storms, still protect inshore fishing boats. Oatmeal mill at eastern end worked continuously for 200 years; closed in 1981.

Strichen Stone Circle Fc
Impressive Buchan stone circle has been dismantled and re-erected many times in traumatic history. Near Mains of Strichen farm, half a mile west of village.

Towie Barclay Castle Db
Unique tower house, now in ruins, dating from 16th century. Upper storeys are no more, but remaining Great Hall is considered one of most imaginative of all tower-house interiors and is Gothic and medieval in inspiration. Visit by prior appointment.

Turriff Db
Bustling, red-sandstone market town, created a burgh of barony in 1511. Ancient ruined church has elaborate double belfry built in 1635 and bell dated 1559.

White Cow Wood Fc
Marked walks through spruce woods noted for badger setts and herons. Beyond, road down to Strichen yields view of Mormond Hill with white horse etched into slope; filled in with stones of gleaming white quartz.

Whitehills Cd
Small fishing village built around thriving harbour. Harbour road leads east to Boyndie Bay, and stony track continues to Banff. Chalybeate spring just off track once part of fashionable 19th-century circuit for visitors 'taking the waters' around Banff.

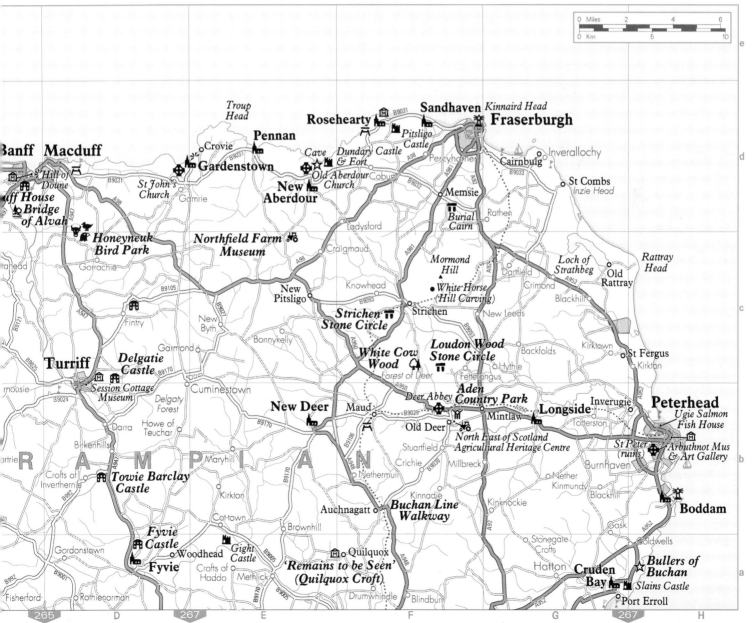

Arnol 🏠📷 Fh
Traditional *tigh dubh*, or black house on Lewis with 6ft thick walls and thatched roof tied down with rope and weighted with stones, now houses folk museum. Crofters' furniture includes straw-filled box beds.

Balranald 🦆 Ki
Waymarked paths lead through Hebridean marsh, machair and along North Uist shoreline, offering chance to see birds such as corncrakes, red-necked phalaropes, oystercatchers and mute swans that visit and nest here.

Barra 🏯⛩⚜ Jc
Castle, dating from 1120 and restored in 1930s, home to the piratic MacNeils of Barra. A thousand species of wild flower have been identified on island.

Benbecula ✳ Lh
Reuval Hill, 408ft high, gives views of whole of Benbecula, North and South Uist and neighbouring islands. On southern slope of hill is cave where Bonnie Prince Charlie waited for Flora MacDonald to bring suitable clothing for him to travel disguised as her maid to Skye. Good beaches at Culla though sea is cold.

Callanish ⛩ Eg
Standing stones erected on Lewis about 4000 years ago. A 270ft avenue of 19 stones leads off from circle of 13 stones, with other avenues heading east, west and

THE RUGGED WESTERN ISLES

The Outer Hebrides stretch in a chain 130 miles long, and act as a break against Atlantic storms heading for the Inner Hebrides and the Western Highlands. The rugged landscape of moorlands, mountains, deep sea lochs, splashing rivers and huge skies is as dramatic as any on the mainland. Against this background lies a wealth of prehistoric standing stones, graves and brochs.

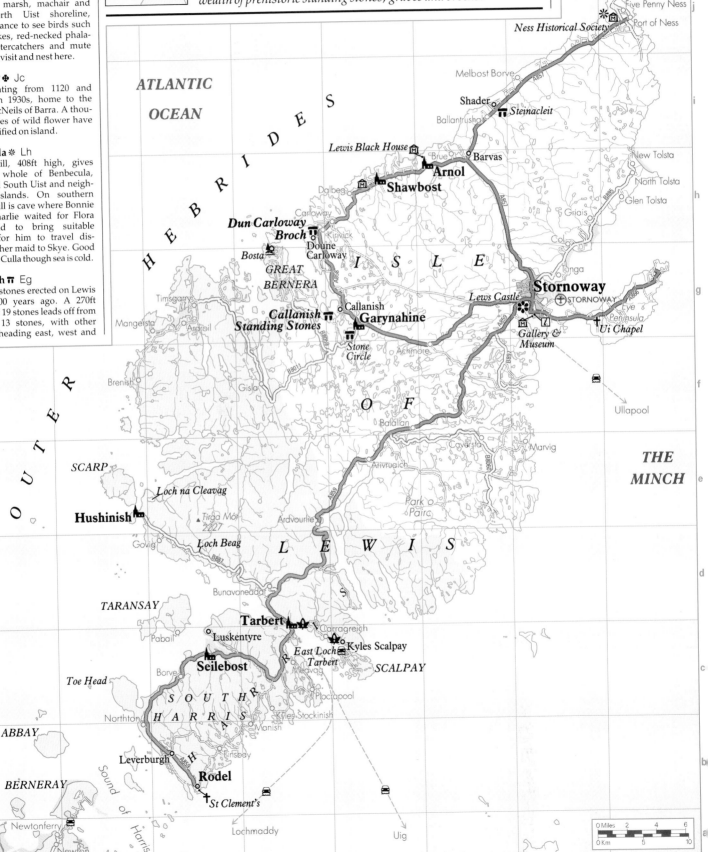

south. Inside the circle is a small chambered tomb. Reasons for its construction not known.

Cille Bharra ✚ Jc
Ruined Church of St Barr and restored Chapel of St Mary once formed part of Barra's medieval monastery. Carved stone in graveyard has Celtic cross on one side and Norse runes on other.

Dun Carloway Broch ⊓ Dh
Iron Age stone fort, built on Lewis 1700 years ago, still has 30ft high walls standing. Courtyard, 25ft across, is surrounded by double walls, between which are chambers, galleries and stairs.

STONE STRONGHOLD *The Iron Age Dun Carloway Broch, on Lewis.*

Eriskay Ld
Island of 'love lilt' and setting of novel *Whisky Galore*, which was based on 1941 event when SS *Politician* foundered off coast with 243,000 bottles of whisky. Pink sea convolvulus flowers supposed to have been planted by Bonnie Prince Charlie when he landed on island on way to Scotland.

Garynahine ⊓ Eg
Bronze Age stone circle on Lewis comprising stone slab surrounded by ring of boulders, in turn surrounded by ring of upright stone slabs; tallest is 9ft.

Hushinish Be
From pier opposite Scarp, walk leads north-east over Harris hills to beach. Inland lies Loch na Cleavag. Hushinish road passes near 19th-century Amhuinnsuidhe Castle and salmon leap at Loch Beag.

North Uist ⊓ Lj
Ancient forts, ruins and standing stones are everywhere on island. Stone group 3 miles north-west of Lochmaddy is called Na Fir Breighe, 'The False Men', said to be either wife deserters turned to stone or gravestones of spies buried alive.

Rodel ✝ Cb
St Clement's Church, built on Harris 1500 and restored in 18th and 19th centuries, finest example of church architecture in Hebrides. Contains monuments to members of Macleod family.

Seilebost Cc
Harris sand dunes sheltering hamlet are populated by rabbits and sea birds. Carpets of bright flowers emerge in early summer.

Shawbost ⌂ 🏛 Eh
Shawbost Museum, housed in disused Lewis church, illustrates old methods of fishing, croft farming and weaving. Restored 19th-century water mill.

South Uist ⚓ Kf
Nature reserve at Loch Druidibeg is breeding ground of greylag goose. Statue of Madonna and Child, 30ft high, carved by Hew Lorimer in 1957. Birthplace of Flora Macdonald now just a tumble of stones near Mingary.

Stornoway ❀ 🏛 ⧉ Gg
Lews Castle, built 1844, now a technical college surrounded by largest wooded park in Hebrides. Ruin of 14th-century Ui Chapel at Point peninsula. Gaelic culture celebrated at An Lanntair Gallery.

HEBRIDES HAVEN *Harbour of Stornoway, capital of Lewis.*

Tarbert ⌂ ⚓ Dd
Harris countryside offers opportunities for walking. Otters, red deer, golden eagles and swans in area. Scenic route runs eastwards from village to Kyles Scalpay. Cairns on road to Luskentyre mark prehistoric funeral routes.

Trinity Temple ✚ Lh
Ruins of medieval college and monastery on North Uist founded in early 13th century. Theologian Duns Scotus studied there. Beside it is Teampull Clan A'Phiocair, chapel of the MacVicars.

BIRDWATCHER'S PARADISE *Shoreline of the Balranald bird reserve is a breeding ground and stopover point for many rare birds.*

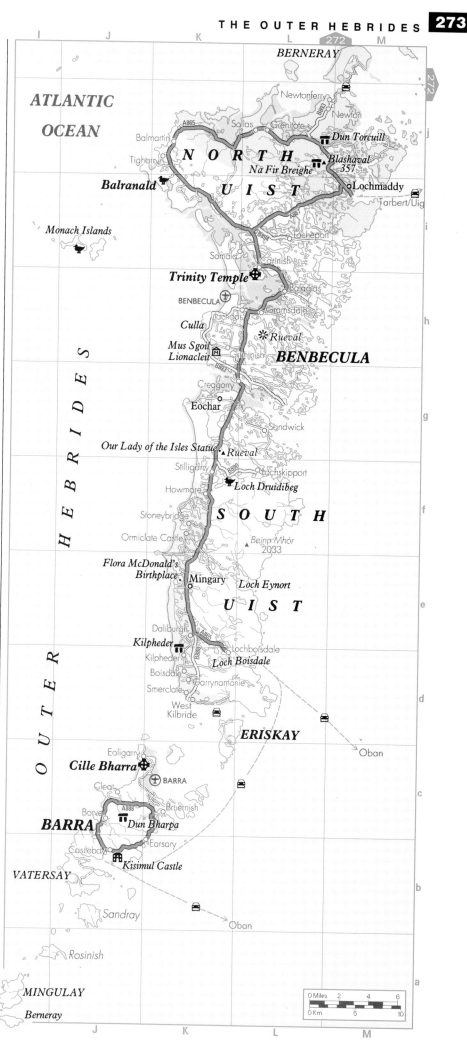

ATLANTIC OCEAN

BERNERAY

NORTH UIST

Balranald

Monach Islands

Trinity Temple

BENBECULA

Culla

Rueval

Mus Sgoil Lionacleit

Eochar

Our Lady of the Isles Statue · Rueval

Loch Druidibeg

SOUTH UIST

Stoneybridge

Ormiclate Castle

Beinn Mhór 2033

Flora McDonald's Birthplace · Mingary

Loch Eynort

Daliburgh

Kilpheder · Loch Boisdale

Boisdale

Smerclate

West Kilbride

ERISKAY

Oban

Eoligarry

Cille Bharra ✚

BARRA

Cleat

Borve A888

Dun Bharpa

BARRA

Castlebay · Earsary

Kisimul Castle

VATERSAY

Sandray

Oban

Rosinish

MINGULAY

Berneray

Newtonferry · Newton

Dun Torcuill

Na Fir Breighe · Blashaval 357

Lochmaddy

Tarbert/Uig

Locheport

Sollas · Grenitote

Balmartin

Tigharry

Samalie

Carinish

Balagias

Gramsdale

Creagory

Sandwick

Stilligarry

Howmore

Lochskipport

0 Miles 2 4 6
0 Km 5 10

Armadale ⛴🏰🏛❀ Fb
Armadale Castle, built in the 19th century, houses museum telling story of MacDonald clan. Forty acres of woodland gardens, guided walks, nature trails. Armadale is ferry link from Mallaig on mainland.

Broadford 🏠 Fd
Red granite Beinn na Caillich dominates this crofting village on bay. Bonnie Prince Charlie took refuge with the MacKinnons after his 1746 defeat at Culloden. He left them his secret recipe for what is now called Drambuie.

Canna Bb
Fertile island, 5 miles long, with small but thriving farming and fishing community. No accommodation on island but campers can stay with permission from the National Trust for Scotland. Deep-water harbour attracts many yachtsmen.

Crusader's Grave Df
Tomb found in a graveyard on a small island in the Skeabost river. Notable for unusual effigy of a warrior in armour.

Cuillin Hills Dd
Semicircular range of bare, black, volcanic peaks, many over 3000ft high. These peaks are for experienced climbers only and provide some of Britain's best and toughest climbing.

Dun Fiadhairt 🜨 Bg
Iron Age broch, or fort, 2000 years old. Walls 12ft thick enclose an area 31ft in diameter. Guardrooms within walls on each side of the entrance.

Dun Hallin 🜨 Bg
Iron Age fort 12ft high with walls 11ft thick surrounded by outer wall. Two wall chambers and a stair lobby remain.

Dunscaith Castle 🏰 Ec
One of oldest fortified headlands of the Hebrides, a home of MacDonald clan until the late 16th century. Well preserved.

Dun Suladale Broch 🜨 Cg
Iron Age dwellings of this type, dry-stone towers with thick walls, are only found in Scotland. This example's walls are 12ft thick and enclose an area 42ft across.

GALLERIED GRANDEUR *Kinloch Castle on the island of Rhum, built in Edwardian days, is a reflection of the elegance of the period.*

CLIMBERS' PARADISE

Skye and its smaller neighbours that make up the Inner Hebrides are known for their wild, beautiful landscapes of deep lochs and jagged mountains, which provide a challenge for the most experienced climbers. The islands have a harsh history, with Norse invasions, fierce clan feuds and the forcible eviction of much of the population during the Highland Clearances of the last century.

SKYE MOUNTAIN GIANTS *Clouds cap the wild Cuillins, a jagged semicircle of peaks, 20 of them over 3000ft high.*

Duntulm Castle 🏰 Di
Ruin of 17th-century castle perched on cliff which falls sharply on three sides. Built by MacDonalds on site of Celtic fort.

Dunvegan Castle 🏛 Bf
Castle on Loch Dunvegan has been stronghold of Clan MacLeod since 1200. Packed with pictures, books and various relics of 20 MacLeod generations.

Elgol 🏠 Ec
Fishing hamlet below Cuillin mountains on southern peninsula of Straithaird. Soay, Canna and Rhum islands visible from here.

Kilmuir 🏛 Ci
Seven thatched cottages hold museum of 19th-century Skye

crofting life. Graveyard's Celtic cross marks the burial place of heroine Flora MacDonald, who helped the fugitive Bonnie Prince Charlie during his flight from the English in 1746.

CROFTING DAYS *Island life a century ago is graphically displayed at Kilmuir on Skye.*

Kinloch Castle 🏛 Ca
Early 20th-century mansion, now a hotel, on Rhum, built for Sir George Bullough. Many original fittings remain. Entire island was Bullough family's private estate from 1888 to 1957.

Knock Castle 🏰 Fb
One of many MacDonald clan strongholds in the 16th and 17th centuries, castle was successfully defended from a 15th-century attack by Clan MacLeod.

Kyleakin ⛴🏠❀🏰 Gd
Seafront village and ferry port on strait that separates island from mainland. Castle Moil, MacKinnon stronghold from the 13th century, set on bluff.

Kyle House ❀ Gd
House's 3 acre garden warmed by mild Gulf Stream throughout

winter. Set by Loch Alsh, site gives views of the Cuillins and Island of Raasay.

Loch Bracadale 🜨 Be
Sea loch where Hakon of Norway's fleet sheltered after defeat at 13th-century Battle of Largs. Dun Beag, one of Skye's best-preserved brochs, is nearby.

Loch Coruisk ☆ Dd
Remote sea loch at foot of the Cuillins, accessible by boat or difficult hike. Name translates as 'cauldron of water'.

Loch Harport ⚓ Ce
Malt-drying kilns of Talisker distillery, Skye's only malt whisky producer, sit beside sea loch.

Loch Mealt ☆ Dh
Water from loch flows 50yds before spilling over a sharp cliff to the sea 600ft below. Nearby is Kilt Rock, a formation with shape and strata resembling a kilt.

Loch Sligachan ✕ Ee
Sligachan Hotel famous as climbing centre for the Cuillins since Victorian times. In Glen Sligachan is Bloody Stone, site of last clan battle between MacDonalds and MacLeods in 1601.

Old Skye Crofter's House 🏛 Ed
Local croft has been converted to Old Skye Crofter's House folk museum, displaying tools and illustrating crofting life.

Portree ✉ Df
Neat whitewashed houses and small hotels line harbour of town, 'capital' of Skye. Royal Hotel is on

site of inn where Bonnie Prince Charlie bade farewell to Flora MacDonald in 1746 before exile in France. Highland Games held here in summer.

Quiraing ☆ Dh
Gaelic name means 'pillared stronghold', describing an extraordinary glacier-created cluster of pinnacles and peaks.

Raasay ⛴🏰⚓🏕 Ee
Isle of Raasay, 13 miles long, lies between Skye and the mainland. Brochel Castle was home to MacLeod of Raasay, whose 1745 support of the Jacobite cause brought severe retribution upon island after defeat of Bonnie Prince Charlie.

Rhum 🏛⛴ Ca
Island with peaks rising to 2659ft. Now a Scottish Natural Heritage reserve, abundant with red deer. The sea eagle has been successfully reintroduced to island, previously extinct in Britain. Centre for botanical research.

WELL PROTECTED *Shaggy-coated Highland cattle on Rhum.*

Staffin 🏠☆ Eh
Rocky coast with crofting and fishing village around Staffin Bay. Reached by narrow road crossing Stenscholl river.

The Storr ☆ Dg
Area of rock cliffs and columns to the south of Trotternish peninsula. Area's highlight is Old Man of Storr, black basalt column 160ft tall and 40ft in diameter, surrounded by lesser pinnacles.

Strollamus Fd
Coastal crofting settlement, centre for sea angling and pony trekking. Sheltered from northerly winds by Scalpay Island.

Trumpan ✚ Bh
Ruined church is site of 1579 fight between MacLeods and MacDonalds. The invading MacDonalds killed all but one of many MacLeods worshipping in the church. The sole survivor raised the alarm and the rest of the clan arrived and killed the MacDonalds before they could escape.

Uig 🏠⛴☆🏕 Ch
Ancient-looking tower overlooking bay is 19th-century folly, built by a Captain Fraser. Car ferry to North Uist and Harris.

Ullinish Point ☆ Ce
Headland gives views of twin flat-topped hills called MacLeod's Tables. At low tide, point is connected to sheep-inhabited islet of Oronsay by sand bar.

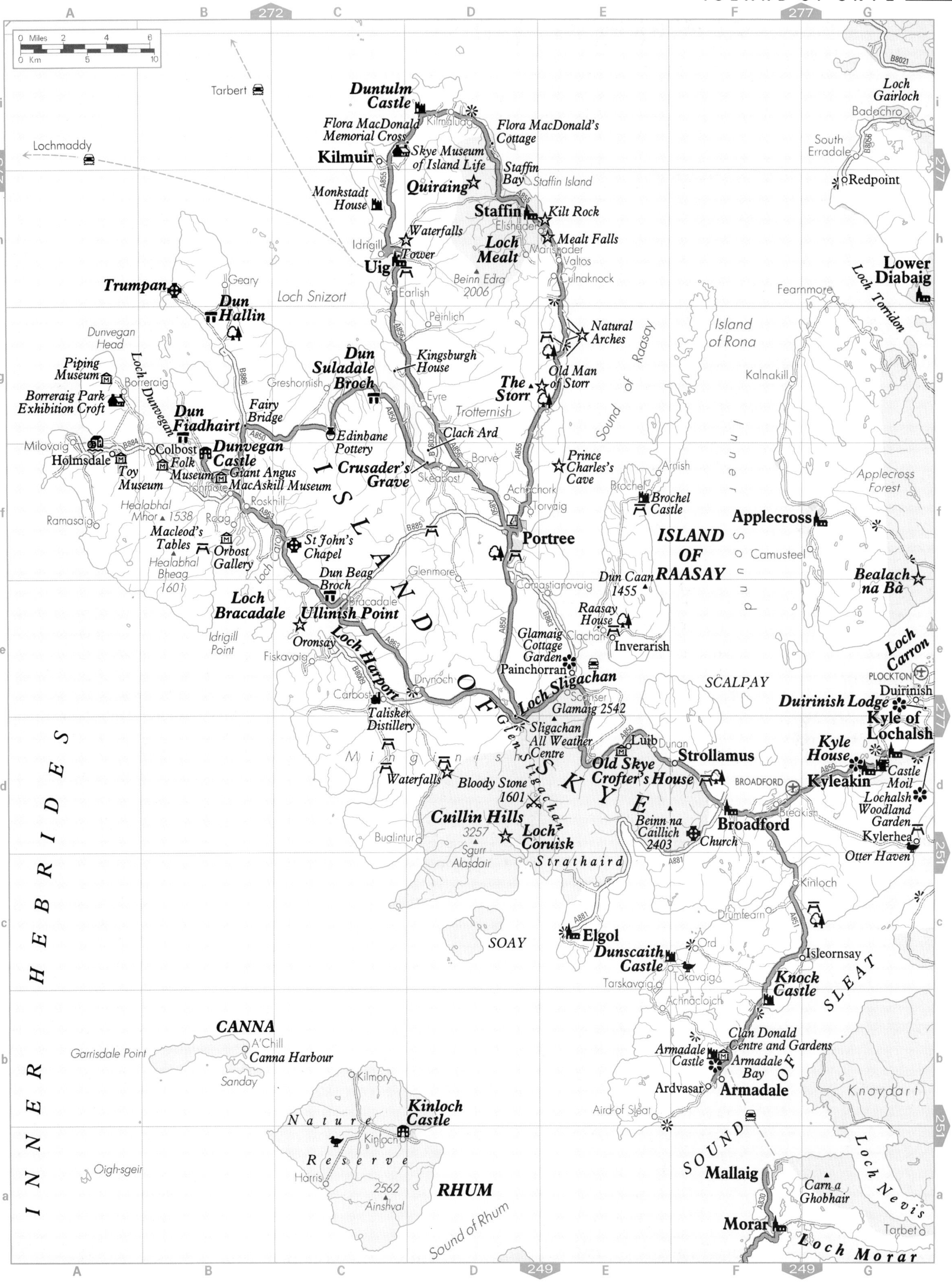

0 Miles 2 4 6
0 Km 5 10

A   B   272   C   D   277   E   F   277   G

Tarbert

Lochmaddy

Duntulm Castle
Kilmaluag
Flora MacDonald Memorial Cross
Kilmuir
Monkstadt House
Skye Museum of Island Life
Quiraing
Flora MacDonald's Cottage
Staffin Bay
Staffin Island
Staffin
Kilt Rock
Elishader
Idrigill
Waterfalls
Tower
Uig
Loch Mealt
Mealt Falls
Marishader
Valtos
Culnaknock

Loch
Gairloch
Badachro
South Erradale
Redpoint

Trumpan
Dun Hallin
Geary
Loch Snizort
Beinn Edra 2006
Peinlich
Earlish

Lower Diabaig
Loch Torridon
Fearnmore

Dunvegan Head
Piping Museum
Borreraig
Borreraig Park Exhibition Croft
Dun Fiadhairt
Dun Suladale Broch
Fairy Bridge
Greshornish
Kingsburgh House
Eyre
Trotternish
Clach Ard
The Storr
Natural Arches
Old Man of Storr

Island of Rona
Kalnakill

Milovaig
Colbost
Folk Museum
Holmsdale
Toy Museum
Dun Fiadhairt
Dunvegan Castle
Giant Angus MacAskill Museum
Edinbane Pottery
Crusader's Grave
Skeabost
Borve
Achachork
Torvaig
Portree
Prince Charles's Cave
Arnish
Brochel
Brochel Castle
Sound of Raasay

Applecross Forest
Applecross

Healabhal Mhor ▲ 1538
Ramasaig
Macleod's Tables
Healabhal Bheag 1601
Orbost Gallery
St John's Chapel
Dun Beag Broch
Loch Bracadale
Ullinish Point
Bracadale
Glenmore
Camastianavaig
ISLAND OF RAASAY
Dun Caan 1455
Raasay House
Clachan
Inverarish
SCALPAY

Bealach na Bà
Camusteel
Loch Carron
PLOCKTON
Duirinish

Oronsay
Fiskavaig
Loch Harport
Drynoch
Scoriser
Glamaig Cottage Garden
Painchorran
Loch Sligachan
Glamaig 2542
Duirinish Lodge
Kyle of Lochalsh

Carbost
Talisker Distillery
Sligachan All Weather Centre
Luib
Dunan
Strollamus
Old Skye Crofter's House
BROADFORD
Kyle House
Kyleakin
Castle Moil
Lochalsh Woodland Garden
Kylerhea
Otter Haven

Waterfalls
Bloody Stone 1601
Cuillin Hills
3257
Sgurr Alasdair
Loch Coruisk
Strathaird
Beinn na Caillich 2403
Church
Broadford
Breakish
Kinloch
Drumfearn

INNER HEBRIDES
SOAY
Elgol
Dunscaith Castle
Tarskavaig
Tokavaig
Ord
Isleornsay
Knock Castle
SLEAT

CANNA
A'Chill
Canna Harbour
Sanday
Garrisdale Point
Kilmory
Nature
Kinloch Castle
Kinloch
Reserve
Harris
Oigh-sgeir
2562
Ainshval
RHUM
Sound of Rhum

Achnacloich
Clan Donald Centre and Gardens
Armadale Castle
Armadale Bay
Ardvasar
Armadale
Aird of Sleat
Knoydart

Mallaig
Carn a Ghobhair
Morar
Loch Nevis
Tarbet
Loch Morar
SOUND OF SLEAT

A   B   249   C   D   249   E   F   G

BRITAIN'S WILD OUTBACK

In this particularly rugged area of the western Highlands, red-sandstone peaks rise above a landscape of moors and hundreds of lochs. Several nature reserves protect the area's wildlife and terrain. Traditional ways of life are retained in the crofting and fishing villages that lie along the shores of the sea lochs. Warm currents of the North Atlantic Drift allow exotic plants to flourish.

Achiltibuie ⚓✿❀ Eh
Boat trips around Summer Isles available from here. Hydroponicum, experimental garden without soil, open to visitors. Smokehouse by the sea has a viewing gallery for watching fish curing.

Applecross ○ Bb
St Maelrubha built a monastery on this bay in AD 672, declaring it a sanctuary for all fugitives. Until new road was built in 1970s, one of the most inaccessible areas of mainland Britain.

Ardvreck Castle 🏰 Gj
Three-storey tower ruin on shore of Loch Assynt, built 1597 for MacLeods of Assynt. Marquis of Montrose fled here in 1650 but was betrayed by Neil MacLeod and taken to Edinburgh for execution.

Bealach na Bà ☆ Bb
This 'Pass of the Cattle', an old drovers' road, was only road to Applecross until 1970s. It leads from Loch Kishorn through ascending hairpin bends and skirts steep precipices on its way.

Beinn Eighe National Nature Reserve ❤✿🆔 Ed
Britain's first national nature reserve (1951). It covers some 10,000 acres of mountain, moorland and forest, including the 3188ft Beinn Eighe. On one side, jagged peaks rise from the surrounding terrain; on the other, gentler slopes with woodland lead down to Loch Maree. Aultroy Cottage Visitor Centre located on A832 north of Kinlochewe.

HIGHLAND CRAFT *Spinning wheel in Gairloch Heritage Museum.*

Corrieshalloch Gorge ☆❤⚓ Ge
Suspension bridge spans gorge 200ft above river. River runs a mile down rocky chasm to plunge over 150ft Falls of Measach.

Diabaig ⚓ Bd
Cottages of Lower Diabaig group around Loch Diabaig, rocky cliffs rise straight up from shore. Exhilarating road along northern side of Upper Loch Torridon.

Dundonnell ⚓ Ef
Village at south-east end of Little Loch Broom is the ideal starting point for exploring remote mountain scenery here. Streams tumble into head of loch from heights of An Teallach, 3484ft. Nearby is Loch Toll an Lochain, 2000ft above sea level.

Dun Lagaidh ✳ Fg
Iron Age fortress on isolated ridge along Loch Broom. Rocks vitrified when its timber walls burnt down.

Eas a Chùal Aluinn Falls ☆ Gj
Glas Bheinn peak is source for 658ft falls, longest fall in Britain. Easily seen by regular boat trips on Loch Glencoul.

Enard Bay Ei
Sandy beaches backed by empty moorland and distant mountains. Narrow switchback road that skirts bay gives views.

Gairloch ⚓🏛🆔 Ce
Village at head of Loch Gairloch has quarter mile of safe, sandy beach where windsurfing and sailing are popular. Sea-angling boats for hire.

Gruinard Bay ✝✳ Dg
Road along bay's western shore passes ruined chapel built where St Columba supposedly founded a church. Bay best viewed from atop Gruinard Hill.

Inchnadamph ⚓❤ Gj
Village at head of Loch Assynt, near 3273ft Ben More Assynt. Nature reserve has wildcats, red deer and limestone caves, where prehistoric animal bones have been found. Salmon and trout fishing in loch.

NORTHERN TROPICS *Exotic plants and shrubs flourish at Inverewe Gardens.*

Inverewe Gardens ❀ Cf
Northern headland garden started by Osgood Mackenzie in 1862. North Atlantic Drift allows exotic shrubs, trees and bamboos to flourish.

Loch Ewe Cf
Broad sea loch where ships assembled for North Atlantic convoys during World War II. A number of pillboxes and gun emplacements still survive. Loch fishing, sea-angling boats for hire.

Lochinver ⚓ Ej
Whitewashed fishing village at head of Loch Inver. Suilven, 2399ft high, stands in Glencanisp Forest 4 miles south-east.

Loch Maree De
Loch with many islands set amid mountainous terrain. Isle Maree was thought to be home to Celtic god Mourie. Later, St Maelrubha established hermitage there, eventually replaced by chapel. Slioch peak at south-eastern end.

Oykel Bridge ☆ Hh
River Oykel flows down slopes of Ben More Assynt and through ice-gouged valley to Oykel Bridge. Single hotel stands by road nearby. Bridge just east of waterfall.

to entice people to live there. Roads from village provide views of Highlands.

Stoer ⚓ Ej
Crofting, fishing villages line each side of peninsula. Safe white sands at Achmelvich Bay and Bay of Clachtoll. Road along peninsula ends at lighthouse on sandstone cliff. Walk to Point of Stoer along cliffs with nesting birds.

Strathcarron ⚓ Db
A890 leads along Loch Carron, up steep grades and down into South Strome Forest. Viewpoint over loch and Stromeferry near forest. Forest walk from Stromeferry to lochside viewpoints.

Suilven Fi
Seen from east or west, 2399ft Suilven appears cone-shaped; from elsewhere it reveals three separate peaks. Unstable cliff faces make it a dangerous climb.

Summer Isles Dh
Islands were once lived on by fishermen, but herring shoals diminished, leaving just one isle currently inhabited. They can be visited by boat from Ullapool or from Achiltibuie.

Torridon ⚓🏛 Dc
Torridon, owned by National Trust for Scotland, has visitor centre giving introduction to walks through area of red-sandstone peaks. Wildlife from red deer to pygmy shrew.

REMOTE FISHING HAMLET *Lower Diabaig is found at the end of a single-track road running from Torridon.*

SILENT SPLENDOUR *Water, rock and pines in harmony at Loch Assynt.*

Inverpolly National Nature Reserve ❤ Fi
Over 26,000 acres of bog, moorland and woodland with sandstone peaks of Cul Mor, Cul Beag and Stac Pollaidh. Loch Sionascaig has good fishing. Information centre and car park in Knockan.

Kinlochewe ❤ Ed
Town at Loch Maree is popular centre for walkers, climbers and anglers. Area dominated by Slioch, 'the spear', 3217ft.

Loch Carron Ca
Sea loch dotted with islands. Strome Castle, overlooking loch, blown up during 1603 clan feud. Nearby town of Lochcarron known for its ties and tartans.

Poolewe ⚓ Cf
Village lies between Loch Ewe and Loch Maree. River Ewe, joining lochs, flows through village. Boats for hire, walks along Loch Maree's wooded banks, loch and river fishing.

Rubha Reidh 🐾 Bg
Peninsula ending in headland of Rubha Reidh extends north from Gairloch into the Minch. Ocean views from lighthouse at tip of promontory. Road over moors to Melvaig passes ruined cottages.

Shieldaig ⚓ Cc
Village founded by Admiralty in 1800 when Britain was short of seamen. Intended as 'nursery' for Royal Navy, grants were offered

Ullapool 🏛 Fg
Planned town developed by British Fisheries Society for local herring industry, founded 1788. Lochbroom Highland Museum houses some local artefacts in one of the original town buildings. Boat trips to Summer Isles, sea and river angling available.

Upper Loch Torridon Cc
Small crofting hamlets dot sea loch's shore. Waters from Loch Damh to south drop down to Upper Loch Torridon through Falls of Balgy.

Victoria Falls ☆ Ce
Waterfall near Slattadale on Loch Maree. Named after visit to loch by Queen Victoria in 1877.

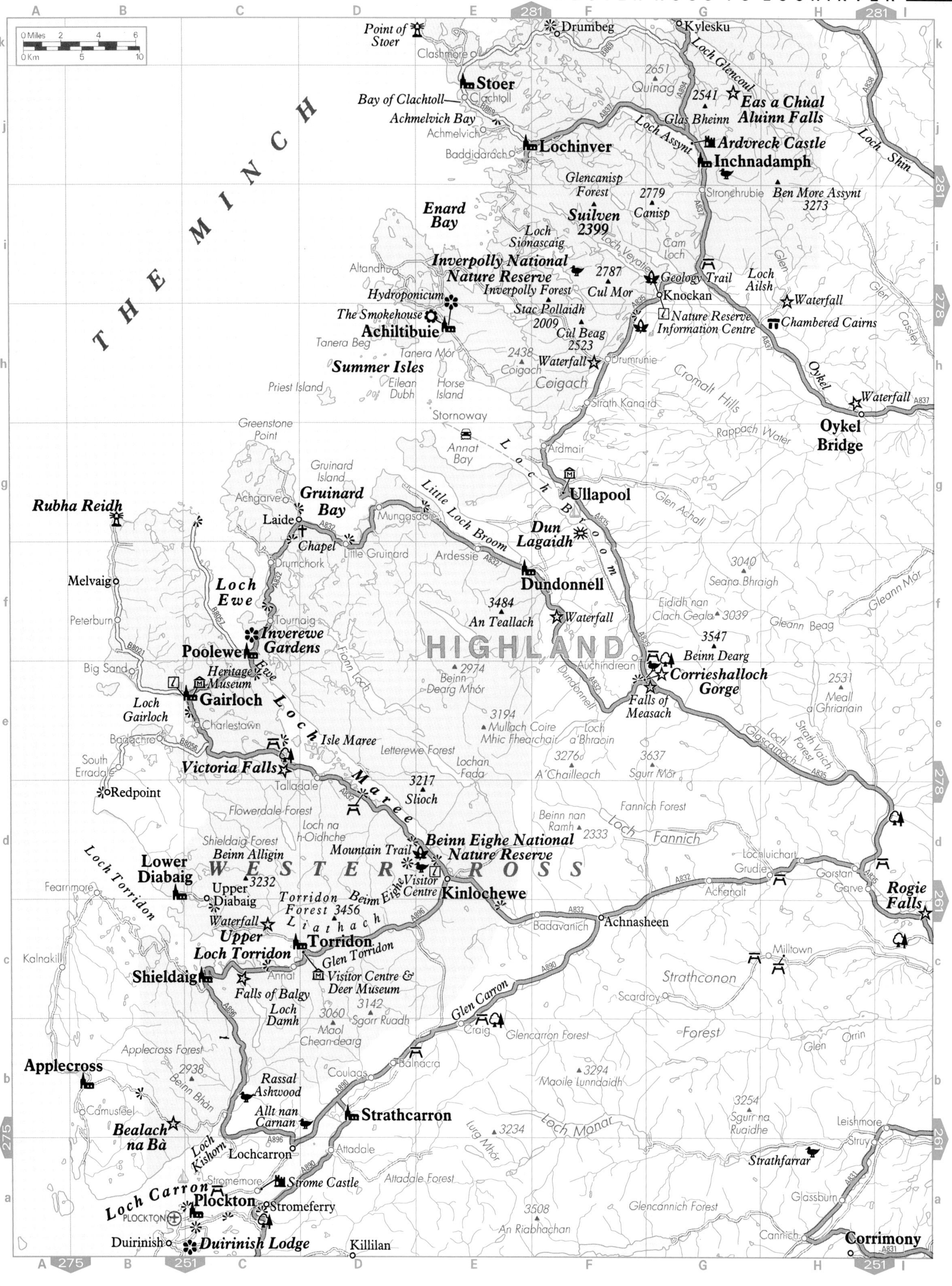

281 281

THE MINCH

0 Miles 2 4 6
0 Km 5 10

Point of Stoer
Drumbeg
Kylesku
Loch Glencoul
Clashmore
Quinag 2651
Loch Assynt
Stoer
Clachtoll
2541
Glas Bheinn
Eas a Chùal Aluinn Falls
Bay of Clachtoll
Achmelvich Bay
Achmelvich
Ardvreck Castle
Inchnadamph
Lochinver
Baddidarach
Stronchrubie
Ben More Assynt 3273
Loch Shin
Enard Bay
Glencanisp Forest
2779 Canisp
Suilven 2399
Loch Sionascaig
Inverpolly National Nature Reserve
2787 Cul Mor
Cam Loch
Geology Trail
Loch Veyatie
Knockan
Loch Ailsh
Waterfall
Glen Cassley
Altandhu
Hydroponicum
Inverpolly Forest
Stac Pollaidh
Nature Reserve Information Centre
Chambered Cairns
The Smokehouse
Achiltibuie
2009
Cul Beag 2523
Drumrunie
Oykel
Tanera Beg
2438
Tanera Mór
Waterfall
Coigach
Strath Kanaird
Cromalt Hills
Waterfall
Oykel Bridge A837
Summer Isles
Eilean Dubh
Horse Island
Coigach
Rappach Water
Priest Island
Greenstone Point
Stornoway
Annat Bay
Loch Broom
Ardmair
Rubha Reidh
Gruinard Island
Achgarve
Little Loch Broom
Ullapool
Glen Achall
3040
Seana Bhraigh
Gruinard Bay
Laide
Chapel
Mungasdale
Dun Lagaidh
Glen Douchary
Melvaig
Drumchork
Little Gruinard
Ardessie A832
Dundonnell
Eididh nan Clach Geala 3039
Gleann Mòr
Peterburn
Loch Ewe
Tournaig
3484 An Teallach
Waterfall
3547
Beinn Dearg
Gleann Beag
Inverewe Gardens
Fionn Loch
HIGHLAND
Auchindrean
Corrieshalloch Gorge
2531 Meall a Ghrianain
Poolewe
Big Sand
Heritage Museum
2974
Beinn Dearg Mhór
Dundonnell
Falls of Measach
Gairloch
Loch Gairloch
Charlestown
Isle Maree
Letterewe Forest
3194
Mullach Coire Mhic Fhearchair
Loch a'Bhraoin
Loch Glascarnoch
Strath Vaich Forest
Badachro
Loch Maree
Lochan Fada
3276
A'Chailleach
3637
Sgurr Mòr
South Erradale
Victoria Falls
Talladale
3217 Slioch
Loch Fannich
Lochluichart
Redpoint
Flowerdale Forest
Shieldaig Forest
Loch na h-Oidhche
Beinn nan Ramh 2333
Fannich Forest
Grudie
Rogie Falls
Lower Diabaig
Beinn Alligin
3232
Mountain Trail
Beinn Eighe National Nature Reserve
Gorstan
Garve
Loch Torridon
Upper Diabaig
Beinn Eighe
Visitor Centre
Kinlochewe
Achanalt
A832
Fearnmore
Torridon Forest 3456
Badavanich
Achnasheen
A890
Milltown
Upper Loch Torridon
Waterfall
Liathach
Torridon
Glen Torridon
Strathconon
Kalnakill
Visitor Centre & Deer Museum
3142 Sgorr Ruadh
Glen
Orrin
Shieldaig
Annat
Falls of Balgy
3060
Maol Chean-dearg
Scardroy
Forest
Loch Damh
Glen Carron
Glencarron Forest
Applecross
2938 Beinn Bhàn
Rassal Ashwood
Coulags
Balnacra
3294 Maoile Lunndaidh
3254 Sgurr na Ruaidhe
Camusteel
Allt nan Carnan
Strathcarron
Leishmore
Bealach na Bà
Loch Kishorn
Attadale
Loch Monar
3234
Strathfarrar
Struy
Lochcarron
Attadale Forest
Lurg Mhòr
Loch Carron
Stromemore
Strome Castle
PLOCKTON
Plockton
Stromeferry
3508 An Riabhachan
Glencannich Forest
Glassburn
Duirinish
Duirinish Lodge
Killilan
Cannich
Corrimony
A831

WESTER ROSS

275 251 251
278 278 261 261

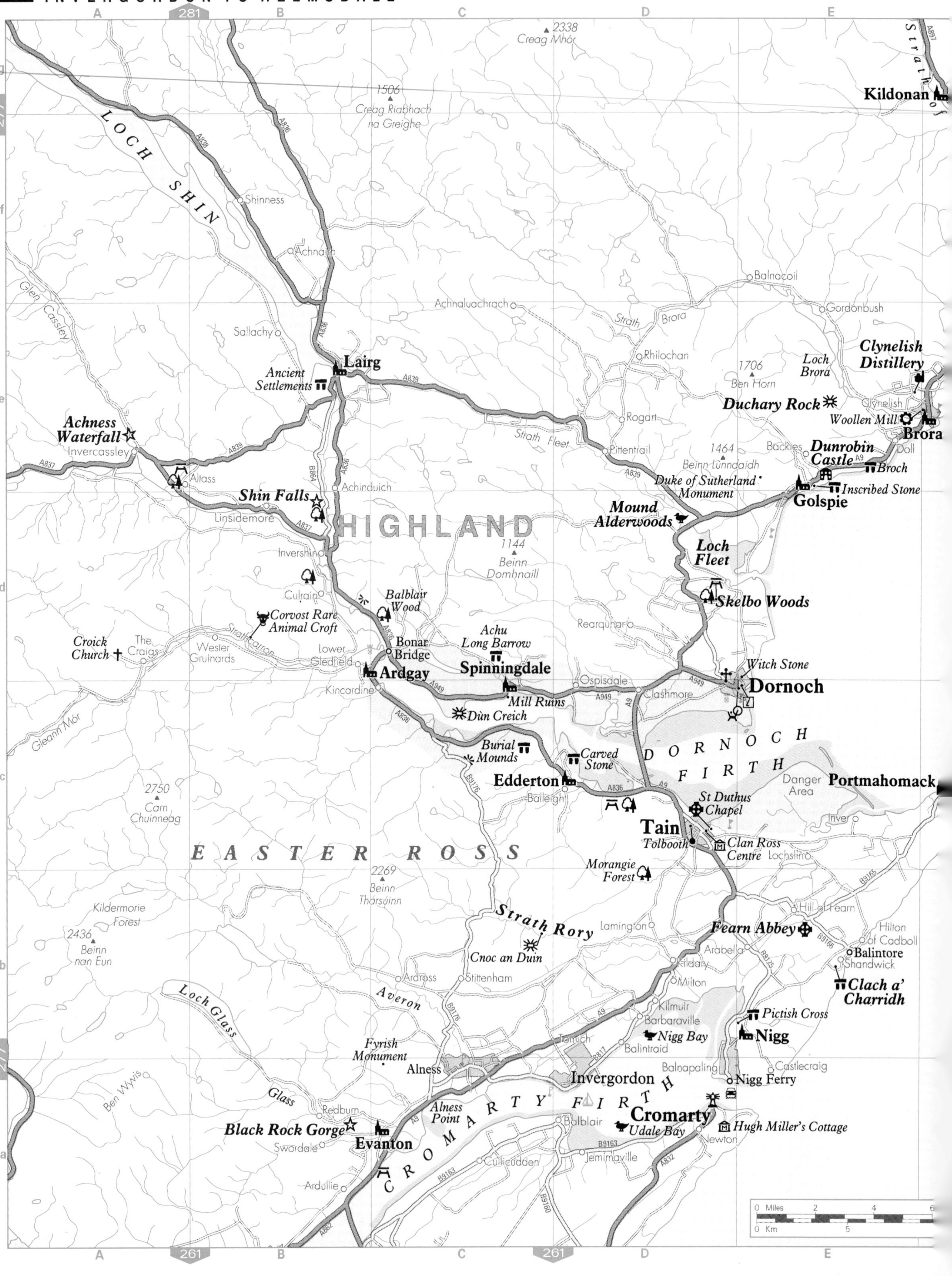

A · B · C · D · E

g

▲ 2338
Creag Mhór

· 1506
Creag Riabhach
na Greighe

Kildonan

f

LOCH SHIN

○ Shinness

○ Achna...

○ Balnacoil

○ Achnaluachrach

Strath · Brora ○

○ Gordonbush

e

Sallachy ○

○ Rhilochan

Loch
Brora

**Clynelish
Distillery**

Lairg

· 1706
Ben Horn

Clynelish ○

*Ancient
Settlements*

Strath Fleet

○ Rogart

Duchary Rock ☀

Woollen Mill

Brora

**Achness
Waterfall** ☆

○ Achinduich

○ Pittentrail

· 1464
Beinn Lunndaidh

Backies ○

**Dunrobin
Castle**

Doll ○

Invercassley

A839

Altass

Shin Falls ☆

Linsidemore

○ Achinduich

Duke of Sutherland
Monument

Broch

HIGHLAND

Golspie

Inscribed Stone

Invershin

· 1144
Beinn
Domhnaill

**Mound
Alderwoods**

**Loch
Fleet**

d

Culrain ○

*Balblair
Wood*

Rearquhar ○

Skelbo Woods

*Corvost Rare
Animal Croft*

*Croick
Church* ✝

The
Craigs

Wester
Gruinards

Lower
Gledfield

**Bonar
Bridge**

*Achu
Long Barrow*

○ Ospisdale

Witch Stone ✝

Dornoch

Gleann Mór

○ Strathcarron

Ardgay

Spinningdale

Clashmore ○

Kincardine

Mill Ruins

A949

A9

**DORNOCH
FIRTH**

c

· 2750
Carn
Chuinneag

☀ *Dùn Creich*

*Burial
Mounds*

*Carved
Stone*

Danger
Area

Portmahomack

Edderton

A836

A9

Inver ○

Balleigh ○

*St Duthus
Chapel*

Lochslin ○

EASTER ROSS

· 2269
Beinn
Tharsuinn

Tain

Tolbooth

*Clan Ross
Centre*

*Morangie
Forest*

Hill of Fearn ○

· 2436
Beinn
nan Eun

Kildermorie
Forest

Strath Rory

○ Lamington

Fearn Abbey ✚

Hilton
of Cadboll

b

☀ *Cnoc an Duin*

Arabella ○

Balintore

Shandwick ○

Loch Glass

Averon

○ Ardross

○ Stittenham

Kildary ○

**Clach a'
Charridh**

Milton ○

Kilmuir ○

Pictish Cross

Fyrish
Monument

Barbaraville ○

Nigg

Nigg Bay

Balintraid ○

Invergordon

Balnapaling ○

Nigg Ferry

Ben Wyvis

Glass

Redburn ○

Alness

Cromarty

Castlecraig ○

a

Black Rock Gorge ☆

Evanton

Alness
Point

Balblair ○

Udale Bay

Hugh Miller's Cottage

Swordale ○

CROMARTY FIRTH

Ardullie ○

○ Culicudden

Newton ○

○ Jemimaville

A · B · C · D · E

| 0 Miles | | 2 | | 4 | | 6 |
| 0 Km | | | 5 | | | |

INLAND FROM DORNOCH FIRTH

Forests and heather-covered hills, sea cliffs and sandy beaches: the east coast may not have the high drama of the west, but it offers beauty, solitude and a wealth of history. It takes the visitor from the ruined brochs of the Iron Age people to the carved stones left by the mysterious Dark Age Picts and on to the bitter memories of the Highland Clearances and the desolation they caused.

Achness Waterfall ☆ Ae
A mile of falls and rapids tumbling over rocks and between wooded banks as River Cassley runs down through pine forest. Good walks and salmon fishing.

Ardgay Bd
Snug setting where Dornoch Firth narrows and hills crowd onto shoreline. Eitag Stone marks site of 19th-century cattle market. Red deer and other species at Corvost rare animal croft, 4 miles west.

Black Rock Gorge ☆ Ba
Precipitous paths are perched 200ft above a narrow ravine carved by waters of River Glass, which snake through clefts little more than 10ft wide. Glen Glass approached down track, left of road from Evanton. A wooden bridge spans gorge where river foams some 70ft below.

Brora Fe
Thriving golf and fishing resort, straddling mouth of river from which it takes its name. Fine mountain and moor scenery; sandy bays indent rocky coast. Pictish remains in surrounding area. Beside road 5 miles north of Brora stands Wolf Stone, said to be site of the shooting of Scotland's last wolf about 1700.

Clach a' Charridh Eb
'Stone of Sorrow', 10ft Pictish stone carved with cross and animals, including stags, wolves and entwined serpents. Traditionally it marks spot where unbaptised infants were buried, but excavation has failed to find any trace.

Clynelish Distillery Ee
Visitors who go on guided tours of Sutherland's only malt whisky distillery are rewarded at the end with a distinctive peaty dram.

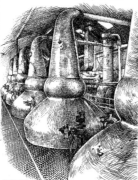

HIGH SPIRITS *The copper stills in which the whisky is distilled glow warmly at Clynelish Distillery.*

Cromarty Da
Cromarty Firth used during both world wars as Royal Navy harbour. Gun emplacements guarding firth entrance still exist. Birthplace cottage of Hugh Miller, area folklorist and geologist, in Church Street, now in hands of National Trust for Scotland.

Dornoch Dc
Mellow stone houses stand in broad, tree-lined streets. Cathedral of 1224 was destroyed in 1570 and later restored, though much ancient stonework remains. Safe bathing, golf on a course that was in use in the 17th century, and tartan weaving in what was once the local jail.

Duchary Rock ✳ Ee
High cliff above Loch Brora, on which stands 2000-year-old Iron Age hill-fort. Natural defences of rock and steep slopes were improved by building a massive wall. Splendid setting with magnificent views.

Dunrobin Castle Ee
Glowing, white-stone chateau; once a grim 13th-century keep. Transformed in 1840 by Sir Charles Barry, architect of the Houses of Parliament. Gardens set out in formal French style of Versailles. Early 20th-century steam fire engine on display.

ROMANTIC SETTING *Dunrobin Castle overlooks lush, formal gardens.*

Edderton Dc
Side road leading north through village passes 10ft high Pictish stone in middle of a field, inscribed with a fish symbol. Beyond Edderton, tree-lined main road twists and turns, skirting placid waters of Dornoch Firth. Local church dates from 1793.

Evanton Ca
Small village of neat houses sheltering under massive hills. Unusual monument on top of Cnoc Fyrish is replica of an Indian gate; erected by General Sir Hector Munro, who gained distinction at Relief of Negapatam in India, 1781. Series of paths and lanes from Evanton lead down to muddy foreshore; excellent place to watch sea birds and waders.

Fearn Abbey ✚ Eb
Founded 13th century, converted into parish church. Brahan Seer, a 16th-century prophet, foretold that disaster would strike. It came true in 1742, when lightning hit during service and the roof fell in, killing 42 people. Nave and choir restored, rest remains in ruins.

Golspie Ee
Busy holiday village with old private station for 3rd Duke of Sutherland. Massive statue on summit of Beinn á Bhragaidh

mountain to ruthless 1st Duke, who evicted 15,000 tenants between 1810 and 1820 to make way for more profitable sheep.

Helmsdale Gf
Fishing village at mouth of River Helmsdale, claimed to be best salmon river in Scotland. Ice house built 1840s to preserve fish; Thomas Telford's stone bridge dates from 1812. Timespan Heritage Centre and guided exploration tours.

Kildonan Fg
Scene of 1869 gold rush among magnificent hills and tumbling streams. Prospectors may still find a little gold in their pans.

Kilphedir Ff
Iron Age tower or broch with 32ft diameter enclosure within walls 15ft thick. Around it are stone circles showing sites of huts, and an eerie underground passage or earth house. Outer enclosure protected by bank and ditches.

Lairg Be
Resort and salmon-fishing village of neat stone houses on shores of Loch Shin. In August streets fill with sheep for biggest sale in Britain. Many ancient sites to be seen in surrounding hills.

Loch Fleet Dd
Birdwatcher's paradise. Separated from sea by narrow channel, it attracts waders and ducks. Seals can often be spotted. Access to pine woodland restricted.

Mound Alderwoods Dd
Thomas Telford built the Mound embankment across River Fleet to control the flow of sea water. In season, salmon queue up waiting for sluices to open and allow them to continue upstream. Woodland reserve grew up in estuary. Good viewpoint from road.

Nigg Eb
Village church has 9th or 10th-century carved Pictish cross. In churchyard is Cholera Stone, where according to legend a 'cholera cloud' was buried after being caught in linen bag during 1832 epidemic. Stone is never moved in case plague escapes.

Portmahomack Fc
Fishing boats and yachts moor in harbour created by Thomas Telford early in the 19th century. Sandy beach.

Shin Falls ☆ Bd
Spectacular falls through rocky gorge famous for salmon leaping, as they return to rivers to spawn. Car park nearby has display about life cycle of the salmon.

Skelbo Woods Dd
Gaunt ruins of 14th-century castle (not open to public) guard Loch Fleet entrance. Network of trails from car park through Forestry Commission plantation.

Spinningdale Cc
Remains of 1790 cotton mill, burnt down 1806. Ancient fort tops Dùn Creich hill. Nearby lies Achu long barrow with passage to roofed chamber, from New Stone Age.

Strath Rory ✳ Cb
Road joining Cromarty Firth and Dornoch Firth crosses Strathrory River in heart of wild moorland, with magnificent views. Good walks from car park by bridge.

Tain ✚ Dc
Ruined chapel built on birthplace of 11th-century St Duthus to house his remains, which were later moved to 1360 church. The 17th-century tolbooth was administration centre for infamous Highland Clearances, when tenants were thrown off their land. Clan Ross centre is town museum.

LOCH SHIN *The village of Lairg lies on the shores of Sutherland's largest loch, which stretches for 17 miles. The loch provides excellent fishing for anglers.*

Armadale 🏠⛪☑⛵ If
Hamlet of crofters' cottages heated in winter by peat fires. Set in Armadale Bay with fine view of sandy beach and sweep of shallow water. Main road leads over two burns, Allt Beag and Armadale, both with twin stone bridges, old and new.

Auckengill 🏠⚱ Of
John Nicholson, 19th-century antiquarian, extensively studied this region's ancient remains. Old school house opposite his home now a museum of region's early human history, a useful starting point for visiting brochs and other area sites.

Balnakeil ⛪✿ Ef
Old Ministry of Defence early warning station is unlikely setting for craft centre; visitors can watch various crafts, ranging from bookbinding and weaving to jewellery and candle-making. The ruined church of 1619 has monument to Celtic bard Rob Donn.

Bettyhill 🏠⚱⚱ If
Crofting centre and resort above Torrisdale Bay. To north is Farr Bay, where precious stones can be found. Salmon fishing in River Naver and trout in Loch Naver, 15 miles inland. Church dating from 18th century houses museum of local history. Outside museum is Farr Stone, an early Christian Celtic stone.

ANCIENT TOMBS *The Grey Cairns of Camster date back to Neolithic times, 6000 years ago.*

Canisbay 🏠 Og
Village with 19th-century church. Inside church is 1558 memorial to Jan de Groot, who started ferry service to Orkney in 1496. When residing in nearby Castle of Mey, the Queen Mother attends services at Canisbay Church.

Cape Wrath ⚑☆ Dg
Red-rock headland rising 360ft from sea, topped by 70ft lighthouse. The Parbh – 100 square miles of peat-bog, heather, scrub and rock – lies inland. Only link to cape from outside world is ferry across Kyle of Durness. Cleit Dhubh, or 'Black Cliff', rises 850ft from sea south-east of cape.

Castletown 🏠✿ Mf
Well-ordered village built for men working in nearby quarries. Castletown's stone has paved the streets of Glasgow and Edinburgh; stone was sent out from neighbouring harbour of Castlehill – also built of this stone.

Dounreay ✿ Kf
Experimental nuclear power station's 135ft steel dome dominates flat coastal area. It was world's first fast reactor to provide power for public use. Dounreay Exhibition tells story of nuclear power and has guided tours.

Dunbeath 🏠⚱ Mc
Harbour is home to small fishing fleet. Dunbeath Castle still lived in but closed to public. Lhaidhay Caithness Croft Museum displays typical 18th-century complex with house, byre and stable all under one roof. Old village school houses heritage centre.

Duncansby Head ⚑☆✿ Pg
Far north-eastern tip of mainland where lighthouse stands high above entrance to Pentland Firth.

THE FAR NORTH'S LONELY COAST

The northern coast offers a rich variety of scenery, from tall storm-swept cliffs to gentle sandy bays. The interior offers equally dramatic contrasts between low-lying windswept bogs and dramatic mountain peaks. Fishing boats shelter in the area's many harbours. Numerous nature reserves protect the moorland's rich plant and animal life, with sea birds to the fore.

Dunnet Head ✿⚑ Mg
Most northerly point of British mainland. Viewing platform provides 360° view over 300ft cliffs, taking in Cape Wrath and Duncansby. Lighthouse stands below viewpoint, its walls battered by stones thrown up by Pentland Firth in rough weather.

Durness 🏠☆ Ff
Crofting village spread out along coast. Along shore is three-chambered Smoo Cave. Its main chamber, over 200ft deep and 110ft wide, is accessible by foot. Allt Smoo burn flows from moorland and drops 80ft into deep pool inside second cavern.

Grey Cairns of Camster ⚱ Nd
Well-preserved burial chambers 2 miles north of Camster date from New Stone Age, beginning 6000 years ago. Visitors can crawl down passage into chambers. Long cairn is nearly 200ft. Legless skeletons found in round cairn.

Halkirk 🏠⚱ Me
Village based on local quarries that mined stone for street paving. The Fossil Centre at Mybster has displays on local flagstone industry.

Handa Island Nature Reserve ✈ Cd
Steep cliffs on three sides of island packed with sea birds in summer.

Moorland interior is also home to variety of birds, from skuas to golden plovers.

Harrow ✿ Ng
Area's best-known building is Castle of Mey, the Queen Mother's summer residence. Its gardens open occasionally in summer. Castle Arms Hotel, Mey, has royal photographs display. Quarries shipped flagstones from harbour a century ago.

Hill o' Many Stanes ⚱ Nc
Bronze Age stone formation on hillock. Rows of small stones form a fan-like formation possibly for astronomical purposes.

Invernaver ✈⚱ Hf
Nature reserve with notable dwarf shrubs. Skelpick long barrow is 200ft long with two burial chambers blocked by massive capstones. Remains of Iron Age settlement with tower stand on rocky slope.

John o' Groats 🏠⚱ Og
Claims to be mainland Britain's most northerly village, named after founder of ferry service to

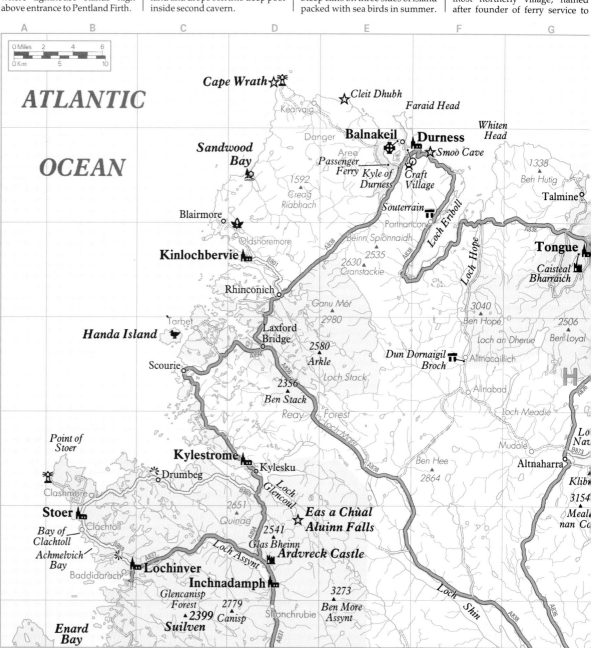

BIRD ISLAND *Kittiwakes, shags and fulmars pack the cliffs of Handa Island in summer.*

---

century castle. Three-mile stretch of sand on Sinclair's Bay lies south.

Kinlochbervie 🏠☸ De
Area's busiest fishing port has double harbour. Nearby Blairmore starts trail to Sandwood Bay.

Kylestrome 🏠☆ Dc
Village at meeting point of three lochs, Kylesku is across water. Boat trip on Loch Glencoul gives views of Britain's highest waterfall, 650ft Eas a Chùal Aluinn.

Lybster 🏠⚓ Nc
Active fishing community; broad street runs down to harbour with octagonal lighthouse at its entrance. Church has finely carved Celtic cross.

Noss Head 🏰 Oe
Rocky point north of Wick is crowned by two ruins. Castle Girnigoe, 15th century, has keep on cliff edge. Castle Sinclair dates from 17th century.

Sandside Bay Kf
Broad bay, with harbour of Fresgoe to one side and village of Reay

sheltering behind dunes. Small whitewashed church of 1740 has gallery for laird and family.

Sandwood Bay Df
Pink, pale sand and grassy dunes, usually deserted except for sea birds and, legend has it, mermaids. Beach lies 4 miles north of Blairmore, accessible by rough track. Swimming not advised.

Scrabster 🏠🚗☀ Lf
Begun as port for loading flagstones, town is now main ferry port for Orkney. Path leads up past lighthouse to cliffs of Holborn Head. Sailing club, sea angling.

Skirza 🏠⛪ Of
Iron Age broch stands on a spur thrusting out from cliffs. Its hollow walls are 14ft thick and enclose an interior 22ft across.

Thurso 🏰⚓🏛 Mf
Britain's most northerly mainland town was laid out as Georgian 'new town' by Sir John Sinclair. Ruined Church of St Peter dates back to 13th century. Thurso Castle, largely rebuilt, dates from 17th century. Heritage museum.

Orkney in 1496, Jan de Groot. Water mill established 1750 operates under original family.

Keiss 🏠 Of
Harbour is important crab and lobster centre. Keiss Castle, 16th century, stands near private 18th-

SANDY INLET *Grassy limestone bluffs surround the sandy beach at Sango Bay, one of several safe ones which lie a short distance from Durness.*

Tongue 🏠🏰 Ge
Village has gabled church, built 1680. Its boxed wooden gallery was once used by Mackay clan. Angling in Loch Loyal, 4 miles south. Ruined 14th-century Caisteal Bharraich, built on Viking lookout spot.

Wick 🏰🌸🏠☐ Oe
Ancient settlement, Vikings once sheltered here. Name comes from Norse *Vik*, 'bay'. Town plan is medieval, but buildings are mostly 18th century. Visitors can watch handmade glass being blown at Caithness Glass.

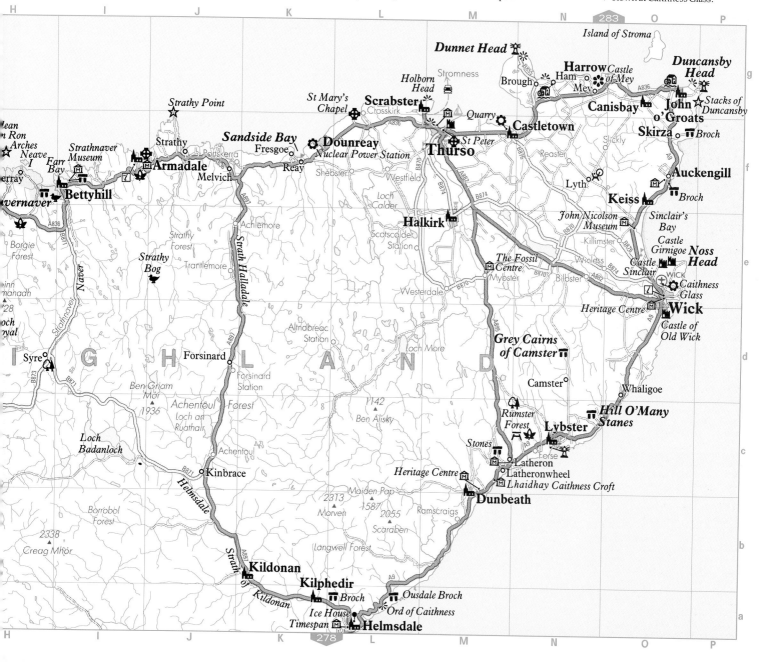

Birsay ⌂ ☆ ⌘ Bf
Ruins of palace built by Earls of Orkney in late 16th century. Remains of 7th and 8th-century Pictish settlement stand on Brough of Birsay island, reached by foot at low tide. Ruins of Thorfinn the Mighty's Romanesque church, shoreline ruins of his hall and outlines of Norse longhouses.

Blackhammer ⊓ Df
One of several Neolithic cairns on Rousay. Its megalithic burial chamber is 47ft long and is split into seven separate stalls by standing slabs.

Burgar Hill ✿ ▲ ▢ Cf
Atlantic winds provide energy to power three wind turbine generators on windswept Mainland hilltop. Visitor centre in summer.

Churchill Barriers Dc
Churchill ordered these concrete causeways to be built in 1939 to block off eastern approach to naval base at Scapa Flow. Some 250,000 tons of material were used, linking largest island of Mainland with islands of Lamb Holm, Glims Holm, Burray and South Ronaldsay.

Click Mill ⌘ Cf
Small turf-roofed building on Mainland houses Orkney's only working corn mill, with wheel set horizontally, not vertically. Based on Norse design, this type was used by islanders for centuries. Signposted off B9057.

Cubbie Roo's Castle ⌂ ✿ Df
Small keep on Wyre, surrounded by circular ditch, said to be Scotland's earliest stone castle. Built in 12th century by Norse chief. In graveyard is ruined chapel, possibly built by chief's son.

Cuween Hill Cairn ⊓ Ce
Bones of dogs and oxen were found along with human remains inside this hillside Neolithic burial tomb, south of Finstown on Mainland. Passage 18ft long leads to central chamber with adjoining smaller cells.

Dwarfie Stane ⊓ Bd
Stone Age rock tomb cut into slab of sandstone, on Hoy. Passage leads to two chambers. Legend says it is home to malevolent dwarf of Norse sagas.

ISLAND HOMES OF EARLY MAN

A tour of Orkney's 18 inhabited islands takes the traveller back through man's history. Scattered across the fertile, flat land are countless reminders of the people who have lived here. Stone Age communities buried their dead in skilfully constructed tombs. Iron Age families inhabited underground earth houses. Celtic Christians founded monasteries, and Norse earls designed great halls.

Egilsay ✚ Dg
Round tower of 12th-century Church of St Magnus soars above roofless nave. Islanders prayed here well into 19th century.

Gurness Broch ⊓ Cf
Dry-stone tower, 2000 years old, stands on Mainland headland overlooking Rousay. It had underground well-chamber, still visible today, and upper gallery and floor. Later settlers built houses around tower.

Holm of Papa ⊓ Ei
Tiny island with huge megalithic tomb. Main chamber over 75ft long is adjoined by 14 smaller cells. No signs of life on island since tomb was built.

Italian Chapel ✝ Dd
In 1943 Italian prisoners-of-war built unique chapel inside two Nissen huts on Lamb Holm using scrap metal, driftwood and concrete. Interior has medieval-style wall paintings and altarpiece. Façade in traditional Italian style even has belfry.

Kirkwall ⌂ ▢ ✝ ⌘ ⌖ De
Busy harbour on Mainland is capital of Orkneys. St Magnus's Cathedral built in 1137 by Norse leader Rognvald, in memory of his murdered uncle, Magnus. Nearby is 17th-century Earl's Palace, built for 2nd Earl of Orkney. Tankerness House is a 16th-century merchant's home, now a local museum. Public library, founded 1683, is Scotland's oldest.

Knap of Howar ⊓ Di
Whalebone mallets and spatula have been unearthed on site of two well-built stone structures on Papa Westray. About 5500 years old, they are considered to be oldest standing dwellings in north-western Europe.

PRISONERS' ARTISTRY *Chapel on Lamb Holm was built in Nissen huts by Italian prisoners-of-war in World War II.*

Loch of Stenness ⊓ Be
Remains of three stone circles dominate Mainland horizon between Loch of Harray and Loch of Stenness. Encircling ditch still visible at Ring of Bookan. Ring of Brogar has 36 tall thin stones forming a circle 2½ acres in extent.

Maes Howe ⊓ ⌘ Ce
Massive Mainland tomb, 115ft in diameter, with vaulted stone chamber and adjoining smaller cells, built about 2500 BC. Later, Viking raiders scratched messages into walls; one message alludes to finding treasure.

Martello Tower Cc
Guarding entrance to Longhope Sound at Harkness, Hoy, one of a pair of towers built 1813 to protect British convoys in Longhope Sound against French and American privateers.

Marwick Head 🐦 Bf
Cliff-top Mainland RSPB reserve supporting flocks of breeding cormorants, kittiwakes, guillemots and razorbills. Reserve overlooks the spot where Lord Kitchener's boat was sunk by German mines in 1916. Monument to Kitchener within reserve.

Mid Howe ⊓ Cg
Largest of Orkneys' stalled cairns, on Rousay. Main chamber, 76ft long, is divided into 12 stalls with central passage. Benches held human remains, including 23 people buried about 2000 BC.

Noltland Castle ⌂ Dh
Castle on Westray was mainly built by Gilbert Balfour in 16th century. Its 71 gun loops in walls and Z-shape were intended to protect it from all sides.

North Hoy Nature Reserve 🐦 Bd
Windswept moorland and sea cliffs of this RSPB nature reserve make ideal habitat for hundreds of birds, from kittiwakes to Arctic skuas. Cliff formations include 450ft stack called Old Man of Hoy.

North Ronaldsay ⊓ Gi
Most northerly of isles of Orkneys is ringed by 6ft stone wall to protect crops from sheep. Sheep survive on seaweed yet produce fine wool. Prehistoric fort remains on southern coast.

Orkney Farm and Folk Museum ⌘ Ce
Two Mainland farmsteads show evolution of Orkney farm buildings over centuries. Kirbuster is the only surviving farmhouse with hearth in middle of floor. Corrigal's 19th-century house has gable fireplace and wooden box beds. Traditional breeds of sheep and poultry.

Orkney Wireless Museum ⌘ Dc
Cottage museum at St Margaret's Hope, South Ronaldsay; exhibits range from early crystal set to modern transistor radio; wireless sets from 1930s and old records.

Orphir Church ✚ Cd
Ruin of 12th-century circular Mainland church overlooks Scapa Flow's northern shore. Probably built by returned Crusader; only one of its type in Scotland. Apse remains – rest used to build 18th-century Presbyterian structure.

Pierowall ⌘ ⌂ Dh
Village set in curve of sheltered bay on east coast of farming island of Westray. The Norse leader Rognvald sailed here in 1136. Ruins of medieval church has tombstones with finely carved inscriptions.

Rennibister Earth House ⊓ Ce
Iron Age earth house was discovered on Mainland in 1926. Its roof collapsed under weight of farm threshing machine and revealed a floor strewn with human bones. Corbelled roof was supported on four stone slabs.

Sanday ⊓ Gh
Green island fringed by golden beaches. Human bones found in chambered tomb at Quoyness suggest that people were living here over 4000 years ago.

Scapa Flow Cc
Eighty square miles of sea enclosed by Mainland's south coast and isles of Burray, South Ronaldsay, Flotta and Hoy. This natural harbour was naval base during both world wars.

Skara Brae ⊓ Be
Buried by sand for 4500 years, Stone Age Mainland village was discovered in 1850 when storm tore sand away. Its roofless houses, linked by covered passages, have central hearths, stone bed-frames and a stone dresser. Paved courtyard where village council probably met.

NEOLITHIC HOME LIFE *Skara Brae Stone Age village, Mainland.*

Stromness ⌂ 🎣 Bd
Port town in sheltered Mainland harbour. Single, narrow street whose seaward houses have little jetties of their own. Fishermen offload catches of lobster and crab. Museum illustrates maritime history and island wildlife. Hudson's Bay Company recruiting site now Pier Arts Centre.

Taversoe Tuick ⊓ Df
Room for many bodies in this split-level Neolithic burial mound on southern coast of Rousay. Upper entrance is at ground level, lower one found through a 19ft sunken passage.

STONES OF MYSTERY *Brogar prehistoric stone circle, near the Loch of Stenness, has 36 stones covering more than 2 acres.*

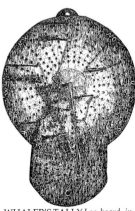
WHALER'S TALLY *Log-board, in Stromness Museum, was used to mark sightings of whales by hunters.*

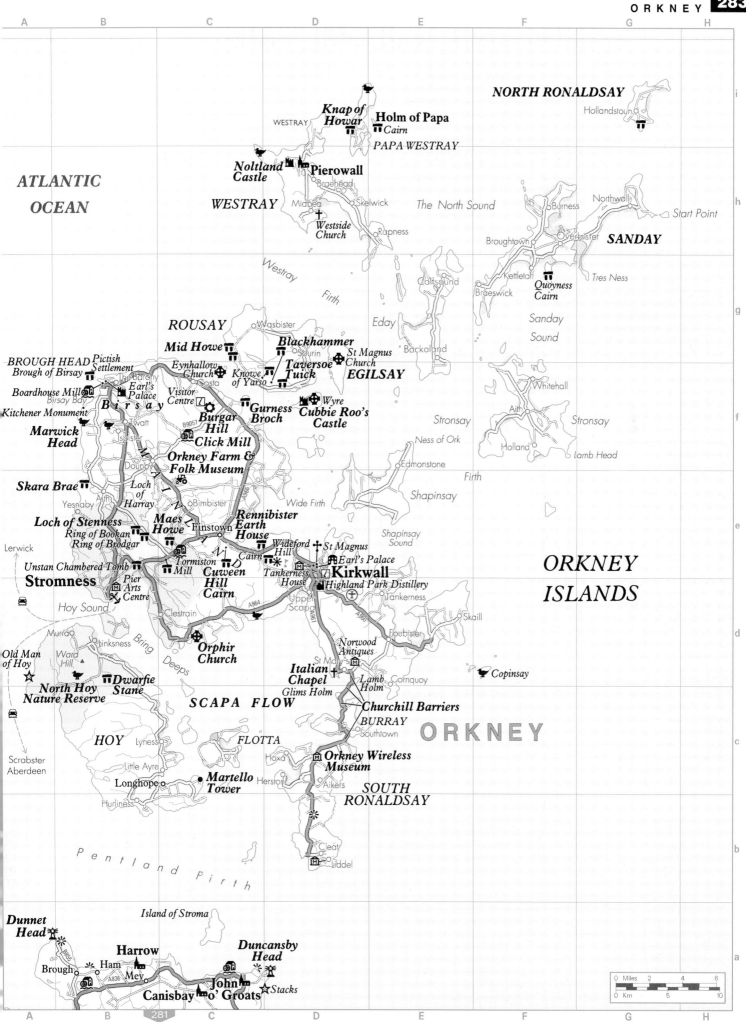

NORTH RONALDSAY

Hollandstoun

**ATLANTIC
OCEAN**

**Knap of
Howar**

WESTRAY

Holm of Papa
Cairn
PAPA WESTRAY

**Noltland
Castle**

Pierowall

Braehead

WESTRAY

Midbea
Skelwick

The North Sound

Northwall

Burness

SANDAY

Start Point

Broughtown
Overbister

**Westside
Church**

Rapness

Kettletoft

Tres Ness

Westray

Firth

Coltsound

Backaland

Braeswick

**Quoyness
Cairn**

ROUSAY

Wasbister

Eday

*Sanday
Sound*

Whitehall

Mid Howe

Blackhammer

Sourin

**Taversoe
Tuick**

St Magnus
Church

Aith

Stronsay

BROUGH HEAD
Brough of Birsay

Pictish
Settlement

The Barony

**Eynhallow
Church**

**Knowe
of Yarso**

EGILSAY

Stronsay

Boardhouse Mill

Birsay Bay

**Earl's
Palace**

Visitor
Centre

**Gurness
Broch**

Wyre
**Cubbie Roo's
Castle**

Stronsay

Ness of Ork

Holland

Lamb Head

Kitchener Monument

Birsay

Twatt

**Burgar
Hill**

Isbister

**Marwick
Head**

Dounby

Click Mill

B9057

Edmonstone

**Orkney Farm &
Folk Museum**

A966

Firth

Shapinsay

Skara Brae

Yesnaby

Aith

**Loch
of
Harray**

Bimbister

Wide Firth

*Shapinsay
Sound*

Loch of Stenness

Ring of Bookan
Ring of Brodgar

**Maes
Howe**

Finstown

**Rennibister
Earth House**

Wideford
Hill

St Magnus

Lerwick

Unstan Chambered Tomb

**Tormiston
Mill**

**Cuween
Hill
Cairn**

Cairn

**Tankerness
House**

Kirkwall

Earl's
Palace

A965

A964

Stromness

**Pier
Arts
Centre**

Clestrain

Upper
Scapa

Highland Park Distillery

Tankerness

Skaill

Hoy Sound

A961

Foubister

**ORKNEY
ISLANDS**

Murra

Linksness

Bring

Scapa Flow
SCAPA FLOW

A960

Norwood
Antiques

St Mary's

Copinsay

**Old Man
of Hoy**

Ward
Hill

**Dwarfie
Stane**

Deeps

**Italian
Chapel**

Lamb
Holm

Cornquoy

**North Hoy
Nature Reserve**

Glims Holm

Churchill Barriers

ORKNEY

Scrabster
Aberdeen

HOY

Lyness

FLOTTA

Hoxa

BURRAY
Southtown

Little Ayre

Herston

**Orkney Wireless
Museum**

**SOUTH
RONALDSAY**

Longhope

**Martello
Tower**

Aikers

Hurliness

Pentland Firth

Cleat
Liddel

Island of Stroma

**Dunnet
Head**

B855

Harrow

Ham

Mey

**Duncansby
Head**

Brough

A836

Canisbay

**John
o' Groats**

Stacks

| 0 | Miles | 2 | | 4 | | 6 |
| 0 | Km | | 5 | | | 10 |

Böd of Gremista 🏛 Fd
Fully restored 18th-century booth for fish curing. One room devoted to Arthur Anderson, founder and developer of the Peninsular and Oriental Steam Navigation Company, who was born here.

Clickimin Broch ⊓ Fd
One of best-preserved brochs in Scotland. Round stone tower built during Bronze Age.

THE CROFTING LIFE *Visitors take a step back in time at Shetland's Croft House Museum, Boddam.*

Croft House Museum 🏛 Ea
Restored, thatched croft house equipped with 19th-century furniture and utensils, showing typical crofting life. Outbuildings include kiln where corn was dried. Nearby lies preserved water mill, still in use.

Esha Ness ❄ Cg
One of few cliff-top viewpoints in Shetland accessible by car. Fulmars and puffins nest in cliffs. Good walking country.

Fetlar Nature Reserve ❦ Hi
This nature reserve's bird life includes Arctic skuas, storm petrels, whimbrels and snowy owls. Otters, common seals and grey seals abound. Bronze Age stone circles at Hjaltadans.

SEA LOCHS, SEALS AND SEA BIRDS

Britain's northernmost islands are home to wildlife of all sorts – gulls, skuas, puffins and seals crowd the shorelines, and inland domestic sheep and the diminutive Shetland ponies outnumber people. Sparsely populated though the Shetlands are, they have a long history of human occupation as the remnants of Bronze Age, Iron Age and Norse buildings testify.

Foula ❄ ☆ Ac
Most westerly Shetland isle with population of 45. Kame Cliff, at 1220ft, second only to St Kilda in height. The Sneug, at 1370ft, has views of surrounding countryside. Gaada Stack has impressive natural arch. Area abundant with sheep, Shetland ponies, fulmars and razorbills.

Hamnavoe 🛖 Fg
Fishing village on attractive natural harbour. Nearby cliffs, called Villians of Hamnavoe, have views of eroded lava rocks with blowholes, arches and caves. Good walking area.

Haroldswick 🛖 Hk
Northernmost post office in Britain can be found here. Special card and letter franking available. Island heritage centre at nearby village of Clibberswick.

Herma Ness ☆ ❦ Gk
Most northerly tip of Britain. Hermaness Nature Reserve is home to great skuas and gannets. Views take in offshore lighthouse on Muckle Flugga and the tiny island of Out Stack, final fragment of Great Britain.

Hjaltasteyn ⬦ Ed
Jewellery centre includes showroom and workshop. Visitors choose from silver, gold and enamel settings. Viking, Celtic and wildlife designs are produced at Shetland Silvercraft workshops, in nearby Weisdale.

Jarlshof ⊓ Ea
Remarkable archaeological site – ancient homestead for over 3000 years. Earliest remains date from Stone Age, later settlements occupied during Bronze Age and Iron Age. Stone rectangular houses remain from Viking community, spanning 200 years. Ruined 'Laird's House' dates from 17th century – the 'Jarlshof' of the novel *The Pirate* by Sir Walter Scott.

Lerwick 🏛 ☑ Fd
Town set around old but busy harbour. Some of merchants' houses have 'lodberries' – loading piers built out over the harbour. Rides around harbour in replica Viking ship on summer evenings. Shetland Museum has displays on archaeology, folk life, textiles, shipping and seafaring – illustrating history of Shetland. Ramparts of 17th-century Fort Charlotte give view over harbour to Bressay and Noss. In January, town celebrates Norse fire festival, Up-Helly-Aa. Replica Viking longship hauled through streets then ceremonially burned as prelude to night of revelry.

Loch of Spiggie ❦ Ea
Whooper swans, ducks, waders, gulls, terns and skuas inhabit this reserve. Nearby lies Scousburgh Sands where visitors can picnic and swim.

Lunna Ness ✝ ☆ Gg
Rugged, ice-moulded headland of Lunna Ness provides good walks,

JARLSHOF HOMES *Circular stone-walled houses replaced defensive brochs during the Iron Age.*

with views of otters, near Ice Age Stanes of Stofast. Lunna Kirk, dating from 1753 is still in use. Hole in wall allowed lepers to see and hear church services.

Mousa Broch ⊓ Fb
Winner of Castle of the Year award in 1989. Most complete Iron Age broch in country. Circular tower rises 43ft above outer rampart. View of seals from white sand beach at West Voe. Boat to island from Sandwick. Evening sea trips view storm petrels in natural habitat.

Muness Castle 🏰 Hj
Ruins of Britain's northernmost stronghold. Castle was built by Laurence Bruce in 1598, but was abandoned within a century. Sections of original three-storey Z-plan design can still be seen. Circular tower also remains.

Noss Nature Reserve ❦ Gd
Sheer cliffs rise 600ft in 774 acre bird reserve, which includes gannets, gulls, skuas and waders. Sea campion, scurvy grass and roseroot thrive here, amongst 150 species of flowering plants. Interpretive display at 17th-century house. Remains of 19th-century croft houses, mausoleum and a pre-Reformation chapel. Restored pony-pund is where Shetland ponies were bred for work in Durham coalfields.

Old Haa of Burravoe 🏛 Gg
Oldest building on island of Yell contains exhibition of local plants, animals, arts, crafts and history. Also has photographic collection and video and tape recordings of local musicians and storytellers. Nearby Hoose of Burravoe has sea-bird colony of puffins, guillemots, shags and fulmars, as well as common seals.

Papa Stour ☆ Cf
Rocky coastline reveals stacks, arches and caves, including Kirstan's Hole – vast sea cave. Archaeological trail takes in recently discovered foundations of medieval house.

Quendale 🏭 Ea
Site of restored water mill with large vertical wheel. Beach at Bay of Quendale is Shetland's largest at almost a mile long.

St Ninian's Isle ✚ Eb
Connected to mainland only by narrow beach. Hoard of ancient Celtic treasure found beneath remains of 12th-century chapel.

Scalloway 🏰 🏛 Fc
Former capital of Shetlands named after Norse *skali*, or hall. Houses cluster around the well-preserved remains of castle – built 1660. Local artefacts and old photographs in converted shop museum. Also on show is the story of Norwegian Resistance's 'Shetland Bus' boat shuttle to and from Norway during World War II, smuggling saboteurs and refugees out of their homeland.

Stanydale ⊓ De
Foundations of large Neolithic house surrounded by domestic remains, field boundaries and clearance cairns. Further finds at nearby Bridge of Walls.

Sumburgh ⊓ Fa
Guillemots, razorbills, kittiwakes and puffins breed near 1821 lighthouse. Grey seals share waters with dolphins and killer whales. Car park display board details breeding sea birds.

Symbister 🛖 Gf
Beside harbour lies Pier House, a Hanseatic Böd where German merchants stored bartered goods.

Tingwall Agricultural Museum ⚒ Fd
Museum has a collection of old crofting tools. Display housed in Victorian farm buildings.

Tingwall Church ✝ Fd
Built 1790 on site of towered Church of St Magnus, dating back to early period of Norse Christianity. Old kirk's burial vault still stands in graveyard.

Unst ✝ 🏛 ❦ ☆ 🏭 Gj
Remains of piers and huts at Baltasound and spoil heaps at Nikka Vord are reminders of former herring and chromite industries. Island also has restored Norse water mill, Shetland ponies and Celtic fish carving in old Kirk of Lund. Caves and islets surround Burra Firth in north – a dramatic sea inlet flanked by cliffs of Saxa Vord (935ft) and the hills of Hermaness. Austere rocks of Muness Castle in south-east.

Whalsay ⊓ Gf
Britain's most northerly golf course lies at Skaw. Coastal walks to south and east reveal breeding seals and birds. Ruined Iron Age blockhouse stands beside Loch of Huxter. Remains of Neolithic houses lie at Isbister. Out Skerries have Bronze Age stone circle and 1857 lighthouse.

Yell ⊓ 🏛 Fi
Ruins of Iron Age fort at Aywick, and White Lady – wrecked ship's figurehead at Otterswick. Shell sand beach at Wick of Breakon, near Gloup Memorial to 58 drowned men. Otters and Shetland field mice abound.

DISTANT SUMBURGH *The rocky headland, seen on the horizon across West Voe of Sumburgh, supports a huge variety of wildlife. Looking out towards Fair Isle, visitors can sometimes catch sight of dolphins and killer whales.*

ATLANTIC

OCEAN

SHETLAND

ISLANDS

ST MAGNUS BAY

MUCKLE ROE

Papa Stour

NORTH

SEA

Point of Fethaland

Ibister

The Faither

Housetter

Collafirth

Yell
Sound

West
Sandwick

West Yell

Ulsta

YELL

FETLAR

Fetlar
Nature Reserve

Turra Field
Aerodrome

Hoube

Aith

Funzie

Broch
Aywick

Otterswick

Horse of
Burravoe

Burravoe

Old Haa
of Burravoe

Lunna
Ness

Stanes of Stofast

Hamnavoe

Lunna

Kirk

Vidlin

Laxo

Mossbank

SCATSTA

Sullom

Roesound

Esha Ness

Stenness

Wick of
Breakon

Gloup

Cullivoe

Westing

Colvister

Sellafirth

Gutcher

Kirk of
Lund

BALTASOUND
AERODROME

Baltasound

Keen of Hamer
Nature Reserve

UNST

Haroldswick

Clibberswick

Norwick

Burrafirth

Saxa Vord

Herma Ness

Out
Stack

Muness Castle

Uyeasound

Out Skerries

Skaw

SKAW

Homesteads

Isbister

Symbister

Fort **WHALSAY**

Neap

Moul of Eswick

Gletness

Stanydale

Dale

Aith

Bixter

Tresta

WEISDALE

Clousta

Walls

Vaila

Culswick

Reawick

White
Ness

Sandness

Wats Ness

Hjaltasteyn

Tingwall Church

Loch of Tingwall

LERWICK
(TINGWALL)

Tingwall Agricultural Museum

Böd of Gremista

BRESSAY

Fort
Charlotte

Noss Nature Reserve

Isle of Noss

Shetland Museum

Lerwick

Clickimin Broch

Scalloway

Scalloway Castle

Easter
Quarff

Hamnavoe

Grunasound

West Burra

East
Burra

Fladdabister

Starkigarth

Helli Ness

Kame
Cliff

Gaada Stack

The Sneug

FOULA

Maywick

Sandwick

Mousa

Mousa Broch

St Ninian's Isle

Church Remains

Northpunds

Stromness
Aberdeen

Loch of Spiggie

Quendale

Fitful Head

Boddam

Scousburgh

Croft House Museum

Mill

Exnaboe

SUMBURGH AIRPORT

Jarlshof

Sumburgh

Ness of
Burgi

0 Miles	2	4	6
0 Km		5	10

Alderney ⌂ ☑ Ef
Small island, only 3½ miles long
and 1½ miles wide. Pleasing mixture of colour-washed houses and
cobbled streets.

Battle of Flowers Museum
⌂ Bc
Flower floats from Jersey's annual
carnival are preserved in this
museum. Arctic, alpine and African scenes among them.

Bonne Nuit Bay Cc
On north coast of Jersey; small and
sandy with fishing harbour at foot
of cliffs. Around the headland of
Fremont Point a steep footpath
leads to Wolf's Caves at low tide.

Burhou ☙ Dg
Boat trips from Alderney to this
bird sanctuary island. Breeding
sea birds include puffin, razorbill,
guillemot and storm petrel.

Corbière Point ✳ ☘ Aa
Barren peninsula on Jersey's
western corner. Jagged rocks and
causeway to 1874 lighthouse
exposed at low tide. Siren sounds
before high tide covers causeway.

Devil's Hole ☆ Bc
Natural phenomenon where sea
has cut through rock. At high tide,
water boils as if in a rocky cauldron. Alongside footpath from car
park, giant effigy of the Evil One
sets a sinister mood.

Elizabeth Castle ☛ Ca
Rugged 16th-century fortress is
reached by amphibious craft or on
foot at low tide. Named after
Elizabeth I by Sir Walter Raleigh.
Contains relics of the German
occupation during World War II.

Fermain Bay Cd
This small sheltered bay is best
approached by motor launch from
St Peter Port. Trees cloaking steep
cliffs tumble to the water's edge.
Stretches of firm sand at low tide.

**German Military
Underground Hospital** ☛ Cb
Excavated out of solid rock over
3½ years by slave workers. Used
for German soldiers wounded in
France after Allies' invasion in
June 1944. Re-created wards and
operating theatre. Relics include
wartime newspapers.

FLOWER POWER *Castle ramparts
loom over peaceful Gorey seafront.*

Gorey ⌂⌂ ⌂ Db
Village is overlooked by Mont
Orgueil Castle with magnificent
13th-century keep and Elizabethan tower. Built as bastion
after King John lost Normandy

ISLANDS OF THE CONQUEROR

*Britain's most southerly islands lie some 14 miles off the French
coast, yet they have never been owned by France, though they once
belonged to William the Conqueror. Each has it own appeal.
Alderney's only town has the character of a Normandy village;
Guernsey displays its links with fishing and the sea; Jersey has two
proud castles; Herm and Sark are places to wander on foot.*

RACE AGAINST TIME *Siren warns when tide is about to cut off the lighthouse at Corbière, Britain's first concrete one.*

to France; restored by Raleigh
among others. Small harbour and
beach bordered by gardens and
golf course.

Grève de Lecq ⛟ ☛ Bc
Sandy beach sheltered by grassy
cliffs. It is reached by road through
a wooded valley and passes Le
Moulin de Lecq, water mill inn
where wheel still turns.

Guernsey Folk Museum ⌂ Be
Life in a farmhouse more than a
century ago recalled with reconstructed kitchen, the traditional
centre of family activities.

Guernsey Museum ⌂ ✿ Ce
Founded by Frederick Corbin
Lukis and his sons – all archae-
ologists. Art gallery has works by
local 19th-century painters. Set in
exotic Candie Gardens.

Guernsey Tomato Centre
☘⌂ Be
The story of the tomato cultivation
industry – introduced in early
17th century – is told using films
and displays. Tomato wine can be
seen in the making.

Herm ✝ De
Tiny island of 600 acres, yet with a
surprising variety of natural
scenery. Towering cliffs, wooded
valleys, sandy beaches, enough
pastureland to support 100
Guernsey cows. Coastal walk
around island; no cars or roads.
Millions of tiny shells washed up
on Shell Beach; some from as far
away as Gulf of Mexico.

Icart Point ✳ Bd
Rocky headland with some of the
finest views in Guernsey. Cliff
path, running entire length of
south coast, can be joined here.

Jersey Zoo ☙ Db
Founded in 1959 by naturalist
Gerald Durrell. More than 1500
endangered animals. Breeding is
a feature here, with the aim of
returning some to the wild.

Kempt Tower Centre ☙ Bb
Nature area which overlooks St
Ouen's Bay. Sand dunes, scrub
and ponds are home for variety of
birds and 5000 insect species.

La Hougue Bie ⛟ ☛ Db
Stone Age site on east of Jersey
island with giant burial mound
thought to be 7000 years old. Passage 33ft long leads to central
burial chamber. Two chapels, one
12th century and the other 16th,
stand on top. German forces set
up underground communications
bunker here in 1940; now housing
museum of German occupation.

La Mare Vineyards ✿ Bc
Tranquil home where the Blayney
family have made wine for 150
years. Gardens and cider orchard,
as well as avenues of vines. Fine
18th-century Jersey farmhouse.

L'Ancresse Bay Cf
Horseshoe of jagged rock and
golden sands, with one of the best
bathing beaches on the island. It is
scattered with defensive Martello
towers built in 1780s.

Little Chapel ✝ Bd
Tiny church at Les Vauxbelets on
Guernsey, decorated with shells,
pebbles and broken glass. Built
1923 by French monk, Brother
Déodat, based on grotto at Lour-
des. Interior only 19ft by 10ft.

Moulin Huet Bay Cd
Bay with three sandy, sheltered
beaches in Guernsey's south-east
corner: Moulin Huet approached
by lane ending at car park; Petit
Port by flight of 365 steps; Saint's
Bay through wooded vale.

Perelle Bay Ae
Small, rocky bay dominated by
German lookout tower from
World War II. Causeway to Lihou
Island – crowned by ruined 12th-
century priory – accessible at low
tide. Megalithic tomb is linked
with 17th-century legend; devil
said to have sat on capstone while
warlocks worshipped.

Portelet Bay ✳ Ba
Rocky bay where wooded hills
rise steeply from foreshore. Sandy
beach exposed at low tide. Off
shore, islet of Ile au Guerdain is
crowned by 18th-century tower
known as Janvrin's Tomb, after
Jersey sea captain buried 1721.

Quetivel Mill ⛟ Bb
Only working water mill in St
Peter's Valley. Milling began on
this site in 1309, continued until
19th century, and began again in
1940s when fine new wheel was
crafted. Recently restored by
National Trust for Jersey.

Rocquaine Bay ⚓ Ad
Bay curving around Guernsey'
largest beach, containing fishin
harbour of Portelet and Fort Grey
Maritime Museum of local ship
wrecks. Pezeries Point, with view
to the offshore Hanois lighthouse
juts into bay at southern end.

St Anne ⌂ ☑ Ef
Charming little town with tin
squares, pastel-shaded cottage
and cobbled streets. History since
Iron Age in Alderney Museum.

St Brelade's Bay Ba
Popular beach backed by prom
enade with palm-fringed garden
and fountains. Seaside attraction
and water sports.

St Helier ⌂ ☕ ☛ ☑ Cb
Jersey's capital and chief port
Colourful pavement cafés, bar
and squares. Fort Regent built fo
defence in Napoleonic wars; now
leisure complex. Jersey Museum
has room devoted to actress Lil
Langtry. Seafront road to S
Aubin, small harbour built 167
with fine merchants' houses.

St Ouen's Bay Ab
Vast stretch of golden sand. Sur
fing, bathing for strong swim
mers, and golf among the dunes.

St Peter's Bunker ☛ ☛ Bb
Built by Germans in 1942 to guard
access to Jersey Airport; now
houses Occupation Museum with
uniforms and equipment. Oppo
site, Jersey Motor Museum ha
Rolls-Royce used by Genera
Montgomery before D-Day.

St Peter Port
✝ ☘⌂ ☑ Ce
Guernsey capital where island
parliament sits in 18th-century
Royal Court. Cobbled streets and
granite buildings clamber up hill
side: 13th-century Castle Corne
houses art gallery and military
museums. Hauteville House
bought by French novelist Victo
Hugo in 1856, is where he wrote
Les Misérables; now museum with
china, paintings and tapestries.

APPLE CRUSHER *Old cider press
at La Seigneurie residence, Sark.*

Sark ☆ ✿ Ed
Island 3 miles long by 1½ wide
almost cut in two but linked by La
Coupée causeway. Enchanting
bays, caves and pools. Since 1565
Sark has been a feudal state
governed by seigneur; gardens of
residence, La Seigneurie, open
some summer days. Cars banned,
travel by bicycle, tractor or horse-
drawn carriage.

Sausmarez Manor ⌂ Cd
Fine example of hereditary feuda
home, still occupied by de Saus
marez family who have had long
association with Channel Islands
Built on site of a Norman house
Richly added to in Queen Anne
and Regency times.

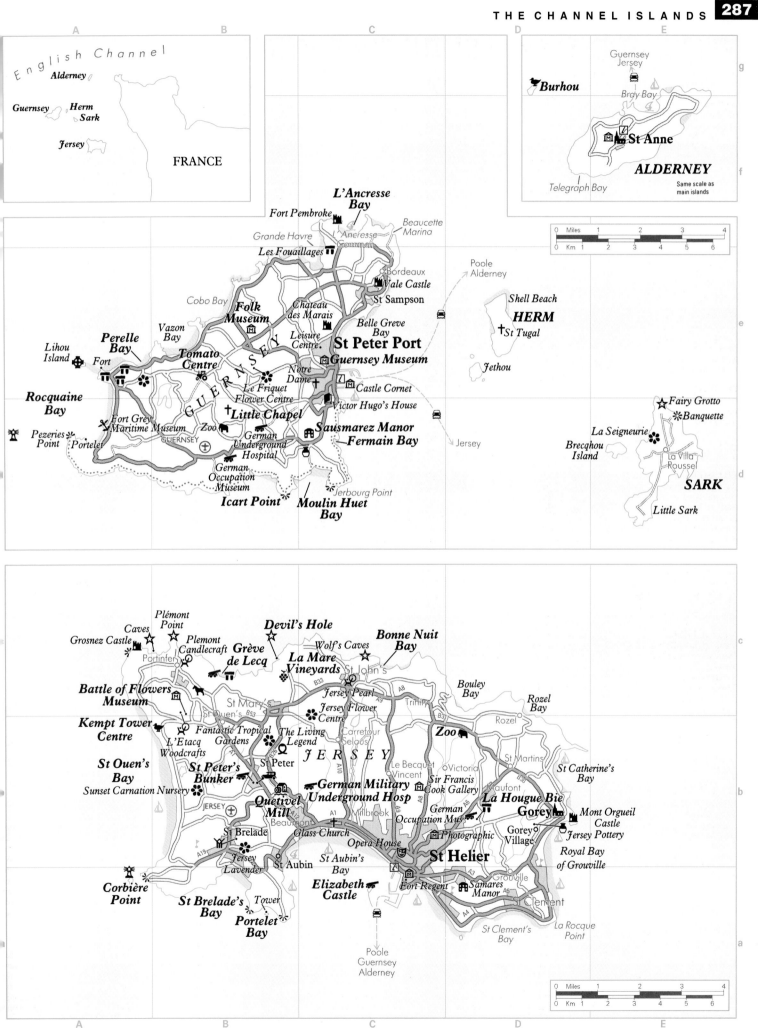

English Channel

Alderney

Guernsey Herm
Sark

Jersey

FRANCE

Burhou

Guernsey
Jersey

Bray Bay

St Anne

Telegraph Bay

ALDERNEY

Same scale as
main islands

L'Ancresse Bay

Fort Pembroke

Grande Havre

L'Ancresse
Common

Beaucette
Marina

Les Fouaillages

Bordeaux

Cobo Bay

Vale Castle

St Sampson

Folk Museum

Château des Marais

Leisure Centre

Belle Greve Bay

Poole
Alderney

Shell Beach

HERM

St Tugal

Vazon Bay

St Peter Port

Guernsey Museum

Jethou

Perelle Bay

Tomato Centre

Notre Dame

Le Friquet Flower Centre

Castle Cornet

Victor Hugo's House

Fairy Grotto

Banquette

Lihou Island

Fort

Little Chapel

Rocquaine Bay

Fort Grey Maritime Museum

Zoo

GUERNSEY

Sausmarez Manor Fermain Bay

La Seigneurie

Brecqhou Island

La Villa Roussel

Pezeries Point

Portelet

German Underground Hospital

German Occupation Museum

Jersey

SARK

Icart Point

Moulin Huet Bay

Jerbourg Point

Little Sark

Miles 0 1 2 3 4
Km 0 1 2 3 4 5 6

Plémont Point

Devil's Hole

Caves

Bonne Nuit Bay

Grosnez Castle

Plémont Candlecraft

Grève de Lecq

Wolf's Caves

Battle of Flowers Museum

Portinfer

La Mare Vineyards

St John's

Jersey Pearl

Bouley Bay

Rozel Bay

Kempt Tower Centre

St Mary's

Jersey Flower Centre

Trinity

Rozel

L'Etacq Woodcrafts

St Ouen's

Fantastic Tropical Gardens

The Living Legend

Carrefour Selous

Zoo

St Martins

St Ouen's Bay

St Peter's Bunker

St Peter

JERSEY

Le Becquet Vincent

Sir Francis Cook Gallery

St Catherine's Bay

Sunset Carnation Nursery

Quetivel Mill

German Military Underground Hosp

Victoria

Maufont

La Hougue Bie

JERSEY

Beaumont

Millbrook

German Occupation Mus

Gorey

Mont Orgueil Castle

St Brelade

Glass Church

Photographic

Gorey Village

Jersey Pottery

Corbière Point

Jersey Lavender

St Aubin

Opera House

St Helier

Royal Bay of Grouville

St Brelade's Bay

Tower

St Aubin's Bay

Elizabeth Castle

Fort Regent

Samares Manor

Grouville

St Clement

Portelet Bay

St Clement's Bay

La Rocque Point

Poole
Guernsey
Alderney

Miles 0 1 2 3 4
Km 0 1 2 3 4 5 6

GAZETTEER

This gazetteer yields a wealth of information about places worth a visit, as well as being an index to the maps. Entries in **bold type** refer to places described in the text. To find a place on the maps use the two-letter map reference that follows the page number. Key to symbols: ⓟ – Parking; ✕ – Refreshments available; £ – Admission charge; ⓰ – Facilities for the disabled. Use telephone numbers for more detailed information, such as opening times. Other symbols are explained on the bookmark and on pages 6 and 7

Abberley 123Ed ○
Abberley Hall 123Ed ⌂
Abberton Reservoir 113Eb ⬥
Abbess Roding 113Ab ⌂
Abbey Cwmhir 119Db ⌂ ⚘
Abbey Dore 119Gb ○ ⚘ ⚘
Abbey Dore Court 119Gb ⚘ ⚘
ⓟ✕⓰☎ 0981 240419
Abbey Gardens 9Bb ⚘
✕⓰☎ 0720 22849
Abbey Mills 61Db ⌂ ⚘
ⓟ✕⓰☎ 081 542 5035
Abbey St Bathans 233Db ⌂
Abbey Wood 63Cc
Abbeydale Industrial Hamlet 173Ac ⚘ ○ ⌂ ⓟ✕£
☎ 0742 367731
Abbeystead 183De ⌂
Abbeytown 207Ce ⌂ ⚘
Abbot Hall, Kendal 197Bc ⌂
ⓟ⓰☎ 0539 722464
Abbots Bromley 147Cd ⌂ ⚘ ⬥
Abbot's Cliff 43Cc ☀ ☆
Abbot's Fish House 45Cc ⌂
Abbots Leigh 45Df ○
Abbot's Wood, E Ssx 39Cb ⬥ ⬥
Abbot's Wood, Glos 97Bd ⬥
Abbotsbury 25Bc ⌂ † ⚘ ⚘ ⌂
Abbotsford 221Be ⌂
ⓟ✕⓰☎ 0896 2043
Abbotstone Down 53Ea ⊓
Aber Falls 161Aa ☆
Aber Valley Reserve 161Ab ⬥
Aberaeron 117Cc ⬥
Aberarth 117Cc ○
Aberavon 91Ac ○
Abercastle 87Be ⌂ ⊓
Aberchirder 271Cc ⌂ ⚘
Aberconwy House 161Bb ⌂
£☎ 0492 592246
Abercynon 91Dd ○
Aberdare 91De ○
Aberdaron 155Ba ⌂
Aberdeen 267Cd
† † ⌂ ⚘ ○ ⬥ ⚘ ⌂ ⌂
Aberdour 247Aa ⌂
Aberdour Castle 247Aa ⌂ £
☎ 031 2443101
Aberdulais Falls 91Ae ☆
Aberdyfi 117Ef ⬥
Aberedw 119Dc ○
Abereiddy 87Ae ○
Abererch 155Db ⌂
Aberfeldy 255Fd ⚘ ⚘ ⬤
Aberfeldy Watermill 255Fd ⌂
ⓟ✕£☎ 0887 20803
Aberffraw 155De ⌂ † ⌂
Aberford 187Ec ○
Aberfoyle 241Cf ⌂ ⚘
Abergavenny 93Ce † ⌂ ⌂
Abergorlech 89Df ○ ⌂
Abergwesyn 119Bd ○ ☆
Abergwesyn Pass 119Bd ☆
Abergwyngregyn 161Ab
⌂ ⬥ ☆ ⬥
Abergynolwyn 117Eg ○ ⬥ ⌂ ⌂
Aberlady 233Ac ⌂ ☆
Aberlady Bay 233Ad ⬥
Aberlemno 259Be ⌂ ⊓
Aberllefenni 157Da ○
Abernant 89Df ⬥ ⬥
Abernethy 247Ad ⌂ ⌂
Aberporth 87Fg ○
Abersoch 155Ba ⬥
Abertarff House 261Ce ⌂ £
☎ 0463 232034
Abertillery 93Bd ○
Aberystwyth 117De ⌂ ⬥ ⌂ ⌂

Aberystwyth Yesterday 117De ⌂
ⓟ⓰☎ 0970 617119
Abingdon 103Ba ⚘ ⚘ ⌂ ⌂
Abinger Common 37Cf ⌂ ⚘
Abington 227Ec ○
Ablington 101Cc ○
Abney 171Cc ○
Aboyne 265Cc ⌂ ⌂
Aboyne Castle 265Cc ⌂
Accrington 185Ab ⌂
Achamore House Gardens 237Be ⚘
ⓟ£☎ 058 35253
Achallader 277Ah ⌂ ⚘ ⚘
ⓟ⓰☎ 0981 240419
Achillibuie 277Eh ⌂ ⚘ ⚘
ⓟ⓰ 085482 353
Achmelvich Bay 277Ej
Achnaba 239Dh ⬥ †
Achnabreck 239Cd ⊓
Achnacarry 251Ee ○
Achnacloich Woodland Garden 239Dh ☆ ⓟ⓰£☎ 0631 71221
Achnasheen 277Fc ○
Achness Waterfall 278Ae ☆
Achray Forest 241Cf ⬥ ☀ ⌂
Achu Long Barrow 278Cd ⊓
Ackling Dyke 27Be ⚘ ☀
Acland Barton 21Ae ○
Acle 141De ○
Aconbury Camp 97Af ☀
Acorn Bank 197Cf ⚘
Acton 167Aa ○
Acton Beauchamp 123Dc ○
Acton Burnell 145Cb ○ ⌂
Acton Burnell Castle 145Cb ⌂
ⓟ⓰ 0902 765105
Acton Round 145Da ○ ⌂
Acton Round Hall 145Da ⌂
ⓟ£☎ 046 31203
Acton Scott Working Farm and Museum 123Bf ⬥
Acton, Suffolk 113Dc ○
Adcote 145Bc ⌂ⓟ⓰
☎ 0939 260202
Adderbury 103Be ○
Adderley 145De ○
Addington 63Bb ○
Addinston 221Bg ☀
Addlethorpe 153Ef ○
Adel 187Cc †
Aden Country Park 271Fb ⬥
ⓟ✕☎ 0771 22857
Adgestone Vineyard 31Cb ⬥
ⓟ☎ 0983 402503
Adisham 43Ce ○
Adlestrop 101De ○
Adlington Hall 167Dd ⌂
ⓟ✕£☎ 0625 829206
Admiral Blake Museum 23Cf ⌂
ⓟ£☎ 0278 456127
Adur Estuary 37Db ⬥
Adwick le Street 173Ce †
Ae 219Ac ○
Aeropark 149Cc ⌓ⓟ£⓰
☎ 0332 810621
Aerospace Museum 145Eb ⌓
ⓟ✕⓰☎ 0902 374872
Afan Argoed Country Park 91Bd ⬥
⬥ ⌂ ⓟ✕⓰☎ 0639 850564
Affleck Castle 259Ac ⌂
Affpuddle 25Ed ○
Afon Cwm-llechan 157Cc
Afon Gamlan Wetlands 157Dc ⬥ ⬥
African Violet Centre 137Df ⚘
ⓟ✕⓰☎ 0553 828374
Agglestone 27Bb ☆

Agricultural & Folk Museum, Havering 85Ad ⬥ ⓟ⓰
☎ 04024 47535
Aigas Dam Fish Lift 261Ae
Aigas House Garden 261Ae ⚘
ⓟ✕⓰☎ 0463 782443
Ailsa Craig 215Bh ⌂
Ainsdale 163Bg ⬥
Ainsdale Sand Dunes 163Ag ⬥
Aira Force 207Fb ☆ ⌂
Airborne Forces Museum 57Cc ⌓
ⓟ⓰☎ 0252 349619
Aird Castle 237Dd ⌂
Airdrie 241Eb ⌂
Airds Moss 227Ac ✕
Aisgill Summit 197Dc
Aisholt 23Bf ⌂ ⬥
Aisholt Common 23Bf ⬥
A La Ronde 15Df ⌂ⓟ⓰£✕£
☎ 0395 265514
Alauna 207Bc ⬥
Albury 37Bf ○ ⌂
Albury Park 37Bf ⌂ⓟ£
☎ 048641 2964
Alby Crafts 143Gb ⬥ⓟ✕⓰
☎ 0263 761590
Alcester 125Cc
Alciston 39Cb ○
Alconbury 135Dc ○
Aldborough 187Ef ○
Aldbourne 53Be ○
Aldbury 107Cc ○
Aldeburgh 115Ee † ⌂
Aldenham Country Park 61Ce ⬥
ⓟ£☎ 081 953 9602
Alderbury 27Cf ○
Alderford 139Ef ○
Alderholt Mill 27Ce ⌂ⓟ✕
☎ 0425 653130
Alderley Edge 167Cc ☆ ⓟ⓰
☎ 0625 584412
Aldermaston 53Ed ⌂
Aldermaston 53Ed ○
Alderney 287Df ⌂
Aldershot 57Cb ⌓ ✕
Aldingham 195Db ○ ⌂
Aldwincle 135Cd ○
Aldworth 53Ee ○
Alexander Keiller Museum 49Df ⌂
ⓟ£ 0672 3250
Alexandra Palace 61De
Alford, Grampian 265Ce ⬥ ⌂ ⌂
Alford, Lincs 177Db ⌂ ⌂
Alford Manor House Museum 177Db ⌂ⓟ£☎ 0507 466514
Alford Mill 177Db ✕ⓟ✕£
☎ 0205 352188
Alford Valley Railway 265Ce ⬤
ⓟ✕£☎ 09755 62326
Alfred's Castle 53Bf ☀
Alfred's Tower 49Ab ⌂
Alfriston 39Cb ⌂ ⌂ ⌂ ⌂ ⌂
Alice Holt Forest 57Cb ⬥ ☀ ⌂ ⌂
Alisby's Castle 93Be ⌂
Alkborough 175Cg ⌂ ☀
Alkham 43Cd ○
All Stretton 145Ba ○
Allan Ramsay Library 227Db ⌂
☎ 065974326
Allen Banks Wood 209Ed ⬥
Allen Gorge 209Dd ⬥
Allendale Town 209Ec ⌂
Allensford Country Park 211Cc ⬥
Allerthorpe Common 189Dd ⬥ ⌂
Allerton Park 189Ae ⌂
ⓟ✕£☎ 0423 330927
Allgreave 167Db ○
Allgreave 171Ab ○
Allhallows Museum, Honiton 23Bc
⌂ £☎ 0404 35851
Allied Forces Museum 153Cf ⬤
ⓟ☎ 0205 480317
Allonby 207Bd ○
Allonby Bay 207Bd
Alloway 225Cb ⌂ ⌂ ⌂
Alloway Kirk 225Cb ⚘
☎ 0292 41252
Allt Coire Eoghain 251Ec ☆
Allt Ddu 91Dg
Allt nan Carnan 277Db ⬥
Almeley 119Gd ○
Almond Aqueduct 229Cf ⚘
Almond Valley Heritage Centre 229Be ⌂ ⓟ✕⓰☎ 0506 414957
Almondell & Calderwood Country Park 229Be ⬥ ⓟ✕⓰
☎ 0506 882254
Alne 189Af ⌂
Alness 278Ca

Alness Point 278Ca
Alnmouth 223Ec ○
Alnwick 223Dc ⌂
Alnwick Castle 223Dc ⌂
ⓟ£ 0665 510777
Alport 171Db ○
Alresford Creek 115Aa
Alresfords, The 29De ⌂ ⌂ ○
Alrewas 147Dc ⌂
Alston 209Db ⌂ ⬤ ⚘ ⌂
Alstonefield 147Dg ○
Altarnun 11Ef ⌂
Altens Haven 267Cd
Alton 57Ba ⬤ ⌂
Alton Towers 147Cf ⌂ ☯
ⓟ✕⓰£☎ 0538 702200
Alum Bay 31Ab ☀ ☆ ⚘
Alva Glen 245Be ⬥
Alvchester 129Bg ⚘ ⬥ ⌂
Alveley 123Ef ○
Alvescot 101Dc ○ ⚘
Alvingham 177Cd ⌂ ⌂
Alvingham Mill 177Cd ⌂
ⓟ£☎ 0507 327544
Alwen Reservoir 159Af ⬥ ☀ ⌂
Alwinton 223Bb ○
Alyth 257Dd ⌂
Alyth Folk Museum 257Dd ⌂
ⓟ☎ 0738 32488
American Adventure Theme Park 149Cc ☯ ⓟ✕£⓰☎ 0773 531521
American Monument, Islay 235Bb
Amersham 107Ca † ⌂
ⓟ✕⓰☎ 0889 270294
Amerton Working Farm 147Bd ⬥
Amesbury 49Ec ⌂
Amble 223Eb ○
Amberley 37Bc ⌂ ⌂ ⚘
Ambleside 195Ee ⌂ ⌂
American Adventure Theme Park
An Sgurr 249Fh
An Teallach 277Ef
Ancaster 151Ce ⌂ ⌂
Ancient High House, Stafford 147Bd ⌂ ⌂☎ 0785 40204
Ancient House Museum, Thetford 139Bc ⌂☎ 0842 752599
Ancroft 223Bf ⬥
Ancrum 221Cd ⌂ ✕
Anderton 167Ac ○ ⚘
Andover 53Cb ⬤ ⚘
Andoversford 101Bd ○
Andreas 181Dd ⌂
Andrew Cotterill Furniture 117Dc
⬤ ⓟ⓰☎ 0570 470120
Angiddy Ironworks 93Ed ⚘
Angle 87Bb ○
Angle Tarn 207Fa ☆
Anglesey 155Ef
Anglesey Abbey 109Eg ⌂
ⓟ✕£☎ 0223 811200
Anglesey Sea Zoo 155Ee ⬥
ⓟ✕⓰☎ 0284 430411
Angletarn Pikes 207Fa
Anglezarke Moor 183Ea
Angmering-on-Sea 37Bc ○
Angora Workshop & Farm 155Ef ⬥
£☎ 0248 750297
Angus Folk Museum 257Ed ⌂
ⓟ£☎ 030 784288
Animalarium, Borth 117Ee ⬥
ⓟ✕£☎ 0970 871224
Annan 219Da
Annard Woollen Mill 125Cc ⬥
ⓟ⓰☎ 0386 870270
Annaside 195Bc ○
Anne Hathaway's Cottage 129Ab ⌂
ⓟ✕£☎ 0789 204016
Anstey, Herts 109Dd ○
Anstey, Leics 133Bf ⌂
Anstey's Cove 15Cd ☆
Anstiebury Camp 37Cf ☀
Anstruther 247Ec ⌂ ☀ ⬤ ⌂
ⓟ✕£☎ 0752 812191
Antonine Wall 241Dc ⬥
Antony 13Bc ⬥
Antony House 13Cc ⌂ ⚘
ⓟ✕£☎ 0752 812191
Anvil Point 27Ba
Ape Dale 123Bf
Apethorpe 135Ce ○

Appleby 175Df ○
Appleby Magna 149Bb ○
Appleby-in-Westmorland 197Cf ⬤ ⌂ ⌂
Applecross 277Bb ⬥
Appledore, Devon 17De ⬥
Appledore, Kent 41Dd ⬥
Appleton-le-Moors 201Eb ○
Appletreewick 185Df ⬥
Appley Park 31Dc ⚘
Appuldurcombe House 31Ca ⌂
ⓟ£☎ 0983 852489
Apuldram 33Cc ⌂
Aran Benllyn 157Ec
Aran Fawddwy 157Ec
Arbeia Roman Fort 213Bd ⬤
Arbigland 217Eb ⬥ ⓟ✕£
Arbor Low 171Cb ⊓
Arbory Hill 227Ec ☀
Arbroath 259Cd ⬥ ⌂ ⬥ ⌂ ⌂ ⌂
Arbury Hall 129Ce ⌂ⓟ✕£
☎ 0203 382804
Arch, The 117Fd ⬥ ✕ ⌂ ⌂
☎ 0970 85233
Archiestown 269Eb ⌂ ⬥
Ard Crags 207Da
Ardanaiseig Gardens 239Eg ⚘
ⓟ✕☎ 0866 3333
Ardbeg 235Db ○
Ardchattan Priory & Gardens 239Dh ☎ 031 2443101
Ardclach Bell Tower 269Bb
Ardeley 109Cd ○
Ardencraig Gardens 237Gg ⚘
ⓟ✕⓰☎ 0700 4225/504644
Ardestie 259Ac ⊓
Ardfern 239Cc
Argyll Wildlife Park 239Ee ⬥
ⓟ✕⓰£☎ 049 92264
Arinagour 249De ○ ⌂
Arisaig 249Hh ⌂
Ariundle 251Bc ⬥ ⬥
Arkengarthdale 199Bd
Arkesden 109Dd ○
Arkholme 183Dg ⌂
Arkle 281Ed
Arkwright's Mill 149Af ⚘
ⓟ✕⓰£☎ 0629 824297
Arley 167Ad ○ ⌂ ⚘
Arley Hall 167Ad ⌂ ⓟ✕£⓰
☎ 0565 777353
Arlington Court 21Bf ⌂
ⓟ✕£⓰☎ 0271 850296
Arlington, E Ssx 39Cb ○
Arlington Mill 101Cc ⌂ £
☎ 0285 740368
Armadale Bay 275Fb
Armadale Castle 275Fb ⌂
ⓟ✕£⓰☎ 04714 305/227
Armadale, Highland 281If ⌂ ⚘ ⚘ ⌂ ⌂
Armadale, Skye 275Fb ⌂ ⌂ ⚘ ⌂
Armathwaite 209Bb ⌂ ⚘
Arne Nature Reserve 27Ab ⬥ ⬥
☎ 0929 553360
Arnesby 133Cc ○
Arnol 272Fh ⌂ ⌂
Arnside 197Aa ⌂ ⬥ ⚘
Arnside Knott 197Aa ☀

Aros Castle 249Gd
Aros Cott 249Gd
Aros Park 249Ge
Arran Heritage Museum 237Fd
☎ 0770 2636
Arran, Isle of 237Ed
Arreton Country Crafts Village 31Cb ☎ 0983 528353
Arreton Manor 31Cb
☎ 0983 528134
Arrochar 239Ge
Arrow Valley Park 125Cd
Art Lover's House 241Cb
☎ 041 427 6884
Arthog 157Cb
Arthog Bog 157Cb
Arthur's Seat 229Df
Arthur's Stone 119Gc
Artisan 167Df
☎ 0457 874506
Arundel 37Bb
Arundel Vineyard 37Bb
☎ 0903 883393
Ascot 57Dd
Ascott 107Bd
☎ 0296 688242
Ash End House Farm 129Af
☎ 021329 3240
Ash End House Farm 147Da
☎ 0213 293240
Ashbourne 147Df
Ashburnham 41Ac
Ashburnham Park 41Ac
Ashburnham Place 41Ac
Ashburton 15Ad
Ashbury 53Bf
Ashby Canal 129Cf
Ashby cum Fenby 177Be
Ashby St Ledgers 133Bb
Ashby-de-la-Zouch 149Bb
Ashclyst Forest 21Fa
Ashdon 109Ee
Ashdown Forest 39Be
Ashdown House 53Bf
☎ 0488 72584
Ashe, Hants 53Eb
Ashenhill Barrows 45Dd
Ashford, Derbys 171Cb
Ashford, Kent 41Ef
Ashington 213Af
Ashleworth Tithe Barn 97De
☎ 0452 70241
Ashley, Hants 27Dc
Ashley, Staffs 145Ee
Ashmore 27Ae
Ashness Bridge 207Da
Ashorne Hall 129Cb
☎ 0926 651444
Ashover 149Bg
Ashprington 15Bc
Ashridge Park 107Cc
☎ 044284 3491
Ashton Court Estate 45Df
☎ 0272 639174
Ashton Gardens 183Bb
☎ 0253 725610
Ashton Keynes 101Bb
Ashton Memorial & Butterfly House 183Cf
☎ 0524 33318
Ashton Mill 45Cd
Ashton Mill Museum 135Cd
☎ 0832 272264
Ashton under Hill 101Af
Ashurst 37Cc
Ashwell 109Bd
Askam in Furness 195Db
Askham 197Bf
Askham Fell 197Af
Askrigg 199Bc
Astbury 167Cb
Asthall 101Dd
Astley 129Ce
Astley Hall 183Da
☎ 0257 262166
Aston Abbotts 107Bc
Aston Cantlow 129Ac
Aston Clinton Ragpits 107Bc
Aston Hall 125Cg
☎ 021 3270062
Aston Munslow 123Cf
Aston on Clun 123Af
Aston Rowant 103Ea
Aston Upthorpe 53Ef
Aston Wood 103Ea
Atcham 145Cb
Athelhampton 25Dd
☎ 0305 848363
Athelstan Museum 49Cg
☎ 0666 822143
Athelstaneford 233Bc
Atherington 21Ad
Atholl Country Collection 255Ff
☎ 0796 81232
Atkinson Art Gallery 183Ba
☎ 0704 533133
Attermire Cave 185Bf
Attingham Park 145Cb
☎ 0743 77203
Attleborough 139Dd
Atwell-Wilson Motor Museum 49De ☎ 0793 520866
Aubourn Hall 151Cg
☎ 0522 788095
Auchagallon 237Dd
Auchen Castle 219Be
Auchenblae 265Ea
Auchencairn 217Cb
Auchencairn Bay 217Db
Auchenmalg Bay 215Dd
Auchindoir 265Bf
Auchindoun Castle 269Fa
☎ 031 2443101
Auchindrain 239Ee
Auchindrain Open Air Museum 239Ee ☎ 049 95235
Auchinleck 227Ac
Auchmithie 259Cd
Auchnagatt 271Fb
Auchtermuchty 247Bd
Auckengill 281Of
Auckland Castle 199Eg
☎ 0388 601627
Audley End 109Ed
☎ 0799 522399
Audley End Miniature Railway 109Ed ☎ 0799 41354
Aughton 163Bf
Auld Brig, Ayr 225Cc
Auld Brig o'Doon 225Cb
Auld Kirk, Ayr 225Cc
☎ 0292 262938
Auld Kirk Museum, Kirkintilloch 241Dc ☎ 041 7751185
Auldearn 269Bc
Ault Hucknall 149Cg
Aultdearg 269Fc
Automobilia, Cornwall 11Bc
☎ 0726 823092
Automobilia, W Yorks 185Db
☎ 0422 844775
Avebury 49De
Avebury Manor 49Df
☎ 06723 203
Aveley 85Ac
Aveline's Hole 45Cd
Avenue Cottage 15Bc
☎ 080 423 769
Averon 278Cb
Aviation Heritage Centre 153Cf
☎ 0790 3207
Avich Falls 239Df
Aviemore 263Ae
Aviemore Centre, The 263Ae
☎ 0479 810624
Avington 29De
Avington Park 29De
☎ 0962 78202
Avoch 261Df
Avon Beach 27Cc
Avon Forest Country Park 27Cd
☎ 0425 478470
Avon Gorge 45Df
Avon Valley Railway 45Ef
☎ 0272 327296
Avoncroft Museum of Buildings 125Bd ☎ 0527 31886
Avondale Glass 87Eb
☎ 0834 813345
Avonmouth 45Df
Axbridge 45Cd
Axminster 23Db
Axmouth 23Cb
Aydon Castle 211Cd
☎ 0434 632450
Aylesbeare Common 15Dg
Aylesbeare Common 23Ab
Aylesbury 107Bc
Aylesford 85Ca
Aylestone 133Bf
Aylsham 141Af
Aynho 103Ce
Ayot St Lawrence 109Ab
Ayr 225Cc
Ayres, The 181De
Ayscoughfee Hall 153Bb
☎ 0775 725968
Aysgarth 199Cb
Aysgarth Falls 199Cb
☎ 0969 663424
Aythorpe Roding 113Ab
Ayton Castle, Borders 233Fb
☎ 0890 781212
Ayton Castle, N Yorks 205Cb
Aywick 285Gh
Babbacombe Model Village 15Cd
☎ 0803 38669
Babington 45Fd
Babington Wood 45Fd
Bablock Hythe 103Bb
Babraham 109Ef
Bach Camp 123Cd
Bachelor's Club 225Dc
☎ 0292 541940
Backbury 123Ca
Baconsthorpe Castle 143Fb
☎ 0223 455520
Bacton, H&W 119Gb
Bacton, Nflk 143Hb
Bacton Wood 143Hb
Bacup 185Bb
Badbury Hill 101Db
Badby 133Ba
Baddesley Clinton 129Bd
☎ 0564 783294
Bader Garden for Disabled 247Cd
☎ 0334 53722
Badgeworth 97Ed
Badgworthy Water 21Cf
Badingham 115Df
Badminston 29Cb
Badminton 49Bg
Badsell Park Farm 41Af
☎ 0892 832549
Bag Enderby 177Cb
Bagborough Vineyard 45Eb
☎ 0749 831146
Baggeridge 125Ag
☎ 0902 882605
Baggy Point 17Df
Baginton 129Cd
Bagmore Common 57Db
Bagpipe Museum 211Df
☎ 0670 519456
Baile Mór 249Db
Bailey Hill 161Ga
Bainbridge 199Bc
Bainton 192Be
Baird Institute Museum 227Ac
☎ 0290 22111
Bakewell 171Db
Bala 157Fd
Bala Lake 157Fd
☎ 06784 666
Bala Lake Railway 157Ed
☎ 06784 666
Balbirnie Craft Centre 247Bc
☎ 0592 755975
Balblair Wood 278Cd
Balcarres 247Dc
☎ 0333 34205
Balcaskie 247Ec
☎ 0333 311202
Balcombe Viaduct 37Ed
Balcomie Castle 247Fc
Baldersby 201Aa
Baldock 109Bd
Baldoon Castle 215Fd
Baledgarno 257Dc
Balephuil 249Ad
Balerno 229Ce
Balgonie Castle 247Cc
☎ 0592 750119
Balintore 278Eb
Ballaglass Glen 181Dc
Ballantrae 215Bg
Ballard Down 27Bb
Ballasalla 181Bb
Ballater 265Ac
Ballaugh 181Cd
Ballinluig Island 255Ge
Balloch 241Ad
Balloch Castle Country Park 241Ad
☎ 0389 58216
Ballone Castle 278Fc
Ballowall Barrow 9Ad
Ballure Walk 181Dd
Ballygowan 239Cd
Balmacara 251Bi
Balmedie 267Ce
Balmedie Beach 267Ce
Balmedie Country Park 267Ce
☎ 0358 42396
Balmerino 247Ce
Balmerino Abbey 247Ce
☎ 031 3362157
Balmoral Castle 263Ec
☎ 03397 42334
Balnain 261Ad
Balnakeil 281Ef
Balquhidder 255Cb
Balranald 273Ki
☎ 031557 3136
Balsham 113Af
Baltasound 285Hj
Balvenie Castle 269Fb
☎ 031 2443101
Bamburgh 223De
Bamburgh Castle 223De
☎ 066 84208
Bampton 21Ed
Banavie 251Ed
Banbury 103Bf
Banchory 265Dc
Banff 271Cd
Bangor 155Ff
Bangor-is-y-coed 159Ee
Banham 139Dc
Banham Zoo 139Dc
☎ 095387 476
Bankfield Museum 187Ab
☎ 0422 354823
Bannerdale 197Ae
Bannock Heritage Centre 245Ae
☎ 0786 812664
Bannockburn 245Be
Bannockburn 1314, Battle of 245Be
Banquette, Sark 287Ed
Bantham 13Eb
Bantock House 147Aa
☎ 0902 312132
Banwell 45Bd
Barbara Hepworth Museum 9Ce
☎ 0736 796226
Barber Institute 125Cf
☎ 021 472 0962
Barbon 197Cb
Barbon High Fell 197Cb
Barbury Castle 49Ef
Barby Beach 161Ec
Barcaldine 239Di
Barcaldine Forest 239Di
Barclodiad y Gawres Burial Chamber 155Df
Barcombe Mills 39Bc
Barden Fell 185De
Barden Tower 185De
Bardfield End Green 113Bd
Bardfield Saling 113Bc
Bardingley Vineyard 41Cf
☎ 0580 892264
Bardon Hill 149Cb
Bardsea 195Eb
Bardsea Country Park 195Db
Bardsey Island (Ynys Enlli) 155Ba
Bardwell 139Cb
Barfold Copse 33Df
Barford Park 23Cf
☎ 0278 671269
Barford St Michael 103Be
Barfrestone 43Ce
Bargain Wood 93Ed
Bargany Gardens 225Ba
☎ 046 587227
Barguillean Garden 239Dg
☎ 0866 2333
Barham 135Dc
Barkham Manor 39Bd
☎ 0825 722103
Barking 63Cd
Barkway 109Cd
Barlaston 147Ae
Barley 185Bd
Barleylands Farm Museum 85Be
☎ 0268 282090
Barmeckin Hill 265Ed
Barmekin of Echt 265Ed
Barmouth 157Cb
Barmston 192De
Barnack 135Cf
Barnard Castle 199Ce
Barnet 61De
Barnet 1471, Battle of 61De
Barnet Museum 61De
☎ 081 440 8066
Barney Water 217Bd
Barnfield Cider Mill 101Bf
☎ 0386 853145
Barns Ness 233Dc
Barnsdale Drought Garden 135Af
☎ 0780 86321
Barnsgate Manor 39Bd
☎ 0825 713366
Barnsley 173Ae
Barnsley House 101Bc
☎ 0285 74281
Barnstaple 17Ee
Barnwell 135Cd
Barnwell Park 135Cd
☎ 0832 273435
Barons Haugh Nature Reserve 227Cf
Barony Chambers Museum 241Dc
☎ 041 7751185
Barr 215Dh
Barr Beacon 147Ca
Barra 273Jc
Barra 1307, Battle of 267Af
Barrack Street Museum 257Fc
☎ 0382 23141 ext 65136
Barrie's Birthplace Museum 257Ee
☎ 057 572646
Barrington Court 23Ed
☎ 0460 40601
Barrow Gurney 45De
Barrowden 135Bf
Barrow-in-Furness 195Da
Barr's Hill 219Bc
Barry 91Ea
Barry Hill 257De
Barsalloch Fort 215Ec
Barston 129Bd
Bartley Mill 39De
☎ 0892 890372
Barton Farm Country Park 49Be
☎ 0225 753641
Barton Hills 107Dd
Barton Manor 31Cc
☎ 0983 292835
Barton Turf 141Cf
Barton upon Irwell 167Be
Barton Waterside 175Eg
Barton-upon-Humber 175Eg
Barvas 272Fh
Barwick in Elmet 187Dc
Bashall Eaves 183Ed
Basildon Park 53Fe
☎ 0734 843040
Basing House 57Ac
☎ 0256 467294
Basingstoke 57Ac
Basingwerk Abbey 161Fb
Baslow 171Dc
Bass Museum 147Ed
☎ 0283 42031
Bass Rock 233Cd
Bassenthwaite 207Dc
Bassenthwaite Lake 207Db
Bassetlaw Museum 175Bc
☎ 0777 706741
Basset's Cove 9De
Batcombe, Dorset 25Ce
Batcombe, Somerset 45Eb
Bateman's 41Ad
☎ 0435 882302
BATH 49Ae Town plan 51
Abbey 51Cb ☎ 0225 330289
Abbey Church House 51Bb
Assembly Rooms 51Bd
☎ 0225 461111 ext 2785
Building of Bath Museum 51Bd
☎ 0225 333895
The Circus 51Bc
Cross Bath 51Bb
East Gate 51Cb
Fashion Research Centre 51Bc
☎ 0225 461111 ext 2752
Great Pulteney Street 51Cc
Guildhall 51Cb
☎ 0225 461111 ext 2785
Henrietta Park 51Cc
☎ 0225 461111
Herschel House & Museum 51Ab ☎ 0225 311342
Holburne Museum 51Dc
☎ 0225 466669
Industrial Heritage Centre 51Bd
☎ 0225 318348
Market 51Cb
Museum of Bookbinding 51Ca
☎ 0225 466000
Museum of Costume 51Bd
☎ 0225 461111 ext 2785
Museum of English Naive Art 51Bd ☎ 0225 446020
Parade Gardens 51Cb
☎ 0225 461111 ext 2785
Postal Museum 51Bc
☎ 0225 460333
Pulteney Bridge 51Cc

Pump Room 51Bb ✕
Queen Square 51Bc
River Avon Towpath 51Cb
Roman Baths & Museum 51Bb
✿ ☎ 0225 461111 ext 2785
Royal Crescent, No.1 51Ad 🏛
🅿£ ☎ 0225 428126
Royal Victoria Park 51Ac
🅿☎ 0225 425066
RPS National Centre of
Photography 51Bc
🅿✕£& ☎ 0225 462841
Sally Lunn's House 51Cb 🏛
✕£ ☎ 0225 461634
Saracen's Head 51Bc
Sydney Gardens 51Dd
🅿& ☎ 0225 461111
Theatre Royal 51Bb ♉
🅿✕& ☎ 0225 448844
Upper Borough Walls 51Bb
Victoria Art Gallery & Museum
51Cb 🏛 &
☎ 0225 461111 ext 2772
Bathampton 49Be ♥ 🕿
Batsford Arboretum 101Cf ❀
🅿✕£ 0608 50722
Battery Point 45Cf ✳
Battle & Farm Museum 133Cc 🏛
Battle 41Bc ✕ ✚ 🏛
Battle Abbey 41Bc ✚ 🅿£
☎ 0424 63792
Battle of Britain Memorial Flight
153Be Ɏ 🅿✕£& 🕿 0526 44041
Battle of Flowers Museum 287Bc 🏛
🅿✕£ 0534 82408
Battlefield Line 149Ba 🚂
🅿✕£ 0827 880754
Battlefield of Bosworth Park 129Df
✕ Ɏ 🅿✕£
☎ 0455 290429
Battlefield Steam Railway 129Cg 🚂
🅿✕£ 0827 880754
Battlesbury 49Bc ✳
Baulking 53Cg ♉
Bawburgh 139Ee 🏚
Bawdsey Quay 115Dc
Baxters Visitor Centre 269Fc ✿
🅿✕& 0343 820393 ext 241
Bay of Clachtoll 277Ej
Bay Pond 39Ag ♥
Bayham Abbey 39De ✚
🅿£& 0892 890381
Bayhurst Wood Country Park
61Bd ♉ ✳ ✿ 🏠 🅿✕&
☎ 0895 250111 ext 3651/2450
Baynards Castle 15Bc 🏰
Bayr ny Skeddan 181Bb
Baysgarth Museum 175Eg 🏛
🅿£ 0652 32318
Bayton 123De ♉
Beach Park 225Cd ✳ ♒
Beachley 93Ec ♉
Beachy Head 39Ca ✰ 🏰 ⚓
Beacon Country Park 163Df ♉ ✳
🅿£ 0509 890048
Beacon Fell Country Park 183Dd ♉
✳ 🅿£ 0695 622794
Beacon Hill, Cumbria 209Ba
Beacon Hill, Gwent 93Eb ♉ ✳ 🏠
Beacon Hill, W Ssx 33Cd ✳
Beacon Hill Country Park 149Db Ɏ
✳ 🅿£& 0509 890048
Beacon Hill, Durham 213Cb ✰
Beacon Hill, Hants 53Dc ✳ 🏠
Beacon Hill, Somerset 23Bg
Beacon Point, Durham 213Cb ✰
Beaconsfield 57Dg ✿ ♉
Beadnell 223Ed 🏚
Beaford 17Dd
Beal 223Cf ♉
Bealach na Bà 277Bb ✰
Bealach Ratagain Pass 251Ch ✰
Beale Bird Park 53Fe ♥
🅿✕£& 0734 845172
Beaminster 25Ae 🏛 ✿
Beamish Open Air Museum 213Ac 🏛
🅿✕£& 0207 231811
Bearley Aqueduct 129Ac ✿
Bearsden 241Cc ♉
Bearsted 85Ca 🏚
Bearsted Vineyard 85Da ❧
🅿£ 0622 36974
Beatrix Potter Gallery 195Ed 🏛
£ 05394 36355
Beattock 219Be ♉ ✳
Beattock Hill 219Be ✳
Beauchamp Roding 113Ab 🏚
Beauchief Abbey 173Ac ✚

☎ 0742 369886
Beaulieu 29Bb 🏚 🚂 🏛 ✿ ✕ 🚗 ☑
Beaulieu Heath 29Bb 🏠
Beauly 261Be ✚ 🏠
Beauly Firth 261Be
Beauly Priory 261Be ✚
Beaumaris 155Gf 🏰 🏛 ♉
Beaumont Quay 115Bb
Beauport Park 41Bc ♒
Beaupre Castle 91Db 🏰 🏛
☎ 0446 773034
Beccles 141Db ♉
Beck Hole 205Bd ♉
Becka Falls 15Af ✰
Beckbury 101Be ✳
Beckfoot 207Bd ♉
Beckford 101Af ♉ ✳
Beckford Silk 101Af ♉
🅿✕& 0386 881507
Beckford's Tower 49Ae 🏛
🅿£ 0225 312917
Beckley 103Cc ♉ ♒
Beckley Children's Farm World
41Cd 🏚 🅿✕£& 0797 26250
Bedale 199Eb ✝ 🏚 🏛
Beddgelert 157Be 🏠 ✿
Beddgelert Forest 157Bf ♉ ✿ ✳ 🏠
Beddington Park 61Db
Bede House 135Ae 🏛 🅿£
☎ 0572 822438
Bede Monastery Museum 213Bd 🏛
🅿✕£& 091 4892106
Bedford 107Df ♉ 🏛 🏛
Bedford Park 61Dc
Bedford Purlievs 135Ce ♉ ♥
Bedgebury National Pinetum 41Be
❀ 🅿✕£& 0580 211044
Bedgreave New Mill 173Bc ✿
🅿✕£ 0742 471452
Bedingfield 115Bf ♉
Bedlington 213Af ✝
Bedlington Country Park 213Af 🏚
🅿& 0670 814444
Bedlow Cross 103Eb ⊛
Bedruthan Steps 11Ad ✰
Beech Hurst 39Ad ✿ 🅿✕&
☎ 0444 412178
Beeches Farm 39Bd ✿
☎ 0825 762391
Beecraigs Country Park 229Af Ɏ
🅿✕£& 0506 844516
Beecroft Art Gallery 85Dd 🏛
☎ 0702 347418
Beeny Cliff 11Dg ✰
Beer 23Ca 🏚 ♉
Beesands 15Bb ♉
Beeston, Nflk 139Cf ♉
Beeston, Cheshire 163Da 🏚 🏰 🏰
Beeston Castle 163Da 🏰
🅿✕£ 0829 260464
Beeston Hall 141Cf 🏚
🅿✕£ 0692 630771
Beetham 197Aa 🏚 🏚 🏠
Beinn a' Bhacaidh 261Ab
Beinn a' Chaolais 235De
Beinn Alligin 277Cd
Beinn an Oir 235De
Beinn Bheigeir 235Dc
Beinn Dearg 277Gf
Beinn Eighe National Nature
Reserve 277Ed ♥ ♥ ☑
Beinn Ime 239Ge ✰
Beinn Mhór 239Fc ✰
Beinn na Caillich 275Ed
Beinn nan Gudairean 235Cg ✳
Beinn Narnain 239Ge
Beinn Nuis 237Ed
Beinn Reithe 239Gd
Beinn Shiantaidh 235Ee
Beinn Tarsuinn 237Ee
Bekonscot Model Village 57Dg ✿
🅿✕£& 0494 672919
Belas Knap 101Be 🏚
Belgrave Hall 133Bf 🏚 🏛
☎ 0533 666590
Belhus Woods Park 85Ad Ɏ
🅿£& 0708 865628
Belle Greve Bay 287Ce
Belleisle Park 225Cc ✿ 🅿✕
☎ 0292 42331
Bellever 13Ee ♉
Bellfoundry & Museum,
Loughborough 149Db ♉
🅿£ 0509 233414
Bellingham 209Ef 🏚
Bell's Blair Atholl Distillery 255Ge
🅿✕& 0796 2234
Bell's Cherrybank Gardens 257Cb
✿ 🅿✕£& 0738 27330

Belmont 85Ea 🏚 🅿✕£ &
☎ 0798 59202
Belper 149Be
Belsay Hall 211Ce 🏚 🏚 ✿
🅿✕£& 0661 881636
Belton House 151Cd 🏚
🅿✕£& 0476 66116
Belvoir Castle 151Bd 🏚
🅿✕£ 0476 870262
Bembridge 31Db ✕ ✰
Bembridge Down 31Db ✳
Bempton Cliffs 192Dg ♥
Ben Aigan 269Fb
Ben Cleuch 245Cf ✳
Ben Cruachan 239Eh ✳
Ben Klibreck 281Hc
Ben Lawers 255Dd ♉ ✳ ♥ ✳
Ben Lomond 241Af ✰
Ben Macdui 263Bc ✳
Ben More 255Bb
Ben More Assynt 277Hj
Ben Nevis 251Ed
Ben Stack 281Dd
Benacre Ness 141Eb
Benbecula 273Lh
Bencroft Wood 109Ca ♉
Benderloch 239Dh ♉ ♉
Benenden 41Ce ♉ ♥
Beningbrough Hall 189Be 🏚
🅿✕£& 0904 470666
Benington Lordship Gardens 109Bc
✿ 🅿✕£& 043885 668
Benllech 155Fg ♉
Benmore 239Fc 🏚 ✿ ✳ ♉
Benmore Forest 239Fc ♉
Bennachie 1733 265Df ✳ 🏚 🏠 ✳
Bennachie Forest 265De ♉ 🏠
Bennan Viewpoint 217Bd ✳ 🏠
Benthall Hall 145Db 🏚
🅿£& 0952 882159
Bentley Wildfowl Collection and
Motor Museum 39Bc 🚗 ✿
🅿✕£& 0825 840573
Beoley 125Cd ♉
Bere Ferrers 13Cd 🏚
Bere Regis 25Ed 🏚
Berengrave 85Db ♥
Berkeley Castle 97Bb 🏚
🅿✕£ 0453 810332
Berkhamsted 107Cb 🏚 ✝ 🏛
Berkswell 129Bd 🏚 🏛
Berkswell Mill 129Bd ✕ 🅿£
☎ 0676 33403
Bernera Barracks 251Bh
Berneray 272Bb
Berners Roding 113Bb 🏚
Berney Arms Mill 141Dd ✕
✕£ ☎ 0223 455523
Berriew 119Ei 🏚
Berrington Hall 123Cd 🏚
🅿✕£ 0568 615721
Berry Head 15Cc ✳ Ɏ
Berry Pomeroy 15Bd ♉ 🏰
Berry Pomeroy Castle 15Bd 🏰 &
Berry Ring 147Ad 🏚
Bersham 159Ee ♉ ✿
🅿✕£ 0978 315151
Berwick 39Cb ♉
Berwick-upon-Tweed 233Fa
🏰 🏚 🏛 🏛 ♉
Berwyn 159Bd
Besford 125Bb ♉
Bessels Leigh 103Bb ♉
Bessie Surtees House 213Ad 🏚
☎ 091 2611585
Bestwood Colliery 149De ✿
Bestwood Country Park 149De Ɏ
Betchworth 37Df ♉
Beth Chatto Gardens 115Ab ✿ 🅿£
Bethersden 41Df ♉
Bethesda 155Ge 🏚
Bethnal Green 63Bd ♉
Bethnal Green Museum of Childhood
63Bd 🅿£ 081 980 3204
Betley 145Ef ♉
Bettisfield 145Be ♉
Bettyhill 281If 🏚 ✳ 🏚 🏠
Betws Garmon 155Fd 🏚
Betws-y-Coed 157Df 🏚 🚂 🏛 🏛 🏠
Bevercotes 175Ab ♉
Beverley 192Cc ✝ 🏛 🏚 ♉
Beverstone 97Db ♉
Bewcastle 209Be 🏚 🏚
Bewl Water 41Ae ✳ ✳ 🏠 ☑
Bexhill 41Bb ✳ 🏛 🏛 🏠
Bexley 63Cc ♉ ♉
Bibury 101Cc 🏚 🏚
Bicclescombe Mill 17Ef 🅿✕£
Bicclescombe Park 17Ef 🏚 🅿✕£
Bicester 103Cd

Bickleigh 21Eb 🏚 🏚 🏠
Bickleigh Castle 21Eb 🅿✕£
☎ 0884 855363
Bickleigh Mill 21Eb 🏚 🅿✕£
☎ 0884 855572
Bicknoller Hill 23Bf 🏚 🏠 ✳
Bicton Park 15Df ✳ ✿
🅿✕£ 0395 68465
Bidborough 39Cf ♉
Biddenden 41Ce 🏚
Biddenden Vineyard 41Ce ❧
🅿✕& 0580 291726
Biddenham 107Df 🏚
Biddestone 49Bf ♉
Biddle Combe 45Dc ♣
Biddulph 167Ca ✳
Biddulph Grange 167Ca ✳
🅿✕£ 0743 77649
Biddulph Moor 167Da ♉
Bideford 17Dd
Bidford-on-Avon 125Dc 🏚
🅿✕£ 0495 790311
Big Pit Mining Museum 93Bd ✿
🅿✕£& 0495 790311
Big Strand, The 235Cc
Bigby 175Ee ♉
Biggar 229Bb ✝ 🏚 ♉ 🏛
Biggar Puppet Theatre 229Bb ♉
🅿✕£ 0899 20631
Biggin Hill 63Cb
Biggleswade 109Ae ✳ Ɏ
Bignor 33Dd 🏚 🏠
Bildeston, Sflk 113Ee ♉
Billesdon, Leics 133Df 🏚
Billesley 129Ab ♉
Billing Aquadrome 133Eb ♒
🅿✕£ 0604 408181
Billing Mill Museum 133Eb ✿
🅿✕£ 0604 408181
Billingborough 151Ed 🏚
Billinge 163Df
Billingford Windmill 139Eb ✕ 🅿£
Billingham 201Bf
Billinghay 151Ef 🏚 🏛
Billingshurst 37Bd 🏛
Binbrook 177Bd 🏚
Binchester Fort 211Ea ♉
🅿£& 0388 663089
Bingley 187Bc ♉ 🏛
🅿£& 0223 455520
Binham Priory 143Dc ✚
Binley 129Cd ♉
Binns, The 229Bf 🏚 🅿£
☎ 0506 834255
Birch Green 113Eb ♉ ✝
Bircher Common 123Bc ♉
Birchills Canal Museum 147Ca 🏛
🅿£ 0922 645778
Birchover 171Db 🏚 ✰
Bird Rock (Craig yr Aderyn)
117Eg ♥
Bird World, Anglesey 155Ee 🐾
🅿✕£& 0248 79627
Birdham 33Cc 🏚
Birdland Zoo Gardens, Bourton-on-
the-Water 101Ce 🅿✕£&
☎ 0451 20480
Birdlip Hill 97Ed ✳ ⊛
Birdoswald Roman Fort 209Cd ♉
Birdworld, Farnham 57Cb 🐾
🅿✕£& 0420 22140
Birkhall 265Ac ♉
Birkhill Clay Mine 229Af ✿
Birkin 189Bb ♉
Birks of Aberfeldy 255Fd ♣ ✰
Birling 85Bb 🏚
Birling Gap 39Ca 🏚
Birlingham 125Bb ♉
Birmingham & Midlands Museum
of Transport 125Ce 🏛 🅿✕£
BIRMINGHAM 125Cf
Town plan 127
   Assay Office 127Bc
   Birmingham and Fazeley
   Canal 127De
   Bull Ring 127Cc
   Broad Street 127Bc
   Central Library 127Bc
   ✕&☎ 021 2354511
   Council House 127Cc
   Curzon Street Station 127Dc
   Gas Street Basin 127Bc
   Great Western Arcade 127Cc
   Gun Barrel Proof House 127Dc
   Hall of Memory 127Bc
   Hippodrome 127Cb ♉
   🅿✕£& 021 6227486
   Iron Gallery 127Cb 🏛 &
   ☎ 021 6430708
   International Convention Centre

127Bc 🅿✕&
☎ 021 2002000
James Brindley Walk 127Bc
Jewellery Quarter 127Bd
🅿✕£& 021 2365918
Museum and Art Gallery 127Cc
🏛 🅿✕£& 021 2352834
Museum of Science and
Industry 127Bc 🏛
🅿✕£& 021 2351661
National Indoor Arena 127Bc
🅿✕£& 021 2002202
Old Crown 127Bc
🅿✕£& 021 4214611
Repertory Theatre 127Bc ♉
🅿✕£& 021 2366771
St Chad's Cathedral 127Cd
St Martin's Church 127Cc ✝
&☎ 021 6435428
St Martin's Rag Market 127Cb
St Paul's Square 127Bd
St Philip's Cathedral 127Cc
Stratford House 127Da
Town Hall 127Cc &
☎ 021 2353942
Worcester and Birmingham
Canal 127Ba
Birmingham Botanical Gardens
125Cf ✳ 🅿✕£& 021 327 0062
Birmingham Nature Centre 125Cf Ɏ
🅿✕£& 021 472 7775
Birmingham Railway Museum
125Df 🏛 🅿✕£& 021 707 4696
Birnam 257Bc ♉
Birnam Wood 257Bc ♉
Birsay 283Bf 🏚 🏚 ✰ 🏛
Birtsmorton Wildfowl Sanctuary
97Cf ✳
Bisham 57Cf ♉
Bishop Abury's Cottage 125Cg 🏚
☎ 021 569 3374
Bishop Auckland 199Ef ✝ 🏚
Bishop Bonner's Cottages 139Cf 🏚
☎ 0362 693534
Bishop Burton 192Bc 🏚
Bishop Wilton 189De 🏚
Bishopbriggs 241Dc 🏛
Bishops Cannings 49De ♉
Bishop's Castle 119Gg 🏚 🏰 🏚
Bishop's Cleeve 97Ee ♉
Bishop's Glen 239Fb ✰
Bishop's House Museum,
Abbeydale 173Ac 🏚 🏛 £&
☎ 0742 557701
Bishop's House, Sheffield
173Ac 🏚
Bishop's Lydeard 23Be ♉ 🏚
Bishop's Stortford 109Dc 🏛 🏛 🏚
Bishop's Waltham 29Dc 🏰
Bishop's Wood 89Da 🏚
Bishopsbourne 43Be ♉
Bishopscourt Glen 181Cd ♣
Bishopstone, E Ssx 39Bb ♉
Bishopstone, H&W 123Bb ♉
Bishopstone, Wilts 27Bf ♉
Bisley, Glos 97Ec ♉
Bitton 45Ee 🏚 🏚
Black Castle, Lothian 233Bb ✳
Black Country Museum 125Bg 🏛
🅿✕£& 021 557 9643
Black Down, Dorset 25Cc ✳
Black Down, W Ssx 33Df ♉
Black Down Hills 23Bd
♉ ✳ ✳ 🏠
Black Head 11Cb ✳
Black Isle 261Cf
Black Middens Bastle House
209Dg 🏚
Black Mountain 91Af 🏚 🏠
Black Park 61Bd Ɏ ♉ ♥
🅿✕£& 0753 511060
Black Rock, Derbys 149Af ✰
Black Rock, Gwent 93Eb ✰
Black Rock Gorge 278Ba ✰
Black Rock, Somerset 45Cd ♣ ♥
Black Ven 23Db ✰
Black Watch Museum 257Cb 🗡
☎ 0738 21281 ext 8530
Blackbrooks Farm 147Cg Ɏ
🅿£ 0538 308293
Blackburn 183Eb ✝ 🏛
Blackbury Castle 23Bb ✳
Blackdown Common 23Bd
Blackfriars, Newcastle upon Tyne
213Ad 🏚
Blackgang 31Ba 🏰 🏛 ✰ ♒
Blackgang Chine 31Ba ✰ ♒
Blackhammer 283Df 🏚

Bridlington 192Df ✕ ⚓ ☑
Bridport 25Ad ⚓ ⌂ ☑
Brierley Crystal 125Bf ✿
☏✕⚕ 0384 70161
Brig o' Turk 241Cf ○
Brig o'Balgownie 267Cd ⚓
Brigg 175Ee ☑
Brighstone 31Bb ⌂
Brighstone Down 31Bb ✿ ❋
Brighstone Forest 31Bb ♤
Brightling 41Ad ⌂
Brightlingsea 115Aa †
Brighton 37Eb ⚓ ✕ ⛱ ⌂ ☑
Brightwalton 53De ○
Brightwell Baldwin 103Da ○
Brigstock Park 135Bd ☙
☏⚕ 0536 373625
Brill 103Dc ⌂ ○
Brimham Rocks 187Cf ☙ ☆
☏✕⚕ 0423 780688
Brimmond & Elrick Country Park
267Bd ☙ ♤ ❋ ⚓
Brimstone Wildlife Centre 117Ec ☙
☏✕⚕ 097423 439
Brindle 183Db ⌂
Brindley Water Mill 167Da ⚙
☏ 0538 381446
Bringewood Forge 123Be ○
Brinkburn Priory 223Da ✚
☏✕⚕ 0665 570628
Brinsop 123Bb ○ ❋
BRISTOL 45Df Town plan 47
  All Saints Church 47Cc †
  Arnolfini Gallery 47Bb
  ☏✕⚕ 0272 299191
  Bank of England, Bristol
  Branch 47Cc
  Brandon Hill 47Ab
  Broad Street 47Cc
  Cathedral 47Bb
  Christchurch 47Cc †
  ☏ 0272 277977
  Christmas Steps 47Bc
  City Museum and Art Gallery
  47Ac ☏✕⚕ 0272 223571
  Corn Street 47Cc
  Edward Everard Building 47Bc
  Exploratory Hands-on Science
  Centre 47Ac ☏✕⚕
  ☏ 0272 252008
  Floating Harbour 47Aa
  Foster's Almshouses 47Bc
  Georgian House 47Ab ⚓
  ☏ 0272 211362
  SS Great Britain 47Aa ✕
  ☏✕⚕ 0272 260680
  Harvey's Wine Museum 47Bb
  ⚓ ☏ 0272 277661
  Industrial Museum 47Ba
  ☏⚕ 0272 251470
  Jacob's Well 47Ab
  John Wesley's Chapel 47Cc †
  ☏ 0272 264740
  King Street 47Cb
  Lewins Mead Unitarian Chapel
  47Bc †
  Lloyds Bank 47Cc
  Llandoger Trow 47Cb
  ✕⚕ 0272 260783
  Lord Mayor's Chapel 47Bb †
  ☏ 0272 294350
  Maritime Heritage Centre 47Aa
  ✕⚕ 0272 260680
  Neptune Statue 47Bb
  Queen Square 47Cb
  Red Lodge 47Bc ⚓ ⚕
  ☏ 0272 211360
  St Bartholomew's Hospital
  47Ac
  St George's, Brandon Hill 47Ac
  St John's Gate 47Bc
  St Mary Redcliffe Church 47Ca
  † ☏✕⚕ 0272 291962
  St Michael's Hill 47Bc
  St Nicholas Market 47Cc
  Temple Church 47Db †
  Temple Meads Station 47Db
  Theatre Royal 47Cb ☙
  ✕⚕ 0272 277466
  University Tower 47Ac
  Victoria Rooms 47Ac
  The Watershed 47Bb
  Welsh Back 47Cb
Britford 27Cf ○
British Commercial Vehicle
Museum 183Db ⚓ ✕⚕⚕
☏ 0772 4510111
British Engineerium 37Db ⚙
☏✕⚕ 0273 559583

British Golf Museum 247Ed ⚓
☏✕⚕⚕ 0334 78880
British In India Museum 185Bc ✕
☏ 0282 870215
British Red Cross Museum 37Bf ⚓
☏✕ 0483 898595
Brixham 15Cc ⚓ ☑
Brixton Windmill 63Bc ✕ ⊡
☏ 081 673 5398
Brixworth 133Dc ⌂
Broad Down 123Ea ☆
☏ 0780 51226
Broad Haven 87Bc ○
Broadclyst 15Cg ○
Broadclyst 21Ea ○
Broadfield Court 123Cc ✿
☏✕ 0568 84483
Broadfield House Glass Museum
125Af ⚓ ☏ 0384 273011
Broadford 11De ○
Broadford 275Fd ⌂
Broadhembury 23Bc ⌂ ❋
Broadlands 29Bd ⚓ ☏✕⚕⚕
☏ 0794 516878
Broadleas Gardens 49Dd ✿
☏⚕ 0380 722035
Broadsands 15Bc
Broadwater 37Cb
Broadway 101Bf ⌂ ○
Broadway Hill 101Cf ☙ ❋
Broadway Tower 101Cf ✿
Broadway Tower Country Park
101Cf ☙ ☏✕⚕ 0386 852390
Broadwindsor 23Ec ⌂
Brobury Gardens 119Gc ✿
☏⚕ 09817 229
Brochel Castle 275Ef ⚔ ⊞
Brockenhurst 29Bb ○ ❋
Brockham 37Cf ⌂
Brockhall 133Cb ○
Brockhampton 97Af ○
Brockhill Country Park 43Bc ☙
☏ 0222 465511
Brockhole 195Ee ✿ ☑
☏✕⚕ 0539 46601
Brockley Combe 45Ce ✤
Brocolitia 209Ee ⚓
Brodick 237Fd ⚓ ⚓ ⌂ ☑
Brodick Castle & Country Park
237Fd ⚓ ☏✕⚕⚕
☏ 0770 2202/2462
Brodie Castle 269Bc ⚓
☏✕⚕⚕ 0309 4371
Brogborough Hill 107Ce ⊞
Bromfield 123Be ⌂
Bromham Mill 107Dg ⚙
☏✕⚕ 0234 228330
Bromley 63Cb
Brompton Regis 21Ee ⌂ ✤ ✤
Bromsgrove 125Be † ⚓ ☑
Bromyard 123Dc ⚓ ☑
Bromyard Downs 123Dc ○
Bronllys 119Eb ⌂
Bronllys Castle 119Eb ⚔
Brontë Parsonage 185Dc ⚓ ⚓
☏⚕ 0535 642323
Brook & Compton Downs 31Ab
Brook 31Ab ✿ ☆
Brook Chine 31Ab ✿ ✿
Brook Cottage 103Af ✿
☏✕⚕ 029587 303 01590
Brooke 135Af ○
Brookland 41Dd ○
Brooklands Museum & Circuit 61Bb
⚓ ☏✕⚕ 0932 857381
Broombriggs Farm 149Db ⚓
☏⚕ 0509 890048
Broomend of Crichie 267Ae ⊞
Broomfield 23Cf ⚓ ✤
Broomhill Sands 41Dc
Brora 278Fe ⌂ ○
Brora Woollen Mill 278Ee ✿
☏⚕ 0408 21366
Brough, Cumbria 197De ⌂ ⌂
⚔ ⚓ ☑
Brough, Derbys 171Cd ○ ✿
Brough Head 283Bf ⌂
Brough, Highland 281Ng ○
Brough of Birsay Island 283Bf ⊞
Brougham Castle 197Bf ⚔
Broughton, Borders 229Cb ⌂ ⌂
Broughton, Humberside 175De
Broughton, Oxon 103Be ○ ⚓ ⊞
Broughton, Staffs 145Ce ○
Broughton Castle 103Be ⚓
☏⚕ 0295 262624
Broughton House 217Bb ⚓
☏⚕ 0557 30437
Broughton in Furness 195Dc ⌂

Broughty Castle Museum 259Ac ⚓
☏ 0382 23141 ext 65136
Broughty Ferry 259Ac ⚓
Brounlie Wood 25Cf ♤
Brown Caterthun 259Bf ❋
Brown Clee Forest Trail 123Df ♤
Brown Clee Hill 123Cf
Brown Knowl 163Ca ⌂ ❋
Brown Moss 145Ce ⌂
Browne's Hospital 135Cf ⚓
☏✕⚕ 0780 51226
Brownhill Visitor Centre 171Af ☑
☏⚕ 0457 872598
Browns Folley Nature Reserve
49Ae ♤
Brownsea Island 27Bb ✿ ✤
Browsholme Hall 183Ed ⚓
☏⚕ 0254 826719
Broxburn 229Bf
Broxhead Common 57Ca ✤
Bruce Castle Museum 63Be ⚓
☏ 081 808 8772
Bruce's Camp 267Ae ❋
Bruce's Cave, near Gretna Green
219Db ☆
Bruce's Stone 215Fg ✕ ❋ ⊓
Bruce's Stone 217Ad
Brueton Park 125De ☙
Bruicheach Crannog 261Ad
Bruichladdich 235Bd ○ ⚓
Bruisyard 115Df ○ ☙
Brunel Atmospheric Railway 15Cf
✿ ☏⚕ 0626 890000
Bruton 45Eb
Bryanston 25Ee ○
Bryher I 9Bb
Brympton d'Evercy 25Bf ⚓ ✿
☏✕⚕ 0935 862528
Bryn Brâs Castle 155Fe ⚓
☏✕⚕ 0286 870210
Bryn Celli Ddu 155Ff ⊞ ⊡
☏ 0222 465511
Bryn Tail Lead Mine 119Cg ✿
☏⚕ 0222 465511
Brynbach Park 93Ad ☙
☏✕⚕ 0495 711816
Bryngarw Park 91Cc ☙
☏✕⚕ 0656 725155
Brynkir Woollen Mill 157Bd ✿
☏⚕ 0766 75236
Brynsiencyn 155Ee ○ ☙
Buchan Line Walkway 271Fb ⊓
Buchan Park 37De ☙ ☏✕⚕
☏ 0293 542088
Buckbarrow Crag 197Ad
Buckden 135Db ○
Buckden Pike 199Ba ❋
Buckenham 141Cd ○
Buckfast Abbey 15Ad ✚
☏✕⚕ 0364 42519
Buckfast Butterfly Farm 15Ad ☙
☏⚕ 0364 42916
Buckenham 247Cb ○
Buckie 269Gd † ✕
Buckingham 103De ✚
Buckingham Canal Reserve
103Ee ☙
Buckland 37Dg ○
Buckland Abbey 13Cd ⚓
☏✕⚕ 0822 853607
Buckland Beacon 13Fe
Buckland, Glos 101Bf ○ ❋
Buckland in the Moor 13Fe ⌂
Buckland Monachorum 13Cd
⌂ ✿ ⌂
Bucklebury 53Ee ○
Bucklebury Common 53Ed
Buckler's Hard 29Ca ⌂ ✕
Buckley's Museum 41Bc ⚓
☏✕⚕ 0424 64269
Bucknell 119Gf ⌂ ❋
Bucknell Wood 103Df ♤ ✤
Bucks Goat Farm Centre 107Bb ⚓
☏✕⚕ 0296 612983
Buck's Mills 17Cd
Buddhapadipa Temple 61Dc ☙
Bude 17Bb ○ ☑
Bude Canal 17Bb ✿ ☏✕⚕
☏ 0288 353576
Budle Bay 223De
Budleigh Salterton 15Df ○
Buildwas Abbey 145Db ✚ ⚕
☏ 0952 433274
Builth Wells 119Dd ⌂ ✕ ☙
Bulbarrow Hill 25De ⊓
Bull Bay 155Eh ○
Bull Point Lighthouse 17Db ⚓
Bullers of Buchan 271Ha ☆
Bulverhythe 41Bb ○

Bulwarks Camp 93Ec ⊓
Bunbury 163Da ⌂ ⚓
Bunessan 249Eb ○
Bungay 141Cb ⌂ ⚓
Bungay Castle 141Cb ⚔
Bunnahabhain 235De ○ ⚓
Bunster Hill 147Dg
Buntingford 109Cc ○
Bunyan's Meeting House 107Df ⚓
✕⚕⚕ 0234 358870
Burbage Common 129Df ☙ ⚓
☏✕⚕ 0455 633712
Bure Valley Railway 141Bf ✕
☏✕⚕ 0263 733858
Bures 113Ed ○
Burfa Camp 119Fe ❋
Burford, Oxon 101Dd ✿ †
✿ ✕ ✤ ☑
Burford, Shrops 123Cd ⌂ ✿
Burford House 123Cd ✿
☏✕⚕ 0584 810777
Burg 249Fb ☆
Burgar Hill 283Cf ✿ ⚓
Burgh by Sands 207Ee ⌂
Burgh Castle 141Dd ☙
☏ 0223 462608
Burgh le Marsh 153Ef ⌂ ✕ ⚓
Burgh le Marsh 153Ef ✿
☏⚕ 0205 870641
Burghclere 53Dd ⌂ †
Burghead 269Df ⌂
Burghley House 135Cf ⚓
☏✕⚕ 0780 52451
Burham Marsh 85Cb ☙
Burhou Island 287Dg ☙
Buriton 33Be ⌂
Burleigh Castle 245Ef ⚔
Burley, Hants 27Dd ⌂ ❋ ❋
Burley, Leics 135Ag ⌂
Burley Wood 13Df ♤
Burnby Hall 192Ad ✿
☏✕⚕ 0759 302068
Burnham 57Df ○
Burnham Market 143Cc ○
Burnham Museum 85Ee ⚓
☏⚕ 0621 782767/783444
Burnham Norton 143Cc ○
Burnham Overy Staithe 143Cc
⌂ ☙
Burnham Thorpe 143Cc ⌂
Burnham-on-Crouch 85Ee ⚓
Burnham-on-Sea 45Bc † ○ ☑
Burnley 185Bc ⚓ ⌂ ☑
Burnmoor Tarn 195Ce
Burnmouth 233Fb ○
Burns Cottage, Alloway 225Cb ⚓
☏✕⚕ 0292 41215
Burns House 217Ed ⚓ ✕
☏ 0387 55297
Burns House Museum,
Mauchline 225Dc ○ ⚕
☏ 0290 50045
Burns Mausoleum 217Ed ✚
☏ 0387 53374
Burns Monument, Alloway 225Cb
⚓ ☏✕⚕ 0292 41215
Burns Monument, Kilmarnock
225Dd ⚓ ☏ 0563 26401
Burns Museum, Irvine 225Cd ⚓
☏⚕ 0294 74511
Burnsall 185Df ○
Burnswark 219Cb ❋ ☙
Burntisland 247Ba † ⌂ ☑
Burntstump Country Park 149Df ☙
☏⚕ 0602 670067 ext 358
Burpham 37Bb ○
Burrafirth 285Hk ☆ ☆ ☙
Burrator Reservoir 13Dd
Burravoe 285Gg ○ ⚓
Burray 283Ec
Burrell Collection 241Cb ⚓
☏✕⚕ 041 6497151
Burrington 21Bc ○
Burrington Combe 45Cd
❋ ⚓ ☆ ☆
Burrough Hill 133Dg ☙ ❋
☏⚕ 0533 656918
Burrow Mump 45Bb ⚔
Burry Holms 89Cb ❋
Burry Port 89Cc
Burscough Priory 163Cf ✚
Burslem 147Af
Burstow 37Ef ○
Burton, Ches 161Hb ⌂ ✿
Burton, Lincs 175Db ○
Burton Agnes 192Df ⌂
Burton Agnes Hall 192Df ⚓
☏✕⚕ 0262 89324

Burton Beach 25Ac
Burton Bradstock 25Ac ○
Burton Constable Country Park
192Dc ☙ ☏✕⚕
☏ 0964 562400
Burton Constable Hall 192Dc ⚓
☏✕⚕ 0964 562400
Burton Court 123Bc ⚓
☏✕⚕ 0544 7231
Burton Dasset Hills Park 103Bg ☙
☏⚕ 0544 7231
Burton Dassett 103Ag † ☙ ❋
Burton upon Trent 147Ed ⌂ ⚓ ☑
Burton-in-Kendal 197Ba ⌂ ☆
Burtree Crafts 197Cc ✿
☏✕⚕ 0539 623342
Burwash 41Ad ⌂ ☙ ⚓
Burwell 137Da ⌂
Bury, Gtr Man 167Cg ⌂ ✕ ⚓
Bury, W Ssx 37Bc ○
Bury Hill 53Cb ○
Bury St Edmunds 139Ba
† ⚓ ⚓ ☙ ✕ ☑
Buscot 101Db ○ ⚓
Buscot Park 101Db ⚓ ☏✕⚕
☏ 0367 240786
Bushmead Priory 135Db ✚
☏⚕ 0230 76214
Bute, Island of 237Fg
Bute Museum 237Fg ⚓
☏⚕ 0600 502248
Butler's Hangings 107Ba ❋
Butley Priory 115Dd ✚
Butser Ancient Farm 33Bd ⚓
Butser Hill 33Be ✿
Butt of Lewis 272Hj
Butter Tubs 197Ec ☆
Butterfly Centre, Newent 97Ce ☙
☏⚕ 0531 821800
Butterfly Centre, The 43Cd ☙
☏✕⚕ 0303 83244
Butterfly World 31Cc ☙
☏✕⚕ 0983 883430
Buttermere 207Ca ⌂ ☙
Buttermere Lake 207Ca
Buttrums Windmill 115Cd ✕
☏⚕ 0473 265162
Buxton 171Bc ✿ ⚓ ☑
Buxton Country Park 171Bc ☙
☏⚕ 0629 580000
Bwlch 93Af ⌂ ⌂
Bwlch Nant Yr Arian Forest 117Fe
♤ ✿ ☏⚕ 0974 37404
Bwlch y Clawdd Pass 91Cd ❋ ☆
Bwlch y Ddeufaen 161Bb ☆
Bwlch y Groes 157Fc ☆
Bwlchgwyn 159Df ⌂
'By Beat of Drum' 233Ga ⚓
☏⚕ 0289 304493
Bygone Village 141De ⚓
☏✕⚕ 0493 369770
Bygones 15Cd ⚓ ☏✕⚕
☏ 0803 326108
Bygones of Holkham 143Cc ⚓
☏⚕ 0328 710806
Byland Abbey 201Ca ✚
☏✕⚕ 03476 614
Byrgwm 89Df ⊓
Byways Water Garden 137Db ✿
☏✕⚕ 0353 721608
Bywell 211Cd ⌂
Caban Coch Reservoir 119Ce ☙
Cacham Manor 33Bb ⌂
Cadair Idris 157Db
Cadair Idris Nature Reserve
157Db ♤
Cadbury Camp 45Cf ❋
Cadbury Castle 25Cg ❋
Cadbury Hill 45Ce ❋
Cadbury World 125Cf ☙
☏✕⚕ 021 433 4334
Cademuir Hill 229Db ❋
Cadgwith 9Eb
Cadhay 23Ab ⚓ ✕⚕
☏ 0404 812432
Cadnam 29Bc ○
Cadney 175Ee ○
Cadzow Castle 227Cf ⚔
Cae Carn Beag 263Eb ❋
Cae Pwtto 91Cc
Caenlochan Nature Reserve 263Da
☏ 0307 68715
Cae'n-y-Coed 157Df ♤ ✤ ⌂
Caeo 89Ef ○
Caer Caradoc 119Gf ❋
Caer Caradoc 145Ba ❋
Caer Lêb 155Ee ⊞
Caerau Fort 91Dc ❋
Caerhun 161Bb ○ ⚓ †

Caerlaverock Castle 219Ba 🏰
✕✘£☎ 0387 77244
Caerlaverock Nature Reserve
219Ba ✿
Caerleon 93Cc 🏰 🏰
Caernarfon 155Ee 🏰 🏰 ✕ 🚂
✕£☎ 0286 830800
Caernarfon Air Museum 155Ed ✈
✕£☎ 0286 830800
Caerphilly 93Ab 🏰 🏰
Caerphilly Castle 93Ab 🏰
£☎ 0222 883143
Caersws 119Dh ⊙ 🏰
Caerwent 93Dc 🏰 🏰
Caesar's Camp, Easthampstead
57Cd ✻
Cairn Baan 237Ec ⏚
Cairn Gorm 263Cd ✻
Cairn o' Mount 265Db ✻ ☆
Cairn Toul 263Bd
Cairnbaan 239Cd ⏚
Cairnbulg 271Gd ⊙
Cairngorm Mountains 263Bd
Cairngorm Reindeer Centre 263Bd
✔ 🅿 £☎ 0479 861228
Cairngorm Whisky Centre 263Be ⊿
✕🅿 £☎ 0479 810574
Cairngorms National Park 263Bc
Cairnholy 217Ab 🏰
Cairnpapple Hill 229Af ✻
Cairnryan 215Be ⊙
Cairnsmore of Fleet 215Fe
Cairnwell, The 263Da ✻
Caisteal Abhail 237Ee
Caisteal Bharraich 281Ge 🏰
Caisteal Grugaig 251Bi ⏚
Caister Castle 141Ee 🏰
Caister St Edmund 141Bd ⊙
Caister-on-Sea 141Ee 🏰 🏰 🚂
Caistor 175Fe ✝
Caithness Crystal 137Ef ✿
✕£☎ 0553 765111
Caithness Glass, Perth 257Bb ✿
✕£☎ 0738 37373
Caithness Glass, Wick 281Oe ✿
✕✘£☎ 0995 2286
Calbourne 31Bb 🏰
Calbourne Mill 31Bb 🏰
✕🅿 £☎ 0983 78227
Calceby 177Cb ✻
Caldbeck 207Ec 🏰 🏰
Caldbeck Fells 207Ec
Calder Abbey 195Be ✚
Calder Bridge 195Be ✚
Calderdale Industrial Museum
187Ab 🏛 🅿 £☎ 0422 359031
Calderglen Country Park 227Bf ✿
✕🅿 £☎ 03552 36644
Caldey Island 87Ea ✚
Caldicot 93Db 🏰 🏰 ✿
Caldicot Castle 93Db 🏰 ✿
✕🅿 £☎ 0291 420241
Caldon Canal 147Bf
Caledonian Canal 251De
Caledonian Railway 259Ce 🚂
✕🅿 £☎ 0334 55965
Calf of Man 181Aa ✿
Calgary 249Ee
Calgary Bay 249Ee
California 141Ee ⊙
California Country Park 57Bd ✿
✕🅿 £☎ 0734 730028
Calke Abbey 149Bc 🏰 ✿
✕£☎ 0332 863822
Callander 241Df
Callanish 272Eg ⊙
Callanish Standing Stones 272Eg ⏚
☎ 031244 3101
Calleva Roman Town 57Ad 🏰 🏰
£☎ 0734 700362/700322
Callibury Hump 31Bb ⏚
Callington 13Bd ⊙ ⏚
Calne 49Df ✝ 🏰 🏰
Calshot 29Cb 🏰 🏰 🏰
Calshot Castle 29Cb 🏰
✕£☎ 0703 892023
Calstock 13Cd ⊙
Calverleigh 21Ec ⊙
Calvert Jubilee 103Dd ✿
Calverton 149Ee ⊙
Calverton Folk Museum 149Ee 🏛
🅿 £☎ 0602 652836
Camas Sgiotaig 249Fh
Camber 41Dc
Camber Castle 41Dc ✕
Camberwell 63Bc 🏛
Cambo 211Cf 🏰
Cambo Country Park 247Ed ✿
✕🅿 ☎ 0333 50810
Cambo Gardens 247Fd ✿

🅿 £☎ 0333 50313
Camborne 9De ✻ ⊙ 🏰 🏛
Camborne School of Mines 9De 🏛
🅿 ☎ 0209 714866
Cambrian Factory 119Bc ✿
✕£☎ 05913 211
CAMBRIDGE 109Df Town plan 111
The Backs 111Ad
Cambridge and County Folk
Museum 111Ad 🏛 £
☎ 0223 355159
Christ's College 111Bc
& ☎ 0223 333900
Clare College 111Ac &
& ☎ 0223 333900
Corpus Christi College 111Bc
Downing College 111Cb
& ☎ 0223 334800
Eagle Inn 111Bc
Emmanuel College 111Cc
& ☎ 0223 334200
Fitzwilliam Museum 111Bb 🏛
✕£☎ 0223 332900
Gonville and Caius College
111Bc & ☎ 0223 332400
Great St Mary's Church
111Bc ✝
Hobson's Conduit 111Ba
Jesus College 111Cd &
☎ 0223 357626
Kettles Yard Art Gallery 111Ad
🏛 ☎ 0223 352124
King's College 111Ac &
☎ 0223 350411
King's College Chapel 111Ac ✝
& ☎ 0223 350411 ext 250
King's Parade 111Bc
Little St Mary's Church 111Bb
✝ ☎ 0223 350733
Magdalene College 111Ad
& ☎ 0223 332100
Mathematical Bridge 111Ab
Pembroke College 111Bb
& ☎ 0223 338100
Pepys Library 111Bd 🏛
☎ 0223 332100
Peterhouse 111Bb &
☎ 0223 338200
Queen's College 111Ac
& ☎ 0223 335511
Round Church 111Bd ✝
St Bene't's Church 111Bc ✝
☎ 0223 353903
St Botolph's Church 111Bb ✝
☎ 0223 63529
St John's College 111Bd
& ☎ 0223 338600
Scott Polar Research Institute
111Ca & ☎ 0223 336540
Sedgwick Museum of Geology
111Bc 🏛 ☎ 0223 333456
Senate House 111Bc
Sidney Sussex College 111Bd
& ☎ 0223 338800
Trinity College 111Bd
& ☎ 0223 338400
Trinity Street 111Bd
University Botanic Gardens
111Ca ✿ ✕& ☎ 0223 336265
University Museum of
Archaeology and Anthropology
111Bc 🏛 & ☎ 0223 333516
University Museum of Zoology
111Bc 🏛 & ☎ 0223 336650
Whipple Museum 111Bc 🏛
& ☎ 0223 334540
Cambridge University Botanic
Garden 109Df ✿ ✕&
☎ 0223 336265
Cambuskenneth 245Be ✚
Cambuskenneth Abbey 245Be ✚
Camden Town 61Dd
Cameley 45Ed ✝
Camelford 11Df 🏛
Camelot 183Da ✿ 🅿 ✕&
☎ 0257 50433044
Camer Park 85Bb ✿ ✕
☎ 0474 813062
Cameron Stone 227Bc ✕
Cameronian's Regimental Museum
227Cf 🏛 ☎ 0698 428688
Cammachmore Bay 267Cc
Campbeltown 237Cc 🏰 🏛
Camperdown House & Country Park
257Ec ✿ ✔ 🅿 ✕&
☎ 0382 621993
Camperdown Wildlife Centre
257Ec ✔ 🅿 ✕&☎ 0382 623555

Camphill Village Trust 267Bd ✿
✕🅿 ☎ 0224 88701
Canada Hill 237Gg ☆
Canal Centre, Devizes 49 De ✿
🅿 £☎ 0380 729489/721279
Candacraig Gardens & Gallery
265Ae ✿ 🅿 ✕£& ☎ 09756 51226
Candlecraft Centre 141De ✿
🅿 ☎ 0493 750242
Canisbay 281Og 🏰
Canisp 277Gi
Cann Wood 13Dc ✿
Canna 275Bb
Canna Harbour 275Bb
Cannock Chase 147Bc ✿ 🏰 ✔ 🏰
🅿 & ☎ 0543 871773
Cannock Wood 147Cc ⊙ ✻
Cannon Aquarium 167Ce ✿
🅿 & ☎ 061 2752634
Cannon Hall 171Df 🏰 🏰 🅿
☎ 0226 790270
Canon Pyon 123Bb ⊙
Canons Ashby 103Cg ⊙ 🏰
Canons Ashby House 103Cg 🏰
✕🅿 £☎ 0327 860044
Canonteign Falls Park 15Bf ✔
✕🅿 £☎ 0647 52666
Canovium 161Bb ⊙
Canterbury 43Be 🏰 🏰 ✝ ✿ 🏛
Canterton Glen 27De 🏰
Cantlop Bridge 145Cb ⏚ 🏰 🏰
Cantref Reservoir 91Cf
Caol Ila 235De ⊿
Cape Cornwall 9Ad
Cape Wrath 281Dg ☆ ⛴
Capel Curig 157Ef ⏚
Capel Garmon 157Ef ⏚
Capel Manor 63Be ✿ 🏰
✕🅿 £☎ 0992 763849
Capel Manor Farm 109Ca 🏰
✕🅿 £☎ 0992 763849
Capel Mounth 263Eb
Capel Newydd 155Cb ✝
Capel-le-Ferne 43Cc ✻ ☆
Capesthorne Hall 167Cc 🏰 🏰
✕🅿 £☎ 0625 861221
Capler Camp 97Af ✻
Capstone Park 85Cb ✔
✕🅿 £☎ 0634 812196
Captain Cook Birthplace Museum
201Ce 🏛 🅿 ✕£& ☎ 0642 311211
Capton 15Bc ⊙ 🏰
Caratacus Stone 21De ⏚
Carbis Bay 9Cd ⊙
Cardhu Distillery Visitor Centre
269Db 🅿 £☎ 03406 204
CARDIFF 93Aa Town plan 95
Bute Park 95Ac &
☎ 0222 751235
126 Bute Street, Cardiff Bay
94Eb
Cardiff Arms Park 95Ba
🅿 & ☎ 0222 390111
Cardiff Bay Visitor Centre 94Fa
🏛 🅿 & ☎ 0222 463833
Castle 95Bb 🏰 🏰 ✕£
☎ 0222 822083
Cathays Park 95Bc &
☎ 0222 751235
City Hall 95Cc &
☎ 0222 822101
Gorsedd Gardens 95Cc
& ☎ 0222 751235
Kingsway Underpass 95Cb
Morgan Arcade 95Ca
National Museum of Wales
95Cc 🏛 🅿 ✕& ☎ 0222 397951
New Theatre 95Cc 🎭
✕& ☎ 0222 394232
Q Shed, Cardiff Bay 94Ea
🅿 ✕& ☎ 0222 481919
Queen's Dragoon Guards
Museum 95Bb 🚂 ✕£
☎ 0222 822088
Queen's West Centre 95Cb
Railway Gallery, Cardiff Bay
94Eb 🅿 ✕& ☎ 0222 481919
Royal Arcade 95Ca
St David's Centre 95Cb
St John's Church 95Cb ✝
Sophia Gardens 95Ab
Techniquest, Cardiff Bay 94Ea
🅿 ✕£& ☎ 0222 460211
War Memorial 95Cc
Welch Regiment Museum 95Bb
🚂 ✕£ ☎ 0222 229367
Welsh Industrial and Maritime
Museum, Cardiff Bay 95Ea 🏛
🅿 ✕£& ☎ 0222 481919

Cardigan 87Ef ✝ 🏰
Cardigan Wildlife Park 87Ef ✔
✕🅿 ☎ 0239 614449
Carding Mill Valley 145Ba 🏔
Cardington 145Ca ✿
Cardinham Woods 11Dd ✿
Cardoness Castle 217Ab 🏰 🅿
☎ 031 5568400
Carew 87Db ⊙ 🏰 🏰
Carew Castle and Tidal Mill 87Db 🏰
🏰 🅿 £& ☎ 0646 651657
Carfin Grotto 241Ea
Carie 255De ✿
Carillon Tower, Loughborough
149Db 🏛
Carisbrooke Castle 31Bb 🏰 ✿ 🏰
✕🅿 £☎ 0983 522107
Carl Wark 171Dd ✻
Carleton Castle 215Cg 🏰
Carling Knott 207Cb
Carlisle 207Ee 🏰 🏰 ✿
Carlisle Castle 207Ee 🏰 🚂 £
☎ 0228 31777
Carlton Hall 151Bg 🏰 🅿 £
☎ 0636 821421
Carlton in Cleveland 201Cd 🏰
Carlton Marsh 173Af ✔
Carlton Towers 189Cb 🏰
✕🅿 £☎ 0405 861662
Carlungie 259Bc ⏚
Carlyle's Birthplace 219Cb 🏰
£☎ 041 5528391
Carmarthen 89Ce 🏰 🏰 🏛
Carmel Head 155Ch ☆
Carmyllie 259Df ✿
Carn a Ghobhair 249Ii
Carn Bàn 261Ca
Carn Boduan 155Db ✻
Carn Brae 9De ✻
Carn Euny 9Ac ⏚ 🅿
Carn Fadryn 155Cb ✻
Carn Goch 89Ee ✻
Carnasserie Castle 239Ce 🏰
☎ 031 2443101
Carnbane Castle 255Dd 🏰
Carnedd Dafydd 157Cg
Carnedd Llewelyn 157Cg
Carnedd Moel-siabod 157Df
Carnegie Museum 245Dd 🏛
🅿 & ☎ 0383 724302
Carnfield Hall 149Cf 🏰 🅿 £
☎ 0773 520084
Carnforth 183Cg 🏰
Carningli Common 87De ✻
Carnoustie 259Bc
Carr Taylor Vineyards 41Cc ✿
🅿 ☎ 0424 752501
Carradale 237Dd 🏰 🏰 🏰 ✿ ✿
Carradale House Gardens
237Dd ✿
Carradale Point 237Dd ✻
Carrbridge 263Bb 🏰 ✿
Carreg Cennen Castle 89Ed 🏰
Carreg Coetan 87De ⏚
Carreg Samson 87Be ⏚
Carrick Castle 239Ed ⊙ 🏰
Carrock Fell 207Ec
Carron Valley Forest 241Ed ✿ 🏰
Carron Valley Reservoir 241Dd
Cars of the Stars Museum 207Db 🚗
£& ☎ 07687 73757
Carsaig 239Bc ⊙
Carsaig Arches 249Fa ☆
Carshalton 41Db ✿
Carstairs 227Ee 🏰
Carswell House 87Db 🏰
Carter Bar 221Cb ✻
Carter Plot 151Ee 🏰
Carthew 11Cc ⊙ ✿
Cartland Bridge 227De ✿
Cartland Crags 227De ☆
Cartmel 195Eb 🏰 🏰
Cartmel Fell 195Fc ✿
Cartmel Priory 195Eb ✚ &
☎ 05395 36602
Cartwright Hall 187Bc 🏛
🅿 ✕& ☎ 0274 493313
Cashtal yn Ard 181Dc ⏚
Cassiobury Park 107Da 🏔
Castell Blaenllynfi 93Af 🏰
Castell Coch 93Ab 🏰 🅿 £
☎ 0222 810101
Castell Collen 119De ✿
Castell Dinas Bran 159De ✻
Castell Henllys 87Ee ✻
Castell Odo 155Ba ✻
Castell y Bere 117Eg 🏰 🅿
☎ 0222 465511

Castell-mawr 155Fg
Caster Hanglands 135Df ✔
Castle Acre 139Bf 🏰 🏰 ✚ 🏰
Castle Acre Castle 139Bf 🏰
✕£& ☎ 0760 755394
Castle an Dinas 11Bb ✻
Castle Ashby 135Aa 🏰 🏰
Castle Bolton 199Cc 🏰
Castle Bromwich Hall 125Df ✿
☎ 021 749 4100
Castle Campbell 245Ce 🏰
Castle Cary 45Eb ✿ 🏰
Castle Combe 49Bf 🏰
Castle Cornet 287Ce 🚂 🏰
✕£☎ 0481 721651
Castle Ditches 163Db ✻
Castle Donington 149Cc 🏰 ✈ 🚗
Castle Dore 11Dc ✔
Castle Douglas 217Cc 🏛
Castle Drogo 13Fg 🏰
✕🅿 £& ☎ 0647 433306
Castle Eden Dene 213Ca 🏔 ✔ ✿
Castle Eden Walkway 201Bf ✔
🅿 & ☎ 0740 30011
Castle Fraser 265Ee 🏰 🏰
✕🅿 £& ☎ 0330 3463
Castle Gaol, Jedburgh 221Cd 🏛
✕🅿 £☎ 0835 63254
Castle Girnigoe 281Oe 🏰
Castle Hedingham 113Cd 🏰 🏰 🏰
Castle Hill, E Ssx 39Ab ✔
Castle Hill, Hampshire 27Cd ✻
Castle House, Dedham 115Ac 🏰
🅿 £& ☎ 0206 322127
Castle Howard 189Dg 🏰
🅿 £☎ 0653 84333
Castle Kennedy Gardens
215Ce ✿
Castle Lachlan 239Ed 🏰
Castle Loch 219Bc ✔
Castle Menzies 255Fd 🏰
✕🅿 £☎ 0887 20982
Castle Moil 275Gd 🏰
Castle Museum, York 189Ce 🏛
✕£& ☎ 0904 653611
Castle Neroche 23Cd ⏚ ✿
Castle O'er 219Dd ✻
Castle O'er Forest 219Dd ✻ 🏰
Castle of May 281Ng ✿
☎ 0955 2596
Castle of Old Wick 281Od 🏰
Castle of Park 215Cd 🏰
Castle Rising 137Eg 🏰 🅿 £
☎ 0553 631330
Castle Rock 207Ea ☆
Castle Rushen 181Ba 🏰 🏰
☎ 0624 823326
Castle Semple Collegiate Church
225Cg ✚
Castle Semple Country Park & Loch
225Cf ✿ 🅿 £☎ 0505 842882
Castle Sinclair 281Oe 🏰
Castle Spynie Broch 261Be ⏚
Castle Stalker 239Di 🏰 🅿 £
☎ 088 3622768
Castle Stuart 261De 🏰
🅿 £& ☎ 0463 790745
Castle Sween 239Bb 🏰
☎ 031 2443101
Castle Tioram 249Hg 🏰
Castlecary 245Ac ✚
Castlegate House Gallery 207Cc 🏰
☎ 0900 822149
Castlehill Point 217Db ✻
Castlelaw 229De ✻
Castlemartin 87Ca ⊙
Castlemorton Common 123Ea ✔
Castlerigg Stone Circle 207Db ⏚
Castles, The, Lothian 233Bb ✻
Castleton 171Cd 🏔 🏰 ✿
Castletown, Highland 281Mf 🏰 🏰
Castletown, IoM 181Ba 🏰 🏛 ✕ 🏛
Castor 135De 🏰
Caswell Bay 89Da
Catcliffe 173Bc ✿
Cater Museum, Billericay 85Be 🏛
☎ 0277 211250
Caterham 63Ba ⊙
Cathcart Castle 241Ca 🏰
Cathcartston Visitor Centre 225Da
🅿 £☎ 0290 550633
Cathole Cave 89Db ☆
Catterick 199Ec
Catterline 267Ba 🏰
Cauldron Snout 197Ef ☆
Cauldside Burn 217Ab ⏚
Causey Arch 211Ec ✿
Cautley Crag 197Cc ☆
Cautley Spout 197Cc ✿

Cavendish 113De ⌂♨⚓✦⛪
Cawdor 261Ee ⌂♨
P✕⛽☎ 06677 615
Cawfields 209Dd ♨☞
Cawsand 13Cc ○
Cawston 143Fa ○
Cawthorn 205Ac ♨
Cawthorne 171Df ⌂☞⚓
Caynham Camp 123Ce ✳
Caythorpe 151Ce ⌂
Cayton Bay 205Db
Cefn Bryn 89Da ✳
Cefn Carn-Fadog 91Af
Cefn Coed Colliery Museum 91Ae
⚙⌂⚓ 0639 750556
Cefncarnedd 119Dg ✳
Cefni Reservoir 155Ef ♀☞
Cei-bach 117Cb ○
Ceiriog Valley 159Dd ⚙
Cemaes 155Dh ○
Cemaes Head 87Eg ☆
Cemlyn Bay 155Dh
Cemmaes 119Bi ○
Cenarth 87Ff ⌂♨⚓
Centre for Alternative Technology 117Fg ⚙
Ceredigion Museum 117De ⚓
P⛽☎ 0970 617911
Ceres 247Dd ⌂♨⚓
P⛽☎ 0792 295438
Ceri Richards Gallery 89Eb ⚓
P☎ 0792 655438
Cerne Abbas 25Ce ⌂♨
Cerne Giant 25Ce ☞
Cerrig-y-Gof 87De ☞
Cessford 221Dd ○
Chaceley 97Df ○
Chacewater 9Ee ⌂○
Chaddesley Corbett 125Ae ⌂
Chaddesley Wood 125Be ☞
Chadlington 101Ee ○
Chadshunt 129Cb ○
Chagford 13Ff ⌂
Chailey 39Ac ○
Chailey Mill 39Ad ✕⛽£
☎ 0825 723007
Chaldon 63Ba ⌂
Chalfont Shire Horse Centre 107Da
🐴 P✕⛽☎ 02407 2304
Chalfont St Giles 107Ca ⌂♨
Chalford 97Dc ○
Chalgrave 107Dd † ▣
☎ 0525 714111
Chalgrove 1643, Battle of 103Da ✳
Chalk Pits Museum 37Bc ⚙
P✕⛽£☎ 0798 831370
Chalkdell Wood 107Cb ☞
Chalkney Wood 113Dc ♀☞
Chambercombe Manor 17Ef ♨
P✕£☎ 0271 862624
Chambers Farm Woods 177Ab ☞
Chanctonbury Ring 37Cc ✳
Chanonry Point 261Df
Chanters House 23Ab ⚓
Chantry Chapel 103 De ♨
Chapel Brampton 133Db ○⛴
Chapel Farm 37Cg ▣£
☎ 0306 882865
Chapel Finian 215Dc †
Chapel of Garioch 265Ef ○
Chapel Porth 9Dc ❀✳⚙
Chapel St Leonards 177Eb
Chapel Wood 17Df ☞
Chapel-le-Dale 197Da ○
Chard 23Dc ⚓☞
Chargot Wood 21Ee ♀
Charing 41Df ⌂
Charlbury 103Ac ☞⚓
Charlecote 129Bb ♨⌂
Charlecote Falconry Centre 129Bb
🐦 P£⛽☎ 0789 470387
Charlecote Mill 129Bb ⚓£
☎ 0789 842072
Charlecote Park 129Bb ♨
P✕⛽£☎ 0789 470277
Charles Burrell Museum 139Bc ⚓
P£☎ 0842 752599
Charles Dickens Centre 85Cb ⚓
£☎ 0634 844176
Charles Rennie Mackintosh Society 241Cb ⚓P✕☎ 041 9466600
Charleston Farmhouse 39Bb ♨
P£⛽☎ 0323 811265
Charleston Manor 39Cb ❀
☎ 0323 870617
Charlestown, Cornwall 11Cc ○
Charlestown, Fife 245Dd ⌂

Charlestown of Aberlour 269Eb ⚓
Charlton Marshall 27Ad ○
Charlton Park 97Ea ♨▣£
Charlton-on-Otmoor 103Cc ○
Charminster 25Cd ○
Charmouth 23Db ⌂☆
Charney Bassett 103Aa ○
Chart Gunpowder Mills 85Fb ⚓
☎ 0795 534542
Charterhouse 45Cd ○
Chartwell 39Bg ♨P✕£
☎ 0732 866368
Chasewater Light Railway 147Cb ⛴
P✕⛽☎ 0543 452623
Chastleton 101De ○
Chateau des Marais 287Ce ♨
P☎ 0481 726518
Chatelherault Country Park 227Cf
♨P✕⛽£☎ 0698 426213
Chatelherault House 227Cf ♨
P£⛽☎ 0698 426213
Chatham 85Cb ☞
Chatham Historic Dockyard 85Cb
✕P✕⛽£⚓☎ 0634 812551
Chatley Heath Semaphore Tower 61Ba ✕£⛽☎ 0932 862762
Chatsworth House 171Dc ♨
P✕£☎ 0246 582204
Chatteris 137Bc ⚓
Chatterley Whitfield Mining Museum 147Ag ⚙P✕£
☎ 0782 813337
Chavenage 97Db ♨P£
☎ 0666 502329
Chawton 57Ba ⌂♨
Chawton Park Wood 57Aa
♀⛽☞
Cheadle 147Cf
Chearsley 103Ec ○
Checkendon 57Af ○
Checkley 147Ce ○
Cheddar 45Cd ☆ ⌂
Cheddar Gorge 45Cd ❀☆☞
P✕£ 0934 742343
Cheddar Valley Vineyard 45Cd ❀
P✕☎ 0934 732280
Cheddleton 147Bg ⌂☞⛴⚙
Chedworth 101Bd ○⚙
Chedworth Roman Villa 101Bd ♨
P£⛽☎ 0242 89256
Cheeswring 11Ee ☆
Chelmorton 171Cb ⌂♨
Chelmsford & Essex Museum 85Cf
Chelmsford 85Cf ✕⚓☑
Chelsea 61Dc
Chelsworth 113Ee ⌂
Cheltenham 97Ee ⚓☑
Chenies 107Da ○
Chenies Manor House 107Da ♨
P✕£☎ 0494 762888
Chepstow 93Ec ☞♨⚓❀⚙⌂
Chequers Reserve 107Bb ☞
Cherhill Down 49De
Cheriton 1644 29Dd ✕
Cheriton Bishop 15Ag ○
Cheriton Fitzpaine 21Db ○
Cherry Trees Farm 107Db ♨
P✕£⛽☎ 0923 268289
Cherry Willingham 175Eb ○
Chertsey 61Bb ○
Cheshire Workshops 163Da ⚓
P✕⛽☎ 0829 70401
Chester 163Cb
⚓♨○†⌂⚓⚙☑
Chester Zoo 163Cc ○
P✕⛽£☎ 0244 380280
Chesterfield 173Ab †♨⚓☑⌂♨
P✕⛽☎ 0434 344277
Chester-le-Street 213Ac
Chesters Roman Fort 211Bd ⚙♨
P✕⛽£☎ 0434 681379
Chesters, The, Lothian 233Bc ✳
Chesterton 135De ○
Cheswardine 145Ed ○
Cheswick 223Cf ○
Chettle 27Ae ○♨
Chetwode 103Dd ○
Chevin Forest Park 187Bd ☞
P☎ 0943 465023
Chevin, The 187Cd ☞✳
Cheviot Hills 223Ac
Cheviot, The 223Bd
Chew Green 221Db ♀

Chew Magna 45De ⌂☞
Chew Valley Lake 45De
Chewton Cheese Dairy 45Dd ♨
P✕☎ 0761 21666
Chichele College 135Bb ⌂
P☎ 023065 252
Chichester 33Cc ♨○†⌂♨☑
P☎ 0767 315674
Chiddingfold 37Ae ⌂
Chiddingly 39Cc ○
Chiddingstone 39Bc ♨⌂
Chiddingstone Castle 39Bf ♨
P✕£☎ 0892 870347
Chidham 33Bc ○
Chilbolton 53Ca ○
Chilcomb 29Dd ○
Chilcombe 25Bd ○
Childhood & Costume Museum 145Ea ⚓⌂⛽☎ 0476 764636
Childswickham 101Bf ○
Chilford Hall Barns 109Ee ❀
P✕£⛽☎ 0223 892641
Chilgrove 33Cd ○
Chilham Castle 43Ae ❀
P✕£☎ 0227 730319
Chillenden 43Ce ○✕
Chillingham 223Cd ⌂♨☞
Chillington 15Ab ○
Chillington Hall 147Ab ♨
P£⛽☎ 0902 850236
Chilmark 27Ag ○
Chilsdown Vineyard 33Cd ❀
P£☎ 0243 63398
Chiltern Brewery 107Bb ⛱
P✕☎ 0296 613647
Chiltern Open Air Museum 107Da
⌂P✕£☎ 02407 71117
Chilworth 29Cc ○
Chilworth Manor 37Bf ❀P✕£
Chingford 63Be ♨○
Chingle Hall 183Dc ♨P✕£
☎ 0772 861082
Chinnor Hill 103Eb ☞
Chipman Strand 17Aa ☆
Chippenham, Cambs 137Ea ⌂
Chippenham, Wilts 49Cf †♨○⌂
Chipperfield 107Db ○
Chipping 183Ed ⌂♨
Chipping Campden 101Cf ♀⚓☑
Chipping Norton 101Ee ♨
Chipping Ongar 109Ea ⌂
Chipstead 61Da ○
Chirbury 119Fh ⌂
Chirk 159Dd ⌂♨♀○
Chirk Castle 159Dd ♨♀
P✕£☎ 0691 777701
Chisbury 53Bd ○✳
Chisbury Hill Fort 53Bd ✳
Chisbury Thatched Chapel 53Bd †
Chiselbury 27Bf ✳
Chisenbury Priory Vineyard 49Ed
❀P✕£☎ 0980 70406
Chislehampton 103Ca ○
Chislehurst Caves 63Cb ☆
P✕£☎ 081 467 3264
Chiswick 61Dc ♨⚓
Chiswick House 61Dc ♨
P✕£☎ 081 995 0508
Chittlehampton 21Bd ○
Chobham Common 57Bd ☞
Cholderton Rare Breeds Farm 53Bb
☞P✕£⛽☎ 098064 438
Cholmondeley Castle Gardens 145Cg ❀P✕☎ 0829 720383
Cholsey & Wallingford Railway 53Ef ⛴P✕☎ 0491 35067
Cholsey 53Ef ☞⌂
Cholsey Marsh 53Ef ☞
Chopwell Wood 211Dc ♀☞
Chorley 183Da ⚓
Chorlton Water Park 167Ce ☞
P£☎ 061 8815639
Christ Church-over-Wyresdale 183De †
Christchurch 27Cc
❀☞†☞⚓⌂
Christchurch Mansion 115Bd ♨
✕£☎ 0473 258070
Christ's Hospital, Horsham 37Cd
P✕£☎ 0403 211297
Chudleigh 15Be ○⌂
Chulmleigh 21Bc ⌂
Claydon 103Bf ⌂♨
Claydon House 103Ed ♨
P✕£☎ 0296 730349/730693
Claydons, The 103Ed ⌂♨
Chun Castle 9Bd ✳
Church Brough 197De ○
Church Cove 9Eb ○
Church Eaton 147Ac ○

Church Farm Museum 153Ef ♨
P£☎ 0754 766658
Church Farm Workshops, Edwinstowe 173Da ☞P♨
☎ 0623 823767
Church Hanborough 103Bc ○
Church Hill 45Bf ✳
Church Laneham 175Cb ⌂
Church Stretton 145Ba ☑
Church Wood 43Bf ☞
Churche's Mansion 167Aa ♨
P✕£☎ 0270 625933
Churchill 45Cd ○
Churchill Barriers 283Dc
Churchill Gardens 123Cb ⌂
P£☎ 0432 267409
Chwarel Wynne Mine 159Dd ⚙
P✕£☎ 0691 72343
Chysauster 9Bd ☞£
☎ 0736 61889
Cider Press Centre 15Ad ☞
P✕⛽☎ 0803 864171
Cilgerran 87Ef ♨⌂
Cilycwm 119Ac ○
Cinn Trolla Broch 278Fe ☞
Cirencester 101Bc ♨♀⚓☑
Cirencester Workshops 101Bc ☞
P✕☎ 0285 61566
Cissbury Ring 37Cb ✳
Clach a' Charridh 278Eb ☞
Clach Ard 275Df
Clachan Bridge 239Bf ⚙
☎ 0631 63122
Clachnaharry 261Ce ⚙
Clackmannan Tower 245Ce
Clack's Farm 123Fd ❀P£♨
☎ 0905 620250
Clacton-on-Sea 115Ba ☞☑
Claerwen Reservoir 119Be ♨
P✕£☎ 0983 78396
Clamerkin Farm 31Bc ☞
Clan Cameron 251Ee ⚓
P✕£☎ 0397 772473
Clan Donald Centre and Gardens 275Fb ☞⚓£♨
☎ 04714 305/227
Clan Donnachaidh Museum 255Ff ⚓
P♨☎ 0796 83264
Clan Gunn Heritage Centre & Museum 281Nc ⚓ ☎ 0955 4771
Clan Macalister Centre 237Bd ⚓
P£☎ 058 32247
Clan Macpherson Museum 255Ei ⚓
P☎ 0540 673332
Clan Ross Centre 278Dc ⚓
P£☎ 0862 893054
Clan Tartan Centre 229Df ☑
P✕£☎ 031 5535100
Clandon Park 37Bg ♨
P✕£☎ 0483 222482
Clanfield 101Dc ○
Clapham, N Yorks 185Af ⌂♨☆♀
Clapham, Beds 107Dg ○
Clapper Bridge 11De ☞
Clapton Court 23Ec ❀P✕
☎ 0460 73220
Clarach 117Ee ○
Clarach Bay 117De
Clare 113Ce ⌂♨
Clare Castle Park 113Ce ☞
P£☎ 0787 277491
Claremont 61Cb ♨❀P£♨
☎ 0372 467841
Claremont Landscape Garden 61Cb
❀P✕£⛽☎ 0372 469421
Clatterin Brig 265Da
Clatteringshaws Forest Wildlife Centre 217Ad ☞
Clatteringshaws Loch 217Ad
Clatto Country Park 257Ec ☞
P✕£☎ 0382 89076
Clatworthy Reservoir 23Af
Clauchland Hills 237Fd ♀
Clava Cairns 261Dd ○
Clavell Tower 27Aa
Clavering 109Da ♨
Claverley 145Ea ⌂
Claverton Manor 49Ae ♨
P✕£☎ 0225 460503
Clay Bank 201Cd ❀♀☞
Claybrooke Parva 133Ad ○
Claycocks 43Bc ♨
Claydon 103Bf ⌂♨
Claydons, The 103Ed ⌂♨
P£☎ 0382 736420

Claythorpe Watermill 177Db ⚓♀
P✕£☎ 0507 450687
Clayton 37Ec ♀
Cleanhill Wood 271Cc ♀
Clearbury Ring 27Cf ✳
Clearwater Leisure Park 175Bf
Clearwell Caves 97Ac ☞
P✕£☎ 0594 32535
Clee St Margaret 123Cf ○
Cleethorpes 177Ce †☞
Cleeve Abbey 23Ag ♨
Cleeve Cloud 101Ae ✳
Cleeve Hill 101Ae ○✳☞
Cleeve Prior 125Cb ○☞
Cleit Dhubh 281Eg ♀
Clent Hills 125Be ☞✳☞£
☎ 0562 710392
Cleobury Mortimer 123Dde ○
Clevedon 45Cf ♨❀✳⚙
Clevedon Court 45Cf ♨P✕£
☎ 0272 872257
Clevedon Craft Centre 45Cf ☞
P✕£ 0272 872867
Cleveland Gallery 201Be ⚓
P£☎ 0642 225408
Cleveland Way 205Db-Ae
Cleveleys 183Bd
Clewer Village 57De †
Cley Hill 49Bc
Cley next the Sea 143Ec ⌂♨
Cley Windmill 143Ec ✕P£
☎ 0263 740209
Clibberswick 285Hk ○
Click Mill 283Cd ⚓
☎ 031 244 3107
Clickimin Broch 285Fd ☞
Cliff End 41Cc ○
Cliffe 85Cc ○
Cliffe Castle 185Dd ⚓
P✕£☎ 0535 618230
Clifford 189Ad ⌂
Clifford's Tower 189Ce ♨
P£☎ 0904 646940
Cliffs Nature Trail 258Cd ☞
Clifton Campville 147Ec ○
Clifton Hampden 103Ca ○
Clifton Park Museum, Rotherham 173Bd ⚓▣
☎ 0709 382121 ext 3628
Clifton Reynes 107Cg ○
Clifton upon Teme 123Ed ○
Cliftonville 43Dg ○
Climping Sands 37Bb
Clink, The 247Bd ☞☞
Clipsham 151Cb ○
Clipsham Park Wood 151Cb ♀☞
Clipstone Forest 149Eg ♀☞
Clitheroe 185Ad ⚓♨☑
Clive House 145Bc ⚓£
☎ 0743 354811
Cliveden 57Df ♨P✕£♨
☎ 0628 605069
Cliveden Reach 57Df ☞
Clocaenog Forest 159Bf
♀✳☞
Cloch Point 239Gb ☞
Clock Mill Heritage Centre 245Ce ⚓
P£☎ 0259 52176
Clocks & Watches Museum, Bury St Edmunds 139Ba ⚓☞
☎ 0284 757072
Clodock 93Cf ○
Cloud, The 167Db ✳
Cloud's Hill 25Ed ♨P£
☎ 0929 463824
Cloughton Wyke 205Dc
Cloutsham 21Ef ☞
Clova 257Eg ○
Clovelly 17Cd ⌂♨✳
Clovelly Dykes 17Cd ✳
Cloverleaf Fibre Stud 271Cb ☞
P£☎ 0466 780879
Clows Top 123Ee ○
Cluanie Deer Park 261Ae ☞
P✕£☎ 0463 782415
Clumber Park 173Db ☞☑
P✕£☎ 0909 476592
Clun 119Gg ⌂♨⚓⌂
Clun Forest 119Fg
Clungunford 123Be
Cluny Gardens 255Fe ❀P£
☎ 0887 20795
Clydach Gorge 93Be ♨
Clydebank 241Cb
Clyffe Pypard 49Df ○
Clyne Valley Park 89Eb ☞
Clynelish Distillery 278Ee ♨
P£☎ 0408 621444

Crossraguel Abbey 225Ba
☎ 031 2443101
Crosthwaite 195Fd
Croston 183Ca
Crovie 271Ed
Crowborough 39Ce
Crowcombe 23Bf
Crowdy Reservoir 11Df
Crowhurst 39Af
Crowland 135Eg
Crowland Abbey 135Eg
☎ 0733 210499
Crowle, H & W 125Bc
Crowle, Humberside 175Bf
Croxden 147Ce
Croxteth Hall 163Ce
P X ☎ 051 2285311
Croy Brae (Electric Brae) 225Bb
Croyde 17De
Croydon 63Bb
Cruden Bay 271Ga
Crug Hywell 93Bf
Cruickshank Botanic Gardens
267Cd ☎ 0224 272704
Crummock Water 207Ca
Crundale Downs 43Ad
Crusader's Grave 275Df
Cruwys Morchard 21Dc
Crychan Forest 119Bc
Crymlyn Bog 89Fb
☎ 0792 459255
Crystal Palace 63Bc
Crystal Palace Park 63Bc
Crystal Visitor Centre 229De
P X ☎ 0968 75128
C.S. Lewis Reserve 103Cb
Cubbie Roo's Castle 283Df
☎ 031 244 3101
Cubert 9Ef
Cuckfield 37Ed
Cuckmere Haven Ca
Cuckney 173Cb
Cuddesdon 103Cb
Cudmore Grove Park 115Aa
P X ☎ 0237 216297/0206 383865
Cuillin Hills 275Dd
Cùl Beag 277Fh
Cul Mor 277Fi
Culbin Forest 269Bd
Culbin Sands 269Bd
Culbone 21Df
Culla 273Kh
Cullen 269Hd
Cullen Old Church 269 Hd
Cullercoats 213Be
Cullerlie 267Ad ☎ 031 2443101
Culloden Muir 1746 261De
Cullompton 21Fb
Cull-pepper's Dish 25Ed
Culm Valley 23Ad
Culmstock Beacon 23Bd
Culross 245Cd
Culross Abbey 245Cd
☎ 031 244 3101
Culross Palace 245Cd P £
☎ 031 244 3101
Culsh Earth House 265Cd
Culver Cliff 31Db
Culverthorpe Walks 151Dd
Culzean Castle 225Bb
P X ☎ 065 56274
Cumberland Pencil Museum 207Db
P X £ ☎ 07687 73626
Cumbernauld 241Ec
Cuming Museum 63Bc
☎ 071 701 1342
Cumnock 227Ab
Cumnor 103Bb
Cupar 247Cd
Curbridge 29Dc
Curlew Weavers 117Ba
P X ☎ 0239 75357
Curraghs Wildlife Park 181Cd
P X ☎ 0624 897323
Curtis Museum 57Ba
☎ 0420 82802
Cusworth Country Park 173Ce
P ☎ 0302 782342
Cusworth Hall Museum 173Ce
P ☎ 0302 782342
Cuween Hill Cairn 283Ce
Cuxham 103Da
Cwm Afan 91Bd
Cwm Bychan 157Cd
Cwm Celyn 93Bd
Cwm Clydach 89Ec
Cwm Einion 117Ff
Cwm Garw 91Bd
Cwm Hirnant 159Ad

Cwm Idwal 157Cf
Cwm Lliedi Country Park 89Dc
P £
Cwm Lliedi Reservoir 89Dc
Cwm Ogmore 91Cd
Cwm Penmachno 157De
Cwmbran 93Bc
Cwmcarn Forest Drive 93Bc
P X ☎ 0495 272001
Cwmmau Farmhouse 119Fd
P X £ ☎ 04973 251
Cwmtillery Reservoirs 93Bd
Cwmtudu 117Bb
Cwm-yr-Eglwys 87De
Cwm-y-Rhaiadr 119Ac
Cyfarthfa Castle & Park 91De
P £ ☎ 0685 723112
Cymer Abbey 157Db
Cynwyl Elfed 89Be
Dacre 197Af
Daglingworth 97Ec
Dairsie Castle 247Dd
Dairyland Farm Park 11Ac
P X £ ☎ 0872 510246
Daisy Nook Park 167Df
P X £ ☎ 061 3083909
Dalavich 239Df
Dalbeattie 217Dc
Dalbeattie Forest 217Db
Dalby 181Bb
Dalby Forest 205Bb
Dale 87Bb
Dale Abbey 149Cd
Dale of Menteith 241Cf
Dalemain 197Af P X £
☎ 07684 56450
Daleslife Visitor Centre 185Cf
P £ ☎ 0756 752150
Dalgarven Mill 225Ce
P X £ ☎ 0294 52448
Dalgety Bay 245Ed
Dalkeith 229Ee
Dalkeith Country Park 229Ee
P £ ☎ 031 6635684
Dallas 269Dc
Dallas Dhu Distillery 269Cc
P X £ ☎ 031 2443101
Dalmally 239Fg
Dalmellington 225Da
Dalmellington Ironworks Museum
225Da ☎ 0292 53144
Dalmeny 229Cf
Dalmeny House 229Cf
P X £ ☎ 031 3311888
Dalness 251Eb
Dalston 207Ee
Dalton Crags 197Ba
Dalton-in-Furness 195Db
Dalveen Pass 227Ea
Dalwhinnie 255Dh
Damside Garden 259Dg
P X £ ☎ 0561 61498
Danbury 85Cf
Danbury Common 85Cf
P X ☎ 0245 412669
Danbury Park 85Cf
☎ 0245 412350
Danby 201Ed
Danby Rigg 201Ed
Dancersend 107Cb
Danebury Ring 53Ca
Danes' Dyke 192Eg
Danes Graves 192Cf
Daniel's Mill 145Ea P X £
☎ 0746 762753
Danny House 37Dc P £
☎ 0273 833000
Dan-yr-Ogof Caves 91Bf
Dare Valley 91Ce P X £
☎ 0685 874672
Daresbury 163Dd
Darley Abbey 149Bd
Darlington 199Ee
Darlington Railway Centre &
Museum 199Ee P X £
☎ 0325 460532
Darnaway Farm Visitor Centre
269Bc P X £ ☎ 0309 72213
Darnaway Forest 269Bc
Darnaway Forest Walks 269Cc
Darrington 189Ab
Dart Valley Railway 15Ad
X £ ☎ 0703 553760
Dartford 63Dc
Dartington Crystal 17Dc
Dartington Hall 15Ad
P X £ ☎ 0803 862271

Dartmeet 13Ee
Dartmoor Wildlife Park 13Dc
P X £ ☎ 0755 37209
Dartmouth 15Bc
Dartmouth Castle 15Bb
P £ ☎ 0803 833588
Daventry 133Bb
Daventry Park 133Bb
P X £ ☎ 0327 77193
David Evans Craft Centre of Silk
63Dc P X £ ☎ 0322 559401
Dawlish 15Ce
Dawlish Warren 15Ce
☎ 0626 863980
Dawlish Water 15Ce
Dawnay House 25Dd
Dawyck Botanic Garden 229Cb
P £ ☎ 072 16254
De Grey Mausoleum 107De
☎ 0223 455520
Deal 43De
Deal Castle 43De P X £
☎ 0304 372762
Dean 135Cb
Dean Castle & Country Park 225Dd
P X £ £
☎ 0563 26401
Dean Forest Railway 97Bc
P X £ ☎ 0594 843423
Dean Heritage Trust 97Bd
P X £ ☎ 0594 822170
Dean Village 229Df
Dean's House, Dunblane 245Af
P £ ☎ 0786 824254
Debden 109Ed
Deddington 103Be
Dedham 115Ac
Dedham Vale 115Ac
Dee Valley Confectioners 265Ac
P X ☎ 03397 55499
Deene 135Cb
Deene Park 135Be
P £ ☎ 078085 278361
Deep Hayes Park 147Bg
P ☎ 0538 387655
Deepdale Forest 205Cc
Deephayes Park 171Aa
P £ ☎ 0785 223121
Deer Abbey 271Fb
☎ 031 2443101
Deer Range 215Gf P £
☎ 0556 3626
Deerhurst 97De
Deerpark Wood 11Dc
Deil's Caldron 255Eb
Deil's Heid, The 259Cd
Delabole 11Cf
Delamere Forest 163Dc
Delapre Abbey 133Da P £
☎ 0604 34734
Delgatie Castle 271Dc
P X £ ☎ 0888 63479
Dell Quay 33Cc
Delph Locks 125Bf
Denant Mill Inn 87Cc
Denbigh 161Ea
Denbigh Friary 161Ea
Denbury 15Bd
Dendron 195Db
Denge Wood 43Ae
Denholm 221Bc
Denmans 33Dc
Denmead 33Ad
Dennington 115Cf
Denny Abbey 137Ca P £
☎ 0223 720333
Denny Ship Model Experiment
Tank 241Bc P £ ☎ 0389 63444
Dent 197Db
Dent Crafts Centre 197Cb
P X ☎ 058 75400
Dentdale 197Db
Denton 151Bd
Denver Windmill 137Ee
P £ ☎ 0603 222706
Deptford 63Bc
Derby 149Bd
Derby Fort and Battery 181Ba
Derby Haven 181Ba
Derby Industrial Museum 149Bd
£ ☎ 0237 441369
Derby Museum and Art Gallery
149Bd £ ☎ 0332 255586
Dervaig 249Fe
Derwent Edge 171Cd
Derwent Reservoir, Derbys 171Ce
Derwent Reservoir, Northld 211Bc

Derwent Walk 211Dc
Derwent Walk Country Park 211Dc
P £ ☎ 091 3864411
Derwent Water 207Db
Desford 133Af
Deskford Church 269Hd
Devil's Arrows 187Df
Devil's Beef Tub 219Bf
Devil's Bellows 9Db
Devil's Bridge 117Fd
Devil's Chimney 97Ed
Devil's Ditch 137Da
Devil's Dyke 37Dc
Devil's Frying Pan 9Eb
Devil's Hole 287Bc
Devil's Kitchen 157Cf
Devil's Pulpit 97Ab
Devil's Punch Bowl 57Ca
Devil's Spittlefield 123Be
Devil's Staircase 119Bd
Devizes 49De
Devizes Castle 49Ce
Dewar's Distillery 257Bb
☎ 0738 21231
Dewerstone Rock 13Dd
Dewlish 25Dd
Dewlish House 25Dd
Dewsbury Museum 187Cb
P £ 0924 468171
D.H. Lawrence's Birthplace 149Ce
£ ☎ 0773 763312
Dhoon Bay 181Dc
Dhoon Glen 181Dc
Diabaig, Lower 277Bd
Diabaig, Upper 277Cc
Dial Cottage 213Ae
☎ 091 2160252
Dick Institute, Kilmarnock 225Dd
£ ☎ 0563 26401
Dickens' Birthplace 33Ac
£ ☎ 0705 827261
Dickens House Museum 43Df
£ ☎ 0843 62853
Didcot 53Eg
Didcot Railway Centre 53Eg
P X £ £ ☎ 0235 817200
Didmarton 97Da
Didsbury 167Ce
Diffwys 157Cc
Dilton Marsh 49Bc
Dilwyn 123Bc
Din Lligwy 155Eg
☎ 0222 465511
Dinas Dinlle 155Ed
Dinas Dinorwig 155Fe
Dinas Head 87Df
Dinas Reserve 117Fa
Dinas-Mawddwy 157Eb
Dinedor Camp 123Ca
Dingwall 261Bf
P X £ ☎ 0432 71322
Dinnet Oakwood 265Bc
Dinorwic Quarry 157Bg
Dinorwig 157Bg
Dinosaur Museum 25Dd
£ ☎ 0305 269880
Dinton 27Bg
Dinton Pastures 57Be
P X £ ☎ 0734 342016
Dirleton 233Bd
Dirleton Castle 233Bd £
☎ 031 2443101
Disley 167Dd
Diss 139Eb
Disserth 119Dd
Dittisham 15Bc
Ditchling 39Ac
Ditchling Beacon 39Ac
Ditchling Common 39Ac
P £ ☎ 0273 477851
Divach Falls 261Ac
Dobwalls Park 11Ed
P X £ ☎ 0579 20325
Docker Park Farm 197Ba
P X £ ☎ 0524 221331
Dockray 207Eb
Docton Mill 17Bd P £
☎ 0237 441369
Docwra's Manor 109Ce
☎ 0763 260235
Dodd Wood 207Db
Doddington, Lincs 175Da
Doddington Moor, Northld 223Ce
Doddington, Northld 223Ce

Doddington Place 85Ea
P X £ ☎ 0798 586385
Doddiscombsleigh 15Bf
Dodington Hall 23Bg
Dodman Point 11Ca
Dog Falls 251Fi
Dogdyke 153Be
Dogton Cross 247Bb
Dolaucothi Gold Mines 89Ef
P X £ ☎ 05585 359
Dolbadarn Castle 157Bf
Dolebury Warren 45Cd
Dolforwyn Castle 119Eh P
Dolgellau 157Db
Dolgoch 117Eg
Dolgoch Falls 117Eg
Doll & Toy Museum, IOW 31Db
£ ☎ 0983 407231
Dollar 245Ce
Dolphin Sailing Barge Museum
85Eb X £ ☎ 0795 423215
Dolphinholme 183De
Dolwyddelan 157Df
Dolwyddelan Castle 157Df
Doncaster 173Ce
Donington 153Bc
Donington Collection 149Cc
P X £ ☎ 0332 810048
Donington le Heath 149Cb
Donington on Bain 177Bc
Donna Nook Nature Reserve
177Dd
Donnington Castle 53Dd
Donview Visitor Centre 265De
☑ P £ ☎ 0466 794161
Doon Hill 233Cc
Doon of May 215Cd
Doon, The 217Ba
Doonies Farm 267Cd
P £ ☎ 0224 276276
Dorchester, Berks 103Ca
Dorchester, Dorset 25Cd
☎ 0270 625245
Dorfold Hall 167Aa P £
Dorking 37Cf
P £ ☎ 0642 813781
Dorman Museum 201Be
Dornoch 278Dc
Dornoch Firth 278Dc
Dorothy Clive Garden 145Ee
P X £ ☎ 0630 81233
Dorset Cursus 27Ae
Dorset Heavy Horse Centre 27Be
P X £ ☎ 0202 824040
Dorstone 119Gc
Dorusduain 251Ci
Double Waters 13Cd
Douch Wood 217Cb
Douglas, IoM 181Cb
£ P £
Douglas, Strathclyde 227Dd
Doune Castle 241Ef P £
☎ 031 2443101
Doune Motor Museum 241Ef
P X £ ☎ 0786 841203
Dounreay 281Kf
Dove Cottage 195Ee
P X £ ☎ 05394 35544
Dove Dale 147Dg
Dover 43Dd
Dover Castle 43Dd P X £
☎ 0304 201628
Dover's Hill 101Cf
Dowdeswell 101Bd
Down Ampney 101Cb
Down Field Windmill 137Eb
P £ ☎ 0353 720333
Down House Museum & Gardens
63Cb £ ☎ 0689 859119
Down St Mary Vineyard 21Cb
P £ ☎ 0363 82300
Downderry 13Bc
Downe 63Cb
Downham 185Ad
Downholme 199Dc
Downies 267Cc
Downland Farm 17Cd
P X £ ☎ 0237 431255
Downlands Cliffs 23Ca
Downside Abbey 45Ed P X
☎ 0761 232205
Downton 27Cf
Dowsborough 23Bf
Doyden Castle 11Bf
Dozmary Pool 11De
Dracula Experience 205Be
£ ☎ 0997 601923/0904 658775
Dragon Hill 53Cf

Draper's Windmill 43Df ✗
☎ 0843 291696
Draycote Water Park 129Dc ☸
☎ 0827 872660
Drayton Manor 129Ag ☸ ♨
✗☎ 0827 260260
Dreamland-Bembom Brothers 43Dg
✗☎ 0843 227011
Drem 233Bc ⌂ ☀
Drewsteighton 13Fg ⌂
Dried Flower Workshop 145Df ♪
☎ 0270 841336
Drift Reservoir 9Bc
Drimsynie 239Fe ☆ ⌂
Droitwich 125Ad ♨ ☑
Druchtag Motte 215Ec
Druidibeg Loch 273Kf ♥
☎ 0870 238/206
Druidston 87Bc ○
Drum Castle 267Ad ♨ ✗£
☎ 0330 8204
Drumbeg 281Cc ○ ☀
Drumburgh 207Df ○
Drumclog 227Bd ○
Drumclog 1679, Battle of
227Bd ✗
Drumcoltran Tower 217Dc
Druminnor Castle 265Cc ⌂
Drumlanrig Castle 217Df ♨ ✗£
✗£☎ 0848 31682
Drumlithie 267Ab ○
Drummond Castle Gardens 255Fa ❀
☎ 0764 81257
Drummore 215Cb ⌂
Drummuir Castle 269Fb ♨
✗£☎ 054 281225
Drumnadrochit 261Bc ⌂ ⌂ ⌂
Drumpellier Country Park 241Eb ☸
✗☎ 0236 422257
Drumtroddan 215Ec ○
Drumtroddan Marked Rocks &
Standing Stones 215Ec
Druridge Bay 223Ea
Druridge Bay Country Park 223Ea
☸ ☎ 0670 760968
Drusillas Zoo 39Cb ♠
✗£☎ 0323 870234
Dry Hill 39Bf ☀
Dryburgh Abbey 221Be ✚
☎ 031 2443101
Dryhope 219Dg ○
Dryhope Tower 219Dg ⌂
Drymen 241Bd ○
Dryslwyn 89De ○ ⌂
Dryslwyn Castle 89De ⌂ P
☎ 0222 465511
Duart Castle 249lc ♨ ✗£
☎ 06802 309
Duchary Rock 278Ee ☀
Duchess of Gordon's Monument
263Ad
Duckpool 17Bc ☀
Duddon Sands 195Cb
Dudley 125Bg ⌂ ⌂ ⌂ ⌂
Dudley Castle 125Bg ⌂
Dudley Zoo 125Bg ♠
✗£☎ 0384 52401
Dudmaston 123Ef ♨
✗£☎ 0746 780866
Duff House 271Cd ♨ P£
☎ 031 2443101
Duffield Castle 149Be ⌂
Dufftown 269Fa ✚ ⌂ ⌂ ⌂
Duffus 269Dd ⌂ ⌂
Duffus Castle 269Dd ⌂
☎ 031 2443101
Dufton 197Cf ○
Duggleby Howe 192Af
Duirinish 251Aj ○ ⌂ P
Duirinish Lodge 251Aj ❀ P
☎ 059 984268
Duke of Gordon's Monument
263Ad
Duke of Sutherland Monument
278Ee
Dukes Theatre, Lancaster 183Cf ☸
✗£☎ 0524 67461
Duloe 11Ec ⊺ ⌂
Duloe Stone Circles 11Ec
Dulverton 21Ed ❀ ☑
Dulwich 63Bc ⌂
Dulwich Picture Gallery 63Bc ⌂
£☎ 081 693 5254
Dumbarton 241Bc ⌂ ○
Dumbarton Castle 241Ac ⌂
✗£☎ 0389 32167
Dumfries 217Ed ✚ ⌂ ⌂ ⌂
Dumgoyne 241Cd ♥
Dumpdon Hill 23Bc ☀

Dumyat 245Be
Dun Beag Broch 275Ce
Dun Bharpa 273Jc
Dùn Bhruichlinn 235Cd ☀
Dun Caan 275Ee
Dun Carloway Broch 272Dh
Dùn Creich 281Cc ☀
Dun Dornaigil Broch 281Fd
Dun Fiadhairt 275Bg
Dun Ghallain 235Cg ☀
Dun Grugaig 251Bh
Dun Hallin 275Bg
Dun Lagaidh 277Fg ☀
Dùn Nosebridge 235Cd ☀
Dun Skeig 237Cf
Dun Suladale Broch 275Cg
Dun Telve 251Bh
Dun Torcuill 273Lj
Dun Trodden 251Bh
Dunadd Hill Fort 239Cd ☀
Dunaverty Rock 237Ba ☆
Dunbar 233Cc ⌂ ⌂ ☀ ⌂
Dunbar 1650, Battle of 233Cc ✗
Dunbeath 281Mc ⌂
Dunblane 245Af ✚ ⌂ ☑
Duncansby Head 281Pg ☀ ☀ ⚓
Dunchideock 15Bf ○
Duncombe Park 201Db ♨
Duncryne Hill 241Bd ☀
Dundary Castle & Fort 271Ed ⌂
Dundee 257Fc ☀ ⌂ ♨ ⌂ ☑ ⌂
✗£☎ 0890 2834
Dundee Law 257Ec ☀
Dundock Wood 221Ee ❀
✗£☎ 0890 2834
Dundonald 225Cd ⌂
Dundonnell 277Ef ☀
Dundrennan 217Ca ○
Dundrennan Abbey 217Ca ✚
Dunfermline 245Dd ❀ ❀ ⌂
Dungary 271Cb ☀
Dungeness 43Aa ⌂ ○
Dungeness Power Station 43Aa ○
✗☎ 0679 21815
Dungeon Ghyll Force 195De ☆
Dungeon Hill 25Ce ☀
Dunglass Collegiate Church 233Dc
✚ ☎ 031 2443101
Dunham Massey 167Bd ♨ ♨
✗£☎ 061 9411025
Dunkeld 257Bd ✗ ❀ ✚ ⌂
P£☎ 0544 7653
Dunkery Beacon 21Df ☀
Dunkery Hill 21Ef
Dunkerton's Cider 123Ac ⌂
Dunnerdale Forest 195Dd ♥ ⌂
Dunnet Head 281Mg ☀ ⚓
Dunnottar Castle 267Bb ⌂
P£☎ 0569 62173
Dunollie Castle 239Ch ⌂
Dunoon 239Fb ⌂ ☀ ☆
Dunrobin Castle 278Ee ♨
✗£☎ 0408 633177
Duns 233Da ☀ ⌂
Duns Law 233Da ☀
Duns Tew 103Bd ○
Dunscaith Castle 275Ec ⌂
Dunsfold 37Bc ○
Dunsford 15Bf ⌂
Dunsinane 257Dc ☀
Dunskey Castle 215Bd ⌂
Dunsmore 107Bb ○
Dunsop Bridge 183Ee ○
Dunstable 107Dd ☑
Dunstable Downs 107Dc ♥ ☀
Dunstaffnage Castle 239Ch ⌂
P£☎ 031 2443101
Dunstall Castle 125Ab ⌂
Dunstanburgh Castle 223Ed ⌂
✗£☎ 0665 576231
Dunster 21Ef ♨ ⌂ ⌂ ⌂
Dunster Castle 21Ef ♨
P£☎ 0643 821314
Dunsyre 229Bc ○
Duntisbournes, The 97Ec ⌂
Duntulm Castle 275Di ⌂
Dunure 225Bb ⌂
Dunvegan Castle 275Bf ♨
✗£☎ 047022 206
Dunwich 115Eg ⌂ ⌂
Dunwich Heath 115Ef ♥ ⌂
Dunyvaig Castle 235Db ⌂
Dupath Well 13Bd ❀
Dura Den 247Dd ☀
Durdle Door 25Ec ☆
Durham 213Ab ✚ ⌂ ✚ ⌂ ⌂
Durham Castle 213Ab ♨ £
☎ 091 3743800

Durham L.I. Museum 213Ab ⚔
P£☎ 091 3842214
Durisdeer 217Dg ⌂
Durlston Country Park 27Ba ☸
P£☎ 0929 424443
Durn Hill 271Bd ☀
Durness 281Ff ⌂ ☆
Durrington Walls 49Ec ⌂
Dursley 97Cb
Dutch Cottage Museum, Canvey
Island 85Cd ⌂ P£☎ 0268 794005
Duthie Park 267Cd ❀
P£☎ 0224 583155
Dutton Viaduct 163Dc ❀
Duxford 109De ⌂ Y
Duxford Chapel 109De ✚
P☎ 0223 455520
Dwarfie Stane 283Bd
Dwyfor Rabbit Farm 155Eb ⌂
P£☎ 0766 523136
Dyce 267Be ⌂
Dyffryn Ardudwy 157Bc ○ ⌂
Dyffryn Crawnon 91Ef
Dyffryn Gardens 91Db ❀
P£☎ 0222 593328
Dyffryn Tywi 89Ee
Dyffryn Wood 119Ce ♥ ♥
Dyfi Furnace 117Ef ❀ P£
☎ 0222 465511
Dyfnant Forest 159Bb ♥
Dylan Thomas's Boathouse 89Bd ⌂
✗£☎ 0994 427420
Dylife 119Bh ○
Dymock 97Cf ○
Dynevor Castle 89Ee ⌂
Dyrham 49Af ⌂
Dyrham Park 49Af ♨
✗£☎ 02475 822501
Dysart 247Cb ⌂
Dyserth 161Eb ⌂ ☀

Eaglesham 225Ef ⌂
Eardisland 123Bc ⌂
Eardisley 119Gc ⌂
Earl Soham 115Cf ○
Earl Stonham 115Be ○
Earle Hill Museum 223Bd ⚔
P£☎ 0668 81243
Earls Barton 135Ab ✚ ⌂
Earl's Hill 145Bb ☀ ✚
Earl's Palace, Birsay 283Bf ⌂
Earl's Palace, Kirkwall 283De ♨
☎ 031 244 3101
Earlsferry 247Db ⌂
Earlshall Castle 247De ♨
✗£☎ 0334 839205
Earlston 221Be
Earlshall Castle 247De ♨
Earnley 33Cb ○ ⌂
Earnley Butterflies 33Cb ⌂
P£☎ 0243 512637
Earn's Heugh 233Eb ☀
Eas a Chùal Aluinn Falls 277Gj ☆
Eas Fors 249Fd ☆
Eas Urchaidh 239Gh ☆
Easby Abbey 199Dd ✚
☎ 0904 622902
Easdale 239Bf
Easdale Island Folk Museum 239Bf
⌂ £☎ 0852 3370
Easington 192Fa ○
Easingwold 189Bf ✚
Eassie 257Ed ⌂
Eassie Stone 257Ed
East Anglia Transport Museum
141Eb ⌂ P£☎ 0502 518459
East Anglian Railway Museum
113Ec ⌂ P£☎ 0206 242524
East Bank Farm Museum 137Cg ⌂
P✗☎ 0406 351127
East Bergholt 115Ac ⌂
East Burra 285Ec
East Carlton 133Ed ○ ☀ ♪
East Carlton Park 133Ed ☀ ❀ ♪
P✗☎ 0536 770977
East Chiltington Forge 39Ac ♪
East Clandon 37Bg ○
East Coker 25Bf ⌂
East Cowes 31Cc
East Dereham 139Cf ✚ ✗ ⌂
P☎ 0608 737414
East Fortune 233Bc Y
East Garston 53Ce ⌂
East Grinstead 39Ae ♨ ⌂
East Guldeford 41Dd ○
East Hagbourne 53Ef ○
East Ham 63Cd ✚
East Harling 103Af ○
East Harptree 45Dd ○ ⌂
East Harting 33Bd ○

East Head Nature Trail 33Bb ♥
East Hendred 53Df ⌂
East Ilsley 53Df ○
East Kennett Long Barrow 49Ee
East Lambrook Manor 23Ed ❀
P✗☎ 0460 40328
East Linton 233Cc ⌂
East Loch Tarbert 272Dc
East Lomond Law 247Bc ☀ ☀ ⌂
East Looe 11Ec ⌂
East Lulworth 25Ec ○
East Malling 85Ca ⌂
East Markham 175Bb ○
East Meon 33Ae ⌂
East Mount Lowther 227Db ☀
East Park Zoo, Hull 192Dc ♠
P£☎ 0482 594796
East Quantoxhead 23Bg ⌂ ❀ ☆
East Riddlesden Hall 185Dd ♨
P✗£☎ 0535 607075
East Runton 143Gc ○
East Somerset Railway 45Ec ⌂
P✗£☎ 0749 88417
East Surrey Museum 63Ba ⌂
✗£☎ 0883 340275
East Wellow 29Bd ○ ❀
East Wemyss 247Cb ⌂ ⌂ ☆
East Wheel Rose Mine 11Ac ○
P£☎ 0872 510317
East Wittering 33Bb ○
East Wretham Heath 139Cc ♥
East Yar 31Cb ☀
Eastbourne 39Da ☸ ☸ ⌂ ☸ ⌂ ⌂
✗£☎ 0449 612229
Eastbury 53Ce ○
Eastchurch 85Ec ○
Eastdean 39Ca ○ ⌂
Easter Aquhorthies 265Ef
Eastgrove Cottage 123Ed ❀
P£☎ 0299 896389
Eastham Woods 161Hc ☸ ☀
Easthope Wood 145Ca ♥
Eastleach Martin 101Dc ○
Eastleach Turville 101Cc ○
Eastleigh 29Cc ☑
Eastney 33Ab ♥
Eastney Industrial Museum 33Ab ♥
P£☎ 0705 827261
Eastnor 123Ea ○ ♨
Eastnor Castle 123Ea ♨
P✗£☎ 0684 567103
Easton 25Cb ⌂
Easton Farm Park 115Ce ⌂
P✗£☎ 0728 746475
Easton Grey 97Ad ○
Eastrington 189Db ⌂
Eastry 43De
Eastwood, Gtr Man 167De ♥
Eastwood, Notts 149Ce ♪ ⌂
Eastwood Craft Centre 149Ce ♪
P£☎ 0602 254891
Eaton Bishop 123Ba ○
Eaton Bray 107Cd ○
Eaton Socon 109Af ○
Eaves Wood 197Aa ♥
Ebberston Hall 205Bb ♨ P£
☎ 0723 859057
Ebbor Gorge 45Dc ❀ ☆ ♥
Ebbw Vale 93Ad
Ebchester 211Dc ⌂ ⌂
Ebernoe 33De ○
Ebrington 101Cg ○
Ecclefechan 219Cb ♨
Ecclesfield 173Ad ○
Eccleshall 147Ad ○ ⌂
Eccleshall Castle 147Ad ⌂ ❀
P✗£☎ 0785 850250
Eccleston 183Da
Eckington 173Bb
Edale 171Cd ⌂ ☑
Edderton 278Dc ⌂
Eddleston 229Dc ○
Eden Camp 189Dg ⌂
P✗£☎ 0653 697777
Eden Farm Insight 189Dg ⌂
P£☎ 0653 692093
Edenbridge 39Bf
Edenham 151Dc ○
Edensor 171Db ○
Edgbarrow Woods 57Cd ♥
Edgbaston 125Cf ☀ ☸ ⌂
Edgcote 1469, Battle of 103Cf ✗
Edge Hill 103Af ☆
Edge Hill 1642, Battle of 103Af ✗
Edge Hill Museum 103Bf ⚔

P✗£☎ 0926 428109
Edinbane Pottery 275Cg ⌂
P£☎ 047082 234
EDINBURGH 229Df Town plan 231
  Brass Rubbing Centre 231Dc
    ☎ 031 556 4364
  Calton Hill 231Dc
  Camera Obscura 231Bb
    £☎ 031 226 3709
  Canongate Kirk 231Dc ✚
    £☎ 031 556 3515
  Canongate Tolbooth 231Dc
  Castle 231Bb ⌂ P✗£⌂
    ☎ 031 244 3101
  Chambers Street 231Cb
  City Art Centre 231Cb ⌂
    ✗£☎ 031 556 670
  Edinburgh Dungeon 231Ab
    £☎ 031 225 1331
  Floral Clock 231Bc
  Georgian House 231Ac ♨
    P£☎ 031 225 2160
  Gladstone's Land 231Cb ♨
    £☎ 031 226 5856
  Greyfriars Kirk 231Ca ✚
    £☎ 031 225 1900
  Holyrood Abbey 231Ec ✚
    P£☎ 031 556 1096
  Huntly House Museum 231Db
    ⌂ ☎ 031 225 2424 ext 6689
  John Knox House 231Db ⌂
    ✗£☎ 031 556 9579/2647
  Lady Stair's House 231Cb ⌂
    ☎ 031 225 2424 ext 6593
  Magdalen Chapel 231Cb ✚
    £⌂ 031 220 1450
  Mercat Cross 231Cb
  Museum of Childhood 231Db ⌂
    £⌂ 031 225 2424 ext 6645/6647
  National Gallery of Scotland
    231Bb ⌂ £☎ 031 556 8921
  National Monument 231Dc
  Nelson Monument 231Dc
  North Bridge 231Cc
  Old Tolbooth 231Cb
  Palace of Holyroodhouse 231Ec
    ♨ P✗£⌂ 031 556 7371
  Parliament House 231Cb
    ✗£☎ 031 225 2595
  Princes Street 231Bc
  Regimental Museum of The
    Royal Scots 231Bb ⚔
    P£☎ 031 310 5014
  Register House 231Cc ⌂
    ☎ 031 556 6585
  Royal Museum of Scotland,
    Chambers Street 231Cb ⌂
    ✗£☎ 031 225 7534
  Royal Museum of Scotland,
    Queen Street 231Cc ⌂
    ✗£☎ 031 225 7534
  Royal Scots Dragoon Guards
    Display Room 231Bb ⚔
    P✗£☎ 031 225 9846
  St Cecilia's Hall 231Db ⌂
    £☎ 031 650 1000
  St Giles' Cathedral 231Cb ✚
  St John's Church 231Ab ✚
    ✗£☎ 031 229 7565
  St Mary's Cathedral 231Cd ✚
  Scotch Whisky Heritage Centre
    231Bb £⌂ 031 220 0441
  Scott Monument 231Cc
  Scottish National Portrait
    Gallery 231Cc ⌂ ✗⌂
    ☎ 031 556 8921
  Scottish United Services
    Museum 231Bb ⚔
    ☎ 031 225 7534
  Traverse Theatre 231Cb ☸
    ✗£☎ 031 226 2633
  University Collection of
    Historic Musical Instruments
    231Ca ⌂
    ☎ 031 447 4791/650 2805
  Water of Leith 231Ad
  West Register House 231Ac
    ⌂£ 031 556 6585
  White Horse Close 231Ec
Edinburgh Crystal 125Bf ❀
P✗⌂☎ 0968 72244
Edinburgh Royal Botanic Garden
229Df ❀ P✗❀ 031 5527171
Edinburgh Royal Observatory 229Df
☑ P£⌂ 031 6688405
Edinburgh Zoo 229Df ♠
P✗£☎ 031 3349171
Edington 49Cd ⌂
Edin's Hall 233Db

Edith Weston 135Bf
Edlesborough 107Cc
Edlingham 223Db
Edlingham Castle 223Db
Edmondsham House 27Be
☎ 0725 4207
Edmondthorpe 151Bb
Edradour Distillery 255Ge
☎ 0796 2095
Edrom 233Ea
Edrom Church Norman Arch 233Ea
☎ 031 2443101
Edwinstowe 173Da
Edworth 109Be
Edzell 259Cf
Edzell Castle & Gardens 259Bf
☎ 031 2443101
Eggardon Hill 25Bd
Eggesford 21Bc
Egginton 147Ed
Egglestone Abbey 199Ce
Egilsay 283Dg
Egleton 135Af
Eglinton Country Park 225Ce
☎ 0294 51776
Egloskerry 11Ef
Eglwyseg Mountain 159De
Egmanton 175Ba
Egton Bridge 205Bd
Egyptian House 9Bc
Eigg 249Fh
Eildon Hills 221Be
Eilean Donan Castle 251Bi
Eilean nan Ron 281Hf
Elan Valley 119Ce
☎ 0686 626678
Elan Village 119Ce
Elcho Castle 257Cb
☎ 031 2443101
Elegug Stacks 87Ca
Elfin Glen 181Dd
Elford 147Dc
Elgar's Birthplace 123Fc
☎ 0905 333224
Elgin 269Ed
Elgol 275Ec
Elham Valley 43Bd
☎ 0227 831266
Elie 247Db
Eliock House 227Ca
Eliseg's Pillar 159De
Elizabeth Castle 287Ca
☎ 0534 23971
Elizabethan House, Great Yarmouth 141Ed
☎ 0493 855746
Elkstone 97Ed
Ellenden Wood 43Bf
Ellesmere 145Ae
Ellesmere Port 161b
Ellis' Mill 175Db
☎ 0522 541824
Ellisland Farm 217Ee
☎ 0387 74426
Ellister Bird Sanctuary 235Bc
Elmbridge Museum 61Bb
☎ 0932 843573
Elmley Castle 101Ag
Elmley Marshes 85Eb
Elms Cross Vineyard 49Be
☎ 02216 6917
Elmswell 139Ca
Elsdon 223Ba
Elsham Hall Country Park 175Ef
☎ 0652 688698
Elsing 139Df
Elston 151Ae
Elstow 107Df
Elterwater 195Ee
Eltham 63Cc
Elton Hall 135Ce
☎ 0832 280468
Elvaston Castle 149Cd
☎ 0332 571342
Elvaston Castle Estate Museum 149Cd
☎ 0332 571342
Elvington Brickyard Windpump 189Cd
☎ 0904 608255
Elworthy 23Af
Ely 137Dc
Emberton Country Park 107Bg
☎ 0234 713325
Embleton 223Ed
Embleton Bay 223Ed
Embsay Steam Railway 185De
☎ 0756 4727

Emmetts Garden 39Bg
☎ 073 275429
Empingham 135Bf
Emsworth 33Bc
Enard Bay 277Ei
Endsleigh House 13Be
☎ 0872 87248
Enfield 63Be
Englemere Pond 57Dd
English Oak Furniture 119Gd
☎ 0544 230208
English Wine Centre 39Cb
☎ 0323 870164
Ennerdale Forest 207Ca
Ennerdale Water 207Ca
Enstone 103Ad
Eochar 273Kg
Epperstone 149Ee
Epping Bury Fruit Farm Centre 109Da
☎ 0378 78400
Epping Forest 63Ce
☎ 081 508 2266
Epping Forest District Museum 63Bf
☎ 0992 716882
Epsom 61Db
Epsom Common 61Cb
Epsom Racecourse 61Da
Epworth 175Be
Erbistock 159Ee
Ercall Woods 145Db
☎ 0978 355314
Eredine 239De
Eredine Forest 239De
Eriskay 273Ld
Erith Museum 63Dc
☎ 0322 336582
Ermington 13Ec
Errwood Hall 171Bc
Errwood Reservoir 171Bc
Escomb 199Dg
Escrick 189Cd
Esgairgeiliog 117Fg
Esha Ness 285Dg
Esher 61Cb
Esk Dale 201Ed
Eskdale 195Ce
Eskdale Mill 195Ce
☎ 0946 723335
Essenden 109Ba
Essendine 135Cg
Essex Aviation Museum 115Aa
☎ 0255 231312
Etal 139Bb
Etal Castle 223Be
Etchingham 41Bd
Etherow Park 167De
☎ 061 4276937
Ettington 129Ba
Ettrick 219Df
European Sheep & Wool Centre (Leisure Complex) 239Fe
☎ 03013 247
Eurotunnel Exhibition 43Bc
☎ 0303 270111
Euston 139Bb
Euston Hall 139Cb
Evanton 278Ca
Evenlode 101De
Everdon Stubbs 133Ca
Evesham 125Cb
Evesham 1265, Battle of 125Cb
Ewelme 57Ag
Ewenny Priory 91Cb
Ewerby 151Ee
Ewes 219Ed
Ewhurst 37Bf
Ewloe Castle 161Ga
Ewyas Harold 93Cf
Exbury Gardens 29Cb
☎ 0703 891203
Exeter 15Cg
Exeter Canal 15Cg
Exford 23Ae
Exmoor Ales 23Ae
☎ 0984 23798
Exmoor Bird Gardens 21Bf
☎ 0398 83352
Exmouth 15Df
Exton 135Bg
Eyam 171Dc
Eye 139Eb
Eye Castle 139Eb
Eyebrook Reservoir 135Ae
Eyemouth 233Fb
Eyeworth Pond 27De

Eynsford 63Db
Eynsford Castle 63Db
☎ 0892 548166
Eynsham 103Bb
Eype Mouth 23Eb
'F' Pit Mining Museum 213Bc
☎ 091 5140235
Faggs Wood 41De
Failford 225Dc
Fair Maid of Perth's House 257Cb
Fairbourne Railway 157Cb
☎ 0341 250362
Fairburn Ings 189Ab
Fairfield Halls 63Bb
Fairford 101Cc
Fairhaven Garden Trust 141Ce
☎ 0605 49449
Fairlands Valley Park 109Bc
Fairlie 225Bf
Fairlop Waters Country Park 63Ce
☎ 081 500 9911
Fairlynch 15Df
☎ 03954 2666
Fairways Heavy Horse Centre 257Cb
☎ 0738 32561
Fairy Bridge 275Bg
Fairy Glen, Gwynedd 157Ef
Fairy Glen, Highland 261Df
Fairy Grotto, Sark 287Ed
Fakenham 143Db
Falconer Museum 269Cc
☎ 0309 673701
Falconry Centre, West Hagley 125Ae
☎ 0562 700014
Falkirk 245Bd
Falkirk 1298, Battle of 245Bc
Falkland 247Bc
Falkland Palace 247Bc
☎ 0337 57397
Falling Foss 205Bd
Falling Foss Forest Trail 205Bd
Falls of Acharn 255Ed
Falls of Balgy 277Cc
Falls of Bruar 255Ff
Falls of Clyde 227De
Falls of Cruachan 239Cc
Falls of Dochart 255Cc
Falls of Falloch 255Ab
Falls of Foyers 261Ac
Falls of Glomach 251Di
Falls of Leny 241Cf
Falls of Lochay 255Cc
Falls of Lora 239Dh
Falls of Measach 277Ge
Falls of Moness 255Fd
Falls of the Braan 257Bd
Falmer 39Ab
Falmouth 9Fd
Fan Brycheiniog 91Bg
Fantastic Tropical Gardens, Jersey 287Bb
☎ 0534 81585
Fantasy Park, IoW 31Ba
Faraid Head 281Eg
Fareham 29Db
Farigaig Forest Centre 261Bc
☎ 0463 791575
Faringdon 101Db
Farleigh Hungerford 49Bd
Farlesthorpe 177Db
Farley Mount Country Park 29Cd
☎ 0962 846034
Farlington Marshes 33Ac
Farmworld, Wrexham 159Ee
☎ 0978 840697
Farnborough 57Cc
Farnborough Hall 103Bf
☎ 0684 850051
Findhorn 269Cd
Farndale 201Dc
Farne Islands 223Ee
☎ 0665 720651
Farnham 57Cb
Farnham Castle 57Cb
☎ 0252 721194
Farnham Potteries 57Cb
☎ 0252 715318
Farningham 63Db
Farnworth 163Dd
Farr Bay 281lf
Farway Countryside Park 23Bb
☎ 040 487 224
Fasque 259Cg
☎ 0330 45227
Fast Castle 233Ec
Faversham 85Fb
Fearn Abbey 278Eb
Feckenham 125Cd

Feering & Kelvedon Museum 113Db
☎ 0376 570307
Felbrigg 143Gb
Felbrigg Great Wood 143Gb
Felbrigg Hall 143Fb
☎ 0263 75444
Felin Crewi Mill 117Fg
☎ 0654 703113
Felin Geri 89Bg
☎ 0239 710810
Felin Isaf Watermill 161Cb
☎ 0492 580646
Felin yr Aber 117Da
☎ 0570 480956
Felixkirk 201Bb
Felixstowe 115Dc
☎ 05395 31273
Felmersham 135Ba
Fenny Bentley 147Dg
Fenside Dairy Goat Centre 153Df
☎ 0790 52452
Fenstanton 137Ba
Fenton 147Af
Fenton House 61Dd
☎ 071 435 3471
Feock 9Fd
Fermain Bay 287Cd
Fermyn Forest 135Bd
Ferniehirst Castle 221Cc
☎ 0835 62201
Fernwood 23Ab
☎ 0404 812820
Fernworthy 13Ef
Fernworthy Reservoir 13Ef
Ferring 37Bb
Ferry Meadows Country Park 135De
☎ 0733 234443
Ferryside 89Bd
Fetlar 285Hi
Fetlar Nature Reserve 285Hi
Fettercairn 259Cg
Ffestiniog 157De
Ffestiniog Railway 157Ce
☎ 0766 512340
Ffestiniog Railway Museum 155Fb
☎ 0766 512340
Fforest Fawr 91Fg
Ffridd Faldwyn 119Fh
Ffrith Beach 161Ec
Fiddleford 25Ef
Fiddleford Manor 25Ef
☎ 0258 72597
Fidra Island 233Bd
Fife Folk Museum 247Dd
☎ 0334 82380
Fifield Bavant 27Bf
Figsbury Ring 27Cg
Filching Manor 39Cb
☎ 0323 487838
Filey 205Eb
Filkins 101Cc
Finavon Castle 259Ae
Finch Foundry 21Ba
☎ 0837 840046
Finchale Priory 213Ab
☎ 091 3863828
Fincharn Castle 239Ce
Finchcocks 41Be
☎ 0580 211702
Finchingfield 113Bd
Findhorn 269Cd
Findhorn Foundation Community 269Cd
Findlater Castle 269Hd
Findochty 269Gd
Findon, W Ssx 37Cb
Findon, Gramp 267Cc
Fineshade Woods 135Be
Fingal's Cave 249Ec
Fingest 57Bg
Fingle Bridge 15Af
☎ 0647 21287
Fingringhoe Wick 115Aa
Finkley Down Farm Park 53Cb
☎ 0264 352195
Finlaggan Castle 235Cd
☎ 049 681254
Finlarig Castle 255Cc
Finlaystone House & Gardens 241Ac
☎ 047554 285
Finnarts Bay 215Bf
Finsthwaite 195Ec
Finstown 283Ce
Finzean 265Dc
Finzean Bucket Mill 265Cc

☎ 0330 45633
Fionnphort 249Eb
Fire & Iron Forge 61Ca
☎ 0372 375148
Fire Defence Museum 49Cd
☎ 0380 3601
Firestone Copse 31Cc
Firle Beacon 39Bb
Firle Place 39Bb
☎ 0273 858335
Firth of Forth 247Ca
Firth of Tay 247Ce
Fish & Water Gardens, Mickfield 115Bf
☎ 0449 711336
Fishbourne 33Cc
Fisheries & Community Museum, Lossiemouth 269Ee
☎ 034 3813772
Fishers Pit Farm 147Cd
Fishertown Museum 261Ef
☎ 0667 53331
Fishguard 87Ce
Fishlake 173Df
Fishnish Bay 249Hd
Fishtoft 153Cd
Fishtown of Usan 259De
Fittleworth 37Bc
Fitz House 27Ag
☎ 0722 716257
Fitz Park Museum 207Db
☎ 0768773263
Fitzwilliam Museum 109Df
☎ 0223 332900
Five Knolls 107Dd
Five Pond Wood 23Ce
Five Sisters 251Ch
Five Wells 171Cc
Fladbury 125Bb
Flag Fen Excavation 135Ee
☎ 0733 313414
Flambards 9Dc
☎ 0326 574549
Flamborough 192Eg
Flamborough Head 192Eg
Flamingo Gardens & Zoo Park 107Bg
☎ 065 386287
Flamingo Land 201Ea
☎ 0983 612153
Flamingo Park, IOW 31Dc
☎ 0983 612153
Flamstead 107Dc
Flamstone Pin 199Db
Flashdown Wood 21Bc
Flatford Mill 115Ac
Flax Bourton 45De
Fleece Inn, Bretforton 125Cd
☎ 0386 831173
Fleet, Dorset 25Cc
Fleet, Lincs 153Cb
Fleet Air Arm Museum 25Bg
☎ 0935 840565
Fleet Forest Trails 217Bb
Fleet Pond 57Cc
Fleetwood 183Bd
Fletcher Moss Botanical Gardens 167Ce
☎ 061 4341877
Fletching 39Ab
Fleur de Lis Heritage Centre 85Fb
☎ 0795 534542
Flimwell Bird Park 41Be
☎ 0580 87202
Flint 161Gb
Flint Castle 161Gb
Flint Mill 167Da
☎ 0782 502907
Flodden Field 223Ae
Flodden Monument 221Ad
Flookburgh 195Eb
Floors Castle 221De
☎ 0573 23333
Flora MacDonald Memorial Cross 275Di
Flora MacDonald's Birthplace 273Ke
Flora MacDonald's Cottage 275Di
Flora MacDonald's Monument 261Ce
Flore 133Cb
Flotta 283Cc
Flowerdown Barrows 29Ce
Flowerdown Barrows 53Da
Flushing 9Fd
Flying Buzzard 207Bc
☎ 0900 815954
Fochabers 269Fc
Foel Farm Park 155Ee
☎ 0248 430646
Foel-Cwmcerwyn 87De
Fogo Church 221Df

Holly Hill, Kent 85Bb
Hollycombe Steam Collection 33Ce
☎ 0420 474740
Holm of Papa 283Ei
Holmbury Hill 37Cf
Holmbury St Mary 37Cf
Holme Cultram Abbey 207Ce
Holme Lacy 97Af
Holme next the Sea 143Bc
Holme Pierrepont 149Ed
Holme Pierrepont Hall 149Ed
☎ 0602 332371
Holme Pierrepont Park 149Ed
☎ 0602 821212
Holme Wood 207Cb
Holmen's Grove 57Da
Holme-on-Spalding-Moor 189Ec
Holmfirth 171Cf
Holmrook 195Bd
Holmsdale 275Af
Holst's Birthplace Museum 97Ee
☎ 0242 524846
Holsworthy 17Cb
Holsworthy Beacon 17Cb
Holsworthy Woods 17Cb
Holt, Clwyd 163Ca
Holt, Dorset 27Bd
Holt, H & W 125Ad
Holt, Nflk 143Eb
Holt Heath 27Bd
Holt Woodlands 143Fb
☎ 0263 824329 ext 4288
Holton Mill 141Da
☎ 0986 872367
Holtye 39Be
Holy Austin Rock 123Ff
Holy Bush Vineyard 29Bb
☎ 0590 23054
Holy Island, Anglesey 155Cf
Holy Island, Northld 223Df
☎ 0289 89273
Holy Island, Strathclyde 237Fd
Holy Loch 239Fc
Holy Loch Farm Park 239Fc
☎ 0369 6429
Holyhead 155Cg
Holyhead Mountain 155Cg
Holystone 223Bb
Holystone Forest 223Bb
Holywell, Cornwall 9Ef
Holywell, Clwyd 161Fb
Holywell Bay 9Ef
Home of Rest for Horses 107Ba
☎ 0494 488464
Homeston Farm Trail 237Bb
Homildon Hill 1402, Battle of 223Bd
Honeybourne Domestic Fowl Trust 101Cg ☎ 0386 833083
Honeychurch 21Bb
Honeyneuk Bird Park 271Dc
☎ 02616 262
Honeypot Wood 139Cf
Honington Camp 151Ce
Honington Hall 101Dg
☎ 0608 61434
Honister Pass 207Da
Honiton 23Bc
Hook 87Cc
Hook Nature Reserve 29Cb
Hook Norton 103Ae
Hooton Pagnell 173Be
Hop Pocket, The 123Db
☎ 0531 86323
Hope Valley 171Cd
Hopeman 269Dd
Hopes, The, Lothian 233Bb
Hopesay Common 123Af
Hopetoun House 229Bf
☎ 031 3312451
Hopetoun Monument 233Bc
Hopton Castle 119Gf
Hopton Heath 1643, Battle of 147Bd
Hopton-on-Sea 141Ec
Horam 39Cc
Hordle Beach 27Dc
Horkstow 175Df
Horley Reserve 103Bf
Hornby 183Df
Horncastle 153Bf
Hornchurch 63Dd
Horner Wood 21Df
Horne's Place Chapel 41De
Horniman Museum 63Bc
☎ 081 699 1872
Horning 141Ce

Horninghold 133Ee
Horningsham 49Bc
Hornsbury Mill 23Dd
☎ 04606 3317
Hornsea 192Ed
Hornsea Mere 192Dd
Horse Isle 225Be
Horsell Common 57Dc
Horseshoe Falls 159Ce
Horseshoe Pass 159Ce
Horseway Herbs 119Ge
Horsey 141Df
Horsey Wind Pump 141Df
☎ 0263 733471
Horsforth 187Cc
Horsforth Hall Park 187Cc
☎ 0532 478362
Horsham 37Ce
Horsmonden 41Af
Horsted Keynes 39Ad
Horton Country Park 61Cb
☎ 0372 741191
Horton Court 49Ag
Horton in Ribblesdale 197Ea
Horton Park Farm 61Cb
☎ 0372 743984
Horwood 17Ed
Hothfield Common 41Df
Hough-on-the-Hill 151Ce
Houghton 137Ab
Houghton Conquest 107Df
Houghton Hall 143Ba
☎ 0485 22569
Houghton House 107De
☎ 0223 455520
Houghton Lodge 53Ca
☎ 0264 810177
Houghton Mill 137Ab
☎ 0480 301494
Houghton St Giles 143Db
Houghton-le-Spring 213Bc
Hound Tor 13Fe
House of Dun 259Cf
☎ 067 481264
House of Keys 181Cb
☎ 0624 685500
House of Treshnish 249Ed
☎ 06884 249
Household Cavalry Museum 57De
☎ 0753 868222 ext 5203
Housesteads Roman Fort 209Dd
☎ 0434 344363
Hove 43Ac
Hovingham 201Da
How Caple Court 97Bf
☎ 098986 626
How Hill 141Ce
How Stean Gorge 199Ca
Howden 189Db
Howden Reservoir 171Ce
Howe of the Mearns 259Cg
Howell 151Ee
Howell Wood Country Park 173Be
☎ 0302 873401
Howff Burial Ground 257Fc
Howick 223Ec
Howick Hall 223Ec
☎ 0665 577285
Howletts Zoo Park 43Be
☎ 0227 721286
Howtown 197Ae
Hoxne 141Ad
Hoy 283Bc
Hubbards Hills 177Cc
Hubberholme 199Ba
Huddersfield 187Ba
Hugh MacDiarmid Memorial Sculpture 219Ec
Hugh Miller's Cottage 278Da
☎ 03817 245
Hugh Town 9Bb
Hughenden Manor 107Ba
☎ 0494 532580
Humber Bridge 192Cb
☎ 0482 647161
Humber Bridge Country Park 192Cb
☎ 0482 641989
Hummersea Scar 201Ef
Hungerford 53Cd
Hungerford Chalk Stream 53Cd
Hunsbury Hill 133Da
☎ 0858 89216
Hunstanton 143Ac
Hunter's Inn 21Bf
☎ 0805 23832
Hunter's Quay 239Fb

Hunterston Castle 225Af
Huntingdon 135Ec
Huntingtower Castle 257Bb
☎ 031 2443101
Huntly 269Ha
Huntly Castle 269Hb
☎ 031 2443101
Hurlers, The 11Ee
Hurley Chalk Pit 57Cf
Hursley 29Cd
Hurst Castle 29Ba
☎ 0590 42344
Hurst Green 183Ec
Hurstbourne Tarrant 53Cc
Hurstwood 185Bc
Hurworth-on-Tees 199Fe
Hushinish 272Be
Husthwaite 201Ca
Huttoft Bank 177Eb
Hutton Roof Crags 197Ba
Hutton-in-the-Forest 209Aa
☎ 085 34449
Hutton-le-Hole 201Eb
Hyde Hill 85Ce
☎ 0245 400256
Hydon's Ball 37Ae
Hydropathic 239Cg
Hydroponicum 277Eh
☎ 085482 202
Hylands Park 85Bf
Hylton Castle 213Bc
☎ 091 5480152
Hynish 249Ac
Hythe, Hants 29Cb
Hythe, Kent 43Bc
Hythe Marsh 29Cb
Icart Point 287Bd
Iceni Village & Museums 139Ae
☎ 0760 721339
Ickleton 109De
Ickwell Green 109Ae
Ickworth House 139Ba
☎ 0284 735270
Ide Hill 39Bg
Iden Croft Herb Garden 41Bf
☎ 0580 891432
Idless Woods 11Ab
Idridgehay 149Ae
Idsworth 29Bd
Iffley 103Cb
Iffley Meadows 103Cb
Iford Manor Gardens 49Bd
☎ 02216 3146
Ifron Forest 119Bd
Ightham Mote 39Cg
☎ 0732 810378
Iken 115Ee
Iken Cliff 115De
Ilam 147Dg
Ilam Park 147Dg
☎ 0335 29295
Ilchester 25Bg
Ilford 63Cd
Ilfracombe 17Ef
Ilkeston 149Ce
Ilkley 187Bd
Ilkley Moor 187Bd
Ilmington 101Dg
Ilminster 23Dd
Imber (deserted village) 49Cc
Immingham Museum 177Af
☎ 0469 577066
Imperial War Museum, Duxford 109De ☎ 0223 833963
Inchcolm Abbey 245Ed
Inchcolm Island 245Ed
Inchinnan 241Bb
Inchmahome Priory 241Cf
☎ 031 2443101
Inchmurrin 241Ad
Inchnacardoch Forest 251Gg
Inchnadamph 277Gj
Inchree 251Dc
Ingatestone 85Be
Ingestre 147Bd
Ingleborough 197Da
Ingleborough Show Cave 185Ag
Inglesham 101Db
Ingleton 197Ca
Ingleton Glens 197Ca
Inglewhite 183Dd
Inigo Jones Slateworks 155Ed
☎ 0286 830242
Inishail 239Eg

Inkberrow 125Cc
Inkpen 53Cd
Inkpen Common 53Cd
Inkpen Hill 53Cd
Innerleithen 229Eb
Innerpeffray 255Ga
☎ 0764 2819
Innerwick 233Dc
Innerwick Castle 233Dc
Innis Chonnell Castle 239Df
Insh Church 261Ea
Instow 17De
Intelligence Corps Museum 41Df
☎ 0233 625251
Intime Designs 43Ac
Inveraray 239Ee
Inverarish 275Ee
Inverawe Smokery & Fisheries 239Eh ☎ 0866 2446
Inverbervie 259Eg
Inverchaolain Church 239Eb
Inveresk Lodge Garden 229Ef
☎ 031 6656181
Inverewe Gardens 277Cf
☎ 0445 86200
Inverfarigaig 261Bc
Invergarry 251Gg
Invergarry Castle 251Gg
Invergordon 278Da
Inverkeithing 245Ed
Inverkeithny 271Cb
Inverkip 239Gb
Inverliever Forest 239De
Invermoriston 261Ab
Invernaver 281Hf
Inverness 261Ce
Inverness Castle 261Ce
Inverness Sea Lock 261Ce
Inveroran Hotel 239Gi
Inverpolly Forest 277Ei
Inverpolly National Nature Reserve 277Fi
Inversanda 251Cb
Inversnaid 241Af
Inverugie 271Hb
Inverurie 267Af
Iona 249Db
Iona Abbey 249Db
☎ 06817 404
Ipswich 115Bd
Irchester Park 135Bb
☎ 0933 76866
Ireshopeburn 209Ea
Irnham 151Dc
Iron-Bridge 145Db
Irvine 225Cd
Isel 207Cc
Island Davaar 237Cc
Island Hall 135Ec
☎ 0480 459676
Island of Mull 249Gc
Islay 235Cc
Isle Abbotts 23De
Isle Maree 277De
Isle of Grain 85Dc
Isle of Man Steam Railway 181Cb
☎ 0624 663366
Isle of Man Steam Railway Museum 181Aa ☎ 0624 663366
Isle of May 247Fb
Isle of Portland 25Cb
Isle of Purbeck 27Ab
Isle of Whithorn 215Fb
Isle of Wight Steam Railway 31Cc
☎ 0983 882204
Isle of Wight Zoo 31Db
☎ 0983 403883
Isleham 137Db
Isleornsay 275Fc
Isles of Scilly 9Bb
Isleworth 61Cc
Islington 63Bd
Islip 103Cc
Italian Chapel 283Dd
Ivinghoe Beacon 107Cc
Ivington Camp 123Bc
Ivy Hatch 85Aa
Ivythorne Hill 45Cb
Iwerne Courteney 25Ef
Iwerne Minster 25Ef
Ixworth 139Cb
Izaak Walton's Cottage 147Ad
☎ 0785 760278/40204
Jack & Jill Mills 37Ec
☎ 0273 843263
Jackfield Tile Museum 145Db
☎ 0952 882030
Jamaica Inn 11De

☎ 0566 86250
James Dun's House 267Cd
☎ 0224 646333
James Hogg Monument 219Df
James White Cider 115Cf
☎ 0738 685537
Jane Austen's House 57Ba
☎ 0420 83262
Jane Welsh Carlyle Museum 233Cc
☎ 0620 823738
Janet's Foss 185Cf
Jarlshof 285Ea
Jarn Mound 103Bb
Jarrow 213Bd
Jaywick 115Ba
Jedburgh 221Cd
Jedburgh Abbey 221Cd
☎ 031 2443101
Jedforest Deer & Farm Park 221Cc
☎ 0835 4364
Jenkyn Place 57Bb
☎ 0420 22109
Jenner Museum 97Bb
☎ 0453 810631
Jennycliff Bay 13Cc
Jephson Gardens 129Cc
☎ 0926 311470
Jerome K. Jerome Birthplace 147Ca
☎ 0922 653175
Jersey 287Bd
Jersey Flower Centre The, 287Cb
☎ 0534 65665
Jersey Lavender 287Bb
☎ 0534 42933
Jersey Motor Museum 287Bb
☎ 0534 82966
Jersey Pearl 287Cc
☎ 0534 62137
Jersey Pottery 287Db
☎ 0534 51119
Jersey Shire Horse Farm Museum 287Bc ☎ 0534 82372
Jersey Zoo 287Db
☎ 0534 64666
Jervaulx Abbey 199Db
☎ 0677 60226
Jethou 287De
Jevington 39Cb
Jewry Wall Museum 133Bf
☎ 0533 544766
Jim Clark Memorial Trophy Room 233Da
☎ 0361 82600 ext 36
Jinney Ring Craft Centre 125Bd
☎ 0527 84272
Jock's Road 263Ea
Jodrell Bank 167Bc
☎ 0477 71339
John Buchan Centre 229Cb
☎ 0899 20150
John Doran Gas Museum 133Bf
☎ 0533 535506
John Hansard Gallery 29Cc
☎ 0703 592158
John Hastie Museum 227Be
☎ 0357 21257
John Moore Museum 97Df
☎ 0684 297174
John Muir Country Park 233Cc
☎ 031 6653711
John Muir House 233Cc
☎ 0368 63353
John Nicolson Museum 281Oe
☎ 0995 3761 ext 242
John o' Groats 281Og
John Walker & Sons 225Dd
☎ 0563 23401
John Webb's Windmill 113Bd
☎ 0371 830366
John Western Reserve 115Cb
John Wood Collection 233Fb
☎ 0890 771259
Johnnie Armstrong Memorial 219Fe
Johnny Wood 207Da
Johnshaven 259Df
Johnston Tower 259Df
Joicey Museum 213Ad
☎ 232 4562
Jonah's Journey 267Cd
☎ 0224 647614
Jorvik Centre, York 189Ce
☎ 0904 643211
Joseph Parry Cottage 91De
☎ 0685 83704
Jubilee Maze 97Ad
☎ 0600 890360
Jubilee Way 151Ad
Judges' Lodging 183Cf
☎ 0524 32808

Julian's Bower 175Cg
Jullieberries Grave 43Ae ⊓
Jumbles Reservoir 185Aa ☂
☎ 0204 853360
Junction Cottage Canal Centre
93Bd ✿
Jungleland 17Ee ✿🄿✕&
☎ 0271 43884
Jura 235Ef ✿※✿✿☆♨
Jura Distillery 235Ed ♫🄿✕
☎ 049 682240
Jura House Walled Garden 235Dd ✿
🄿☎ 049 682315
Kailzie Gardens 229Db ✿
🄿✕&☎ 0721 70007
Kame Cliff 285Ad ☆
Kearsney Abbey 43Cd ✿
🄿✕&☎ 0304 821199
Keathbank Mill 257Cd 🏛
🄿✕&☎ 0250 872025
Keats' House 61Dd 🏛
☎ 071 435 2962
Kedington 113Ce ○
Kedleston Hall 149Be 🏛
🄿✕£☎ 0332 842191
Keen of Hamer Nature Reserve
285Hj ☂
Kegworth 149Cc ○
Keighley & Worth Valley Railway
185Dc 🚂
Keighley 185Dd 🏛🚂
Keil Point 237Ba ☆
Keillmore 239Ac ○✿
Keinton Mandeville 45Db ○
Keir Hardie Statue 227Ab
Keir Mill 217Df ○
Keiss 281Of 🏛
Keith 269Gc ✿♫
Kelburn Country Centre 225Bf ☂
🄿✕&☎ 0475 568685
Keld, Cumbria 197Be ○†
Keld, N. Yorks 199Ad ○
Kelham 151Af ○
Kellie Castle 247Ec 🏛🄿✕£
☎ 0333 38271
Kelling Aviaries 143Ec 🐦
🄿✕&☎ 0263 711185
Kelmscot 101Db 🏠
Kelso 221De ✿🏛🏛
Kelso Abbey 221De ✿
☎ 031 2443101
Kempley 97Be ○
Kempock Stone 239Gb ○
Kempsford 101Cb ○
Kempt Tower Centre 287Bb ☂
Kempton Park Racecourse 61Cc ○
Kemsing Downs 63Da ☂
Kendal 197Bc ✿🏛🏛
Kenfig Pool & Dunes 91Ac ☂
Kenick Burn 217Bc ♨🗚
Kenilworth 129Bd ✿🏛🗚
Kenilworth Castle 129Bd 🏰
🄿£☎ 0926 52078
Kenmore 255Ed 🏛
Kenmure Castle 217Bd 🏰
Kennack Sands 9Eb
Kensington 61Dd ○
Kent & East Sussex Railway 41Cd 🚂
🄿✕&☎ 05806 5155
Kent Battle of Britain Museum
43Cc 🄵
Kent Rural Life Museum 85Ca 🏛
🄿✕&☎ 0622 763936
Kent Viaduct 197Aa ✿
Kentchurch 93Df ○🏛
Kentisbeare 23Ac ○
Kentmere 197Ad 🏛🏛※
Kent's Cavern 15Cd ☆£
☎ 0803 294059/215136
Kentwell Hall 113De 🏛
🄿✕£☎ 0787 310207
Kenwood House 61Dd 🏛🄿✕
☎ 081 348 1286
Kerrera 239Cg 🏛
Kerries, The 223Bd ※
Kerr's Miniature Railway 259Cc 🚂
£☎ 0241 79249
Kerry 119Eg ○
Kersey 113Fe 🏛
Kessingland 141Eb 🏛🄵
Keswick 207Db 🏛🏛🏛
Kettering 135Ac 🏛🗚
Ketteringham 139Ee ○
Kettleness 205Be ✿
Kettlewell 199Ba ○
Ketton 135Bf ○
Kew 61Cc 🏛✿
Kew Bridge Steam Museum 61Cc 🏛
🄿✕&☎ 081 568 4757

Kew Gardens 61Cc 🏛✿
🄿✕&☎ 081 940 1171
Kewstoke 45Be ○♨
Keyhaven 29Ba 🏛☂
Keynes Park 101Bb ☂🄿&
☎ 0285 861459
Kibworth Harcourt 133Ce ○
Kidbrooke Park 39Be ✿
🄿£&☎ 0342 822275
Kidderminster 123Fe 🏛🏛🗚
Kidlington 103Bc
Kidsgrove 167Ca
Kidwelly 89Cc †✿🏛🏛
🄿✕&☎ 0934 73242
Kielder 209Cg ○🏛♨🗚🏛
Kielder Forest 209Cg ♨♨※🗚
Kielder Water 209Cf 🗚
🄿✕&☎ 0485 533576
Kiftgate Court 101Cg ✿
🄿✕&☎ 0386 438777
Kilbarchan 241Bb 🏛
Kilberry 237Cg ○
Kilbo Path 257Dg
Kilburn 201Ca 🏛🏛
Kilburn White Horse 201Cb ⊓♨※
🗚🄿✕
Kilchattan 235Cg †
Kilchattan Church 237Be ✿
Kilchiaran 235Bd ✿
Kilchiaran Bay 235Ac
Kilchoan 249Ff ○
Kilchoman 235Bd ○⊓🏛
Kilchrenan 239Eg ○
Kilchurn Castle 239Fg 🏰
Kilconquhar 247Dc ○
Kilcreggan 239Gc ○
Kildalton 235Dc ✿
Kildonan 237Fc 🏛
Kildonan 278Fg 🏛
Kildoon 225Ba ※
Kildrummy Castle 265Be 🏰✿
🄿£&☎ 09755 71264
Kildwick 185Dd ○
Killerton 21Eb 🏛🄿✕&
☎ 0392 881345
Killhope Wheel Lead Mining Centre
209Eb ✿🄿£
☎ 0388 537505
Killiecrankie 255Gf ○
Killiecrankie 1689, Battle of
255Gf ※
Killilan 251Cj ○
Killin 255Cc 🏛🏛☆
Killington 197Cb ○
Killingworth 213Ae 🏛
Killochan Castle 215Di 🏰
Kilmarnock 225Dd 🏛♨🗚🏛
🗚🏛🏛
Kilmartin 239Cd 🏛🏛
Kilmersdon 45Ed ○
Kilmichael Chapel 237Eh ○
Kilmory, Strathclyde 239Bb ✿
Kilmory, Arran 237Ec ○⊓
Kilmory Cairns 237Ec ⊓
Kilmory Castle Gardens 239Cc ✿
🄿☎ 0546 602127
Kilmuir 275Ci 🏛
Kilmun Arboretum 239Fc ✿
🄿☎ 039 684666
Kiln Wood 41Cg ☂
Kilnaughton Bay 235Cb
Kilnave 235Be ○
Kilnsea 192Ga ○
Kilnsey 185Cf 🏛☆🗚
Kilnsey Crag 185Cf
Kiloran 235Cg ○✿
Kiloran Bay 235Cg
Kiloran Gardens 235Cg ✿
🄿☎ 095 12312
Kilpeck 123Ba 🏛
Kilpheder 273Ke ⊓
Kilphedir 278Ff 🏛
Kilravock Castle 261Ee ✿
🄿✕&☎ 066 78258
Kilsyth 241Ec 🏛🏛
Kilt Rock 275Eh ☆
Kilve Chantry 23Bg ☆
Kilve Pill 23Bg ☆
Kilvert Gallery 119Fc 🏛🄿£
☎ 0497 820831
Kilwinning 225Ce ✿
Kimbolton 135Cb 🏛
Kimmeridge 27Aa ○🏛
Kimmeridge Bay 27Aa 🏛
Kinbrace 281Jc ○
Kincardine 245Cd ○
Kincardine Bridge 245Cd ○
Kinder Scout 171Bd ☆
Kindrochit Castle 263Dc 🏛🗚🄿

Kindrogan 257Bf ♨🐾※
Kindrogan Hill 257Bf ※
King Arthur's Cave 97Ad ☆
King Arthur's Round
Table & Mayburgh 197Bf ⊓
King Charles' Castle 9Bb 🏛
King Constantine's Cave
247Fd ☆
King Doniert's Stone 11Ed ⊓
King Harry Ferry 11Aa 🏛
☎ 0872 72463
King John's Hunting Lodge 45Cd 🏛
🄿☎ 0934 732012
Kingairloch 251Bb
Kingdom of the Sea 143Ac 🐟
🄿✕£&☎ 0485 533576
Kingdom of the Sea, Great
Yarmouth 141Ed 🐟🄿✕£&
☎ 0493 330631
Kinghorn 247Ba 🏛
Kingley Vale 33Cd ※☂
King's Cave 237Dd ☆
King's Lynn 137Eg †🏛🏛🏛
King's Mill, Clwyd 159Ee 🏛
King's Mill, W Ssx 37Cd ✕🄿£
☎ 0403 783188
King's Norton, Leics 133Cf ○
King's Norton, W Midlands
125Ce ○
King's Own Royal Border Regiment
207Fe ✕£
☎ 0228 327790
King's Own Scottish Borderers
Regimental Museum 233Ga 🄶
£☎ 0289 307426
King's Quoit Burial Chamber
87Da ⊓
King's Sedge Moor 45Cb ✕
King's Standing 39Be ※
King's Sutton 103Be ○
King's Weston Roman Villa 45Df 🏛
🄿☎ 0272 506789
King's Wood, Kent 43Ae ☂
King's Wood, Somerset 45Cd ☂
Kings Wood, W Yorks 173Dd
♨☂
King's Worthy 29Ce ○
Kingsbridge 15Ab ○🏛
Kingsburgh House 275Cg
Kingsbury Water Park 129Bf ☂
🄿✕£&☎ 0827 872660
Kingsbury Watermill 109Ab
🏛🄿✕£&☎ 0727 53502
Kingsclere 53Ec 🏛🏛
Kingscross Point 237Fc
Kingsdale 197Db
Kingsdown 43Dd
Kingsford Park 123Ff ☂
🄿£&☎ 0562 851129
Kingsgate 43Dg
Kingston, Dorset 27Aa ○
Kingston, Grampian 269Fd 🏛
Kingston House 103Ba 🏛
🄿✕£☎ 0865 820259
Kingston Lacy House 27Ad 🏛
🄿✕£&☎ 0202 883402
Kingston Lisle 53Cf ○
Kingston upon Hull 192Cb †🏛🏛
✕♨🗚
Kingston upon Thames 61Cb
🏛🗚
Kingswear 15Bc ✿○
Kingswood Abbey Gatehouse 97Cb
✿☎ 0272 734472
Kingswood, Glos 97Cb ○✿
Kingswood Junction 129Ad ✿
Kington 119Fd ✿✿🏛
Kingussie 255Ej ○🏛
Kinkell Church 267Ae ✿
☎ 031 2443101
Kinlet 123Ef ○
Kinloch Castle 275Ca 🏛✕£
☎ 0687 2037
Kinloch Hourn 251Cg ○
Kinloch Rannoch 255De 🏛
Kinlochaline Castle 249Hd 🏛
🄿☎ 0967 421288
Kinlochbervie 281De 🏛🏛
Kinlochewe 277Ec ☂
Kinlochlaich House Gardens 239Di
✿🄿☎ 0631 73342
Kinlochmoidart 249Ig ○
Kinlochmore 251Ec ○☆🗚
Kinnaird 257Db 🏛
Kinnaird Head 271Gd 🚢
Kinneff 259Eg ○
Kinneil Museum 229Ag 🏛
🄿£&☎ 0324 24911
Kinnesswood 245Ef 🏛🏛

Kinnoull Hill 257Cb ※
Kinross 245Ef ○
Kinross House Garden 245Ef ✿
🄿£&☎ 0577 63416
Kintail Country Park 251Ci ☂
🄿☎ 059 981219
Kintail Visitor Centre 251Ci
Kintore 267Ae 🏛🏛
Kintraw 239Ce ○⊓
Kintyre 237Cd
Kinver 123Ff ☂※☆✿
Kinver Crystal 123Ff ✿🄿
☎ 0384 872833
Kinver Edge 123Ff ※※☆
Kiplin Hall 199Ec 🏛🄿✕£
☎ 0748 818178
Kippen 241De ○
Kippford 217Db 🏛
Kirby Hall 135Be 🏛🄿£&
☎ 0536 203230
Kirby le Soken 115Cb ○
Kirby Misperton 201Ea ○♨
Kirby Muxloe 133Bf 🏛
Kirby Muxloe Castle 133Bf 🏛
Kirk Dale 201Db †☆
Kirk Hammerton 189Ae ○
Kirk Michael 181Cd 🏛🏛
Kirk of Lund 285Gj †
Kirk Sandall 173De ○
Kirk Yetholm 221Ed 🏛
Kirkandrews 217Ba ○
Kirkbean 217Eb 🏛
Kirkby Lonsdale 197Ca †※🗚
Kirkby Malham 185Bf ○
Kirkby Stephen 197Dd †🏛
Kirkby Thore 197Cf ○♨
Kirkbymoorside 201Db 🏛
Kirkcaldy 247Bd ✿♨🏛🗚
Kirkcudbright 217Bd †🏛🏛♨
Kirkham, Lancs 183Cc ○
Kirkham, N Yorks 189Df ○♨
Kirkham House 15Cd 🏛£
Kirkham Priory 189Df ✿
🄿£&☎ 0653 81768
Kirkharle 211Cf ○
Kirkleatham 201Cf ○🏛
Kirkley Hall 211De 🏛
🄿✕£&☎ 0661 860808
Kirkliston 229Cf 🏛🏛
Kirkmadrine Church 215Bc †
Kirkmaiden 215Cb ○🗚
Kirknewton 223Be 🏛
Kirkoswald, Cumbria 209Bb 🏛🏛
Kirkoswald, Strathclyde 225Ba
○🏛
Kirkpatrick Durham 217Cd 🏛
Kirkstall Abbey 187Cc ✿
Kirkstead Abbey 153Af †✿
🄿£☎ 0526 52554
Kirkstone Pass 195Fe
Kirkton 239Bf ○
Kirkton of Glenisla 257Df 🏛
Kirkton of Maryculter 267Bc
🏛✿
Kirktown of Deskford 269Hd
○✿
Kirkwall 283De †🏛♫🏛🗚
Kirkwhelpington 211Bf 🏛
Kirriemuir 257Ee 🏛
Kirroughtree Visitor Centre 215Fe
✿🄿✕£&☎ 0671 2420
Kirtling 113Bf ○
Kirtlington 103Bc ○
Kirton in Lindsey 175Dd †✕🏛
Kisdon Gorge 199Dd ☆
Kisimul Castle 273Jb 🏛
£&☎ 08714 336
Kit Hill 13Be ○✿
Kitchener Monument 283Bf
Kitley Caves 13Dc ☆
Kit's Coty House 85Cb ⊓
Knap Hill 49Ee
Knap of Howar 283Di ⊓
Knapdale Forest 239Bd ♨
Knapp & Papermill Reserve
123Ec ☂
Knapton 143Hb ○
Knaresborough 187De 🏛☆
Knaresborough Castle 187De 🏛
£☎ 0423 503340
Knebworth House 109Bc 🏛☂🏛
🄿£&☎ 0438 812661
Knebworth Park 109Bc ☂
🄿✕£&☎ 0438 812661
Knepp Castle 37Cd 🏛
Knettishall Heath Park 139Cc ☂
🄿£&☎ 0953 818265
Knightley Way 133Ca

Knighton 119Ff 🏛
Knights Templar Church 43Dd †
Knightshayes Court 21Ec 🏛
🄿✕£&☎ 0884 254665
Knightwood Oak 29Ab ☂
Knock Castle, Grampian 265Ac 🏛
Knock Castle, Skye 275Fb 🏛
Knockan 277Hc ○☂🗚🏛
Knockin 159Ec 🏛
Knole 63Da 🏛🄿✕£
☎ 0732 450608
Knoll Gardens 27Bc ✿
🄿✕£&☎ 0202 873931
Knott End-on-Sea 183Bd ○
Knovacks, The 9Ce ☆
Knowe of Yarso 283Cf ⊓
Knowle 129Ad ○
Knowlton Circles 27Be ⊓
Knowsley Safari Park 163Ce 🦁
🄿✕£&☎ 051 4309009
Knutsford 167Bc 🏛🏛
Kyle House 275Gd ○
Kyle of Lochalsh 251Ai 🏛🏛※
Kyleakin 275Gd 🏛🏛○
Kylerhea 275Gd
Kyles of Bute 237Eh
Kyles Scalpay 272Ec ○☂
Kylesku 281Dc ○
Kylestrome 281Dc 🏛☆
Kymin, The 97Ad ※
Kynance Cove 9Db ☆
Kynaston's Cave 145Ac ☆
🄿☎ 0785 223121
Kyson Hill 115Cd ☂
La Hougue Bie 287Db ⊓🚢
🄿✕£☎ 0534 53823
La Mare Vineyards 287Bc ✿
🄿✕£☎ 0534 811178
La Seigneurie 287Ed ✿
£&☎ 048183 2017
Lace Centre, The 149Dd ✿
☎ 0602 413539
Lace Hall, The 149Dd 🏛✕£
☎ 0602 413539
Lacey Green Windmill 107Bb ✕
£☎ 08444 3560
Lackham Agricultural Museum 49Cf
🏛🄿✕£&☎ 0249 443111
Lacock 49Ce 🏛🏛🏛
Lacock Abbey 49Ce 🏛
🄿✕£&☎ 024 973227
Ladder Hills 263Fe
Ladham House 41Be ✿
🄿✕£☎ 0580 211203
Ladle Hill 53Dc ✿
Lady Gifford's Well 229Cd
Lady Herbert's Gardens 129Cd ✿
☎ 0203 832351
Lady Isabella Waterwheel 181Dc ✿
🄿£&☎ 0624 675522
Lady Isle 225Bc ☂
Lady Lever Art Gallery 161Hc 🏛
🄿✕£&☎ 051 2070001
Ladybower Reservoir 171Cd ♨
Ladycroft Agricultural Museum
269Eb ☂🄿£&☎ 03406 274
Ladykirk 223Af 🏛
Lagavulin 235Db ○🏛♫
Laggan Bay 235Bc
Laide 277Cg ○†
Laing Museum 213Ad 🏛✕&
☎ 091 2327734
Laing Museum 247Bd 🏛
☎ 0334 53722
Lairg 278Be 🏛🏛
Lake Vyrnwy 159Ac ☂☂
Lakeland Motor Museum 195Eb 🚗
🄿✕£&☎ 05395 58509
Lakeside & Haverthwaite Railway
195Ec 🚂🄿✕£&☎ 05395 31594
Lakeside 195Ec ○🏛
Lamb Holm 283Dd
Lamb House 41Dd 🏛£
☎ 0892 890651
Lamberhurst 41Ae 🏛✿🏛
Lambert's Castle 23Db ※
Lambourn 53Ce 🏛
Lambourn Downs 53Cf ⊓☂
Lamb's House 229Df 🏛&
☎ 031 5543131
Lamington 227Ed 🏛
Lamlash 237Fd 🏛☆🏛
Lammer Law 233Bb
Lammermuir Hills 233Bb ※♨☂
Lamorna Cove 9Bc
Lampeter 117Da
Lamphey Bishop's Palace 87Db ✿
Lamport Hall 133Dc 🏛🏛
🄿✕£&☎ 060 128272

Piercebridge Fort 199Ee
☎ 0904 622902
Pierowall 283Dh
Pilch Field 103Ee
Piles Mill 21Ef
☎ 0643 862318
Pilgrim Fathers' Memorial 153Cd
Pilkington Glass Museum 163De
☎ 074 4692014
Pill 45Df
Pilsdon Pen 23Ec
Pilton 45Dc
Pin Mill 115Cc
Pinchbeck Engine 153Bb
☎ 0775 725468
Pinchbeck Marsh 153Bb
Pineapple, The 245Bd
☎ 0738 31296
Pines, The 43Dd
☎ 0304 852764
Pioneers' Memorial Museum 185Ba
☎ 0706 524920
Piping Museum, Island of Skye 275Ag ☎ 047081 213
Pirton 109Ad
Pistyll Cain 157Dc
Pistyll Rhaeadr 159Bc
Pitagowan 255Ff
Pitcairngreen 257Bb
Pitch Hill 37Bf
Pitchford 145Cb
Pitlochry 255Ge
Pitlochry Power Station, Dam & Fish Ladder 255Ge
☎ 0796 4111
Pitmedden Forest 247Ad
Pitmedden Garden 267Bf
☎ 06513 2352
Pitmuies 259Bd
☎ 0241 2245
Pitsford Reservoir 133Dc
☎ 0604 781350
Pitshanger Manor 61Cd
☎ 081 567 1227 or 081 579 2424
Pitsligo Castle 271Fd
☎ 0261 812419/812789
Pitstone 107Cc
Pitstone Hill 107Cc
Pitstone Windmill 107Cc
☎ 0296 668227
Pittencrieff House Museum 245Dd
☎ 0383 722935/721814
Pittencrieff Park 245Dd
☎ 0383 731066
Pittenweem 247Ec
Pittington 213Bb
Pittville Pump Room Museum 97Ee
☎ 0242 512740
Pixley 123Da
Place Mill 27Cc
☎ 0202 486321
Pladda 237Fb
Plantasia 89Eb
☎ 0792 474555
Plas Brondanw 157Ce
☎ 0766 771136
Plas Gogerddan 117Ee
Plas Newydd, Anglesey 155Fe
☎ 0284 714795
Plas Newydd, Clwyd 159De
☎ 0978 780277
Plassey, The 159Ee
☎ 0978 780277
Plas-yn-rhiw 155Ca
Platt Hall 167Ce
☎ 061 2245217
Pleasaunce, The 143Gc
☎ 0263 78212
Pleasurewood Hills 141Ec
☎ 0502 513626
Plemont Candlecraft 287Bc
☎ 0534 82146
Plemont Point 287Bc
Pleshey 113Bb
Plessey Woods Country Park 213Ae
☎ 0670 824793
Plockton 251Bj
Plompton Rocks 187De
Pluckley 41Df
Plumpton 39Ac
Plumpton Rocks 187De
Pluscarden Abbey 269Dc
Plym Valley Railway 13Dc
Plymouth 13Cc
☎
Plympton 13Dc
Plynlimon 117Fe

Pocklington 189Ed
Poddington 135Bb
Point Clear 115Aa
Point Lynas 155Eh
Point of Ardnamurchan 249Ff
Point of Ayr 161Fc
Point of Ayre 181De
Point of Lag 215Eb
Poldark Mine 9Dd
☎ 0326 575173
Polden Hills 45Cb
Poldhu Cove 9Dc
Poldrate Mill 233Bc
Polegate 39Cc
Polegate Mill 39Cc
☎ 0323 484763
Polesden Lacey 37Cg
☎ 0372 453401
Police Museum, Ripon 187Dg
☎ 0765 3706
Polkemmet Country Park 245Cb
☎ 0501 43905
Polkerris 11Cc
Pollok Country Park 241Cb
☎ 041 6329299
Pollok House 241Cb
☎ 041 6320424
Polmassick 11Bb
Polperro 11Ec
Polruan 11Dc
Polstead 113Ed
Polstreath 11Cb
Polzeath 11Be
Pont Melin-Fâch 91Cf
Pont y Pair 157Df
Pont-Cysyllte 159De
Pontefract 189Ab
Ponteland 211De
Ponterwyd 117Fe
Pont-Llogel 159Bb
Pontneddfechan 91Ce
Pontrhydfendigaid 117Fc
Pontrilas 93Cf
Pontsticill 91Df
Pontsticill Reservoir 91Df
Pontypool & Blaenavon Railway 93Be
☎ 0495 772200
Pontypool 93Dd
Pontypridd 91Dd
Poole 27Bc
Poole's Cavern 171Bc
Poolewe 277Cf
Pooley Bridge 197Af
Poosie Nansie's 225Dc
Porchester Castle 29Eb
☎ 0705 378291
Porlock 21Df
Porlock Bay 21Df
Porlock Weir 21Df
Port Appin 239Di
Port Askaig 235Dd
Port Charlotte 235Bc
Port Cornaa 181Dc
Port Ellen 235Cb
Port Erin 181Aa
Port Erroll 267Dg
Port Glasgow 241Ac
Port Isaac 11Bf
Port Logan 215Bc
Port Logan Bay 215Bc
Port Lympne Zoo Park 43Bc
☎ 0303 264646
Port Mooar 181Dd
Port Mulgrave 205Ae
Port of Menteith 241Cf
Port Soderick Glen 181Cb
Port St Mary 181Ba
Port Sunlight 161Hc
Port Talbot 91Ad
Port Wemyss 235Ac
Port William 215Ec
Portchester 29Eb
Portdinorwic 155Fe
Portelet Bay 287Ba
Portencross 225Ae
Port-Eynon 89Ca
Portgaverne 11Cf
Portgordon 269Fd
Porth 11Ad
Porth Dinllaen 155Cc
Porth Joke 9Eg
Porth Iago 155Bb
Porth Neigwl or Hell's Mouth 155Ca
Porth Nevas 9Ec
Porth Oer 155Bb
Porth Trecastell 155Df
Porth Tywyn Mawr 155Cg

Porth Yr Ogof Caves 91Cf
Porth Ysgadan 155Cb
Porth Ysgo 155Ca
Porthcawl 91Bb
Porthcothan Beach 11Ae
Porthcurnic Beach 11Aa
Porthcurno 9Ac
Porthgain 87Be
Porthkerry 91Da
Porthkerry Country Park 91Da
☎ 0446 733589
Porthleven 9Dc
Porthluney Cove 11Bb
Porthmadog 155Fb
Portholland 11Bb
Porthoustock 9Fc
Porthpean 11Cc
Porthstinian 87Ad
Porthtowan 9De
Portishead 45Cf
Portknockie 269Gd
Portland Bill 25Ca
☎ 0305 820495
Portland Castle 25Cb
☎ 0305 820539
Portlethen Village 267Cc
Portloe 11Ba
Portmahomack 278Fc
Portmeirion 155Fb
Portmellon 11Cb
Portminian Model Village 192Df
☎ 0262 606414
Portnacroish 239Di
Portnahaven 235Ac
Portobello 229Ef
Portpatrick 215Bd
Portquin 11Bf
Portreath 9De
Portree 275Df
Portscatho 11Aa
Portsea 33Ac
Portslade-by-Sea 37Db
PORTSMOUTH 33Ab Town plan 35
 Australian Settlers Memorial 35Ab
 Cathedral 35Bb
 Charles Dickens' Birthplace Museum 33Ac
 ☎ 070 5827261
 City Museum 35Cb
 ☎ 0705 826261
 Commissioner's House 35Bd
 D-Day Museum and Overlord Embroidery 33Ab
 ☎ 0705 827261
 Dockyard Apprentice Museum 35Ce
 Double Ropehouse 35Ad
 Garrison Church 35Bb
 ☎ 0705 527667
 Guildhall 35Cd
 ☎ 0705 834158
 HMS Victory 35Ae
 ☎ 0705 819604
 HMS Warrior 35Ad
 ☎ 0705 291379
 High Street 35Bb
 Landport Gate 35Bc
 Lombard Street 35Bb
 Mary Rose Exhibition 35Ad
 ☎ 0705 750521
 Mary Rose Ship Hall 35Ae
 ☎ 0705 750521
 Nelson Statue 35Ca
 Porter's House 35Ad
 Quebec House 35Ab
 Round Tower 35Ab
 Royal Naval Museum 35Ad
 ☎ 0705 733060
 Lumps Fort
 Natural History Museum 33Ab
 ☎ 0705 827261
 Pyramids Centre
 ☎ 0705 294444
 Royal Marines Museum 33Ab
 ☎ 0705 819385
 St Mary's Church
 Sea Life Centre 33Ab
 ☎ 0705 734461
 Southsea Castle 35Ab
 ☎ 0705 827261
 Spitbank Fort ☎ 0329 664286
 St George's Church 35Bd
 Sally Port 35Ab
 Spice Island 35Ab
 Square Tower 35Ab
 Unicorn Gate 35Ce
 Victoria Park 35Cd
 ☎ 0705 822251

Portsonachan 239Eg
Portsoy 271Bd
Portwrinkle 13Bc
Posingford Wood 39Be
Postbridge 13Ee
Potter Heigham 141De
Potteries Centre, The 147Af
Potters Museum, Bolventor 11De
☎ 0566 86838
Poulton-le-Fylde 183Bc
Poultry Park 175Eb
☎ 0507 578633
Pow Hill Park 211Cc
☎ 091 3864411
Powderham Castle 15Cf
☎ 0626 890243
Power of Wales 157Bf
☎ 0286 870636
Power Station Visitor Centre, Strathclyde 239Eg
☎ 0866 2673
Powerstock 25Bd
Powfoot 219Ca
Powis Castle 159Da
☎ 0938 554336
Powysland Museum & Canal Centre 159Da
☎ 0938 554656
Praa Sands 9Cc
Prawle Point 15Aa
Precipice Walk 157Dc
Prescot 163Ce
Preservation Trust Museum, St Andrews 247Ed
☎ 0334 77629
Pressaddfed Burial Chamber 155Dg
Pressmennan Wood 233Cc
Prestatyn 161Ec
Prestbury 167Dc
Presteigne 119Ge
Preston, Lancs 183Db
Preston Hall Museum 201Be
☎ 0642 781184
Preston, Leics 135Af
Preston Manor 37Eb
☎ 0273 603005
Preston Mill, Lothian 233Bc
☎ 0620 860426
Preston, Northld 223Dd
Preston Tower 229Ef
Preston Tower, Northld 223Dd
☎ 066 589227
Prestonpans 229Ef
Prestonpans 1745, Battle of 229Ff
Preston-under-Scar 199Cc
Prestwick 225Cc
Pretty Corner 143Gc
Prickwillow 137Dc
Prickwillow Drainage Engine 137Dc
☎ 0353 88230
Priddy 45Dd
Priddy Circles 45Dd
Prideaux 11Be
Priest House Museum 39Ae
☎ 0342 810479
Priest's House, Muchelney 23Ee
☎ 0458 250672
Priests Mill 207Ec
Priest House Museum 275Ef
☎ 06998 369
Prince Charles's Cave 275Ef
Prince Charlie's Cave, Highland 249Hh
Prince Charlie's Cave, Highland 251Eh
Prince Charlie's Cave, Highland 255Cf
Prince's Cairn, The 249Ih
Princes Risborough 107Bb
Prinknash Abbey 97Dd
☎ 0452 812455
Prinknash Bird Park 97Dd
☎ 0452 812727
Prinsted 33Bc
Prior Crauden's Chapel 137Dc
☎ 0353 662837
Prior's Hall Barn 109Ed
☎ 0799 41047
Prior's Park 23Cd
Priorwood Garden 221Be
☎ 089682 2555
Priory Park 107Df
☎ 0234 211182
Priory, The, H & W 97Ef
☎ 0386 89258
Priston Mill 45Ee
☎ 0225 423894/429894

Prittlewell Priory 85Dd
☎ 0702 342878
Privett 33Ae
Probus 11Ab
Provost Ross's House 267Cd
☎ 0224 585788
Provost Skene's House 267Cd
☎ 0224 641086
Prudhoe Castle 211Cd
☎ 0661 833459
Prussia Cove 9Cc
Puck's Glen 239Fc
Puddletown 25Dd
Puffin Island 155Gg
Pulborough 37Bc
Pulpit Hill 107Bb
Pumsaint 89Eg
☎ 0283 840348
Purbeck Hills 27Ab
Purbeck Marine Reserve 27Aa
☎ 0305 264620
Purse Caundle 25Cf
Purton Museum 49Dg
☎ 0793 770567
Pusey 103Aa
Putney 61Dc
Putney Heath 61Dc
Putsborough Sand 17Df
Puzzle Wood 97Ac
Pwllberia Bay 87Be
Pwllduu Bay 89Da
Pwllheli 155Db
Pwllperian 117Fd
Pyecombe 37Dc
Pyrton 103Da
Pythouse 27Af
☎ 0747 870210
Quainton 103Ed
Quainton Railway Centre 103Ec
☎ 0296 75450
Quantock Hills 23Bf
Quantock Pottery 23Bf
☎ 0823 433057
Quantock Weavers 23Bf
☎ 0278 671687
Quarley Hill 53Bb
Quarry Bank Mill 167Cd
☎ 0625 527468
Quarry Caves 23Ca
Quarry Steam Museum 41Bd
☎ 0580 830670
Quarrymill Woodland Park 257Cb
Quart's Moor 23Bd
Quatt 123Ef
Quebec House 63Ca
☎ 0959 562206
Queen Alexandra's Royal Army Nursing Corps 57Cc
☎ 0252 349301
Queen Bower 29Ab
Queen Camel 25Bg
Queen Charlton 45Ee
Queen Down Warren 85Db
Queen Elizabeth Country Park 33Bd
☎ 0705 595040
Queen Elizabeth II Jubilee Park 213Af
☎ 0670 814444
Queen Mary's House, Jedburgh 221Cd
☎ 0835 63331
Queenborough 85Ec
Queen's Park, Glasgow 241Cb
☎ 041 6329299
Queen's View, Central 241Cd
Queen's View, Tayside 255Fe
Queen's Way, The 215Ff
Queen's Wood Arboretum 123Cc
Queen's Wood, H & W 97Be
Queensberry Aisle 217Dg
Queensferry 229Cf
Quendale 285Ea
Queniborough 133Cg
Quenington 101Cc
Quetivel Mill 287Bb
☎ 0534 83193
Quex House 43Cf
☎ 0843 42168
Quilquox 271Fa
Quince Honey Farm 21Cd
☎ 0769 572401
Quiraing 275Dh
Quoyness Cairn 283Fg
Raasay House 275Ee
Raasay, Island of 275Ef

Raby Castle 199Df
☎ 0833 60202
Radbourne 149Ad
Radcot Bridge, Battle of 101Db
Radford Farm 45Ed
☎ 076170106
Radipole Lake 25Cb
Radnor Forest 119Ee
Radway 103Af
RAF Valley 155Df
Raglan Castle 93Dd
☎ 0291 690228
Ragley Hall 125Cc
☎ 0789 762090
Raiders' Road 217Ad
Railway Museum, Wylam 211Dd
☎ 0661 852174
Rainbow Wood 49Ae
☎ 0225 466366
Raindale 205Bc
Rainham 63Dd
Rainham Hall 63Dd
☎ 0402 754908
Rainsbarrow Wood 195Cd
Rainsborough Camp 103Ce
Rainthorpe Hall 141Bc
☎ 0508 470618
Rait Castle 269Ac
Rame Head 13Cb
Rammerscales 219Bb
☎ 0387 811988
Ramparts Field 139Ab
Rampside 195Da
Ramsbury 53Be
Ramsdown Hill 27Cc
Ramsey, Cambs 137Ac
Ramsey, IoM 181Dd
Ramsey Abbey Gatehouse 137Ac
☎ 0284 735480
Ramsey Island 87Ad
Ramsey Mill 115Cc
☎ 0473 890264
Ramsey Rural Museum 137Ac
Ramsgate 43Df
Ramsgill 187Bg
Ramsholt Quay 115Dd
Ramster 33Df
☎ 0428 64422
Randolph's Leap 269Bb
Ranmore Common 37Cg
Rannerdale 207Ca
Rannoch Forest 255Dc
Rannoch Moor 255Ae
Ranworth 141Ce
Ranworth Broad 141Ce
Rare Breeds Park, IOW 31Ca
☎ 0983 852582
Rassal Ashwood 277Cb
Ratcliffe on Soar 149Cc
Rattery 15Ad
Rattray 257Cd
Rattray Head 271Hc
Ravenglass & Eskdale Railway 195Cd
☎ 0229 717171
Ravenglass 195Bd
Raveningham Gardens 141Cc
☎ 0508 46206
Ravensburgh Castle 107Dd
Ravenscar 205Cd
Ravenscraig Castle 247Bb
☎ 031 2443101
Ravenshill Woodland Reserve 123Ec
Ravenstone 107Bg
Ravenstonedale 197Dd
Rawtenstall 185Bb
Reach 137Da
Reading 57Be
Readymoney Cove 11Dc
Reasty Bank 205Cc
Reay 281Kf
Reculver 43Cf
Red Castle 259Ce
Red Head 259Dd
Red Hill, Lincs 177Bc
Red House Museum 187Cb
☎ 0202 482860
Red Wharf Bay 155Fg
Redbourn 107Dc
Redcar 201Df
Redditch 125Cd
Redgrave 139Db
Redhill 37Dg
Redhouse Castle 233Ac
Redhouse Cone 125Af
☎ 0384 71101
Redmire 199Cc
Redmires Reservoirs 171Dd
Redpoint 277Bd

Redruth 9De
Redwing's Horse Sanctuary 141Be
☎ 0603 737432
Reedham 141Dd
Reekie Linn 257De
Reepham 143Fa
Reeth 199Cc
Reg Taylor's Swan Sanctuary 149Ff
Regent's Canal 61Dd
Regent's Park 61Dd
Regimental Museum (Q.O.H.) 261Df
☎ 0463 224380
Regulbrium Fort 43Cf
Reigate 37Dg
Reigate Heath Mill 37Df
☎ 0737 221241
'Remains to be Seen' 271Ea
☎ 0358 7229
REME Museum, Arborfield 57Bd
☎ 0734 763567
Rendcomb 101Bc
Rendlesham Forest 115Dd
Rennibister Earth House 283Ce
☎ 031 244 3101
Rennie's Bridge 221De
Renton 241Ac
Repton 149Bc
Rest and be thankful 239Ge
Restenneth Priory 259Ae
☎ 031 2443101
Restormel Castle 11Dd
☎ 0208 872687
Reuval 273Lh
Revesby 153Cf
Revesby Abbey 153Cf
Revesby Reservoir 153Cf
Revolution House 173Ab
☎ 0246 231224
Rey Cross Roman Camp 199Be
☎ 0833 690606
Reynoldston 89Ca
Rhaeadr Mawddach 157Dc
Rhaeadr y Cwm 157De
Rhaeadr y Cynfal 157De
Rhaiadr Du 157Dc
Rhandirmwyn 119Ac
Rhayader 119Ce
Rheidol Falls 117Fd
☎ 0970 84667
Rheidol Power Station 117Fd
☎ 0970 84667
Rhinconich 281De
Rhinog Fawr 157Cc
Rhobell Fawr 157Dc
Rhodes Memorial Museum 109Dc
☎ 0279 651746
Rhondda Fach 91Cd
Rhondda Fawr 91Cd
Rhondda Heritage Centre 91Dd
☎ 0443 682036
Rhoscolyn 155Cf
Rhosneigr 155Df
Rhôs-on-Sea 161Cc
Rhossili 89Ca
Rhossili Bay 89Ca
Rhossili Down 89Cb
Rhôs-y-llan 155Cb
Rhu 239Gc
Rhubodach 237Fh
Rhum 275Da
Rhyl 161Ec
Rhymney Valley 91Ed
Rhynie 265Bf
Ri Cruin 239Cd
Riasg Buidhe 235Dg
Ribble Head 197Da
Ribblesford 123Ee
Ribchester 183Ec
Ribchester Museum of Roman Antiquities 183Ec
☎ 0254 878261
Riber Castle Wildlife Park 149Bf
☎ 0629 582073
Riccarton Junction 221Ba
☎ 0450 77001
Richard Jefferies Museum 49Eg
☎ 0793 526161 ext 4526
Richards Castle 123Be
Richborough Castle 43Df
☎ 0304 612013
Richborough Port 43Df
Richmond Castle, N Yorks 199Dd
☎ 0748 822493
Richmond, N Yorks 199Dd

Richmond Park, Gainsborough 175Cd
Richmond Park, Surrey 61Cc
Richmond upon Thames 61Cc
Richmondshire Museum 199Dd
☎ 0748 825611
Richmont Castle 45Dd
☎ 0748 822493
Rickinghall Superior 139Db
Riddlesden 185Dd
Ridges, The 57Cd
Ridley Wood 27Dd
Rievaulx 201Cb
Rievaulx Abbey 201Cb
☎ 04396 228
Rievaulx Terrace 201Cb
☎ 04396 340
Rigsby Wood 177Db
Ring of Bookan 283Be
Ring of Brodgar 283Be
Ringmer 39Bc
Ringstead Bay 25Dc
Ringwood 27Cd
Rinns Point 235Ac
Ripley Castle 187Cf
☎ 0423 770152
Ripley, N Yorks 187Cf
Ripley, Surrey 61Ba
Ripon 187Dg
Ripple 97Df
Risley Moss 167Ae
☎ 0925 824339
Rispain Camp 215Fb
Rivelin Nature Trail 171Dd
Rivenhall 113Db
River Dart Country Park 15Ae
☎ 0364 52511
River Wey Navigation 61Bb
Riverhill House 39Cg
☎ 0732 452557/458802
Riverside Country Park 85Db
☎ 0634 378987
Riverside Mill 15Be
☎ 0626 832223
Rivington 183Ea
Rivington Pike 183Ea
Roa Island 195Da
Roaches, The 171Bb
Roadford Reservoir 13Cg
Rob Roy's Cave 241Ag
Rob Roy's Grave 255Cb
Rob Roy's Statue, Peterculter 267Bd
Robert Burns Centre 217Ed
☎ 0387 64608
Robert H. Lewin Furniture 101Dc
☎ 0993 842435
Robert Owen Museum 119Eh
☎ 0686 625544
Robert Thompson 201Ca
☎ 03476 218
Robertsbridge 41Bd
Robertson Museum & Aquarium 225Af
☎ 0475 530581
Robin Hill Park 31Cb
Robin Hood's Bay 205Cd
Robin Welch Ceramics 141Ba
Robin's Wood Hill 97Dd
Robinswood Hill Country Park 97Dd
☎ 0453 413029
Rochdale 185Ba
Roche 11Bd
Roche Abbey 173Cc
☎ 0709 812739
Roche Rock 11Bc
Rochester, Kent 85Cb
Rochester, Northld 223Aa
Rochford, Essex 85De
Rochford, H & W 123Dd
Rock 11Be
Rock Lodge 39Ad
☎ 0444 831567
Rock Wood Ponds 261Ea
Rockbourne 27Ce
Rockbourne Roman Villa 27Ce
☎ 07253 541
Rockcliffe 217Db
Rockingham 135Ae
Rockingham Castle 135Ae
☎ 0536 770240
Rocky Valley 11Cf
Rocquaine Bay 287Ad
Rodbridge Park 113De
Rode Hall 167Ca
Rode 167Ca
Rode Tropical Bird Gardens 49Bd
☎ 0373 830326
Rodel 272Cb

Roderick Mackenzie Memorial 251Fh
Rodmell 39Bb
Rodmell 39Bb
Roehampton 61Dc
Roewen 161Bb
Rogie Falls 261Af
☎ 0833 37334
Roker 213Cc
Rollesby 141De
Rolleston 147Ed
Rollright Stones 101Df
Rolvenden 41Ce
Romaldkirk 199Bf
Roman Army Museum 209Cd
☎ 0697 747602
Roman Signal Stations 255Ga
Romany Museum 33Bf
Romney, Hythe & Dymchurch Railway 43Aa-Bc
☎ 0679 62353/63256
Romsey 29Bd
Ronachan Bay 237Cf
Rookley Country Park 31Cb
Ros Castle 223Cd
Rosa Shafto Nature Reserve 213Aa
Rose Ash 21Cd
Roseberry Topping 201Ce
Rosedale Abbey 201Ec
Rosehearty 271Fd
Roseisle Forest 269Dd
Rosemarkie 261Df
Rosemoor Garden 17Ec
☎ 0805 24067
Rosemullion Head 9Ec
Roslin 229De
Rosneath 239Gc
Ross Priory 241Bd
Ross-on-Wye 97Be
Rossendale Museum 185Bb
☎ 0706 217777
Rossett 163Ba
Rossie Law 245Cg
Rostherne 167Bd
Rosthwaite 207Da
Rosyth 245Ed
Rothbury 223Cb
Rother Valley Country Park 173Bc
☎ 0742 471452
Rotherfield 39Cd
Rotherfield Greys 57Bf
Rotherfield Park 33Af
☎ 0420 58204
Rotherham 173Bd
Rothersthorpe 133Da
Rotherwas Chapel 123Ca
☎ 0902 765105
Rothes 269Eb
Rothesay 237Fg
Rothiemurchus Estate 263Be
Rothley 133Bg
Rothwell, Lincs 177Ad
Rothwell, Northants 133Ed
Rottingdean 39Ab
Rotunda Theme Park 43Cc
☎ 0303 56361/53461
Rougemont House 15Dc
☎ 0392 265858
Rough Castle 245Bc
☎ 031 2443101
Rough Island 217Db
Rough Tor 11Df
Roughting Linn 223Be
Rouken Glen Park 225Ef
☎ 041 6386511
Rousay 283Cg
Rousham 103Bd
Rousham Park 103Bd
☎ 0869 47110
Row Tor 171Db
Rowardennan Forest 241Ae
Rowhedge 115Ab
Rowhill Copse 57Cb
Rowley's House Museum 119Dd
☎ 0743 354811
Rowlstone 93Cf
Rowney Warren 109Ae
Rowsley 171Db
Roxburgh 221De
Roxburgh Castle 221De
☎ 0573 23333
Royal & Ancient 247Dd
Royal Air Force Museum 61De
☎ 081 205 9191
Royal Albert Museum 15Cb

☎ 0392 265858
Royal Army Dental Corps Museum 57Cb
☎ 0252 347782
Royal Army Medical Corps Historical Museum 57Dc
☎ 0252 340212
Royal Army Ordnance Corps Museum 57Dc
Royal Army Veterinary Corps Museum 57Cc
☎ 0252 348527
Royal Bay of Grouville 287Db
Royal Corps of Transport Museum 57Cc
☎ 0252 348837
Royal Crown Derby Museum 149Bd
☎ 0332 47051
Royal Engineers Museum 85Cb
☎ 0634 406397
Royal Leamington Spa 129Cc
☎ 0926 47051
Royal Lochnagar Distillery 263Ec
☎ 03397 42273
Royal Marines Museum 33Ab
☎ 0705 819385
Royal Military Canal 43Ac
Royal Pavilion, Brighton 37Eb
☎ 0273 603005
Royal Pioneer Corps Museum 133Da
☎ 0604 762742 ext 4734
Royal Pump Room Museum 187Ce
☎ 0423 503340
Royal Signals Museum 27Ad
☎ 0258 482248
Royal Tunbridge Wells 39Ce
Royal Victoria Country Park 29Cb
☎ 0703 455157
Royal Welsh Showground 119Dd
☎ 0982 553683
Royalty & Empire Exhibition, Windsor 57De
☎ 0753 857837
Rozel Bay 287Dc
Rozelle House 225Cb
☎ 0292 45447
RRS Discovery 257Fc
☎ 0382 201175
Ruabon 159Ee
Ruan Minor 9Eb
Rubers Law 221Bc
Rubha nan Gall 249Ge
Rubha Reidh 277Bg
☎ 0445 85263
Rudbaxton 87Cd
Ruddington 149Dd
Rudgwick 37Be
Rudston 192Cf
Rudyard 167Da
Rufford 183Ca
Rufford Country Park 173Da
☎ 0623 824153
Rufford Old Hall 183Ca
☎ 0704 821254
Rufus Castle 25Cb
☎ 0305 821804
Rufus Stone 29Ac
Rûg Chapel 159Be
Rugby 133Bc
Rugby Football Museum 133Bc
☎ 0788 536500
Rugby School Museum 133Bc
☎ 0788 543054
Rumbling Bridge 245De
Rumbling Bridge Gorge 245De
Rumster Forest 281Nc
Runcorn 163Dd
Runnymede 61Bc
Runston Chapel 93Dc
Runswick 205Be
Runswick Bay 205Be
Rushbeds Wood 103Dc
Rushen Abbey 181Bb
Rushton 135Ad
Rushton Triangular Lodge 133Ed
☎ 0536 710761
Ruskin Museum 195Dd
☎ 05394 41387
Rustington 37Bb
Rutherglen 241Db
Ruthin 159Cf
Ruthven Barracks 255Ei
☎ 031 2443101
Ruthwell 219Ca
Rutland Farm Park 135Af
☎ 0572 756789
Rutland Museum 135Af

Sennen 9Ac ○
Session Cottage Museum
271Db 🏛
Settle 185Bf 🏠🏤
Seven Barrows 53Cf ⚱
Seven Barrows Nature Reserve
53Cf ⚘
Seven Sisters 91Be ○ ○
Seven Sisters Country Park 39Ca ♈
☎ 0323 870280
Seven Sisters Sheep Centre 39Ca 🐑
P✕£☎ 0323 423302
Sevenoaks 63Da 🏠🛥🖼
Severn Beach 45Dg ○
Severn Road Bridge 97Ab
Severn Valley Railway 123Ef 🚂
P✕£☎ 0299 403816
Sewerby 192Df 🏠
Sewerby Hall 192Ef 🏠🏛
P✕£☎ 0262 673769
Sezincote 101Cf 🏠🏛
Sgurr a' Choinnich 239Fd
♈ ☆ ♣ ☶
Shackerstone Railway Museum
149Ba P✕£☎ 0827 880754
Shader 272Fi ○
Shaftesbury 25Eg ☀🏛🏠
Shakespeare Cliff 43Dc ☀ ☆
Shaldon 15Ce 🏠
Shaldon Wildlife Trust 15Ce ♈
☎ 0626 872234
Shalford Mill 37Af £
☎ 03724 53401
Shallowford 147Ad 🏠
Shambellie House 217Ec 🏠
P☎ 031 2257534 ext 219
Shambles Museum 97Ce 🏛
✕£☎ 0531 822144
Shandy Hall 201Ca 🏠
P✕£ 03476 465
Shanklin 31Cb ☆ 🖼
Shanklin Chine 31Cb ☆
Shap 197Be ○ ✚
Shap Abbey 197Be ✚
Shapwick Heath 45Cc ♥
Shardlow 149Cd ○
Sharpenhoe Clappers 107De ♈ ☶
Sharpitor 15Aa ✿P£☶
☎ 054884 2893
Shatterford 123Ef ○ ♥
Shatterford Lakes 123Ff ♥
P✕£☎ 0299 7403
Shaw 167Df
Shawbost 272Eh 🏠🏛
Shaw's Corner 109Ab 🏠P£
☎ 0438 820307
Shaw's Sweet Factory 257Ec ○
P✕£☎ 0382 610369
Shawsgate Vineyard 115Cf ♣
P✕£☎ 0728 724060
Shebbear Pottery 17Dc ♠P
☎ 0409 28271
Sheep Milking Centre 23Bf 🐑
P✕£☎ 0278 732385
Sheepwash 17Db ○
Sheerness 85Ec 🖼
Sheffield 173Ac ✚ ○ 🏛
Sheffield City Museum 173Ac 🏛
✕£☎ 0742 367731
Sheffield Industrial Museum 173Ac
🏛P✕£☎ 0742 722106
Sheffield Park 39Bd ♣🏛
P✕£☎ 0825 790655
Sheldon 171Cb 🏠
Sheldon Manor 49Bf 🏠
P✕£☎ 0249 653120
Sheldon Park 125Df ♥
P✕£☎ 021 742 0226
Shell Bay 27Bb
Shell Beach, Herm 287De
Shell Grotto, Margate 43Dg ✿
£☎ 0843 220008
Shell Island 157Bc ☆ ♥
Shell Ness 85Fb ♥
Shelley Museum 27Cc 🏛P
☎ 0202 303571
Shellingford 101Eb ○
Shelsley Walsh 123Ed ○
Shelton 141Bc ○
Shepherd Wheel 173Ac ○
☎ 0742 367731
Sheppy's Cider 23Be ♠
P✕£☎ 0873 461233
Shepton Mallet 45Ec ○
Sherborne, Dorset 25Cf ✚🏛
🏛✿☶🏤
Sherborne, Glos 101Cd 🏠
Sherburn in Elmet 189Ac 🏠

Shere 37Bf 🏠🐑🏛
Sheriff Hutton 189Cf 🏠🏛 ✿
Sheriffmuir 1715, Battle of
245Bd ⚔
Sheringham 143Fc ♈🏛🚂🖼
Sheringham Park 143Fc ♈
Sherington 107Bf ○
Sherston Earl Vineyard 49Bg ♣
P✕☎ 0666 840030
Sherston Vineyard 97Da ♣
P✕☎ 0666 840030
Sherwood Forest Country Park
173Da ♈♥🖼P☶
☎ 0623 823202
Sherwood Forest Farm Park 173Ca
🐑P✕£☶ 0623 823558
Sherwood Forest Visitor Centre
173Da 🏠🖼P✕☶
☎ 0623 823202
Shetland Museum 285Fd 🏛
P£ 0595 5057
Shibden Hall 187Bb 🏠
P✕£☎ 0422 352246
Shiel Bridge 251Ch ○
Shieldaig 277Cc 🏠
Shifnal 145Eb ✚🏛
Shifnal Manor 145Eb 🏤
Shildon 199Ef 🏠
Shimpling 139Ec ○
Shin Falls 278Bd ♈ ☆
Shingle Street 115Dd ○
Shining Tor 171Ac ♈♥
Shipley 37Cd ○
Shipley Art Gallery, Gateshead
213Ad 🖼P☶☎ 091 4771495
Shipley Park 149Ce ♈
P✕£☎ 0773 719961
Shipton Hall 123Cg 🏠P£
☎ 074636 225
Shipwreck Centre 11Cc ⚓
P✕£☎ 0726 69897
Shire Horse Farm & Carriage
Museum 9Dd 🐴🐑P✕£☶
☎ 0209 713606
Shirley 125De
Shobdon 123Ad ○
Shoeburyness 85Ed ☀
Shoreham-by-Sea 37Db ♥ ☀
Shorne Wood Park 85Bb ♥
P✕£☎ 0622 696411
Short Heath Park 147Bb ♥
Shortwood Dairy Farm 123Cc ♥
P✕£☎ 0885 400205
Shotley 115Cc ○
Shotley Bridge 211Cc 🏠
Shotley Gate 115Cc ○ ☀
Shotover Park 103Cb ♥ ♈
☎ 0865 715830
Shottery 129Ab 🏠
Shotwick 161Hb 🏠
Shouldham Warren 137Ef
♈ ☶ 🏠
Shrewsbury 145Bc ✚🏛🏤
🛥🐑
Shrewsbury, Battle of, 1405
145Cc ⚔
Shrewsbury Castle & Museum
145Bc 🏛🛥£☎ 0743 354811
Shugborough 147Bd 🏠♥🖼
P£☎ 0889 881388
Shute Barton 23Cb 🏰
Shuttleworth Collection 109Ae ✈
P✕£☎ 076727 288
Siblyback Reservoir 11Ee
Sibsey Trader Mill 153Ce ✕P
£☎ 0246 822621
Sidbury 23Bb ○
Sidbury Hill Fort 53Bc ☀
Sidmouth 23Ba 🏛
Sidney Wood 37Be ♈
Signal Tower Museum 259Cd 🏛
P£ 024175598
Silbury Hill 49De ⚱
Silchester 57Ad 🏠
Silecroft 195Cc ○
Silent Pool 37Bf ♈
Silkstone 171Df ○
Sillerhole 247Cc ○⚒
Silloth 207Ce
Silsoe 107De ○🏠✿
Silton Forest 201Bc ♈
Silverdale 197Aa
Silverdale Glen 181Bb ♈
Silverstone 103Df
Simonburn 211Ae ○
Simons Wood 57Cd ♈
Simonsbath 21Ce ♥
Simonsburrow 23Bd ○ ♥
Simonside 223Ca ♈ ☶

Simonside Hills 223Ca ♈♥☶
Sinclair's Bay 281Oe
Sindon Hills 107De ♈
Singleton, Lancs 183Bc ○
Singleton, W Ssx 33Cd 🏠✿🛥
Sir Francis Cook Gallery 287Cb 🖼
P✕£☎ 0534 63333
Sir George Staunton Park 33Bc
♈ ♥
Sir Max Aitken Museum 31Bc 🏛
☎ 0983 295144
Sir Tatton Syke's Monument 192Bf
Sir Walter Scott's Courtroom,
Selkirk 221Ad 🏛P£☎ 0750 20096
Sirhowy Valley 93Ac
Sissinghurst Castle Gardens 41Ce ✿
P✕£☎ 0580 712850
Sittingbourne & Kemsley Light
Railway 85Eb P✕£
☎ 0634 852672/0795 424899
Sittingbourne 85Eb ♥ ✕
Sixpenny Handley 27Ae ○
Sizergh Castle 197Ab 🏠✿
P✕£☎ 0539 560070
Sizewell Visitor Centre 115Ef ○ 🖼
P£☎ 0728 642139
Skara Brae 283Be ⚱P£
☎ 031 244 3101
Skegness 153Ef ☀ ♥ 🐑🖼
P✕£☎ 0754 763333
Skelbo Woods 278Dd ♈
Skelmorlie 239Fa ○
Skelmorlie Aisle 225Bf
Skelton 187Df ○
Skelton 189Be 🏠
Skelwith Force 195Ee ☆
Skenfrith 93Df ○ 🏰
Skerray 281Hf ○
Skidby Windmill Museum 192Cc ✕
✕£☎ 0482 882255
Skiddaw 207Db
Skinburness 207Ce ○
Skinningrove 201Ee 🏠 ○
Skipness 237Df 🏰 ✚
Skipsea 192De ○
Skipton 185Ce ✚🏛🏰
Skipton Castle 185Ce 🏰P£
☎ 0756 792442
Skirza 281Of 🏠
Skokholm Island 87Ab ♥
Skomer Island 87Ab ♥
Skye, Island of 275
Skye Museum of Island Life 275Ci
🐑P✕£☎ 047052 279
Skyreburn 217Ab ♣P£☶
☎ 0671 82403
Slade, The 103Be ♥
Slaidburn 183Fe ○
Slains Castle 267Eg 🏰P
☎ 0261 812419/812789
Slapton Ley 15Bb ♥ ♈
Slapton Sands 15Bb
Slate Cavern 11Dd ○
Slaughan 37Dd ○ 🏰🏠
Slaugham Common 37Dd ♥
Slaugham Place 37Dd 🏰
Slaughter Bridge 11Df ⚱
Slaughters, The 101Ce 🏠
Sleaford 151De ✚ 🏰🏠
Sledmere House 192Bf 🏠
P✕£☎ 0377 86208
Sligachan All Weather Centre
275Dd P✕£☶ 047852 204
Slimbridge Wildfowl and Wetlands
Trust 97Cc ♥
Slindon 33Dc ○
Slinfold 37Ce ○
Slingsby 201Da ○
Slioch 277Ed
Sma'Shot Cottages 241Bb 🏠
✕£☎ 041 8891708
Smailholm Tower 221Ce 🏠
P£☎ 031 2243101
Smail's Print Works 229Eb ○
£☎ 0896 830206
Small Hythe 41Ce ○♣🏛
Small Water 197Ad
Small World Pony Centre 89Cb ♥
P✕£☎ 0792 390995
Smallcombe Wood 49Ae ♈
Smallhythe Place 41Cd 🏠
☎ 05806 2334
Smarden 41Cf ♥ ✈
Smedmore 27Aa 🏠P£☶
☎ 0929 480719
Smethwick 125Cf
Smirisary 249Hg
Smith Art Gallery 245Ae 🖼
P✕£☎ 0786 71917
Smithbrook Kilns 37Be ✿
P✕☎ 0483 276455

Smithills Hall 167Bg 🏠
P✕£☎ 0204 41265
Smoo Cave 281Ff ☆
Smuggling Experience Museum
205Cd 🏛£☎ 0847 880010
Snaefell 181Dc ○
Snaefell Mountain Railway 181Dc
🚂P✕£☎ 0624 663366
Snailbeach 119Gi ○ ○
Snainton 205Cb 🏠
Snaith 189Cb 🏠
Snake Pass 171Bc ☆
Snape, N Yorks 199Eb ○🏠
Snape, Suffolk 115De 🏠♥🖼
Snape Maltings 115De ♥🖼
P✕£☎ 0728 88303
Snarford 151Ec ✚
Snelsmore Common Country Park
53De ♥ ♥P☎ 0635 42400
Snettisham Nature Reserve
143Ab ♥
Snettisham Watermill 143Ab 🏛
P£☎ 0485 542180
The Sneug 285Ac ☀
Snibston Discovery Park 149Cb 🏛
P£☎ 0530 510851
Snipe Dales 153Df ✕ P
☎ 0522 552222
Snowdon 3560 157Cf 🏔♈
P✕£☎ 0286 870549
Snowdon Mountain Railway 157Bf
🚂P✕£☎ 0286 870223
Snowdonia Visitor Centre 157Df ○
P£☎ 0492 531731
Snowshill Manor 101Bf 🏠
P£☎ 0386 852410
Soar Chapel 117Fb ✚
Soar Mill Cove 13Ea
Soay 275Dc
Soberton 29Ec 🏠
Soham 137Db
Soldier's Leap, The 255Gf
Solihull 125De 🏠 ♥🖼
Solva 87Bd ○
Solva Nectarium 87Bd ♥
✕£☎ 0437 721323
Solway Firth 207
Somerleyton Hall 141Dc 🏠
P✕£☎ 0502 730224
Somersby 177Cb 🏠
Somerset Rural Life Museum 45Db
🏛P✕£☎ 0458 31197
Somerton 45Ca ✚
Sompting 37Cb 🏠
Sorn 225Ec 🏠
Sotterley 141Db ○
Soulby Fell 197Af
Soulseat Loch 215Cd ✿
Sound of Arisaig 249Hh
Sound of Gigha 237Be
Sound of Sleat 249Hi
Sound, The 13Cc
Source of Thames 101Ab ☆
Sourmill Gill Waterfall 207Da ☆
Souter Johnnie's Cottage 225Ba ○
P£☶☎ 065 56603
South Ballachulish 251Db 🏠
South Beach 13Eb
South Cadbury 25Cg ○ ☀
South Creake 143Cb 🏠
South Dalton 192Bd ○
South Downs 39
South Foreland 43Dd
South Gare Breakwater 201Cf ☀
South Gower Coast Reserve 89Ca ♥
P☎ 0792 390320
South Harris 272Cc
South Harting 33Bd 🏠
South Hayling 33Bb ○
South Hill Park 57Cd ♥
South Lancing 37Cb
South Landing 192Ef ☆
South Leaze Sheep Farm 49Eg 🐑
P✕£☎ 0793 523134
South London Art Gallery 63Bc 🖼
P☎ 071 703 6120
South Molton 21Cd ✚🏛🏠
South Petherton 23Ed ○
South Pool 15Ab ○
South Port 239Eg ○
South Ribble Museum & Exhibition
Centre 183Db 🏛P☎ 0772 422041
South Ronaldsay 283Db
South Shields 213Bd ♥🏛🏛
South Stack 155Cg ♥ P✕
☎ 0407 763043
South Stoke 37Bb ○
South Swale 85Fb ♥
South Tidworth 53Bb

South Tyneside Railway 209Db ♥
P✕£☎ 0434 381696
South Uist 273Kf
Southam 129Dc ✚
Southampton 29Cc ♥✕♥🏛🖼
Southchurch Hall 85Dd 🏠
P☎ 0702 467671
Southend, Strathclyde 237Ba
🏠♥
Southend-on-Sea 85Dd 🏛🏠🖼
Southerndown 91Bb 🏠🖼
Southerness 217Eb ○
Southey Wood 135Df ♈ ♥
Southport 183Ba 🏤♥🏛🖼
Southsea 33Ab 🛥
Southsea Castle 33Ab £
☎ 0705 827261
Southside House 61Dc 🏠£
☎ 081 946 7643
Southwater Park 37Cd ♥
P✕£☎ 0403 731218
Southwell 149Ff ✚ ♥
Southwick 29Eb ○
Southwick Hall 135Ce 🏠
P✕£☎ 0832 274064
Southwold 85Fg ○
Sowerby Bridge 185Db
Spalding 153Bb 🏠✿🖼
Sparkford 25Cg ○
Sparkford Motor Museum 25Cg 🚗
P✕£☎ 0963 40804
Sparrowpit 171Bd ○
Spean Bridge 251Fe 🏠
Speedwell Cavern 171Cd ☆
Speke Hall 163Cd ♥P✕£☶
☎ 051 4277231
Speke's Mill Mouth 17Bd ☶
Spelthorne Museum 61Bc 🏛
£☶☎ 0784 461804
Spetchley Park 125Ac ✿
P✕£☎ 0905 65213
Spey Bay 269Fd 🏠🏛
Speyside Heather Garden Centre
263Bf ✿P✕£☶☎ 0479 85359
Speyside Way 269Fc ♥ ☆ ☶
Spilsby 153Df ○
Spinners 29Ba ✿£☎ 0590 673347
Spinningdale 278Cc ♥ ⚱
Spitend Marshes 85Eb ♥
Spittal 233Ga
Spode Museum 147Af ♠🏛
P£☎ 0782 744011
Spofforth Castle 187De 🏰
☎ 0912 611585
Spooyt Vane 181Cc ☆
Spout Force 207Cb ☆
Spring Hill Wildfowl Park
39Be ♥
Springburn Museum 241Db ○
P£☎ 041 5571405
Springfields Gardens 153Bb ✿
P✕£☎ 0775 724843
Springwell 213Ac 🏠♥
Sprivers 41Ae ✿P£
☎ 0892 723553
Sproatley 192Dc ○
Sprotbrough 173Ce 🏠
Spurn Head 192Fa ♥
Squerryes Court 39Bg 🏠
P£☶☎ 09595 62345/63118
Stac Pollaidh 277Fi
Stackpole 87Ca ○ ☆ ♥
Stackpole Reserve 87Ca ♥
Stacks of Duncansby 281Og ♥
Staffa 249Ec ☆
Staffin 275Dh 🏠 ☆
Staffin Bay 275Dh
Stafford 147Bd 🏛🏰🏠🖼
Stafford Castle 147Bd 🏰
Stafford Doxey Marshes 147Bd ♥
Staffordshire Peak Arts Centre
147Cf ♣P✕£☶ 0538 308431
Staffordshire Regiment Museum,
The 147Db 🛡£
☎ 0785 40204
Stagsden 107Cf ○ ♥
Stagsden Bird Gardens 107Cf ♥
P✕£☎ 02302 2745
Stagshaw 195Ee ✿£
☎ 05394 35599
Staindrop 199Df ○
Stained Glass Studio, The 219Cb ○
✕£☎ 0387 84688
Stainforth 185Bf 🏠 ☆
Stainforth Force 185Bf ☆
Stainton 197Bb ○
Stair 225Dc ○
Stair House 225Dc
Staithes 201Ee 🏠

Stalybridge 167De 🏛
Stamford 135Cf ♦🏛🏛 ☑
Stamford Bridge 189De 🏠♦ 🏕
Stamford Bridge, Battle of 189De ✕
Stamfordham 211Ce 🏠
Stanage Edge 171Dd ☆
Stanbury Mouth 17Ac ☆
Stand 167Bf
Standalone Farm Centre 109Bd 🐑
P✕&☎ 0462 686775
Standen 39Ae 🏕 P✕&£
☎ 0342 323029
Standish 163Dg
Stane Street 33Dd ⚓
Stanes of Stofast 285Gg 🗼
Stanford Hall 133Bc 🏕 🏛
P✕&£ ☎ 0788 860250
Stanford in the Vale 103Aa ○
Stanford on Avon 133Bc 🏠🏕🏛
Stang, The 199Cd ⛳ ☀
Stanhope 211Ca
Stanley 257Cc
Stanley Abbey 49Cf ♣
Stanley Force 195Cd ☆
Stanley Park Model Village 183Bc ♣
P✕&☎ 0253 63827
Stanley Spencer Gallery 57Cf 🏛
&☎ 06285 20890/20043
Stanmer 37Eb ○
Stanmore 61Ce †
Stanner Rocks Reserve 119Fd
⛳ ❧
Stanpit Marsh 27Cc ❧
Stanstead Abbots 109Cb ○
Stansted Mountfitchet 109Ec
♣✕🏛
Stansted Park 33Bd 🏕
P✕&£ 0705 412265
Stanton by Bridge 149Bc ○
Stanton, Glos 101Bf ○
Stanton Harcourt 103Bb 🏠🏛
Stanton Moor 171Db 🗼♨
Stanton St John 103Cb ○
Stanway 101Bf ○
Stanway House 101Bf 🏕
P£☎ 0386 73469
Stanwell 61Bc †
Stanwick-St-John 199De ○☀
Stanydale 285De 🗼
Stapeley Water Gardens 145Dg ♣
P&☎ 0270 623868
Staple 43Ce ○♣
Staple Plantation 23Bg ⛳
Stapleford 151Bb 🏠
Star Castle 9Bb 🏰
Starcross 15Cf ○○
Start Point 15Ba ☆
Staughton Farm 133Cf 🐑
P✕&☎ 0533 710355
Staunton in the Vale 151Be 🏠
Staunton Park 119Ge ♣
P✕&☎ 05447 474
Staunton Stables 149Bc ⚘
P✕&☎ 0332 86337
Stawley 23Ae ○
Steall 251Ec ☆
Steamboat Museum 195Fd 🚢
P✕&☎ 05394 45565
Steamport Transport Museum 183Ba P✕&☎ 0704 530693
Steamtown Railway Centre 183Cg 🚂 P✕&£☎ 0524 732100
Stebbing 113Bc 🏠
Steep 33Be 🏠
Steeple Aston 103Bd ○
Steeple Claydon 103Dd 🏠
Steeple Langford 49Db ○
Steetley 173Cb †
Steeton Hall Gateway 189Ac 🏕
P£&☎ 0904 658626
Steinacleit 272Fi 🗼 P
☎ 031244 3101
Stelling Minnis 43Bd ✕ P£
☎ 0227 87627
Stembridge Tower Mill 45Cb ✕ P£
☎ 0458 250818
Stenton 233Cc 🏠
Stephenson Railway Museum 213Bd 🏕 P£&☎ 091 2622627
Stevenage 109Bc 🏛&☑
Stevens Windmill 137Da ✕
☎ 0638 741689
Stevenson House 233Bc 🏕
P✕&☎ 0620 823376
Stevenston 225Be
Steventon 53Dg ○🏕
Stevington 107Cg ○✕

Stewartby Lake 107Df 🏕 P
☎ 0234 228160
Stewarton 225De
Stewartry Museum 217Bb 🏛
P£☎ 0557 31643
Stewkley 107Bd ○
Steyning 37Cc 🏛
Stichill 221De ○
Stickford 153Ce ○♦
Sticklepath 21Ba ○
Stiffkey 143Dc 🏠
Stilton 135Dd ○
Stinchar Bridge 215Eh ⛳🏕
Stinchcombe Hill 97Cb ☀
Stinsford 25Dd ○
Stiperstones 119Gh ☆ 🏠
P☎ 05887 618
Stirling 245Ae 🏕○○🏛
Stirling Castle 245Ae 🏕🏛
P✕£☎ 031 2443107
Stirling Guildhall 245Ae 🏛
☎ 0786 62373/79000
Stithians Reservoir 9Ed
Stob Binnein 255Bb
Stobo 229Cb ○
Stock 85Be ○✕
Stockbridge 53Ca ○
Stockbridge Down 53Ca
Stockghyll Force 195Ee ☆
Stockgrove Park 107Cd ❧
P✕&☎ 0234 228160
Stocking Pelham 109Dc ○
Stockley Farm 167Ad 🐑
Stocks Mill 41Dd ✕ £
☎ 0797 270537
Stocks Reservoir 185Ae ⛳
Stockton-on-Tees 201Be 🏛
Stockwith Mill 153Cf🏛
P✕&☎ 0507 588221
Stockwood Craft Museum 107Dc 🏛
P✕&£☎ 0582 38714
Stodmarsh 43Cf ❧
Stoer 277Ej ☆
Stogursey 23Cg ○🏰
Stogursey Castle 23Cg 🏰
Stoke 17Bd ○
Stoke Abbott 23Ec ○
Stoke Bruerne 103Eg 🏠🏛
Stoke Charity 53Da ○
Stoke D'Abernon 61Ca 🏠†
Stoke Doyle 135Cd ○
Stoke Dry 135Ae ○
Stoke Edith 123Db ○
Stoke Ferry 137Fe ○
Stoke Field 1487, Battle of 151Ae✕
Stoke Fleming 15Bb ○
Stoke Gabriel 15Bc 🏠
Stoke Pero 21Bf 🏠☀
Stoke Pero Common 21Df
Stoke Prior 125Bc ○🏛
Stoke Sub Hamdon 25Af ○
☀✕🏛
Stoke Woods 15Cg ⛳☀🏕
Stoke Woods 21Ea ⛳
Stoke-by-Nayland 113Ed ○
Stoke-on-Trent 147Af ♣♦🏛☑
Stokes Bay 29Da
Stokesay 123Bf ○🏕
Stokesay Castle 123Bf 🏕 P£
☎ 0588 672544
Stokesley 201Cd
Stolford 23Cg ○
Stone, H & W 125Ae ○
Stone, Kent 85Ac ○🏠🐑
Stone, Staffs 147Be
Stone Castle 21Cc 🏰
Stone Creek 192Ea
Stone House Cottage 125Ae ♣
P✕&☎ 0562 69902
Stone in Oxney 41Dd 🏠
Stone Lodge Farm 85Ac 🐑
P✕&☎ 0322 343456
Stone Science, Anglesey 155Ff 🏛
P✕&£☎ 0248 70310
Stoneacre 85Da P£
☎ 0622 862871
Stonebarrow Hill 23Db
Stonefield Castle Hotel Gardens 239Cb ♣P✕&☎ 0880 820836
Stonehaven 267Bb ⛳🏠✕
Stonehenge 49Ec 🗼 P✕&£
Stoneleigh 129Cd 🏠
Stonethwaite 207Da
Stoney Middleton 171Db 🏠
Stoneybrook Pools 147Cc ⛳❧
Stonor Park 57Bf 🏕🏕 P✕£
☎ 0491 63587
Stony Littleton 49Ad 🗼

Stony Stratford Reserve 107Af ❧
Stopham 37Bc 🏠
Stormont Loch 257Cd ❧
Stornoway 272Gg ♣🏛☑
Storr, The 275Dg ☆
Storybook Glen 267Bc 🦆
P✕&☎ 0224 732941
Stott Park Bobbin Mill 195Ec 🏛
P✕&☎ 091 2611585
Stottesdon 123Df ○
Stoughton 33Cd ○
Stoupe Beck Sands 205Cd
Stour Wood 115Bc ❧
Stourbridge 125Bf ○🏛☑
Stourhead 49Ab 🏕♣
P✕&£☎ 0747 840348
Stourport-on-Severn 123Fe ☆❧
Stourton 49Ab ○🏕
Stover Park 15Be 🐎
Stow, Borders 221Af ○
Stow, Lincs 175Cc 🏠✕
Stow Windmill 143Hb ✕£
☎ 0263 720298
Stow-Bardolph 137Ee ○
Stowe 103De 🏕 P£&
☎ 0280 813650/822850
Stowlangtoft 139Ca 🏠
Stowmarket 115Ae 🏛☑
Stow-on-the-Wold 101Ce †☑
Stracey Arms Windpump 141Dd ✕
£☎ 0603 222706
Strachur 239Ee ○
Straiton 225Ca ○🏕⛳
Strand, The 235Cg ☆
Strangers Hall 141Bd 🏛£
☎ 0603 667229
Stranraer 215Be 🏕🏠
Strata Florida 117Fc ○
Stratfield Saye House 57Ad 🏕
P✕&£☎ 0256 882882
STRATFORD-UPON-AVON129Bb
Town plan 131
  American Fountain 131Ac
  Bancroft Gardens 131Bb
  P£& ☎ 0789 267575
  Brass Rubbing Centre 131Ba
  P£& ☎ 0789 297671
  Bridge Street 131Bb
  Butterfly and Jungle Safari
  131Ca ❧P&☎ 0789 299288
  Church Street 131Ab
  Clopton Bridge 131Cb
  Falcon Hotel 131Bb
  P✕&☎ 0789 205777
  Great Garden 131Bb ♣
  £ ☎ 0789 204016
  Guild Chapel 131Bb †
  ☎ 0789 266316
  Guildhall 131Bb £
  ☎ 0789 293351
  Hall's Croft 131Aa 🏕
  ✕£☎ 0789 204016
  Harvard House 131Bb 🏕
  P£& ☎ 0789 204507
  Holy Trinity Church 131Aa †
  P£& ☎ 0789 266316
  Judith Quiney's House 131Bb
  Knott Garden 131Bb
  £& ☎ 0789 204016
  Nash's House 131Bb 🏛
  £☎ 0789 204016
  New Place 131Bb £
  ☎ 0789 204016
  The Other Place 131Ba 🎭
  P✕&☎ 0789 205301
  Royal Shakespeare Company
  Collection 131Bb 🏛✕&
  ☎ 0789 296655
  Royal Shakespeare Theatre
  131Bb 🎭 P✕&
  ☎ 0789 205301
  Shakespeare Centre 131Bc 🏠
  P£ ☎ 0789 204016
  Shakespeare Hotel 131B
  P✕&☎ 0789 294771
  Shakespeare's Birthplace 131Bc
  🏕🏛P✕&£☎ 0789 204016
  Stratford Canal 131Bc
  P✕&☎ 0926 492192
  Stratford New Lock 131Ba
  P✕&☎ 0386 870526
  Swan Theatre 131Bb 🎭
  ✕£&☎ 0789 205301
  Teddy Bear Museum 131Ac 🏛
  £☎ 0789 293160
  Town Hall 131Bb
  Tramway Bridge 131Cb
  White Swan 131Ac
  P✕&☎ 0789 297022

World of Shakespeare 131Bb
  P✕&☎ 0789 269190
Strath Halladale 281Ke
Strath of Kildonan 278Ff
Strath Rory 278Cb ☀
Strathaird 275Ec
Strathaven 227Ce 🏠
Strathcarron 277Db 🏠
Strathclyde Country Park 227Cf 🐎
P✕&☎ 0698 66155
Strathcoil 249Hc ○
Strathdon 265Ae 🏠♣
Strathfarrar 277Ha ❧
Strathisla Distillery 269Gc ♦
P☎ 05422 7471
Strathnaver Museum 281If 🏛
P£☎ 0641 2303
Strathpeffer 261Af 🏠🗼🏛
Strathspey 263Dg
Strathspey Railway 263Be 🚂
P✕&£☎ 0479 810725
Strathy 281Jf ○
Strathy Bog 281Je ❧
Strathy Point 281Jf ☆
Strathyre 241Cg ⛳🏠○
Strathyre Forest 241Cg ⛳🏕○
Stratton 17Bb
Streatley 53Ef 🏠☀
Streens 269Aa
Street 45Cb 🐎🏛
Street Shoe Museum 45Cb 🏛&
☎ 0458 43131
Strelley 149De ○
Strensham 97Eg ○
Stretham 137Db 🏠○
Stretham Old Engine 137Db ♦
P☎ 0223 277346
Stretton 147Ac ○
Stretton Hills 145Ba ☆
Stretton Mill 163Ca 🏛P£
☎ 0606 41331
Stretton-on-Dunsmore 129Dd 🏠
Strichen 271Fc ○🗼
Strichen Stone Circle 271Fc 🗼
Strid Wood 185De ⛳❧
String Road, The, Arran 237Ed
Stroan Loch 217Bc ⛳🏕
Strollamus 275Fd
Stroma, Island of 281Og ○
Strome Castle 277Ca 🏰
Stromness 283Bd 🏕✕
Strone 251Ee ○⛳
Strone House Gardens 239Ff ♣
P£☎ 049 96284
Stronmilchan 239Fg ○
Strontian 251Bc 🏠❧✕🏕
Stroud 97Dc 🏛☑
Strumble Head 87Bf ☀☆
Strumpshaw Fen 141Cd ❧
Stuart Strathearn Crystal 255Fb ♦
P£☎ 0764 4004
Studham 107Dc ○
Studland 27Bb 🏠☆🐎
Studland Heath 27Bb ❧
Studley Royal 187Cf 🐎
P✕&£☎ 0765 620333
Stump Cross Caverns 187Af ☆
Stumpshaw Hall Steam Museum 141Cd 🏛P&☎ 0603 714535
Sturminster Newton 25Df 🏕🐑
Styal 167Cd 🏠🐎♣
Suck Stone 97Ad ☆
Sudbrook 93Eb ○
Sudbury, Derbys 147De 🏠🏕
Sudbury, Suffolk 113De
†🏕🐎☑
Sudbury Hall 147De 🏕
P✕£&☎ 0288 55305
Sudeley Castle 101Be 🏕
P✕&£☎ 0242 602308
Sudley Art Gallery 163Bd 🏛
P✕&☎ 051 2070001
Sue Ryder Foundation 113De ○
P✕&☎ 0787 280252
Sueno's Stone 269Cc 🗼
Suffolk Regiment Museum 139Ba 🐎
P☎ 02843 752394
Suffolk Wildlife & Rare Breeds Park 141Eb ❧🐑
☎ 0502 740291
Sugar Loaf 93Be ☀
Suie Hill 217Cb ☀
Suilven 277Ei ☆
Sulgrave 103Cf ○🏕
Sulgrave Manor 103Cf 🏕
P✕&☎ 0295 760205
Sullington Warren 37Bc ❧
Sullom Voe 285Eg

Sumburgh 285Ea
Summer Isles 277Dh
Summerhouse Point 91Ca
Summerlee Heritage Trust 241Eb ⚒
P✕&☎ 0236 431261
Summerwell Forest Trail 17Bd ❧
Sunderland, T & W 213Cc 🏛
Sunderland, Lancs 183Ce ○
Sunnyhurst Wood 183Eb 🏛
☎ 0254 701545
Sunset Carnation Nurseries 287Bb
♣P✕&☎ 0534 82090
Surlingham Marsh141Cd ❧
Surprise View 207Da ☆
Surrey Heath Museum 57Cd 🏛
P&☎ 0276 686252
Sussex Farm Museum 39Cc 🐑
P✕&☎ 0435 32597
Sutton Bank 201Cb ☀☑
Sutton Bingham Reservoir 25Bf ❧
Sutton Bridge 153Db ○
Sutton Cheney 129Dg ○
Sutton Coldfield 147Da 🐎☑
Sutton Common 115Dd 🏕
Sutton Courteney 53Ce ○
Sutton Hoo 115Cd 🗼
Sutton on Sea 177Ec
Sutton Park, N Yorks189Bf 🏕
P✕£& 0347 810249
Sutton Park, W Midlands 147Ca 🐎
☑P✕&☎ 0213 556370
Sutton Scarsdale Hall 173Ba 🏰
P☎ 0246 850705
Sutton Valence 41Cf ○🏰
Sutton Waldron 25Ef ○
Sutton Walls 123Cb ☀
Sutton Windmill 141Cf ✕
P£&☎ 0692 581195
Swaffham 139Be
Swaffham Bulbeck 137Da 🏠
Swaffham Prior 137Da ○
Swaffham Warren 139Af ⛳🏕
Swainby 201Bd ○
Swalcliffe 103Ae ○
Swaledale 199Bc
Swaledale Folk Museum 199Cc 🏛
P£☎ 0748 84373
Swallow Falls 157Df ♣♨🏕
Swallowfield Park 57Bd 🏕
P£&☎ 0734 883815
Swanage 27Ba 🐎🏕
Swanbourne 107Bd ○
Swanbourne Lake 37Bb ❧
Swanscombe 85Bc
Swansea 89Eb 🏕♣♦🏛☑
Swansea Bay 89Eb
Swansea Valley 91Ae
Swanton Mill 43Ac ✕ P
☎ 0233 720223
Swarkestone 149Bc ○○
Swarkestone Bridge 149Bc ♦
Sweetheart Abbey 217Ec ♣
Swell Wood 23De ❧
Swettenham Mill 167Cb 🏛
Swimbridge 21Be ○
Swinbrook 101Dd ○
Swindon & Cricklade Railway 101Ca 🚂P✕&☎ 0793 771615
Swindon 49Eg 🏕🐎☑
Swindon Railway Museum 49Eg 🏛
✕£☎ 0793 493189
Swine 192Dc ○
Swinsty Reservoir 187Be 🏕
Swiss Garden 109Ae ♣
P✕£&☎ 0234 228330
Swynnerton 147Ae 🏠
Sydling St Nicholas 25Cd ○
Sygun Copper Mine 157Ce ♦
P✕£☎ 0766 86595
Symbister 285Gf🏠
Symonds Cider 123Db ♦
P£☎ 0855 490211
Symonds Yat 97Ad ☀☆
Syon House 61Cc 🐎❧🚜
P✕£&☎ 081 560 0881
Syon Park 61Cc 🐎🚜 P✕£&
☎ 081 560 0881
Syre 281Hd ○⛳
Sywell Park 133Eb 🐎
P✕&☎ 0604 810970
Tabley House 167Bc 🏕
P✕£&☎ 0565 650888
Taddington Moor 171Cc ✕
Taf Fawr Valley 91Cd ⛳⚘❧
Taf Fechan Forest 91Df ⛳❧
Taf Fechan Valley 91Df ⛳☀❧
Taff Vale 91Dd
Tain 278Dc ♣🏛

Talgarth 119Eb 🏰 †
Talisker Distillery 275Ce ⚓
☎ 047842 203
Talkin Tarn Country Park 209Bc ⚲
P✕🅖☎ 0697 73129
Tall Trees Walk 29Ab ⚘
Talland Bay 11Ec
Talley 89Ef ✿ ✤
Talley Abbey 89Ef ✤ P£
☎ 0222 465511
Talmine 281Gf ○
Talybont 93Af 🏠
Tal-y-bont, Dyfed 117Ee 🏠
Tal-y-bont, Gwynedd 157Bc
○ 🏠
Talybont Reservoir 91Ef
Talybont Valley 91Df ⚘ ☀ 🎋
Talyllyn Railway 117Eg 🚂
P✕🅖☎ 0654 710472
Tam O'Shanter Museum
225Cc 🏛
Tamar Lakes 17Bc ⚓
Tamar Otter Park 13Ag 🦦
P✕🅖☎ 0566 85646
Tamdhu Distillery 269Db
P☎ 03406 486
Tamnavulin-Glenlivet Distillery
263Ef ⚓ P☎ 08073 442
Tamworth 129Bg 🏰🏠
Tan Hill 199Bd
Tanat Valley 159Cc
Tandle Hill Park 167Df ⚲
P✕☎ 061 6272608
Tanfield 211Dc ○
Tanfield Railway 211Ec 🚂
P✕🅖☎ 091 2742002
Tangmere 33Dc ⦿ P✕🅖
☎ 0243 775223
Tankerness House 283De 🏛
£☎ 0856 873191
Tannadice 259Ae 🏠
Tantallon Castle 233Bd 🏰
P£ 031 2443101
Tap o' Noth 265Bf ☀
Tapeley Park 17Dc ✿
P✕🅖☎ 0271 860528
Tarbat Ness 278Fc 🔆 🏠 ⚓
Tarbert, Lewis 272Dd 🏠 ⚓
Tarbert, Strathclyde 237Dg
🏠 🏠 🏰
Tarbet, Strathclyde 241Af ○
Tarbolton 225Dc 🏠 ○
Tardebigge Locks 125Bd ✿
P☎ 0527 72572
Tarfside 265Ba ○
Tarnbrook 183De ○
Tarnbrook Wyre 183De
Tarporley 163Db 🏠
Tarr Steps 21De 🏛
Tarves 267Bg 🏠 🏰
Tattershall 153Be ⊚ 🏰 🏰
Tattershall Castle 153Bf ⊚ 🏰
P£🅖 0526 42543
Tattershall College 153Bf ⊚
☎ 0246 822621
Tattershall Park 153Bf Ω
P✕£ 0526 43193
Tatton Park 167Bd 🏰 🎋
P✕🅖☎ 0565 750250
Taunton 23Ce ⚓ ⚓ 🏛 🎠
Taunton Cider 23Be ⚓
P£🅖 0823 332211
Taversoe Tuick 283Df 🏛
Tavistock 13Cc
Tay Bridges 247Ce and De
Taynuilt 239Eh 🏠
Tayport 247De
Tayvallich 239Bc 🏠
Tealby 177Ad 🏠
Tealing 257Fc 🏠 🏛
Techniquest 93Aa ✿
P✕£☎ 0222 460211
Teddy Bear Museum, Broadway
101Bf 🏛 P£🅖☎ 0386 858323
Teffont Evias 27Ag 🏠 ✿
Tegg's Nose Park 167Dc 🎋 ☀ 🎋
P✕🅖☎ 0625 614279
Tehidy Woods 9De ⚲ 🎋
Teifi Valley Railway 89Bg 🚂
P✕£🅖 0559 371077
Teigh 151Bb ○
Teignmouth 15Ce 🏛
Telford Horsehay Steam Trust
145Db 🏠 P✕🅖☎ 0952 244919
Telford Memorial 219Ec
Tellisford 49Bd ✿
Telscombe 39Bb 🏠
Temple 229Ed ○

Temple Guiting 101Be ○
Temple Manor 85Cb 🏰 P£
☎ 0634 402276
Temple Newsam 187Dc 🏰 🎋 🎋
P✕🅖☎ 0532 647321
Temple Sowerby 197Cf ✿ ✿
Temple Wood 239Cd 🏛
Templecombe 25Dg ○
Tenbury Wells 123Cd 🏛 🗓
Tenby 87Eb † 🏠 🏠 ⚓ 🏛
Tennis Museum 61Dc 🏛 P£
☎ 081 946 6131
Tennyson Down 31Ab ☀ 🏛
Tenterden 41Ce † 🏠 🏛
Tenterden Vineyards 41Ce ✿
P✕£☎ 0580 63033
Tentsmuir Point 247De ✿ 🎋
Terling 113Cb ○
Terrington St Clement 137Dg
○ ✿
Terrington St Clement 153Eb ○
Tetbury 97Db 🏛 🗓
Tetford 177Cb 🏠
Tetney Haven 177Ce ⚓
Tetney Marshes 177Ce ⚓
Teversal 149Cg ○
Teviothead 219Fe 🏠
Tewkesbury 97Df ✕ ✤ 🏰 🏰
Tewkesbury 1471, Battle of
97Df ✕
Teynham 85Eb ○
Thainstone Agricultural Centre
267Ae 🏠 P✕🅖☎ 0467 23700
Thame 103Eb ○
Thamesmead 63Cd
Thatcham Reed Beds 53Ed
Thaxted 113Bd 🏠 🌾
Theatr Ardudwy 157Bd 🎭
P✕£🅖☎ 0766 780667
Theatr Mwldan 87Ef 🎭
P✕£🅖☎ 0239 621200
Theddlethorpe All Saints
177Dc ○
Theddlethorpe St Helen 177Dc ○
Thelnetham Windmill 139Db 🌬
Therfield 109Cd ○
Therfield Heath 109Ce 🏛
Thetford 139Bc 🏠 🏰 🏰
Thetford Forest 139Bc ⚲
Thetford Forest 139Bc ⚲
Thetford Priory 139Bc ✤
P☎ 02234 55520
Thetford Warren Lodge 139Bc 🏰
☎ 0223 455550
Thieves Wood 149Df ⚲ ⚓ 🎋
Thirlestane Castle 221Bf 🏰
P✕£ 05782 430
Thirlmere 207Ea ☀ 🎋
Thirsk 201Bb ○
Tholt-e-Will 181Cc ⚓ ☆
Thomas Bewick Museum 211Cd 🏛
P£🅖 0661 843276
Thomas Muir Museum 241Db 🏛
P🅖☎ 041 7751185
Thomason Foss 205Bd ☆
Thompson's Bottom Visitor Centre
151Df P☎ 0529 414155
Thomson Memorial Seat 237Fd ✿
Thornborough Circles 199Ea 🏛
Thornbury, Avon 97Bb ✿
Thornbury, Devon 17Db 🏠 🏰
Thorndon Park 85Be ⚓
P✕🅖☎ 0277 211250
Thorner 187Dc 🏠
Thorney 137Ae 🏠 🏠
Thorney Island 33Bc
Thornhill 217Df 🏠
Thornthwaite 207Db 🏛
Thornthwaite Galleries 207Db 🏛
P✕🅖☎ 0596 82248
Thornton, Lancs 183Bd 🌾
Thornton, Leics 149Ca ○
Thornton Abbey 175Ff ✤
P£🅖 0469 40357
Thornton Dale 205Bb 🏠
Thornton Force 197Ca ☆
Thorpe Cloud 147Dg ○
Thorpe Market 143Gb ○
P£🅖☎ 0209 218198
Thorpe Park 61Bb Ω
P✕£🅖☎ 0932 562633
Thorpe Perrow Arboretum
199Eb ✤ P£
Thorpe Salvin 173Cc 🏠
Thorpeness 115Ee 🏠 🌬
Threave Castle 217Cc ⚓ 🏰
Threave Garden and Wildlife Centre
217Cc 🏠 ⚓ P£🅖☎ 0556 2575
Three Choirs Vineyard 97Ce ✿
P✕🅖 053185 223
Three Corners Vineyard 43De ✿

P✕🅖☎ 0304 812025
Three Shire Heads 171Bb ☀
Three Tuns Brewery 119Gg ⚓
P✕🅖☎ 0588 638797
Threecliff Bay 89Da 🏛
Threekingham 151Dd 🏠
Threlkeld 207Eb 🏠
Throwley 85Ea 🏠
Thrumpton Hall 149Dd 🏰
P£🅖 0602 830333
Thrunton Wood 223Cb ⚲ ⚓ 🏛
P✕🅖☎ 0709 850353
Thrybergh Country Park 173Bd 🎋
Thurgarton, Nflk 143Fb ○
Thurgarton, Notts 149Ee ○
Thurlbear 23Ce ○
Thurlestone 15Eb ○
Thurne Dyke Wind Pump 141De ✕
☎ 0603 222706
Thurrock Local History Museum
85Bc 🏛 P✕🅖🅖☎ 0375 390000
Thursford Collection 143Db 🏛
P£🅖 0328 878477
Thursford Green 143Db ○ 🏛
Thursley 57Da ⚓
Thursley Nature Reserve 57Db ⚓
Thurso 281Mf ⦿ 🏠 🏛
Thurstaston 161Gc 🏠 ☀
Thurstaston Hill 161Gc ☀
Thwaite 199Ac ○
Thwaite Mills 187Dc 🏛
P£🅖 0532 496453
Ticehurst 41Ae ○
Tichborne 29De ○
Tickencote 135Bf ○
Tickhill 173Cd † 🏠
Tickmore Pottery 159Dc ⚲
P£🅖 0601 661842
Ticknall 149Bc 🏠 🏰 ✿
Tickover 135Bf ○
Tideswell 171Cc ○
Tighnabruaich 239Db 🏠
Tilbury Fort 85Bc ⚓ P£
☎ 0375 858489
Tilford 57Cb 🏠 🏛
Tilgate Forest Park 37Dc
⚲ 🎋 ⚓ P✕
Tillicoultry 245Ce ⚓ 🏛
Tilshead 49Dc ○ 🏛 🗓
Tilty 113Ac ○
Time Ball Tower 43De 🏛 £
☎ 0304 360897
Timespan Heritage Centre 278Gf 🏛
P£🅖 04312 327
Tingwall Agricultural Museum
285Fd 🏠 P£🅖 0595 84344
Tingwall Church 285Fd †
Tinkinswood 91Db 🏛
Tintagel 11Cf 🏠 🏰
Tintern Abbey 93Ed ✤ P£🅖
☎ 0291 689251
Tintinhull 25Bf ○ ✿
Tintinhull House 25Bf ✿
P£🅖 0985 847777
Tinto Hill 227Ed ☀
Tintwell Marsh 143Bc ⚓
Tisbury 27Af 🏠
Tissington 147Dg 🏠 🏛
Titchfield 29Db 🏠 ✿
Titchfield Abbey 29Db ✤
P£🅖 0329 43016
Titchfield Haven 29Db ⚓
Titchwell Marsh 143Bc ⚓
Titterstone Clee Hill 123Ce ☀ ☀
Tittleshall 139Bg ○
Tiverton 21Ec 🏠 † 🏛
Tobermory 249Ge ⚓ 🏛
Toby's Walks 141Da 🎋
Tockett's Mill 201De 🏛 P£
☎ 0287 639285
Tockholes 183Eb ○
Toddington, Beds 107Dd ○ †
Toddington, Glos 101Bf ○ 🏠
Todmorden 185Cb
Toe Head 272Bc
Tolgus Tin Mill 9De ⚓
P✕🅖☎ 0209 218198
Tollard Royal 27Ae 🏠
Toller Down 25Be
Tollesbury 113Eb ○
Tolleshunt D'Arcy 113Eb 🏠
Tolleshunt Major 113Db ○
Tolpuddle 25Dd 🏠
Tolquhon Castle 267Bf 🏰
P£🅖 031 2443101
Tolquhon Gallery 267Bf 🏛
P🅖 06513 2343
Tolsey Museum 101Dd 🏛 £
☎ 0993 823647

Tolson Museum 187Ba 🏛
P£🅖 0484 530591
Tom Brown's School Museum 53Cf
P£🅖 0367 820675
Tomatin 261Ec ○ ⚓
Tomen-y-Mur 157Dd 🔆
Tomintoul 263De 🏠 🏛
Tomnaverie Stone Circle 265Bd 🏛
Tomnavoulin 263Ef ○ ⚓
Tonbridge 39Cf 🏰 🏛
Tong 145Eb 🏠
Tonge 85Eb ○
Tonge Moor Textile Museum 167Bg
🏛🅖 0204 21394
Tongland 217Bb ✿
Tongue 281Gf 🏠 🏛
Topcliffe 201Ba ○
Topsham 15Cf 🏛
Torbay Aircraft Museum 15Bd 🔆
Torcross 15Bb ⚓
Torhouse Stone Circle 215Ed 🏛 🏛
Tormiston Mill 283Ce 🏛 P✕
☎ 031 2443107
Torness Power Station 233Dc ✿
P✕🅖☎ 0368 63500 ext 3871
Torosay Castle 249Ic 🏰
P✕£🅖 06802 421
Torphichen 229Af ○ 🏛
Torpoint 13Cc ⚓
Torquay 15Cd ✿ ☀ ⚓ 🏛
Torre Abbey 15Cd ✤ P£
☎ 0803 293593
Torrent Walk 157Db 🎋
Torridon 277Dc 🏠 🏛
Torridon Forest 277Dc
Torridon Visitor Centre & Deer
Museum 277Dc 🏛 £
☎ 044581 221
Torrs Park 17Ef ⚓
Torthorwald 219Bb ○ 🏠
Torthorwald Castle 219Bb 🏰
Tortington 33Bb 🏠
Tosson Hill 223Ca
Totland 31Ab 🏠
Totnes 15Bd 🏠 ⚓ 🏛
Totnes Motor Museum 15Bc ⚓
P£🅖 0803 862777
Tottenham House 53Bd 🏰
P£🅖 0672 870331
Totternhoe 107Cd ○ 🎋
Totternhoe Knolls 107Cd 🎋
Towan Beach 11Aa
Toward Castle 239Fa 🏰
Towbury 97Df ☀
Towcester 103Df † 🏛
Towie Barclay Castle 271Db 🏰
P£🅖 0888 4347
Town Yetholm 221Ed 🏠
Towneley Hall 185Bc 🏰
P✕☎ 0282 24213
Townend 195Fe 🏰 P£
☎ 05394 32628
Towton, Battle of 189Ac ✕
Toy's Hill 39Bg ○ 🏠 ⚓
Trading Places Gallery 109Cb 🏛
P£🅖☎ 0920 469620
Traeth Bychan 155Fg
Traeth Lligwy 155Eg
Traeth yr Ora 155Eg
Traith Penllech 155Cb
Traprain Law 233Bc ☀
Traquair House 229Eb 🏰
P✕£🅖☎ 0896 830323
Trawsfynydd 157Dd ○ ✿ ○
Trawsfynydd Nuclear Power
Station 157Dd ✿ P✕🅖
☎ 0766 87331
Treak Cliff 171Cd ☆
Trearddur 155Cf ○
Treasurer's House, York 189Ce 🏰
✕£☎ 0904 624247
Trebah Gardens 9Ec ✿
P✕£🅖☎ 0326 250448
Trebarwith 11Cf ○
Trebarwith Strand 11Cf
Trebetherick 11Be ○
Trebinshwn House 93Af 🏰
P£ 0874 730653
Trecastle 119Ba ○
Tredegar House 93Bb 🏰 ⚓
P✕£🅖☎ 0633 815880
Tredinnick 11Be 🎋 ○
Tredunnock 93Cc ○
Treffgarne Gorge & Mill 87Cd ☆ 🏰
✕£☎ 0437 87671
Treffry Viaduct 11Cc 🎋
Trefignath 155Cg 🏛
☎ 0222 465511
Trefor 155Dc ○

Trefriw 161Ba 🏠 🏰 ✿
Tregardock Beach 11Cf
Tregaron 117Eb
Tregaron Bog 117Ec ⚓ 🦦
Tregrehan 11Cc ✿ P£🅖
☎ 0726 812438
Tregwynt Woollen Mill 87Be ⚓
P✕🅖☎ 03485 225
Trelissick Gardens 9Fd ✿ ⚓
P✕🅖☎ 0872 862090
Trelleck 93Ed ○
Trelowarren House 9Ec 🏰
P£🅖☎ 0526 22366
Tremadog 155Fc ○
Trenance Park 11Ad Ω
Trenarren 11Cb 🏠
Trencrom Hill 9Cd 🏛
Trendle Ring 23Bf ☀
Trengwainton Gardens 9Bd ✿
P£🅖☎ 0736 63021
Trent 25Bf ○
Trent and Mersey Canal 149Cc
Trent Country Park 61De ⚲ 🎋
P✕£🅖☎ 081 449 8706
Trentham Gardens 147Af ✿
P✕£🅖☎ 0782 657341
Tre'r Ceiri 155Dc ☀ ☀
Tre'r-ddol 117Ef ○ 🏠
Trerice 11Ac 🏰 P✕£🅖
☎ 0637 875404
Tresaith 117Ab ○
Tresco I 9Bb
Trethevy Quoit 11Ed 🏛
Tretower 93Af 🏠 🏰 🏰
Trevaunance Cove 9Ef ☆
Trevellas Porth 9Ef ✿ P
☎ 0872 573368
Trevone 11Ae ○
Trevose Head 11Ae ☀ 🏛
Trevose Lighthouse 11Ae ☀
P£☎ 0841 520494
Trewithen 11Bb 🏠 P✕£🅖
☎ 0726 882418
Treyarnon 11Ae ○
Tri Thŷ 159Df ⚓ P✕
☎ 0352 771359
Tring 107Cc 🏛
Tring Zoological Museum 107Cc 🏛
P✕£🅖☎ 044282 4181
Trinity Hill 23Db ⚲
Trinity Temple 273Lh ✤
Troller's Gill 185Df ☆
Troon 225Cd ☀ 🏛
Tropical Bird Park, IoW 31Ca 🏰
P✕£🅖☎ 0983 853752
Tropical World 187Dc ✿ ⚓ 🦋
P£🅖 0532 661850
Tropiquaria 23Ag ⚓ P✕£
☎ 0984 40688
Trosley Park 85Bb ⚲ P£
☎ 0732 823570
Trossachs, The 241Bf ⚲ 🏠
P✕£🅖☎ 0877 30342
Trottiscliffe 85Bb ○
Trough of Bowland 183Ee ☆
Troup Head 271Ed
Troutbeck 195Fe 🏠
Trouts Dale 205Cb ⚲ ☀ 🎋
Trowbridge 49Bd 🏛
Trowlesworthy Warren 13Dd 🏛
Trumpan 275Bh ✿
Trumpington 109Df ○
Trunch 143Gb 🏠
Truro 9Fe † ✿ 🏛 🗓
Tuckenhay 15Bc 🏠
Tucker's Maltings 15Be ⚓
P£🅖☎ 0626 334734
Tudeley 39Df 🏠
Tudor Crystal 125Af ✿ P£🅖
☎ 0384 393325
Tudor House, Margate 43Dg 🏰
£☎ 0843 225511
Tudor House Museum 29Cc 🏛
🅖☎ 0703 224216
Tuetoes Hills 175Ce ⚲ ⚓ 🎋
Tugnet Ice House 269Fd 🏛
P£🅖 0309 73701
Tullibardine Chapel 245Cg †
Tullibody 245Be †
Tullie House 207Ee 🏛
P✕£🅖☎ 0228 34781
Tummel Bridge 255Ee ○
Tummel Forest 255Ef
Tummel Forest Visitor Centre 255Fe
⚲ P✕🅖☎ 0350 2284
Tunstall 147Ag
Tunstall Forest 115De
Turin Hill 259Be ☀

ACKNOWLEDGMENTS

The illustrations in this book were provided by the following artists, photographers and agencies. Those commissioned by Reader's Digest appear in *italics*.

The position of illustrations on each page is indicated by letters after the page number:

T=top; B=bottom; L=left; C=centre; R=right.

This book contains material from the following titles originally published by Drive Publications Limited and The Reader's Digest Association Limited.

Discovering Britain, Hand-picked Tours in Britain, Illustrated Guide to Britain, Book of British Villages, Illustrated Guide to Country Towns and Villages, 250 Tours of Britain, Book of British Coasts, Town Tours in Britain, Nature Lover's Library.

Cover *Patrick Thurston; Neil Holmes; Andrew Lawson; Trevor Wood.* 1 Arcaid/Lucinda Lambton. 2-3 *John Sims.* 4-5 *Nigel Cassidy.* 6 Images Colour Library. 8 TL Artist, *Colin Emberson;* TR Artist, *Richard Bonson;* BL Landscape Only. 10 TL John Cleare/Mountain Camera; BL Artist, *Richard Bonson;* BR Artist, *Richard Bonson.* 12 T Tim Woodcock; BL Artist, *Barbara Walker;* BR Artist, *Richard Bonson.* 14 L Biofotos; TR Artist, *Richard Bonson;* B Artist, *Richard Bonson.* 16 TC Andy Williams; BL Artist, *Colin Emberson;* BR Artist, *Nicolas Hall.* 18 T Artist, *Ivan Lapper;* BL Mary Evans Picture Library. 18-19 Robert Estall/Malcolm Aird. 19 T Mary Evans Picture Library; BL The National Trust/Nick Meers; BR Artist, *Gill Tomblin.* 20 T Artist, *Richard Bonson;* L Tim Woodcock; BR Artist, *Richard Bonson.* 22 TR Artist, *Richard Bonson;* CL Artist, *Barbara Walker;* B Neville Fox-Davies 24 TR Artist, *Colin Emberson;* C Landscape Only; BR Artist, *Nicolas Hall.* 26 T Artist, *Colin Emberson;* BL John Cleare/Mountain Camera; BR Artist, *Nicolas Hall.* 28 BL Artist *Richard Bonson;* TL Neil Holmes; TC Neil Holmes; TR Neil Holmes; BR John Cleare/Mountain Camera. 29 Artist, *Nicolas Hall.* 30 T Tim Woodcock; CR Artist, *Nicolas Hall;* BL Sheila & Oliver Mathews. 31 Artist, *Barbara Walker.* 32 TR Artist, *Nicolas Hall;* CL John Cleare/Mountain Camera; BR Sheila & Oliver Mathews. 33 Artist, *Kevin Dean.* 34 TL Sheila & Oliver Mathews; TR Artist, *Richard Bonson;* CL Artist, *Nicolas Hall;* BL Adam Woolfitt; BR Neil Holmes. 35 T *Neil Holmes;* C Neil Holmes; B *Neil Holmes.* 36 T Patrick Thurston; BL Artist, *Nicolas Hall;* BR Artist, *Barbara Walker.* 38 T Sheila & Oliver Mathews; CL Artist, *Nicolas Hall;* CR Artist, *Barbara Walker;* BL Sheila & Oliver Mathews. 40 L Sheila & Oliver Mathews; B Artist, *Nicolas Hall.* 41 Artist, *Barbara Walker.* 42 TL Artist, *Nicolas Hall;* CR Sheila & Oliver Mathews; B Artist, *Barbara Walker.* 44 TR & B Artist, *Richard Bonson;* L Tim Woodcock. 46 T *John Vigurs;* TR Artist, *Richard Bonson;* BR *John Vigurs.* 47 L *John Vigurs;* C Artist, *Nicolas Hall;* R *John Vigurs.* 48 T Tim Woodcock; CR Artist, *Nicolas Hall;* BL Artist, *Barbara Walker.* 50 TL Artist, *Richard Bonson;* TR Artist, *Nicolas Hall;* CL *Neil Holmes;* BR *Neil Holmes.* 51 *Neil Holmes;* TR Tim Woodcock. 52 TL Artist, *Richard Bonson;* BL Tim Woodcock; BR Artist, *Nicolas Hall.* 54 TL Tim Woodcock; TR Mary Evans Picture Library; C *Reader's Digest;* BR Artist, *Peter Barrett.* 54-55 Southampton City Art Gallery. 55 Full page, Images Colour Library; inset, English Heritage. 56 TL Landscape Only; TR Artist, *Leonora Box;* BL Tim Woodcock; BR Artist, *Nicolas Hall.* 58 TL Neil Holmes; TR Artist, *Richard Bonson;* BL Artist, *Barbara Walker;* BR Jeremy Whitaker. 59 L *Neil Holmes;* R Robert Harding Picture Library/Philip Craven. 60 TL Neil Holmes; TR Artist, *Barbara Walker;* BR Artist, *Nicolas Hall.* 62 TL Tim Woodcock; TR Artist, *Nicolas Hall;* BL Tim Woodcock; BR Artist, *Richard Bonson.* 64 TL Tim Woodcock; CR The Image Bank/Terry Williams; BC Michael Holford. 65 TL Barbara *Walker;* TR Magnum/Erich Lessing. 66 TC Arcaid/Mark Fiennes/1988; BR Michael Jenner. 67 TR Neil Holmes; CL Neil Holmes; C Neil Holmes; CR Artist, *Colin Emberson;* BL Artist, *Nicolas Hall;* BR Neil Holmes. 68 TL Tim Woodcock; CR *Neil Holmes;* BL Artist, *Colin Emberson.* 69 Neil Holmes. 70 TL *Neil Holmes;* R Tim Woodcock; BL *Neil Holmes.* 71 TL Arcaid/Robert O'Dea; CL Artist, *Barbara Walker;* C Artist, *Richard Bonson;* BR Tim Woodcock. 72 TL Artist, *Barbara Walker;* CL Tim Woodcock. 73 BR Artist, *Richard Bonson.* 74 T Neil Holmes; CL Artist, *Barbara Walker;* CR Michael Jenner; BL Copyright the Historic Royal Palaces. 75 TL Arcaid/Richard Bryant; BL Artist, *Nicolas Hall;* BR Derek Forss. 76 Syndication International. 77 L Artist, *Richard Bonson;* R *Neil Holmes.* 78 L Artist, *Richard Bonson;* TL Neville Fox-Davies; BR Tim Woodcock. 79 T Neil Holmes; TR Artist, *Richard Bonson;* BL Tim Woodcock; BR Tim Woodcock. 80 C Arcaid/Richard Bryant/1991; BC Artist, *Colin Emberson.* 81 TL Artist, *Nicolas Hall;* TR Arcaid/Jeremy Cockayne/1989. 82 TL Tim Woodcock; CR Michael Jenner; BL Arcaid/Martin Jones. 83 TL Artist, *Colin Emberson;* TR London Docklands Development Corporation; CL Neil Holmes; BR Tim Woodcock. 84 T Sheila & Oliver Mathews; CL Artist, *Nicolas Hall;* BL Tim Woodcock; BR Artist, *Richard Bonson.* 86 T Artist, *Nicolas Hall* CL Sheila & Oliver Mathews; BR Artist, *John Rignall.* 88 T Tim Woodcock; BL Artist, *Colin Emberson;* BR Artist, *Nicolas Hall.* 90 TL Artist, *Nicolas Hall;* TR Artist, *Richard Bonson;* B John Vigurs. 92 TL Artist, *Nicolas Hall;* TR Neville Fox-Davies; BL Artist, *Colin Emberson.* 94 TL & TR Arcaid/Lucinda Lambton; BR *Barbara Walker.* 95 TL *John Vigurs;* TL Wales Tourist Board; CL *Richard Bonson.* 96 TL Artist, *Barbara Walker;* TR Susan Lund; BR Artist, *Nicolas Hall.* 98 TL English Heritage; TR *Richard Bonson;* BL *John Vigurs;* BR John Vigurs. 99 TL Sheila & Oliver Mathews; TR John Heseltine; C *Richard Bonson;* BL John Vigurs. 100 TL The National Trust/Michael Allwood-Coppin; R Artist, *Colin Emberson.* 101 Artist, *Nicolas Hall.* 102 TL Artist, *Colin Emberson;* C Artist, *Nicolas Hall;* BL Sheila & Oliver Mathews. 104 T Oxford Picture Library/Chris Andrews; BL Oxford Picture Library/Chris Andrews; BR Artist, *Nicolas Hall.* 105 L Artist, *Barbara Walker;* TR Oxford Picture Library. 106 T Artist, *Nicolas Hall;* BL Patrick Thurston; BR Artist, *Barbara Walker.* 108 T Tim Woodcock; CR Artist, *Barbara Walker;* BL Artist, *Nicolas Hall.* 110 L The Image Bank/Colin Molyneux; TR Artist, *Colin Emberson;* BR Neil Holmes. 111 TL The Image Bank/Obremski; TR The Image Bank/Colin Molyneux; B Artist, *Richard Bonson.* 112 TL Neville Fox-Davies; R Artist, *Barbara Walker;* B Artist, *Nicolas Hall.* 114 TL Sheila & Oliver Mathews; CR Artist, *Kevin Dean;* B Artist, *Nicolas Hall.* 116 T Neville Fox-Davies; BL Artist, *Colin Emberson;* BR Artist, *Nicolas Hall.* 118 TL Artist, *Richard Bonson;* BL Tim Woodcock; BR Artist, *Richard Bonson.* 120 TL John Cleare/Mountain Camera; TC Images Colour Library; TR *John Vigurs.* 120-121 Images Colour Library. 121 TL Artist, *Victoria Goaman;* TL F.C.Morgan/The Dean & Chapter of Hereford; BR Trustees of the British Museum (Natural History). 122 T Tim Woodcock; CR Artist, *Colin Emberson;* B Artist, *Nicolas Hall.* 124 T Artist, *Richard Bonson;* B Andy Williams. 125 Artist, *Richard Bonson.* 126 T Impact/Bruce Stephens; TR Artist, *Nicolas Hall;* BL *John Vigurs;* BR Artist, *Richard Bonson.* 127 *John Vigurs.* 128 T Visionbank Library Limited & England Scene; CL Artist, *Nicolas Hall;* B Sheila & Oliver Mathews. 129 Artist, *Colin Emberson.* 130 T *John Vigurs;* CR The Image Bank; BL *John Vigurs.* 131 TL Artist, *Nicolas Hall;* TR *John Vigurs;* C Artist, *Colin Emberson;* BL *John Vigurs.* 132 T Sheila & Oliver Mathews; B Artist, *Richard Bonson.* 133 Artist, *Richard Bonson.* 134 TL Artist, *Nicolas Hall;* TR Artist, *Richard Bonson;* B Lucinda Lambton. 136 T Neville Fox-Davies; BL Artist, *Colin Emberson;* BR Artist, *Richard Bonson* 138 T Neville Fox-Davies; C Artist, *Barbara Walker;* CR Artist, *Nicolas Hall;* BL Robert Estall. 140 TL Neville Fox-Davies; TR Artist, *Robert Moreton;* C Artist, *Nicolas Hall;* B Sheila & Oliver Mathews. 142 L Artist, *Nicolas Hall;* R Artist, *Richard Bonson.* 143 Tim Woodcock. 144 T Neil Holmes; CL Artist, *Nicolas Hall;* CR Artist, *Barbara Walker;* B Sheila & Oliver Mathews. 146 TL Swift Picture Library; TR Artist, *Nicolas Hall;* B Artist, *Colin Emberson.* 148 TL Artist, *Nicolas Hall;* TR Artist, *Nicolas Hall;* BL Syndication International. 150 T *Jason Shenai;* TR Artist, *Colin Emberson;* B Artist, *Nicolas Hall.* 152 TL Artist, *Richard Bonson;* TR Artist, *Peter Barrett;* BR *Tim Woodcock.* 154 T Artist, *Nicolas Hall;* CR Artist, *Barbara Walker;* B John Cleare/Mountain Camera. 156 T John Cleare/Mountain Camera; BL Artist, *Nicolas Hall;* BR Artist, *Richard Bonson.* 158 TL Artist, *Nicolas Hall;* TR Neville Fox-Davies; B Artist, *Colin Emberson.* 160 T Andy Williams; B Artist, *Richard Bonson.* 161 Artist, *Colin Emberson.* 162 TL Artist, *Colin Emberson;* TR Artist, *Nicolas Hall;* BL Neil Holmes. 164 *John Vigurs;* BL Artist, *Richard Bonson;* BR *John Vigurs.* 165 TL John Vigurs; TR Syndication International; BL Artist, *Colin Emberson.* 166 TR Artist, *Richard Bonson;* B The National Trust. 167 Artist, *Barbara Walker.* 168 TL *John Vigurs; John Vigurs;* CL *John Vigurs;* C Artist, *Richard Bonson;* BR *John Vigurs.* 169 Artist *Richard Bonson;* TR *John Vigurs.* 170 TL Artist, *Colin Emberson;* TR Tim Woodcock; C Artist, *Nicolas Hall;* BL *Richard Surman.* 172 L Artist, *Colin Emberson;* R Tim Woodcock. 173 Artist, *Nicolas Hall.* 174 TL Neville Fox-Davies; TL Artist, *Richard Bonson;* BL Artist, *Richard Bonson;* BR Neil Holmes. 176 TL Artist, *Richard Bonson;* C Artist, *Tim Hayward;* BR Tim Woodcock. 178 TL Patrick Thurston; C Neville Fox-Davies; B Tim Woodcock. 179 Aerofilms; TR Permission of the Board of the British Library; BR Artist, *Ronald Maddox.* 180 TL Patrick Thurston; CL Artist, *Brian Hawkes;* BL Patrick Thurston. 181 Artist, *Nicolas Hall.* 182 T The National Trust/Mike Williams; CL Artist, *Richard Bonson;* B Artist, *Richard Bonson.* 184 TR Mike Freeman; BL Artist, *Colin Emberson;* TC Artist, *Nicolas Hall.* 186 TL Sheila & Oliver Mathews; TR Artist, *Nicolas Hall;* B Artist, *Colin Emberson.* 187 TL Artist, *Richard Bonson;* TR Artist, *Nicolas Hall;* B Images Colour Library. 190 TC Patrick Thurston; C *Nicolas Hall;* BL *Susan Elwes;* BR Arcaid/Jeremy Cockayne/1991. 191 TL *Neil Holmes;* TR Artist, *Colin Emberson.* 193 *Jon Wyand;* CR & BL Artist, *Richard Bonson.* 194 TL Artist, *Nicolas Hall;* CR Artist, *Richard Bonson;* B Jon Wyand. 196 T The National Trust/David Noton. 198 T Images Colour Library; CL Artist, *Nicolas Hall;* CR Artist, *Colin Emberson;* BL Tim Woodcock. 200 L & TR Artist, *Richard Bonson;* B Syndication International/Roger Scruton. 202 T Reader's Digest; B Sheila & Oliver Mathews. 202-203 Tim Woodcock. 203 TL *Martyn Chillmaid;* TR Tim Woodcock; BR Artist, *Ken Wood.* 204 TL The National Trust/Joe Cornish; TR Artist, *Richard Bonson;* BC John Cleare/Mountain Camera; BR Artist, *Nicolas Hall.* 206 T Jon Wyand; TL Artist, *Gill Tomblin;* BR Artist, *Richard Bonson.* 208 TL Artist, *Colin Emberson;* TR Images Colour Library; B Artist, *Richard Bonson.* 210 T Artist, *Nicolas Hall;* BL Neil Holmes; BR Artist, *Richard Bonson.* 212 TL Artist, *Richard Bonson;* TR Tim Woodcock; BL Artist, *Richard Bonson;* BR Simon Fraser. 214 TL Artist, *Barbara Walker.* 214 BL Impact/ Penny Tweedie; BR Artist, *Nicolas Hall.* 216 TR Scottish Tourist Board/Paul Tomkins; CL Artist, *Nicolas Hall;* B Artist, *Colin Emberson.* 218 TL Artist, *Nicolas Hall;* TR Artist, *Barbara Walker;* B Scotland in Focus/J Forsyth. 220 TL Artist, *Colin Emberson;* TR Artist, *Nicolas Hall;* B Images Colour Library. 222 TR Images Colour Library. 222 CL Artist, *Nicolas Hall;* BR Artist, *Graham Allen.* 224 TL Artist, *Colin Emberson;* TR Jon Wyand; CR Artist, *Richard Bonson;* B Jon Wyand. 226 TR Artist, *Richard Bonson;* CL Images Colour Library; BR Artist, *Colin Emberson.* 228 T Neil Holmes; BL Images Colour Library; BC Artist, *Nicolas Hall;* BR Artist, *Gill Tomblin.* 230 T Woodmansterne Ltd; BL Artist, *Richard Bonson;* BR Neil Holmes. 231 TL Artist, *Barbara Walker;* TR Doug Corrance. 232 T John Cleare/Mountain Camera; BL Artist, *Richard Bonson;* BR Artist, *Colin Emberson.* 233 Doug Corrance. 234 T Artist, *Nicolas Hall;* BL The Edinburgh Photographic Library Photographer; BR Artist, *Stephen Adams.* 236 TL Artist, *Nicolas Hall.* 236 TR Artist, *Colin Emberson;* B David Paterson. 238 TL Artist, *Richard Bonson;* TR Images Colour Library; CR Artist, *Barbara Walker;* BL Neville Fox-Davies 240 TL Artist, *Nicolas Hall;* TR Artist, *Richard Bonson;* B Swift Picture Library/ Mike Read. 242 T Doug Corrance; B Artist, *Colin Emberson.* 243 Artist, *Richard Bonson.* 244 TL Artist, *Barbara Walker.* 244 CR Artist, *Nicolas Hall;* BL Neil Holmes. 246 T Artist, *Nicolas Hall;* B Neil Holmes. 247 Artist, *Colin Emberson.* 248 T Neville Fox-Davies; BL Artist, *Colin Emberson;* BR Artist, *Richard Bonson.* 250 T Artist, *Colin Emberson;* CL Images Colour Library/Derry Brabbs; BL Artist, *Nicolas Hall.* 252 TL Artist, *Jim Robins;* TC David Paterson; CR Patrick Thurston; BL Glasgow Museums. 252-253 Neville Fox-Davies; Artist, *Peter Barrett;* B Biofotos. 254 T Images Colour Library; BL Artist, *Colin Emberson;* BR Artist, *Richard Bonson.* 256 L Gordon C.Henderson; TR Artist, *Nicolas Hall;* B Artist, *Barbara Walker.* 258 TL Artist, *Nicolas Hall;* CR Images Colour Library; BL Artist, *Colin Emberson.* 260 TR Tim Woodcock; CL Artist, *Nicolas Hall;* CR Artist, *Colin Emberson;* BL Scotland in Focus. 262 T Artist, *Colin Emberson;* CL Artist, *Nicolas Hall;* BR Images Colour Library. 264 TL Artist, *Richard Bonson;* TR Artist, *Barbara Walker;* B Images Colour Library. 266 R Artist, *Nicolas Hall;* B Scotland in Focus/R.G.Elliott. 267 Artist, *Shirley Hooper.* 268 Tim Woodcock. 269 L Artist, *Nicolas Hall;* R Artist, *Colin Emberson.* 270 L Artist, *Nicolas Hall;* R Colin Molyneux. 271 Artist, *Colin Emberson.* 273 TL Artist, *Nicolas Hall;* Artist, *Colin Emberson;* B Scotland in Focus/L Campbell. 274 TL Images Colour Library; TR Artist, *Richard Bonson;* C Artist, *Nicolas Hall;* BL David Paterson. 276 T Artist, *Barbara Walker;* CL Artist, *Nicolas Hall;* CR Images Colour Library; BL Andy Williams. 279 Artist, *Barbara Walker;* CL Artist, *Richard Bonson;* BR David Paterson. 280 Artist, *Richard Bonson.* 281 L Artist, *Colin Emberson.* 281 R Images Colour Library. 282 T Gordon C.Henderson; CR Artist, *Colin Emberson;* BL Gordon C.Henderson; BR Artist, *Nicolas Hall.* 284 TL Artist, *Barbara Walker;* TR Artist, *Nicolas Hall;* BL Charles Tait. 286 T Andy Williams; BL Artist, *Barbara Walker;* BR Artist, *Nicolas Hall.*

The publishers would also like to thank English Heritage, the National Trust, the National Trust for Scotland, Cadw (Welsh Historic Monuments) and Scottish Historic Buildings and Monuments for their help in the preparation of this book; also local authorities, Tourist Boards and owners of properties for the information they provided and their cooperation throughout the production of the book.

Cartography by:
Thames Cartographic Services Limited; Map Data Management Limited; Colourmap Scanning Limited.

Separations:
Scantrans Overseas Co Pte, Singapore; Studio One Origination, London.
Paper: Townsend Hook Ltd, Snodland.
Printing and Binding: Jarrold & Sons Ltd, Norwich.